ILLUMINATING THE RENAISSANCE

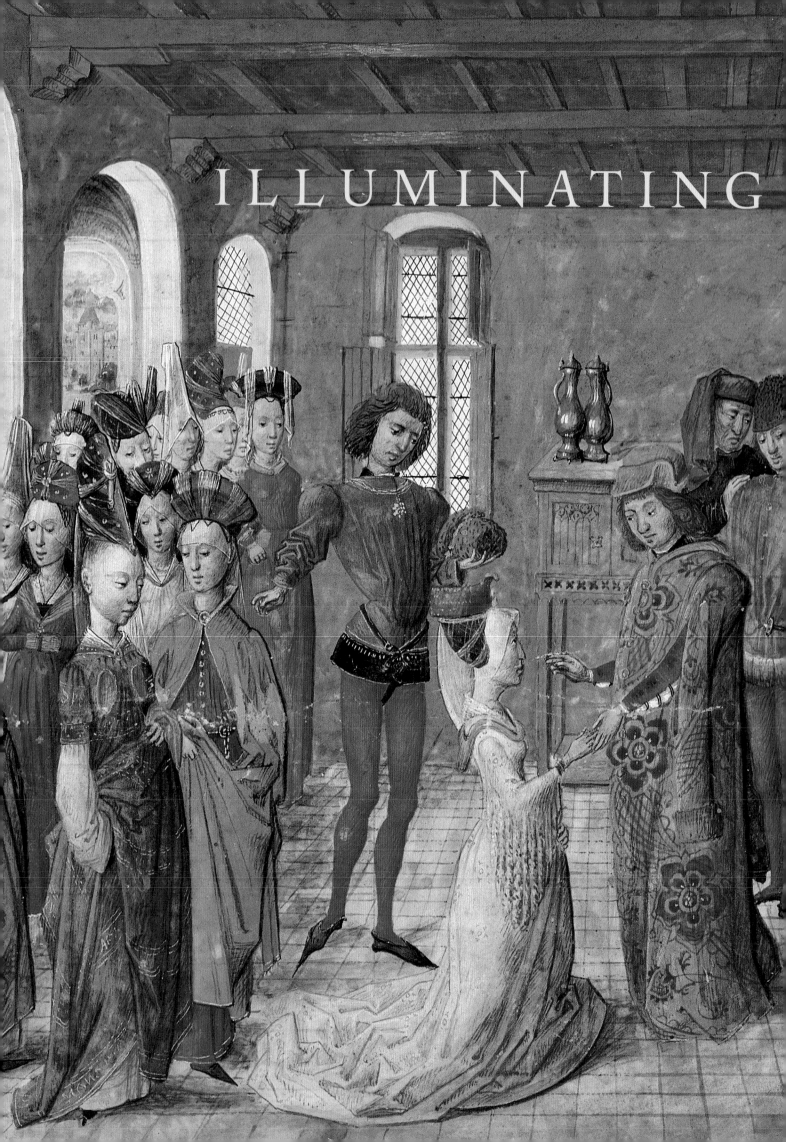

ILLUMINATING

THE RENAISSANCE

THE TRIUMPH OF FLEMISH MANUSCRIPT PAINTING IN EUROPE

THOMAS KREN AND SCOT MCKENDRICK

with contributions by

Maryan W. Ainsworth, Mari-Tere Alvarez, Brigitte Dekeyzer,
Richard Gay, Elizabeth Morrison, Catherine Reynolds

THE J. PAUL GETTY MUSEUM · LOS ANGELES
ROYAL ACADEMY OF ARTS · LONDON

First published on the occasion of the exhibition *Illuminating the Renaissance: The Triumph of Flemish Manuscript Painting in Europe*

The J. Paul Getty Museum, Los Angeles, 17 June – 7 September 2003
Royal Academy of Arts, London, 29 November 2003 – 22 February 2004

The Royal Academy of Arts is grateful to Her Majesty's Government for agreeing to indemnify this exhibition under the National Heritage Act 1980, and to Resource, The Council for Museums, Archives and Libraries, for its help in arranging the indemnity.

Exhibition Curators: Thomas Kren and Scot McKendrick with Norman Rosenthal, MaryAnne Stevens, and Cecilia Treves

Royal Academy of Arts
Exhibition Organisation: Lucy Hunt and Emeline Max
Photographic and Copyright Coordination: Andreja Brulc

Getty Publications
Christopher Hudson, *Publisher*
Mark Greenberg, *Editor in Chief*
Ann Lucke, *Managing Editor*
Dinah Berland, *Project Editor*
Karen Jacobson and Nomi Kleinmuntz, *Manuscript Editors*
Kurt Hauser, *Designer*
Anita Keys, *Production Coordinator*

Typeset by Diane L. Franco and G & S Typesetters
Separations by Professional Graphics Inc., Rockford, Ill.
Printed and bound in England by Butler & Tanner Limited

HALF-TITLE PAGE: Master of James IV of Scotland, *The Last Judgment* (detail, ill. 111); FRONTISPIECE: Vienna Master of Mary of Burgundy, *Alexander Takes the Hand of Roxanne* (detail, ill. 54); TITLE PAGE: The Spinola Hours, fol. 269 (detail; see cat. no. 124); PAGE ix: Master of the Dresden Prayer Book, *Crossing of the Red Sea* (detail, ill. 93); PAGES x, xi: Simon Bening and workshop, Stein Quadtriptych (detail, ill. 146)

British Library Cataloguing-in-Publication Data

A catalogue record for this book is available from the British Library

ISBN 1-903973-28-7 (paperback)
ISBN 1-903973-25-2 (hardback)

Distributed outside the United States and Canada by Thames & Hudson Ltd, London

CONTENTS

FOREWORD

Manuscript illumination, the quintessential medieval art form, enjoyed its final triumph during the Renaissance. In the wake of the invention of printing, Flemish illuminators created extravagant and lavish manuscripts in which their art was revitalized and given new direction. These manuscripts were collected by rulers, their consorts, and their courtiers across Europe: the dukes of Burgundy in Flanders; their Hapsburg successors in Spain, Germany, and Flanders; the Yorkist and Tudor monarchs in England; and the Aviz dynasty of Portugal. The art and achievements of these illuminators are the subject of *Illuminating the Renaissance: The Triumph of Flemish Manuscript Painting in Europe.*

This publication accompanies the first exhibition to bring together the greatest works produced by Flemish illuminators during this exceptional period. Some of the objects included have never been exhibited previously, and most have been seen only rarely. *Illuminating the Renaissance* encompasses works that reveal the full range of sizes and formats in which illuminators worked: from a monumental genealogy to diminutive private altarpieces on parchment, from huge folio-size volumes to tiny prayer books, and from single, independent miniatures to books containing one hundred or more illustrations. The types of texts also vary: from histories, chronicles, and romances to Christian devotional writings, breviaries, and books of hours. The exhibition presents manuscript illumination within the broader context of painting in oil on panel and explores the close relationship between the two media, including objects by artists who worked in both.

Thomas Kren, curator of manuscripts at the J. Paul Getty Museum, and Scot McKendrick, curator of manuscripts at The British Library, conceived the exhibition and catalogue. The Getty Museum's Flemish manuscripts, some of the finest in the world, are among the high points of its collection. The British Library's holdings, founded on the manuscripts purchased by King Edward IV more than five hundred years ago, are arguably without rival. With these strengths, the Getty and The British Library were ideal collaborators for this exhibition. For the presentation in London, this collaboration required a third partner. In 2001, when given the opportunity of providing the London venue, the Royal Academy of Arts was delighted to participate. With its own successful history of exhibiting illuminated manuscripts, including the 1994–95 exhibition *The Painted Page*, which showed the highest achievements of Italian Renaissance book illumination, the Royal Academy offered its full commitment to the realization of this project. The British Library continued to support the exhibition through unprecedented and generous loans and through the participation of Scot McKendrick as co-curator of the exhibition.

No previous exhibition or catalogue of Flemish manuscript illumination of this period matches the scope and ambition of the present undertaking. We are most grateful to Thomas Kren and Scot McKendrick for their vision, determination, and scholarship. They undertook the task of selecting objects for the exhibition. Aided by their colleagues in the fields of manuscript illumination and northern Renaissance art, they pursued the relevant manuscripts, paintings, and drawings, securing loans with tenacity and diplomacy. As they did so, they took the opportunity both to explore the broad themes of this era and to approach the more perplexing problems of connoisseurship. This catalogue is a testament to their achievement. We extend our gratitude to the many institutions and private individuals, both named and anonymous, whose generosity has made this exhibition possible. It is our privilege to present these precious objects to a larger public.

Deborah Gribbon, Director, J. Paul Getty Museum
Professor Phillip King, C.B.E., President, Royal Academy of Arts
Lynne Brindley, Chief Executive, The British Library

LENDERS TO THE EXHIBITIONS

Alnwick Castle, The Duke of Northumberland

Antwerp, Museum Mayer van den Bergh

Arundel Castle, The Duke of Norfolk

Baltimore, The Walters Art Museum

Basel, Kunstmuseum

Berlin, Staatliche Museen zu Berlin, Preussischer Kulturbesitz, Gemäldegalerie

Berlin, Staatliche Museen zu Berlin, Preussischer Kulturbesitz, Kupferstichkabinett

Berlin, Staatsbibliothek zu Berlin, Preussischer Kulturbesitz, Handschriftenabteilung

Bibermühle, Heribert Tenschert

Birmingham Museums and Art Gallery

Blackburn Museum and Art Gallery

Brussels, Bibliothèque royale de Belgique

Cambridge University Library

Cambridge, The Fitzwilliam Museum

Cambridge, St John's College

Cambridge, Mass., Fogg Art Museum, Harvard University

Cambridge, Mass., The Houghton Library, Harvard University

Chatsworth, The Duke of Devonshire and the Chatsworth Settlement Trustees

The Cleveland Museum of Art

Copenhagen, Det Kongelige Bibliotek

Darmstadt, Hessisches Landesmuseum

Dublin, Chester Beatty Library

El Escorial, Real Biblioteca del Monasterio de El Escorial (Patrimonio Nacional)

Glasgow University Library

The Hague, Koninklijke Bibliotheek

Hatfield House, The Marquess of Salisbury

Holkham Hall, The Earl of Leicester and Trustees of the Holkham Estate

Kingston Lacy (The National Trust)

Lisbon, Fundação Calouste Gulbenkian, Museu Calouste Gulbenkian

London, The British Library

London, The British Museum

London, The Courtauld Institute Gallery

London, Her Majesty Queen Elizabeth II, The Royal Collection Trust

London, Lambeth Palace Library

London, The National Gallery

London, Public Record Office

London, Sir John Soane's Museum

London, Victoria and Albert Museum

Los Angeles, The J. Paul Getty Museum

Madrid, Biblioteca de la Fundación Lázaro Galdiano

Madrid, Biblioteca Nacional

Manchester, The John Rylands University Library of Manchester

Montserrat, Biblioteca de l'Abadia de Montserrat

Munich, Bayerische Staatsbibliothek

Naples, Biblioteca Nazionale "Vittorio Emanuele III"

New York, The Metropolitan Museum of Art

New York, The Pierpont Morgan Library

Nová Říše, The Premonstratensian Abbey of Nová Říše

Oxford, Bodleian Library

Oxford, Christ Church

Oxford, Magdalen College

Paris, Bibliothèque de l'Arsenal

Paris, Bibliothèque nationale de France

Paris, École nationale supérieure des Beaux-Arts

Paris, Musée du Louvre

Philadelphia Museum of Art

San Marino, The Huntington Library

Stonyhurst College

Toronto, Art Gallery of Ontario

Valencia, Colección Serra de Alzaga

Vatican City, Biblioteca Apostolica Vaticana

Vienna, Österreichische Nationalbibliothek

Waddesdon Manor (The National Trust)

Ware, St Edmund's College

Wilton House, The Earl of Pembroke

Windsor Castle, Her Majesty Queen Elizabeth II, The Royal Library

Wormsley Library, Sir Paul Getty, K.B.E.

and other collectors who wish to remain anonymous

Secundum iohannem.

In illo tempore venit ihs in civitatem samarie que dicitur sychar: iuxta predium quod dedit iacob ioseph filio suo. Erat autem ibi fons iacob. Ihs ergo fatigatus ex itinere: sedebat sic super fontem. Hora erat quasi sexta. Venit mulier de samaria: haurire aquam. Dicit ei ihs: Da michi bibere.

ACKNOWLEDGMENTS

Illuminating the Renaissance is the result of years of research, negotiations, and planning. It is with pleasure and great appreciation that we thank those institutions and individuals who have made both the exhibition and this publication possible. In Los Angeles John Walsh, former director of the Getty Museum, and Deborah Gribbon, the Museum's current director, lent enthusiastic support to this project from the outset. Lynne Brindley, chief executive at The British Library, offered critical and generous support for a project that showcases the Library's remarkable holdings of Flemish Renaissance manuscripts, and the Royal Academy of Arts greeted the prospect of this exhibition with enthusiasm. We are deeply grateful to them all.

We wish to thank all the individuals on the staffs of the J. Paul Getty Museum, the Royal Academy of Arts, and The British Library who collaborated on the preparation of this exhibition. It has been a privilege to work with such experienced and dedicated teams. Their commitment, resourcefulness, patience, and good humor have been a source of inspiration and have made our tasks easier in every respect. In particular we want to thank, at the Getty, William Griswold, assistant director for collections; Quincy Houghton, head of exhibitions and public programs; Amber Keller, senior exhibitions coordinator; Sally Hibbard, chief registrar; and Cory Gooch and Betsy Severance, registrars. At the Royal Academy of Arts we especially thank Norman Rosenthal, exhibitions secretary; MaryAnne Stevens, collections secretary and senior curator; Cecilia Treves, exhibitions curator; Emeline Max, head of exhibitions organization; and Lucy Hunt, exhibitions organizer. At The British Library, thanks are extended to Jill Finney, director of strategic marketing and communications; Pam Porter, head of manuscripts loans; and Barbara O'Connor, registrar.

The study of Flemish manuscripts is a tremendously complex undertaking due to the ambitious nature of the books themselves, their far-flung locations, and the technical nature of manuscript studies. Inevitably this survey of a great era of Flemish illumination rests on foundations built over several generations by an army of talented scholars whose contributions we have endeavored to recognize specifically where appropriate here. Flemish manuscripts remain to this day a lively field of research. In particular we would like to thank our colleagues who contributed essays and entries to this catalogue and also offered many valuable suggestions regarding content and presentation: Mari-Tere Alvarez, Brigitte Dekeyzer, Richard Gay, Susan L'Engle, Elizabeth Morrison, and especially Maryan W. Ainsworth and Catherine Reynolds. Janet Backhouse and Lorne Campbell offered many thoughtful suggestions as the project first took shape, and Christiane van den Bergen-Pantens, Patricia Stirnemann, and Elizabeth Teviotdale conducted extensive research toward the identification of escutcheons in many of the books. John Plummer and Margaret Scott have generously shared the results of their own ongoing, long-standing research for many of the catalogue's entries to help us with problems of locating books of hours and the dating of illuminations on the basis of fashion, respectively. Justine Andrews, Agnes Bertiz, Rita Keane, and Christopher Lakey have devoted countless hours to the references for this volume, which represent only a portion of their work.

Richard Gay has tirelessly administered the project on behalf of the Getty Manuscripts Department. Elizabeth Morrison has taken responsibility for all gallery materials and the editing of the descriptive data for the individual catalogue entries. Rita Keane has assisted in the administration of loans. In addition, we extend our thanks to Kurt Barstow, Elizabeth Caldwell, Kristen Collins, Tulis McCall, Christina Nielsen, Stephanie Porras and Elizabeth Teviotdale in the Department of Manuscripts at the Getty. Further, we would like to acknowledge the assistance of the Research Library of the Getty Research Institute, especially Jay Gam, Ross Garcia, Aimee Lind, Joyce Ludmer, Amelia Wong—and with it the great importance and value of the Research Library's large Photo Study Collection of illuminated manuscripts, ably staffed by Tracey Schuster and Mark Henderson.

At The British Library we would like to thank Claire Breay, Greg Buzwell, Kathleen Houghton, Jacqui Hunt, and Peter Kidd, who provided invaluable administrative and research support. We are also indebted to Alixe Bovey, Hugh Cobbe, Laura Nuvoloni, Ann Payne, Alice Prochaska, David Way, and Christopher Wright. In addition we acknowledge our debt both to the rich research collections of The British Library and to the dedicated staff members who make these remarkable collections both accessible and a pleasure to consult.

Deep thanks for her conservation of key manuscript loans and guidance on issues related to the books' installation and safekeeping go to Nancy Turner, associate conservator of manuscripts at the Getty. We also thank those conservators whose appraisal and treatments of objects in the exhibition made their display possible: Priscilla Anderson, Liudmila Lidon Arnal, Nancy Bell, Laurence Caylux, Alan Derbyshire, Teresa Lignelli, Teresa Martin, John Mumford, Deborah Novotny, Sabrina Pugh, Catherine Rickman, Jean Rosston, Helen Shenton, Pilar Ineba Tamarit, Jiří Vnouček, Lieve Watteeuw, Deborah Willis, and Akiko Yamazaki-Kleps. The imaginative installation at the Getty is due to Ann Marshall, as well as Reid Hoffmann, Leon Rodriguez, and Nicole Trudeau, all working under the direction of Merritt Price, and at the Royal Academy to Ivor Heal.

In the production of this splendid catalogue, we express our gratitude to Getty Publications, in particular Mark Greenberg, editor in chief; Dinah Berland, project editor; Kurt Hauser, designer; Anita Keys, production coordinator; Cecily Gardner, photo researcher; and Brandi Franzman, now staff assistant in the Department of Manuscripts; along with the invaluable contributions of editorial consultants Desne Ahlers, Mary Gladue, Karen Jacobson, Nomi Kleinmuntz, Sarah Koplin, and Jean Wagner. The indexes were produced by Charles W. Berberich of Coughlin Indexing Services, Inc. The Getty manuscripts were newly photographed for this publication by Christopher Foster; new digital images of The British Library manuscripts were produced by Laurence Pordes.

We hope that *Illuminating the Renaissance* also reflects the many insights generously provided by the following colleagues: Elisabeth Antoine, Alain Arnould, O.P., Anne Magreet As-Vijvers, François Avril, Janet Backhouse, Holm Bevers, Chrystèle Blondeau, Bernard Bousmanne, Bodo Brinkmann, Michelle Brown, Stephanie Buck, Thomas Campbell, Hubert Cardon, Dawson Carr, Christina Ceulemans, Kate Challis, Gregory Clark, Elizabeth Cleland, Melissa Conway, Dominique Cordellier, Christopher De Hamel, Antoine de Schryver, Consuelo Dutschke, Dagmar Eichberger, Noel Geirnaert, Ketty Gottardo, Barbara Haggh-Huglo, Lee Hendrix, Eva Irblich, Chiyo Ishikawa, Lynn Jacobs, Susan F. Jones, Ronda Kasl, Martin Kauffmann, Ann Kelders, Elisabeth Klemm, Akiko Komada, Anne Korteweg, Michaela Krieger, Anne-Marie Legaré, Claudine Lemaire, Teresa Lignelli, Philippa Marks, James Marrow, Maximiliaan Martens, Masami Okubo, Mark Meadow, Susie Nash, Ina Nettekoven, Ludovic Nys, the late Myra Orth, Katarzyna Płonka-Bałus, Patti Reyes, Richard and Mary Rouse, Cécile Scailliérez, Stephanie Schrader, Katharina Smeyers, Frauke Steenbock, Kay Sutton, Dagmar Thoss, Maria da Trindade Mexia Alves, Anne Van Buren, Dominique Vanwijnsberghe, Roger Wieck, Hanno Wijsman, Jacob Wisse, and Anne Woollett.

In addition we would like to thank most warmly His Excellency Baron Thierry de Gruben, Belgian ambassador to Great Britain, and Baroness Françoise de Gruben, as well as the following people who have helped us in so many ways: Julián Martin Abad, Jean-Pierre Angremy, Bruce Barker-Benfield, Peter Barnet, Clare Baxter, Holm Bevers, Pauline Birtwell, Vincenzo Boni, Christopher Brown, Michelle Brown, Emmanuelle Brugerolles, Ina Busch, João Castel-Branco Pereira, Julien Chapuis, Mary Clapinson, Pierre Cockshaw, Monique Cohen, Katherine Coombs, Miguel Ángel Recio Crespo, Peter Day, Richard Deutsch, Mark L. Evans, Everett Fahy, Manuela Fidalgo, Stephen Fliegel, Susan Foister, Philippa Glanville, Juan Carlos de la Mata González, Antony Griffiths, Rainald Grosshans, Richard Hamer,

Robert Harding, Jonathan Harrison, Lee Hendrix, Chris Hoornaert, Charles Horton, David T. Johnson, Theo Jülich, Laurence Kanter, Christopher Lloyd, Katherine Crawford Luber, Bryan Maggs, Susy Marcon, Richard Marks, Hope Mayo, Bernhard Mendes Bürgi, Václav Milek, Ulrich Montag, Theresa-Mary Morton, Danielle Muzerelle, Mark Nicholls, Hans Nieuwdorp, William Noel, Eef Overgaauw, Richard J. Palmer, Susan Palmer, Stella Panayotova, Michael Parke-Taylor, Allegra Pesenti, Erik Petersen, Wolfgang Prohaska, Suzanne Reynolds, Joseph Rishel, the Hon. Jane Roberts, Mary Robertson, John Martin Robinson, William B. Robinson, Damià Roure, Martin Royalton-Kisch, Scott Schaefer, Scott C. Schwartz, Wilfried Seipel, Angela Starling, William P. Stoneman, Sarah Tyacke, Françoise Viatte, William Voelkle, Kate Warren, Rowan Watson, Robin Harcourt Williams, Juan Antonio Yeves, David Zeidberg, and Patrick Zutshi.

It is the private collectors (including several who wish to remain anonymous) and the curators, directors, and trustees of the institutions who so willingly lent works that in many instances have never been lent previously, to whom we owe our greatest debt of gratitude.

The Getty is also most grateful to the Federal Council on the Arts and Humanities for their support of this exhibition.

Finally we thank Bruce Robertson and Alison, Iona, Alexander, and the late Imogen McKendrick for enduring a frequently absent and distracted partner or parent over the past few years along with the endless interruptions of telephone calls. We dedicate this catalogue to Iona, Alexander, and the memory of Imogen.

Thomas Kren
Scot McKendrick

NOTES TO THE READER

This catalogue contains the following types of manuscript illuminations: books, leaves or cuttings from books, and illuminations that may or may not have been made for books. Also included are drawings, paintings, and printed books.

Measurements refer to the size of a leaf or cutting, not to the binding.

Illuminations are tempera on parchment unless otherwise indicated; "tempera" refers to any water-soluble medium of which the usual binding media are gum arabic or glair. Some illuminations contain added gold and silver leaf, or gold paint.

Text blocks are one column unless otherwise indicated.

For some books that are temporarily bound or cut up and their individual leaves dismounted in scrapbooks, only selected leaves or bifolia have been borrowed; the catalogue entry data provides information on the complete manuscript from which the work was taken.

In provenances, "to" indicates that the work passed directly to the next owner. "Full-page miniature" refers to any fully illuminated page whether a miniature with a full border or one without a border.

Due to limitations of space, bibliographies for the catalogue items are extensive but not exhaustive.

Comparative illustrations are referred to as "figures" and are numbered consecutively, beginning in the introduction; catalogue illustrations are referred to as "ills." and correspond to the catalogue entry numbers.

KEY TO ABBREVIATIONS:
fol. / fols. = folio / folios
Ms. / Mss. = manuscript / manuscripts
r = recto (rarely used; a folio number not followed by r or v indicates a recto page)
v = verso

Contributions to the catalogue are by Maryan W. Ainsworth (M. W. A.), Mari-Tere Alvarez (M.-T. A.), Brigitte Dekeyzer (B. D.), Richard Gay (R. G.) Thomas Kren (T. K.), Susan L'Engle (S. L'E.), Scot McKendrick (S. McK.), and Elizabeth Morrison (E. M.).

INTRODUCTION

Thomas Kren and Scot McKendrick

This exhibition celebrates the great era, between about 1470 and 1560, when Flemish manuscript painters created, on the pages of illuminated books, some of the most stunning works of art of the Renaissance. During this period manuscript illuminators radically transformed the appearance of the illustrated page. First, they introduced into their miniatures the mastery of light, texture, and space that Jan van Eyck (1390–1441) and Rogier van der Weyden (ca. 1400–1464) had achieved in their devotional images, altarpieces, and portraits painted in oil on panel. Indeed, the finest of the new generation of illuminators rivaled the painters in the expressiveness and subtlety of their best miniatures. Second, the decorated border of the page, the area that surrounds a painted image or text, grew comparable in its richness to the miniature it framed. Superseding the two-dimensional border concept of the past (e.g., cat. nos. 2, 15), the framing flora and fauna were more three-dimensional and closer to actual size. Flowers and insects cast their own painted shadows, teasing the eye with their apparent veracity. The wonder inspired by the scrupulous observation of nature in its endless variety reflects the Renaissance's startling marriage of art and science.[1] The exquisite naturalism that infuses both miniatures and borders places Flemish manuscripts among the artistic achievements of this time.

Flemish manuscript illumination from the 1470s on was an art that maintained medieval traditions, such as depending on workshop pattern books as sources, yet consistently succeeded in rethinking and refreshing standardized imagery. This period gave rise to many illuminators of genius, including Simon Marmion, the Vienna Master of Mary of Burgundy, the Master of the Houghton Miniatures, the Master of the Dresden Prayer Book, Gerard David, the Master of the Prayer Books of around 1500, the Master of James IV of Scotland, and Simon Bening. These and others enjoyed a continuous demand for sumptuous works from many of the great courts of Europe, especially those linked with the Burgundian and Hapsburg dynasties. Their manuscripts served as opulent symbols of the courts' power. The innovations of these illuminators included one of the most widely popular and influential styles in the history of manuscript illumination, involving the miniature, the border, and the integration of the two. The new style was embraced across western Europe, and not only by collectors but by other artists as well. It was an art that drew much from the newly refined medium of painting in oil on panel and that also gave something back to it. Together painters and illuminators explored the visual world, and each discovered sources of wonder that encouraged mutual emulation.

THE ROLE OF COURT CULTURE

The Renaissance was an era of great princely libraries. The patronage of the dukes of Burgundy, a powerful duchy located in parts of present-day Belgium and eastern France, and their courtiers played a fundamental role in the great flowering of Flemish manuscript illumination during the fifteenth century.

MASTER OF JAMES IV
OF SCOTLAND
The Last Judgment
(ill. 111a)

The dukes formed one of the largest and most splendid of these libraries. The Burgundian dynasty's political exploitation of extravagant display was one of its essential contributions to modern European statecraft. The lavish new style of Flemish manuscript painting mirrored the glamour of the court, and the court politics of splendor sometimes shaped the illumination itself. For example, during the 1470s some borders in the new style meticulously reproduced the finely woven brocades worn ceremonially only by members of the ducal household. Others display tidy arrangements of jewelry with pearls, rubies, and gold, or colorful arrays of peacock feathers (e.g., ill. 42). Both these borders and the objects they depict are manifestations of the Burgundian dynasty's taste for splendor and its display.

As an art of the court, the new Flemish manuscript illumination was first and foremost a vehicle of piety, politics, and status. The patronage of such luxurious arts inspired emulation on the part of both nobles and merchants and at other courts. In Flanders the tradition of manuscript illumination was already centuries old. As one of a range of costly goods for which the Flemings developed a reputation throughout western Europe—they included painting, tapestry, embroidery, sculpture, jewelry, and metalwork—illuminated manuscripts established a strong presence within the bustling European marketplace. The new type of illusionistic borders adopted by Flemish illuminators during the 1470s became the hallmark of these books for several generations and may even have served as a form of branding.

The triumph of Flemish manuscript illumination in Europe was made possible by this commercial tradition; by this art form's close ties to the Burgundian dynasty, whose love of art and display was so influential; and by the Burgundian house's marriages with the Hapsburg and Spanish ruling families. Flemish Burgundian visual culture held in its thrall the imaginations of both the Hapsburg successors to the Burgundian dukes and their loyal courtiers.

THE BURGUNDIAN DUKES AND THE NORTH

The Burgundian state of the fifteenth century, what came to be called the "Grand Duchy of the West," had its roots in the previous century. In 1369 Duke Philip of Burgundy—called "the Bold" (r. 1363–1404), who was the younger brother of King Charles V (r. 1364–80) and first peer of France—married Margaret of Mâle (r. 1384–1405), the daughter and heir of Louis, count of Flanders (r. 1346–84). The union of Philip and Margaret eventually brought under the control of the dukes of Burgundy significant parts of Flanders and northern France, including the prosperous urbanized Artois. These territorial acquisitions, which permanently transformed the character of life in the already prosperous region of Flanders and its neighboring territories, secured a place for the Burgundians in European history. It marked the beginning of an expansion of Burgundian hegemony into two physically distinct regions, the first centered in the north—encompassing Brabant, Hainaut, Holland-Zeeland, Guelders, Utrecht, and Liège—and the second in Burgundy.[2] (Dijon, the capital of Burgundy, is four hundred kilometers [250 miles] south of Bruges.) Philip the Bold and his successors, most importantly his grandson Philip the Good (r. 1419–67), stewarded this growth through a policy of territorial acquisition via inheritance, purchase, treaty, and conquest. The latter Philip consolidated one of the most powerful sovereignties in Europe, often a rival to the kingdom of his Valois cousin and feudal overlord, Charles VII of France (r. 1422–61). In the course of his reign, Philip the Good abandoned Paris for the commercial centers of Flanders, where he ruled with pomp and ceremony. His court was peripatetic, moving among administrative centers he had set up in the region.

During the fourteenth century Flemish towns enjoyed great mercantile prosperity. They developed local political and cultural traditions, including public festivals that engaged the talents of artists, musicians, and performers. Flemish artistry abetted the Burgundians' taste for splendor and display. The dukes staged magnificent feasts, pageants, and other celebrations that exploited the hypnotic appeal of grandiose ceremony and demonstrated the power of visual symbolism. Philip the Good used these means strategically in his larger ongoing efforts to centralize authority and strengthen the administration of his principalities. Conscious of his growing power and prestige on the European stage, he may also have wished to elevate the duchy to a kingdom, a goal that his son Charles (r. 1467–77) would take up in earnest some decades later.[3] By the second half of the fifteenth century, the splendor and magnificence of the Burgundian court had become legendary, influencing the way other European states presented themselves to their subjects and the world. The Burgundians had created an idealized image for the public expression of secular power.

As noted earlier, the dukes of Burgundy, whose closest relations among the Valois line were renowned for their bibliophilia, became important patrons and collectors of illuminated manuscripts. Philip the Bold—residing for long stretches of his rule in Paris, the most important center of artistic and manuscript production at that time—laid the foundations of a library of finely illuminated books.[4] During the 1440s Philip the Good turned to manuscript illumination as a central component of his politics of splendor. He commissioned at least sixty manuscripts. Although not all were illuminated, they included some of the most beautiful and lavish books produced in the Flemish territories up to that time.[5] Philip commissioned books not only for their countless miniatures painted with rare and costly minerals and with gold but also for their political significance. Through several literary works that recounted the exploits of his glorious forebears (e.g., cat. no. 55), the duke strove to demonstrate his belief in his descent from the Lotharingian kings.[6] Histories of territories that he had brought under his rule, such as the *Chroniques de Hainaut* (cat. no. 3), explicitly justified his claims to power. Other literary works offered illustrious political-military leaders, such as Alexander the Great, as exemplars for his rule; devotional manuscripts, including sumptuously illuminated breviaries (e.g., cat. no. 10), were suited to a Christian prince of his status and aspirations.[7]

The secular texts and their stunning imagery were particularly important for Philip and contributed actively to court life. Presentation miniatures (illustrations depicting the presentation of a book to its patron or donor) show the book itself as a focus of ceremony that engaged the most prominent officials of the ducal household (e.g., ill. 3).[8] With their potent political underpinnings, the chronicles helped to shape the imaginations and thinking of the ruler and his courtiers. These books often had lengthy cycles (twenty, fifty, one hundred miniatures), including many subjects not previously illuminated. Their physical presence alone, as the presentation miniatures also suggest, conveyed authority.

The art of manuscript illumination was not new to Flemish cities. Bruges and Ghent had been producing luxury devotional books since the early thirteenth century, while medieval Tournai, Hainaut, and Brabant also were centers of production. Like other producers of luxury goods in Bruges and Ghent, Flemish illuminators developed an export market for their work.[9] But manuscript illumination in Flanders before the period of Philip's patronage was generally less distinguished than the production of the other great European centers, especially Paris. From midcentury, however, it would equal and even surpass them.[10]

Almost certainly Philip the Good's demand for books of the highest quality to rival those acquired by his grandfather and his other Valois forebears—including the legendary bibliophile John, duke of Berry—helped to foster the growing refinement of Flemish illumination. The finest artists of the day gravitated to the medium as court patronage created fresh opportunities. Both Philip and his son Charles, the young count of Charolais, retained illuminators as court artists.[11] Duke Philip's library had lasting historical importance. The roughly 867 books that he had acquired through inheritance, commission, purchase, and gift would become a cornerstone of one of the great national libraries, the Bibliothèque royale de Belgique in Brussels.[12]

When Philip died at the age of seventy-one, many of his bibliophilic projects were left incomplete. During the years immediately after his death, his son Charles spent substantial sums on the illumination of a particularly ambitious group of books (including cat. nos. 10, 55) that his father had originally commissioned. Many had been produced with spaces for miniatures but were left only partially illuminated or not at all. Charles also personally commissioned other significant books (see cat. nos. 16, 54, 56, 64).[13] Meanwhile the period of Charles's rule witnessed a flowering of patronage among his courtiers. They ordered books suited to a ruling class and a chivalric culture: the life of Alexander the Great, newly translated and critically revised by Vasco da Lucena (cat. no. 63); and Valerius Maximus (cat. no. 73), a collection of rhetorical exercises that had been popular since the time of the French king Charles V.

Among the leading patrons of this era were many of Charles's family members, courtiers, and/or allies: the loyal ducal councillor Louis of Gruuthuse, stadtholder of Holland and Zeeland (see cat. nos. 58, 59, 60, 62); Duke Charles's illegitimate half brother Anthony of Burgundy; his third wife, Margaret of York (see cat. nos. 13, 14, 22, 27–29, 43, 51, 85); and Edward IV of England (see cat. nos. 66, 80–83, 87), his brother-in-law through Margaret. They each developed collections of luxury volumes. Significantly, Edward's holdings, though much more modest than those of the Burgundian rulers, are among the most important surviving works of the early English royal collections and, as such, today constitute a cornerstone of the British Library's collections.

Philip and Charles favored several illuminators who played a key role in the transformation of Flemish manuscript illumination during the 1470s. They included Simon Marmion (ca. 1425–1489), who had long been a favorite court painter and illuminator; and a much younger artist, the Vienna Master of Mary of Burgundy, whose earliest datable miniatures, from 1470 and shortly thereafter appear in books made for Charles the Bold (cat. nos. 16, 54).

As a painter himself, Marmion introduced to miniatures some of the luminous pictorial qualities seen in Flemish painting, while the Vienna Master introduced the pictorial values and powerful emotional expression of the Ghent painters, especially Joos van Ghent (act. 1460–75). The Vienna Master was also among the first to paint a border in the new style, with its strongly spatial character (ill. 19a). Perhaps led by his example, or under his influence, Flemish illuminators found a way of uniting the area of the decorated border and the miniature by imbuing both with complementary naturalistic forms. His greatest miniatures appear in the Hours of Mary of Burgundy (cat. no. 19), which was probably made for Charles the Bold's daughter, Mary, the heiress to the Burgundian domains. The 1470s saw the production of a number of highly luxurious manuscripts, primarily devotional books, featuring the new border style. Examples were made for members of the ducal family (see cat. nos. 19, 22, 44), in honor of them (cat. no. 23), or for their courtiers (cat. no. 20).

Charles the Bold sought to unite his vast domains in Flanders with his dynasty's older territories to the south by conquering the duchy of Lorraine and adjoining areas (fig. 1). Initially these efforts enjoyed some success, but they ultimately led to catastrophe. A series of defeats beginning in 1475 culminated in Charles's death on the battlefield at Nancy in January 1477. Since Charles had failed to produce a male heir, his territories passed to his daughter, the twenty-year-old Mary, and on her death in a riding accident five years later, they passed to her young son, Philip the Handsome (1478–1506). The era of Flanders as the base for Burgundian rule gradually came to an end.

FLEMISH ILLUMINATION AFTER CHARLES THE BOLD

The tragic and premature death of Duke Charles created political upheaval. The king of France immediately invaded the Low Countries to reclaim territory. Following Mary of Burgundy's untimely death in 1482, her husband, the Hapsburg prince Maximilian (1459–1519), archduke of Austria and later Holy Roman emperor, endured a stormy regency from 1482 to 1494 as the Flemish towns chafed against his rule. While the besieged Maximilian devoted his energies to keeping his head above water, sustained patronage of Flemish manuscripts no longer came from the ruling family.

Burgundian courtiers nevertheless continued to commission opulent secular manuscripts. Such distinguished bibliophiles as Engelbert II, count of Nassau and Vianden (1451–1504), and John II, lord of Oettingen and Flobecq (d. 1514), commissioned masterpieces such as the lavish illuminated copies of the

*North
Sea*

Leiden
Utrecht

Rhine

BRABANT

Antwerp

Bruges
Ghent
Mechelen
Calais
FLANDERS
Leuven
Cologne

Maas

St. Omer
Brussels
Lille
Tournai
Liège
HAINAUT
Namur
Hesdin
ARTOIS
Mons
Valenciennes
Cambrai

NASSAU

Moselle

Amiens
PICARDY

Luxembourg

Seine
Marne
Meuse

Paris

Nancy

FRANCE

LORRAINE

Loire

Dijon

BURGUNDY

0   50 mi
0   50 km

Roman de la rose (cat. no. 120) and Ludolph of Saxony's *Vie du Christ* (cat. no. 96).[14] Despite this high-caliber patronage, the place of secular manuscripts in the overall production of books dwindled in importance as the end of the century approached. The focus of illuminators had shifted back to devotional books, which had been a mainstay of Flemish production long before the era of Philip the Good. Yet the patronage of the duke, the duchess, and members of their household in the 1470s had a lasting impact.

During the years between the deaths of Duke Charles and Duchess Mary, interest in the new style of illumination grew rapidly. Not only were miniatures closely linked to the lustrous aesthetic of painting in oil, but they were sometimes derived directly from paintings by well-known artists such as Hugo van der Goes (1440–1482) and Dieric Bouts (1415–1475). Between the mid-1470s and 1483 illuminators quickly assembled a large body of patterns for miniatures. In addition to those by Van der Goes and Bouts, these patterns were designed by or derived from the Vienna Master, Marmion, Lieven van Lathem, and the Master of the Houghton Miniatures.[15] Thus the new style of illumination was rapidly subjected to the Flemish artists' powerful entrepreneurial instincts. The use of patterns on the part of illuminators was hardly new, but now they were used in a more systematic way. In fact, many of these new patterns came to be used for several generations or more, ensuring the longevity of the new fashion in Flemish illumination. Coupling the new style of naturalism in the borders with the miniatures themselves, the illuminators created a system of production of surpassing artistry. The luxurious and refined Hours of Mary of Burgundy and Maximilian (cat. no. 38) from the early 1480s, with its seventy-five miniatures, is just one example of this type of production in these years. Most of its miniatures appear to be derived from patterns, yet it is a dazzling and engaging work. Other examples include the two books of hours made for William Lord Hastings (ca. 1430–1483; cat. nos. 25, 41).[16]

With patterns likely available for the flowers, acanthus leaves, and other motifs in the borders as well, highly skilled artisans (including the Master of the First Prayer Book of Maximilian, his prolific workshop, and the Ghent Associates) began to produce sumptuous books of hours and devotional books for the European market. This practice of using patterns did not so much discourage innovation and creativity as help to meet the demand for richly decorated books in the new style without sacrificing the high level of quality that the most discerning patrons demanded. Indeed, several outstanding illuminators—including the Vienna Master, Simon Marmion, and the brilliant Master of the Houghton Miniatures—contributed completely original miniatures and borders to some of these books. The Houghton Master's brief career around 1480 rivals in invention that of the Vienna Master (see cat. nos. 32–35). Thus original and copy often graced the pages of the same book. Other established illuminators—such as the Master of the Dresden Prayer Book, whose witty style was largely independent of the new naturalism (see cat. no. 49)—adapted the borders and worked regularly in manuscripts where they were featured (see cat. nos. 20, 32, 33). By the mid-1480s virtually all Flemish illuminated manuscripts, no matter their quality or miniature style, featured the new illusionistic border with flowers and insects painted on solid-colored grounds.[17]

The 1480s saw several other major developments. First Simon Marmion, by then active for more than four decades, created his most innovative and influential cycle of miniatures, mostly half-length "close-ups," for a devotional book (cat. no. 93). Second, Gerard David settled in Bruges and started to execute both paintings and miniatures (cat. nos. 99–107). Third, a new generation of illuminators emerged, led by the Master of James IV of Scotland (cat. nos. 124–28), who might well be identifiable with Gerard Horenbout of Ghent (cat. nos. 129, 130). The Master of James IV was a brilliant narrative artist with a poet's eye for outdoor settings. He was active in Flanders for four decades, rarely relying on models, although when he did, as in his famous calendar for the Grimani Breviary (cat. no. 126), he completely reinvented his source.[18]

FLEMISH ILLUMINATION AND PATRONAGE UNDER THE HAPSBURGS

As noted earlier and as Scot McKendrick makes clear in his essay "Reviving the Past: Illustrated Manuscripts of Secular Vernacular Texts, 1467–1500" in this volume, the popularity of the luxury illuminated secular text declined with the demise of the Burgundian dynasty, though some of the most memorable examples appeared during the 1480s and 1490s with the new border style (see cat. nos. 86, 96, 104, 120). Certainly one factor in this decline was the rise of the printed book (see cat. nos. 67, 72). A princely library had become an essential instrument of the authority, learning, and splendor at rulers' courts across Renaissance Europe, and the printed book would increasingly play a prominent role within such libraries. Flemish illuminated manuscripts would nevertheless remain of importance at court for decades to come.

During the years of his marriage to Mary of Burgundy and subsequently, during his regency in the Netherlands (1482–94), Maximilian of Austria enjoyed intimate, ongoing involvement with Charles's

Figure 2
Hapsburg Empire under
Charles V, ca. 1556

courtiers. He certainly would have beheld the splendor of the ducal and courtiers' libraries. He also acquired over the years a few superb Flemish illuminated manuscripts (including cat. nos. 38, 104). The luxury volumes he commissioned much later to glorify his reign—most notably the *Theuerdank*, *Der Weisskunig*, and *The Triumphs of Maximilian*—were published by the great German printers and illustrated by Germans: Albrecht Dürer (1471–1528), Hans Burgkmair (1473–1531), and others.[19] Since Maximilian returned to his German territories at the end of his regency, it is perhaps inevitable that he would turn to the established German printing industry to create the volumes particularly suited to the Hapsburg legacy. The ability to make multiple copies of any one luxury book also enabled him to reach a much wider audience than had his Burgundian forebears.

Nevertheless the new tradition of Flemish illumination prospered, largely in the form of increasingly lavish devotional books and breviaries. Two ruling households, their wealth augmented by the bounty of the age of exploration, quickly stepped into the fray in the closing years of the fifteenth century. They were the Spanish and Portuguese monarchs and their courtiers. The Spanish nobility had long been enamored of Flemish art, importing not only major works by such prominent artists as Rogier van der Weyden, luxurious manuscripts by Willem Vrelant (1430–1481/82), and tapestries but also works by Flemish (and other northern European) painters, illuminators, sculptors, and architects.[20] Part of the great wealth of the major Castilian cities, such as Burgos and Valladolid, was derived from the wool trade and other commerce with the Low Countries. Already by the middle of the fifteenth century, the splendor of the Burgundian court provided a model for the Spanish nobility. The marriage of the children of Isabella of Castile and Ferdinand of Aragon (Joanna and Juan) to those of Mary of Burgundy and Maximilian (Philip the Handsome and Margaret of Austria), only served to heighten this predilection. Two of the finest Flemish manuscripts from the decades just before and after 1500 were made for Isabella, one apparently presented by her ambassador Francisco de Rojas in 1497 (cat. no. 100), the other somewhat later, a book of hours, perhaps also commissioned for presentation to her (cat. no. 105). In addition, she drew to Spain, among other artists, the Flemish painter Juan de Flandes (act. 1496–1519), who was perhaps also an illuminator, and the Flemish-trained painter Michael Sittow (ca. 1469–1525). A number of other particularly lavish books of hours produced around the turn of the century were made for Isabella's daughter Joanna of Castile (see cat. no. 114), consort of Philip the Handsome (r. 1494–1506). He assumed the rule of the Netherlands upon Maximilian's return to Germany. Further lavish books were made for Spanish patrons who have not been firmly identified (e.g., cat. nos. 109 and the Rothschild Book of Hours).[21]

The Master of James IV of Scotland, who contributed a cycle of miniatures to Isabella's breviary, was one of the artists who benefited from Iberian patronage.[22] Other books that he and his workshop likely illuminated for Iberian patrons include a book of hours (cat. no. 109) and the little-studied prayer book in Lisbon made for a member of the Portuguese royal family (Museu Nacional de Arte Antiga, Ms. 13). It was probably during the first decades of the sixteenth century, under such patronage, that the Master of James IV explored the potential of illusionism on the page and found new ways to integrate miniature, border, and text (see the Lisbon prayer book and cat. no. 124).

Born and raised in Ghent, the Hapsburg emperor Charles V (r. 1519–56), son of Philip and Joanna, continued to rule the Netherlands (see fig. 2). He did so, however, primarily from Spain and largely through first his aunt Margaret of Austria and subsequently his sister Mary of Hungary. A splendid rosarium illuminated by Simon Bening (1483/84–1561), the leading artist of the third generation of Flemish illuminators, was made for Charles or his son Philip (cat. no. 156). Charles's consort, Isabella of Portugal, had a book of hours with miniatures by Bening (cat. no. 151). One of Charles's courtiers probably commissioned one of Bening's finest books of hours (cat. no. 154). A distinctive Mannerist school of Flemish illumination is linked with the patronage of Charles V from the 1520s through the 1540s (e.g., cat. nos. 166, 167).

The ongoing connection between manuscript illumination and Burgundian traditions is exemplified not only by such books of hours and breviaries but also by Bening's commission from the Order of the Golden Fleece of a copy of its statutes (Madrid, Instituto Don Juan de Valencia).[23] It is the most beautiful of the many copies created by Flemish illuminators over the previous hundred years.

The Portuguese royal family also had married into the Burgundian line, having provided a duchess, Isabella (1397–1471), for Philip the Good. The humanist Vasco da Lucena (c. 1435–1512) was a courtier of Isabella's and the author of texts that were favored for luxury production (cat. nos. 54, 63). He owned a painting by Simon Marmion.[24] The Portuguese interest in manuscript illumination accelerated by the 1490s, part of a larger and expanding taste for Flemish tapestries, paintings, and other works of art. Two of the most luxurious breviaries of the turn of the century were made for Portuguese patrons (cat. nos. 91, 92), and one of them quickly became the property of Queen Eleanor of Portugal (1458–1525). Less than a generation later, the first truly sumptuous commission received by the young Bening derived from the Sá family of Portugal (cat. no. 140). This was the first of a series of major commissions Bening enjoyed from high-ranking Portuguese, including the royal family, over many decades (see cat. nos. 147, 150). This generous patronage, which stemmed from the interrelationship among the courts and the upper nobility of Spain and Portugal, would result in many of the most splendid Flemish illuminated manuscripts produced during the remainder of the century. Elsewhere, within the Hapsburgs' sphere of influence, Cardinal Albrecht of Brandenburg (1490–1545), a great prince and voracious art patron, commissioned several costly devotional books. One of these, among the finest Flemish manuscripts of the 1520s, was by Bening himself (cat. no. 145). During the sixteenth century most of the great commissions for Flemish manuscript illumination came from outside Burgundian Flanders.

Simon Bening was innovative in the art of narrative; in the development of new formats for illumination, such as the triptych and quadriptych (see cat. nos. 146, 157); and in the depiction of nature. He was also a skilled portraitist. In these diverse areas his art seemed to grow continuously, from his earliest works (see cat. nos. 139, 140) through the end of his career (see cat. nos. 159, 161). His illumination reflected recent developments in the art of painting, as that of his forebears had, and like the art of his forebears, it gave something back, especially in the arena of landscape painting. By midcentury Bening was the last Flemish illuminator of the first rank who was still working.

Ultimately the printing press brought about the decline of Flemish manuscript illumination. That this sad result took nearly a century to achieve attests to the continued vitality of the medium of manuscript illumination in Flanders from the 1470s through the middle of the sixteenth century. With the death of Simon Bening in 1561 the tradition of Flemish manuscript illumination was no longer an important part of Netherlandish artistic culture. Yet it produced one more gifted figure, George Hoefnagel (1545–1600/1601), a full two generations after Bening. Hoefnagel's relatively circumscribed activity as an illuminator appears to have been largely at the pleasure of a Hapsburg emperor, Rudolf II. Thus Flemish manuscript illumination remained an art of the court even in its waning years.

HISTORIOGRAPHY AND ORGANIZATION

The literature on the period of Flemish manuscript illumination covered by this exhibition is staggering in its volume and continues to expand at a breathtaking pace, as the bibliography at the end of this book attests.[25] Flemish manuscript illumination from the period discussed here has been the subject of intensive research and scrutiny since the mid-nineteenth century. During the second half of the nineteenth century, scholarly investigation of the Grimani Breviary led to an interest in those manuscripts related to it artistically.[26] In the same decades, archival research in Bruges, Ghent, Antwerp, and other centers revealed the names, guild memberships, patrons, and some of the artistic projects of Simon Marmion, Alexander Bening, Gerard Horenbout, Simon Bening, and other illuminators.[27] Indeed, research on the art of this period has focused strongly on areas of traditional art-historical concern: connoisseurship, the identification and localization of artists, the reconstruction of their careers, and the matching of artists mentioned in surviving documents with specific works and even entire oeuvres.[28]

The intent of this catalogue is to review critically what has come before, assess the progress of scholarly research, and build on the most secure foundations. Exploiting the full range of methodologies employed over the past two generations, we have brought to bear the evidence of codicology, textual transmission, liturgical content, and, for the knotty problems of dating, costumes depicted in the illuminations. To achieve a fresh appraisal of the evidence available, the authors have endeavored to examine personally all the manuscripts and other works of art illustrated here.[29] With the aid of his expansive computer database, John Plummer analyzed the calendars of most books of hours in the exhibition to identify evidence of shared exemplars that would assist in grouping and localizing them. Margaret Scott has provided evidence for the dating of images and books based on costume.

Given the wide-ranging investigation of individual manuscripts and artists from the period, it is remarkable that no single study has attempted a proper overview of the period considered here. Both Paul Durrieu and Friedrich Winkler treated it within the broader parameters of the entirety of fifteenth- and sixteenth-century Flemish manuscript illumination.[30] More recently, Maurits Smeyers addressed the period within the context of an epic survey of the history of Flemish manuscript illumination, from the eighth to the sixteenth century, organized under diverse themes.[31] L. M. J. Delaissé, in the exhibition of 1959 and its influential accompanying catalogue, focused on the era of Philip the Good, or that immediately preceding the period considered here.[32]

The present volume is conceived as a sequel to Delaissé's catalogue. Delaissé focused attention on the considerable interest of secular manuscript illumination and other deluxe bibliophile volumes created for members of the court after the death of Philip the Good, especially during the 1470s.[33] In his introductory essay, McKendrick explores this important topic in much greater depth and draws particular attention to the extraordinary and often poorly studied examples in the British Library, many of which were passed down to it directly through the descendants of the most prominent patron of such manuscripts, Edward IV.

Like the catalogue of the 1959 exhibition, this book is organized roughly chronologically. It is divided into five parts, including one for works of art that largely predate the time frame of the exhibition but announce some of its themes. Unlike the earlier catalogue, which organized its material around workshops of book production and their locations, this publication is organized by illuminator. As a number of illuminators enjoyed extended careers—including Marmion, the Master of the Dresden Prayer Book, and the Master of James IV of Scotland—their activity is represented in more than one part of the book. Following in the spirit of Delaissé's inquiry, an appendix by Richard Gay, with an introduction by McKendrick, discusses some of the scribes whose work is represented here.

Other studies, such as those of Otto Pächt and G. I. Lieftinck, have focused on a much narrower time frame of about fifteen to twenty years, circa 1470–90, during which the new style emerged.[34] Indeed, the bias of research on Flemish manuscripts in general has been weighted heavily toward the first decades of the new style. This exhibition argues for a reassessment of the entire period, based on the intensive research on its early decades that has dominated scholarship of the last generation and also on the belief that some achievements of the sixteenth century have not received due recognition, mostly because a number of major works came to light only recently. This exhibition endeavors both to demonstrate the importance of secular and other bibliophile manuscripts and to illustrate the many ways in which illumination remained a continuously inventive and significant art form well into the sixteenth century.

Modern criticism has viewed the art of the Master of Mary of Burgundy as setting the standard against which all subsequent Flemish illumination should be measured. A reevaluation of the artist over the past several decades has led to a diminished critical appraisal, however, both aesthetically and in terms of invention, of a significant component of his oeuvre.[35] At the same time scholars have uncovered several of his works only recently, including some introduced in this exhibition (cat. nos. 16, 54). Even as this catalogue was being written, Anne Korteweg rediscovered one of these and kindly brought it to our attention (cat. no. 17). We have also adopted Bodo Brinkmann's proposal to rename the artist the Vienna Master of Mary of Burgundy. Thomas Kren identified another illuminator, the Master of the Houghton Miniatures, as belonging to the new generation whose art was strongly linked to the aesthetic of the Ghent painters. An artist with a very brief career, he is named after the Emerson-White Hours (cat. no. 32) in the Houghton Library. His work shows exceptional originality, and his artistic inventions were influential.

Viewing manuscript illumination of this period largely through the filter of the great Flemish painters has obscured its accomplishments and its place within the history of Flemish art. In an age of public museums, where paintings are more readily and regularly displayed than manuscripts, and within a discipline long influenced by Italian painter and art historian Giorgio Vasari (1511–1574), modern art-historical scholarship has shown an overwhelming bias toward the history of painting on panel and canvas. While it is true that Hugo van der Goes, Joos van Ghent, and other painters, such as Dieric Bouts, strongly influenced the compositions of Flemish illuminators, the relationship was more complex and more dynamic than has generally been recognized. Historically artists working in the diverse media that formed the full range of medieval art had always engaged in mutual exchange of ideas and artistic models. Without denying the influence of painters on illuminators, which is well documented, Thomas Kren and Maryan W. Ainsworth, in their introductory essay, "Illuminators and Painters: Artistic Exchanges and Interrelationships," clarify the varied ways in which illumination provided sources and points of departures for painters, whether in style, composition, individual motifs, subject matter, or through an artist's practice of both media. Accordingly, the catalogue includes paintings and drawings independent of manuscript illumination to the extent that they are pertinent to the understanding of the illuminators, their originality, and their working methods. Kren and Ainsworth reconsider some of the painters who executed illuminations, such as Petrus Christus and Simon Marmion. Ainsworth also closely examines the work of Gerard David, a master whose art comfortably straddles the two disciplines. Although he executed a relatively small number of miniatures, his oeuvre exemplifies this vital interchange of artistic ideas.

Within this context Catherine Reynolds, in her essay, "Illuminators and the Painters' Guilds," casts a fresh eye on the rules of the painters' guilds and the role of the Bruges confraternity of book producers. Reynolds offers fresh insights into the status of illuminators, the interrelationship among the arts, and the limits on trade. She reexamines widely held assumptions about the commerce in illuminations, in particular the single-leaf miniature, the staple of devotional books.

Other recent advances in scholarship include Brinkmann's demonstration of the originality and high level of artistic achievement of the Master of the Dresden Prayer Book, long regarded as a secondary figure.[36] His influential study of this artist casts its net widely over the period, raising broader questions concerning artistic innovation, connoisseurship, and dating in the 1470s. François Avril and Nicole Reynaud have advanced our understanding of the illuminators of northern France working in the Burgundian orbit.[37] Janet Backhouse's recent discovery of the scintillating Hours of Charlotte of Bourbon-Montpensier (cat. no. 44), in which the Dresden Master was the lead artist, has also prompted further thought on several key issues. As the earliest known manuscript to include illusionistic borders in the new style (datable before 1476), the Bourbon-Montpensier Hours challenges assumptions about the origins of the new border. We are fortunate to be able to display this book of hours publicly for the first time. Another book of hours that dates from the mid-1470s (cat. no. 37) suggests that Marmion's contribution was integral to the emergence of the new style. Long recorded, but rarely seen by specialists and poorly published, this manuscript is discussed here in detail for the first time.

For the sixteenth century, recent major discoveries concerning the Master of James IV of Scotland (including cat. nos. 124, 125, 127) have greatly enriched our understanding of his originality and of the duration of his activity in Flanders.[38] The exhibition also introduces several little-known manuscripts by his important follower, the Master of the David Scenes in the Grimani Breviary (cat. nos. 115, 116). Several sixteenth-century illuminators overlooked by Friederich Winkler and Georges Dogaer are defined here for the first time by Elizabeth Morrison, who also helps to clarify the place of Mannerism in Flemish illumination of the time. In recent years Judith Testa and Thomas Kren have reconstructed several key books by Simon Bening, a number of which have been disassembled over the centuries. The exhibition offers an in-depth survey of Bening's lengthy and highly varied career.

Finally, the reader familiar with the period will note that the phrase "Ghent-Bruges school" has generally been avoided here. It is true that Bruges and Ghent remained major centers of production and played a central role in the birth of the new style. It is also clear that they were not alone as centers of artistic creativity and that a number of significant illuminators came from other towns or created books in collaboration with artisans from other locations. Many of the finest books from the period were produced in a cosmopolitan way with a scribe in one center and an illuminator in another, as, for example, David Aubert in Ghent and Marmion in Valenciennes for Margaret of York's *Les Visions du chevalier Tondal* (cat. no. 14). Her husband's documented prayer book (cat. no. 16) featured illuminations by Van Lathem from Antwerp and script by Nicolas Spierinc from Ghent. Remarkably, the Trivulzio Hours (cat. no. 17) includes the work of Marmion, Van Lathem, and Spierinc between the same covers, artisans from three different towns represented in a single book. Although Marmion resided in Valenciennes, he belonged to the painters' guild in Tournai, a center whose connection to the new style of book illumination otherwise remains to be demonstrated.[39] Yet given the mobility of the Burgundian court, it is not surprising that such a situation arose.[40]

In this context of ongoing interurban collaboration, the international case of the Genealogy of Dom Fernando of Portugal is compelling. An artist residing in Portugal, António de Holanda (1518–1551), supplied drawings that Bening illuminated in Bruges (cat. no. 147). The Portuguese trade secretary in Antwerp, Damiao de Gois, coordinated the work (cat. no. 147). He not only provided historical content and guidance to the draftsman but also ensured that the drawings found their way to the illuminator. A form of interurban production appears to have been common practice for the most luxurious Flemish manuscripts of the period, but collaboration on manuscript production across the continent also occurred (see also cat. no. 151).[41]

In light of the many recent discoveries and of international scholarly research of the past half century, the time has come to reconsider some of the larger questions. What is the contribution of the Vienna Master of Mary of Burgundy? Did he act alone in the development of the new style? Did he invent the new style of border? Which artists made original contributions in the succeeding generations? What is the relationship between painters and illuminators? What is the place of copying and imitation? What is the real contribution of Flemish manuscript illumination to the history of art of this period? Here we argue that the origins of the new style are more complex than was once thought and attributable to more than one master. Moreover, with the establishment of the new style, the rapid development of a large body of patterns—literally scores of them from the mid-1470s to the early 1480s—contributed greatly to its success. Even the generation of these patterns was a collaborative undertaking. It facilitated the production of exceptionally lavish books at a very high level of quality in an efficient and reasonably systematic manner. For the next several decades most of the truly lavish books were collaborative productions involving three or more gifted masters with wholly distinctive styles.

The ensuing decades show continuous innovation in style and iconography along with the use and reuse of patterns in inventive and often surprising ways. Illuminators of the sixteenth century also broke new ground in the depiction of landscape, in narrative, and in the domain of the portrait miniature. Right up to its last years, Flemish manuscript illumination exhibited a dynamic relationship to tradition and to innovation, often looking backward, always looking ahead.

Notes

1. The carefully arranged flowers and other naturalia anticipate the emergence of the Baroque genre of still-life painting.

2. In this volume the term Flanders is used in the broadest sense, to refer to the larger Burgundian holdings in the southern Netherlands and northern France.

3. Blockmans and Prevenier 1999: 106–7, 188.

4. De Winter 1985.

5. Blockmans 1998: 7, 10–15, although his calculations are probably conservative, not taking into account evidence of all the inventories.

6. Blockmans 1998: 15.

7. Because of their fragile nature, illuminated manuscripts may have been reserved for display to a more select audience than were tapestries, plates, and other luxurious objects that were subject to inclusion in public ceremony. The audience for the display of luxurious books was relatively circumscribed but powerful and politically significant nonetheless.

8. In the *Chroniques de Hainaut*, Van der Weyden portrayed these high-ranking officials and family members, as did Marmion in the frontispiece miniature of the *Grandes Chroniques de France* (Saint Petersburg, National Library of Russia, Ms. Erm. 88, fol. 1; Paris 1993: 81).

9. Smeyers et al. 1993: 45–65; Louvain 1993.

10. France remained a great center for manuscript illumination throughout the fifteenth century; see Paris 1993.

11. See Thomas Kren and Maryan W. Ainsworth, "Illuminators and Painters: Artistic Exchanges and Interrelationships," (this volume).

12. About 400 of these books survive today, 247 in the Bibliothèque royale de Belgique (Blockmans 1998: 7).

13. See Brussels 1977a. Charles commissioned many fewer books than his father did; the length of his reign was only a bit more than a fifth of that of his father. Moreover Philip began commissioning luxury books seriously only at the age of about fifty, while Charles died when he was forty-four.

14. Both of these books contain texts copied from printed books. See cat. nos. 96, 120.

15. For examples, see cat. nos. 20, 25, 37, 38, 41.

16. The Madrid Hastings Hours likely includes both entirely original miniatures and miniatures based on patterns (see cat. no. 25). The illuminators of this book and the Voustre Demeure Hours (cat. no. 20) show how great talents could use strong patterns in highly original ways.

17. Although illuminators of secular manuscripts had also used pattern drawings (cf. Van Buren 1983: 57, 61, 65), this was much less common than it was in devotional books during this period.

18. There he took the courtly, elegant calendar of the renowned *Très Riches Heures* of the duke of Berry, perhaps the most celebrated cycle of miniatures of the later Middle Ages, and turned it to something entirely his own—earthy, picturesque, and direct. On the presence of the *Très Riches Heures* in the Netherlands and the artist's access to it, see the biography of the Master of James IV of Scotland, part 4, this volume.

19. Landau and Parshall 1994: 206–11.

20. On Spanish patronage of Flemish arts and artists, see Yarza Luaces, in Toledo 1992: 133–50, and Yarza Luaces 1993.

21. Trenkler 1979. Often called the Rothschild Prayer Book, it is in fact a book of hours.

22. On this illuminator's connection to the Hapsburg court of Margaret of Austria, regent of the Netherlands, see the biography of Gerard Horenbout, part 5, this volume.

23. Bening appears to have been paid for this manuscript in 1538, as recorded in the Chambre des Comptes at Lille. See Hulin de Loo 1925: 104–5. It was created following the twentieth assembly of the Order of the Golden Fleece, convened by Emperor Charles V at Tournai in 1531. See also Valencia 1999.

24. At his death in 1512 he bequeathed a *Virgin and Child* by Simon Marmion to the hospital in Louvain (De Ram 1861, 2: 870).

25. Following our use of the term Flanders (see note 2), the phrase "Flemish illumination" is used to describe not only manuscripts produced solely in Bruges, Ghent, or other towns of the county of Flanders but also miniatures and books produced entirely or in part in such centers as Valenciennes, Antwerp, and Brussels.

26. Michiels 1845–49, 2: 571–75; Reichhart 1852; Zanotto 1862; Förster 1867; Chmelarz 1889; Durrieu 1891; Destrée 1894a; Destrée 1894b; Coggiola 1908.

27. De Busscher 1859b; Weale 1864–65a; Pinchart 1865; De Busscher 1866; Weal 1872–73a; Hénault 1907.

28. Antoine de Schryver has made a number of significant identifications of illuminated manuscripts described in the Burgundian ducal accounts. See, for example, de Schryver 1957; de Schryver 1969b; de Schryver 1979b; and cat. no. 16.

29. We have not seen the Trivulzio Hours (cat. no. 17), which came to our attention after the writing of the catalogue was well under way.

30. Durrieu 1921a; Durrieu 1927; Winkler 1925. See also Dogaer 1987a, an attempt to update Winkler 1925; and Cambridge 1993.

31. Smeyers 1998.

32. Brussels 1959.

33. Here we distinguish secular volumes and learned religious tracts as bibliophile works, in contrast to devotional books, which appealed to collectors of artistic objects and to collectors of more modest means who might possess no other book than their own book of hours. The great court bibliophiles collected both, often including devotional books of great quality.

34. Pächt 1948; Lieftinck 1969.

35. For example, Lieftinck 1969; Van Buren 1975; Brinkmann 1997; and Brinkmann 1998: 133–47.

36. Brinkmann 1997.

37. Paris 1993: 71–103, 389–92.

38. See also under the biography of the Master of James IV of Scotland, part 4, this volume.

39. Vanwijnsberghe 2001: 25–29.

40. Cf., for example, Charron and Gil 1999.

41. Dürer met with Gerard Horenbout, a member of the Ghent painter's guild, who owned property there, in Antwerp. Horenbout was also the court artist of the regent Margaret of Austria, who resided in Mechelen (Winkler 1943: 55). The importance of Antwerp in particular for "Ghent-Bruges" manuscript illumination, also suggested by the growing understanding of the influential role of the Antwerp illuminator Lieven van Lathem, deserves closer study. See also under cat. no. 139.

ILLUMINATORS AND THE PAINTERS' GUILDS

CATHERINE REYNOLDS

The records generated by the painters' guilds are an important source of information on painters, illuminators, and the relationship between them. Because of religious upheavals and the long series of European wars fought over the Netherlands, records and works have survived in a particularly fragmentary and random fashion. Although books have a much higher survival rate than paintings, surviving documents and surviving objects seldom mesh. The especially rich Tournai archives survived until 1940, and earlier publications preserve much material on the painters' guild there and its members. Because of the relative wealth of documentary evidence, Tournai is frequently cited in this discussion, based on published records, yet what Tournai illuminators produced during the century following 1460 seems not to have been of high quality and is not represented in this exhibition.[1] When studying guild regulations such as the particularly informative set from Tournai in 1480, it is important to remember that regulations are framed to achieve a certain state of affairs and not to record what was actually happening. Although legal records can be a better indicator of the guilds' success in realizing their aims, lawsuits inevitably document conflict and so are unlikely to reveal the amicable cooperation and fruitful interchange between painters and illuminators that surely also existed.

Interpretation of documentary evidence is often difficult and sometimes has to remain tentative; crucial phrases are given in the original language in the notes to this essay so the validity of the translations can be assessed. This is particularly important for the Confraternity (Ghilde) of Saint John the Evangelist, founded by the book artisans in Bruges by 1454, since it was a religious confraternity honoring Saint John the Evangelist and not a trade guild, as it is usually represented by art historians. No guilds exclusively for the book trades, embracing scribes and illuminators, are known in the Netherlands in the fifteenth century, probably because writing and illumination were too widely practiced to be easily susceptible to the monopolistic control on which guild authority depended. With the exception of Bruges, it seems to have been only in the second half of the fifteenth century that painters' guilds attempted to bring illuminators under their control. The Bruges painters' guild, which was challenging illuminators from at least 1403, was perhaps activated earlier than its neighbors because of the profits to be made from the town's flourishing export trade in illuminations and illuminated books.

The trade in illuminations was a particular feature of the efficient production that evolved in the Netherlands to supply the huge markets at home and abroad for standard devotional texts, particularly books of hours. Instead of leaving spaces for miniatures on leaves with text, as was done for books not based on the liturgy (e.g., cat. nos. 54, 60, 62; and see Scot McKendrick, "Reviving the Past: Illustrated Manuscripts of Secular Vernacular Texts, 1467–1500," this volume), artists prefabricated miniatures on blank

SIMON MARMION
*Saint Luke Painting
the Virgin* (detail, ill. 12a)

single sheets to be inserted wherever a book's producer or purchaser wished. So entrenched was this method of production that even specially commissioned prayer books with specially commissioned miniatures usually have the miniatures on inserted leaves (e.g., cat. nos. 25, 37, 41). These single-leaf miniatures particularly aroused the painters' concerns because they could be used in other ways, beyond their insertion in books, and so compete with the painters' market in independent paintings on panel or cloth. Illuminated sheets were also specifically designed for independent use. Some independent illuminations were principally text, some combined text and image, and others were purely pictorial. This last category again encroached on the painters' territory.

The expansionist painters' guilds were confronting illuminators just as printing was gradually undermining the manuscript book. Woodcuts and then engravings imitated and ultimately replaced independent illuminations and fulfilled the functions found for single-leaf miniatures outside books; printers learned how to articulate texts without colored headings and initials and to illustrate them with woodcuts or metalcuts instead of miniatures. Having previously produced work at all price levels, from cheap color-washed drawings on paper (fig. 3) to lavish miniatures in gold and expensive pigments on fine parchment, creative illuminators were driven by the printers to concentrate on the luxury end of the market, where, for a limited workforce, fame and fortune remained possible. At the other extreme, those with less talent and ambition could make a modest living coloring prints. The middle market had virtually disappeared. By the end of the period covered by the exhibition, the printer and the painter had left little room for the illuminator.

THE PAINTERS' GUILDS

In 1480 the painters' guild of Tournai stated that new regulations were required because its members were suffering from competition from those outside the town and outside the guild who were selling shoddy products and, moreover, importing works made elsewhere for sale. Good workers were therefore leaving, and profits that could be made in Tournai were going elsewhere.[2] These were the concerns common to the trade or craft guilds that had developed in Netherlandish towns from the thirteenth century. In addition to protecting their members from outside competition—whether from fellow citizens, foreigners, or foreign imports—the guilds tried to eliminate unfair competition between members and to ensure a good reputation for their products. Only a master could make and sell on his own account or employ others to make and sell in his name, and to become a master, it was usually necessary to be a burgess of the town, to have completed an apprenticeship, and to have paid an entry fee to the guild. *Burgess* expresses the terms *bourgeois* and *poorter* better than *citizen*, with its connotations of all members of a community, since only the burgess enjoyed full municipal rights, usually participation in government, judicial and fiscal benefits, and freedom to trade. Other dwellers in the town, perhaps the majority, were described as natives or residents depending on origin. Fees to become a burgess or to enter a trade guild were usually less for natives of the town or, as in the Bruges and Lille painters' guilds, for those who had served their apprenticeship in the guild.[3] Restrictions on the right to sell were removed or weakened during the free fairs, annual or twice-yearly events in the larger towns.

Exemption from guild control was open to clerics and to those employed full-time by the ruler. The Bruges painters' guild in 1444 exempted from the yearly fee journeymen employed by the duke of Burgundy, as count of Flanders. (A journeyman was a qualified craftsman working for a master from lack of finance or inclination to set up as a master himself.) In 1473 the guild accepted that Charles the Bold's painter, Pierre Coustain, was exempt from membership.[4] In Ghent the painter and illuminator Lieven van Lathem succeeded in obtaining letters from Philip the Good demanding exemption from the balance of his mastership fee, owed to the guild from 1454, and that the installments already paid should be returned. The guild agreed in 1459, with evident ill feeling, since Van Lathem and his descendants were banned from ever becoming members in the future.[5] While membership offered the advantages of corporate strength and protection, there were balancing disadvantages of regulation and cost. Mastership would be necessary in every town where the painter wanted to work or sell his work in his own name, which is perhaps why Simon Marmion, resident in Valenciennes, became a member of the painters' guild of Tournai. It was especially expensive to become a master of the Ghent guild, even for a native, who paid the equivalent of about 288 days' wages of a journeyman painter, whereas in Bruges the full fee was equivalent to about 125 days' wages.[6] The practitioners of crafts not controlled by guilds had the benefits of a freer market to compensate for the lack of protection. While economists still debate whether freedom or control most favors prosperity, it is clear that Netherlandish artists, whether helped or hindered by the guild system, were successfully dominating Europe with their products.

The guilds were run by the masters, whose elected officials framed and enforced the guild regulations in conjunction with the town government. Inevitably the masters benefited more than the salaried journeymen. Self-interest was most blatant in the reduced fees paid by masters' sons to become masters. Since it was less expensive for a master's son to serve an apprenticeship with his father, the incentives for professions to become hereditary were considerable, as the many dynasties of painters and illuminators demonstrate. Requirements for becoming a master were central to guild regulations, which usually covered training and apprenticeship, the employment of journeymen, marketing, and standards of materials and workmanship. The Bruges painters' guild seems to have been especially jealous of its rights, even asserting its authority outside the town when it fought a legal battle to make painters in Sluys observe the edict of 1441 that limited their numbers. In September 1487 their costly lawsuit had already lasted nine years and seemed likely to last a lot longer.[7] This is one demonstrable instance of a regulation being a misleading guide to what was actually happening.

Although it is usual to refer to painters' guilds, the painters were never sufficiently numerous to constitute guilds on their own. They are found with various crafts—allied by materials, tools, or skills—in combinations that varied from town to town.[8] In Tournai, for instance, the other major craft was that of the glaziers, as was the case in Antwerp, Bruges, Brussels, Lille, and Mons; painters were associated with wood sculptors in Antwerp, Bruges, Ghent, Ypres, and Mechelen. The comparatively new trade of printmaking was included in the Antwerp guild regulations of 1442, while the departure of the Antwerp goldsmiths by that year for their own guild enhanced the painters' importance among the remaining crafts. This seems part of a general trend. In Bruges the guild of image makers and saddlers was increasingly referred to as the guild of painters and saddlers, once the image cutters, or wood carvers, had left in 1432 for the carpenters' guild. In 1462 the other crafts in the guild—cloth painters, glaziers, and mirror makers as well as saddlers—had to call in the town government to stop the painters from monopolizing the guild offices.[9] The painters' predominance is evident in the coat of arms generally used by painters' guilds—three silver shields on an azure field—and the guilds frequently had as their patron Saint Luke, painter of the Virgin.

TRADE GUILDS AND CONFRATERNITIES

The guilds fostered their members' spiritual welfare and expressed their corporate identity by financing a chapel where masses were offered for the members, living and dead. In Antwerp the painters were among the trade guilds who contributed to the rebuilding of the Church of Our Lady and by 1442 had there a richly decorated chapel of Saint Luke.[10] In Bruges in 1450 the painters' guild was sufficiently wealthy to erect an independent chapel near the ducal palace of the Prinsenhof. This chapel of Saint Luke and Saint Eligius, the patron of goldsmiths, provides striking instances of the integration of Netherlandish nobles into urban life. In 1455 Philip the Good moved the daily mass for his household there at the request of the painters and of "some of our very special servants."[11] From 1468 one ducal servant, Guillaume de Montbléru, councillor and maître d'hotel of Charles the Bold, was buried there in a handsome tomb, so an armored knight lay in effigy in a trade guild's chapel.[12] An epitaph commemorated de Montbléru and his bequests, and he was recorded in the painters' obituary, as was another Burgundian courtier, Jean de Montferrand, councillor and chamberlain to Philip the Good and Charles the Bold (see cat. nos. 69, 70).[13] Although de Montbléru commissioned paintings and de Montferrand owned illustrated copies of his own poetry and of Boccaccio's *Fall of Princes*,[14] it was probably the chapel's location that attracted their benefactions. De Montferrand's house, purchased in 1469, adjoined the painters' hall and had an oratory opening into the chapel, presumably reached by a gallery, since it necessitated exterior columns. A similar, though grander arrangement survives between Louis of Gruuthuse's palace and oratory and the Church of Our Lady.[15]

Some religious confraternities were associated with particular crafts but had a legal identity independent of any trade guild. In Valenciennes, where a guild of painters and related crafts existed by 1367, the painters, embroiderers, and sculptors in 1462 established a confraternity dedicated to the Virgin and Saint Luke in the chapel behind the high altar of Notre-Dame-la-Grande. Simon Marmion painted the altarpiece, which is inadequately described as including grisailles that looked like real statues and a candle that seemed truly to burn.[16] Craftsmen who were not united in a trade guild could also form a confraternity. The Confraternity of Saint John the Evangelist, founded by members of the Bruges book trades at the Abbey of Eeckhout by May 1454, falls within this category: when they founded the confraternity, the book traders were plying a craft but did not have and did not acquire the status of a trade guild.[17]

In Bruges *ambocht* was the usual word for a trade guild. The painters' guild allocated its fees between the *ambocht*, meaning its professional functions, and the *gilde*, meaning its religious functions. In 1457, to ensure the funding of the Confraternity of Saint John, those plying the book crafts—that is, scribes, illuminators, bookbinders, and painters of miniatures—obtained a ruling from the town government that in future all practitioners of these crafts must become members of the confraternity.[18] From about 1470 Saint Luke was being honored as a copatron, perhaps indicative of the influence of the illuminators within the confraternity. Successful lawsuits extended obligatory membership to those dealing in printed books in 1489 and to schoolteachers in 1557.[19] Despite the obligatory membership, the confraternity had none of the regulatory functions of a trade guild, so that the court illuminators Dreux Jean and Philippe de Mazerolles apparently enrolled willingly, in contrast to the court painter Pierre Coustain's successful refusal to join the painters' guild. Although all those in the book trades had to belong, members were not necessarily masters of a trade guild, and so no qualifications for mastership were laid down, just as apprentices had to join without there being any rules on apprenticeship as such. In 1532, when Jan van Dale was prosecuted for not paying two apprentices' dues, he argued that they were not true apprentices since they had brought no premium and had not been placed with him by a responsible adult. His defense was not questioned, but he was ordered to pay anyway because the sum was not large and it was all for divine service.[20] Trade guilds kept records of apprentices because it was essential to certify that apprenticeships had been duly served to establish eligibility for mastership. The confraternity clearly had no official records of apprenticeship, which would have settled the question, only records of what dues had been paid to fund its chapel and its services.

Anyone could join the confraternity by paying the appropriate fee, including Philibert Poitevin, "barber of my lord of Montferrand," in 1471–72.[21] While Poitevin possibly shared de Montferrand's interest in books, he perhaps acted from devotion to Saint John, since he paid only a half fee. By the sixteenth century the nonprofessionals were being termed "brothers of devotion" or "of grace," at the half fee also required of women, but it is clear that the category, if not the name, had existed much earlier.[22] The distinction between the two sorts of membership did not make the professionals a trade guild. When the Bruges painters complained about the book men in 1457, the dispute was not between the officials of two trade guilds but between, on the one side, the officials of the painters' guild and, on the other side, Maurice de Hac "and others practicing the book trades, as scribes, illuminators and makers of little pictures in books or rolls," a necessary circumlocution because there was no corporate body of book traders equivalent to the painters' guild. Indeed, during this lawsuit, the book traders successfully submitted to the aldermen that the book trades were a *poorters neeringhe*—that is, a craft free of regulation by a trade guild, for which the only qualification was to be a *poorter*, or burgess.[23]

ILLUMINATION OUTSIDE THE GUILDS

Illuminators remained largely outside guild control until the second half of the fifteenth century, and several reasons for this can be suggested. In the Netherlands, where levels of literacy were exceptionally high, no attempt seems to have been made to regulate scribes through trade guilds. The techniques and materials of writing were too widespread to be easily brought under control. Even in 1463 the Ghent painters' guild accepted that those who used the pen, not the brush, were free of guild regulation, and in 1510 the Lille illuminators successfully asserted that illumination was not a controlled craft and that illuminators had never come under the painters' guild.[24] When colored letters or decoration were more important than spacing for differentiating the various sections of a text, anyone writing, amateur or professional, would have found illuminating skills desirable and useful, without necessarily aspiring to paint miniatures. Furthermore, the techniques of writing, and its attendant illumination, were not easily separated from creative scholarship or literary activity. In 1450 Jean Miélot's service to Philip the Good was summarized as making translations, then writing and illustrating them—that is, the entire production of a book, not just its composition. Although Miélot seems never to have worked on anything more ambitious than sketches for miniatures, he declared on the preparatory copy of one of his works that he had made the translation, then illustrated it and flourished the letters with his own hand.[25]

Had any guild tried to force membership on Miélot, he could have resisted on two grounds: not only was he in ducal service, but he was also a cleric. Clerical exemption from guild control was an important factor in the relative freedom of the book trades. Religious houses were still major centers of scholarship and commercial book production in the fifteenth century. The Convent of Sion in Bruges, founded in 1488 for Carmelite nuns, provides one example. The products of the nuns skilled as scribes was enhanced when the illuminator Margriet Sceppers began decorating a gradual "out of charity" and also taught illumination to Cornelia van Wulfschkercke, a resident since 1495 and a nun from 1501 until her death in 1540. Cornelia passed on her skills to another sister, and books were written and illuminated "in house" for the convent's own use and for other patrons (as a new foundation, Sion needed sources of revenue).[26] Many secular clergy, those not within a monastery or convent, supplemented their libraries or incomes by writing and illuminating. In the university town of Louvain in 1452, a woodblock cutter argued that he should not be forced into the joiners' guild because his craft of printing letters and images belonged more to the clergy; he lost, since other block cutters had enrolled, but his claim won him exemption from the entry fee.[27] Clerics could choose to join a guild so they could enjoy the benefits of membership and avoid the resentment of members. In Tournai the priests Jean du Buret, Alexandre David, and Guillaume Godefroy became master illuminators in 1464, 1471, and 1488, respectively, and Godefroy registered another priest as an apprentice.[28]

ILLUMINATORS AND PAINTERS

Compared with other forms of painting, illumination was more easily learned and more widely required. Across Europe more manuals have survived for illumination than for other painting techniques. This is probably a result not of arbitrary destruction but of the impracticality of putting the complexities of oil painting into a teach-yourself manual. Moreover, few would have needed, or attempted, to learn in such a way.[29] The relative complexity of illuminating and painting techniques is demonstrated by the lengths envisaged for apprenticeships as guilds began to devise regulations for illuminators: in Brussels and Tournai it took four years to become a painter and two to become an illuminator.[30] A painter would inevitably have acquired the skills to allow him to illuminate, using gum and glair for colored sketches and designs, whereas someone trained only in illumination might not be equipped to work in the demanding medium of oil. Gerard Horenbout, active as a painter and illuminator, took on an apprentice specifically to learn illumination, only one part of his master's skills.[31] Technically, illumination represented only one aspect of the painter's craft, but the survival of many more illuminations than panel paintings has distorted knowledge of their relationship.[32] Although the possibilities for innovation were the same in all media — oil on panel or wall, glue size on cloth, or gum and glair on parchment — it was oil that offered the greatest potential for the exploration of tone, one of the key developments in early Netherlandish painting.

According to most regulations, only full masters of a painters' guild could paint in oil or sell oil paintings. In Ghent in 1441 a Jean Le Tavernier, who may have been the illuminator from Oudenaarde, had to pledge that he would not undertake works of painting in the town without joining the painters' guild.[33] In 1477–78, when the illuminator Willem Vrelant presented an altarpiece to the Bruges Confraternity of Saint John, he did not paint it himself but instead commissioned it from the painter Hans Memling. In 1499 the abbot of the Eeckhout carefully stipulated that, if the altarpiece were ever removed, it must be replaced by another oil painting.[34] If Simon Bening indeed produced panel paintings in oil (see cat. no. 142), he either had to contract his services to a master painter or run the risk of being brought before the Bruges authorities to be fined by a painters' guild that was demonstrably ready to protect its privileges. Bening may have taken the risk or been able to exploit the relaxed trading regulations applying to fairs; it is hard to imagine someone who had achieved wealth and status as an illuminator letting a master painter take a percentage on his work in a different medium.

There were people engaged in both illuminating and painting, but the balance of their activities is hard to ascertain from the fragmentary records. The apparently disproportionate representation of illuminators among the court painters reflects either the fuller documentation available from the court or the particular demands of court service, where illuminators could provide more than books. Court painter-illuminators often headed teams of artists in the preparation of festivities or the heraldic trappings of court and battlefield, so colored designs employing illuminating techniques may have been a vital part of their work. In addition, painters were often required to design for other media. The painter-illuminator Jean Hennecart, for instance, was paid by Charles the Bold in 1457 for designs for an elaborate gold cross and two alternative designs for a silver falcon and, in 1470, for thirty alternative designs for coins, from which the duke selected four to be worked up in color and delivered to the mint. With Pierre Coustain, not known as an illuminator, Hennecart supervised the huge team of artists recruited from all over the Netherlands to prepare for the fantastically lavish celebrations at the marriage of Charles and Margaret of York in 1468.[35] With both court and other painter-illuminators, payments do not prove authorship, only responsibility. In addition to taking an apprentice in illumination, Horenbout, a full master in the Ghent painters' guild, took on a journeyman for four years specifically to illuminate. The master himself need not have worked in both forms of painting if he could employ the necessary specialists. When Horenbout entered the service of Margaret of Austria, governess of the Netherlands, in 1515, he remained based in his own workshop in Ghent, where he could continue to offer the range of painting that had presumably helped to attract her patronage.[36]

The range of Horenbout's activity may have been unusual by the fifteenth century in larger towns with the markets to support specialized workers. If so, the existence of illuminations and panel paintings in the style of the Master of James IV perhaps encourages his identification with Horenbout. Jean Molinet, a contemporary of Simon Marmion, apparently thought his versatility noteworthy, recording books, panels, "chapels" (perhaps mural paintings), and altars among his works.[37] That most painters were not much concerned with illumination in the fifteenth century is suggested by the fact that the known apprentice lists for Tournai show only six illuminators apprenticed to painters, of whom two were with Mille Marmion, who perhaps shared his brother Simon's versatility. At least twenty were apprenticed to master illuminators.[38] In Bruges in 1457 the painters' guild did not refute the book traders' assertion that none of its members was engaged in making pictures for books. This marks a notable change from 1426, when, of the sixteen makers of images for books, three or four were members of the guild, among them the dean, Jan Coene, who had made miniatures for years before joining.[39] They may have become members to practice other forms of painting, or they may have remained specialist illuminators.

Masters were usually admitted to a guild for a specific craft, and in 1491 in Amiens, where painters and illuminators were among the craftsmen obliged to join, they were explicitly restricted to the craft for which they had been admitted.[40] Some crossover was allowed in the Bruges painters' guild, since a master could practice another craft but could not employ others to do so and could not display such works for sale; prosecutions show that these restrictions were enforced.[41] Some guilds gave limited rights in a craft for a reduced fee, as the Bruges guild envisaged when it claimed in 1426 that all makers of miniatures should be "free" or "half-free" of the guild, presumably paying either the full fee for full master's rights or a half fee for limited rights to illuminate. The guild did not succeed in forcing membership on illuminators, although the town government did require that all makers of miniatures should register a mark for their products with the painters' guild for a single payment.[42] This arrangement was unusual, for in other towns illuminators were increasingly listed among the craftsmen expected to join the painters' guilds, usually at a lesser fee: in Brussels from 1453 the fee was reduced by half, in Ghent from 1463 by three-quarters, and in Tournai from 1480 by about two-thirds. Although the 1480 Tournai regulations were reported largely to repeat those of 1423, the first known illuminator enrolled only in 1431; before 1480 membership may, as in Bruges, have been possible but not obligatory for illuminators.[43]

The Tournai regulations established a hierarchy of painters: those able to practice all forms of painting, who paid five Tournai pounds if they had been trained in the town and seven Tournai pounds if trained elsewhere; the illuminators, playing-card makers, painters on paper (whose work perhaps consisted largely of coloring woodcuts), and makers of polychromed paper reliefs, who all paid two Tournai pounds; the painters of toys, parrot perches, and flowerpots, as well as housepainters, who paid one Tournai pound.[44] No provision for a lower fee for illuminators is evident in Antwerp, where illuminators as a class first appear in the preamble to the establishment of the guild chapel in 1442[45] or in the founding guild regulations of Mons in 1487 and Amiens in 1491, which both required membership of illuminators.[46] Even when membership was officially essential, it was probably only large-scale operators who were made to enroll. The one attempted enforcement recorded for Antwerp involved a scribe in 1462 who was not illuminating himself but buying miniatures for books and employing illuminators.[47] In Ghent in 1464 the painters' guild successfully challenged a scribe, Gerard van Crombrugghe, who had been importing miniatures as well as having them made.[48] In Bruges in 1457 the painters unsuccessfully claimed that the right to illuminate was strictly personal: an individual could make and sell his own work but could not employ anyone else. The aldermen accepted the book traders' reasonable riposte that without apprentices the craft would die and that all craftsmen had to employ assistants to meet demand.[49]

The lower fees presumably reflected the expected profitability of illumination in relation to painting, as well as its restricted techniques and materials, although illumination could bring wealth and fame, as shown by both Simon Bening and his daughter Levina Teerlinc. Both the likelihood of lesser rewards and ease of practice are possible factors in explaining why more female illuminators than painters are recorded: illumination could be practiced at home without assistants and never demanded unfeminine adjuncts such as trestles and ladders. Although the Tournai guild specifically allowed for female apprentices in general, it seems that women usually learned the full craft of painting only if they could do so within the family. Many towns provided fourteenth- and fifteenth-century precedents for the painter Katharina van Hemessen, born in 1527/28, who was trained by her father, Jan Sanders van Hemessen. After the general clauses on apprenticeship in the Tournai regulations, the feminine form is added only for the two categories of painters who paid lower fees. They were all banned from working in oil and, except for the illuminators, restricted to cheaper pigments. Illuminators could use fine colors and gold and silver. The masters in these two categories were envisaged as employing journeywomen as well as journeymen, and reduced fees for mastership are specified for the sons and daughters of masters; full masters of painting were conceded special rates only for sons and sons-in-law.[50] As was so often the case, it was at the potentially less lucrative end of the market that women were expected to be active.

The first woman to appear in the Antwerp guild lists, which survive from 1453, is an illuminator, Magriete van Mere, in 1470.[51] The lists of the Bruges Confraternity of Saint John show many female illuminators and female apprentices learning with both women and men, including leading illuminators such as Mazerolles and Vrelant.[52] One female illuminator lived in the *béguinage* of the Wijngaerde.[53] (*Béguinages* were communities of women who lived in chastity to further spiritual improvement but retained their own property.) During the fifteenth century the houses of the Sisters of the Common Life also became centers of female education and commercial activity. As the case of Cornelia Wulfschkercke shows, religious communities of all types were important sources of instruction and opportunity for women.

THE PAINTERS' GUILDS AND INDEPENDENT ILLUMINATIONS

Bruges was the center of a huge export market, and the sheer number of book traders there helps to explain their partial success in resisting the encroachments of the painters' guild. The legal records generated by the conflict between the book traders and the painters offer some insight into the painters' anxieties, particularly over who should profit from producing and dealing in single-leaf miniatures, arguably part of the guild's remit of image making. In the first dispute to emerge, in 1403, the guild procured a ruling that scribes and book dealers, who could not themselves paint, should not contract with purchasers to provide miniatures. In 1426 the guild complained that this was continually contravened by the book dealers, who were, moreover, importing miniatures from Utrecht and elsewhere, which were sold in the town both with and without books—that is, bound into books and as loose single leaves. In response, the town government decreed that, as the guild demanded, miniatures could be sold only in books or rolls and single-leaf miniatures were neither to be exhibited for sale nor imported; home products would bear identifying marks, which the illuminators would register with the guild. Like many regulations, this seems to have been erratically enforced. Given the volume of Bruges production, marks occur on surprisingly

Figure 4
QUENTIN MASSYS
Detail of central panel
of Saint Anne Triptych,
1509, showing infant
apostle reading.
Oil on wood panel,
224.5 × 219.1 cm
(88⅜ × 86¼ in.).
Brussels, Musées royaux
des Beaux-Arts de
Belgique, inv. 2784

few miniatures, and in 1457 the book traders could claim ignorance of the requirement. The first surviving list of marks, from 1501, includes Simon Bening's, which has yet to be found on any of his works.[54]

The miniatures "without books," or single-leaf miniatures, which challenged the painters' own productions most closely, were the guild's overriding concern. The nature of the challenge is less clear. In 1426 the guild could be seen as acting in the interests of its illuminating members, but this was not the case in 1457, when it sued the book traders for breaking the 1426 regulations. In 1457 the assertion that no guild member made miniatures went undisputed. The book traders further claimed that far from importing single-leaf miniatures, they were actually exporting, to Ghent, Ypres, Antwerp, and elsewhere. In other words, they were fostering, not depressing, production in Bruges. The emphasis in the disputes on exhibition for sale suggests that the painters feared that the illuminators were attracting purchasers away from their own products. They cannot have been pleased when the aldermen confirmed the provisions of 1426 with the important change that independent miniatures made in Bruges, and marked to prove it, could now be displayed for sale.[55]

The same concern with independent miniatures and their exhibition for sale is evident in regulations made by the Ghent painters' guild. In 1463 the Ghent guild obtained a ruling in a dispute with an illuminator that narrowly defined the rights of illuminators in language that has been variously interpreted since it appears to leave them virtually nothing to do. It can be paraphrased as follows: whoever illuminates beyond the use of the pen, that is, with the brush, must pay a quarter fee to the guild; such an illuminator will be able to make and illuminate all that one does not put or shut in missals and other books; if an illuminator wants to exhibit work for sale or to work more widely in the craft in any way, he must pay the remaining three-quarters fee for full mastership.[56] In Bruges the phrase "little pictures to put in books" was routinely used in the lawsuits to describe single-leaf miniatures; in 1522 Simon Bening gave the Confraternity of Saint John a Crucifixion "to put in a missal."[57] All that one does *not* put in missals and other books, therefore, signifies the opposite of a single-leaf miniature: illumination that is integral to the volume. The same is probably meant by what is *not shut* in missals and books, since what is *shut*, as opposed to *put*, or bound, is presumably loose, unbound leaves like those spilling from a book and its bag in Quentin Massys's Saint Anne Triptych of 1509, in which an infant apostle pretends to read by holding a text leaf sideways (fig. 4). Prayer cards and pictures are still kept in prayer books, and this was probably a widespread function of independent illuminations and single-leaf miniatures. A quarter fee allowed the illuminator to paint in books but not to compete with the painters' products by exhibiting for sale and making single-leaf miniatures and independent illuminations.

When, in 1464, the scribe Gerard van Crombrugghe was charged under the 1463 ruling, his main defense, that he had been selling illustrated books and not dealing in single-leaf miniatures, was presumably deemed the central issue.[58] The admittedly scanty evidence, reviewed above, suggests that the regulations on illumination were actually invoked only against entrepreneurs like Van Crombrugghe. The Ghent guild may well have tolerated illuminators profiting from their own work beyond the limits imposed by the quarter fee. The tentative identification of Alexander Bening, Simon's father, with the Master of the First Prayer Book of Maximilian is not made impossible by the apparent incompatibility of Alexander's enrollment in the guild at a quarter fee and the Maximilian Master's production of single-leaf miniatures.

The Tournai guild in 1480 attempted to draw up a detailed definition of "all the work of illumination," which could be made by those paying the lesser fee for illuminating rights. Illumination included miniatures, borders, illuminated and flourished initials, and gilding books. Although the full range of fine colors and gold and silver were open to illuminators, supports were restricted to paper and parchment. The size of an illumination was limited to nine or ten *pouces* in height (approximately 24.3 to 27 cm [9½ to 10⅝ in.]), and illuminations had to be in books or on other things with writing.[59] Independent illuminations were thus permitted but under restrictions that made them more distinguishable from other independent paintings. The article on illuminators is not immediately followed by the orderly sequence of playing-card makers, painters of paper, and painters of molded paper, as might be expected. The next article interrupts the sequence by banning those who are not master painters or glaziers from producing "tables"—no modern term covers the same diversity of forms of image—of painted glass, mounted in wood or otherwise.[60] What is an interpolation, in terms of materials, follows logically in terms of the guild's concerns about independent images that rival those of the full masters.

This interpretation is confirmed by the recently published documents on the Lille painters' guild. In 1510 the guild tried to force illuminators to join because they were making "tables" by the dozen and sending them for sale "in baskets." The town authorities responded by banning the illuminators from making or gilding "tables," from gluing their "images of illumination," presumably to panels, and from selling "tables," whether by the dozen or otherwise. Only if illuminators violated the new ruling would they have to join the guild. The illuminators could continue to illuminate outside the guild, as long as they produced wares that did not emulate those of the painters.[61]

VARIETIES OF INDEPENDENT ILLUMINATIONS AND SINGLE-LEAF MINIATURES

The painters' guilds were worried by independent illuminations never intended for books as well as by single-leaf miniatures "with or without books" by the purchaser's choice. Truly independent paintings on parchment or paper in the illuminators' media of gum and glair date from at least the thirteenth century: the Beguine Beatrice of Nazareth from Tienen, in Brabant, who died in 1268, had a crucifix painted on parchment.[62] Yet independent illuminations have received little attention outside the context of *Nonnenarbeit*, the often amateurish productions of German nunneries.[63] Their existence in the Netherlands before around 1500 is seldom credited since attention has focused either on the extant examples or on their role in the prehistory of collecting manuscript cuttings.[64] Earlier independent illuminations have usually survived only by ceasing to be independent through being mounted in books, as with the sheets added during the fifteenth century to the prayer book of Philip the Bold, among them a striking parallel to the leaf with the Holy Face depicted by Petrus Christus in his portrait of a young man in the National Gallery, London (fig. 5).[65] Books also preserve parallels to the leaves "to be shut in a book" shown by Massys (see fig. 4).[66] When the few survivors are considered alongside other visual and documentary evidence, some deductions can be made about this almost vanished art form that so concerned the painters' guilds.

It is instructive to compare the depicted leaf with the Holy Face with another version of the same subject by Petrus Christus in oil on parchment, once securely glued to a panel (ill. 4). These suggest that Tournai's notions of what constituted an illumination were shared elsewhere. The depicted illumination shows the Holy Face above text, a long verse prayer to be said in front of the image; inscriptions on the oil

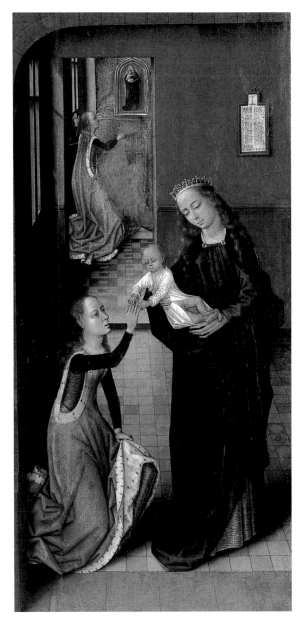

Figure 5
PETRUS CHRISTUS
Portrait of a Young Man,
ca. 1450. Oil on wood
panel, 35.4 × 26 cm
(13¹⁵⁄₁₆ × 10¼ in.). London,
National Gallery, NG 2593

Figure 6
MASTER OF THE SAINT
CATHERINE LEGEND
Detail of *Scenes from the
Life of Saint Catherine*,
ca. 1485, showing
mystic marriage of
Saint Catherine. Oil on
wood panel, 120 × 100 cm
(47¼ × 39⅜ in.).
Brussels, Musées royaux
des Beaux-Arts de
Belgique, inv. 12.102

were apparently limited to a signature. Without very minute examination, the oil on parchment would have been indistinguishable from a panel painting, whereas the parchment of the depicted illumination remains obvious. The sheet has been nailed to its panel support through a red ribbon, which then acts as a frame, a convention employed for cloth but not panel paintings.[67] Many depictions of interiors, both ecclesiastical and secular, include such mounted sheets where the centralized layout, not weighted to the exterior margin as the recto or verso of a leaf, shows that the leaves were never intended to be bound in books. The independent sheet affixed to the wall at the right in the eponymous panel by the Master of the Saint Catherine Legend of about 1485 (fig. 6) is even more emphatically centralized. The indentation of the miniature is more extreme and is emphasized by the trimming.[68] This leaf looks glued to its board, which, like that of the young man's *Holy Face*, hangs from a hole in the top projection; otherwise its molded wooden framing is closer to the conventions for panel painting. It is hardly surprising that the Lille painters' guild thought the producers of such "tables" should come under its control.

Specifically independent illuminations could cover a wide range of formats and functions. In many, illumination served text: informative sheets for public buildings, for instance, or liturgical or didactic texts for churches. In 1505, when regulations for the Great Council at Mechelen were written on two sheets of parchment, illuminated, and then mounted on panels to be hung in the council rooms, conventions were sufficiently established for the joiner to be paid for doing so in the customary fashion.[69] For short texts, mounted sheets were probably a cheaper way of ensuring safe accessibility than the binding and chaining or caging of a book. To the left of the church interior of Van der Weyden's Triptych of the Seven Sacraments (fig. 7), a ribbon-framed leaf is seen on a pier, and a caged book is set against the screen. Two large "tables," made "for the instruction of all Christian men and women of whatever rank," with the text of Jean Gerson's *Doctrinal* were put up by Matthieu or Regnault de Bapaume, bishop of Thérouanne from 1404 to 1414, in his cathedral, on the outer side of the choir enclosure. The bishop's intentions were fulfilled beyond his imagining when his benefaction, directly or indirectly, provided the text of the incunable printed in Bruges by Jan Brito.[70] The two "tables" might have formed a diptych; a late-fifteenth-century Austrian diptych of two illuminated sheets with indulgence prayers mounted on wood survives in the Metropolitan Museum of Art, New York.[71] In some, text and image might play a more equal role. For the Church of Our Lady, Antwerp, in 1474, Lieven van Lathem was paid for a "table" with the Incarnation. Since this involved writing and flourishing, the table was presumably an illumination.[72] Touching a combination of words and image was usually required for oaths, a very specific function for some illuminated sheets.[73] Parchment could be used for records of burials and endowments, although brass plaques were more durable and more common. In 1463 the tablet in Cambrai cathedral with the arms of Pierre d'Ailly, bishop from 1397 to 1411, was renewed by a scribe and illuminator.[74]

Specially commissioned combinations of text and images are most likely to have generated written records than sheets produced for the open market. The speculative production of single-leaf miniatures, whether exclusively or potentially for independent use, is indirectly documented by the anxieties of

Figure 7
ROGIER VAN DER
WEYDEN
Detail of central panel of
Triptych of the Seven
Sacraments, ca. 1445–50,
showing church interior.
Oil on panel, 200 × 97 cm
(78¾ × 38¼ in.). Antwerp,
Koninklijk Museum voor
Schone Kunsten, inv.
393–395

the painters' guilds. Their determined efforts to limit their display for sale—the 1457 lawsuit in Bruges was prompted by the guild's attempt to fine book traders for exhibiting unmarked miniatures for sale—suggests that they feared that buyers wanting an image might settle for an illumination instead of a panel or cloth painting. Before border decoration defined the intended destination of a miniature—asymmetrical for a book, omitted or symmetrical for independent use—a miniature could be deployed however its purchaser wished. If not eventually placed in a book, its chances of survival were minimal, and it is impossible to know how many miniatures suitable for books were diverted to other functions. Inevitably, the first certainly independent miniatures can be discerned only because they were designed to be independent, like the sheets associated with the Master of the Lübeck Bible (cat. no. 113) or the triptychs associated with Simon Bening (e.g., fig. 9 and cat. no. 157).

What must have been earlier diptychs or polyptychs of illumination were owned by Philip the Bold in 1367 and by his brother Charles V of France in 1380.[75] Jan van Woluwe in 1384 may have illuminated a diptych or triptych for his employer, Joanna, duchess of Brabant, and a "table" for Joanna to give to Philip.[76] In 1516 Margaret of Austria owned, among many independent illuminations, "a little table of an Our Lady and of Madame de Charolais of illumination put in a case together," which presumably dated from before the death in 1465 of the last Madame de Charolais, Isabella of Bourbon.[77] Some idea of its

Figure 9
SIMON BENING
AND WORKSHOP
Virgin and Child with
Saints Catherine and
Barbara, ca. 1520.
Tempera on parchment
on wood panel: central
panel, 25.1 × 18.4 cm
(9⅞ × 7¼ in.); left wing,
24.8 × 7 cm (9¼ × 2¾ in.);
right wing, 24.2 × 7 cm
(9⁹⁄₁₆ × 2¾ in.). Houston,
Museum of Fine Arts,
Edith and Percy S. Straus
Collection, inv. 44.529

possible appearance can be gained from the miniatures incorporated in the binding of the Prayer Book of Philip the Good, now in Vienna (fig. 8).[78] Since the framed miniatures appear to date from the 1430s and the book from about 1450, it is possible that Philip already owned the miniatures as a diptych. The broad, molded frames correspond to those often represented around single sheets (see fig. 6). Arguably, the surviving sixteenth-century illuminated triptychs without text follow an established format (fig. 9; see also fig. 15 and ill. 157), and earlier single-leaf miniatures could have been mounted for independent display.

Antecedents can also be deduced for the illuminated portraits in Margaret of Austria's collection by 1516.[79] The Rhineland mystic Henry Suso had a picture painted on parchment of the Eternal Wisdom, Christ, whom he had chosen as his beloved, which went with him to Cologne in the 1320s.[80] Much of Suso's devotional practice, which was extremely influential in the Netherlands,[81] was a repetition of the rituals of earthly lovers, suggesting that portraits of the beloved may already have been fashionable in the Rhineland; in Provence, Petrarch's portrait of Laura by Simone Martini on paper or parchment may be exceptional only in being recorded.[82] The 1471/72 inventory of René of Anjou's château at Angers lists a parchment roll with the portrait of the queen of Sicily, presumably René's second wife and beloved by convention, Jeanne de Laval.[83] René's chief painter and illuminator was the Netherlander Barthélemy d'Eyck. In the sixteenth century illumination was the accepted technique for portrait miniatures (e.g., cat. nos. 153, 161).

A folding triptych or diptych resembles the sheltered environment of a book, which allowed illuminators to use pigments derived from light-vulnerable dyes and the less resilient media of gum and glair. A displayed single sheet was difficult to protect. The nature and expense of crystal probably largely restricted its use to illuminations incorporated into metalwork. Glass was possible only for small works, like the little image under glass of the Sweet Name of Jesus by Cornelia Wulfschkercke in the Convent of Sion in 1537.[84] An illuminated triptych attributed to Simon Bening (see fig. 9), now in the Houston Museum of Fine Arts, was reported to have been in about 1855 "in a sixteenth-century frame protected by talc" (i.e., hydrated silicate of magnesium, although the term was also used loosely for mica).[85] Unprotected, Petrus Christus's depicted leaf with the *Holy Face* (see fig. 5) already has a curling corner, to the apparent unconcern of its owner, who could always reuse the wooden panel for a new sheet.

INDEPENDENT ILLUMINATIONS AND PRINTS

Parchment and paper were cheaper supports than a panel prepared with a chalk ground, and illuminators could work economically in cheaper pigments, quickly applying thin washes of color instead of creating the elaborately finished paint surfaces deploying fine pigments and precious metals. Illumination in cheaper pigments was suitable for ephemeral images. In 1477 the Abbey of Saint Waudru at Mons paid Jehan Kenon for painting images of its patron on half sheets of paper to be attached to abbey buildings to deter military arson.[86] The saint's image would act as an identifying badge, like a coat of arms. The repetitive nature of much heraldic work made it an obvious area for prints to replace hand-drawn illumination.[87] Without a preexisting market for cheaper images on parchment and paper as well as cloth, there would have been little stimulus to mass-produce them through printing. The relationship between independent illuminations and prints is encapsulated in the random accumulation of objects preserved under the woodwork of the choir and summer refectory of the nunnery at Wienhausen in Lower Saxony. Thirty-five miniatures on parchment or paper, dating from the mid-thirteenth century onward, were found alongside twenty woodcuts dating from the late fourteenth century onward, together with a few metalcuts and engravings. Some of the miniatures had been glued to oak panels, and one prayer sheet had been tacked to its panel through a framing strip of leather.[88] Similar deposits are unlikely to survive in the Netherlands, where few religious houses have escaped devastation by warfare or reform.

As would be expected, woodcuts drew on the conventions established by independent illuminations, in particular the centralized layouts and the incorporation of texts. With the introduction of the more expensive and refined technique of engraving, which made less use of text, prints came to be available across a range of prices, from the crudest woodcuts to elaborately colored and gilded engravings, mirroring the scale from outline drawings to lavishly finished illuminations. When makers and owners of books sometimes added prints to manuscript books, they made a choice that was presumably already familiar from their treatment of handmade images. Sets of engravings may have been inspired by sets of illuminations so that there could have been much earlier precedents for the set of illuminations associated with the Master of the Lübeck Bible, which have the centralized, symmetrical layout and inscriptions appropriate to independent illuminations (e.g., cat. no. 113). As with Simon Bening's Stein Quadriptych (cat. no. 146), their original arrangement is unknown; possibly they were not formally arranged but kept loose to be viewed in whatever combinations were desired, just as Isabella of Castille kept in a cupboard forty-seven little panels in oil by Juan de Flandes and Michael Sittow.[89]

In written records, it is often impossible to know whether illuminations or prints are meant. While the "one leaf" bequeathed by a Tournaisienne in 1303 was probably an independent illumination,[90] the "painted papers" supplied by a Ghent painter in 1404–5 could have employed printed designs.[91] In Dutch, as in German, various forms of the term *brief*, originally indicating any two-dimensional image on paper or parchment, not necessarily with text, were eventually restricted to prints by the sixteenth century, with Dutch increasingly using forms of the term *prenten*. When the musician Richard de

Bellengues died in 1470 in Brussels, he had hanging on the walls of his dining room a portrait on panel, a vernicle, and many other "briefkens ende beschreven berdekens."[92] The *berdekens* are little panels, described as *beschreven*, literally "written," but also meaning "painted," suggesting that the *briefkens* too deployed imagery. The *briefkens* were probably small, although diminutive forms are not reliable indicators of size, and may have been prints, probably colored, or entirely handmade sheets. The fact that a more precise vocabulary was not immediately required is indicative of the ease with which prints took their place alongside, and then supplanted, an existing form of imagery.

The imprecision of language is particularly frustrating when trying to assess the impact of independent illuminations on the export trade. Few records are as clear as the Lille dispute of 1510, when the painters' guild complained of the illuminators making "tables" by the dozen and sending them for sale in baskets as far afield as Paris. The "tables" are subsequently termed "images of illumination." Entire books of hours were made in quantity for the English market, and the English customs rolls between 1404 and 1485 reveal imports from Antwerp of loose sheets, possibly handmade images as well as prints.[93] Similarly, Netherlandish miniatures made their way into Italian books,[94] and the Roman customs records show imports of pictures on *carta*, paper or parchment, by the bundle, particularly of the Virgin; "Germans," a term that included Netherlanders, were heavily involved in the trade.[95] Some painted *carte* may have been of considerable quality and ambition. Alessandra Strozzi, writing from Florence in 1460 to her son in Bruges, first described pictures he had sent as painted *carte* and then had to correct herself to *panni*, cloths; among them were an image of a peacock, an *Adoration of the Magi*, and a *Holy Face*.[96]

PRINTERS, PAINTERS, AND ILLUMINATORS

The vigilant painters' guilds were alert to the dangers of competition from prints. In 1447 the Bruges painters' guild obtained a ruling that nonmembers could not use oil, gold, and silver for coloring prints but must instead use watercolor, *water vaerwe*.[97] Their intention was presumably to prevent any "painting by numbers" challenge to their oils, although an example survives in the National Gallery, London, in which a print on paper from Martin Schongauer's engraved *Entombment* long remained undetected between a panel and a Bruges-style oil painting.[98] The 1510 regulations of the Lille painters' guild, which to an unknown extent repeated earlier rules, obliged "makers of colored works on papers" to pay an annual fee and banned them from using fine gold, fine blue, and other fine colors. By 1520 the Bruges guild was no longer content to allow colorers of prints to remain outside its control since, the guild claimed, print colorers had to join the painters' guilds in Brussels, Mechelen, Ghent, Tournai, and many other places. It was again a large-scale entrepreneur who had attracted the painters' wrath, since the challenge in this case was against someone directly employing painters' journeymen to color prints and thereby depriving master painters of their cut as middlemen. The guild argued, albeit unsuccessfully, that print colorers, who used "thin" colors, could not claim exemption from the guild as illuminators, since illuminators used exclusively "thick" colors.[99] The gum washes employed for prints had actually been adopted from the conventions for low-cost illuminations, also usually on paper. Such a division between prints and illuminations was only possible once printing had priced illumination out of the lower end of the market, reducing its clientele to the upmarket patrons who had always been willing to pay for quality.

The illuminators and the print colorers were not the only artisans to suffer from the jealous attentions of the painters' guilds. In the same lawsuit the Bruges guild tried to force membership on makers of cartoons for tapestries and embroideries. The Tournai guild had regulated to control designing in 1480, and the Brussels guild had achieved, at least on paper, a virtual monopoly over tapestry cartoons in 1476.[100] Earlier, in the 1450s, the Brussels guild had secured very favorable terms for painters at the expense of wood carvers in the marketing of polychromed altarpieces.[101] The painters' monopolistic instincts encouraged the process of definition that replaced the broad category of "tables," covering many art forms and combinations of art forms, with the more narrowly defined "pictures," which owners increasingly expected to hang on their walls. Little scope was being left for independent illuminations, apart from portrait miniatures, and they, like most surviving independent illuminations, conform closely to panel paintings in type. The surviving examples inadequately represent the earlier conventions for independent illuminations, which saw them frequently, indeed in Tournai compulsorily, associated with texts. The conventions for prints developed from, and then interacted with, those for independent illuminations; eventually prints usurped the place of illuminations in the market. Printing also undermined the chief function of single-leaf miniatures, as their insertion in books became an impractical procedure with the increased pace and quantity of book production. In printed books, illumination and even the hand-coloring of printed decoration eventually became exceptional. Thus the printers were eroding demand for illuminated books and independent illuminations at the same time that the painters were extending their jurisdiction.

The painters' guilds were not trying to suppress illumination. On the contrary, what they wanted was some control over its profits, while limiting competition with their own products. They resented scribes and book dealers making money from illuminations, which were reasonably perceived as a craft allied with painting. Town governments apparently agreed, and illuminators were required to join many painters' guilds or, as in Bruges, to accept some guild control. That this happened only in the later fifteenth century, outside Bruges, may partly be explained by the difficulty of separating illumination from writing in the highly literate Netherlands and by the strength of clerical book production. These factors also underlie the book crafts' apparent avoidance of guild organization in the fifteenth century. The book men valued their freedom from guild control and guild expense. The Bruges Confraternity of Saint John the Evangelist expressed the book traders' desire for a corporate identity within a devotional framework, not their desire for a trade guild. In Antwerp in 1557 they unsuccessfully but stubbornly opposed their incorporation into the painters' guild, which recorded that great costs had been incurred in enforcing the new decree that all printers, booksellers, and binders must become members, "because they were all ingenious men and the guild authorities had astonishing difficulty with them."[102]

No trade guild could have protected the illuminators and scribes from the consequences of the printing press. By 1548 there were only three illuminators in the Confraternity of Saint John: the great Simon Bening, distinguished by the title of master; Thomas de Raet, a member since 1527; and Pieter Claeissens, a member since 1544.[103] This may be the Pieter Claeissens who had been apprenticed to a cloth painter in 1516 and become a master in the painters' guild in 1530, although no works of illumination by him are recorded. The difficulties of distinguishing him from his painter son and grandson of the same name render attributions of paintings uncertain, and illuminations have yet to be associated with the Claeissens family.[104] The listing of Pieter Claeissens as an illuminator is currently an isolated fact, hard to interpret in the absence of visual evidence. As is generally the case, the written sources offer only incomplete insights into the varied and varying relationships between painters and illuminators and between painting and illumination. The visual results of these crucial interactions can be sampled and assessed in the exhibition and in this catalogue.

Notes

This subject was first explored in one of the 1995 Linbury Renaissance Lectures at the National Gallery, London, and I thank the Linbury Trust for its valued support. I am also grateful for information and comments from Fr. Alain Arnould O.P., Lorne Campbell, Thomas Kren, Scot McKendrick, and Susie Nash.

1. For written and visual evidence on Tournai illumination, see Vanwijnsberghe 2001.

2. Goovaerts 1896; Charron 2000: 735.

3. Schouteet 1989: 16.

4. Van de Casteele 1866: 23; Weale 1863–65, pt. 1: 205–6.

5. Duverger 1969: 97–98.

6. Cornelis 1987: 104; Campbell 1981a: 46.

7. Weale 1863–65, pt. 1: 214–21.

8. For the working of the guilds, see Campbell 1976 and Campbell 1981a, with references to published sources on individual guilds; for Lille, see Charron 2000.

9. Van de Casteele 1866: 30–32.

10. Van der Straelen 1855: 4–7.

11. The mass was funded by the town in reparation for the 1436–38 revolt (Weale 1863–65, pt. 1: 118).

12. Vermeersch 1976: 249–51, no. 254, pl. 117; Van den Gheyn (G.) 1889: 31–33, pls. 3, 7; Weale 1863–65, pt. 1: 145–52, 202–3, 222; Feys and De Schrevel 1896; the most informative of the foundation documents is transcribed with English translation in New York 1994: 203–6, with comments on 19, 22, n. 50, where the 1466 permission to amortize—to give in perpetuity to a religious foundation, thus diminishing ducal rights and revenues—is misunderstood as a ducal grant.

13. Van den Haute 1913: 196–97; Chavannes-Mazel 1992: 140–42.

14. An *Annunciation* with de Montbléru's arms in the rebuilt church at Coulanges-la-Vineuse might come from the high altarpiece he presented to the original church in 1463; his will charged his heirs to give a picture to Auxerre Cathedral (Carton 1966: 172–87); de Montferrand's Boccaccio manuscript is London, British Library, Add. Ms. 11696 (Branca, in Turin 1999, 3: 155–57), illuminated by a hand close to the Master of the Harley Froissart, who also worked for Louis of Gruuthuse (Sotheby's, London, December 6, 2001, lot 67).

15. Gilliodts-van Severen 1899, 2: 351; more summarily in Weale 1863–65, pt. 1: 202; in 1475 his widow, Isabelle de Machefoing, by 1479 remarried to Olivier de la Marche, endowed an annual distribution to the poor by the Painters' Chapel (Weale 1863–65, pt. 1: 208–9; Chavannes-Mazel 1992: 142); for the Gruuthuse oratory, see Bruges 1992: 39–41, 58–59, ills. on 35, 38.

16. Nys and Salamagne 1996: 422–23; Hénault 1907, pt. 1: 414–15.

17. As pointed out in Trio 1995: 727; "de meeste menichte van den ghonen die hemlieden nu gheneeren van de voorseide neeringhe van der librarie, houden eenen ghilde ter eeren van Sint Ian Evangeliste int cloostere ten Eechoute in Brugghe" (Weale 1872–73a: 251–52).

18. Weale 1872–73a: 251–52.

19. Gilliodts-van Severen 1897: 253–54; Schouteet 1963: 237.

20. Gilliodts-van Severen 1897: 293–94.

21. Weale 1872–73a: 284.

22. De Schrevel 1902: 181–83.

23. "Tusschen den deken ende ghezworne van den beildemakers ende zadelaers binnen de voorseide stede van Brugghe, an deen ziide, ende Morissis de Hac ende andere hemlieden gheneerende met librarien, als boucscrivers, verlichters ende die beildekins in bouken of in rollen maken, an dander ziide" (Weale 1872–73a: 245–46); "librariers ende boucscrivers ende datter an cleift poorters neeringhe es" (Weale 1872–73a: 249).

24. "Par lesdits illumineurs avoit esté dict que illuminer ne estoit stil et que jamais ne avoient esté comprins sousz ledit mestier de paintres et voiriers" (Charron 2000: 738); De Busscher 1859a: 207–8.

25. Pinchart 1860–81, 3: 46; Brussels, Bibliothèque royale de Belgique, Ms. 9249-50 (Dogaer 1987a: 87–88).

26. Weale 1866–70: 320, 323; see Arnould 1998.

27. "Van letteren ende beeldeprynten te snyden . . . ginghe eensdels meer der Clerkgien aen den voirscreven ambachte [scrynmakers]" (Even 1866–69, pt. 1: 286–87).

28. Pinchart 1860, 3: 73–75.

29. For a fifteenth-century north Netherlandish treatise on illumination, see Cologne, Historisches Archiv, W 80 293; published in Leloux 1977: 11–31; discussed and partially translated in Wallert 1991: 447–56.

30. Mathieu 1953: 221–35; Goovaerts 1896.

31. Campbell and Foister 1986: 719.

32. For some consequences of the differential rate of survival for art history, see Reynolds (C.) 2000b: 10–12.

33. Vanwijnsberghe 1995: 34.

34. Weale 1872–73a: 299, 336.

35. Laborde (L.) 1849–52, 1: 467–69, 2: 223–24; Van der Velden 2000: 184–85, 210, 309.

36. Campbell and Foister 1986: 719–20.

37. Dehaisnes 1892: 72–74.

38. Pinchart 1860–81, 3: 73–75.

39. "Ian Coene, die nu deken van den voorseiden beildemakers es, menich iaer beilden maecte binnen der stede van Brugghe, zonder eenighe vryhede of halfvryhede int voorseid ambocht te hebbene . . . van alden ghesellen die ieghenwoordelicke beilden maecken in boucken of in rollen, wel wesende in ghetale van zestiene, en esser metten voorseiden Ian Coene maer drie of viere vryhede hebbende in tvoorseid ambocgt" (Weale 1872–73a: 247, 242; the French translation misprints *seize* as *treize*, reducing the number of illuminators to thirteen).

40. Thierry 1835: 5.

41. Van de Casteele 1866: 30–32.

42. Weale 1872–73a: 239–45.

43. Illuminators are not mentioned in the first Brussels statutes of 1387; see Favresse 1946: 76–79; Mathieu 1953; De Busscher 1859a: 207–8; Goovaerts 1896: 171; Grange and Cloquet 1887–88: 27.

44. Goovaerts 1896.

45. Illuminators were not specified in the first regulations of 1382; see Van der Straelen 1855: 1–4, 7.

46. Devillers 1880: 289–522; Thierry 1856–70.

47. Van der Straelen 1855: 11–12.

48. Diericx 1814–15, 2: 111–12; earlier Van Crombrugghe had been Van Lathem's representative in his disputes with the guild (see note 5).

49. Weale 1872–73a: 245–51.

50. Goovaerts 1896: 174–78, 158–59.

51. Rombouts and Lerius 1864–76, 1: 20.

52. Weale 1872–73a: 253–74.

53. "De verlichteghe in den Wingaert, Babekin Boons" (Weale 1872–73a: 278).

54. Weale 1872–73a: 239–51; Weale 1863–65, pt. 2: 298–319; attention was first drawn to illuminators' marks by Farquhar (1980: 371–83); for further discussion, see Smeyers and Cardon 1990; Cambridge 1993: 116–21.

55. Weale 1872–73a: 240, 245–51.

56. "Dat so wie van nu voortan binnen der voors. Stede van Ghend verlichten sal breeder werckende dan met pennen, te wetene met pinchelen, twelcke der neeringhe vanden scilders van ouden tijden toebehoort heeft, dat hij gehouden sal zijn te coopene deen vierde vander vrijhede vander neeringhe vanden scilders . . . dies zullen sulcke verlichters moghen maken ende verlichten al tgheundt dat men in missalen ende andre boeken niet en stelt of sluut . . . toogh van sulken werken thoudene of andersins de voors. neeringhe breeder te moghen doene, in einiger wijs" (De Busscher 1859a: 207–8).

57. In 1457 "beildekins omme in boucken te stellen" had been illegally exhibited for sale, showing that these must have been single-leaf miniatures; Bening "heeft der ghilde ghesconken een groot crucifix om te stellen in een missael" (Weale 1872–73a: 246; Weale 1863–65, pt. 2: 311).

58. Diericx 1814–15, 2: 111–12.

59. "Lesquelz enlumineurs, aiant paié ledit droit, poront faire tout ouvraige d'enlumineur: c'est assavoir ymaiges, istoires, vingnettes, tourner lettres d'or et d'asur et les floreter et champier, dorer et lister livres, et ouvrer de toutes coulleurs fines, de fin or et d'argent, et de toutes autres coulleurs servans à ladite enluminure, pourveu que icelle enluminure soit faicte sur pappier, parchemin, vellin ou avortin, et non autrement, et que lesdits ouvraiges . . . ne soient que de noef ou dix pos

de hault, et non plus; car qui feroit lesdictes ymaiges plus grandes que dit est, ou qui les feroit sur autres fons que dessus n'est déclaré, ou qui ouveroit de ladicte enluminure ou feroit ouvrer autrement que sus livres ou autres choses où il y oroit escripture. . . . Il encheroit en l'amende de dix solz tournois" (Goovaerts 1896: 171).

60. Goovaerts 1896: 172.

61. "Ilz faisoient tableaux et iceulx par XIInes et en paniers envoioient vendre . . . interdict aux dits enlumineurs de non doresenavant faire aulcuns tabliaux ne iceulx faire dorer ne y faire coler leurs ymages de enlumineres ne aussi les vendre ou faire vendre par douzaines ou aultrement, a peine que se ainsy le faisoient, ils seroient tenus paier les droix et franchises dudit mestier de paintre et subgetz aux ordonnances de icelluy" (Charron 2000: 737–38).

62. "Dominice crucis signaculum, in pargameni cedula depictum" (Hamburger 1997: 178).

63. E.g., Spamer 1930; Hamburger 1997.

64. Single leaves traceable "at least to the fifteenth century" (Wieck 1996: 233); "single leaves date as early as the fifteenth and sixteenth centuries" (Hindman et al. 1997: xi).

65. Brussels, Bibliothèque royale de Belgique, Ms. 11035-7, fol. 98; see Köster 1979: 87–95; Bousmanne and Van Hoorebeeck 2000: 264–72; London, National Gallery, inv. 2593; see Campbell 1998: 104–9.

66. E.g., in Vienna, Österreichische Nationalbibliothek, Ms. s.n. 12897, a compilation from the Rooclooster, near Brussels; see Pächt, Jenni, and Thoss 1983, 1:114–15, 2: figs. 8, 9.

67. Reynolds (C.) 2000a: 94.

68. Friedländer 1967–76, 4: no. 47; see also Sotheby's, London, sale, July 12, 2001, lot 13.

69. "Pour avoir fait deux tableaux et mis lesdits deux rolles dessus, fermés en tel estat et forme qu'il est accoustumé faire en telles choses, pour les mettre ou pendre es chambres où l'on tient ledit grand conseil" (Pinchart 1860–81, 1: 103).

70. Gilliodts-van Severen 1897: 66–67.

71. New York 1999a: 193, no. 234.

72. "Meester Lieven heeft verdient van der tafelen te maken daer incarnacioen in staet met scriven ende floren tsamen" (Asaert 1972: 68).

73. See Nys 1991: 47–56.

74. Houdoy 1880: 194; the record of a late-thirteenth-century foundation in the priory of Rabestens, Toulouse, survives as a diptych of parchment glued to wood with two miniatures on each wing (Périgueux, Musée de Périgord; see Paris 1998: 326–27, no. 226).

75. "Un trableaux [sic] de enluminure et de pourtraire" (Prost 1902–13, 1: 122); "ungs autres petits tableaux de parchemin paints, c'est assavoir d'un crucefix et de plusieurs ymages" (Labarte 1879: 242, no. 2218; the parchment is unlikely to have been detectable unless it was illuminated).

76. Payments to Jan van Woluwe apparently call him illuminator or painter depending on the work produced; he was paid as "illuminatori pro una tabuleta cum duobus foliis facti, pendente in parva camera domine" and as "pictori pro ymaginibus in curia facti in via qui de aula itur ad capellam" (Pinchart 1860–81, 3: 96–99); payment was made to Hennequin de Bruxelles as "enlumineur de madame la duchesse de Brabant pour ce qu'il a presenté un tablel au duc" (Prost 1902–13, 2: 159).

77. "Ung petit tableau d'une Notre Dame et de Madame de Charolais de illuminure mis en ung estuy ensemble" (Finot 1895: 212).

78. Vienna, Österreichische Nationalbibliothek, Ms. 1800; Pächt, Jenni, and Thoss 1983, 1: 19–23, pls. 24–7; Mazal and Thoss 1991.

79. Finot 1895: 210; for early portrait miniatures, see Campbell 1990: 62–64.

80. "Gemalet an ein bermit" (Seuse 1907: 103).

81. See Wolfs 1966; Axters 1966.

82. Martindale 1988: 50, 183; the references' consistency and attribution to a known artist make it unlikely that the portrait was a literary conceit; see Mann 1998: 18–19.

83. Lecoy de la Marche 1873: 256.

84. "Een beeldeken met eenen glaes daer voore, de zoete naame Jhesus, gemaect by der hant van . . . suster Cornelie van Wulfskercke" (Weale 1866–70: 92).

85. Edith A. and Percy S. Straus Collection, inv. 44,529, Weale 1895: 47; Bruges 1998, 1: 166, no. 71, 2: 102.

86. Devillers 1880: 441.

87. For the functions of armorial prints, see London 1995: 59, 138–39.

88. Appuhn and Heusinger 1965: 157–238.

89. Campbell 1998: 260–66.

90. "I fuellait" (Grange 1897: 39).

91. "Ghescrevenen pampieren" (Cornelis 1987: 114); these could have been "written," but "painted" is more likely since they were supplied by a painter.

92. Huybens 1975: 330.

93. Charron 2000: 737–38; Asaert 1985; in addition, some "paper poynctes" or "poyntes" are perhaps painted papers, not "spelde brieven," papers of pins or needles, as there translated, see Kurath et al. 1952.

94. E.g., The Hague, Koninklijke Bibliotheek, Mss. 135 E 23, 133 D 15 (The Hague 1980: 144–45, 138–39, no. 59); Rome, Biblioteca Vaticana, Ms. Vat. lat. 6259 (Morello, in Vatican City 1988: 92, fig. 16).

95. Esch and Esch 1978: 211–17; Esch 1995: 72–87.

96. "Le carte, o vero panni dipinti . . ." (Macinghi negli Strozzi 1877: 223–24, 229–31, 245–46).

97. Weale 1872–73a: 244–45.

98. Inv. 1151 (Lehrs 28); Billinge 1998: 81–90.

99. Charron 2000: 738; "de verlichter moet wercken met dicke ende luneghe vaerwe ende de scildere of prenter in zodanich werc up papier met dorschineghe vaerwe" (Gilliodts-van Severen 1905: 517–20).

100. Goovaerts 1896; Wauters 1878: 47–49.

101. See Jacobs 1998: esp. 152–55.

102. Rombouts and van Lerius 1864–76, 1: 206.

103. De Schrevel 1902: 181–83.

104. In 1557 he was paid for painting and illuminating the letters of an epitaph, but this was specifically in oil (Weale 1911: 29–35); for a recent survey, see Bruges 1998, 1: 216–23, 2: 147–50, nos. 116–20.

ILLUMINATORS AND PAINTERS: ARTISTIC EXCHANGES AND INTERRELATIONSHIPS

Thomas Kren and Maryan W. Ainsworth

There is no disputing that the innovations of Flemish painters in oil on panel helped to shape the new style of manuscript illumination during the 1470s and for the next several generations. Hugo van der Goes and Joos van Ghent provided inspiration for illuminators through their handling of light and color, texture and space. Their paintings became sources for compositions and specific motifs in illuminations. Van der Goes's workshop may also have provided drawings for the use of book painters (see cat. no. 30), while the illuminators probably created workshop model sheets after his panel paintings. Simon Marmion's activity as a panel painter informed his extensive production as an illuminator and inevitably made his illuminations more sophisticated.

The relationship between the arts of painting and manuscript illumination in the years from around 1467 to 1561 was far more complex and creatively interactive, however, than these few examples indicate. The common tendency to view Flemish manuscript illumination after 1470 largely through the conceptual filter of a golden age of Flemish painting is misleading. It has obscured the high level of interdependence between illumination and painting. A flow of artistic ideas among media has long been recognized in the art of the medieval era, as has the role of manuscript illumination as an inspiration for other media during this period. The relationship between painters and illuminators and between their respective media was often an intimate one.[1] This was due in part to the central importance of illumination throughout much of the Middle Ages. On a more practical level, it may have depended on two facts: on the one hand, illuminators and other artists were often skilled in more than one medium, while, on the other hand, the different media were employed to represent many of the same themes, using similar conventions, in the service of a common faith. An exploration of the relationships between manuscript illuminators and panel painters, and the different ways in which they shared ideas, reveals many instances in which the art of manuscript illumination, contrary to commonly accepted notions, helped to shape the language of painting in oil on panel.

BEYOND SPECIALIZATION

In the Netherlandish tradition of the fifteenth century, most artists specialized in one medium, a result in part of the restrictions set up by the guilds and their method of training.[2] Panel painters were primarily painters in oil, and illuminators were largely masters of tempera on parchment.[3] The exceptions to the rule are interesting, however, and illustrative of the ways in which the arts of painting and manuscript illumination intersected. Illuminators received particularly favorable treatment from the dukes Philip the Good and Charles the Bold, and at least four of them had titles at court. One who did not, Simon

Marmion, nevertheless enjoyed generous patronage from the ducal family over two decades. He executed both manuscripts and paintings for the family (see cat. nos. 10, 11, 13, 14) and for at least one of its courtiers, Guillaume Fillastre. Although the illuminator Jean Hennecart held the title of painter to Charles (see cat. no. 56), he also designed for his employer coins and objects in metalwork and silver.[4] Lieven van Lathem was painter to both Philip and Maximilian, but of the art he executed for the ducal household, only manuscripts survive (e.g., cat. no. 16). Margaret of Austria paid the illuminator Gerard Horenbout, her court painter, for paintings, including portraits; illuminations; and a design for a window, presumably stained glass; and for collaborating with a group of nuns on an embroidered *jardinet*.[5] His only securely documented surviving work, however, is an illuminated manuscript (cat. no. 129). While in the service of Henry VIII between 1528 and 1531, Horenbout was also described as "paynter."[6] Indeed, he is more often mentioned as painter than as illuminator, but he received numerous commissions for both types of work (and others too).[7] He was also paid to design "petits patrons" for ten tapestries for the Confraternity of Saint Barbara in the church of Saint Pharahildis in Ghent in 1508 and 1509. His artistic talents ultimately served a range of projects, from the commanding scale of wall hangings to the intimacy of devotional books.[8] As Catherine Reynolds has shown, some illuminators—including Horenbout, Van Lathem, and Marmion—enjoyed full membership in painters' guilds and thus also had the appropriate professional training and credentials to work in oil on panel.[9]

The range of talents required of an official artist usually included the painting or fabrication of ephemeral works for lavish court weddings, triumphal entries, chivalric banquets, and various other festivities. Such events, which contributed significantly to the fabled magnificence of the Burgundian court, entailed the collaboration of artists from throughout the region. Indeed, the documents make clear that many artists not attached to the court were brought in to work on these events. For example, in 1454 the painter Jacques Daret of Tournai and painter-illuminator Jean Hennecart worked alongside the young Simon Marmion at Philip the Good's Feast of the Pheasant in Lille.[10] In 1468 Van der Goes, Daret, Van Lathem, and a Tournai illuminator named Jan van der Straet all worked under Hennecart's supervision at Bruges for the wedding of Charles the Bold and Margaret of York.[11]

Such festivities provided circumstances where artists with different specialties interacted and might become acquainted with one another's art. Inevitably the practice of working in more than one medium broadened not only the range of the artist's professional contacts but likely his colleagues' exposure to his art as well. The prominence of so many illuminators under Philip and Charles—other court illuminators included Dreux Jean and Philippe de Mazerolles—helped to ensure the dissemination of their ideas. The highly specialized nature of the art-historical discipline—and indeed of modern collecting— has encouraged scholars to approach the different media separately, as narrow specialties. In so doing, however, we may overlook the complex nature of the artistic culture that painters and illuminators shared. Flemish illuminators, especially those associated with the court, could have broad responsibilities, which likely brought with them extensive interactions with the wider artistic culture.[12]

FAMILY TIES AND GUILD TIES AMONG PAINTERS AND ILLUMINATORS

Various spheres of activity outside the court also brought the arts of painting and illumination into regular or intensive contact. Prominent among them were the guilds and families of artists, both of which included practitioners of the two arts. Certain painters' guilds, such as those in Ghent and Tournai, required (or allowed) illuminators to join.[13] Simon Marmion was the son of a painter, the brother of a painter, the father of an illuminator, and the uncle of a painter. His brother Mille belonged to the painters' guild in Tournai, where he took two apprentices in the art of illumination.[14] Like his more successful brother, he may have practiced in both media. Simon's widow married Jan Provost, a painter.[15] The range of Simon's activities included painting, illumination, and the decorations for court festivities, as well as the polychroming of statues and the painting of armorials. Jan van der Straet, who earned the title of master illuminator in Tournai in 1463, was trained by the painter Louis le Duc, the nephew of Rogier van der Weyden. As noted, Van der Straet was among the artists who worked on the ducal marriage festivities in 1468. In 1515 a Jan van der Straet is described as a painter working on the decorations for the triumphal entry of Charles V into Bruges. If this was not the same Jan as the Tournai illuminator, he was almost certainly the artist's son. Lorne Campbell has recently raised the question of whether he might be identified with Juan de Flandes, the Flemish painter at the court of Isabella of Castile, whose paintings, as we shall see, owe a strong debt to manuscript illumination.[16]

As is frequently remarked, Alexander (or Sanders) Bening, the successful illuminator who belonged to the Ghent painters' guild, married Catherine van der Goes, who was likely a sister or niece of the painter Hugo van der Goes. Van der Goes and another painter, Joos van Ghent, sponsored Bening's entrance into the Ghent painters' guild in 1469. Their close ties to the trade of illumination have long been recognized.[17] Bening in turn sponsored the membership of one Jan van der Goes in the same guild in 1481.[18] The painter-illuminator Van Lathem's sons were, respectively, a painter and a goldsmith, and like him, they obtained official positions at court.[19] Horenbout, who was equally active as a painter and as an illuminator, took both a journeyman illuminator and an apprentice illuminator into his shop at Ghent. His children Susanna and Lucas, whose work is still poorly understood, both enjoyed reputations after their deaths as painters and illuminators, although Lodovico Guicciardini was careful to remark about Susanna: "She was an excellent painter, above all in very small works . . . and superb in the art of illumination."[20]

It is intriguing that the Italian historian distinguished between illumination and "very small" paintings. Carel van Mander credited Lucas Horenbout, who is first mentioned in the accounts of Henry VIII as "pictor maker," with teaching Hans Holbein the Younger the technique of illumination.[21] Holbein seems to have used that knowledge mainly to paint portrait miniatures. The similar techniques of manuscript illumination and the painting of the portrait miniature, both done in tempera on parchment, made the new art a natural heir to the older one. Alexander Bening's son Simon became a successful illuminator, while Simon's daughter Levina Teerlinc, like the children of Gerard Horenbout, took up the ascendant art of the portrait miniature.

In sum, families of professional artists plied their trades in a range of interrelated media. Family ties made the connections between the arts of painting and illumination intimate; extensive and regular contact often took place between these specialists. Illuminators belonged to painter's guilds and, in some cases, enjoyed the full rights and status of master painters, while painters trained illuminators and illuminators trained painters. Even those artists who stuck faithfully to one specialty were often related to and in contact with individuals who practiced the other. Via such paths, many painters of the period became acquainted with new illumination as it was being produced, just as illuminators would have gained familiarity with the work of certain painters. It was undoubtedly the success of illuminators that caused the painters' guilds to legislate to control their production.[22]

PAINTERS AS ILLUMINATORS

Despite this complex network of professional, familial, and social connections among painters, illuminators, and even some masters working in other media, most remained specialists. Jan van Eyck, Rogier van der Weyden, Petrus Christus, Joos van Ghent, and Gerard David are known to us today solely or largely as painters of works on panel (and sometimes canvas). If these artists worked as illuminators, that activity is undocumented. Yet some scholars have argued, on the basis of stylistic or technical evidence, that each of them also executed a small number of illuminations. Although no illuminations survive from the hands of Robert Campin (ca. 1375/79–1444) or Ambrosius Benson (d. before 1550), Campin is documented as an illuminator,[23] and Benson, according to court records, had two trunks containing patterns "for painting or illumination."[24] At one point Gerard David, his employer, confiscated them. Although David, whose illuminations are featured in this exhibition (cat. nos. 92, 99, 100, 103, 105, 107), is not mentioned in the registers or accounts of the confraternity of booksellers and illuminators, he must have had a close relationship with illuminators. At the time of his death in 1523,[25] his wife, Cornelia Cnoop, paid the book producers' confraternity for mortuary debts, a burial cloth, and for a mass to be said in her husband's honor.

Newly recognized details of the painting technique of certain panel painters suggest the specific nature of their association with illumination. A case in point is Petrus Christus, perhaps Jan van Eyck's most noted follower, although never his direct pupil.[26] A difference can be observed between the delicate, jewel-like quality of Christus's small oil paintings, rendered with the refined brushwork of a miniaturist, and his large-scale works, which are broadly painted. Max J. Friedländer once described his larger paintings as including stiff, geometrically conceived figures "turned out on a lathe."[27] It would appear that Christus's painting technique was more effective on a diminutive scale. Close study of the small-scale panel paintings reveals a remarkable resemblance to the technique and handling of manuscript illumination. Christus achieved the modeling of flesh tones by the application of extremely fine brushstrokes built up in an additive way over an underpainting that is usually in a flat, pinkish color (e.g., cat. nos. 4, 5). The modeling of draperies is not fully blended, as we would expect in oil painting, but rather shows the placement of contrasting strokes side by side and the definition of forms through black contour lines. G. J. Hoogewerff thought that Christus could be identified with Hand H of the Turin-Milan Hours,[28] and some have suggested that the heart-shaped mark that is part of the signature on his *Portrait of a Goldsmith* (New York, Metropolitan Museum of Art, Lehman Collection) is an illuminator's mark that had by law to be registered with the painters' guild. In light of the documentation presented here concerning the training of painters and illuminators and the evidence of Christus's own technique, one cannot help but wonder whether he was trained by an illuminator. While he is not recorded as a member of the confraternity of illuminators, it was not formed until about 1454, ten years after he had arrived in Bruges. By the early 1450s his focus may have shifted largely to panel painting, where he earned his reputation. Viewed against this background, the survival of a splendid illumination by Christus (cat. no. 6) has considerable significance.

Where some scholars have made persuasive or at least tantalizing attributions of illuminations to Van Eyck, Van der Weyden, and Christus, they are instances of a single miniature or a handful of miniatures within books that contain extensive campaigns of illumination. It appears that some artists active principally as panel painters were enlisted to paint miniatures that played a special role within the program of illumination, in the case of Van der Weyden, the spectacular frontispiece for Duke Philip's *Chroniques de Hainaut* (cat. no. 3). Despite the miniature's delicate state of preservation, the intelligence, dignity, and authority of Van der Weyden's individual portrayals of Philip and members of his court are apparent. The remaining miniatures of volume one of the *Chroniques* are by a team of anonymous illuminators; volumes two and three are, respectively, by the well-known if conventional Bruges illuminators Willem Vrelant and Loyset Liédet.

Although there is no direct evidence that Hugo van der Goes painted manuscript illuminations, a drawing probably from his workshop came to serve as a pattern for illumination (cat. no. 30). An assistant of the artist copied this design, showing a seated female saint, from one of his paintings, apparently as a *ricordo*. A Ghent illuminator used it at least once while the painter was still alive (cat. no. 32); other illuminators used it repeatedly many times after Van der Goes's death. It served usually as the model for miniatures of Saint Barbara and Saint Catherine, two of the most popular female saints in this time. They invariably figure prominently within illuminated cycles accompanying the suffrages of female saints. Given the drawing's large dimensions, it was probably intended for use in his own workshop. In light of his friendship and apparent familial relationship with Alexander Bening, however, it is possible that Bening or another illuminator colleague asked to borrow (or perhaps rent) it.

Many of Van der Goes's other motifs were copied by or entered the vocabulary of illuminators within his lifetime. Two of the better-known examples are the pair of shepherds greeted by an angel in the background of the Berlin *Adoration of the Shepherds* (see fig. 58). They reappear, with a change of outfit but little alteration in their complex poses, in *The Annunciation to the Shepherds* in the Voustre Demeure Hours (cat. no. 20).[29] Van der Goes's influence remained strong in manuscript illumination long after his death, but it is most clearly seen between 1475 and 1485 in illuminations by the Master of the First Prayer Book of Maximilian, the Master of the Houghton Miniatures, and the Ghent Associates. The Madrid Hours of William Lord Hastings (cat. no. 25), datable before 1483, derives a number of its miniatures from Goesian prototypes, notably from *The Trinity* in the Edinburgh panels and from a curious but revealing reconsideration of the painter's Vienna *Lamentation* (fig. 16).[30] Among Van der Goes's other paintings, the Portinari Altarpiece, the Edinburgh panels, and the Berlin *Adoration of the Shepherds* seem to have been particularly influential. The echoes from these paintings include conceptions of interior space, a store of physical types (especially the distinctive male peasants), and specific quotations. Since Van der Goes's influence on manuscript illumination was so strong within his own lifetime, it is reasonable to surmise that he played an active role, even if not a hands-on one, in the transformation of Flemish manuscript painting from the mid-1470s.[31]

The pattern of Gerard David's participation in manuscript illumination is perhaps more interactive than that of Van der Goes. He painted miniatures in only a few extant books of the 1480s and 1490s, but these include two ambitious volumes that eventually became the property of Queen Isabella of Castile (cat. nos. 100, 105). After about 1500 his activity in the medium increased somewhat, and he seems to have been enlisted to provide one or two miniatures each for several of the most luxurious books of the day, including the Mayer van den Bergh Breviary (cat. no. 92) and the Grimani Breviary (cat. no. 126).[32] His participation in these books for eminent patrons was limited but usually involved illuminations that are arguably among the most important in the book. They include the full-page miniature of the Virgin and Child in the Hours of Margaretha van Bergen (cat. no. 103) and the *Virgin and Child* and *Salvator Mundi* miniatures in the Escorial Hours (cat. no. 99). The last is the first full-page miniature after the calendar and a subject that often received special treatment. Other examples by David include miniatures of a patron saint or name saint of a book's intended owner, such as Saint Elizabeth of Hungary in Isabella's hours (cat. no. 105); of particularly beloved saints, such as Saint Catherine in the Mayer van den Bergh Breviary; or simply of the subjects in which he specialized or for which he was known, such as the Virgin and Child, the Adoration of the Magi, the Nativity, and the Virgin among Virgins (e.g., cat. nos. 100, 107). Moreover, in some of these miniatures he painted only the figures or some portion of the figures, so that his participation was even more exclusive and, as it were, rationed than might appear at first glance (see cat. no. 99).

David approached each illumination as a panel painter working on a small scale. He had readily available workshop patterns for compositions and motifs from which he could draw for the job at hand. Indeed, the attributions of some illuminations to David were initially based on their close relationship to identical compositions known from the artist's panel paintings. A closer look reveals a similar treatment in terms of handling and execution and serves to confirm the attribution in each case. David's characteristic attention to enlivening his compositions with carefully rendered faces and hands studied after life (see cat. no. 106) and the remarkable subtlety of his modeling of flesh tones come from his experience as a panel painter.

Take, for example, the *Saint Catherine* from the Mayer van den Bergh Breviary (ill. 92b and fig. 10), here attributed to David. Although the background is by another hand, the figure, by David, follows the aforementioned pattern drawing after Hugo van der Goes (cat. no. 30), adhering to the woman's pose and nearly exactly duplicating the configuration of drapery folds in her dress. Informing David's rendering, however, was a study after life probably inspired by the Goesian model. This is the head of a young girl that shares the same sheet with a study of a man's head (fig. 11). Immediately apparent is the similarity between the metalpoint drawing and the illumination in the attention given to the modest inclination of the head, so evocative of the figure's purity and mood of contemplation. Even more striking is

Figure 10 (near right)
GERARD DAVID
Saint Catherine. In the
Mayer van den Bergh
Breviary, fol. 611v (detail;
see cat. no. 92)

Figure 11 (far right)
GERARD DAVID
Four Heads, 1495.
Metalpoint over traces
of black chalk on
prepared paper,
12.8 × 9.2 cm
(5¹⁄₁₆ × 3⅝ in.), recto.
Frankfurt, Städelsches
Kunstinstitut

Figure 12 (below)
GERARD DAVID
*The Virgin and Child with
the Milk Soup,* ca. 1515.
Oil on panel, 33 ×
27.5 cm (13 × 10¹¹⁄₁₆ in.).
New York, Aurora Trust

the extremely close correspondence in the modeling
of the faces in diagonal parallel strokes across the
foreheads of the two. The delicate position of the
saint's hands was also individually studied in metalpoint drawings. A study of four girls' heads and two
hands (cat. no. 106) likely provided a model for Saint
Catherine's proper left hand, its bony structure characteristically emphasized by David.

David understood the technique of illumination, which required that he model the draperies in
contrasting colors and use disengaged brushstrokes
on the surface of the forms. In a sense, he simply
reversed his panel painting technique. The conventions of hatching and cross-hatching that he applied
in the modeling of draperies in the meticulous underdrawings of his panel paintings, he also employed
on the surface of the draperies of his illuminations.[33]

In *The Visitation* in the Mayer van den Bergh
Breviary (ill. 92c), the entire illumination, possibly
including the border, is by David. The composition is
a close-up view of the focal point of *The Visitation* in
the London Hastings Hours (cat. no. 41), a pattern in
regular use in the workshop of the Master of the First
Prayer Book of Maximilian. The large figures—unparalleled elsewhere in the book—are reminiscent

Figure 13
JAN VAN EYCK
*Saint Francis Receiving
the Stigmata*, 1430s. Oil
on parchment on wood
panel, 12.4 × 14.6 cm
(4⅞ × 5¾ in.).
Philadelphia Museum
of Art, John G. Johnson
Collection, inv. 314

of David's paintings of the Virgin and Child with the Milk Soup of around 1515 (e.g., fig. 12).[34] The pose of
the Virgin's head and its distinctly chiaroscuro treatment parallel the same features in the Aurora Trust
Virgin, and the view past city houses to a pond surrounded by trees appears in both. Elizabeth finds an
antecedent in the type of the older Virgin in paintings by David representing Christ Taking Leave of His
Mother.[35] In these respects—composition and technique—David merged his activities in the crafts of
panel painting and manuscript illumination.

As the techniques of painting and illumination evolved, artists in both media experimented to
a degree with materials and techniques. One of these areas of experimentation was painting in oil or in
tempera on parchment supports that were pasted down or tacked to secondary panel supports, producing in effect small easel paintings, diptychs, or triptychs. The Philadelphia *Saint Francis Receiving the Stigmata* attributed to Van Eyck (fig. 13) and the *Head of Christ* by Christus (cat. no. 4) are two early examples
of paintings in oil on parchment mounted on panel. In these cases, as well as in others where the rendering approximates the art of illumination, one can imagine that the parchment was simply used because,
like a good white ground preparation on panel, it provided a smooth, solid, and white reflective surface
on which to apply the thin glazes of a Flemish oil painting. In other words, the parchment was a good
substitute in its properties for the application of a white ground preparation and was perhaps more
easily used.

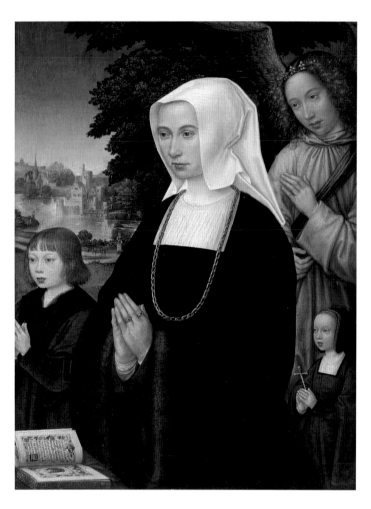

Figure 14
MASTER OF JAMES IV
OF SCOTLAND
*Portrait of Livina de
Steelant*, ca. 1500–1510. Oil
on panel, 43 × 33.5 cm
(16¹⁵⁄₁₆ × 13³⁄₁₆ in.). Ghent,
Museum voor Schone
Kunsten, inv. 1937-A

PAINTING IN OIL BY ILLUMINATORS

As noted above, those artists whom one might describe today more as illuminators than as painters—such as Lieven van Lathem, the Master of James IV of Scotland, and Simon Marmion—are so described on the basis of incomplete evidence. While we have no paintings for Van Lathem, scholars have adduced at least one surviving painting and one drawing as evidence for his activity as a painter.[36] If one worked on the basis of the documentary evidence alone, one would assume that Marmion was more active as a painter than as an illuminator, yet the patterns of survival suggest otherwise.[37] The quantity of surviving manuscripts makes it clear that, even with the collaboration of assistants, he spent a great deal of time on illumination throughout his career. For the painter and illuminator Gerard Horenbout, no paintings survive, but a pair of portraits on panel have been attributed to the Master of James IV of Scotland (see below), with whom he may be identified.[38] Although the painters' guilds promoted clear boundaries between the painters' and illuminators' respective crafts, the records also show that some illuminators did earn the full guild credentials of a painter.[39] Indeed certain painters, such as Christus and Juan de Flandes, may have started their careers as illuminators.

By way of contrast to the example of painters such as David, technical evidence shows the carryover in the tempera technique of Simon Marmion's illuminations to his work as a panel painter.[40] As in the case of Christus, the characteristics of Marmion's panel paintings indicate the methods of an artist trained in illumination: greater proficiency in small-scale works; the chalky, matte-looking, rather than enamel-like, quality of the paint; and the clearly visible, individual, unblended brushstrokes of flesh tones. Marmion's underdrawings are very summary indeed, the modeling taking place in the upper paint layers, as is the case with illumination.

Some paintings in oil have been persuasively attributed to illuminators not only because the figure types, motifs, and compositions bear similarities to the work of illuminators but also because the handling calls to mind the more additive technique employed by manuscript illuminators, in which modeling is built up largely in the upper paint layers. A good example is *The Destruction of Jerusalem by the Armies of the Emperor Titus* (Ghent, Museum voor Schone Kunsten), the epic predella panel on which hordes of small soldiers, brilliantly orchestrated, surge across a tremendous expanse, giving the panel the feel of a greatly elongated manuscript illumination. The artist appears to rely less on glazes than on relatively opaque paint layers to achieve his effects, modeling much more on the surface than in depth. Bodo Brinkmann has remarked rightly that the poses of some of the compact figures owe much to the Vienna Master of Mary of Burgundy, but the handling of the medium here is less subtle and graceful than in the master's miniatures.[41]

A pair of portraits of Lievin van Pottelsberghe and his wife, Livina de Steelant (fig. 14), alluded to above, are correctly attributed to the Master of James IV of Scotland (Gerard Horenbout?).[42] The facial types and proportions of the angels and the painting of the wings recall prominent features of the illuminations of the Master of James IV, especially as found in the Spinola Hours (cat. no. 124). And the glassy surface of the water in the background also evokes a distinctive effect used by this artist.

The mid-sixteenth-century Bruges historian Denis Harduyn identified Simon Bening, who has been known in recent times only as an illuminator, as a panel painter, too—an assertion also made by Antonius Sanders (1586–1664).[43] Included in this exhibition is an oil painting that is probably by him or by his workshop (cat. no. 142). One of two paintings in oil of the Virgin and Child that have been attributed to him,[44] it features his familiar type of the Virgin, along with landscape motifs that recall his miniatures. Here too the oil technique owes much to manuscript illumination, and, not surprisingly, the painting is less subtle and refined than the artist's illuminations.

For Bening the opportunity to create small altarpieces and independent devotional images had a strong appeal. He seems to have specialized in a hybrid form, the illuminated altarpiece in tempera on parchment mounted on board, which he almost certainly produced in larger numbers than survive today (see cat. no. 157). Due to the inherent fragility of freestanding parchment and the fugitive behavior of certain of the artist's vegetable-based pigments when exposed to sunlight, it is likely that some were destroyed. When he began to paint such independent works in tempera, it made practical sense perhaps to use the support that he was accustomed to employing in his daily work as an illuminator. The largest and finest of these, the Saint Jerome Triptych in the Escorial (fig. 15), at 39 centimeters (ca. 15 inches) in height,[45] is fairly well preserved and shows Bening succeeding on a much larger scale than he customarily undertook. It features his largest and one of his most accomplished landscape settings, which unfolds continuously over the three panels of the triptych, reminiscent of his composing of pairs of calendar miniatures over the expanse of a two-page opening. The technique here is the same, tempera on parchment. He and his workshop painted some smaller triptychs in the same format (see cat. no. 157), including one probably from his workshop (Houston, Museum of Fine Arts; see fig. 9).[46] In this way he succeeded in widening the range of his artistic production without abandoning the medium for which he had genius.

One of Bening's most original and dramatic works, the Stein Quadriptych (cat. no. 146), deserves mention in this context. It shows sixty-four scenes that tell the story of the lives of the Virgin and Christ, from Joachim and Anne at the Golden Gate to the Last Judgment. The very small miniatures, each less

Figure 15
SIMON BENING
The Penitent Saint Jerome with *The Flight into Egypt* and *Saint Anthony of Padua*, triptych, 1530s. Tempera on parchment, 39 × 64 cm (15⅜ × 25³⁄₁₆ in.). El Escorial, Spain, Monasterio de San Lorenzo

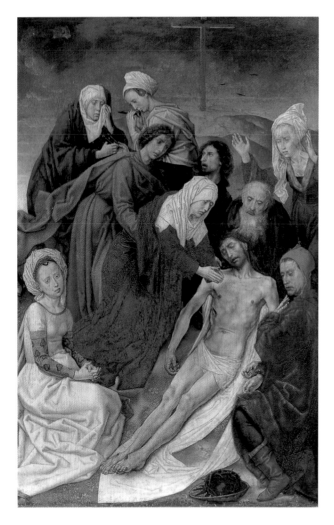

Figure 16
HUGO VAN DER GOES
The Lamentation, ca. 1469.
Oil on wood panel, 34.4
× 22.8 cm (13⁹⁄₁₆ × 9 in.).
Vienna, Kunsthistorisches
Museum, inv. 5822

than three inches tall, are currently arranged in four panels, with six-teen on each. Some specialists have wondered whether the very lengthy cycle was originally illuminated for a devotional book. There are many reasons to think that Bening conceived it as a freestanding altarpiece, however, notably the existence of various precedents, including his other impressive forays into the illumination of altar-pieces as well as altarpieces by Flemish panel painters that consisted of many small scenes from the life of Christ.[47]

MANUSCRIPT ILLUMINATIONS AS SOURCES FOR PAINTERS

Whereas the influence of Van der Goes on Flemish manu-script illumination of the last quarter of the fifteenth century is undisputed, the possibility that the relationship between painters and illuminators was more reciprocal in this period has received less con-sideration.[48] While Van der Goes himself left us no trace of his own hand in a manuscript painting, we have argued for his intimate rela-tionship with the new generation of Ghent illuminators, a link docu-mented by family and guild ties. Here we offer evidence of ways in which such contact might have inspired his work. Friedrich Winkler identified the figure of John the Evangelist supporting the sorrowful Virgin Mary in the painter's Vienna *Lamentation* (fig. 16) as a source for John holding back the Virgin Mary, who is wailing in grief over the prone Christ as he is nailed to the cross, in the Vienna Hours of Mary of Burgundy (fig. 17 and cat. no. 19).[49] In fact, the motif in the minia-ture is more likely the antecedent since John's action is more logical and integral to the narrative. John is a poignant figure in the painting, but his action is awkward. Along with most of the other figures, he seems isolated in his own world of grief. Van der Goes's Virgin, with fingers joined in prayer, seems to hover over the body of Christ, while John weakly restrains her. Moreover, the underdrawing of the Vienna *Lamentation* shows John in a closer, more forward-leaning position holding up the Virgin, as in the miniature.[50] While the dating of both manuscript and painting is controversial, it is plausible that the painting is later.[51]

Another miniature by the Vienna Master of Mary of Burgundy that may have served as a source for Van der Goes is *Alexander Takes the Hand of Roxanne* of 1470 (ill. 54a). The pose of the elegant Roxanne kneeling before her prince, with both accompanied by attendants, anticipates that of Abigail kneeling be-fore King David in Van der Goes's lost painting, which is preserved in many copies.[52] That Van der Goes might have seen such a miniature by the Vienna Master before it entered the ducal library is suggested by his friendship with Joos van Ghent, the Vienna Master's lasting source of inspiration.[53]

An artist sometimes cited as following the example of Flemish manuscript illumination of the last quarter of the fifteenth century is Hieronymus Bosch. He was from Brabant, and s'Hertogenbosch, his home, was under Burgundian and then Hapsburg rule. Indeed the assembly of the Order of the Golden Fleece was held there in 1481, and Bosch received a commission for a huge altarpiece of the Last Judgment from Philip the Handsome in 1504. *The Garden of Earthly Delights* (Madrid, Museo del Prado) was by 1517 in the possession of the art patron and Hapsburg chamberlain Henry III of Nassau (see cat. no. 149), who was the nephew of the bibliophile and ranking Burgundian official Engelbert II of Nassau (see cat. nos. 18, 120). Engelbert, in the eyes of some, commissioned the painting.[54] So it is conceivable that Bosch, through such contacts, had knowledge of the Burgundian/Hapsburg court libraries. Walter S. Gibson has shown how much Bosch's early art is steeped in Dutch manuscript illumination.[55] His unusual iconography had

Figure 17 (opposite)
VIENNA MASTER OF
MARY OF BURGUNDY
Christ Nailed to the Cross.
In the Hours of Mary of
Burgundy, fol. 43v
(see cat. no. 19)

Figure 18
SIMON MARMION
Adam and Eve in Paradise.
In *Les Sept Âges du monde*,
ca. 1460. 43.5 × 30.5 cm
(17⅛ × 12 in.). Brussels,
Bibliothèque royale
de Belgique, Ms. 9047,
fol. 1v (detail)

Figure 19
HIERONYMUS BOSCH
Adam and Eve, interior
left wing of *The Garden
of Earthly Delights*,
triptych, 1503–4. Oil
on wood panel, 220 ×
97 cm (86⁹⁄₁₆ × 38³⁄₁₆ in.).
Madrid, Museo del
Prado

countless antecedents in late medieval manuscript illumination, although it is often difficult to ascertain whether the manuscript motifs were actual sources for the artist.

The opaque, tempera-like character of Bosch's paint material sometimes calls to mind Flemish manuscript illumination.[56] Indeed the somewhat pale and pastel tonalities of Marmion's illuminations in particular anticipate the wholly distinctive palette of Bosch. Here again, scholars have cited examples of Marmion's illuminations as antecedents for Bosch's art without viewing them necessarily as specific models.[57] Marmion executed the only surviving illuminated copy of *Les Visions du chevalier Tondal* (cat. no. 14), a widely read text that Bosch may have drawn upon. The delicate, spindly physiques and pale flesh of Marmion's nudes, such as Tondal himself or Adam and Eve in *Adam and Eve in Paradise* in *Les Sept Âges du monde* (fig. 18), are remarkably similar to Adam and Eve in the left wing of Bosch's *Garden of Earthly Delights* (fig. 19) and to the naked souls in the triptych's central panel.[58]

In a comparable way the emaciated Christ of the Last Judgment, a figure type that Marmion treated in many similar full-page miniatures of this subject (see ill. 44b and cat. nos. 33, 37) in the 1470s and 1480s, closely anticipates the Christ in Judgment of Bosch's Vienna triptych (Akademie der Bildenden Künste).[59] Van der Weyden's Christ of the Last Judgment in the Beaune Altarpiece is sometimes cited as an influence on Bosch, yet both the pose of Christ in Bosch's painting and the arrangement and coloring of the figures on either side of him more closely resemble those in Marmion's miniatures. While Bosch ultimately brought greater nuance and fireworks to the flames and darkness of hell, the matte quality of the paint, the depiction of tortured souls in a half-light, and the way the flames spout and spark also call to mind Marmion's inferno from the Tondal (ill. 14b). Finally, the low, round trees with narrow trunks that carry the eye into the distance are features of both artists' work, as, for example, in the painter's *Saint John the Baptist in Meditation* (Madrid, Museo Lazaro-Galdiano) and in the illuminator's Adam and Eve in *Les Sept Âges du monde* (fig. 18).[60]

Thus, in various aspects, Bosch's art recalls the illumination of Marmion, certainly more so than the work of any Flemish painter and in formal aspects more so than the work of Dutch illuminators who came before Bosch.[61] The painter may have had access to Marmion's books through his links to the Hapsburg Burgundian court. It may also be that the illuminator's paintings, many of which are lost, were known to Bosch.

The activity of Gerard David illustrates the ongoing interchange between painters and illuminators. Documentation survives pertaining to a court case between David and his workshop assistant, Ambrosius Benson. As noted earlier, David had held in escrow two trunks of workshop paraphernalia on the condition that Benson repay a debt to David by working it off three days a week until the sum of seven *livres de gros* was met. Among the items in the trunks were the aforementioned patterns for panel painting or manuscript illumination.[62] In addition there were unfinished paintings, a small sketchbook, a box of pigments, diverse patterns that David had taken from the house of Adriaen Isenbrandt but that apparently belonged to Benson, and patterns that Benson had borrowed from Aelbrecht Cornelis for a fee. It is not known who designed the patterns or whether David had plans for their use, other than holding onto them until the debt was paid. As noted above, it is intriguing that certain patterns were considered usable for both media. As striking is the fact that all those named, who at one time or another might have enjoyed access to the patterns, were strictly or primarily painters.

Furthermore, evidence may be adduced for the existence of patterns that David created for the use of illuminators, one of which he subsequently used for a painting of his own, even though the drawings themselves do not survive. *Saint Anthony of Padua and the Miracle of the Host* and *Saint Bernard's Vision of the Virgin and Child* in the Hours of Isabella of Castile (cat. no. 105) are Davidian but not painted by David. In the former miniature (fig. 20), the crowd of male onlookers, arrayed in a narrow horizontal band, is evocative of such masterworks of the 1490s as David's *Flaying of Sisamnes* from the *Justice of Cambyses* panels (Bruges, Groeningemuseum). The facial types are specifically Davidian. The face of the tonsured Saint Anthony recalls the more lined, hirsute visage of the enthroned Sisamnes, while a hoary version of Cambyses himself, wearing a virtually identical fur-brimmed cap, appears in the miniature behind the kneeling donkey.

David's lost pattern for the Saint Anthony of Padua composition seems to have entered the repertoire of models of the Maximilian Master as a pattern thereafter and is among those patterns to which Simon Bening also enjoyed access.[63] David himself took up the composition, mirror reversed, on panel (fig. 21). It is an awkwardly cropped variation, ca. 1500–1505, that has the quality of a condensation of the more open, carefully thought-through pattern reflected in the miniature of the Isabella Hours.[64] In this instance it seems likely that the painting is based either upon the miniature or, more likely, on the artist's own pattern for the miniature. *Saint Bernard's Vision* is comparably Davidian, especially in the pose and drapery of Saint Bernard, which correspond remarkably to those of Saint Anthony of Padua, and in the compact Virgin and Child.[65] This composition also entered the repertoire of patterns passed down by illuminators over the next generation.

David's paintings show that he was familiar with the compositions and motifs of the leading illuminators of the day and borrowed from them often.[66] His assimilation of patterns used by illuminators is evident even in his earliest paintings. Among these is his *Crucifixion* of ca. 1475 (Madrid, Thyssen-Bornemisza Collection), which borrows a group of standing soldiers from a Crucifixion in the Hours of

Catherine of Cleves of the 1440s (New York, Morgan Library, Ms. 945, fol. 66v) and refers to landscapes by another Utrecht illuminator, the Master of Evert Zoudenbalch.[67] Later, David borrowed from the work of illuminators for unusual subjects that appeared more often in miniatures than in panel painting. He assimilated features from *The Judgment of Cambyses* by Loyset Liédet from the manuscript of Antoine de la Sale, *La Sale* (Brussels, Bibliothèque royale de Belgique, Mss. 9287–88, fol. 132) into his *Flaying of Sisamnes*.[68] He looked at *The Marriage at Cana* by the Master of Edward IV in Jean Mansel's *Vie, passion, et vengeance de nostre seigneur Jhesu Christ (Vie du Christ)* (fig. 23) for the arrangement of figures around the table and the general composition of his *Marriage at Cana* (figs. 22, 23).[69] Moreover, one may find the source for David's *Christ Carrying the Cross* of ca. 1505 (New York, Metropolitan Museum of Art, Lehman Collection) in an illumination by the Master of the First Prayer Book of Maximilian in a book of hours (ca. 1497–98; cat. no. 90, fol. 112v). The companion piece, *The Resurrection*, is likewise influenced by a pattern that circulated among illuminators and was later employed in the Grimani Breviary (cat. no. 126, fol. 162v).[70]

The miniatures that David contributed to the Isabella Breviary in the 1480s (cat. no. 100) are based in part on illuminations in the London Hastings Hours (cat. no. 41) by the Master of the First Prayer Book of Maximilian, sometimes thought to be Alexander Bening, who joined the illuminators' confraternity in Bruges in 1486, not long after David's arrival there. In fact, quite a number of paintings and illuminations by David are connected to patterns that first appeared in miniatures by the Master of the First Prayer Book of Maximilian. In turn, a number of these patterns were employed later in miniatures by Simon Bening, testifying perhaps to the ongoing ownership of these specific patterns by the Bening workshop.[71] They demonstrate that by the late fifteenth century certain painters routinely drew upon patterns and other compositions created by illuminators.

Some of the examples of the painter David's appropriations from manuscripts indicated here illustrate a particularly important role that illuminators played for painters. Manuscript illuminators tackled a much broader range of subject matter, especially secular themes but also certain devotional and Old Testament subjects. The writings of eminent theologians and clerics, such as Ludolph of Saxony (see cat. no. 96), were particularly useful textual sources for painters for a wide range of biblical subject matter, while illuminated copies of their writings usually included representations of a greater range of subjects than was customarily found in independent paintings.[72] The series of forty-seven small panels in oil painted for Queen Isabella of Castile by Juan de Flandes in collaboration with Michael Sittow offers further instances of manuscript illuminations as artistic models for particular subjects.[73] For these paintings

Figure 22
GERARD DAVID
AND WORKSHOP
The Marriage at Cana,
ca. 1503. Oil on wood
panel, 100 × 128 cm
(39¼ × 50½ in.). Paris,
Musée du Louvre,
inv. 1995

Figure 23
MASTER OF
EDWARD IV
The Marriage at Cana.
In Jean Mansel, *Vie,
passion, et vengeance de
nostre seigneur Jhesu
Christ,* vol. 1, between
1486 and 1493. 35.5 ×
24.7 cm (14 × 9¾ in.)
(cat. no. 97). Paris,
Bibliothèque de
l'Arsenal, Ms. fr. 5205,
fol. 23

Figure 24
MICHAEL SITTOW
The Coronation of the Virgin, between 1496 and 1504. Oil on wood panel, 24.5 × 18.3 cm (9⅝ × 7¼ in.). Paris, Musée du Louvre, inv. RF 1966-11

Figure 25
MASTER OF JAMES IV OF SCOTLAND
The Coronation of the Virgin. In the Breviary of Isabella of Castile, fol. 437 (detail; see cat. no. 100)

scholars have already noted precise sources in Flemish manuscripts that were likely at hand, such as Juan's patron's own breviary (cat. no. 100). *The Temptation of Christ* (Washington, D.C., National Gallery of Art) follows the breviary's version by the Master of the Dresden Prayer Book not only in the pose of Christ but also in the massing of the landscape features, down to the arrangement of certain rocks, trees, and buildings.[74] Juan exquisitely adapted his version to the vertical format and exploited fully the nuances of the oil technique to fashion a work that is even more compelling.

Scholars have consistently linked other images in this cycle, including Sittow's *Assumption of the Virgin* (Washington, D.C., National Gallery of Art), to miniatures by the Master of the Dresden Prayer Book.[75] Sittow's *Coronation of the Virgin* (fig. 24) from the cycle illustrates a theme that was more popular in devotional books than in panel paintings.[76] Sittow's composition reflects particular features of the version in Isabella's breviary illuminated by the Master of James IV of Scotland (fig. 25), such as the pose of the Virgin and her white mantle, the billowing clouds along the perimeter of the image, the tiaraed God the Father, and the red robes of Christ and God the Father. Even closer, although in mirror reflection, is a detached miniature of the same subject by the Master of Edward IV from a book of hours (fig. 26). Most of the basic elements recur in Sittow's version: Christ and God the Father both seated on the diagonal, the Virgin dressed in white kneeling before them, an angel crowning her, the dove of the Holy Spirit hovering over the other members of the Trinity, and clouds along the outer edges of the miniature.[77] From Sittow's early years in Bruges during the 1480s, when the Master of Edward IV was also active there, he

Figure 26
MASTER OF EDWARD IV
*The Coronation of the
Virgin*, 1480–90. 17.3 ×
13.7 cm (6¹³⁄₁₆ × 5⅜ in.),
detached leaf. Baltimore,
The Walters Art
Museum, inv. W.443f

Figure 27
JUAN DE FLANDES
*Christ Appearing to the
Virgin with the Redeemed
of the Old Testament*,
before 1505. Oil on oak
panel, 21.2 × 15.4 cm
(8⅜ × 6¹⁄₁₆ in.). London,
National Gallery,
NG 1280

was exposed to manuscript images of this type. When he painted *The Coronation*, he probably had such illuminations in mind, including the Coronation from his patron's breviary.

Overall, the Isabella panels consistently reflect the compositional simplicity and iconic character of the full-page miniatures in devotional books of the era, the Vienna Master of Mary of Burgundy's subtle handling of light, and that illuminator's distinctive atmospheric veiling of the horizon that coalesces individual form into a larger whole. In those panels that feature a sea of individuals, such as *The Multiplication of the Loaves* and *Christ Appearing to the Virgin with the Redeemed of the Old Testament* (fig. 27), Juan de Flandes also seems to have been inspired by the Vienna Master of Mary of Burgundy. The illuminator's Last Judgment miniature (ill. 18b) shows an assembly of souls enveloped in a comparably even, diaphanous light; they are articulated individually only by pale contours. As in the miniature, the pale forms in the painting meld into a unified whole.[78] The Vienna Master's handling of the flickering torchlight in his nocturnal *Arrest of Christ* (cat. no. 18, fol. 56v) may also have provided inspiration for the panel of this subject.[79]

Neil MacLaren drew attention to a pair of inscriptions on the back of two of the Isabella panels in Madrid—"Juan Astrat" and "Juᵒ Astrat"—which might offer clues to the painter's identity.[80] As noted above, Lorne Campbell identified a Jan van der Straet as a master illuminator in Tournai in 1463 and a Jan van der Straet as a painter at Bruges in 1515.[81] Was Juan de Flandes strongly influenced by the latest trends in Flemish illumination during the 1470s because that was his trade at the beginning of his career? Did he only later become a painter? Was he therefore Jan van der Straet of Tournai? If both documents refer to the same person, then he enjoyed a long career that stretched over fifty years.[82] This is unusual for the time, but then Simon Bening had a career that extended nearly sixty years. If the illuminator of 1463 was instead the father of the painter mentioned in 1515, was the former the father of Juan de Flandes? In either case a plausible explanation for the artist's connection to manuscript illumination is at hand. It seems very possible that Juan de Flandes was one of the two documented Jan van der Straets, or both, but more than that is difficult to say. Whether one agrees with these theses or not, manuscript illumination clearly helped to form the style of the painter Juan de Flandes.

Both for the scale of its small panels, mostly about 21 by 16 centimeters (8¼ by 6⁵⁄₁₆ inches), and for certain Gospel narratives more distinctive to manuscripts, the Isabella cycle suggests various reasons painters might look to book painting for inspiration. A more complex and intriguing case concerns landscape as artistic subject matter. The wide-ranging secular themes more readily demanded of illuminators, from the cycle of twelve (or even more) calendar illustrations in devotional books to diverse historical narratives, created opportunities to explore a tremendous variety of outdoor settings in ways that painters in oil rarely pursued. Manuscript illuminators anticipated specific themes of the landscapes of Cornelis Massys in the 1540s. For example, Massys's *Mary and Joseph at the Inn* of 1543 (cat. no. 164) treats a theme that was particularly popular in Flemish manuscript illumination, due largely to a pattern dating to the late 1470s (cf. cat. no. 21). The arrangement of Joseph and Mary met by the female proprietor at the door of the inn closely resembles the much-copied manuscript source. Moreover, the subtle handling of the seasonal foliage is anticipated in calendar miniatures by Simon Bening of the preceding decade.[83] Massys might have known the Mary and Joseph composition through the Master of James IV of Scotland, who also copied it in his manuscripts (cat. no. 128).

The influence of illuminators in the domain of landscape likely began much earlier. One of the Antwerp painter Joachim Patinir's clearest forebears in the development of the deep-set vista was the Antwerp illuminator Lieven van Lathem (figs. 28, 29). Van Lathem used rivers and seas in particular to create atmospheric and winding recessions, even in miniatures that, like those in the Prayer Book of Charles the Bold (cat. no. 16), are only a couple of inches tall. Starting with the Master of the Dresden Prayer Book, an artist of the generation after Van Lathem, illuminators began to make the annual cycle of climatic changes a subject to rival and sometimes eclipse the labors and the zodiacal signs that traditionally (and perpetually) illustrated the calendar. For illuminators the focus was not only a landscape's scope and expanse, the true and in a sense the only theme of Patinir's work, but also its atmosphere and texture. Beginning with the Voustre Demeure Hours, circa 1475–80 (cat. no. 20 and fig. 30), calendar cycles developed narratives that, whether figures predominated or not, traced the slow but deliberate course of a year's continuous climatic change. In certain calendars the Dresden Master doubled the number of miniatures and expanded the variety and character of the figural narratives (cat. nos. 32, 33). The story of a year might encompass a snowstorm; a cold, damp, and blustery winter's day; a foggy spring day with abundant signs of new growth; the sunny summer days that nurture crops and lead to harvest; the changing colors of autumn; and the barren landscape at the onset of winter.

By the time such artists as the Master of James IV of Scotland and Simon Bening took up the brush, multiple narratives gave calendar cycles a level of interest and novelty rarely equaled elsewhere in a book's decoration (fig. 31).[84] These narratives range from the story of the annual cycle of ever-changing seasonal weather to those of the steadily expanding variety of aristocratic leisure activities. Other cycles gain immediacy by setting the traditional labors in vividly characterized topographies, including urban settings, and depicting figures in contemporary costume while mixing peasants and aristocrats to suggest everyday life. From the vantage point of the fully developed landscapes of the months, the inspiring, often vast perspectives of Patinir (which strongly influenced Simon Bening) seem narrower in their ambitions. Perhaps more surprising, by the time Pieter Bruegel the Elder began to paint his cycle of the seasons (or months), during the 1560s, sophisticated landscapes in manuscript calendars had flourished for several generations, to the point of overshadowing a book's devotional imagery. Bening's winter scene in the

Figure 28
LIEVEN VAN LATHEM
Saint Christopher. In the
Prayer Book of Charles
the Bold, fol. 26
(see cat. no. 16)

Figure 29
JOACHIM PATINIR
*Landscape with Saint
Christopher*, early 1520s.
Oil on wood panel,
127 × 172 cm (50 ×
67¾ in.). El Escorial,
Spain, Monasterio
de San Lorenzo

Figure 30
MASTER OF
THE DRESDEN
PRAYER BOOK
January. In the Voustre
Demeure Hours, fol. 2
(see cat. no. 20)

Figure 31
MASTER OF JAMES IV
OF SCOTLAND
November. In the Breviary
of Cardinal Domenico
Grimani, fol. 11v
(see cat. no. 126)

Da Costa Hours (ill. 140a) predates Bruegel's by two generations; one finds no equal to it in the interim.[85] In the end Bruegel drew not only upon the iconography of Bening's calendars but also upon the variety of their presentation, including the high vantage points, the sensitivity to light and varied atmospheres, and, we suspect, also upon the flecklike brushwork of the later Bening cycles. This technique lent itself well to creating particularly dense and charged atmospheres. Bruegel did not use it often, but it is most compelling in the autumnal *Landscape with a Magpie on the Gallows* (cat. no. 165). The more conservative character of independent painting is highlighted by panel painters' slow embrace of the iconography of the seasons. Bruegel was far from the first to paint such subjects, but earlier painters had not treated them as boldly and originally as the illuminators had.[86]

The professional cultures of painters and manuscript illuminators intersected and overlapped to such a degree that the exchange of ideas and imagery between the two media was natural and inevitable. In many cases illuminators and painters were related by blood or marriage, they often belonged to the same guilds, they sometimes trained one another, and they shared a body of subject matter and iconography. Some of the finest illuminators were also painters. Many of the best painters executed illuminations or worked closely with illuminators. Indeed, court documents register a dispute between painters over a trunk that contained patterns for "painting or illumination." Surviving examples also show that artists experimented with oil on parchment. And visual evidence suggests that some painters may have begun their careers as illuminators. While many painters appear to have been specialists in oil on panel, as suggested by the guild regulations and surviving work, the boundaries between the media were probably less rigid in practice than this body of evidence indicates. Accordingly, the flow of ideas may have been greater than has generally been thought.

Many of the artists connected to the court were painter-illuminators for whom the art of illumination was one of their strengths and a key part of their practice even as they demonstrated their versatility to meet the needs of the court. The large number of illuminators who held court positions—such as Van Lathem, Hennecart, and Horenbout—or enjoyed ongoing, generous court patronage over decades—such as Marmion and Simon Bening—indicates the prominence that this art form held within the artistic culture. Indeed, it is intriguing that one of the few known works that Rogier van der Weyden executed for Philip the Good, besides portraits on panel, is a manuscript illumination. This favor in turn lent the art of illumination a certain eminence and prestige within the wider artistic culture. Well established is the fact that painters from Ghent strongly shaped the character of Flemish manuscript painting from the 1470s. Hugo van der Goes was related by marriage to a successful illuminator, and during his lifetime a style of illumination emerged that drew extensively upon his pictorial ideas. For the next generation, the art of Gerard David would contribute to the nourishment and renewal of Flemish illumination under the brush of Simon Bening. At the same time the range of subject matter that regularly confronted illuminators replenished the vocabulary of Flemish art, making book illumination a fertile source for painters from Bosch to David to Bruegel the Elder. David seemed to draw from manuscript illumination as much as he gave. More complex are the cases of Petrus Christus and Juan de Flandes, whose paintings are so clearly informed by the technique of tempera on parchment that one suspects that they began their training in the art of illumination.

The priority given to the study of painting in the modern era has to a degree encouraged its study within an art-historical vacuum. Most major art museums concentrate on the collecting and display of paintings. Even museums that focus on medieval art rarely feature significant collections of manuscript illumination. At the same time the complexities of manuscript studies and the relatively poor documentation of the art of major illuminators often discourage historians of paintings from exploring the role of illumination in the larger artistic culture. Clearly this situation deserves redress. While arguments concerning the direction of influence are subject to debate, we have attempted to outline a well-documented historical perspective for considering the interactions between illuminators and painters. Manuscript illumination provided a broad array of sources and inspiration for painters. Under the Flemish Burgundian dukes and well into the post-Burgundian era, manuscript illumination retained a prominent position in the hierarchy of the arts. Even as the importance of painting in oil and the illustrated printed book rose among the elite, manuscript illumination remained an aristocratic art with an ever more cosmopolitan audience. Even when the number of first-rate illuminators in Flanders declined dramatically, especially by the second quarter of the sixteenth century, a leading artist such as Simon Bening continued to enjoy patronage from the loftiest and most discerning circles across Europe.

Notes

We would like to acknowledge the many fruitful comments and suggestions provided for this essay by Catherine Reynolds, Scot McKendrick, Elizabeth Teviotdale, Elizabeth Morrison, Chiyo Ishikawa, Lynn Jacobs, and Myra Orth.

1. Examples go back to early Christian art. Concerning the San Marco mosaics and the Cotton Genesis, for example, see Kitzinger 1975: 22–31. Weitzmann (1975: 22–31) cites examples of illuminations copied into other media. Pächt (1961: 166–75) discusses a famous example of an English Romanesque illuminator whose work anticipates a style of fresco in Siena. Some have seen French manuscript illuminators of the early fifteenth century as crucial forerunners of Van Eyck (for example, Meiss 1968: 72–74).

2. On this topic, see Catherine Reynolds, "Illuminators and the Painters' Guilds" (this volume).

3. Tempera is the term for the water-soluble medium of manuscript illumination. Its binding medium is usually egg white or gum arabic.

4. Reynolds, "Illuminators and the Painters' Guilds" (see note 2).

5. Campbell and Foister 1986: 720.

6. Campbell and Foister 1986: 719–21.

7. See esp. Campbell and Foister 1986: 720–21.

8. Van der Haeghen 1914: 30–35.

9. Reynolds, "Illuminators and the Painters' Guilds" (see note 2); for more on painters who also worked as illuminators, see Duclos 1910: 385.

10. Significantly for the prominence of illuminators in the court milieu, three of the seven most highly paid artists (out of a total of thirty-four) engaged for the Feast of the Pheasant were illuminators. See Martens (M.) 1999: 405.

11. Reynolds, "Illuminators and the Painters' Guilds" (see note 2).

12. The evidence from France is similar, and even more striking. During the fifteenth century, such major artists as Jean Fouquet, Barthélemy d'Eyck, Enguerrand Quarton, Jean Bourdichon, Jean Poyet, and Jean Perréal executed both paintings and illuminations (Paris 1993: 130–31, 224–25, 238, 293, 306–8, 365–66). Here too most of these figures were official court artists or enjoyed continuous service at a major court. In the sixteenth century Noël Bellemare from Antwerp was active in Paris as a "master painter," a designer of stained glass, and an illuminator (Leproux 1998: 125, 142; Leproux 2001: 111–40). Indeed, some scholars place the painter-illuminator Marmion firmly within the French tradition (Ring 1949b: 219–22, 246; Reynaud, in Paris 1993: 80). Born in Amiens when it was still under French rule, and almost certainly trained there, he lived most of his adult life in French-speaking Valenciennes, a town that nevertheless did not become part of the kingdom of France until the seventeenth century.

13. Reynolds, "Illuminators and the Painters' Guilds" (see note 2).

14. Pinchart 1860–81, 3: 73–75. Catherine Reynolds kindly drew this reference to our attention.

15. In the minds of some scholars today, Provost was also an illuminator; see Brinkmann 1997: 173–76; Weniger 2001: 143–51; and the biography of the Master of the Houghton Miniatures, this volume.

16. Campbell 1998: 260.

17. On Joos Van Ghent's connections, see the biography of the Vienna Master of Mary of Burgundy, this volume.

18. Winkler 1943: 263

19. Significantly, however, Van Lathem married the daughter of a book dealer, a connection that held greater value for his practice as an illuminator.

20. Guicciardini [1567]: 98.

21. Campbell and Foister 1986: 721–22. The authors take pains to point out that Lucas is never referred to in the royal accounts as an illuminator and is not described there as an illuminator. The accounts, however, are incomplete.

22. Reynolds, "Illuminators and the Painters' Guilds" (see note 2).

23. Dumoulin and Pycke 1993: 301. We are grateful to Catherine Reynolds for helping us locate this reference.

24. Parmentier 1937: 92–94.

25. First published in Weale 1864–65b: 293–94.

26. On the relationship between Jan van Eyck and Petrus Christus and the latter's painting technique, see Ainsworth, in New York 1994a: 26–65.

27. Friedländer 1967–76, 1: 89.

28. Hoogewerff 1936–47, 2: 8–9

29. Alexander 1988: 124–26; Dhanens 1998: 158, 160.

30. Fols. 14v and 59v, respectively (Lieftinck 1969: figs. 165, 175). For *The Lamentation* the illuminator shrewdly removed the figure of the Evangelist from behind the Virgin altogether and had him support the body of Christ instead.

31. It is intriguing that a couple of manuscripts with miniatures influenced by Van der Goes were written at the monastery of Rooclooster in or around 1477 (cat. nos. 24, 39). This is the Windesheim house to which the painter eventually retreated in 1475 and where he remained until his death in 1482.

32. Hulin de Loo 1939b: 169.

33. For further discussion of David's underdrawing technique, see Ainsworth 1998.

34. For these versions, see Ainsworth 1998: 295–305, figs. 284–87.

35. For illustrations, see Ainsworth 1998: figs. 256b, 257b, 262.

36. Campbell (1998: 297–98) has argued that a *Virgin and Child with Saints and Donor* (London, National Gallery) on panel may have been begun by Van Lathem and completed by his son Jacob, while Buck (in Berlin 2001: 79–85) has argued that a drawing in the Kupferstichkabinett in Berlin (inv. KdZ 1975) is a copy after a lost painting by the artist.

37. Cf. Hénault 1907: 412, 414ff., 423. There are still further examples of painting if one takes into account commissions to paint sculpture, coats of arms, and other decorative work (Hénault 1907: 411, 412; Deshaisnes 1892: 135ff.).

38. Martens (M.) 2000: 52–56.

39. Reynolds, "Illuminators and the Painters' Guilds" (see note 2).

40. Ainsworth 1992. Gas chromatography analysis of pigment samples taken from the Simon Marmion *Saint Jerome and a Donor* (cat. no. 46) showed the presence of both oil and egg as binding media, in a mixed-media approach. We are very grateful to Ken Sutherland and Beth Price, who carried out this analysis in the Analytical Laboratory of the Philadelphia Museum of Art.

41. Brinkmann, in Berlin 1998: 143–47.

42. Hulin de Loo (1939a: 12–13, 19–20) considered the Master of James IV to be Horenbout; see also Martens (M.) 2000: 52–56.

43. Ainsworth 2002: 1–2.

44. The other is in the Museo del Prado, Madrid (inv. 1537). See Ainsworth 1997; New York 1998: 312; and Ainsworth 2002: 1–25.

45. Scailliérez (1992: 18) gives the dimensions of the central panel as 39 × 35 cm (15⅜ × 13¾ in.).

46. Bruges 1998: 102, no. 71.

47. See the entry on the Stein Quadriptych (cat. no. 146) for further discussion of the cycle's original form.

48. In this section we survey selected examples from throughout the period. A number of scholars have seen the miniatures of Vrelant, an illuminator who himself relied extensively on pattern books for his miniatures, as a source for painters such as Dieric Bouts, Hans Memling, and others. See, for example, Schestag 1899: 215–16; and Lorentz, in Paris 1995: 28–29. See also Bousmanne 1997: 103.

49. Winkler 1915: 288; Oettinger 1938: 43ff.; Van Buren, in DOA 1996, 20: 926; Dhanens 1998: 148.

50. The underdrawing is visible in infrared reflectograms of the Vienna *Lamentation* made by Maryan W. Ainsworth. The figure of John the Evangelist is further anticipated in two other miniatures by the Vienna Master of Mary of Burgundy: *The Deposition* in the Prayer Book of Charles the Bold (cat. no. 16) and *The Crucifixion* in the Trivulzio Hours (cat. no. 17).

51. See Dhanens (1998: 224–25) for a summary of views of the painting's dating. The dendochronological dating of *The Lamentation*'s support to circa 1469 ensures that the painting does not date before the mid-1470s because of time needed to season the wood. On the dating of the Vienna Hours, which may be as early as ca. 1470–75, see cat. no. 19 and Pächt and Thoss 1990: 69, 79–80.

52. All three are illustrated in color in Dhanens 1998: 108.

53. On the relationship between the Vienna Master and Joos van Ghent, see the biography of the former, this volume.

54. Gerlach 1969: 155–60, for example, points out the close relationships of the Nassau family of Breda to s'Hertogenbosch.

55. Gibson 1973: 19–27.

56. For a range of examples from manuscripts in this exhibition and closely related works, see esp. Hammer-Tugendhat 1981: 15–16, 31, 33.

57. For example, Gibson (1973: 64–65) cites the echoing sequence of circles within a circle of zodiacal signs (*Les Sept Âges du monde*, Brussels, Bibliothèque royale, Ms. 9047, fol. 12) as the type of conical form that Bosch adapted in the Venice *Ascent of the Blessed* (Palace of the Doges). The delicate shadings that characterize Marmion's miniatures in this volume might be a formal characteristic that the painter responded to in rethinking the form.

58. For the former, see Delaissé, in Brussels 1959: 153, and for the latter, see Buzzati and Cinotti 1966: pl. 25–27. On Bosch and *Les Visions du chevalier Tondal*, see also McGrath 1968: 46–47.

59. Friedländer 1967–76, 5; pls. 66–67.

60. Delaissé, in Brussels 1959: 153; Buzzati and Cinotti 1966: pl. 41.

61. An intriguing, though perhaps not entirely convincing, example of a Flemish source is the Brussels *Mass of Saint Gregory* from the Emerson-White Hours (ill. 32c), which Sulzberger (1962a: 46–49) has identified as the inspiration for the grisaille outer panels of Bosch's *Epiphany* altarpiece in Madrid. She pointed out more convincingly that the Flemish illuminator's narrative style, especially in the new type of historiated border, looks forward to the arrangements around the altar in the Bosch painting. See also Sulzberger 1962b: 119–20. See also Ainsworth 2003.

62. See note 24.

63. The Maximilian Master copied it in the Mayer van den Bergh Breviary (cat. no. 92, fol. 651v), while he or a member of his workshop copied it in the Breviary of Eleanor of Portugal (cat. no. 91, fol. 411v). Simon Bening seems to have painted it in the Rothschild Prayer Book (Paris, private collection, fol. 240v) and in the Grimani Breviary (cat. no. 126, fol. 579v).

64. De Winter 1981: 401, 418, fig. 125.

65. De Winter 1981: 418, fig. 163.

66. Ainsworth 2003 discusses this issue further.

67. Scillia 1975: 81–95.

68. Van der Velden 1995: 55–59.

69. We are grateful to Scot McKendrick for calling this example to our attention. Equally influential may have been *The Temperate and the Intemperate* (cat. no. 73) by the Master of the Dresden Prayer Book.

70. Martha Wolff in Begemann 1998: 110–12.

71. See Ainsworth 2003.

72. Winkler (1921) cited the example of a Valerius Maximus illuminated in part by the Master of the Dresden Prayer Book as an important forerunner of the genre themes of Pieter Bruegel the Elder. See also the exhibited version of this manuscript illuminated by the same artist (cat. no. 73).

73. The panels, now in various collections, are often referred to erroneously as an oratorio.

74. Wolff, in Washington 1986b: 133–34. See also Backhouse (1993b: 50), who agrees and further suggests persuasively that *The Last Supper* in the Isabella Breviary may have been a source for the panel of this subject in the cycle (Madrid, Palacio Real). Backhouse (1993b: 15, 19, 20) also argues, somewhat less persuasively, that a similar relationship exists for the *Entry into Jerusalem* in the two works (London, Lord Wellington Collection; Bermejo 1962: pls. 7, 8).

75. Compare, for example, Reynaud 1967: 349–51; Vandevivere, in Bruges 1985: 53; and Brinkmann 1997: 11–12.

76. The dimensions of this panel and several others are larger than most in the Isabella Altarpiece, prompting some scholars to doubt that it belonged to the series, including Chiyo Ishikawa, in her forthcoming book on the altarpiece.

77. Baltimore 1997, 2: 436–38, no. 282.

78. Vandevivere and others before him consider Juan de Flandes to have been trained in Ghent in the 1470s, when the new style of manuscript illumination seems to have emerged there. For a history of this view, see Bruges 1985: 17–19, and Ishikawa (1989: 13–16, 95–100), who considers the relationship of Juan's technique to manuscript illumination and the inspiration for the artist's *Christ Nailed to the Cross* (among the altarpiece panels) in the miniature of the same subject by the Vienna Master of Mary of Burgundy.

79. Vandevivere, in Bruges 1985: 17. In addition, the figure of Malchus with his arm raised over his head in the panel is likely derived from *The Betrayal of Christ* in the Prayer Book of Charles the Bold (cat. no. 16, fol. 71) or a pattern based on it. The miniature seems to be by the young Vienna Master of Mary of Burgundy or perhaps by an assistant. The facial type—with wide, low jaw—along with the pose of Malchus's body, is very similar in the two works. In the miniature Malchus's arm is raised to his head as Christ restores his ear. In Juan de Flandes's painting the raised arm protects Malchus from Peter's sword, even though Christ already holds the ear in his hand. Similarities between miniature and painting are also found in the facial type of the bearded Judas and the pose of Christ, who gathers up his robe in his proper left hand.

80. MacLaren and Braham 1970: 43.

81. London 1998: 260.

82. In this instance, as Campbell implies, Juan would have interrupted his work on the Palencia *retablo*—which is consistent with Spanish documents, though not demonstrable—to make the trip to work on the project for the future emperor Charles V in Bruges (London 1998: 260).

83. Kren, in Kren and Rathofer 1988: 254, 256–57.

84. Indeed, they ultimately took their inspiration from the tradition of manuscript illumination, in this case, looking back to the example of the *Très Riches Heures* of the duke of Berry, which may have been in the collection of Margaret of York in these years. See Kren, in Kren and Rathofer 1988: 225–31, 235–36, 241–44, 248–49, 253, 258–59, 262–64.

85. Malibu 1983: 81, 84.

86. Vöhringer (2002: 44–79) analyzed precedents for Bruegel's *Fall of Icarus* (Brussels, Musée royaux des Beaux-Arts) in Flemish manuscript illumination and especially in Bening's work.

REVIVING THE PAST: ILLUSTRATED MANUSCRIPTS OF SECULAR VERNACULAR TEXTS, 1467–1500

SCOT McKENDRICK

On December 1, 1480, a deal was struck for the production of a book.[1] On one side of the agreement was Colard Mansion,[2] by then established at Bruges as an exponent of the new technology of printing with movable type, but here contracting to produce the much older form of a book, the handwritten manuscript. On the other side of the agreement was Philippe de Hornes, lord of Gaasbeek, who up until the death of Charles the Bold three years earlier had been one of the duke's most trusted generals and courtiers. He was also to become a notable collector of manuscripts.[3] The text to be transcribed and illustrated was an account of the virtues and vices of the Romans by the ancient author Valerius Maximus, a text that was often illuminated in the fifteenth century (e.g., fig. 32). It had been translated into French and commented on for two earlier bibliophiles, Charles V of France and his brother John, duke of Berry.[4] Philippe de Hornes's copy of this text was to be divided into two large volumes[5] and written out by Mansion or an equally good scribe. As part of an age-old tradition of production of deluxe manuscripts, Mansion's book was to be illustrated with nine large illuminated miniatures. Each miniature was to be accompanied by an illuminated border that included the arms and devices of Philippe de Hornes. For all this, Mansion was to be paid twenty Flemish groat pounds, five of which he received then and there and the rest due on delivery of the finished book in six months' time. Because Mansion failed to fulfill his part of the deal until October of the following year, however, the manuscript taking just under one year to produce, he was paid in installments from June until the completion of his work.

The commercial production and lay consumption of manuscripts of secular texts within western Europe has a long history, stretching back into classical antiquity.[6] The contribution of artists to, and the interest of individual owners in, the illustration of these texts may have similarly ancient origins.[7] In the fourth century, however, the adoption of Christianity by the rich and powerful severely disrupted the creation of secular manuscripts. Production and sponsorship of Christian texts, including those intended for use within communal and personal devotional and sacramental acts, took precedence.[8] Most secular texts were produced by monastic scribes and artists for clerics and Christian communities; these texts were decorated—sometimes on a grand scale—but rarely included narrative illustrations. Only from the thirteenth century onward did professional producers consistently create fine illustrated copies of secular texts for noble individuals. Most notable among such texts were the vernacular romances that became so popular with the upper nobility. Many illuminated copies of these were produced in northern France and Flanders. Thereafter, histories and philosophical, moral, and advisory texts also came to be illustrated by commercial book producers in both France and Italy.

MASTER OF THE
PRAYER BOOKS OF
AROUND 1500
Scenes from the Aeneid
(detail, ill. 118a)

By the fifteenth century, however, a distinct divergence of practice had developed in book production between northern and southern Europe. Because of the decorative sobriety of their models, Italian humanistic manuscripts—including those of the revived texts of classical authors—largely eschewed narrative illustration. Even those destined for the grandest of libraries and made for the wealthiest of clients had few narrative scenes. Meanwhile, in Paris the luxury book trade and its aristocratic consumers had joined together to create a distinctive type of book, in which a secular vernacular text was often lavishly illustrated. Paralleling the shift of political power away from Paris to the Burgundian Low Countries during the fifteenth century, production of manuscripts of secular vernacular texts came to flourish further north. Philip the Good's court is justly famous for its patronage of such production.[9] Although illuminated manuscripts of secular vernacular texts made up a relatively small proportion of the books produced in northern Europe, they came to be a distinctive and important factor in its cultural development.[10] They continued to be produced in significant numbers even after the invention of printing with movable type and the introduction of commercial production of printed books into the Low Countries.

Colard Mansion's deal with Philippe de Hornes was far from unusual for the time. Mansion was just one of several professional book producers based in Bruges in the late fifteenth century who made fine copies of Valerius Maximus and similar texts; Philippe de Hornes was just one of many members of the nobility in the southern Netherlands who came to own such texts. Philippe's manuscript survives, as do many others like it.[11] These manuscripts were the product of a northern European culture that was distinct from that of the southern Renaissance. By outlining their origins and contemporary purpose, I hope to illuminate the importance of such manuscripts in the development of western European culture at the end of the Middle Ages.

PRODUCERS AND CONSUMERS

As illustrated by the deal struck between Colard Mansion and Philippe de Hornes, a manuscript is the product of an interaction between at least two parties. On the one hand, there are those responsible for the production of manuscripts; on the other, there are those who wish to own them. I will explore the evidence of surviving works and contemporary documents within the context of this broad division between the producers and the consumers of manuscripts. Surviving manuscripts are material witnesses to a complex series of interactions among authors, scribes, illuminators, miniaturists, binders, booksellers, readers, advisers, and librarians. Broadly speaking, all of these individuals fall into one of these two categories: some organize and promote production; some organize and promote consumption. Production and consumption also took place on distinctly different social levels. One was an activity of the artisan and commercial classes; the other was an aspect of life in the upper echelon of society.[12]

Production and consumption of manuscripts of secular vernacular texts cannot be viewed in complete isolation from the production and consumption of devotional manuscripts. In their respective roles, many of the same people were involved in both.

Producers   The production of manuscripts of secular vernacular texts formed part of a bigger picture of economic and artistic activity in the Low Countries during the second half of the fifteenth century. The production of these manuscripts was one facet of a thriving commercial book trade, in which the participants were highly trained, well organized, and long established in such urban centers as Bruges and Brussels. Materials, labor, capital, and entrepreneurial skill were readily available. Distribution networks were in place, established as part of the complex nexus of economic, political, and dynastic ties that bound the Burgundian Low Countries to the rest of Europe. Production of illuminated manuscripts also formed part of the trade in luxury goods, which flourished in the Low Countries and to which many of its inhabitants contributed. Together with panel paintings, metalwork, jewelry, textiles, and woodwork,

Figure 32
MASTER OF
THE DRESDEN
PRAYER BOOK
The Temperate and the Intemperate. In Valerius Maximus, *Faits et dits mémorables des romains,* translation by Simon de Hesdin and Nicolas de Gonesse of *Facta et dicta memorabilia,* ca. 1470–75. 41 × 31 cm (16⅛ × 12³/₁₆ in). Leipzig, Universitätsbibliothek, Ms. Rep. I.ɪɪ.b, fol. 137v

illuminated manuscripts have contributed considerably to the reputation of that region as a center of high artistic achievement.[13]

Documents from the ducal archives include many accounts of the production of manuscripts of secular vernacular texts. Indeed, many more relate to these texts than to devotional ones. Most important, we have a series of payments made by Charles the Bold to scribes and illuminators in the early years of his rule.[14] Typical examples are those that relate to a copy of Quintus Curtius Rufus's *History of Alexander the Great* (cat. no. 54), as translated into French by Vasco da Lucena. In this case, the documents tell us who was involved in the production of the manuscript, the relative cost of their contributions, and the rates of pay for each miniature and initial.[15] Separate consideration of such documentary evidence offers deeper insights than the well-trodden path of matching document and manuscript. Because the manuscript survives in this case (cat. no. 54), however, we can also compare what was produced with what was paid for.[16] Most surprisingly, the strongest artistic contribution to the surviving work was from the Vienna Master of Mary of Burgundy, whose payment is completely subsumed into the payment to the principal illuminator for the project, the much less accomplished Loyset Liédet.

Taken on their own, the documents that have survived can be deceptive. Almost exclusively, they relate to the purchases of the dukes of Burgundy. The contract between Mansion and Philippe de Hornes offers a very rare insight into the mainstream of production for other members of the nobility, a production that is adequately reflected by the significant number of surviving manuscripts that bear the marks of ownership of other nobles. Consequently, a fair picture of production needs to take into account the evidence of both documents and surviving works.

The documents concerned with the production of manuscripts of secular vernacular texts reveal the costs of both materials and labor. Moreover, the concentration of a significant group of payments from the late 1460s and the 1470s allows for easy comparison of relative rates of pay among contemporary miniaturists,[17] and between miniaturists and other book producers. The most extensive series of payments to one miniaturist, those to Loyset Liédet of Bruges, suggests that he established a scale of three rates for miniatures of different sizes. Small miniatures cost 12 Flemish groats, average-sized ones 32, and large ones 36 or even 40.[18] Several contemporary miniaturists seem to have worked for similar rates of pay. In 1470 the Brussels miniaturist Jean Hennecart was paid 48 Flemish groats for each miniature accompanied by a large decorated initial in two copies of Guillebert de Lannoy's *Instruction d'un jeune prince* made for Charles the Bold (cat. no. 56). Two years earlier Willem Vrelant was paid the same amount for miniatures in the second volume of the duke's copy of the *Chroniques de Hainaut*.[19] In 1469 Nicolas Spierinc received either 32 or 36 Flemish groats for each miniature in nine copies of the duke's Hotel ordinances.[20]

The only significant divergence from such rates of pay was in 1459, when Liédet was paid 120 Flemish groats for each of the fifty-five miniatures he produced for a copy of Jean Mansel's *Histoires romaines*.[21] Indeed, such a high rate finds a sustained parallel only in the exceptional and extravagant production of the Breviary of Charles the Bold (cat. no. 10), for which Simon Marmion painted ninety-five miniatures at the rate of 120 or 180 Flemish groats each.[22] The similar rate of 120 Flemish groats was paid to Jean Le Tavernier in 1455 for his miniature of the Crucifixion in a book of hours made for Philip the Good; most of the other miniatures contributed by him to this book of hours were paid for at a much lower rate.[23] No similarly high payments for a specified miniature appear to have been made in the case of manuscripts of secular vernacular texts. The fact that lower rates were paid for miniatures that did not employ full color[24] suggests that a significant proportion of the cost lay in the pigments used.[25] Comparison of salaries suggests that most miniaturists were paid for their labor alone at rates similar to those of other artisans, including painters.

In the case of two ducal manuscripts (see fig 23 and cat. no. 63) for which we know the price of all components,[26] the miniatures account for 34 and 54 percent of the total cost of each book, respectively; adding in the remaining illumination, the percentages rise to 37 and 62. The script accounts for 58 and 32

percent, respectively. These figures reflect the much higher density of illumination found in one of the manuscripts.[27] In each case, however, illumination together with script made up nearly the full cost of the volume. The other principal component, the binding, cost a mere 5 and 6 percent, respectively.

The total price paid for a manuscript varied greatly. Much depended on the length of the text and thereby on the cost of its transcription. (Scribes were regularly paid per quire of sixteen pages, a rate that was intended to cover the cost not only of the work but also of the writing materials, most notably the parchment.)[28] Colard Mansion charged Philippe de Hornes more than twice as much for his Valerius Maximus as he charged Philip the Good for an illuminated *Romuléon* (fig. 33),[29] principally because the first text required about twice as many pages.[30] The extent of the illumination was also an important factor. Especially lavish manuscripts cost the most. Charles the Bold's Quintus Curtius (cat. no. 16), for example, cost no less than 5,382 Flemish groats. The cost of most manuscripts of secular vernacular texts, however, was small in comparison with the cost of important devotional manuscripts such as Charles's breviary. For this the text alone cost more than all the elements of his Quintus Curtius, and the illumination four times that of the illumination of the secular text.[31] Given that the daily wage of a master mason was 12 groats and that 4 to 6 groats of that sum were spent on basic foodstuffs,[32] it is clear that none of these costs could be borne by anyone other than the rich nobility or urban elite. The total cost of Mansion's two-volume Valerius Maximus was equal to the entire earnings of a master mason for four hundred days. The three illustrations in Charles the Bold's copy of *L'Instruction d'un jeune prince* (see cat. no. 56) would have cost the master mason his earnings for fourteen days.

What then of the social and economic structures that supported the production of manuscripts of secular vernacular texts? Setting aside the wider issue of trade guilds, a subject discussed elsewhere in this volume by Catherine Reynolds, I would like to explore some of the evidence for the smaller unit of artisans responsible for production for particular volumes or sets of volumes. In the first place, it is clear that the manuscripts were the result of the collaboration of several persons. Comparison of surviving manuscripts with corresponding contemporary documents suggests that subcontracting was commonplace. At least two volumes for which Liédet was paid include significant contributions by artists whose artistic styles are unrelated to his.[33] Although Spierinc received the money for the miniatures produced for Charles the Bold's Hotel ordinances, he did not paint them.[34] These observations are hardly surprising, given that both Liédet and Spierinc—despite not being binders—were also paid for the binding of each of these volumes. In each case they acted as coordinators of the work of several people.

The role of coordinator—at least of the production of miniatures, decorated initials, and binding—appears to have been one taken on by illuminators.[35] By contrast, scribes were most frequently paid merely for the transcription of text.[36] They sometimes copied the text of a volume in a center different, and sometimes distant, from that in which the rest of the work was done. As a ducal secretary, David Aubert followed his peripatetic masters. His manuscripts were copied at the current residence of the court and then dispatched to the illuminators.[37] While the scribe Jan Du Quesne remained at Lille, many of the manuscripts he transcribed passed up to Bruges for decoration and binding.[38] By contrast, many illuminators worked in important artistic centers such as Bruges and were thus central to the production of such manuscripts and in the best position to coordinate these projects. As illustrated by the example of Mansion, however, some scribes did assume the role of *libraire*, which encompassed the activities of coordination, bookselling, and more. Their relatively low profile is probably to be explained in terms of the unfortunate dearth of documents that deal with purchases made by nobles other than the duke.

The production of most manuscripts of secular vernacular texts followed the traditional order of a professionally produced volume but also conformed to a distinctive aesthetic.[39] First the text was copied in one or two columns,[40] employing almost without exception a script known as *littera bastarda, lettre bâtarde,* or *lettre bourguignonne.*[41] The vast majority of pages presented a spare but calculated look. The black ink of the script was set against the white of heavily chalked parchment and the red or violet of the ruling. The principal decorative element was provided in the right-hand margin by the ragged edge of the unjustified text. Then the subsidiary decoration of initials, paragraph marks, and borders was added. Decorated initials varied greatly, from those that occupied many lines, were fully painted, were lavished with gold or, more rarely, historiated[42] to those that occupied only one line and were executed with pen and ink. Most commonly, the minor decoration of a volume comprised large illuminated initials marking the main divisions of a text and small penwork initials marking smaller divisions such as chapters. Chapter titles were written or underlined in red ink.

The margins of pages were treated in various ways. Sometimes borders were consciously omitted altogether or for all but the opening miniature. Full borders were usually intended to accompany full- or three-quarter-page miniatures. Partial borders usually accompanied smaller miniatures, most frequently those that were only the width of one column on a two-column page; they were regularly placed either in the outer margin or above and below the column occupied by the miniature. Once the borders were completed, miniatures were added, sometimes in tandem with the major illuminated initial that accompanied them. Although the shape of miniatures varied greatly, their position was largely defined within the text block, and the margins were encroached upon only by elements in the image, rather than being fully occupied by marginal miniatures. Historiated borders[43] and borders with roundel miniatures[44] were rarities. Full-page miniatures were also relatively rare (see cat. nos. 120, 123); most miniatures were accompanied by text on a page.

On completion of their decoration, all the leaves were gathered together and sewn onto leather bands, and the bands were attached to wood boards. The whole structure was then covered in skin or fabric and embellished with metalwork bosses, corner pieces, clasps, and title pieces.[45] The metalwork fittings frequently bore the arms or devices of the owner (fig. 34), and the most common coverings were blind-stamped calf—plain or dyed—or dyed velvet.[46] The most elaborate volumes also had an additional fabric cover and a leather pouch.[47]

One of the most consistent features of manuscripts of secular vernacular texts was their adherence to integrated miniatures (miniatures integrated with text). In this they followed traditional manuscript practice but took a very different approach from manuscripts of devotional texts produced in the Low Countries, in which it was standard practice to insert miniatures on individual leaves.

Figure 34
Binding made for Anthony of Burgundy's copy of Jean Froissart, *Chroniques,* 1468. Berlin, Staatsbibliothek, Ms. Dep. Breslau 1, vol. 4, front cover

Because producers of manuscripts of secular vernacular texts eschewed this new practice, all of the decorative elements for these manuscripts were usually produced at the same center. This also bound miniaturists more tightly into the production of the volumes they illustrated; the fact that the miniatures were integrated with the text meant that these miniaturists would almost always have at least part of the text before them.[48] In contrast, miniaturists who contributed to books of hours and other devotional manuscripts need never have seen the texts they illustrated or the pages that came to face their illustrations. Consequently, there was much less need for such miniaturists to be literate. The standardization of religious iconography and the plentiful supply of patterns for such images greatly helped miniaturists engaged in illustrating devotional texts.

Illustrators of secular vernacular texts did not always contribute to a volume immediately after its text was written or its subsidiary decoration was completed. Several surviving volumes appear to have been started speculatively and only illustrated fully after a client had been found.[49] Some, like Jan Crabbe's Virgil (cat. no. 118) and the Herbert Lydgate (cat. no. 130), merely had illustrations added; others, like Edward IV's copy of the poems of Charles d'Orléans (cat. no. 119), required more significant changes, including the alteration or replacement of original leaves.[50] Some remain only partly illustrated or totally unillustrated to this day.[51] In some cases, it is clear it was the choice of a buyer not to have any more illustrations, or any illustrations at all, added.[52]

As stated earlier, manuscripts of secular vernacular texts were the product of collaboration among several persons. Such collaboration involved not only those with different skills but also those with the same skills. For example, many volumes contain miniatures painted by more than one hand (see cat. nos. 16, 66, 68, 71, 77, 79, 87). The balance of such contributions varied greatly; it was even possible for a miniaturist to contribute only one miniature to an extensive campaign of illustrations. Explanations for such collaboration vary. When, as often happens, the most accomplished artist contributed the opening or principal miniatures (see cat. nos. 79, 87), the planners probably intended to highlight the work of that artist. When a more accomplished hand appears buried within a volume (see cat. no. 54), however, it is more difficult to find an explanation. In some cases, an otherwise incomplete volume was being finished. In others, an otherwise inactive coordinator may have decided to contribute to a volume.

In any manuscript in which collaboration is evident, the cooperation between master and apprentice is only one of several possible explanations. Collaborations could continue from one volume to another or could occur only once. They sometimes produced stylistic juxtapositions that are startling to a modern eye (see cat. nos. 16, 66, 68, 71, 79); given how frequently this contrast of styles within a single volume occurs, however, this was apparently acceptable to a contemporary eye. Collaboration also created the opportunity for artists to influence one another, either directly as partners in a project or indirectly as successive contributors to a volume.

Miniaturists employed several different strategies for creating their illustrations.[53] Some illustrations were based on a fresh reading of the text by either the miniaturist or a coordinator of production. Such a practice was not limited to new or uncommon texts but was also employed in profligate manner for each manuscript of such relatively popular texts as Raoul Lefèvre's *Recueil des histoires troyennes* (see cat. no. 123) and Lucena's translation of Quintus Curtius (see cat. no. 63).[54] Illustrations often appear at different points in the text in different manuscripts, and even when the illustrations appear at the same points, they are often of different subjects. Occasional use of written instructions to miniaturists within a manuscript suggests that a coordinator of production has given fresh thought to the text.[55] Complete sequences of instructions within a manuscript may suggest the same, or they could indicate the existence of a separate sequence of instructions that were intended to be reused in other manuscripts.[56] Another aid to the illustrator were rubrics or chapter headings, many of which did not form part of the text when it was first written; these seem to have been compiled for this purpose by coordinators of the production of manuscripts of secular vernacular texts.[57]

Another aid in the illustration of a text was the visual model. In some cases, the similarity of the illustrations of two manuscripts is so great that it is evident that either one was copied from the other or they shared a common visual source that not only was complete in all its parts but was also fully colored. This copying occurred in the closely contemporaneous production of manuscripts, such as in the Yale and London copies of the *Commentaries* of Caesar (New Haven, Conn., Beinecke Library, Ms. 226, and cat. no. 74),[58] and also as a sort of replication of earlier manuscripts.[59] Some sequences of illustrations, although visually connected and inadequately explained in terms of shared textual guides, were clearly not copied from each other directly but were based on a shared set of visual models. Two examples of this are the Getty Quintus Curtius (cat. no. 63)[60] and some contemporary copies of the same text, and the Cambridge and Paris copies of *Les Douze Dames de rhétorique* (cat. nos. 69, 70). Sometimes these models must have consisted only of outlines of each composition. Such models appear to have traveled into and out of the Low Countries, thereby disseminating further their impact and influence.[61] In some cases, as with Charles the Bold's *L'Instruction d'un jeune prince* (see cat. no. 56), the models probably accompanied a text in its transmission from one center to another. In other cases, the models may have traveled separately. In this way, images developed for one text came to be used again for another.[62] As in other contemporary artistic media, the reuse of patterns—including either whole compositions, figure groups, individual figures, landscapes, or architectural structures—was common practice within particular centers of illumination and for particular miniaturists and their assistants and followers.[63] The reuse of modules in woodblock illustrations of contemporary printed editions built upon strategies for image creation employed by miniaturists. Strikingly, however, the artists illustrating secular vernacular texts made little use of patterns developed and employed in other artistic media.[64]

Producers of manuscripts of secular vernacular texts were capable of making volumes that differed considerably from the mainstream of production in their overall appearance (see cat. nos. 85, 86). For the most part, however, these producers created recognizably similar works.[65] When change occurred, it was adopted quickly and consistently by producers. Thus, for example, flower borders, which first appeared in devotional manuscripts in the mid-1470s, came later to secular vernacular manuscripts but were a regular feature of them from the mid-1480s on (see cat. nos. 76, 119–22). Miniatures without borders were a hallmark of Liédet's manuscripts (see cat. nos. 54, 55) and came to be considered appropriate for a high-status volume in the 1460s.[66] In the 1470s borders returned as a consistent part of such manuscripts, and only in the 1480s did miniatures without borders make a reappearance.[67] From the late 1470s onward, producers became less and less concerned about placing miniatures at the top of the page, or even at the start of the relevant chapter and above the corresponding rubric (see cat. nos. 84, 96). Although there were practical and financial advantages in less careful placement of miniatures, not least that of less need for meticulous planning, the resulting look seems also to have chimed in with a contemporary fashion and the taste for a more jumbled appearance.[68] Such considerations of taste lead us to the role of the consumers of secular vernacular manuscripts.

Consumers   Consumption of illuminated manuscripts of secular vernacular texts formed part of a bigger picture of the consumption of both books and luxury goods. During the period under consideration, books remained relatively rare by modern standards but were becoming more common and affordable. The increasing availability of books printed with movable type made a significant impact in this respect. And just as woodcuts and engravings widened access to images, so printing broadened awareness and reading of texts. Literacy increased among both the upper and the middle classes. Among the upper classes, however, this literacy seems mainly to have been restricted to the court vernacular of French.[69] Luxury goods produced in the Low Countries had a dependable consumer base in the ducal court. They also had an important export market based on strong economic, dynastic, and political relations with the rest of Europe.[70] Within this market, goods from the Low Countries came to

have a significant cachet among the rich and powerful. With the demise of the Burgundian court around the end of the fifteenth century, consumers based in Spain, Portugal, and the Italian and German states—with their increasing financial resources, partly funded from the New World—were to prove invaluable to producers in the Netherlands.

Looking at the full range of available evidence, it becomes obvious that there were many different ways of obtaining an illustrated manuscript of a secular vernacular text.[71] Most obviously, but probably least frequently of all, consumers could commission a volume and specify exactly each element that would make up the manuscript. At the other end of the scale, they could, and many did, buy a manuscript off the shelf. Many such manuscripts had few subsequent additions or alterations made to them. Some had no illustrations inserted in the spaces left for them; others had no marks of ownership added.

The person with whom the consumer dealt also varied. As we have already seen, several important purchases made by Charles the Bold were made through illuminators, and it was they who arranged even the delivery of the finished work to the duke.[72] In these cases the copying of the text was an entirely separate activity and one apparently organized within the duke's own household.[73] A person who initiated or promoted a contemporary text was also someone through whose agency a consumer might obtain such a manuscript. Such persons promoted works by circulating texts in manuscript within a circle of potential readers and offering to have fine copies made for those who showed an interest. When soliciting the patronage of Isabelle of Bourbon, countess of Charolais and second wife of Charles the Bold, the Portuguese noble Vasco Quemada de Villalobos listed the characteristics of the volume on offer as fine parchment, fine script, pictures, illuminated letters of gold, and a rich binding. Its proper destination, according to Vasco, was the duchess's chamber.[74]

A note recording the purchase in 1475 (by Hospitaller knight Philippe de Cluys) of an illuminated copy of Lucena's translation of Quintus Curtius appears to record an "off-the-shelf" sale (fig. 36a).[75] At this date the text was certainly much sought after by nobles, and it would certainly have been sensible for producers to have copies in stock. The fact that this copy of Curtius includes a minimum of personalization, clearly added post factum, and that it is one of several surviving copies to have been written and illustrated by the same scribes and artists, appears to confirm this as a likely scenario.[76]

Occasionally, written evidence of a consumer's link with a volume and its producers is provided by additional words, supplied by the scribe, at the end of the text. Of all the colophons that survive, relatively few include the name of the person for whom the volume was made.[77] Several manuscripts that include consistent and integral marks of ownership in their illumination have a colophon that provides details of one or more of the following: the date, the scribe, and the place of writing (but not the name of the owner).[78] Even fewer contain colophons that state that someone commissioned both script and illumination.[79]

Consumers of illuminated manuscripts of secular vernacular texts were mostly members of the nobility (fig. 35). Many were from the upper nobility and part of the ruling class; others were their close dependents from the lower nobility.[80] Almost none was a member of the mercantile class. At the very most, a merchant owned fine illuminated copies of printed editions of these texts;[81] any aspiration on his part to read and display them appears not to have required the acquisition of a manuscript copy.[82] The practice of these merchants contrasts sharply with that of such noble collectors as Raphael de Mercatellis, who had manuscripts and illustrations copied after printed editions and woodcuts.[83]

Although this difference in practice might lead one to believe that the inhibiting factor for the merchants was lack of money, this almost certainly was not the case;[84] many merchants and other members of their class were as rich as contemporary nobles, and the price of an average illuminated manuscript was not beyond their financial means.

The evidence of surviving manuscripts suggests that owners were almost exclusively male. When arms, ex libris, and other marks of ownership occur, most are of a man, not a woman. Contemporary documents appear to confirm this imbalance. It is, however, probably incorrect to assume that consumers of such manuscripts were exclusively male. Throughout the Middle Ages, women owned far fewer books than men, and even the grandest of women had relatively small amounts of money to spend on books.[85] Yet their interest in books is generally acknowledged, as is their important role in the education of children.[86] It is therefore unsurprising to find some evidence of female interest in secular vernacular texts and female use of manuscripts owned by and created for men.[87] In addition to collecting devotional texts, Margaret of York, for example, added her signature to a manuscript of Jean Mansel's *Fleur des histoires* that belonged to the Burgundian ducal library.[88] Presumably she did so when she had the volume on loan. In 1420 Margaret of Bavaria had on loan from her husband's library seventeen volumes, including copies of *Lancelot*, *Guiron le Courtois*, *Propriétés des choses*, Boccaccio's *Des cas des nobles hommes et femmes*, *Renart*, *Miroir historial* in three volumes, *Chroniques de France*, *Voeux du Paon*, and *Saint Graal*.[89]

Given that most texts were written in French, and assuming that most people who acquired manuscripts containing them wished to engage with the text, consumers were generally limited to those who understood French. Whereas in the fourteenth century, or even early in the fifteenth century, French was the common language of most western European courts, by the latter half of the fifteenth century its use and familiarity as a literary language were restricted to a much narrower field. Across Europe, local vernaculars had risen in use and become more and more frequently employed in literature. Thus, although French remained popular among the upper nobility in England, it suffered a serious decline in Spain, Italy, and Germany. Despite such shrinkage in the consumer base for texts in French, very little attempt was made to produce illuminated copies of texts in either Latin or other vernaculars.[90] The lavish illuminated copy of Jean de Wavrin's *Chroniques d'Angleterre* owned by Pietro Villa, a Piedmontese resident of Bruges,[91] is a rare example of a Flemish manuscript of a secular text in French owned by a foreigner.

Collectors were most active in their middle and later years. Anthony of Burgundy, Wolfart VI van Borssele, Louis of Gruuthuse, and Engelbert of Nassau made their most significant acquisitions from around the age of forty.[92] Edward IV began his collecting at around the same age.[93] Baudouin II de Lannoy may not have begun until he was forty-five years old.[94] Even Philip the Good was most active from his mid-forties onward.[95] In each case, greater financial security made collecting possible. Was greater leisure also a factor? Did more intense social interaction at court encourage collecting for contemporary prestige? Was collecting an activity more fitting for the middle-aged? Or was it viewed as an investment for future enjoyment and reputation? The life span of each collector beyond the age of forty certainly explains, in part, the size of each collection. Those who enjoyed a long life often continued to collect into their later years. Louis of Gruuthuse, who died around the age of seventy, certainly took the opportunity of his long life to form one of the most substantial collections of manuscripts. Those who, like Charles the Bold, did not survive beyond forty-five years of age had correspondingly less opportunity to build large personal collections.

Collections of manuscripts varied greatly in size. Those that included secular vernacular texts could be extremely large. Most commonly, such large collections were the product of more than one generation of collectors and often derived not only from purchase but also from inheritance and gifts. Within the collections formed during the period in question, vernacular texts were an important part. By far the largest collection was that of the dukes of Burgundy.[96] By 1469 it contained between 850 and 900 volumes, of which Philip the Good had acquired some 600.[97] More than half of the manuscripts in that collection

Figure 36b
Signature of Philip
of Cleves, lord of
Ravenstein. In Jean
Mansel, *La Fleur des
histoires*, ca. 1480. 38 ×
36.6 cm (15 × 10½ in.).
London, British Library,
Royal Ms. 16 F.vii,
fol. 314 (detail)

were of secular vernacular texts. The next largest collections were that of Louis of Gruuthuse, with around 190 volumes, principally of secular vernacular texts, and that of Philip of Cleves, lord of Ravenstein, with around 140 volumes (fig. 36b).[98] More than half of Louis of Gruuthuse's collection, which was largely formed by him alone, comprised contemporary illuminated manuscripts.[99] A collection of at least 45 volumes was formed by Philip the Good's illegitimate son, Anthony of Burgundy; of these, around 30 were contemporary illuminated copies.[100] Edward IV of England seems to have formed a collection of similar size.[101] Smaller but significant collections of between 10 and 20 manuscripts of secular vernacular texts include those formed personally by Jean de Créquy; Antoine Rolin; Wolfart VI van Borssele; Philippe de Hornes; John II, lord of Oettingen and Flobecq; and Engelbert of Nassau.[102] Successive counts of Chimay—Jean, Philippe, and Charles de Croÿ—came to own more than 90 manuscripts.[103] Jean III de Berghes, Sir John Donne, and the Burgundian ducal equerry Guillaume de Ternay appear to have owned only a handful of volumes.[104] Many of these collections were formed by known patrons of other contemporary forms of art and luxury goods.

The secular vernacular texts collected reflect very similar choices on the part of these nobles. The texts that were illuminated were largely the same as those produced in more modest copies. Some were contemporary; others were much older. Several contemporary texts proved very popular among consumers. Some—such as Guillaume Fillastre's *Histoire de la toison d'or*, Raoul Lefèvre's *Recueil des histoires troyennes* (cat. no. 123), Lucena's translations of Quintus Curtius's text (cat. nos. 54, 63) and of Xenophon, and Jean Miélot's *Romuléon*—were consistently produced in deluxe copies. Older texts such as Froissart's *Chroniques* (see fig. 34 and cat. nos. 68, 71, 79) and the *Faits des romains* enjoyed significant but short-lived popularity.[105] Others, including Pierre Bersuire's translation of Livy and the *Grandes Chroniques de France*, were never revived in the Low Countries,[106] despite contemporary awareness of them and the availability of these texts in other centers of production. Earlier copies of these texts seem to have supplied any demand for them.[107] Prose texts greatly outnumbered those in verse. History was consistently favored over other subjects.[108] Advisory literature, particularly of the mirror-of-princes type, continued in popularity. Both history and advisory texts frequently received lavish illumination. Even extremely long texts, such as the chronicles of Froissart and of Jean de Wavrin (cat. no. 75), which filled up several large folio volumes each, were repeatedly collected in deluxe editions.

Many manuscripts of secular vernacular texts were intended for reading aloud.[109] Both Philip the Good and Charles the Bold enjoyed hearing such texts.[110] They were read to the duke alone and in the presence of his court, in his chamber when in residence, and in his tent when on campaign.[111] Together with his other goods, books could travel with the duke; they were delivered on completion to his current residence and, when required, formally removed from the ducal library to be used and stored wherever suited his personal convenience.[112] How such noble owners responded to or interacted with the illustrations in their manuscripts is difficult to assess and never explicit in contemporary records. Like owners of panel paintings,[113] they almost never expressed an opinion on the works they owned. Yet the very sophistication of the illustrations and their popularity must reflect considerable interest on the part of the noble owners of such manuscripts. Although some critics have claimed that illustrations in these manuscripts serve merely to mark out major divisions in the text or to enrich the volumes, I find this explanation unsatisfactory and incomplete. Illustrations were also vehicles of further meaning; they commented on, explained, and highlighted aspects of narrative or argument in a text.[114] At least one contemporary noted the improvement to be gained by the daily hearing and seeing of ancient deeds, old chronicles, and wonders.[115]

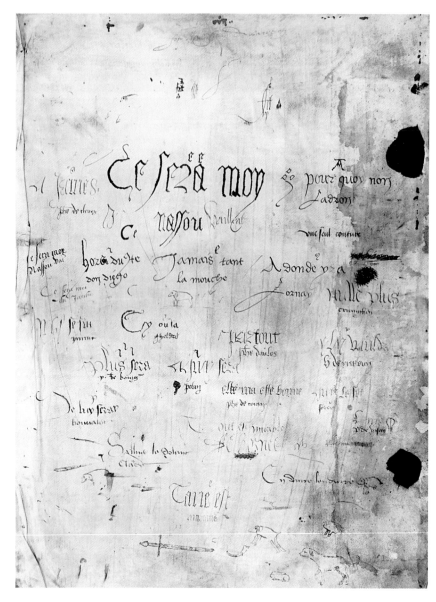

Figure 36c
Signatures and devices of
Engelbert II of Nassau
and other nobles. In
Quintus Curtius Rufus,
*Livre des fais d'Alexandre
le grant*, translation by
Vasco da Lucena of
Historia Alexandri magni,
ca. 1475–90. 51 x 37 cm
(20 1/16 x 14 9/16 in.), leaf
123. Oxford, Bodleian
Library, Ms. Laud misc.
751, lower pastedown
(detail)

It is difficult to quantify or make general statements about the influence of consumers on the
visual appearance of manuscripts of secular vernacular texts. The Mansion document cited at the opening
of this essay suggests that Philippe de Hornes was not involved in the selection of either artists or
illustrations. The agreement certainly appears to have allowed Mansion considerable scope in these areas.
This scope may, however, have been understood by both parties to be within certain clear limits and
restricted to the creation of volumes similar to ones shown to the buyer. The repeated contribution of certain artists to manuscripts made for particular nobles suggests that at least some consumers had aesthetic
preferences or were at least satisfied with a particular aesthetic. The Masters of Margaret of York and of
Anthony of Burgundy, for example, contributed to many of the manuscripts of Louis of Gruuthuse (cat.
nos. 61, 69, 71). If, as I argued earlier, the illuminator was often the coordinator, he would also have been
the consumer's point of contact with production. Through dealings with this illuminator-cum-
coordinator, the consumer would have had a clear idea of the likely appearance of the decoration. His
choice would thereby have been an informed one.

The influence of one consumer on another is easier to determine. The noble sponsors of texts
often secured further patronage for an author. Most frequently, this sponsorship worked upward in society; for example, Jean de Créquy repeatedly secured the formal dedication of a text to Philip the Good.[116]

From that point, the influence worked back down the social scale, the open approval of one member of the ruling class encouraging interest from others at the court.[117] This interest on the part of social superiors and inferiors led formally to the sponsorship of a further manuscript of the text. If a superior chose to invest in a fine copy, an inferior might well consider investing in one also. The very frequent inclusion of a presentation scene at the opening of each copy of a text seems intentionally to reinforce both the authority of and link to the dedicatee.[118] Communal reading, and perhaps also communal viewing, not only would have encouraged wider interest in the text but also would have stimulated others to want their own copies. Several of the nobles who added their names and mottoes to two manuscripts owned by Engelbert of Nassau (fig. 36c) themselves came to own similar manuscripts.[119] Some acquired the very same text, and one close dependent of Engelbert commissioned a copy partially based on a manuscript belonging to Engelbert, to which he had previously added his name.[120]

Manuscripts of secular vernacular texts made an impact on the social milieu in several other significant ways. First of all, they were lent by one noble to another. Several manuscripts that formed part of the library of the dukes of Burgundy were lent in this way.[121] Borrowers of books were sometimes stimulated to have a copy made for themselves, as in the case of Jean de Wavrin, who came to own a manuscript of *Gilles de Chin*, probably as a result of having borrowed the draft manuscript from Jean de Créquy.[122] Contemporary consumers attributed a positive value to faithful copies of other works, and thus several manuscripts very closely resemble their models. Going one stage further, a collector could make a gift of such a manuscript, either by extracting a volume from his own collection or by commissioning one for the purpose.[123] A dependent could seek favor by presenting a fine manuscript to a social superior who was a bibliophile.[124] Finally, parents could pass on books to their children before or upon their deaths.[125]

Successive owners took pride in what they had acquired from others. Some, such as Paul de Baenst after he had acquired Jan Crabbe's Virgil (see cat. no. 118), made substantial additions to the illumination of their manuscripts. Philip the Handsome paid for the careful restoration of several books he had inherited from the Burgundian ducal library and also added his signature to some.[126] Adolph of Burgundy took great care to add his name and motto next to those of his bibliophile grandfather, Anthony of Burgundy (fig. 36d).[127] Louis XII lavished great expense on imposing his marks of ownership on manuscripts previously owned by Louis of Gruuthuse and on suppressing Gruuthuse's arms, devices, and portraits.[128] Although many noble collections were subsequently dispersed, the principal princely collections remained virtually intact and came to form the foundations of the national libraries of England, Belgium, the Netherlands, and France.

Figure 36d
Signatures and devices of Anthony and Adolph of Burgundy. In Diego de Valera, *Espejo de verdadera nobleza*, ca. 1470. Brussels, Bibliothèque royale de Belgique, Ms. II 7057, fol. 72v (detail)

ORIGINS AND MOTIVATION

Commercial production of manuscripts of secular vernacular texts prospered in the Low Countries beyond the death, in 1477, of the last Valois duke of Burgundy. In the late 1480s, however, a significant decline set in.[129] Illustrated manuscripts of such texts became a rarity, and their creation was clearly led by consumers on an ad hoc basis (see cat. nos. 119, 120, 123). Text and image took on greater specificity and a direct relation to the consumer. A manuscript, if created, was a more self-conscious choice on the part of the consumer. This trend is particularly clear in the manuscripts of secular texts illuminated by the Master of the Prayer Books of around 1500. Notably, it worked in the opposite direction for other luxury goods produced in the Low Countries during the same period, in which case speculative production increased steadily and came to dominate the market.[130]

It is worth pausing to consider the reasons for the demise of illustrated manuscripts of secular vernacular texts. One explanation is that several book producers in the Low Countries, including Colard

Mansion, quickly perceived the commercial advantages of printed books.[131] Most important, printed books offered a wider range of texts to a broader market. As a result, the numbers of scribes and illuminators engaged in the commercial production of books declined, the necessary skills became less common, and the visual models were forgotten. In addition, the stability of the larger princely collections and the decreasing cost of secondhand manuscripts made the creation of further copies of the same texts less advantageous commercially. Newer collections, such as that of Charles II, count of Lalaing (1506–1558),[132] came to include more printed books, with a focus on humanistic texts.

The demise of deluxe copies of secular vernacular texts in the Low Countries is, however, best explained by the contemporary shift of power and the court's movement away from the Low Countries under the Habsburgs, resulting in a lack of an influential demand for such manuscripts. Less exalted and less permanent social groups, such as those formed among the nobility of Hainaut or around Engelbert of Nassau,[133] were unable to sustain an adequate demand. As more people of Spanish and German background became members of the court, there was a decline at the center of power in the interest in texts not only written in French but also Francocentric in their subject matter and cultural origins. It is interesting to note that during the same period, illuminated manuscripts of liturgical and devotional texts in the Low Countries continued to be produced on a significant scale and came to enjoy wide ownership among the upper nobility of Europe.[134] At the same time, in France, fine manuscripts of devotional, liturgical, and secular vernacular texts continued to flourish.

Why then did manuscripts of secular vernacular texts come to be fostered and sought after within the Burgundian court in the first place, long before their demise? Most modern critics view these manuscripts—both individually and in the form of libraries—as created and viewed as emblems of prestige and cultivation, as well as a means to glory.[135] According to these critics, the books spoke to contemporaries through visible luxury and constituted signs of a ruler's or noble's magnificence. Within noble circles these books were a necessary part of the outward signs of the courtly cultivation of an individual or group. Independently or as a collection, the manuscripts were also a permanent monument representing a grand achievement for which a noble might hope to be celebrated in the future.

Two further factors may have influenced the development and promotion of manuscripts of secular vernacular texts. First, a crucial role was played by contemporary patterns of friendship and patronage. The influence of such relationships in the dissemination of preference and taste was undoubtedly very great. Second, we need to look again and more closely at the persistent and often elaborate personalization of such volumes through the addition of the arms, devices, and mottoes of the owner.[136] Most modern critics view these features merely as welcome clues to the identity of the owner of a particular volume and therefore regard them as the decorative counterparts of written ex libris. Few have considered this virtual meeting point of text and owner, past and present, as a conscious link, binding each to the other as part of a joint hypertextual statement. In this context I would suggest that many such manuscripts were conceived as markers in the life of a particular social class. Throughout this period members of the nobility sought ways to redefine themselves, distinguish themselves from other social classes, and bind together their upper and lower tiers. The creation, possession, and enjoyment of illuminated manuscripts of secular vernacular texts were certainly distinguishing pursuits, and ones that seem to have become a shared passion of many nobles.

At the same time that these manuscripts were being produced and consumed in the Low Countries, Italy was experiencing a major cultural change. Most prominently, in Florence the Renaissance was in full swing. The rediscovery of both the artistic and the literary heritage of classical antiquity was injecting new vigor into artistic, intellectual, and political life. Artists sought to emulate and imitate classical forms; humanist scholars and their patrons recovered, collected, and read texts written in classical times. Neither protohumanism nor a Northern Renaissance can, however, fully explain the cultural origins of illuminated manuscripts of secular vernacular texts. Professional book producers for, and consumers within, the luxury market in the Low Countries did show some interest in humanistic texts.[137] New and sensitive translations of ancient authors such as Quintus Curtius and Xenophon did have significant successes.[138] Such texts, however, formed a very small part of those copied and consumed. Older medieval and contemporary nonhumanistic texts—such as Froissart's *Chroniques* and Lefèvre's *Recueil des histoires troyennes*—formed a much larger proportion and were sought after as part of a consistent approach to and interest in the past. Underpinned by and in parallel with the more intellectual interests of important court officials such as Charles's chancellor Guillaume Hugonet,[139] this interest in the past—and the reading of secular vernacular texts—offered nobles practical benefits in terms of political skill and knowledge and also examples of virtuous and noble action through which they might achieve honor.[140] Northern nobles sought to understand the present and their position in it by reference to the past. They were not principally interested in truth but in a credible and involving account of the link between past and present. The past could be best understood couched in contemporary terms. It needed to be revived in contemporary dress so that it would strike home with power and immediacy. Thus, contemporary miniaturists in the Low Countries made no attempt at *all'antica* reconstruction, and consumers showed no signs of wanting such an approach. Alexander the Great could thus be compared with Charles the Bold with ease, and readers could become engaged in the story of a Macedonian king who had ruled nearly two thousand years before. In this respect, illustrations to secular vernacular texts share the same concerns as those of contemporary illustrations to liturgical texts. The latter sought to bring an immediacy to images of heaven and to the lives of Christ and Christian saints and to enable the devout to share in the joys and sorrows, elation and suffering of Christ, the Virgin, and other saints. The former sought to enable contemporary nobles to become Charlemagne, Julius Caesar, or Alexander the Great.[141]

MODERN RECEPTION

Illustrated manuscripts of secular vernacular texts produced in the southern Netherlands have provided a particularly rich store of images for the illustration of modern texts on various aspects of medieval history and for medieval merchandise for the modern public. Colorful and naturalistic, the images in such manuscripts have been seized upon with enthusiasm by picture researchers, antiquarians, and historians of medieval costume, warfare, and daily life. As a result, these images have reached a wider audience than they ever obtained or were intended to obtain during their own time. Through their direct appeal to a modern audience and repeated popular reproduction, some have become modern icons of late medieval European culture. They have thus done much to shape our perceptions and understanding of the cultural history of the Middle Ages and early Renaissance, of the meeting point of these two periods in western European history, and of the development of the secular domain in Western civilization.

Modern exposure, however, has a price. The miniatures in manuscripts of secular vernacular texts are frequently discussed or reproduced without a context or an understanding of the means by which—and reasons for which—they were created. Their naturalistic detail often distracts from their idealism and artifice. The text they illustrate is very often ignored, or at least not reproduced. To unwary viewers, these images offer simple views of medieval life, "photographs" of the age before photography. The abuse of these images is commonplace and has a long history.[142]

Let us take three examples. First, two miniatures from Engelbert of Nassau's beautiful manuscript of *Le Roman de la rose* (cat. no. 120)—*The Garden of Pleasure* and *The Dance of Sir Mirth* (ill. 120)—have been used repeatedly as the quintessential image of late medieval courtly love and ease.[143] The costumes of their figures do indeed reflect contemporary court fashion. Their subjects, however, are particular episodes from the text of *Le Roman de la rose*. This text was written in an era very different from that of Engelbert of Nassau. It was hardly ever illustrated in the southern Netherlands and never in such an extravagant fashion as in Engelbert's manuscript. The illustrations therefore require a particular explanation. Important factors for the creation of the miniatures in Engelbert's manuscript include a nostalgia on his part for the lost days of Burgundian splendor. Seen in this light, these miniatures appear to echo images such as *The Hunting Party of Philip the Good* (Versailles). They also form part of a fin de siècle retrospection and antiquarianism that revived interest in the *Roman.*

The second example is the *Bathhouse* miniature of the Breslau Valerius Maximus (fig. 37), which has been reproduced repeatedly in modern times as offering insight into the underbelly of late medieval life—of what lay under all the splendor and pageantry. As the Breslau manuscript and other contemporary copies of Valerius Maximus (see cat. no. 66) show, however, this subject was frequently used to illustrate a particular story offered by the Roman author as an illustration of physical indulgence. In that story, of Hannibal's army at Capua, he lists among their wasteful pleasures "wine, meats, prostitutes, gaming, and doing nothing." Since the artists were both illustrating their text and drawing on what they knew of their own world, the image needs to be understood as reflecting both sources. It is not an undistorted peek through the keyhole at medieval life.

The third example is the image of the Canterbury pilgrims taken from the Herbert Lydgate (fig. 38), which has been frequently reproduced since the nineteenth century. Not only is this an image of John Lydgate—not his more famous predecessor Geoffrey Chaucer (it illustrates Lydgate's *Siege of Thebes,* not Chaucer's *Canterbury Tales*)—it also dates from the early sixteenth century (not the fourteenth) and is by Flemish, not English, hands. Knowing this detracts considerably from the image's power as a British cultural icon.

The present volume provides the opportunity to consider together a generous selection of illustrations in manuscripts of secular vernacular texts. My hope is that it offers insight into the culture that gave rise to the illustrations, the artists who created them, and the nobles who paid for and viewed them. To understand the origins and contemporary purpose of these illustrations is to understand more fully the aspirations of artists who added beauty to our world. It also helps us understand more fully the powerful patrons who did so much to shape western Europe at the end of the Middle Ages and the beginning of the modern era. Put simply, understanding how illustrations revived the past for producers and consumers of these manuscripts illuminates the Renaissance centuries later.

Figure 37 (opposite)
MASTER OF ANTHONY
OF BURGUNDY
Bathhouse. In Valerius
Maximus, *Faits et dits
memorables des romains,*
translation by Simon de
Hesdin and Nicolas de
Gonesse of *Facta et dicta
memorabilia,* ca. 1470.
44.2 × 33.4 cm (17⁷⁄₁₆ ×
13³⁄₁₆ in.) Berlin,
Staatsbibliothek, Ms.
Dep. Breslau 2, vol. 2,
fol. 244

Notes

1. This documentation was first published in Carton 1847: 370–71. See also Dubois 2002: 615–19; and Pinchart 1865: 13–14.

2. On Mansion, see Brussels 1973: 212–38.

3. Thirteen manuscripts and one printed copy of secular vernacular texts were recorded in his residence at Antwerp in 1488 (Génard 1875: 21–30). Of these, at least eight were written on parchment and illuminated. As indicated by the presence of incomplete works (there was only one of the two volumes of Valerius Maximus), Philippe de Hornes had had a much larger collection than was listed in 1488. Surviving manuscripts that belonged to him include three volumes of Froissart's *Chroniques* (Denucé 1927: 13–16); a *Chroniques de Charlemagne* (Dresden, Sächsische Landesbibliothek, Ms. Oc. 81); and vol. 4 of Mansel's *Fleur des histoires* (Copenhagen, Kongelige Bibliotek, Ms. Thott 568 2°). He may also have owned, and had updated, a fine illuminated book of hours (Leeds, University Library, Brotherton Ms. 4; see Ker 1969–92, 3: 30–34; and Brussels 1959, no. 57).

4. See Di Stefano 1963: 403–6; and Di Stefano 1965: 210–13. On the outstanding popularity of Valerius Maximus, see Guénée 1980: 250.

5. Volume 2 was described in 1488 as "un ouvrage en parchemin, avec figures, relié en velours bleu avec fermoirs et clous en cuivre doré et portant pour titre 'Le 2d volume du grand Valere'" (Génard 1875: 25). Dubois (2002: 616–23) has identified the two volumes as Paris, Bibliothèque de l'Arsenal, Mss. 5194–5195.

6. For an outline of this history, see De Hamel 1994.

7. For a cautious view of the origins of secular manuscript illustrations, see Pächt 1986: 22–28.

8. For the early stages of this process, see Petrucci 1977: 5–26.

9. See Brussels 1967a.

10. These include principally romances, histories, and advisory, moral, and philosophical texts.

11. Contemporary copies of the same translation of Valerius Maximus were illuminated at Bruges for Jean Gros (Leipzig, Universitätsbibliothek, Ms. Rep. I fol. 11b), Anthony of Burgundy (Berlin, Staatsbibliothek, Dep. Breslau 2), Jan Crabbe (Bruges, Grootseminarie, 157/188, 158/189, 159/190), Louis of Gruuthuse (Paris, Bibliothèque nationale de France, Mss. fr. 288, 289), and Edward IV (London, British Library, Royal Mss. 18 E.iii, 18 E.iv); several copies of the text as printed by the Josephus printer in the 1470s were also illuminated at Bruges (see Brussels 1973: 188; Lenger 1985; and Brinkmann 1997: 91–102). Four further copies (Berlin, Staatsbibliothek, Ms. 94; Jena, Universitätsbibliothek, Ms. El. fol. 88; London, British Library, Royal Ms. 17 F.iv; Paris, Bibliothèque de l'Arsenal, Ms. 5196) had their illumination completed around the same time in either the north of France or Flanders. In 1464 Jehan III de Hangest, lord of Genlis (d. 1490), even passed his captivity in Paris writing an abridged version of the French translation of Valerius Maximus, printed by Vérard in 1497 (Contamine 1997: 264; Lucas 1970: 247, n. 227).

12. My division does not imply that there is anything mechanistic about this process or that one part of the dynamic necessarily precedes or leads the other. I do not wish to promote a teleological explanation and prefer to see book production and consumption as a circle of self-renewing activity. Putting one before the other in the following text is merely necessary, not significant.

13. For more on the book trade and the production of luxury goods in the Low Countries, see Prevenier and Blockmans 1986: 282–372.

14. Pinchart 1865: 3–10.

Figure 38
GERARD HORENBOUT
*John Lydgate and the
Canterbury Pilgrims.*
In John Lydgate,
Siege of Thebes, fol. 148
(see cat. no. 130)

15. Pinchart 1865: 7, 9–10.

16. De Schryver 1979b: 472–73.

17. See Martens (M.) 1999: 412–13.

18. Based on Pinchart 1865. Twelve groats were paid for the small miniatures in Charles's Quintus Curtius and *Bible moralisée*; 32 groats for miniatures in the *Chroniques de France*, vols. 1 and 2 of the *Songe du viel pelerin*, and vols. 3, 4, and 5 of *Renaut de Montauban*; 36 groats for miniatures in the *Vie du Christ*, vol. 3 of the *Chroniques de Hainaut*, vols. 1 and 2 of *Renaut de Montauban*, vols. 3 and 4 of *Charles Martel*, and the large miniatures in the *Bible moralisée*; and 40 groats for the large miniatures in the Quintus Curtius.

19. Pinchart 1865: 6; de Schryver, in Van den Bergen-Pantens 2000: 75.

20. De Schryver 1969b: 456–57 nn. 6, 7; Pinchart 1860–81, 2: 207.

21. Dehaisnes 1881: 209 (B 2037).

22. Pinchart 1860–81, 2: 202–3.

23. Dehaisnes 1881: 197 (B 2018).

24. Jean Le Tavernier, for example, was paid 24 groats for average-sized miniatures in grisaille in a book of hours for Philip the Good, and probably also in his *Chroniques et conquestes de Charlemagne* (Dehaisnes 1881: 197 [B 2018], 209–10 [B 2037]).

25. Van Uytven 1992: 110–11.

26. For details, see Pinchart 1865: 5, 7, 9–10.

27. The *Vengeance* contains twenty miniatures in 304 folios; the Quintus Curtius, eighty-six miniatures in 270 folios.

28. Comparison of surviving manuscripts suggests that page size was an important factor in these costs. Yvonnet Le Jeune was paid 32 groats per quire for Charles the Bold's *Vengeance* (Chatsworth, Duke of Devonshire, Ms. 7310) and 48 groats per quire for his Quintus Curtius (Paris, Bibliothèque nationale, Ms. fr. 22547). The pages of the former (37 × 26 cm [14⁹⁄₁₆ × 10¼ in.]) are around half the size of those of the latter (48 × 38 cm [18⁷⁄₈ × 14¹⁵⁄₁₆ in.]). Earlier Jacotin du Bois and Jacques Pilavaine were paid at the rate of 50 groats per quire (Cockshaw 2000: 45–46).

29. On the *Roముléon*, see Pinchart 1860–81, 2: 190; also McKendrick 1994: 153 n. 23. The *Roముléon* cost 2,160 groats, and the Valerius Maximus 4,800 groats.

30. The *Roముléon* survives as Besançon, Bibliothèque municipale, Ms. 850, a large folio parchment manuscript of 287 folios (see McKendrick 1994: 153, 167). Philippe de Hornes's copy of Valerius Maximus (Paris, Bibliothèque de l'Arsenal, Mss. 5194–5195) comprises about 544 folios. Estimating the cost of the *Roముléon* at a rate of 50 groats per quire and 48 groats per miniature produces a total of 2,232 groats, a figure remarkably close to that paid by Philip the Good.

31. The text of the breviary cost 5,440 groats, and the illumination 13,310 groats. For the Quintus Curtius, the illumination cost 3,376 groats.

32. Van Uytven 1992: 103–4.

33. Paris, Bibliothèque de l'Arsenal, Mss. 5087, 5088 (see Paris 1993: no. 44), and cat. no. 54.

34. De Schryver 1969b: 448.

35. The dominant role of the *libraire* in Paris (see Rouse and Rouse 2000) does not seem to have pertained in the Low Countries. At the 2002 Annual Palaeography Lecture in London, Malcolm Parkes argued that the same is true for England.

36. An apparent exception is the payment to David Aubert for having a manuscript for Jacques de Bourbon illustrated and bound (Straub 1995: 311; Charron and Gil 1999: 84). Aubert may not, however, have been the scribe of this manuscript; he may merely have been coordinating work on the duke's behalf. Charron and Gil (1999: 84–85) propose that Aubert's colophon in Anthony of Burgundy's copy of the *Roman de Gillion de Trazegnies* states merely that the patron had ordered both the transcription and the decoration. This proposal is supported by Aubert's more explicit colophon in Louis of Gruuthuse's copy of the same text (Wolf [E.] 1996: 252).

37. Charron and Gil 1999: 96–98.

38. Those illuminated at Bruges include cat. no. 63; London British Library, Royal Mss. 17 F.i, 17 F.vi–vii; and former Longleat, Marquess of Bath, Botfield Ms. 2. See McKendrick 1996a: 30–31, 44, 46.

39. See Hasenohr 1990: 349–52.

40. Even in large-format volumes, one column was more commonly used in the time of Philip the Good (Hasenohr 1990: 349). During the rule of Charles the Bold, and in contrast to humanistic book practice, the more traditional two-column format returned to favor.

41. See Brown (M.) 1990: 42; also Bruinsma 1992: 156–64.

42. Rare sequences of historiated initials occur in cat. no. 58; Paris, Bibliothèque nationale, Ms. 137 (Jung 1997: 102–3; Scott [K.] 1976: 15, pl. 6a); and Baltimore, Walters Art Museum, Ms. W.307.

43. In contrast, borders with figural or animal elements were relatively common. See, for example, cat. nos. 57–59, 68, 71, 75.

44. Rare examples occur in the frontispieces of a Josephus (Paris, Bibliothèque de l'Arsenal, Ms. 5082, fol. 3v) and a *Guiron le Courtois* (Oxford, Bodleian Library, Douce Ms. 383, fol. 17). Both date from the 1480s, are from the same artistic circle, and are probably influenced by earlier Parisian manuscripts.

45. For the documented binding on a *Chroniques de France* made for Charles the Bold, see Legaré 1999.

46. Notable survivals include the bindings of Anthony of

Burgundy's four-volume set of Froissart's *Chroniques* (see fig. 34, this chapter) and Philip of Cleves's Quintus Curtius (Wieselgren 1925: 81, fig. 1). See also Lemaire 1983: 7–16.

47. Charles the Bold, for example, had these made for his *Vita Christi* and his Quintus Curtius (Pinchart 1865: 6, 9).

48. Significantly, and in contrast to earlier practice (cf. Rouse and Rouse 2000), many miniaturists worked solely or almost entirely on the illustration of secular vernacular texts.

49. Of a four-volume set of the *Miroir historial*, now divided between London and The Hague, only the first volume was illuminated for Edward IV; the other three were completed for Philip of Cleves (see Chavannes-Mazel 1988: 106–10).

50. See also cat. no. 121.

51. One volume in which only the opening miniature of a much longer campaign was executed is Wolfart VI van Borssele's *Ovide metamorphose* (Saint Petersburg, Russian National Library, Ms. Fr.F.v.XIV.1; see Jung 1997: 103–4). His *Faits des romains* (Paris, Bibliothèque nationale, Ms. fr. 20312 bis) has a similar opening miniature but did have the other miniatures added (McKendrick 1990: 124, pl. 7).

52. In, for example, a manuscript of the *Faits des romains* (Paris, Bibliothèque nationale, Ms. fr. 281), spaces were left for the same campaign of illustrations as those executed in three other manuscripts (see McKendrick 1990: 116, 129).

53. See Alexander 1992: 52–71.

54. See Aeschbach 1987: 24–57; McKendrick 1996a: 53, 101–3. For similar treatment of Jean Miélot's translation of the *Romuléon*, see McKendrick 1994: 160.

55. See, for example, the few traces of instructions in volume 3 of Jean de Wavrin's *Chroniques d'Angleterre* made for Edward IV (McKendrick 1994: 163, n. 86).

56. Shared written instructions are a sufficient explanation for the similar illustrations in two contemporary manuscripts of Petrus de Crescentiis from the same artistic circle (cat. no. 65, and Paris, Bibliothèque de l'Arsenal, Ms. 5064), as well as the very similar illustrations in the Flemish manuscripts of the French translation of the *Fortalitium fidei* of Alfonso de Spina (see Fifield 1972: 98–111).

57. For four closely related copies of the *Faits des romains* with identical rubrics, see McKendrick 1990: 115–16.

58. See also the two large miniatures in Louis of Gruuthuse's copies of Gaston Phébus's *Livre de la chasse* and Frederick II of Hohenstaufen's *De arte venandi cum avibus* in French translation (Geneva, Bibliothèque publique et universitaire, Mss. fr. 169, 170) and two contemporary miniatures in Philip of Cleves's copies of the same two texts (Stuttgart, Württembergische Landesbibliothek, Ms. HB XI.34a). See Wood and Fyfe 1955: lxxiii–lxxv, pls. 16, 17, 21, 22. For color reproductions of these miniatures, see Walz 1994: pls. 18, 19. Another pair of manuscripts owned by Gruuthuse and Cleves comprise two contemporary copies of Jean de Beuil's *Jouvencel* (Paris, Bibliothèque nationale, Ms. fr. 192, and Munich, Bayerische Staatsbibliothek, Ms. gall. 9). Two contemporary manuscripts of Jan Du Quesne's translation of Caesar's *Commentaries* share the same compositions in all their large miniatures (see cat. no. 74); two others (London, British Library, Egerton Ms. 1065; Oxford, Bodleian Library, Douce Ms. 208) share some compositions.

59. For such a replication (of a Quintus Curtius), see McKendrick 1996b: 141–44.

60. See McKendrick 1996a: 50–62.

61. The dissemination of such models may be the best explanation of why compositions produced by Jean Hennecart to illustrate Guillebert de Lannoy's *L'Instruction d'un jeune prince* reappear in manuscripts illuminated in Tours (see cat. no. 56), as well as why compositions produced by Rouen artists to illustrate Jean de Courcy's *Bouquechardière* (see Chancel 1987: 224–28) came to be reused in two copies illuminated by the Master of Fitzwilliam 268 and the Master of Margaret of York (New York, Morgan Library, Mss. M.214, M.224; Paris, Bibliothèque nationale, Mss. fr. 65–66; de Chancel 1987: 247–49, 270–72). In contrast, direct descent from the original manuscript appears to explain why compositions produced in Provence for René d'Anjou's *Livre des tournois* reappear in three Bruges manuscripts of the same text (Paris 1993: 236).

62. The Rambures Master's opening miniature in a copy of Valerius Maximus (Paris 1993: no. 47) is clearly based on a composition devised by Lieven van Lathem (cf. Bruges 1992: pls. on 114, 115; see also cat. nos. 58, 59).

63. In an illustrated manuscript of the *Miroir historial*, for example, the same figure group is used in a miniature by the Master of Edward IV and by one of his assistants, the Master of the Trivial Heads (The Hague, Koninklijke Bibliotheek, Ms. 128 C.i, vol. 2, fol. 58, and vol. 3, fol. 268). For the reuse of other figure groups of the Master of Edward IV, see the biography of this master, this volume; see also cat. no. 84. For more on the reuse of patterns in other artistic media, see Van Uytven 1992: 109–10.

64. *Pace* Van Buren (1979: 368–70) argues that patterns originally created for a monumental work of art were used as models for manuscript illustrations.

65. Delaissé (in Brussels 1959: 182–85) notes a move to greater uniformity from around 1475.

66. De Schryver (in Van den Bergen-Pantens 2000: 89 n. 19) correctly notes that Liédet did contribute some borders.

67. Most notably in the manuscripts illuminated by the Master of 1482 and his assistants. These include The Hague, Koninklijke Bibliotheek, Ms. 133 A.5; London, British Library, Add. Ms. 19720 and Egerton Ms. 1065; Lyons, Bibliothèque municipale, Ms. 1233; New Haven, Beinecke Library, Ms. 230; Oxford, Bodleian Library, Douce Ms. 208; and Paris, Bibliothèque nationale, Ms. fr. 1837.

68. Scott (M.) 1980: 190–205.

69. See Guénée 1980: 314–18; Hasenohr 1989: 245, 255; and Contamine 1997: 274–77.

70. Prevenier and Blockmans 1986: 342–47; also Van Uytven 1992: 107–8 (with extensive bibliography).

71. For a different interpretation of the evidence from that which follows, see Sutton and Visser-Fuchs 1995: 61–98.

72. On deliveries, see Charron and Gil 1999: 88–90. On the reception and retention of manuscripts by the *garde des joyaux*, see de Schryver, in Van den Bergen-Pantens 2000: 83–89.

73. On David Aubert in this role, see Charron and Gil 1999: 96–98. Other scribes who were probably attached to a household include Yvonnet Le Jeune for Charles the Bold, described as "clerc escripvain" (Pinchart 1865: 5, 7); Jacotin de Ramecourt, secretary to Isabella of Portugal (Lieberman 1970, p. 470; Sommé 1998: 325, 326, 360, 362, 446, 458); and Thierion Anseau, described as Baudouin II de Lannoy's "serviteur et escripvain" (see cat. no. 97). Jean Paradis described himself twice as Louis of Gruuthuse's "indigne escripvain" (see Paris 1992: no. 50; and Bruges 1992: 126).

74. On Vasco Quemada, see Gachard 1845: 147–48; also Brussels 1991: 121–23. Jean de Créquy was another who promoted texts by circulating them (Gil 1998b: 69–93; see also Willard 1996: 55–62). Probably also serving this role was Jean de Montferrant, for the *Douze Dames de rhétorique* (see cat. no. 70).

75. London, British Library, Burney Ms. 169; see McKendrick 1996a: 24.

76. McKendrick 1996b: 137 n. 21. Other volumes profusely illustrated by the same artists and lacking any early marks of ownership include Jean de Wavrin's *Chroniques d'Angleterre* (Vienna, Österreichische Nationalbibliothek, Ms. 2534; see Pächt and Thoss 1990: 39–45) and Raoul Lefèvre's *Recueil des histoires troyennes* (Wolfenbüttel, Herzog August Bibliothek, Ms. A.1. Aug. fol.).

77. Such colophons are preserved in only 12 of the 190 volumes collected by Gruuthuse (see Bruges 1992: 126) and 7 of the 45 surviving from the collection of Anthony of Burgundy (Van den Bergen-Pantens 1993: 324).

78. See, for example, cat. no. 83.

79. Two such rare manuscripts are Anthony of Burgundy's and Louis of Gruuthuse's copies of the *Roman de Gillion de Trazegnies* (see Wolf [E.] 1996: 252, 258).

80. See Hasenohr 1989: 246.

81. On such copies of the French translation of Valerius Maximus, see note 11 in this essay and cat. no. 67; on fine illuminated printed copies of Boethius, see Cambridge 1993: nos. 57–59, and Arnould 2002. See also cat. no. 73.

82. For more on the aspirations of merchants and their desire to imitate the practice of the nobility, see Van Uytven 1992: 106.

83. Derolez 1979: 16, 294, 305–6; also Arnould 1988.

84. Further research needs to be undertaken to clarify what the inhibiting factor was. One possibility is the differences in class culture.

85. Buettner 2001: 9–12.

86. Bell 1988: 149–87.

87. Although when discussing women's collections in general, Hasenohr (1989: 248) considered this interest marginal, she later (p. 248) admitted to the recorded use of men's books by "princesses."

88. Brussels, Bibliothèque royale, Ms. 9233; see Lemaire 1994: 298.

89. Doutrepont 1906: nos. 68, 69, 81, 82, 134, 149–51, 154, 170, 204; Doutrepont 1909: 466. The swift incorporation into her nephew's library of books delivered to Margaret of Burgundy from her late husband's library suggests that they were not delivered for her use (see Derolez 2001: nos. 96, 97).

90. Rare exceptions in Latin include two volumes owned by Jan Crabbe (cat. no. 118 and Boccaccio's *Genealogia deorum* [Bruges 1981: no. 88]); two copies of Virgil (The Hague, Koninklijke Bibliotheek, Ms. 76 E.21; Edinburgh, University Library, Ms. 195); and the *Historia de Preliis* (Aberystwyth, National Library of Wales, Peniarth Ms. 481). The Latin manuscripts illuminated for Raphael de Mercatellis form a library totally distinct from contemporary libraries. For a rare example in English, see cat. no. 84; for an Italian translation of Livy with illustrations by Flemish artists, see Limentani Virdis 1981: no. 9.

91. Paris, Bibliothèque nationale, Ms. fr. 87. Pietro Villa also owned a copy of Valerius Maximus in Latin (London, British Library, Burney Ms. 210).

92. On these collectors, see Van den Bergen-Pantens 1993, Bruges 1992, and Korteweg 1998.

93. Some consider circa 1478 to be the crucial turning point of his collecting; see Backhouse 1987: 25–28; McKendrick 1992: 153; McKendrick 1994: 164; and Sutton and Visser-Fuchs 1995: 80.

94. See cat. no. 97.

95. Brussels 1959: 12; see also Doutrepont 1909: 467.

96. On the library of the dukes of Burgundy, see Brussels 1967a; see also Blockmans 1998: 7–18. A useful statistical breakdown of the types of text in the Burgundian library is given in Hasenohr 1989: 278.

97. Hasenohr (1989: 278) counts 831–ca. 880 volumes; Blockmans (1998: 7) counts 867.

98. The figures for Gruuthuse are based on Bruges 1992: 198–99 (to which I add an additional manuscript: London, British Library, Cotton Ms. Vespasian B.i, a copy of Guillebert de Lannoy's *Instruction d'un jeune prince*, bearing the arms of Gruuthuse and illuminated by the Master of the Harley Froissart, McKendrick 2003: pl. 20). The figures for Philip of Cleves are based on Finot 1895: 433–34. In each case, I count the total number of volumes, not texts.

99. Lafitte 1997: 248.

100. Van den Bergen-Pantens 1993.

101. Backhouse 1987.

102. See, respectively, Gil 1998b; Legaré 1991: 91–93; McKendrick 1990: 124, 137, n. 48 (to this list, I now add two further volumes in Jena, noted in Knaus 1960: col. 576, n. 16); Génard 1875; Lemaire 1993; Korteweg 1998.

103. Debae, in Brussels 1996: 201–5.

104. Thoss 1987: nos. 58, 61; Backhouse 1994: 48–53. Two manuscripts illuminated for Guillaume de Ternay are Darmstadt, Hessische Landesbibliothek, Ms. 133 (Olschki 1932: pl. 60), and Kraków, Biblioteka Czartoryskich, Ms. Czart. 2919 V (Płonka-Bałus 2002 and Płonka-Bałus 2002b).

105. See Le Guay 1998 and McKendrick 1990.

106. An exceptional copy of volume 1 of Bersuire's translation was copied and illustrated for Louis of Gruuthuse merely to complete a set with much earlier copies of volumes 2 and 3 (Lafitte 1997: 251).

107. Earlier manuscripts formed an important part of many contemporary collections—including those of Louis of Gruuthuse, Philip of Cleves, and the Croÿ family—and there was a buoyant market in such manuscripts.

108. Hasenohr 1989: 246–47.

109. Coleman 1996: 109–47.

110. On Philip, see Doutrepont 1909: 466–67; on Philip's reader, see Doutrepont 1909: 141, 228, 236. Contemporary observers—including Charles Soillot, Guillaume Fillastre, Olivier de la Marche, Philippe Wielant, and Raymondo de Marliano (see Brussels 1977a: 15, n. 39; Smeyers 1998: 355; and Paravicini and Paravicini 2000: 287, n. 159)—noted Charles's passion for having accounts of the past read to him. Charles's favorite reader was Guy de Brimeu, lord of Humbercourt (see Paravicini 1975: 89).

111. On Charles's reading in camp before Neuss in 1475, see Vaughan 1973: 163.

112. See de Schryver 2000: 83–89; Charron and Gil 1999: 96–98.

113. See Campbell 1976: 189.

114. For a good discussion of these issues, see Lawton 1983: 41–52; see also McKendrick 1996b: 136.

115. Brussels 1977a: 15, n. 39. Jean de Créquy was also "given to looking at, studying and possessing books" (Gil 1999: 73).

116. Gil 1998b.

117. See cat. no. 74.

118. See Stroo 1994: 285–98; and Dubois, in Van den Bergen-Pantens 2000: 119–24.

119. For the names and mottoes added in the first manuscript owned by Engelbert of Nassau, see McKendrick 1996b: 148, fig. 11. For the names and mottoes added in Engelbert's second manuscript, a copy of *Isaie le Triste* dated 1445 (Darmstadt, Hessische Landes- und Hochschulbibliothek, Ms. 2524), see Knaus 1960: col. 573.

120. McKendrick 1996b: 141, 144.

121. In 1469 a manuscript of *Perceforest* was on loan to Louis of Luxembourg, count of Saint Pol (Doutrepont 1909: 466), and a manuscript of Jean Lebègue's translation of Bruni's *De primo bello punico* was on loan to Anthony of Burgundy (de Schryver 2000: 85).

122. Gil 1998b: 83–84.

123. See cat. no. 85. Around 1477 Guillaume de la Baume appears to have supplied Margaret of York and Mary of Burgundy with a manuscript from his collection to present to Sir John Donne (Backhouse 1994: 50–51); in 1489 Louis of Gruuthuse had his manuscript of René of Anjou's *Livre des tournois* copied for presentation to Charles VIII (Paris 1992: no. 51).

124. Such a motivation may lie behind the apparent transfer of ownership of Jacques le Grand's *Livre de bonnes moeurs* (transcribed by Aubert) from the ducal financier Guillaume Bourgeois to Anthony of Burgundy. On this manuscript, see Van den Bergen-Pantens 1993: 353; Straub 1995: 90.

125. For an English perspective, see Rosenthal 1982: 535–48. For information on women who passed on books, see Buettner 2001: 12–16.

126. Dehaisnes 1881: 299 (B 2173); Pinchart 1860–81, 1: 61–62; Pinchart 1865: 37.

127. Van den Bergen-Pantens 1993: 324.

128. Bruges 1981: 207–8; Paris 1992: 195.

129. There was, however, less of a decline in France.

130. Campbell 1976: 198; Van Uytven 1992: 108–9.

131. Brussels 1973.

132. Mestayer 1991: 199–216.

133. See Legaré 1992: 209; and Korteweg 1998: 17–22.

134. See the introduction to part 4, this volume.

135. See, for example, Boudet 1997: 271–73.

136. See Pastoreau 1989: 196–200.

137. Monfrin 1967: 285–89; Monfrin 1972: 143–44.

138. Bossuat 1946; Gallet-Guerne 1974.

139. Vanderjagt 1995: 267–77; Paravicini and Paravicini 2000.

140. See Vale 1981: 14–32.

141. On such models of noble conduct, see Heitmann 1981: 97–118; see also Franke 1997a: 113–46.

142. Backhouse 1997b.

143. See, for example, the reproduction of *The Garden of Pleasure* on the cover of *The Art of Courtly Love* (1973), an EMI recording of performances by the Early Music Consort of London, directed by David Munrow.

CATALOGUE

PART I

FROM PANEL TO PARCHMENT AND BACK: PAINTERS AS ILLUMINATORS BEFORE 1470

THOMAS KREN

Around 1470 the Vienna Master of Mary of Burgundy imbued the illuminated page with the verisimilitude found in Flemish painting in oil on panel (see part 2). This event marks a turning point in the history of manuscript illumination as artists began to develop qualities of naturalism in book painting. Yet the Vienna Master's bold new style was not the first instance in which the visual aesthetic of Flemish oil painting appeared in miniatures. A range of examples were executed before 1470 by painters in oil, who for the most part illuminated manuscripts sporadically and sparingly. (Simon Marmion, who worked in both media regularly, is the notable exception to this.) The painters' miniatures that survive are few; here and there a single miniature in tempera that captures the subtle effects achieved by the painters in oil shows up in a book with other miniatures that display a more traditional, less naturalistic style.[1]

The earliest, most celebrated instance of the naturalistic style is the series of miniatures in the Turin-Milan Hours that are generally attributed to Jan van Eyck (ca. 1390–1441) or his workshop (fig. 39). They are usually dated to the 1420s, though occasionally as much as a decade later. Georges Hulin de Loo called the painter of the miniatures "Hand G."[2] This artist is often identified with Jan van Eyck because Hand G perfected the illuminator's technique of tempera on parchment in a way that parallels Van Eyck's much-heralded perfecting of the technique of oil on panel.[3] In the truthfulness of his miniatures, Hand G raised manuscript illumination to a new level of refinement and subtlety. Moreover, he had a gift for pictorial invention comparable to Van Eyck's. The originality of Hand G's miniatures rests in their boldness in the depiction of interior space and landscape, their subtlety in the handling of light in different environments, their quality of observation, and their monumentality.[4] Since the Burgundian court particularly appreciated manuscript illumination and illuminators, it is tempting to think that Van Eyck, who was Duke Philip the Good's favorite artist, also executed miniatures for him, including those assigned to Hand G. Whatever the case, Hand G's miniatures represent milestones in the history of Flemish painting.

In addition to the illuminations of Hand G and the closely associated Hand H, the Van Eyck workshop's involvement with manuscript illumination is further evidenced by subsequent campaigns in the Turin-Milan Hours, in particular those of Hands I and J (cat. no. 1). Van Eyck's legacy to manuscript illumination is arguably as significant as that to his signature medium of oil on panel.

Given the important role of illumination at court, it is not surprising that the single surviving commission for a miniature that Rogier van der Weyden received came from Duke Philip. Van der Weyden's frontispiece for the *Chroniques de Hainaut* (cat. no. 3) represents the apogee of court portraiture of this era and enjoyed a wide influence.

Petrus Christus may have begun his career as an illuminator, though only a single illumination from his hand has come down to us (cat. no. 6). His technique in the oil medium betrays strong affinities with illuminators' working methods (see cat. nos. 4, 5). Presumably he learned the tempera medium early in his career. His art also shows familiarity with the Eyckian miniatures of the Turin-Milan Hours.[5]

Of all the painters active before 1470, Simon Marmion is the most important forerunner of the new style of illumination. A full generation older than the Vienna Master, he learned early in his career the skills of both the oil painter and the illuminator. He was the first artist to introduce the naturalism of the oil painter's aesthetic to the art of the miniature, employing the style consistently from one book to the next. His artistic practice enabled him to draw upon innovations in both media, so that his work in each medium informed that in the other (see cat. nos. 7, 14, 46, 93).

The evidence from these four artists and their workshops confirms what was likely often, though not always, the case throughout the Middle Ages. Painters also illuminated manuscripts, and the boundaries within the different practices were not invariably rigid. Many painters worked in various media. At the same time, the rarity of surviving examples also indicates what was equally true in fifteenth-century Flanders: most painters in oil on panel—with the exception of Marmion, who moved easily from panel to parchment and back—illuminated manuscripts only occasionally if at all. Yet the examples discussed here show that the painters themselves contributed to introducing the new naturalism of the medium of oil on panel to the illuminated page.

Figure 39
HAND G
The Birth of Saint John the Baptist, ca. 1440–45. In the Turin-Milan Hours, 28 × 20 cm (11 × 8 in.). Turin, Museo Civico d'Arte Antica, Ms. 97, fol. 93v

Notes

1. The work of Willem Vrelant exemplifies the more traditional but still highly successful style of miniature that is illustrative of a broad segment of book painting in Bruges and Flanders before 1470 (see cat. no. 15; cf. also the Llangattock Hours [cat. no. 2], where the older and newer traditions meet). Examples of this more conservative style, though not by Vrelant, are also found in cat. nos. 3 and 6.

2. Hulin de Loo 1911: 27–36.

3. Regarding the chronology of Hand G, see "Flemish Artists of the Turin-Milan Hours," following.

4. See Marrow's comments on these innovations and their significance for their religious subject matter in Van Buren, Marrow, and Pettenati 1996: 227–31.

5. Ainsworth, in New York 1994a: 58–59, 60, 81–82, 148, 173.

FLEMISH ARTISTS OF THE TURIN-MILAN HOURS

Until the Hours of Mary of Burgundy (cat. no. 19), no manuscript had captured the verisimilitude of Flemish painting—especially its innovations in the use of light, texture, and space—as brilliantly as a select group of miniatures in the Turin-Milan Hours. The manuscript represents a portion of the prayers and masses from the *Très Belles Heures* of John, duke of Berry, which, still unfinished, was separated from the core of the book. It subsequently entered the possession of William VI of Bavaria (d. 1417), count of Holland, Zeeland, and Hainaut; of his brother and successor, Count John (d. 1425); or of both. Under these and subsequent patrons, its program of illuminations, begun toward the end of the fourteenth century by Parisian and other French illuminators, was finished by Flemish artists working in the first half of the fifteenth century.

The Flemish portion, known today as the Turin-Milan Hours, has a rich history. It was divided into two separate volumes, one in the Biblioteca Nazionale in Turin, the other in the Trivulzio collection in Milan. Tragically, in 1904 the Turin portion was gravely damaged by fire. Subsequently, in 1935, the Museo Civico d'Arte Antica in Turin acquired the Trivulzio portion. Both volumes contained miniatures that have long been associated with Jan van Eyck and have often been attributed to him. Although the attributions remain a topic of considerable controversy, most scholars agree that certain miniatures assigned by Georges Hulin de Loo to Hand G represent some of the most advanced expressions of the new style of painting that Van Eyck himself perfected. They include, in the surviving volume in Turin (ex Trivulzio), *The Birth of Saint John the Baptist* (see fig. 39), *The Mass for the Dead*, *The Discovery of the True Cross*, and the famous bas-de-page scenes that accompany the first two of these miniatures—*The Baptism of Christ* and *A Procession to the Grave*—along with a group of miniatures in the destroyed companion volume.[1] These illuminations to a degree represent an even more advanced and complex handling of interior spaces and of landscape than appears in the paintings of Van Eyck. Hulin de Loo called them "the most marvelous that had ever decorated a book and, for their time, the most stupefying known to the history of art. For the first time we see realized, in all of its consequences, the modern conception of painting. . . . For the first time since antiquity, painting recovers the mastery of space and light."[2] Nevertheless, Hulin de Loo considered Hand G to be Hubert van Eyck, while Albert Châtelet, Anne van Buren, and others believed him to be Jan.[3] Still others have argued that Hand G was a follower of Jan.[4] The dating of the miniatures ascribed to Hand G has meanwhile also remained a subject of debate, with dates ranging from the end of the lifetime of Count William to the last years of the life of Count John, when Jan van Eyck was in his service (1422–25), to the late 1430s.

What is important, and seems to be generally agreed, is that the miniatures by Hand G are wholly original, even progressive compositions within the Eyckian idiom. They present a revolutionary visual language long considered perfected in the medium of oil on panel yet here employed in tempera on parchment. If one follows the older and more traditional arguments that place the miniatures before the death of Count John, then they date earlier than any surviving Eyckian works in oil on panel.[5] As such their existence raises provocative questions about the role that manuscript illumination may have played in the emergence of the vaunted verisimilitude of Eyckian oil painting.

Hulin de Loo identified several styles among the Flemish illuminators who helped to finish the book after Hand G. He assigned these styles to illuminators he called Hands H through K. Their work seems to have taken place over many decades, into the 1440s, carrying on even after Jan van Eyck's death in 1441. The miniatures continued to show Van Eyck's stylistic influence and to employ a body of motifs from the workshop. The evidence suggests that manuscript illuminators were counted among Van Eyck's workshop assistants, a fact that appears to be corroborated by technical features in his own paintings.[6] Above and beyond the question of whether Jan van Eyck himself illuminated manuscripts, which seems more than likely, his workshop probably trained assistants with the ability to practice both media. Represented in this catalogue are several of these illuminators (or their workshops), such as the ones Hulin de Loo identified as Hands I, J, and K (see cat. nos. 1, 2). Hands I and J worked together in one phase of the book's execution, probably during the early 1440s. Hand K, working in the second half of the 1440s, is usually identified as the Master of the Llangattock Hours or as related to him.[7]

Hulin de Loo grouped Hands I and J together as illuminators whose styles are closely related and who executed a group of bas-de-pages in the existing Turin volume and the volume that was destroyed. Their style is Eyckian and accomplished. They draw closely upon Eyckian models.[8] He related the miniatures of Hand J narrowly to a frontispiece miniature in Saint Augustine's *La Cité de Dieu*, made for Jean Chevrot, bishop of Tournai (Brussels, Bibliothèque royale de Belgique, Ms. 9015, fol. 1), without explicitly identifying them as by the same artist.[9] Châtelet believed that the miniatures ascribed to Hands I and J were all by the painter of the Chevrot frontispiece, whom he called the Master of Augustinus.[10] Van Buren argued that only certain miniatures within the I and J group are by this painter, whom she called the Master of Jean Chevrot, after the same manuscript in Brussels.[11] Van Buren believed one of the illuminators in the Hand J group to be a panel painter. She renamed him the Master of the Berlin Crucifixion, after a painting in Berlin (Staatliche Museen, Gemäldegalerie, inv. 525F).[12] The Brussels manuscript is dated 1445, while Van Buren assigned the Chevrot Master's contribution to the Turin-Milan Hours to around 1441. Like the other Flemish artists who contributed to completing the Turin-Milan Hours, Hands I and J appear to have worked in Bruges.[13]

Hand K was the last and the weakest of the illuminators in the Flemish group; his style is still Eyckian, but he was probably painting outside the workshop environment. He borrowed extensively from various of his predecessors among the Flemish illuminators of the Turin-Milan Hours, especially Hand G. Nevertheless, his contribution to the manuscript was considerable, especially in the bas-de-page scenes and the now-destroyed calendar.[14] Châtelet identified Hand K as the Master of the Llangattock Hours, a Bruges book of hours from the 1450s (cat. no. 2).[15] Van Buren believed that Hand K can be divided into several hands, the primary one of which she named the Master of Folpard van Amerongen and identified as the main painter of the Llangattock Hours.[16] The Hand K illuminators were probably active around 1445–50.

While the interactions between painters and illuminators around and including Van Eyck remain to be clarified (a daunting task), it is clear that manuscript illuminators, some possibly trained in his workshop as both painters and illuminators, continued to follow Eyckian models into the 1450s. The influence of Van Eyck on the art of the book was strong. The Turin-Milan Hours, the Llangattock Hours, and the Hours of Paul van Overtvelt (cat. no. 6) indicate the importance of the new style of painting but also raise questions about the ongoing interaction between painting and illumination in these years.   T. K.

Notes

1. *The Betrayal of Christ*, historiated initial, and bas-de-page; *Saint Julian on the Water; The Virgin as the Queen of Heaven* and bas-de-page; and *Duke William of Bavaria at the Seashore*, historiated initial, and bas-de-page; Hulin de Loo 1911: 30–31.

2. Hulin de Loo 1911: 31 (author's translation). For a very thoughtful and compelling analysis of the miniatures' broader importance for the history of painting and the history of art, see the remarks by Marrow in Van Buren, Marrow, and Pettenati 1996: 227–31.

3. Hulin de Loo 1911: 30–39; Châtelet 1993: 68–73; Van Buren, Marrow, and Pettenati 1996: 313–23, 385. While Châtelet accompanies his attribution with a question mark, he offers particularly telling observations about the conceptual and stylistic links between Hand G and Jan van Eyck. Van Buren gives Hand G's *Discovery of the True Cross* (Turin, Museo Civico d'Arte Antica, inv. 47, fol. 118) to Hubert and the rest of Hand G's miniatures to Jan.

4. E.g., Lyna 1953: 7–20; Dhanens 1980: 350–53; Campbell 1998: 174; Reynolds (C.) 2000b: 6–12.

5. These arguments include Durrieu 1902: 16–17; Hulin de Loo 1911: 26–29; and more recently Van Buren, Marrow, and Pettenati 1996: 298–307, 313–23.

6. Buck (1995: 67–72; see also New York 1998: 89) observed that the technique of the Metropolitan Museum's *Last Judgment* panel suggests that it may have been finished by an illuminator. Marigene Butler offered a close comparison of the technique of the Turin-Milan Hand H, the painter of *The Agony in the Garden*, with that of the painter of the

Philadelphia *Ecstasy of Saint Francis*, a work certainly painted in the Van Eyck workshop (Van Asperen de Boer et al. 1997: 41–42, see also 47–50 for evidence localizing the latter's production to the Van Eyck workshop). It is pertinent in the present context that the latter is executed in oil on parchment, further evidence of the Van Eyck workshop's employment of the illuminator's traditional painting support.

7. Not discussed here, because he was not represented in the exhibition, is the important Hand H, whom Hulin de Loo thought to be the young Van Eyck, and others have considered to be Petrus Christus or Jan Coene. Cf., e.g., Hulin de Loo 1911: 36–38, and Châtelet 1993: 74–76. Châtelet identified the artist as possibly Coene; Van Buren, Marrow, and Pettenati (1996: 330–31) believe that he is the Master of the Philadelphia Saint Francis, hence an artist who worked in both oil and tempera.

8. Cf., e.g., Smeyers, in Van Asperen de Boer et al. 1997: 65–74.

9. The Hand J miniatures in the surviving volume, in the opinion of Hulin de Loo (1911: 40–43), included the following bas-de-page scenes: *Moses with the Tablets of the Law, Confession and Communion, Jonah and the Whale,* and *The Sacrifice of Isaac,* along with the initials on the pages with the second and the third of these.

10. Châtelet 1993: 77–78.

11. Van Buren, Marrow, and Pettenati 1996: 332–33, 386. Van Buren also attributed to the Chevrot Master one of the miniatures Hulin de Loo attributed to Hand F (ex Biblioteca Nazionale, Turin [destroyed], fol. 77v; Châtelet 1967: pl. 43). Châtelet considered his Master of Augustinus to have been a member of Van Eyck's atelier, while Van Buren believed that her Chevrot Master was not. For the Brussels manuscript and also for the Turin-Milan Hours, the I and J artists had access to Van Eyck workshop drawings.

12. Jones (2000: 203) has suggested that the miniatures of Hand J are closely related to certain Eyckian paintings, such as *The Fountain of Life* (Madrid, Museo del Prado; and Oberlin, Ohio, Allen Memorial Art Museum).

13. Châtelet (1999) argued that the Master of Augustinus could be identified with Jean de Pestinien, who enjoyed the positions of "varlet de chambre et enlumineur" to Duke Philip the Good. He attributed to this artist a substantial and diverse body of works that also includes miniatures in the Hours of Philip the Good (Cambridge, Fitzwilliam Museum, Ms. 3-1954) and the Hours of René of Anjou (London, British Library, Ms. Egerton 1070). His view of the artist's activity is quite different from that of Van Buren. The Master of Jean Chevrot/Master of Augustinus/Hands I and J of the Turin-Milan Hours deserve to be the subject of a fuller investigation. Bernard Bousmanne (1997: 72–74) discussed the Chevrot Master's influence on Vrelant.

14. Hulin de Loo 1911: 45–49; Van Buren, Marrow, and Pettenati 1996: 386.

15. Châtelet 1993: 80–85.

16. Van Buren, Marrow, and Pettenati 1996: 346–49, 386. Schilling (1961: 232–34) believed that the Llangattock Master was at best a follower of Hand K. On the Master of Folpard van Amerongen, see cat. no. 2, note 2. König (1998b: 354–65, no. 26) identified a book of hours on the art market not long ago as by the Master of the Llangattock Hours. It is certainly from the artist's workshop.

I

MASTER OF THE BERLIN CRUCIFIXION OR CIRCLE AND MASTER OF JEAN CHEVROT OR CIRCLE

Christ Blessing
Leaf from the Turin-Milan Hours
Bruges, ca. 1440–45

One leaf, 27.2 × 17.6 cm (10¹¹⁄₁₆ × 6¹⁵⁄₁₆ in.); justification: 16.7 × 11.1 cm (6⁹⁄₁₆ × 4⅜ in.); recto: 20 lines of *textura*; verso: 1 half-page miniature, 1 bas-de-page miniature

COLLECTION: Los Angeles, J. Paul Getty Museum, Ms. 67 (2000.33)

PROVENANCE: John, duke of Berry (1340–1416); William VI, count of Holland, Zeeland, and Hainaut (d. 1417), and/or John of Bavaria, count of Holland (d. 1425); dukes of Savoy, by seventeenth century; private collection, Ostende; acquired 2000

JPGM and RA

This miniature from the Turin-Milan Hours shows a full-length iconic figure of Christ holding rounded tablets with a passage from John 14:6, *Ego sum via [et] veritas [et] vita* [I am the way and the truth and the life]. He appears before a background of exceptionally fine diapering (repetitive geometric pattern), raising his hand in blessing. James Marrow has argued convincingly that the unusual round-topped tablets he holds, in place of an open book, allude to Moses and the Old Law. The Gospel inscription on the tablets represents the New Law. Marrow has further suggested that the figure is derived from a lost prototype by Van Eyck that other illuminators also drew upon.[1] Particularly Eyckian is the modeling of the face and the facial type of Christ, including the handling of the hair, along with the conception of the drapery folds. The Eyckian refinements extend to such details as the large jewel that secures the figure's mantle, the quietly shimmering fine white and yellow rays of the halo painted over the intricate diapering, and even the floor tiles. In the mantle differing shades of red are applied in thin, semitransparent layers. While executed in tempera, they recall the glazes of the oil painter's technique.

The style recalls that of Hand J in the Turin-Milan Hours as defined by Georges Hulin de Loo and appears to be closest to one miniature in the damaged volume from Turin (fig. 40).[2] The facial type and hair of Christ, along with the bunching of the drapery folds (and the resulting zigzag pattern of the hemline), in the Getty leaf resemble closely these features in the same figure in *Christ Teaching the Pater Noster to the Disciples* (see fig. 40), attributed by Hulin de Loo to Hand J. In both depictions Jesus' hands and feet have a similar boneless quality. Anne van Buren isolated the Pater Noster miniature from the Hand J group and ascribed it instead to the panel painter who executed the Eyckian Crucifixion in Berlin (Staatliche Museen, Gemäldegalerie, inv. 525F).[3] Although the facial types there are quite different from those in the Pater Noster miniature, the handling of the drapery is similar. The columnar treatment of the robe and the handling of its folds are similar in the figures of Saint John the Evangelist in Berlin and in the Getty Christ. Likewise, the organization of the man-

tles of both John and the Virgin in bunches of inverted V-shaped folds with zigzag hemlines is comparable to that of the Getty Christ's mantle.[4] In both, the drapery conveys breadth and monumentality. Another telling detail is the continuous straight line that links the front edges of Christ's toes in both works. It is not certain that the Getty *Christ Blessing* and the Pater Noster miniature are by the Master of the Berlin Crucifixion, but the miniatures and painting are closely related. The link confirms this illuminator's close ties to the Van Eyck workshop.[5]

Many of the miniatures and marginal vignettes executed for the Turin-Milan hours in the 1440s evoke the words of the text they accompany, and the bas-de-page composition of Ms. 67 may do so as well. The prayer "Savoureus Ihesucrist tres debonnaires sires" is directed to Christ, begging him to pardon the supplicant's persecutors and grant them paradise through his pity, and asking the same compassion for himself, that he might pardon his enemies and so receive pardon for his sins.[6] The subject matter of the bas-de-page miniature may be more difficult to pin down than that of the main miniature, yet it appears to embody closely the words of the prayer and may at the same time have had a contemporaneous association. At center, a cleric presents two kneeling knights to an elegantly dressed aristocrat. The lord raises his left hand in greeting and extends his right to clasp the right hand of the foremost knight, who places his left hand on his heart and gazes meekly forward. The second, wearing an empty scabbard on his belt, crosses his arms on his chest in a gesture of submission; his unsheathed sword and a helmet lie discarded on the grass. The humble gestures and postures of the knights imply that they are beseeching pardon for some deed; the lord, with his proffered hand, conveys his forgiveness. Susan L'Engle, in a perceptive unpublished paper, has related the action to the expiatory ritual known as the *amende honorable*, which was popular with Burgundian authorities as a means to shame political offenders without physically punishing them.[7]

The bas-de-page miniature is not by the same hand as the large miniature, and its technique is quite different, featuring a thicker, more opaque medium, especially in the costumes. Distinctive features are the gently rolling terrain, the green color of the grass, and the architecture, which call to mind the celebrated frontispiece miniature in Jean Chevrot's *La Cité de Dieu* manuscript (Brussels, Bibliothèque royale de Belgique, Ms. 9015, fol. 1). Marrow attributed the bas-de-page to the painter of the frontispiece, the Master of Jean Chevrot, to whom Albert Châtelet also attributed all of the miniatures by Hands I and J and to whom Van Buren attributed some of the miniatures by Hand J, some by Hand I, and one by Hand F.[8] The figures show the same squat proportions and round facial types, and the settings display similar architecture to that found in the work of the Eyckian Hand F, who painted many bas-de-page and historiated initials in the Turin-Milan Hours. Yet the Getty bas-de-page is not by the same hand.[9] Nor do the figure types or details of the landscapes compare closely with those bas-de-pages ascribed by Hulin de Loo to Hand J.[10]

I
MASTER OF THE
BERLIN CRUCIFIXION
OR CIRCLE AND
MASTER OF JEAN
CHEVROT OR CIRCLE
Christ Blessing

Figure 40
MASTER OF THE
BERLIN CRUCIFIXION
OR CIRCLE
*Christ Teaching the Pater
Noster to the Disciples.*
In the Turin-Milan
Hours, 28 × 20.2 cm
(11 × 8 in.). Turin,
Biblioteca Nazionale,
Ms. K IV 29, fol. 60v
(prior to 1904)

fol. 48v), features very similar coloring in the drapery of Saint John the Evangelist. He wears an orange-red mantle with a green lining. Hand H, whose drawing of hands and other details is finer than that of the painter of the Getty leaf, has been identified at various times with the young Jan van Eyck (Hulin de Loo 1911: 36–38), Petrus Christus (Hoogewerff 1936–47, 2:8–9), and Jan Coene, an assistant in the workshop of Van Eyck (Châtelet 1993: 74–76). Van Buren believed that the Chevrot Master painted *The Crucifixion* but that the miniature was then repainted by the Master of the Philadelphia Saint Francis (Van Buren, Marrow, and Pettenati 1996: 330–31).

5. Moreover, the artist of the Getty *Christ Blessing* employs the distinctive Van Eyck workshop pattern for the light-colored floor tiles. They also appear in the painting *Virgin and Child with Saints Barbara and Elizabeth and Jan Vos* (New York, Frick Collection), which seems to have been finished in the artist's workshop in the years immediately after Van Eyck died (Marrow 2002: 70). This is further evidence of our painter's close association with painters in oil on panel. For a thoughtful discussion of the use of workshop patterns for architectural details in Van Eyck's workshop paintings, including the Frick *Virgin and Child*, see Jones 2000: 197–207.

6. Sonet 1956, no. 1884: "Savoureus Ihesucrist tres debonnaires sires se il est nul ne nulle qui mal me vueille ne qui mal me cacent qui soient mes anemis mes contraires ne mes persecuteurs, sire pardonnes leur et leur donnez paradys par nostre pitie."

7. Marrow (2002: 72–74) has proposed several alternative interpretations for the scene, of which the most intriguing is a depiction of an Old Testament event described in Exodus 18:1–7. Jethro, priest and father-in-law of Moses, brings Moses' two sons and his wife, Sephore, back to him. This would connect the subjects of miniature and bas-de-page through the person of Moses. Quite a few of the bas-de-page scenes in the Turin-Milan Hours have Old Testament subjects.

8. Châtelet (1993: 77–78) called the Chevrot Master the "Master of Augustinus."; Van Buren, Marrow, and Pettenati 1996: 332–33, 386. Hulin de Loo (1911: 40) associated the style of Hand J with the *La Cité de Dieu* frontispiece but did not go further than that.

9. The miniatures by Hand F may have belonged to an earlier campaign. They include initials and bas-de-pages on folios 57, 57v, 58, and 80v in the destroyed Turin volume (Châtelet 1967: pls. 31–33, 45) and the initials and bas-de-pages on fols. 1v and 20v in the current Turin volume (Hulin de Loo 1911: pls. 9, 10). See Hulin de Loo 1911: 24.

10. See Hulin de Loo 1911: 39–40.

11. The Turin volume was gravely damaged in a library fire in 1904.

12. The large miniature above "Pardurables diex gouveneres" shows God the Father enthroned, blessing, crowned and holding a scepter (Sonet 1956: nos. 1660, 1661). It belonged to the destroyed volume and hence is known only in a poor black-and-white reproduction (Durrieu 1902: pl. 41). Hulin do Loo also attributed it to Hand J, and it shows similarities to the Getty leaf's large miniature in the facial type and hair, the boneless fingers, the treatment of certain folds, and the tiles in the floor. The prayer "O Intemerata" begins on the verso of the Louvre leaf.

The leaf is one of eight removed, probably in the seventeenth century, from the portion of the book now in the Biblioteca Nazionale in Turin.[11] It followed folio 75 and bears the conclusion of the prayer "Pardurables diex gouverneres," which began on the verso of that leaf. The prayer that begins below the miniature, which is on the leaf's verso, is completed on the recto of one of the removed leaves (Paris, Musée du Louvre, Cabinet des Dessins, R.F. 2024).[12]   T. K. and S. L'E.

Notes

1. Marrow 2002: 68–72.

2. Hulin de Loo 1911: 39–40; this is known today only in mediocre black-and-white reproductions (Durrieu 1902: pl. 36; Châtelet 1967: pl. 36).

3. Van Buren, Marrow, and Pettenati 1996: 331–32.

4. *The Crucifixion,* attributed to Hand H by Hulin de Loo in the well-preserved volume (Turin, Museo Civico d'Arte Antica, inv. 47,

2a
WILLEM VRELANT
AND MASTER OF THE
LLANGATTOCK HOURS
The Annunciation, fol. 53v

2b
MASTER OF JEAN
CHEVROT WORKSHOP
The Trinity, fol. 25v

2

WILLEM VRELANT, MASTER OF THE LLANGATTOCK
HOURS, MASTER OF THE LLANGATTOCK EPIPHANY,
MASTER OF WAUQUELIN'S ALEXANDER OR
WORKSHOP, AND WORKSHOP OF MASTER OF
JEAN CHEVROT

Llangattock Hours
Use of Rome
Bruges, 1450s

MANUSCRIPT: i + 169 + i folios, 26.4 × 18.4 cm (10⅜ × 7¼ in.);
justification: 12.8 × 8.2 cm (5 × 3¼ in.); 18 lines of *textura*; 14 full-page
miniatures, 13 historiated initials

INSCRIPTIONS: Binder's signature *Stuvart Lieuin me lya ainsin A gand*,
fifteenth century

BINDING: Lievin Stuvaert, Ghent, 1450s; brown calf, blind-tooled with
foliage, zoomorphic decoration, and inscription *liuinus stuuaert me
ligauit*; two silver-gilt clasps with round glass-filled mounts flanked
by pearls (lower clasp reverse: the arms of Folpard van Amerongen,
Utrecht; upper clasp reverse: the arms of Folpard van Amerongen
impaling those of Themseke of Bruges)

COLLECTION: Los Angeles, J. Paul Getty Museum, Ms. Ludwig IX 7
(83.ML.103)

PROVENANCE: Folpard van Amerongen, mayor of Utrecht, and
Geertruy van Themseke (?); second baron Llangattock [his sale,
Christie's, London, December 8, 1958, lot 191]; [H. P. Kraus,
New York]; to Peter and Irene Ludwig, Aachen; acquired 1983

JPGM and RA

The Llangattock Hours is well known for the derivation
of some of its major compositions from the work of
Jan van Eyck and the probable participation of artists active
in the Turin-Milan Hours. Its miniatures, which vary in
refinement, represent the work of as many as eight artists,
and some were collaborative efforts.[1] The face and hands of
the Virgin in *The Annunciation* (ill. 2a), for example, are by
Willem Vrelant, while the rest of the miniature is by an
artist dubbed the Master of the Llangattock Hours, who is
the book's main illuminator.[2] The artists modeled the composition—especially the poses and gestures of the figures
and, in many cases, the folds of the garments—after a
panel of the Annunciation by Van Eyck (fig. 41). The figures
in the miniature, however, unlike those in the panel, appear
in a domestic interior with everyday objects of iconographic significance. Its niche with ewer and towel, symbols of Mary's purity, originates in paintings such as the
Mérode Altarpiece by Robert Campin (ca. 1375–1444) and
The Annunciation of the Ghent Altarpiece.

Although Anne van Buren attributed the miniature of
the Trinity in the Llangattock Hours (ill. 2b) to the Master
of Jean Chevrot, it is more likely from his workshop.[3] It is
unusual in its depiction of the Holy Spirit as a winged,
bearded man (see ill. 2b). This variation is found in other
Flemish devotional books produced in Bruges, including
the Hours of Paul van Overtvelt (cat. no. 6) and a book of

Figure 41
JAN VAN EYCK
(Flemish, ca. 1390–1441)
The Annunciation,
ca. 1434/36 (detail). Oil on
canvas transferred from
panel, 92.7 × 36.7 cm
(36½ × 14⁷⁄₁₆ in.).
Washington, D.C.,
National Gallery
of Art, Andrew W.
Mellon collection
(1937.1.39.[39]/PA)

hours with miniatures by the Master of Jean Chevrot (New York, Morgan Library, Ms. M.421, fol. 15v).[4] In the Overtvelt miniature—which is by Petrus Christus, the panel painter—the order of the figures is reversed and the canopy omitted.[5] Ursula Panhans-Bühler proposed a lost Eyckian model as the probable source for the Christus miniature.[6] Following this supposition, the Llangattock *Trinity* would similarly share an Eyckian prototype.

Scholars have associated several artists believed active in the Llangattock Hours—including the Master of Jean Chevrot, the Master of the Llangattock Hours, and the Master of the Llangattock Epiphany—with work in the final campaigns of the Turin-Milan Hours.[7] They were perceptibly aware of figural groupings found there and at times rearranged them to create new compositions in the Llangattock Hours.[8] These artists were apparently not members of the Van Eyck workshop but were more likely illuminators familiar with his work and that of his workshop. The Eyckian compositions, the familiarity with the Turin-Milan Hours, and the participation of Vrelant all suggest that the Llangattock Hours was produced in Bruges in the generation following Van Eyck.[9]   R. G.

Notes

1. Van Buren, Marrow, and Pettenati 1996: 346, 352, n. 27. Van Buren identifies among others the hands of the Master of Wauquelin's Alexander, fol. 43v; the Master of Jean Chevrot, fol. 25v; and a hand active in Philip the Good's Valerius Maximus (Paris, Bibliothèque nationale de France, Ms. fr. 6185), fol. 37v. Smeyers (1998: 262) believed that nine artists participated in the book's illumination.

2. Delaissé (1968: 77) noted that Vrelant painted part of this miniature. Euw and Plotzek (1979–85, 2:115–41), who call the manuscript the Hours of Folpard van Amerongen, argue that Willem Vrelant, as director of a workshop, hired artists to illuminate and to bind the book. Its clasps, which bear the arms of Van Amerongen and his wife and date to the fifteenth century, are not original to the manuscript. Recent X rays of the boards by Elizabeth Mention of the Paintings Conservation Department at the J. Paul Getty Museum show that the book originally had a different set of endpieces. Since the clasps themselves are too large for the book, they may have been appropriated from another book, perhaps well after the lifetime of Van Amerongen. The book's original owner therefore remains unknown, and I prefer Master of the Llangattock Hours to Van Buren's Master of the Folpard van Amerongen (in Van Buren, Marrow, and Pettenati 1996: 346). Van Buren's Master of the Van Amerongen Epiphany, named after a miniature of the Epiphany in the Llangattock Hours, ought likewise to be renamed. On the clasps, see Euw and Plotzek 1979–85, 2:119–20, and Lemaire 1983: 9, 11–12. Schilling (1961: 211) believed that the arms of the clasps are probably those of the original owner.

3. Van Buren, Marrow, and Pettenati 1996: 346, 352, n. 27.

4. This iconography for the Trinity is also found in the Trivulzio Hours (cat. no. 17, fol. 13v) and the Prayer Book of Charles the Bold (cat. no. 16, fol. 14). In addition, the Llangattock *Virgin and Child with Donor* (fol. 43v) shares its composition with the donor miniature by the Master of Wauquelin's Alexander in the Overtvelt Hours (fol. 21). For Morgan M.421, see Wieck 1997: 106–7, and Smeyers 1998: 260, 263.

5. New York 1994a: 176–80.

6. Panhans-Bühler 1978: 18–25. See also Gorissen 1973: 1053–57. Another Eyckian composition in the Llangattock Hours is an inhabited initial depicting the Holy Face on fol. 13v, reminiscent of Van Eyck's lost *Vera Icon*, which is known only through copies; see Belting and Eichberger 1983: 95–96. Schilling (1961: 219–20) suggested that *The Crucifixion* (fol. 31v) may ultimately rely on a Van Eyck panel painting.

7. Van Buren (Van Buren, Marrow, and Pettenati 1996: 332, 346–49) argued that the Master of Jean Chevrot (whom she linked with miniatures by Hands I and J) and the Masters of the Llangattock Hours and the Llangattock Epiphany (artists traditionally identified with Hand K) produced miniatures in both manuscripts. Delaissé (1968: 76–77) noted that the artist completing the Turin-Milan Hours, identified by Hulin de Loo (1911) as Hand K, collaborated with Vrelant and other artists in the Llangattock Hours. For Schilling (1961: 232–34), by contrast, the Llangattock Master is neither Hand K nor Vrelant, and she sees the hand of the Llangattock Master both alone and in collaborations in the Llangattock Hours. On the Chevrot Master, see Châtelet 1999, who proposed that the artist is Jean Pestinien; see also Bousmanne 1997: 72–75.

8. Elements derived from the Turin-Milan Hours include the Magdalene's costume and raised hands, Longinus on a horse, and the body type of Christ in *The Crucifixion* (fol. 31v), which copy miniatures on fols. 34v and 48v of the Turin-Milan Hours; see Schilling 1961: 217–18, 220, and Gorissen 1973: 1057–58. *The Massacre of the Innocents* (fol. 96v) is derived from a bas-de-page by Hand J in the Turin-Milan Hours (Paris, Musée du Louvre, RF no. 2023), as noted in Schilling 1961: 217–18. Schilling (1961: 217) and Marrow (1966: 67–69) noted similarities between the Llangattock *Office of the Dead* (fol. 131v) and elements in the Turin-Milan Hours.

9. John Plummer (in Baltimore 1988: 153) indicated that the Llangattock calendar is specific to Bruges, whereas Clark (2000: 112, 126 n. 8) suggested that it is more complicated, ascribing it to the diocese of Tournai. Plummer calculated that the calendar agrees 94.89 percent with a dismembered book of hours illuminated by the Gold Scrolls group (ex Philip Duschnes, New York); see Baltimore 1988: 150.

ROGIER VAN DER WEYDEN

The son of Henri de la Pasture, a cutler, and Agnès de Watreloz, the Tournai native Rogier van der Weyden (ca. 1399–1464) became one of the most renowned and influential painters of the fifteenth century. By about 1426 he had married Elisabeth Goffaert, the daughter of a wealthy shoemaker, and in 1435 he settled in Brussels, becoming the official town painter the following year and adopting the now well-known Dutch form of his family name.[1] He continued for a while, however, to maintain a workshop in Tournai.[2] His post demanded a variety of tasks, such as designing decorations for civic celebrations and the town hall.[3] He may have visited Rome in 1450.[4] In 1462 he was a member of the Confraternity of the Holy Cross at Saint-Jacques-sur-Coudenberg. He died in June 1464 and was buried in the Church of Saint Gudule, Brussels.

The documents pertaining to Van der Weyden's artistic training are much debated. On March 5, 1427, a "Rogelet de la Pasture, natif de Tournai" registered as an apprentice to Robert Campin with that city's Guild of Saint Luke, and he would have completed his training in 1431. The following year, "Maistre Rogier de la Pasture, natif de Tournay" became a master in the guild. It seems probable that Rogelet and Rogier are the same person and that Van der Weyden was a pupil of Campin, a notion supported on stylistic grounds.[5]

Three works by the artist, which are mentioned in early documents, form the basis for all attributions. *The Descent from the Cross* (Madrid, Museo del Prado), described in sixteenth-century sources as by Rogier, displays the deep emotionalism characteristic of his work.[6] In 1445 the Miraflores Altarpiece (Berlin, Staatliche Museen) was described as by "the great and renowned Fleming, Rogel."[7] Finally, in 1555, the charterhouse of Scheut sold *The Crucifixion*, now in the Escorial, describing it as donated by "Maister Rogere, pictore."[8]

Van der Weyden's patrons included the Burgundian dukes, and he was a favorite portraitist of the court. For Philip the Good he polychromed funerary statues in 1439, illuminated a frontispiece in 1448 (cat. no. 3), and presumably painted portraits of the duke, Isabella of Portugal, and Charles the Bold, which survive only in workshop copies. Among the portraits by the artist are those of Anthony of Burgundy (Brussels, Musées royaux des Beaux-Arts de Belgique); Jean Gros, secretary to Charles the Bold and treasurer of the Golden Fleece (Art Institute of Chicago); Francesco d'Este, who was raised at court with young Charles (New York, Metropolitan Museum of Art); Philippe de Croÿ (Antwerp, Koninklijk Museum voor Schone Kunsten); and Laurent Froimont (Brussels, Musées royaux).[9] Lorne Campbell has justifiably credited the artist with reviving the half-length devotional portrait.[10]

Van der Weyden's reputation and influence extended beyond his native land. "After that famous man from Bruges, Jan [Van Eyck], the glory of painting," wrote the Italian humanist Cyriacus of Ancona in 1449, "Rogier in Brussels is considered the outstanding painter of our time."[11] The German cardinal Nicholas of Cusa described him in 1453 as "the greatest of painters," and in 1460/61 the duchess of Milan sent her court painter to study with him in Brussels, demonstrating his international reputation as a leading artist.[12] Even today, most critics would agree with Cyriacus's assessment.

R. G.

Notes

1. Campbell 1998: 392.

2. "Maistre Rogier le pointre" was paid for work in Tournai in 1432–33, 1434–35, 1436, 1437; see Dhanens and Dijkstra 1999: 156–67, which quotes the primary documents associated with his life. In 1441 he received a lifetime annuity for property in Tournai; see Dhanens and Dijkstra 1999: 158, 159.

3. A workshop drawing of a capital on the town hall, for example, survives (New York, Metropolitan Museum of Art, Robert Lehman collection). In 1441 he was paid for painting a dragon for a procession at Nivelles; see Dhanens and Dijkstra 1999: 159. For the town hall he painted four celebrated panels depicting the Justice of Trajan and the Justice of Herkinbald, which were destroyed by the French in 1695. One of the panels was dated 1439. They are known from descriptions and a copy in tapestry (Bern, Historisches Museum); see De Vos 1999: 345–54.

4. In his *De viris illustribus*, Bartolommeo Fazio, writing ca. 1456, states that Van der Weyden visited San Giovanni in Laterano in Rome; see De Vos 1999: 60–61.

5. Although Van der Weyden, finishing in his early thirties, would have been older than the typical apprentice, an example of another student past the usual age, Jacques Daret, completing his training with Campin may be cited; see Campbell 1998: 392. Friedländer (1924–37, 2:11–12, 76–80) suggested that Van der Weyden was a master in another craft, such as sculpture, because he is mentioned as a master in 1426.

6. Friedländer 1924–37, 2:92–93, no. 3; De Vos 1999: 10–41, 185–88; Davies (M.) 1972: 223–26

7. Campbell 1998: 394. See also De Vos 1999: 226–33.

8. "Nobis donata a magistro Rogere pictore" (Dhanens and Dijkstra 1999: 172). The painting was replaced with a copy by Anthonis Mor; see De Vos 1999: 291–94.

9. For the various portraits, see De Vos 1999: 298–313, 323–27, 372–75, which includes additional bibliography.

10. Campbell 1979: 17.

11. Campbell 1998: 18, 33 n. 1.

12. See Campbell 1979: 5, and De Vos 1999: 418.

3

ROGIER VAN DER WEYDEN AND OTHERS

Jacques de Guise, *Chroniques de Hainaut*, translation by Jean Wauquelin of *Annales historiae illustrium principum Hannoniae*, part 1

Mons, Brussels, or Tournai, 1447–48

MANUSCRIPT: ii + 295 + ii folios, 43.9 × 31.6 cm (17 ⁵⁄₁₆ × 12 ⁷⁄₁₆ in.); justification: 29.2 × 20.1 cm (11 ½ × 8 ¼ in.); 33 ruled lines with 32 lines of *bastarda* in two columns by Jacquemin du Bois and Jean Wauquelin (?); 41 miniatures

HERALDRY: Escutcheon with the arms of Philip the Good, those of his numerous estates, his cry *mon yoie*, fol. 1; device *Aultre narey* and briquets of the Order of the Golden Fleece, fols. 1, 20v

BINDING: Nineteenth century; red morocco over pasteboard, stamped with the arms of France

COLLECTION: Brussels, Bibliothèque royale de Belgique, Ms. 9242

PROVENANCE: Philip the Good, duke of Burgundy (1419–1467) (his *inventaire dressé*, ca. 1467); Paris, Bibliothèque du roi, 1746–70; restituted to Bibliothèque de Bourgogne, Brussels, in 1770; Bibliothèque nationale de France, Paris, 1795–1815; restituted to Bibliothèque royale de Belgique in 1815

JPGM and RA

By 1433 Duke Philip the Good had conquered the territories of Hainaut, Holland, and Zeeland. Some years later—at the instigation of Simon Nockart, his councillor and clerk of the bailiff's court in Hainaut[1]—he commissioned from Jean Wauquelin a French translation of the most ambitious history of that province. Jacques de Guise (d. 1399), Franciscan confessor to the second count of Hainaut, compiled the original work, *Annales historiae illustrium principum Hannoniae*, between 1390 and 1396. Importantly, the translation, with a preface added by Wauquelin, presents the duke as the legitimate heir in a long line of rulers who trace their origins to the fall of Troy. As such, it epitomizes the politically charged texts that supported the duke's dynastic ambitions.[2] The present luxurious volume, the first of three, is part of Philip's own historic copy.[3]

Wauquelin, who is mentioned in the Burgundian accounts for the first time in 1445, completed the first volume of the translation by 1446, the year given in its prologue. Hainaut accounts record that by February 4, 1447, a portion of the translation was transported from Mons to Bruges for the duke's approval and that by March 1448 the transcription by Jacquemin du Bois and perhaps by Wauquelin as well was delivered to the duke.[4] No record of payment for its decoration survives. L. M. J. Delaissé distinguished four artists active in this volume, whereas Anne van Buren recently proposed that there were six working in two teams.[5]

The book's frontispiece, one of the most celebrated of all Flemish miniatures, shows Wauquelin presenting his translation to Philip (ill. 3). One of the most imposing and influential portrayals of the Burgundian court, it dramatically evokes the quality of court ritual.[6] The duke, elegantly attired in black damask, stands under a cloth of honor; at his right side are the chancellor Nicholas Rolin and Jean Chevrot, bishop of Tournai. The young Charles the Bold stands on the other side of the duke, observing as Wauquelin kneels.[7] Philip and Charles both wear the collar of the Order of the Golden Fleece, as do at least five of the courtiers, who stand beside or behind the book's presenter.[8] The importance of this particular iconography of Philip and his court is evident from its frequent repetitions and derivations in ducal manuscripts such as the frontispiece to *Le Livre du Gouvernement des princes* (Brussels, Bibliothèque royale de Belgique, Ms. 9043, fol. 2), illuminated by the Master of the Ghent Privileges in 1452. It copies closely the design but accommodates the growth of Charles in the intervening years from adolescent to young man. The frontispiece to the *Chroniques de Hainaut*, moreover, features the armorials of the ducal territories, underscoring Philip's authority by emphasizing the scope of his sovereignty.

First attributed to Rogier van der Weyden by G. F. Waagen, the miniature has attracted wide attention among scholars of both painting and illumination, but there is little agreement as to whether it is by the painter or his workshop.[9] Most concede that it is the work of a painter and at least from the workshop of Van der Weyden.[10] Even though the miniature is damaged,[11] the intelligence, force, and sympathy of the individual portrayals remain apparent, a fact that argues for an attribution to Van der Weyden rather than his workshop. The subtlety of the painting of the garments, particularly the exceptional handling of the knights' gowns of diverse damasks, also supports an attribution to him. The transparency of the shadows and the delicate quality of light betray the hand of an exacting master of these effects in oil, working, perhaps not for the first time, in an egg-based medium.[12] The miniature was probably painted in 1448, shortly before or perhaps just after du Bois delivered the portion of the manuscript that contained this page.

R. G. and T. K.

Notes

1. The preface of the manuscript mentions "honnorable et saige homme Symon Nockart, a son tampz clerc du baillieuwaige de Haynnau et consillier de mon dit tres redoubté seigneur"; for a complete transcription of the preface, see Cockshaw, in Van den Bergen-Pantens 2000: 40–41. On Nockart's role, see Delaissé 1955a: 31–32; De Vos 1999: 251 n. 4; and de Schryver 1974: 57–60.

2. Beginning around 1442 the duke commissioned a variety of politically motivated texts, including a chronicle of Brabant that stressed his right of succession. From Wauquelin he also commissioned an Alexander manuscript (Paris, Bibliothèque nationale de France, Ms. fr. 9342) and a Girart de Roussillion in prose (Vienna, Österreichische Nationalbibliothek, Ms. 2549), both of which stress the protagonists' rule of France and Flanders. See Hagopian-van Buren 1996b: 49–64. See also cat. no. 55.

3. The second and third volumes (Brussels, Bibliothèque royale de Belgique, Mss. 9243, 9244) contain, respectively, sixty and twenty-two half-page miniatures; see Bousmanne, in Van den Bergen-Pantens 2000: 179–87.

4. For a detailed investigation of the *Chroniques de Hainaut* by an international team of scholars, see Van den Bergen-Pantens 2000. In 1445 Wauquelin was paid for "la translation de pluseurs hystoires des païs de mon dit seigneur." On February 4, 1447, the bailiff of Hainaut paid Josee Hanotiau for transporting "pluiseurs grans livres des Cronicques de Haynnau, lesquelx Jehan Waucquelin avoit translatez, au command de mon dit seigneur le duc, de latin en franchoix." This copy may have been on paper; see Bousmanne, in Van den Bergen-Pantens 2000: 75. Jean de Croÿ was reimbursed in 1448 for payment "a maistre Jehan Wauquelin et Jaquemin dou Boix son clerq, demorans a Mons

. . . pour avoir escript et coppijét en velin pluiseurs livres . . . comme: la premiere partie des cronicques de Belges." The archival documentation of Wauquelin's activities is substantial; see Cockshaw, in Van den Bergen-Pantens 2000: 37–49.

5. Delaissé discerned artists working in the style of the Master of Mansel, the Master of the Chroniques de Hainaut, the Master of Wauquelin's Alexander, and the young Loyset Liédet; see Delaissé 1955a: 23–30. According to Van Buren, the first team was led by the Master of the Tiny Prayer Book of Philip the Good and included the Master of the Coronation of Ursus, and the Master of the Chroniques de Hainaut. The second team, associated with the workshop of the Master of Wauquelin's Alexander, included the Master of the Commodus and the Senate, the Master of the Reconstruction Scenes and an assistant; see Van Buren, in Van den Bergen-Pantens 2000: 65–73. Dirk de Vos suggested that Dreux Jean was active in the manuscript; see De Vos 1999: 251. In July 1468 Willem Vrelant was paid for illuminating the second volume and Loyset Liédet for the third.

6. Other examples derived from Van der Weyden's miniature include the frontispieces to the Alexander produced by Wauquelin (Paris, Bibliothèque nationale de France, Ms. 9342, fol. 6) and cat. no. 56, fol. 5. See Dubois, in Van den Bergen-Panteus 2000, 121–22.

7. Delaissé (1955a: 37) argued that the presenter of the book is Simon Nockart rather than Wauquelin. Van Buren is also of that opinion; see Van Buren 1996b: 58, and Van Buren, in Van den Bergen-Pantens 2000: 112.

8. Dubois (in Van den Bergen-Pantens 2000: 119–23) discussed the meaning of this miniature in relation to its text and political background. Van den Bergen-Pantens (2000: 124–31) explained the frontispiece's elaborate heraldry and the symbolism of the hammer that the duke holds in his hand.

9. Waagen 1847: 177; Waagen 1862: 110–11; and bibliography for this catalogue entry. Most recently Van Buren suggested that the composition is Van der Weyden's invention but doubted that the painting is by Van der Weyden himself (though she notes both its subtlety and its technical closeness to Van der Weyden). Not visible to our eyes are her suggestions of "stiffly drawn" noblemen. She asserted that the lack of pentimenti in the underdrawing and the dissimilarity of the underdrawing technique to his work on panel argue against an attribution to the master (in Van den Bergen-Pantens 2000: 65–66). These criteria are insufficient to dismiss the attribution, however, since the approach to working on a much smaller scale on parchment might well differ from that on panel. By contrast, Verougstraete and Van Schoute (in Van den Bergen-Pantens 2000: 150) marshal evidence of dramatic pentimenti that indicate, potentially, a different placement of both the presenter and the duke. See also their remarks about changes in the legs of the duke (in Van den Bergen-Pantens 2000: 151). Most recently Kemperdick (1999: 58–59) and De Vos (1999: 249–50) have both argued cogently in favor of the attribution to Van der Weyden.

10. Cf., e.g., De Vos 1999: 249, and Van Buren, in Van den Bergen-Pantens 2000: 66.

11. For an assessment of the damage, along with superb macrophotographs that illustrate it, see Verougstraete and Van Schoute, in Van den Bergen-Pantens 2000: 149–53, 274–82.

12. While no further examples of illuminations by Van der Weyden are known, the level of mastery he exhibits in this miniature makes it probable the he painted others.

PETRUS CHRISTUS

Petrus Christus (ca. 1410–1475/76) was born in Baerle, a village in Brabant not far from Breda. In 1444 he purchased the rights of citizenship in Bruges. Since such privileges could also be acquired by residing there for one year and one day, it is clear that the artist had arrived there more recently.[1] Christus's art shows a strong debt to the paintings of Jan van Eyck, whose individual works provided him with important models. Since Van Eyck died in 1441, Christus's acquaintance with his work and his techniques must have come from members of the master's workshop. The strong influence of Eyckian miniatures in the Turin-Milan Hours, underscored by the close parallels between Christus's technique and the working methods of illuminators, suggests that he may have trained or studied with illuminators. The view that the young Christus was Hand H of the Turin-Milan Hours is not widely accepted, however, and only one miniature by him is known (cat. no. 6). Christus had a good understanding of Van Eyck's working methods, but his paint handling is broader and his light effects are more restrained.[2]

Although a number of signed paintings by Christus survive, all of his dated works fall early in his activity, between 1446 and 1457. He seems to have worked in Bruges until his death in 1475 or 1476. His membership in two prominent confraternities there, Our Lady of the Dry Tree and Our Lady of the Snows, indicates his financial success and his access to both the urban and the court elite. Still, relatively few of his patrons have been firmly identified. Some commissions have been linked to Bruges confraternities (cat. no. 5) and guilds. The ducal courtier Paul van Overtvelt, who was dean of the Confraternity of Our Lady of the Dry Tree in 1469, when Christus was a member of its board, had earlier been a patron of the artist (see cat. no. 6). Like Van Eyck before him and Hans Memling (ca. 1440–1494) afterward, Christus enjoyed the patronage of eminent foreign clients, including Englishmen and apparently also Italians and Spaniards. The artist is known for his innovative handling of light and setting in portraiture and as perhaps the first artist in the north to master one-point perspective.

T. K.

Notes

1. For the facts of his life within their cultural context, see Martens's excellent account in New York 1994a: 15–23. Published monographs on the artist include Friedländer 1967–76, vol. 1; Schabacker 1974; Panhaus-Bühler 1978; Upton 1990; and New York 1994a.

2. On Eyckian influence on Christus, his relationship to manuscript illumination, and the matter of Hand H in the Turin-Milan Hours, see Ainsworth, in New York 1994a: 33–39, 53–62, 78–91, 105, 112–16, 162–65, 174–80.

3
ROGIER VAN
DER WEYDEN
Presentation Scene,
fol. 1

4

PETRUS CHRISTUS

Head of Christ
Bruges, ca. 1445

Oil on parchment, laid on wood panel; parchment: 14.6 × 10.5 cm
(5¾ × 4⅛ in.); panel: 14.9 × 10.8 cm (5⅞ × 4¼ in.)

INSCRIPTIONS: *Petr...*, on simulated frame, bottom

COLLECTION: New York, The Metropolitan Museum of Art,
Bequest of Lillian S. Timken, 1959, 60.71.1

PROVENANCE: Private collection, Spain; [Lucas Moreno, Paris, until
1910]; [Francis Kleinberger, Paris, 1910–31]; Mr. and Mrs. William R.
Timken, New York, 1931–49; Lillian Timken, New York, 1949–59; her
bequest, 1959

JPGM

With furrowed brow and an expression of deep
pathos, Christ engages the viewer from behind a
trompe l'oeil frame, a device of contemporary portraiture
that served to reinforce the physical presence of the suffering man. Crowned with thorns and wearing a purple robe,
this is the pitiful figure described in the Gospels (Mark
15:17–18 and John 19:1–5), mocked by the soldiers as "King
of the Jews" and presented by Pilate to the Jews for judgment with the words "Ecce Homo" (Behold the man). The
tripartite floriated nimbus, frontal aspect, and fictive frame
of this Christ link the work to the famous lost painting of
the Holy Face by Jan van Eyck, now known only through
later copies.[1] These copies reproduce Van Eyck's inscriptions on the original frame, including his signature and the
date of the painting. This practice was emulated by Petrus
Christus, whose partial signature, *Petr*, may be deciphered
at the lower damaged edge of the painted frame.[2]

The remarkable refinement of the execution in paint
indicates Christus's intention to make a portrait of Christ
rather than the generic and formulaic Christ type found in
the artist's other paintings. Even so, there are certain similarities in treatment, for example, with the head of the
Pantocrator in *The Last Judgment* (Berlin, Gemäldegalerie)
or the face of God the Father in the Trinity miniature
(ill. 6): the vertical wrinkles in the brow and comparable
morphological details of the facial features, such as the
heavy-lidded eyes, long triangular nose, and full lips.
Details of the handling also link these works: the modeling

of the flesh tones was achieved in each with extremely fine brushstrokes built up in an additive way over underpainting in a broadly applied pinkish tone. To this, disengaged, not fully blended strokes were added in gray for the shadows and white for the highlights of the modeling of forms. Such a technique may indicate an artist who was initially trained as an illuminator.[3]

It is unlikely that this portrait of Christ was ever intended as a leaf of an illuminated book. Although painted on parchment, the medium is oil, not tempera.[4] Moreover, the heads of Christ in contemporary devotional books tend to follow the Eyckian Holy Face model, not the suffering Christ type. The regularly placed nail holes (later restored) at the top and left and right edges of the trompe l'oeil frame suggest that it may have been tacked to a panel early on and hung in a chamber for daily private devotions.[5] Tiny slivers of an oak panel can be detected between the parchment and the present mahogany support, on which it was remounted.[6] Alternatively, in keeping with the sacrificial essence of this Christ, who suffers for the redemption of humankind, a connection with the Eucharist is possible. Perhaps this image adorned the door of a small host reliquary; such host shrines were usually decorated with an image of the Salvator Mundi, Man of Sorrows, a monstrance, or a chalice.[7] Whatever its original function, in its diminutive size, parchment support, and details of handling and execution, the *Head of Christ* manifests the close relationship between panel painting and illumination in the middle of the fifteenth century.   M. W. A.

Notes

1. One in the Gemäldegalerie, Berlin, dated 1438, and three others dated 1440 in the Bayerische Staatsgemäldesammlungen, Munich; the Groeningemuseum, Bruges; and the Swinburne collection, Newcastle-upon-Tyne, England.

2. The reading of this inscription has remained somewhat controversial. The formation of the letters in Christus's signature in the Berlin Gemäldegalerie *Nativity*, however, provides a convincing parallel for the script type, which is also common in manuscript illumination.

3. For further discussion about the development of Christus's painting technique, see Ainsworth in New York 1994a: 33–49.

4. Other examples of diminutive paintings in oil on parchment include *Saint Francis Receiving the Stigmata* attributed to Jan van Eyck (Philadelphia Museum of Art) and the *Virgin and Child* by Geertgen tot Sint Jans (Milan, Pinacoteca Ambrosiana).

5. As in the case of the image of Christ's head that appears tacked onto a panel and hung on the back wall in *Portrait of a Young Man* by Petrus Christus (London, National Gallery). A find of some one hundred similar images was made at the convent of Wienhausen, near Celle (see Amsterdam 1994: 163, fig. 75).

6. This was discovered by Peter Klein (Department of Wood Biology, University of Hamburg) during the course of his dendrochronology investigations of panel paintings attributed to Petrus Christus preceding the 1994 exhibition at the Metropolitan Museum of Art, *Petrus Christus: Renaissance Master of Bruges*. For more on this issue, see Klein, in New York 1994a: 213–15.

7. See Braun 1924, 2:628–39; Gottlieb 1971: 30–46; and Lane 1984: 129–30.

5

PETRUS CHRISTUS

The Man of Sorrows
Bruges, ca. 1450

Oil on wood panel, 11.2 × 8.5 cm (4⅜ × 3⅜ in.)

INSCRIPTIONS: Seal of Empress Maria Theresa embossed in paper and affixed with red sealing wax; *Rougier van der Weyde*, in ink, underneath, both on reverse

COLLECTION: Birmingham, Birmingham Museums and Art Gallery, P.306.35

PROVENANCE: Empress Maria Theresa (1717–1780) (?); Rev. Henry Parry Liddon (1829–1890); Mary Ambrose (niece of H. P. Liddon); Major M. R. Liddon; Trustees of the Feeney Charitable Trust; gift to the Birmingham Museums and Art Gallery in 1935

R A

Heavenly attendants carrying lilies and a sword, symbolic of divine mercy and justice, hold open the canopied curtains to reveal Christ as the Man of Sorrows. Crowned with thorns and a cruciform nimbus, Christ boldly displays the wounds of the cross. Blood streams from his forehead down his shoulders and gushes from the wound in his side toward the flowing waters below. According to Christian belief, Christ presents his body and blood as a reminder of his sacrifice for humankind in the Crucifixion and in reference to the sacraments of Holy Communion and baptism. In this regard, it is intriguing that the most important relic in Bruges, where Christus worked his entire career, was that of the Holy Blood. It was brought back from a crusade to the Holy Land by Count Thierry of Alsace in 1150 and inspired the formation of an elite confraternity in 1405 that included thirty-one noblemen of Bruges, with the dukes of Flanders as honorary members.[1]

The relic is still kept on the Burg Square in the Chapel of the Holy Blood, where a replacement nineteenth-century mural on the east wall depicts the mystery of the Holy Blood and reflects the traditional iconography associated with the relic and with the Birmingham picture.[2] Before a landscape depicting Jerusalem and Bethlehem, God the Father supports the crucified Christ, who sheds his blood into dishes held by angels above a fountain of life. Below, twelve lambs (symbolic of the disciples) drink from the restorative waters at the base of the cross, which merge into a river. The diminutive Birmingham painting serves as a condensed version of the mural's themes of redemption through the sacraments of Communion and baptism. Given its fine state of preservation, the panel most likely served as an object of private devotion, perhaps made for a member of the confraternity.[3]

In several ways Christus's *Man of Sorrows* approximates the art of illumination. In its diminutive size and composition, for example, the panel relates to miniatures such as *The Man of Sorrows* in a book of hours in the Morgan Library, New York (Ms. M.46, fol. 99v),[4] and to folio 14 by Hand H in the Turin-Milan Hours (showing an enthroned God the Father revealed by two angels, who hold back the curtains of a canopied enclosure). Moreover, as with

Christus's other paintings of the 1450s,[5] details of the handling and execution parallel those of manuscript illumination. Instead of fully blending passages of the angels' draperies, Christus here juxtaposed strokes of pure color. The flesh tones reveal a pink underpainting typical of illumination, over which there are thin, disengaged, and rather matte-looking applications of darker hues.[6] As such, the panel may be compared with the exquisite Trinity miniature in the Overtvelt Hours (cat. no. 6), which shows evidence of the craft where Christus may have first earned his fame.   M. W. A.

Notes

1. On the confraternity, see Cuvelier 1900: 5–7.

2. The original decoration was destroyed during the Beggar's Revolt and the French Revolution.

3. The embossed seal of Maria Theresa appears on the reverse of the panel. Along with Francis I, Maria Theresa had dominion over Flanders from 1740 to 1790. The couple is depicted in stained-glass windows decorating the upper level of the Chapel of the Holy Blood in the company of the other rulers of Flanders, beginning with Philip the Bold and Margaret of Male (1384–1404). The Birmingham painting may have come into the collection of Maria Theresa through a connection with Bruges's revered relic or the Confraternity of the Holy Blood, although there is no known record of a visit by the empress to Bruges during her reign or of her devotion to this cult. I am grateful to Gottfried Mraz, archivist of the state archives in Vienna, for this information about Maria Theresa.

4. See New York 1994a: 114, fig. 122.

5. Also dating the painting to the 1450s are Rowlands 1962: 420; Gellman 1970: 204; and Schabacker 1974: 105. Upton (1972: 109) dates it to 1444–45.

6. On Christus's painting technique, see Ainsworth, in New York 1994a: 33–53.

5
PETRUS CHRISTUS
The Man of Sorrows

6

PETRUS CHRISTUS AND
MASTER OF WAUQUELIN'S ALEXANDER

Hours of Paul van Overtvelt
Use of Tournai
Bruges, 1450s

MANUSCRIPT: 299 folios, 15.8 × 10.4 cm (6 3/16 × 4 1/16 in.); justification: ca. 8.8 × 5.8 cm (ca. 3 7/16 × 2 1/4 in.); 18 lines of *bastarda*; 15 half-page miniatures

HERALDRY: Escutcheon with the arms of Overtvelt, fol. 21

BINDING: Nineteenth century; red morocco; the arms, motto, and monogram of Henry of Orléans, duke of Aumale

COLLECTION: Brussels, Bibliothèque royale de Belgique, Ms. IV 95

PROVENANCE: Paul van Overtvelt; probably Jean-Louis Bourdillon (1772–1856); A. C. Chesnet [his sale, Techner, Paris, May 4, 1853, lot 16]; Henri d'Orléans, duc d'Aumale (1822–1897), by June 1853; gift to Edouard Bertin (1797–1871); [F. Tulkens, Brussels, by 1959]; acquired 1959

JPGM and RA

This book of hours was written for Paul van Overtvelt, whose coat of arms appears on folio 21. A reference to him, "famulo tuo paolo" (your servant Paul), appears in the prayers to Saint Bernard (fol. 154v).[1] A leading citizen of Bruges, he served as secretary to Isabella of Portugal from 1435 and later on, in 1442, as her collector of finances in Flanders. He became a member of the Council of Flanders in 1454 and traveled as an ambassador on behalf of Philip the Good both to Lübeck and to London to negotiate with the Hanseatic League during 1457–58. In 1460 he became bailiff of Bruges.[2] He served as dean of the elite Confraternity of Our Lady of the Dry Tree in 1469, at the same time that Petrus Christus was also a member of this group.[3]

This book of hours was illuminated by at least two artists active in Bruges: Christus, who painted *The Trinity*, and the Master of Wauquelin's Alexander, who was responsible for the best if not all of the remaining miniatures in the book.[4] The borders and decorated initials appear similar to those from the Bruges workshop of Willem Vrelant.[5] Further connecting *The Trinity* with Bruges, and specifically with Eyckian manuscript production around 1450, is its unusual representation of the third member of the Trinity not as a dove, but as a winged male figure with a beard.[6]

Specific details of handling and execution in this miniature support an attribution to Petrus Christus. *The Trinity* is set within an illusionistic blue-gray stone frame that is illuminated, as are the figures, from the left. A similar framing device and system of lighting may be found in Christus's *Head of Christ* (cat. no. 4) and *Portrait of a Carthusian*, around 1445 and 1446, respectively (both New York, Metropolitan Museum of Art). The facial types are reminiscent of Christus's conventional representations: the broad and flat forehead, furrowed brow, prominent nose, and heavy-lidded eyes are familiar from the heads in Christus's *Head of Christ* or *Man of Sorrows* (cat. no. 5). Furthermore, the juxtaposition of lime green and orange-red hues in God the Father's mantle and the aureole behind the

6

PETRUS CHRISTUS
The Trinity, fol. 155v

nated two of the ducal copies of texts Jean Wauquelin produced for Philip the Good.[10] She suggested that the black gown of Van Overtvelt in the Virgin and Child miniature belongs to circa 1455, while independently Margaret Scott suggested a dating early in the decade.[11] A dating for this volume in the 1450s is also consistent with the evidence of the Alexander Master's artistic activity and the theory that Christus may have been active as an illuminator at the beginning of his career.   M. W. A. and T. K.

Notes

1. Van Buren 1999: 17, n. 32.
2. Vermeersch 1976, 2: 284–86, no. 291.
3. See New York 1994a: app. 1, doc. 16.
4. Van Buren 1983: 64; Van Buren 1999: 17, n. 32.
5. New York 1994a: 179 n. 8; Smeyers and Cardon 1991: 99–104.
6. Two illuminations that are stylistically close relate to the Eyckian portion of the Turin-Milan Hours, namely the Trinity miniature found in the Llangattock Hours (see ill. 2b) and in a Book of Hours in the Pierpont Morgan Library, New York (Ms. M.421, fol. 15v), both of which date to around 1450. The Van Overtvelt composition is very similar to these, except for the mirror-image positions of the figures placed in a heavenly sphere rather than seated beneath a baldachin. It bears mentioning that while the patron and illuminators of the book are from Bruges, the calendar does not point very strongly to that city. Donatian is not present in October, and Basil (June 14) is not in red. Both saints are especially venerated in Bruges.
7. Compare the wings of Gabriel in the *Annunciation* in the Gemäldegalerie, Berlin, or in the Friedsam *Annunciation* in the Metropolitan Museum of Art, New York. Even the specific form of the triforium halo behind the head of Christ and the translucent gold-banded globe at his feet find parallels in Christus's panel paintings. The halo may be found in the Metropolitan Museum of Art *Head of Christ* and the globes in such paintings as *The Madonna of the Dry Tree* (Lugano, Thyssen collection), *The Holy Family in a Domestic Interior* (Kansas City, Nelson-Atkins Museum), or *The Virgin and Child* (Budapest, Fine Arts Museum; Madrid, Museo del Prado).
8. For further discussion of Christus's technique, see New York 1994a: 25–65 and passim.
9. The Virgin and Child miniature reflects a pattern also used in a miniature attributed by Van Buren (see cat. no. 2 n.1) to the artist in the Llangattock Hours (cat. no. 2, fol. 43v), though the latter is not by the same painter. Note that the subjects of the David and the Virgin before the Altar miniatures are unusual and that the book has several distinctive prayers in French (see also Bruges 1981: 273, no. 116).
10. The artist was first identified by Delaissé (1955a: 24–25), who attributed miniatures in the two Wauquelin books to him. The other is the *Chroniques de Hainaut* (cat. no. 3, fols. 75, 175v, 267, 274v, 277, 281, 284v, 286v, 291). Van Buren also attributed to him miniatures in the Llangattock Hours (cat. no. 2, fol. 43v), the Hours of Philip the Good (Cambridge, Fitzwilliam Museum, Ms. 3-1954), and another book of hours (Getty Museum, Ms. 2, fols. 31v, 115v, 243v). See Van Buren 1983: 64, and her unpublished expertise on Getty Ms. 2 on file. Van Buren (1999: 17) has suggested that the Alexander Master may have been Vrelant's teacher in Bruges. He has still not been the subject of systematic investigation.
11. Van Buren (1999: 17, n. 32) and Margaret Scott have pointed to links with Duke Philip's garment in the famous frontispiece miniature of the *Chroniques de Hainaut* from the late 1440s (see ill. 3), among other examples (Scott, correspondence with the authors, May 27, 2002). Van Buren's dating is in response to the previous date of about 1470–75 (de Schryver and Lemaire, in Bruges 1981: 273, no. 116, and Ainsworth, in New York 1994a: 176, 179).

figures is typical of Christus's palette, as is the colored stippling on the inside of the wings of the Holy Ghost.[7] Characteristic of Christus's execution in both panel painting and illumination are his use of pinkish flesh tones and impasto touches on fingertips to suggest three-dimensional form, and the brown outlining of contours. Perhaps most convincing is the identical manner by which Christus modeled draperies in the underdrawing of his panel paintings and on the surface of his illumination, in parallel hatching at an oblique angle to the main folds.[8]

Among the finest of the book's miniatures painted by the Master of Wauquelin's Alexander (or close to his style) are *David Writing* (fol. 104), *The Virgin and Child Reading before an Altar* (fol. 86), and *Paul van Overtvelt Kneeling in Adoration before the Virgin and Child* (fol. 21).[9] Anne van Buren, who considers the Overtvelt Hours an important work by the artist, localized his activity to Bruges. He also illumi-

SIMON MARMION (A)

Simon Marmion (ca. 1425–1489) enjoyed a career rich with significant commissions over four decades. The documentary evidence shows that the dukes of Burgundy, high-ranking officials at court and other nobles, the city of Amiens, and other urban institutions commissioned work from him. From 1449 Marmion enjoyed a succession of projects from Amiens, where he lived, including an altarpiece with Christ, the Virgin, Saint John, and other figures for the court of justice in 1454. The same year Philip the Good enlisted him as a member of the team of more than thirty artists called to contribute to the decorations for the Feast of the Pheasant in Lille. By 1458 the artist had settled in Valenciennes, where he lived for the next three decades. In 1462 he played a role in founding the city's Confraternity of Saint Luke, and the next year he painted an altarpiece for the confraternity's chapel. In 1463 he painted a sculpture of the Virgin for the cathedral at Cambrai. He also painted a portrait of Charles the Bold, the count of Charolais, with one of his spouses.[1] The artist himself married Jeanne Quaroble, the daughter of a prominent and wealthy citizen of Valenciennes, in 1465.[2]

Ducal accounts show further that Philip the Good commissioned from Marmion an elaborate breviary with ninety-five miniatures and twelve calendar vignettes (cat. no. 10) in 1467, the year of the duke's death. The work was completed three years later for the duke's successor, Charles. In 1468 Marmion joined the painters' guild in Tournai, but there is no evidence that he resided there. The last two decades of his artistic activity are much less well documented. In 1484 he painted a Virgin, perhaps in a diptych, as an epitaph for Pierre Dewez (Devado), canon of Cambrai cathedral, who had died the previous year. The artist himself died on Christmas Day in 1489. His documented paintings and painted sculptures are today largely untraced.[3]

Marmion belonged to a family of artists. He was the son of Jean, also a painter, who was active in Amiens as early as 1426, and whom Simon assisted there in 1449. He had a brother, Mille, who became a master in the painter's guild in Tournai in 1469 and was residing there in 1473. Further, Jean Lemaire de Belges sang the praises of a Marie Marmion, who was Simon's daughter. A nephew, Michel Clauwet, also a painter, is documented in Valenciennes from 1492 to 1519. Upon Simon's death his widow married a young painter from Hainaut, Jan Provost.[4] The fact that Marmion had relatives who were painters and illuminators may help to explain the range in execution among his manuscripts and paintings. It is the likely result of workshop collaboration that often involved family members. Unfortunately, among the aforementioned artists, only the art of Provost is known. It bears little relationship to that of the master from Valenciennes.

Despite the wealth of documentation, the only surviving works reliably identifiable as Marmion's are two leaves from the breviary begun for Philip the Good. Since the nineteenth century most scholars have, however, accepted the circumstantial evidence that he painted the large wings for the elaborate altar with silver-gilt sculpture made for the Abbey of Saint Bertin at Saint-Omer (see cat. no. 7), which was completed in 1459.[5] A substantial body of manuscripts and paintings may be grouped around these works, which greatly enrich our understanding of his career.

While residing most of his life in Picardy, Marmion maintained a favorable relationship with the Burgundian ducal family and the ducal household, which led to some of his most important commissions. This relationship, indicated by the documents, is fleshed out by the attributed works. The patron of the Saint Bertin Altarpiece was Guillaume Fillastre, the bishop of Verdun, Toul, and Tournai. In the same years Fillastre also commissioned from the artist the lavish *Grandes Chroniques de France* for presentation to the duke (Saint Petersburg, National Library of Russia, Ms. Erm. 88). Philip himself acquired—in addition to the previously mentioned breviary—devotional writings, a miniature in a book of hours, and a treatise on health illuminated by Marmion. Besides the lost portraits and the breviary, Marmion painted for Margaret of York a *Lamentation* panel in or after 1468, when she wed Charles the Bold (cat. no. 11). For Margaret he also illuminated three distinctive works: *Les Visions du chevalier Tondal* (cat. no. 14), *La Vision de l'âme de Guy de Thurno* (cat. no. 13), both from 1475, and probably at the same time *L'Histoire de madame sainte Katherine* (France, private collection).

Besides Fillastre, other patrons from the court circle included the humanist Vasco da Lucena, a favorite of Philip's consort, Isabella of Portugal; Jean Gros, secretary and *audiencier* of Charles the Bold; Walpurga de Moers, wife of Philippe de Croÿ; and Guillaume Rolin, son of the ducal chancellor Nicholas.[6] Lucena left Marmion's *Virgin and Child* to the Hospital in Louvain at his death in 1512.[7] The chronicler Jean Molinet wrote in his epitaph for the artist that emperors, kings, counts, and marquesses admired his work.[8] To judge from documents and surviving art, at least through the 1470s the Burgundian court and its retainers commissioned or were the intended first owners of many of his most important works.

Marmion painted books of hours for much of his career, and they dominate his production from the mid-1470s on. Unfortunately we know much less about the patrons or first owners of these. In the same period he collaborated with many illuminators from Bruges and Ghent, such as the Master of the Dresden Prayer Book (cat. nos. 32, 33, 53), the Master of the Houghton Miniatures (cat. nos. 32, 33), the Vienna Master of Mary of Burgundy (cat. nos. 17, 20), and others (cat. nos. 20, 32, 37), along with the Antwerp illuminator Lieven van Lathem (cat. nos. 17, 19, 20). He moved quickly to adopt the new style of illusionistic strewn-pattern border and was the lead illuminator for a number of projects with the new border (e.g., cat. nos. 32, 33, 37, and the Gros Hours in Chantilly, Musée Condé).[9] Yet he belonged to the painters' guild in Tournai, rather than those in Bruges and Ghent. The meaning of this connection merits exploration. Did it facilitate collaborations with his brother Mille, a painter and illuminator, on Simon's projects; or did it result from former ties with the workshop of Rogier van der Weyden, whose art influenced his; or both?

Both Molinet and Jean Lemaire de Belges, writing not long after his death, attested to Marmion's success and reputation as an illuminator.[10] He exercised a strong influence on the art of manuscript illumination, specifically in the Hainaut region through the art of the Master of Antoine Rolin, who used and reused many of his compositions and other artistic ideas (cat. nos. 94, 123).[10]   T. K.

Notes

1. Hénault (1907, 9: 137) believed the spouse was his second wife, Isabella of Bourbon, while Châtelet (in Nys and Salamaghe 1996: 155) identified her as his third wife, Margaret of York.

2. The documents, mostly published by Maurice Hénault, were conveniently assembled by Edith Hoffman in her dissertation of 1958 (98–124). See also Hénault 1907, 9: 411–15, and Deshaisnes 1892: 135–36. Hoffman's dissertation is to this day the only monograph on the artist.

3. Hénault 1907, 9: 419, 10: 128 n. 4, 110.

4. Hénault 1907, 9: 118–24, 410, 190–97, 10: 113; Reynaud, in Paris 1993: 80.

5. Dehaisnes 1892.

6. Gros owned the book of hours in Chantilly, Musée Condé, Ms. 85 (Clark 1992: 197, 206, n. 6). De Moers owned a Valerius Maximus, a leaf from which Bodo Brinkmann recently discovered in the Oskar Reinhart collection, Winterthur. He will publish it in the forthcoming catalogue of that collection. The Rolin Hours, Madrid, Biblioteca Nacional, Ms. Res. 149 (Clark 1992: 196, 206–7, n. 10, and Reynaud, in Paris 1993: 89, under no. 40).

7. De Ram 1861, 2: 870.

8. Dehaisnes 1892: 74.

9. I argue in the catalogue entries that these books are all earlier than has generally been thought.

10. Stecher 1882–91, 4: 162; Dehaisnes 1892: 74.

11. Also particularly influential is the cycle of his half-length miniatures incorporated into the book of hours called La Flora (cat. no. 93).

7

SIMON MARMION AND WORKSHOP

Fragments from the Saint Bertin Altarpiece
Valenciennes, 1459

A Choir of Angels, interior; *A Stone Canopy,* exterior

Oil on oak panel, 59.9 × 23.2 cm (23⁹⁄₁₆ × 9⅛ in.); painted surface, interior: 57.6 × 20.9 cm (22¹¹⁄₁₆ × 8¼ in.); painted surface, exterior: 57.9 × 20.8 cm (22¹³⁄₁₆ × 8³⁄₁₆ in.)

COLLECTION: London, National Gallery, NG 1303

The Soul of Saint Bertin Carried Up to God, interior; *A Stone Canopy,* exterior

Oil on oak panel, 59.9 × 22.7 cm (23⁹⁄₁₆ × 8¹⁵⁄₁₆ in.); painted surface, interior: 57.7 × 20.5 cm (22¹¹⁄₁₆ × 8⅛ in.); painted surface, exterior: 57.8 × 20.5 cm (22¾ × 8⅛ in.)

COLLECTION: London, National Gallery, NG 1302

PROVENANCE: Abbey church of Saint Bertin at Saint-Omer, until 1791; a baker in Saint-Omer; a "local art lover"; Louis Francia (1772–1839), England, by 1822; offered to the Royal Academy and for sale at 27 Leicester Square, London; offered for sale at Hôtel Bullion, Paris; Lambert-Jean Nieuwenhuys (1777–1862), Paris, 1824; Nieuwenhuys family; to Edmond Beaucousin, Paris, ca. 1847; purchased 1860

R A

In 1447 Guillaume Fillastre became abbot of the Benedictine abbey of Saint Bertin at Saint-Omer, in northern France. Highly regarded by Dukes Philip the Good and Charles the Bold, he also held important posts as bishop of Verdun, Toul, and Tournai and was chancellor of the Order of the Golden Fleece. Fillastre was a noted patron of the arts, and among his most important commissions was a "silver *tabula* for the high altar" of the abbey church of Saint Bertin. Extant accounts list four separate payments for this elaborate altarpiece, which comprised a central shrine of silver-gilt statuettes and gems from the treasury of the abbey, and painted wings. The work was completed and installed in 1459, when the final payment was made.[1]

Although no document confirms an attribution to Marmion (we know only that Fillastre had the altarpiece "made at Valenciennes"),[2] there is substantial circumstantial evidence to support this. Marmion had relocated to Valenciennes from Amiens by 1458 and was the preeminent painter there. Furthermore, according to the chronicler Jean Molinet, Marmion was favored by emperors, kings, counts, and marquesses, and he moved in the same exalted social circles as Fillastre, who commissioned the work.

A Choir of Angels (ill. 7a) originally formed the upper part of the left side of the left wing of the altarpiece, directly over the scene of the portrait of Fillastre kneeling in prayer (fig. 42). *The Soul of Saint Bertin Carried Up to God* (ill. 7b) completed the scene at the right side of the right wing, above *The Death of Saint Bertin* (see fig. 42). The two stone canopies found on the reverses of the two panels covered the top part of *The Crucifixion,* the central sculptural group of the altarpiece, and appeared above a grisaille of the Annunciation when the wings were closed.

In style, the London fragments recall some of the most lavish manuscripts of the 1450s that were commissioned

by Fillastre for presentation to Philip the Good, namely the *Fleurs des histoires* (Brussels, Bibliothèque royale de Belgique, Ms. 9231-9232) and the *Grandes Chroniques de France* (Saint Petersburg, National Library of Russia, Ms. Erm. 88).[3] They also relate to the later production of Marmion and his workshop, especially to the leaf with *The Holy Virgins Entering Paradise* (ill. 10b), which may have come from a breviary begun for Philip the Good in 1467 and completed for Charles the Bold in 1470. The trumpeting angels at the windows and the specific forms of the flamboyant Gothic architecture in the miniature are similar to analogous features in the London fragments.[4] Marmion's forte was portraying emotion through directional glances and gesture. In this regard, the figures of *A Choir of Angels* are more expressive and more refined in technique than those of *The Soul of Saint Bertin Carried Up to God*, raising the question of workshop participation in the latter. Support for this suggestion is provided by the fact that the former shows more alterations in the poses and musical instruments of the angels from the underdrawing to the final paint layer than can be found in the working stages of the latter.[5]

The characteristics of Marmion's technique suggest his participation in the sister arts of panel painting and manuscript illumination. On close inspection, the paint applications of the London fragments have a matte, chalky appearance, and individual brushstrokes are evident in the flesh tones as well as in the draperies, just as in Marmion's miniatures. The palette of subtly varied reds (tending toward salmon tones), yellows, and acid greens was favored by Marmion in panel painting and illumination alike.[6]

M. W. A.

Notes

1. C. Dewitte, "Le Grand Cartulaire ou Recueil général des chartes et titres de l'abbaye de Saint-Bertin," Bibliothèque communale, Saint-Omer, Ms. 803, vol. 3, fol. 6, in Dehaisnes 1892: 39, 45. In 1793, during the French Revolution, the abbey church was desecrated. The central shrine of the altarpiece was melted down, while the wings, apparently considered of little importance, came into the possession of a local baker of Saint-Omer. Later the London fragments were separated from the main portions of the shutters by Lambert-Jean Nieuwenhuys, who sold the latter to the prince of Orange in 1823, from whence they entered the Kaiser Friedrich Museum in Berlin. The dismembered fragments were purchased in 1860 by the National Gallery, London. For more on the provenance, see Campbell 1998: 303.

2. Dewitte, "Le Grand Cartulaire" (see note 1), fol. 6.

3. Campbell 1998: 300.

4. Hindman, 1992: 226–27, and Hindman 1997: 66.

5. Ainsworth 1992: 244–45; Campbell 1998: 305.

6. For further information on Marmion's painting technique, see Ainsworth 1992: 243–55.

7a (opposite, left)
SIMON MARMION
A Choir of Angels

7b (opposite, right)
SIMON MARMION
AND WORKSHOP
The Soul of Saint Bertin Carried Up to God

Figure 42
SIMON MARMION
Scenes from the Life of Saint Bertin, 1459. Interior panels from the Saint Bertin Altarpiece. Tempera on panel, 56 × 147 cm (22 × 57⅞ in.) each. Partial reconstruction of the altarpiece wings with fragments in place (see opposite). Berlin, Staatliche Museen zu Berlin, Gemäldegalerie (1645, 1645a)

8

SIMON MARMION

The Mass of Saint Gregory
Valenciennes, ca. 1460–65

Oil on wood panel, 45.1 × 29.4 cm (17¾ × 11⁹⁄₁₆ in.)

INSCRIPTIONS: *Ou tamps que Saint Gregore pappe celebra[n]t messe a Rom[m]e en l'eglise nom[m]ee pantheo[n]. n[ost]r[e] seigneur s'aparut a luy e[n] telle se[m]bla[n]ce. do[n]t po[u]r la gra[n]de co[m]passion qu'il ot le voya[n]t ainsy. Otroya a to[u]s cheulx qui po[u]r la Revere[n]ce de luy diront deuotem[en]t e[n] genoulz v fois p[ate]r n[oste]r [et] ave m[ari]a XIIII m[il] a[n]s de vrais p[ar]do[n]s [et] d'aultr[e]s pappes [et] evesq[ue]s XII c[ent] a[n]s [et] XLVI fois xl jo[u]rs de i[n]dulge[n]ces . . . et ce p[ar]do[n]s a estably le IIIIᵉ pappe Clemens,* bottom

COLLECTION: Toronto, Art Gallery of Ontario, Inv. 79/121

PROVENANCE: Private collection, Switzerland; [sale, Thomas Agnew and Sons, London, November 2–December 10, 1971, lot 24]; [sale, Thomas Agnew and Sons, London, June 7–July 27, 1979, lot 13]; purchased 1979

At the very moment that the kneeling Pope Gregory the Great (ca. 540–60) elevates the host to bless it, Christ as the Man of Sorrows miraculously appears before him. The Toronto *Mass of Saint Gregory* is derived not from the popular model associated with Robert Campin, of which there are many copies,[1] but from a formula found in illuminations, some of which are accompanied by the indulgence granted by Pope Clement to those who pray before the image. At least two manuscripts from Amiens, produced around the time Marmion was in residence there in the 1450s, show a similar composition, with Christ standing in a sarcophagus on the altar, but with his body twisted and his hands raised to reveal his wounds.[2] Both Marmion's painting and these miniatures present an obliquely positioned altar before which the celebrant, accompanied by an acolyte, kneels and raises the host. In a later version of the theme in the Huth Hours from the early 1480s (London, British Library, Add. Ms. 38126, fol. 125v), which is attributed to Marmion and his workshop, a full-length Christ stands on the altar with no tomb, pressing the wound in his side with his right hand. Here, as in the Toronto panel, the instruments of the Passion are displayed on the back wall.

The inspiration for the Christ in the Toronto painting and at least one close copy on panel[3] appears to come from an earlier type of around 1400, in which Christ is shown standing with his head somewhat lowered to the side and his hands crossed before him at his groin.[4] A Byzantine mosaic icon of Christ in Santa Croce in Gerusalemme, Rome (fig. 43), thought to have been commissioned by Gregory the Great to commemorate the miraculous appearance of Christ at the Mass, is considered the source of this Man of Sorrows. The icon dates later, however, from the late thirteenth or early fourteenth century, and was not acquired by the Carthusians in Santa Croce until the late fourteenth century.[5] The popular legend of the miraculous appearance of Christ led to the development of various versions of the image as well as diverse accompanying indulgence texts composed to directly suit their readership. Some French indulgences indicate, as does the text for the Toronto panel, that the event took place in the Pantheon instead of in Santa Croce.[6] As Sterling noted, the text on the Toronto panel is written in the Picard dialect, which suggests that the work was commissioned either in Amiens, where Marmion lived from 1449 to 1454, or in Valenciennes, where he settled in 1454 and remained until his death in 1489.[7]

Certain details of style and effects of color, however, support a date during the Valenciennes period. The body type of Christ—with its pronounced chest cavity, tapered midriff, and long, thin arms—is found both in the Toronto painting and in *The Lamentation* of around 1470 in the Lehman Collection, Metropolitan Museum of Art, New York (see ill. 11a). The marvelously individualized heads of Christ, the pope, and the acolyte are similar to those found in the Saint Bertin Altarpiece, dedicated in 1459 (see cat. no. 7 and fig. 45). The striking effect of the diaphanous surplice of the acolyte over his orange-pink garment is one that Marmion used in the Saint Bertin Altarpiece (for the attire of the chaplain attendant to the donor, Guillaume

Figure 43
The Man of Sorrows, early
fourteenth century.
Mosiac mounted in a
reliquary frame, 28 ×
23 cm (11 × 9¹/₁₆ in.) with
frame. Rome, Santa
Croce in Gerusalemme

Fillastre, fig. 44), for the donor in *Saint Jerome and a Donor*
(see cat. no. 46), and for the costume of one of the Marys in
The Lamentation. Moreover, the Toronto panel, the Saint
Bertin Altarpiece, and *The Lamentation* share a pasty, matte-
paint quality, as well as similar details of execution and handling on a small scale. These similarities indicate that *The
Mass of Saint Gregory* is close in date to the Saint Bertin
Altarpiece and *The Lamentation*; it was probably painted
around 1460–65.   M. W. A.

Notes
1. See Stroo and Sypher-d'Olne 1996: 65–75.
2. Châtelet 1996: 163. These manuscripts are in Waddesdon
Manor, James de Rothschild collection (Ms. 6, fol. 21v), and British
Library (Ms. Add. 31835 fol. 33v); both are illustrated in Nash 1999, pls.
9, 10. Both are accompanied by indulgence prayers.
3. This panel in Burgos Cathedral, Capilla del Condestable, is
ascribed to a follower of Marmion around 1500 (illus. in Sterling 1981b:
6, fig. 2).
4. See Lewis (F.) 1992: esp. 185, pl. 3: *Man of Sorrows*, Boulogne,
Bibliothèque municipale, Ms. 93, fol. 10.
5. Boston 1995: 34–36.
6. For example, British Library, Ms. Add. 29433, fol. 107v, and
Florence, Biblioteca Riccardiana, Ms. Ricc. 466, fol. 140, as in Lewis
(F.) 1992: 186.
7. Sterling (1981b: 8) thus favors a late date for the painting, while
Châtelet (1996: 163) favors an earlier date, when Marmion was in
Amiens.

9

SIMON MARMION AND WORKSHOP

Cuttings from a Book of Hours
Valenciennes, late 1460s

Saint John on Patmos, leaf A
Saint Luke Painting the Virgin, leaf B
Saint Matthew, leaf C
David in Prayer, leaf J

Four cuttings, each 16.8 × 13.8 cm (6⅝ × 5⁷/₁₆ in.); justification:
10.5 × 7.9 cm (4⅛ × 3⅛ in.); 18 lines of *bastarda*; 4 three-quarter-page
miniatures with architectural borders painted in early sixteenth
century

HERALDRY: Split double cord punctuated by linked letters *W* and *M*,
or joined double cord without those letters, each accompanied
by repeated letter *I* and shells, leaves Av, Cv, Dv, etc.; shells accompanied by pilgrim staffs, leaf Ev; all added in early sixteenth century
to text pages

COLLECTION: London, The British Library, Add. Ms. 71117, leaves A,
B, C, J

PROVENANCE: [Tomás Harris (1908–1964), managing director of
the Spanish Art Gallery, London]; to his sister Miss Violeta Harris
(1898–1989), ca. 1945–50; accepted by HM Treasury in lieu of
inheritance tax from estates of Miss Violeta Harris and her sister,
Mrs. Conchita Wolff; to British Library 1992 through National Art-
Collections Fund

RA

Figure 44
SIMON MARMION
*Scenes from the Life of
Saint Bertin*
(detail, fig. 42)

This group of cuttings contains eight half-page miniatures by Simon Marmion and his workshop from a
large book of hours that originally held at least nineteen
miniatures.¹ The group includes individual depictions of
the four Evangelists and two miniatures from the Hours of

the Virgin (*The Presentation in the Temple* and *The Flight into Egypt*), along with *David in Prayer*, illustrating the Penitential Psalms, and *The Raising of Lazarus*. The latter, a subject that Marmion depicted often and that usually illustrated the Office of the Dead, illustrates here an unusual pair of Memorials for All Deceased and for the Souls of Family Members.[2] Another four miniatures from the series—*The Annunciation to the Shepherds*, *The Adoration of the Magi*, *The Crucifixion*, and *The Martyrdom of Saint Apollonia*—are in the Rijksmuseum, Amsterdam.[3] Although the miniatures from both groups have suffered some fading, their quality is apparent, especially in the lovely landscapes of *Saint John on Patmos* and *David in Prayer* and in the colorful monastic enclosures of the writing Evangelists.

Although Marmion rarely used patterns in his workshop or repeated himself, these miniatures are striking for their correspondence to compositions in the Berlaymont Hours (cat. no. 12), especially *Saint Luke Painting the Virgin*,[4] *The Presentation in the Temple*, and *The Adoration of the Shepherds*. Also, in the two cycles the narrow cells of the Evangelists are broadly similar in their furnishings and architectural detail. This close relationship suggests that the London/Amsterdam miniatures belong not far in date from the Berlaymont Hours of around 1470–75. The fact that the conceptions of interior space and landscape are less ambitious in the former than those evident in the Berlaymont Hours indicates that the artist painted them some-

what earlier, perhaps in the late 1460s.[5] At the same time these works are not as accomplished as the Berlaymont miniatures and were likely executed in part by assistants.

The group of British Library cuttings also contains another eight fragments of text, all incipits or portions of lower borders from the same manuscript. Seven belong to the miniatures in the series (to all except *David in Prayer*), while one contains the incipit for Terce that the Amsterdam *Annunciation to the Shepherds* illustrated before the leaf was cut up.[6]

In the early sixteenth century a French illuminator crudely overpainted the book's leaves with brown borders of engaged columns and Renaissance putti. He also added to the borders of the reverses personal insignia of a subsequent owner, including the initial *I*, the double *cordelière* of the royal Order of Saint Michael, and the shell and pilgrim's staff associated with Saint James the Greater. Thus, these additions were likely made for a noble close to the French crown named Jacques. Interlaced letters *M* and *W* accompany the other insignia in some of the borders. This evidence makes possible the identification of the original codex, now stripped of all of its miniatures, in the Biblioteka Czartoryskich in Kraków (Ms. Czart 2945 II).[7] The book's pages, written by the same scribe as the leaves catalogued here, with the identical number of lines per page and justification, have the same body of heraldic motifs added by the same sixteenth-century painter.   T. K.

9c
SIMON MARMION AND
WORKSHOP
Saint John on Patmos,
leaf A

Notes

1. The book was certainly larger than the largest dimensions of the reconstructed cuttings, 16.8 × 13.7 cm (6⅝ × 5⅜ in.), since the leaves are all trimmed to the edges of the painted areas.

2. The incipits for the two memorials are, respectively, "De profundis clamavi" (Psalm 129), and "Deus venie largitor." The memorials feature a sequence of psalm, versicle, responsory, versicle, responsory, concluded by prayers. They appear to derive from the Office of the Dead itself. Lauds of the Office of the Dead for the use of Paris has the same texts in a slightly different sequence and concludes with some of the same prayers (Baltimore 1988: 167). *Deus venie largitor* (a prayer, not a psalm) is found in first Vespers of the same office.

3. Nos. 61.100, 70.44, 70.45, 70.46 (Boon 1978: 3–4, nos. 4–7; Ainsworth 1992: 243–44).

4. The *Saint Luke* features an odd detail. The Evangelist paints the Virgin and Child arranged in the mirror image of their actual pose, a curiosity not found in the Berlaymont version. Although the painting of light and the interior is particularly beautiful in this miniature, it is perhaps painted with workshop collaboration.

5. Kren 1996: 215–16.

6. All illustrated in Kren 1996.

7. The book came to my attention in the recent publication of Katarzyna Płonka-Bałus (2001: 354–56). She establishes that the book was in Poland by the seventeenth century, perhaps brought there by someone in the circle of Queen Maria Ludwika (1611–1667). I am grateful to Isabella Zuralski for translating the text. The justification of the detached leaves is 10.8 × 8 cm (4¼ × 3⅛ in.), while the justification of the leaves in the codex measures 11 × 8 cm (4⁵⁄₁₆ × 3⅛ in.). Peter Kidd and Katarzyna Płonka-Bałus kindly supplied this information.

10

SIMON MARMION AND WORKSHOP

Leaves from the Breviary of Charles the Bold
Valenciennes, ca. 1467–70

Scenes from the Life of Saint Denis

One leaf, 15.2 × 11.3 cm (6 × 4⁷⁄₁₆ in.); justification: 10.7 × 7.3 cm (4³⁄₁₆ × 2⅞ in.); recto: 1 full-page miniature with historiated border; verso: 27 lines of *textura*

COLLECTION: Private collection

PROVENANCE: Charles the Bold, duke of Burgundy (1433–1476); private collection

JPGM and RA

The Holy Virgins Entering Paradise

One leaf, 16 × 11.9 cm (6⁵⁄₁₆ × 4¹¹⁄₁₆ in.); justification: 10.7 × 7.1 cm (4³⁄₁₆ × 2¾ in.); recto: unruled, 13 lines of *textura* (remainder of text area blank); verso: 1 full-page miniature with historiated border

COLLECTION: New York, The Metropolitan Museum of Art, Robert Lehman Collection, 1975.1.2477

PROVENANCE: Charles the Bold, duke of Burgundy (1433–1476); [A. S. Drey, Munich (no. 07041)]; to Robert Lehman (1891–1969), February 1, 1930

JPGM and RA

The iconography of these two devotional miniatures, derived from a now-lost breviary probably made for Charles the Bold, is unusual. One shows, on a recto, scenes from the life of Saint Denis. On the verso is the beginning of the office for the Feast of Saints Denis, Eleutherius, and Rusticus, which falls on October 9. The miniature shows the three saints beheaded, with Denis, bishop of Paris, returned to his feet, holding his head in his hands. The fully historiated border represents Saints Paul and Denis approached by a blind beggar; the baptism of Saint Denis; Saint Denis kneeling before Pope Clement I prior to their departure for Gaul; and the three imprisoned missionaries taking Communion in a Parisian jail.[1]

The second miniature, on a verso, is a rare illustration to the Common of Virgins. The miniature shows Christ at the gate of paradise—conceived as a Late Gothic palace—receiving the Wise and Foolish Virgins, one of whom moves to the front as the bride of Christ. The historiated border illustrates, at the left in an enclosed garden, the virgins holding hands in a circle around Christ, the bridegroom; below, the virgins appear seated in a garden as an angel beckons: *Venite, omnes virgines* [Come, all virgins].[2] In each scene, one of the virgins is dressed in a black habit with a wimple and hood, marking her as a nun, and in the bas-de-page she is depicted as an abbess, holding the staff of her authority. The other virgins wear plain white dresses (though some with fashionable high belts), some holding lamps, some wearing crowns.[3] The wimpled figure in each miniature must have given the narrative a more immediate meaning for the book's courtly audience. The text on the recto of this miniature is the conclusion of the Common of Confessors, which precedes the Common of Virgins.

Although lavish illuminated breviaries were not rare in the later fifteenth and early sixteenth centuries, they were

the faces in the miniature of the virgins have fine brush-strokes in red applied to give ruddiness to the flesh, but in a manner so repetitive and clumsy that it muddies the features.[9] The style is Marmion's, but the execution is often weaker than his. Since the miniatures for these two offices were full page, many of the other ninety-three miniatures were also probably full page. So, even if it took the illuminator three years to complete the work, as the documents suggest, he would have required assistance.   T. K.

Notes

1. See Hindman 1992: 224–25, also for the account of the iconography of the virgins miniature.

2. As Hindman (1992: 224) notes, this is the response to the third nocturne in the Common of Virgins.

3. Hindman argues that the iconography is derived from the Common of Virgins itself. It refers to the bride of Christ taking the crown and to ten virgins with lamps going to meet the bride and bridegroom (cf. the response to the first nocturne at Matins and the seventh lesson of the third nocturne at Matins). The inscription *Venite, omnes virgines* does not, however, as she suggests, appear in the Common of Virgins, or at least not in the modern edition.

4. Brussels, Bibliothèque royale de Belgique, Mss. 9511, 9026 (Gaspar and Lyna 1984–89, 3:305–11, 462–63, nos. 319, 319.2).

5. Hindman 1992; Hindman et al. 1997: 61–72.

6. One may add to her argument that the subject of the martyrdom of Saint Denis and his companions is illustrated in both the winter and summer portions of the first breviary that Philip ordered (see note 2), a book less richly decorated than that commissioned from Marmion (Brussels, Bibliothèque royale de Belgique, Ms. 9511, fol. 510, and Ms. 9026, fol. 452v (Gaspar and Lyna 1984–89, 3: 307, 308).

7. The borders are unusual for the menacing, grotesque profile also found in the margin of the verso of the Saint Denis leaf.

8. Paris, Bibliothèque nationale de France, Ms. n. a. fr. 3214; cf. Gil 1998a: 44, figs. 1–3.

9. I am grateful to Laurence Kanter and Akiko Yamazaki-Kleps for facilitating a closer study of the miniatures' technique with the aid of high-magnification microscopy.

10a

SIMON MARMION
*Scenes from the Life
of Saint Denis*

10b

SIMON MARMION AND
WORKSHOP
*The Holy Virgins Entering
Paradise*

most often made for individuals at the highest level of society. Examples include breviaries made for Philip the Good,[4] presented to Isabella of Spain (cat. no. 100), perhaps owned by King Manuel I of Portugal (cat. no. 92), and acquired by Eleanor of Portugal (cat. no. 91). Sandra Hindman has argued that both leaves are by Marmion and that they could date to the late 1460s, when the artist created the celebrated but otherwise untraced breviary with ninety-five miniatures and a dozen calendar vignettes commissioned by Philip the Good in 1467 and completed for his son, Charles the Bold, in 1470.[5] Although the evidence is circumstantial, Hindman's hypothesis has considerable merit.[6] Marc Gil has shown that decorative borders similar to these appear in a book of hours from the Marmion workshop.[7] The latter perhaps also dates from the 1460s.[8]

The leaf with Saint Denis was certainly painted by Marmion, while the other may be only his invention. The modeling of flesh areas differs in the two leaves; only that in the Saint Denis leaf is characteristic of the artist. It shows his deft handling, creating expression in the figures with carefully placed strokes and an economy of means. Most of

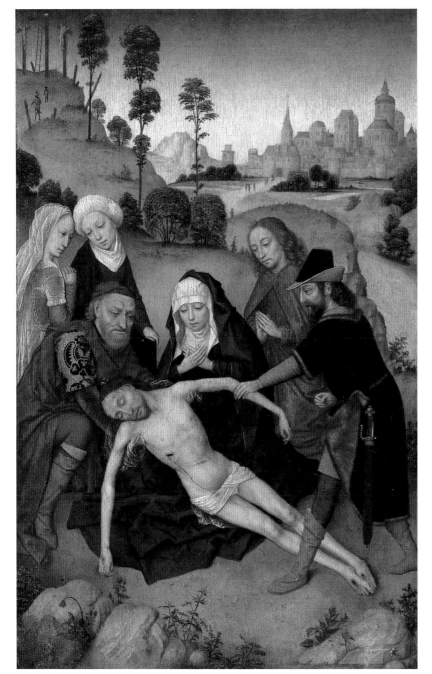

11b
SIMON MARMION
Arms (reverse of panel
in ill. 11a)

Figure 45
SIMON MARMION
*Scenes from the Life
of Saint Bertin*
(detail, fig. 42)

II

SIMON MARMION

**The Lamentation; on the reverse: Coat of Arms of Margaret
of York and Interlaced Initials of Charles the Bold and Margaret
of York**

Valenciennes, ca. 1470

Oil and tempera (?) on oak panel, 51.8 × 32.7 cm (20⅟₁₆ × 12⅞ in.)

COLLECTION: New York, The Metropolitan Museum of Art, Robert
Lehman Collection, 1975.1.128

PROVENANCE: Margaret of York, duchess of Burgundy (1446–1503);
Charles and Eliza Aders, London, by 1831 [their sale, Christie's,
London, April 26, 1839, lot 23]; Henry Crabb Robinson (1775–1867);
[Christie's, London, July 27, 1917, lot 128]; Langston Douglas; Philip
Lehman, New York, by 1922; to Robert Lehman (1891–1969),
New York

JPGM and RA

11a
SIMON MARMION
The Lamentation

The Lamentation joins the elaborate breviary completed
in 1470 for Charles the Bold (cat. no. 10) and various
illuminated books made for Margaret of York in 1475 (cat.
nos. 13, 14) as premier examples of Simon Marmion's commissioned work for the ducal couple. The coat of arms on
the reverse of the panel indicates that it once belonged to
Margaret (ill. 11b). Her marriage to Charles in 1468 signals a
terminus post quem for the painting, which may have been
commissioned around that time or later, in early May of
1473, when with great fanfare the couple attended the meeting of the Order of the Golden Fleece in Valenciennes. In
residence at the time, Simon Marmion was likely employed
to provide decorations for various festivities associated
with the meeting.[1]

The attribution of *The Lamentation* to Marmion and
a date between 1468 and the early 1470s accord well with

stylistic and technical considerations. *The Lamentation* is painted in the same style and technique as the Saint Bertin Altarpiece (see cat. no. 7), an elaborate altarpiece commissioned by Guillaume Fillastre and dedicated in 1459. Both works include similar figure types and an expression of mood and psychological content that is conveyed effectively through directional glances (fig. 46) and meaningful gestures of the protagonists (see fig. 43). In terms of technique, the relatively matte finish and disengaged brushstrokes characteristic of these paintings are features of execution that suggest an artist who was trained in manuscript illumination. Marmion's palette of lime greens, salmon pinks, and pale tones of red and blue in *The Lamentation* is frequently encountered in his miniatures and paintings alike, and his particular rendering of the gauze-like material over Mary Magdalene's dress is a feature of the costumes of Saint Omer and the chaplain in the Saint Bertin Altarpiece (see fig. 44) and the donor in *Saint Jerome and a Donor* of around 1475 (cat. no. 46). Marmion's later works reveal the influence of south Netherlandish artists, hinting at a sojourn in Ghent and Louvain, where he would have encountered the art of Hugo van der Goes, Joos van Ghent, and Dieric Bouts. The composition, specific arrangement of landscape and architectural forms, and the sense of psychological detachment of the stiffly posed figures in *The Lamentation* in particular recall Bouts's *Abraham and Melchizedek*, the upper-left wing of the Holy Sacrament Altarpiece (Louvain, Saint Peter's Church), which was painted between 1464 and 1468.

The Lamentation is essentially a Pietà, a subject especially favored by French panel painters and illuminators. As Joseph of Arimathea and Nicodemus gently lower the body of Christ onto the lap of the Virgin, she crosses her hands over her heart in acceptance of her son's fate and in veneration of him. Two Marys and Saint John prayerfully look on with quiet and restrained sorrow. A master of naturalistic detail, Marmion echoed the empathic response of the figures through the bent-over red poppy, a symbol of sleep and death, at the lower left.

The Pietà was a theme that Marmion treated with full-length figures, as in the present panel, and as a close-up excerpt, concentrated solely on the interaction between the figures of the Virgin and the dead Christ. The immediate relationship between Marmion's miniatures—namely, the single leaf in the Philadelphia Museum of Art (cat. no. 20) and folio 165v in the La Flora Hours (cat. no. 93)—and his panel paintings is indicated further by the underdrawing of *The Lamentation*.[1] In addition to a number of adjustments in the positions and poses of the figures, this preliminary sketch in brush shows that the Virgin's hands were clasped in prayer and her head further lowered beneath a single, rather than a double, veil. These details are found in the miniatures and in a metalpoint drawing (cat. no. 30) that served as a workshop model for panel painting and illumination alike.   M. W. A.

Note

1. Ainsworth 1992: 246–48, fig. 238; Sterling and Ainsworth 1998: 4–5, fig. 1.1.

12

SIMON MARMION

Leaves from the Berlaymont Hours
Use undetermined
Valenciennes, ca. 1470–75

Saint Luke Painting the Virgin, fol. 15v
The Crucifixion, fol. 24
The Flight into Egypt, fol. 56

MANUSCRIPT: iii + 126 folios, 20.5 × 14.5 cm (8⅛ × 5¹¹⁄₁₆ in.); justification: 10 × 6.8 cm (3¹⁵⁄₁₆ × 2¹¹⁄₁₆ in.); 18 lines of *bastarda*; 17 three-quarter-page miniatures

HERALDRY: Full-page escutcheon with the arms of Charles de Berlaymont impaled by those of his wife, Adrienne de Ligne, encircled by wreath, fol. 13; full-page escutcheon with the arms of Berlaymont encircled by collar of the Order of the Golden Fleece, fol. 13v

INSCRIPTIONS: *Lan mil cincq cent xvj le xxiii jo[u]r de jullet e[n]tre trois et quatre heures apres midi trespassat de ce . . . me[sei]g[neu]r michiel de berlaymont seign[eu]r de floyon kernixt et haultpen[ne] en la ville de huy duquel le corps fut portez en terre en leglise dung kernixt pries dieu pour son ame*, fol. ii; *Trespas de feu ma fe[m]me le xv.e doctobre 1558 entre lez iii et iiii heures du matin et ung sabmedi au chateau de berchies*, entered in the calendar on October 15, fol. 10; *Le xvii le corps fut menez a birleymo[n]t et le xviii.e mons.r de crespin soufragen de cambray fit la benediction de legl[is]e et le terrat au coir dicelle Dieu par sa bontez ayt avis lame en son paradis*, bottom, fol. 10; *Le xviii.e octobre 1558 legl[is]e de berlaymont fut dediee*, fol. 10v; *faictes pour moy com[m]e eusse / faict pour vous*, fol. 12v

BINDING: Disbound; original red velvet back cover in the Huntington Library files

COLLECTION: San Marino, The Huntington Library, HM 1173

PROVENANCE: Michel de Berlaymont or a member of his family, by 1516; Charles de Berlaymont (1510–1578) and his wife, Adrienne de Ligne (d. 1563); [Alexander Storch, Prague, by November 1896]; [Ellis and Elvey *Catalogue 96*, 1901]; E. Dwight Church (1835–1908); to Henry E. Huntington (1850–1927) in 1911

JPGM

The Berlaymont Hours is a routine book of hours without unusual iconography or surprises among its devotions. It has only standard offices and no suffrages or extra prayers.[1] Despite its basic devotional content, its miniatures rank with the most beautiful among Simon Marmion's many books of hours. *Saint Luke Painting the Virgin* (ill. 12a) shows the Virgin and Child posed behind a parapet draped with a cloth of honor in an arched opening. Working at a tall easel, Saint Luke captures their features on a gold-ground panel, fittingly also arched; Luke paints the classic small-scale private devotional image of the later Middle Ages. The scene is both contrived and remarkably intimate, with the Evangelist's symbol, the ox, watching as his master works. Previously Marmion may have painted an altarpiece with this subject when he created the altar retable for the newly founded Confraternity of Saint Luke at the Church of Notre-Dame in Valenciennes in 1463.

The Berlaymont cycle is noteworthy for the strongly axial compositions, established by symmetrical architectural settings whose outer edges or columns are sometimes congruent with the frame, by a standing figure, or by a pair of figures flanking an implied central vertical. Among its other arresting features are the evocative golden sky lined

with dark clouds in *The Crucifixion* (ill. 12b); the elaborate spatial recession of the landscape in *The Flight into Egypt* (ill. 12c); and the expressiveness of gaze and gesture in *The Presentation in the Temple*, *The Nativity*, *The Crucifixion*, and *The Raising of Lazarus*. Also distinctive are the novelty and subtlety of the miniatures' color harmonies.

The book has a rare style of decorative border that appears only in manuscripts illuminated by Marmion, notably *Les Visions du chevalier Tondal* (cat. no. 14), *La Vision de l'âme de Guy de Thurno* (cat. no. 13), *L'Histoire de madame sainte Katherine* (France, private collection), *L'Instruction d'un jeune prince* (Cambridge, Fitzwilliam Museum), and a book of hours, now preserved in only a single leaf, made for a young nobleman.[2] These borders feature golden brown and dark blue acanthus in the corners, with stems, leaves, and vines in a similar golden brown relieved by a few flowers in red or blue. A flowering thistle is a typical motif

in this border type. Since the two *Visions* are dated 1475, the Berlaymont Hours is generally dated to the first half of the 1470s, given the rapid further development of the artist's style later in the 1470s.[3]

The book features an added leaf with the coats of arms of Charles de Berlaymont (1510–1578) and his wife, Adrienne de Ligne (d. 1563). Under Emperor Charles V (1500–1558), Berlaymont served as regent of the Netherlands following the departure of Mary of Hungary. He was inducted into the Order of the Golden Fleece on January 28, 1555 (n.s. 1556), and was the first count of Berlaymont. Thus, the inserted armorials date between 1556 and 1563.[4] They show the great pride in the Flemish Burgundian artistic heritage among the lieutenants of the Hapsburg court and perhaps also a regional pride in Marmion himself. In the same years Louis de la Fontaine, the historian of Valenciennes, praised the illuminator's achievements.[5]

I2b

SIMON MARMION
The Crucifixion, fol. 24

I2c

SIMON MARMION
The Flight into Egypt,
fol. 56

The book was certainly in the Floyon branch of the Berlaymont family a full generation before it was acquired by Charles. It contains a death notice for Charles's father, Michel, lord of Floyon, Kernt, and Haultepenne, which was written within days of his passing, in Huy on July 23, 1516.[6] Probably the book was owned by Michel or a close relative at the time of his death. Since the book's calendar points to Amiens[7] and it has an "Obsecro te" that includes an Amiens variant, it is of interest that a cousin of Michel, Gillette de Berlaymont (d. 1545), was related by marriage to one of the greatest of Amiens families. Through her nuptials with Louis Rolin d'Aymeries, the grand marshal and first viscount of Hainaut (d. 1528), Gillette became the daughter-in-law of Marie d'Ailly, the daughter of Raoul d'Ailly, vidame of Amiens. Raoul d'Ailly was a patron of manuscript illumination in Amiens.[8] Marie d'Ailly and Antoine Rolin (ca. 1424–1497) were also important patrons of manuscript illumination, notably of the Master of Antoine Rolin, Marmion's prolific follower (cf. cat. no. 94).[9] Thus, perhaps the book discussed here was originally created for a member of the Rolin/d'Ailly family (or of their circle) and then passed to the Floyon branch of the Berlaymont. Gillette de Berlaymont, who died without issue, must have been close to her cousin Michel; she ultimately left her estate to Charles.[10]

T. K.

Notes

1. Clark (1992: 206 n. 7) points out that the uses of the Office of the Dead and Hours of the Virgin have not been determined. See Dutschke et al. 1989, 2:523–24, for a description of the contents.

2. Paris, École nationale des Beaux-Arts, M. 130; Reynaud, in Paris 1993: 89, no. 41. The donor, in a costume and bowler hat not unlike those of the donor in a diminutive book of hours discussed in cat. no. 37, is shown presented to the Virgin by a bishop saint. In the Fitzwilliam manuscript, the border appears only around the single miniature painted by Marmion, not around other miniatures in the same volume painted by Loyset Liédet.

3. Kren, in Malibu 1983a: 31, under no. 4; Clark 1992: 201.

4. A note dated October 15, 1558, written in a frail hand, records the passing of "feu ma femme" at four o'clock in the morning at the château of Berchies. This does not refer to Charles's spouse, who died five years later. The woman was buried two days later in the choir of the church of Berlaymont by the suffragan bishop Crespin of Cambrai. Nor does the inscription refer to Marie de Gavre, wife of Charles's older brother, Louis de Berlaymont, who was lord of Floyon and Haultepenne before him and who died in 1567. She was the daughter of Geoffroy, lord of Fresin. Although her death date is unknown, she was still alive in 1559. I am grateful to Elizabeth Teviotdale for her research on de Gavre's life and to Scot McKendrick, who transcribed the inscriptions on the flyleaves. I have not been able to confirm the identity of the owner of the château of Berchies.

5. See Dehaisnes 1892: 122, and Ainsworth 1992: 243. They draw on de la Fontaine's *Antiquitez de la ville de Valenciennes* of 1551–54.

6. Fol. ii. He was buried in the church at Kernixt (Kernt).

7. Honoratus (May 16) and Firminus (September 25) are both featured as red-letter feasts.

8. Nash 1999: 47, 56 n. 90, 364–69.

9. On the library of Antoine Rolin and Marie d'Ailly, see Legaré, in Nys and Salamagne 1996: 204–9, and Maurice-Chabard 1999: 56–60. Earlier Marmion had illuminated a book of hours for Guillaume Rolin (1411–1488), the uncle of Louis Rolin, who served, among his various offices, as governor of Artois (Madrid, Biblioteca Nacional, Res. 149; see Reynaud, in Paris 1993: 88–89, under no. 40, and Vaivre, in Maurice-Chabard 1999: 53–55).

10. According to Poplimont (1863: 552), he was her adopted son.

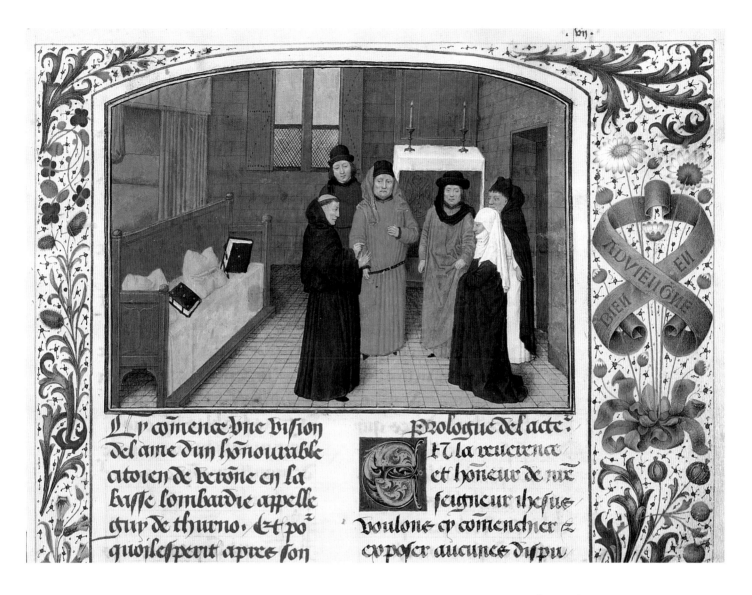

13

SIMON MARMION
*A Priest and Guy's Widow
Conversing with the Soul
of Guy de Thurno, fol. 7
(detail)*

13

SIMON MARMION

La Vision de l'âme de Guy de Thurno, **translation of** *De spiritu
Guidonis*
Valenciennes and Ghent, 1475

MANUSCRIPT: ii + 34 + ii folios; 36.3 × 25.7 cm (14 ¹⁵⁄₁₆ × 10 ⅛ in.);
justification: 24.4–24.9 × 16.3–16.8 cm (9 ⅝–9 ¹³⁄₁₆ × 6 ⁷⁄₁₆– 6 ⅝ in.);
28 lines of *bastarda* in two columns by David Aubert; 1 two-column
miniature

HERALDRY: Initials *CM* (for Charles the Bold and Margaret of York)
and motto of Margaret of York *Bien en adviengne,* fol. 7; the arms of
the marquis de Ganay, front flyleaf

INSCRIPTIONS: *Cy fine le livre intitule Vision le l'âme de Guy de Turno.
lequel livre a este escript et ordonne par le commandement et ordonnance de
treshaulte et tresexcellente princhesse Madame marguerite de yorch. Par la
grace de Dieu. duchesse de bourgoigne. de lothriik. de brabant. de lembourg.
de luxembourg et de guerles. Comtesse de flandres. Dartois. de Bourgoingne.
Palatine de haynnau. de holla[n]de. de zeelande. de namur et de zuutphe[n].
marquise du saint empire. Dame de salins et de malines. A este escript en sa
ville de gand par david. son escripvain Lan de grace mil cccc soixante et
quatorse. le p[re]m[ier]s du mois de fevrier,* colophon, fols. 34–34v

BINDING: Trautz-Bauzonnet, France, probably ca. 1850–60; brown
morocco over pasteboard; the arms of Burgundy on both covers
and pastedowns; mottoes of Margaret of York *Bien en adviengne* and
je l'ai emprins

COLLECTION: Los Angeles, J. Paul Getty Museum, Ms. 31 (87.MN.152)

PROVENANCE: Margaret of York, duchess of Burgundy (1446–1503);
Marquis de Ganay, in 1853 [his sale, Hôtel Drouot, Paris, May 12–14,
1881, lot 38]; Comte de Lignerolles [his sale, Charles Porquet, Paris,
1894, lot 17]; Baron Vitta; Baron de Brouwer, Manoir du Relais,
Pommeroeul (Hainault); [to F. Tulkens, Brussels, ca. 1944];
[to H. P. Kraus, New York]; to Philip Hofer (1898–1984), Cambridge,
Mass., in 1951 (his Ms. Type 234H); private collection, United States;
acquired 1987

JPGM and RA

This book is a French translation of a Latin text of 1323,
De spiritu Guidonis, which deals with Church doctrine
on purgatory. As Nigel Morgan and Roger Wieck have
pointed out, *La Vision de l'âme de Guy de Thurno* is an appropriate companion to the more spectacular and dramatic
Visions du chevalier Tondal (cat. no. 14), which treats matters
of heaven and hell.[1] The colophon of this book establishes
that it was written in Ghent for Margaret of York, duchess
of Burgundy, by "David, son escripvain" (David, her
scribe), or David Aubert, who signed the text February 1,
1474 (n.s. 1475).[2] The text, already translated into French in
the fourteenth century, seems to have been especially popular in England.[3]

The story concerns Guy de Thurno, a wealthy citizen of Verona, or more specifically his ghost, who returns to haunt his spouse. She engages a priest to aid her, and a debate on the nature of the afterlife ensues between the priest and the spirit of the dead man. In one of the most psychologically acute paintings of the second half of the fifteenth century, Simon Marmion engages the viewer directly in the supernatural event. It is apparent that the priest alone can perceive the ghost, with whom he is shown actively debating. The bystanders show their unease. The figures of the priest, the widow, and the others define three sides of the space occupied by the ghost. The viewer, by implication, occupies the fourth side. Through the symmetry and clarity of this grouping, Marmion invites the viewer into the enclave, resulting in a remarkably immediate experience of the invisible, as the viewer shares with most of the others the inability to see the ghost at this dramatic moment. The miniature, the book's frontispiece, is the only one in the book. It is also, to this writer's knowledge, the only depiction of this subject in fifteenth-century Flemish art.   T. K.

Notes

1. Wieck 1992: 126; Morgan 1992: 67. The book may have had an additional companion in the form of *L'Histoire de madame sainte Katherine* (France, private collection; discussed in cat. no. 14), also written by Aubert and illuminated by Marmion for Margaret of York.

2. The leaf containing the colophon (fol. 34) is a replacement leaf that was taken from blank ruled pages that followed the original written text of *Les Visions du chevalier Tondal* (based on the evidence of shared stains at the lower edge). Another replacement leaf appears in *Les Visions du chevalier Tondal* (fol. 41), this one removed from before the original written portion of the manuscript. Both replacement leaves closely follow the style of the original calligraphy and capture it successfully. On close examination, however, the letters appear drawn—that is, outlined with a pen and then filled in, either with a wash or a more opaque medium, often rather unevenly. It appears that an effort was made to imitate the degree of wear and abrasion of the original text pages, although the replacements are not written with a split-nib quill, as the others are. In short, it appears that a painstaking effort was made to copy the original, in this case what were probably damaged leaves. (Folio 41 also has a decorated initial that is painted faithfully in the style of the book's other initials, though with pigments that vary slightly in color and texture from the originals.) This raises the possibility that the colophon of the Guy de Thurno manuscript is false, even modern, but it appears to copy carefully and reasonably accurately a leaf that was damaged. That folio 41 is based closely on the lost original text is suggested by the text itself. Although no other version of this translation is known, Roger Wieck kindly advised me that the text on folio 41 is continuous with the rest and omits nothing from the Latin narrative. Thus, there is no reason to doubt that folio 34 copies faithfully the text of the original colophon too. Whether this is the case or not, the Getty Guy de Thurno text was undoubtedly written by the same scribe as the Tondal manuscript. The latter also has a colophon identifying the scribe as Aubert and was made for Margaret of York, whose initial (with that of her spouse) and motto appear in the book's single decorated border (fol. 7). Scot McKendrick, who believes that these substitute leaves are modern, points out that the foliation in red is modern. It copies the form and calligraphic style of Aubert's original foliation, which is partially erased and partially trimmed away along the upper edge at the right side. I am grateful to Nancy Turner for a helpful microscopic analysis of the scribal technique.

3. Morgan (1992: 67) cites a printed English translation from as early as 1492.

14a (opposite)
SIMON MARMION
*Tondal Suffers a Seizure
at Dinner*, fol. 7

14

SIMON MARMION

Leaves from *Les Visions du chevalier Tondal*, translation of
Visio Tugdnali
Valenciennes and Ghent, 1475

MANUSCRIPT: 45 folios, 36.3 × 26.2 cm (14⁵⁄₁₆ × 10⁵⁄₁₆ in.); justification: 24.4–24.9 × 16.3–16.8 cm (9⅝–9⁹⁄₁₆ × 6⁷⁄₁₆–6⅝ in.); 28 lines of *bastarda* in two columns by David Aubert; 15 two-column miniatures, 5 one-column miniatures

HERALDRY: Initials *CM* (for Charles the Bold and Margaret of York) and motto of Margaret of York *Bien en adviengne* in borders accompanying each miniature

INSCRIPTIONS: *Cy fine le livre intitule les Visions que recheu l'esperit d'un chevallier des marches d'Irlande nomme monsieur Tondal, lequel livre a este escript et ordonne par le commandement et ordonnance de treshaulte et tresexcellente et trespuissante princesse madame Marguerite de Yorch, par la grace de Dieu Duchesse de Bourgoingne, de Lothriik, de Brabant, de Lembourg, de Luxembourg et de Guerles, Comtesse de Flandres, d'Artois, de Bourgoingne, Palatine de Haynnau, de Hollande, de Zeelande, de Namur et de Zuutphen. Marquise du Saint Empire, dame de Salins et de Malines. A este en sa ville de Gand par David, son trespeut indigne escripvain, escript ou mois de mars lan de grace mil cccc soixante et quatorse*, colophon, fols. 43v–44

BINDING: Aquarius, London, 1987; brown calfskin over wood boards; bifolia split at gutter and leaves individually mounted on guards; formerly in the binding of cat. no. 13

COLLECTION: Los Angeles, J. Paul Getty Museum, Ms. 30 (87.MN.141)

PROVENANCE: Margaret of York, duchess of Burgundy (1446–1503); Marquis de Ganay, in 1853 [his sale, Hôtel Drouot, Paris, May 12–14, 1881, lot 39]; Comte de Lignerolles [his sale, Charles Porquet, Paris, 1894, lot 17]; Baron Vitta; Baron de Brouwer, Manoir du Relais, Pommeroeul (Hainault); [to F. Tulkens, Brussels, ca. 1944]; [to H. P. Kraus, New York]; to Philip Hofer (1898–1984), Cambridge, Mass., in 1951 (his Ms. Type 234H); private collection, United States; acquired 1987

JPGM and RA

The *Visio Tugdnali* was the most popular and elaborate text in the medieval genre of visionary infernal literature. Written around 1148–49 by an Irish monk named Marcus at Regensburg, it had been translated into fifteen languages by the fifteenth century. There were many French translations, and the particular example contained in the Getty volume appears to be unique.[1] This volume is further distinguished as the only surviving fully illustrated example of the text and contains the most original cycle of illumination in the library of Margaret of York, duchess of Burgundy.[2] Its existence owes much not only to the duchess's taste for spiritual literature, especially of a visionary nature, and for luxurious manuscripts, but also to the Burgundian ducal families' enduring admiration for the art of Simon Marmion.

As Roger Wieck has demonstrated, the illustrations are faithful to the translation at hand, responding to additions and errors of the translator.[3] This is corroborated by the evidence of infrared reflectography, which reveals a pentimento of a mountain nearly as tall as the beast Acheron. It illustrates the passage comparing the size of the beast to a mountain (ill. 14b, fig. 47).[4] In the end the illuminator changed his mind and painted out the mountain, a modification undertaken for aesthetic reasons, to darken hell. The

Cy commence le liure
dun chãllier et grant
seigneur en yrlande et
fut nõme messire tondal
Et est contenu en cestuy
liure coment son ame
part de son corps coment
elle vey et sent les tour
mene denfer. Et ainsi
les peines de purgatoire
Et apres langele luy
moustra la gloire et la
noblesse de paradie. Et
puis luy fut lame remise
ou corps. Et luy fut ce
moustre pour le doubter

et vitoire de sa peruerse
vye. Le prologue.
Que ceulx qui
leur courage et
affection ont et
arrestent en lamour de
ce monde present Trop
voulentiers escoutent et
racomptent fables et to
exemples de vanitez Si
en oublient souvent les
grans biens de paradie
et les tourmens denfer
pardurables dont ilz sont
malement decheus maiz
ceulx qui ayment dieu

que bien y entraffent de
front a vne fois dix mille
cheualliers armez tous
acheual. Celle horrible
befte auoit en fa gueule
deux grans diables tres
hideulz et cruelz a beoir
dont lun auoit fichee fa
tefte ene ce dens de hault
Et ce dens de bas eftoiet
fes pies fichnes Et laut
quy famouftroit plus en
parfont eftoit au contraue
Car il auoit fa tefte atta
che ce dens de bas et fes
pies fe fichoient parmy
les dens deffenne. Et la

eftoient ces deux Diables
en la gueule de celle befte
enfement come deux cou
lombes Et faifoient en
Icelle gueule trois portes
Vng merueilleux feu en
grandeur quy iamais ne
pouoit eftaindre yffoit de
icelle gueule quy fe depar
toit en trois parties. Et
les ames dempnees entroi
ent en celle gueule tout
parmy la flambe La pu
anteur fi grande en ptoit
que il nen eftoit nulle pa
reille Et fi ouoit lefperit
du cheualier les doloureufe

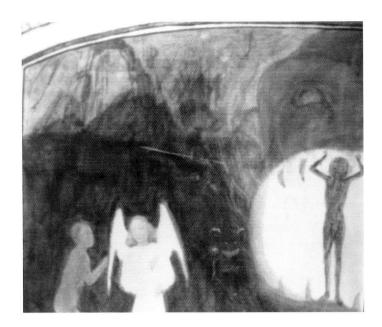

14b (opposite)
SIMON MARMION
The Beast Acheron, fol. 17

Figure 46 (above)
Infrared photograph
of *The Beast Acheron*
(detail, ill. 14b)

14c
SIMON MARMION
*The Joy of the Faithfully
Married*, fol. 37 (detail)

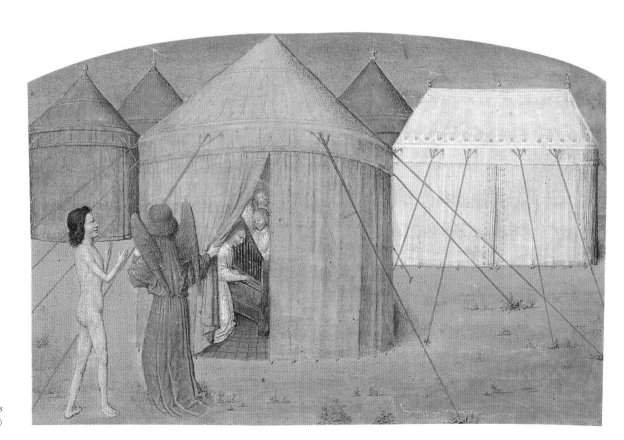

14d
SIMON MARMION
*The Glory of Good Monks
and Nuns*, fol. 39 (detail)

artist made the story immediate for Margaret by show-ing the young knight Tondal in the garb of her courtly contemporaries, wearing a gold necklace somewhat remi-niscent of the glistening chain of the Burgundian duke's fabled Order of the Golden Fleece. *Tondal Suffers a Seizure at Dinner* (ill. 14a) shows the elegant woman at his side in court costume that Margaret herself might have worn. As Tondal becomes ill, only a few of those present in the room take notice.

The miniatures of hell convey the intense glow and solidity of hellfire, its diaphanous vapors, and the murky darkness. Although both Flemish and French art of this time focused on the representation of light and its diverse effects, the evocative character of Marmion's inferno is without parallel up to this time. For the flames, the illumi-nator layered saturated reds to enhance their vibrancy and gave their tips a brilliant yellow that spews sparks, convey-ing the spectrum of color visible in such intense fire. By contrast, the subdued chromatics of purgatory and para-dise seem placid, although the subtle color harmonies and simplified palette of such miniatures as *The Joy of the Faith-fully Married* (ill. 14c) and *The Glory of Good Monks and Nuns* (ill. 14d) convey a serene beauty and optimism.

Signed by "david son trespeut indigne escripvain," this text is one of half a dozen written by the peripatetic David Aubert in the library of the duchess (cf. cat. nos. 27–29, 43). Another is *La Vision de l'âme de Guy de Thurno* (cat. no. 13), which was bound with it in the nineteenth century, though each text has its own colophon. Aubert completed the writ-ing of *Les Visions du chevalier Tondal* in March 1475 (n.s.), and it appears that he completed the Guy de Thurno text a bit earlier, on February 1 of the same year.[5] Whether or not he conceived them as companions, it is likely that, given their slim proportions, they were joined together from early in their history. In this connection it bears mentioning that a third volume of a spiritual nature written for the duchess by Aubert and illuminated by Marmion was likely executed at the same time; perhaps it was also once bound with the others. It is *Vie de sainte Catherine* (France, private collec-tion) in the French translation by Jean Miélot.[6] It has two miniatures of two columns and eleven one-column minia-tures. It also has a style of border that is virtually identical to those of the Tondal and Thurno volumes with the motto of Margaret in the margins and her and Charles's initials in the bas-de-page. It was described with the other two man-uscripts in the 1881 auction catalogue of a single collection. Although bound separately from the others then, this book was probably created with them as part of a set of spiritual texts gathered together in one volume.[7]   T. K.

Notes

1. Dinzelbacher 1992: 116.

2. François Avril has kindly drawn to my attention a cycle of sev-enteen historiated initials that may have been inspired by the story of Tondal. They appear in the Office of the Dead of the Hours of Louis of Savoy (Paris, Bibliothèque nationale de France, Ms. lat. 9473, fols. 114–31) and show an angel and a soul observing various infernal pun-ishments. See Paris 1993: 208–9, no. 114, and Leroquais 1927, 1:297.

3. Wieck 1992: esp. 120–23.

4. See Kren and Wieck 1990: 44.

5. Regarding the colophon of the Thurno volume, which appears to be a later but faithful copy of the original, see under cat. no. 13.

6. The colophon gives the date of the translation as "mil cccc lvii," which is clearly not the date of Margaret's copy, and it identifies Miélot as canon of Saint Peter's in Lille "en Flandre." Unlike the other colophons, this one apparently does not mention the patron or the scribe. See also de Schryver 1992: 175–76, 180, n. 35.

7. *Catalogue d'un choix de livres rare et précieux manuscrits et imprimés composant le cabinet de feu M. le Marquis de Ganay*, Paris, May 12, 1881, cf. esp. 27 and 107. By the late nineteenth century *L'Histoire de madame sainte Katherine* was in a Trautz-Bauzonnet binding similar to the one containing the two *Visions*.

WILLEM VRELANT

The earliest mention of Willem Vrelant occurs in 1449, when he registered as a citizen of Utrecht as Willem Backer, an illuminator from Vrede-lant, explaining the origin of the surname he generally used henceforth.[1] From 1454 he is mentioned, sometimes as "from Utrecht," in various archival records for Bruges, where he appears to have spent the rest of his life. He was involved with the Confraternity of Saint John the Evange-list, the civic organization for those involved in book pro-duction, from the time of its establishment in 1454 and may have been one of its founders. He paid his dues regularly through 1481, with the exception of a period between 1456 and 1459. He registered two apprentices with the guild, both female, during the 1460s and two others, Adrien de Raet and Betkin Scepens, who may have been his children, in the 1470s.[2]

A document in the ducal archives records a payment to Guillaume Wyelant in July 1468 for sixty miniatures in the second volume of the *Chroniques de Hainaut* that he had illu-minated for Philip the Good. Long the basis for recon-structing the artist's oeuvre, while also a topic of debate and uncertainty due to the odd spelling, the document can now be accepted without question as referring to Vrelant. Pascale Charron and Marc Gil have recently shown that a payment by the duke of Burgundy in 1469 to "Guillaume Vrelant" for a *Vita Christi* applies to the *Miroir d'humilité* (Valenciennes, Bibliothèque municipale, Ms. 240), a manu-script whose first portion, now lost, was demonstrably a *Vita Christi*.[3] The Valenciennes volume is clearly by the same hand as the aforementioned miniatures in the *Chroniques de Hainaut*. In 1478 Vrelant acted on behalf of the Confraternity of Saint John in commissioning Hans Mem-ling to paint a pair of wings for a retable. Now lost, the wings seem to have included portraits of Vrelant and his wife Mary as donor figures.[4] A mass said in his honor on June 19, 1481, indicates that Willem Vrelant was deceased by this date.[5]

Bernard Bousmanne has identified more than seventy manuscripts as illuminated entirely or in part by Vrelant, who must have been one of the most prolific illumina-tors of the fifteenth century. Moreover, many other manu-scripts, especially books of hours, survive in his style. The Vrelant manner represents the conservative strain of Bruges illumination for the third quarter of the fif-teenth century. His art features carefully drawn but stiff, frequently expressionless figures; strong areas of local, matte color; little interest in light effects; and deep-set but schematic, airless landscapes. He favored ultramarines and rich burgundies. While he derived little aesthetic-ally from French manuscript painting, he seems to have enjoyed access to pattern books derived from the art of the Boucicaut Master and other Parisian illuminators of the first quarter of the fifteenth century.[6] The tremendous scale of his production, including many books with several score miniatures or more, necessitated the extensive use and reuse of models.

Besides enjoying the active patronage of both Duke Philip and Duke Charles, Vrelant produced luxury books for ducal family members, courtiers, and functionaries such as Anthony of Burgundy, Louis of Gruuthuse, Charles de Croÿ, Ferry de Clugny, Jean IV d'Auxy, and Jacques de Bregilles. His ambitious commissions from foreign patrons epitomize the growing international character of the book trade in Bruges. Prominent foreign patrons included Juana Enriquez, consort of King Juan II of Aragon, the powerful Breton noble and bibliophile Jean de Malestroit, lord of Derval, and the Genoese noble Paolo Battista Spinola. Liturgical and linguistic evidence suggests that he also produced books of hours for customers from England (see cat. no. 15).   T. K.

Notes

1. Utrecht 1989: x.
2. See Van Buren 1999: 22–23.
3. Charron and Gil 1999: 90–95. See also Liebermann 1970: 367–75.
4. Bousmanne 1997: 52–53.
5. Bousmanne 1997: 39.
6. See cat. no. 15 and Bousmanne 1997: 37, 48, 108–9, 117, and so on. See also Van Buren 1999: 16–17.

15

WILLEM VRELANT AND WORKSHOP

Arenberg Hours
Use of Sarum
Bruges, early 1460s

MANUSCRIPT: iii + 265 + iii folios, 25.6 × 17.3 cm (10 1⁄16 × 6 13⁄16 in.); justification: 13.5 × 7.8 cm (5 15⁄16 × 3 1⁄8 in.); 20 lines of *textura*; 47 half-page miniatures, 30 quarter-page miniatures, 12 small calendar miniatures

BINDING: Early nineteenth century; purple velvet over wood boards; eight corner bosses; silver clasps with filigree; gilt edges

COLLECTION: Los Angeles, J. Paul Getty Museum, Ms. Ludwig IX 8 (83.ML.104)

PROVENANCE: Intended for an English owner; dukes of Arenberg, Brussels; Otto Schäfer (d. 2000), Schweinfurt, by 1970; [H. P. Kraus, New York]; to Peter and Irene Ludwig, Aachen; acquired 1983

JPGM

In the variety of its devotions and in both the complexity and number of its miniatures, this large book of hours is one of the most elaborate illuminated by Vrelant. For example, the eight half-page miniatures in the Hours of

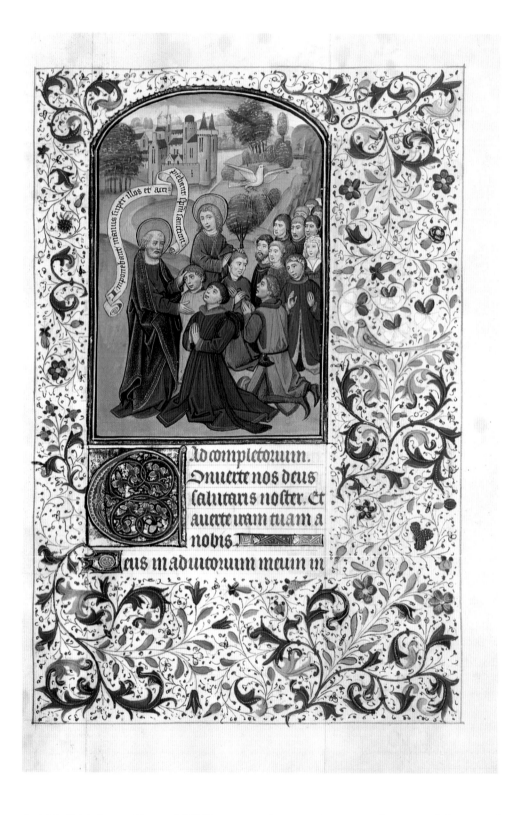

15
WILLEM VRELANT
*Saints Peter and John
Baptizing the Samarians,*
fol. 30.

the Holy Spirit feature New and Old Testament and non-biblical subjects with biblical inscriptions on prominent banderoles.[1] The Hours of the Virgin is mixed with twenty-one memorials, the Hours of the Passion, and those of the Compassion of the Virgin. The memorials each have eight-line miniatures, while half-page miniatures illustrate the Virgin's and Passion hours. Comparably large miniatures also accompany the Holy Face, a group of Passion prayers and individual prayers to the Trinity, five saints' suffrages, a sequence of prayers to the Virgin, a salutation to the Holy

Sacrament, the Hours of the Virgin for Advent, the Penitential Psalms, the litany, Office of the Dead, Commendation of Souls, Passion Psalms, and Psalter of Saint Jerome. A prayer to the wood of the cross and salutations to the Head of Christ and the five wounds of Christ, to the Virgin, and to John the Evangelist each feature eight-line miniatures.[2]

Vrelant painted the majority of the book's half-page miniatures, including the cycle for the Hours of the Holy Spirit, the large miniatures of saints, and — except for a few works specified here — the Hours of the Virgin, the Hours of the Passion, and possibly the calendar. Others include *The Virgin and Child in Glory, David in Prayer, All Saints, The Adoration of the Eucharist, Mass of the Dead*, and *The Last Judgment*. They are close in modeling and color to the documented *Chroniques de Hainaut* (Brussels, Bibliothèque royale de Belgique, Ms. 9243) for the duke, who paid the artist for it in 1468; the costumes in the Getty hours suggest that the book may date from earlier in the 1460s.[3] At least two other workshop hands contributed to the book. *The Annunciation, The Visitation, The Nativity*, and *The Betrayal of Christ*, among the finest miniatures, lack the fine, dark contours typical of Vrelant. They feature smoother surfaces and are generally more colorful and luminous than his work and are probably by a gifted assistant.[4] A weaker collaborator painted the remainder of the cycle for the Hours of the Passion, possibly *Saint Jerome in His Study*, and the small miniatures of saints.

The Arenberg Hours illustrates the pattern-driven nature of even Vrelant's finest devotional books. *The Adoration of the Eucharist* shows a devout gentleman and lady, dressed in courtly costume, kneeling at the altar. They are surrogates for the book's patrons. The indoor scene closely follows *Duke Philip and Duchess Isabella Adoring the Cross*, set out-of-doors, in the Breviary of Philip the Good (Brussels, Bibliothèque royale de Belgique, Ms. 9026, fol. 443).[5] The figures in *The Visitation* are closely based on a pattern the young Vrelant employed while still in Utrecht.[6] The Labors of the Months and the Signs of the Zodiac in the calendar are derived from a pattern book much used in Flanders, which originated two generations earlier in the circle of the Boucicaut Master in Paris.[7] The book contains many other examples of miniatures based on workshop patterns.[8]

While the book's Hours of the Virgin and Office of the Dead are for Sarum use, its calendar represents a Bruges type with a few English saints added (Wulfstan on January 19, Queen Bathilda on January 30, translation of Swithun on July 15, and Hugh of Lincoln on November 17) to accommodate the foreign customer.[9] The litany also has a strongly Flemish character and follows closely the form of other books of hours made in Bruges but includes some English saints and others popular with English patrons (Thomas Becket [canceled], Edmund, Swithun, Chad, Cuthbert, Patrick, Richard, Sitha).[10] The youthful noble couple represented in *The Adoration of the Eucharist* and in the miniature at the memorial for Peace, however, follow loosely the Burgundian costume types of the duke and duchess from Philip's breviary.[11] They do not wear particularly English costume. And the illuminated cycles of prayers and memorials for saints lack any particularly English character, except for that of Saint Thomas Becket.[12] Despite the elaborate liturgical and iconographic program of this book, its texts are only partially personalized for its English patron and its illumination not at all.   T. K.

Notes

1. Plotzek (in Euw and Plotzek 1979–85, 2: 142–43) has transcribed all the inscriptions and given their sources. The cycle is copied in at least one other elaborate book of hours from the circle of the artist (Paris, Bibliothèque nationale de France, Ms. lat. 10548). The book has the arms of Brittany on fol. 44v and is illuminated by the Master of the Lee Hours, an artist from the Vrelant circle.

2. See Euw and Plotzek 1979–85, 2: 142–46, for an excellent description of the book's contents. Bousmanne (1997: 98–99, 110, 114–15, 121) drew parallels between the rich iconography of this book and that in Madrid (Biblioteca Nacional, Ms. Vit. 24-2)

3. Plotzek (in Euw and Plotzek 1979–85, 2: 157–58) and Bousmanne (1997: 42–43) both attributed most of the miniatures of this manuscript to the main painter of the second volume of the *Chroniques de Hainaut*, the artist now identified as Vrelant. One feature distinguishes the miniatures in the Hours of the Holy Spirit and the large suffrage miniatures from the rest here attributed to Vrelant. They lack the deep, rich blues and lush burgundies of the others. Plotzek dated the book to around 1460, a suggestion corroborated by the costumes and men's hairstyles (in the view of Margaret Scott, correspondence, March 3, 2002) and the fact that there seems to be relatively little development in Vrelant's style in the 1460s (Euw and Plotzek 1979–85, 2: 142).

4. Plotzek, in Euw and Plotzek 1979–85, 2: 149. *The Coronation of the Virgin* may also be by this hand.

5. Bousmanne 1997: 174

6. Vienna, Österreichische Nationalbibliothek, Ms. s.n. 12878 (Vienna 1975, plates volume, fig. 50). Bousmanne (1997: 100–101) pointed out that the figures of *The Annunciation* are derived from Jan van Eyck's Ghent Altarpiece.

7. The earliest manuscript in the sequence is the Hours of Saint Maur (Paris, Bibliothèque nationale de France, Ms. n.a.lat. 3107; Meiss 1968: 128–30), while those in the Flemish group include a book of hours, use of Sarum, ca. 1440 (priv. coll., Belgium); the Hours of Charles the Bold and Margaret of York (ex collection Lee), before 1465; and books of hours in Tours, ca. 1450 (Bibliothèque municipale, Ms. 218); Baltimore, ca. 1460 (Walters Art Museum, W.197); Los Angeles, ca. 1450 (Getty Museum, Ms. 2); and the Escorial (Avril 1989). Further, Bousmanne (1997: 109–10) indicated that the images in the calendar are "nearly entirely identical" to those in Vrelant's earlier so-called Hours of Isabella the Catholic (Madrid, Biblioteca del Palacio) and also shows strong parallels with that in the Missal of Ferry de Clugny (Siena, 10.5.1).

8. For example, some of the other large miniatures are based on Vrelant's earlier so-called Hours of Isabella the Catholic (Bousmanne 1997: 106–15, 189–92, figs. 95, 96). Bousmanne also offered examples of many other Vrelant books with which the Getty manuscript shared patterns.

9. It follows closely the model Bruges calendar compiled by John Plummer (in Baltimore 1988: 153–56) and is particularly close to a diverse group of Bruges manuscripts, including the Llangattock Hours (cat. no. 2) and the Black Prayer Book of Galeazzo Maria Sforza (Vienna, Österreichische Nationalbibliothek, Ms. 1856), neither apparently made for an Englishman.

10. Plummer (in Baltimore 1988: 152) also cited parallels to other Bruges manuscripts in the form of its "Obsecro te," especially Walters Art Museum W.240, and the Black Prayer Book. He suggests that all three "in all probability" were written in the same scriptorium.

11. A devout figure at the head of the apostles in the *Saints Peter and John Baptizing the Samarians* also appears in contemporary costume, though somewhat less fashionable than that of the "donor" figures mentioned. Margaret Scott kindly discussed the costumes with me.

12. Illustrated in both instances by his martyrdom. The name of Saint Thomas was effaced throughout the book (in the calendar, prayer, memorial, and litany), confirming the book's presence in England in the sixteenth century.

PART 2

REVOLUTION AND TRANSFORMATION: PAINTING IN DEVOTIONAL MANUSCRIPTS, CIRCA 1467–1485

THOMAS KREN

The appeal to the French royal household of luxury books of hours and prayer books (generally referred to as devotional books) during the later Middle Ages cannot be overstated. The book of hours was the most popular and common type of devotional book, organized to foster private meditation and prayer throughout the day. It was also an important vehicle for artistic innovation, as the unrivaled collection of lavish books of hours assembled by John, duke of Berry (1340–1416), shows. Luxury devotional books were simultaneously a means to communion with God, physical evidence of personal piety, and testaments to the wealth and taste of their patrons. From the Flemish and northern French territories of the Burgundian dukes, Philip the Good's prayer book, illuminated by Jean Le Tavernier at midcentury, is one of the artist's masterpieces, originally containing as many as 230 miniatures (The Hague, Koninklijke Bibliotheek, Ms. 76F2). In the course of his relatively short life, Charles the Bold acquired at least four books of hours and prayer books. Furthermore, books of hours had been a feature of Flemish export production since the fourteenth century.[1]

Although only two of Charles's devotional books survive, we know enough about the other two to see both a distinctive taste and considerable variety among them. The earliest datable one is a book of hours made for Charles and Isabelle of Bourbon, his second spouse. Completed before 1465, the year of her death, within the conservative Bruges circle of Willem Vrelant, it has forty-six miniatures (ex Lee collection).[2] A bit later, in 1466, the magistrates of the Franc de Bruges presented to Charles a book of hours written in gold and silver on black parchment, the illumination of which was still not complete. The duke selected Philippe de Mazerolles, who shortly thereafter became his *enlumineur en titre* and *valet de chambre*, to finish the job (at the expense of the Vrije of Bruges).[3] In 1469 the duke himself paid his late father's court painter, Lieven van Lathem, for illumination of the small but highly inventive prayer book in the Getty Museum (cat. no. 16). The book's exuberant and elaborate calligraphy is a tour de force by Nicolas Spierinc, a favorite scribe of the Burgundian court. In the same years Simon Marmion completed a breviary for the ducal chapel with ninety-five miniatures (cat. no. 10). Although not strictly speaking a devotional book, it was a sumptuous witness to the duke's piety and almost certainly intended for his devotional use. In 1476 or 1477, following one of their routs of the Burgundian armies, the Swiss captured from Charles another small prayer book, luxuriously illuminated with gold calligraphy on purple parchment.[4] As with the book presented by the Franc de Bruges, its current location is unknown.[5]

The new style of Flemish manuscript illumination that emerged during the 1470s appeared first in illuminated books of hours. Several artists associated with the emergence of the new style enjoyed Charles's patronage, including Marmion and the Vienna Master of Mary of Burgundy, who contributed at least one miniature to the surviving prayer book as well as to Charles's Alexander manuscript (cat. no. 54). During the 1470s Van Lathem and Spierinc would collaborate with the Vienna Master several times (cat. no. 17), notably on the celebrated eponymous book, probably made for Charles's daughter (cat. no. 19).[6] Further, the Getty prayer book introduced at least one feature that would become part of the new vocabulary of Flemish illumination, a richly colored border that simulates brocade. Since much is lost, it is difficult to ascertain precisely the role of the young duke's patronage in the emergence of the new style. Nevertheless, it is significant that he supported some of its innovators. Moreover, ducal family members and high-ranking courtiers were among the first to commission manuscripts in the new style.

The new style of illumination transformed both miniature and border. These changes seem to have occurred separately but probably within a few years of each other, perhaps around 1470 and not later than the mid-1470s. The change in approach to the miniatures probably occurred first and is signaled by two phenomena. First is the participation of painters or their workshop members in manuscript illumination, evidenced by the Eyckian miniatures in the Turin-Milan Hours (see cat. no. 1), the miniature by Rogier van der Weyden in the *Chroniques de Hainaut* for Philip the Good (cat. no. 3), and that by Petrus Christus in the Overtvelt Hours (cat. no. 6). The second is the activity of the painter-illuminator Marmion, whose work in oil on panel reflected his study of the great Flemish painters and also shaped the style of his miniatures.

Marmion's vivid Rogierian portraits, found in the dedication miniature to the *Grandes Chroniques de France* (Saint Petersburg, National Library of Russia, Ms. Erm. 88) of the late 1450s and in the detached miniature from a devotional book, *Saint Bernard's Vision of the Virgin and Child* (cat. no. 45), show just how the illuminator learned not only subtleties in the depiction of light, texture, and space but psychological expression as well. (The latter miniature also features a Rogierian female.) The raging, translucent hellfire of the Tondal manuscript (cat. no. 14), Marmion's one major project from the 1470s not for a devotional book, and the delicate, austere landscapes of purgatory in the same volume show further ways he imbued his miniatures with some of the nuanced effects he had mastered in oil. Indeed, for an altarpiece of the 1460s Marmion earned praise expressly for the way he depicted a candle "that seems to truly burn."[7] He pursued this approach to miniatures in the various vernacular and liturgical texts he illuminated in the 1450s and 1460s; his miniatures in the Kraków/London, Berlaymont, and Trivulzio Hours (cat. nos. 9, 12, 17)— that is, those pieces likely painted before 1475—helped to establish the aesthetic direction for miniatures in books of hours. After 1467 Marmion turned almost entirely to the illumination of books of hours, foretelling their growing dominion within Flemish book production.[8]

The Vienna Master of Mary of Burgundy, who was probably trained by a painter and was perhaps a painter himself, was younger than Marmion but followed a parallel path. Long considered the most important and influential—even the greatest—of the Flemish illuminators, the Vienna Master owed a profound artistic debt to the Ghent painter Joos van Ghent (fl. ca. 1460–80), an equally rare master. Indeed, the two artists have even been identified with each other. A preponderance of the Vienna Master's miniatures are scenes of the Passion, and in one way or another, they evoke Van Ghent's Crucifixion triptych in Saint Bavo's cathedral (fig. 48). The miniatures have a depth of feeling and a delicate, ethereal atmosphere that appears to extend and develop the themes of the triptych. Marmion collaborated with the Vienna Master on two lavish books of hours during the 1470s: the Trivulzio Hours (cat. no. 17) and the Vienna Hours of Mary of Burgundy (cat. no. 19).

The masterpieces of the Vienna Master of Mary of Burgundy are the full-page miniatures *Mary of Burgundy (?) Reading Her Devotions* (see fig. 65), *Christ Nailed to the Cross* (fig. 17), and *The Crucifixion* (ill. 19a) in the Vienna Hours. They surpass Marmion's miniatures in their sophisticated pictorial character and rival Flemish oil painting of the same period in their pictorial complexity, dense descriptive quality, and limpid atmosphere. They offer a level of nuance and subtlety in light and texture that is distinctly their own. Moreover, the first two miniatures feature a complex spatial configuration, with the central devotional scene viewed through a window from a niche that itself is part of the miniature. Simultaneously the niche acts as a frame, and the decorative border is eliminated. The interior scene is pictorially one with the exterior view. The early dates for two of the Vienna Master's works, 1470 and shortly after 1470, show that the new Ghent style of illuminating miniatures probably took root even earlier than mid-decade, when it is usually thought to have started.[9] Finally, the artist's earliest known miniatures appear in Charles's Alexander manuscript (cat. no. 54), but he supplied all his other illuminations to books of hours. Taken together with the shift in the character of Marmion's production in these years, the Vienna Master's work shows the ascendancy of the new style and with it the heightened importance of devotional books.

In the wake of the Vienna Master of Mary of Burgundy, illuminators turned to the style of the new generation of Ghent painters for inspiration, in particular to Van Ghent's friend and contemporary Hugo van der Goes. The best of these illuminators, the Master of the Houghton Miniatures, qualifies as a true heir of Van der Goes in his sensitive rendering of peasant types, the psychological depth of his characterizations, and his lyrical, even exhilarating, response to landscape and place. He seems to have favored full-page miniatures without borders. Unfortunately, fewer than a dozen miniatures from three prayer books (cat. nos. 32–34) and only one drawing (cat. no. 35) survive from his hand. He appeared, seemingly fully mature, in the late 1470s or early 1480s and disappeared just as suddenly. Perhaps he was a painter who turned to manuscript illumination for only a short while.

By the time the Master of the Houghton Miniatures appeared, the new style of border illumination, the other key innovation, was firmly established. Equally enduring in its appeal, the new style of borders shared with the fresh approach to the miniatures the concern with verisimilitude, especially qualities of light, texture, shadow, and color. The borders also have a spatial component that is rare in Flemish border illumination up to this time. The objects cast their own shadows against backgrounds that are now solid colored. The origins of the new type of border are generally dated to the mid-1470s, but the lack of precise dating for most devotional books makes a chronology difficult to sketch. At least four manuscripts with the new border likely date to the year of Charles's death, 1477, or earlier (cat. nos. 22–24, 44).

The most fully developed and varied borders appear in the recently discovered book of hours made for Charlotte of Bourbon-Montpensier (cat. no. 44), wife of the prominent Burgundian courtier Wolfart van Borssele[10] and cousin of the late Isabelle of Bourbon. There most borders surround splendid miniatures by the Master of the Dresden Prayer Book (ills. 44b, 44c). One such border has two dozen small violets lightly scattered across the page with a butterfly alighting on a blossom, an angel bearing an armorial in the bas-de-page, and a small vignette in the area at the right (fol. 23). Others feature a greater variety of flowers—irises, thistles, columbine, daisies, and so on—and also the heraldic insignia and device of Wolfart and the couple's initials *en lac* (e.g., fols. 31, 40, 84, 148v). Many, though not all, such borders feature acanthus in white, gold, or blue. The border of the page with *The Annunciation* has several dozen white seashells arranged in a lozenge pattern, while the border of the page with *The Coronation of the Virgin* features a collection of rose-colored peacock feathers arranged to highlight the blue and green eye on each. The page with *The Massacre of the Innocents* features a border that consists of a brocade of flowers and thistles in gold and burgundy, reminiscent of the finest Flemish textiles of the time.[11] Although relatively flat, the fictive textile is cropped off-axis, as if placed there casually. In a few instances in this book, the new style of border appears on both pages of an opening, with matching gold backgrounds for a memorably luxurious and radiant effect. The Bourbon-Montpensier Hours shows the earliest datable examples of many of the new Flemish border types that would enjoy currency for the next seventy years. They include the signature borders with acanthus and a variety of flowers that appear to be randomly strewn. Still other kinds feature borders painted as costly textiles or with seashells or exotic plumage.

It is intriguing that the painter of the miniatures within most of these borders is the Master of the Dresden Prayer Book of Bruges. Was he the artist of the borders as well? Some of the figures that appear in the borders are clearly by him, though the technique for the flowers and other motifs is different from that employed in the miniatures, and it is difficult to judge. The answer matters because the invention of the illusionistic border is usually assigned to the Vienna Master of Mary of Burgundy and the Ghent illuminators around him.[12] In fact, the early Ghent borders of this type are distinctive from those just described. The border of the Vienna Master's *Crucifixion* from the eponymous book (ill. 19a) has an independent spatial character, with both a depth and a scale distinct from the miniature. The golden acanthus is dense and thick, filling the space, casting deep and large shadows, yet it is not naturalistically colored. Its pods feature pearls rather than peas, and its flowers are also jewel-like rather than true to life. It has the immediacy, vivid textures, and spatial quality of the new borders, with more fantasy and less verisimilitude. This is to a degree true of other borders by the Vienna Master or his circle, including one datable to 1477 (cat. no. 23) and another datable around then (cat. no. 22). These borders combine carefully observed flowers with human figures, nonnaturalistic color, and, sometimes, jarring contrasts of scale.[13] Finally, the Vienna Master or a member of his circle introduced yet a further variation on the new border with a spatial character, a narrative border whose continuous space wends around the page (ill. 20b). It is occasionally linked via an illusionistic device to the text block or central miniature, as in the celebrated example of the Passion border in the Voustre Demeure Hours (cat. no. 20).

By the mid-1480s, if not earlier, the new types of spatial borders—especially those with "strewn" flora and acanthus, luscious textures, and occasional illusionism—were a feature of nearly all Flemish illuminated manuscripts, not only books of hours and prayer books but liturgical and vernacular texts, too.[14] Marmion, the Master of the Houghton Miniatures, and the Master of the Dresden Prayer Book all eventually adopted them (see cat. nos. 32, 33, 37, 49, 117). From the outset they proved especially popular with artists associated with Ghent, such as the Master of the First Prayer Book of Maximilian, who was less gifted than the three artists just named but more productive. He was active by 1477 and worked for the ducal court (see cat. nos. 41, 86, 88), and he quickly codified in his miniatures the pictorial values of Hugo van der Goes. Like Vrelant, he had a large workshop and produced many works for export, and he appears to have lived a long life, into the second decade of the sixteenth century. Characteristic of his books are an extensive reliance on patterns, a great deal of collaboration with other workshops, and the luxurious new style of border.

A distinctive feature of the early manuscripts in the new style of illumination, especially those closely based on painting of the Ghent school, is the number of anonymous hands that appear to have painted miniatures at a fairly high level of refinement. The artists used patterns, sometimes suites of them, while exploiting the effects of light, atmosphere, color, and space in ways consistently reminiscent of painting in oil on panel. While the Maximilian Master offers one of the best examples of this work, another group of illuminators who are more difficult to define individually, called the Ghent Associates by Anne van Buren, collaborated on such books as the diminutive hours in a private collection (cat. no. 37), the Madrid Hours of William Lord Hastings (cat. no. 25), the Hours of Mary of Burgundy and Maximilian (cat. no. 38), and a book of hours made for a German cleric (Kraków, Biblioteka Czartoryskich, Ms. 3025).[15] These artists looked not only to Van der Goes and Van Ghent but also to Dieric Bouts (ca. 1415–1475) and Rogier van der Weyden for compositional sources. They too played a role in spreading the new naturalism of Flemish manuscript illumination by producing manuscripts—especially books of hours, prayer books, and breviaries—of an elaborate, costly, and refined character.

Notes

1. Since the mid-fifteenth century illuminators such as Willem Vrelant had produced devotional books for English, Spanish, German, Italian, and French patrons. The Arenberg Hours (cat. no. 15), made for the use of Sarum, hence for an English patron, offers an indication of their elaborate artistic character.

2. Known sometimes as the Lee Hours (Farquhar 1976: 88–96, 141–44).

3. See de Schryver 1999: 62–63 for the documents.

4. Deuchler 1963: 349, no. 316; see also de Schryver 1999: 51–52.

5. De Schryver (1999: 50–58) argued recently that the book given by the Vrije of Bruges and that lost to the Swiss are one and the same and identical with the so-called Black Hours (Vienna, Österreichische Nationalbibliothek, Ms. 1856), but I do not find his argument convincing.

6. A recent, particularly cogent argument for Mary as the book's intended owner is offered by Inglis (1995: 14–16).

7. Louis de la Fontaine, *Les Antiquitez de la ville de France*, Valenciennes, Bibliothèque communale, Ms. 529, fol. 288 (quoted in Hénault 1907: 414–15).

8. Examples that he executed likely between about 1467 and 1480 include the Kråkow/London hours (cat. no. 9), the Trivulzio Hours (cat. no. 17), the Berlaymont Hours (cat. no. 12), the Salting Hours (cat. no. 53), a diminutive book of hours in a private collection (cat. no. 37), and the Hours of Jean Gros (d. 1484), the secretary and *audencier* of the Golden Fleece (Chantilly, Musée Condé, Ms. 85). In this period Marmion also contributed a miniature to the Vienna Hours of Mary of Burgundy. In the process his circle of patrons probably did not shift dramatically but rather remained at the court and close to it, as indicated by the Vienna Hours, the Gros Hours, and others. The Berlaymont Hours may have been made for a member of the Rolin family, the diminutive hours might have been for a Burgundian courtier, and the Trivulzio Hours was put together by a group of artists and artisans who enjoyed the duke's favor.

9. Pächt 1948: 20; Inglis 1995: 14. The Vienna Hours is traditionally dated to the latter half of the 1470s (cf. Pächt and Thoss 1990: 69–84). In my view it may be earlier.

10. His father, Hendrick, had been stadholder general and a captain of the Burgundian naval forces.

11. A similar pattern appears in certain costumes in Flemish miniatures around this time. See, for example, folios 14v and 99v in the Vienna Hours of Mary of Burgundy (fig. 63 and ill. 19a).

12. Some artists used the new style of border only sporadically at the beginning, for example, the Master of the Dresden Prayer Book. Following the stunning appearance of the borders in the Bourbon-Montpensier Hours and the inclusion of some examples in his Hours of Colard Pingret of 1478 (Brussels, Bibliothèque royale, Ms. II 7604), the Dresden Master eschewed them in the Nová Říše Hours (cat. no. 36) of 1480 and in the Psalter of Petrus Vaillant of 1482 (cf. Bruges 1981: 195–96). The Nová Říše Hours has such borders, but they are connected to a miniature by another illuminator. They do not appear there around any of the miniatures by the Dresden Master, the book's main illuminator. He is nevertheless an intriguing figure because border decoration interested him greatly. Especially during the 1470s, in books such as the Hours of Jean Carpentin (cat. no. 48) and the Salting Hours (cat. no. 53), he experimented with figures and acanthus on various colored grounds in his borders. In this he is heir to the example by Van Lathem in the Prayer Book of Charles the Bold (cat. no. 16). The fine textile border in the Bourbon-Montpensier Hours also has an antecedent in those in Charles's prayer book (fols. 24v, 46). The latter manuscript is important as well for its early use of traditional border elements, mostly figures and acanthus in monochrome on solid-colored grounds, usually of gold or silver (fols. 14, 17, 19v, 22, 29, 33, 36, 39v, 43, 49v).

13. Limitations of space do not allow further discussion on the origins and meanings of the new style of borders, but some ideas on these topics are put forward by Pächt (1948: 29–32); Büttner (1985: 197–233); and Kaufmann and Kaufmann (1991: 43–64).

14. See Scot McKendrick, "Reviving the Past: Illustrated Manuscripts of Secular Vernacular Texts, 1467–1500" (this volume). Pächt (1948: 29) called the new type "strewn" borders because the objects appeared to him as if casually dropped there, yet as often as not they appear to be carefully arranged.

15. Van Buren 1975: 291–92, 307–8. On the Kråkow example, see Brinkmann 1998: 147–53.

VIENNA MASTER OF MARY OF BURGUNDY (A)

The activities of few fifteenth-century artists have provoked more discussion and disagreement than those of the illuminator once known as the Master of Mary of Burgundy. He was named for two different manuscripts: the Hours of Mary of Burgundy in Vienna (cat. no. 19), which is traditionally considered to have been intended for the young duchess, and the Hours of Mary of Burgundy and Maximilian in Berlin (cat. no. 38). Friedrich Winkler grouped around these two books a body of manuscripts whose miniatures featured the new style of naturalism inspired largely by the Ghent painters Hugo van der Goes and Joos van Ghent.[1] Many of the same books also feature the new style of borders with finely observed flora and acanthus that cast shadows on solid-colored grounds. Although not always naturalistically colored, the border motifs have the sparkling surfaces and carefully observed textures one associates with Flemish oil painting. Otto Pächt believed that the Master of Mary of Burgundy invented the new styles of both border and miniature.[2]

Pächt's 1948 publication on the artist was the first monograph on a Flemish illuminator. Eloquently written, it inspired widespread interest in and affection for its subject, but it has not stood the test of time. Starting in 1964 with G. I. Lieftinck, who rejected half of Pächt's attributions, most specialists have taken a revisionist approach.[3] Among the books Lieftinck removed from the Master's oeuvre was the Berlin Hours, one of the eponymous manuscripts. Anne van Buren has since named the artists of Lieftinck's rejected series the Ghent Associates, to whom she assigned further manuscripts.[4] Bodo Brinkmann proposed a still more radical approach, returning to the artist's two most impressive groups of miniatures as the building blocks for all other attributions.[5] They are found in the Vienna Hours of Mary of Burgundy and the Hours of Engelbert of Nassau (cat. no. 18). Brinkmann was prudent in suggesting using them as the foundation for further attributions to this artist, whom he rechristened the Vienna Master of Mary of Burgundy. As a result of this revisionist criticism, the original Master of Mary of Burgundy in effect no longer exists. His entire oeuvre has been reassigned to different artists or to the broadly defined group of the Ghent Associates.

Using the Vienna and Engelbert Hours as the foundation for reconsidering the achievement of this illuminator, I propose to add here a few significant miniatures overlooked in the literature or until now unknown.[6] They include ten miniatures in the Quintus Curtius of Charles the Bold, paid for in 1470 (cat. no. 54); a single miniature in the cycle added to the duke's Getty prayer book (cat. no. 16) shortly after the completion of the book's first campaign in 1469; and one miniature in the recently rediscovered Trivulzio Hours (cat. no. 17). The illuminations of the

Vienna Master of Mary of Burgundy constitute an art of profound emotion; subtle atmospheric effects; abundant, richly textured detail; and the most delicate draftsmanship. His miniatures convey a powerful sense of the moment.

To illustrate these characteristics as they appear in our new attributions, consider three of the artist's famous full-page miniatures in the Vienna Hours of Mary of Burgundy. *The Crucifixion* (ill. 19a), *Christ Nailed to the Cross* (fig. 17), and *Mary of Burgundy (?) Reading Her Devotions* (fig. 65) help to justify the attribution of these additional miniatures.[7] The first two miniatures present impressive spectacles in which all participants from Christ and the Virgin to the most peripheral onlookers are intensely engaged in the emotional narrative. In both miniatures some look out, even back over their shoulders, to catch our eye. The effect is enhanced by the thickness of the crowd and the telescoping spatial recession. In *Christ Nailed to the Cross*, the spectators surge or stare or swoon or debate or holler. The artist dramatizes the pain of the Virgin, who reaches out to Christ as he is nailed on the cross. Her emotional distress is physically palpable, as it is in the Getty *Deposition* (ill. 16b) and the Trivulzio *Crucifixion* (ill. 17a), where she collapses under the cross.

In the Vienna *Crucifixion*, Christ and the two thieves tower over the vast crowd, the emaciated savior's chest heaving heroically against the sky. The quality of drawing of Christ's anatomy—particularly the upward motion of the expanded chest, the figure's delicate proportions, and the fine muscles of the legs—reveals the illuminator's skill to be far superior to that of his contemporaries. The same characteristics are found in the superb figure of Christ in the Getty *Deposition*, in the Christ and the writhing thieves in the Trivulzio *Crucifixion*, and in the bound Saint Sebastian and the perished souls of the Engelbert Hours *Last Judgment* (ill. 18b). In the art of the Vienna Master of Mary of Burgundy, immediacy is lent by numerous figures in motion—writhing, gesturing, stepping, or just listening with head attentively inclined. Movement is keenly observed: the weight of the Virgin's body as John restrains her in *Christ Nailed to the Cross*, the delicate footwork of the figures lowering the body of Christ in the Getty *Deposition*, or the stride of Philotes, his body tensed, led before Alexander in the duke's Alexander manuscript (cat. no. 54, fol. 155).[8]

The poetry of the artist's drawing is further evidenced by the idealized beauty of his young female types, as in the presumed portrait of Mary of Burgundy in the Vienna Hours. The exquisite, courtly girl, seated with a view of the Virgin and Child in a church, has an oval head, whose purity of form is emphasized by the high forehead and small features. Although seen from above, with down-turned glance, the face seems perfectly symmetrical and calls to mind the faces and inventive costumes of the female figures in *Alexander Takes the Hand of Roxanne* from Charles's Alexander manuscript (ill. 54a).[9] In the Engelbert Hours, Saint Barbara, shown seated on the ground reading her devotions; the Virgin in *The Adoration of the Magi*; and the nurse attending the Virgin in *The Presentation in the Temple* (fols. 41, 145v, 152v) all show similar facial types.

One of the Vienna Master's most compelling yet least imitated innovations was the use of framing niches in two of the Vienna miniatures. In the first of these, Mary of Burgundy is seated in the area that would have been the border in most Flemish miniatures, now a developed, inhabitable space. What is traditionally the space occupied by the miniature is now the view through her window. The artist seamlessly melded the traditionally separate domains of miniature and border into a complex and continuous physical domain. The decorative border has been eliminated, and the miniature completely fills the page. *Christ Nailed to the Cross* offers a similar structure, although in this work the foreground niche is left uninhabited. Instead the rosary, prayer book, and other aids to meditation and prayer are arrayed along the sill and ledge as if for the viewer's use. Although Pächt heralded this innovation as the hallmark of the new type of illusionistic border, relatively few images of comparable spatial complexity were attempted by the next generations of Flemish illuminators (see cat. no. 117, fol. 280v). The concept of a miniature that fills the page, lacking the traditional decorative border, would, however, enjoy favor among artists working in the new style (see, for example, cat. nos. 32, 33, 37).

Several other manuscripts seem to represent a later phase or continuation of the style of the Vienna Master of Mary of Burgundy as defined here. Unlike the examples discussed previously, all of these manuscripts feature the new style of border strewn with finely textured flora and acanthus as part of their original decoration. They represent either the next phase in the development of the Vienna Master or perhaps extraordinary works by a student or follower. Two of these are the Breviary of Margaret of York (cat. no. 22) and the Voustre Demeure Hours (cat. no. 20). Their miniatures, also once attributed to the Master of Mary of Burgundy, are here attributed to the Vienna Master, his workshop, and/or followers.[10] They show many similarities in motifs, composition, and lighting to the work of the Vienna Master as defined in the first five manuscripts. The distinctive torch-bearing soldiers, bathed in nocturnal darkness, approaching the garden in the Voustre Demeure *Crucifixion* (ill. 20c) recall those in the Engelbert Hours *Betrayal of Christ* (fol. 56v). The miniatures in the breviary and the Voustre Demeure Hours feature similar emotionally expressive figures, such as the image of the crucified Saint Andrew in the former and the Christ in *The Crucifixion* in the latter. But in these miniatures the figures are taller, more angular, and weightier, and the women are blander in expression and plainer in type than those found in earlier works by the Vienna Master. The brushwork also has more variety, the artist sometimes using a more angular stroke or fine points of color to build up a velvety surface.

The Voustre Demeure Hours has an intriguing place in the sequence of the Vienna Master's work. Here the illuminator (or his workshop or follower) collaborated with Lieven van Lathem and Nicolas Spierinc on the book, as he did on the Prayer Book of Charles the Bold, the Trivulzio Hours, and the Vienna Hours of Mary of Burgundy. The difference from the Voustre Demeure Hours is that the Vienna Master and his workshop appear to be the lead artists, whereas Van Lathem was the lead artist in the earlier projects.

Although the evidence is modest, it seems likely that the Vienna Master was based in Ghent. As Georges Hulin de Loo and Antoine de Schryver recognized, he owes a strong debt to Joos van Ghent, especially to *The Crucifixion* in his Calvary triptych in Ghent (fig. 48).[11] Further, Nicolas Spierinc, the scribe for most of the books illuminated by the Vienna Master, lived in Ghent. Neither relationship is sufficient to prove that the Vienna Master was from Ghent, but the weight of evidence supports this notion. For his earliest project, the Alexander manuscript, he was working for Loyset Liédet, who was based in Bruges at the time. Yet even here the Vienna Master shows a stylistic debt to Van Ghent.

The close relationship between Van Ghent and the Vienna Master merits careful consideration. Many features of the two magnificent paintings attributed to Van Ghent during his time in Ghent, *The Crucifixion* in the Calvary triptych and the Metropolitan Museum of Art *Adoration of the Magi*, show links to the art of the Vienna Master. They include the device of lining up crowds of figures leading back into space on one side of the composition; figures that look out toward the viewer from over a shoulder; the tall, exotic profiles of the women's headgear; the V-shaped landscape of the Calvary triptych's central panel;[12] the subtle contrapposto of courtly male figures clad in tights; the drooping hands of the sorrowing Virgins; and hoary males with bifurcated beards. Both artists also show a strong preference for historical figures dressed in gold brocades. Is the Vienna Master identical with Joos van Ghent? Eberhard Schenk zu Schweinsberg proposed that the illuminator of the Engelbert Hours might be Joos van Ghent, who left Flanders in 1473 to work in Urbino.[13] The similarities between the Vienna Master and Van Ghent are sometimes startling, but questions remain. The Alexander manuscript shows that the Vienna Master was active by 1470, if not a year or two earlier. His other four securely assigned works are undated, although the Engelbert Hours and the Vienna Hours are usually placed later than 1473. Nevertheless, if Margaret's breviary and the Voustre Demeure Hours are by the Vienna Master, then his Flemish career continued into the later 1470s. Van Ghent's own career is shadowy and his activity after 1475 is untraced.[14] Thus there are a number of unresolved questions regarding the proposed identification.   T. K.

Notes

1. Winkler 1915: 282–87; Winkler 1925: 102–15; Winkler 1942: 262–71.

2. Pächt 1944, 1948. Winkler (1942: 264) saw the naturalism of the miniatures as an older phenomenon, but he too saw the Master of Mary of Burgundy as the inventor of the new type of border.

3. Lieftinck 1964b and 1969. Less convincingly, Lieftinck also sought to localize the activity of the artist to the Windesheim monastery of Rooclooster, near Brussels (to which Van der Goes himself eventually withdrew).

4. Van Buren 1975: esp. 289–93, 307–8. One of the identifiable masters within Van Buren's Ghent Associates is the Master of the First Prayer Book of Maximilian (cat. nos. 41–43, 86, 88).

5. Brinkmann 1998: 133–47.

6. The only other work that Brinkmann (1998: 143–47) attributed to the Vienna Master is a predella panel in the Museum voor Schone Kunsten, Ghent, which has the qualities of being painted by an illuminator and some of the proportions of the Vienna Master's figures, aspects of their movement, and some similar postures. Yet I am not convinced it is the same hand; the quality of painting itself is much less fluid and expressive. Is it the work of an illuminator in a foreign medium? A cleaning and technical examination might lead to a better understanding of this important and unusual work. Cf. Verhaegen 1961: 6–10; de Schryver and Marijnissen 1961: 11–23.

7. In this manuscript the illuminator painted, in addition to the fifteen small miniatures in the cycle of the suffrages, parts of two large miniatures, *The Way to Calvary* (fol. 94v) and the *Annunciation* (fol. 19v); border motifs on folios 19v, 121, 121v, 123, and 123v; and perhaps the grisaille initials on folios 15 and 16v. For a detailed analysis of the manuscript and complete bibliography, see also Pächt and Thoss 1990: 69–85.

8. The Vienna *Crucifixion* and *Christ Nailed to the Cross* show the artist's predilection for composing crowds of people in long, narrow lines that move back swiftly into depth. This appears also in the *Roxanne* miniature, the Trivulzio *Crucifixion*, and *The Death of the Virgin* and *The Last Judgment* in the Engelbert Hours (fols. 171, 182). Here heads tightly overlap one another, with only the eyes, mouths, or some portion of a face visible.

9. Other examples of the exotic headgear on his female characters appear in the foreground of *Christ Nailed to the Cross* and inside the church in *Mary of Burgundy (?) Reading Her Devotions* (see fig. 65) in the Vienna Hours, at the foot of the cross in the Getty *Deposition*, and in *The Presentation in the Temple* (fol. 152v) in the Engelbert Hours.

10. In the Voustre Demeure Hours there seem to be several hands working in this style. See cat. no. 20.

11. Hulin de Loo 1939b: 178; de Schryver 1969a: 115–28.

12. Compare, for example, *Christ Nailed to the Cross* and *The Way to Calvary* in the Vienna Hours (fols. 44v and 94v).

13. Schenk zu Schweinsberg 1975: 155; cf. also Brinkmann 1998: 174.

14. See Campbell (1988: 267) on Joos van Ghent.

16

VIENNA MASTER OF MARY OF BURGUNDY AND WORKSHOP, AND LIEVEN VAN LATHEM AND WORKSHOP

Prayer Book of Charles the Bold
Ghent and Antwerp, 1469 and ca. 1471

MANUSCRIPT: ii + 159 + ii folios, 12.4 × 9.2 cm (4⅞ × 3⅝ in.), justification: 6.3 × 4.6 cm (2½ × 1¹³⁄₁₆ in.); 13 lines of *bastarda* by Nicolas Spierinc; 5 full-page miniatures, 32 three-quarter-page miniatures, 2 quarter-page miniatures, 42 historiated borders; 8 small miniatures added, fols. 126–159v, probably Paris, ca. 1480–90

INSCRIPTIONS: *Je suys a Mademoiselle de Marles*, front flyleaf

BINDING: French(?), late fifteenth or early sixteenth century; purple velvet over wood boards; silver corner pieces inscribed *sg*, silver central medallion inscribed *Non Terra Dissolvet Unita Celis*; German(?) silver clasps; gilt edges

COLLECTION: Los Angeles, J. Paul Getty Museum, Ms. 37 (89.ML.35)

PROVENANCE: Charles the Bold, duke of Burgundy (1433–1477); Marie of Luxembourg, countess of Marle (ca. 1464–1546); possibly Jeanne d'Albret, queen of Navarre (1528–1572); Marie Jeanne de Chaussy; Delaroche(?), nineteenth century; Count Paul Durrieu (1855–1925), Larrivière; to Jean Durrieu, Paris; acquired 1989

JPGM and RA

The Burgundian accounts for January 1469 record payment to Nicolas Spierinc "for having written . . . some prayers for my lord."[1] The accounts for August show payment to Lieven van Lathem for twenty-five *histoires* (miniatures) and their borders, for eighty-eight smaller borders, and for two hundred initials in gold or in color in "a small booklet for my lord containing many prayers made for his devotions." Although full publication of the documents is still eagerly awaited, Antoine de Schryver has connected these documents to the prayer book catalogued here, an identification accepted by most scholars.[2]

The Prayer Book of Charles the Bold was executed in two campaigns, and the payment of 1469 applied only to the portion extending from folios 9 to 66. This is the portion described in the documents as a "petit livret."[3] The texts originally began with several Marian prayers, followed by twenty-four suffrages, the Athanasian Creed, the Verses of Saint Bernard, and several prayers in Latin and in French—all in all, a disarmingly modest program. The only full-page miniature in the first campaign is that dedicated to Saint Hubert, the patron of the city of Liège, which had surrendered to Charles in November 1467.[4]

Unexpected is the paucity of references in the first campaign to the august patron himself, who is named only in the suffrage to Saint Christopher (fol. 26v).[5] He is completely absent from the decorative program—which does not include his image, device, heraldry, or any other symbol—although the full border around the miniature of the Virgin and Child, the opening miniature of the first campaign, originally contained a series of armorials.[6] It was repainted, either as the selection of heraldry grew inaccurate over time or by a subsequent owner.

Van Lathem's second campaign includes devotions to the Holy Face and to the Virgin added at the front of the volume. Both are illustrated with miniatures of the duke

16a
LIEVEN VAN LATHEM
*Christ Appearing to Saint
James the Greater*, fol. 22

16b
VIENNA MASTER OF
MARY OF BURGUNDY
The Deposition, fol. 111v

presented by Saint George. Van Lathem added a full-page suffrage to Saint George at the back of the volume, again accompanied by the image of Charles kneeling in veneration.[7] Also included in the second campaign is a long Hours of the Passion. Since Charles is not represented at all in the original portion of the book, the longer version, which contains sixty-seven additional leaves and an entirely new pictorial cycle, has quite a different character. The second campaign features four full-page, eight half-page, and two small miniatures plus extensive historiated rather than decorated borders, in what amounts to a twofold increase in the devotional iconography. The additional miniatures are for the most part not as finely painted as those in the first campaign, almost certainly because Van Lathem was working quickly or relying on assistants. The background of *Saint Veronica* is fully sketched in but still unpainted.[8]

The original portion of the book represents a landmark in the illumination of devotional books, not so much for the quality of the miniatures, which is often superb, but for the novelty and variety of the borders.[9] The ducal prayer book represents a summa of the artist's favored motifs: hunters, wild men, centaurs and other anthropomorphic hybrids, griffins, birds, monkeys, and lions (ill. 16a), usually

paired off or engaged in wrestling, face-offs, swordplay, tournaments, or other forms of combat. A few of these creatures are shown playing instruments, and one border features musical angels (fol. 43). Van Lathem usually painted these motifs in color, embellished with acanthus and rinceaux, on bare vellum, as he did here, but in the prayer book he also introduced these motifs against colored, gold, or silver backgrounds (ills. 16a, 16d) or in grisaille on gold or silver. The result is a suite of borders of uncommon inventiveness, with a broad variety of effects of light and color. Sometimes the exuberance and vitality of a marginal griffin or chimera seems to overwhelm the pious subject matter, as seen, for example, in the image of a somewhat weary Saint Margaret emerging from the belly of a dragon (oddly enough, in the form of a griffin[10]) or in the soldier, hybrid creatures, and griffins engaged in vigorous combat beneath the iconic *Trinity* (fol. 14). Although more modest variations of the borders with colored backgrounds appear in at least one other book of hours that Van Lathem illuminated, they seem to have had no real succession in his own work. Nevertheless, they do presage the popularity of solid-colored grounds in the illusionistic borders of the 1470s and beyond (see cat. nos. 48, 52, 53). Four

16c
WORKSHOP OF
VIENNA MASTER
OF MARY OF
BURGUNDY
The Agony in the Garden,
fol. 70v

16d
LIEVEN VAN LATHEM
Saint Stephen, fol. 24v

of the borders (ill. 16d; fols. 10, 19v, 46v) are decorated with flat designs inspired by enamels or textiles, probably fabrics imported from Italy, which feature intricate patterns of gold or silver acanthus and griffins on black, red, or brown.[11] This type anticipates the illusionistic borders with Flemish silk brocade that became popular during the 1470s and early 1480s (see cat. nos. 20, 44).

The illuminations of the second campaign offer a striking contrast to the first not only in the donor's presence but also in the persistent association of Charles with Saint George. The historiated borders of the second campaign also represent a conceptual departure. The vignettes all expand or embellish the narrative of the miniature itself. Some of these narratives, such as the sacrifice of Isaac accompanying *The Crucifixion* and the whale swallowing Jonah accompanying *The Entombment,* function typologically. Several of these leaves—including those with *The Agony in the Garden* (ill. 16c), *The Flagellation,* and *The Deposition* (ill. 16b)—are not by Van Lathem but have strong echoes of the Vienna Master of Mary of Burgundy.[12] *The Deposition,* which is superior to the other two, is likely by the Vienna Master's hand. The long torso and narrow limbs of the dead Christ recall closely the graceful, elongated male nudes among the damned souls of *The Last Judgment* in the Hours of Engelbert of Nassau (ill. 18b). The sensitive

rendering of the musculature finds no equal in the work of any contemporary illuminator—not even Marmion. The three men lowering the body of Christ strain under the weight of their burden. Typical also of the Vienna Master of Mary of Burgundy are the broad, bearded facial type of Joseph of Arimathea, with high cheekbones and without mustache; the lost profile of the Magdalene at the left; and the culmination of the Virgin's robe on the ground in a pool of drapery.[13] Finally, the miniature packs an emotional punch unlike any other in the prayer book; the artist conveys the Virgin's grief quietly, internally, along with the sadness of the men as they perform their grim task. Only the miniatures by the Vienna Master in the Vienna Hours of Mary of Burgundy (cat. no. 19) and the Engelbert Hours display a comparable depth of feeling.

Charles's prayer book and the Vienna Hours have much in common despite the considerable difference in their devotional content, iconographic programs, scale, and scope. In both the scribe was Nicolas Spierinc, and in both he offered virtuoso performances. Indeed, Spierinc's reputation as the greatest of Burgundian scribes rests primarily on his sustained performances in this book and the Vienna Hours. While pen flourishes and cadelles are hallmarks of his calligraphy, in these two manuscripts he shows greater artistry, exuberance, and inventiveness than in any other work. Many of his pen flourishes culminate in the wispy contours of acanthus, griffins, and human and animal profiles. The text pages give nearly as much pleasure as the illuminated ones. Few other luxury books from this period show cadelles and flourishes to a comparable extent.[14] Moreover, Lievin van Lathem was the primary illuminator of both manuscripts. A few individual compositions and numerous border motifs are also shared between them. Finally, the Vienna Master of Mary of Burgundy made small but important contributions to both.[15]

The twenty-five miniatures at the core of the book were completed by August 1469, when Van Lathem delivered it to the duke and was paid. The second campaign was painted somewhat later, probably after 1470. Van Lathem (or an assistant) seems to have based a small miniature of Saint George presenting Charles the Bold to the Virgin (fol. 6) from the second campaign on the famous *Saint George Presenting Charles the Bold* by Gerard Loyet (d. 1502/3).[16] Charles presented it to the cathedral in Liège on Valentine's Day 1471, but given Van Lathem's dealings with the court, he may well have seen the completed work in Bruges beforehand.

An exlibris on the flyleaf at the front identifies a subsequent owner as "Mademoiselle de Marles." She was Marie (ca. 1464–1546), the granddaughter of Louis de Luxembourg, who was executed by Louis XI in 1475 for his intrigues with Charles the Bold.[17] She had thirty-four leaves and eight miniatures added to the prayer book, probably during the period of her second marriage, to François de Bourbon, count of Vendôme (1470–1495), a confidant and companion of Charles VIII.[18]   T. K.

Notes

1. Pinchart 1861–62, 2: 208. Author's translation.

2. De Schryver 1957: 340–42. The documents will be published in their entirety and analyzed by de Schryver in his facsimile *The Prayer Book of Charles the Bold* (forthcoming).

3. De Schryver, *Prayer Book of Charles the Bold* (see note 2).

4. The city would rise up against him again in 1468, only to suffer a second defeat (Van der Velden 2000: 95–97). In 1463 Philip the Good had commissioned an exquisite illuminated *Vie de Saint-Hubert* (The Hague, Koninklijke Bibliotheek, Ms. 76 F 10), and in 1470 Louis de Gruuthuse commissioned an illuminated copy for himself (Paris, Bibliothèque nationale de France, Ms. fr. 424).

5. Unless one takes into account the full-page miniature of Saint Hubert mentioned above and in note 5. The suffrages include some surprising choices, such as Saints Gatian and Fiacre, both associated with Tours, and Saint Eutropius of Saintes, further to the southwest in France.

6. Perhaps it was an arrangement of the arms of Charles's various territories, as found in an illuminated volume of his military ordinances (cat. no. 64) or like those within the miniature in the Register of the Guild of Saint Anne (cat. no. 23). Scot McKendrick kindly pointed this out to me.

7. Van der Velden (2000: 122–53) has assembled extensive evidence of Charles's particular veneration of Saint George throughout his career but especially in the years before these miniatures were painted.

8. In September 1469, not long after the first portion of the book was delivered to the duke, Ernoul de Duvel, a goldsmith in The Hague, was paid for the gold clasps for two small devotional books, one of which may have been made for the Getty manuscript. A payment was made in the same month for binding a prayer book for the duke, and another was made two months later for a black velvet cover for the duke's prayer book. See de Schryver, *Prayer Book of Charles the Bold* (see note 2).

9. Van Lathem's skill at painting drolleries earned him an early commission to decorate some of the borders of a Utrecht book of hours illuminated by the Master of Catherine of Cleves (The Hague, Rijksmuseum Meermanno-Westreenianum, Ms. 10 F 50).

10. The dragon is also shown as winged in the votive reliquary of Charles the Bold created by Gerard Loyet in 1471 (Liège, Trésor de la Cathédrale; Van der Velden 2000: 83, fig. 47).

11. A similar type of border to this on a black ground appears in a book of hours that Van Lathem partially illuminated (Paris, Bibliothèque nationale de France, Ms. n.a.lat. 215).

12. Pächt and Thoss (1990: 83) first noted that *The Agony in the Garden* and "several" other miniatures in the second campaign recall the style of the Master of Mary of Burgundy.

13. For a facial type similar to Joseph's, see the Christ in *Christ Carrying the Cross* (fol. 94v) and the figure in profile at the lower left in *The Crucifixion* (ill. 19a) in the Vienna Hours of Mary of Burgundy (cat. no. 19). For similar females seated on the ground, see the *Saint Barbara* and the Virgins of *The Annunciation* and *The Nativity* in the Hours of Engelbert of Nassau (Alexander 1970: nos. 36, 72, 77).

14. For some of the others, see Wolf (E.) 1996: 237–40, 249–51, 280–82, 293–98, nos. 1, 3, 12, 15, and the Voustre Demeure Hours (cat. no. 20), to which Van Lathem contributed a miniature.

15. The same three figures also collaborated on the Trivulzio Hours (cat. no. 17).

16. Durrieu (1916: 121–22) thought both images were derived from Van Eyck's *Madonna with Canon George van der Paele*. It seems more likely, as Marian Campbell (in London 1980: [6]) and Van der Velden (2000: 124) have suggested, that the sequence was Van Eyck-Loyet-Van Lathem.

17. Durrieu 1916: 123–24.

18. The additions include an excerpt from the Passion according to John and another from that according to Pope John, seven illuminated suffrages, and several prayers. Its modest miniatures were painted in a Parisian manner derived from the Maître François (active ca. 1460–80).

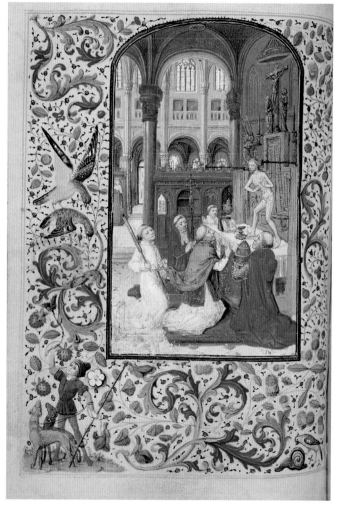

17

VIENNA MASTER OF MARY OF BURGUNDY, LIEVEN VAN LATHEM, AND SIMON MARMION

Trivulzio Hours
Ghent, Antwerp, and Valenciennes, ca. 1470–75

MANUSCRIPT: 319 folios, 13.5 × 9 cm (5 5/16 × 3 1/2 in.); justification: 7.8 × 4.5 cm (3 1/16 × 1 3/4 in.); 16 lines of *bastarda* by Nicolas Spierinc; 28 full-page miniatures, 16 historiated initials

BINDING: Eighteenth century; gold-tooled red morocco

COLLECTION: The Hague, Koninklijke Bibliotheek, Ms. SMC1

PROVENANCE: Gian Giacomo Trivulzio, prince of Milan (1839–1902) (his Ms. 472); by descent to Luigi Alberico Trivulzio (1868–1938); private collection, the Netherlands; gift to the Koninklijke Bibliotheek in 2002

JPGM and RA

17a
VIENNA MASTER OF
MARY OF BURGUNDY
The Crucifixion, fol. 94v

17b
LIEVEN VAN LATHEM
The Mass of Saint Gregory,
fol. 103v

The three most talented artists who collaborated on the Vienna Hours of Mary of Burgundy (cat. no. 19) illuminated this book, while Nicolas Spierinc, the scribe of the Vienna Hours, wrote it. Simon Marmion, who illuminated only a single miniature in the Vienna Hours, here illuminated the entire Life of the Virgin cycle and the miniature of King David. The Vienna Master of Mary of Burgundy painted only *The Crucifixion* (ill. 17a). Lieven van Lathem

painted the remaining eighteen large miniatures—including those of the four Evangelists, an unusual sequence of masses to illustrate a cycle of the liturgical celebrations, and *Pentecost* (fol. 44v)—along with most, if not all, of the sixteen historiated initials in the suffrages. Here—as in the Vienna Hours and the Prayer Book of Charles the Bold (cat. no. 16), on which Spierinc and the Vienna Master also collaborated, and the Prayer Book of Philip the Good (Paris, Bibliothèque nationale de France, Ms. n. a. lat. 16428)—he was the main artist.

Marmion's cycle is distinctive because the compositions seem to reflect a pattern book. Nearly all of the nine miniatures are close siblings of the same subjects in the Berlaymont Hours (cat. no. 12), a key work of the 1470s whose links to a pattern book have already been demonstrated.[1] Such an extensive set of corresponding miniatures is completely unknown within Marmion's corpus. Between the related Trivulzio and Berlaymont cycles, the poses of the main protagonists are identical or at least similar, while their costumes are often quite different. Sometimes the architectural elements, such as the sheds in *The Nativity* and *The Adoration of the Magi*, also correspond closely. Moreover, though never identical, the landscapes are often similar, with many like components put together in corresponding ways. The landscapes in the Trivulzio Hours are

17c
LIEVEN VAN LATHEM
David in Prayer, fol. 248v

Figure 47
SIMON MARMION
David in Prayer. In the
Berlaymont Hours,
fol. 65 (see cat. no. 12)

somewhat more sophisticated, as a comparison between
the two versions of King David in prayer demonstrates. In
both versions (ill. 17c and fig. 47) the artist leads the eye over
David's shoulder gradually down a hillside to a lake. In the
Trivulzio version, however, the descent is more dramatic,
the transitions smoother, and the background itself more
picturesque and arresting. The format of the Trivulzio
miniatures is narrower than that found in the Berlaymont
Hours, resulting in intriguing differences in the configuration of space.

Van Lathem's cycle of miniatures illustrating the masses
that conclude each of the offices for the Days of the Week
is striking for including a male devout observing or in sup-
plication at the event (fols. 22v, 55v, 67v, 76v, 86v, 120v,
271v).[2] For the most part these figures wear the costumes
fashionable at the Burgundian court, though several different physical types are represented, suggesting that none
portrays the owner. This cycle is also distinctive for the spatially complex views of church interiors, as, for example, in
The Mass of Saint Gregory (ill. 17b) and *The Mass of the Virgin*
(fol. 120v). Here the artist leads the viewer through a
sequence of contiguous spaces, for example, from chapel to
choir or from nave and aisle to chapel. The glimpse of the
choir in the Pentecost miniature calls to mind the setting of
Mary of Burgundy (?) Reading Her Devotions in the Vienna

Hours (see fig. 65). The novel iconography anticipates a
subject that the Master of James IV of Scotland made popular: the image of the devout at prayer in a church, usually
at mass. Examples appear in the latter's Vatican Hours (cat.
no. 111), Lisbon prayer book (Museu Nacional de Arte
Antiga, Ms. 13), Rothschild Book of Hours (private collection), and other works.[3]

Van Lathem's *Trinity* (fol. 13v), *All Saints* (fol. 59v), *Virgin and Child with Musical Angels* (fol. 110v), *Saint John on
Patmos* (fol. 157v), and *Saint George and the Dragon* (fol. 128)
are all close variations on compositions in the Prayer Book
of Charles the Bold (cat. no. 16, fols. 10, 14, 18, 43, 67). The
versions in the book catalogued here are generally more
spacious and the effect more monumental. Many of the
splendid border vignettes are by Van Lathem or his assistants (ills. 17a, 17b). They feature such signature motifs of
the artist as comic dueling figures (fol. 159v), music-making
hybrids (fol. 44v), and monkeys mimicking humans (fols.
67v, 157v). They draw upon the same patterns as those in
Charles's prayer book but are not as vigorously drawn.

Like other miniatures by the Vienna Master of Mary of
Burgundy, especially in the eponymous hours, the magnificent *Crucifixion* echoes *The Crucifixion* in the Calvary
triptych of Joos van Ghent (see fig. 48) in many ways: the
swooning Virgin, her arms limp; the writhing figures on

the cross; the facial types, such as the man with the bifurcated white beard in the left foreground; and the brooding
sky. The figure of the crucified Christ, his chest heaving its
last breath, is virtually identical to that in the Vienna Hours
Crucifixion (ill. 19a). The composition, with a tight enfilade
of figures arranged along the right border, recalls features
of the Vienna Master in both the Alexander manuscript's
Alexander Takes the Hand of Roxanne (ill. 54a) and the Vienna
Hours *Crucifixion*.

The book offers few obvious indications of its original
patron or owner. The illustrated sequence of suffrages is
virtually identical to that found in the Vienna Hours, including Saint Bavo of Ghent and the unusual, colorful Saint
Ontcommer (Wilgefortis), the bearded woman whose cult
originated in Flanders in the fourteenth century.[4] This
striking link between the two manuscripts is perhaps an
indication that their patrons shared devotional interests.
The books' litanies and calendars, however, are not similar.
The one distinction between the two sets of suffrages is
that the Trivulzio Hours includes Saint Nicholas of Tolen-
tino after Nicholas of Bari. Thus the book may have been
made for a man named Nicholas.

The presence of Spierinc as scribe suggests that the
book was written in Ghent, but since its three major
illuminators almost certainly lived in three different towns,
the rest of the book was not necessarily all painted there.
The style of the book's miniatures falls chronologically
between the Prayer Book of Charles the Bold and the
Vienna Hours of Mary of Burgundy, so a date in the early
to mid-1470s seems likely. This is supported by the evidence
of costume. The tall, furry bowler-style hats worn or carried by some of the supplicants were out of fashion by the
mid-1470s. The split sleeves and padded shoulders of the
noble supplicant in *The Mass of the Virgin* (fol. 120v) are also
consistent with this dating.[5]   T. K.

Notes

1. Kren 1996: 211–16. I am grateful to Anne Korteweg for generously providing me with reproductions and a careful description of the
Trivulzio Hours.

2. One is lacking for the Mass for the Dead, between folios 39 and
40, while the example on folio 271v, in a separate section of the book,
illustrates the Office of the Dead.

3. Cf., e.g., Santos 1930: 26–27; Trenkler 1979.

4. Not only are the subjects of the suffrages virtually identical, but
the devotions themselves seem to be the same.

5. I am grateful to Margaret Scott for her research and analysis of
the dating of these costume elements, on which I have drawn extensively. She also pointed out that the hairstyles are longer in the frontispiece to Charles's Ordinance (cat. no. 64, fol. 5), which was painted
between 1473 and 1475, so that the Trivulzio Hours would appear to be
earlier in date.

18

VIENNA MASTER OF MARY OF BURGUNDY

Hours of Engelbert of Nassau
Dominican use
Ghent, mid-1470s and early 1480s

MANUSCRIPT: iii + 286 folios in 2 continuously foliated volumes
(vol. 1, 158 folios; vol. 2, 127 folios), 13.8 × 9.7 cm (5⁷⁄₁₆ × 3¹³⁄₁₆ in.),
justification: 7.1 × 4.2 cm (2¾ × 1⅝ in.); 14 lines of *bastarda* by
Nicolas Spierinc; 7 full-page miniatures, 31 half-page miniatures,
1 full-page hunting scene, and marginal vignettes

HERALDRY: Escutcheons with the arms of Philip the Handsome,
sometimes surmounted by helm and archducal coronet and encircled
by collar of the Order of the Golden Fleece, fols. 19v, 36, 42v, etc.;
motto of Engelbert of Nassau *Ce sera moy*, fol. 214; repeated letter *e*
filling borders, fol. 33, and on unicorn's trappings, fols. 96, 128, 132v,
141; birds holding initials GG in their beaks, fols. 151v, 158v, 269

INSCRIPTIONS: *l'ornay*, fol. 132v; *de la bibliothèque de Charles Adrien
Picard, 1767*, erased, fol. 1

BINDING: Nicolas-Denis Derôme (Derôme le Jeune), Paris, before
1788; gold-tooled dark blue morocco; the arms of the Paris family

COLLECTION: Oxford, Bodleian Library, Mss. Douce 219–20

PROVENANCE: Engelbert II, count of Nassau and Vianden
(1451–1504); Philip the Handsome, duke of Burgundy (1478–1506);
Charles Adrien Picard, by 1767 [his sale, Mérigot, Paris, January 31,
1780, lot 37]; to the Paris family [their sale, Edwards and Sons,
London, March 28, 1791, lot 15]; to the duke of Newcastle; Francis
Douce (1757–1834); his bequest, 1834

JPGM (Douce 220) and RA (Douce 219)

This book of hours represents one of the great achievements of Flemish manuscript illumination, the most
ambitious surviving pictorial cycle by the era's greatest illuminator, the Vienna Master of Mary of Burgundy. Despite
its modest dimensions, its narrative and pictorial scope place
it among the monuments of Flemish fifteenth-century
painting. The miniatures bring an epic character to biblical
narrative while simultaneously drawing the viewer close
to the events depicted.[1] The artist created a grand stage
for many of his stories, sometimes populating them with
seemingly endless, densely massed crowds (see ill. 18b and
fol. 74v). In their breadth and depth of space the miniatures
are a tour de force, a supreme expression of the illuminator's ability to depict the most complex narratives. The
artist could shift effortlessly from the intimate character of
a miniature showing the Virgin alone on her way to visit
Elizabeth, an unusual subject that is introduced between
The Annunciation and *The Visitation* (ill. 18a), to the grand
sweep of *The Last Judgment* (ill. 18b). The pictorial narratives include a Passion cycle of eight miniatures, a Life of
the Virgin cycle of sixteen miniatures, a King David cycle
of seven miniatures, and, in the bas-de-pages, separate
extended cycles devoted to falconing and a joust.

More than any of his other projects, the Engelbert
Hours shows the Vienna Master's prodigious range of
invention. His originality resides in such features as the
exquisitely observed anatomy in *The Last Judgment* and *The
Martyrdom of Saint Sebastian* (ill. 18c) as well as his expressive depictions of movement, exemplified by the Annunciate Virgin's graceful upper torso and, in the hunting
sequence of the bas-de-pages (fols. 47–68v), the superbly

18a
VIENNA MASTER OF
MARY OF BURGUNDY
The Visitation and *Mary
and Joseph at the Inn*,
fols. 114v–115

18b
VIENNA MASTER OF
MARY OF BURGUNDY
The Last Judgment and
David Wrestling a Bear,
fols. 181v–182

or rethinks some of its more unusual themes and motifs.[3] This means that the Engelbert Hours was probably executed in the mid-1470s.[4] The manuscript's illusionistic borders feature the new type of naturalistically painted flowers and insects on gold and colored grounds, along with others featuring peacock feathers, jewelry, seashells, pilgrimage medals, patterns of initials, or architectural niches with majolica or skulls. However, these borders of the new type are not part of the book as originally completed, which consisted of the script, a prior set of borders, and all of the miniatures.[5] The original borders were of the Ghent type associated with the 1470s, consisting of blue and gold acanthus with spray, raised gold dots, flowers, and birds. This type is found in a group of books written in Ghent for Margaret of York in the 1470s (cat. nos. 28, 29, 43). Most of the illusionistic borders were painted over this older type.[6] The new borders are comparable to those in the Berlin Hours of Mary of Burgundy and Maximilian (cat. no. 38), so they may have been added in the early 1480s.[7]

The borders appear to have been requested by Engelbert of Nassau; his motto, *Ce sera moy*, appears in an architectural niche border of the added type at the Office of the Dead along with his initial *e*, repeated in a checkerboard pattern, in a border added to the suffrage of Saint Sebastian (ill. 18c). This follows, given Engelbert's prominence in the Burgundian household and his military service to the ducal family.[8] There is also ample evidence of his arms being overpainted (fols. 16v, 182, 194, 197v, 200).[9] He may have presented the book to his liege Philip the Handsome, as the latter's arms were added in many places, including over some erased armorials that were probably Engelbert's.

Nevertheless, a question remains regarding the book's original owner. G. I. Lieftinck noted minute coats of arms, which have not been identified securely, on the collars of three hounds.[10] Perhaps Engelbert acquired the book from this person.[11] The fanciful jousting scene, however, which was certainly painted by the Vienna Master, features the caparison of a unicorn covered with the letter *e*, a pattern that anticipates the one added to the Saint Sebastian border for Engelbert himself. Is it possible that the book was originally made as a present for Engelbert and that he had it modernized not long after he received it? Engelbert had exquisite taste and acquired some of the most beautiful manuscripts of the time (see cat. no. 120).

Other features of the manuscript support the idea that Engelbert was the original owner. Certainly the manuscript was created for a knight, as the emphasis on Saints Sebastian and Christopher makes clear. The unusual narrative cycle of the life of King David emphasizes David's strength and his roles as both combatant and warrior. The chivalric interest of the David cycle is unquestionable, as is its appeal to rulers and their most influential lieutenants. The hunting and jousting sequences epitomize elements of the chivalric life, depicting the exalted pastimes of the Burgundian court. Finally, it is clear that both the book's brilliant scribe, Nicolas Spierinc, and the Vienna Master had enjoyed Charles the Bold's patronage, so one can imagine them working for a prominent aide to the duke. All this evidence still does not prove that Engelbert was the book's

drawn postures of the falconers and maidens. The Vienna Master brought immediacy and continuity to the narrative of the Virgin's life by inserting scenes that emphasize travel and movement. In addition to the scene of the Virgin on her way to visit Elizabeth are depictions of Mary and Joseph arriving at the inn (see ill. 18a), the three kings en route, and the soldiers pursuing the Christ child into Egypt. In pairing the solders' pursuit with the Flight into Egypt, the former miniature was surpisingly given the larger format. Figures viewed from behind in the immediate foreground help to draw in the viewer. The artist also employed axiality and subtle symmetries, such as the multiple pairings of frontal and rear views in *The Crucifixion*, to structure some of his compositions and the viewer's experience of them. Finally, he imbued his landscapes with extraordinarily variegated and picturesque terrain (see ill. 18a) and gave both rural and urban scenes a great depth of recession. Orthogonals are used for dramatic effect, providing some of the most emotionally charged narratives (*The Annunciation, Christ Led before Pilate, Ecce Homo, The Death of the Virgin*) with grand-scale settings. These very small miniatures are consistently conceived monumentally.[2]

The history of the book's execution is complex. The contemporary costumes featured in the falconing and jousting scenes date them to the 1470s. The sophisticated development of landscape and setting in the miniatures beyond that found in Duke Charles's Alexander manuscript (cat. no. 54), finished by 1470, and in *The Deposition* in Charles the Bold's prayer book (see ill. 16b), completed only a year or two later, indicates that the Engelbert Hours dates later than either one. Yet it probably precedes the Voustre Demeure Hours of ca. 1475–80 (cat. no. 20), which adapts

intended first owner. It could have been someone else in the household or circle of Burgundian dukes, but Engelbert remains a strong candidate, especially considering the use of the letter *e* in the joust scene.[12] Closer study of the book's distinctive iconography may offer further clues to the identity of its original patron.[13]

One piece of evidence that still requires explanation in relationship to the Engelbert identification is the book's French calendar. John Plummer reported that it strongly agrees with Perdrizet's Parisian calendar and with those of books of hours written in Paris.[14] The full calendar is fairly unusual in a Flemish book of hours, yet it appears in the Voustre Demeure Hours, another book written by Spierinc and illuminated by the Vienna Master or a follower. Since Spierinc resided in Ghent and the Vienna Master probably did too, the book was almost certainly created there.   T. K.

Notes

1. In two volumes today, the book may have been divided as late as the eighteenth century but was probably produced as one.

2. These features point to the modernity of this book's miniatures in their psychological and spatial dimensions. This is further illustrated by the miniature *The Martyrdom of Saint Sebastian*, whose pictorial sophistication and psychological subtlety are underscored by comparison with Hans Memling's two roughly contemporaneous versions of the subject (Paris, Musée du Louvre, and Brussels, Musées royaux des Beaux-Arts de Belgique). See Friedländer 1967–76, 6, pt. 1: no. 45, pl. 96, and Lorentz and Borchert in Paris 1995: 14.

3. These themes include Mary and Joseph at the inn, Saint Anthony Abbot with the lions, and the Agony in the Garden, in which Christ stretches his praying arms high into the sky.

4. Van Buren (in DOA 1996, 20: 724) argued that the costumes in the bas-de-page cycles point to a dating in the late 1470s. Margaret Scott suggested to me in conversation that a date in the mid-1470s would be consistent with the costumes depicted.

5. Alexander (1970: 13–14) noted that these borders were added.

6. Alexander (1970: 14, 92–93, pl. 27) pointed out that folios 181v–182 constitute an exception to this and that on folio 16v the outer margin has been cut off and replaced (see also Backhouse 1973b: 685).

7. Van Buren 1975: 288–89. An excellent analysis of the physical evidence of the book's production, along with a discussion of major literature on the subject, can be found in Backhouse 1973b.

8. He was a knight of the Golden Fleece.

9. Alexander 1970: 93, 97–99, pl. 27.

10. Fols. 50, 53, 56 (Lieftinck 1969: 380). Van Buren (1975: 289, n. 19) identified these with the Picard family Bollioud de Saint-Julien, but Alexander (1970: 9, pls. 45, 49, 63) doubted their authenticity.

11. Another unexplained piece of evidence, often connected to the book's mysterious first owner, is the appearance of sets of paired Gs (fols. 151v, 158v). While this might be a set of initials of the owner, it might also refer to Engelbert in another way, as the opposed letter *e* refers to Philip the Good. (These are commonly found in Philip's books; see Thomas M. 1976: 86, and Van Buren 1975: 289, n. 18.)

12. An alternate hypothesis might be that the Vienna Master returned in the early 1480s to add the jousting scenes, but some of the costumes in these vignettes were likely out of date by then.

13. Novel and compelling treatments of the life of David were particularly popular in Parisian books of hours around this time. See, for example, Kren 2002: 158–59, nn. 8, 9.

14. The litany has popular French saints such as Saints Denis, Maurice, Louis, and Martha, but none of these is particularly unusual in Flemish books of hours at this time. Plummer (report, Department of Manuscripts files, JPGM) found agreement with the Perdrizet calendar at 82.21 percent, with the Pierpont Morgan Library's book of hours by the Boucicaut Master and other artists (M.1004) at 78.70 percent, and with the Getty's book of hours by the Boucicaut Master and his workshop (Ms. 22) at 67.92 percent.

19

LIEVEN VAN LATHEM AND WORKSHOP, VIENNA MASTER OF MARY OF BURGUNDY, SIMON MARMION, AND WORKSHOP OF WILLEM VRELANT

Hours of Mary of Burgundy
Use of Rome
Ghent, Antwerp, Valenciennes, and Bruges(?), ca. 1470–75

MANUSCRIPT: 190 folios, 22.5 × 16.3 cm (8⅞ × 6⁷⁄₁₆ in.); justification: 11 × 7.5 cm (4⁵⁄₁₆ × 2¹⁵⁄₁₆ in.); 17 lines of *bastarda* by Nicolas Spierinc; 20 full-page miniatures, 16 quarter-page miniatures, 14 historiated initials, 24 calendar roundels, drolleries in the margins of most pages

COLLECTION: Vienna, Österreichische Nationalbibliothek, Ms. 1857

BINDING: Vienna, nineteenth century

PROVENANCE: Mary, duchess of Burgundy (?) (1457–1482); Emperor Matthias I (1557–1619); obtained by 1795

R A

For more than a century the Hours of Mary of Burgundy has rightly occupied a central position in the study of the great period of Flemish manuscript illumination that began in the 1470s. Three of its miniatures are seminal works: *Mary of Burgundy (?) Reading Her Devotions* (fig. 65), *Christ Nailed to the Cross* (fig. 17), and *The Crucifixion* (ill. 19a). They are the greatest paintings by the Vienna Master of Mary of Burgundy, who is named for this book, and the most ambitious and accomplished miniatures of their day. In these works the conventions of miniature and border are integrated in a way that had no equal previously or subsequently.[1] The rest of the book, which represents an older tradition, is ambitious and innovative on its own terms. The book as a whole merits greater attention, not only for this reason but also because the Vienna Master's collaborations reveal so much about the working methods of the time.

As is the case with the Trivulzio Hours (cat. no. 17), the Prayer Book of Charles the Bold (cat. no. 16), and perhaps the Voustre Demeure Hours (cat. no. 20), this book represents a collaboration among the Vienna Master, Lieven van Lathem, and the scribe Nicolas Spierinc.[2] As in all but the last of the three examples, Van Lathem was the lead artist. In the Vienna Hours he and members of his workshop illuminated the brilliant cycle of small roundels in the calendar, the half-page Evangelist miniatures, six of the full-page miniatures in the Passion cycle of the Hours of the Virgin (ill. 19b), and all but one of the historiated initials in the parallel cycle of the life of the Virgin that appears on facing pages to the full-page miniatures. He also provided a full-page miniature and facing historiated initial in other major openings, such as the Hours of the Holy Spirit, the Penitential Psalms, and the Office of the Dead.[3]

The ambitious Passion cycle is not entirely from Van Lathem's hand. There are two miniatures by the Vienna Master: *The Road to Calvary* (fol. 94v), in which Van Lathem may have played a role, and *The Crucifixion*. In addition, *The Agony in the Garden* (fol. 56v), illustrating Matins of the Hours of the Virgin, lacks the fluid brushwork and lively color characteristic of Van Lathem. His best miniatures in the cycle include *Christ Led before Pilate* (see ill. 19b) and *The Flagellation* (fol. 89v). *The Agony in the Garden* (fol. 56v) is no

19a
VIENNA MASTER
OF MARY OF
BURGUNDY
The Crucifixion,
fol. 99v

Figure 48
JOOS VAN GHENT
The Crucifixion, central
panel of the Calvary
Triptych, ca. 1465.
Oil on wood panel,
216 × 170 cm (85 1/16
× 66 15/16 in.). Ghent,
Saint Bavo Cathedral

less detailed but duller in its palette and more linear in the treatment of faces, hands, and feet.[4] Otto Pächt and Dagmar Thoss called its style "unclassifiable,"[5] but it seems to have been painted under the influence of Van Lathem himself. Finally, there is a variable level of quality in Van Lathem's own execution, which becomes apparent when one compares miniatures within the Passion cycle or in the sequence of drolleries in the border and bas-de-page which extend for the length of the book.[6]

The book has long been considered a complex production. It was possibly executed in stages, given the exaggerated number of illuminators long thought to have participated, shifts in the character of decorated borders, modifications to borders, peculiarities of the collation, and the striking contrast between the style of the Vienna Master and those of the other artists, along with the placement of his miniatures.[7] Yet the book's genesis was probably neither as problematic nor as discontinuous as this evidence suggests. As noted, Van Lathem, Spierinc, and the Vienna Master collaborated on other occasions, and the three of them also collaborated previously with Simon Marmion (see cat. no. 17), who contributed one miniature to this book. Moreover, the Vienna Master was called upon consistently to execute Passion subject matter, so his engagement on the full-page miniatures here, seemingly randomly chosen, may reflect the choice of Van Lathem or of a patron, based on an appreciation of the illuminator's talents (see ills. 16b, 16c, 17a, and cat. no. 16, fol. 71).[8]

The book's countless drolleries, all by Van Lathem and his workshop, constitute one of the most ambitious and distinctive programs of such vignettes at this time.[9] Van Lathem probably did not execute all of them, but even those that appear to be by assistants are derived largely from his designs.[10] The finest, almost certainly by him, are the colorful bas-de-page motifs in the calendar, which were drawn and modeled with great refinement and attention to detail.[11] Many of the bas-de-pages of the remaining text pages feature finely drawn angels, beasts, wild men and women, hunters, farmers, prelates, beggars, musicians, gymnasts, jugglers, and courtly ladies-in-waiting. The ape parodies of human behavior are particularly amusing and were influential (see cat. nos. 36, 49).[12] An intriguing feature of the border decorations is that Van Lathem or a workshop member collaborated with other illuminators on the same page, sometimes on the same border.[13]

Marmion painted the full-page miniature *Virgin and Child with Musical Angels* (fol. 35v). With its elaborate gilt throne of Gothic tracery, it is a variation on a composition in the Berlaymont Hours from the same period (cat. no. 12, fol. 20). The workshop of Willem Vrelant contributed a single small initial *D* with *The Throne of Mercy* (fol. 51) and the border on the same page, the only one of its type in the book. Van Lathem may have illuminated the unusual half-length *Apocalyptic Virgin and Child* (fol. 24), which is perhaps derived from a Rogierian model filtered through a miniature by Vrelant.[14] The facial type of the angels and their drapery, wings, and hair are reminiscent of the work of Van Lathem, who also painted the more characteristic (for him) border vignettes.

The book's devotions are largely conventional, but the treatment of those in the front of the book is unusual in a number of ways. A sequence of devotions, including the Marian prayers ("Obsecro te" and "O Intemerata," fols. 20–27) that often appear later in the book, are placed close to the beginning. Moreover, the first text, an account of Saint Thomas Becket's vision of the Virgin and Child, is rare. It is illustrated by the extraordinary frontispiece miniature *Mary of Burgundy (?) Reading Her Devotions* (fig. 65). The patron's inclusion in the miniature and her physical prominence in relation to the Virgin and Child underscore the importance of this text. The front section, which starts with the calendar and continues through the Gospel extracts (fols. 2–34), is distinguished by another unusual feature. On these pages the parchment within the text block is painted black, while the script is in white and gold.[15] From folio 36 to the end, the text block assumes the traditional form of brown script on unstained prepared parchment, but with a number of rubrics in white or gold on black. The reason for the sudden switch is unclear, unless it was to underscore the importance of the opening devotions.

Given the striking prominence of the beautiful girl in prayer on folio 14v, the identity of the book's patron has long been a topic of debate. W. H. James Weale and others have endeavored to show that the book is the documented one written on black parchment for Charles the Bold in 1466 and later illuminated by Philippe de Mazerolles, but most scholars have rejected that notion.[16] Yet even when

the view held sway, scholars considered the young woman dressed in the garb of the Burgundian court to be Charles's daughter Mary. Antoine de Schryver, in arguing decisively against identifying the book with the document of 1466, suggested that Mary herself was perhaps the intended owner.[17] Since then Pächt and Thoss, Anne van Buren, and Bodo Brinkmann have all argued that the book was made for Margaret of York, Mary's stepmother.[18] This is based largely on the inclusion and prominence of the text of the vision of Becket. Brinkmann went further, suggesting that the setting of the accompanying miniature features at the east end of the choir a chapel conceived in a more typically English architectural idiom that would have been familiar to Margaret and included to suit her tastes.[19] Little else points to Margaret, however, and since nearly all of her other books from this period featured her arms or motto, it would be surprising for such an elaborate book to lack them.[20] The female devout in the Vienna Master's miniature, admittedly an idealized depiction, has the character of an adolescent more than that of a woman in her middle or late twenties, so it makes more sense to identify the figure with the young Mary than with her stepmother.[21] Nevertheless, even this evidence is circumstantial and the present interpretation but a hypothesis.

The litany, suffrages, and rather full calendar show a predominance of well-known saints from Flanders and northern France—especially the dioceses of Utrecht, Tournai, and Cambrai—although in the calendar, for example, few of these are actually highlighted. One that does appear in gold is Saint Lievin (November 13), a saint with strong ties to Ghent. Saint Amalberga, another distinctively Ghent saint, appears in the litany, while Saint Bavo, who has a long association with Ghent, is found in the illustrated suffrages, although he more commonly appears in the calendar. Whether these inclusions indicate that Ghent was the location of production—Spierinc resided there, and the Vienna Master probably did, too—or that Ghent was the residence of its intended patron, or both, is hard to say.[22]

The book has generally been dated to the second half of the 1470s on the theory that the new-style Flemish border,[23] a variation of which is found on folio 99v, first appeared around this time and on the basis of the book's association with Charles and Mary.[24] This does not preclude a somewhat earlier dating, however, which is suggested (though not dictated) by the fact that Van Lathem, the Vienna Master, and Spierinc had been collaborating since the early 1470s (see cat. no. 16). A dating in the mid-1470s (or even earlier) is further suggested by the profound connection of *Christ Nailed to the Cross* and *The Crucifixion* to Joos van Ghent's Calvary Triptych of the late 1460s (see fig. 48).[25]

T. K.

Notes

1. The historical place of these miniatures is analyzed in greater detail in the introduction to part 2 of this volume and in the biography of the Vienna Master of Mary of Burgundy.

2. Two leaves from a book of hours in Berlin (Kupferstichkabinett, nos. 1754, 1755) may result from another collaboration among Van Lathem, the Vienna Master, and Spierinc (Lieftinck 1969: figs. 56, 57).

3. In the openings for the Mass of the Virgin and the Hours of the Cross, he painted only the historiated initials.

4. *The Deposition* and *The Entombment* are much closer in execution to the best miniatures in the Passion cycle—*Christ Led before Pilate*, *The Crowning with Thorns*, and *The Flagellation*—but they are more awkward and less expressive than these, perhaps the result of the artist working more rapidly and less carefully.

5. "Kann keinem bestimmten Stil zugeordnet werden"; Pächt and Thoss 1990: 81. They correctly group with this miniature the vignettes in the borders of the same leaf and the facing page. They are also right in thinking that the historiated initial on the facing page, *The Annunciation*, is not by Van Lathem.

6. This is also apparent in the miniatures in the Van Lathem style in the Prayer Book of Charles the Bold, most strikingly between the first and second campaigns of the book but even within the first campaign.

7. Winkler 1915: 304–6; Pächt 1948: 64; Van Buren 1993: 1189; de Schryver (1969a: 159), by contrast, believed that the book was completed relatively quickly.

8. *Christ Nailed to the Cross* is a relatively unusual subject to illustrate the Hours of the Cross, but its popularity had grown in Flemish art. Van Lathem himself had employed it earlier in his career for one of his finest miniatures in the Sachsenheim Hours (Stuttgart, Würtembergisches Landesmuseum, Ms. brev. 162, fol. 26; Wolf (E.) 1996: 48–53, pl. 1). Since the Vienna Master was treating *The Crucifixion*, the traditional illustration for the Hours of the Cross, elsewhere in the Hours of the Virgin, *Christ Nailed to the Cross* was a reasonable alternative to illustrate it.

9. He also illuminated the other major example from this time (cat. no. 16).

10. Pächt and Thoss (1990: 83, figs. 62, 63) pointed out the links in subject matter and style to the drolleries in a book of hours that

Van Lathem decorated in collaboration with the Master of Catherine of Cleves (The Hague, Museum Meermanno-Westreenianum, Ms. 10 F 50).

11. Also particularly beautiful are other drolleries toward the front of the book, such as those from folios 15 to 30, though the quality is generally good from front to back.

12. The ape parodies and hybrids found in this book are also common in the Trivulzio Hours (cat. no. 17). The lovely winged griffins and hybrids also appear in the Prayer Book of Charles the Bold (cat. no. 16). Pächt and Thoss (1990: 83) noted that the ape subjects are also found in the Dutch book of hours for which Van Lathem furnished some drolleries (see note 10).

13. In the short sequence of suffrages (fols. 116–20) illustrated with small miniatures by the Vienna Master, drolleries like those elsewhere in the book appear in the borders, illuminated mostly by Van Lathem and his workshop. The figures of angels in the borders of folios 121, 121v, 122, and 123 must, however, be by the Vienna Master. Further, certain of the miniatures in this cycle, such as *Saint George and the Dragon*, look as though they were designed or conceived by Van Lathem but executed by the Vienna Master. In the full-page *Annunciation* (fol. 19v) Van Lathem seems to have painted the right side of the miniature while the Vienna Master painted the angel Gabriel and perhaps most of the left side, also supplying the figure of the prophet in the border (see also Brinkmann 1997: 25–26). Van Lathem or a member of his workshop painted the musical angels in the border of the single miniature by Marmion (fol. 35v) (Pächt and Thoss 1990: 80). The miniatures in the suffrages have been attributed to the Master of Mary of Burgundy since Winkler (1915: 286). Two small historiated initials in grisaille (fols. 15, 16v) are also by the Vienna Master.

14. Winkler (1915: 290, n. 1) first suggested the Rogierian source. An example that shows a virtually identical type of the Christ child and a similar Virgin, but in mirror image, is in the Musée des Beaux-Arts, Brussels, no. 667 (as Rogierian; Friedländer 1967–76, 2: 83, pl. 108a).

15. Several other examples show them in calendars of Flemish books of hours from the last quarter of the fifteenth century: Budapest, National Széchényi Library, Ms. lat. 396 (Soltész 1985), and excollection Heribert Tenschert (König 1991: 270–302).

16. Weale 1872–73a: 111–19; Winkler 1915: 279–81, 304–6; Pächt 1948: 64.

17. In Unterkircher and de Schryver 1969: 23–33. See also Van Buren 1975: 294–95.

18. Pächt and Thoss 1990: 69–70; Van Buren 1993: 1189–90; Brinkmann 1997: 22–24.

19. Brinkmann 1997: 23–24. Brinkmann also pointed out that the only other example of the text of Becket's vision appears in a book of hours for the use of Sarum.

20. Thus, as Van Buren has suggested, the book may have been commissioned by Margaret as a present to Mary, to whom she was close (1993: 1189–90). See also Inglis 1995: 14–16.

21. Moreover, a long-standing iconographic tradition suggests that a figure shown reading his or her devotions before the Virgin in a miniature is also the book's intended owner. Following this interpretation, the courtly, devout couple shown inside the church may represent or allude to Mary's father and stepmother.

22. Both Margaret of York and Mary resided in Ghent from late 1474. The suffrages also include another uncommon saint, the apocryphal bearded female martyr Ontcommer (Wilgefortis or Uncumber). She is included in the calendar (February 4) as well but not highlighted (her feast day is normally July 20). She is also included in the nearly identical sequence of illustrated suffrages in the Trivulzio Hours.

23. For a discussion of the dating of the earliest borders of the new style, see the introduction to part 2 of this volume.

24. Pächt (1948: 64) dated the miniatures he ascribed to the Vienna Master ca. 1480; de Schryver, in Unterkircher and de Schryver 1969: 159, as ca. 1475–77; Pächt and Thoss 1990: 69, as late 1470s; Inglis 1995: 16, as late 1470s.

25. Moreover, Margaret Scott (1980: 176–78) has argued that the elegant dress on the figure of Mary of Burgundy (fol. 14v) is closer in style to the fashion of the late 1460s than to that of the late 1470s.

20a
VIENNA MASTER OF
MARY OF BURGUNDY (?)
*The Disputation of Saint
Barbara,* Berlin album,
no. 18

20b
VIENNA MASTER OF
MARY OF BURGUNDY (?)
*The Martyrdom of Saint
Barbara,* fol. 48

20

VIENNA MASTER OF MARY OF BURGUNDY
AND/OR WORKSHOP/FOLLOWERS, SIMON
MARMION, MASTER OF THE DRESDEN PRAYER
BOOK, AND LIEVEN VAN LATHEM

Voustre Demeure Hours
Use of Rome
Ghent, ca. 1475–80

MANUSCRIPT: i + 298 folios, 13.1 × 9.2 cm (5⅛ × 3⅝ in.); justification:
6.5 × 4.5 cm (2⁹⁄₁₆ × 1¾ in.); 15 lines of *bastarda* by Nicolas Spierinc;
2 half-page miniatures, 20 small miniatures or historiated initials,
5 historiated borders, 24 small calendar miniatures

HERALDRY: Motto *voustre demeure*, fols. 129, 144; two(?) initials, the left
black, the right white, readable as *v, n,* or *ii,* inside decorated initials,
fols. 50, 114, 144, etc.

INSCRIPTIONS: *1513* in right border, fol. 14; letter *L* added in lower right
corner of miniature, fol. 238

BINDING: Fifteenth(?) century; green leather over beech boards
covered with green silk velvet; missing central metalwork; yellow
silk flyleaves; gilt edges

COLLECTION: Madrid, Biblioteca Nacional, Ms. Vit. 25-5

PROVENANCE: Cardinal Zelada (1717–1801); to the Chapter of the
Cathedral, Toledo

JPGM and RA

Album of Miniatures from the Voustre Demeure Hours

MANUSCRIPT: 20 folios, 13.2 × 9.5 cm (5⁵⁄₁₆ × 3¾ in.); 20 full-page
miniatures trimmed to their outer borders and pasted on modern
parchment

HERALDRY: Initials *CM* (for Charles the Bold and Margaret of York)
twice on carpet in miniature of the Elevation of the Host, fol. 16,
initials appearing to be original

INSCRIPTIONS: Letter *L* added to nine miniatures; *AD* added to two
miniatures

COLLECTION: Berlin, Staatliche Museen zu Berlin, Kupferstichkabinett,
Ms. 78 B 13

PROVENANCE: Alexander Hamilton, tenth duke of Hamilton (1767–
1852) (no. 437); to the Prussian state in 1882

JPGM and RA

The Pietà
Miniature from the Voustre Demeure Hours

One full-page miniature, 11.9 × 8.9 cm (4¹¹⁄₁₆ × 3½ in.); back: blank

COLLECTION: Philadelphia, Philadelphia Museum of Art, no. 343

PROVENANCE: [Böhler, Munich]; John G. Johnson, ca. 1910; bequeathed
1917 to the City of Philadelphia (housed at the Philadelphia Museum
of Art since 1933)

JPGM

This small manuscript originally contained only twenty-
two or twenty-three full-page miniatures[1] to go with
its two half-page miniatures, five historiated borders, and
various smaller miniatures. The book is now divided, with
the full-page miniatures kept in an album in Berlin, while
the remaining illumination and the text are in the original
codex in Madrid. Despite its modest size, the Voustre
Demeure Hours is one of the most innovative books of the
new style of Flemish illumination.[2] This results from the
sophistication of the miniatures, the pictorially dramatic
way some are paired with historiated borders, and the
sculptural and spacious character of the decorated borders.

20c
VIENNA MASTER OF
MARY OF BURGUNDY (?)
The Crucifixion, Berlin
album, no. 10

20d
SIMON MARMION
The Pietà

The major illuminators involved are Simon Marmion, Lieven van Lathem, and the Vienna Master of Mary of Burgundy and/or his workshop or followers. Some artists painted miniatures based on models created by other artists in this group. And in a number of openings, miniatures by one artist face illumination by another.

The largest and most important group of miniatures is one we associate with the Vienna Master of Mary of Burgundy and his assistants or followers: a total of fourteen full-page miniatures, two half-page miniatures, five historiated borders, and the small miniatures and historiated initials.[3] The celebrated Passion border unfolds from the Entry into Jerusalem to the Ecce Homo behind a text suspended illusionistically from cords bound to the edge of the painted image.[4] The eloquent *Crucifixion* (ill. 20c), originally opposite it, hovers within an ellipse like a bright vision over the nocturnal *Agony in the Garden* and *The Betrayal of Christ*. The illuminator situated the *Agony* and the *Betrayal* in the border and bas-de-page, but they fill much of the page. He integrated them pictorially with the looming *Crucifixion* in an entirely original and moving manner. The distinct scenes are melded by nuances of hue and value and by the flecklike brushwork that gives the entire image an unusual velvety texture. In a particularly novel and touching vignette, the artist shows the troubled Christ returning to the apostles as they gently and absently emerge from their slumber.[5]

Forming the first opening after the calendar, this pair of leaves made a powerful introduction to the book's devotions. Four other historiated borders would have been combined with full-page miniatures to create additional highlights throughout the book.[6] These include the full-page, borderless *Disputation of Saint Barbara* (ill. 20a), opposite a historiated border with scenes from her martyrdom (ill. 20b). The *Disputation* offers a setting that is both intimate and spacious, rendered in muted grays and browns yet crisply detailed. Behind Saint Barbara a large palace stands beside a lagoon. Her tower, the topic of her discourse, is under construction behind the philosophers, her brightly dressed antagonists. A massive church and a city gate appear in the distance, and blocks of stone, presumably related to the tower's construction, line the immediate foreground. The importance of this miniature in the book's program is underscored not only by its originality and its large size but also by the placement of its suffrage toward the front of the book, before all but one of the others.[7]

The treatment of the settings is surprisingly novel in other miniatures, such as *The Mass of Saint Gregory*, a poetic interpretation of a stolid subject. The artist emphasizes the elevation of the high altar in the church choir. A candle-bearing acolyte stands on the other side of the altar and several steps beneath it, while the base of the columns on the other side also reaches well below it. Meanwhile the youthful praying cardinal seems oddly placed; his gaze turns away from the vision of Christ. Yet his body's awkward pose, tilted forward, focuses the eye on the cavernous church beyond, drawing the viewer into it.[8] *The Mass of the Dead* has both a dignity and an intimacy often lacking in renditions of the subject (see ill. 20e). In fact, the figures and furnishings are closely based on a composition by Van Lathem (cat. no. 17 and fig. 49). At the same time, the copyist eliminated several figures, gave focused expression to the central figure of the priest, and simplified the church setting, achieving a concentration and psychological clarity atypical of Van Lathem. *The Flight into Egypt*, with figures also based on an older pattern,[9] features a sun-drenched landscape whose sky, filled with billowing clouds, is laced with golden light.[10] Despite the pervasive naturalism, the artist has subtly enveloped the Virgin in a golden supernatural light via the coloring of the mound behind her passing donkey. In *The Adoration of the Magi* all three kings are viewed in three-quarters from behind, a rare device. It heightens the focus on the Virgin, who occupies the visual center of a large circle described by the inward-gazing figures of Joseph, the standing Magi, and the shepherds seen in the window.

Although these miniatures were long regarded as a major late work of the Master of Mary of Burgundy, G. I. Lieftinck along with some others questioned whether they were all by this artist, and indeed whether any miniatures other than the Passion border and *The Disputation of Saint Barbara* were by him.[11] Bodo Brinkmann, in reducing the corpus of the artist and renaming him the Vienna Master of Mary of Burgundy, omitted these miniatures from his body of work.[12] Yet it is clear that the Saint Barbara miniature has many of the characteristics of the work of the Vienna Master, especially the facial types of the saint's antagonists—with their distinctive beards, strong cheeks, and long, straight noses—and the care given to individualizing the faces in a crowd. Certain details of costume—such as the robe of gold brocade over a dress with velvet sleeves,[13] the hats with tall fur brims, the rich red or blue cloth caps, and the soft boots—are common in his work going as far back as the Paris Alexander manuscript (cat. no. 54). The saturated colors of the costumes are used to make the figures stand out from the setting, a technique employed by the Vienna Master of Mary of Burgundy.

Nevertheless, in this manuscript young women's faces are flatter and plainer than those in earlier miniatures by the Vienna Master. While the *Crucifixion* departs from the *Saint Barbara* in its brushwork and facial types, it has other hallmarks of the Vienna Master's style: the internalized yet powerful emotions of Christ and Saint John, the finely articulated body of the nude Christ on the cross, the subtle handling of torchlight and nocturnal effects, and the sleeves that extend beyond arm's length. The handling of landscape—including the gently reflective stream, the use of different greens to define spatial recession, and the role of trees and other natural growth in it—finds a close parallel in miniatures by the artist from the Engelbert Hours (cat. no. 18).[14] Likewise the facing border with Passion scenes, though not always as subtle as the illumination in the Engelbert Hours, echoes it in the handling of crowds, specific postures, and details of costume. In its acutely observed rendition of the male nude, along with the figures' gestures of despair, the border with hell (see ill. 20e) is comparable to the Engelbert *Last Judgment* (ill. 18b). If not actually representative of a later phase of the Vienna Master's art,

these miniatures strongly show his influence. Moreover, familiar motifs of his work repeatedly show up throughout the other miniatures.[15]

The variety of facial types and compositions in the rest of the series—including works such as *The Mass of Saint Gregory, The Mass of the Dead*, and *The Adoration of the Magi*—may result from workshop collaboration, a liberal use of patterns from diverse sources, or collaboration with a still unidentified master.[16] What many of the miniatures share, even when individual passages or motifs betray some awkwardness, is a sustained level of invention and exploration—especially of light effects, landscape, and interior space—that secures the book's position not only in the history of Flemish book illumination but also in the language of Flemish painting.

Marmion executed only full-page miniatures—*The Virgin and Child, Noli me tangere, The Ascension*, and *The Raising of Lazarus*—in the Voustre Demeure Hours. Georges Hulin de Loo rightly suggested that Marmion's *Pietà* now in Philadelphia once belonged to the book, too, though it is the only miniature in the cycle with a gold background (ill. 20d).[17] The subject of the pietà is common to the second half of Marmion's career. This version may have been the most influential of his many treatments of the subject. The figure of the dead Christ rises stiffly from the lap of the Virgin, his thin arms meekly crossed. The latter motif is likely an awkward adaptation of the physiognomically similar Man of Sorrows in Marmion's diptych pietà (Strasbourg, Musée de la Ville), which tightly fills the frame and more dramatically confronts the viewer. As in the diptych, the heads of both Christ and the Virgin incline toward each other, and the figures appear before a gold ground modeled with parallel hatching that offers a suggestion of a shallow space behind the figures. In the *Pietà* in La Flora (see cat. no. 93), Marmion relieved some of the stiffness by allowing Christ's proper right arm to rest on the frame, as in the diptych. He also tilted the Virgin's head in the opposite direction and added a landscape, without entirely omitting the gold backdrop.[18]

Although Eva Wolf does not agree,[19] it seems likely that Van Lathem, a regular collaborator of the Vienna Master of Mary of Burgundy (e.g., in cat. nos. 16, 17, 19), painted *The Annunciation* and *The Visitation* as well as providing the design for *The Mass of the Dead*.[20] If this is correct, then these are the latest miniatures from his hand. The Master of the Dresden Prayer Book illuminated most, if not all, of the twenty-four calendar miniatures.[21] Some display great originality in reducing the role of staffage so dramatically that the figures are barely visible. Here the subject is the landscape itself—its climatic character, its textures, and its mood.[22] The script may be attributed to Nicolas Spierinc, the brilliant Ghent scribe.

Hulin de Loo suggested that the book was made for a woman on the grounds that the motto *Voustre demeure* has the character of a woman's motto and that the suffrage and splendid miniature for Saint Barbara are prominently placed. This thesis is supported by the prominence of four women among the suffrages; Saint Catherine also has a full-page miniature. Other books executed in the late 1470s

and 1480s (see cat. nos. 32, 33, 37) give one or the other of these saints particular distinction either within the devotional sequence or within the decorative program, though they were not necessarily illuminated for women. Perhaps more revealing for the book's origins are the Mass for Saint Benigne and the initials *C* and *M en lac* on the carpet in *The Mass of the Dead*. Benigne was particularly venerated by the Burgundians and was associated with Dijon. The initials *C* and *M* probably refer to the duke and duchess, as their initials often appear in this form, even though the book was not made for them. It was probably made for an individual attached to the court with the aforementioned device,[23] perhaps a member of the Guild of Saint Barbara in Ghent, to which Margaret belonged from 1472. Does the presence of the initials of the duke and duchess constitute evidence that the book was completed before 1477 (or under way by then)?

Some parallels to the distinctive illusionistic borders are evident in the Register of the Guild of Saint Anne (cat. no. 23), which was in progress at the beginning of 1477. The Voustre Demeure Hours features a text block that is framed on three sides by branches, as on folio 3 of the register (fig. 53 and ill. 23).[24] The alternation of white acanthus with naturally colored flowers common in the Voustre Demeure Hours is also found in the register (fol. 2v), where in one border the acanthus curls back in a symmetrical pattern much as it does in this volume (fol. 41).[25] The stylistic links to the register and Margaret's breviary (cat. no. 22) confirm that the Voustre Demeure Hours dates from around the same period.[26]   T. K.

Notes

1. Likely missing among the full-page miniatures is one to accompany the suffrage of Saint Anthony and perhaps one to accompany the Mass of the Nativity. The Gospel sequence for Saint John the Evangelist is also lacking a miniature, but it is not clear that it was full-page.

2. Brinkmann (1997: 185–91) has convincingly reconstructed its original program, from a proposal by Lieftinck (1969: 98–105).

3. Berlin, Kupferstichkabinett, nos. 4, 5, 6, 7, 8, 10, 12, 13, 14, 15, 16, 17, 18, 19; Madrid, Biblioteca Nacional, Ms. Vit. 25-5, fols. 214, 238; 14, 48, 68, 191, 238; and 41, 44, 45, 49, 59v, 86, 97, 104, 144, 185, 186, 188, 189, 190, 192, 193, 194, 196, 197, 208.

4. Madrid, Biblioteca Nacional, Ms. Vit. 25-5, fol. 14.

5. In subtle ways the very sketchy *Agony in the Garden* added to the Prayer Book of Charles the Bold (ill. 16c) by the workshop of the Vienna Master anticipates features of this composition, including the posture of Christ with arms raised high, the sleeping disciple with his face in his hand, the use of foliage to screen this scene from that with the approaching soldiers, and the use of golden highlights to articulate the group of soldiers.

6. Madrid, Biblioteca Nacional, Ms. Vit. 25-2, fols. 48, 68, 191, 238.

7. The other, dedicated to Saint Apollonia, is illustrated with a small miniature.

8. This composition probably served as the model for a pattern, yet none of the other versions (see, for example, cat. no. 93, fol. 307v) is as successful as this one in conveying the church's imposing scale.

9. A book of hours with miniatures from around the 1470s and influenced by both Van Lathem and Marmion contains a *Flight into Egypt* with figures based on the same design (Oxford, Bodleian Library, Ms. Gough 15, fol. 59; Pächt and Alexander 1966–73, 1: 26, no. 353, pl. 27).

10. Hulin de Loo (1939b: 177) emphasized the quality of the landscape in *The Annunciation to the Shepherds*.

11. Lieftinck 1969: 92–93.

12. Brinkmann 1997: 190–91; Brinkmann 1998: 139–43.

13. In the miniature *Alexander Founding Alexandria* in the Paris Alexander manuscript (cat. no. 54, fol. 195v), Alexander is shown wearing a similar gold brocade robe with green velvet sleeves.

14. Especially *The Virgin Going to Visit Elizabeth* (fol. 98) and *The Visitation* (fol. 114v).

15. The distinctive profile and rumpled garment of the acolyte viewed from the back closely reflect characteristics of the small child in the foreground of the Vienna *Crucifixion*, while the massing of the souls in the middle distance of *The Last Judgment*, an otherwise Marmionesque miniature, recalls the souls in the middle distance of the Engelbert Hours *Last Judgment*. The pose of the king kneeling before the Virgin in *The Adoration of the Magi* resembles the pose of the male supplicant before the Virgin in the Vienna *Mary of Burgundy (?) Reading Her Devotions*.

16. A number of other miniatures seem to reflect the input of several artists. Both *The Coronation of the Virgin* and *The Last Judgment* show compositional and figure types associated with Marmion yet were painted by an artist in the Vienna Master group.

17. Hulin de Loo 1939b; Brinkmann (1997: 188, n. 155) proposed that it could illustrate the Stabat Mater (fol. 64). The leaf's dimensions, trimmed of any painted border or fictive frame that may have existed, closely approximate those of Marmion's other miniatures in this book (only slightly less tightly trimmed). Most telling, the pattern of red hatching modeling the upper edge of the *Pietà* curves up and inward along the central axis, suggesting that the miniature originally culminated in a short peak. Thus, although it is currently trimmed, it likely appeared similar to two of the Marmion miniatures with the unusual peak in the Berlin-Madrid manuscript.

18. The placement of Christ's arms in the Huth version anticipates this development, while the tilt of the Virgin's head most closely resembles the Philadelphia version. The Huth *Pietà* is likely from the artist's workshop, as it displays weaker drawing and modeling of the anatomy, but it may nevertheless represent an intermediate stage between the Philadelphia and La Flora versions. A small, badly damaged painting, described in a sales catalogue as tempera on panel, copies closely the type of the Philadelphia Virgin with her tightly clasped hands and the type of Christ, though his head turns a bit away from her. It is known to me only in reproduction and from a photograph, but it appears to be a workshop piece; 20.5 × 13 cm (8⅛ × 5⅛ in.), Sotheby's, New York, January 17, 1985, lot 29. A Flemish miniature by the Master of Antoine Rolin (Baltimore, Walters Art Gallery, W. 431, fol. 77v), apparently based on the Philadelphia composition, departs from it mainly in also using the motif of Christ's arm resting on the lower edge of the miniature (Legaré 1992: 215, fig. 201). A faithful but broadly painted Flemish copy of the Philadelphia miniature is currently pasted into a book of hours from Zwolle with a figure of John the Evangelist introduced behind the figure of Christ (Brussels, Bibliothèque royale, Ms. IV 858, see Brussels 1975: 1 [ill.], 92–94).

19. Wolf (E.) 1996: 316.

20. In *The Annunciation* the church interior, the drapery of both the angel and the Virgin, and even the angel's wing are typical of Van Lathem, but Brinkmann is likely correct that the face of Gabriel was repainted. It is much closer to the long, flat, small-featured faces found elsewhere in the book, such as the face of Saint Barbara. The angel in *The Visitation* is very close to that in Van Lathem's *Saint John on Patmos* in the Trivulzio Hours (cat. no. 17, fol. 157v).

21. See Brinkmann 1997: 191–94, for the history of the cycle's attribution.

22. See esp. Brinkmann's (1997: 191–94) analysis.

23. Cf. Hulin de Loo 1939b: 177.

24. On the register border the trunk itself is inhabited, as is often the case in the Voustre Demeure Hours (Ms. Vit. 25-5, fol. 56).

25. The Voustre Demeure Hours features some of the most distinctive and dramatic examples of the illusionistic borders of the school. They include some unusual motifs, thicker and heavier naturalia (not just branches but also trunks and roots), and also denser acanthus rendered more sculpturally. The scale is magnified by the inclusion of very small figures located at the bases of the trunks and among the roots. Many of the full borders feature deep shadows that rake across the painted areas, dividing the borders sharply into lighter and darker areas, enhancing the illusions of space behind the text block. The book has a preponderance of borders with dark gray and blue grounds.

26. Still, the Voustre Demeure Hours is a bit later in date than the breviary (see cat. no. 22). Lieftinck (1969: 89) also noted parallels between the borders in both volumes. It is also clear that the Voustre Demeure manuscript predates at least one manuscript painted before 1482 (see cat. no. 32).

21

VIENNA MASTER OF MARY OF BURGUNDY (?)

Mary and Joseph at the Inn
Ghent, ca. 1475–80

Point of the brush in black ink with gray wash heightened with lead white on gray prepared paper, 11 × 7.9 cm (4⁵⁄₁₆ × 3⅛ in.)

COLLECTION: London, The British Museum, 1883.7.14.78

PROVENANCE: Buonfiglio family, Bologna; Sagredo; John Udney; Sunderland Collection [sale, Christie's, London, June 15, 1883, lot 41]; acquired 1883

JPGM and RA

As its format suggests, this drawing is a study for a manuscript border. Its shape follows the convention of a design intended for a recto, which is usually a text page in a Flemish book of hours. The drawing features three interlocked narrative vignettes. In the bas-de-page, the main scene, Joseph and Mary stop at an inn. Above and behind the inn the stable appears. Its large window openings glow with white heightening, and there is a gathering of angels immediately above. The Christ child has been born. At the upper left an angel announces the good tidings to the shepherds in the fields.

At least eight Flemish manuscripts with historiated borders feature the main vignette and a component or close variant of the setting. Several feature most of the vignettes. One version, in the Voustre Demeure Hours (fig. 50), appears to be by an assistant of the Vienna Master of Mary of Burgundy and may date to the mid- to late 1470s. Others appear to be by the Master of the Prayer Books of around 1500 or his workshop,[1] the Master of the First Prayer Book of Maximilian or his workshop,[2] Simon Bening or his

workshop,[3] and the workshop of the Master of James IV of Scotland (cat. no. 128).[4] The drawing may nevertheless have begun its life as a study for the Voustre Demeure border. Its measurements are remarkably close to those of the painted area of the manuscript's pages (the full page is 13.2 × 9.5 cm [5 3/16 × 3 3/4 in.]).

The drawing features nearly all the figures shown in the illumination, starting with the shepherds at the upper left and proceeding clockwise to the donkey and steer at the lower left. Other shared motifs include the two distant peasants seen from the back, gazing at the glowing stable, and the fellow in the doorway. But the border departs from the drawing in a number of significant ways. The illuminator added an angel at the upper right, moved the annunciatory angel closer to the shepherds, and spread out the other angels. He expanded the flock of sheep, barely indicated in the drawing, into the area of the initial, altered the character and placement of windows and doors, and exaggerated the upper contour of the donkey's hindquarters dramatically, making them lower than the line of the neck.

Some changes, such as moving the appropriate angel closer to the shepherds, are followed consistently in later miniatures, suggesting that they are based on a different model.[5] The London drawing may have continued to serve as a model for several generations. The miniature that follows the details of Bethlehem's architecture most closely, especially the conception of doors and windows, is a border in a Chatsworth book of hours (fig. 51 and cat. no. 128), a relatively late work by the workshop of the Master of James IV from the 1520s.[6]

Both A. E. Popham and Otto Pächt attributed the drawing to the Master of Mary of Burgundy. Although not as fine as the *Pentecost* attributed here to the Vienna Master of Mary of Burgundy (cat. no. 26), it is related in the use of white heightening on gray prepared paper. There is also a resemblance in the way the eyes and mouth are blocked in and in the long, drapery folds on standing figures. Thus, it may well be by the same illuminator.[7]   T. K.

Notes

1. Rothschild Book of Hours, fol. 108v (private collection; Trenkler 1979: facsimile 108v).

2. Breviary of Eleanor of Portugal, fol. 32v (cat. no. 91) and the Mayer van den Bergh Breviary, fol. 158v (cat. no. 92; Nieuwdorp and Dekeyzer 1997: 38).

3. Book of hours, Rouen, Bibliothèque municipale, Ms. 3028 (Leber 142), fol. 116; book of hours, Stockholm, Kungliga biblioteket, Ms. A227, fol. 73.

4. In the Croÿ Hours (Vienna, Österreichische Nationalbibliothek, codex 1858, fol. 55). The border is not by Bening or his workshop but by a lesser artist, although Bening executed a number of the book's full-page miniatures. See Thoss, in Mazal and Thoss 1993: 81, 83, 85.

5. There is further evidence that another version of this drawing existed. The border in the Rothschild Book of Hours shows a developed flock of sheep, a feature of the Voustre Demeure border but not of the London drawing.

6. The Chatsworth border follows closely these details of the drawing: the tall, narrow dormer windows of the inn; the door to the left, behind Mary and Joseph; and the house with a door and three narrow windows in the left margin. None of these details appears in the Madrid historiated border.

7. Lieftinck (1969: 91, n. 6) questioned the attribution to the Master of Mary of Burgundy on the grounds that the drawing has too many weak passages. Van Buren (in DOA 1996, 20: 727) considered the drawing to be a copy after the Master of Mary of Burgundy.

Figure 50
ASSISTANT OF VIENNA MASTER OF MARY OF BURGUNDY(?)
Border with *Mary and Joseph at the Inn*. In the Voustre Demeure Hours, fol. 68 (see cat. no. 20)

Figure 51
WORKSHOP OF THE MASTER OF JAMES IV OF SCOTLAND
Border with *Mary and Joseph at the Inn*. In a book of hours, fol. 39 (see cat. no. 128)

22a

22

VIENNA MASTER OF MARY OF BURGUNDY OR WORKSHOP / FOLLOWER

Breviary of Margaret of York
Use of Sarum
Ghent, ca. 1475–80

MANUSCRIPT: i + 264 + ii folios, 26.4 × 18.5 cm (10⅜ × 7⁵⁄₁₆ in.); justification: 17.4 × 12.3 (6⅞ × 4¹³⁄₁₆ in.); 30 lines of *textura* in two columns; 6 miniatures

HERALDRY: Initials *CM* (for Charles the Bold and Margaret of York) and motto of Margaret of York *Bien en aviegne* throughout

INSCRIPTIONS: *Ex bono thomae Gardiner Armigeri*, inside front cover

BINDING: Gold-tooled brown leather over pasteboard; marbled edges

COLLECTION: Cambridge, Saint John's College, Ms. H. 13

PROVENANCE: Margaret of York, duchess of Burgundy (1446–1503); Thomas Gardiner "Armigero"; his gift, ca. 1618

JPGM and RA

This breviary, which has lost many of its leaves, was perhaps made in two campaigns.[1] The second campaign shows that it was intended for Margaret of York, as the presence of her motto and arms in the borders attests. Moreover, the book was written for Sarum use, so it was always intended for an English patron. The litany contains many saints of Flemish origin, but it corresponds very closely to the Sarum litany published by Francis Procter.[2] While many other miniatures may be lost, six splendid one-column examples from the second campaign remain inside the book.[3] A seventh, now mutilated and removed, but with most of its border intact, shows David taunted by a devil (fig. 52).[4] All the miniatures are painted with a freedom, breadth, and deft touch that place them among the eye-catching examples of the new naturalism that emerged in the 1470s.

The miniatures were attributed to the Master of Mary of Burgundy by Otto Pächt. In streamlining the illuminator's oeuvre, G. I. Lieftinck retained this group of minia-

tures as by the master. Bodo Brinkmann, who reduced the artist's corpus further and renamed him the Vienna Master of Mary of Burgundy, did not include Margaret's breviary in his discussion.[5] Nevertheless the miniatures have several features that call to mind Brinkmann's Vienna Master, such as the distinctive crouching poses of certain figures, who seem to be not quite kneeling and not quite sitting: for example, David and Joachim in *The Annunciation to Joachim*, and Simeon in *The Presentation in the Temple* (ill. 22a). Also typical of the Vienna Master is the interest in gold brocades with red patterns, often with sleeves in green or another contrasting color, and the preference for strong reds in the foreground, often combined with violet or green. And, as in the case of *The Crucifixion of Saint Andrew* (ill. 22b) and *The Presentation in the Temple*, the figures have a quiet dignity that is emotionally expressive, a quality reminiscent of the Vienna Master. The settings for *The Presentation in the Temple*, *The Annunciation*, and *The Annunciation to Joachim* are spacious, finely proportioned, and conceived with a coherent system of receding orthogonals, like those of the Vienna Master.

At the same time the breviary artist's handling of the brush is different from what one sees in either the Engelbert Hours (cat. no. 18) or the Vienna Hours (cat. no. 19), the key manuscripts by the Vienna Master. It is broader and shows less attention to detail, as is evident in the women's faces. They are noble and idealized in the art of the Vienna Master of Mary of Burgundy and narrow and plain in Margaret's breviary. The breviary's landscapes are spacious and evocative, too, but more simply and broadly painted. Some of the miniatures stylistically closest to the breviary are those in the Voustre Demeure Hours (cat. no. 20), a late work by the Vienna Master and/or his workshop or brilliant followers. The use of a golden yellow in place of grassy green in the foreground of some landscapes, such as *The Crucifixion of Saint Andrew* and *The Ascension*, recalls the use of this device in the Voustre Demeure *Flight into Egypt*. In these three miniatures the sky is also painted in a similar atmospheric blue laced with patches of golden light. The *Flight*, however, is painted more tightly, with greater attention to detail. An illuminator of the Voustre Demeure Hours copied both the breviary's *Presentation in the Temple* and its *Annunciation to Joachim* fairly carefully but in both cases added detail while sacrificing subtlety.[6]

The breviary includes some of the earliest roughly datable borders in the new style with strewn flora.[7] Based on the similarity of one border (fol. 103) to one in the Register of the Guild of Saint Anne (cat. no. 23), illuminated probably at the beginning of 1477 (or the end of 1476), this campaign of illumination might date as early as middecade.[8] Most scholars have argued that Margaret's breviary dates before 1477 because it contains her initial with that of Charles *en lac* and her arms impaling his.[9] This conclusion assumes, however, that she ceased to use such heraldry after his death. Given the book's relationship to the Voustre Demeure Hours, a broader dating within the second half of the decade seems prudent.   T. K.

Notes

1. Lieftinck (1969: 1) held the view that the book may have been begun in the first half of the fifteenth century due to the older style of initials and decoration. It is clear that there are older-style borders (cf., e.g., fols. 62, 63v) that preceded the two types that belong to the 1470s: the new style of naturalistic borders with strewn flora and acanthus and a type with gold and blue acanthus on plain grounds that is usually associated with Ghent.

2. Procter and Wordsworth 1879: cols. 255–60, esp. cols. 259–60, which correspond closely to the surviving litany (fols. 102–102v), although Margaret's breviary includes Sirus (immediately after Mamerte), which is not in Procter and excludes Ausberte (immediately before Mamerte in Procter).

3. M. Brown (1998: 287–90, pls. 8, 9, figs. 169–71) also identified accurately for the first time all the other surviving fragments of the book and corrected previous errors made by Pächt and Wright. The accurate accounting includes Cotton Ms. Tiberius A.ii, fol. 1; Cotton Ms. Galba A.xviii, fol. 2; Cotton Ms. Vespasian A.i, fol. 160v; Cotton Ms. Titus C.xv, fol. 1; Ms. Nero A.ii, fol. 2. Note that these fragments are usually combined with fragments from other manuscripts.

4. All the text has been erased, the center of the leaf excised, and part of the text-block area overpainted for Cotton. M. Brown (1998: 289, pl. 9) noted that an eighth miniature, also from a Cotton pastiche and showing David kneeling in a landscape, "might be from the breviary." Although it is badly damaged, Scot McKendrick expressed his belief that it likely did come from the breviary, noting that the offset script, which is partially overpainted beneath the miniature, comes from the breviary. The border accompanying the first David miniature also includes the arms of England impaling Burgundy in a lozenge, the initials *C* and *M en lac*, and a discolored device: *Bien en aviengne*.

5. Pächt 1948: 64, no. 6; Lieftinck 1969: 1–7; Brinkmann 1998: 133–43.

6. The *Presentation in the Temple* in the Voustre Demeure Hours has a more crowded composition than that in Margaret's breviary, with some awkward passages (the curtain and the additional heads) but richer color effects.

7. On its borders, see the introduction to part 2 of this volume and note 1.

8. Arnould (in Cambridge 1993: 150–51, no. 49) and Smeyers (1998: 416, no. 61) dated it to around 1470.

9. See also Lieftinck 1969: 5; Pächt (1948: 64) dated it "before 1477?"

23

CIRCLE OF VIENNA MASTER OF MARY OF BURGUNDY

Register of the Guild of Saint Anne
Ghent, 1477

MANUSCRIPT: 82 folios, 27.7 × 20.2 cm (10 ¹⁵⁄₁₆ × 8 in.); justification: 18 × 9.9 cm (7 ⅛ × 3 ⅞ in.); 20 lines of *bastarda*; 1 full-page miniature

HERALDRY: Escutcheons with the arms of Margaret of York and Mary of Burgundy, same arms on fabric draped over prie-dieux, escutcheons with the arms of the territories of Burgundy, in miniature, fol. 2v; initials CM (for Charles the Bold and Margaret of York) and motto of Margaret of York *bien en aviengne*, in border, fol. 2v

INSCRIPTIONS: *Int jaer ons heeren ciiii.c ende lxxvij zo was gemaect dezen bouc ter eeren der edlre vorss princessen und gheducter vrouwen. En louf. vornt. En es te wetene binnen den termine dat dit weert begonst was. eer dat volmaect was zo quam binnen dess vorssstede van ghendt de lare meeste jammerlixste. ende ont faermlixste tydinghe. Die noyt man hoorde. [et]c hoe dat Karele [ ]ider gracien gods wylen hertoghe van Bourg. Ende heere van alle den vorsslanden. bleef omtrent Nancy bidt xpm datti sim helighe passie. Wille sijnre siele deelachrich maken en verleenen die hemelsce glorie. Amen,* fol. 6

BINDING: Black morocco, grained; silver cartouches on both covers; silver clasps

COLLECTION: Windsor Castle, RCIN.1047371

PROVENANCE: Guild of Saint Anne, Ghent; entered the Royal Library by 1894

JPGM and RA

The deacon, bailiff, and stewards (*proviserers*) of the prominent Guild of Saint Anne in Ghent ordered and paid for this register.[1] It was begun in honor of Margaret of York, duchess of Burgundy, who joined the guild in 1473. Her device and her initial *en lac* with that of her husband appear in the border surrounding the book's single miniature (ill. 23). The miniature portrays Margaret and her stepdaughter Mary of Burgundy, who joined the guild in 1476, along with their arms. The volume contains a list of the guild's members through the middle of the seventeenth century. Although the writing was likely begun in 1476, the illumination was probably completed the following year. An inscription (see above) establishes that the book's production was in progress when the guild learned of the death of Charles the Bold in the battle at Nancy on January 5, 1477.

The register is one of the earliest datable examples of manuscript illumination to feature the new style of Flemish borders with flowers and acanthus that cast their own shadows. Although these borders are celebrated for their naturalism, the flora is not always accurately colored, as in the border on the frontispiece (fol. 2v), where the tightly wound acanthus is white. A close variation of this border appears in Margaret's breviary (cat. no. 22, fol. 103), which was likely painted not long before or after it. Both feature the white acanthus alternating with naturalistic flowers, among which violets and strawberries figure prominently, with birds resting on the acanthus. Given the abraded condition of the register's border, it is difficult to tell if it is by the same hand as the borders in the breviary, but it might well be.

23
CIRCLE OF VIENNA
MASTER OF MARY
OF BURGUNDY
*Margaret of York and Mary
of Burgundy in Prayer,*
fols. 2v–3

Figure 53
VIENNA MASTER OF
MARY OF BURGUNDY,
WORKSHOP, OR
FOLLOWER
Decorated border. In
the Voustre Demeure
Hours, fol. 156
(see cat. no. 20)

In the register the facing border (ill. 23) surrounds text written in gold on reddish prepared parchment.[2] This border, also superb (and better preserved), combines close observation with whimsy. A pair of thick, knobby branches, tautly twisted together, frame the text. The branches themselves, faithfully described on the surface, are nonetheless modeled in blue and gold for a decided fantasy effect. The thickness of the branches heightens the sense of depth in the border, and the diminutive figure of a monkey in a red jacket comforting a hermit at the lower right further exaggerates the scale of the branches.[3] The rest of the border combines gold acanthus modeled in blue with accurately colored violets, roses, and other flowers. Although uncommon, some of the distinctive motifs of this border find correspondences in the Voustre Demeure Hours, where the hermit under an ancient tree and the text framed by thick, knobby branches recur (fig. 53).[4]

In the miniature, Margaret and Mary kneel at priedieux before a painted altarpiece with *The Annunciation to Joachim and Anne.* Above this altarpiece is a sculptural group in gray stone with a towering Saint Anne cradling in one arm the Virgin and Child.[5] The armorial shields that frame the altar represent Charles's five duchies and his twelve other territories.[6] The dean, bailiff, and two other board members appear among the guild members in the bas-de-page. As the faces and garments in the miniature are abraded, a firm attribution is difficult to venture. Scholars have voiced opinions both in favor of and against assigning it to the illuminator once called the Master of Mary of Burgundy. The quality of the modeling of folds, the use of light and color, and the expressive handling of grisaille situate the work within the circle of artists who illuminated both Margaret's breviary and the majority of the miniatures in the Voustre Demeure Hours.   T. K.

Notes

1. It contains a long list of the register's commissioners, including the deacon Jacob Coubrake and the bailiff Arent van Mechelen, starting on folio 6v.

2. This tinted parchment was almost certainly intended to imitate a luxurious purple page associated with emperors and kings. Charles the Bold owned a prayer book written in gold on purple parchment that no longer survives (Deuchler 1963: 349, no. 316). For a similar example of the use of such parchment in an imperial book, see cat. no. 151.

3. The motif of the thick, twisted branches finds a suite of successors in the Breviary of Isabella of Castile (cat. no. 100), but the branches there lack the finesse of those in the register's border (cf. fols. 37, 81v, 86, 211; see Backhouse 1993b: figs. 8, 12, 13, 38).

4. Fols. 156 and 150, respectively. Significantly, in both books the ancient, thick trees at the bottom of the page rest on areas of earth, which further enhances the suggestion of depth.

5. Blockmans (1992: 38) identified the altar as that in the Church of Saint Nicholas in Ghent, where the guild had its chapel. The relics of Saint Anne were brought to Ghent from the Holy Land at the beginning of the twelfth century.

6. Per Blockmans (1992: 38), these present his holdings in late 1475.

24

VIENNA MASTER OF MARY OF BURGUNDY
OR WORKSHOP / FOLLOWER

Rooclooster Breviary
Monastery of Saint Paul (the Rooclooster), near Brussels, and Ghent, 1477

MANUSCRIPT: 306 folios, 11.5 × 7.5 cm (4½ × 2¹⁵⁄₁₆ in.); justification: 8 × 5 cm (3⅛ × 1¹⁵⁄₁₆ in.); 28 lines of *hybrida*; 1 miniature

INSCRIPTIONS: *Deo gratias, Anno Domini 1477*, fol. 304; *Pertinet monasterio Rubeevallis iste liber, et concessi ego frater cornelius prior eiusdem fratri henrico confessori in monasterio sancte elizabeth ad vitam suam teste signo meo manuali*, later hand

BINDING: Sixteenth century; brown calf over wood boards with blind-stamped initials *MM*

COLLECTION: Brussels, Bibliothèque royale de Belgique, Ms. IV 860

PROVENANCE: Monastery of Saint Paul (the Rooclooster), near Brussels; dukes of Arenberg, Brussels; Ph. J. van Alfen, Doorn, 1962; [Maggs Brothers]; acquired 1972

R A

This breviary, with a single small miniature, was written at the monastery of Rooclooster, a foundation of the Windesheim congregation. Because the volume is dated 1477, it has some art-historical importance. The book contains several of the earliest borders of the new type with naturalistically observed flowers that cast their own shadows on solid-colored grounds.[1] G. I. Lieftinck demonstrated that these borders are related to those found in some of the finest manuscripts in the group attributed here to the Vienna Master of Mary of Burgundy and his circle.[2] He went further still, though less persuasively, in suggesting that the illuminator of this manuscript must have resided at the monastery, where the painter Hugo van der Goes settled before his death in 1482.[3]

The miniature shows the standard iconography of King David kneeling in prayer looking up to the heavens, where the clouds open to reveal a golden light that shines upon him. He is depicted at the edge of a hilly shoreline with a view of a magnificent palace across the water. Lieftinck emphasized the artist's skillful painting of hands, epitomized by the cupped fingers of David's right hand. He is correct that this feature is found in the celebrated miniatures of the Vienna Hours of Mary of Burgundy (e.g., cat. no. 19, fol. 43v) and in other manuscripts that Lieftinck grouped around these miniatures. A particularly close relationship is apparent with the best miniatures in the Voustre Demeure Hours (cat. no. 20). *The Disputation of Saint Barbara* in the latter (ill. 20a) shows similar finely drawn hands, pale bearded heads in profile, with hair that is fine but a bit straggly. The patch of golden light in the sky is treated in a comparably luminous way, and both miniatures capture the reflections of the architecture in the water. Finally, David's distinctive red cap with a tall fur brim is virtually identical to one worn by Saint Barbara's father. The Voustre Demeure Hours also contains a similar border type that features white acanthus alternating with naturalistically colored flowers against a gold background (e.g., Madrid, fols. 41, 194).[4]

The profile head, hands, and drapery of David are anticipated at the beginning of the decade in the man kneeling in prayer before the shrine in the Vienna Master's *Apulians Killing the Ambassador of the Etholes* in Duke Charles's Alexander manuscript (fig. 54). The fur-brimmed red crown also recalls the one Alexander wears while ordering the slaughter of the Branchides in the same volume (fol. 168v).

Although the book must have been written at Rooclooster, it was probably decorated in Ghent, where the Vienna Master of Mary of Burgundy and his workshop seem to have been based. The book also features the 1470s-style borders of blue and gold acanthus with flowers and spray on white vellum that one associates with Ghent production.   T. K.

Notes

1. See also Lieftinck 1964a, 1: pl. 232A.

2. Lieftinck 1964b and Lieftinck 1969, 13–14, 18–20. He named him the Master of Rooclooster and identified him as Nicholas van der Goes, Hugo's brother. Neither the name-of-convenience nor the identification has gained acceptance in the literature.

3. Lieftinck 1964b; for fuller discussion of why this is not likely to be so, see Kren, in Malibu 1983a: 18–20, and Brinkmann 1997: 343 n. 2.

4. As discussed in cat. no. 20, it is not entirely clear whether the *Disputation* miniature represents a second phase in the work of the Vienna Master of Mary of Burgundy or the work of a brilliant workshop member or follower.

24
VIENNA MASTER OF
MARY OF BURGUNDY
OR WORKSHOP /
FOLLOWER
David in Prayer, fol. 36

Figure 54
VIENNA MASTER OF
MARY OF BURGUNDY
*The Apulians Killing the
Ambassador of the Etholes*.
In Quintus Curtius
Rufus, *Livre des fais
d'Alexandre le grant*,
translation by Vasco
da Lucena of *Historia
Alexandri magni*, fol. 128
(detail; see cat. no. 54)

25

VIENNA MASTER OF MARY OF BURGUNDY (?)
AND WORKSHOP / FOLLOWERS

Madrid Hours of William Lord Hastings
Use of Sarum
Ghent, late 1470s

MANUSCRIPT: 296 folios, 12.4 × 9 cm (4⅞ × 3½ in.); justification:
7.3 × 4.7 cm (2⅞ × 1⅞ in.); 17 lines of *bastarda*; 33 full-page
miniatures; 1 full-page miniature, 2 smaller miniatures added,
fols. 286–296, England, end of fifteenth century

HERALDRY: Full-page escutcheon with the arms of William Lord
Hastings, surmounted by helm, mantling or doubled gules, and
crest with coronet and bull's head sable and encircled by the Garter
with motto *Hony soit qui mal y pense*, fol. 1v; escutcheon with arms
of the earls of Arundel, in bas-de-page, fol. 287

INSCRIPTIONS: *Conventus Anglo-Bornhemiensis, Dono datus ab
Generosissimo[?] Domino cardinali de norfolcia Fundatori eiusdem
Conventus 1659*, first flyleaf; *When yow your prayer doo rehers Remembrer
Henry Mawtrevers*, fol. 84; *Myne owne good kate as ofte as you can not se
me bodyly wyth your prayrs I pray you vysyte me, and wyth thys specially,
because it is to the hole trynyte, wherin you shall doo a great pleasure unto
me, whyche ame your loving mystres and ever wyll be / marye*, fol. 286;
*Queen of Scotland whose booke this was as appears by her own hand as
above is*, seventeenth-century hand, fol. 286

BINDING: Seventeenth century; rose velvet over pasteboard; four
metal corner pieces incised with putti and grotesque masks

COLLECTION: Madrid, Fundación Lázaro Galdiano, Inv. 15503

PROVENANCE: William Lord Hastings (ca. 1430–1483); probably Henry
Fitzalan, twelfth earl of Arundel (1512–1580); to Katherine Grey; by
descent to Philip Howard, fourteenth earl of Arundel (1585–1646); to
the English Dominican friars, Bornhem, in 1659; Lady Stourton, by
1862, and therefore perhaps from the Clifford of Chudleigh library;
Rodolphe Kann, Paris (his objet d'art no. 73), by 1907

JPGM and RA

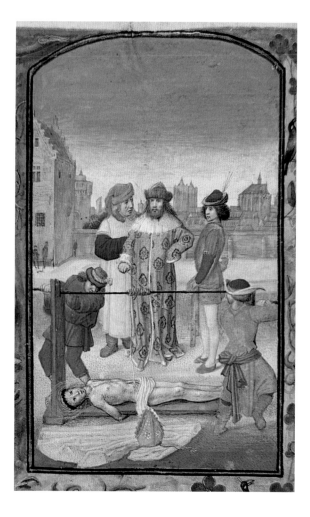

The program of miniatures in this book commences dramatically after the calendar, with eighteen full-page illuminations illustrating the suffrages, the book's largest pictorial cycle.[1] Among the more unusual ones is that devoted to the Magi, while another, even rarer miniature is devoted to Saint Sitha.[2] Among the more distinctive illustrations in the suffrages are narrative miniatures that show the beheading of Saint John the Baptist and the martyrdom of Saint Erasmus (ill. 25a). The Hours of the Virgin is illustrated by a Life of the Virgin cycle that features both *The Circumcision* and *The Presentation in the Temple* but not the usual *Adoration of the Magi,* perhaps because it appears earlier, illustrating the suffrage of the Magi.[3]

The most original miniatures appear to be inspired by the Vienna Master of Mary of Burgundy and his workshop and/or followers, although one might be by the Vienna Master himself. *The Annunciation,*[4] *The Agony in the Garden,*[5] *The Nativity,*[6] *The Presentation in the Temple,*[7] *Saint Sitha,*[8] and perhaps *The Death Vigil* (ill. 25b) are based on one or more miniatures by the Vienna Master group. Most striking and beautiful is the dimly lit *Death Vigil*, which features the type of interior that the Vienna Master painted throughout his career and one of his characteristic motifs, the figure in the foreground right, viewed from the back, about to exit the scene (cf. cat. no. 18, fol. 170v; cat. no. 54, fol. 223v; and ill. 54a).[9] The figures are so graceful, the light

so expressive that one is tempted to suggest that *The Death Vigil* is a late work by the Vienna Master. Other miniatures, such as the nocturnal *Agony in the Garden* (ill. 25c) and *The Nativity*, are influenced by him but fail to capture fully the sophistication and subtlety of their pictorial sources.

The Vienna Master or his workshop and/or followers also provided patterns for border motifs. Some of the idiosyncratic branch motifs and distinctively posed peacocks in the borders of the Madrid Hastings Hours repeat closely motifs from the pages of the Voustre Demeure Hours (cat. no. 20); the Hastings volume also mimics the marked chiaroscuro effects of the latter's borders.[10] The Vienna Master's followers, who illuminated most of the Madrid Hastings Hours, must have been apprenticed in his workshop in the late 1470s, when the Voustre Demeure Hours was likely being produced.[11]

The book is remarkable in another way. Finely painted, sumptuous in its effect, and long considered an important example of the new style of illumination, the manuscript derives its appeal largely from the effect of the whole rather than from the originality of its parts. Nearly every one of its miniatures can be linked to the pattern of an illuminator, such as the Vienna Master or the Master of the Houghton Miniatures, or to a source in the work of a Flemish painter, such as Hugo van der Goes or Dieric Bouts.[12] *The Annunciation to the Shepherds* shows the composition of the Houghton Master's version of this subject in mirror

25a
VIENNA MASTER
OF MARY OF
BURGUNDY (?)
AND WORKSHOP
*The Martyrdom of Saint
Erasmus*, fol. 36v (detail)

25b

VIENNA MASTER
OF MARY OF
BURGUNDY (?)
The Death Vigil, fol. 223v
(detail)

25c

WORKSHOP OR
FOLLOWER OF THE
VIENNA MASTER OF
MARY OF BURGUNDY
The Agony in the Garden,
fol. 243v

image (ill. 32d). *The Trinity* and *The Man of Sorrows* are both closely adapted from Van der Goes's *Trinity* in Edinburgh, while *The Martyrdom of Saint Erasmus* is based upon Bouts's altarpiece of this subject (fig. 60).[13] The evidence of other miniatures whose compositions closely correspond to those in other manuscripts implies that patterns existed for them.[14] Thus this book of hours epitomizes the commodification of the new naturalistic style of manuscript illumination.

While the use of patterns, and even pattern books, was common in the creation of Flemish manuscripts before this time, the Madrid Hastings Hours and the London Hastings Hours (cat. no. 41), both executed before 1483, represent early examples of the systematized use of patterns for the new type of miniature in the production of luxury devotional books.[15] Since the present book is an early example of such systematic copying following the invention of the new style during the 1470s, the identity of the patterns' designers deserves to be addressed. As suggested above, one of the Vienna Master's followers probably conceived some of the miniatures by adapting compositions from miniatures by the master and from paintings by Bouts and Van der Goes. Since the Vienna Master seems to have participated in the illumination of a miniature, perhaps he also designed some of the patterns used in this book, which his assistants and/or followers then copied.[16]

The Madrid Hours was produced for William Lord Hastings, the great chamberlain of the household of Edward IV and one of several prominent English patrons of Flemish manuscript illumination in the late 1470s and early 1480s. His death in June 1483 establishes a terminus ante quem for this book. That it was not produced before the late 1470s is suggested by its derivations from the Voustre Demeure Hours, but the costume in *The Death Vigil* indicates that it was probably painted no later than 1480.[17] The calendar was intended for an English patron, with an emphasis on Saint Edward the King and Saint Richard de Wyck, while the Hours of the Virgin was for the use of Sarum. In light of Hastings's close relationship with Edward IV, it is not surprising to find such prominence given to the name saints of the king and his brother, the future Richard III. The litany is essentially a Flemish litany with a few English saints, notably Saints Swithin and Sitha.

Insofar as the book draws heavily upon the example of Ghent painters and illuminators, it may have been made in Ghent. Its bar borders belong to a Ghent type that was popular in the 1470s,[18] and its calendar compares closely with another Sarum calendar in a Flemish prayer book probably made in Ghent.[19]   T. K.

Notes
1. It is characteristic of books of hours for the use of Sarum that the suffrages come at the beginning of the book.

2. This may have been intended to be Saint Osith, an English saint with whom Saint Sitha (i.e., Zita of Lucca) is sometimes confused. Saint Sitha is included not only in the suffrages and litany of both this and the London Hastings Hours but also in the litany of the Hours of Katherine Bray, another English patron (cat. no. 88).

3. For more on the devotional content of the book, see cat. no. 41.

4. *The Annunciation* adapts the complex spatial arrangement of the Virgin's bedchamber and the pose of Gabriel, though not that of the Virgin, in the Engelbert Hours (cat. no. 18, fol. 97v).

5. *The Agony in the Garden* is derived from several versions of this subject by the Vienna Master of Mary of Burgundy or his workshop. The general arrangement of the figures in the landscape, especially Christ on the hilltop, and the gate to the garden at the back right recall the version of this subject in the Prayer Book of Charles the Bold (ill. 16c), which is probably an early version by the Vienna Master or an assistant. The pose of Christ with his hands reaching toward the heavens recalls the treatment in the Voustre Demeure Hours (ill. 20c).

6. The illuminator of *The Nativity* adapted awkwardly the architecture and basic compositional elements from the ambitious version of this subject in the Voustre Demeure Hours (cat. no. 20, Berlin, no. 4), introducing ambiguity, especially in the placement of Joseph in the foreground.

7. *The Presentation in the Temple* is adapted from the Voustre Demeure Hours (cat. no. 20, Berlin, no. 7), using a similar architectural setting of an apse or a side chapel hung with a curtain and the same number of figures as in Margaret's breviary (ill. 22a).

8. For the Voustre Demeure Hours model, see the miniature of Saint Apollonia, (cat. no. 20, fol. 56) (Lieftinck 1969: figs. 126, 173).

9. *The Death Vigil* recalls the interior of the Engelbert Hours *Death of the Virgin* (cat. no. 18, fol. 170v) but is more spacious and more dramatically and atmospherically lit.

10. Compare, for example, the branches in the lower border of folio 48v of the Madrid Hastings Hours with the same motif on folio 114 of the Voustre Demeure Hours (Lieftinck 1969: figs. 173, 140) or the peacock on folio 134v of the Madrid Hastings Hours and on Berlin, no. 5, of the Voustre Demeure Hours (Lieftinck 1969: figs. 184, 160).

11. Pächt (1948: 68, no. 17) attributed the Hastings volume to the Master of Mary of Burgundy. De Winter (1981: 353, 424 n. 20) unpersuasively ascribed it to the Master of the First Prayer Book of Maximilian.

12. Lieftinck (1969: 113–24) identified other manuscripts that have miniatures from the same patterns, although his suggestion that the Berlin Hours of Mary of Burgundy and Maximilian is an important source for this book is unconvincing.

13. *The Trinity* comes directly from Van der Goes. The illuminator copied the basic figures and their gestures, adding a miter for God the Father and adapting some throne features while simplifying them (Lieftinck 1969: fig. 165; Friedländer 1967–76, 4: no. 12, pl. 21).

14. Some examples include *The Annunciation*, *The Raising of Lazarus*, *The Last Judgment*, *The Martyrdom of Saint Barbara*, *The Virgin and Child*, *Saint Anthony Abbot*, *The Mass of Saint Gregory*, *Saint Jerome in His Study*, *Saint Catherine of Alexandria*, and *Saint Elizabeth of Hungary*.

15. For example, the Hours of Philip of Cleves (Vienna, Österreichische Nationalbibliothek, Ms. s.n. 13239) features five miniatures in its Life of the Virgin cycle that are based on patterns also used in the Madrid Hastings Hours (Pächt and Thoss 1990: 90–98, figs. 176–80; Lieftinck 1969: figs. 166, 177, 179, 180, 182).

16. The Madrid *Nativity*, which appears to be derived from the Voustre Demeure Hours, may have become the model, in particular for the figures of Mary and Joseph in the Vienna Hours of Philip of Cleves (cf. Lieftinck 1969: figs. 157, 179; Pächt and Thoss 1990: fig. 177). *The Man of Sorrows* is probably the earliest of the many known versions of this subject. On other versions, see Brinkmann, in König et al. 1998: 119, 125–26, figs. 23, 24, 38. The Vienna Master probably designed *The Martyrdom of Saint Erasmus* (ill. 41a).

17. Van Buren (1975: 307; in DOA 1996, 20: 727) has argued that the book could be as early as 1470 on the basis of the costume in *The Death Vigil*. Margaret Scott, however, feels that certain details, such as the absence of pleating and the unbelted gown and jackets, suggest a date later in the 1470s. The long-toed shoes disappear by the 1480s.

18. See cat. nos. 18, 36, and Lieftinck 1969: fig. 176.

19. W. 436 in the Walters Art Museum, ca. 1500 (Randall 1997: 509–21, no. 295). John Plummer reported agreement of 87.3 percent and a close relationship to this manuscript in the confessor saints of the litany (report, Department of Manuscripts files, JPGM).

26

VIENNA MASTER OF MARY OF BURGUNDY

Pentecost

Ghent, ca. 1480

Silverpoint heightened with white on prepared paper, 6.8 × 5.3 cm (2 11/16 × 2 1/16 in.)

COLLECTION: Paris, École des Beaux-Arts, Masson 664

PROVENANCE: J. Masson

JPGM

The tiny dimensions of this elaborate compositional drawing indicate that it is a study for a miniature.[1] It shows the Virgin seated at the right in a church, reading from a devotional book. Nine disciples gather around her, several of them looking up at the ceiling. In the side aisle, farther back, two apostles are seated; one of them looks toward the ceiling, too. A chapel or transept with a tall lancet window can be seen through the archway behind the Virgin. Although drawn in a free, sketchy manner with elements of the architecture only thinly blocked out and the facial features indicated broadly, the sheet presents a subtle and cohesive figural composition. The white heightening lends the figures a strongly sculptural presence. The deep, cavernous interior—which shows a side aisle, a taller vessel, and the chapel or transept—contributes to the scene's drama.[2]

Long associated with a miniature in the Berlin Hours of Mary of Burgundy (fig. 55) for which it probably served as a model, the drawing is not by the same artist. In the miniature some heads were added to the main grouping. They are out of scale, and they diminish the subtle interconnection of the core groups of figures, weakening the coherence of the composition. Nevertheless, the relationship of the drawing to the miniature demonstrates that the drawing must date before 1482. As such, it is the earliest datable drawing by an artist working in the new Flemish style of manuscript illumination.

Figure 55
MASTER OF THE FIRST
PRAYER BOOK OF
MAXIMILIAN
Pentecost. In the Hours
of Mary of Burgundy
and Maximilian, fol. 31v
(see cat. no. 38)

The bifurcated spatial composition was more common in large horizontal miniatures in princely secular vernacular volumes.[3] The interior calls to mind, in particular, a very similar setting in *Alexander Takes the Hand of Roxanne* in Charles the Bold's Alexander manuscript (ill. 54a). The tall arcade that leads the eye back into the interior at the right and the tall column in the foreground (cut off at the top) that demarcates the side aisle and the main space of the drawing seem to mirror the arrangement in the Alexander miniature, in which the arcade appears on the left rather than the right of the main hall. Further, although the two images show spaces with entirely different purposes, in both works the main hall has a flat, beamed ceiling, while the ceiling of the narrower space is vaulted.[4]

Following A. E. Popham, scholars have consistently associated the drawing with the Master of Mary of Burgundy. Otto Pächt did this, while G. I. Lieftinck attributed it to the Master of Rooclooster, the artist to whom he ascribed the finest manuscripts formerly assigned to the Master of Mary of Burgundy, including the Vienna Hours of Mary of Burgundy (cat. no. 19) and the Engelbert Hours (cat. no. 18).[5] I assign the finest works in the Vienna and Engelbert Hours, along with the aforementioned miniature from Charles's Alexander, to the Vienna Master of Mary of Burgundy. The Vienna Master excelled at imbuing similar tight groupings of figures with variety and interest.[6] Moreover, certain details, such as the jagged patterns of drapery folds that rest on the ground, appear in other works by this artist,[7] and the broad handling of the white highlights recalls the elegant treatment of white in the gown of the seated *Saint Barbara* in the Engelbert Hours (fig. 56).

T. K.

Notes

1. Popham (1928: 139) identified this drawing as the work of the Master of Mary of Burgundy even before he could associate the composition with a particular miniature.

2. The dove of the Holy Ghost, the focus of the drama, is not depicted.

3. For example, *The Interview between the Pope and Charles Martel* in the *Histoire de Charles Martel* (Brussels, Bibliothèque royale de Belgique, Ms. 7, fol. 62v; Van den Gheyn [J.] 1910: pl. 55).

4. The composition and setting represented in the drawing also appear in several later Flemish manuscripts. One such miniature, by the Master of Edward IV, appears in the Blackburn Hours (cat. no. 98, fol. 40v), and another, from the workshop of the Master of the First Prayer Book of Maximilian, appears in the Munich Hours (cat. no. 90, fol. 88v).

5. Pächt 1948: 70, no. 26; Lieftinck 1969: 136; see also Van Buren 1975: 292.

6. Such as the virgins in *Alexander Takes the Hand of Roxanne* (ill. 54a) or the figures gathered under the cross in the Vienna *Crucifixion* (fol. 99v)

7. Such as *The Apulians Killing the Ambassador of the Etholes* in Charles's Alexander manuscript (fig. 54) or the previously mentioned Vienna *Crucifixion.*

Figure 56
VIENNA MASTER OF
MARY OF BURGUNDY
Saint Barbara. In the
Hours of Engelbert
of Nassau, fol. 41
(see cat. no. 18)

MASTER OF THE MORAL TREATISES

This artist illuminated several vernacular spiritual texts that were made for Margaret of York or acquired by her during the 1470s. They include an Apocalypse (cat. no. 27), a *Somme le roi* (Brussels, Bibliothèque royale de Belgique, Ms. 9106), and two manuscripts of moral treatises in the Bibliothèque royale (cat. nos. 28, 29). The artist's work was defined by Frédéric Lyna.[1] The painters and illuminators of Ghent—such as Hugo van der Goes, the Vienna Master of Mary of Burgundy, and book painters of the latter's circle—shaped the master's artistic development. Certain figure types are distinctly Goesian, such as the noblewoman kneeling in prayer (ill. 28a) or the square-shouldered male nudes. The weightiness of the figures, the quality of gesture, and the drawing of hands, which are usually cupped, with the fingers tightly placed, are also features of the work of the Vienna Master and illuminators of his circle. The Master of the Moral Treatises imitated the delicate washes in the Vienna Master's landscapes, as well as the way he painted flames and smoke in, for example, Charles the Bold's Quintus Curtius manuscript of 1470 (cat. no. 54). At his best, the Master of the Moral Treatises could create delicate and dramatic light effects, as is especially evident in Margaret's Apocalypse. Yet his painting lacks the richness of color found in the illuminations of the Vienna Master, and it exhibits much broader handling.[2] The bulky figures sometimes have disproportionately small heads and large hands, and they move or stand stiffly.

Typical of the miniatures of the Master of the Moral Treatises are lightly tinted, transparent washes and crisp, white highlights, often calligraphically applied along the ridges of folds or in short, parallel dashes. In particular, the artist used washes in the landscape, creating atmospheric perspective by painting skies a rich blue in the top half and nearly white in the bottom half, as if the thick air has washed away the color. He showed less attention to detail than his Ghent contemporaries and also used less expensive pigments. In each of the small number of manuscripts to which he contributed, there is a variation in quality and technique that suggests the possibility of workshop participation or collaboration.   T. K.

Notes

1. Gaspar and Lyna 1984–89, 3: 169–70, 173, 175–76. I do not agree that either the manuscript of moral treatises in the Bodleian (cat. no. 43) or the *Chronique de Flandres* (cat. no. 85) is by this artist.

2. Cf., e.g., the burning cities in the Quintus Curtius (cat. no. 54, fol. 168v) and in the Apocalypse (cat. no. 27, fol. 89).

27

MASTER OF THE MORAL TREATISES

Apocalypse with Commentary, in French
Ghent, ca. 1475–79

MANUSCRIPT: 121 folios, 36.2 × 26.5 cm (14¼ × 10⁷⁄₁₆ in.); justification: 23.7–24.7 × 8–1.6–7.9 cm (9⁵⁄₁₆–9¾ × 3⅛–⅝–3⅛ in.) with slight variations; 27–28 lines of *bastarda* in two columns by David Aubert; 79 two- and one-column miniatures

HERALDRY: Escutcheon with the arms of Margaret of York, fol. 10

BINDING: C. Lewis, England, nineteenth century; gold-tooled light brown morocco; quatrefoil filled with linked-chain motif in central panel of front cover; initials *J. W.* (for John Wilks), on back cover

COLLECTION: New York, The Morgan Library, Ms. M.484

PROVENANCE: Margaret of York, duchess of Burgundy (1446–1503); Prince Michel Petrovich Galitzin (1764–ca. 1835) [his sale, Paris, March 3, 1825, lot 8]; [to Payne]; [Longman]; to Rev. Theodore Williams [his sale, Stewart, Wheatley and Adlard, London, April 5, 1827, lot 114]; to Philip Hurd [his sale, Evans, London, March 29, 1832, lot 170]; [to Payne]; [Philip Augustus Hanrott sale, Evans, London, July 16–29, 1833, lot 214]; to J. Wilks [sale, Sotheby's, London, March 12–24, 1847, lot 417]; [to Joseph Lilly]; [Manuel John Johnson sale, Sotheby's, London, May 27, 1862, lot 29]; [to Joseph Lilly]; Henry Huth (1815–1878); to Alfred H. Huth [his sale, Sotheby's, London, November 5–24, 1911, lot 232]; [to Quaritch, London]; purchased 1911 by J. P. Morgan (1837–1913)

JPGM

This Apocalypse has the most extensive narrative cycle among Margaret of York's books.[1] Within the tradition of medieval Apocalypses its visual conception is striking for its sensitivity to the new pictorial interest in light. The drawing is not particularly refined, nor is there the attention to detail found in other illumination that emulated Flemish oil painting, but the artist shows an overriding interest in both spiritual and natural light. Exemplified by the marked aerial perspective in many miniatures and a supernatural radiance in others, the exploration of light effects gives the cycle a quirky poetry. In general, the finest and most original miniatures in the book are those dealing with purely celestial visions: *Christ Adored by the Elders* (fol. 26v), *Christ and the Four Beasts* (fol. 27v), *The Woman Standing on the Crescent Moon* (fol. 59v), *The Last Judgment* (ill. 27), and *Christ in Glory Holding the Book* (fol. 117v).

The heavenly backdrop of *The Last Judgment* radiates a pure white light, while the diaphanous glow from the golden mandorla enveloping Christ dematerializes the leaves of the large open books recording the deeds of the judged. The artist painted transparent glazes over underdrawing in portions of the books to achieve this effect. The miniature offers new iconography within a fresh visual framework for a theme that late medieval illuminators rarely rethought. As Suzanne Lewis has noted, the cycle,

in the Apocalypse. For example, in the sequence of miniatures of Christ and Saint John with the Seven Bishops (fols. 17, 18v, 19, 20, 21, 22v, 23v), the composition, the palette, and the handling of the landscape setting remain fairly consistent from one scene to the next, but the facial type (not just the expression) of John shifts several times, along with the technique for modeling his bulky robe.[3] Thus, individual miniatures themselves may also be collaborative efforts. The style of such miniatures as *The Woman Standing on the Crescent Moon*, among the strongest in the book, resembles that of the much-admired miniatures that show the devout in prayer in one of the collections of devotional writings in Brussels (cat. no. 28). The dank, infernal depths of *The Fifth Trumpet* (fol. 47) evoke the hell scene in the other Brussels devotional texts (ill. 29), and at its best, the treatment of landscape and atmospheric affects compares favorably with that in the single miniature by this artist in the Brussels *Somme le roi*.[4]

The Apocalypse has strong codicological links with other books made for Margaret of York by David Aubert. Although this book, like some of the illuminator's other volumes (cat. nos. 28, 29), is unsigned by the scribe, the style of its script is that of Aubert, whether it be by him or an assistant. Moreover, the distinctive style of the borders, with black and gold acanthus in the corners and rinceaux with small strawberries, daisies, pansies, and other flowers, is similar to the other manuscripts illuminated by this artist (cat. nos. 28, 29) and to Margaret's moral treatises in the Bodleian (cat. no. 43), which Aubert in the colophon dates to March 1476 (n.s.) and to Ghent.[5] All but the Apocalypse have blue and gold acanthus in the corners of the borders. The unusual gray and gold acanthus of the Apocalypse was perhaps judged appropriate to the harrowing theme. It complements the pale, grayish hues of many of the miniatures.

Pascale Charron and Marc Gil have argued that Aubert's activity for Margaret took place in Ghent, where she moved only in mid-December 1474, so that the Apocalypse does not date before 1475 and belongs to the two years before her husband died.[6] Nevertheless, since she seems to have commissioned work from Aubert even after her husband's death and could have continued to use the Burgundian arms, the book might also have been executed within the next few years. Both she and Aubert continued to live in Ghent through 1479.   T. K.

which illustrates closely the Morgan volume's particular translation, including its errors and departures, emphasizes the book itself as a vehicle of revelation.[2]

The miniatures' palette is generally muted and limited to blues, greens, and grays, with the sky and water blue, the earth green or greenish, and costumes various grays tinted with blue, green, violet, gold, or a faint red. This range of hue and value and the washlike technique that dominates much of the execution are characteristic of the work of the Master of the Moral Treatises. A curious exception to the coloration of the rest of the cycle are the first two miniatures, the rather bleak *Saint John the Evangelist and Saint Paul* (fol. 10) and *Saint John in a Vat of Boiling Oil* (fol. 13), both painted in a gray monochrome overall relieved by touches of green in the landscape and flesh tones in the figures.

As appears to be the case with the Master of the Moral Treatises's other projects, more than one hand was at work

27
MASTER OF THE
MORAL TREATISES
The Last Judgment,
fol. 103v

Notes

1. It features the mid-thirteenth-century, non-Berengaudus French gloss that first appeared in an Anglo-Norman text (Paris, Bibliothèque nationale de France, Ms. fr. 403). Its appeal for an English patron is enhanced by the brief coda of events from the life of Saint Edmund drawn from *The Golden Legend*.

2. Lewis (S.) 1992: 80–81.

3. The most dramatic shift occurs from folio 20 to folio 21 to folio 22v, a change also apparent, though less dramatically, in the figure of Christ. A further shift occurs in the facial type of Saint John on folio 25.

4. Ms. 9106 (Gaspar and Lyna 1984–89: pt. 1, 171–74, no. 289, and pt. 2, 440; Smeyers 1998: 377–78, color ill.).

5. Barstow 1992: 260; for a reproduction of the Oxford full border in color, see Hassall 1976: 143.

6. Charron and Gil 1999: 96–97, 100; see also Lewis (S.) 1992: 77.

28

MASTER OF THE MORAL TREATISES
AND WORKSHOP

**Pseudo-Thomas à Kempis, *Une bonne et necessaire doctrine*;
Thomas à Kempis, *L'Imitation de Jésus-Christ*, translation of
De imitatione Christi, books 1–3; Jean Gerson, *Traictie de mendicité
spirituelle*; Jean Gerson, *La Medicine de l'âme*; Saint John
Chrysostom, *Réparation du pécheur*, translation by Alard de Leuze
of *De reparatione lapsi*; and other devotional writings**
Ghent, ca. 1475–79

MANUSCRIPT: ii + 308 + ii folios, 38.7 × 27.5 cm (15¼ × 10¹³⁄₁₆ in.);
justification: 27.6 × 17.9 cm (10⅞ × 7¹⁄₁₆ in.); 30–31 lines of *bastarda*;
5 large miniatures

HERALDRY: Escutcheon with the arms of England impaling those of
Burgundy, fol. 9

BINDING: Nineteenth century; gold-tooled brown calfskin; the arms
of Belgium and title *Traités de Morale*, back cover

COLLECTION: Brussels, Bibliothèque royale de Belgique, Ms. 9272-76

PROVENANCE: Margaret of York, duchess of Burgundy (1446–1503);
Margaret of Austria (1480–1530), at least until 1523; in France by 1793;
Bibliothèque nationale de France, Paris (1794–1815); restituted 1815 to
the Bibliothèque royale de Belgique

JPGM and RA

This miscellany of ten treatises of spiritual instruction
and devotion includes three by the Parisian theologian
Jean Gerson (1363–1429), one by the fourth-century ascetic
Saint John Chrysostom,[1] and one by the advocate of the
Devotio Moderna, Thomas à Kempis, along with one other
that is sometimes ascribed to him. The five two-column
miniatures illustrate the first four writings in the volume
and the last one. *The Creation of Eve* illustrates *Une bonne et
necessaire doctrine* (fol. 9). *The Celebration of the Mass* (ill. 28a)
includes a devout nobleman kneeling in prayer at the
left. He wears a gold chain without a pendant. This miniature illustrates Kempis's *L'Imitation de Jésus-Christ*. Gerson's
Traictie de mendicité spirituelle is accompanied by *A Man Debating His Soul* (fol. 165), in which the soul is portrayed as a
youthful nude in a loincloth. The miniature *A Woman Kneeling before an Altar with a Sculpture of the Trinity* (ill. 28b),
a sort of visual complement to the second miniature, accompanies Gerson's *Medicine de l'âme*, which treats the art of
dying well. *Saint John Chrysostom* shows the saint at his desk

with a friend in attendance, the latter mentioned in the
rubric of the treatise, *Réparation du pécheur* (fol. 254).

While the woman on folio 182 is usually identified as
Margaret of York and the man on folio 55 as Charles the
Bold, Frédéric Lyna and Christiane van den Bergen-Pantens
have rightly expressed reservations about this, due to the
lack of official trappings.[2] Margaret's arms were added to
the book, suggesting that it was not necessarily a commission for her.[3]

Although the artist called the Master of the Moral Treatises takes his name from this book, he may not have been
the sole illuminator. The second, fourth, and fifth miniatures show a lightness of touch and distinctive rapid brushwork that set them apart from the others, calling to mind
some of the best miniatures in Margaret's Apocalypse (cat.
no. 27), such as *The Woman Standing on the Crescent Moon*.
The other two miniatures were probably painted by an
assistant. Georges Doutrepont considered the book's script
to be by the scriptorium of David Aubert, and this has been
accepted by most subsequent writers.[4] The volume has
virtually identical justification to a copy of *Somme le roi*
(Brussels, Bibliothèque royale, Ms. 9106), a manuscript
illuminated by the same workshop for Margaret, which
was signed by Aubert in Ghent in 1475. While the present
book has generally been dated broadly to the nine-year
period of Margaret's marriage to Charles, it was probably
executed late in their alliance, in the period when both Margaret and Aubert were residing in Ghent, between 1475 and
1479, though perhaps before the death of Charles.[5]   T. K.

Notes

1. Morgan (1992: 67) believed that this was probably the translation that Alard le Fèvre undertook for Philip the Bold.

2. Van den Bergen-Pantens, in Bousmanne and Van Hoorebeeck
2000: 121–22.

3. Barstow 1992: 261, no. 21; Van den Bergen-Pantens, in Bousmanne and Van Hoorebeeck 2000: 12.

4. Doutrepont 1909: 235–36.

5. Van den Bergen-Pantens (in Bousmanne and Van Hoorebeeck
2000: 122) dated the volume to around 1470 on the basis of the border
decoration and the fact that Jean V de Créquy (d. 1473) counseled Philip
the Good to commission the translation of the Chrysostom text, the
original copy of which is lost. Charron and Gil (cf. 1999: 95–100) do not
include the book in their discussion of the illuminators of Aubert's
manuscripts.

28a (right)
MASTER OF THE
MORAL TREATISES
*The Celebration of the
Mass*, fol. 55 (detail)

28b (opposite)
MASTER OF THE
MORAL TREATISES
*A Woman Kneeling before
an Altar with a Sculpture
of the Trinity*, fol. 182

Orison sur la premiere partie de la paternostre auec
la premiere demande. Pater nr et c.

Ous aues voulu sire tout puissant que en nostre
priere nous nommons vous et apellons nre pere
Or soit se vous suplie ce nom sanctifie et conferme
en moy Cest que perseueramment Je soie vre fille car aul
trement ne me seriez vous me pere se Je ne vous sui fille
sun nom laultre requiert O quel meschief est perdre
vnng tel pere quele honte est le tour:ouchier ou non ser
uir O quant porray Je veoir cestui pere en son pays Je qui
suis en cest present exil quant Jouray Je de son heritage
qui mest garde Quant seray Je mise en sa salle royale en
son palais imperial Je qui suis durement emprisonnee
et de toutes pars de guerre auuronnee Je qui sui fille de Roy
et de tel Roy comment oseray Je dorenauant oublier mon
lignage et ma noblesse Comment moseray Je habando/
ner en guise de garce auc corzompeurs de toute chastete
les traites aduersaires de mon pere et de moy Mais aus
si quele fiance doy Je prendre de recourir a vng bel pere
si Riche si large et si benng hardiement lui doy Je deman
der qui par auant sans mes desfertes me daigne apeller

This collection of eleven texts of religious instruction and devotion is illustrated by two double-column miniatures, followed by a pair of single-column miniatures. *The Crossing of the Red Sea* (fol. 9) illustrates a passage from Exodus extracted from a *Bible moralisée*. It shows the exiles safely on shore as the ruddy waters close over the Egyptian armies. *Honorius and His Disciple* (fol. 161) marks the opening of the popular *Lucidaire*, adapted from an excerpt from the *Elucidarium* by Honorius Augustodunensis. *La Passion Jhesus Christ* opens with the miniature *Christ before Pilate* (fol. 129), while *Hell* shows a murky scene of the nether world, evoked atmospherically with layers of dark wash. The naked, floating damned and the sparks and trails of flame recall Simon Marmion's closely contemporaneous *Valley of the Homicides* from Margaret's *Les Visions du chevalier Tondal* (cat. no. 14). Like the *Tondal*, the *Purgatoire* is a twelfth-century Irish tale that enjoyed wide popularity in Europe, having been translated into a number of tongues from the original Latin.

Executed rapidly, in broad strokes, often with a wet brush, the miniatures recall especially another volume of devotional treatises in the Bibliothèque royale de Belgique (cat. no. 28) and the miniature in a copy of *La Somme le roi* (Brussels, Bibliothèque royale, Ms. 9106). They are likely by the artist identified by Frédéric Lyna as the Master of the Moral Treatises. Here, as in the master's other works, the painting varies in quality.[1] In the miniature of the Red Sea, the weakest of the cycle, he or an assistant employed a wetter brush and broader handling in the trees and rocks than one generally finds in either the Apocalypse or the other Brussels devotional collection.

The book has the arms and device of Margaret of York (fol. 9) but lacks the colophon found in some of her books. The script has been attributed to David Aubert, who seems to have worked for Margaret at least from the time of her move to Ghent, toward the end of 1474.[2] Given that Margaret's arms and motto were added and given the absence of either for Charles, Christiane van den Bergen-Pantens has suggested that Margaret may have acquired the book after his death.[3] As Pascale Charron and Marc Gil have suggested, the book's manufacture likely belongs to the period when both Margaret and Aubert were in Ghent, that is, through ca. 1479.[4]   T. K.

Notes

1. Gaspar and Lyna 1984–89, 3: 169, 176. It is not clear that Lyna actually coined the name; it may have come from Delaissé.

2. Delaissé, in Brussels 1959: 155–56, no. 197; Charron and Gil 1999: 100.

3. Van den Bergen-Pantens, in Bousmanne and Van Hoorebeeck 2000: 93.

4. Even though they date it ca. 1475 (Charron and Gil 1999: 100).

29

MASTER OF THE MORAL TREATISES

Bible moralisée, Exodus; *La Passion Jhesus Christ*; *Lucidaire*, extracts; Henry of Saltrey, *Le Purgatoire de Saint Patrice*, translation of *Tractatus de purgatorio sancti Patricii*; and other moral writings
Ghent, ca. 1475–79

MANUSCRIPT: iii + 269 folios, 37.3 × 26.8 cm (14⅞ × 10⁹⁄₁₆ in.); justification: 24.6 × 7–1.8–7.2 cm (9¹¹⁄₁₆ × 2¾–¹¹⁄₁₆–2¹³⁄₁₆ in.); 28 lines of *bastarda* in two columns by David Aubert; 2 half-page miniatures, 2 small miniatures

HERALDRY: Escutcheon with the arms of England impaling those of Burgundy, fol. 9; motto of Margaret of York *bien en aviengne*, fols. 2, 9

BINDING: Red chamois; rebacked with gold-tooled brown morocco; large brass corner pieces and clasps; crowned monogram of Léopold I

COLLECTION: Brussels, Bibliothèque royale de Belgique, Ms. 9030-37

PROVENANCE: Margaret of York, duchess of Burgundy (1446–1503); Margaret of Austria (1480–1530), at least until 1523; Bibliothèque de Bourgogne, Brussels; Bibliothèque nationale, Paris (1794–1815); restituted 1815 to the Bibliothèque royale de Belgique

JPGM

HUGO VAN DER GOES

Hugo van der Goes (ca. 1440–1482) was among the most influential Flemish painters of the second half of the fifteenth century. Born in Ghent, he became a master in the painters' guild there on May 5, 1467, sponsored by Joos van Ghent.[1] Between 1468 and 1473 Van der Goes provided ephemera for a variety of celebrations, including the sumptuous festivities in Bruges celebrating the marriage of Margaret of York and Charles the Bold in 1468 and the entry of Charles the Bold into Ghent in 1468/69. With Joos van Ghent, Van der Goes sponsored the membership of the illuminator Alexander Bening in the Ghent painters' guild in 1469. Van der Goes was related to Bening by marriage, and the illuminator in turn sponsored the guild membership of Cornelius van der Goes, a relation of Hugo's. By 1474 Van der Goes had been elected dean of the painter's guild, a post he held until August 1475.[2] From about 1475 he painted as a lay brother at Rooclooster, near Brussels, a house of the Windesheim congregation, where Gaspar Ofhuys chronicled the last year of his life.[3]

Van der Goes's early works, such as *The Adoration of the Magi* (Berlin, Staatliche Museen), exhibit Eyckian attention to detail combined with single-point perspective. Later paintings, such as *The Death of the Virgin* (Bruges, Groeningemuseum) show distortions of space and figures and feature innovative color combinations.[4] Although none of his paintings is signed or dated, Van der Goes's body of work has been constructed around the Portinari Altarpiece (Florence, Galleria degli Uffizi), which is recorded in two sixteenth-century Italian accounts as by "Ugo."[5] Datable to between 1473 and 1478,[6] the altarpiece was commissioned for Saint Egidio in Florence by Tommaso Portinari, a wealthy Italian banker who represented the Medici at the Burgundian court and acted as counselor to Charles the Bold. The work was particularly admired for its sympathetic, finely observed depictions of the coarse-featured shepherds. The realism and emotional concentration evident in the Portinari Altarpiece, which arrived in Florence in 1483, was emulated by Italian artists such as Filippino Lippi, Sandro Botticelli, and Domenico Ghirlandaio, who quoted its shepherds' faces in his *Nativity* (Florence, Santa Trinità).[7]

Van der Goes also influenced artists working in a variety of other media, including tapestry and manuscript illumination (see cat. no. 30). His distinctive physical types and compositions and, to a degree, his artistic sensibility were carried forward by such illuminators as the Master of the First Prayer Book of Maximilian, the Master of the Houghton Miniatures, and the Ghent Associates, through whose work Van der Goes's artistic ideas lasted well into the sixteenth century.   R. G.

Notes

1. The figure of Saint Anthony in the Portinari Altarpiece shares physiognomy with Joos van Ghent's Joseph in *The Adoration of the Magi* (New York, Metropolitan Museum of Art, 41.190.21), giving evidence of the artists' friendship.

2. Dhanens 1998: 36. Jean Hey (Master of Moulins) may have trained with Van der Goes; see New York 1998: 181.

3. See Stechow 1966: 15–18.

4. New York 1998: 395. Much of his oeuvre was known through copies; see Winkler 1964: 95–246.

5. Vasari in 1550 noted that a picture in Santa Maria Nuova, Florence, was by "Ugo d'Anversa." Ludovico Guicciardini mentions "Ugo d'Anversa, who made an extremely beautiful painting which can be seen in Santa Maria Nuova, Florence" (author's translation); see, among other early editions, Guicciardini 1588: 128. Catherine Reynolds (in DOA 1996, 12: 845) noted that, in sixteenth-century Italy, Antwerp may have been synonymous with the entire Netherlands.

6. Dhanens 1998: 257–60.

7. New York 1998: 49.

30

AFTER HUGO VAN DER GOES

A Seated Female Figure
Ghent, ca. 1475

Brush and ink heightened with white on green prepared paper, 22.8 × 18.8 cm (9 × 7 7/16 in.)

INSCRIPTIONS: *Sandro scrive che sicuro sia* on backing sheet, top center, in ink, sixteenth-century (?) hand; *Pietro Perugino* below, different hand

COLLECTION: London, Courtauld Institute Gallery, Princes Gate Collection 314 (D1978.PG.314)

PROVENANCE: Italian (?) collection, sixteenth century; private collection, France; M. L. Rosenthal, Bern, in 1935; L. V. Randall, Montreal [his sale, Sotheby's, London, May 10, 1961, lot 4]; [to Colnaghi, London]; Count Antoine Seilern, Princes Gate; bequeathed 1978

R A

Although this superb large chiaroscuro drawing is one of only two drawings that have generally been accepted as by Hugo van der Goes himself, Stephanie Buck argues that it is a copy by a close associate of the artist.[1] The drawing shows a young woman seated on the ground with her hands resting on a book. She grasps the ring finger of her right hand with the thumb and index finger of her left hand. She wears the archaic but courtly costume of *robe royale* with a circlet with attached net (*crespine*) in her hair. The figure is probably based on Van der Goes's lost panel *The Virgin and Child with Female Saints*.[2] A copy attributed to Adriaen Isenbrandt (Munich, Alte Pinakothek) may provide the best record of the painting's character.[3] The drawing copied the figure in the left foreground of the original.

30

AFTER HUGO
VAN DER GOES

A Seated Female Figure

The drawing, remarkably well preserved, almost certainly functioned as a model for manuscript illuminators.[4] Van der Goes's pervasive influence on the first and subsequent generations of Flemish illuminators in the new style is widely acknowledged, and the drawing offers the most direct and intimate evidence of his role. The earliest known copy after it—the *Saint Barbara* (fig. 57) in the Emerson-White Hours (cat. no. 32) by one of the Ghent Associates—may have been painted within the Ghent artist's lifetime. It follows the drawing closely in the details of the costume and its elaborate folds. Overall, the richness and subtlety of modeling in the *Saint Barbara* seem to owe their integrity to the nuanced example of the Courtauld drawing, especially the distinctive highlights on the faces, hands, and sleeve.

The miniature may have been executed as early as 1480, not long after the drawing was completed. In the drapery on the ground to the left and right of the figure at the back, the few passages where the drawing itself is a bit ambiguous, the illuminator's own depiction of the folds is also weakest. The miniature is also noteworthy for the artist's attempt to elaborate the skirt, which is cut off in the drawing in its present state. That the drawing itself is not significantly trimmed at the right or left is confirmed by the fact that nearly all the other manuscript copies of the drawing are comparably cropped in design.[5]

The illuminator gained access to the drawing when he was working on the Emerson-White *Saint Barbara*. Thereafter the Master of the First Prayer Book of Maximilian or

Figure 57
GHENT ASSOCIATES
Saint Barbara. In the
Emerson-White Hours,
fol. 112v (see cat. no. 32)

members of his workshop copied it several times,[6] though always in illuminations executed as much as two decades later. Thus, the Maximilian Master eventually gained possession of it. Since Alexander Bening was related to Van der Goes by marriage, this helps to support the identification of Bening with the Maximilian Master. It was probably through Gerard David's collaboration with the Maximilian Master on the Mayer van den Bergh Breviary (cat. no. 92, fol. 611v) that the Bruges painter also gained access to the pattern.[7] By the sixteenth century many artists were using it or a faithful version of it, including Simon Bening,[8] the Master of the David Scenes in the Grimani Breviary,[9] and an artist from the circle of the Master of Charles V.[10] At least thirteen miniatures of this figure are known, not all demonstrably based on the Courtauld drawing, but likely all ultimately derived from it. The drawing seems to have been most widely copied in the first two decades of the sixteenth century, but several examples are known from as late as the 1530s, well over half a century after Van der Goes's original invention.[11]

While the figure in Van der Goes's lost original painting appears to have represented Saint Catherine,[12] the miniatures represent either her or Saint Barbara. They were the two most popular female saints in northern Europe during the late Middle Ages and are often the most prominent women in pictorial cycles of the suffrages. Thus the model's distinguished pedigree may have ensured its use for significant illumination within a given prayer book. Many of the miniatures in question, starting with the Emerson-White *Saint Barbara*, show the saint's robe made of an elaborate brocade, which is lacking entirely in the drawing.

Nevertheless, the nature of the brocade ornament and its arrangement on the skirt vary to a considerable degree among the versions, suggesting that it is an interpolation of the illuminators. David and the Master of the David Scenes are among the few who omitted the brocade.

Another version of the drawing itself, now missing, was in the Kupferstichkabinett in Dresden.[13] Although probably an early copy after the Courtauld drawing, it was less elaborate, lacking the heightening in white and many details, including parts of the hair, the brooch, and portions of the border at the hem, while adding other details, including small beads along the edges of the book cloth. It is not likely that this drawing served as a model for any of the surviving miniatures, but its existence raises a question. Did the admiration for the Courtauld drawing lead to a series of careful copies that facilitated the propagation of the design in so many Flemish manuscripts? If this is the case, then the Courtauld drawing's exquisite condition is less surprising.

T. K.

Notes

1. Friedländer 1935: 99–104; Seilern 1969: 39–42, Campbell 1985: 49; Braham, in London 1991: 82; Buck 2003. The other drawing by Hugo is the large *Jacob and Rachel* at Christ Church, Oxford.

2. Some specialists have considered it a *ricordo*, Van der Goes's own copy after this figure; see Seilern 1955: 118, no. 167; Winkler 1964: 166, n. 2.

3. For a useful summary of the early versions and variants after the lost painting, see Campbell 1985: 49–51, under no. 32. Winkler (1964) thought that the Munich painting was a copy after a lost work by Gerard David based on the lost painting by Van der Goes.

4. Given its dimensions, it was not likely conceived for this purpose, and hence it was not necessarily drawn by an illuminator.

5. Two others date much later, a *Saint Catherine* by the Master of the David Scenes in Douce 112 (cat. no. 137, fol. 165) and a *Saint Catherine* in one of the prayer books for Charles V of 1533 (cat. no. 166, fol. 61v). The skirt is particularly awkward at the far left and right.

6. *Saint Barbara* in the La Flora Hours, Naples (cat. no. 93, fol. 341v) and, from his workshop, *Saint Barbara* in the Breviary of Eleanor of Portugal (cat. no. 91, fol. 558v).

7. Winkler (1964: 161, 164, fig. 124) believed that David may have copied the lost painting by Van der Goes with this figure type, but the corresponding figure there, known only in a copy after David, seems at best to be a variant of that in the Courtauld drawing. See also Campbell 1985: 49–50. David may have painted part of the *Saint Barbara* in the Grimani Breviary (cat. no. 126, fol. 828v), which is also based on the drawing.

8. *Virgin and Child with Five Female Saints* in the Grimani Breviary (cat. no. 126, fol. 719v). This miniature, which seems to reflect Hugo's lost painting, might therefore also be based on a larger, more complex model. Another example, by Simon Bening or his workshop, is *Saint Catherine* in the *Hortulus animae* (Vienna, Österreichische National-bibliothek, codex 2706; Dömhöffer 1907, 2; pl. 608).

9. *Saint Catherine* in the Hours of Joanna of Castile (cat. no. 114, fol. 417v) and the example from Douce 112 cited in note 5.

10. See note 5.

11. *Saint Catherine* in the Prayer Book of Antoine de Berghes (cat. no. 168, fol. 49) and *Saint Catherine* in the Prayer Book of Charles V of 1533 (cat. no. 166, fol. 61v).

12. This is based on Buck's 2003 interpretation of the Courtauld drawing. Campbell (1985: 49) believes that the figure in Van der Goes's lost painting represented Saint Ursula.

13. Woermann 1896: no. 5 (ill.). In brush, it measured 19.7 × 11.4 cm (7¾ × 4½ in.).

31
FOLLOWER OF
HUGO VAN DER GOES
The Nativity

31

FOLLOWER OF HUGO VAN DER GOES

The Nativity
Ghent, 1480s

Oil on wood panel, 32.5 × 32.5 cm (12¾ × 12¾ in.)

INSCRIPTIONS: [false] *Jan van Eyck [1]410*, lower front edge, side of manger

COLLECTION: Salisbury, Wilton House, Earl of Pembroke Collection, no. 309

PROVENANCE: Perhaps bought by Philip, fourth earl of Pembroke, before 1650, or Thomas, eighth earl, before 1730

R A

Although the Wilton House *Nativity* was accepted early on as an autograph work by Hugo van der Goes,[1] Joseph Destrée and Georges Hulin de Loo, followed by Friedrich Winkler, considered it to be a copy,[2] and Erwin Panofsky acknowledged the possibility that it was the work of an imitator.[3] Recently scholars have noted differences in the handling and execution of the Wilton House *Nativity* in comparison to Van der Goes's generally accepted works, and they now uniformly assign the panel to a follower.[4] The execution of the work is uneven—compare, for example, the angels at the left with those of poorer quality and condition at the right—and it is possible that the artist more proficiently rendered forms when following workshop patterns than when relying on his own invention.

There can be no disputing the derivation of the Wilton House painting from Van der Goes's *Adoration of the Shepherds* in Berlin (fig. 58).[5] In particular, the faces of the Virgin and Joseph are akin in each, as are the general pose and red robe of Joseph. Both show the angels, shepherds, and the ox and the ass pressing toward the Christ child, who, lying in a manger, turns his head to address the viewer directly. Even the centrally placed background stable wall and open-air vistas to the left and right (revealing the Annunciation to the Shepherds) bear direct comparison.

But the Wilton House *Nativity* is a condensed version of the Berlin painting, essentially a whittled-down account of the Adoration of the Shepherds.[6] It heralds a new treatment of narrative with which Van der Goes experimented during his relatively brief artistic career.[7] His followers found the dramatic close-up especially effective for themes such as the Nativity, the Adoration of the Magi, the Deposition, and the Descent from the Cross. This format became popular as well with manuscript illuminators beginning in the 1480s, when it was used especially effectively by Simon Marmion and his workshop in works such as the La Flora Hours (cat. no. 93) and the Huth Hours (cat. no. 33). Considerably later, in the late 1520s, the Stein Quadriptych (cat. no. 146) by Simon Bening and his workshop shows the continued efficacy of the half-length format and the potential of the dramatic close-up for enhanced emotional power. In addition to this new compositional formula, illuminators revealed their indebtedness to Van der Goes's style through their assimilation of certain types. The worldly and crude-looking shepherds at the left in the Wilton House *Nativity* are similar to those that appear, for example, in *The Annunciation to the Shepherds* attributed to the Master of the Houghton Miniatures (ill. 32d). Such types, as well as the use of varied hand gestures in order to heighten the expression of the narrative, are conventions inspired by Van der Goes's example, as the Wilton House *Nativity* so effectively conveys.   M. W. A.

Notes
1. Schöne 1939: 120; Van Puyvelde 1948: pl. 70; Van Puyvelde 1953: 225; Winkler 1964: 212; Friedländer 1967: 33, 70–71; Ringbom 1984: 99.
2. Hulin de Loo, cited in Destrée 1914: 119; Winkler 1964: 212.
3. Panofsky 1953: 501.
4. Sander 1996: 255; Dhanens 1998: 162. Lorne Campbell suggested "an early imitator who had a fairly comprehensive knowledge of Van der Goes's work" (correspondence with the author, September 24, 2002).
5. Friedländer 1967–76, 4: 33; Ringbom 1984: 99.
6. There are three known variations on the Wilton House *Nativity*: Matuschke à Biechów collection, Museum of Nysa (PA 105) (Białostocki, in Warsaw 1960: no. 23); Mayer collection, Kötzchenbroda; and Rueda collection, Riehen (near Basel).
7. This was pointed out by Friedländer (1967–76, 4: 33) and discussed by Ringbom (1984: 99).

Figure 58
HUGO VAN DER GOES
The Adoration of the Shepherds, ca. 1480. Oil on wood panel, 97 × 246 cm (38³⁄₁₆ × 96⅞ in.). Berlin, Staatliche Museen zu Berlin, Gemäldegalerie (1622A)

MASTER OF THE HOUGHTON MINIATURES

A group of miniatures in the Emerson-White Hours in the Houghton Library (cat. no. 32) have long been associated with the style of the Master of Mary of Burgundy but not attributed to him.[1] Some in this group may be early works by the Ghent Associates, but one full-page miniature, *Saint Anthony Abbot in the Wilderness* (ill. 32a), is by a superior hand. The same artist painted several of this book's historiated borders, notably *Scenes from the Life of Saint Anthony* (see ill. 32a), *The Funeral Procession of the Virgin* (ill. 32b), and *Two Pilgrims in a Church Portal* (fol. 166). These four illuminations help to define his style and provide a foundation for adding other miniatures to his slender oeuvre (cat. nos. 33–35). *Saint Anthony Abbot* represents the elderly desert saint as distinctively Goesian, with bald dome and full, hoary beard. The miniature is distinctive for the refinement of the handling of the landscape—not only in texture, as in the varied and often wispy foliage, but also in the vista, where the recession has a measured quality and an imposing depth and scale. Within the confines of the border with the funeral procession, the artist conveyed depth through nuances of color, value, relative size, and even the direction of movement.

In recent years two detached miniatures have been identified as originally belonging to the Emerson-White Hours. Both are by the painter of the full-page Saint Anthony miniature. *The Annunciation to the Shepherds* shows a rural hilltop in the foreground, with Bethlehem set on a knoll in the middle distance (ill. 32d). The hilltop and knoll are peaks in an undulating topography. At the bottom right a moated castle occupies a valley; the orthogonal lines defined by its architecture demarcate the distance between the hills. Flemish illuminators regularly used a variegated landscape as a setting for sequential narratives. Few conveyed rolling terrain with comparable majesty and conviction. In the Brussels *Mass of Saint Gregory* (ill. 32c), also from the Emerson-White Hours, the imposing scale of the choir and muted overall tonality lend drama and coherence to a ponderous subject that confounded even the best of artists. Similar architecture, precisely measured and distinctly textured, serves as a backdrop to *The Visitation* (fig. 59) and *The Disputation of Saint Barbara* in the Huth Hours (ill. 33a), both attributable to the Master of the Houghton Miniatures. The same handling is evident in the magnificent palatial setting of *David in Prayer*, one of two miniatures from a lost devotional book with Dominican iconography (ill. 34a). The architecture in the small group of miniatures by this artist is painted neutrally, in muted browns and grays. The contours and moldings of the structures define orthogonals that are relieved by horizontals in the middle distance. The

artist achieved equilibrium in the discreet interplay of horizontal, vertical, and orthogonal elements.

One of this illuminator's strengths is crisp, precise draftsmanship. He achieved particular subtlety and freshness in his facial types, ranging from the properly virginal Mary to the coarse-featured shepherds to the elderly figures of Saint Elizabeth, Saint Anthony, and Saint Gregory. A fine, wiry line is evident in the painting of hair, especially beards. A drawing in Berlin with various head studies (ill. 35) shows the same fidelity of observation and control of line. Other hallmarks of his technique and taste include attention to the smallest details, such as the feet of the disciples carrying the Virgin's bier. The soles of the feet are lighter in color than the rest. In *The Annunciation to the Shepherds* (ill. 32d) the illuminator's use of light is resourceful, in particular the column of golden angels hovering like a beacon above the stable. Only the golden light in the windows otherwise offers a suggestion of the stable's identity.[2] He articulated his narratives crisply, even in the most constricted formats, such as the gray archivolts of an architectural border in the Emerson-White Hours that features biblical subjects. The artist occasionally used a highly dilute medium, a wet-on-wet technique, found in the robe of the kneeling monk in the foreground of the Saint Gregory miniature (ill. 32c), in the skirt of Saint Barbara in *The Disputation*, and in the skirt of Elizabeth in *The Visitation*. Another characteristic is an affinity for animals stretching their torsos, such as the lions in the Saint Anthony border, the leaping dog in the foreground of *The Disputation*, and the dog in the foreground of *The Annunciation to the Shepherds*.

Friedrich Winkler, G. I. Lieftinck, and Anne van Buren attributed *The Mass of Saint Gregory* to the Master of Mary of Burgundy.[3] J. J. G. Alexander attributed *The Annunciation to the Shepherds* to the same famous illuminator, and Brinkmann compared *Saint Anthony*, with its partly pointillist brushwork, with the Agony in the Garden vignette in the Voustre Demeure Hours *Crucifixion* (ill. 20c), also usually attributed to this master.[4] There are numerous parallels between the work of the Vienna Master of Mary of Burgundy, who may have painted the latter, and the Master of the Houghton Miniatures: a light-filled aesthetic shared with oil painting, occasional use of a fine pointillist technique, similarity in certain facial types, superb draftsmanship, and microscopic brushwork. The differences between the two are, however, substantial. The figure types in the work of the Master of the Houghton Miniatures have greater physical breadth and weight. Facial outlines are rounder and less attenuated. The male figures especially are more Goesian—with strong noses, deep-set or even

sunken eyes, strong cheekbones, and bony foreheads—
while the facial types of the Vienna Master in general owe
more to Joos van Ghent. In the Saint Anthony border the
Houghton Master constructed a rhythmic spatial recession
that exists behind the text block, while the Vienna Master
of Mary of Burgundy (or an associate) closed off the far distance in his rendition of the same border subject in the
Voustre Demeure Hours. The Master of the Houghton
Miniatures was more adventurous in the depiction of space
and often used a low vantage point. He relied on orthogonals that converge toward a proximate center in a measured recession.

Since so little of this artist's work has been identified,
localizing the illumination is difficult. His debt to Van der
Goes may indicate Ghent as a possible base of operation.
Although he collaborated with Marmion on the only two
surviving books with his miniatures, his fully formed artistic style has little to do with the art of this time in Hainaut.
He was active around 1480.[5]   T. K.

Notes

1. Hulin de Loo (1939b: 179) assigned the miniature of Saint
Anthony Abbot, along with the *Saint Barbara*, to the "groupe Marie de
Bourgogne"; Pächt (1948: 71–72, no. 31) placed the same miniatures
under "doubtful attributions" to the Master of Mary of Burgundy. On
the Master of Mary of Burgundy, whose oeuvre has continually been
revised by scholars over decades, see the biography of the Vienna Master of Mary of Burgundy in this volume. As a result of this revisionism,
works formerly assigned to the Master of Mary of Burgundy have been
attributed to the Vienna Master of Mary of Burgundy and other artists.

2. This invention was imitated by later illuminators, for example,
by the Master of the First Prayer Book of Maximilian in the Hours of
Isabella of Castile (cat. no. 105, fol. 131v; cf. De Winter 1981: 386, fig. 88).

3. Winkler 1925: 113, 168; Lieftinck 1969: 37–38; Van Buren, in DOA
1996, 20: 725.

4. Alexander 1988: 123; Brinkmann 1997: 199.

5. Brinkmann (1997: 173–76) has suggested, and Weniger (2001:
143–51) has argued forcefully for, the identification of the illuminator
with the painter Jan Provost, but their arguments are unconvincing, as
is the attribution of *The Birth of the Virgin* in the Mayer van den Bergh
Breviary (cat. no. 92) to this book painter. See also cat. no. 92; Winkler
1957: 285–89; and Nieuwdorp and Dekeyzer 1997: 9.

32

SIMON MARMION, MASTER OF THE DRESDEN PRAYER BOOK, MASTER OF THE HOUGHTON MINIATURES, GHENT ASSOCIATES, AND ANOTHER ARTIST

Emerson-White Hours
Use of Rome
Valenciennes, Bruges, and Ghent, late 1470s/early 1480s (before 1482)

MANUSCRIPT: vi + 248 folios in 2 continuously foliated volumes
(vol. 1, 118 folios; vol. 2, 130 folios), 14.5 × 10.2 cm (5 11/16 × 4 in.),
justification: 7.2 × 4.9 cm (2 3/16 × 1 15/16 in.); 20 lines of *gotica rotunda*;
7 full-page miniatures, 28 historiated initials, 13 historiated borders,
24 roundels in calendar

HERALDRY: Initials *YY*, fols. 5v, 6, 10v, 196

BINDING: Joseph William Zaehnsdorf (1853–1930), London, 1891;
blue morocco; gilt

COLLECTION: Cambridge, Massachusetts, Houghton Library,
Typ. 443–443.1

PROVENANCE: [Quaritch Cat. 3460, 1886, no. 35696]; to William
Stirling Maxwell; [Quaritch again, who divided the manuscript in
two volumes]. Vol. 1: William A. White, in 1892; by descent to
Mrs. William Emerson; presented 1958 by Harold T. White, Donald
Moffat, and Mrs. Jon Wiig. Vol. 2: Alfred T. White, in 1892; inherited
by his son-in-law Adrian van Sinderen, Brooklyn; deposited 1966 by
Mrs. Adrian van Sinderen, Washington, Connecticut

JPGM

The Annunciation to the Shepherds
Miniature from the Emerson-White Hours

One full-page miniature, 12.5 × 9 cm (4 7/8 × 3 1/2 in.); back: blank

COLLECTION: Los Angeles, J. Paul Getty Museum, Ms. 60 (95.ML.53)

PROVENANCE: Mrs. M. Williams, Great Britain [on deposit at the
Bodleian Library (Ms. Dep. D. 417), Oxford]; [sale, Sotheby's,
London, June 20, 1995, lot 24]; acquired 1995

JPGM and RA

The Mass of Saint Gregory
Miniature from the Emerson-White Hours

One full-page miniature, 12 × 8.4 cm (4 3/4 × 3 5/16 in.); back: blank

COLLECTION: Brussels, Bibliothèque royale de Belgique, Ms. II 3634-6

PROVENANCE: Joseph Gielen; his donation, September 24, 1906

JPGM and RA

The Houghton Library's once lavish devotional book—
one of the most important of the era that featured the
new aesthetic of partially illusionistic borders of flowers,
insects, and other naturalia—has lost most of its full-page
miniatures. Nevertheless, its high artistic ambitions are
evident in the contributions of four of the finest illuminators of the day: Simon Marmion, the Master of the
Houghton Miniatures (named for this book), the Master of
the Dresden Prayer Book, and one of the Ghent Associates.
Marmion illuminated three of the nine surviving full-page
miniatures and five of the twenty-eight historiated initials.[1]
Further, a full-page *Ascension* by him in a Belgian private
collection perhaps illustrated this volume's Mass of the
Ascension.[2] The Master of the Dresden Prayer Book
painted the twenty-four highly inventive calendar roundels
of the Emerson-White Hours and twenty historiated initials but none of the surviving full-page miniatures. The
most gifted of the Ghent Associates painted the full-page

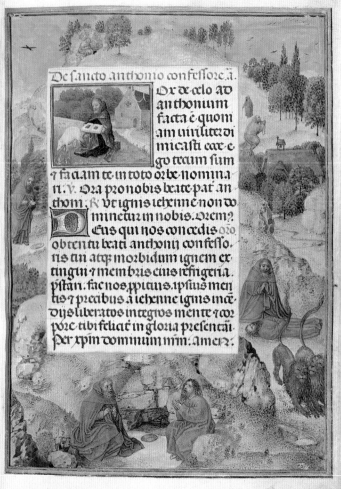

32a

MASTER OF THE
HOUGHTON
MINIATURES
*Saint Anthony Abbot in the
Wilderness* and *Scenes
from the Life of Saint
Anthony Abbot,* border,
fols. 99v–100

miniatures *Saint George and the Dragon, Saint Catherine of Alexandria* (ill. 32f), and *Saint Barbara* and at least three of the historiated borders.[3] A fifth artist probably illuminated the border with Judas leading the soldiers into Gethsemane and its historiated initial with the soldiers falling before Christ. He executed the spirited figures' garments in a painterly, distinctive white-on-white.

The Master of the Houghton Miniatures painted *Saint Anthony Abbot in the Wilderness* (ill. 32a), the historiated border with the life of Saint Anthony, the historiated border with *The Funeral Procession of the Virgin* (ill. 32b), the historiated border with pilgrims in the portal of a church, a damaged border with a cemetery, a historiated initial, and possibly several borders with camaïeux of biblical subjects. In addition, the artist painted the bold *Annunciation to the Shepherds* (ill. 32d) in the Getty Museum that originally illustrated Terce of the Hours of the Virgin, where the border features an Adoration of the Shepherds (ill. 32e) that is perhaps by a lesser hand of the Ghent Associates. The Master of the Houghton Miniatures also painted *The Mass of Saint Gregory* (ill. 32c) now in Brussels, which illustrated the "Adoro te."

The Emerson-White Hours is a textual twin of the Huth Hours (cat. no. 33). The two books were written by the same scribe, and the majority of their extensive offices and devotions are nearly identical, an occurrence that is not unknown but is uncommon for such elaborate books.[4] Their calendars, based on the same model, agree strongly, by 84 percent, and their litanies are nearly identical, save for a saint or two in either.[5] Besides the core texts and the Psalter of Saint Jerome, which appeared frequently at the time, further texts in common include dominical prayers for Advent, a Psalter of the Passion, an Office of the Passion, an Office for Good Friday, a long group of suffrages that differ by only two, and certain prayers. Significantly, both lack the Gospel sequences, a common feature of Flemish books of this time.

Further, the two books' three main illuminators are the same: Marmion, the Master of the Houghton Miniatures, and the Master of the Dresden Prayer Book. The Dresden Master illuminated the calendar in both with comparably elaborate, though not identical, cycles of twenty-four roundels. Marmion illuminated the suffrages of Saint Jerome, Saint Christopher, and Saint Apollonia in the two books, all with full-page miniatures, with the exception of Apollonia in the Huth Hours. And the books share a similar type of illusionistic border, in which flowers and painted gold grounds are dominant. The borders extend to every writ-

32b
MASTER OF THE
HOUGHTON
MINIATURES
*The Funeral Procession of
the Virgin*, border, fol. 171

32c
MASTER OF THE
HOUGHTON
MINIATURES
The Mass of Saint Gregory

ten page. Bar borders appear where full borders do not, and the full borders also feature other similar motifs: a border of red brocade, another with children playing tops, one that features camaïeux and jeweled flowers, and one with columns wrapped in banderoles that flank a shallow niche.[6] The main difference between the two is that the Emerson-White Hours features a greater variety of border types.[7]

Thus it appears that the two books were created for the most part by the same team (whose members, significantly, resided in different towns) and likely produced either back-to-back or simultaneously, a conclusion further supported by the closeness of Marmion's miniatures from one book to the other.[8] But there are striking differences in the programs of illumination and in the division of labor among the artists. While we do not know the original number of full-page miniatures in the Emerson-White Hours, it was likely as many as in the Huth Hours and perhaps a few more. Yet the Emerson-White has fourteen historiated borders where the Huth has three, but only twenty-eight historiated initials where the Huth has fifty.[9] While the books have the same number of lines per page, twenty or nineteen, each is laid out slightly differently, giving certain offices more emphasis through illumination. Whereas Marmion painted most of the lavish Huth Hours, including all but

two of the large miniatures and historiated initials, it is less certain that he was the main artist here. As noted, the Master of the Dresden Prayer Book illustrated the Huth calendar, but there he provided no other miniatures or initials. And the Master of the Houghton Miniatures enjoyed a larger role in this book than he did in the Huth Hours, where he painted only two full-page miniatures and no initials or borders.

The Emerson-White Hours has been associated with the Voustre Demeure Hours (cat. no. 20), another luxury prayer book from roughly the same period that also features the new style of partially illusionistic borders, pictorially ambitious historiated borders, inserted full-page miniatures by Marmion, and illuminations by an innovative artist from Ghent.[10] Despite the exquisite quality and originality of some of the borders in the Emerson-White Hours—especially *The Funeral Procession of the Virgin*, *Scenes from the Life of Saint Anthony Abbot*, and *Two Pilgrims in a Church Portal*—others, including *The Life of Saint Barbara* and *Scenes from the Passion*, are copies, most likely after the Voustre Demeure Hours. Thus the manuscript under discussion here is probably later in date than the latter book, which belongs to the second half of the 1470s.[11]

32d
MASTER OF THE
HOUGHTON
MINIATURES
*The Annunciation to
the Shepherds*

32e
GHENT ASSOCIATES (?)
*The Adoration of the
Shepherds*, border, fol. 157

The Emerson-White Hours probably dates to the late 1470s or early 1480s and certainly was completed before 1482. The border with the funeral procession of the Virgin, which illustrates Complines of the Hours of the Holy Spirit, is copied in part in the Berlin Hours of Mary of Burgundy and Maximilian (cat. no. 38). There, in the form of a full-page miniature, the design illustrates the Monday Hours of the Dead.[12] The Berlin Hours was likely largely complete by the death of Mary of Burgundy in 1482. Moreover, the motif of the two shepherds in the Getty *Annunciation to the Shepherds* (ill. 32d) is imitated in mirror image in the Hours of William Lord Hastings (cat. no. 25), which was completed by the noble's death in 1483.[13]

The evidence of prayers written in Spanish by two different hands, both apparently of the late fifteenth century, suggests that at a very early moment in its history the book belonged to a Spaniard. The initials *YY* have been connected with the Spanish names Juana and Isabella, but this has not led to a convincing identification of the book's first owner. Neither the calendar nor the litany points in any particular way to a Spanish patron.[14] Indeed, the extreme similarity of the calendar and litany to those in the Huth Hours, which was apparently made for a French-speaking patron, raises interesting questions about their relative liturgical significance. They were certainly derived from

the same models. One notable distinction between the two *horae* is that the Emerson-White Hours includes Saint Apollonia both in the litany and in a full-page miniature in the suffrages, while the Huth Hours shows only a modest historiated initial of Apollonia in the suffrages, and there is no mention of her in the litany.[15]

T. K.

Notes

1. Three of the historiated borders (fols. 111, 113, 181) open into the space where historiated initials generally appear in this book. Thus these spaces are historiated, but I have not counted them here since they are part of historiated borders.

2. Collection of Sir Dominique de Hertoghe, Antwerp (provenance: sale, Hôtel Drouot, Paris, June 11, 1954, lot 12; to Princess Monique de Croÿ-Solve; to Pascal Ruys Raquez, Brussels). The leaf measures 14.3 × 9.8 cm (5⅝ × 3⅞ in.), the approximate dimensions of the leaves of the Emerson-White Hours. Moreover, the dimensions of the painted area, 12 × 8.2 cm (4¾ × 3¼ in.), correspond closely to those for the Saint Christopher miniature in the Emerson-White Hours (fol. 115v; 11.9 × 8.2 cm [4¹¹⁄₁₆ × 3¼ in.]). Although the miniature fits stylistically with Marmion's late work, it is less finely painted than those by the artist still in the book. I am grateful to Sir Dominique for providing access to the leaf and its history.

3. The artist's hand is subtler and finer than that of the Master of the First Prayer Book of Maximilian, though there is some similarity in the small-featured facial types of the female saints, the bright blue skies with wispy white clouds, and the painting of trees with oval boughs and fine points of color. Particularly striking and sophisticated is the

Haven, Connecticut (Beinecke Library, Ms. 287, fol. 38). For a facsimile of the former, see Brinkmann 1992c.

7. In the Emerson-White Hours this includes a large number of full and bar borders with Passion iconography.

8. On the relationship between the miniatures, see Kren, in Malibu 1983a: 33–34, 38–39, n. 18.

9. The books also complement each other in eccentric ways. For example, the Hours of the Virgin in the Huth Hours has small miniatures to illustrate the first six hours but not the last two. In the same office the Emerson-White Hours has small miniatures that illustrate the last two but not the first six.

10. Clark 1992: 207, n. 18; Brinkmann 1997: 196–98.

11. Both books give particular prominence to Saint Barbara, with a full-page miniature and a historiated border, and it seems likely that both gave prominence in a similar way to Saint Anthony Abbot, although the full-page miniature for this saint is now lacking from the Voustre Demeure Hours.

12. It is changed into a different subject, a generic funeral procession rather than that of the Virgin. See König et al. 1998: 45.

13. Alexander 1988: 123–25; also imitated is the relationship of the flanking houses to the plateau of the foreground.

14. The book was long called the Hours of Joanna of Castile ("Juana la Loca"; since Quaritch 1887: 3458, col. 35696), but in recent years some scholars have correctly been skeptical about this (Hindman 1977: 189). The suggestion that the book was made for Hippolyte de Berthoz and Isabeau van Keverwijk (Hulin de Loo 1939b: 179; Pächt 1948: 71–72; Wieck 1983: 50, no. 24) also seems unlikely (Van den Bergen-Pantens 2002: 18). They have been connected to the book through the initials *YY*.

15. See also note 5.

handling of the prone body of the emperor under Saint Catherine (ill. 32f), his shoulders flat against the ground, his long, elegant legs twisted to the side. He is more finely drawn, fully developed, and richly modeled than other versions of this subject from the period around 1475–85 (see cat. no. 40), including those by the Maximilian Master (see cat. no. 41). Does this result from the influence of the Houghton Master? The facial type of Saint Catherine—with oval face, narrow pursed lips, long nose, and small eyes with rounded brow—is reminiscent of the half-length *Virgin and Child* in the Berlin Hours of Mary and Maximilian (cat. no. 38, fol. 284v). *Saint George and the Dragon* is the finest of the early versions of this composition that were derived from or became patterns (cf. cat. nos. 37, 38). *Saint Barbara* is based on the well-known drawing by Hugo van der Goes (cat. no. 30).

4. The devotions are not in the same sequence in the two books, however, which may be the result of the division of the Emerson-White Hours into two volumes during the late nineteenth century. Hindman (1977: 189–91) was the first to explore in detail some of the codicological similarities between the two books.

5. The percentage is derived from a computerized analysis of Flemish and French calendars of the later Middle Ages by John Plummer, a process he describes in Baltimore 1988: 149–52. The Emerson-White omits Adrian and Denis among the martyrs in the Huth Hours litany, while the Huth Hours omits Saint Apollonia among virgins. Among the confessors Anthony comes earlier in the Huth sequence, between Augustine and Nicholas. The Emerson-White Hours also switches the order of Catherine and Barbara.

6. In the Emerson-White Hours the banderoles are blank, while in the Huth Hours they carry the initials *MY/YM* (fol. 12). Other books of hours that feature the same or a similar pattern and the initials *MY/YM* are in the Vatican Library (Ms. Vat. Lat. 10293, fol. 13v) and in New

This elaborate book of hours contains the most ambitious devotional program by Simon Marmion and his workshop. He and his assistants painted not only twenty-two of the twenty-four surviving inserted full-page miniatures[1] but also the majority of the fifty small miniatures.[2] Marmion's full-page illuminations—including *The Temptation of Saint Anthony*, *Saint Jerome in the Wilderness*, *Saint Christopher*, and *The Annunciation to the Shepherds*—are noteworthy for their highly developed landscapes, which represent the culmination of a careerlong interest.[3] Six of Marmion's large miniatures show half-lengths, a format he helped to popularize among book painters, and seventeen of the full-page miniatures have no borders whatsoever, a striking development.[4] The book has strong visual unity, the result of the coherence of the cycle of miniatures by a single painter and his workshop and also of the uniformity of the borders. The quality of the decorated borders, most of them with flowers and insects on gold-colored grounds, is remarkable, and every text page has a bar border of this type.

The Master of the Houghton Miniatures, the youngest of the three artists who collaborated on this book and the one with the most naturalistic style, painted *The Visitation* (fig. 59) and *The Disputation of Saint Barbara* (ill. 33a). The Master of the Dresden Prayer Book illuminated the unusually expansive cycle of twenty-four roundels in the calendar, one of several ambitious calendar decorations by this artist in these years.

The iconographic program emphasizes the Passion, commencing immediately after the calendar with a full-page miniature of the Sacrifice of Isaac, the typological antecedent of the Crucifixion, illustrating the opening of the Office of the Passion. Eight small initials also illustrate the hours of this office. Additional Passion themes include the individual wounds of Christ and—illustrating the Penitential Psalms, Masses and/or Offices of the Cross, Good Friday, Easter, and the Ascension—*The Last Judgment*, *The Crucifixion* (ill. 33b), *The Adoration of the Cross*, *Three Marys at the Tomb*, and *The Ascension*. The Office of the Virgin features both a cycle of full-page miniatures of the life of the Virgin and a contiguous cycle of six small historiated initials.[5]

Particularly striking visually are the fifteen suffrages, all of which are illustrated. Seven of them have full-page miniatures, and eleven have seven-line miniatures. The suffrages for Saint James the Greater, Saint Catherine, and Saint Barbara each have both. There are not only two miniatures of Saint Catherine but also a pair of suffrages for her. Nevertheless, visually Saint Barbara is emphasized above all others with the further complement of a full historiated border, the only one in the suffrages and the most dramatic of the three in the book. It contains scenes from her martyrdom.[6] Like the slightly earlier Voustre Demeure Hours (cat. no. 20), the Huth Hours features for the full-page miniature *The Disputation of Saint Barbara*, a relatively unusual subject at this time in Flemish manuscripts. The Voustre Demeure Hours also depicts scenes from Barbara's martyrdom in its historiated border. These miniatures of the Disputation were painted by different artists using different compositions, but each is pictorially prominent

33

SIMON MARMION AND WORKSHOP,
MASTER OF THE HOUGHTON MINIATURES,
AND MASTER OF THE DRESDEN PRAYER BOOK
AND GHENT ASSOCIATES (?)

Huth Hours
Use of Rome
Valenciennes, Bruges, and probably Ghent, early 1480s

MANUSCRIPT: viii + 252 folios, 14.8 × 11.6 cm (5¹³⁄₁₆ × 4⁹⁄₁₆ in.); justification: 7.3–7.4 × 4.9–5.1 cm (2⅞ × 1⅞–2 in.); 20 lines of *gotica rotunda*; 24 full-page miniatures, 50 small miniatures, 1 historiated border, 24 calendar roundels

INSCRIPTIONS: Initials *MY* and *YM* as part of decorated border, fol. 12

BINDING: Ghent or Bruges, ca. 1500; blind-stamped leather

COLLECTION: London, The British Library, Add. Ms. 38126

PROVENANCE: Probably Gian Antonio Baldini (1654–1725), Piacenza; Baldini Museum, Piacenza, by 1752 (handwritten description in Italian inserted in manuscript); Henry Huth (1815–1878), in 1857; Alfred H. Huth (1850–1910); bequeathed 1912 to the British Museum

JPGM and RA

33a
MASTER OF THE
HOUGHTON
MINIATURES
The Disputation of Saint Barbara, fol. 145v

33b
SIMON MARMION
The Crucifixion, fol. 39v

Ascension, The Raising of Lazarus, and *The Pietà*) are also variations, sometimes a bit simplified, of compositions belonging to the Voustre Demeure Hours.⁹ A number also anticipate Marmion's influential cycle of half-length miniatures in the La Flora Hours (cat. no. 93): *The Annunciation to the Shepherds, Noli me tangere, Saint James the Greater Preaching,* and also *The Pietà.*¹⁰

The manuscript is linked with a book of hours (cat. no. 40) made for a cleric, which is not illuminated by Marmion but is nevertheless a related production. Its scribe is very likely that of both the Huth and the Emerson-White Hours. A Ghent artist, perhaps from the group known as the Ghent Associates, loosely copied the Huth *Nativity* in this manuscript. The binding of the Huth Hours is also similar to that of the cleric's manuscript, which has been associated with both Ghent and Bruges.¹¹ Since Marmion was clearly the lead artist for the Huth manuscript, it is tempting to suggest that the book was also written in Valenciennes. Yet it is also conceivable that the Huth Hours was written in Bruges or Ghent, since he sometimes worked with scribes living in other cities (see cat. nos. 13, 14), and his collaborating artists on this book resided in Bruges and probably Ghent.¹² Further, John Plummer has cited liturgical connections for this manuscript with both Bruges and Ghent.¹³

A group of prayers added in French at the end in a late-fifteenth-century hand, including one to Saint Louis, suggest that the book might have been made for a French person or someone close to the Flemish Hapsburg court.¹⁴ The fact that a group of miniatures by different artists in the Huth Hours, along with one of its most unusual borders, were all copied in the Soane Hours (cat. no. 138), which dates to the second decade of the sixteenth century, suggests that the book was still in Flanders a generation or two after its manufacture.¹⁵   T. K.

Notes

1. Only one miniature, *The Annunciation*, illustrating the opening of the Hours of the Virgin, appears to be lacking. Brinkmann (1997: 179, fig. 54) suggested that the lost miniature was copied in the Soane Hours, giving an idea of its character.

2. The eight small miniatures of the Man of Sorrows, Cross, Crown of Thorns, and Wounds of Christ (fols. 32–34) do not appear to be by Marmion. They are closer in style to the work of the Ghent Associates, perhaps the same artist who painted the borders with children playing tops and the *Martyrdom of Saint Barbara* (fols. 46, 146).

3. See Kren, in Malibu 1983a: 31–36, under no. 4.

4. The six full-page miniatures with full borders, all of the illusionistic type, have strips added at the left, suggesting that the original designs were too narrow, a curious error given that the size of the miniatures matches the text block well and that the same illuminator produced other miniatures on sufficiently large sheets of parchment. Borderless miniatures seem to have gained in popularity during the 1470s. See also cat. nos. 20, 32, 37, 44.

5. The cycle of smaller miniatures consists of subjects that either expand the narrative of the full-page miniature or relate to it typologically. They illustrate only the first six of the hours. Vespers and Compline lack smaller miniatures.

6. The border at Lauds of the Hours of the Virgin (fol. 67) features a couple of Old Testament scenes in cameos: *David Harping* and *Baalam and the Donkey*. The other historiated border, at the Hours of the Holy Spirit (fol. 46), shows a nonreligious scene with children playing tops before a church facade. These two openings are the only others besides

within its book. In the Huth Hours the miniature is set off visually by the unique combination of full-page miniature with both historiated initial and historiated border. In the Voustre Demeure Hours the miniature (and hence suffrage) is situated much closer to the front of its devotions, wholly apart from the other suffrages, which are illuminated and joined in sequence. The special treatment of Saint Barbara in these manuscripts reflects a particular reverence for this saint on the part of each book's patron.⁷

The Huth Hours was likely painted at roughly the same time as, or shortly after, the Emerson-White Hours (cat. no. 32), its textual twin, which was also written by the same scribe. The Emerson-White Hours probably dates to the late 1470s or early 1480s.⁸ The two books share their three main illuminators, some iconography, some unusual border motifs, a strong interest in landscape settings, and their overall visual style, including very similar partly illusionistic strewn borders that favor flowers. Marmion's *Saint Jerome* and *Saint Christopher* are also variations of those in the Emerson-White Hours. Several of the Marmion miniatures in the Huth Hours (*The Virgin and Child, The*

the Saint Barbara with a full-page miniature, a historiated initial, and a historiated border.

7. The Emerson-White Hours (cat. no. 32) also highlights Saint Barbara within its decorative scheme via a figure of the saint copied after a drawing by Hugo van der Goes and with the addition of a historiated border, but it is not otherwise distinguished within that manuscript's decorative program. As the Huth Hours and the Voustre Demeure Hours may well have been made for patrons close to the Burgundian court, it is possible that the patrons had connections to a confraternity of Saint Barbara, such as the one in Ghent to which Margaret of York and Mary of Burgundy belonged (Blockmans 1992: 39).

8. This is earlier than I had dated the manuscript previously (Malibu 1983a: 37, no. 4), but the new evidence put forward here is more convincing. See Clark (1992: 200–201), who also dates it later but acknowledges the difficulty of dating the book under his hypothetical framework. In an extended analysis of costume in the Huth Hours, focused on the many secular costumes in the calendar, Margaret Scott suggested a date broadly in the late 1470s (correspondence with the author, March 4, 2002).

9. *The Raising of Lazarus* in the Huth Hours was either finished or repainted at a much later date, probably in the mid- or late sixteenth century, but the composition is essentially Marmion's. Brinkmann (1992a: 189–90; 1997: 176–81) advanced the hypothesis that the Master of the David Scenes repainted part of this miniature and *The Martyrdom of Saint Catherine* and also painted some borders (e.g., fol. 27) in the book. His argument founders on the visual evidence.

10. On these links, see Kren, in Malibu 1983a: 32, 36, 37, though I am no longer inclined to argue that the Huth miniatures are derived from those in La Flora. The Huth's full-length *Sacrifice of Isaac* is a variation on the half-length now in the Munich Hours (cat. no. 90, fol. 117v), which may originally have belonged with the La Flora series.

11. Also similar is the binding of a book of hours with miniatures by the Master of the Dresden Prayer Book (Berlin, Kupferstichkabinett, Ms. 78 B 11), per Brinkmann 1997: 181, nn. 120–21. Brinkmann believed that the binding type should be localized to Ghent, while De la Mare (in Oxford 1984: 49–50, no. 78) called the binding "of Bruges type."

12. Brinkmann (1992a: 188–91) analyzed in detail some of the codicological peculiarities of the Huth Hours to show that Marmion painted his miniatures on single leaves for insertion in the book in another location, which he unconvincingly argued was Ghent. He ignored the fact that Marmion painted nearly all of the book's miniatures, including the many small ones, so that he must have had most, if not all, of the volume in his possession most of the time. On the matter of single leaves produced for export to Bruges, see Catherine Reynolds's essay "Illuminators and the Painters' Guilds" (this volume).

13. Plummer (in Randall 1997: 258, 304) indicated that some forms in the suffrages are characteristic of Bruges, while he included its litany in a "probably Ghent group." Its calendar also has a high level of agreement, 74.09 percent, with that of a small book of hours illuminated by his collaborator from Bruges, the Master of the Dresden Prayer Book (New York, Morgan Library, Ms. 1077), whose litany also belongs with the "probably Ghent group" (liturgical analysis, Department of Manuscripts files, JPGM, and in Randall 1997: 304). On the Morgan manuscript, see also Ryskamp 1989: 26–27, who assigned it to Bruges.

14. The latter possibility is perhaps corroborated by the view of Clark (1992: 207, n. 18), who felt that the calendar points to a German patron. The Emerson-White Hours—the apparent twin, with a calendar that correlates with that of the Huth Hours at 84 percent—has all of the relevant saints mentioned by Clark (Quintianus, Servatius, Erasmus, Gallus, Elizabeth), except Erasmus, but they are mostly not written in blue ink as special feasts.

15. The miniatures are copied not only in outline but also in color. While this evidence does not guarantee that the Huth manuscript itself was the model, given the combination of sources by different artists in this case, it seems more than likely. Two other miniatures from the Huth Hours are also copied in color into the Hours of Joanna of Castile (cat. no. 114).

34

MASTER OF HOUGHTON MINIATURES

Two Leaves from a Devotional Book
Probably Ghent, ca. 1480

David in Prayer
One leaf, 12.5 × 7.75 cm (4⅞ × 3¹/₁₆ in.); 1 full-page miniature mounted on cardboard

The Vision of Saint Dominic
One leaf, 12.8 × 7.75 cm (5 × 3¹/₁₆ in.); 1 full-page miniature mounted on cardboard

COLLECTION: Private collection

PROVENANCE: [Fankhauser?]; to current owner, ca. 1963

JPGM and RA

These little-known miniatures—despite their pale tonalities, due in part to fading[1]—are among the most beautifully drawn works in the new style of Flemish manuscript illumination. Both reflect the size and subject matter of a small private book of hours or prayer book, which was intended for a devout with Dominican affiliations. The iconography of David is traditional (ill. 34a). He kneels in prayer, his harp on the ground, while his gaze turns to the Lord in the clouds. God the Father holds the globe of the Salvator Mundi in his right hand, tightly gripping an arrow with the other. The powerful curve of David's back, sweeping up from the tip of the long train of his robe, gives him a magisterial weight and dignity. Adding to the king's earthly glory is the enormous complex of palaces and court

buildings behind him, including a towering church belfry. They line a moat that, with the sweeping orthogonals of the architecture, draws the eye in a steady and measured manner deep into the miniature.

The companion miniature depicts a celestial space (ill. 34b), but its geometry is no less imposing. The Virgin, crowned, kneels beside a seated God the Father, his right hand raised in blessing, his left holding a scepter. He wears the papal tiara and is the largest figure in the miniature and the only one whose robe is richly colored. The aureole that radiates out behind him underscores his position as the anchor of the composition. Beneath them, rows of saints, including the Doctors of the Church, are arrayed in sweeping curves, some of which define horizontal ellipses within the composition. All turn to behold the Lord. In the center the kneeling Saint Dominic, with his back to the viewer and his hands uplifted, beholds the Virgin and the Lord.

Friedrich Winkler, in an expertise, attributed both miniatures to the Master of Mary of Burgundy, whose illuminations are now assigned to several different artists.[2] Bodo Brinkmann attributed *David* to the Master of the First Prayer Book of Maximilian, but his argument is unpersuasive.[3] The two miniatures are by the same artist, and both display a sophisticated use of geometry and figures imbued with a level of intelligence and psychological alertness that are uncharacteristic of the Maximilian Master. Although the beard is trimmed differently, the facial type of David

closely resembles that of Saint Barbara's father in the miniature of this subject in the Huth Hours (ill. 33a). Akin are the eyes, mouth, strong nose, and aged, slightly hollow cheeks. The distinctive modeling of David's golden sleeve in blue is identical to that of Elizabeth's sleeve in the Huth *Visitation* (fig. 59). The handling of the architecture behind David— with its crisply drawn details, finely modeled brick surfaces, beautifully proportioned recession into depth, and execution in transparent washes—calls to mind both of these miniatures from the Huth Hours, which are by the Master of the Houghton Miniatures.

In the companion miniature, Saint Gregory, seated below God the Father, resembles in facial type the kneeling Saint Gregory in the miniature of his mass, now in Brussels, by the Houghton Master (ill. 32c).[4] Indeed, the treatment of the hair, in curling wiry lines, strongly recalls the Berlin drawing also attributed to the Master of the Houghton Miniatures (ill. 35). Similar to the drawing, too, are the strong contour lines of the mouth, nose, and eyes and the deft use of white highlights to give both three-dimensionality and texture to the flesh. The long, thin, tubular folds of the drapery, seen in Saint Gregory's robe and in the Emerson-White *Funeral Procession of the Virgin* (ill. 32b) are also characteristic of the Houghton Master.

As with the Berlin drawing, given the paucity of works by this illuminator that survive, it is difficult to date *David in Prayer* and *The Vision of Saint Dominic* with much

34b
MASTER OF
THE HOUGHTON
MINIATURES
*The Vision of Saint
Dominic*

Figure 59
MASTER OF
THE HOUGHTON
MINIATURES
The Visitation. In the
Huth Hours, fol. 66v
(see cat. no. 33)

precision. These miniatures, along with his other roughly datable work in the Huth and Emerson-White Hours, almost certainly belong to the period from 1475 to 1485. *David in Prayer* is likely the original of a composition that was repeated at least five more times.[5]   T. K.

Notes

1. Following his examination of the miniatures in the laboratories of the Getty Conservation Institute in 1994, Arie Wallert suggested that the robes of both David and God the Father were originally red, as is typical for these subjects.

2. The expertise (November 8, 1962) was written for Fankhauser before the leaves entered a private collection. In a subsequent letter to the present owner (January 12, 1963), Winkler stated that the miniatures "emerged" around 1942.

3. Brinkmann 1997: 310–11. He did not comment on the other miniature.

4. In a letter to the author, April 2, 1994, Brinkmann linked the two miniatures to this *Mass of Saint Gregory*, which he associated with the Maximilian Master and the two Hastings books of hours.

5. Brinkmann (1997: 310–11, nn. 96, 97) listed several versions. A particularly brilliant variation on the pattern, in mirror image, by Simon Bening develops the elaborate architectural setting in a novel and compelling manner (sale, Christie's, London, July 11, 2002, lot 13: 24, color). Another, weaker version is in cat. no. 109, fol. 135.

35

MASTER OF THE HOUGHTON MINIATURES

Fourteen Heads
Probably Ghent, ca. 1475–85

Brush and pen in black heightened with white on paper, 7.4 × 11.1 cm (2⅞ × 4⅜ in.)

COLLECTION: Berlin, Staatliche Museen zu Berlin, Kupferstichkabinett, KdZ 12512

PROVENANCE: John Thane; Sir Thomas Lawrence; William Esdaile; John Postle Heseltine; Wendlandt; [Paul Cassirer, Berlin]; acquired 1927

JPGM and RA

This drawing shows studies of the heads of fourteen men of different ages, facial types, and ethnicities. They are intricately arranged, shown gazing in different directions and with widely varying expressions, from angry and wary to curious, wistful, and sad. While the heads look up, down, sidelong, or at an angle, the eyes carry the feeling and give the figures a remarkable psychological depth. As is the case with the Paris *Pentecost* (ill. 26), the drawing's small dimensions and the scale of the figures indicate that it is the work of a manuscript illuminator. As Stephanie Buck has pointed out, the dimensions of the heads resemble closely those of Flemish illuminators of the new style, especially the Master of the First Prayer Book of Maximilian.[1] The drawing also displays the outline of the type of decorative border space that would flank a text block, reinforcing the link to manuscript painting.

Like the Paris drawing, *Fourteen Heads* has been attributed to the Master of Mary of Burgundy, the Maximilian Master's precise contemporary.[2] Buck made a cogent argument for instead attributing the drawing to the Maximilian Master,[3] and some of the heads do resemble those in this artist's work. Rarely, however, did the Maximilian Master convey the depth of feeling displayed here, and the draftsman of the Berlin sheet is a subtler artist. More refined technique, greater psychological acuity, and more similar facial types appear in the art of the Master of the Houghton Miniatures. For example, the dark-haired, densely bearded man second from the left in the middle row is the facial type of Saint Barbara's father in the Huth Hours' *Disputation of Saint Barbara* (ill. 33a). The intensity of her father's gaze; the dense, dark, wiry quality of the hair (with the beard trimmed a bit differently); the suggestion of bags under the eyes; the lines that run from the nose to the mouth; and the mouth itself all find counterparts in the drawing. The gentle, bald, bearded older man two heads to the right in the same row, a classic Flemish type for Saint Anthony Abbot, finds his counterpart in the miniature of Saint Anthony Abbot in the Emerson-White Hours (cat. no. 32). Here too the mouth and nose and the lines between them are similar, as are the strong arch of the brow and the distinctive way the lower beard culminates in individual wiry curls. The two younger men in the central vertical row of the drawing, each with a distinctive jaw, resemble one of the heads in the aureole around Christ in the Houghton Master's *Mass of Saint Gregory* (ill. 32c). I refer to the figure in a pointy red cap to the right of Christ, the cap itself being similar to the one in the drawing. The densely bearded man two heads above this figure in the miniature also recalls the one mentioned above, two heads from the left in the middle row of the drawing.

Using the approximate dates of the Huth and Emerson-White Hours as a point of departure, the drawing may be assigned to the period from 1475 to 1485.   T. K.

Notes

1. Buck 2001: 161–62.
2. Pächt 1948: 71, no. 29.
3. Buck 2001: 161–62.

GHENT ASSOCIATES

The loosely associated manuscripts that Anne van Buren grouped under the Ghent Associates consisted of works she believes are by either the Master of the First Prayer Book of Maximilian or the artists of the Berlin Hours of Mary of Burgundy.[1] She constructed this group by starting with illuminations attributed to the Master of Mary of Burgundy by Friedrich Winkler, Otto Pächt, and others but rejected by G. I. Lieftinck in his pivotal study of 1969.[2] Van Buren then ascribed his list of works not by the Master of Mary of Burgundy to the Ghent Associates. She also assigned to the Ghent Associates other manuscripts from the period from roughly 1470 to 1490 that she considered to be by the same artists. She described this group as "more diversified," noting that "the several illuminators seem to have adapted their manner to a polished and impersonal style."[3] The virtue of this grouping was that it isolated a body of works, mostly of high quality, that carried forward the style of the artist here called the Vienna Master of Mary of Burgundy and that of Hugo van der Goes.

The category "Ghent Associates" will be provisional until closer examination leads to more constructive groupings. For example, I argue here that the Madrid Hours of William Lord Hastings (cat. no. 25) may have been illuminated by the Vienna Master of Mary of Burgundy (a single miniature) and his workshop (the remainder of the book) and that the master himself played a role in the book's genesis. Additionally, the illuminations ascribed to the Maximilian Master deserve to be treated as a separate category. This is because his style continued for more than two decades after 1490 and because the Maximilian Master group, which presents its own substantial problems of connoisseurship, can be studied more profitably apart from the work of the other Ghent Associates. He and his workshop are treated here in a separate biography.[4]

The remaining volumes in the Ghent Associates group include the Berlin Hours of Mary of Burgundy and Maximilian (cat. no. 38); the book of hours for the use of Saint Peter's, Ghent (cat. no. 40); a book of hours in Kraków (Biblioteka Czartoryskich, Ms. 3025);[5] the very small book of hours with some miniatures by Simon Marmion (cat. no. 37); some of the miniatures in the Emerson-White Hours (cat. no. 32); the frontispiece of the Nová Říše Hours (cat. no. 36); and the London breviary written at Rooclooster (cat. no. 39).[6] They clearly represent a range of hands along with a range of quality and even of technique. It is difficult to believe that the miniatures in the Emerson-White Hours, which are among the most beautifully painted in the group, are by either the painter of the Berlin Hours or the Maximilian Master.[7] The miniatures by the Ghent Associates in the small book of hours also seem to represent several hands,[8] or at least a range of quality, as do those in the hours for Saint Peter's.

Nevertheless, all of these artists share a style of painting steeped in the naturalism of the Flemish oil painters. Their primary sources of artistic inspiration appear to have been the Vienna Master of Mary of Burgundy and Van der Goes, both of whom provided patterns and models for the artists.[9] This suggests that the artists were active in Ghent. Marmion, Dieric Bouts, and the Master of the Houghton Miniatures probably also provided models and patterns for the Ghent Associates, although the role of these three creative personalities in the formation of their art appears less decisive. The larger question concerning the Ghent Associates and the Maximilian Master is the degree of their originality. Were they primarily copyists? Is their work based entirely on patterns? Did they design any of the patterns that they illuminated? It is still unclear which artists designed the bulk of the patterns used by the Ghent Associates. The question is intriguing in part because such a large body of new patterns, literally scores of them, emerged in a fairly short period of time, apparently between roughly 1475 and 1480. The Maximilian Master and the Ghent Associates shared many of these patterns.

The use of the new style of Flemish borders with colored grounds, naturalistically painted flowers, white or gold acanthus, and cast shadows—the so-called strewn patterns—is a standard feature of their manuscripts. Along with the Maximilian Master, the Ghent Associates succeeded in producing lavish books with rich color and sparkling light effects that offered tremendous luxury and even a high degree of personalization for an owner, although at the same time relatively little that was original or new. In essence they commodified the style of the Vienna Master of Mary of Burgundy and the new naturalism of manuscript illumination steeped in the aesthetic of Flemish painters in oil on panel.   T. K.

Notes

1. Van Buren 1975: 307–9.

2. The books rejected by Lieftinck are cat. nos. 25, 38, 40, 42; the *Chronodromon Antiquitates* (Brussels, Bibliothèque royale de Belgique, Ms. II 1169); and the two prayer books of Philip of Cleves (Brussels, Bibliothèque royale, Ms. IV 40, and Vienna, Österreichische Nationalbibliothek, Ms. s.n. 13239). See Lieftinck 1969: vii–xi, xxiii–xxvi, 109–70.

3. Van Buren 1975: 291.

4. Van Buren's list includes the First Prayer Book of Maximilian (Vienna, Österreichische Nationalbibliothek, Ms. 1907), the London Hastings Hours (cat. no. 41), the *Légende de Saint Adrien* (cat. no. 42), the Chronicle of the Princes of Cleves (cat. no. 86), the Brussels Hours of Philip of Cleves (Bibliothèque royale, Ms. IV 40), the Hours of Louis Quarré (Oxford, Bodleian Library, Ms. Douce 311), and the Stonyhurst Hours (cat. no. 88).

5. Brinkmann proposed that the illuminator of the Berlin Hours also illuminated the Kraków hours (in König et al. 1998: 147–53).

6. The single miniature in the Nagonius manuscript (cat. no. 104) can also be excluded from Van Buren's list because its miniature is certainly by Gerard David.

7. The miniatures in the Emerson-White Hours ascribed to the Ghent Associates are on folios 102v, 110v, 112v.

8. The miniatures by the Ghent Associates in this book are on folios 148v, 160v, 162v, 164v, 170v, 172v.

9. Manuscripts such as the Brussels and London Rooclooster breviaries (cat. nos. 24, 39) indicate the close relationship between the Vienna Master and the Ghent Associates.

36

MASTER OF THE DRESDEN PRAYER BOOK
AND GHENT ASSOCIATES

Book of Hours
Use of Rome
Bruges and Ghent, 1480

MANUSCRIPT: 158 folios, 17.5 × 12.5 cm (6¹⁵⁄₁₆ × 4⅞ in.); 18 lines of *bastarda*; 14 full-page miniatures

HERALDRY: Escutcheon with unidentified arms, argent a chevron between three mullets gules, pierced, the mullets having eight points, fols. 18v, 25v, 33, etc.; escutcheon with wife's arms, or a chevron sable, between three annulets gules, impaling the former, fols. 19, 26, 32v, etc.; fol. 17, arms are painted by different artist, husband's side of escutcheon is or rather than argent but a darker, less yellow shade of or than wife's side; initials IA and motto *Tous iours ioieuls*, fol. 16v; initials IA en lac and motto *Je ne puis*, with hedgehog (porcupine?) chained to banderole and large egg nearby, fol. 17

INSCRIPTIONS: *Anna van Gatzf[eld?] a Wyckh*, sixteenth-century hand; *serriara a Wich possidet*, different hand; *Un bel morire tutta la vita honor . . .* , same hand as immediately preceding (?); *Inclita mors vita est ingloria vita sepulcrum*, probably same hand as immediately preceding, although much smaller lettering; *Sum Io:Schelverij*, another hand; *Poco giova il stato Dove non e contentamento del cuore*, all on recto of first flyleaf; date *1480*, in painted border, fol. 17

BINDING: Modern; black leather; clasps

COLLECTION: Nová Říše, The Premonstratensian Abbey of Nová Říše, Ms. 10

PROVENANCE: Anna van Gatzf[eld?], Wijck, near Maastricht

JPGM

The devotions of this book, referred to here as the Nová Říše Hours, open with a dramatic full-page miniature with a full-length double portrait that accompanies a prayer in Dutch verse to the Virgin (ill. 36a). It serves as an eloquent frontispiece honoring the patrons and their devotion to Mary. They are shown kneeling in veneration on a knoll beneath the Virgin and Christ child in the sky. Mary and Jesus are set against a gold backdrop and framed by an oval of clouds. The valley below reveals an elaborate walled enclosure dominated by a church with an imposing tower.[1] The patrons are dressed elegantly in black and gray, the man vividly portrayed with small, bulging eyes; long, frizzy hair; and bangs that cover his forehead. His long velvet gown, worn over a bright red doublet, folds under his knees.[2] The woman's short steeple headdress and gown are reminiscent of the costume of ladies-in-waiting at the Burgundian court. The couple's dramatic presence dominates the miniature and even the lovely, tenderly integrated figures of the Virgin and Child. The pair's coats of arms

hang from a nearly barren tree behind them, and their armorials appear again in the border, along with their initials and devices.[3] Based on costume, the noble couple appears to have been close to the court.

This ambitious miniature belongs to the new style of illumination that reflects the pictorial values of the painters in oil on panel. It may be assigned to the somewhat heterogeneous group called the Ghent Associates, book painters inspired by the Vienna Master of Mary of Burgundy and Hugo van der Goes, who shared their pictorial ideas and patterns. The artist is one of the better hands within this group, and the miniature echoes in some respects the work of the Vienna Master.[4] The miniature and facing page feature a border in the new style with gilt acanthus alternating with truthfully observed flowers. These borders are especially reminiscent of those in such manuscripts as the Madrid Hours of William Lord Hastings (cat. no. 25) and the Berlin Hours of Mary of Burgundy and Maximilian (cat. no. 38).

The remaining thirteen miniatures are by the Master of the Dresden Prayer Book. They represent for the most part standard iconography but include some unusual themes and storytelling features. The illumination accompanying the Mass for the Dead shows a parishioner kissing the paten in the celebration of the Eucharist (ill. 36b).[5] In *The Presentation at the Temple* (fol. 79v)—which is set outdoors, at the entrance to the temple—a frowning, heavy-lidded woman behind the Virgin looks directly at the viewer.[6] In *The Flight into Egypt* (fol. 92v), Joseph walks toward the viewer, foreshortened.

Although the book has a calendar that follows closely a Bruges model, it has other connections with Ghent besides the illuminator of its frontispiece.[7] The borders of the Dresden Master's miniatures—with their distinctive blue and gold acanthus, butterflies, and flowers on a plain ground—correspond to a type uncommon in his work but popular during the 1470s in Ghent. They appear in illuminated books written there, and probably also illuminated there, that Margaret of York acquired (see cat. nos. 28, 29, 43). Indeed, the main border artist of the Nová Říše Hours was also responsible for some of the borders in Margaret's breviary (cat. no. 22).[8] Moreover, in the years shortly before and after this book was painted, the Master of the Dresden Prayer Book was collaborating actively with artists and scribes from Ghent (see cat. nos. 20, 32, 33). A charming feature of the borders of the Dresden Master's miniatures is monkeys engaged in parodies of human activities.   T. K.

Notes

1. The architecture is specific in character, with a large open area within the enclosure. Might it represent a monastic foundation supported by the book's patrons?

2. He also wears a gold necklace, but its pendant is not legible.

3. Perhaps this is a reference to the Confraternity of the Dry Tree in Bruges, to which many of the urban and court elite, along with wealthy foreigners, belonged. The confraternity was devoted to the Immaculate Conception of the Virgin.

4. It is clear that this artist is neither the Maximilian Master nor the Master of the Houghton Miniatures and is probably not the Vienna Master of Mary of Burgundy. He appears to be neither the painter of the Berlin Hours of Mary and Maximilian (cat. no. 38) nor that of the

36a
GHENT ASSOCIATES
*A Couple in Prayer before
the Virgin*, fol. 16v

36b
MASTER OF THE
DRESDEN PRAYER
BOOK
Kissing the Paten, fol. 115v

Madrid Hastings Hours (cat. no. 25). Brinkmann (1997: 124, 127) compared the artist with the Maximilian Master, but the Nová Říše Master was a better draftsman and more attentive to detail. The angels call to mind the angel in the *Annunciation to Joachim* in the Voustre Demeure Hours (cat. no. 20, Berlin no. 17), and the quality of tenderness between mother and child, along with the facial types, also recalls some of the miniatures in this manuscript (Berlin nos. 6, 7), although they are not necessarily by the same hand. The features of the female patron in the miniature recall those of Saint Barbara in *The Disputation of Saint Barbara* (ill. 20a). Pächt (1948: 65, no. 8), without having seen the miniature, assigned it to the Master of Mary of Burgundy, while Lieftinck (1969: x, xxv), after examining the same photograph, dismissed it as of inferior quality.

5. See Wieck 1999: 438–39, 463.

6. She wears a black mantle, as does, atypically, a female mourner below the cross in *The Crucifixion* (fol. 25v) and a entirely draped figure seen only from the back in *Pentecost* (fol. 32v).

7. John Plummer, in an unpublished analysis (Department of Manuscripts files, JPGM), reported very high agreements with Bruges books of hours of the Llangattock group, including 94.6 percent for the Llangattock Hours (cat. no. 2), 95.97 percent for the ex Duschnes Hours, and 94.6 percent for a Bruges book of hours in the Walters Art Gallery, Baltimore (W.190). On the Bruges calendar linked to the Llangattock and ex Duschnes manuscripts, see Plummer, in Baltimore 1988: 149–56.

8. In the breviary, see especially folio 57v, where the drawing and painting of the acanthus, birds, and daisies, along with the handling of the gold, are virtually identical. Brinkmann (1997: 128, fig. 41) identified a small book of hours as having borders by the same hand. It was, however, bound in Bruges (Bruges, Onze Lieve Vrouwe ter Potterie). Manuscripts were often bound in towns other than those in which they were produced (cf., e.g., cat. no. 16). Brinkmann attributed the miniatures in this book to the Pseudo-Alexander Bening (the Master of the Flemish Boethius), an artist who was active in Ghent.

37

SIMON MARMION AND GHENT ASSOCIATES

Book of Hours
Use of Rome
Ghent and Valenciennes, mid- to late 1470s

MANUSCRIPT: iv + 250 + iii folios, 7.5 × 5.2 cm (2¹⁵⁄₁₆ × 2¹⁄₁₆ in.);
justification: 4.3 × 2.1 cm (1¹¹⁄₁₆ × ¹³⁄₁₆ in.); 14 lines of *bastarda*; 14 full-page miniatures

BINDING: Early nineteenth century; red morocco; double-headed eagle at center of both covers; cross and MISSALE / MS / MEMP. / SAEC. 15 on spine; green morocco doublures; gilt and goffered edges

COLLECTION: Private collection

PROVENANCE: Philip Augustus Hanrott (1776–1856) [his sale, Evans, London, July 16, 1833, lot 2408]; to William Knight [his sale, Sotheby's, London, August 2, 1847, lot 1335]; to William Stuart, Tempsford Hall; to his wife, Henrietta Maria Sarah (d. 1853), in 1847; by descent to William Dugdal Stuart; to his widow [her sale, Sotheby's, London, June 4, 1934, lot 25]; [to Tancred Borenius]; Lord Moyne [sale, Sotheby's, London, May 4, 1953, lot 68]; [to H. Eisemann]; to parent of present owner

JPGM and RA

This tiny volume holds the distinction of being the smallest of the first books of hours that were fully outfitted with the new type of Flemish border that is partially illusionistic and strewn with flowers, acanthus, and other motifs.[1] Simon Marmion painted half of its miniatures, including those illustrating all of its major devotions: the Hours of the Cross, of the Holy Spirit, and of the Virgin, along with the Penitential Psalms and the Office of the Dead.[2] Although he illustrated only one of the suffrages, it is the most important one in the book, the miniature devoted to Saint Catherine (ill. 37a). The miniature and its suffrage are distinguished from the other illuminated suffrages by the particular and original character of the iconography, by the singular presence of the book's patron as a witness to the narrative, and by their unusual location, within the sequence of male saints.

The subject is Saint Catherine's vision of the Virgin in the company of Christ, patriarchs, prophets, and saints, as recounted by the cleric Jean Miélot, a favorite translator, scribe, and illuminator of Philip the Good. The Virgin permits Catherine to choose a spouse, and she selects Christ. In Miélot's account the Virgin refers to him as "L'Empereur de Gloire" [the emperor of glory], and Marmion depicted him in an imperial crown; of the others she says, "tous ceux-ci sont les rois" [all of them are kings], and the painter showed them crowned.[3] Marmion himself had illuminated a copy of Miélot's *Vie de sainte Catherine* for Margaret of York only a few years earlier, so he was acquainted with Miélot's text (1475, private collection; see cat. no. 14). Since the only two copies of Miélot's *Vie de sainte Catherine* to come down to us from this era were created for a Burgundian duke and a Burgundian duchess, a high-ranking Burgundian courtier probably would be among the first to own a book of hours that specifically reflected its text.[4] The Burgundian dukes' relationship to the Holy Roman Emperor was an ongoing issue under both Philip the Good and Charles the Bold.[5] In the miniature the patron wears a bowler-shaped hat, a fashion of headgear popular at the court of Charles the Bold, particularly during the early to mid-1470s.[6] It is slung over the man's shoulders.

Another of Marmion's more original miniatures shows a corpse lying in an open field with an angel expelling a devil from its soul. The seven remaining miniatures were once attributed to the Master of Mary of Burgundy but are more likely by one or more of the Ghent Associates group.[7] All occur between folios 148 and 172, while six are inserted into a single gathering with suffrages of the saints. The seven are uneven in quality, but two, the half-length *Virgin and Child* (ill. 37b) and the atmospheric *Saint Michael Expelling the Demons*, rank with the most beautiful works in the new Ghent style of illumination of the 1470s. The artist repeated the strongly Goesian half-length *Virgin and Child* (ill. 38a) with greater attention to detail in the Berlin Hours of Mary and Maximilian, also a comparatively small book.

37a
SIMON MARMION
The Mystic Marriage of Saint Catherine,
fol. 168v–169

The gold highlights that lend radiance to the drapery there are lacking in the version under consideration here. The Saint Michael miniature anticipates the composition from the Berlin Hours *Saint Michael Expelling the Fallen Angels*, but the former is executed with greater subtlety, the gold of the background dissolving into the darkness of hell, chillingly embodied by a dank pile of monsters.[8] In the Hours of Mary and Maximilian (fol. 65), one of the Ghent Associates copied from this manuscript Marmion's *Virgin and Child in an Interior* (fol. 35). This relationship offers the primary evidence for dating the book, since the Berlin Hours was substantially completed by 1482, the year of Mary's inauspicious death. The patron's courtly Burgundian attire suggests an approximate dating for this book of hours somewhat earlier, in the mid- to late 1470s.[9]   T. K.

Notes

1. All the miniatures in the book are on inserted single leaves with full borders of the strewn type, with the exception of *The Virgin and Child*, which lacks a border.

2. Brinkmann's (1992c: 135) attribution of all the miniatures to the Master of the David Scenes in the Grimani Breviary is untenable.

3. This identification is owed to Susan L'Engle. I quote from a modern edition of the text drawn from the copy in the library of Philip the Good (*Vie de Sainte Catherine d'Alexandrie*, Paris, Bibliothèque nationale de France, Ms. 6449; Miélot 1881: 69–71).

4. Brussels 1959: 121, no. 139

5. Blockmans and Prevenier 1999: 79–81, 105–7.

6. Margaret Scott (correspondence, April 22, 2002) indicated that the bowler hat was popular at the Burgundian court from the late 1460s through the mid-1470s but that it is not clear precisely when it went out of fashion there. Consider, for example, miniatures in cat. nos. 17, 64.

7. The miniatures are *The Virgin and Child* (fol. 148v), *Saint Peter* (fol. 160v), *Saint George* (fol. 162v), *Saint Michael* (fol. 164v), *Saint Christopher* (fol. 166v), *Saints Anthony and Paul* (fol. 170v), and *Saint Barbara* (fol. 172v).

8. The figure of Saint Michael in the book discussed here resembles closely the angel with raised arms in front of Saint Michael in the Berlin Hours (cat. no. 38).

9. Clark (1992: 200–207, n. 10) dated it around the same time as the Gros Hours, which he placed ca. 1480.

37b
GHENT ASSOCIATES
The Virgin and Child,
fol. 148v (detail)

38a
GHENT ASSOCIATES
The Virgin and Child,
fol. 284v

38

GHENT ASSOCIATES

Leaves from the Hours of Mary of Burgundy and Maximilian
Use of Rome
Ghent, ca. 1480–82

The Trinity, fol. 13v
Pentecost, fol. 31v
The Man of Sorrows, fol. 56v
The Virgin and Child, fol. 284v
Saint Sebastian, fol. 327v
Saint Michael, fol. 351
A Noblewoman in Prayer before Her Guardian Angel, fol. 355

MANUSCRIPT: 362 folios, 10.3 × 7 cm (4 ¹⁄₁₆ × 2 ¾ in.); justification: 6.2 × 4.2 cm (2 ⁷⁄₁₆ × 1 ⅝ in.); 16 lines of *bastarda*; 27 full-page miniatures, 12 three-quarter-page miniatures, 36 small miniatures

HERALDRY: Escutcheon with the arms of Maximilian I of Austria, in bas-de-page, fol. 340v; escutcheon with the arms of Mary of Burgundy, fol. 341; motto of Maximilian I *Halt Mas*, fol. 327v; initials *MM* in many borders from fol. 158 onward

INSCRIPTIONS: *de toutes autres plus / a vous lealle margo / vo[s]tr[e] maxi[milian] Leal // A . . . mains que [?] . . . Engelber // vre gr.s bes..e / esuhturgl,* signed by Maximilian, Engelbert of Nassau, and presumably Louis of Gruuthuse, fol. 13; *1513 / A tort seuffre / A swartzenberch,* f. 284

BINDING: Temporarily disbound; former binding: nineteenth century; red velvet; silver-gilt clasp

COLLECTION: Berlin, Staatliche Museen zu Berlin, Kupferstichkabinett, Ms. 78 B 12

PROVENANCE: Mary, duchess of Burgundy (1457–1482), and Emperor Maximilian I (1459–1519); Margaret of Austria (1480–1530) (?); Adolf von Schwarzenberg (?), by 1550–60; William Beckford (1759–1844), Fonthill Abbey; to his son-in-law, Alexander Hamilton, tenth duke of Hamilton (1767–1852); to the Prussian state in 1882

JPGM and RA

hours in Kraków created for a German cleric (Biblioteka Czartoryskich, Ms. 3025).[7] In my view another work by him appears in this exhibition (cat. no. 39).

The book seems to have been largely under way, perhaps even complete, by the time of Mary of Burgundy's death in 1482, and thus it belongs to the first decade of the new style of Flemish manuscript illumination, with miniatures inspired in part by panel painting and with naturalistic borders. At the same time there is substantial evidence that a number of miniatures are based on patterns, and significantly, they appear to be derived from diverse artists. At least one drawing exists that almost certainly served as a model for a miniature. The subject of both is Pentecost, and the drawing (cat. no. 26) is here attributed to the Vienna Master of Mary of Burgundy. Another miniature, *The Virgin with Musical Angels,* copies a typical interior as well as the figures, down to particularities of color, in a miniature by Simon Marmion from a tiny book of hours in a private collection (cat. no. 37, fol. 34v). Hugo van der Goes indirectly provided the model for the Berlin Hours' *Man of Sorrows* (ill. 38b). The latter miniature is copied from a pattern that was used at least once previously (cat. no. 25, fol. 252v), but the pattern closely follows Van der Goes's monumental *Trinity* panel in Edinburgh. The full-page, borderless Goesian *Virgin and Child* (ill. 38a), one of the most beautiful miniatures in the book, repeats another miniature in the aforementioned tiny book (ill. 37b). They are very similar in technique, except that the Berlin version features more generous highlights in gold.[8] They were painted by the Ghent Associates, perhaps by the same artist within this group. But who ultimately designed the pattern? One candidate is the Vienna Master, but might Van der Goes have provided it? The model for the funeral procession that illustrates the Monday Hours of the Dead in Mary's hours is *The Funeral Procession of the Virgin* in a bas-de-page in the Emerson-White Hours (ill. 32b), a larger and more ambitious composition illuminated by the Master of the Houghton Miniatures. The Houghton Master certainly designed the latter and is thus the source of the pattern.[9]

Other examples could be cited of compositions that were reused from books that were only a few years older than the Berlin Hours. What is intriguing is that the models for the miniatures here were designed by or based closely on the work of many artists, including the Vienna Master of Mary of Burgundy, the Master of the Houghton Miniatures, Simon Marmion, and Hugo van der Goes. A systematic study of all the book's sources remains to be undertaken, but the evidence suggests that the availability of a sizable body of new patterns, most apparently generated during the 1470s, greatly facilitated production by the late 1470s and early 1480s of books such as this and the two Hastings books of hours (cat. nos. 25, 41).[10] Circumstantial evidence suggests further that some patterns may have been organized in complete pictorial cycles.[11]

The book's illuminations extensively personalize the devotions. The female figure among the living in the miniature *The Three Living and the Three Dead* (ill. 38e), which illustrates the Office of the Dead, represents Mary; the initials

Few Flemish manuscripts have had the kind of abundant praise heaped upon them that this regal, copiously illuminated little book has. It has parallel Passion and Life of the Virgin cycles in the Hours of the Virgin, fully illustrated Penitential Psalms, and no fewer than thirty-four illustrated suffrages and Marian prayers. The book features two depictions of the fabled Mary, duchess of Burgundy, one of them unusual and perhaps posthumous.[1] It is personalized with the arms of Mary and her consort, Maximilian, and with their initials *en lac* generously distributed in the margins.[2] The artist thought to be the seminal figure of the new style of Flemish book painting, the Master of Mary of Burgundy, was named for this manuscript and a book of hours in Vienna (cat. no. 19).[3] The volume has long occupied a central position in the study of Flemish late medieval manuscript illumination.

Despite its celebrity and the critical attention it has received over the past century, its reputation has diminished considerably in the last five decades, initiated by the skepticism of G. I. Lieftinck. He doubted that the book was indeed painted by the same innovative artist who executed the celebrated full-page miniatures in the Vienna Hours (cat. no. 19, fols. 14v, 43v, 99v).[4] He considered the artist to be among the followers of the Master of Mary of Burgundy, a group that Anne van Buren called the Ghent Associates.[5] Recently Bodo Brinkmann proposed that the book's illuminator was just a copyist with a decorator's eye for color and a skillful brush.[6] He also connected his miniatures to those of another of the Ghent Associates' manuscripts, a book of

38c
GHENT ASSOCIATES
The Trinity, fol. 13v

38d
GHENT ASSOCIATES
A Noblewoman in Prayer before Her Guardian Angel,
fol. 355

38e
GHENT ASSOCIATES
The Three Living and the Three Dead, fols.
220v–221

MM appear on her horse's harness. The female devout in prayer before a guardian angel (ill. 38d) is clearly a courtly surrogate for Mary. Maximilian and Mary's arms appear in the opening with the miniature of the Old Testament heroine Susanna at her bath accompanying the relatively rare suffrage to her. The tribulations of Susanna would have particularly spoken to the young duchess.[12] Maximilian's motto *Halt Mas* appears in the elaborate border of the miniature of Saint Sebastian, a martial saint he particularly venerated. Other signs of ownership appear with the suffrages to his other patron saints, Christopher and Gregory, and beside miniatures emphasizing Christ's sovereignty over earthly rulers.[13]

The manuscript was almost certainly begun after the marriage of Maximilian and Mary in 1477 and, as noted, was substantially complete, if not entirely so, by Mary's death in 1482. It is later than the very small hours now in a private collection (cat. no. 37) and the Emerson-White Hours (cat. no. 32), works that can themselves be dated only approximately, to the late 1470s or early 1480s.[14]   T. K.

Notes

1. Since E. Bock, as cited by Winkler, some scholars have concluded that the female rider shown among the living in the miniature *The Three Living and the Three Dead* represents Mary herself. According to Bock's interpretation, the miniature (which is inserted) was created shortly after her death as a result of a riding accident (Winkler 1925: 158; Hulin de Loo 1939b: 176; Anzelewsky, Brinkmann, and König, in König et al. 1998: 31–37). It is very unusual to show any of the living as other than male. Van Buren (1975: 308, n. 6) proposed that the book was only half complete when Mary died and that her husband saw to its completion and reshaping after her death. Nevertheless, illustrations for the Office of the Dead often alluded to a book's living patron.

2. The initials of the couple in the decorated borders start to appear only about halfway through the book, on folio 158, though they appear commonly thereafter. This may be an indication that the book was already under way before the ducal couple became its intended owners. Their full armorials appear only at the very end of the book, on folios 340v–341.

3. Winkler 1925: 103–5.

4. Lieftinck 1969: vii–xxi, 134–47.

5. Van Buren 1975: 291, 307.

6. See König et al. 1998: 124–32.

7. See König et al. 1998: 147–53. Brinkmann proposed to rechristen the illuminator of the Berlin Hours the Master of the Berlin Hours of Mary of Burgundy. De Winter (1981: 424, n. 20) argued that the Berlin Hours is by the Master of the First Prayer Book of Maximilian. I disagree.

8. Brinkmann's (in König et al. 1998: 129) suggestion that the miniature in the tiny book is by the Master of the David Scenes is untenable. There is no evidence that he was active at this very early date or even during the lifetime of Simon Marmion, the book's main illuminator (d. 1489). The brushwork in the two versions of the Virgin and Child is remarkably similar in its delicacy and precision. The differences between the two include the extensive use of gold highlights in the drapery of the Berlin miniature, a feature lacking in the other version; a subtly warmer overall tonality in the Berlin miniature; and yellow sleeves in the Berlin miniature, with red in the other. Also, perhaps most striking, the Virgin and half moon are placed off center within the miniature in the tiny book of hours, suggesting perhaps that both it and the Berlin version were based on the same pattern rather than the latter being based on the former.

9. The Berlin artist, however, used only the left half of the design.

10. For further examples of miniatures linked to patterns, see Lieftinck 1969: 134–47, and Brinkmann, in König et al. 1998: 119, 124–32.

11. For example, eight compositions from the Berlin Hours reappear in the Hours of Isabella of Castile (cat. no. 105), including six from the Passion cycle, while five miniatures from the Passion cycle reappear in the Brussels Hours of Philip of Cleves (Brussels, Bibliothèque royale de Belgique, Ms. IV 40). Moreover, four (or parts of four) compositions show up in the Passion cycle in the La Flora Hours (cat. no. 93), out of a total of seven patterns that the two books shared. This suggests that the patterns given to the illuminator of the Berlin hours may well have been organized in complete pictorial cycles.

12. König, in König et al. 1998: 105–6.

13. *Christ's Entry into Jerusalem* (fol. 177v) and *Augustus and the Tiburtine Sibyl* (fol. 178). See Van Buren 1975: 308, n. 6.

14. While identifying the original in a series of miniatures related to a common pattern is very difficult, in my view *The Funeral Procession of the Virgin* in the Emerson-White Hours is the original (ill. 32b), so that the Berlin Hours must postdate it. Since *The Virgin with Musical Angels* is an invention of Marmion and he rarely repeated himself precisely, the version of this subject in the small book of hours (cat. no. 37) probably predates the version in the Berlin Hours.

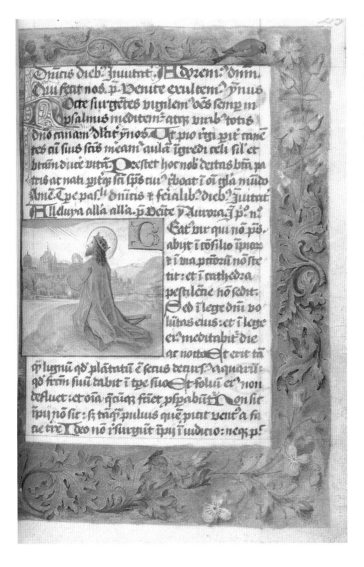

39

GHENT ASSOCIATES

Rooclooster Breviary

Monastery of Saint Paul (the Rooclooster), near Brussels, 1477 or a little later

MANUSCRIPT: 400 + vii folios, 12.7 × 8.9 cm (5 × 3½ in.); justification: 8.8 × 5.2 cm (3⁷⁄₁₆ × 2¹⁄₁₆ in.); 24–29 lines of *hybrida*; 1 small miniature

INSCRIPTIONS: *Liber monasterii rubee vallis in zonia iuxta bruxellam in brabancia* and *Pertinet liber iste monasteri sancti pauli dicti rubeevallis in zonia iuxta bruxellam*, fol. 1

BINDING: Probably Rooclooster, late fifteenth century; blind-tooled pink-stained calf; rebacked

COLLECTION: London, The British Library, Add. Ms. 11863

PROVENANCE: Monastery of Saint Paul (the Rooclooster), near Brussels; probably H.-J. Van Campenhout [his sale, Berthot, Brussels, June 21, 1830, lot 164]; Samuel Butler, bishop of Lichfield (1774–1839) [his sale catalogue, Christie's, London, June 1, 1840, part of lot 307; the sale did not take place because Butler's son sold the entire contents]; [to Payne and Foss]; purchased 1841 by the British Museum

RA

39
GHENT ASSOCIATES
David in Prayer, fol. 23

This breviary has a single miniature of King David and four borders of the colorful new type of border with naturalistically rendered flowers on solid-colored grounds (fols. 23, 140, 234, 336). It is one of three breviaries of modest dimensions that were written at the monastery of Rooclooster for its members but illuminated in Ghent.[1] Another (cat. no. 24) is dated 1477 and, like it, has a single miniature that shows David in prayer, the new type of decorated borders, and the 1470s Ghent-style border of blue and gold acanthus with spray and flowers on plain vellum (fol. 35, etc.). A third breviary written at the same monastery, also in the British Library (Add. Ms. 11864), lacks a miniature or the newer style of border but has the 1470s-type border.[2] The similarity of borders especially suggests that the three books were decorated for the most part by the same team in Ghent, even though different hands painted the two miniatures of David (see ills. 24, 39). The difference in the quality and quantity of illumination in otherwise quite similar, and decidedly modest, books probably reflects a difference in the size of their patrons' purses.[3]

This breviary's miniature of King David represents the subject from roughly the same angle as the Brussels miniature does, from behind yet nearly in profile. His harp lies in the same place, to his side on the ground, and the massing of the foreground landscape is similar. But the London David rests less firmly on the ground, his flesh tones are ruddier, and the lakeside background in the Brussels version has been replaced with a view across a field to a town. The London miniature was not painted by the same artist as the Brussels miniature. The latter is by the Vienna Master of Mary of Burgundy or a close follower. The London David miniature resembles more closely the work of artists in the circle of the Vienna Master, such as the painter of the Berlin Hours of Mary and Maximilian, who composed views in a similar way and whose figures appear sometimes to hover over the ground (see cat. no. 38, fol. 178).[4] The painter of the Berlin Hours is one among a group of illuminators called the Ghent Associates who worked in the new style. Significantly, the illusionistic borders in this manuscript are particularly subtle and fine, certainly equal in quality to those in the Brussels example and perhaps better.[5] The three related breviaries were probably produced around the same time, with the present example painted not long after the Brussels one. T. K.

Notes

1. The Österreichische Nationalbibliothek in Vienna owns eighty late-fourteenth- and fifteenth-century manuscripts from the library at Rooclooster. Most are not decorated or are only very modestly illuminated (Pächt, Jenni, and Thoss 1983, 1: 109–30; 2: figs. 7–12, 179–88).

2. Lieftinck 1969: 22–23.

3. The success of the painter Hugo van der Goes, who was a lay brother from the mid-1470s, shows that some lay brothers would certainly have had the means to purchase books of this relatively modest character.

4. Kren, in Malibu 1983a: 17, fig. 2c.

5. Cf. also Kren, in Malibu 1983a: 17.

40

GHENT ASSOCIATES

Book of Hours
Use of Saint Peter's, Ghent
Ghent, ca. 1480–85

MANUSCRIPT: 198 folios, 16 × 11.5 cm (6 5/16 × 4 1/2 in.); justification:
7.4 × 4.9 cm (2 7/8 × 1 15/16 in.); 20 lines of *gotica rotunda*; 10 miniatures

BINDING: Bruges (?), fifteenth century; blind-stamped panel binding
rebacked; gold-tooled on spine: *Officium B. Mariae Virginis* and device
of tree with *F.X.2*; gold-tooled spine

COLLECTION: Oxford, Bodleian Library, Ms. Douce 223

PROVENANCE: A cleric connected with abbey of Saint Peter, Blandin,
Ghent (Philippe de Conrault [?], abbot 1471–1490); still at Saint Peter's
in sixteenth century when a proper liturgical calendar replaced
original calendar; Francis Douce (1757–1834); his bequest, 1834

JPGM

40a
GHENT ASSOCIATES
Saint Amalberga, fol. 22v

Although books of hours are considered the quintessential prayer books of the laity, considerable evidence indicates that the present example was intended for a cleric. Some of the book's devotions are specific to the Abbey of Saint Peter's, Blandin, in Ghent. The mass "De sanctis huius locis" (fol. 151v) makes reference to a group of saints' relics (those of Ansbert, Wulfram, Gudwalt, Bertolph, Floribert, Winwaloe, and Amalberga) that were housed in Saint Peter's.[1] All but one of these saints (Wulfram) appears in the litany, along with others who may be associated with Saint Peter's.[2] The book's current calendar, which is not original but probably early sixteenth century, is a liturgical calendar for the use of Saint Peter's, suggesting that the well-worn book was, within a generation or so after its creation, still in the hands of a monk there, if not of its abbot. The first illustrated suffrage of the book's sequence is dedicated to Saint Peter, though its full-page miniature is now missing; a splendid full-page illumination of Saint Amalberga, a patron of the city of Ghent, adorns the last of the suffrages (ill. 40a).[3]

Derek Turner proposed that the book's patron might have been Philippe II Conrault, the abbot of Saint Peter's, Blandin (1471–90).[4] The abbot of Saint Peter's had long enjoyed a close relationship with the Burgundian dukes. The evidence within the book for the identification of its patron as an abbot or bishop includes a rare petition on behalf of bishops and abbots in the litany. Within the sequence of effaced coats of arms found in the lower borders, one shows traces of the crook of a bishop's or abbot's crosier (fol. 107), recalling the ecclesiastical accoutrements that appeared in the books of Philippe's bibliophile uncle and predecessor, Philippe Conrault. Perhaps also pertinent to this argument is the presence of two dozen benedictions, a rare feature of books of hours.[5] Given Philippe II's strong court connections, evidenced by his role as confessor of Archduke Maximilian as well as that of court adviser,[6] he is the most likely figure connected with Saint Peter's to have commissioned this book.

Once adorned with twenty full-page miniatures, the book retains only half this complement today. The most beautiful are easily the four at the front of the book representing female saints—Veronica, Catherine, Barbara, and Amalberga—along with one representing Saints Peter and Paul. They are probably by one or more of the Ghent Associates. The handling of landscapes and other aspects of settings for the individual saints recalls the Master of the First Prayer Book of Maximilian, but the brushwork is not his. The shape of the face, the eyes, and the narrow, pouty mouth of the superb Saint Catherine (ill. 40b) recall especially the figures in the half-length *Virgin and Child* (ill. 38a) in the Hours of Mary of Burgundy and Maximilian, which Van Buren ascribed to the Ghent Associates.[7] Distinctive features are the use of color in the miniatures of Saint Veronica (fol. 7v), Saint Amalberga, and Saint Catherine and the beautifully drawn folds of Amalberga's habit. The rest of the miniatures are weaker than these five and are certainly workshop productions.

Notes
1. De Schryver, in Ghent 1975: no. 616, 378–79.

2. In a psalter that Clark (2000: 230) connected with the Abbey of Saint Peter's, a remarkably similar list of confessors continues with the same three rare saints: Erembert, Ermelande, and Condede.

3. Both Saint Amalberga and a fellow Ghent patron, Saint Bavo, appear in the litany.

4. D. Turner cited in Van Buren 1975: 308, n. 19. Conrault succeeded as abbot at Saint Peter's a bibliophile uncle of the same name.

5. Fols. 156v–170v. Van Buren (1975: 308, n. 19) cited D. Turner as describing these as papal benedictions, but it is unclear why papal benedictions would appear in a book that was not made for the pope. The book originally contained a colophon in a cartouche on the lower margin of the December calendar page (fol. 6v), but it has proved illegible even with the aid of raking and ultraviolet light. I am grateful to Martin Kauffmann for his help with this investigation.

6. Derolez, in Ghent 1997: 46–48.

7. Van Buren (1975: 289–93, 307) coined the term following Lieftinck 1969: 157–64. Brinkmann (1998: 147–54) called the artist of cat. no. 38 the Berlin Master of Mary of Burgundy.

8. The pose of Saint Catherine of Alexandria is the mirror image of that of the same figure in the Emerson-White Hours (ill. 32f), though the proportions differ, the drapery is handled differently, and the figure of the emperor is also handled differently.

9. Other miniatures also follow patterns well known from the repertoire of the school of illuminators who emerged in the shadow of Hugo van der Goes in Ghent during the 1470s, including those for Saint Veronica, Pentecost, the Mass of the Dead, the Virgin in Glory, and the half-length Virgin and Child. Miniatures based on the patterns for both Saint Veronica and the half-length Virgin and Child appear in the Berlin Hours of Mary and Maximilian and in a very small book of hours from the 1470s (cat. nos. 38, 37), and one for the Assumption of the Virgin appears in the Berlin Hours. A miniature of the Mass of the Dead based on the same pattern appears in the London Hastings Hours (cat. no. 41). All reappear in other manuscripts from around the same time, the early 1480s.

10. Lieftinck (1969: 164) also dated the book before 1485 on the basis of the border types, which he compares with those of other prayer books of this period (e.g., cat. nos. 25, 38).

This book of hours belongs to the family of production of the Huth Hours (cat. no. 33) and the Emerson-White Hours (cat. no. 32) and was almost certainly written by the same scribe. It has the same number of text lines and the same justification, shares some conventions of border decoration, derives several of its figural compositions from one or the other, and has some miniatures closely related in style. *The Nativity* (fol. 57v) is a loose copy after the one by Simon Marmion in the Huth Hours. The figures of Saints Anthony and Paul and another figure in the background of that miniature (fol. 12v) are based closely on the historiated border in the Emerson-White Hours depicting the life of Saint Anthony Abbot (ill. 32a).[8] The latter was painted by the Master of the Houghton Miniatures.[9] The borders of strewn flowers and gold or white acanthus recall both the Huth and Emerson-White Hours in type, although they are less finely painted. Further, the binding of the clerical book of hours resembles that of the Huth Hours. The former is probably also the latest in the sequence of the three books, although given its close links to the Huth and Emerson–White Hours, it was probably made not much later. I would date it broadly to ca. 1480–85.[10]   T. K.

40b

GHENT ASSOCIATES
Saint Catherine, fol. 18v

MASTER OF THE FIRST PRAYER BOOK OF MAXIMILIAN (A)

One of the most complex and still inadequately studied groups of manuscripts in late medieval Flemish illumination is the very substantial one associated with the Master of the First Prayer Book of Maximilian.[1] The eponymous manuscript, the First Prayer Book of Maximilian (Vienna, Österreichische Nationalbibliothek, Ms. 1907) from 1486, includes only eight illuminations, all by one hand. Georges Hulin de Loo placed this book's illumination at the center of what he called the second style of the Master of Mary of Burgundy, in essence the second phase of the latter's work.[2] He attributed to him or associated with his style the *Légende de Saint Adrien* (cat. no. 42), the Brussels Hours of Philip of Cleves (Brussels, Bibliothèque royale de Belgique, Ms. IV 40), the Vienna Hours of Philip of Cleves (Österreichische National-bibliothek, Ms. s.n. 13239), the Munich Chronicle of the Princes of Cleves (cat. no. 86), the Hours of Louis Quarré (Oxford, Bodleian Library, Ms. Douce 311), and even the Grimani Breviary (cat. no. 126). He also indicated that the artist's oeuvre included a large body of manuscripts that Friedrich Winkler had grouped, in Hulin de Loo's view erroneously, around the *Hortulus animae* in Vienna (Öster-reichische Nationalbibliothek, Ms. 2706).[3] The last consists mostly of manuscripts of later date. They are the Brussels Cleves Hours and five manuscripts in this catalogue (cat. nos. 90, 92, 93, 109, 111).[4]

Subsequently, however, a debate emerged over whether this artist's production represented a second phase in the career of the Master of Mary of Burgundy or indicated a separate artistic personality.[5] Otto Pächt argued strongly for distinguishing them, an effort culminating in his celebrated 1948 monograph on the Master of Mary of Burgundy, the figure to whom most attention shifted for a long time. He also added to the list of attributions to the Maximilian Master the London Hastings Hours (cat. no. 41), the Bray Hours (cat. no. 88), and the Glasgow Breviary (cat. no. 89).[6] Following the example of Pächt, Wolfgang Hilger asserted in his monograph on the Vienna Prayer Book that the Max-imilian Master should be treated as a separate personality, replacing the Hortulus Master.[7] Patrick de Winter focused on one of the master's key works, the Hours of Isabella of Castile (cat. no. 105), and added a group of miniatures in the Spinola Hours (cat. no. 124).[8] I added to his oeuvre a rare secular manuscript, the Chronicles of the Counts of Flan-ders of 1477 (cat. no. 85), and the Carondelet breviary (cat. no. 112), and in this publication I attribute to him a minia-ture in the newly discovered Hours of Charlotte of Bour-bon-Montpensier (cat. no. 44).[9]

It is not possible to do justice to the complex issues raised by the corpus of manuscripts assigned to the Maxi-milian Master group in the space available here. Suffice it to say that comparisons between particular manuscripts in this group and the eponymous book often yield contrasts that are as striking as the similarities. The Vienna book's miniatures are dull in comparison with the finest minia-tures assigned to the artist. The latter appear, for example, in the Chronicle of the Princes of Cleves, the London Hast-ings Hours, La Flora (cat. no. 93), and the much later Grimani Breviary (cat. no. 126). Yet, like the earlier produc-tion of the prolific and financially highly successful Bruges illuminator Willem Vrelant, the manuscripts of the Maxi-milian Master group have the character of a great enter-prise. Some of the latter's books have lengthy pictorial cycles in which finely painted miniatures are side by side with clumsier work.[10] The workshop of the Maximilian Master involved a number of collaborators who shared pat-terns, similar figure types, and often a similar palette, but they produced variable results. Frequently the Maximilian Master himself seems but a shadowy presence.

A number of the most luxurious commissions with miniatures in the style of the Maximilian Master, such as the Breviary of Eleanor of Portugal (cat. no. 91) and the Munich Hours (cat. no. 90), were painted largely by mem-bers of the workshop. The most distinctive and original of these artists I have named the Master of the Munich *Annun-ciation* after that miniature (ill. 90). This artist favored half-length figures inspired by Marmion, though they are fuller-bodied than Marmion's and feature abundant spit curls. Another distinctive workshop personality, influenced by the same Marmion cycle, along with the male peasant types of Hugo van der Goes, appeared in the decade imme-diately before and after the turn of the century. This artist featured relatively broad, short figures. The men have a strong brow; loose, wavy hair; and an upper lip that pro-trudes slightly and is sometimes flared. The female types have moon faces with bland features. This style appears in some miniatures in the Munich Hours, the Eleanor Bre-viary, and the breviaries in Berlin and Glasgow (cat. nos. 112, 89). The quality of the Maximilian Master's workshop production was sometimes very high, as in the miniatures, mostly of single figures, illustrating the suffrages in the Spinola Hours (cat. no. 124), where the quality of the brush-work and modeling is exceptional. Yet even here the differ-ent components of the figure and drapery are not fully integrated pictorially.

Despite the range in their quality and handling, individ-ual miniatures in the Maximilian Master style share certain features. First and foremost is the dependence on a large body of patterns that originated during the 1470s with the Vienna Master of Mary of Burgundy, his workshop, and Van der Goes.[11] Other artistic sources include Dieric Bouts and Simon Marmion. Although the Maximilian Master's miniatures are often beautifully and brightly colored and have handsome landscape settings (see ills. 41a, 41b), they lack atmospheric effects and subtleties of psychological expression. Sometimes, in repeating a pattern, the workshop used an entirely different palette or interchanged the placement of particular hues. A feature common to the modeling of faces is a mixture of gray and pink used in the flesh, with distinctive pink (or white) highlights on the nose and chin (see cat. no. 41, fols. 20v, 40; and cat. no. 105, fols. 10v, 154v).[12] Particularly characteristic are Goesian types, especially the male peasants, who are characterized by strong brows, sloping foreheads, and pointed jaws.

The degree of the illuminator's own contribution to the invention of the large body of patterns he employed remains unclear but was probably quite limited. One of the rare secular manuscripts he illuminated with complex multifigure compositions shows remarkably stiff and awkward movement (cat. no. 85), and sometimes a figure from one composition is inserted into an entirely different composition in the same book with awkward results (see cat. no. 41, fols. 55v, 139v).[13] Occasionally a gesture or figural movement in a composition based on a pattern is altered in an unconvincing way (see cat. no. 105, fol. 97v; and cat. no. 92, fols. 97v, 520v). Another common feature is the appearance of disproportionate heads and limbs, as if a pattern was copied clumsily or carelessly (cat. no. 112, fol. 7v; cat. no. 91, fol. 555v; and cat. no. 92, fol. 558). This may reflect the illuminator's own shortcomings, but it resulted from the reliance upon assistants as well.

The extended artistic career of the Maximilian Master has prompted scholars to identify him with Alexander Bening (d. 1519), the illuminator whose membership in the Ghent painters' guild was sponsored by Hugo van der Goes and Joos van Ghent in 1469.[14] Bening married Catherine van der Goes, who was likely the sister or niece of Hugo. Scholars have long associated him with a number of the aforementioned works, as some of them once identified him with the Master of Mary of Burgundy (when they also believed that the latter's career extended for several more decades).[15] The virtue of his identification with the Maximilian Master rests on a variety of circumstantial and stylistic factors. Key among them are the relationship of his work to that of Van der Goes and the circumstance that the artist spent the early years of his career in Ghent, where many of those books are thought to have been made. Bening also belonged to the confraternity of the book trade in Bruges, an important center for the production of such books in the sixteenth century, while the Maximilian Master workshop produced a number of books in collaboration with artists from there (cat. nos. 90, 93, 105, 124). Also important are the facts that Bening lived until 1519, by which point evidence of the artistic activity of the Maximilian Master ceases, and that the large body of patterns that the Maximilian Master used were passed to the celebrated Bruges illuminator Simon Bening, the son of Alexander. Finally, Erik Drigsdahl's plausible argument that Alexander Bening's signature appears in the Grimani Breviary heightens the probability of this identification.[16] A renewed study of the famous breviary offers an appropriate point of departure for revisiting the question of the Master of the First Prayer Book of Maximilian.

T. K.

Notes

1. In the literature he is sometimes called the Master of the Older Prayer Book of Maximilian.

2. Hulin de Loo 1931: 41–42; Hulin de Loo 1939b: 162, 170–76.

3. Winkler 1925: 119–20.

4. The Master of the *Hortulus animae* no longer makes sense as an artistic personality. The Maximilian Master has assumed the majority of the works on Winkler's list, and Hulin de Loo was right to omit the *Hortulus animae* from this group. Winkler (1925: 119–21) included the Grimani Breviary in his list for the Hortulus Master, while De Winter (1981: 424, n. 20) omitted it from his list for the Maximilian Master. Many of the compositions in the Grimani Breviary are based on those used by the Maximilian Master as many as three decades earlier in the Hastings Hours in London. Examples include *Christ Washing the Feet of the Disciples* (fol. 219v), *The Office of the Dead* (fol. 58), *The Blessed Carried to Heaven* (fol. 469), *The Visitation* (fol. 610v), *Saint Elizabeth of Hungary* (fol. 812), and *Saint Jerome* (fol. 751v). The technical superiority of these Grimani miniatures to those by the Maximilian Master is clear, yet their authorship deserves closer examination.

5. See Hilger 1973: 47–52; Pächt 1976.

6. Pächt, in London 1953: 160–61, nos. 598–599, 602.

7. Pächt, in London 1953: 160–61, nos. 598–599, 601–602; Hilger 1973: 52–54, n. 94.

8. De Winter 1981: 424, n. 20. De Winter erroneously included in this list the Madrid Hastings Hours (cat. no. 25), the Berlin Hours of Mary of Burgundy and Maximilian (cat. no. 38), and a book of hours in Kraków (Biblioteka Czartoryskich, Ms. 3025).

9. On the first of the three, see Kren, in Malibu 1983a: 23, 26, 39, n. 30, and Pächt and Thoss 1990: 101.

10. De Winter (1981: 356–57, 361–63, 396–97) remarked on the visual evidence of extensive workshop participation in the Hours of Isabella of Castile (cat. no. 105) and other works. Dekeyzer proposed that as many as four artists assisted the Maximilian Master in the execution of his portion of the Mayer van den Bergh Breviary (see cat. no. 92). The differences in quality that suggest workshop participation are seen by comparing the miniatures in the London Hastings Hours (cat. no. 41) with those based on the same patterns in the Bray Hours (cat. no. 88). Or one can compare the finest miniatures by this artist in the Isabella Hours (cat. no. 105), such as *Saint Michael* (fol. 167v), with the *Virgin and Child* (fol. 159v) or *Saint John the Baptist Preaching* (fol. 169v), or those in the Mayer van den Bergh Breviary, such as *The Trinity* and *The Beheading of a Martyr* (cat. no. 92, fols. 100, 590v). Brinkmann (1988: 91) considered the stylistic variety within this group to be so large as to suggest the participation of more than one master, with "the attributions urgently in need of revision."

11. The influence of the patterns used by the Maximilian Master on painters such as Gerard David is discussed in Thomas Kren and Maryan Ainsworth's essay "The Interrelationship and Artistic Exchanges between Illuminators and Painters, ca. 1467–1561," in this volume.

12. This feature is less common in his later works (see cat. nos. 124, 126).

13. This manuscript shows him reusing the figure of an assassin at the right in both *The Martyrdom of Saint Thomas Becket* and *The Massacre of the Innocents*. See Turner (D.) 1983: figs. 55b, 139b.

14. Hulin de Loo 1931: 41; De Winter 1981: 353–57; Kren, in Malibu 1983a: 29.

15. Winkler 1915: 282–88; Winkler 1925: 102–13; Pächt 1948.

16. Drigsdahl 1997: 38–40.

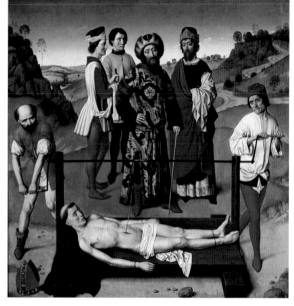

41a
MASTER OF THE FIRST
PRAYER BOOK OF
MAXIMILIAN
*The Martyrdom of Saint
Erasmus*, fol. 53v

Figure 60
DIERIC BOUTS
(ca. 1415–1475)
*The Martyrdom of Saint
Erasmus*, central panel
of the Triptych of Saint
Erasmus, ca. 1450–60.
Oil on wood panel, 82 ×
80 cm (32⅛ × 31½ in.),
central panel. Leuven,
Collegiate Church of
Saint Peter

41

MASTER OF THE FIRST PRAYER BOOK
OF MAXIMILIAN

London Hours of William Lord Hastings
Use of Sarum
Ghent, before 1483

MANUSCRIPT: 300 + iii folios, 16.5 × 12.3 cm (6½ × 4¹³⁄₁₆ in.);
justification: 8.5 × 6 cm (3⁵⁄₁₆ × 2⅜ in.); 16 lines of *bastarda*; 28 full-
page miniatures, 4 half-page miniatures, 4 historiated borders

HERALDRY: Escutcheon with the arms of William Lord Hastings,
encircled by the Garter with motto *Hony soit qui mal y pense*, fols. 13,
74, 151, 184v; escutcheons with the royal arms of England overpainted
by those of Hastings, two banners with coats of arms (one *or*, a
chevron sable, and three martlets sable, the others not fully legible),
and a banner of red and gold, fol. 184v; standard with first word of
motto of the Order of the Garter and colors of England, banners
bearing the royal arms, fol. 126

BINDING: Modern; red morocco, richly tooled; gilt and goffered edges

COLLECTION: London, The British Library, Add. Ms. 54782

PROVENANCE: William Lord Hastings (ca. 1430–1483); [Bernard
Quaritch, London]; to C. W. Dyson Perrins (1864–1958), in
January 1910 (his Ms. 26, later renumbered Ms. 104); bequeathed by
his widow to the British Museum in December 1968

JPGM and RA

The devotional contents of this book are very similar to
those of a Flemish book of hours in Madrid also owned
by William Lord Hastings (cat. no. 25). The latter includes
the same eighteen suffrages before the Hours of the Virgin
in nearly the same sequence.¹ In both books these suffrages
are illustrated by full-page miniatures, and the London

hours also has a nineteenth suffrage illustrated by a full-
page miniature, dedicated to Saint Thomas Becket.² In
addition, the London hours has a group of four suffrages
illustrated by half-page miniatures that seem to have been
added after the book had been planned and its production
was under way but prior to its completion. They are dedicated to Saint Paul, Saint Leonard, Saint David of Wales,
and Saint Jerome. In both books the devotions that follow the Hours of the Virgin are identical and in the same
sequence.³ Both manuscripts have Hours of the Virgin for
the use of Sarum, which is to be expected in a book of hours
made for an English patron. They also have English calendars, although they are different from each other.⁴

In aspects of their production and their pictorial character, the London and Madrid books show further com-
monalities. Originally, prior to the late addition of four
suffrages, they had the same number of full-page miniatures, give or take one or two, along with a roughly identical pattern of facing full borders of the new illusionistic
style. Moreover, the scribal hands are similar, and if Derek
Turner was correct, the same scribe may have written
both.⁵ Finally, although the books were unquestionably
illuminated by different artists, the artists nevertheless
occupied the same milieu, probably Ghent, and they had
artistic sources in common. For example, in both books
The Martyrdom of Saint Erasmus is derived from Dieric
Bouts's altarpiece devoted to this subject (ill. 41a and fig.
60). The illuminators of the two books also shared at least
one pattern⁶ as well as other sources such as specific paintings by Hugo van der Goes and miniatures by the Vienna
Master of Mary of Burgundy and his immediate circle.⁷ The

41b
MASTER OF THE FIRST
PRAYER BOOK OF
MAXIMILIAN
Saint Anthony, fol. 50v

hues.[12] Despite the two books' iconographic similarities, entirely different subjects and compositions illustrate many of their devotions. So Hastings, even while acquiring a couple of devotional books of nearly identical spiritual content from essentially the same artistic environment, obtained ones that are nonetheless quite distinct from each other visually.

Along with the Madrid hours, this manuscript is important for its large body of compositions in the new naturalistic style of illumination that came to be handed down by means of patterns over the next several generations. In many instances these two books contain the earliest roughly datable examples, and as such they show the new style being codified for efficient production. Sometimes these patterns migrated in groups, perhaps gathered in a pattern book or in an artist's chest.[13] There is no doubt that the Master of the First Prayer Book of Maximilian himself returned to them regularly (cf. cat. no. 105). As for who designed the patterns, we know that the Vienna Master of Mary of Burgundy, or someone close to him, provided models for some, but who conceived the rest?[14] Such miniatures as *The Martyrdom of Saint Erasmus*, which takes some liberties with its masterful source, are remarkably successful, and the secular borders are also bold and original. Nevertheless, it is possible that someone else adapted Bouts's composition so that the Maximilian Master could copy it.

The dependence of some of the pictorial ideas in the London Hastings Hours on such innovative books as the Voustre Demeure Hours (cat. no. 20), suggests that it was not made earlier than the late 1470s. This date is consistent with Hastings's own visits to Flanders and the active collecting of his good friend Edward IV.[15] That the book was produced in Ghent is suggested by the accepted localization of the illuminator, the numerous links to the Ghent-produced Madrid Hastings Hours, and particular liturgical features shared with Ghent manuscripts.[16]   T. K.

London hours was illuminated by the Master of the First Prayer Book of Maximilian,[8] whereas I believe that one miniature in the Madrid hours may be by the Vienna Master of Mary of Burgundy and the rest by his workshop.[9] Further evidence of artistic exchange between the London and Madrid artists is provided by the Hours of Katherine Bray (cat. no. 88), another Flemish book made for an English patron. It was illuminated in the workshop of the Maximilian Master and contains many miniatures based on patterns used previously in either the London or the Madrid Hastings Hours.

The artists of the London and Madrid codices, who also shared a naturalistic aesthetic derived from Flemish oil painting, nevertheless had clearly distinguishable styles. For example, in *The Martyrdom of Saint Erasmus* both illuminators reconfigured Bouts's composition and the landscape, but they did so in different ways.[10] The proportions of the figures are slenderer in the Madrid hours, in keeping with the style of the Vienna Master's work, while in the London Hours the figures are subtly broader and the facial types more consistently reminiscent of Goesian models. The London Hastings Hours is more colorful overall. Its miniatures are brighter and more evenly lit, especially in their settings, while in the Madrid Hours the settings are more atmospheric, with stronger chiaroscuro in both miniatures and borders.[11] The London Hastings Hours also features five full borders with secular themes and drolleries, all of which depict a unified three-dimensional space that is, by implication, continuous behind the text block. These distinctive, highly original borders heighten the book's pictorial variety and enhance the overall effect of saturated

Notes

1. Both books also contain, before the Hours of the Virgin, the Gospel extracts, the "Obsecro te," "O Intemerata," the Verses of Saint Bernard, and the prayer "Deus propicius esto michi peccatori," though they are not in the same sequence.

2. In the London Hastings Hours five full-page miniatures have been removed from the section of suffrages (John the Baptist, Adrian, George, Sebastian, and Anne), while another is missing, for the "Obsecro te," as is possibly one for the Gospel extracts.

3. They are, in order, the Penitential Psalms, the Office of the Dead, Commendation of Souls, Psalms for the Passion, Fifteen Prayers on the Passion, and the Psalter of Saint Jerome. The last four texts also appear in another book of hours made for an English patron in this catalogue (cat. no. 15).

4. A much-discussed feature of this manuscript is the Hastings armorials, which are painted over completed decorative borders (fols. 13, 74, 151) and over the English royal arms in the miniature of the Office of the Dead. This fact has sparked a debate over whether or not the book was actually begun for Hastings himself. D. Turner (1983: 115–19) argued persuasively that two of the four suffrages that the Maximilian Master added prior to the book's completion specifically reflect Hastings's requirements. Saint Leonard was Hastings's father's name saint. Hastings was chamberlain of north Wales, and Saint David of Wales was the patron saint of that region. This does not, however, prove that the book was begun for Hastings, and the possibility remains that it was not. Also, although this book and the Madrid

Hastings Hours remain in most respects textual twins, their calendars and litanies, where they might be most expected to agree, are not especially similar. While both calendars are English with an admixture of Flemish and northern French saints, John Plummer reports that they agree by only 71 percent (Department of Manuscripts files, JPGM). (On some types of textually twin French and Flemish manuscripts in the fifteenth century, see Kren 2002: 167–75.) For different views on the question of the book's first owner, see Turner (D.) 1983: 115–19; Kren, in Malibu 1983a: 21; Tudor-Craig 1987; Brinkmann 1988: 90–91; and Backhouse 1996: 43–54.

5. Turner (D.) 1983: 123.

6. The shared pattern was the source for the figure of Saint Margaret in the London Hastings Hours (fol. 62v) and the Virgin of the Annunciation in the Madrid Hours (fol. 73v). Brinkmann (1997: 154 n. 24) rightly questioned my assertion of the primacy of the Madrid version of this figure on the basis of the erroneous inclusion of the dove in the narrative of Saint Margaret (Kren, in Malibu 1983a: 27). It is thus possible that the London version is earlier, although it remains to be demonstrated.

7. See Kren, in Malibu 1983a: 27–29; Lieftinck 1969: 116–23; and cat. no. 25 in this volume.

8. This attribution goes back to Pächt (in London 1953: 601, no. 598). While it seems to have stood the test of time, Brinkmann (1988: 100–104) rightly pointed out the heterogeneous character of the oeuvre associated with this artist, especially as conceived by De Winter (1981: 353–417, 424, n. 20), and endeavored to link the illuminator of the London Hastings Hours with the Master of 1499—to my mind, unconvincingly.

9. See cat. no. 25.

10. In the London version the designer fit the composition to the vertical format by adjusting the landscape and the figures' relationship to it. Here the setting is a unifying element. Fully characteristic of the Vienna Master of Mary of Burgundy, who probably designed the Madrid miniature (ill. 25a), is the way the two executioners are symmetrically disposed but one faces the viewer while the other has his back to us. The Vienna Master subtly strengthened the structure of Bouts's composition.

11. In the London hours the artist took greater care to harmonize the color of the miniature and border.

12. The spatial character of these borders distinguishes them from those illuminated by the Vienna Master of Mary of Burgundy and his workshop, who treated the historiated border quite differently.

13. Brinkmann (1988: 93–95) provided a useful and extensive list of examples from this manuscript.

14. See my remarks under cat. no. 38.

15. Kren, in Malibu 1983a: 26–27, figs. 3d, 3e.

16. Plummer pointed out in correspondence with the author the connection of some textual models, such as that for the "Obsecro te," to Ghent (Department of Manuscripts files, JPGM).

42 (opposite)
MASTER OF THE FIRST
PRAYER BOOK OF
MAXIMILIAN
*Louis XI and Charlotte
of Savoy before the Altar
of Saint Adrian*, fol. 3v

42

MASTER OF THE FIRST PRAYER BOOK OF MAXIMILIAN AND GHENT ASSOCIATES

Légende de Saint Adrien
Ghent, between 1477 and 1483

MANUSCRIPT: 17 folios, 28.4 × 20.2 cm (11¼ × 8 in.); justification: 15.5 × 10.3 cm (6⅛ × 4 in.); 17 lines of *bastarda* by Patoul' Agilson (?); 1 full-page miniature, 1 historiated initial, 4 historiated roundels in borders

HERALDRY: Escutcheons with the arms of France, fols. 3v, 4; lozenge with the arms of France impaling those of Savoy, fol. 3v

BINDING: Flanders, late fifteenth century; black velvet over wood boards

COLLECTION: Vienna, Österreichische Nationalbibliothek, Ms. s.n. 2619

PROVENANCE: Louis XI, king of France (1423–1483), and his wife, Charlotte of Savoy (1439–1483), or Abbey of Saint Adrian, Grammont; Schloss Ambras, Innsbruck; Kunsthistorisches Museum, Vienna (inv. 4996); transferred 1936 to the Nationalbibliothek

JPGM

In 1458 the dauphin of France, the future King Louis XI (r. 1461–83), visited the Abbey of Saint Adrian at Grammont (Geraardsbergen), in east Flanders, and the following year he returned, appointing its abbot, Nicaise de Frasnes, as his counselor. The abbey housed the relics of the saint and as such was an important pilgrimage site, enjoying many visits from the Burgundian dukes and the patronage of Guillaume Hugonet, Charles the Bold's chancellor, and of Margaret, countess of Poitiers and wife of Antoine de Croÿ.[1] Louis's contacts with the abbey were renewed many years later, toward the end of his life. In 1482, in ill health, he donated the sum of 22,500 crowns to commission four bells for the church, but his interest was perhaps rekindled as early as 1477, when the death of Charles the Bold caused him to return to the Burgundian lands and regain territory.[2] It was during this period that this slim but exquisite volume was commissioned either by Louis or by the abbey itself. In the latter instance it would have served either as a thank-you to the king and queen or as a testament to the abbey's allegiance to its benefactors.[3]

The full-page frontispiece shows angels presenting the kneeling king and queen before a tall carved and polychromed altar (ill. 42). Saint Adrian, brandishing his sword and astride a lion, is flanked by Saint John the Baptist and Saint Louis of France. Louis XI is dressed in armor and draped with a mantle decorated with fleurs-de-lis and an ermine collar.[4] Although the composition is coherent and imposing, each of the three main figures and the angels may have been constructed from distinct patterns. This is in keeping with the practice of the Master of the First Prayer Book of Maximilian, to whom the miniature is attributed.[5] Louis's pose and costume were employed in the figure of Maximilian I in his prayer book of a few years later, which was illuminated by the same workshop (fig. 61). The angel, whose presenting hand is awkwardly cut off by Louis's ample collar, reappears behind the female patron in the dedication miniature in the Breviary of Eleanor of Portugal (ill. 91b). The same pattern that served for the

Notes

1. Also in 1458 Jean Miélot, who translated texts and wrote and illustrated books for Duke Philip, prepared an edition of the legend of Saint Adrian, also in French but distinct from the text of the Vienna volume.

2. De Smet 1845: 156–58; *Monasticon belge* 1890–1993, 7/2: 99. The king and his queen, Charlotte of Savoy, were both patrons of manuscripts and of illumination, and Charlotte in particular strongly favored spiritual texts (Delisle 1868–81, 1: 74–79, 91–96; Legaré 2001). The painter and illuminator Jean Bourdichon was his court artist. Van Buren (1975: 307, no. 2) observed that the costume of Charlotte of Savoy argues for a dating earlier in this period, i.e., 1477/78. While this dating seems a bit narrow, it would not surprise me if the miniature were painted before 1480.

3. For the third alternative proposed here, see Van Buren 1993: 1189. For evidence of the abbey's own patronage in the early sixteenth century of a missal and of an altarpiece by Jan Gossaert, see the sales catalogue *Printed Books and Manuscripts from Longleat*, Christie's, London, June 13, 2002, 30. In addition, there is no record of the book ever having been in the French royal library.

4. Lieftinck (1969: 155) considered the altarpiece a faithful depiction of the retable at the abbey in Grammont.

5. Hulin de Loo (1939b: 162) grouped the Saint Adrian frontispiece with other manuscripts around the Berlin Hours of Mary and Maximilian and the First Prayer Book of Maximilian, while Winkler (1925: 113, 208) initially attributed it provisionally to the Master of Mary of Burgundy, and Pächt (1948: 66, no. 12) also initially attributed it to this artist. Since many saw the First Prayer Book as a key to the group, Hilger (1973: 53–54, n. 54) suggested renaming the artist the Master of the First Prayer Book of Maximilian. See also Kren, in Malibu 1983a: 21–29; Pächt and Thoss 1990: 98, 101. De Winter (1981: 423–24, n. 16) attributed the Vienna Saint Adrian to "The Master of the Nassau Hours."

6. Lieftinck 1969: 155, fig. 238. A variation of the pose of Saint Adrian appears in the Madrid Hastings Hours (cat. no. 25, fol. 26v); they might share a source rather than copy the same pattern (Lieftinck 1969: fig. 192).

7. The facial type of Louis is typical of this illuminator and not so different from that of Maximilian (fig. 61), so it was likely not intended as a true portrait. Charlotte is also shown as much younger than she actually was.

8. In this book even the illusionistic borders have narrative vignettes, one of which is shared with a book of hours in Kraków (Biblioteka Czartoryskich, Ms. 3025). See Pächt and Thoss 1990: 100, fig. 104, pl. 14.

9. The delightful drolleries may represent a special category within the group. They perhaps descend from the simian and other animal escapades in the borders of the Vienna Hours of Mary of Burgundy (cat. no. 19), and they appear to be by a different hand from the small miniatures and historiated initial. See Pächt and Thoss 1990: 100–101.

10. Pächt 1948: 66; Lieftinck 1969: 153.

figure of the queen probably served as the source for the devout Mary of Burgundy in her prayer book painted around the same time by one of the Ghent Associates (cat. no. 38, fol. 354).[6] The elegant finish of the costumes and the gray underpainting of the face of the king call to mind miniatures in the Maximilian Master's London Hastings Hours (cat. no. 41), which is probably close to this volume in date.[7]

The book features four narrative scenes from the saint's life and nineteen drolleries in the borders that—with their much rounder heads, paler flesh, and indistinct fold patterns—have less in common with the work of the Maximilian Master.[8] They probably should be attributed to the Ghent Associates, anonymous practitioners of the new Ghent style of illumination.[9] The participation of the Maximilian Master and the inclusion of the older Ghent-style borders with blue and gold acanthus on plain grounds suggest the localization of the manuscript to Ghent. Otto Pächt identified Patoul' Agilson as the scribe on the basis of the signature at the bottom of folio 16v. G. I. Lieftinck commented on the French quality of the script.[10] Nothing else is known of Agilson.   T. K.

Figure 61
MASTER OF THE FIRST PRAYER BOOK OF MAXIMILIAN
Maximilian Kneeling before Saint Sebastian. In the First Prayer Book of Maximilian. 19 × 13.3 cm (7½ × 5¼ in.). Vienna, Österreichische Nationalbibliothek, Ms. 1907, fol. 61v

43

MASTER OF THE FIRST PRAYER BOOK
OF MAXIMILIAN (?)

L'Abbaye du Saint Esprit, translation of *Abbacia de Sancto Spiritu*;
Saint Peter of Luxembourg, *Livret; Les Douze Fleurs de tribulation*,
translation of *De XII utilitatibus tribulationis*; **Pseudo-Seneca,**
***Remèdes de fortune**, translation by Jacques Bauchant of *De remediis*
fortuitorum; and other devotional writings
Ghent, 1475

MANUSCRIPT: 267 folios, 36 × 28 cm (14 ³⁄₁₆ × 11 in.); justification:
24.8 × 15.8 cm (9¾ × 6³⁄₁₆ in.); 28 lines of *bastarda* by David Aubert;
4 half-page miniatures

HERALDRY: Escutcheon with the arms of Margaret of York, fol. 155;
unidentified coat of arms overpainted with black, fol. 1

INSCRIPTIONS: Colophon *Cy finent aucuns moult devots traitties moralz*
et aultrement comme par la table des rubrics de ce volume appert en brief,
lequel volume a este escript et ordonne comme il s'ensieult par le commande-
ment de tres haulte, tres excellente et tres puissante princesse et ma tres
redoubtee et souveraine dame, Madame Marguerite de Yorke, duchesse de
Bourgoingne, de Lothrijk, de Brabant, de Lembourg, de Luxembourg, de
Gueldres et de Loheraine, contesse de Flandres, d'Artois, de Bourgoingne,
de Zutphen, palatin de Haynou, de Hollande, de Zeellande, de Namur et
de Vaudemont, marquise du Saint Empire, dame de Frise, de Salins et de
Malines, en sa ville de Gand ou mois de mars l'an de grace nostre seigneur
mil CCC soixante et quinze, par David Aubert son escripvain indigne,
fol. 267v

BINDING: Probably a binder who later worked in London with
William Caxton, Flanders, fifteenth century; blind-stamped leather
over wood boards; rebacked; corner pieces and bosses; missing clasps

COLLECTION: Oxford, Bodleian Library, Ms. Douce 365

PROVENANCE: Margaret of York, duchess of Burgundy (1446–1503);
Bellingham Inglis [his sale, Sotheby's, London, June 1826, lot 1650];
[Cochran Catalogue, 1829, no. 73]; to Francis Douce (1757–1834),
June 1829; his bequest, 1834

RA

43a

MASTER OF THE FIRST
PRAYER BOOK OF
MAXIMILIAN (?)
Seneca Presenting a Book
to Calyo, fol. 155 (detail)

This book is the most splendid of the various collections
of spiritual writings that entered the library of Margaret of York (see cat. nos. 28, 29). Its nine treatises are illustrated by four miniatures. *Truth, Chastity, Humility, and*
Poverty—with the virtues embodied by four courtly, youthful women—illustrates the first, *L'Abbaye du Saint Esprit*
(fol. 1). The second treatise concerns organizing one's life in
order to devote it to God. The miniature shows Saint Peter
of Luxembourg, identified as the text's author in the rubric,
with his sister Jeanne of Luxembourg—to whom he sent
the treatise, according to the rubric—in an interior (fol. 17).[1]
Les Remèdes de fortune, attributed to Seneca,[2] is prefaced by
an illumination showing the translator receiving the treatise from Seneca (ill. 43a) and, in the background, the former presenting it to the dedicatee. A depiction of Duchess
Margaret in prayer before her ladies-in-waiting (ill. 43b)
illustrates the fifth selection, *Les Douze Fleurs de tribulation*
(fol. 115).

The four miniatures are by the same hand. Although
they share with the other collections of spiritual writings
that David Aubert wrote out for Margaret (cat. nos. 28, 29,
and Brussels, Bibliothèque royale de Belgique, Ms. 9106; Jena,
Thüringer Universitäts- und Landesbibliothek, Ms. El. Fol.
85) a tinted grisaille technique, the execution here is quite
different, relying on stronger contours; highly structured
modeling with short, mostly parallel dashes; and a drapery
style with thin, tubular folds. The facial types with gray
modeling over a flesh-toned underlayer (with some flesh
highlights) and the style of slightly stiff drapery with elaborate tubular fold patterns are strongly reminiscent of the
work of the Master of the First Prayer Book of Maximilian.[3]

43b

MASTER OF THE FIRST
PRAYER BOOK OF
MAXIMILIAN (?)
Margaret of York in Prayer,
fol. 115 (detail)

Both male and female facial types find correspondences in the artist's early works.[4] The disproportion between heads and bodies or between sleeves and the rest of a costume, most striking in the miniature with the female virtues, along with the occasional skewed orthogonal in the rendering of an interior, is typical of this illuminator's production throughout his career. The disproportion may result from the construction of parts of the figures from different patterns. At the same time both the contours and the modeling of the faces are more precise and subtle here than they are in the work of the Maximilian Master, and the device of parallel dashes for modeling the architecture is more developed here.[5] If this manuscript is by the Maximilian Master, it is his earliest dated miniature cycle, and *Margaret of York in Prayer* is one of his finest miniatures. If not, then the artist was important for the formation of the Maximilian Master.

Although the book has a colophon in which Aubert dedicated the volume in March 1476 (n.s.) to Margaret of York and in which her arms also appear, the colophon itself was partly effaced and rewritten.[6] This is probably the result of scribal error, conceivably because of the titles that the duke and duchess continued to accumulate in those years. Even though the armorials seem to be painted out of the margin on the page with Margaret's portrait, yet another alteration, the book was likely still intended for her originally.[7] The traditional identification of the elegant woman in prayer with the duchess is confirmed by her ermine-lined robe and the retinue that attends her. The facial type, though probably not a good likeness, nevertheless compares closely with other portrayals of her in her books.[8] In this period she was already a client of Aubert's for similar illuminated books of religious texts (cat. nos. 13, 14, 28, 29).

Binding specialists have noted a connection between the fleur-de-lis and dragon stamps on the book's original binding and those on some Caxtons bound in London. The latter bindings are ascribed to William Caxton's binder, a Bruges artisan thought to have moved to London around 1477 to work for the English printer.[9]   T. K.

Notes

1. Chesney (1951: 18–19) pointed out that the treatise is thirteenth century and so could not have been written by Saint Peter of Luxembourg, only amended by him. Moreover, the text repeatedly addresses "fille," not "soeur."

2. Chesney 1951: 28–29.

3. Pächt (1944a: 295) attributed the miniatures to the Master of Mary of Burgundy.

4. Lieftinck 1969: 154; Kren, in Malibu 1983a: 28–29. Both made comparisons between the facial types in this book and those found in the manuscripts illuminated by the Master of the First Prayer Book of Maximilian.

5. One might, for example, compare the depiction of Margaret of York (ill. 43b) with that of Charlotte of Savoy (ill. 42). The treatment of the drapery, including the disposition of the folds, is similar. The differences may result from the monochrome technique, but the Douce miniature has greater crispness overall, and the statuesque male attendant on folio 115 finds no counterpart in the Maximilian Master's miniatures.

6. This caused Delaissé (in Brussels 1959: 153–54, no. 192) to wonder if the book was originally intended for Margaret. Scot McKendrick advised me that the erasures belong to the second half of the colophon and are most noticeable from the title "Dame de Frise." During the period following the completion of *Les Visions du chevalier Tondal* (cat. no. 14) in March 1475, Margaret had gained the titles of "Palatin de Vaudemont" and "Dame de Frise" and had been elevated from "Palatin de Zutphen" to "Contesse de Zutphen." Charles the Bold took Vaudemont only in October 1475 (Vaughn 1973: 356).

7. Her armorials appear on folio 155, painted over the border decoration, in the same position where the armorials had originally appeared on folio 115. Here the charges are preserved. The armorials are overpainted in black on folio 1.

8. She wears a virtually identical outfit and is also attended by ladies-in-waiting in the frontispiece to the Jena Boethius (Thüringer Universitäts- und Landesbibliothek, Ms. El. Fol. 85, fol. 13; Smeyers 1998: 385, figs. 41, 42), which is dated 1476 (old style). On the depictions of Margaret in her books, see Smith (J.) 1992: 54.

9. Pollard 1970: 205; see also Lowry 1992: 103–10 for this binding's role as evidence of Caxton's relationship to court circles.

SIMON MARMION (B)

For biography, see part 1

44a
SIMON MARMION
The Last Judgment,
fol. 171v

44

MASTER OF THE DRESDEN PRAYER BOOK,
SIMON MARMION, WORKSHOP OF THE FIRST
PRAYER BOOK OF MAXIMILIAN, AND OTHERS

Hours of Charlotte of Bourbon–Montpensier
Use of Rome
Bruges, between 1474 and January 1477, and 1480s (?)

MANUSCRIPT: 202 + i folios, 21.5 × 15.5 cm (8½ × 6⅛ in.); justification: 10.1 × 7.1 cm (3¹⁵⁄₁₆ × 2¾ in.); 25 lines of *bastarda*; 1 full-page miniature, 22 half-page miniatures, 102 small miniatures or historiated initials, 24 bas-de-page calendar miniatures

HERALDRY: The arms of the Borssele family impaling those of Bourbon-Montpensier at lower margins of seven principal miniatures, fols. 43, 46, 84, etc.; Bourbon-Montpensier arms, fol. 137; linked initials *VC*, fols. 15, 40, 60v, etc.; motto *Nul ny aproche*, fols. 15, 143, 148v; flaming grenade, motto *Nul ny aproche*, and inverted flask issuing drops of liquid, fols. 31, 63; motto *Sans changier*, fols. 74v, 94v; linked initials *b* and *d* (*d* may be an inverse *b*), fols. 34, 65v, etc.; initials *es*, fol. 94v; monogram *wft* with *ch*, fols. 37, 55, 149, etc.

INSCRIPTIONS: *PE selon fortune Montfort*, fol. 14v; *1557 Je men contente Manderschert Je vous suplie de noublier la toute v[ost]re sans varier*, fol. 22v; erased inscription dated 1607, fol. 30v; *GAE 1555 peult estre H. de brederode*, fol. 36v; *Noubliez james v[ost]re tant lealle cousine marie de bou[r]g[og]ne* and *Noblies jamais v[ost]re mauvaise fille phelipote de ghelres*, fol. 39v; *Aymee de vous soit la meilleuse de vos cousines Anne. Sans changier v[ost]re auryl [?]*, fol. 45v; Latin inscription signed *Merode*, fol. 54v; *Sans changier*, fols. 74v, 94v; *Jehan de Merode chevalier Baron de houffalizes, et de Moriamez seigneur de Ham sur Heuze, Malines, Briffeuil, Braffe Wlasines, Quesnoy, etc. se maria a damoiselle Philipotte de Montfort dame desdis lieux le XIe jour du mois juing 1555 et ont ne les enffans nomez comme il sensuit, Premier* (immediately after this inscription, which ends at bottom of fol. 202v, three leaves have been removed)

BINDING: Red velvet over wood boards; gilt pastedowns; traces of two clasps

COLLECTION: Alnwick Castle, duke of Northumberland, Ms. 482

PROVENANCE: Charlotte of Bourbon-Montpensier (d. 1478); possibly Jean de Merode and Philipotte de Montfort, sixteenth century

JPGM and RA

This is the earliest securely datable Flemish book of hours with the illusionistic borders of flowers and golden acanthus on solid-colored grounds that became the hallmark of Flemish manuscript illumination henceforth.[1] It was certainly completed before March 1478, when Charlotte of Bourbon-Montpensier died. If Janet Backhouse is correct regarding an inscription signed by Charlotte's second cousin Mary of Burgundy, then the book was likely completed still earlier, by January 1477, when Mary became duchess.[2] The dated examples with such borders that are closest in time belong to 1477 and were painted by the Vienna Master of Mary of Burgundy or by an artist of his workshop or circle (cat. nos. 22, 23).[3]

44b
MASTER OF THE
DRESDEN PRAYER
BOOK
The Flight into Egypt,
fol. 74v

Further, Backhouse's discovery confirms that the new border style emerged, if not under the auspices of the duke, then at least within his circle of close advisers. Charlotte was a cousin of the Charles the Bold's previous consort, Isabelle of Bourbon (d. 1465). She was the fourth child of Louis de Bourbon and Gabrielle de la Tour, count and countess of Montpensier. When Charlotte's mother died, in 1474, she left a library of two hundred volumes.[4] In 1468 Charlotte married Wolfart van Borssele, who was inducted into the Order of the Golden Fleece in 1478 and was himself a bibliophile.[5] His brother-in-law was the powerful Burgundian courtier and bibliophile Louis of Gruuthuse (see cat. nos. 58, 59, 60, 81).

The book is personalized to a dramatic degree. It includes Charlotte's arms impaling those of her husband; Van Borssele's badge of a flaming grenade doused by drops from an upended vial; and the couple's initials, *V* and *C*, en

lac eight times, often with his motto, *Nul ny aproche*, and twice with another motto, *Sans changier*, which may have been Charlotte's.[6] Also integrated into the decorative borders is another pair of initials *en lac*, *b* and *d*, perhaps meant to be read as mirrored *b*s, probably referring to Van Borssele, Bourbon, or both.[7] There is a monogram that might represent the *W*, *f*, and *t* of Wolfart (ill. 44c). Finally, Charlotte is mentioned in a short verse that concludes a suffrage to her namesake Charlemagne, a devotion likely added when the book was near completion or even shortly after its completion.[8]

Although the book's offices and prayers are fairly conventional, accessory texts worthy of note are the votive offices for the days of the week, the Seven Verses of Saint Bernard, the Psalter of Saint Jerome, and most remarkably, more than ninety suffrages to individual saints and for feast days.[9] These include many well-known and less often

rior in *The Annunciation*, the crowded square that features the Massacre of the Innocents, the cloister graveyard for the burial scene, and the sequence of interiors, reminiscent of those of Jan Crabbe's Valerius Maximus (cat. no. 73), that show David in prayer. Also distinctive are some of the courtly costumes and the choice of color in costumes overall, remarkable even for an artist known for a highly varied palette: gold, red, blue, yellows shot with red, pinks shot with blue, violet, teal, white, and a variety of greens. The Master of the Dresden Prayer Book often used black to dramatic effect in costume (see cat. no. 36), but here he used white for a comparably original and striking effect. Typically, he told familiar biblical narratives in new ways, as in *The Visitation* (ill. 44c), where Elizabeth and Mary are seated while Joseph and Zechariah stand quietly at their sides; in *The Flight into Egypt* (ill. 44b) the Virgin walks with the Child beside the donkey.[12] A second, more conservative and less accomplished artist, of much lesser stature but probably also from Bruges, painted a total of 102 historiated initials and smaller miniatures in the suffrages. Nearly all appear after folio 150.

Revisions to the decorative program seem to have begun while the Master of the Dresden Prayer Book was still working on the manuscript, with the addition of the full-page *Pietà* and the prayer that it illustrates, "Stabat mater." This opening was thus probably the first to have facing full borders of the new type with strewn flora. Perhaps at the same time, or at least before Charlotte's death, a group of suffrages for Charlemagne and Saints Louis of Toulouse and his uncle Louis of France were added. Joined with them was an inserted full-page miniature that apparently portrays Saint Louis of France but might be a representation of Charlemagne (fol. 169v).[13] The border includes Wolfart's flaming grenade along with the inverted vial above. The miniature is placed opposite a suffrage of Saint Louis of Marseilles (fol. 170) that has a historiated initial by the painter of the initials and small miniatures in the sequence of suffrages. The suffrage to Saint Louis of France appears only on the verso of this page, while that of Charlemagne appears on the recto of the leaf preceding the miniature. *Saint Louis of France* is related to the style of the Master of the First Prayer Book of Maximilian.

The added prayer in French, "Le tetre mort," is accompanied by a full-page, borderless *Last Judgment* by Simon Marmion (ill. 44a). This may be the earliest and arguably the most beautiful version of a composition that would reappear in distinctive variations in a diminutive book of hours of a few years later (cat. no. 37), in the Huth Hours (cat. no. 33), and in La Flora (cat. no. 93). While the border of the text page closely imitates others in this book, its decorated initial is unique in style, its script is by an entirely different hand, and the leaf is unruled, the last a most unusual feature in a written page in a fifteenth-century Flemish illuminated manuscript. Still, the initials of Wolfart and Charlotte appear within the border, suggesting that it too was painted before March 1478, when Charlotte died.

Finally, the oddest addition of all is a page with a Goesian *Lamentation* with a full border, which was designed as a recto but inserted as a verso.[14] It is located opposite an

invoked saints (among the latter Caprasius, Dicentius, Gislenus, Catherine of Siena, Bridget of Ireland, Susanna,[10] and Gummar) and also major church feasts such as Christmas, Epiphany, Easter, and Ascension. One rare devotion in rhymed verse with ten-line stanzas—"Le tetre mort le lieu caligineux Le prem beat et lextreme lumiere . . ."—was added probably not long after the book's completion.[11]

The Master of the Dresden Prayer Book was the book's main illuminator, responsible for twenty-four calendar miniatures, a single full-page miniature, and twenty-two half-page miniatures. This book confirms the 1470s as a period both of major commissions for him and of a major flowering of his art. The ambition of his celebrated calendar landscape settings in the Voustre Demeure Hours (cat. no. 20) is rivaled by the eloquent, deep settings of *Saint Augustine Meditating on the Trinity*, *The Visitation*, *The Annunciation to the Shepherds*, *The Flight into Egypt* (ill. 44b), and *The Pietà*. The architectural settings, too, are among his most ambitious. They include the cavernous cathedral inte-

indulgence prayer whose text and border seem to be original to the book. Here only the style and motifs of the full border on the text page fit well with the original book. The facing illumination is not of a piece with the rest, yet the initials *V* and *C* are inserted in a space where the incipit to the devotion would normally appear. Was this leaf hastily adapted to fit an almost finished book, the result of a misunderstanding between artist and patron? Or, as the style suggests, was it added posthumously and adapted heraldically to fit the book's original patron? The golden sky in the miniature is more common in Flemish prayer books from the 1480s. It is certainly the weakest of the additions, following a pattern from the workshop of the Maximilian Master but inferior to his work and not in his technique.

T. K.

Notes

1. On the importance of this manuscript in the origins of the new border style, see the introduction to part 2 of this volume.

2. Backhouse 2002: 87. I am grateful to Janet Backhouse for drawing this manuscript to the attention of the exhibition organizers and for sharing with me the fruits of her research well before its recent publication.

3. Backhouse (2002: 88) also pointed out that the book was probably begun no earlier than early 1474, when Charlotte's spouse's father, Hendrik van Borssele, died.

4. De Boislisle 1880: esp. 271–74, 297–309.

5. His father, Hendrick, had been stadholder general and "captain of the duke of Burgundy at sea." For some of Wolfart's books, see Backhouse 2002: 86, n. 23, and Scot McKendrick's essay, "Reviving the Past: Illustrated Manuscripts of Secular Vernacular Texts, 1467–1500," this volume.

6. *Sans changier* appears twice but neither time with Van Borssele's coat of arms, once with a coat of arms with Bourbon-Montpensier impaling a Bourbon heraldry with red fleur-de-lis (fol. 74v), and elsewhere with the initials *E* and *S en lac* (fol. 94v). The same arms appear on folio 23 but without *Sans changier*.

7. One border, which features the device *Sans changier* on a banderole, also features the initials *E* and *S en lac* (fol. 94v).

8. "Deffens nous de tout erreur / Et hors de tout pechie oste/ Ton charlot et ta charlotte" (Backhouse 2002: 83).

9. See Backhouse 2002: 72, for the sequence and location of the offices and prayers.

10. Susanna, who was not a saint but an Old Testament heroine, seems to have been especially popular within the suffrages of female patrons of a certain rank. See under cat. no. 105. Susanna also appears in the litany.

11. The book's calendar points strongly toward Liège, following Clark's (2000: 293–327) model of its regional feasts, including Gudule (January 8), Hadelinus (February 3), Ursinarus (April 18), Domitian (May 7), Servatius (May 13), Monulphus and Gondulphus (July 16), Magdalberte (September 7), Theodard (September 10), Lambert in red (September 17), Maternus (September 19), Ode (October 24), Rumoldus (October 27), Hubert in red (November 3), and Perpetuus (November 4). Liège saints who also appear in the litany include Hubert, Maternus, Servatius, and Domitian.

12. For an interesting variation on this iconography, also novel, see the version of this subject by the illuminator in cat. no. 49, fol. 114v.

13. The suffrage to Saint Louis appears only on the verso of the facing page. As Backhouse (2002: 83) has noted, the crown, scepter, and royal robe with fleurs-de-lis could certainly refer to Louis IX, from whom the Bourbon traced descent, but the fleur-de-lis robe might equally apply to Charlemagne, who was not only Charlotte's name saint but that of several other family members as well.

14. A miniature based on the same pattern appears in the Hours of Isabella of Castile (cat. no. 105, fol. 261v; De Winter 1981: 415, fig. 157).

45
SIMON MARMION
*Saint Bernard's Vision of
the Virgin and Child*

45

SIMON MARMION

Saint Bernard's Vision of the Virgin and Child
Miniature from a devotional book
Valenciennes, ca. 1475–80

One full-page miniature, 11.6 × 6.3 cm (4⁹⁄₁₆ × 2½ in.); back: blank

COLLECTION: Los Angeles, J. Paul Getty Museum, Ms. 32 (88.MS.14)

PROVENANCE: La Béraudière, comte de la Béraudière [his sale, Escribe and Paul Chevallier, Paris, May 18–30, 1885]; Edouard Aynard [his sale, Galerie Georges Petit, Paris, December 1–4, 1913, lot 154]; Martine, comtesse de Béhague; by descent to the marquis of Ganay (d. 1974); to his heirs [their sale, Sotheby's, Monte Carlo, December 5, 1987, lot 151]; acquired 1988

JPGM and RA

This miniature, removed from an unidentified devotional book, represents a subject that became popular in northern Europe in the second half of the fifteenth century. Netherlandish examples frequently show Saint Bernard as an abbot with his crosier.[1] Distinctive about this version is Bernard's richly appointed bishop's cope, which he wears in place of the Cistercians' traditional white habit.[2] Embroidered in gold, the garment bears across the shoulders a depiction of the Annunciation, the event that made Bernard's vision possible. The cope, along with Bernard's portraitlike features, suggests that the miniature may also depict the book's patron.[3]

Simon Marmion exploited the half-length format so that the viewer does not merely contemplate the scene but experiences it directly. Bernard's back is turned to the viewer, who looks over Bernard's shoulder to witness the miracle very nearly from his intimate vantage point. Unusual for Flemish devotional books of this time, and less easy to explain, is the strongly vertical format of the miniature, its height nearly twice its width.

The half-length format is generally associated with the last decade of the artist's career. Since Marmion admired the work of Rogier van der Weyden, he may have begun to adapt this convention from the older master earlier. In particular, the long, thin fingers of the Virgin, as well as the attenuated body of Christ, call to mind Rogier's Huntington *Virgin and Child*, while the Virgin's full lips, wide eyes, and rolling tresses recall his Froimont *Virgin and Child* (Caen, Musée des Beaux-Arts). Both are half-lengths.[4]

The distinctive background showing God the Father on high, rendered only in blues and golds, recalls the heavenly presence in the miniature of King David in the Berlaymont Hours (fig. 47), likely executed in the first half of the 1470s.[5] An even closer comparison is the half-length Virgin in *The Virgin and Child* from the Voustre Demeure Hours (cat. no. 20), in which he models similarly with long brushstrokes. Thus, the Getty miniature may date as early as 1475–80.   T. K.

Notes

1. Dupeux 1991: 165, 174–75, esp. figs. 5, 6, 8.

2. While unusual, it is not unique. Dupeux (1991: 180–81) mentioned several other examples from around 1500 and later.

3. Dupeux (1991: 180) indicated that in other paintings of this subject in which the white Cistercian habit is not represented, the depictions of Saint Bernard are also portraits of patrons.

4. De Vos 1999: 321–24.

5. Clark 1992: 201.

46

SIMON MARMION

Saint Jerome and a Donor
Valenciennes, ca. 1475–80

Oil and tempera on wood panel, 65.1 × 49 cm (25¹¹⁄₁₆ × 19⁵⁄₁₆ in.)

HERALDRY: Escutcheon bearing an unidentified coat of arms, azure a 1 fess or between 3 cinquefoil or, surmounted by cardinal's hat and tassels; fragment of motto *Placet* in a banderole; initials *JB* at lower right, all in stained-glass window behind donor

COLLECTION: Philadelphia, Philadelphia Museum of Art, Johnson Collection, Inv. 1329

PROVENANCE: E. P. Morrell, Oxford; [to Colnaghi, London, in 1913]; John G. Johnson, in 1914; bequeathed 1917 to the City of Philadelphia (housed at the Philadelphia Museum of Art since 1933)

JPGM

Saint Jerome and a Donor most likely formed the left wing of a diptych or triptych whose right wing or central panel perhaps displayed *The Virgin and Child*. The oblique angle of the left wall of the interior space inhabited by the saint and donor suggest a perspective scheme that would have united these figures in the same room with the Virgin and Christ child. Such an arrangement is found, for example, in Hans Memling's Nieuwenhove Diptych (Bruges, Memlingmuseum) or in his Portinari Triptych (Berlin, Staatliche Museen, and Florence, Galleria degli Uffizi), both of 1487.[1] Unfortunately, no suitable candidates for panels that might be linked to the Philadelphia painting are known.

Since John G. Johnson acquired the panel in 1914, it has been attributed to Simon Marmion. The large scale of the figures within the composition, however—indeed a significant leap from those in Marmion's miniatures—and the broad brushwork of their execution beg the question of the dating of the panel within his oeuvre. Certain issues of style and technique are helpful in solving this riddle. Marmion especially favored the half-length format in the miniatures he produced in the last decade of his life. Furthermore, the facial types of the Philadelphia painting—the high cheekbones, broad-bridged noses, and large, dark, expressive eyes—are found within his late illuminations, such as those of the La Flora Hours of the 1480s, especially *Saint James the Greater Preaching* (cat. no. 93, fol. 318v). The border of the illuminated page of the donor's open book—with its illusionistic array of leaves, flowers, and fruits—is typical of those in books produced in Marmion's workshop after about 1475.

Despite the difference in date, antecedents of the details of handling and execution of *Saint Jerome and a Donor* are found in Marmion's Saint Bertin Altarpiece and *Lamentation* (cat. nos. 7, 10). The matte, opaque quality of the paint, suggesting a mixed technique of oil and tempera, is characteristic of the illuminator's panel paintings.[2] Individual brushstrokes are visible, not blended to the fine, enamel-like finish that one generally encounters in early Netherlandish panel painting of similar date. Moreover, the mannerisms of modeling the flesh are similar, as can be noted in the form-defining daubs of paint at the ears, in the folds of flesh beneath the eyes and creases at the outside edges of the eyes, and in the long, straight brushstroke that accents the broad nose above Jerome's slightly off-center mouth. A trademark of Marmion's paintings is the extraordinary execution of transparent garments, with the highlights of the narrow folds appearing to have been drizzled on, like a glaze on a delicious confection. This effect is achieved with great mastery in the dalmatic worn by the kneeling canon in the present panel, in the garments of several figures in the Saint Bertin Altarpiece, and in those of one of the Marys in the Lehman *Lamentation*. Similar landscape features may also be found in all three paintings— winding roads dotted with single trees and wandering figures as markers, studied rocky cliffs, narrow rivers flowing past villages and castles. But the accomplished landscape view of the Philadelphia painting shows a more natural recession into depth than those of the earlier paintings, in which individual features are superimposed on top of one another.[3]

What also separates the Philadelphia panel from Marmion's earlier paintings is the influence of the works of Hugo van der Goes. This is evident in the illuminations of the La Flora Hours, namely, *The Death of the Virgin* (cat. no. 93, fol. 150v). As in *Saint Jerome and a Donor*, here is a new

sense of quiet pathos, a bold use of ruddy flesh tones, and carefully studied veined and bony hands. Especially reminiscent of Van der Goes's *Death of the Virgin* (Bruges, Groeningemuseum) is the expressive use of hand gestures, a likely influence on the hands of Marmion's canon, which slowly come together in an incipient attitude of prayer. Sterling noted that Marmion is not mentioned in Valenciennes between 1475 and 1478 and suggested that he made a trip at the time to Ghent, where he could well have seen works by Hugo van der Goes, dean of the painter's guild there from 1474.[4] This would support the suggested date of around 1480 for *Saint Jerome and a Donor*.

What is less clear than the panel's attribution and date is the identification of the commissioner of the work. The coat of arms in the stained-glass window is surmounted by a cardinal's hat and tassels and accompanied by a banderole with the motto *Placet* and the initials *JB*. The kneeling donor is dressed as a canon, however, not a cardinal, and perhaps served a cardinal or pope in some capacity.[5] Georges Hulin de Loo dismissed the notion that, because of the initials *JB*, the coat of arms can be identified as that of the Busleyden family. Henri Bouchot, followed by Grete Ring, later suggested the French family Baradat, also a match based on the initials.[6] More recently, the coat of arms has been linked with the Nicholaus Vierling family (he was count of Nassau and baron of Breda), but there was no known cardinal in this family.[7] Albert Châtelet proposed that among the rare cases of a cardinal attached to the Burgundian court is one Philipert Hugonet, bishop of Mâcon, who was elevated to cardinal by Sixtus IV on May 7, 1473. Hugonet's family coat of arms, however, is different from that shown here, and although the cardinal could have created his own heraldry, this identification remains to be proved.[8]

There is one intriguing document that should be brought into consideration here. Dated May 28, 1484, it is an entry in the account of the testament of one Pierre Dewez (Devado), chaplain of the cathedral of Cambrai, who died on May 9, 1483: "A Symon Marmion demorant a Valenchiennes ad cause de reste de son mestier de pointerie, pour ung tablet de Nostre-Dame a II feulles en maniere de ung epitaphe, paye pour l'aportage et a le demande du deffunct xiij l" [To Simon Marmion, residing at Valenciennes for the remainder of his work of painting, for a "tablet" of Our Lady with (or on) two wings in the manner of an epitaph, paid for the delivery and at the request of the deceased, 13 livres].[9] Could this description of either a triptych or a diptych by Marmion, intended as an epitaph for Pierre Dewez and including a panel of the Virgin, refer to the Philadelphia wing and its lost panel(s)? The entry is close in date to that suggested here for the Philadelphia panel, but this identification must remain hypothetical in the absence of further evidence. M. W. A.

2. Gas chromatographic analysis of paint samples from the Philadelphia painting indicated the presence of both oil and egg as binding media. Thanks to Ken Sutherland and Beth Price for these results (report, Analytical Laboratory, Philadelphia Museum of Art, October 29, 2002).

3. X-radiography and infrared reflectography show that Marmion originally planned a higher, more pointed mountain peak in the painting before revising it in paint to its current lower, flatter form with castle. Underdrawing is sparingly used to establish the general placement of forms. My thanks to Katherine Luber, Teresa Lignelli, and Joe Mekuliak for help with the technical examination of the painting. A recent reexamination of the painting reveals that the lower portions of Saint Jerome's beard were removed in an earlier cleaning (see Rosen 1941: 6–7, 10). This area was reconstructed to its original form by Teresa Lignelli in the 2001–2 cleaning and restoration of the painting at the Philadelphia Museum of Art.

4. Sterling 1981b: 14, n. 37. Van der Goes's *Death of the Virgin* was likely in the vicinity of Bruges or Brussels. See Martens 1992: 347, and Dhanens 1998: 333, 336, for various theories.

5. Carl Strehlke has pointed out that although the hat is dark gray instead of red, one finds at this period cardinal's hats of various colors, including blue, red, and darker gray. Lorne Campbell has suggested the possibility that the donor was a protonotary, who would have worn a black hat of this type. My thanks to Carl Strehlke, adjunct curator at the Philadelphia Museum of Art, and Lorne Campbell of the National Gallery, London, for this information.

6. Hulin de Loo 1902: no. 101; Bouchot, cited in Ring 1949: no. 181.

7. My thanks to Elizabeth Morrison for her investigation of this matter.

8. Châtelet (1996: 166–67, n. 27) further suggested that if his theory is right, the canon represented could be Étienne de Longvy. Close scrutiny of the coat of arms under a microscope reveals that the paint here is intact and original. All the more troubling, therefore, is the fact that there appear to be too many tassels for the identification of a cardinal.

9. Hénault 1907: 63, no. 65.

47

ATTRIBUTED TO SIMON MARMION

The Pietà
Valenciennes, ca. 1470

Metalpoint over black chalk (?) on white prepared paper, 15.3 × 11.6 cm (6 × 4⁹⁄₁₆ in.)

COLLECTION: Cambridge, Massachusetts, Harvard University Art Museums, 1941.343

PROVENANCE: Lewis Gilberson, London; Henry Oppenheimer; Fogg Art Museum

JPGM

This rare drawing of the pietà is the only surviving sheet attributed to Simon Marmion (ill. 47). Restricted to the figural group of the Virgin and dead Christ, it served as a workshop model for both Marmion's paintings and his illuminations. The details of the drawing are not copied exactly in the Lehman *Lamentation* (cat. no. 11) or in Marmion's miniatures of the same subject (cat. nos. 20, 33); instead the sheet served as a model that could be adjusted to suit multiple purposes. The underdrawing of the Virgin in *The Lamentation*, for example, follows the motif of the drawing, in which the head of the Virgin is further lowered and covered by a simple rather than a double-layered veil and the Virgin's hands are clasped in prayer rather than crossed over her chest, as in the final painted version.

46
SIMON MARMION
Saint Jerome and a Donor

Notes
1. These are illustrated in De Vos 1994: 280–81, 284–85. A triptych of similar format by a follower of Marmion, dated ca. 1480, is discussed and illustrated in Campbell 1998: 310–15.

47
ATTRIBUTED TO
SIMON MARMION
The Pietà

Figure 62
Infrared reflectogram of
The Pietà (detail)

Figure 63
Infrared reflectogram
assembly of *The Pietà*
(detail)

The rigid lines and summary nature of the underdrawing of the Fogg sheet (as revealed by infrared reflectography; figs. 62, 63)[1] indicate that the Virgin and the dead Christ were traced in black chalk (?) from a template. The pattern served as a foundation for the delicate metalpoint rendering over it, in which the artist further elaborated the folds of drapery and the modeling of forms and experimented with the placement of the body of Christ, as evidenced by the shifted left contour of his torso.

The authorship of the drawing may never be determined unequivocally because of the lack of comparative autograph sheets. In favor of an attribution to Marmion is the apparent high quality of the drawing and the directness of the handling and execution. At once striking are the similarities in form between the drawing and the Lehman *Lamentation* in the general types of the Virgin and Christ; the pose of the head of Christ; the articulation of his torso, with its pronounced chest cavity; the narrow folds of flesh at the navel and at the groin; and the long, tubular folds of the Virgin's drapery adjacent to broad, flat areas. As with a *Crucifixion* assigned to a follower of Marmion in the Philadelphia Museum of Art,[2] the heads and the facial features in the drawing appear to be more angular, the arms of Christ more elongated, the hands larger, and the fingers more attenuated in comparison to the same features in the Lehman painting. It is perhaps best to designate the drawing as attributed to Marmion—that is, intimately connected with his workshop production but not verifiably by his own hand.

M. W. A.

Notes
1. The drawing was studied with infrared reflectography on May 22, 1990, by Jeffrey Jennings and Maryan Ainsworth, with the kind permission of William Robinson, curator of prints and drawings, Fogg Art Museum. Alison Gilchrest processed the image.
2. Ainsworth 1992: 251–53.

MASTER OF THE DRESDEN PRAYER BOOK (A)

Friedrich Winkler named the Master of the Dresden Prayer Book for an early masterwork by the artist, an unusual book of hours of small dimensions (Dresden, Sächsische Landesbibliothek, Ms. A 311), datable to about 1470.[1] The calendar illuminations in the Dresden manuscript are the first examples of full-page miniatures in a calendar since the famous cycle in the duke of Berry's *Très Riches Heures* sixty years earlier. Winkler christened the illuminator the Bruges Master of the Dresden Prayer Book after his presumed artistic base.[2] He was probably born during the 1440s and became active in Bruges by the late 1460s. Initially he worked with the Master of Anthony of Burgundy, who influenced the types and bearing of his figures, including their plain features and certain postures that call to mind dolls or string puppets.

During the first ten years of his activity, the Dresden Master was the sole illuminator of, or collaborated on, books for such eminent Burgundian courtiers and bibliophiles as Louis of Gruuthuse (cat. no. 71); Jean Gros, first secretary of Charles the Bold; Jan Crabbe, the abbot of Duinen; and Guy de Brimeu, lord of Humbercourt and one of the duke's most trusted associates. Sir John Donne, one of Edward IV's retainers on the Continent, was another patron in these years. For the humanist Crabbe, the Dresden Master illuminated a Valerius Maximus (cat. no. 73), another masterwork from the 1470s. Significantly, the most fully developed example of the new style of illusionistic, strewn-pattern border appears first in the Hours of Charlotte of Bourbon-Montpensier (cat. no. 44), where the Master of the Dresden Prayer Book was the lead artist. While he was one of the first illuminators to use these borders in his books, he did not employ them consistently until the 1480s. Even so, another book of hours that he illuminated is among the earliest dated examples (Brussels, Bibliothèque royale de Belgique, Ms. II 7604, dated 1478).[3]

For the next three decades a wealth of aristocratic and ecclesiastic patrons from Flemish and northern French Burgundian towns such as Bruges (cat. no. 71), Tournai, Cambrai, Mons, and Amiens, and also from Normandy (see cat. nos. 48, 117) and other parts of France, commissioned or acquired illuminations by the Master of the Dresden Prayer Book. Although perhaps not the initial patron, the Spanish courtier Francisco de Rojas saw to the completion of a now-famous breviary as a present for Queen Isabella of Castile. The Dresden Master was the lead illuminator of this epic work (cat. no. 100). Still, like most Flemish illuminators active during the last quarter of the century, he produced mostly books of hours.[4]

The Master of the Dresden Prayer Book was the sole or lead illuminator of many manuscripts (including cat. nos. 36, 44, 48, 49, 72, 100, 117), but he collaborated often and as a result worked on some of the best books produced during his lifetime (see cat. nos. 20, 32, 33, 53, 93, 124). Simon Marmion, the Master of the Houghton Hours, the Vienna Master of Mary of Burgundy, the Master of James IV of Scotland, and the Master of the First Prayer Book of Maximilian all shared responsibilities with him. Working with such masters often brought out the best in him. During the 1470s and early 1480s, for example, the Dresden Master specialized in particular features of devotional books, such as cycles of small calendar miniatures (see cat. nos. 20, 32, 33) that were much imitated (see cat. nos. 93, 105). From the 1490s until his retirement or death, perhaps as late as the second decade of the sixteenth century, he fashioned historiated borders for such important devotional books as the La Flora Hours and the Spinola Hours (cat. nos. 97, 124). In those manuscripts he lucidly staged a wealth of incident within the awkward and constricted format of the historiated border and used a raised angle of vision effectively as a dramatic device.

The Dresden Master is one of the most original Flemish artists of the second half of the fifteenth century. In the calendar cycle of the Dresden hours, he conveyed a new breadth and depth of space while still painting fairly loosely, with a systematized brushwork that paid greater attention to overall texture than to detail. The calendar cycle in the Voustre Demeure Hours (cat. no. 20) features some of the earliest landscapes without figures and has an atmospheric quality that helped to establish new ways of seeing landscape. The Dresden Master's exploitation of the expressive character of different conditions of weather was of profound importance for Simon Bening[5] and probably also Joachim Patinir. In a rare cycle of illuminations to the infernal *Visions of Lazarus* (Paris, Bibliothèque nationale de France, Ms. lat. 16428), the Master of the Dresden Prayer Book developed tonal landscapes, including a bleak winter scene, that remain distinctive even following the emergence of the new genre of winter scenes in sixteenth-century Flemish illumination and seventeenth-century Dutch painting.[6]

The Master of the Dresden Prayer Book also displayed originality in his cheerful, often witty retellings of familiar biblical narratives and stock secular themes. He located humor, irony, and unexpected tensions in narratives, sometimes choosing to depict an unconventional episode (see cat. nos. 49, 73). As a result, both his interpretation of character and his iconography can surprise the viewer. To symbolize the months, he introduced new activities, such as swimming, that reflect his sympathy for the events of daily life (see cat. no. 32). Long ago Winkler aptly observed that the Dresden Master's affection for the lowly and the down-trodden anticipated the art of Pieter Bruegel the Elder (ca. 1525/30–1569).[7] This may also be said of his humor and of his concern with both climate and mood in his depictions of the months and the seasons.   T. K.

Notes

1. Winkler 1913a: 276–77, n. 5.

2. Brinkmann (1997: 245–60) proposed a sojourn for the artist in Amiens in the first half of the 1490s. There are different views of the illuminator's origins. Brinkmann (1997: 356–69) suggested that he came from Utrecht, while de Schryver (1979a: 144) argued that he was French-born and could be identified with the illuminator Didier de la Rivière, who became a citizen in Bruges in 1475.

3. The Dresden Master was one of the first illuminators to paint borders on solid-colored grounds, starting in the first half of the 1470s (see cat. nos. 48, 53).

4. Brinkmann (1997: 383–97) attributed all or part of more than three dozen to him.

5. Bening added historiated borders to the versos of leaves with calendar medallions by the Dresden Master in a book of hours in The British Library, London (Egerton Ms. 1147). See Brinkmann 1997: 388–89.

6. Kren 1992b: 143, 149, fig. 94.

7. Winkler 1921: esp. 7–12.

48

MASTER OF THE DRESDEN PRAYER BOOK
AND WORKSHOP

Hours of Jean Carpentin
Use unidentified
Bruges, mid-1470s

MANUSCRIPT: iv + an inserted postmedieval oblong leaf, folded twice, + 300 + iii, 14.5 × 10.5 cm (5 ^{11}/₁₆ × 4 ⅛ in.); justification: 7.4–5 × 4.9–5.2 cm (2⅞–2 ^{15}/₁₆ × 1 ^{15}/₁₆–2 ¹/₁₆ in.); 14 lines of *textura*; 22 full-page miniatures, 42 historiated initials, 24 calendar miniatures

HERALDRY: Escutcheons with the arms of Jean Carpentin and his forebears, fols. 1v, 2, 17v, 183; motto *Encore mieux*, fols. 1v, 2, 17v, etc.; initials *LK* joined by love knot, fol. 18; initials *IJ* joined by love knot, fol. 194; initials *IK* joined by love knot, fol. 283v

INSCRIPTIONS: *Jean de Carpentin, Seig[neu]r de Gravile*, fol. 1; notes concerning the Carpentin family, leaf inserted seventeenth or eighteenth century

BINDING: Sixteenth century; worn red velvet over pasteboard; silver niello corner pieces, clasps, and catches dated 1553. Corner pieces (front cover): the Creation (upper left), Noah in the Ark (upper right), Abraham and Isaac (lower left), and Joseph Taken from the Well and Sold (lower right); corner pieces (back cover): Moses Receiving the Tablets of the Law (upper left), Samson and the Lion (upper right), David with the Head of Goliath (lower left), and the Judgment of Solomon (lower right). Clasps (obverse): monogram *DCLA* and, to its right, half-length depictions of Saint Anne and the Virgin and Child (upper clasp) and Joseph and Joachim (lower clasp); clasps (reverse): half-length personifications of Justice and Fortitude (upper clasp) and Prudence and Temperance (lower clasp). Catches: inscription from Psalm 99:3, ISPE / FECIT / NOS / 1553 (upper catch) and ET NON / IPSI / NOS / PSAL. 99 (lower catch)

COLLECTION: Private collection

PROVENANCE: Jean Carpentin, lord of Gravile; the Carpentin family by descent until 1841; Comte Adrien de Louvencourt, nephew of the last Carpentin [his sale]; to the Wildensteins, Abbeville, 1927 (?); to Sam Fogg Rare Books, 2000; to current owner

JPGM and RA

48a (opposite, top)
MASTER OF THE
DRESDEN PRAYER BOOK
The Agony in the Garden,
fols. 135v–136

48b (opposite, bottom)
MASTER OF THE
DRESDEN PRAYER BOOK
David in Prayer,
fols. 199v–200

This book of hours combines a relatively modest and straightforward collection of devotions with a lavish program of illumination.[1] The few somewhat uncommon features are the Gradual Psalms and the Long Hours of the Cross and Hours of the Holy Spirit (rather than the usual short hours). The suffrages section has only fourteen items. The manuscript opens with a diptych without text, an unusual feature of Flemish manuscript illumination of this time, which features *The Crucifixion* opposite *The Lamentation* and a depiction of the book's patron, Jean Carpentin, kneeling in devotion in the border, with his coat of arms and those of his forebears filling out the borders. Another diptych without text, featuring bust-length figures of Saint John the Baptist and the Salvator Mundi (fols. 15v–16), prefaces the Hours of the Virgin.[2] Such diptychs are more common in French manuscripts from the second half of the fifteenth century, which probably explains their appearance here, especially given that this book's patron, Jean Carpentin, lord of Gravile, was Norman.[3]

Most of the narrative cycles are exceptionally elaborate, giving free reign to the Master of the Dresden Prayer Book's gifts as a storyteller. For example, the Hours of the Virgin has an Infancy cycle of full-page miniatures, each opposite a historiated initial of mostly typologically linked Old Testament scenes. Throughout the book the illustrated borders mix large, leafy acanthus, flowers, birds, and insects with drolleries, angels, and narratives scenes, many biblical. The pictorial cycle of the long Hours of the Cross is constructed in a similar way for a comparably rich effect. The long Hours of the Holy Spirit opens at Matins with the same combination of full-page miniature, historiated border, and borders filled with figures, but for the remaining seven hours features only historiated initials and full borders with vignettes. The Penitential Psalms, Gradual Psalms, and Office of the Dead each have openings that combine full-page miniature, historiated initial, and full borders, while the prayers to the Virgin and each of the suffrages feature only a historiated initial with a full border.

It is the borders that hold the greatest visual interest in the manuscript, and this is the area where the illuminator himself seemed to take the greatest pleasure, often displaying great inventiveness and attention to detail. On some leaves, such as the page with the Last Judgment in the initial, the border becomes an extension of the pictorial field of the historiated initial; in the bas-de-page the condemned souls endure their miserable fate. Another page shows the Emperor Augustus and the Tiburtine Sibyl in the initial, but the apparition of the Virgin and Child is actually painted in the upper border. The artist frequently combined rich color with *camaïeu gris* and other types of monochrome, sometimes within a border or miniature, sometimes in the various elements of a page. On the page with the Emperor Augustus and the Tiburtine Sibyl, the scene in the initial is in rose monochrome, while the figures in the border are treated in white against a bright blue ground. These borders are siblings of those painted by the Dresden Master in the Salting Hours (cat. no. 53). In both, drolleries, biblical vignettes, and plush acanthus, the last often in

camaïeu gris, are depicted against colored grounds. Here, however, in contrast to the Salting Hours, all of the borders in the book or nearly all of them were painted by the Dresden Master.[4] The ensemble shows an astonishing variety of color and motif.

In some miniatures, such as *The Agony in the Garden* (ill. 48a), the figures wear white robes in a fully colored landscape. In contrast, the borders of this miniature have narrative vignettes and acanthus in delicate yellow against a red ground. In the nocturnal *Betrayal of Christ* all the figures except Judas wear black robes bathed in a golden light against a deep blue sky. Facing borders often feature the same color or color combination, so that they have a striking unity even when the palette of the border and miniature contrast. In their spatial character and colored backdrops these pages are comparable to the illusionistic borders in the new style, though they lack the latter's verisimilitude. Although the style of border illumination in the Carpentin Hours did not have the extraordinary afterlife of the new border style, it remains an artistic tour de force and has helped secure the importance of the Dresden Master in the history of Flemish manuscript illumination.

Carpentin not only had himself depicted in this volume but also had it liberally decorated with his own coats of arms, his device, and his initial *I en lac* with *J*, presumably the initial of his wife. Based on the similarity of its borders to those of the Salting Hours, this book probably dates to the same period, roughly the 1470s. Based on details of costume, it should date to the first half of the decade.[5] In this context it bears noting that the miniature *Christ Nailed to the Cross* (fol. 166v) has several striking features in common with the version of this subject in the Vienna Hours of Mary of Burgundy (see fig 17).[6] The latter was executed in the mid-1470s or perhaps earlier.   T. K.

Notes

1. Brinkmann (1997: 264–65) pointed out that the calendar is for the use of Rouen, appropriate to a Norman patron; that the Office of the Dead is for Dominican use; and that that of the Hours of the Dead is unidentified.

2. Like the opening diptych, this one clearly honors the book's patron by its focus on his name saint.

3. For example, Jean Fouquet's *Simon de Varie in Prayer before the Virgin*, the frontispiece to the Hours of Simon de Varie, where both the diptych and the miniatures on the reverse feature the patron's armorials and device (J. Paul Getty Museum, Ms. 7, fols. 1v–2; Marrow and Avril 1994). A second example by Fouquet is the diptych with the patron and the Virgin and Child in the Hours of Étienne Chevalier (Chantilly, Musée Condé). A northern French example is the diptych without text of Jacques de Chatillon II and his spouse in the Hours of Jacques II of Chatillon (Paris, Bibliothèque nationale de France, Ms. n. a. lat. 3231, fols. 58–59). It was illuminated by the Master of Raoul d'Ailly of Amiens in the second quarter of the fifteenth century.

4. Certain borders—for example, those on folios 89v, 106, 178v, 239v, 298, 299—have birds and exotic creatures painted in saturated colors with little modeling, motifs that are atypical of the Dresden Master. Brinkmann (1997: 271–73) related some of these borders to the Master of Fitzwilliam 268. While it is not clear that they are by the Master of Fitzwilliam 268, the Dresden Master may have had a collaborator on some of the borders.

5. Margaret Scott expressed to me the view that the men's costumes in the calendar bas-de-pages (fols. 6, 7)—especially the wide shoulders, overlong sleeves, and tall caps—belong to the first half of the 1470s.

6. The foreshortening of Christ is a mirror image of that in the Vienna miniature. The posture of the figure nailing at the far right resembles that of the executioner in the same location in the Vienna miniature. The repoussoir figures of onlookers seen from the back are similar, and the equestrian figures in the background echo those of the Vienna miniature.

49

MASTER OF THE DRESDEN PRAYER BOOK AND WORKSHOP

Crohin–La Fontaine Hours
Use of Rome
Bruges, ca. 1480–85 (?)

MANUSCRIPT: iii + 214 + i folios, 13.3 × 9.4 cm (5¼ × 3¹¹⁄₁₆ in.); justification: 6.8 × 4.1 cm (2¹¹⁄₁₆ × 1⅝ in.); 17 lines of *bastarda*; 12 half-page miniatures, 21 historiated initials; 2 full-page coats of arms added, fols. 13, 29, sixteenth century

HERALDRY: Full-page armorial comprised of a lozenge with the arms of Marguerite de Crohin held by winged female figure and escutcheons with the arms of the Crohin, Hannemau, Perssant, and Joie families, fol. 13; full-page armorial comprised of an escutcheon with the arms of Louis de la Fontaine surmounted by helm and crest with swan and escutcheons with the arms of the La Fontaine, Crestien, Lois, and Crohin families, fol. 29

INSCRIPTIONS: *Demoiselle Margherite Crohin fille de Jan et dernniereme[n]t veuve de feu Jacq[ue]s Chr[est]ien en son ta[m]pz dame de Salmonsart et de la Bassee: laisee par testament ces p[rese]ntes heures a revere[n]d pere e[n] dieu mo[n]s[eigneur] Nicolas abbe de S. Jan en Vallen[ciennes] et trespassa icelle le 20[eme] dece[m]bre a[nn]o 1552*, fol. 13; *Messire Lois de la Fontaine dict Wicart Ch[eva]l[ier] de Hier[u]z[alem], S[eigneu]r de Salmonsart de la Bassee en Ugies*, fol. 29

BINDING: J. Schavye, Brussels, first half of nineteenth century; brown calf over pasteboard; rebacked; blind-tooled panel design; sixteenth-century silver-gilt clasp engraved with *LF* and the La Fontaine arms, with a miniature of Christ's head on parchment under glass; stamped *J. Schavye, relieur de S.M. le roi, Bruxelles* on back flyleaf

COLLECTION: Los Angeles, J. Paul Getty Museum, Ms. 23 (86.ML.606)

PROVENANCE: Marguerite de Crohin, dame de Salmonsart et de la Bassée (d. 1552), Mons; bequeathed to Nicholas de Faulche, abbot of Saint Jean-Baptiste (d. 1553), Valenciennes; to Louis de la Fontaine (1522–1587) called Wicart, seigneur de Salmonsart et de la Bassée, and Jeanne Crestien, Valenciennes, by 1575; William Loring Andrews; Cortlandt F. Bishop (1870–1935) [his sale, Anderson Galleries, New York, April 25–27, 1938, lot 1434]; to Elizabeth P. Martin, Upper Montclair, New Jersey, 1938; bequeathed to Elizabeth K. Robbins, Berkeley, California; by descent to Deborah, Peter, and Daniel Robbins; acquired 1986

JPGM and RA

The illumination of the original portion of this book is entirely from the hand of the Master of the Dresden Prayer Book and, in the case of some miniatures, his assistants. It shows some of the artist's characteristically fresh readings of familiar subjects. The full-page miniature of David and Goliath focuses on an unexpected moment in the confrontation between the boy and the giant and shows the Dresden Master's occasionally wry view of heroic or solemn themes (ill. 49a). The first book of Samuel (17:42) describes Goliath showing disdain for the boy. The Philistine's erect posture, hand on hip, and downcast gaze from shielded eyes evoke this passage. The artist heightened the

49a
MASTER OF THE
DRESDEN PRAYER
BOOK
David and Goliath, 121v

49b
MASTER OF THE
DRESDEN PRAYER
BOOK
*The Three Living and the
Three Dead,* fol. 146v

absurdity of the confrontation by dressing David foppishly and underscoring his youth and innocence. No textual source has been cited for the unusual *Flight into Egypt.* Here the Virgin walks beside the donkey, rather than riding it, while Joseph, rather than Mary, carries the Christ child.[1] The Dresden Master also contributed one of the earliest Flemish depictions of the joyful shepherds dancing in a circle at the appearance of the angels announcing Christ's birth.[2] In a more conventional vein, his retelling of the theme of the three living and the three dead shows three young knights reeling in horror at the sight of the gaunt specters of death (ill. 49b). This is his finest formulation of a subject to which he returned repeatedly.

Although Bodo Brinkmann dated the manuscript to around 1500 on the basis of the style of the miniatures,[3] a date in the 1480s seems more plausible due to several factors, including the similarity of the border types to others of around 1475–85. Typical of the earliest borders of the new style are those densely crowded with a multitude of loose flowers, relieved by the odd moth, or a border that mixes naturalistically placed flowers with golden or silver-white acanthus. Similarly, the elegant *bastarda* script

is especially typical of the 1470s and 1480s. More tellingly, in this book the artist and his assistants repeated a variety of motifs and compositions that belong especially to his work of the 1470s, from the Dresden Prayer Book (Sächsische Landesbibliothek, Ms. A311) to the Nová Říše Hours of 1480 (cat. no. 36).[4] From the latter he and his collaborators redeployed a range of figural and compositional elements, not only from its miniatures but also from its borders. In the Crohin–La Fontaine Hours (fol. 107), the border artist copied a motif from an elaborate marginal cycle of simian escapades in the Nová Říše Hours.[5]

While the book's calendar and litany are strongly characteristic of Bruges, they both feature Saint Walpurgis, a saint venerated in Mons.[6] This may indicate that the manuscript was intended for a customer there. The book's earliest known possessor, Marguerite de Crohin, came from a prominent Mons family.[7] She was the daughter of Jean de Crohin, seigneur des Bois-de Salmonsart and de la Bassée, and married Jacques Chrétien, seigneur de la Tourelle. The book contains two full-page heraldic miniatures, the first commemorating Marguerite, that were added in the sixteenth century. The Valenciennes illuminator Hubert

Cailleau painted it after her death in 1552 (fol. 13). The other (fol. 29) is for her son-in-law Louis de la Fontaine (called Wicart, 1522–1587), the historian of Valenciennes. His *Antiquités de la ville de Valenciennes* is an important source for our knowledge of the painter and illuminator Simon Marmion, an occasional collaborator of the Master of the Dresden Prayer Book (see cat. nos. 32, 33).   T. K.

Notes

1. The Master of Edward IV painted similar iconography about the same time in a Ludolphus of Saxony *Vita Christi* (cat. no. 96), perhaps borrowing from the older artist, as this interpretation bears no relationship to Ludolphus's text. See, for example, Paris, Bibliothèque nationale de France, Ms. fr. 20096, fol. 107v, and the Hours of Bourbon-Vendôme, Paris, Bibliothèque de l'Arsenal, Ms. 417, fol. 46. The latter version of *The Flight*, by a French illuminator from the circle of Bourdichon, is probably very closely contemporaneous.

2. Per Brinkmann 1997: 289; it bears noting that some of these inventions went on to be imitated by other artists. Brinkmann (1997: 289 and ill.) has shown that the composition of *The Annunciation to the Shepherds* was copied by the Master of the Prayer Books of ca. 1500. The Crohin–La Fontaine *Massacre of the Innocents* was copied by a follower of the latter (Brinkmann 1997: 314, fig. 84), while a Psalms miniature in a modest Flemish book of hours in Mount Angel Abbey, Saint Benedict, Oregon (Ms. 67), is based on the David and Goliath miniature. The Dresden Master was probably adapting a French tradition of the dancing shepherds before the angel in the sky.

3. Brinkmann 1997: 290.

4. Other examples of his own work from the period that the Dresden Master drew upon include a book of hours in the Museum Meermanno-Westreenianum, The Hague (Ms. 10 F 1; Brinkmann 1997: 288), and the Morgan Library, New York (M. 1077, e.g., fol. 28v). Note that the Dresden Prayer Book itself is actually a book of hours.

5. According to Maximiliaan Martens (note, July 28, 1989, Department of Manuscripts files, JPGM), the presence of Sixtus in the litany offers corroborating evidence that the book was written within the papal term of Sixtus IV (r. 1471–84), especially as the name saint of his successor, Innocent VIII, does not appear. The former's death date would offer a terminus ante quem for the writing of the text. Thus, although the book may be dated broadly to the 1480s, the evidence of the litany, if correctly interpreted here, would allow us to date its writing to the early 1480s. Confirmation of this hypothesis would, however, be necessarily subject to a systematic investigation of the appearance of these two saints in the litanies of Flemish books of hours in the last quarter of the fifteenth century.

6. Saint Walpurgis is entered on February 23, two days before her death, the date of the celebration of her feast in Mons.

7. She also owned a northern French book of hours datable as early as 1500 (Copenhagen, Kongelige Bibliotek, Ms. Thott 542; Legaré 1998: 60).

DREUX JEAN (A)

Dreux Jean, otherwise known as Dreux Bachoyer, was an artist of Parisian origin who emigrated northward, probably during the English occupation of the city.[1] By 1448 he had entered the service of Philip the Good and was engaged by him to produce "miniatures, illuminations, and writings" and to organize the binding of books. By 1449 he had become a valet de chambre to Philip, and from then until 1454 he received the regular salary of a master craftsman in the duke's service, as well as occasional gifts and reimbursements for expenses. By the end of 1454, however, as part of a drive to economize at court, Dreux Jean's salary was terminated, and the salaried post of court illuminator was left vacant.

Although by 1456 Jean owned property in Brussels near the ducal palace, he was soon drawn to Bruges by the greater commercial opportunities available to him there. In 1457 he obtained citizenship in Bruges, and from 1457 to 1461 he was a member of the town's Confraternity of Saint John. By 1463, however, he appears to have returned to Brussels, and in 1464 he was appointed illuminator and valet de chambre to the future Charles the Bold, then count of Charolais. A final reference in contemporary records to his holding of property in Brussels in 1466, as well as the appointment of Philippe de Mazerolles as court illuminator in 1467, suggest that Jean was dead by 1467.

Crucial to our understanding of the history of illumination in the Low Countries is the relationship between the historical figure of Dreux Jean and the miniaturist known as the Master of Girart de Roussillon. The latter artist is named after his contribution to a deluxe copy of Jean Wauquelin's prose version of the chanson de geste *Girart de Roussillon*, which was transcribed for Philip the Good in 1448 (Vienna, Österreichische Nationalbibliothek, Ms. 2549). His hand is also recognizable in the illustrations of the *Chroniques de Jérusalem abrégées* in roll format, made for Philip shortly after 1455 (Vienna, Österreichische Nationalbibliothek, Ms. 2533). The Girart Master's style is notable for its fusion of the traditions of Parisian illumination and south Netherlandish panel painting, as well as echoes of the work of both the Bedford Master and Rogier van der Weyden. Sophisticated landscapes, fine portraiture, an intense palette, and the distinctive juxtaposition of unblended colors are the hallmarks of the Girart Master's work.

One possible link between Dreux Jean and the Girart Master has been identified in a two-volume book of devotions now divided between Cambridge and Brussels (Fitzwilliam Museum, Ms. 3-1954; Bibliothèque royale de Belgique, Ms. 11035-7). It has been argued that this surviving work is the book of daily hours begun in Paris for Philip the Bold in 1376 by the scribe Jean L'Avenant.[2] If this is the same book, the additions that were evidently made to this work around the middle of the fifteenth century are probably those for which Dreux Jean was paid in 1451. Very clearly, however, these additions are the work of many hands. What then remains an issue is whether the two miniatures in the style of the Girart Master preserved in the Cambridge volume (fols. 238v, 256) are Dreux Jean's own contribution to the volume. The presence of Philip's emblems in only these two miniatures may be explained as marks of his official illuminator. The closely contemporary roles of Dreux Jean as overseer of work on the ducal library and of the Girart Master as a contributor to ducal manuscripts might also suggest that the two were the same person.

The Girart Master's designs were reused and his artistic style perpetuated by several followers. These followers included the talented miniaturist responsible for the illustration of two works of devotion compiled for Margaret of York shortly after 1468 (see cat. no. 51) and a much less accomplished artist who earlier painted the miniatures in Philippe de Crèvecoeur's *Grande Chronique de Normandie* (cat. no. 57).   S. McK.

Notes

1. For the documentary evidence for what follows, see Van Buren 2002: 1377–81. I am grateful to Anne van Buren for allowing me to consult this article in typescript.

2. Van Buren 2002: 1382.

50

DREUX JEAN OR WORKSHOP AND MASTER
OF THE BRUSSELS ROMULÉON AND WORKSHOP

L'Invention et translation du corps de Saint Antoine, translation of
Inventio et translatio corporis sancti Antonii
Probably Brussels or Bruges, ca. 1465–70

MANUSCRIPT: i + 56 + i folios, 24.8 × 17.5 cm (9¾ × 6⅞ in.); justification: 15.6 × 10.8 cm (6⅛ × 4¼ in.); 22 lines of *bastarda* attributed to David Aubert; 2 full-page miniatures with 4 vignettes each, 2 half-page miniatures, 19 historiated initials

HERALDRY: Escutcheon with unidentified arms, sable quartering 1 and 4 double fleurs-de-lis or, 2 and 3 fretty argent and device *du bien delle*, fols. 6v, 10v, 50

INSCRIPTIONS: *Girin Martin p[ro]tho [notaire]*, fol. 5v; *Vinc le cure de Vincent a sont desir / P Martin G Martin*, fol. 56v

BINDING: Eighteenth (?) century; saffron-colored doeskin over pasteboard; two leather ties, removed; gilt edges

COLLECTION: Los Angeles, J. Paul Getty Museum, Ms. Ludwig XI 8 (83.MN.127)

PROVENANCE: Flemish nobleman portrayed on fol. 50; G. Martin (?), late fifteenth century; C. Radoulesco; [H. P. Kraus, New York]; to Peter and Irene Ludwig, Aachen; acquired 1983

JPGM and RA

This manuscript appears to represent a French translation of the *Inventio-Translatio* portion of a life of Saint Anthony Abbot in Latin.[1] The latter text concludes with the narration of the discovery of the saint's relics and their translation to Constantinople through the efforts of Bishop Theophilus in the seventh century.[2] The Getty manuscript's

text appears to have been conceived as an independent text, commencing with an encapsulated vita (fols. 7–10).[3] Its decorative program recounts the life of the saint in four scenes on a single page, and then, in another four scenes on one page, it tells the story of the relics, of the events that led up to their discovery, and of their translation. Nineteen historiated initials follow these large miniatures. The volume concludes with seven prayers in French verse to Saint Anthony.[4] The first features a half-page miniature with the donor kneeling before Saint Anthony Abbot.

L'Invention et translation du corps de Saint Antoine is executed in two styles, both employing grisaille, sometimes heightened with gold and sometimes embellished with landscapes in color. The better hand appears in the final miniature. This illuminator portrays the devout patron as a young knight, in full armor, with handsomely chiseled features (ill. 50). The bearded Saint Anthony, standing before his makeshift cell, stares rapt over the head of the supplicant. The same hand appears in a monochrome miniature in a copy of Saint Augustine's moral treatises that David Aubert wrote out for Philip the Good in 1462 (Madrid, Biblioteca Nacional, Ms. Vit. 25-2).[5] In the miniature showing Saint Augustine witnessing a man on his deathbed (fig. 64), the drawing of the drapery folds with a wiry black contour, the way the folds bend at the ground, the liberal use of white highlighting, and the loose brushwork correspond very closely to what can be found in the Saint Anthony miniature.[6] The Madrid illuminations are attributed to the Master of Girart de Roussillon, who is now identified as Dreux Jean. Significantly, David Aubert or one of his assistants likely was also responsible for the Saint Anthony volume's superb unsigned *bastarda* script.

Less familiar and sophisticated is the style of the remaining miniatures, which resemble the illumination by the main artist of the Brussels *Romuléon* (Bibliothèque royale de Belgique, Ms. 9055).[7] In some cases (e.g., fols. 6v, 29), the miniatures in the Saint Anthony manuscript appear to be by an assistant of the *Romuléon* illuminator. Similar are the stylized figures with their distinctive silhouettes, the orientalizing costumes, and the bluish tinge to the grisaille. Also, the Saint Anthony borders resemble those in the *Romuléon*. David Aubert wrote the latter, in this instance for Anthony of Burgundy, Duke Philip's illegitimate son, in 1468.[8] Although difficult to date closely, the Saint Anthony manuscript probably also belongs to this period. If the miniature with the patron is by Dreux Jean himself, which is not certain, then the book likely dates before 1467, by which date this illuminator appears to have died.[9]

The unusual coat of arms of the manuscript has not been identified, but the motto *Du bien delle* belonged to Fonteny, whose name appears together with the motto in an *album amicorum* of Marie of Cleves.[10] A Guillaume de Fonteny was a member of the household of Charles d'Orléans, Marie's spouse, during the 1450s.[11] Yet, given the links of the two illuminators and the scribe to the Burgundian ducal family—in particular to Philip, Charles, and Anthony—the patron very likely came from their inner circle. Charles d'Orléans had close personal and political ties to his cousin Philip the Good. Each saw to the

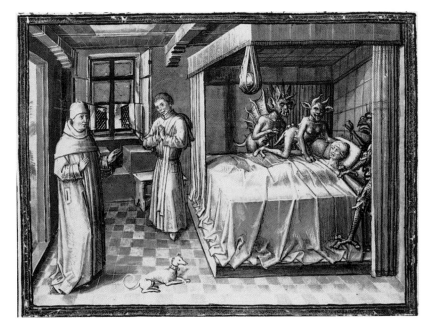

11. He was the duke's *écuyer* (Champion 1911: 518). In 1455 he is described as one of the "gens et officiers" of Charles d'Orléans (Laborde [L. de] 1849–52, 3: 371).

12. Charles d'Orléans was made a knight of the Golden Fleece in Saint-Omer at the end of December 1445, a few days after his marriage to Marie of Cleves in the Abbey Church of Saint Bertin there. Charles offered Duke Philip his Order of the Camail at the same time.

13. The golden lion that holds the standard with the arms recalls the Burgundian lion. It can also be said that the patron particularly venerated Saint Anthony. The wide popularity of Saint Anthony and of confraternities dedicated to him, such as the Order of Saint Anthony in Hainaut, offers another possible context for the creation of such a book.

51

FOLLOWER OF DREUX JEAN

Nicolas Finet, *Le Dialogue de la duchesse de Bourgogne à Jésus Christ*
Brussels, shortly after 1468

MANUSCRIPT: i + 142 folios, 20.4 × 13.8 cm (8 × 5⅜ in.); justification: 10.3 × 7.4 cm (4 × 2⅞ in.); 12 lines of *bastarda*; 1 full-page miniature

HERALDRY: Recumbent shield and lozenge with the arms of Margaret of York, fols. 1v, 2; initials *CM* (for Charles the Bold and Margaret of York), fols. 1v, 5, 11v, etc.; motto of Margaret of York *Ben en aviegne*, fol. 1v

INSCRIPTIONS: Signed *margarete dyork* by Margaret of York; *dyork* later partly erased and overwritten with *de angleterre au done a jane de halevyn dame vessenar et dame de la planc se lyvre lan xv27*, f. 140v

BINDING: Brabant, mid-seventeenth century; parchment over pasteboard, gold-tooled with central oval stamp of the Virgin and Child between stars, inscribed *Santa Maria Ora Pro Nobis*; rebacked with gilt leather[1]

COLLECTION: London, The British Library, Add. Ms. 7970

PROVENANCE: Margaret of York, duchess of Burgundy (1446–1503), probably shortly after 1468; Jeanne de Hallewin (d. 1529), wife of Jan I van Wassenaer, burgrave of Leiden (d. 1494/5); probably Jesuit College, Leuven, mid-seventeenth to eighteenth century; [John Cochran, London]; purchased 1830 by the British Museum

JPGM

induction of the other into their respective chivalric orders.[12] Marie of Cleves, who was Philip's niece, was raised in his household. Is it possible that Guillaume de Fonteny entered the service of one of these powerful Burgundians at some point during the 1460s, perhaps at the death of Charles d'Orléans in 1465? A proper identification of the book's armorials would settle the matter.[13]   T. K.

Notes

1. Fols. 11–49v; it is an expanded French paraphrase of the Latin text found in the Musée archéologique, Namur (Ms. 159), a paper manuscript of saints' lives dating from the fifteenth century (De Smedt et al. 1883: 341–54). I am grateful to Elizabeth Teviotdale for this information.

2. Euw and Plotzek 1979–85, 3: 86. Some of those relics had been translated from Constantinople to Saint-Antoine-de-Viennois in the eleventh century, but this is not addressed in the text.

3. The table of contents confirms this conclusion. It is much shorter than the Greek *Life* of Athanasius of Alexandria and its Latin translations (Bartelink 1994).

4. None of the prayers is in Sonet 1956 or Rézeau 1986.

5. Scot McKendrick drew my attention to the stylistic connection to the Madrid Saint Augustine. See Brussels 1959: 141, no. 172, but see also 142, under no. 174; Straub 1995: 50, fig. 5.

6. Van Buren (in DOA 1996, 17: 455) attributed the Saint Anthony manuscript to Dreux Jean, but she did not specify which miniatures. In my view only the one mentioned here is by him or his workshop.

7. Euw, in Euw and Plotzek 1979–85, 3: 88.

8. Anthony of Burgundy was a powerful figure at the court of his half brother Charles the Bold.

9. Van Buren (2002: 1381) indicated that he was dead by early 1467. Since the miniature with the patron may have been painted by an assistant, the manuscript could also date later than 1467. It was probably made around 1465–70. Margaret Scott pointed out that such a dating fits with the hairstyle of the patron, whose bangs extend down into his eyes (correspondence with the author, March 4, 2002, Department of Manuscripts files, JPGM.); the chronicler Jacques du Clerq remarked in 1467 that men's hair was growing down into their eyes (cited in Scott [M.] 1980: 176). Also, the patron's armor resembles that in Hans Memling's Danzig altarpiece of these years (1467–71).

10. See Champion 1910: 326, 334. Scot McKendrick drew to my attention the presence of *Du bien delle* in Marie's *album amicorum*.

50 (opposite)
DREUX JEAN OR
WORKSHOP
A Knight in Prayer before
Saint Anthony, fol. 50

Figure 64 (above)
DREUX JEAN
OR WORKSHOP
Dying Man's Prayer. In
Saint Augustine, *Moral*
Treatises, 1462; 37 ×
26 cm (14⁹⁄₁₆ × 10¼ in.).
Madrid, Biblioteca
nacional, Ms. Vit. 25-2,
fol. 52 (detail)

Shortly after her marriage to Charles the Bold in 1468, Margaret of York successively requested two texts from her almoner Nicolas Finet.[2] The first and much longer text, entitled *Benois seront les miséricordieux*, draws from scriptural, patristic, and other authorities to teach the power of salvation through acts of mercy and charity. The second text, the *Dialogue de la duchesse de Bourgogne à Jésus Christ*,[3] advises Margaret on how to approach God and achieve spiritual improvement. Notably, Finet had Christ himself offer this advice.

Margaret's unique copies of these two texts form a closely related pair of manuscripts.[4] Not only were they written by the same scribe;[5] they were also decorated in a very similar manner. Comparison of the two pages illustrated for the *Benois* text and the one for the *Dialogue* reveals identical treatment of initials, heraldry, and devices.[6] Close similarities in the treatment of space, color, figures, and costume suggest that the same illuminator was responsible for all three miniatures. That illuminator was previously thought to be Dreux Jean. Given, however, that we now know that Dreux was probably dead by 1468, the miniatures of the *Benois* have been attributed to a follower of

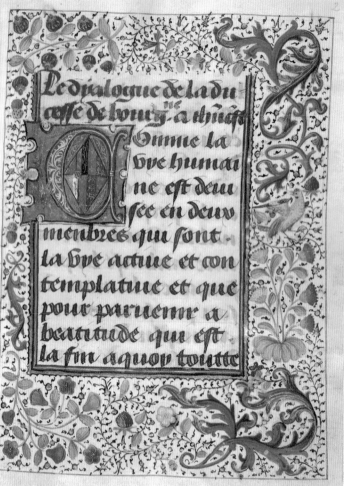

51
FOLLOWER OF
DREUX JEAN
Margaret of York and the Risen Christ, fols. 1v–2

Dreux—known as the Master of Guillebert de Lannoy because he illustrated Philip the Good's copy of de Lannoy's *L'Instruction d'un jeune prince* (Brussels, Bibliothèque royale de Belgique, Ms. 10976).[7] In the two miniatures of the *Instruction*, however, the long-legged figures have an elegance and swing not found in either the *Benois* or the *Dialogue*. Faces in the *Instruction* are treated differently, and the painting has a subtlety of application and palette not found in the other two manuscripts.

The miniatures of the *Benois* and the *Dialogue* are also very closely related iconographically. In the *Benois*, Margaret's acts of mercy are made in the presence of the living Christ. In the *Dialogue*, Margaret kneels in her chamber at her devotions before the resurrected Christ (ill. 51); the artist has evoked scenes of Christ appearing to the Virgin and Christ before Mary Magdalene. Whether using this iconography is programmatic or whether it is dependent on workshop models is difficult to assess. What is certain is that this image was intended to illustrate the text's recommendation to Margaret to contemplate Christ and yearn for his living presence.   S. McK.

Notes

1. Thanks to Claude Sorgeloos for help in identifying the binding and to Philippa Marks for making the identification possible.

2. This dating is suggested by Finet's description of Margaret of York in the preface to the *Benois* as "sister of Edward IV and wife of Charles the Bold." The prominence given to her relationship to Edward is most easily explicable if Finet was writing shortly after her marriage on July 3, 1468. In both the *Benois* and the *Dialogue*, she is also described as "wife of Charles the Bold"—not as "duchess of Burgundy," etc.—as in the manuscripts made for her in the 1470s. For all the relevant dedications and colophons, see Barstow 1992: 257–60.

3. Finet's prologue to the *Dialogue* makes it clear that this work was written after, and as a complement to, his *Benois*. Unlike the *Benois*, which, as Finet stressed, is a translation, the *Dialogue* is an original composition.

4. The *Benois* survives in Brussels (Bibliothèque royale de Belgique, Ms. 9296).

5. The same scribe—possibly a member of Margaret's household—also wrote her copy of devotional texts by Jean Gerson (Brussels, Bibliothèque royale, Ms. 9305-06). Given several careless errors of transcription in the *Dialogue*, it is unlikely the scribe was Finet himself. Their correction, however, suggests that Finet supervised its production.

6. The artist responsible for the border decoration in the *Dialogue* contributed the partial borders throughout the *Benois*, but not the full borders that accompany its miniatures.

7. De Schryver 1974: 67.

MASTER OF MARGARET OF YORK GROUP (A)

The Master of Margaret of York was named by Friedrich Winkler after a manuscript of devotional works by Jean Gerson made for Margaret of York, the wife of Charles the Bold (Brussels, Bibliothèque royale de Belgique, Ms. 9305–06).[1] The manuscript was executed between 1468 and 1477. Winkler also attributed to the Master of Margaret of York the miniatures in copies of the *Ovide moralisé*, Hubert le Prévost's *Vie de Saint Hubert*, and a French translation of Henricus Suso's *Horologium sapientiae*, all of which were made for Louis of Gruuthuse (Paris, Bibliothèque nationale de France, Mss. fr. 137, 424, 455–56). Winkler traced a line of artistic development in manuscript illumination in Bruges leading from Willem Vrelant to the Master of the Dresden Prayer Book, placing the Master of Margaret of York's style somewhere between these two. In his opinion, the Master of Margaret of York employed similar artistic formulas to these two illuminators but did so with more competence than Vrelant and less competence than the Dresden Master. Winkler even wondered whether the works of the Master of Margaret of York might in fact be the immature efforts of the Dresden Master.

Since Winkler's identification in 1925 of the Master of Margaret of York, important questions have arisen concerning the extent of the master's corpus of works and the relationship between the small number of miniatures that Winkler attributed to the master and the much larger number that he did not attribute to him but that are nonetheless stylistically related. As early as 1930, Ottokar Smital noted characteristics closely similar to those of the Master of Margaret of York's work in eight further manuscripts. These manuscripts of vernacular texts, first owned by Louis of Gruuthuse, include Louis's copies of the French translations of Quintus Curtius and Valerius Maximus (Paris, Bibliothèque nationale, Mss. fr. 257, 288–89).[2] Smital named the miniaturist of these eight manuscripts the Master of Louis of Bruges and hypothesized that the Master of Margaret of York and the Master of Louis of Bruges were in fact the same person; the differences between their works, according to Smital, merely reflected the differences between the work of an immature artist and that of a mature artist. Although subsequently rejected by Winkler,[3] Smital's hypothesis has prompted more recent critics, including Georges Dogaer[4] and Maximiliaan Martens,[5] to explore the complexities of a wider corpus of stylistically related works, including those attributed by Smital to the Master of Louis of Bruges. This body of miniatures has continued to expand piecemeal as the miniatures of other manuscripts, such as those in Gruuthuse's copy of the *Remèdes de fortune* (cat. no. 61), are newly attributed to

the Master of Margaret of York. A detailed review of all the relevant manuscripts remains to be undertaken.

Undeniably, miniatures attributed to the Master of Margaret of York share certain distinctive features. Architectural settings, for example, repeatedly include tall, arched windows, often topped by smaller traceried lunettes; sundials in red, blue, and gold; tall marble columns; stonework figures in canopied niches; and beamed wood ceilings. In interiors the lower portions of rear walls are frequently draped with gold cloth hangings, and side walls feature elaborately paneled wood thrones under baldachins of red patterned silk with green valences. Many of the Master of Margaret of York's compositions and artistic formulas are based on those originally created by the Antwerp illuminator Lieven van Lathem.

In addition to the shared details of many of these miniatures, several manuscripts also share the same border decoration and mise-en-page on miniature pages.[6] Almost all of the miniatures attributed to the Master of Margaret of York are illustrations for vernacular texts, and most illustrate secular texts. The cumulative evidence of patronage, subsidiary decoration, and collaborations—such as that with Loyset Liédet and the Master of Anthony of Burgundy on Gruuthuse's copy of Froissart's *Chroniques* (cat. no. 71)—strongly suggests that all the manuscripts were produced in Bruges. Only one manuscript with miniatures attributed to the Master of Margaret of York is securely datable (a copy of Christine de Pisan's *Cité des dames* in Dutch, dated 1475 [London, British Library, Add. Ms. 20698]).[7] Most of the other miniatures in this style appear to date from the 1470s.

Although miniatures attributed to the Master of Margaret of York show so many similarities, a closer examination reveals significant stylistic differences. Such differences are particularly apparent when the miniatures of manuscripts containing the same text are compared. A prime example of this is found in the illustrations of five copies of Quintus Curtius Rufus's *Livre des fais d'Alexandre le grant*,[8] which are clearly related in style, with the illustrations of all but one of the copies based on the same models. It is clear, however, that several different artists were responsible for the execution of these illustrations (see cat. no. 63). The same is also true of related copies of *Livre des profits ruraux*[9] and related copies of the *Bouquechardière*.[10]

Both Martens and Bodo Brinkmann have separated out from the main corpus of works attributed to the Master of Margaret of York the miniatures in Margaret of York's copy of the *Vie de Sainte Colette* (Ghent, Armeklarem, Ms. 8).[11] Martens also distinguished another artist at work in the miniatures of a copy of the *Jardin de vertueuse consolation* (cat. no. 62), to whom I subsequently attributed one of the copies of the *Livre des fais d'Alexandre* (cat. no. 63).[12] Brinkmann attributed a small corpus of manuscripts to an associate of the Master of Margaret of York, whom he named the Master of Fitzwilliam 268 after a book of hours in Cambridge (cat. no. 52).[13] I would suggest that another subgroup could be formed around the miniature at the opening of Jan Crabbe's copy of Boccaccio's *Genealogia deorum* (Bruges, Groot Seminarie, Ms. 154/44) and that the artist could be named the Master of the Bruges *Genealogia deorum*.[14]

Of these various hands, perhaps the most interesting is the Master of Fitzwilliam 268. Starting from the miniatures in the eponymous manuscript, Brinkmann attributed to this artist one miniature in Jan Crabbe's copy of the works of Virgil and another in Charles the Bold's copy of his military ordinances (cat. nos. 118 and 64)—both of which were produced in Bruges, in 1473 and 1475, respectively.[15] Brinkmann also attributed to the Master of Fitzwilliam 268 part of the illumination of the Salting Hours (cat. no. 53), a manuscript to which Willem Vrelant, Simon Marmion, and the Master of the Dresden Prayer Book also contributed. There is some disagreement about whether the Master of Fitzwilliam 268 should be a separate artistic grouping.[16] Moreover, the relationship between this proposed master and the documented miniaturist Philippe de Mazerolles requires further exploration.[17]   S. McK.

Notes

1. Winkler 1925: 86, 165.

2. Smital 1930a: 228; Smital 1930b: 48–49.

3. Winkler rejected Smital's hypothesis in a typescript expertise for H. P. Kraus on the manuscript (cat. no. 63), now at the J. Paul Getty Museum (Department of Manuscripts files, JPGM).

4. Dogaer 1987a: 113.

5. Bruges 1992: 142–44, 169–71, 181, 184–85.

6. E.g., Paris, Bibliothèque nationale de France, Ms. fr. 137; Saint Petersburg, Russian National Library, Ms. Fr. F.v.XIV.1; and cat. no. 65. For additional related borders, see cat. nos. 61–63.

7. Only the first miniature (fol. 2; McKendrick 2003: pl. 31) was completed by the Master of Margaret of York. For the rest of the miniatures, see Brinkmann 1997: 89–91.

8. Geneva, Bibliotheca Bodmeriana, Ms. Bodmer 53; Jena, Thüringer Universitäts- und Landesbibliothek, Ms. El. fol. 89; cat. no. 63; Paris, Bibliothèque nationale, Ms. fr. 257; Vienna, Österreichische Nationalbibliothek, Ms. 2566.

9. Cat. no. 65 and Paris, Bibliothèque de l'Arsenal, Ms. 5064. In May 2002 I had the opportunity to compare, side by side, the miniatures in these two volumes. I am grateful to William Voelkle, Danielle Muzerelle, and Élisabeth Antoine for this opportunity. See Paris 2002, nos. 91, 92.

10. Paris, Bibliothèque nationale, Mss. fr. 65–66, and New York, Pierpont Morgan Library, Ms. M.214, 224.

11. Bruges 1992: 142; Brinkmann 1997: 79. Martens and Brinkmann have dubbed this artist the Master of the Ghent Life of Saint Colette.

12. McKendrick 1996a: 44. The characteristics of this style are noted under cat. no. 62. Martens baptized this artist the Master of the *Jardin de vertueuse consolation*.

13. Brinkmann 1992a: 192 n. 17; Brinkmann 1997: 164–69, 272–74.

14. I would include in this subgroup the large miniature at the opening of Wolfart van Borssele's copy of *De civitate dei* by Saint Augustine (Utrecht, Universiteitsbibliotheek, Ms. 42); the three large miniatures in Anthony of Burgundy's copy of the *Chronique* by Aegidius de Roya (The Hague, Museum Meermanno-Westreenianum, Ms. 10 A 21); and all nine large miniatures in a copy of *Livre des fais d'Alexandre* (Jena, Thüringer Universitäts- und Landesbibliothek, Ms. El. fol. 89). Characteristic of miniatures in this grouping are elongated, hourglass-shaped figures with long, pointed shoes, sharply pleated gowns, and tall bonnets over tightly bunched hair. Also distinctive are an unnecessarily elaborate juxtaposition of colors in small areas, chaotic spatial relationships, and a more emotional treatment of subjects (often effected by the gesture of a raised hand) than in the main corpus of miniatures attributed to the Master of Margaret of York. The horizon is punctuated by castle-topped mounds in atmospheric perspective. Brinkmann (1997: 71 n. 8) attributed to this artist eight small miniatures in Anthony of Burgundy's copy of Valerius Maximus (Berlin, Staatsbibliothek, Ms. Dep. Breslau 2). Probably also by the Master of the Bruges Genealogia Deorum are five large miniatures in Gruuthuse's copy of Quintus Curtius (Paris, Bibliothèque nationale, Ms. fr. 257), the style of which Martens (in Bruges 1992: 184) notes also in the frontispiece of Gruuthuse's Valerius Maximus (Paris, Bibliothèque nationale, Mss. fr. 288–89).

15. I accept Brinkmann's further attribution to the Master of Fitzwilliam 268 miniatures in the book of hours once in the collection of René Héron de Villefosse (see Héron de Villefosse 1959: 56–59). An unpublished book of hours with miniatures by the Master of Fitzwilliam 268 is in the Gulbenkian Museum, Lisbon (L.A.144).

16. De Schryver (1999: 61) proposed the *Ordinance* miniature (cat. no. 64) as a collaboration between the Master of Margaret of York and Philippe de Mazerolles; he implicitly rejected Brinkmann's attribution of this miniature to the Master of Fitzwilliam 268.

17. On this issue, see Brinkmann 1997: 274.

52

MASTER OF FITZWILLIAM 268

Book of Hours
Use of Rome
Bruges, ca. 1475

MANUSCRIPT: 171 + iv folios, 14.7 × 10.5 cm (5¾ × 4⅛ in.);
justification: 9.7 × 6.5 cm (3⅞ × 2½ in.); 18 lines of *gotica rotunda*;
15 full-page miniatures, 24 small calendar miniatures

HERALDRY: Escutcheon with the arms of Aragon surmounted by
coronet, in miniature of Saint Nicholas, fol. 138v

INSCRIPTIONS: Additions, partly in Italian, in an Italian humanist
hand, early sixteenth century; inspected by the inquisitor Pedro del
Suelves in 1575

BINDING: France, seventeenth century; red morocco, gilt-lined;
gold-tooled spine

COLLECTION: Cambridge, Fitzwilliam Museum, Ms. 268

PROVENANCE: Written probably for an Aragonese patron living in
the kingdom of Naples (arms, Italian additions); in Aragon by 1575
(inscription); Don Antonio Villadiego da Montoya, seventeenth
century; [Techener, Paris]; to Henry Yates Thompson (1838–1928),
February 1897 (his Ms. 20) [his sale, Sotheby's, London, May 14, 1902,
lot 21]; [Pickering and Chatto]; to Noel Barwell; presented 1903 to the
Fitzwilliam Museum by a group of members of the university

The miniatures of the present manuscript are the starting point for the identification of the Master of Fitzwilliam 268, who, alongside the Master of Margaret of
York, developed a style of painting based on the artistic
inventions of Lieven van Lathem. The borders—which
are closely related to those found in manuscripts to which
Van Lathem contributed—are by the same hand as the
miniatures in this volume. Both miniatures and borders
reflect the illuminator's dependence on preexisting models.
Almost all the striking borders on dark grounds have their
compositions illogically and inelegantly truncated on the
outer right- or left-hand side, suggesting that the models
used were intended for larger surfaces than were available
in the manuscript. The miniatures, by contrast, must have
been based on models smaller than the spaces provided in
the manuscript. Several miniatures present compositions
that have been stretched vertically, sometimes by filling out
the upper space with towering rocks. In *The Flight into Egypt*
an intrusive wicker fence fills the foreground, and in *The
Presentation in the Temple* a horizontal band in the foreground has been left blank. In each case, a model devised
for a miniature heading a few lines of text has been adapted
to generate a full-page miniature and facilitate the creation
of an impressive opening with matching borders. Unusually for Flemish books of hours, all the miniatures are
painted on integral leaves.

Although largely conventional in its iconography and
liturgical content, Fitzwilliam 268 includes some distinctive
features. The miniature entitled *The Martyrdom of Saint
Catherine* (ill. 52) is clearly based on a model similar to that
used in the *Salting Hours* (cat. no. 53, fol. 15v). The Master of
Fitzwilliam 268 has, however, sought to accentuate the
drama of the scene with a glowing sky reminiscent of *The
Crucifixion* by Simon Marmion in the Huth Hours (ill. 33b).
The drama in *The Martyrdom of Saint Catherine* is further
heightened by the expressionistic palette of green, red, and
orange and by the variety of complicated poses in which
the saint's stricken torturers are shown.

Another distinctive feature of Fitzwilliam 268 is the
customization of a prominent miniature (fol. 138v). In this
illustration a well-dressed man representing the patron
kneels before Saint Nicholas. Nicholas is certainly the only
male saint for whom there is a memorial, and he is featured
prominently at the very end of the litany; clearly the patron
of the manuscript had a particular devotion to him. Liturgical texts added in an Italian hand, and partly in the Italian
language; the appearance of the crowned arms of Aragon
in the miniature of Saint Nicholas; and the manuscript's
later appearance in Aragon suggest that the patron was
a foreigner to the Low Countries from the kingdom of
Naples. Since political, commercial, and artistic relations
between the Low Countries and Aragon were well established and flourishing by the 1470s, such an identification is
entirely plausible.   S. McK.

52
MASTER OF
FITZWILLIAM 268
*The Martyrdom of Saint
Catherine*, fol. 140v

RA

53

SIMON MARMION AND WORKSHOP,
MASTER OF THE DRESDEN PRAYER BOOK,
MASTER OF FITZWILLIAM 268, AND
WILLEM VRELANT AND WORKSHOP

Salting Hours
Use of Rome
Bruges and Valenciennes, early to mid-1470s

MANUSCRIPT: i + 250 + ii folios, 11 × 7.8 cm (4⁵⁄₁₆ × 3¹⁄₁₆ in.);
justification: 6 × 3.9 cm (2⅜ × 1⁹⁄₁₆ in.); 16 lines of *gotica rotunda*;
13 full-page miniatures; 28 historiated or inhabited borders

BINDING: France, ca. 1840–50 (?); red velvet over wood boards; frame
of enameled gold; enameled medallions of the Virgin (front cover)
and Saint John the Baptist (back cover); two foliate enameled clasps

COLLECTION: London, The Victoria and Albert Museum, L.2384-1910
(Salting Ms. 1221)

PROVENANCE: Samuel Addingham, by 1862; Frédéric Spitzer (1815–
1890) [his sale, Paul Chevallier, Paris, April 17–June 16, 1893, lot 3027];
George Salting (1835–1909); his bequest, 1910

RA

With only thirteen full-page miniatures remaining out of an original complement of twenty, this small book of hours is a production of unusual complexity for its modest scope. Four illuminators shared responsibility for the project, often collaborating on the same page. The Master of Fitzwilliam 268 and the Master of the Dresden Prayer Book supplied borders for the nine miniatures by Simon Marmion and his shop, along with others on facing pages. An unusual opening that features a *Last Judgment* with a full border on the left and a full-page *Hell and Paradise* opposite (ill. 53a) reflects the participation of all three of these artists. The Fitzwilliam artist painted *Hell and Paradise*, the only miniature that lacks a decorated or historiated border, and two other full-page miniatures.[1] The Dresden Master, whose seven subtle and delicate historiated borders are the volume's finest and are located at key divisions, supplied none of the large illuminations that survive. It is clear that some of his borders are now missing. A single full-page miniature, *The Martyrdom of Saint Catherine*, and its border are by Willem Vrelant and his shop.[2]

Another unusual feature of the book's production is the sequence of three full-page miniatures that illustrate the Office of the Dead: *The Last Judgment*, *Hell and Paradise*, and *The Raising of Lazarus* (ill. 53b). Devotions in a book of hours were rarely preceded by more than one full-page miniature or a full-page miniature opposite a smaller miniature. The second in the sequence, the book's most unusual miniature, features a dense network of infernal tortures, likely inspired, albeit loosely, by such visionary texts as *Les Visions du chevalier Tondal* (cat. no. 14).[3] The presence of *Hell and Paradise* on the recto of an inserted full-page miniature suggests that the sequence results from an element of improvisation. Full-page miniatures were rarely painted on both sides of a leaf in Flemish manuscripts.[4]

There are few clues to the book's original ownership, but the suffrages—only five in total—are suggestive. Four suffrages appear together at the back; only the Saint Catherine appears at the front, and it alone is illuminated. As such, the placement of the suffrage and its illumination reflects the prominence this saint enjoyed in the programs of even more luxurious books of hours in the 1470s and beyond (see cat. nos. 18, 33, 37). Only Saint Barbara enjoyed a comparably privileged position among female saints during this period (see cat nos. 20, 33, 37). Significantly, these examples appear for the most part to have been made for individuals connected with the Burgundian court.[5] Three of the four suffrages at the very end of the book are familiar—those to John the Baptist, James the Greater, and Sebastian—but one, the suffrage to Reginald, is extremely rare. The eleventh-century Saint Reginald of Picardy was evoked against fever, as he is in this prayer. He appears in neither the calendar nor the litany.

For all its variety of artistic participants, the book shows considerable unity in its approach to the border, and for this it holds some art-historical significance. Although most of the borders show familiar combinations of acanthus, grotesques, narrative figures, and narrative vignettes, these elements are usually set against solid-colored grounds in gold, green, red, blue, and black (ill. 53b). The figures do

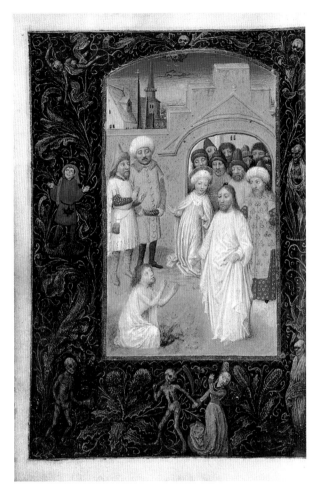

Notes

1. Brinkmann (1997: 160–62, 164–69) first identified and articulated the participation of the Master of Fitzwilliam 268 in this manuscript.

2. Bousmanne (1997: 265) attributed the miniature and its border to Vrelant himself, while Brinkmann (1997: 159–60) ascribed it to an artist from the circle of Vrelant; Rowan Watson, in his thoughtful description of the manuscript, called it "Vrelant style" (Department of Manuscripts files, JPGM).

3. Hindman 1977: 193; Brinkmann 1997: 163.

4. Brinkmann (1997: 171–72) proposed that the book's unusual sequence of three full-page miniatures preceding the Office of the Dead results from Marmion's error in sending two miniatures, *David in Penitence* and *The Last Judgment*, to illustrate the Penitential Psalms. In Bruges it was more common to use the David subject, but some locations also used *The Last Judgment*. Brinkmann suggested that the book's organizer found that *The Last Judgment* could be made to fit thematically with the Office of the Dead, where it is uncommon, by joining it with *Hell and Paradise*. This view has some merit, though it would be surprising for an artist of Marmion's experience to make such an error.

5. Bousmanne (1997: 265) suggested that the prominence of the Saint Catherine suffrage and miniature indicates that the book was made for a woman named Catherine. This is possible but not necessarily true.

6. Lieven van Lathem also experimented with solid-colored grounds in the Prayer Book of Charles the Bold (cat. no. 16), for which he was paid in 1469. See also the introduction to part 2 in this volume.

7. Both Clark (1992: 196–97) and Brinkmann (1997: 59, 159, 169–72), using different criteria, have argued strongly for the localization of the book's production to Bruges.

8. Clark 1992: 196–97, 198, 200, 206, n. 8, as 1475/80; Brinkmann 1997: 389, as 1475/80.

not cast shadows in the manner of those in the illusionistic borders that would began to appear in the same decade, but it is clear that the solid grounds often set off the figures' sculptural qualities more fully than does the neutral ground of the unpainted vellum. The result is not so much illusionism as a playful spatial quality. One wonders whether the colored grounds, which seem to have appealed to both the Master of Fitzwilliam 268 and the Dresden Master in these years (see cat. nos. 52, 48), represent a stage in the evolution of the new border type.[6] The introduction of illusionism appears to be the next step in this development.

Three of the illuminators appear to have been based in Bruges, and Bodo Brinkmann has argued, sensibly, that the Valenciennes-based Marmion most likely shipped his miniatures, all painted on single leaves, to Bruges, where their decorative borders were added and they were inserted in the book.[7] Although the book is difficult to date precisely, most scholars agree that it belongs to the 1470s. I would place it in the middle or first half of that decade, based on the similarities of its borders to those of the Carpentin Hours (cat. no. 48).[8]   T. K.

53b
SIMON MARMION
The Raising of Lazarus,
fol. 153v

PART 3

PAINTING IN MANUSCRIPTS OF VERNACULAR TEXTS, CIRCA 1467–1485

By 1467, when Charles the Bold succeeded his father, Philip the Good, as duke of Burgundy, production of illuminated manuscripts of secular vernacular texts was an established part of the cultural and economic life of the southern Netherlands. Authors, scribes, and illuminators often combined their skills to produce books of the highest quality and sophistication. Many of these books rivaled the finest books made in all of western Europe, during this or any other period. The lavish patronage of Philip the Good, as well as that of significant members of Philip's court, was crucial in encouraging the highest standards of artistic achievement in manuscripts of secular vernacular texts. It also encouraged—among the nobility of the northern territories of the duke of Burgundy—a passion for illuminated manuscripts that Philip the Good and his family had adopted from their French royal ancestors as the presumptive heirs of the cultural capital of Europe, Paris.

During the dukedom of Charles the Bold, production of illuminated manuscripts of secular vernacular texts continued to thrive. Although he commissioned fewer manuscripts of significance than his father had, his completion of several important projects that Philip had begun, such as the four-volume *Histoire de Charles Martel* (cat. no. 55), is worthy of note. Illuminated manuscripts initiated by Charles, such as the twin copies of *L'Instruction d'un jeune prince* (cat. no. 56) and his personal copy of Vasco da Lucena's *Livre des fais d'Alexandre le grant* (cat. no. 54), also constitute some of the finest manuscripts produced in their time. In addition, such courtiers as his illegitimate half brother Anthony of Burgundy and his trusted governor of Holland, Zeeland, and West Frisia, Louis of Gruuthuse (see cat. nos. 58–62, 69, 71, 81), continued to encourage the production of books of the highest quality and sophistication. The patronage of such manuscripts by both of these men greatly increased after 1467, and in the case of Gruuthuse, by far the largest part of his collection was formed after that date. Another courtier of Charles the Bold, Jean de Montferrant, was even a member of the same Bruges confraternity as the miniaturists. This membership must have secured for him a particularly advantageous context in which to work closely with a Bruges illuminator on the illustration of *Les Douze Dames de rhétorique*, a collection of contemporary texts of which he himself was one of the authors (cat. no. 70). Within court circles, Montferrant could also act as an advocate for both the text and its illustrators and seek to promote the production of further copies of the *Douze Dames* (see cat. no. 69).

MASTER OF THE
WHITE INSCRIPTIONS
Samson and the Lion
(detail, ill. 80)

When Charles the Bold died in battle at Nancy at the beginning of 1477, the subsequent collapse of the Burgundian state and dismemberment of its territories seriously threatened the future of production of deluxe manuscripts of secular vernacular texts in the southern Netherlands. Fortunately, however, long-standing economic, cultural, and political relations between the southern Netherlands and England had developed to such a point that a newly invigorated England under Edward IV offered an important market for the very books for which there was now a threateningly low demand in the southern Netherlands. The sequence of illuminated manuscripts produced for Edward IV (cat. nos. 75, 78, 80, 82, 83, 87), particularly those made from 1478 onward, thereby offered a lifeline for young Flemish illuminators such as the Master of Edward IV. The work provided by these manuscripts did much to tide scribes and illuminators over into the next decade, at which point greater political and economic stability allowed the return of significant patronage within the southern Netherlands by such nobles as Baudouin II de Lannoy, John II of Oettingen and Flobecq, Engelbert of Nassau, and Philip of Cleves. Therefore, in or shortly before 1480, when Louis of Gruuthuse enabled Edward IV to acquire a copy of Josephus originally intended for Louis himself (cat. no. 81) and either encouraged or at least facilitated the acquisition by Edward of further such manuscripts, he may well have been prompted to do so as much from concern for the economic position of the scribes and illuminators—whose works he himself so clearly valued— as from a wish to promote cross-channel cultural exchange. Edward's own motivation was at least in part a response to the "great kindness and courtesy" he and his retinue had enjoyed in Bruges during their exile in the Low Countries in the winter of 1470–71.

The careers of some key illustrators of secular vernacular texts straddled the periods before and after 1467. Most notably, the Bruges miniaturist Loyset Liédet produced important manuscripts for both Philip the Good and Charles the Bold (cat. nos. 54, 55). The mainstream of production after 1467 was, however, undertaken by a new generation of miniaturists. These artists included the Master of Margaret of York, the Master of the Vienna *Chroniques d'Angleterre*, the Master of the Soane Josephus, the Master of Edward IV, the Master of the London Wavrin, the Master of the Getty Froissart, the Master of the White Inscriptions, the Master of 1482, the Master of the Flemish Boethius, and the Master of the Dresden Prayer Book. Except for the last miniaturist, all worked almost exclusively on the illustration of secular vernacular texts. Willem Vrelant, who had been one of the artists greatly favored by Philip the Good for the illustration of vernacular texts and did not die until 1481, seems not to have found favor with Charles the Bold.

At least one important style of illustrating secular vernacular texts seems to have been set in motion by the new artist Lieven van Lathem just before 1467. Through his contribution to such manuscripts as Louis of Gruuthuse's copies of the *Roman de Gillion de Trazegnies*, Raoul Lefèvre's *Histoire de Jason*, and the *Secret des secrets* (cat. nos. 58–60), this Antwerp miniaturist both demonstrated the artistic heights to which other miniaturists and patrons might aspire and introduced compositional formulas and even figure types that were repeatedly used during the 1470s by such miniaturists as the Master of Margaret of York, the Master of Fitzwilliam 268, and the Master of the *Jardin de vertueuse consolation* (cat. nos. 61–65). Remarkably, one of the miniaturists of the new generation who contributed most to the illustration of devotional texts, the Vienna Master of Mary of Burgundy illuminated only one secular vernacular text (cat. no. 54). Miniaturists from his circle produced a few outstanding manuscripts, such as the Holkham *Chroniques de Flandres* (cat. no. 85) and the Munich *Chronique des haulx et nobles princes des Cleves* (cat. no. 86), as well as the larger corpus of illuminations by the Master of the Flemish Boethius, including Edward IV's copy of William of Tyre (cat. no. 87). These manuscripts, however, formed only a small part of production in the southern Netherlands.

Such was the renown of the southern Netherlands as a center for the production of manuscripts that many artists migrated there from both the northern Netherlands and France. One such artist was the Master of the Harley Froissart (see cat. no. 68), a miniaturist who appears to have begun his career in Paris in the 1450s and to have moved to Bruges around 1460. Whereas his earliest known illuminations form part of a book of hours, in Bruges he came to specialize in the illustration of secular vernacular texts. Another artist who may have begun his career in Paris before moving to Bruges, around 1460, was Philippe de Mazerolles. The Rambures Master, whose origins may lie in the border town of Amiens, also spent some time in the 1470s working alongside the Bruges artists, as suggested by two copies of Valerius Maximus in French translation (see cat. no. 66).

Artistic continuity was largely brought about by the lingering influence of the training given to contemporary artists by artists of the earlier generation. In some cases, such as the *Grande Chronique de Normandie*, illustrated by a follower of the Brussels court illuminator Dreux Jean (cat. no. 57), the artistic tradition and formulas perpetuated by the follower appear all too obviously exhausted. In other cases, such as the Manchester copy of the first edition of Valerius Maximus in French translation (cat. no. 67), there is a remarkably vigorous continuation of artistic formulas that had their origins in Paris at the beginning of the fifteenth century. Usually the style of the miniaturist of an earlier generation is taken merely as a starting point from which a younger miniaturist develops his own way of illustrating texts. For example, although the Master of the Soane Josephus, and particularly the Master of Edward IV, were dependent on Willem Vrelant for elements of their artistic language, they developed distinctive ways of using color and treating narrative (see cat. nos. 81–84). Illustrations by followers of the Master of Anthony of Burgundy—such as the Master of the Dresden Prayer Book (cat. no. 73), the Master of the Vienna *Chroniques d'Angleterre* (cat. nos. 68, 82), and the Master of the London Wavrin (cat. nos. 74–76)—demonstrate in their differences the independent artistic characteristics of each follower.

Comparison between miniatures painted before 1467 and those painted after this date draws into focus the distinguishing characteristics of some of the most accomplished miniatures painted between 1467 and 1485. One of these characteristics is a heightened interest in naturalism. Greater sophistication in the treatment of landscape is especially evident in miniatures by both Lieven van Lathem and the Master of the London Wavrin. Van Lathem repeatedly experimented with atmospheric perspective and developed landscapes that were built up of a sequence of interlocking planes. The landscapes first fall, then rise in zigzag recessions, often delineated by winding rivers or paths (ill. 74). The Master of the London Wavrin was often so absorbed by his interest in landscape that he pushed the narrative subject into a corner of the miniature. Within the work of both these miniaturists, however, the setting of an episode was viewed by the artist not only as a pleasant backdrop and a means of structuring and highlighting a narrative but also as an aid to placing events from the distant past in a setting that is recognizably Flemish yet also of another world. At the same time the artists mirrored the natural world in their miniatures, either purifying it of unwanted elements or embellishing it with elements that added to the overall intended effect. Thus, regardless of the season in which his narrative took place, the Master of the London Wavrin strewed his miniatures with tall, leafing trees; regardless of the country in which it was set, he consistently marked the far distance with snow-clad mountains (ills. 75a, b). In these ways the miniaturist contributed, on the one hand, to both the naturalism and the immediacy of illustrations and, on the other, to their artifice and timelessness.

Repeatedly reflected in miniatures by the Master of the London Wavrin is the artist's close observation of the effect of both fire and sunlight on figures, landscape, or buildings. The same effect is well known in the work of another artist, the Master of Anthony of Burgundy, the presumed mentor of the Master of the London Wavrin. His *Bal des Ardents* (ill. 71a) is a particularly fine example of this treatment of light—an effect that is also apparent in the work of his other followers, including the Master of the Vienna *Chroniques d'Angleterre* and the Master of the Dresden Prayer Book. The Master of the Getty Froissart (who appears at least to have known the work of the Master of Anthony of Burgundy) was also interested in subtle effects of light—particularly those that help shape interior spaces and heighten the dramatic impact of a particular episode—as seen in his name manuscript and in the London *Trésor des histoires* (cat. nos. 79, 77).

Significant development can also be observed in the choice of texts illustrated. Whereas Flemish illuminators active in the time of Philip the Good had dedicated much of their time to the illustration of late medieval prose romances, those active from 1467 onward worked increasingly on the illustration of chronicles and other historical texts. This change of emphasis reflects a steady shift in the interests of the French-speaking nobility toward the subjects and lessons of ancient and modern history. This movement led to the revival of earlier texts, such as the translation of Valerius Maximus's compilation of anecdotes from history begun for Charles V (see cat. nos. 66, 67, 73, 80), the chronicle of the Hundred Years War written by Jean Froissart between 1370 and 1400 (see cat. nos. 68, 71, 79), and the anonymous biography of Julius Caesar, the *Faits des romains*, compiled as long ago as 1213–14. This shift of interest also made popular among the nobility such new historical texts as Vasco da Lucena's translation of Quintus Curtius Rufus's biography of Alexander the Great (cat. nos. 54, 63), Jan Du Quesne's translation of Julius Caesar's autobiographical account of his military and political successes (cat. no. 74), and Jean de Wavrin's history of England from legendary times to his own (cat. no. 75).

VIENNA MASTER OF MARY OF BURGUNDY (B)

For biography, see part 2

54

LOYSET LIÉDET AND WORKSHOP AND VIENNA MASTER OF MARY OF BURGUNDY

Quintus Curtius Rufus, *Livre des fais d'Alexandre le grant*, translation by Vasco da Lucena of *Historia Alexandri magni*
Bruges, ca. 1468–70

MANUSCRIPT: iii + 269 folios, 43.5 × 33.5 cm (17⅛ × 13¼ in.); justification: 28 × 21 cm (11 × 8¼ in.); 33 lines of *bastarda* in two columns by Yvonnet le Jeune; 74 half-page miniatures, 12 one-column miniatures

HERALDRY: Escutcheon with the arms of Charles the Bold in decorated initial, fol. 1

BINDING: Paris, late eighteenth century; green morocco; gold-tooled spine

COLLECTION: Paris, Bibliothèque nationale de France, Ms. fr. 22547

PROVENANCE: Charles the Bold, duke of Burgundy (1433–1477); Dijon private collection, early eighteenth century; Louis-Jean Gaignat (1697–1768) [his sale, De Bure, Paris, 1769, lot 2875]; Louis-César de La Baume Le Blanc, duke of la Vallière [his sale, De Bure, Paris, January 12–May 5, 1784, lot 4844]; purchased for the Bibliothèque du Roi

JPGM and RA

In 1468 the Portuguese humanist Vasco da Lucena completed his translation of a history of Alexander the Great by the ancient writer Quintus Curtius Rufus. Lucena dedicated it to Charles the Bold, who had inherited the title of duke of Burgundy the previous year. To Lucena, whose patron was Charles's mother, Isabella of Portugal, the dynastic ambitions of the new ruler made him the obvious dedicatee for a new life of the greatest of ancient conquerors. The translator's gesture was not ignored. Although not the earliest copy,[1] the illuminated volume that Charles himself paid for in 1470 is one of the earliest deluxe versions of Lucena's Alexander to come down to us.[2] In November 1470 Loyset Liédet was paid not only for the book's eighty-six miniatures ("74 grandes et 12 petites") but also for the decorated letters, a binding in damask, a white leather case, and the book's delivery from Bruges to Hesdin. Antoine de Schryver has persuasively identified the volume in the Bibliothèque nationale as this copy.[3] It has Charles's armorials prominently displayed in the initial beneath the dedication miniature, corresponds to the documents in the number of large and small miniatures, and is clearly illuminated by the well-documented Liédet.

Seventy-six of the miniatures show Liédet's characteristic style, along with the broad range of finish and quality that one associates with the artist. The finest is the presentation miniature, in which the costumes and furnishings are richly detailed and the modeling full. Vasco da Lucena is shown presenting his tome to Charles while courtiers, including a member of the Golden Fleece, look on or mingle among themselves. One courtier, who wears his initial and that of his spouse *en lac* embroidered on his tights, seems to have just arrived and raises his hat to the others. Indicative of this artist's limitations, the faces of Charles and a number of his courtiers are remarkably similar.

Although Liédet received payment for all of the miniatures, ten display an entirely different style.[4] For all his ability to work fast, he still had to enlist help to finish the job. The second painter was almost certainly a junior colleague, as he was assigned six of the book's twelve one-column miniatures and only four of the double-column miniatures. This artist was not a follower of Liédet, for he displays far greater verisimilitude, a richer and subtler handling of light, and more graceful and integrated figural movement. At the same time his miniatures too represent a range of quality. Easily the finest is *Alexander Takes the Hand of Roxanne* (ill. 54a). The miniature shows the banquet given for Alexander by a Bactrian leader and attended by thirty virgins of noble lineage, including Roxanne, whose beauty was of a sort "rarely found among the barbarians." Vasco describes this event and the subsequent nuptials of the pair only briefly (bk. 7, chap. 10), but the artist gives it a grand treatment. At the far right, in a separate incident, the sycophant Cleon of Sicily kneels before Alexander, who desired to have the Macedonians revere him as a god.

The illuminator of this miniature was likely the young Vienna Master of Mary of Burgundy, the painter of the famous miniatures in the Hours of Mary of Burgundy in the Austrian capital (cat. no. 19). In the geometry of their adolescent features, the two virgins facing right in the foreground of *Alexander Takes the Hand of Roxanne* have the idealized simplicity and purity of the young girl seated at prayer in the Vienna Hours, who is often identified with Mary of Burgundy herself (fig. 65). Within the former pair, the arched eyebrows; small, dark eyes; and narrow but full mouth of the exquisite young woman in a yellow robe with violet mantle correspond to the features of the presumed Mary. The two miniatures reveal a similar interest in Burgundian court costumes and their imaginative variations, especially in the colorful headdresses, the diaphanous veils, and the strong role accorded richly hued and textured drapery.[5] In both scenes the elaborate, enveloping costumes succeed in conveying the delicate physical character and slight proportions of the women. This is especially apparent in the kneeling Roxanne, in the Mary of Burgundy in the Vienna Hours, and in the kneeling Burgundian dame in the cathedral of the latter miniature, each with small limbs, waist, and hands. Moreover, the soft light that bathes Roxanne's gown from the left recalls the palpable light that suffuses the church in the Vienna miniature.

Other features—such as the distinctive type of the retainer in red tights, the dense line of human forms defined by the virgins, and the figure viewed from the back

54a
VIENNA MASTER OF
MARY OF BURGUNDY
*Alexander Takes the Hand
of Roxanne,* fol. 195v
(detail)

54b
VIENNA MASTER OF
MARY OF BURGUNDY
*Darius Giving a Messenger
a Letter for Alexander,*
fol. 53v (detail)

Figure 65
VIENNA MASTER OF
MARY OF BURGUNDY
Mary of Burgundy (?)
Reading Her Devotions.
In the Hours of Mary
of Burgundy, fol. 14v
(cat. no. 19)

in the right foreground—are characteristics of this artist's work also found in the Vienna miniatures.[6] Although the other nine miniatures here attributed to the Vienna Master do not achieve the level of courtly splendor of the miniature just discussed, all show the same or similar figure types and poses, a grace in movement, physically grounded standing figures, expressive hand gestures, and psychologically compelling faces. In *Darius Giving a Messenger a Letter for Alexander* (ill. 54b), typical of the Vienna Master is the psychological concentration not only of the messengers but also of the densely massed troops, whose faces peer out from the sea of helmets. Other characteristics include the long, handsome horses' snouts and their long necks and down-turned heads when shown in profile; the small but finely observed hands; the bulkiness and rumpled character of the messengers' drapery; and the atmospheric quality of the landscape.[7] This miniature is painted more rapidly than those in the Vienna Hours, and one finds awkwardness in the scale of the boy at the right attending the horses, but the scene is filled with passages of great subtlety. The

problems of scale indicate that this cycle of miniatures predates the artist's work in Vienna.

Although Liédet was paid toward the end of 1470 for the book, it is possible that his work was begun not long after Lucena completed his translation. The year 1468 was also marked by the wedding of Charles to Margaret of York, a circumstance that might explain the artistic focus accorded this volume's betrothal theme.[8]   T. K.

Notes

1. McKendrick (1996a: 20) cited a copy made for the duke of Savoy in 1469 (Bern, Burgerbibliothek, Ms. A.25).

2. Blondeau (2001) discussed this copy's iconography in relationship to its patron.

3. De Schryver 1979b: 469–76; for a transcription of the documents, see 478–79.

4. They are on folios 53v, 128, 140v, 155, 167, 168v, 171, 172, 175, and 195v. Two other miniatures, on folios 52 and 192, appear to be designed at least in part by the younger artist but painted by a member of Liédet's workshop. As Scot McKendrick kindly pointed out to me, it is striking thus that most (though not all) of the younger artist's work is localized to one section of the book, between folios 128 and 195v (books 5–7). These are gatherings 17 to 22.

5. For other examples in the Vienna Hours displaying a comparable variety of color and of rich fabrics, see especially *Christ Nailed to the Cross* (fig. 17) and *The Crucifixion* (ill. 19a).

6. For these artistic characteristics, cf., respectively, *The Martyrdom of Saint Sebastian* (fol. 119), *The Crucifixion* (ill. 19a), and *Christ Nailed to the Cross* (fig. 17). The celebrated engraving *Caxton Presenting the Recuyell to Margaret of York*, pasted into William Caxton's printed copy of Raoul Lefèvre's *Recuyell of the Historyes of Troye* (Bruges, ca. 1473–74; San Marino, Calif., Huntington Library; Lowry, in Kren 1992: 104, fig. 67), shows many correspondences to the Roxanne miniature. These include the poses of the central couple (with genders interchanged), the line of courtly women along one side, many architectural details and furnishings of the chamber, and the pose of the male courtier behind Roxanne compared with that of the one behind Margaret. The engraving has long been considered to be from the circle of the Master of Mary of Burgundy. Its intimate connection to the Roxanne miniature raises anew the question of its authorship.

7. Comparable qualities are particularly visible in *Christ Nailed to the Cross* (fig. 17) and *The Crucifixion* (ill. 19a).

8. McKendrick has observed that illuminated copies of Vasco's texts rarely agree in the chapters selected for illustration. In this respect the duke's copy has a twin that McKendrick (1996a: 53) characterized as "slightly humbler and from the same scribal and artistic circle." It is also in the Bibliothèque nationale (Ms. fr. 20311; McKendrick 1996a: 18–19, 53; McKendrick 1996b: 141, n. 34). It appears that there was also a paper copy of the manuscript in the Burgundian library (see McKendrick 1996b: 133, n. 13).

LOYSET LIÉDET

The first mention of Loyset Liédet is found in the 1460 payment documents for the illumination of two volumes containing Jean Mansel's *Histoires romaines*. Although Liédet was paid by Philip the Good for all fifty-five miniatures as well as the borders, initials, and paragraph marks, the evidence of the surviving manuscript (Paris, Bibliothèque de l'Arsenal, Mss. 5087–88) shows that the artist did not undertake this work on his own. Most obviously, one very different artist, now identified as the Rambures Master, painted five of the miniatures.[1] The hand responsible for the vast majority of the miniatures has, however, been identified as that of Liédet. When paid for these miniatures, Liédet was living in Hesdin, in the north of France, and was a fully trained and accomplished miniaturist.

In 1469 Liédet joined the book producers' confraternity in Bruges.[2] Between 1468 and 1472 Charles the Bold paid him for several hundred miniatures in a sequence of manuscripts of vernacular texts, some of which had been transcribed in the time of Charles's father, Philip the Good; the rest were undertaken by scribes working in collaboration with Liédet.[3] Several of the payments indicate that Liédet was then living in Bruges. The miniatures in these documented manuscripts have enabled modern scholars to establish a much larger corpus of works for Liédet than were previously known and to further our knowledge of his career. This larger corpus demonstrates that he illustrated mostly secular texts and almost exclusively texts in the vernacular. It also reveals that he illustrated an important sequence of manuscripts written by David Aubert for Philip the Good in the 1460s and was therefore one of the principal illuminators of books made for the Burgundian library for more than a decade.[4] Surviving manuscripts indicate that Liédet's work for Charles the Bold was even more extensive than is evident from the documents.[5]

Some of the miniatures Liédet painted for the two dukes[6] are more highly finished and inventive than much of his corpus, but he had a tendency to make pretty pictures and repetitive, all-purpose scenes and to handle dramatic action clumsily. His virtues, however, were those of an adept colorist and simple and direct narrator. These skills he first learned in Hesdin under the influence of such miniaturists as the Mansel Master and Simon Marmion.[7] He then refined the application of these skills into a successful formula. In addition to the internal consistency of his later miniatures, he regularly omitted border decoration.[8] This *mise-en-page* became the hallmark of a style favored by both artist and patron.[9]

Liédet's aim in enrolling in the Bruges confraternity may have been to diversify and extend his commercial activity. Under Charles the Bold, he certainly undertook work for patrons other than the duke. Most notably, he contributed to the illustration of several manuscripts made for Louis of Gruuthuse in the 1470s.[10] Still working within the upper circles of the Burgundian court, but now on a liturgical text, Liédet also illuminated the pontifical made for Ferry de Clugny, bishop of Tournai, between 1473 and 1480.[11] In contrast to those made for ducal manuscripts, Liédet's miniatures for all these volumes are accompanied by borders. These borders imitate and codify the type first found in manuscripts illuminated by Lieven van Lathem.[12]

Although there is no documentary evidence of Liédet's having assistants, the vast number of miniatures produced in his style are unlikely to have been the work of one person. The miniatures themselves indicate that almost all his collaborators worked in styles closely similar to his. The most likely explanation for this is that these collaborators were trained by him. The "Huson" Liédet recorded as a member of the Confraternity of Saint John between 1476 and 1484[13] was very probably his son, who sought to continue his father's work beyond the latter's death sometime after 1478.[14] Many miniatures certainly continued to be produced in Liédet's style after 1478.[15] By the mid-1480s, however, demand for the type of manuscripts and texts with which Liédet had enjoyed such success was in serious decline.

S. McK.

Notes

1. Paris 1993: 93–94, no. 44.

2. Also admitted to the confraternity in 1469 was another immigrant, Philippe de Mazerolles. Mazerolles's known activity in Bruges before that date lends support to the possibility that Liédet was also well established in the town before his admission.

3. The earlier works Liédet illustrated for Charles were included in volume 3 of the *Chroniques de Hainaut* (Brussels, Bibliothèque royale de Belgique, Ms. 9244; see also cat. no. 3); a *Songe du viel pelerin* (Paris, Bibliothèque nationale de France, Mss. fr. 9200–9201); a five-volume prose version of *Renaut de Montauban* (Paris, Bibliothèque de l'Arsenal, Mss. 5072–74; Munich, Bayerische Staatsbibliothek, Ms. gall. 7); and a four-volume *Histoire de Charles Martel* (see cat. no. 55). He also illustrated a *Bible moralisée* (untraced), *Vengeance de Notre Seigneur* (Chatsworth, duke of Devonshire, Ms. 7310), and *Livre des fais d'Alexandre le grant* (cat. no. 54), all of which had their texts newly transcribed by the scribe Yvonnet le Jeune. A further new manuscript he illustrated was a *Chronique abrégée de France* (Paris, Bibliothèque nationale de France, Ms. fr. 6463).

4. For a list of volumes written by Aubert and illuminated by Liédet for Philip the Good, see Charron and Gil 1999: 87.

5. Also attributed to Liédet are a *Romuléon* (Florence, Biblioteca Medicea Laurenziana, Ms. Med. Pal. 156); *Recueil des histoires troyennes* (Brussels, Bibliothèque royale, Ms. 9261); *Gérard de Nevers* (Paris, Bibliothèque nationale, Ms. fr. 24378); *Histoire d'Olivier de Castille* (Paris,

Bibliothèque nationale, Ms. fr. 12574); and *Chroniques de Pise* (Brussels, Bibliothèque royale, Ms. 9029).

6. E.g., in the *Vie de Saint Hubert* (The Hague, Koninklijke Bibliotheek, Ms. 76 F 10) and *Histoire de la belle Hélène* (Brussels, Bibliothèque royale, Ms. 9967).

7. For miniatures attributed to Liédet in this early period, see Brussels 1959: nos. 63, 66–70; and Paris 1993: 91–93, no. 43.

8. Apart from the early *Histoires romaines* and three other manuscripts attributed to Liédet's early Hesdin period (Brussels 1959: nos. 66, 68, 69), I know of only one ducal manuscript illuminated by Liédet that includes borders. This miniature at the beginning of an *Arbre des batailles* (Brussels, Bibliothèque royale, Ms. 9079, fol. 10v; Smeyers 1998: 315, fig. 35) is, however, far from typical in its full-page format. The format of the border is also far from standard.

9. De Schryver (2000: 84) considered the motivation to be one of economy rather than aesthetic preference.

10. E.g., a *Somme rurale*, dated 1471 (Paris, Bibliothèque nationale, Mss. fr. 201, 202), and a copy of Froissart's *Chroniques* (see cat. no. 71). For others, see Bruges 1992: 138, 140, 172–74, no. 7.

11. Sotheby's, London, June 18, 2002, lot 34; probably around the same time, Liédet also illuminated two books of hours (Legaré 1999: 36).

12. Bruges 1992: 140, 142.

13. Weale 1872–73a: 278–301.

14. The last references to Liédet in the confraternity records are in 1478 (Weale 1872–73a: 300, 301). His disappearance coincided with that of Philippe de Mazerolles.

15. E.g., two copies of the *Forteresse de la foi*, made for Louis of Gruuthuse (Paris, Bibliothèque nationale, Mss. fr. 20067–20069) and Edward IV (London, British Library, Royal Ms. 17 F.vi–vii). For the latter, see Backhouse 1987: pl. 10; and McKendrick 2003: pl. 68.

55

LOYSET LIÉDET

Cuttings from *Histoire de Charles Martel*
Brussels, 1463–65, and Bruges, 1467–72

The Abduction of Ydoire, leaf 1
The Byzantine Emperor Welcoming Roussillon and Martel, leaf 2
Girart and Bertha Find Sustenance at a Hermitage, leaf 5
Fromont de Lens Receiving News of the Devastation of His Land, leaf 9

Four cuttings, 23.1–23.5 × 18.1–19 cm (9⅛–9¼ × 7¼–7½ in.), trimmed from 41.3 × 29.5 cm (16¼ × 11⅝ in.); justification: originally 26.5 × 17.2 cm (10⁷⁄₁₆ × 6¾ in.); originally 29 lines of *bastarda* by David Aubert; 4 half-page miniatures

COLLECTION: Los Angeles, J. Paul Getty Museum, Ms. Ludwig XIII 6 (83.MP.149)

PROVENANCE: Philip the Good, duke of Burgundy (1419–1467); Charles the Bold, duke of Burgundy (1433–1477); probably Bibliothèque nationale, Paris, 1796; [H. P. Kraus, New York, by 1978]; to Peter and Irene Ludwig, Aachen; acquired 1983

JPGM (leaves 1, 5, 9) and RA (leaves 2, 5, 9)

One of the most prolonged geneses of a manuscript of a secular vernacular text was that of the unique copy of the rewritten stories about Girart de Roussillon, Garin le Loherain, and Charles Martel, an eighth-century Frankish leader and the grandfather of Charlemagne. Begun for Philip the Good in 1463, the manuscript remained undecorated and unbound upon his death in 1467. The final payment for its illustration and binding was not made until 1472 at the instruction of Philip's successor, Charles the Bold.[1] When completed, its four large folio volumes of more than four thousand pages in total, illustrated by no fewer than 117 miniatures, constituted one of the treasures of the Burgundian ducal library. Although the bulk of these volumes remain in Brussels (Bibliothèque royale de Belgique, Mss. 6–9), one leaf is now in Paris (Musée du Louvre, Cabinet des Dessins, R.F. 1345) and fifteen leaves, including those on display, are in Los Angeles.

Despite claims by previous scholars that David Aubert authored these volumes, he seems to have been responsible only for the transcription of the work. According to the text itself, the *Histoire de Charles Martel* was converted into prose in 1448, based on lost verse romances. A compiler's name is not given, but in its content, the text is very much in line with those compiled by Jean Wauquelin around that time. His *Girart de Roussillon* in particular concerns some of the same characters as the *Histoire de Charles Martel* and is an identifiable source for the *Histoire*. Together, all these texts reflect the ambition of Philip the Good to position himself within an illustrious tradition dating back, at the very least, to the time of the Carolingian Empire. The completion by Charles the Bold of the *Histoire de Charles Martel* for the ducal library was not only part of a pious consummation of a project undertaken by his father; it was also consonant with Charles the Bold's own egocentric ambitions and aspirations as a modern-day Charlemagne and true heir of Charlemagne's empire.

Whereas the text was copied by Aubert within the ducal household at Brussels—the first volume in 1463 and the last in 1465—the decoration was undertaken by artists

55a

LOYSET LIÉDET

Girart and Bertha Find
Sustenance at a Hermitage,
leaf 5 (detail)

based in Bruges. In 1468 the illuminator Pol Fruit was paid
for the decorated initials in the third volume, and in 1472 the
miniaturist Loyset Liédet was paid for the forty-three
miniatures in the third and fourth volumes, as well as further initials and the bindings. In confirmation of Liédet's
part in the illumination, his signature is also incorporated
into one of the miniatures at the beginning of the final volume. The echo of Eyckian artistic ambitions found in this
rare signature of a miniaturist is complemented by Eyckian
parallels in the composition of the opening miniature of the
first volume, in which the writer is depicted being visited in
his study.

Throughout the four volumes, Liédet consistently
attended to the details of the narrative. Although many of
his illustrations are generic scenes of battle, processions,
and attendance at court, most highlight and lead the viewer
through episodes particular to this story.[2] In the Getty
miniature depicting the adventures of Girart and his wife,
Bertha, for example, careful use of setting, costume, and
color helps tell in successive scenes how the temporary
plight of these two grand people forces them to seek out
food and water in the countryside like the poorest of peasants (ill. 55a). There is a greater attention to surface detail in

the miniatures of the *Histoire de Charles Martel* than in many
other miniatures attributable to Liédet, in which speed of
execution seems to be of greatest concern. Together with
Aubert's crisp *bastarda* and the plain, borderless margins,
the miniatures establish a pleasing *mise-en-page*. As with
most other works by Liédet, however, there is little drama
or emotion in the miniatures, and many of the narratives
are hindered by a colorful prettiness. Because it is so consistently present, this prettiness detracts from diversity of
episode and achieves a cumulative blandness.   S. McK.

Notes

1. For discussion of the documentary evidence, see Brussels 1959:
nos. 144–47. See also Van den Gheyn (J.) 1910.

2. The work tells first of the childhood of Charles Martel, son of
Pepin of Herstal, then of his battles with the Saracens and eventual
coronation, as well as his adventures with the young Girart, duke of
Burgundy. The second volume then tells the story of Pepin the Short,
son of Charles Martel, and the war between Girart and Charles the
Bald. Most of the rest of the work is concerned with the bitter power
struggle between Garin le Loherain and Fromont de Lens and their
successors.

sentement nest ce pas Justement ober · Si se tuist a tant
deulz listoire · Et retourne a parler du conte fromont de
lens quy pour lors estoit a bourdeaulx sur geronde · [

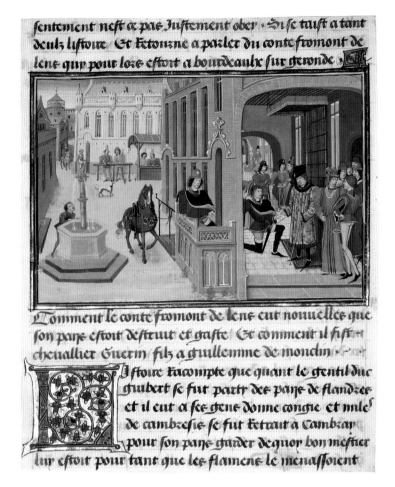

Comment le conte fromont de lens eut nouuelles que
son pays estoit destruit et gaste · Et comment il fist
cheuallier Guerin / filz a guillemme de monclin ·

Istoire racompte que quant le gentil duc
guibert se fut party des pays de flandres
et il eut a ses gens donne congie · et mise
de cambresie se fut retrait a Cambray
pour son pays garder deguor bon mestier
luy estoit pour tant que les flamens le menassoient

deablerie · Mais de tant se poeult il bien vanter que
sil chiet en mes mains · iamais de mort neschappera
que finer ne luy face ses iours par griefz tourmens ·
Touteffois labbe ne luy oza lors riens respondre pour
tant que trop le veoit tourble · Et pour ce que ien par
leray en temps et en lieu plus amplement ie men de
porte pour le present · Et retourneray listoire a parler
des deux nobles princes et vaillans cheualliers · cest
assauoir de gerard de roussillon · et de charles martel ·

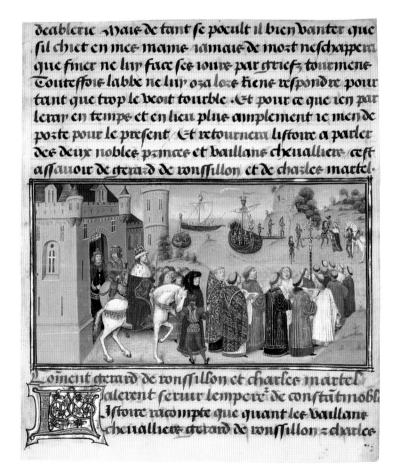

Comment gerard de roussillon et charles martel
alerent seruir lempereur de constantinoble ·

Istoire racompte que quant les vaillans
cheualliers gerard de roussillon z charles

JEAN HENNECART

Jean Hennecart is first documented as one of the artists engaged in the elaborate preparations for the Feast of the Pheasant, held by Philip the Good at Lille on February 17, 1454.[1] He was employed by the duke to work on the decorations for twelve days and was paid at a generous daily rate also paid to the illuminator Jean Le Tavernier. The next mention of Hennecart is in 1467, by which date he is said to be painter and valet de chambre of Charles the Bold, then count of Charolais. The large payment made to him at this point appears to have been for work carried out over several years and stretching back to at least 1457. This work included designs for a gold cross made for Charles at Brussels; a large noted sheet of parchment for a "cymbal"; a long parchment roll of a motet made at the birth of Mary of Burgundy (b. 1457); designs for a silver falcon; black lances and batons for Charles at festivities at Sluys and Bruges; and an illuminated and noted "cymbal" and lute. All these tasks were the staple diet of contemporary court painters. After Charles succeeded his father as duke in 1467, Hennecart continued as his official painter, most notably as one of the coordinators of the decorations for Charles's wedding celebrations in 1468. Between 1468 and 1472 Charles paid Hennecart successively for the following: the painting of arms, designs for new coinage to be made by Gerard Loyet, banners, and more designs for coinage. It is within the context of these payments that Charles also paid Hennecart for the illumination undertaken on two small parchment copies of L'Instruction d'un jeune prince, one of which has survived (cat. no. 56).

Although some doubt has been cast on whether Hennecart personally undertook the illumination of the surviving manuscript of the Instruction,[2] several observations support an attribution to him. In the first place, Hennecart definitely undertook the other work for which he was paid at the same time, namely designs for coinage. Second, as court painter, it would not have been customary for Hennecart simply to coordinate the work of illuminating ducal books. (As garde des joyaux for Charles, Jacques de Brégilles undertook this duty.)[3] Third, although Hennecart may not have been an obvious choice for illuminating the volumes, other artists who were more likely candidates may have been otherwise fully occupied. Charles's illuminator, Philippe de Mazerolles, was still occupied in 1468 on the Black Hours of Charles the Bold.[4] Another of the court's most favored illuminators, Loyset Liédet, was also engaged in an extensive campaign of illuminating ducal books (see separate biography, this part). Finally, as noted in the payment record of 1467 cited above, Hennecart had already undertaken some illumination for Charles.

The illuminations in the surviving copy of the Instruction may provide further support for crediting an attribution to Hennecart. The accomplished heraldic painting in initials and border would be well explained by his documented activity as a heraldic painter. The two marginal roundels also seem to fit well with his contemporary work on the design of coinage. Although miniatures and borders in several contemporary manuscripts are closely related in style to those in the Instruction,[5] none of these illuminations has been convincingly attributed to Hennecart. This sits well with Hennecart's having been a court painter rather than a commercial illuminator. The subtle and new iconography also is well explained as devised by an artist closely linked to the court. A further reflection of Hennecart's court position is his clear knowledge of the famous court portrait at the opening of Philip the Good's manuscript of the Chroniques de Hainaut (cat. no. 3). S. McK.

Notes

1. For this and other cited payments, see Laborde 1849–52, 1: nos. 1549, 1799–1807, 1943, 1944, 1968; 2: nos. 4035, 4039, 4044, 4732, 4794, 4880, 4896, 4898.

2. Dogaer 1987a: 86.

3. De Schryver 2000: 83–89.

4. De Schryver 1999: 50–51.

5. Delaissé (in Brussels 1959: no. 187) noted a connection between the miniature style of the Arsenal Instruction and that of the miniaturist he named Maître de Vasque de Lucène, and more generally with what he perceived as the Brussels tradition of miniature painting. He also found the border style typical of Brussels. The Arsenal miniatures certainly have points of similarity in their style with the work of Dreux Jean, and in particular with that of his follower the Master of Guillebert de Lannoy.

56

JEAN HENNECART

Guillebert de Lannoy, L'Instruction d'un jeune prince and Enseignements paternels
Brussels, 1468–70

MANUSCRIPT: 85 folios, 26.5 × 19.1 cm (10½ × 7½ in.); justification: 17 × 11.5 cm (6¾ × 4½ in.); 19 lines of bastarda; 3 half-page miniatures

HERALDRY: Full achievement of the arms of Charles the Bold encircled by collar and briquets of the Order of the Golden Fleece; motto Je l'ay emprins, all fol. 5; confronted initials CC, fols. 5, 14; linked initials CM (for Charles the Bold and Margaret of York), fol. 66; cross of Saint Andrew, fols. 5, 14, 66

BINDING: France, eighteenth century; red morocco; gold-tooled spine

COLLECTION: Paris, Bibliothèque de l'Arsenal, Ms. 5104

PROVENANCE: Charles the Bold, duke of Burgundy (1433–1477); Benedictine Abbey of Liessies, Hainaut, by 1707; Antoine-René de Voyer d'Argenson, marquess of Paulmy (1722–1787)

JPGM and RA

56a
JEAN HENNECART
*Rudolph of Norway
Receives Foliant de Ionnal's
Text*, fol. 14

On September 20, 1470, Jean Hennecart was paid by Charles the Bold's treasury for illuminating two small parchment books, each containing the text *L'Instruction de josne prince*.[1] In all the elements of their illumination, these two manuscripts were twins. Each had one large miniature accompanied by a decorated border that included roundels bearing the devices of Charles the Bold and by a decorated initial including his devices and arms. Each also had two further large miniatures without borders but with initials bearing the same devices. The number and size of smaller illuminated initials were identical in each volume, as was the number of illuminated paragraph marks.

The present manuscript (now in Paris at the Bibliothèque de l'Arsenal) has long been identified as one of these two manuscripts made for Charles the Bold.[2] Its decorative program and date correspond exactly to those listed in the payment document. Since it bears the initials of Charles the Bold and his wife, Margaret of York, it must date from after their marriage in 1468. The costume worn by figures in its miniatures is also compatible with this date.

Two texts are contained within this manuscript. The first, that named in the document, is an advisory text now thought to have been written by the Burgundian courtier Guillebert de Lannoy around 1439–42. At its core, the text constitutes a set of rules for good conduct to be followed by a young prince. Around this, however, Lannoy has woven an elaborate fiction of the type loved by readers of this period. The central narrative takes place long, long ago in Norway, where the aging King Ollerich—on his deathbed—asks his wise and trusted counselor Foliant de Ionnal to write up some helpful rules to guide his son Rudolph through the temptations and troubles that will face him

after the king's death. Foliant complies, and the advice he has written is discovered many years later by the clerk of a Picard knight and thus becomes a Burgundian court text. The second text, the *Enseignements paternels*, is a more straightforward advisory text by Guillebert de Lannoy and takes the form of a letter from Lannoy to his son.

Although the *Enseignements* did circulate beyond the Lannoy family circle, its text was copied relatively rarely in comparison to that of the more fanciful *Instruction*. Whereas the former is preserved in only four other manuscripts, the latter appears in no fewer than thirteen others. Of the other manuscripts of the *Instruction*, seven are fine illustrated copies. The earliest of these is probably the copy made for Charles the Bold's father, Philip the Good, sometime before Philip's death in 1467 (Brussels, Bibliothèque royale de Belgique, Ms. 10976). Only one other manuscript (Paris, Bibliothèque nationale de France, Ms. fr. 1216) contains both of the texts included in the present volume.

The most important aspect of the present manuscript is the gloss its miniatures offer on Lannoy's texts. Unlike the miniatures in Philip's surviving copy, those in the present manuscript do not merely narrate the principal episodes from the Norwegian fiction but couch these scenes in an explicitly contemporary setting. In its first miniature the dying king reminds contemporary viewers of Philip the Good, then recently deceased; the young Rudolph calls to mind Charles the Bold; and the aged counselor presumably alludes to Lannoy, even though he had died in 1462. In the second miniature (ill. 56a), which shows Rudolph receiving his book of advice, the inclusion of Burgundian devices

within the miniature reinforces the contemporary references. Lannoy's *Enseignements paternels* is prefaced by a miniature (ill. 56b) that visually echoes the famous prefatory miniature to Philip's copy of the *Chroniques de Hainaut* (ill. 3). As this reference to the earlier miniature makes clear, the father who offers the advice is now Philip, and its recipient is Charles. Of all the miniatures, this one offers the clearest reinterpretation of Lannoy's text.

It is interesting to speculate on the intentions behind such visual glosses on Lannoy's texts. By the time the miniatures were painted (after the death of Philip), Charles was not as young as the prince they depict. His character and likely conduct as successor to Philip the Good were, however, a pressing concern of members of the Burgundian court. As a result, several other advisory texts were written and promoted within this circle. What would have seemed more appropriate as a framework for such advice than a work originally commissioned and authorized by Charles's father? Was this, in fact, the very context in which Lannoy's text was created, at a time when Charles was between six and nine years old—closer in age to the young Rudolph? Hennecart could not have produced the present miniatures unaided. Their meaning is too subtle and at the same time too risky. Since the painter had long worked for Charles and his household, it is most likely that someone within that circle provided the program.

The influence of the images created by Hennecart was considerable. In the first place, the illustrations of the only other surviving manuscript to include both the *Instruction* and *Enseignements* (Paris, Bibliothèque nationale, Ms. fr. 1216) are closely based on Hennecart's compositions. The second and third miniatures in this other manuscript reveal only minor differences when compared with those in the Arsenal volume. (This includes the imposition into the image of the initials of the patron of the volume, Louis of Gruuthuse.) The first miniature shares the same setting as that in the Arsenal volume but the scene is reduced to the three principal participants and the poses of two of them were altered. The latter two participants are, however, based on figures created for the same characters in the second and third Arsenal miniatures. These changes were clearly made by a miniaturist from the circle of Hennecart and at a date close to that of the production of the Arsenal volume. One further manuscript (Paris, Bibliothèque de Sainte-Geneviève, Ms. 2218) repeats this simplified version of the first miniature. Two other manuscripts retain the two figure poses in the first miniature of Gruuthuse's manuscript but also include additional figures behind the principal group, as in the Arsenal manuscript.

One of two possible scenarios may explain these divergences from Hennecart's compositions. First, very soon after the Arsenal manuscript left the hands of the artist, part of the right half of the composition of the first miniature, which included the distinctive poses for Foliant and Rudolph, had possibly disappeared. Perhaps that part of a set of sketches was damaged or lost. Alternatively, Hennecart may have introduced—in the untraced twin of the Arsenal manuscript—the two alternate figure poses.

The designs for the first and second miniatures created by Hennecart in the southern Netherlands also traveled with the text of the *Instruction* to the Loire Valley. Sometime in the late 1470s a French artist produced versions of these designs in a manuscript made for a member of the circle of Louis XI (Baltimore, Walters Art Museum, Ms. W.308).[3] Given the very recent creation of these designs at the heart of the Burgundian court, their rapid reuse in the very different artistic milieu of Bourges (in the Loire Valley) is somewhat surprising. One possible means of their transmission is suggested by another copy of the *Instruction* in Paris,[4] which appears to have been made for the young François Phébus, count of Foix (d. 1483). In this manuscript Lannoy's text was pirated by Bernard de Béarn, bâtard de Comminges (d. 1497), for presentation to the young man probably just before he became king of Navarre in 1479. In the late 1460s de Béarn was recorded as a potential client for another Burgundian text,[5] and by his death his library certainly included several such texts, which led some scholars to believe that de Béarn's copy of the *Instruction* had also been produced in Flanders.[6] Contrary to these earlier views,[7] however, Nicole Reynaud attributes the decoration of the *Instruction* in the Foix manuscript to French artists.[8] Also, although the illustrations of both the Foix manuscript and the stylistically related Walters manuscript reveal similarities to the Netherlandish compositions, these points of similarity lie in different areas in each of these two manuscripts. In the deathbed scene, for example, the Walters miniature accurately copies such details as the stick in Foliant's left hand, but the Paris miniature shows his hand without the supporting stick. And yet the Paris miniature includes the window at the rear, which the Walters miniature omits. Such independent use of the same models suggests that either a set of models or a third manuscript traveled to the Loire. One possible way in which a manuscript might have become available is through the defection of a Burgundian courtier to the court of Louis XI before or after the fall of Charles the Bold in 1477.   S. McK.

Notes

1. Hennecart's quittance is most accurately transcribed in Martin 1917: 164–65. The text published by Laborde (1849–52, 2: 223–24) contains several inaccuracies.
2. The other copy is untraced.
3. Randall 1992: no. 151.
4. Paris, Société des manuscrits autographes français, Ms. 80-11.
5. Gachard 1845: 147.
6. Desbarreaux-Bernard and Baudouin 1872: 82–131.
7. Sale cat., Sotheby's, London, December 20, 1980, lot 88.
8. Paris 1993: no. 79a.

DREUX JEAN (B)
For biography, see part 2

57

FOLLOWER OF DREUX JEAN

Grande Chronique de Normandie
Brussels, ca. 1465–68

MANUSCRIPT: 257 folios, 36 × 26 cm (14¼ × 10¼ in.); justification: 22 × 15.5 cm (8⅞ × 6⅛ in.); 25 lines of *bastarda*; 15 large miniatures

HERALDRY: Escutcheons with the arms of Crèvecoeur differenced by a crescent azure, surmounted by helm, mantling, and crest of two arms holding cloven heart dripping blood, fols. 1, 151

BINDING: France, seventeenth or eighteenth century; parchment over pasteboard

COLLECTION: London, The British Library, Yates Thompson Ms. 33

PROVENANCE: Philippe de Crèvecoeur, seigneur des Querdes (d. 1494); Charles-Antoine Bernard, marquess of Avernes, in 1767; by descent to M. de Vauquelin des Chênes (d. 1850), Ailly, by 1839; Ambroise Firmin-Didot (1790–1876) [his sale, Hôtel Drouot, Paris, June 6–15, 1878, lot 64]; [to Messrs. Morgand and Fatout]; to the comte de Toustain, in 1881; [sale, Sotheby's, London, July 9, 1884, lot 175]; [Bernard Quaritch, *Catalogue 369*, 1886, no. 35728, and *Catalogue 103*, 1890, no. 411]; [sale, Hôtel Drouot, Paris, February 27, 1892, lot 112]; to Henri Bordes, Bordeaux; to Henry Yates Thompson (1838–1928), in 1898 (his Ms. XCVIII); bequeathed 1941 to the British Museum

RA

Compiled by an anonymous Norman probably around 1350, the *Grande Chronique de Normandie* is based on a thirteenth-century chronicle of Normandy and the twelfth-century *Roman de Rou* of Wace. It tells the history of the dukes of Normandy from the first duke, Rollo (in the ninth century), to just after the accession of Henry III as king of England in 1216. Unlike another chronicle of Normandy that became, at the Burgundian court, an official chronicle of the origins of Franco-Flemish conflict,[1] the present text was copied mainly in France and found little favor at the Burgundian court.[2]

When, sometime between 1465 and 1468, a Flemish miniaturist illustrated a copy of the *Grande Chronique*, it seems that he had no illustrated exemplar on which to base his miniatures. Instead he fell back on compositions and figure groups that had been created nearly twenty years earlier for the illustration of other chronicles and secular texts. Several of his pastiches, such as *The Marriage of Duke Rollo* (ill. 57), echo compositions found in three manuscripts of texts by Jean Wauquelin produced in 1448.[3] Such dependency is most neatly explained if the illuminator was a follower of Dreux Jean, who is thought to have coordinated work on the Wauquelin manuscripts.[4] Within the pastiches, several of which rely on the same models, the illuminator of the present manuscript employed a distinctive muddy palette, awkwardly elongated his figures, and selectively updated the costumes.

The patron of the manuscript, Philippe de Crèvecoeur (d. 1494), is not well known as a bibliophile.[5] He was, however, raised at the Burgundian court alongside the future Charles the Bold and later became one of his most trusted courtiers.[6] After Philippe's defection to the French king in 1478 upon the death of Charles the Bold, the Bruges book producer Colard Mansion offered him a translation of the *Dialogus Creaturum moralizatus* of Maynus de Mayneriis,[7] and an anonymous writer dedicated to him Cicero's *De amicitia* and a similar text by the Italian humanist Guarino da Verona.[8]

The present manuscript may be datable to before 1468 on the basis of the omission of the collar of the Order of the Golden Fleece from the manuscript's heraldic display; Philippe was granted the collar in that year.   S. McK.

Notes

1. Hasenohr and Zink 1992: 289.

2. Only two paper copies and one parchment copy, in which the illustrations were never executed, belonged to the Burgundian ducal library (Labory 1997–99: 201).

3. Brussels, Bibliothèque royale de Belgique, Ms. 9242; Paris, Bibliothèque nationale de France, Ms. fr. 9342; Vienna, Österreichische Nationalbibliothek, Ms. 2549. The miniature *Duke Rollo* is a pastiche of the composition of *The Altar of Diana* (Brussels, Bibliothèque royale, Ms. 9242, fol. 175v).

4. The further similarity of the opening border with those in the Brussels *Benois* adds to the connections with the work of Dreux Jean.

5. The Crèvecoeur arms are included in illuminated copies of Jean Mansel's *Fleur des histoires* (Thoss 1987: no. 10; Sotheby's, London, June 17, 1997, lot 59, now Ms. 117 in the collection of Lawrence J. Schoenberg) and Christine de Pisan's *Livre des trois vertus* (Paris 1993: 93). Since the arms in these two manuscripts do not include Philippe's mark of difference, however, they cannot be his. Instead they probably relate to his elder half brother Anthony, chamberlain to Charles from 1447. Anthony has recently been identified as the owner of a *Bible historiale* (Paris, Bibliothèque Mazarine, Ms. 312; Komada 2000: 59–62) and a fine book of hours (Leeds, University Library, Ms. 4; Arras 2000: no. 31).

6. De Smedt (R.) 2000: no. 69; see also Harsgor 1980: 1081–87.

7. Mansion's preface, which names Crèvecoeur as the dedicatee, is preserved in Vienna, Österreichische Nationalbibliothek, Ms. 2572 (see Van Praet 1829: 20–22; and Thoss 1987: no. 65). A second manuscript of the *Dialogue des créatures*, the preface of which names Louis of Gruuthuse and is dated 1482, is described in König 1991, no. 15. See, in general, Bruges 1981: 209–10.

8. Sotheby's, London, June 25, 1985, lot 70. The latter manuscript—transcribed just after the text was written—is datable to between 1491 and 1494.

57
FOLLOWER OF
DREUX JEAN
*The Marriage of Duke
Rollo*, fol. 24v (detail)

LIEVEN VAN LATHEM

Lieven van Lathem—from the village of Latem, not far from Ghent—joined the painter's guild in Ghent in 1454. This is the earliest evidence of his life. The year 1456 found him in the service of Philip the Good, a relationship that seems to have continued through 1459. He enjoyed the patronage of the Burgundian dukes and their successors throughout his career, even when not officially attached to the court. A book of hours he illuminated for Philip in the following decade survives (Paris, Bibliothèque nationale de France, Ms. n.a. lat. 16428).[1] From April to July 1468 Van Lathem was one of the most highly paid of a team of artists involved in the decorations for the chapter of the Order of the Golden Fleece held in Bruges in May, followed by the decorations for the "entremets" at the wedding celebration of Charles the Bold held there two months later. The following year Charles paid him for the illumination of a prayer book (cat. no. 16). In the next decade he illuminated the Hours of Mary of Burgundy (cat. no. 19), long thought to be for Charles's daughter, Mary, or for another member of his family. The period 1487 to 1490 witnessed the artist's service to Maximilian I, in the last year as "varlet de chambre" and "paintre du roy." He may have continued in this capacity until his death in 1493.

Given Van Lathem's strong connection to the Burgundian household, it is not surprising that he illuminated a series of secular texts for eminent court bibliophiles: the Roman de Gillion de Trazegnies (cat. no. 58), the Histoire de Jason (cat. no. 59), and the Pseudo-Aristotle Secret des secrets (cat. no. 60), all for Louis of Gruuthuse, and a magnificent Froissart (Berlin, Staatsbibliothek, Ms. Depot Breslau 1) for Anthony of Burgundy. He collaborated with two other favorites of the Burgundian court: the scribes David Aubert (cat. no. 58 and the Berlin Froissart) and Nicolas Spierinc (cat. nos. 16, 17, 19).

According to Alphonse Wauters, Lieven was the son of an artist, Leon van Lathem.[2] His father-in-law, Jacob de Meyster, was a bookseller from Amsterdam who joined the Antwerp guild in 1457. His son Jacob was a painter, served Philip the Handsome as valet de chambre, and traveled with the prince to Spain. Lieven the younger was a goldsmith and engraver, also in the service of Philip.

The documents make clear that Lieven van Lathem spent most of his career in Antwerp, but employment brought him to many cities in northwestern Europe. He resigned from the Ghent guild in 1459 after a dispute involving his dues and the impact of his service to the duke. He may have visited Utrecht around 1460, perhaps the result of a family connection, when he collaborated with the Master of Catherine of Cleves on a book of hours.[3] In 1462 he joined the painters' guild in Antwerp and continued to live in that city until his death. Around 1468 he is recorded in Brussels, and in 1469 he delivered to the duke in The Hague the prayer book that he had illuminated for him. Several decades later he returned to Bruges, where he undertook part of his service to Maximilian.

Despite documentation of his artistic activity over nearly forty years and evidence of his role as a painter,[4] only Van Lathem's manuscript illuminations survive and only from the period of the 1460s to the early 1480s.[5] This lack of later illuminations is a mystery, all the more so given the originality and power of the known examples. The Prayer Book of Charles the Bold of 1469 is the single documented work and the foundation for all attributions. Van Lathem was a gifted narrative artist, as witnessed by his epic narrative cycles for the Roman de Gillion de Trazegnies and the Histoire de Jason. They set the standard for secular narration for the following decades. His figure style and narrative conventions were emulated by such artists as the Master of Margaret of York and his associates (see cat. nos. 61–63), including the Master of Fitzwilliam 268 (cat. nos. 52, 64, 65), all of whom specialized in secular texts. Van Lathem showed a strong interest in landscape perspectives, especially the meandering spatial recessions described by winding rivers and irregular shorelines. In miniatures such as Christ Appearing to Saint James the Greater (ill. 16a) and Saint Christopher (fig. 28) in the Prayer Book of Charles the Bold or the marine subjects in the Chatsworth Gillion, he showed a feeling for both the dense atmosphere of landscape vistas and the scale of landscape that looks forward to the paintings of Joachim Patinir (ill. 16a and figs. 28, 29). Another distinctive feature of Van Lathem's art is the border decoration, especially the battling griffins and hybrids of the Gothic tradition, which he drew with such grace and spirit that the visual appeal of his borders rivaled and sometimes eclipsed that of the miniatures they accompanied.

T. K.

Notes

1. Thomas (M.) 1976.
2. Wauters 1890–91: col. 422.
3. Boon 1964: cols. 247–51.
4. The reputation of the artist lived on for at least a generation in the praises of the poet Jean Lemaire de Belges, in his Couronne Margaretique of 1505, and still later, around 1520, in Marc Antonio Michiel's curious assertion of Van Lathem's participation in the Grimani Breviary (cat. no. 126), which was produced fully a generation after his death (Stecher 1982–91, 4: 163; Frimmel 1888: 104, respectively).
5. Recently Campbell (1998: 298) identified a painting in the National Gallery in London that may have been initiated by Van Lathem or his workshop but that was finished by artists of another generation. Buck (2001: 79–85) has adduced a drawing as a study for a lost painting by the artist.

que de bone elle deult enfanter mcfmement difout
que lenfant mozu lozs que il bint fur terre poquoy
Ieuz telle doulcur au cuer que ic fie ferement de no
Iamais Retoiner pdela Si adumt affes toft apres q̃
au pres de cefte cite le fouldan liura bne moult fierc
bataille alencoutre des fararis lesquelz furent defco
fis et ocis Ceftuy amauttry dont bone me parlez
y laiffa la bie Par ma for fire de ces nonuelles ne
doit nul bon cuer eftre dolant mais ioieulx Selon
fa defferte il a receu fon guerzedon come raifo eftoit

Comment meffire gillion de trafignies pruft con
gie du fouldan pour retourner en fa terre Coment
il luy promuft de aler pardela fil le mandoit Et
coment il amena en hatnau fa feconde feme la belle
gracienne filles du fouldan et fes deur filz ich z grand

58a

LIEVEN VAN LATHEM
*Gillion and Family Take
Leave of the Sultan,*
fol. 188v

58

LIEVEN VAN LATHEM

Roman de Gillion de Trazegnies
Antwerp, after 1464

MANUSCRIPT: iii + 237 + iii folios, 37 × 25.5 cm (14⅝ × 10 in.);
justification: 24.3 × 15.8 cm (9⅝ × 6¼ in.); 27 lines of *bastarda*
attributed to David Aubert; 8 half-page miniatures, 44 historiated
initials

HERALDRY: Escutcheons, partly supported by lion helmed and
bearing collar of the Order of the Golden Fleece, with the arms of
Gruuthuse partly overpainted by the royal arms of France, fols. 9,
21, 36v, 150v; motto *Plus est en vous* and bombard device in decorated
borders, fols. 9, 36v

BINDING: London, ca. 1815; blind-tooled orange morocco; full
achievement of the arms of the sixth duke of Devonshire on both
covers; green silk doublures and endleaves

COLLECTION: Chatsworth, duke of Devonshire, Ms. 7535

PROVENANCE: Louis of Gruuthuse (1422–1492); Louis XII, king of
France (1462–1515) (Blois inventory of 1518 [no. 97]); William George
Spencer Cavendish, sixth duke of Devonshire (1790–1858)

JPGM and RA

The eight miniatures and forty-four historiated initials
that Lieven van Lathem produced for Louis of Gruuthuse's copy of the romance *Gillion de Trazegnies* constitute
his most ambitious narrative cycle. The beauty of this
sequence of illustrations and the subtlety in the handling of
narrative, mood, and human emotion have few parallels
among contemporary manuscripts. Of the spectacular
large miniatures, one that is particularly successful is Van
Lathem's depiction of the hero, Gillion, and his second wife

saying their sad farewells to the sultan of Egypt (ill. 58a).
Even within Gruuthuse's extensive and refined collection,
this volume must have been regarded as a remarkable artistic achievement.

The text Van Lathem illustrated is a typical late
medieval prose romance relating the high adventures of a
bigamist knight from Hainaut in the exotic lands of Egypt
and Persia. Captured on his return from a pilgrimage to the
Holy Land, Gillion de Trazegnies is saved from death by
the intervention of the enamored daughter of the sultan,
Gracienne; in return, he enters the sultan's service. Back in
Hainaut, another noble, Amaury d'Ormais, seeks favor
with Gillion's abandoned wife, Marie, by volunteering to
search for her husband. But once Amaury finds Gillion,
treachery leads him to tell the knight that his wife and twin
sons are dead. But because Amaury fails to return to Hainaut, the twins decide to seek out their father themselves,
and on finding him, reveal Amaury's deception. Having
married Gracienne before the twins' arrival, Gillion finds
himself in an awkward position. To resolve this situation,
both women agree to enter a convent, then die. Gillion
returns to Egypt but is subsequently reunited—in death—
with his two wives; after he has died in battle, his heart is
returned to Hainaut and is buried between the two women
at the Olivet convent in Binche.

According to the work's prologue, it was their three
tombs that prompted the author's interest in Gillion's story.
Intrigued by the unusual burial, he asked for more information and received from the abbot "a small book on
parchment written in very ancient script most unclear in
the Italian language." It was supposedly from that text that

58b
LIEVEN VAN LATHEM
*Gillion's Son in Combat
with the Saracen Lucion,*
fol. 134v

he produced his story in French. The French text reveals little of certainty, however, except that it was composed sometime in the middle of the fifteenth century in Hainaut. The author remains unknown, although for a time David Aubert was erroneously credited with the creation of the *Gillion*. It is unclear to modern critics whether, like other similar prose romances, the *Gillion* is based on an older verse text.

The *Gillion* appears to have had a very limited circulation. The Chatsworth manuscript is one of only four surviving manuscripts of the romance. Of these, the most closely related is the one now in Dülmen, Germany, the text of which was copied by Aubert for Anthony of Burgundy in 1463, only one year before he copied the volume discussed here. Aubert's opening dedication to Anthony is clearly the model for his later dedication of the text to Louis of Gruuthuse in the present volume. The Dülmen and Chatsworth manuscripts, unlike the other two copies, contain the "longer version" of the romance and are deluxe volumes, including fine decoration and illustrations. Interpolations, including the rubrics in the Chatsworth manuscript, show, however, that Aubert did not merely recopy the text of the earlier manuscript, but drew on a second, complementary source.

At first glance, one notices significant differences between the Chatsworth and the Dülmen manuscripts, both in the format and in the style of the border and miniature decoration. Most obviously, the Dülmen manuscript groups its illustrations in tiered blocks of two, three, or four scenes within an overall frame on single pages. As a result, only nine pages bear its thirty illustrations. The Chatsworth manuscript spreads its illustrations more evenly through the text, with large miniatures and historiated initials. The Dülmen manuscript also restricts its border decoration to the outer right- or left-hand margins and never achieves the full decorative impact of the lavish borders of the Chatsworth manuscript. Much of the impact of the Chatsworth manuscript results, of course, from the greater invention and more assured use of color of a much more talented artist. Despite claims to the contrary,[1] the miniatures appear not to be by the same hand as those in the Dülmen manuscript. As was suggested some time ago,[2] the style of the Dülmen miniatures has more in common with that of Dreux Jean than with that of other works attributed to Van Lathem. Dissimilarities of style between the two sets of miniatures are certainly difficult to explain in terms of the same artist if only one year lies between the painting of one and the painting of the other. For example, in his portrayal of the unwitting combat between Gillion's twin sons—depicted in four successive moments—the Dülmen artist adopted a quasi-cinematic presentation that never is evident in the Chatsworth miniatures. His landscapes are also less formulaic than those in the Chatsworth manuscript, and his large crowds of onlookers do not appear in the latter manuscript.

The miniatures of the Dülmen manuscript are, however, linked in subtle ways to those of the volume at Chatsworth. Despite overall differences of format, style, and selection of subjects, a few similarities occur in the composition and choice of subject in particular miniatures. Most notably, the Chatsworth historiated initial that shows Gillion and his wife Marie fishing appears to be based on the same visual model as that for the same subject depicted in the opening miniature of the Dülmen manuscript.

Reconsideration of the decoration of the Chatsworth manuscript may offer an explanation of the significant stylistic differences from that of the Dülmen manuscript. First, it is clear that Van Lathem took great liberties with the space left to him, space in which he introduced historiated initials. In most cases he greatly extended the initials and the picture space into the outer margins, sometimes in two directions, if at the top or bottom of the page. Given that historiated initials are a rarity both in his oeuvre and in Flemish manuscripts of this period in general, it is questionable whether they were part of the original plan for the volume or whether van Lathem was involved in such a plan. Second, the most distinctive aspect of the decorative borders in the Chatsworth manuscript is that they are not full, but three-sided borders (ill. 58a). Three-sided borders are uncommon in Flemish manuscript production as a whole and have not been found in other manuscripts decorated by Van Lathem. Given the obvious practical difficulties of painting an inner border within a bound volume, the three-sided borders may indicate that the volume was already bound when these borders were painted. All of this may suggest that, as happened in other manuscripts, the decoration of the Chatsworth manuscript was not completed as originally envisaged. The spaces occupied by Van Lathem's historiated initials may have been intended merely for decorated initials, the only spaces originally intended for illustrations being those now occupied by his large miniatures. For some reason the original plan may have been abandoned and the manuscript laid to one side. Only when the services of such a talented artist as Van Lathem became available to him did Louis of Gruuthuse return to the manuscript. Strong similarities in format and style of decoration between the Chatsworth manuscript and the Paris *Jason* (cat. no. 59), as well as the evidence that the same border artist worked on both manuscripts, suggest that this resumption of work on the volume took place later in the 1460s—possibly, as in the case of the *Jason*, sometime after 1467.

To argue for such a delayed dating for the illumination of the Chatsworth manuscript may seem to go against the evidence of the text itself. In his preface Aubert explicitly stated that in 1464 Louis not only ordered him to copy the text of the *Roman* but also had that text decorated and bound. Given, however, that these words appear at the very beginning of Gruuthuse's manuscript and that they merely repeat the wording of the colophon to Anthony of Burgundy's earlier copy, there is, I think, scope for skepticism as to whether what Aubert stated in the present manuscript actually took place.

S. McK.

Notes
1. Most notably by Wolf (E.) 1996.
2. Brussels 1959: no. 240.

59

LIEVEN VAN LATHEM

Raoul Lefèvre, *Histoire de Jason*
Antwerp, ca. 1470

MANUSCRIPT: iv + 163 folios, 38.8 × 27.3 cm (15¼ × 10¾ in.);
justification: 24.8 × 16.8 cm (9¾ × 6⅝ in.); 27 lines of *bastarda*
attributed to David Aubert; 18 half-page miniatures

HERALDRY: Escutcheons, partly supported by lion helmed and
bearing collar of the Order of the Golden Fleece, with the arms of
Gruuthuse partly overpainted by the royal arms of France, fols. 1,
2, 29, etc.; overpainted standard and banner, fol. 1; bombard device,
fols. 52v, 83, 132, 153v

BINDING: Paris, seventeenth or eighteenth century; red morocco;
the royal arms of France gold-stamped on both covers

COLLECTION: Paris, Bibliothèque nationale de France, Ms. fr. 331

PROVENANCE: Louis of Gruuthuse (1422–1492); Louis XII, king
of France (1462–1515) (Blois inventories of 1518 [no. 115] and 1544
[no. 1386])

JPGM

Lieven van Lathem was responsible for what is arguably
the finest and most extensive sequence of images illustrating the story of Jason, the hero from classical mythology who became one of the most favored models of
chivalric conduct at the court of Philip the Good. As in the
case of the *Gillion de Trazegnies* (cat. no. 58), Van Lathem
produced this significant and highly accomplished narrative cycle for Louis of Gruuthuse. Here too the text he illustrated had been transcribed by David Aubert.

The *Histoire de Jason* was written probably around 1460
by Raoul Lefèvre, a historically elusive figure who claimed
to be chaplain to Philip the Good but may have been a servant of Jean de Créquy. Like Lefèvre's later work—the
Recueil des histoires troyennes (see cat. no. 123)—the *Jason*
was dedicated to Philip. The *Jason* tells of the adventures of
the young Greek hero Jason and his companions, the Argonauts, on their expedition to Colchis, on the Black Sea, to
recover the Golden Fleece, and of his fatal attraction to
Medea, daughter of the king of Colchis. Interest in this
story has a long history. Its revival as a prequel to the story
of the Trojan War within the highly influential romance
tradition ensured the story's popularity among medieval
nobles.[1] Most significantly, Philip the Good had founded
the chivalric Order of the Golden Fleece in 1430. The members of this order aspired to emulate Jason's example, and
they were presented with a livery collar bearing the device
of the Golden Fleece won by Jason.

Unlike the *Recueil*, the *Jason* appears to have had a very
limited circulation in manuscript form.[2] In addition to the
volume discussed here, only three manuscripts survive,
two of which belonged to Philip the Good himself and
to the Burgundian bibliophile Jean de Wavrin (New York,
Morgan Library, Ms. M.119; Paris, Bibliothèque de l'Arsenal, Ms. 5067; Paris, Bibliothèque nationale, Ms. fr. 12570).
Although they are all illustrated, Louis of Gruuthuse's manuscript is by far the most lavish, Philip's copy having colored miniatures of moderate quality and the two others
only grisaille miniatures. They do not appear to be based

on a common model. Louis of Gruuthuse's manuscript is a
conscious revival of Lefèvre's text after Philip's death. Its
revised dedication to Louis, together with Van Lathem's
fine illustrations, suggests a particular interest in the story.[3]

Except for the opening presentation miniature,[4] all the
miniatures depict episodes from Jason's story. This they do
in spacious settings, the eye frequently led beyond the main
subject in the foreground and through successive planes by
means of winding paths and rivers, featuring rocky out-
crops, tents, and cityscapes along the way. Within this
complex setting, Van Lathem included further episodes
from Jason's story that work together with his sensitive
treatment of the principal subjects to suggest a particularly
careful reading of Lefèvre's text on his part. As ever, the
miniaturist revels in a complex patchwork of color and fine
detail yet consistently maintains a firm grip on the whole
composition. Jason's battles (fols. 29, 83) become a tour de
force of color balance. His dramatic encounters with the
dragon guarding the Golden Fleece and with the avenging
Medea (fols. 106v and ill. 59) reveal the artist's delight in the
monsters' writhing, rainbow-colored forms. Van Lathem's
use of more muted color for the setting of the poignant
scene where the lovesick young girl Mirro leaves home in
pursuit of Jason reveals a sensitivity to the human emotions
that lie behind the actions.   S. McK.

Notes
1. En route to Colchis, Jason and Hercules laid siege to and
destroyed Troy, thus fueling the dispute between Greeks and Trojans
that culminated in the famous Trojan War. Lefèvre himself returned
to this story at greater length in book 2 of his *Recueil*.
2. Its circulation was enhanced by an early first printing at Bruges
between 1476 and 1478 and also by early translations into English
and Dutch.
3. Louis became a knight of the Order of the Golden Fleece in 1461.
By that date, however, Gideon had officially replaced Jason as patron
of the order. It was only after Philip's death in 1467 that some attempt
was made to revive Jason, most notably in the *Histoire de la toison d'or*
by Guillaume Fillastre.
4. The collar of the Order of the Golden Fleece worn by the male
figure receiving the book was—like other marks of Louis's ownership
and Burgundian allegiance in his manuscripts—overpainted after the
Jason was passed on to Louis XII.

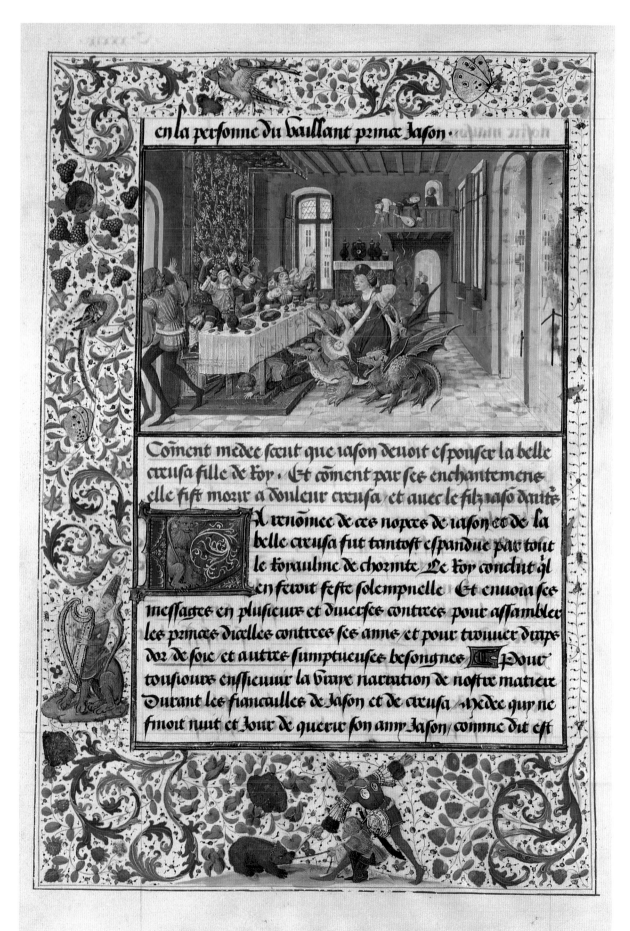

59
LIEVEN VAN
LATHEM
Medea Kills Jason's Son,
fol. 139v

60

LIEVEN VAN LATHEM AND AN
ASSISTANT / FOLLOWER OF MASTER OF
THE HARLEY FROISSART

Pseudo-Aristotle, *Secret des secrets*, translation of *Secretum secretorum*; and Jacob van Gruytrode, *Miroir de l'âme pécheresse*, translation by Jean Miélot of *Speculum aureum animae peccatricis*

Antwerp, ca. 1470

MANUSCRIPT: ii + 121 folios, 35 × 24 cm (13¼ × 9½ in.); justification: 22.5 × 15.2 cm (8⅞ × 6 in.); 25 lines of *bastarda* attributed to David Aubert; 2 half-page miniatures

HERALDRY: Escutcheon with the arms of Gruuthuse supported by lion helmed and bearing collar of the Order of the Golden Fleece, overpainted by the royal arms and crest of France, fol. 7; motto *Plus est en vous* on standard overpainted with same, fol. 7

BINDING: Paris, mid-nineteenth century; blue-green crushed morocco, with gilt-lined compartments in black; initials *JL* crowned and *Zoulre* gold-stamped on spine

COLLECTION: Paris, Bibliothèque nationale de France, Ms. fr. 562

PROVENANCE: Louis of Gruuthuse (1422–1492); Louis XII, king of France (1462–1515) (Blois inventory of 1518 [no. 214])

Ⓞne of the manuscripts illuminated by Lieven van Lathem for Louis of Gruuthuse is a small volume containing two short texts. The first, entitled *Secret des secrets*, relates advice purportedly offered by the philosopher Aristotle to Alexander the Great. Of Near Eastern origin, this text came to enjoy wide popularity among western nobles and was translated into Latin in the thirteenth century by Philip of Tripoli. The present text is a rewriting of one of two French translations that were widely read during the fifteenth century.[1] At the head of this text Van Lathem introduced a miniature depicting Alexander receiving Aristotle's advice (ill. 60). Although embellished with fanciful costumes, and thereby distanced from the contemporary, the miniature also encourages comparison of distant events with contemporary ones. Its clear visual reference to a contemporary presentation scene furthers the parallel commonly made between the Macedonian ruler and the duke of Burgundy. A spacious open loggia setting and landscape—along with the miniaturist's fine handling of color, light, and figure drawing—produce a most impressive opening miniature. The subsidiary decoration and *mise-en-page* are extremely close to those of Louis of Gruuthuse's *Gillion de Trazegnies* (cat. no. 58) and *Histoire de Jason* (cat. no. 59). This close relationship suggests a similar dating for the present manuscript of around 1470.

The second text in the manuscript—added by another scribe—is a translation of Jacob van Gruytrode's *Speculum*. Some attempt was made to match the two parts of the manuscript, but the artistic styles of both border and miniature are very different. The miniature that introduces the second text was apparently painted by an assistant or follower of the Master of the Harley Froissart who illuminated several other manuscripts for Louis of Gruuthuse.[2]

The translation of the *Speculum* was completed by the Burgundian court writer Jean Miélot in 1451.[3] Copies were made for Philip the Good in 1451 and for his wife, Isabella of Portugal, in 1457 (Brussels, Bibliothèque royale de Belgique, Ms. 11123; Lille, Bibliothèque municipale, Ms. 128, fols. 3–95v). Louis himself came to own another, humbler copy that was written at Abbeville in 1473 (Paris, Bibliothèque nationale, Ms. fr. 1001). Jacob van Gruytrode's exposure of worldly vanities in this second text contrasts sharply with the worldly advice of the first.   S. McK.

Notes
1. Monfrin (1982: 91) suggested that this rewriting is the work of Jean Miélot, the translator responsible for the second text in this volume. Monfrin was, however, incorrect in attributing the transcription of the volume to Miélot.
2. See the biography of the Master of the Harley Froissart, this part.
3. Perdrizet 1907: 476, no. 9. Miélot's autograph manuscript is The Hague, Koninklijke Bibliotheek, Ms. 76 E9 (Smeyers 1998: 319–20, fig. 44). For a different translation of the same text, see cat. no. 97.

60
LIEVEN VAN LATHEM
*Alexander the Great
Receives Aristotle's Text.*
In Pseudo-Aristotle, fol. 7

RA

MASTER OF MARGARET OF YORK GROUP (B)

For biography, see part 2

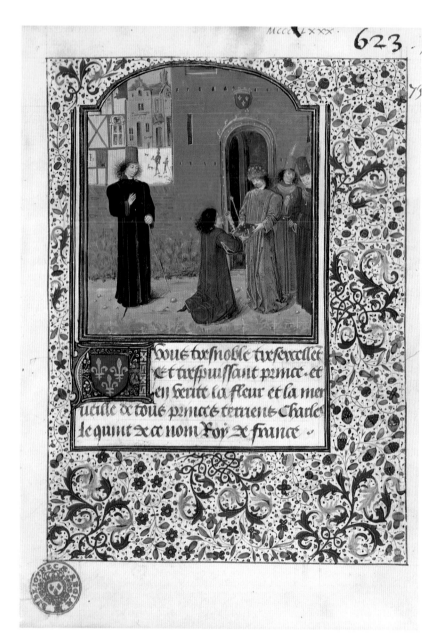

61

MASTER OF
MARGARET OF YORK
*Charles V of France
Receives Jacques
Bauchant's Text,* fol. 1

61

MASTER OF MARGARET OF YORK

Pseudo-Seneca, *Des Remèdes de fortune*, translation by Jacques Bauchant of *De remediis fortuitorum*; and Albertano da Brescia, *Livre de Mélibée et Prudence*, translation by Renaut de Louhans of *Liber consolationis et consilii*

Bruges, ca. 1470

MANUSCRIPT: iii + 98 + i folios, 25.7 × 18.6 cm (10⅛ × 7⁵⁄₁₆ in.); justification: 14 × 10.3 cm (5½ × 4 in.); 17 lines of *bastarda*; 3 half-page miniatures

HERALDRY: Escutcheon in initial with the arms of Louis of Gruuthuse overpainted by the arms of France, fol. 1

BINDING: Paris, seventeenth or eighteenth century; red morocco; the royal arms of France gold-stamped on both covers

COLLECTION: Paris, Bibliothèque nationale de France, Ms. fr. 1090

PROVENANCE: Louis of Gruuthuse (1422–1492); Louis XII, king of France (1462–1515) (Blois inventories of 1518 [no. 216] and 1544 [no. 1395])

JPGM

In this small manuscript two short texts promote the consolation of reason. In the first, *Des Remèdes de fortune*, the ancient Roman author Seneca seeks to console his troubled friend Calyo. In the second, *Livre de Mélibée et Prudence*, the young noble Mélibée is persuaded by his wife, Prudence, to seek reconciliation with, not revenge on, those who have abused his family. Whereas this simplified French version of Albertano da Brescia's scholastic debate was popular with late medieval nobles,[1] the first text is preserved in only four other manuscripts. Each of these was produced in the southern Netherlands; two were made for Philip the Good and one for Margaret of York (see cat. no. 43).[2] Only the present manuscript preserves the original dedication to Charles V of France, in which the translator is identified as the king's sergeant at arms, Jacques Bauchant.[3]

The three miniatures that illustrate these two texts in the present manuscript serve as good examples of how the Master of Margaret of York adapted contemporary formulae for such small-scale works.[4] A simplified presentation scene (ill. 61), for example—in which the figures are placed in a narrow foreground before a flowering hedge and an interior opens up to the right—was easy for him to repeat and for others to imitate. Yet the uniqueness of the first text, *Des Remèdes de fortune*, is complemented by the intrusion into this pictorial formula of a customized detail: appearing in two scenes—both the opening presentation to Charles V and the depiction of Seneca's debate—is none other than the patron of the manuscript, Louis of Gruuthuse. Gruuthuse is identified not only by his collar of the Order of the Golden Fleece but also by the long black robe and red bonnet in which he is portrayed in his copies of *Horloge de sapience* (Paris, Bibliothèque nationale de France, Mss. fr. 455, 456), *Cité de Dieu* (Paris, Bibliothèque nationale, Ms. fr. 17), *Romuléon* (Turin, Biblioteca nazionale, Ms. L.I.4), and *Les Douze Dames de rhétorique* (cat. no. 69).⁵   S. McK.

Notes

1. Thirty-nine copies are noted in Roques 1938: 493–503.

2. For Philip's copies, see Brussels 1967a: nos. 31, 228; see also Gaspar and Lyna 1984–89, 3: no. 277.

3. The others open with a dedication to Philip the Good, in which the translation is claimed by his "orateur." *Pace* Gaspar and Lyna (1984–89, 3: 133), the manuscript discussed here is not the "original." Either the "original," however, or a copy of it must have served as its exemplar. Given Louis of Gruuthuse's known interest in the books of Charles V, it is likely that his acquisition of this text was a conscious one.

4. The volume discussed here is particularly closely related to one other small-format volume and two larger-format manuscripts with miniatures from the circle of the Master of Margaret of York (London, British Library, Add. Ms. 18798; Paris, Bibliothèque nationale de France, Mss. fr. 455, 456; cat. no. 63). The miniature pages of all four of these manuscripts are identical in their *mise-en-page*, border decoration, and major decorated initials. Particularly characteristic of the borders is the extremely contorted blue and gold acanthus.

5. He appears dressed in a similar long gold robe and red bonnet in his copy of the *Vie de Saint Hubert* (Paris, Bibliothèque nationale, Ms. fr. 424). For reproductions of four of these portraits, see Bruges 1992: 12, 17, 31, 131. The portrait in the presentation miniature of the *Cité de Dieu* is particularly close to that in the volume discussed here, and it contains a similarly anachronistic intrusion in the presentation to Charles V.

62

MASTER OF THE *JARDIN DE VERTUEUSE CONSOLATION*

Pierre d'Ailly, *Le Jardin de vertueuse consolation*
Bruges, ca. 1475

MANUSCRIPT: iii + 46 + iv folios, 27.3 × 20 cm (10¾ × 7⅞ in.); justification: 15.1 × 10 cm (6 × 3⅞ in.); 16 lines of *bastarda*; 3 three-quarter-page miniatures

HERALDRY: Escutcheon with the arms of France, fol. 1

BINDING: Paris, seventeenth or eighteenth century; brown morocco; the royal arms of France gold-stamped on both covers

COLLECTION: Paris, Bibliothèque nationale de France, Ms. fr. 1026

PROVENANCE: Louis of Gruuthuse (1422–1492); Louis XII, king of France (1462–1515) (Blois inventory of 1518 [no. 114])

JPGM

This small manuscript made for the library of Louis of Gruuthuse contains an early work in French by the prolific writer and ecclesiastic Pierre d'Ailly (1350–1420). Entitled *Le Jardin de vertueuse consolation*, the text was not commonly included in contemporary noble libraries. It is preserved in several other manuscripts, only one of which is an illustrated deluxe copy like the one discussed here.¹ Even so, sometime in 1475 or 1476 book producer Colard Mansion chose the *Jardin* for his first printing ever at Bruges.² His printed version is very similar to Gruuthuse's roughly contemporaneous manuscript. They both omit the name of the writer. They also both append a *chansonette*

amoureuse and two chapters that are not included in any of the other manuscripts. The two chapters have been considered later additions, written by someone other than d'Ailly.

Contrary to earlier theories, the more recent line of thinking is that Mansion did not base his editions on manuscripts owned by Gruuthuse.³ A book dealer and printer would not have had easy access to such a noble library, and it seems unlikely that Gruuthuse would have taken the risk of lending his fine manuscripts to a printer. In the case of the *Jardin*, significant differences between the printed and manuscript texts offer additional evidence that Mansion did not base his edition on the manuscript made for Gruuthuse. Instead, it is possible that Gruuthuse commissioned his manuscript only after Mansion had printed the *Jardin*. This he would have done with the full knowledge of the availability of Mansion's edition. Like many other nobles, Gruuthuse had a clear preference for fine manuscript copies; despite their ready availability in Bruges, no printed texts appear to have formed part of his library.

The mystical text of Pierre d'Ailly tells how Christ lovingly summoned Âme, a female personification of the human soul, out of the world and into the Garden of Virtuous Consolation. In the first miniature Âme is seen leaving the world dressed as a pilgrim. On entering the beautiful garden, she is received by a grand lady, Obedience, and is introduced to her four ladies in waiting, who personify the four Cardinal Virtues of Prudence, Temperance, Fortitude, and Justice. In the second miniature, Âme is seen within the garden kneeling before the Tree of Life, beside two golden fountains and two bushes filled with birds. D'Ailly's text tells how, overcome by a fervent compassion for the crucified Christ, Âme falls at the foot of the Tree. On hearing her complaint, God sends the three Theological Virtues of Faith, Hope, and Charity to console her. They lead her to the Fountain of Grace and the Fountain of Pity, where she is refreshed by their living waters and the loving song of devoted souls in the form of birds. The third and final miniature illustrates the first chapter appended to the *Jardin*, in which Sapience offers advice to Âme (ill. 62). In each miniature the artist treated his subject with notable freshness and attended closely to the details of d'Ailly's text. Given that only one other illustrated copy of this text survives (Paris, Bibliothèque nationale, Ms. fr. 22922, fols. 153–59) and that it was produced in France, it is likely that the miniaturist created these images especially for the present manuscript.

The style of the miniatures was recently distinguished from that of the oeuvre of the Master of Margaret of York.⁴ While the miniatures adopt the formulas of that master, the execution is distinct and of superior artistic quality. The skillfully modeled and firmly located figures of the present manuscript constitute distant cousins of the stiff and silhouette-like characters of manuscripts illuminated by the Master of Margaret of York. The palette is much richer and more subtly handled, and the attention to surface detail much greater. Other miniatures attributed to this hand are those in the Getty Quintus Curtius (cat. no. 63). Another manuscript that is closely related is Gruuthuse's

63

MASTER OF THE *JARDIN DE VERTUEUSE CONSOLATION*
AND ASSISTANT

**Quintus Curtius Rufus, *Livre des fais d'Alexandre le grant*,
translation by Vasco da Lucena of *Historia Alexandri magni***
Lille and Bruges, ca. 1470–75

MANUSCRIPT: 237 folios, 43.2 × 33 cm (17 × 13 in.); justification:
25.6 × 20.4 cm (10¹/₁₆ × 8¹/₁₆ in.); 32 lines of *bastarda* in two columns
by Jan Du Quesne; 1 full-page miniature, 10 three-quarter-page
miniatures, 3 one-column miniatures

HERALDRY: Effaced and overpainted escutcheon with the arms
possibly of the dukes of Croÿ, fol. 2v

BINDING: Prague(?), eighteenth century; red velvet over wood boards;
two engraved brass clasps

COLLECTION: Los Angeles, J. Paul Getty Museum, Ms. Ludwig XV 8
(83.MR.178)

PROVENANCE: Possibly Charles-Alexandre de Croÿ, marquess of
Havré and count of Fontenoy (1581–1624); Rudolf, sixth prince Kinsky
of Wchinitz and Tettau (1802–1836), Prague; [H. P. Kraus, New York];
to Otto Schäfer (d. 2000), Schweinfurt, 1961; [H. P. Kraus, New York];
to Peter and Irene Ludwig, Aachen; acquired 1983

JPGM and RA

There are at least thirty-five surviving manuscripts of
a French translation of the biography of Alexander the
Great compiled by the Roman writer Quintus Curtius
Rufus in the first century A.D. This translation, completed
in 1468, was by a Portuguese member of the Burgundian
household, Vasco da Lucena. Lucena was encouraged in his
work by the Burgundian courtier and bibliophile Jean de
Créquy, and he dedicated his translation to Charles the
Bold, duke of Burgundy. In his attempt at a straightforward
translation of a classical author, Lucena stood in the
vanguard of developments in literature promoted at the
Burgundian court.

Like most other surviving manuscripts of this text, the
present copy of Lucena's translation is handsomely written
and illuminated. Its text was transcribed by the professional
scribe Jan Du Quesne, probably in his hometown of Lille in
the first half of the 1470s.[1] It was embellished by a miniature
depicting Lucena presenting his translation to the duke of
Burgundy; thirteen other miniatures illustrate episodes
from the life of Alexander. All of these illustrations are
painted in a style related to that of Lieven van Lathem, as
developed at Bruges beginning around 1468 by the Master
of Margaret of York and his associates. Most recently the
miniatures in this manuscript have been attributed to the
same associate of the Master of Margaret of York who
painted the miniatures of Louis of Gruuthuse's *Jardin de
vertueuse consolation* (cat. no. 62).[2] The artists responsible
for the borders collaborated with the Master of Margaret of
York on other manuscripts, including a copy of Pseudo-
Seneca (cat. no. 61).

The miniatures of the Getty manuscript are characterized by fine figure drawing and by the clear and expressive
articulation of narrative through carefully constructed
compositions, subtle use of a rich palette, and skilled handling of human gesture, posture, and facial expression. In
these respects the present manuscript is, together with

copy of the *Romuléon*.[5] Although seriously damaged and
much larger in format than the *Jardin*, this copy of the
Romuléon clearly includes miniatures by the same distinctive hand. It also includes borders with almost exactly the
same dense decoration.[6]   S. McK.

Notes

1. In addition to the four manuscripts listed in Cockshaw and Vanden Bosch 1963: 25, I have noted three further manuscripts (Paris,
Bibliothèque nationale de France, Mss. fr. 22922, 24863, 25548), the first
of which was illustrated in France (see Paris 2002: no. 9).

2. Brussels 1973: 212–13, 216–19, no. 101.

3. Brussels 1973: 213–15; Bruges 1992: 150–52.

4. Bruges 1992: 142–43, 182–84, no. 13.

5. For this volume, see McKendrick 1994: 152–56, 168, pl. 23.

6. Several other manuscripts illuminated in the style of the Master
of Margaret of York have similar border decoration. These include
Gruuthuse's copies of *Cité de Dieu*, Livy, Quintus Curtius, and Valerius
Maximus (Paris, Bibliothèque nationale, Mss. fr. 17, 34, 257, 288–89);
Anthony of Burgundy's *Faits des romains* (Pommersfelden, Gräflich
Schönborn'sche Bibliothek, Ms. 310); and Pietro Villa's Wavrin (Paris,
Bibliothèque nationale, Ms. fr. 87). For some color reproductions, see
Bruges 1992: 130, 131, 185–88.

62
MASTER OF THE
*JARDIN DE VERTUEUSE
CONSOLATION*
*Sapience Instructing Devote
Âme*, fol. 28v

63a (opposite)
MASTER OF THE
*JARDIN DE VERTUEUSE
CONSOLATION*
*Alexander and the Niece
of Artaxerxes*, fol. 123

Er commence le .ve. liure de quinte curfe lequel contient en foy .
xxviii. Chapitres , Prologue du tranflateur .

Ay emprunte
de Juftin et de
ozofe la fin du
quart liure
depuis le lieu
ou il dift aifr

Ze roy dauic en bne charette
perthie de plufieurs places

Jufques a la fin dicellui liure
Pareillement ze prengz defoie
acteurs le commencement du
Chinquiefme liure enfeuant
Jufques la ou il dift . Au my
deftroit de la bataille Allec
mift en pieces zc. Si ne lai
pas feulement tranflate axie

Et commence le quart liure de Quintecurse lequel contient en soy
xxviij. chapittes . Le premier desquelz parle du conseil que le roy
Daire tint / Et de la reddition Darbelle . Et la rescription des ri-
uieres du Tigre / et Deuffrates . Et de la prouince de mesopotanie
gisant entre elles .   Premier Chapittre .   . I.

E N Je vouloie
riconter les
choses faites
soubz la sou
uictamente .
Dalexandre ou temps dessusd

tant en grece comme es Illi-
ens et icelles rendre chascune
a son temps / Il me fauldroit
entreprendre les choses dasye
Lesquelles mettre audeuant de
la fuite et mort du roy Daire

Charles the Bold's own copy (cat. no. 54), exceptional among the twenty-eight surviving copies of Lucena's translation that include illustrations. Most of these were illustrated by artists of average ability, and some were illustrated by artists of extremely limited ability.

Comparison with these other manuscripts is instructive. First of all, the only other manuscript of Lucena's translation copied by Du Quesne (London, British Library, Royal Ms. 17 F.i) was based on a different textual exemplar and contains twenty illustrations depicting subjects entirely different from those found in the Getty miniatures. More important, three other volumes—now in Geneva, Jena, and Paris—include identically placed illustrations that are strikingly similar to the Getty miniatures.[3] Together, these four closely contemporaneous manuscripts stand out among surviving copies of Lucena's translation as a discrete group, closely related by the subject, composition, and artistic style of their miniatures. They are, however, the work of four different scribes, and none of the subsidiary decoration of illuminated borders and initials is the same. Their overall campaigns of illustration are also different in extent.[4]

The link among these four manuscripts is that they were probably based on a common pool of evolving visual models. Written instructions could not have generated what are in some instances very similar compositions that share small details of figural and architectural design. The specificity of the iconography of, for example, the miniatures *The Competition in Sittacene and the Placating of Sisigambis* (ill. 63b) and *Alexander Kills Clitus* (fol. 175) implies that the visual models used were specially created for the illustration of Lucena's text. Direct copying of one set of miniatures from another is unlikely, given significant differences between the Getty set and the others. The fact that there are elements found in the Getty miniatures that are not drawn directly from the text suggests that the models were originally created for a manuscript other than the Getty manuscript. Selective use of these models within the four manuscripts may indicate that some of the models had disappeared before certain manuscripts were illuminated. Differences of color among the manuscripts suggest the models comprised uncolored sketches. Knowledge of the availability of such sketches in Bruges may have prompted Du Quesne to send his manuscript to be illuminated there.

As in the case of the two related copies in Geneva and Jena, no early owner of the Getty manuscript is known. Comparable illuminated copies of Lucena's translation were owned by such prominent bibliophiles at the Burgundian court as Louis of Gruuthuse, Anthony of Burgundy, and Philip of Cleves, as well as by Charles the Bold, as previously noted. It is likely that the first owner of the present copy was a wealthy member of the French-speaking upper nobility within the same circle.[5]   S. McK.

Notes

1. Another copy of the same text written by Du Quesne (London, British Library, Royal Ms. 17 F.i) was certainly written in Lille (McKendrick 1996a: 21, fig. 4). The latest manuscript copied by Du Quesne (ex Longleat, Marquess of Bath, Botfield Ms. 2) is dated 1478/79.

2. McKendrick 1996a: 44.

3. Geneva (Cologny), Bibliotheca Bodmeriana, Ms. Bodmer 53; Jena, Thüringer Universitäts- und Landesbibliothek, Ms. El. Fol. 89; Paris, Bibliothèque nationale de France, Ms. fr. 257 (McKendrick 1996a: figs. 11, 14–20).

4. The Geneva, Jena, and Paris volumes contain twenty-one, nine, and forty-five miniatures, respectively.

5. The arms (fol. 2v), largely obscured by border decoration, were identified as belonging to one of the members of the Croÿ family, who were prominent at the Burgundian court, but this identification was unsustainable. See McKendrick 1996a: 62, n. 3. A later member of the Croÿ family, Charles-Alexandre de Croÿ (1581–1624), marquess of Havré and count of Fontenoy, added almost identical arms to three similar Flemish manuscripts (Geneva, Bibliothèque publique et universitaire, Mss. fr. 85, 182; Warsaw, Biblioteka Narodowa, Ms. 8005).

63b
MASTER OF THE
JARDIN DE VERTUEUSE
CONSOLATION
The Competition in
Sittacene and the Placating
of Sisigambis, fol. 99

64

MASTER OF FITZWILLIAM 268

Military Ordinance of Charles the Bold, in French
Bruges, 1475

MANUSCRIPT: 41 folios, 30.5 × 21.5 cm (12 × 8½ in.); justification: 17 × 10.8 cm (6¼ × 4¼ in.); 21 lines of *bastarda*; 1 three-quarter-page miniature

HERALDRY: Full achievement of the arms of Charles the Bold; escutcheons with the arms of his six duchies, nine counties, one marquisate, and three lordships; linked initials *CM* (for Charles the Bold and Margaret of York); cross of Saint Andrew and flint-and-steel device; mottoes *Je lay en prins* and *Bien en aviengne*, all fol. 5

BINDING: England(?), nineteenth century; crimson velvet over oak boards; gilt bosses and clasps

COLLECTION: London, The British Library, Add. Ms. 36619

PROVENANCE: Charles the Bold, duke of Burgundy (1433–1477); Marc Antoine Martin de Choisey, lord of Barjon, Anet, and Parthenay, second half of seventeenth century; Jean Bouhier (1673–1746), Dijon, in 1721; Haselden or Carter family, ca. 1800 (their heraldic bookplate inside lower cover); William Beckford (1760–1844), Fonthill Abbey [his sale, Phillips Son and Neale, London, September 9, 1823, lot 606]; Joseph Barrois (d. 1855); to Bertram, fourth earl of Ashburnham (1797–1878), in 1849 (his Barrois Ms. 2) [his sale, Sotheby's, London, June 10, 1901, lot 434]; [to Bernard Quaritch]; purchased 1901 for the British Museum

RA

A t Trier in 1473 Charles the Bold, duke of Burgundy, completed an important set of ordinances for the organization of his standing army. Subsequently, at the beginning of each year, his military captains received, with their batons of authority, personal copies of these ordinances. Including the volume discussed here, six copies of these ordinances survive.[1] All are fine manuscripts of similar format written on parchment. The margins of their opening pages are decorated in identical fashion, and their texts are preceded by a depiction of Charles receiving the captains. Whereas the other five surviving copies restrict this scene to the opening initials of the text and feature only three figures, the manuscript discussed here presents a detailed picture of the installation of Charles's captains in a large miniature that fills nearly the whole page (ill. 64).

In August 1475 Charles the Bold paid for twenty-one copies of his military ordinances of 1473.[2] His valet de chambre and illuminator, Philippe de Mazerolles, was paid for both the script and the illumination. One volume, called "the original," was embellished with a large and expensive miniature[3] and a fine box to house the appended seal of Charles.[4] The present manuscript has been identified as that volume and thereby as Charles's own copy of the ordinances.[5] Moreover, its miniature has been considered by de Schryver to be a documented work of the illuminator Philippe de Mazerolles.[6] It is clear, however, that several different hands were responsible for both the writing and the illumination of the six surviving copies; thus Mazerolles was clearly paid for work undertaken by others. Bodo Brinkmann has accordingly attributed the miniature in the present copy to the Master of Fitzwilliam 268.[7]

The opening miniature is a tour de force. The overall composition is based on the same model of authority used by contemporary illuminators to portray Charles as head of the Order of the Golden Fleece.[8] In its detail, however, it also offers an exemplification of the installation of Charles's military captains. Seated on Charles's right are knights of the Order of the Golden Fleece; on his left are lay and clerical members of his council; in the foreground, facing Charles, stand twenty unarmed captains.[9] In the middle an additional two captains receive copies of the ordinances, and another his baton. Clearly, this image is not a photographic record, but a formal template for the ceremony. Like the content of the text, it forms a ducal *ordonnance*. Given its importance, the duke's own illuminator must have been closely involved in the formalization of this image.

S. McK.

Notes

1. Listed in de Schryver 1999: 59. Three further manuscripts preserve household ordinances of Charles the Bold (de Schryver 1969b; Brussels 1977a: 10–11; Thoss 1987: nos. 21, 22).

2. Since red velvet was delivered in July for the covers of the manuscripts, it is likely that the twenty-one copies were nearing completion around that date.

3. It cost five livres or two hundred groats. For prices of contemporary miniatures, see my essay "Reviving the Past: Illustrated Manuscripts of Secular Vernacular Texts, 1467–1500," this volume.

4. This volume was not the exemplar from which the other copies were made. "L'original" referred to the copy intended for Charles. Another "original" was his copy of Jan Du Quesne's translation of Caesar (see cat. no. 74).

5. De Schryver 1999: 59–60.

6. De Schryver 1999: 61–62.

7. Brinkmann 1997: 168.

8. For such miniatures—in manuscripts of the Statutes and Armorial of the Golden Fleece and Guillaume Fillastre's *Histoire de la Toison d'Or*—see Brussels 1996. An earlier model for the armorial border and the figure facing forward at the center of the composition was available in the presentation miniature in Philip the Good's *Girart de Rousillon* (Vienna, Österreichische Nationalbibliothek, Ms. 2549, fol. 6). A later reinterpretation of the ordinance miniature by a follower of the Master of Margaret of York occurs in the presentation miniature of Louis of Gruuthuse's *Quintus Curtius* (Paris, Bibliothèque nationale de France, Ms. fr. 257, fol. A; Bruges 1992: 183, color pl.).

9. These twenty captains were presumably the recipients of the twenty copies made in 1475 in addition to "l'original." Their portrayal may provide further evidence for associating the volume discussed here with Charles's commission of 1475. The three recipients in the middle of the composition merely help exemplify the formal installation and are not necessarily captured at the same moment in time as the twenty captains in the foreground.

64 (opposite)
MASTER OF
FITZWILLIAM 268
Charles the Bold Receives His Military Captains,
fol. 5

65

MASTER OF FITZWILLIAM 268

Pietro di Crescenzi, *Livre des proffits ruraux,* **translation of** *Liber ruralium commodorum*
Bruges, ca. 1470

MANUSCRIPT: 304 folios, 42.8 × 33.5 cm (16⅞ × 13³⁄₁₆ in.); justification: 27.1 × 8.2–2.8–8.7 cm (10¹¹⁄₁₆ × 3¼–1¹⁄₁₆–3⁷⁄₁₆ in.); 36 lines of *bastarda* in two columns; 12 half-page miniatures

HERALDRY: Escutcheon with the arms of Burgundy (azure three bends or), in miniature, fol. 77

BINDING: Southern Netherlands, eighteenth century; gold-tooled mottled calf

COLLECTION: New York, The Morgan Library, Ms. M.232

PROVENANCE: Belgium, eighteenth century (?); earl of Cork and Orrery; [sale, Christie's, London, November 21, 1905, lot 207]; [to Quaritch, *Catalogue 250,* 1906, no. 764]; J. P. Morgan (1837–1913) in 1906

JPGM

This book features the French translation of Pietro di Crescenzi's *Liber ruralium commodorum* that was dedicated to Charles V of France, who commissioned the translation in 1373. Its frontispiece, showing the book presented to the king, is a variation on the type of presentation miniature that the Master of Margaret of York group of artists supplied to similar large, learned volumes.[1] The figure type seen in the miniature—with small, often jutting heads; pointed chins; and black, frizzy hair—is characteristic of the Master of Fitzwilliam 268, an artist of this group.[2] The illustration for book 8, concerning the pleasure garden, shows a well-manicured orchard with round, squat trees of the type painted by the Master of Fitzwilliam 268 to illustrate Virgil's *Eclogues* (ill. 118a).[3] Each of the volume's first eleven books opens with a miniature that follows a set formula: Crescenzi teaching a nobleman in the left foreground, manorial architecture behind them, and the pertinent gardening activities depicted at the right.[4] The conception of the architecture and the painting of the trees in the illustration for book 5 (ill. 65), concerning fruit and shade trees, owe much to the Master of Margaret of York.⁵ The Morgan Crescenzi was perhaps illustrated when the Master of Fitzwilliam 268 was working closely with him.

The volume is one of two copies of Crescenzi's text executed in Burgundian Flanders around 1470, the other closer in style to the work of the Master of Margaret of York himself (Paris, Bibliothèque de l'Arsenal, Ms. 5064).⁶ The architecture in the background of the miniature for book 5 in the Morgan copy finds a variation in book 6 in the Arsenal copy, and the latter also employs the same broad compositional formula described above. The patron of the Arsenal copy was Anthony of Burgundy, a powerful figure at the court of Duke Charles the Bold, his half brother. The Morgan copy was likely intended for a client of a similar station, a view supported by the Burgundian colors that appear prominently on a banner within the miniature for book 4 (fol. 77). Unfortunately the spaces set aside for the book's armorials (fols. 2, 11) were never filled.⁷   T. K.

Notes

1. The frontispiece is a variation on that which appears in the Getty Quintus Curtius manuscript (cat. no. 63, fol. 2), which is by another artist of the Master of Margaret of York group, called the Master of the *Jardin de vertueuse consolation*. Significantly, the costumes in the Morgan Crescenzi suggest that it is slightly earlier in date, that is, of the late 1460s or around 1470. The two miniatures correspond closely, not only in figural groupings but also in the conception and coloring of the architecture. Certain architectural motifs that appear throughout the Morgan manuscript are characteristic of the Master of Margaret of York group: the colored marble columns, the beamed ceilings, and oculi with carved S-shaped bars. Such features were of course easily imitated in a workshop. A similar frontispiece, often given to the Master of Margaret of York but perhaps by the Master of Fitzwilliam 268, is found in a *Cité de Dieu* (Paris, Bibliothèque nationale de France, Ms. fr. 17, fol. 1; Smeyers 1998: 408, fig. 75). Note especially the figure types and the fine, wiry black hair.

2. Brinkmann (1997: 168–69, 399) attributed the miniatures to the Master of Fitzwilliam 268 or his circle.

3. Cf. Calkins 1986: fig. 12; Hassall 1970: color pl. 158.

4. The volume actually has twelve chapters. The twelfth, the shortest, was not intended to be illuminated.

5. Compare, for example, the treatment of the shape of the trees, the geometry of the garden, the tower, and the carved decoration of the doorway to the features in the Master of Margaret of York's *Légende de Saint Hubert* (Paris, Bibliothèque nationale, Ms. fr. 424, fol. 1; Bruges 1992: 31).

6. Brinkmann (1997: 168–69, n. 67) linked the Arsenal manuscript more closely to the style of the Master of Fitzwilliam 268. Scot McKendrick was able to examine the two copies together recently and remarked on the differences in execution between the two.

7. Brinkmann (1997: 168–69) also associated with the Master of Fitzwilliam 268 another book made for Anthony of Burgundy, a copy of the *Faits des romains* in Pommersfelden (Gräflich Schönborn'sche Bibliothek, Ms. 310).

RAMBURES MASTER

Previously named the Master of Amiens 200 by John Plummer,¹ the Rambures Master was renamed by Nicole Reynaud after the patron of the Amiens manuscript, Jacques de Rambures (d. 1488).² Much attention has been given to this miniaturist's work in recent studies of both manuscript illumination in Amiens³ and the patronage of Jean de Créquy (d. 1474), uncle of Jacques de Rambures.⁴ The Rambures Master has also been studied in relation to the Brussels panel painter Rogier van der Weyden.⁵

The earliest and latest miniatures attributed to the Rambures Master appear in a *Fleur des histoires* (Paris, Bibliothèque de l'Arsenal, Ms. 5088)⁶ and a *Faits des romains* (Chantilly, Musée Condé, Ms. 770),⁷ both of which were written in Hesdin—the first in 1454 and the second in 1480. His contribution to the *Fleur* was as a collaborator of Loyset Liédet, who was paid for all the miniatures in 1460 and was then living in Hesdin (see the separate biography of Liédet, this part). Further miniatures attributed to the Rambures Master occur in three books of hours that are datable to between 1460 and 1475 and are linked to the town of Amiens by their liturgical content, subsidiary decoration, and patrons.⁸ Other miniatures by the Rambures Master have been identified in a *Chroniques de Hainaut* made for Jean de Créquy around 1465 (Boulogne-sur-mer, Bibliothèque municipale, Ms. 149), in which the subsidiary decoration and hands responsible for the other miniatures in this volume provide further links with Amiens production.

What has not been noted are several important connections between the work of the Rambures Master and Bruges production of manuscripts of secular vernacular texts in the late 1460s and 1470s. First, the Rambures Master contributed to two copies of Valerius Maximus that appear to be products of Bruges (cat. no. 66; Paris, Bibliothèque de l'Arsenal, Ms. 5196). Moreover, in the Arsenal copy, his sole contribution, the opening presentation miniature (fol. 1), is clearly based on an elaborate composition devised by Lieven van Lathem and found in both the Chatsworth *Gillion* (cat. no. 58) and the Paris *Jason* (cat. no. 59). Given Van Lathem's known impact on manuscript painting in Bruges in the late 1460s, it seems likely that the Rambures Master gained knowledge of this composition through his contact with Bruges artists. In addition, the Rambures Master reused in two manuscripts of the *Faits des romains* (Chantilly, Musée Condé, Ms. 770; Lille, Bibliothèque municipale, Ms. 442) a campaign of illustrations that appears to have been devised in Bruges between 1473 and 1478,⁹ possibly for Charles the Bold's own copy of the *Faits* (untraced). The panoramic landscapes that appear in these two manuscripts also seem to depend on compositions of a Bruges miniaturist, the Master of the London Wavrin.

Other texts illuminated during this period almost exclusively at Bruges—the translation of Quintus Curtius's history of Alexander the Great and Jean de Wavrin's *Chroniques*—were also illustrated by the Rambures Master (London, British Library, Royal Ms. 15 E.iv; Oxford, Bodleian Library, Ms. Laud misc. 653).[10]

The implications of these connections with Bruges merit further consideration. The contribution of the Rambures Master to the Valerius Maximus manuscripts is difficult to explain unless he was working in Bruges with the other artisans responsible for these two volumes. The Rambures Master's collaboration with a follower of Liédet and other Bruges miniaturists on the Wavrin manuscript and its companion volumes also suggests at least a temporary stay in Bruges. Other connections with Bruges illumination may, however, be explained by the Rambures Master's early collaboration in Hesdin with Liédet, who subsequently became one of the leading illustrators of secular vernacular texts in Bruges. Another possible link with Bruges illuminators is the Lille scribe Jan Du Quesne. Du Quesne was almost certainly the scribe responsible for the Wavrin volume, to which the Rambures Master contributed.

S. McK.

Notes

1. New York 1982: 14–15; this master was so named after a book of hours now in Amiens (Bibliothèque municipale, Ms. 200).

2. Paris 1993: 93–97.

3. Nash 1999: 194–204.

4. Gil 1999.

5. Cardon 1991: 43–55; Cardon 1993: 51–57.

6. Paris 1993: no. 44.

7. Paris 1993: 97.

8. Amiens, Bibliothèque municipale, Ms. 200 (the name Ms.); London, British Library, Add. Ms. 19738 (Hours of Marguerite Blondel); New York, Morgan Library, Ms. M.194. See Paris 1993: 95; and Nash 1999: 194–202.

9. On this campaign, see McKendrick 1990: 115–16, 124, 131–32.

10. Laud misc. 653 comprises leaves extracted from The Hague, Koninklijke Bibliotheek, Ms. 133 A 7, vol. 1. The latter volume—together with Mss. 133 A 7, vols. 2–3, and Baltimore, Walters Art Museum, Ms. W.201—forms an incomplete copy of Wavrin's *Chroniques* (vols. 2–5).

66

RAMBURES MASTER AND FOLLOWER OF WILLEM VRELANT

Valerius Maximus, *Faits et dits mémorables des romains*, translation by Simon de Hesdin and Nicolas de Gonesse of *Facta et dicta memorabilia*
Bruges, ca. 1470

MANUSCRIPT: i + 352 + i folios, 49 × 34.8 cm (19¼ × 13¾ in.); justification: 31.6 × 21.2 cm (12⅜ × 8⅜ in.); 53 lines of *bastarda* in two columns; 9 small miniatures

HERALDRY: Escutcheon with the royal arms of England, fol. 3

BINDING: London, mid-eighteenth century; brown morocco; the arms of George II gold-stamped on both covers

COLLECTION: London, The British Library, Royal Ms. 17 F.iv

PROVENANCE: Edward IV, king of England (1442–1483) (?); English royal library, Richmond Palace, in 1535, and Saint James's in 1666; George II, king of England (1683–1760); presented 1757 to the British Museum

R A

The historical text that survives in by far the greatest number of late medieval manuscripts is a compilation of anecdotes drawn from Roman and foreign history by the ancient author Valerius Maximus.[1] Dedicated to the Emperor Tiberius (r. A.D. 14–37), this text offered contemporary students and practitioners of rhetoric a rich and neatly organized quarry of *exempla*. These stories illustrate religious practices, civil and military institutions, virtue and vice, happiness, private and public judgments, and finally luxury and avarice. A commentary written by Dionigi da Borgo Sansepolcro (d. 1342) after 1339 contributed much to the medieval popularity of Valerius Maximus.

The French text in the present manuscript was begun by the Hospitaller Simon de Hesdin (d. 1383) in 1375 for Charles V of France and completed by Nicolas de Gonesse by 1401 for presentation to John, duke of Berry. This text includes not only a translation of Valerius Maximus's Latin text but also an extensive commentary based on the work of Dionigi. Together, the translation and commentary make up a very long work that frequently required two folio volumes. The survival of at least sixty-five manuscripts, however, attests to the popularity of this work.[2] The large number of deluxe and illustrated copies reflects strong interest among the nobility. A significant group of these were produced in the southern Netherlands between 1470 and 1480 (see cat. nos. 67, 73, 80).

The Rambures Master contributed to the illustration of no fewer than three copies of this text. Of these, the present copy in London and one other (Paris, Bibliothèque de l'Arsenal, Ms. 5196) contain the full nine books and were each written and decorated as one campaign.[3] These two volumes share very similar subsidiary decoration[4] and *bastarda* script.[5] Whereas only the opening miniature of the Paris volume is by the Rambures Master, all the miniatures of the London manuscript, except the opening one, are by him. The opening miniature of the London manuscript,

Within the miniatures of the London manuscript, the Rambures Master displayed characteristic assurance in figure drawing. This assurance is evident not only in the many varied and complex poses his characters adopt but also in the pairs of two nudes of *The Bath House* (ill. 66). The miniaturist employed his usual skill in balancing colors from a subtly chosen palette—dominated by blue, red, light green, and violet—and in applying them quickly within a broadly sketched composition. Although some definition was lost in the haste to put paint on the page, the touch is still very assured and under control. If it is accepted that the Rambures Master became increasingly broader and less assured in his later work, the London miniatures are from an earlier phase in his career, possibly around 1470.

We know only that the London manuscript was already a part of the English royal collection by 1535; unfortunately we do not know when it entered the collection. It does not include any of the heraldic devices of Edward IV found in other royal manuscripts, nor does it conform to the style of Edward's other manuscripts. It does, however, contain the same text as one of these other manuscripts (cat. no. 80). If, therefore, Edward was unlikely to have commissioned two copies of this work, it may have entered the English royal library as a gift.   S. McK.

Notes

1. Guénée 1980: 250.

2. Schullian 1981: 695–728; Lucas 1970: 247–48.

3. Paris 1993: no. 47; also Martin and Lauer 1929: pls. 55–56.

4. Borders with almost identical elements also appear in Brussels, Bibliothèque royale, Ms. 9263—a copy of Lefèvre's *Recueil* datable to between 1464 and 1467 and attributed to Bruges (see Smeyers 1998: 369, fig. 23). The *mise-en-page* with full decorated borders in this Brussels volume is also very close to that in both the Paris and London manuscripts.

5. The script is that described by Delaissé (in Brussels 1959: nos. 107, 110, 111, 113, 114, 117) as "la belle courante moyenne" and identified by him in several Bruges manuscripts of the second half of the 1460s. M. Brown (1990: no. 41) described the characteristic features of this script.

6. Breslauer 1965; Wiesbaden 1975: no. 125.

which is attributable to a follower of Willem Vrelant, is by the same hand as the remaining miniatures in the Paris manuscript. The third manuscript to which the Rambures Master contributed (Berlin, Staatsbibliothek, Ms. 94) contains only the first seven books, as completed by Simon de Hesdin, and was begun earlier in the century in Paris.[6] Its opening miniature, subsidiary decoration, and *textualis* script date from that period. In the other six miniatures of the Berlin manuscript, the Rambures Master was able to be more expansive in his treatment of the subjects than in the one-column miniatures of the London manuscript. The smaller miniatures in the Berlin volume (fols. 218v, 283), however, reveal him treating his subject in a manner very similar to that employed in the London volume. Most remarkably, none of the three manuscripts follows the same program of illustration. Even when treating the same subject, such as the wedding scene at the beginning of book 3, the artist employs different compositions. Only in one miniature (*The Suicide of Lucretia*) did the Rambures Master fall back on the same model for use in two different volumes—the Berlin and the London manuscripts. Here the composition of the Berlin miniature, which includes Lucretia holding the dagger in her left hand, is a reversal of that of the London miniature (in which Lucretia holds the dagger in her right).

66
RAMBURES MASTER
The Bath House, fol. 297
(detail)

MASTER OF THE PRIVILEGES OF GHENT AND FLANDERS

The starting point for the oeuvre of an anonymous miniaturist first identified by Friedrich Winkler is a group of fifteen miniatures painted in an unusual deluxe manuscript in which are collected the privileges and statutes of Ghent and Flanders from 1241 to 1453 (Vienna, Österreichische Nationalbibliothek, Ms. 2583).[1] Although it is certain that this volume was made for Philip the Good (d. 1467), the circumstances and place of its production have been the subject of much debate and are still not clear. Most significantly, the miniatures have been variously considered the product of Ghent, Lille, Mons, or Tournai.

The Vienna miniatures are characterized by their predominantly archaic pictorial language. Nonnaturalistic use of color, persistently starry skies, and stylized triangular trees echo the phrases of earlier Parisian painting. Sharply raked floors, high horizons, lack of proportion between figures and architecture, and density of pictorial detail reflect an interest in surface geometry rather than the depiction of space. The Master of the Privileges of Ghent and Flanders (known as Master of the Ghent Privileges) described forms with a nonnaturalistic boldness, uniformity, and weight of detail. His volumetric figures have almost identical facial features, including large eyes and prominent ears.

Based on the style of the miniatures in the Vienna manuscript, several other attributions have been made to the Master of the Ghent Privileges. Most recently Gregory T. Clark has assembled a large corpus of miniatures in both devotional and secular manuscripts that he argues reveals the miniaturist's stylistic development through the 1440s and 1450s.[2] One of the most convincing attributions remains the presentation miniature in the copy of Wauquelin's translation of *De regimine principum*, for which Philip the Good paid the scribe Jacquemart Pilavaine of Mons in 1452 (Brussels, Bibliothèque royale, Ms. 9043, fol. 2). This miniature is a somewhat weakly executed copy of the presentation miniature in Philip's copy of the *Chroniques de Hainaut* (cat. no. 3). Another persuasive attribution remains the dedication miniature in a copy of Valerius Maximus made for Philip the Good (Paris, Bibliothèque nationale de France, Ms. fr. 6185). This volume was probably produced in the 1450s and illuminated mainly by the artists responsible for the miniatures in Philip's copy of Wauquelin's *Histoire d'Alexandre le Grand* (Paris, Bibliothèque nationale, Ms. fr. 9342).[3] The style of the Master of the Ghent Privileges was continued by followers into the 1460s and 1470s, most notably in the designs for a set of four tapestries of the history of Julius Caesar (Bern, Historisches Museum)[4] and an illuminated copy of a printed edition of Valerius Maximus in French translation (cat. no. 67), the artist of the latter having been named by Clark as the Ghent Gradual Master.

As first remarked by Winkler, reiterated by L. M. J. Delaissé, Georges Dogaer, and Maurits Smeyers, and more recently argued at length by Clark, the Master of the Ghent Privileges continued a style of miniature painting first seen in the second decade of the fifteenth century.[5] The chief exponent of this style was the Master of Guillebert de Mets, an anonymous miniaturist named after the scribe of a copy of Boccaccio's *Decameron* in French translation (Paris, Bibliothèque de l'Arsenal, Ms. 5070).[6] This volume was copied at Geraardsbergen (Grammont), in East Flanders, probably in the 1430s and illustrated first by the Master of Guillebert de Mets and later by the Mansel Master. The Master of Guillebert de Mets's earliest work occurs in a psalter added to a breviary made at Paris probably for John the Fearless (d. 1419) (London, British Library, Harley Ms. 2897).[7] It is generally agreed that this illuminator was a Flemish artist trained either in Paris or by Parisian artists. His activity appears to have ended at roughly the point when that of the Master of the Ghent Privileges began.   S. McK.

Notes

1. Winkler 1915: 306–11.

2. Clark 2000.

3. Van Buren (1999: 12, n. 24) dated the frontispiece to the late 1440s and the other miniatures to a second campaign in the early 1450s.

4. Wyss 1955–56: 103–232.

5. Winkler 1915: 323; Winkler 1925: 31; Delaissé, in Brussels 1959: no. 244; Dogaer 1987a: 57; Smeyers 1998: 248, 299; Clark 2000: esp. 18–20, 54–65.

6. On the Master of Guillebert de Mets, see Brussels 1959: nos. 1–13; Dogaer 1987a: 33–37; and Smeyers 1998: 241–49. On the name manuscript, see Paris 1993: no. 32.

7. Meiss 1974: 327. A full account of the production of this breviary remains to be published.

67

GHENT GRADUAL MASTER

Valerius Maximus, *Faits et dits mémorables des romains*, translation by Simon de Hesdin and Nicolas de Gonesse of *Facta et dicta memorabilia*, books 5–9
Bruges(?), 1470–77

PRINTED BOOK: Paper, 236 folios, 38.5 × 27.5 cm (15⅛ × 10⅞ in.); justification: 27 × 17.2 cm (10⅝ × 6¾ in.); 44 lines of type resembling *gotica rotunda* in two columns attributed to the Josephus printer; 5 half-page miniatures

HERALDRY: Various escutcheons (fols. 245, 284, 312v, 352v, 403): (1) vert a chevron or between three escallops argent (also in miniature on fol. 403); (2) argent a fess gules; (3) party per pale (1) and (2); (4) gules a castle argent; (5) unidentified merchant's mark (?) on an argent field; motto *La bien le alle*, fol. 284

BINDING: England, early nineteenth century; gold-tooled mottled brown calf

COLLECTION: Manchester, John Rylands University Library, Inc. 26 A.4 (Inc. 5676, vol. 2)

PROVENANCE: George John, second earl Spencer (1758–1834), probably after 1822; John Poyntz, fifth earl Spencer (1835–1910); Mrs. John Rylands, in 1892; part of her foundation gift

R A

Sometime before 1477, possibly around 1475, an anonymous printer produced the first edition of the *Facta et dicta memorabilia* of Valerius Maximus as translated into French by Simon de Hesdin and Nicolas de Gonesse.[1] This printing was undertaken at the same time that deluxe manuscripts of the text were repeatedly being produced for French-speaking nobles in the Low Countries (see cat. nos. 66, 73, 80). Like these deluxe manuscripts, and unlike most contemporary printed texts,[2] the text in this edition of Valerius Maximus was set so that the opening page of each book could accommodate large illustrations and other substantial decoration. In most copies of this edition, the illustrations and accompanying decoration were executed in full color and at a high artistic level.

Of the seven complete and four incomplete copies of this edition that include such illustrations,[3] the present copy and its companion first volume (Manchester, John Rylands University Library, Inc. 26 A.3) have the most ambitious decorative program. As in the case of most other copies, the text is divided into two volumes, and the beginning of each of its nine books is marked with a large miniature accompanied by a full decorative border and a large illuminated initial. Unlike most other copies, the present copy presents within the large frames of each of its miniatures complex images that combine several smaller scenes. Because these scenes lack explanatory labels and overlap in their pictorial space, the images they present challenge the viewer and require a detailed knowledge of their textual source. In the miniature that heads book 7, for example, the artist illustrates the story of Gyges in a particularly subtle manner (ill. 67). Several contemporary miniaturists chose the same story from Valerius's opening chapter on happiness and selected similar elements, such as the worshipers kneeling before the pagan idol at Delphi and the cattle of the humble but happy Aglaus.[4] Their images, however,

attend more to naturalism and eschew the multiple layers of reference found in both earlier Parisian miniatures[5] and the Manchester miniature. Once understood,[6] the Manchester miniature presents a moral image of great power and clarity that portrays the contrast between Gyges, on the left, and Aglaus, on the right; unhappiness, wealth, and impiety, on the left, happiness, simplicity, and respect for the gods, on the right.

One artist was responsible for all nine miniatures. Previously identified with the Master of the Privileges of Ghent and Flanders—who illustrated the deluxe copy of the statutes and privileges of Ghent made for Philip the Good around 1453 (Vienna, Österreichische Nationalbibliothek, Ms. 2583)—this artist has recently been identified instead as a successor of his, the Ghent Gradual Master.[7] Comparison of the miniatures in the present copy with the two miniatures in this master's name manuscript—a gradual made for Jacob van Brussel (d. 1474), abbot of Saint Bavo's, Ghent, sometime before 1469 (Ghent, Universiteitsbibliotheek, Ms. 14)—is difficult, given their very different subjects.[8] Comparison with other illuminations attributed to the Ghent Gradual Master, however, supports the attribution of the Manchester miniatures to him.[9] Additional close relationships between the manuscripts and the incunable can be established through comparison of the subsidiary decoration, including that of the borders.[10]

Most obviously, the miniaturist responsible for the Manchester illustrations worked in a style that depended heavily on earlier Parisian illumination and was by the 1470s deeply retrospective in character. Even most of the costumes seen in the miniatures are from an earlier generation. Some of this retrospection may derive from the artist's dependence on an earlier exemplar.[11] It may also reflect a client's wish to have a printed book that mimicked a deluxe Parisian manuscript from the early years of the fifteenth century or at least looked much older than it really was, as well as appearing to be a manuscript rather than a printed book.[12] At root it shows the artist's training in an older, Parisian tradition of manuscript illumination promoted by the Master of Guillebert de Mets. It also reflects his attempt to continue that style regardless of how contemporary miniaturists—with the notable exception of the Master of the Harley Froissart, who appears to have been trained in France and only subsequently moved north (see cat. no. 68)—were illustrating similar texts or even the same text in the Low Countries.

In addition to the Manchester volumes, at least one further copy of the translation of Valerius Maximus was illustrated within the same artistic circle.[13]   S. McK.

Notes

1. No date or place of publication is given in this edition. The terminus of 1477 is established by a sixteenth-century manuscript note recording the purchase in 1477 of another illustrated copy of the edition now in the Rosenwald Collection of the Library of Congress, Washington, D.C. (note reproduced in Davies [H.] 1910, 2: 828). As the place of publication, Bruges remains only a working hypothesis (Brussels 1973: 183, 188; Lenger 1985: 99–100).

2. Important exceptions are the editions of Boethius, on which see Arnould 2002.

VII

Icy cõmence le .vij. liure de vale-
rius/lequel contient. ix. chappitres
dont le pmier determine de feliate.

Uolubilis for-
tune ꝛc
Translateur
Icy cõmence
le .vij. liure
lequel felon
mon aduis
a.ix. chappi
tres a traſlater Et eſt le pmier cha
pitre de feliate/prinſe pour bonne
fortune ꝛ eureuſe/pour homme bien
fortune/non pas pour eſtat parfait
pour la cõgregation de tous biens
ſi cõme lappelle boece/Ne pour la vi
ſion ne fruicion diuine/ſi cõme nous
xpiens lattendons/de feliate dont ꝗ
eſt effect de fortune en biens tem
perelz parle icy valerius/Et non
pas auſſi de celle qui eſt en la ſpecu

lacion de la premiere verite/et en la
cognoiſſance des choſes diuines/de
laquelle Ariſtote parle ou .x. liure
de ethicques/A parler dont de ceſte
fortuneuſe mondaine feliate continue valerius ce .vij. liure / au prece
dent .vi. et diſt ainſi / Acteur / Nous
auons racompte ou chappitre pre
cedent pluſeurs exemples de fortu
ne voluble et mirable/Mais nous
en poons peu racompter de fortune
conſtant et eſtable/ pour quoy
il appert quelle a grant couuoitiſe
de largement enuoyer aduerſitez
et baillier largement proſperitez/
Quant elle veult oublier ſa malig
nite elle ne baille pas ſans plus
grant plente de biens/Mais les
baille grans et perpetuelz ꞇ Tranſ
lateur ꞇ Valerius entend perpetu
elz toute la vie dun homme/ſi com
me on diſt yne vicarie ou vng au
tre office perpetuel.

67

GHENT GRADUAL
MASTER
*The Story of Gyges, the
Delphic Oracle, and
Aglaus of Psophis,*
fol. 312v

3. For a list of these volumes and six detached leaves, see Brinkmann 1997: 93.

4. For examples, see Brinkmann 1997: figs. 23, 24, pls. 57, 77, 83, 89.

5. For example, Berlin, Staatsbibliothek, Ms. 94, fol. 1 (Breslauer 1965: pl. 4).

6. *Pace* Clark (2000: 100–101), the image reads simply and as follows: In the left foreground, Valerius Maximus presents Gyges to the Emperor Tiberius; Gyges wears a red robe and is consulting the oracle (who is dressed as a priest). In the foreground to the right, we remain at Delphi, where worshipers kneel before a pagan idol. The scenes farther back to left and right depict what lies behind what Gyges is told by the oracle. Immediately behind Gyges, and as an illustration of why he is an unhappy man, is his murder of his predecessor as king. To the right is the happy man Aglaus, with his wife and cattle.

7. Clark 2000: 39–52.

8. Clark 2000: pls. 21, 189.

9. Particularly close are miniatures in the Kornfeld Hours (Clark 2000: pls. 190–203).

10. Clark 2000: 173–75. Again the Kornfeld Hours is most closely related to the Manchester volumes.

11. As noted by Clark (2000: 47–48), the opening miniature of the Manchester incunable depends on the same model as the corresponding miniature by the Master of the Ghent Privileges in an earlier manuscript copy of Valerius Maximus made for Philip the Good (Paris, Bibliothèque nationale de France, Ms. fr. 6185, fol. 1). Further comparisons need to be made with miniatures produced in Paris earlier in the fifteenth century. On these, see Meiss 1974: 369, 410, 411. One copy begun in Paris and only later completed by the Rambures Master is Berlin, Staatsbibliothek, Ms. 94 (see Breslauer 1965).

12. The first owner of the Manchester incunable remains to be identified. The 4 mark in the initial on folio 284 and the central escutcheon charged with a tower may suggest that he was a merchant of Tournai.

13. As evidence of this, there survive six detached leaves that preserve the opening pages of six books of another copy of this translation (Clark 2000: 49–52, pls. 227–32). Although these pages bear six further large miniatures of high quality, the ambition of their parent volumes was clearly less than that of the Manchester copy. Not only are the detached miniatures executed only in pen and ink and thin colored washes, they also lack the fine illuminated borders and initials that accompany the Manchester miniatures. Comparison of their iconography establishes that each campaign of illustration was conceived independently and that the humbler illustrations are not mere copies or imitations of the grander ones.

MASTER OF THE HARLEY FROISSART

The Master of the Harley Froissart was named by John Plummer in his overview of late medieval French manuscript painting.[1] Yet, despite Plummer's published findings, both the miniaturist and his name manuscript—Philippe de Commynes's copy of book 4 of Froissart's *Chroniques*—have been neglected by subsequent historians of manuscript illumination. Almost certainly he has fallen outside of strict and artificial boundaries set down by many critics. For example, historians of Flemish illumination have deemed him French,[2] while to historians of French illumination he is a Flemish artist.[3] The Master of the Harley Froissart should be of interest to both parties, particularly for what—as an immigrant artist—he brought with him to the artistic melting pot in Bruges. The parallels between his career and that of the documented illuminator Philippe de Mazerolles are worthy of further investigation.[4]

According to Plummer, miniatures in a book of hours for the use of Paris datable to around 1455 (Princeton, University Library, Ms. 87) are the early work of the Master of the Harley Froissart.[5] In this book his illustrations derive from the tradition of miniature painting established in Paris by the Bedford Master. More directly, his style seems related to the art of the Master of Jean Rolin II, one of the leading commercial illuminators in Paris between 1445 and 1465 and a formative influence on subsequent Parisian illumination. Similarities between the style of the Master of the Harley Froissart and that of the Master of Jean Rolin II are likely the result of the former's training in Paris.

The most distinctive interest of the Master of the Harley Froissart was in pattern and surface geometry. Patterned tapestries and tiles create a busy setting in his steeply raked interiors. Lavish heraldic display on banners, standards, and horse trappings enliven armies on the move, jousts, formal entries, and other chivalric events. A generally pale palette is energized by blocks of intense color and a predilection for sharp edges. Formulaically drawn figures with white, childlike features are individually unremarkable but contribute to compositions in which figures and setting form harmonious images of frozen time.

The earliest datable manuscript produced in the Low Countries by the Master of the Harley Froissart is a copy of *Vie, passion, et vengeance de nostre seigneur Jhesu Christ* made for Louis of Gruuthuse sometime after 1461 (Sotheby's, London, December 6, 2001, lot 67). As he did for many Bruges illuminators, Louis became an important client of the Master of the Harley Froissart.[6] The latter's most extensive work, however, was created in the early 1470s for several large manuscript histories—none of which bears any sign of early ownership—that appear to have been produced for the trade. In these long campaigns he worked closely with the Master of the Vienna *Chroniques d'Angleterre*, a Bruges illuminator who came to specialize in the illustration of historical texts.[7] The Master of the Harley Froissart also collaborated on the illustration of one volume of the edition of Valerius Maximus produced by the Josephus Printer probably around 1475 (Antwerp, Museum Plantin-Moretus, o.B.6.9; see cat. no. 67). In the 1470s he contributed to the illustration of manuscripts of secular vernacular texts that were acquired by English patrons.[8] By the late 1470s his personal contribution seems to have become somewhat tired, and much of the work was either allocated to assistants or subcontracted to artists of the younger generation.[9] The miniatures painted by the Master of the Harley Froissart are consistently accompanied by a distinctive type of decorated outer border that includes hybrids and knights, some of whom bear banners or standards.[10] These figurative elements have the same characteristics as the figures in the accompanying miniatures and appear to have been designed and sometimes painted by the master.

S. McK.

Notes

1. New York 1982: 64–65. François Avril prefers the name "the Master of the Froissart of Philippe de Commynes" (Le Guay 1998: 173).

2. There is no mention of him in Durrieu 1921a, Winkler 1925, Brussels 1959, Dogaer 1987a, or Smeyers 1998.

3. There is no mention of him in Paris 1993.

4. In this context it is worth noting that Mazerolles was probably in Paris in 1454, in Bruges by at least 1467, and dead by 1479. A summary of his documented career is offered in de Schryver 1979a: 135–44.

5. Another early work appears to be Geneva, Bibliothèque publique et universitaire, Ms. fr. 164.

6. Manuscripts illuminated for Gruuthuse by this artist include two small-format volumes, *Instruction d'un jeune prince* (London, British Library, Cotton Ms. Vespasian B i) and *Miroir de l'âme* (cat. no. 60). He also illustrated three larger volumes: two romances, *Lancelot* and *Perceforest*, and a history, the *Chronique de Charles VII* (Paris, Bibliothèque nationale de France, Mss. fr. 121, fr. 345–46, fr. 2691).

7. Paris, Bibliothèque de Sainte-Geneviève, Ms. 935; Sotheby's, London, May 31, 1960, lot 2; cat. no. 68. Also, in semi-grisaille, London, British Library, Burney Ms. 169; Vienna, Österreichische Nationalbibliothek, Ms. 2566; cat. no. 82.

8. London, British Library, Add. Mss. 35322–23, Royal Mss. 14 D.ii–vi, 16 G.ix, 18 E.i, 20 C.ii, 20 C.ix; Cambridge, Corpus Christi College, Ms. 91. For the first manuscript, see Reynolds (C.) 1988: 131–35. For the Cambridge volume and a list of attributions to an illuminator called "the Tapestry Master," see Visser-Fuchs 1998: 282–83.

9. In the Thwaytes Froissart (London, British Library, Royal Mss. 14 D.ii–vi), even the frontispieces are by an assistant (Le Guay 1998: figs. 6, 9, 10, 11), and a few smaller miniatures are by the Master of the London Wavrin (Le Guay 1998: figs. 41, 48). Only the opening miniatures of vol. 2 of Edward IV's Froissart (London, British Library, Royal Ms. 18 E.i, fol. 12), *Cyropédie* (London, British Library, Royal Ms. 16 G.ix, fol. 7), and *Bible historiale* (cat. no. 83) are by the Master of the Harley Froissart. Around 1480 he collaborated with the Master of the Soane Josephus on the *Fleur des histoires* of Jean-Louis de Savoie, bishop of Geneva (d. 1482) (see Paravicini Bagliani 1990: pls. 31–34).

10. These figurative elements are also found in the borders of Edward IV's *Bible historiale* (cat. no. 82), and in the borders of the Josephus that passed to Edward by 1480 (cat. no. 81), which may confirm the Master of the Harley Froissart's involvement in the early stages of these volumes. In 1479 Edward made a large payment for books to a foreign merchant called "Philip Maisertuell." I suggest elsewhere (McKendrick 1992: 159 n.91) that this merchant was Philippe de Mazerolles. This payment may offer a further link between the two.

68

MASTER OF THE HARLEY FROISSART AND MASTER OF THE VIENNA *CHRONIQUES D'ANGLETERRE*

Jean Froissart, *Chroniques*, book 4
Bruges, ca. 1470–72

MANUSCRIPT: iii + 184 + ii folios, 42 × 32 cm (16½ × 12⅝ in.); justification: 27 × 19.5 cm (10⅝ × 7⅝ in.); 36 lines of *bastarda* in two columns; 1 three-quarter-page miniature, 10 half-page miniatures, 18 one-column miniatures

HERALDRY: Escutcheon with the arms of Commynes quartering those of Armuyden, surmounted by helm, crest of wolf's head, wreath, and mantling, fol. 3; escutcheons and banners with the same arms, fols. 12v, 23v, 29v, etc.; undeciphered inscription on standard, fol. 99

BINDING: France, ca. 1700; green velvet over pasteboard; rebacked; gold-tooled vellum doublures; two brass clasps

COLLECTION: London, The British Library, Harley Ms. 4379

PROVENANCE: Philippe de Commynes, lord of Argenton (1447–1511); the Château d'Anet (mark on fol. 1), sold after the death of Anne of Bavaria (1648–1723) [her sale, Pierre Gandouin, Paris, November 1724, lot 44 of the vellum manuscripts]; [James Woodman, London]; Edward Harley, second earl of Oxford (1689–1741), first offered to him in 1725; Margaret, duchess of Portland (1715–1785); purchased 1753

R A

The present manuscript and its companion (London, British Library, Harley Ms. 4380) were produced as one volume and together are known as the Harley Froissart. The illustrative program of eighty miniatures was the most ambitious of seven known copies of book 4 of Jean Froissart's *Chroniques* produced in the southern Netherlands between 1460 and 1480. In fact, the Harley Froissart is the most extensively illustrated manuscript of any of the books of Froissart's *Chroniques*. This lavish manuscript exemplifies the particular interest in this text shown by readers associated with the Burgundian court many decades after the work's composition and its initial reception and illustration in Paris.

Most of the illustrations are the work of one artist, the Master of the Harley Froissart, who takes his name from this book. Others are by a Bruges artist known as the Master of the Vienna *Chroniques d'Angleterre*, after one of his most extensively illustrated manuscripts.[1] A few are clearly the collaborative work of both artists,[2] and from these it is evident that the two artists worked very closely on the present volume. Both miniaturists came to specialize in the illustration of secular vernacular texts, many of which were very long and filled several folio volumes.[3] These two artists were also collaborators on at least two further volumes: a *Chroniques d'Angleterre* and a copy of Monstrelet's *Chroniques*.[4]

The Harley Froissart includes some of the most inventive and colorful miniatures produced by its name artist. Interested primarily in surface pattern, he delighted in the pageantry of his subjects, transforming a ship at sea into pleasing shapes and splashes of color. Trained in the old traditions of Parisian illumination, he transmuted walls into pink and green counterpoints to the figures before them. Landscapes are marked out with stubby, triangular trees, and skies are studded with gold stars. The relative freshness

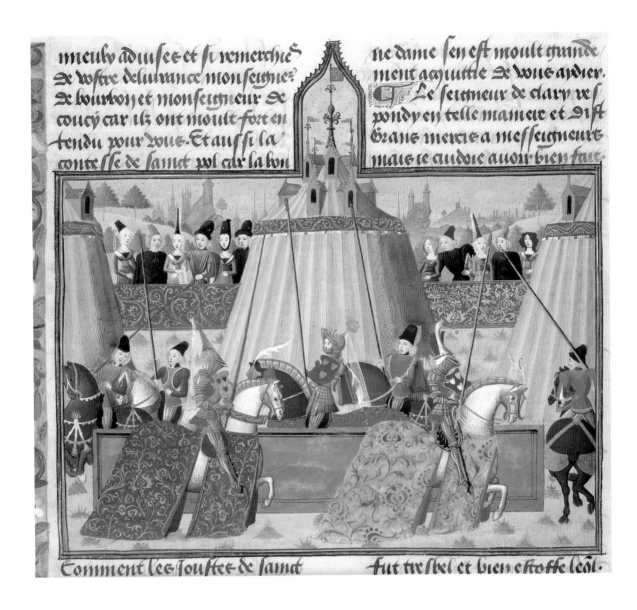

of his painting points to the absence of collaborators and suggests a date early in his career (soon after his move from Paris to Bruges). Other illustrations attributed to the Master of the Harley Froissart are more clearly formulaic than those in his name manuscript and are thus probably imitations by his assistants. Such imitations appear in at least two copies of Froissart's *Chroniques* (other than the Harley volume).[5] One of these copies includes a version of the opening miniature of the Harley volume.[6]

The first owner of this copy of part of Froissart's *Chroniques*, Philippe de Commynes, was himself a significant chronicler and would thus have had a particular interest in this text. How and when he came to acquire the manuscript is less easy to determine. His arms and devices are clearly an addition to the border decoration, but they are integrated in a way that suggests that they were added very soon after the illumination of the borders and form the first marks of ownership. Although Commynes, who was born in 1447, would have been very young at the time and less financially well off,[7] the most likely opportunity for him to have acquired this Flemish manuscript was before 1472, when he transferred his allegiance from Charles the

Bold to the rival Louis XI of France. Commynes had been a close associate of Charles the Bold beginning in 1464, and on the latter's succession to the dukedom in 1468 Commynes became one of his counselors and chamberlains. The inclusion in the present manuscript of the arms of Commynes's Flemish mother, Marguerite d'Armuyden, suggests a dating before 1472. All of his other surviving manuscripts are of French origins and thus seem to belong to a later phase in Commynes's fine manuscript collection.

S. McK.

Notes

1. Thoss 1987: no. 56.

2. The most obvious example of this collaboration is a miniature in Harley Ms. 4380 (fol. 149), in which the overall composition and landscape were contributed by the Master of the Vienna *Chroniques d'Angleterre* and the figures are by the Master of the Harley Froissart. Another obvious collaboration is Harley Ms. 4380, fol. 151.

3. See Pächt and Thoss 1990, 2: 45; and Le Guay 1998: 173. See also Visser-Fuchs 1998: 282–83.

4. Paris, Bibliothèque de Sainte-Geneviève, Ms. 935; Sotheby's, London, May 31, 1960, lot 2.

5. London, British Library, Royal Mss. 18 E.i, 14 D.ii–vi.

6. London, British Library, Royal Ms. 14 D.vi, fol. 5.

7. On his early financial difficulties, see Harsgor 1980: 1605–6.

MASTER OF ANTHONY OF BURGUNDY

The Master of Anthony of Burgundy was named by Friedrich Winkler after three large manuscripts containing secular vernacular texts made for Anthony (1421–1504), the illegitimate half brother of Charles the Bold.[1] Painted around 1470, the miniatures in these volumes are clearly the work of more than one illuminator. The Master of Anthony of Burgundy's miniatures are easy to distinguish,[2] as they are by far the most artistically accomplished. One of his assistants is the much less talented follower of the Master of Margaret of York (see biography of the Master of Margaret of York, part 2), whom I have named the Master of the Bruges *Genealogia deorum*.[3] The collaboration of this artist with the Master of Anthony of Burgundy, together with evidence of the illuminated borders and other subsidiary decoration, suggests that all three manuscripts were produced in Bruges.[4]

Within the miniatures in these three manuscripts the figures are expressive and animated in both gesture and facial expression.[5] Faces are heavily modeled and individualized, sometimes to the point of caricature. Figures are well drawn, varied in their assured poses, and relate well to one another, often establishing a rhythmical chain of linear or even circular movement on the page. Prominent S-shaped paths winding through landscapes or townscapes further animate the surface, as do large-patterned brocade hangings. Wood, stone, and fabrics are crisply delineated and have a tactile reality. Winkler likened the sharply folded drapery to "freshly ironed laundry."[6] The repeated cutting off of figures and other forms by the frame of the miniature gives these works by the Master of Anthony of Burgundy a pictorial breadth. This tactic helped him produce some of his finest work even within the restricted spaces of one-column miniatures.

On the basis of the style of the miniatures in the three manuscripts made for Anthony of Burgundy, Winkler made several further attributions to the Master within roughly contemporaneous manuscripts, including the frontispiece of Louis of Gruuthuse's copy of Bartholomaeus Anglicus (Paris, Bibliothèque nationale de France, Ms. fr. 134), all fifteen miniatures in Philip of Cleves's copy of *Les Douze Dames de rhétorique* (Munich, Bayerische Staatsbibliothek, Ms. gall. 15), and the lavishly illustrated Pembroke Hours (Philadelphia, Free Library, Ms. Lewis E 182). Ottokar Smital added four more volumes to Winkler's corpus, including Gruuthuse's copies of the *Douze Dames* and the final volume of Froissart's *Chroniques* (cat. nos. 69, 71).[7] Recent close comparison of the Gruuthuse and Cleves copies of the *Douze Dames* with another copy made for Jean de Montferrant (cat. no. 70), however, has highlighted subtle but significant differences of execution within this extended corpus of miniatures.[8] These observations suggest that the Master of Anthony of Burgundy had more than one assistant capable of painting in a closely related style.

Most significant for subsequent studies of the Master of Anthony of Burgundy, Winkler also attributed to him the arresting miniatures in the Vienna Black Hours (Vienna, Österreichische Nationalbibliothek, Ms. 1856). As a counterpart to his revisionist interpretation of the Vienna Hours of Mary of Burgundy (cat. no. 19), Antoine de Schryver identified the Vienna Black Hours with a documented book of hours made for Charles the Bold and presented to the duke by the Vrije (Liberty) of Bruges in 1466.[9] Its illumination was completed by Charles's court illuminator, Philippe de Mazerolles, in 1468. De Schryver supported his identification of Philippe de Mazerolles as the miniaturist of the Black Hours through detailed stylistic analysis of the book's illuminations. In particular he emphasized features of the miniatures that he considered reflective of Mazerolles's French origins. Despite his most recent publication on the subject,[10] de Schryver's identification remains contentious and ultimately unproved. Doubts raised separately by Dagmar Thoss and Ulrike Jenni[11] and by Bodo Brinkmann[12] are significant, as are their alternative identifications.

Whatever his origins, the Master of Anthony of Burgundy painted some of the most original miniatures produced at Bruges in the late 1460s and early 1470s. In such major projects as Gruuthuse's copy of Froissart's *Chroniques*, he collaborated as an equal with the leading Bruges miniaturists Loyset Liédet and the Master of Margaret of York. His collaboration with the Master of the Dresden Prayer Book in the same manuscript appears to have been that of a master with an assistant.[13] Part of the outstanding achievement of the Master of the Dresden Prayer Book derives from the training that the artist received from the Master of Anthony of Burgundy.   S. McK.

Notes

1. The three manuscripts are Berlin, Staatsbibliothek, Dep. Breslau 2; The Hague, Museum Meermanno-Westreenianum, Ms. 10 A 21; and formerly Paris, private collection; Winkler 1921: 13; Winkler 1925: 82.

2. The Master of Anthony of Burgundy was responsible for most of the miniatures, including the large ones, in the Berlin and Paris manuscripts, but only the ten small miniatures in the Hague volume (see note 1).

3. The Master of the Bruges *Genealogia deorum* painted the three large miniatures in the Hague volume (Byvanck 1924: 124) and eight small ones in the Berlin Valerius Maximus (Brinkmann 1997: 71 n. 8).

4. The border decoration of the Berlin Valerius Maximus is of the same type continued in several manuscripts illuminated in the 1470s by the Master of the Vienna *Chroniques d'Angleterre*, whose miniature style derives from that of the Master of Anthony of Burgundy.

5. De Schryver (1979: 144) described the Master of Anthony of Burgundy as a "peintre de l'angoisse et de l'inquiétude."

6. Winkler 1921: 12.

7. Smital 1930b: 47, 63–65. The other two volumes noted by Smital are two copies of Lefèvre's *Recueil* (Brussels, Bibliothèque royale de Belgiques, Mss. 9262, 9263). Of these two volumes, the copy made sometime before 1467 for Charles the Bold as count of Charolais (Ms. 9263) includes the earliest miniatures securely attributable to the Master of Anthony of Burgundy. They reveal a fully mature style. The miniatures in the other Brussels *Recueil* are the work of a less talented assistant.

8. Chavannes-Mazel 1992: 144–47.

9. De Schryver 1957, as noted in Brussels 1959: no. 135. See also de Schryver 1979a: 136–41.

10. De Schryver 1999: 50–58.

11. Jenni and Thoss 1982; Pächt and Thoss 1990: 17–38; Thoss 1991. They argue for an origin in Holland for the miniaturist of the Vienna Black Hours.

12. Brinkmann 1997: 22 n. 56, 274; also Brinkmann, in DOA 1996, 20: 618–19; Brinkmann, in DOA 1996, 24: 605–6.

13. Brinkmann 1997: 75–79. Brinkmann wondered if the Master of Fitzwilliam 268 should be identified with Philippe de Mazerolles.

69
WORKSHOP OF
MASTER OF ANTHONY
OF BURGUNDY
*Jean de Montferrant
Receives Letters from
Jean Robertet*, fol. 1

69

WORKSHOP OF MASTER OF ANTHONY OF BURGUNDY

Georges Chastellain, Jean Robertet, and Jean de Montferrant,
Les Douze Dames de rhétorique
Bruges, ca. 1465–75

MANUSCRIPT: iv + 47 + ii folios, 30.2 × 22 cm (11⅞ × 8⅝ in.); justification: 18.6 × 11.6 cm (7⅜ × 4½ in.); 33 lines of *bastarda*; 14 half- to three-quarter-page miniatures

HERALDRY: Escutcheon with the arms of Louis of Gruuthuse, encircled by collar of the Order of the Golden Fleece and surmounted by helm, crest, and mantling, overpainted by the arms of France; banner with the arms of Louis of Gruuthuse, all fol. 1

BINDING: Paris, early nineteenth century; blind-tooled calf over wood boards, in imitation of a medieval blind-stamped binding

COLLECTION: Paris, Bibliothèque nationale de France, Ms. fr. 1174

PROVENANCE: Louis of Gruuthuse (1422–1492); Louis XII, king of France (1462–1515) (Blois inventories of 1518 [no. 76] and 1544 [no. 1400])

JPGM

Les Douze Dames de rhétorique preserves a rare example of literary correspondence from the time of Charles the Bold. Starting with a pleading letter from Jean Robertet, poet and secretary of the duke of Bourbon, to the Burgundian courtier Jean de Montferrant, the text centers on verses attributed to the Burgundian court chronicler and poet Georges Chastellain. These verses, composed in response to flattering praise of Chastellain from both Montferrant and Robertet, describe twelve aspects of rhetoric as personified by twelve ladies.[1] The literary exchange, replete with mutual admiration, reflects the close political, dynastic, and artistic relations that linked the Burgundian and Bourbon courts in the 1460s.

Of the five manuscripts that preserve this text, three of them are deluxe copies, such as this one, made for Louis of Gruuthuse (1422–1492). This manuscript is closely related in its illustrative campaign to the two other fine copies of this text, one made for Jean de Montferrant (cat. no. 70) and the other owned by Philip of Cleves (Munich, Bayerische Staatsbibliothek, Ms. gall. 15). These campaigns are similar not only stylistically but also iconographically, with images based on the same models. Although only Montferrant's copy is closely datable, stylistic comparison suggests that all three copies are roughly contemporaneous.

The artist responsible for the illustration of Gruuthuse's volume is freer in the interpretation of his models than that responsible for Montferrant's copy of *Les Douze Dames* or the slavish but inaccurate copyist of the Cleves version. In the second miniature, for example, which illustrates Montferrant's first encounter with the twelve ladies, the Gruuthuse artist carefully repeated the distinctive features of each lady. At the same time, however, he omitted their identifying titles and arranged the figures in such a tightly packed group that several of them are represented by their heads only. As a result the artist conflated the features of two of the ladies, Multiforme ricesse and Clere invention, thus reducing their number to eleven. That this is a temporary lapse and not merely a reflection of the model is made clear by the next miniature. In this, as in Montferrant's copy, all twelve ladies reappear, correctly distinguished from one another.

Comparison with Montferrant's copy reveals several other important differences. The depictions of the ladies in Gruuthuse's copies are more schematic. The compositions in this volume are also simplified, and some details are either suppressed or included in a labored manner. Settings never equal the beautiful landscapes behind the figure of Eloquence in Montferrant's copy, for example. More frequently the scene is set on a narrow stage, on a loggia, with parted curtains gathered to each side.

Most notably in the case of the illustrations in Gruuthuse's manuscript, the first (ill. 69) and third miniatures prominently feature a figure included in neither the Montferrant (ill. 70) nor the Cleves copy. According to Claudine Lemaire and Antoine de Schryver, this figure represents Montferrant's pupil, the short-lived Jacques de Bourbon (d. 1468).[2] Such an interpretation makes sense, given the reference in the text's rubrics to Montferrant's tutorship of Jacques. Since he had barely been nominated a knight of the Order of the Golden Fleece before he died, however, his depiction wearing the collar of the order is somewhat surprising. His presence in both miniatures is difficult to explain unless this was done sometime between the meeting of the order on May 14, 1468, and his death eight days later.[3] A more plausible argument is that the figure represents Gruuthuse himself. A very similarly dressed figure is introduced into miniatures in several other manuscripts produced for Gruuthuse (see cat. no. 61). As in the present miniatures, this figure frequently introduces a further link between Gruuthuse and his manuscripts.

The differences to be observed between the interrelated campaigns of the three manuscripts of *Les Douze Dames* do not merely reflect three attempts at its illustration by the same artist. They reflect the work of three artists, trained in the same circle but of different levels of artistic ability and with different artistic characteristics. Although this fact is most obvious in the case of the Cleves manuscript, it is also true in the case of the other two. Comparison of palette, figure scale, and treatment of faces, gesture, costume, and landscape suggests that a different artist worked on each. Thus each manuscript of *Les Douze Dames*, although closely related, is the product of an entirely different team of scribe, decorator, and miniaturist.   S. McK.

Notes

1. The twelve are, respectively, Science, Eloquence, Profundité, Gravité de sens, Vielle acquisition, Multiforme ricesse, Flourie memoire, Noble nature, Clere invention, Precieuse possession, Deduction loable, and Glorieuse achevissance.

2. Bruges 1981: 253.

3. De Smedt (R.) 2000: no. 66.

70

MASTER OF ANTHONY OF BURGUNDY

Georges Chastellain, Jean Robertet, and Jean de Montferrant,
Les Douze Dames de rhétorique
Bruges, 1467–68

MANUSCRIPT: 61 folios, 27.5 × 20.3 cm (10⅞ × 8 in.); justification: 17.1 × 11.5 cm (6¾ × 4½ in.); 35 lines of *bastarda*; 14 half- to three-quarter-page miniatures, 1 historiated initial

HERALDRY: Escutcheons with the arms of the Montferrant family of Bugey, fol. 9

BINDING: England, ca. 1700; gold-tooled calf over beveled wood boards; two brass clasps with the arms of the Montferrant family of Bugey, remounted

COLLECTION: Cambridge, University Library, Ms. Nn.3.2

PROVENANCE: John of Montferrant, lord of Bugey; presented 1715 by George I, king of England (1660–1727)

RA

The recent recognition that this deluxe copy of *Les Douze Dames de rhétorique* belonged to the Burgundian courtier Jean de Montferrant establishes it as the only copy closely linked to a participant in the literary correspondence that forms the basis of the text. Whereas the correspondence probably dates from 1463/64, the text of Montferrant's manuscript was copied during the period between 1467 and 1468.[1] It is clearly not an authorial script but a fair copy produced by commercial book producers, the finely written text spaciously laid out and lavishly illustrated by a professional miniaturist. Stylistically and iconographically, the illustrations are closely related to those produced for the only other fine copies of *Les Douze Dames*, one produced for Louis of Gruuthuse (cat. no. 69) and another that came to belong to Philip of Cleves (Munich, Bayerische Staatsbibliothek, Ms. gall. 15). Although of more elevated social status, these two members of the Burgundian court would have been well acquainted with Montferrant as "maître d'hôtel" of Philip the Good and then counselor and chamberlain of Charles the Bold. Such acquaintance almost certainly explains their knowledge of his text. Unlike Montferrant,[2] both Gruuthuse and Cleves had the financial resources to indulge a taste for fine copies of such texts. Their motivation for acquiring copies of *Les Douze Dames* was therefore less personal and more circumstantial than Montferrant's.

As might be expected, the illustrative program preserved in Montferrant's manuscript is the most complete and accurate among the three copies.[3] In comparison, the illustrations of the Cleves manuscript are considerably inferior. They are repeatedly inaccurate in detail and clearly the work of a less accomplished artist. Their similarity to the illustrations in Montferrant's volume is reflective of either a direct but sloppy copy or a less careful and informed version of the same models. The illustrations in Gruuthuse's manuscript reflect the work of a more accomplished artist embellishing the same models, sometimes to good effect and at other times with a freedom that causes the miniatures to deviate from the text (see cat. no. 69).

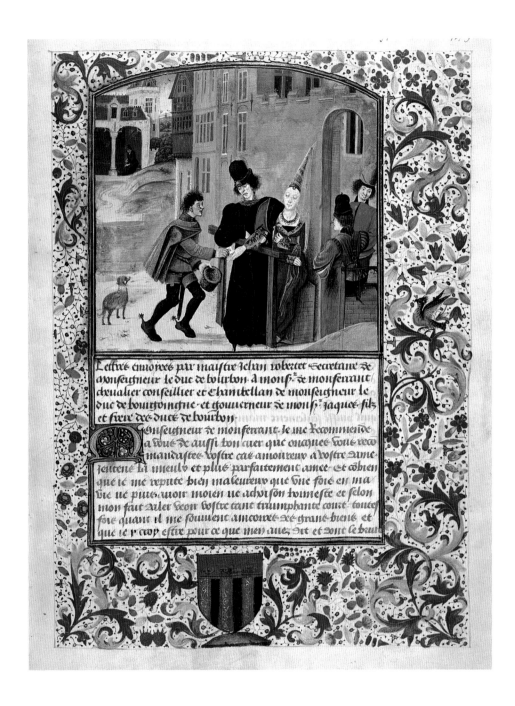

Whatever their exact relationships, the three sequences of illustrations of the twelve ladies are all ultimately based on the same visual models, as they all contain details not found in the text they illustrate. The nature of such models has been given careful consideration elsewhere.[4] One possibility is that these illustrations accompanied the original correspondence. Their greater detail would thus reflect early elaborations on the texts by their authors. An alternative explanation sees the models as created for a monumental work similar to the wall paintings depicting the twelve ladies of rhetoric that survive in Lausanne. As both iconographically related and independent sources, such models could explain differences between the miniatures and their text. A final possibility, little considered, is the influence of mime or drama. The ladies' elaborate costume, their stagelike settings, the inscriptions, and the repeated framing by curtains is very suggestive of such

influence and certainly comparable with descriptions of contemporary *tableaux vivants*. A visual record of such tableaux could have served as a model for the miniatures.[5] Montferrant's direct relations with the Bruges illuminators through the Confraternity of Saint John[6] would certainly have allowed him to provide guidance on how he wished the text of *Les Douze Dames* to be illustrated.   S. McK.

Notes

1. This dating is based on Montferrant's titles in the rubrics.
2. His arms have been recognized in only one other manuscript: London, British Library, Add. Ms. 11696.
3. The absence of a miniature for Flourie memoire is a late loss.
4. Chavannes-Mazel 1992: 147–50.
5. A later example exists in the illustrated record of the entry of Joanna of Castile into Brussels in 1496 (see Berlin 1975: no. 171).
6. See Catherine Reynolds, "Illuminators and the Painters' Guilds" (this volume).

71

MASTER OF ANTHONY OF BURGUNDY, MASTER OF THE DRESDEN PRAYER BOOK, AND MASTER OF MARGARET OF YORK

Jean Froissart, *Chroniques*, books 3 and 4
Bruges, ca. 1470–75

MANUSCRIPT: viii + 379 + i folios and 341 folios, 44 × 33 cm (17⅛ × 13 in.); justification: 28.5 × 20 cm (11¼ × 7⅞ in.); 38 lines of *bastarda* in two columns; fr. 2645: 9 half- to three-quarter-page miniatures, 13 one-column miniatures; fr. 2646: 10 half- to three-quarter-page miniatures, 17 one-column miniatures, 1 historiated initial

HERALDRY: Escutcheons with the arms, helm, wreath, and mantling of Gruuthuse overpainted by the royal arms and crest of France, fr. 2645, fol. 1, and fr. 2646, fol. 6; bombard device, fr. 2646, fols. 14v, 58v, 79, etc.

BINDING: Paris, seventeenth or eighteenth century; yellow morocco; the arms of France gold-stamped on both covers; traces of former blue velvet binding on former pastedowns of fr. 2645

COLLECTION: Paris, Bibliothèque nationale de France, Mss. fr. 2645, 2646

PROVENANCE: Louis of Gruuthuse (1422–1492); Louis XII, king of France (1462–1515) (Blois inventory of 1518 [nos. 94, 95])

JPGM (fr. 2646) and RA (fr. 2645)

The present two manuscripts (books 3 and 4) and their companion volumes (books 1 and 2: Paris, Bibliothèque nationale de France, Mss. fr. 2643, 2644) form a deluxe four-volume set of the full text of the *Chroniques* of Jean Froissart. Made for the Bruges bibliophile Louis of Gruuthuse between 1470 and 1475, these four volumes bear witness to a significant resurgence of interest in Froissart's text, which was written between 1370 and 1400.[1] The author's colorful account of the battles waged across northern Europe between 1327 and 1400 became popular again in the Burgundian Netherlands between the late 1460s and around 1480. Of the manuscripts that this revival spawned (see cat. nos. 68, 79), the present two volumes contain some of the most artistically accomplished illustrations of their time.

The attention of previous scholars has focused on the present two volumes of Gruuthuse's copy of the *Chroniques*. As early as 1925 Friedrich Winkler tentatively attributed some of the illustrations in this copy to one of the most original miniaturists of Gruuthuse's time, the Master of the Dresden Prayer Book.[2] Subsequently L. M. J. Delaissé, Claudine Lemaire and Antoine de Schryver, and Bodo Brinkmann sought to define the contribution of this miniaturist within the present two volumes.[3] All four scholars agree that the Master of the Dresden Prayer Book worked on the illustrations in close collaboration with another Bruges miniaturist, the Master of Anthony of Burgundy. Lemaire, de Schryver, and Brinkmann define that collaboration as one between master and assistant and the role of the Master of the Dresden Prayer Book as that of a talented pupil. Whereas Delaissé noted the hand of the Master of the Dresden Prayer Book in only the final volume of Gruuthuse's set (Ms. fr. 2646), the other three critics correctly observed his hand at work also in the third volume (Ms. fr. 2645). They also note the contribution of a third miniaturist, the Master of Margaret of York.

Despite such critical attention, much remains unclear concerning Gruuthuse's copy of the *Chroniques*. Why in particular are the present two volumes so different from the first two? As has frequently been noted since the time of Winkler, the sixty miniatures of the first two volumes are by the prolific Bruges illuminator Loyset Liédet. As in the case of many other works by Liédet, these miniatures are of adequate but unremarkable artistic quality. As first noted by Delaissé,[4] the border decoration of the first two volumes is very different in character from that of the two final volumes. Moreover, as Delaissé also noted, whereas the border decoration of first two volumes is consistent in character, the border decoration of the third volume is very different from that of the fourth.[5] Given that the scribe of the first two volumes is also not the same as that of the second two,[6] a significant and broad-based division emerges between these two pairs of volumes. Teasing out the possible reasons for this division will help to elucidate the present two manuscripts.

Many contemporary manuscripts bear witness to the contribution of more than one scribe, illuminator, and miniaturist in the production of a deluxe copy of either a devotional or a secular text. Many volumes that make up multivolume sets also differ significantly in artistic character from their companion volumes. Such general observations are, however, an insufficient explanation of the differences observed within Gruuthuse's copy of the *Chroniques*. The distinctions between the first two and the second two volumes are better explained as the result of a very early partition of the project between Liédet and the Master of Anthony of Burgundy.[7] Indeed, the overall differences between these two pairs of manuscripts suggest that in each manuscript the miniaturist was responsible for coordinating every aspect of their production. The greater uniformity of the border decoration in the first two volumes thus reflects Liédet's ready access at this point in time to a border artist inspired by the inventions of Lieven van Lathem,[8] as well as Liédet's consistent and well-developed production methods. The differences between the border decoration of the second two volumes derive from the more fluid collaborations of the Master of Anthony of Burgundy. The border artist for book 3 is frequently linked with the Master of Anthony of Burgundy's first collaborator, the Master of Margaret of York.[9] The border artist for book 4 has been identified as an illuminator who worked elsewhere with the Master of Anthony of Burgundy's other collaborator on the *Chroniques*, the Master of the Dresden Prayer Book. This illuminator has been called the Dresden follower of Willem Vrelant after his collaboration with the Master of the Dresden Prayer Book in his name manuscript.[10]

It is in this context that the miniatures in the present two manuscripts should be considered. For just as other aspects of these two volumes seem to have been coordinated by the Master of Anthony of Burgundy, so the campaign of illustration was ultimately the responsibility of this miniaturist. The imprint of his hand is therefore likely to be pervasive. And so it is. The miniatures that can be attributed to the Master of Margaret of York are notably different

71a (opposite)
MASTER OF ANTHONY OF BURGUNDY
Bal des Ardents, Ms. fr. 2646, fol. 176

176

L'aduenture d'une danse faitte a paris en samblance d'homes sauuaittes la ou le roy fut en grant peril. vvvij.

D uant assez tost ap̄s cesse retemie que vn mariage se fist a lo ster du roy de vn nou ne cheuasser de vermendois et de vne des damoiselles de la vyme sy en fu se roy z sa royme ses f̄ et ses dames et ses damoiselles z tout

softes resiou Et pour ceste cause se roy vost faire ses noepces et furent fauttes dedens softes de samt vosa paris z y ot grant foison de bōnes gens z de seigneurs Et y furet se duc d'siens se duc de berri z se duc de bourgoingne et seurs femmes Tout se iour des noepces que il̄z espouserent on ainsa et mena grit reuel̄z fist se roy se souper auv dames z tint sa royme de frāce sestat. Et sefforceoit chascun de ioye faire pour sa cause de ce que il̄z seroient se roy qui se esmoit

71b
MASTER OF ANTHONY
OF BURGUNDY
*Louis of Anjou Greeted
outside Paris*, Ms. fr. 2645,
fol. 321v (detail)

from other works by that miniaturist, particularly with respect to their treatment of space and landscape.[11] Given that the treatment of these features of the miniatures is more characteristic of the Master of Anthony of Burgundy, it seems likely that an outline of his composition was followed by the Master of Margaret of York. The precise identification of the contribution of the Master of the Dresden Prayer Book has, I think, eluded previous scholars because of important input from the Master of Anthony of Burgundy into all the miniatures in the two volumes. Indeed, the problem of distinguishing the Master of the Dresden Prayer Book's part is much greater than the problem of identifying that of the Master of Margaret of York. However talented he was, the Master of the Dresden Prayer Book still served in the capacity of an assistant to the Master of Anthony of Burgundy.

Two examples serve to illustrate both the remarkable artistic achievement of the Master of Anthony of Burgundy and the academic difficulties presented by the miniatures of the present two volumes. According to Winkler,[12] the miniature of the young Louis of Anjou being greeted outside the city of Paris (ill. 71b) could well be by the Master of

the Dresden Prayer Book. In making this judgment, Winkler was undoubtedly impressed by the ambitious composition of the miniature, through which the artist sought to link the narrative subject with the background setting. The foreground, with its assured figure poses, and the background, with its topographic accuracy, are linked by figures that move from background to foreground. Their presence in a middle ground is signaled by a dissipation of color and detailing. The center point of the composition is artfully left empty by the inclined head of the principal man greeting Louis of Anjou and by a break in the figures joining foreground and background. All aspects of this composition are credible as the work of the Master of Anthony of Burgundy. Moreover, the execution of individual figures is perfectly consistent with that found in miniatures accepted as the work of the Master of Anthony of Burgundy. In my opinion, therefore, there is no need to attribute even part of this miniature to the Master of the Dresden Prayer Book.

A similar attribution to the Master of Anthony of Burgundy can be made in the case of the miniature showing how Charles VI was nearly burned alive at the Hôtel de Saint-Pol in Paris at the so-called *Bal des Ardents* (ill. 71a).

Despite the fading resulting from previous exposure to strong light, this miniature is a veritable tour de force in the handling of space, forms, light, and emotion. Comparison of individual figures and the handling of paint, however, reveals nothing inconsistent with other miniatures attributed to the Master of Anthony of Burgundy. Emotional power is a common distinguishing characteristic of his miniatures. The somber setting and subtly illuminated interior are also within his repertoire. Even within the same volume the miniature of Pierre de Craon assaulting Olivier de Clisson (fol. 146v) shows the Master of Anthony of Burgundy enhancing the emotional impact of his subject though a partly lit night setting.

While I prefer to consider these much-discussed miniatures as the work of the Master of Anthony of Burgundy at his most accomplished, I would distinguish the work of the Master of the Dresden Prayer Book in several other miniatures within the present two manuscripts.[13] These works are distinguished from the others by their startlingly ambitious palette and combination of colors, agitated and vibrantly modeled drapery, an apparently inexhaustible range of well-designed figure poses, and challenging placement of figures within complex spaces. Within the third volume of Gruuthuse's copy of the *Chroniques*, miniatures that include these characteristics are *The Battle of Aljuborrota, Turks in Battle with Serbs, The Capture of Oresne, The Battle of Radcot Bridge,* and *The Flight of Robert de Vere* (Ms. fr. 2645, fols. 62v, 79, 82v, 211v, 244, 245v). Within the fourth and final volume they include *The Battle of Nicopolis* and, most notably, *The Massacre of Christian Prisoners* (Ms. fr. 2646, fols. 220, 255v).

S. McK.

Notes

1. On this revival, see cat. no. 79.
2. Winkler 1925: 98, 192. On the basis of Durrieu 1921a: pl. 49, Winkler suggested an attribution to the Master of the Dresden Prayer Book for the miniature on folio 321v of Ms. fr. 2645.
3. Delaissé, in Brussels 1959: nos. 162–65; Lemaire and de Schryver, in Bruges 1981: no. 109; Brinkmann 1997: 75–79.
4. Brussels 1959: nos. 162–65.
5. In addition, the spray decoration accompanying two-line initials in the two volumes is different in style and apparently by a different hand.
6. To my knowledge no previous critic has considered the scribes of these four volumes.
7. This division of labor was probably intended to increase the speed at which the set was produced for Gruuthuse. The allocation of the third and fourth volumes to the Master of Anthony of Burgundy may be a further reflection of greater interest on the part of the Burgundians in the later parts of Froissart's *Chroniques*.
8. On this border artist, see de Schryver, Dykmans, and Ruysschaert 1989: 69–73.
9. On this border style, see cat. no. 62.
10. Brinkmann 1997: 47–53, 78–79, 397. A further datable example is the border accompanying the dedication illustration in the Boston copy of Colard Mansion's 1476 edition of Boccaccio (see Brinkmann 1997: pl. 92). On this edition and the Master of the Dresden Prayer Book, see cat. no. 73.
11. The miniatures painted by the Master of Margaret of York are Ms. fr. 2645, fols. 282v, 351. Miniatures that also include backgrounds by this artist are Ms. fr. 2645, fol. 1, and Ms. fr. 2646, fol. 58v.
12. Winkler 1925: 192.
13. Previous critics have generally avoided attribution of specific miniatures to the Master of the Dresden Prayer Book.

72

MASTER OF THE WHITE INSCRIPTIONS, MASTER OF THE GETTY FROISSART, AND CIRCLE OF MASTER OF ANTHONY OF BURGUNDY

Giovanni Boccaccio, *De la ruine des nobles hommes et femmes,* translation by Laurent de Premierfait of *De casibus virorum et feminarum illustrium*
Bruges, 1476 or later

PRINTED BOOK: Paper, 289 folios, 34 × 23 cm (13½ × 9 in.); justification: 26.5 × 17 cm (10½ × 6⅛ in.); 33 lines of type in two columns printed by Colard Mansion in black and red; initials and paraphs added by hand in red and blue; 8 pasted-in copper engravings

INSCRIPTIONS: *A la gloire et loenge de dieu et a linstruction de tous a este cestui euure de bocace du dechiet des nobles hommes et femmes. jmprime a Bruges par Colard mansion. Anno. M. CCCC. lxxvj.,* colophon

BINDING: Netherlands, ca. 1700; undecorated vellum over pasteboard; faded early title *Johan Bocace de Certald . . .* and later title *Les OEuvres de J: Bocace* on spine

COLLECTION: Bucks, The Wormsley Library, Sir Paul Getty, K.B.E.

PROVENANCE: Melchoir Lomenius (?); Gualther Schaghius; Pe. Homborch, 1620, 1633, 1637 (inscriptions on first flyleaf and last page); Arnold a Lamzweerde, M.D. 1720; [possibly the copy owned by Edward Harley, second earl of Oxford (1689–1741), bought and sold by Thomas Osborne, London, *Catalogus Bibliothecæ Harleianæ,* part 3, February 14, 1744, lot 3654]; [sale, Varon and Gaillard, The Hague, May 14, 1764, lot 1129]; to Göttingen, Universitätsbibliothek [deaccessioned, April 6, 1958, to H. P. Kraus]; to Otto Schäfer (d. 2000), Schweinfurt, 1960 (his OS 194); [his sale, part 3, Sotheby's, November 1, 1995, lot 42]; to the Wormsley Library

JPGM and RA

The volume now at Wormsley has long been recognized as a landmark in the history of books.[1] Together with two other illustrated copies of the *De la ruine des nobles hommes et femmes* that include the same colophon by the printer Colard Mansion dated Bruges 1476,[2] it is generally considered the earliest book designed to be illustrated with copperplate engravings. It has therefore been studied by many scholars of early printing and engraving. The Wormsley Boccaccio is, however, also significant for the history of Flemish manuscript painting. As has been noted for some time, the style of the eight pasted-in engravings is close to that of illuminated miniatures produced in Bruges in the 1470s and early 1480s.[3] Most recently Bodo Brinkmann has considered at length whether the designs for the engravings can be attributed to the Master of the Dresden Prayer Book.[4] The significance of miniaturists contributing to the illustration of the Mansion Boccaccio cannot be overstated, for the illustrated copies of Mansion's printed edition mark a crucial, if faltering, step in the development of book illustration. This step led to the wider dissemination of images linked to text but ultimately also to the demise of illumination as the principal mode of book illustration. This decline in the fortune of illumination was to be most rapid in the illustration of secular texts. If, as appears likely, miniaturists who specialized in the illustration of secular texts were involved in Mansion's enterprise, a further dimension emerges of what has long been perceived as a paradigm of cultural transition.

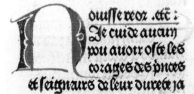

72a
CIRCLE OF THE
MASTER OF ANTHONY
OF BURGUNDY
Marcus Manlius Capitolinus Thrown into the Tiber,
book 4, fol. 103

72b
CIRCLE OF THE
MASTER OF ANTHONY
OF BURGUNDY
The Death of Brunhilde,
book 9, fol. 252 (detail)

The text that the Wormsley volume contains is a French translation of Giovanni Boccaccio's *De casibus virorum et feminarum illustrium* that the Paris protohumanist Laurent de Premierfait completed in 1400. This translation, the first of two undertaken by Premierfait (the second was completed in 1409), is a literal version of Boccaccio's text. Unlike the second, freer version, which proved very popular with French-speaking nobles throughout the fifteenth century, the first version was rarely copied and even more rarely illustrated.[5] Yet of the three manuscripts of Premierfait's translations known by me to have been illustrated in the Low Countries, two produced in Bruges contain this first version of the translation.[6] Clearly an exemplar of the rarer first version was available to Bruges book producers.

That said, why did Mansion ever introduce engravings into his edition of Premierfait's translation of Boccaccio? Six surviving copies of his original issue[7] suggest very strongly that his first instinct was to produce a printed book after the model of a deluxe manuscript.[8] In each of these copies, half-page spaces were left above the dedicatory preface and the opening of all nine books of his text except the first.[9] These spaces were clearly intended for large, two-column illustrations. Following the manuscript model, these spaces were very probably intended for illuminated or at least colored miniatures. Thus far Mansion's intention seems to have been to produce an illustrated edition similar to the closely contemporaneous edition of Valerius Maximus printed by the Josephus Printer (see cat. no. 67) and the 1485 edition of Boethius's *De consolatione philosophiae* printed by Arend de Keyser.[10] As four copies of two later states of Mansion's Boccaccio demonstrate, however, Mansion was not content merely to produce copies in this format.[11]

Much previous discussion has focused on how Mansion came to be in the position of having available to him nine engravings clearly based on Boccaccio's text. One suggested scenario is that the engravings became available to Mansion after the printing of his first issue of the Boccaccio. Being an entrepreneur, the printer then saw the engravings as opening the way for him to offer clients an illustrated edition off the shelf. If such a scenario is to be credited, however, it must offer an explanation of why engravings illustrating Boccaccio's text were ever created—an explanation that would be difficult to formulate outside the context of book illustration, especially given the format of the engravings. One would then have to posit another edition of the same text, of which no copy now survives. An alternative scenario has Mansion as the person who initiated the whole enterprise. According to it, the printer commissioned the engravings as part of a planned reshaping of his edition. What remains difficult to understand about this scenario is why engravings that Mansion commissioned are not uniform in format and do not include an illustration for book 6.[12] Although most critics have envisaged these explanations as the only alternatives available, one further explanation that lies somewhere between these two scenarios should be considered. According to this hypothesis, the engravings were produced as illustrations for Mansion's edition. Instead of being commissioned by Mansion, however, they constituted a response by the miniaturists to the lack of business that had come their way as a result of the original issue of the Boccaccio. It is, after all, the case that the vast majority of the surviving copies of this issue remain unillustrated.[13] Moreover, the only copy of Mansion's original issue to retain hand-painted illustrations (San Marino, Huntington Library, no. 85076) was apparently sold by Mansion unillustrated and was only subsequently illustrated in France at the request of either a bookseller or an owner.[14] Within this third scenario Mansion might well have seized upon whatever the miniaturists offered him and eagerly employed the engravings in further states of his edition, regardless of their manifest deficiencies of consistency and completeness. The desperation of the miniaturists to maintain a trade in illustrated copies of secular texts may have led them to risk undermining any potential market in illuminated copies of the Boccaccio.

Whichever explanation is correct, a much broader question remains to be answered: why did Mansion ever entertain pasting engravings into the Wormsley Boccaccio? Since more copies survive of the Boccaccio than any other edition printed by Mansion, it is difficult to argue that the enterprise of printing Premierfait's translation was ill calculated or that there was no market for his book in an unaltered state. Yet it is worthy of note that Mansion appears not to have taken the risk of offering off-the-shelf illuminated copies of the Boccaccio and that, as outlined above, there does not appear to have been a market for expensive illuminated copies of this text. If, however, clients were prepared to pay for Mansion's edition, but not for illumination, would they still be enticed to buy an illustrated copy? From Mansion's point of view, relatively little additional investment of time and money was required to achieve such an edition. To produce versions illustrated with pasted-in engravings, he needed to make only relatively minor revisions to his text and reprint only a few pages. Also, although the engravings would have required an initial financial outlay from Mansion, a stock of engravings would have enabled the printer thereafter to produce many copies of his illustrated book. From a client's point of view, an off-the-shelf edition illustrated with pasted-in engravings might also have been an attractive proposition, offering an illustrated copy that cost less than an illuminated one. If future research could clarify the identity of those who bought copies of Mansion's Boccaccio illustrated with engravings, or at least ascertain their social position, we would have a much clearer understanding of who in the late fifteenth century, although insufficiently monied to afford illuminations, still deemed illustrations an important part of a book.

Another matter that requires further attention is the identity of those responsible for the engravings. Long classified by historians of engraving as the work of an anonymous Flemish engraver—the Master of the Boccaccio Illustrations[15]—these engravings have more recently been proposed as based on designs produced by Flemish illuminators. The attribution by Fedja Anzelewsky of three of the engravings to the Master of the Dresden Prayer Book remains a sound starting point.[16] Most important, Anzelewsky's attribution located the engravings within the correct artistic circle and established specific links with manuscript illumination. The more recent attribution by Bodo Brinkmann of at least three of the other engravings to the Master of the White Inscriptions forms an important consolidation of the links between the engravings and manuscript illumination.[17] The compositions of the engravings *Marcus Manlius Capitolinus Thrown into the Tiber* (ill. 72a) and *The Humiliation of the Emperor Valerian* have a robust clarity and immediacy and the figures in them a sturdy roughness, all distinctive features found in works by the Master of the White Inscriptions. In my opinion, however, these compositions and that of *The Death of Brunhilde* (ill. 72b) are best attributed more generally to the circle of the Master of Anthony of Burgundy. The opening engraving of Boccaccio presenting his text to Cavalcanti is notably closer in style to the work of the Master of the Getty Froissart, the miniaturist whose work has been so generally, but incorrectly, subsumed within the work of the Master of the White Inscriptions. Facial types and figure drawing particularly close to those in the opening Mansion engraving are to be noted in, for example, the opening miniature of the Baltimore *Fleur des histoires* (Walters Art Museum, Ms. W.305, fol. 1) and the miniature *Pope John XII* in the Cotton *Trésor des histoires* (cat. no. 77, fol. 460). What is clearly needed from future research is a detailed comparison of the engravings with a wider group of works from the circle of the Master of Anthony of Burgundy and his followers.[18] Within any future study, close consideration needs to be given to the long-neglected work of the Master of the Getty Froissart.

S. McK.

Notes

1. According to Lehrs (1902: 128), this volume, then in the University Library at Göttingen, was first noted by W. Meyer in 1897.

2. The other two copies are Amiens, Bibliothèque municipale, Rés. 188-E, and Boston, Museum of Fine Arts, acc. no. 32.458. On the first, see Michel (H.) 1925; on the second, see Laing 1878. The Boston copy, which once belonged to the marquess of Lothian at New Battle Abbey, is distinguished from the Amiens and Wormsley copies principally in that it has all its engravings colored, apparently by a contemporary hand. Unlike the other two copies, it also includes an illuminated border to the right of the opening engraving, an illuminated initial on the same page, and pen-flourished initials at the beginning of each of the books.

3. See, in particular, Boon 1958: 85–88; Anzelewsky 1959: 114–25.

4. Brinkmann 1997: 113–21.

5. For a list of manuscripts, see Bozzolo 1973.

6. The two manuscripts of the first version are London, British Library, Add. Ms. 11696, and Paris, Bibliothèque nationale de France, Ms. fr. 132. For the other manuscript, see cat. no. 78.

7. The six copies of the original issue, generally classified as state A, are now in Bruges, Glasgow, Lille, Providence, San Marino, and Vienna.

8. In the four copies of a subsequent state of the Boccaccio, known as state B, Mansion seems to have made only a slight adjustment to this

overall strategy. State B is identical to state A except that the space above the opening of the preface has been enlarged, the text on the leaf compressed, and the title of the preface printed in red ink. Most critics have interpreted this change as the first stage in an evolutionary progression toward full illustration with pasted-in engravings. As suggested by the large pen and ink drawing within this enlarged space in the only copy of this state to include any illustrations (New York, Morgan Library, 75112), this enlargement was also appropriate for the opening illustration of a more traditional book. On the New York copy, see Kraus 1956: no. 60. It is common practice for the opening illustration of manuscripts of this period to be larger than those that follow it. The other, unillustrated copies of state B are in Bruges, London, and Paris.

9. Whether or not a blank page opposite the opening of book 1 (which begins at the top of a page) was always envisaged, a space for a tenth illustration is open to question. This space was certainly exploited for the inclusion of an engraving in the case of the Boston and Amiens copies. Many contemporary manuscripts do not mark the opening of the core text of a literary work with an illustration, but merely mark the opening of a preface.

10. On the Boethius edition, see Arnould 2002.

11. These four copies are those now in Amiens, Boston, Edinburgh, and Wormsley. State C—of which the Boston copy is the only surviving example—has the same larger space at the opening of the preface as state B, but state C also enlarged the spaces, compressed the text, and introduced titles in red ink at the beginning of books 2–5 and 7–9. State D is identical to state C, except that the space above the opening of book 6 also is enlarged, the text revised, and the title printed in red.

12. The nonexistence of an engraving for book 6 either in the three copies of Mansion's Boccaccio or independently among the print collections that hold examples of the engravings for all the other books is one of the most puzzling problems associated with the engravings. The inclusion of an illustration for book 6 in all subsequent early printings of Boccaccio's text has merely added to the mystery.

13. Van Praet (1829: 29–30) stated that he knew of three illustrated copies. Of these three, one is probably that now at the Huntington Library. The excision of the relevant spaces from the Lille copy makes identification with one of the copies noted by Van Praet difficult to confirm. Lehrs (1902: 127, n. 1) speculated that one of these was the Boston copy with colored engravings.

14. Brinkmann (1997: 121, n. 79) attributed the four surviving miniatures in the Huntington copy to a Rouen illuminator. Independently, but merely on the basis of poor reproductions, I had suspected a French origin.

15. This name was first given in Passavant 1860–64, 2: 275–77.

16. Anzelewsky (1959: 123–24) attributed the engravings for books 2, 5, and 7 to the Master of the Dresden Prayer Book.

17. Brinkmann (1997: 114–15) suggested the attribution of the engravings for the preface and books 4 and 8 to the Master of the White Inscriptions.

18. The bold and assertive draftsmanship of the engravings for books 4, 8, and 9 seems to me to suggest a different artist from that responsible for the other engravings. As I have already suggested, the opening engraving has distinct and clear links to the work of the Master of the Getty Froissart. At present, therefore, I would suggest the presence of three artists at work—one from the circle of the Master of Anthony of Burgundy, close to the Master of the Dresden Prayer Book; another possibly the Master of the White Inscriptions; and the third, the Master of the Getty Froissart.

MASTER OF THE DRESDEN PRAYER BOOK (B)

For biography, see part 2

73

MASTER OF THE DRESDEN PRAYER BOOK

The Temperate and the Intemperate

Miniature from Valerius Maximus, *Faits et dits mémorables des romains*, translation by Simon de Hesdin and Nicolas de Gonesse of *Facta et dicta memorabilia*

Bruges, ca. 1475–80

One half-page miniature, 17.4 × 19.3 cm (6⅞ × 7⅝ in.); justification: originally 28.5 × 20.2 cm (11¼ × 8 in.); originally 39 lines of *bastarda* in two columns

COLLECTION: Los Angeles, J. Paul Getty Museum, Ms. 43 (91.MS.81)

PROVENANCE: Jan Crabbe, abbot of Duinen (1457/59–1488); Library, Abbey of Duinen; [William Schab, New York, *Catalogue 1*, 1939, no. 62]; to Lewis V. Randall, Montreal; his widow; [to Jörn Günther Antiquariat, Hamburg, 1990]; acquired 1991

JPGM and RA

This leaf is one of the missing miniatures from the three-volume set of the *Faits et dits mémorables des romains* illuminated by the Master of the Dresden Prayer Book for Jan Crabbe, the humanist abbot of Ter Duinen, the Cistercian monastery outside Bruges (Bruges, Groot Seminarie, Mss. 159/190, 158/189, 157/188). Loosely organized by moral and philosophical categories (temperance, charity, cruelty, etc.), the *Deeds* served as a textbook of rhetorical exercises during the Middle Ages. The version represented in Crabbe's copy is the popular French translation begun by Simon de Hesdin under King Charles V of France (1338–1380), of which many illuminated copies survive (see cat. nos. 66, 67, 80), mostly of French origin. *The Temperate and the Intemperate* is the frontispiece to book 2.[1]

The iconography of this miniature is uncommon among the numerous fourteenth- and fifteenth-century illuminated manuscripts of this text. Book 2, entitled *Des moeurs et coutumes*, refers to the danger of drinking wine and, in both the text and its gloss, particularly admonishes against intemperance on the part of women.[2] A reading that contrasts the intemperate behavior of the lower classes with the temperate conduct of a higher social caste is not explicit in the text, however, and appears to be an innovation of the Dresden Master.[3] Many of the miniatures in the Bruges volume illustrate their respective texts more literally. In this cutting the artist situates the temperate on a higher level both physically and metaphorically but also relegates them to the background.

The Dresden Master illuminated two manuscript copies of this text, including an earlier one for Jean Gros, first secretary and *audiencier* of Charles the Bold (Leipzig, Universitätsbibliothek, Ms. Rep. I 11b; and fig. 32),[4] yet only the copy in Bruges has miniatures entirely by the artist. He or members of his workshop also illustrated two printed

copies, and all four date to the 1470s.[5] Bodo Brinkmann persuasively argued that Crabbe's copy was the last in the series of four. In a version of *The Temperate and the Intemperate* in one of the printed copies (Paris, Bibliothèque nationale de France, Rés. Z.200), the scope of the setting, its architectural character, the placement and postures of Valerius Maximus and the emperor Tiberius at the left, and especially the arrangement of the figures at the rear table closely anticipate corresponding features of the Getty miniature.   T. K.

73
MASTER OF
THE DRESDEN
PRAYER BOOK
*The Temperate and
the Intemperate*

Notes

1. The entire leaf containing the opening of book 2 from Bruges, Groot Seminarie, Ms. 159/190, is lacking, but the rest of the leaf is untraced. The bibliography for the Bruges volume includes Bruges 1927: 59–61, nos. 62–64; Brussels 1959: 186, no. 256; Huyghebaert 1969: 237–38, 242; Bruges 1981: 203–4, no. 97; Schullian 1981: 699; Dogaer 1987a: 131.

2. Bk. 2, chap. 1, sec. 5.

3. For example, the frontispiece of book 2 of an earlier Valerius Maximus from Mons (Paris, Bibliothèque nationale de France, Ms. fr. 6185, fol. 51) shows drunken and lascivious conduct. It offers neither the sharp class distinctions found in the Getty and Leipzig miniatures nor an example of temperate behavior. See Brussels 1959: no. 34, pl. 17.

4. Winkler 1921: pl. 2a.

5. Brussels 1959: 186, no. 256, largely on the basis of the style of the borders ("On a conservé à Bruges ce genre de décor même au delà de 1480"); Geirnaert dated the manuscript 1470–75 on the basis of initials and borders (see Huyghebaert 1969: 237–38; and Geirnaert, in Bruges 1981: 203–4, no. 97). Brinkmann (1997: 106) dated it around 1480.

MASTER OF THE LONDON WAVRIN

The miniatures painted around 1475 in Edward IV's copy of volume one of Jean de Wavrin's *Chroniques d'Angleterre* (cat. no. 75) are proposed here as the starting point for the reconstruction of the work of a talented miniaturist of the 1470s. The Master of the London Wavrin, named as such for the first time here, made a particularly important contribution to the illustration of secular texts in the Low Countries. Until now his achievement has been largely overlooked.

As seen in the London miniatures (ills. 74, 75a, 75b), the Master of the London Wavrin defined forms with linear clarity and sharpness but softened this linearity through the play of light over figures as well as landscapes. A generally light palette—including violet, slate blue, pale green, and rose—is strengthened by the inclusion of dark brown and black. Dark brown reflects the physical weight of bulky wooden ships; black offsets the tracery-like silhouettes of trees against the light blue sky and water, pale green rolling hills, and varied colors of costumed figures. The Master of the London Wavrin composed varied and elaborate settings for his miniatures, principally in the form of extensive landscapes that have extremely high horizons and conclude in snow-capped mountains. These settings add more to the tranquil atmosphere and poetry of the images than to dramatic impact or narrative clarity. Although the latter characteristics are peculiar to the Master of the London Wavrin, several other features—including manner of composition, crisply defined drapery, and treatment of light—suggest that he was a follower of the Master of Anthony of Burgundy (see separate biography, this part).[1]

Around the same date that he worked on his name manuscript, the Master of the London Wavrin painted three miniatures in a manuscript of the first book of Guillaume Fillastre's *Histoire de la Toison d'Or* (Vienna, Österreichische Staatsarchiv, Archiv des Ordens vom Goldenen Vlies, Ms. 1).[2] The Wavrin Master can therefore be identified as one of the artists that Georges Dogaer grouped under the name of the Masters of the Golden Fleece.[3] This artistic grouping, first made by Friedrich Winkler, is based on the reuse of the compositions of the Vienna miniatures in the illustrations of two contemporary manuscripts of Fillastre's text (Brussels, Bibliothèque royale de Belgique, Ms. 9027; Paris, Bibliothèque nationale de France, Ms. fr. 139).[4] Although stylistically related, the miniatures in these three manuscripts are clearly the work of three different artists.[5] The models for these miniatures were very likely devised in close collaboration with the author around the completion of his text in 1473.[6] So characteristic are they of the Master of the London Wavrin that it is most probable that it was he who devised the models

themselves and thus initiated this sequence of illustrations. The further reuse of the first miniature in the chapter of the Order of the Golden Fleece in manuscripts of the order's statutes underlines the iconographic status given to these images at the heart of the Burgundian court (see cat. nos. 76, 122).

The Master of the London Wavrin seems also to have invented the earliest sequence of illustrations for at least one other text dedicated to Charles the Bold.[7] The illustrations in one of the surviving copies of Jan Du Quesne's translation of Caesar made shortly after 1473/74 (cat. no. 74) reveal very similar preoccupations to those shown in the London Wavrin. Later in the 1470s the Wavrin Master contributed to copies of Jean Froissart's *Chroniques* (London, British Library, Royal Ms. 14 D.vi),[8] *Régime de Santé* of Aldobrandinus of Siena (Lisbon, Biblioteca de Ajuda, 52-XIII-26),[9] and the *Trésor des histoires* (cat. no. 77). The Wavrin Master's collaboration in the latter manuscript with the Master of the Getty Froissart appears to be a further reflection of a close artistic relationship between the two miniaturists, also evident in shared compositional and figure patterns.[10]   S. McK.

Notes

1. In addition to these stylistic links, it is worth noting that the Master of the London Wavrin painted the opening large miniature of a copy of the *Régime de Santé* (Lisbon, Biblioteca de Ajuda, 52-XIII-26) in which some of the smaller miniatures were executed in cameo by a miniaturist from the circle of the Master of Anthony of Burgundy. This volume, which once formed part of the library of Henry VIII of England, bears the arms of Sir Thomas Boleyn, K. G. The opening miniature of the Creation in the Lisbon volume (fol. 1) is closely related to the miniature of the same subject in the London *Trésor des histoires* (cat. no. 77, fol. 18).

2. Telling comparisons are, respectively, London, British Library, Royal Ms. 15 E.iv, fols. 14, 141v, and Vienna, Österreichische Staatsarchiv, Archiv des Ordens vom Goldenen Vlies, Ms. 1, fols. 1, 4v. The landscape on folio 19 of the Vienna manuscript has repeated parallels in the London Wavrin.

3. Dogaer 1987a: 95.

4. Winkler 1925: 137, 163, 191, 208. A fourth manuscript with illustrations based on the same models and made for Charles the Bold is reconstructed in Cockshaw 1984: 201–12.

5. A fourth artist was responsible for the fourth manuscript noted in Cockshaw 1984. For a comparison of four versions of the miniature of Perseus on Pegasus, see Pächt, Jenni, and Thoss 1983: figs. 113–16. Unfortunately figures 115 and 116 are incorrectly captioned: figure 115 is in fact from the Paris manuscript, and figure 116 is from the Vienna manuscript. The differences between the artists responsible for the miniatures of Phryxus and Helle in the Brussels and Vienna volumes are apparent from a comparison of Brussels 1996: color pl. 2, and Brussels 1987b: 27, fig. 2.

6. Bayot 1907: 436.

7. A second text is the *Faits des Romains*. A cycle of miniatures created sometime after 1473 to illustrate this text (McKendrick 1990: 115–16) may not only have been created for a lost manuscript of Charles the Bold but also reflects the original inventions of the Master of the London Wavrin. Surviving copies of these miniatures—Chantilly, Musée Condé, Ms. 770 (1055); Lille, Bibliothèque municipale, Ms. 442; Paris, Bibliothèque nationale de France, Ms. fr. 20312 bis—certainly reflect similar interest in developed landscape settings.

8. Fols. 84v, 161, 268v, 303.

9. See Santos 1930: 14–15, pl. 17.

10. For some initial comparisons, see Sutton and Visser-Fuchs 1999: 268–79. The artist responsible for the miniatures in the Paris copy of the first book of Fillastre's *Histoire de la Toison d'Or* (Paris, Bibliothèque nationale, Ms. fr. 139) worked in a style very close to that of the Master of the Getty Froissart.

74
MASTER OF THE
LONDON WAVRIN
View of Gaul, fol. 86v

74

MASTER OF THE LONDON WAVRIN

Julius Caesar, *Commentaires de César*, translation attributed to Jan Du Quesne of *Commentarii*
Bruges, 1473–76

MANUSCRIPT: 338 folios, 40 × 29 cm (15¾ × 12⅛ in.); justification: 25.1 × 17.7 cm (9⅞ × 7 in.); 30 lines of *bastarda* in two columns attributed to Jan Du Quesne; 10 three-quarter-page miniatures, 13 one-column miniatures

BINDING: London, mid-eighteenth century; brown morocco; the arms of George II gold-stamped on both covers

COLLECTION: London, The British Library, Royal Ms. 16 G.viii

PROVENANCE: Edward IV, king of England (1442–1483); English royal library, Richmond Palace, in 1535, and Saint James's in 1666; George II, king of England (1683–1760); presented 1757 to the British Museum

R A

At least eight manuscripts survive of a biography of the Roman general and dictator Julius Caesar.[1] This text was completed at Lille in 1473/74 by the scribe Jan Du Quesne and dedicated to Charles the Bold, duke of Burgundy. At its core is a fresh translation into French of Julius Caesar's own account of his conquest of Gaul in 58–51 B.C. The first and last of its ten books are Du Quesne's own compilation based on a wide range of Roman and other literary sources. Within the text frequent comparison is made between Charles and his Roman predecessor, and it was Du Quesne's intention to produce a companion text that continued the narrative up to the time of Charles the Bold.[2] Du Quesne often drew on his personal knowledge of the territories through which Caesar moved and at least once referred to his hometown of Lille.

The present volume is the earliest surviving copy of Du Quesne's translation. The models for most of its illustrations had been devised by 1476, when they were copied into a much humbler manuscript made for Charles the Bold's counselor Jacques Donche (New Haven, Beinecke Library, Ms. 226). This manuscript was said in its colophon to have been "copied after the original." By comparison with other signed examples of Du Quesne's script, the text of the present manuscript is identifiable as an autograph. It is therefore likely that the volume is either Charles the Bold's copy or its twin in respect to its illustrations.

The illustrations are the earliest known works of the Master of the London Wavrin. As is most evident in the bird's-eye view of Gaul that forms the illustration at the beginning of Du Quesne's second book and the beginning of his translation of Caesar's *Gallic Wars* (ill. 74), this artist is distinguished by his strong, almost overwhelming interest and delight in landscape. This interest chimes very well with that of Du Quesne in the setting of Caesar's campaigns and also adds a special dimension to such conventional subjects as the surrender or siege of a city or a sequence of battles. Assured figure drawing, handling of color, and compositional skills distinguish his work from that of many of his contemporaries.

The distinctive borders accompanying the large miniatures recur in modified form in two later copies of Du Quesne's translation of Caesar (Copenhagen, Kongelige

Bibliotek, Ms. Thott 544 2°; ex Longleat, marquess of Bath, Botfield Ms. 2). Of these the Botfield copy is dated 1478/79 and is an autograph of Du Quesne. Closer versions are, however, to be found in at least one more manuscript illuminated by the Master of the London Wavrin,[3] as well as one illuminated by a miniaturist with whom Du Quesne collaborated earlier on two other works.[4] As in the case of Du Quesne's copies of Vasco da Lucena's translation of Quintus Curtius (see cat. no. 63), therefore, the scribe sent his manuscripts away from Lille for their illumination.

Six manuscripts of Du Quesne's translation, including the present volume, are deluxe copies written in accomplished *bastarda* script on large folio sheets of parchment and decorated with fine illustrations. Of these the Botfield copy was illuminated for a former captain of Charles the Bold, André de Haraucourt (d. 1484); the Copenhagen copy came to belong to Philip of Cleves; and a third (Paris, Bibliothèque nationale de France, Ms. fr. 38) was written at Ghent in 1482 for Louis of Gruuthuse.[5] Of the present copy all we know for certain is that it was in the English royal collection by 1535. Given Edward IV's acknowledged interest in Roman and imperial history, however, it seems very likely that he would have wanted a copy of Du Quesne's text. In compiling the companion imperial history that survives in the Botfield manuscript, Du Quesne seems to have been aware of and keen to satisfy Edward's interest.[6] By some means, perhaps the agency of his sister Margaret of York or Louis of Gruuthuse, Edward contrived to acquire another copy of Du Quesne's text that did not include the companion text and may have been intended for Charles the Bold himself. Contrary to long-held opinions concerning the direction of influence across the channel, it is probable that Edward acquired his copy of Caesar's history before Gruuthuse acquired his.[7]   S. McK.

Notes

1. In addition to the six listed by Bossuat 1943 are Oxford, Bodleian Library, Douce Ms. 208, and ex Longleat, marquess of Bath, Botfield Ms. 2 (Christie's, London, June 13, 2002, lot 2). A ninth (lost) manuscript was noted between 1577 and 1731 in the Bibliothèque de Bourgogne in Brussels (Barrois 1830: no. 2235).

2. Bossuat 1943: 275. Du Quesne's companion text, significantly modified after the death of Charles the Bold, is preserved uniquely in ex Longleat, marquess of Bath, Botfield Ms. 2, fols. 247–317 (see note 1).

3. Vienna, Österreichische Staastarchiv, Archiv des Ordens vom Goldenen Vlies, Ms. 1.

4. The first with related borders is The Hague, Koninklijke Bibliotheek, Ms. 133 A 3, vols. 1–2. The two du Quesne volumes are New Haven, Beinecke Library, Ms. 129, and Turin, Biblioteca Nazionale, Ms. L I 6, and Archivio di Stato, Ms. B III 12 J (dated 1466).

5. The remaining two, in Oxford (Douce 208) and London (British Library, Egerton 1065), are a closely related pair, produced by the Master of 1482 and other artists in the mid-1480s. Little is known of the first owner of the Oxford manuscript and nothing of that of the Egerton copy.

6. In modification of what is stated in his preface, the Botfield text ends with Edward, not Charles. Before that it also repeatedly concerns itself with the kings of England.

7. For a revised view of Gruuthuse's influence on Edward, see Backhouse 1987: 25–26; McKendrick 1992: 153–54; Backhouse 2001: 151–52.

75

MASTER OF THE LONDON WAVRIN

Jean de Wavrin, *Recueil des croniques et anciennes istoires de la Grant Bretaigne*
Bruges, ca. 1475

MANUSCRIPT: i + 350 folios in two continuously foliated volumes, 46 × 34.5 cm (18⅛ × 13⅝ in.); justification: 27.3 × 21 cm (10¾ × 8¼ in.); 36 lines of *bastarda* in two columns; 1 three-quarter-page miniature, 6 miniatures of 23–24 lines, 22 half-page miniatures

HERALDRY: Full achievement of the arms of Edward IV; escutcheon with the royal arms of England encircled by the Garter, surmounted by helm, cap, and crest of lion passant and fleur-de-lis, supported by two white lions; banner with motto *Honny soit qui mal y pense*, all fol. 14

BINDING: London, ca. 1960; blind-tooled maroon morocco

COLLECTION: London, The British Library, Royal Ms. 15 E.iv

PROVENANCE: Edward IV, king of England (1442–1483); English royal library, Richmond Palace, in 1535, and Saint James's in 1666; George II, king of England (1683–1760); presented 1757 to the British Museum

JPGM (vol. 1) and RA (vols. 1, 2)

The present manuscript apparently forms the first volume of a third edition of Jean de Wavrin's *Recueil des croniques et anciennes istoires de la Grant Bretaigne*. This edition was to comprise seven volumes and continue Wavrin's narrative up to Edward IV's return to the throne in 1471. A new prologue dedicates the edition to Edward.[1] Omission of any mention of Wavrin as author suggests that someone else compiled the edition after Wavrin's death.[2] As the heraldry on the opening page makes clear, the present volume was illuminated for its text's dedicatee, Edward IV.

Encouraged by his nephew Waleran, Jean de Wavrin, lord of Le Forestel, completed around 1445 the first edition of his lengthy *Recueil* in four volumes. As openly stated in the title, this work was compiled from earlier chronicles. Among these were the *Chroniques* of Jean Froissart and Jean Chartier (d. 1464) and the *Mémoires* of Jacques Du Clercq (1420–1501). Although his work began with the legendary Albion and concluded with the death in 1413 of Henry IV of England, the subject of his text from the fourteenth century on was as much France and Burgundy as England. In a second edition comprising six volumes, the author extended his narrative to 1469. Two years before, Wavrin had visited England as part of a Burgundian delegation and witnessed the tournament between Anthony of Burgundy and Anthony Woodville.

Despite its great length, the second edition survives in one complete set, made for Louis of Gruuthuse,[3] and another almost complete set that came to belong to the Nassau library.[4] Both are deluxe editions, profusely illustrated by Flemish artists, the first around 1475 by a team of artists led by the Master of the Vienna *Chroniques d'Angleterre* and the second probably assembled around 1480 from volumes decorated by several unrelated Bruges artists at different dates.[5] In addition to these sets, two separate volumes—a deluxe copy of volume 1[6] and a paper copy of volume 2[7]—were also illustrated by Flemish artists around the same date. The first was illuminated by the same team as Gruuthuse's set and the second by a follower.

Out amfi cōme   quelle famble aproi auoir efte

75a
MASTER OF THE
LONDON WAVRIN
Landscape, vol. 1, fol. 24v

In terms of artistic quality, the twenty-nine large miniatures that illustrate Edward's manuscript of the *Recueil* are
the finest of all those included in his collection of Flemish
manuscripts. In striking contrast to the overblown border
decoration that accompanies them,[8] these miniatures are
of outstanding delicacy and clarity. Although frequently
repeating both figure and larger compositional models,[9]
the miniaturist treated Wavrin's account of the early history of Britain with consistent freshness and poetic respon-
siveness to setting and atmosphere. His success is largely
the result of an ability to suggest the contemporary
through costume and architecture, on the one hand, and
through an enhanced and idealized depiction of the natural
world, particularly landscape, on the other. His skill is evident in the precocious independent landscape that marks

the beginning of his account of the Trojan descent of Brutus (ill. 75a) and also in the panoramic setting for his miniature *The Marriage of Edward II* (ill. 75b). Overall his
miniatures are fine examples of the revival of the past
undertaken within the best manuscripts of secular vernacular texts during this period.

Like the London Caesar (cat. no. 74), the present volume 1 of Wavrin's *Recueil* was probably acquired by Edward
IV earlier than his principal acquisitions of Flemish illuminated manuscripts between 1478 and 1480. The copy of volume 3 of Wavrin's work that also bears his arms (London,
British Library, Royal Ms. 14 E.iv) was almost certainly
acquired in that later phase of his collecting and therefore
independently from the present volume 1.[10] It is therefore
possible that the seven-volume edition signaled in the

prologue to the present volume was aborted and that no volume other than the first was ever produced. Despite the beauty of the miniatures of that volume, it seems likely that Edward was not enticed to order further volumes to complete the set.   S. McK.

Notes

1. By mistake the Flemish copyist referred to him as Edward V.

2. Wavrin died sometime between 1472 and 1475.

3. Paris, Bibliothèque nationale de France, Mss. fr. 74–85.

4. This set is now dispersed. Volumes 2, 3, and 5 are The Hague, Koninklijke Bibliotheek, Mss. 133 A 7 1–3; and volume 4, Baltimore, Walters Art Museum, Ms. W. 201. Ten illustrated pages detached from volume 2 before 1636 are Oxford, Bodleian Library, Ms. Laud misc. 653. The last were earlier intended for Anthony of Burgundy, whose devices are overpainted in the borders.

5. Volume 2 is illuminated in part by the same miniaturist as the principal artist in London, British Library, Royal Ms. 14 E.iv; volume 3, by the same miniaturist as London, British Library, Royal Ms. 17 F.i, datable between 1468 and 1479; and volumes 4 and 5 principally by another Flemish miniaturist working around 1475–80.

6. Vienna, Österreichische Nationalbibliothek, Ms. 2534.

7. San Marino, Huntington Library, Ms. 28562.

8. An earlier version of this type of border appears on the opening folio of Anthony of Burgundy's Froissart dated 1468 (Berlin, Staatsbibliothek, dep. Breslau 1, vol. 1, fol. 1). Roughly contemporaneous versions accompany the later miniatures in Engelbert of Nassau's Quintus Curtius (Oxford, Bodleian Library, Ms. Laud misc. 751, fols. 32, 45, 103, 152, 165, 172, 179, 208, 230).

9. The setting of the opening miniature of Edward receiving the book (fol. 14) repeats that of the miniature Phrixos and Helle in the Vienna Toison d'Or (Vienna, Archiv des Ordens vom Goldenen Vlies, Ms. 1, fol. 4v).

10. The principal miniaturist is the same one responsible for Guillaume de Ternay's Chroniques de Pise (Darmstadt, Hessische Landes- und Hochschulbibliothek, Ms. 133). A finishing hand is that of an assistant of the Master of the White Inscriptions (see McKendrick 1994: 163).

75b

MASTER OF THE
LONDON WAVRIN
The Marriage of Edward II,
vol. 2, fol. 295v (detail)

76

CIRCLE OF MASTER OF THE LONDON WAVRIN

Statutes and Armorial of the Order of the Golden Fleece
Bruges, between 1481 and 1486

MANUSCRIPT: iii + 77 + xv (+ 6 folios after fol. 56), 26 × 18.8 cm
(10¼ × 7⅜ in.); justification: 16.2 × 12 cm (6⅜ × 4¼ in.); 23 lines of
bastarda; 3 full-page miniatures, 1 three-quarter-page miniature;
24 illuminated panels with the arms of members of the Order of
the Golden Fleece

HERALDRY: Escutcheon with the arms of Jean de Lannoy as abbot;
escutcheon with the arms of Abbey of Saint Bertin; escutcheon with
the arms of Maximilian as archduke of Austria impaled by those of
Burgundy, surmounted by archducal bonnet; escutcheon with the
arms of Maximilian as king of the Romans, all fol. 7

BINDING: France, early eighteenth century; red morocco; device of
three interlaced crescents and monogram *DDLLM* encircled by
collars of the Orders of Saint Michael and the Holy Spirit and
surmounted by ducal coronet on spine

COLLECTION: London, The British Library, Harley Ms. 6199

PROVENANCE: Jean de Lannoy, abbot of Saint Bertin and chancellor
of the Order of the Golden Fleece; Jean Antoine II de Mesmes, count
of Avaux (1661–1723); [James Woodman, London]; purchased for
Edward Harley, second earl of Oxford (1689–1741), in 1725; Margaret,
duchess of Portland (1715–1785); purchased 1753

JPGM and RA

Its creation is very closely tied to the history of the
order. The heraldry in the border of its opening miniature
makes it clear that the book was made for Jean de Lannoy
(d. 1492), abbot of Saint Bertin and chancellor of the order
from 1480. The text recounts the order's meetings up to
and including the first one, at Bois-le-Duc on May 9, 1481,
at which Lannoy served as chancellor. Its opening depiction of a meeting of the order updates a composition
devised sometime after 1473 as an opening illustration for
the *Histoire de la Toison* by Lannoy's predecessor as chancellor, Guillaume Fillastre.[4] This composition depicted Fillastre standing at its center dressed in his episcopal miter
and chasuble, reading his book to Charles the Bold at the
1468 meeting of the order.[5] The artist responsible for the
invention of this composition was the Master of the
London Wavrin.

The omission of any account of the meeting at Mechelen, which took place on May 26, 1491, and any heraldic
reference to or portrait of the order's new patron, Philip
the Handsome, suggests that the volume was produced
before 1491. The subsequent updating of Maximilan's arms
to those of the Roman king narrows the dating to before
1486. The absence of any updating of the text is probably
explained by Lannoy's death in 1492.   S. McK.

Notes

1. The other deluxe copies are Brussels, Bibliothèque royale de
Belgique, Ms. FS IX 93 LP; Vienna, Österreichische Nationalbiblio-
thek, Cod. 2606; Waddesdon Manor, Ms. 17 (see cat. no. 122); and
Madrid, Instituto de Valencia de Don Juan, Ms. 26 I.27.

2. Their model would appear to be the standing portraits of each
member of the order devised for the armorial presented to Charles the
Bold in 1473 (The Hague, Koninklijke Bibliotheek, Ms. 76 E 10).

3. On this tradition, see cat. no. 122.

4. This updated version reappears in the later statutes and armorial at Waddesdon (see cat. no. 122).

5. See Brussels, Bibliothèque royale, Ms. 9028, fol. 6; Copenhagen,
Kongelige Bibliotek, Ms. Thott 465 2°, fol. 1; Dijon, Bibliothèque
municipale, Ms. 2948; Paris, Bibliothèque nationale de France, Ms. fr.
139, fol. 4; Vienna, Österreichisches Staatsarchiv, Archiv des Ordens
vom Goldenen Vlies, Mss. 1, fol. 1, and 2, fol. 1.

76a
CIRCLE OF MASTER OF
THE LONDON WAVRIN
Maximilian I, fol. 73v

76b
CIRCLE OF MASTER OF
THE LONDON WAVRIN
Philip the Good, fol. 57v

Very few surviving manuscripts contain both the
statutes and the armorial of the Order of the Golden
Fleece. Of these, the present volume is the earliest of only
five deluxe copies.[1] It is also the earliest manuscript to commemorate successive patrons of the Order of the Golden
Fleece in a series of full-length portraits[2] and thus begin a
long tradition of dynastic portraiture in such books that
continued well into the seventeenth century.[3]

MASTER OF THE GETTY FROISSART

An important miniaturist who has received almost no attention thus far from scholars of Flemish manuscript illumination is the artist responsible for most of the large miniatures in a copy of book 3 of Jean Froissart's *Chroniques* now held by the J. Paul Getty Museum (cat. no. 79). The omission of this miniaturist from scholarly discussions is largely the result of his principal works having been overlooked by or unknown to such influential critics such as Paul Durrieu, Friedrich Winkler, L. M. J. Delaissé, Georges Dogaer, and Maurits Smeyers.[1] A review of this artist's part in revitalizing the illustration of secular texts around 1480 is long overdue. Since the Getty manuscript includes the most extended sequence of miniatures that I consider attributable to this artist, I hereby propose to name him the Master of the Getty Froissart.

In his name manuscript, which was produced in Bruges around 1480, the Master of the Getty Froissart revealed a distinctive and accomplished style of manuscript painting (ills. 79a, 79b). In contrast to the Master of the White Inscriptions, to whom miniatures in this volume have previously been attributed,[2] this artist took delight in the subtle handling of light, space, and color. Interiors—although dominated, like those of the Master of the White Inscriptions, by gray stone walls—are subtly lit and reveal a persistent interest on the part of the miniaturist in the spatial relationships of figures within them. Several landscapes reveal a keen interest in the definition of larger spaces, as well as in their contribution to the dramatic setting of a particular subject. Both male and female figures, although each broadly similar in their facial features, reveal a variety of poses, costumes, and gestures, as well as an assured figure drawing; none of these characteristics is found in the works of the Master of the White Inscriptions. Male facial features, although somewhat broad and roughly hewn, as in miniatures by the Master of the White Inscriptions, are lacking in brooding aggression. The Master of the Getty Froissart is also distinguished from his contemporary by the use of a much wider palette and by an interest in fine details of costume and surface patterns.

Next in importance within the corpus of the artist is a most imaginatively illustrated copy of the *Trésor des histoires*, produced in Bruges around 1475–80 (cat. no. 77). Collaborating closely on the illumination of this manuscript with the contemporary miniaturist most comparable in innovative pictorial ability—the Master of the London Wavrin—the Master of the Getty Froissart produced another sequence of miniatures that injected new life into the illustration of a secular text.[3] A third series of miniatures, produced for Edward IV's copy of Boccaccio (cat. no. 78)—although in some cases difficult to separate from the contribution of the Master of the White Inscriptions—also treats the subjects with a remarkable freshness. The compositions of some of the miniatures painted in this volume[4] suggest that part of this achievement was due to a knowledge on the part of our artist of the work of the Master of Anthony of Burgundy, and perhaps also of the early work of the Master of the Dresden Prayer Book. Further research needs to be undertaken to establish how the Master of the Getty Froissart gained such knowledge and whether he can be considered a follower of the Master of Anthony of Burgundy.

Further detailed consideration also needs to be given to the relationship of the Master of the Getty Froissart to several large miniatures in manuscripts of secular texts produced in Bruges around 1480. The style of the large miniature at the beginning of a copy of the *Fleur des histoires* (Baltimore, Walters Art Museum, Ms. W.305, fol. 1)[5] and of the opening engraving of Colard Mansion's edition of Boccaccio (cat. no. 72) is very close to that of several miniatures in the *Trésor des histoires*. Two further miniatures in book 4 of Edward IV's Froissart, a possible companion of the Getty Froissart (London, British Library, Royal Ms. 18 E.ii, fols. 7, 206); one further miniature in Edward IV's *Bible historiale* (cat. no. 82, fol. 66v); and two marking the openings of copies of the *Livre d' Eracles* (cat. no. 87, fol. 16) and of the *Des proffits ruraux* (London, British Library, Royal Ms. 14 E.vi, fol. 10)[6] have many stylistic features in common with the Getty miniatures and those in Edward IV's copy of Boccaccio. Even if none of these miniatures can be securely attributed to the Master of the Getty Froissart, their close stylistic relationship to the work of the Getty Master requires further explanation.   S. McK.

Notes

1. The Getty Froissart was completely unstudied until around 1974, when it emerged from the Rothschild collections. Despite forming part of a public collection from the middle of the eighteenth century, the Cotton *Trésor* appears to have remained unknown to art historians until noted by Ross in 1963 (Ross [D.] 1963: 21).

2. Von Euw and Plotzek 1979–85, 3: 265–66.

3. If, as I am inclined to believe, the miniatures of Louis of Gruuthuse's copy of book 1 of Fillastre's *Histoire de la Toison d'Or* (Paris, Bibliothèque nationale de France, Ms. fr. 139) can also be attributed to the Master of the Getty Froissart, a further link with the Master of the London Wavrin is provided by this manuscript. See the separate biography of the Master of the London Wavrin, this part.

4. E.g., London, British Library, Royal Ms. 14 E.v, fols. 64, 113v.

5. Randall 1997: no. 267, fig. 504.

6. For reproductions of four of these miniatures, see, respectively, McKendrick 2003: pl. 64; Komada 2000: pl. 238; Backhouse 1997a: pl. 180; Sutton and Visser-Fuchs 1999: fig. 15.

les gens de ce pais sont plꝰ beaulx · prouincie de savone · chap v̄·xlv·

avone est vne pro ou plat pais si va mo
ult de

77

MASTER OF THE GETTY FROISSART AND MASTER
OF THE LONDON WAVRIN AND ASSISTANTS

Trésor des histoires
Bruges, ca. 1475–80

MANUSCRIPT: i + 481 folios, 48 × 35.5 cm (18⅞ × 14 in.); justification:
28.8 × 20.2 cm (11⅜ × 8 in.); 37 lines of *bastarda* in two columns;
1 three-quarter-page miniature, 54 half-page miniatures

BINDING: London, mid-eighteenth century; brown morocco; the
arms of Sir Robert Cotton gold-stamped on both covers; rebacked

COLLECTION: London, The British Library, Cotton Ms. Augustus A.v

PROVENANCE: English royal library, Richmond Palace, in 1535; Sir
Robert Cotton (1571–1631) in 1616; to the nation in 1702; to the British
Museum in 1753

JPGM and RA

The *Trésor des histoires* formerly in the Cotton Library
is one of the most remarkable manuscripts of a secular
vernacular text to have been produced in the last quarter
of the fifteenth century. The fifty-five large miniatures of
the volume are of the very highest visual sophistication in
the illustration of such a text. In particular, a refined and
ambitious treatment of light and landscape defines the
unique contribution of the miniaturists who painted these
miniatures.

In outline, the text that the Cotton manuscript contains
is far from unusual. The *Trésor des histoires* or *Trésor de sapience* is one of several vernacular world chronicles that were

repeatedly copied for and read by French-speaking nobles
from the thirteenth century onward. A first version was
compiled between 1275 and 1282 for Baudouin d'Avesnes
(1219–1289), son of Bouchard d'Avesnes and Margaret of
Flanders, countess of Hainaut. Stretching from Creation to
the anonymous author's own time, this work's narrative
was based in part on two earlier histories: the *Histoire ancienne* compiled between 1206 and 1230, and the *Faits des
romains*, written in 1213–14. As a result, much of the *Trésor*
relates events from ancient, particularly Roman, history.

The particular version of the *Trésor* text that the Cotton
manuscript contains is, however, rare and worthy of note.[1]
Within its 763 chapters, material from several fourteenth-
century texts have been interpolated. Included among
these are Jean de Vignay's *Jeu des échecs*, compiled shortly
before 1350; Jean Corbechon's translation of Bartholomaeus
Anglicus (1372); and Guillaume de Tignonville's *Dits moraux
des philosophes*, completed sometime before 1402.[2] A passage of text that forms part of these interpolations compares Paris to Athens as the mother of the arts and sciences
(fol. 345), which suggests that the Cotton version of the
Trésor was compiled in Paris in 1416.[3] Although several
other manuscripts of the *Trésor* were produced in the Low
Countries,[4] none contains this version. It therefore seems
likely that the text of the Cotton manuscript was copied
directly from a much earlier manuscript, probably of
Parisian origin and dating from the first quarter of the
fifteenth century.

Although some dependence on earlier models has been discerned,[5] the illustrations of the Cotton manuscript are largely the result of a new and independent response to the text.[6] These illustrations were clearly planned with much care. The miniatures, which punctuate the text in a strikingly regular manner throughout the volume, work together to form an impressive visual summary of the narrative of the *Trésor*. Within that campaign their faithful illustration of the interpolated texts proves that all of the miniatures were devised for this uncommon version of the *Trésor*. To facilitate this, detailed instructions to the miniaturists outlining the principal elements of each illustration were written in the lower margins of each page on which a miniature was to be painted.[7]

Two main artistic styles are discernible in the Cotton miniatures. The first style has much in common with that of the miniatures in the London Wavrin (cat. no. 75), including the palette, the style of drawing, and complex and novel landscapes. One of the two miniaturists working in this style in the Cotton manuscript may indeed be the Master of the London Wavrin. The second style has many points of connection with the majority of miniatures in the Getty Froissart, especially in their subtle depiction of the play of light within interiors and in their accomplished figure drawing. Thus, one of the two artists who worked in this second style in the Cotton manuscript seems to be the Master of the Getty Froissart. The four artists working in these two styles were responsible jointly for almost all of the miniatures, and separately for around a quarter of the miniatures each. Three of the most beautiful miniatures in this manuscript illustrate the interpolation of Bartholomaeus's description of different parts of the world. The first is one of the earliest independent views of the Flemish countryside (fol. 345v).[8] The second is a dramatic and fanciful landscape intended to represent Mauritania, in Africa (fol. 354v).[9] In the third the miniaturist delighted in the depiction of Saxons busily extracting iron in a large cauldron of water heated over a blazing fire and of the contrastingly still landscape in which they work (ill. 77). The only other artist involved in the campaign was a follower of Loyset Liédet. Fortunately, the limited abilities of this artist were applied to only two miniatures in the volume (fols. 22, 30v).   S. McK.

Notes

1. D. Ross (1969) noted only one other copy of this text, namely Paris, Bibliothèque nationale de France, Ms. n. a. fr. 14285.

2. Ross (D.)1969: 179.

3. The passage is quoted in full in Meiss 1974: 345–46, from Paris, Bibliothèque nationale de France, Ms. n. a. fr. 14285. It seems likely that this version of the *Trésor* was intended for one of the bibliophile members of the Valois hierarchy in Paris.

4. E.g., Brussels, Bibliothèque royale de Belgique, Ms. 9069, datable to ca. 1473 (Brussels 1987a: no. 27; Debae 1995: 53–56, no. 31), and London, British Library, Royal Ms. 18 E.v, dated 1473 (Warner [G.] and Gilson 1921, 2: 315–16).

5. Ross (D.) 1969: 178.

6. On this new aspect of the Cotton miniatures, see Pächt 1978: 3–5.

7. Instructions are still visible on folios 94v, 99v, 142, 293v, 302, 319, and 398v.

8. Malibu 1983a: 7, fig. 2.

9. McKendrick 2003: pl. 35.

78

MASTER OF THE GETTY FROISSART (?) AND MASTER OF THE WHITE INSCRIPTIONS (?)

Giovanni Boccaccio, *Des cas de nobles hommes et femmes*, translation by Laurent de Premierfait of *De casibus virorum et feminarum illustrium*
Bruges, ca. 1480

MANUSCRIPT: 513 + i folios, 48 × 34 cm (18⅞ × 13⅜ in.); justification: 29 × 20.4 cm (11⅜ × 8 in.); 37 lines of *bastarda* in two columns; 9 three-quarter-page miniatures, 67 one-column miniatures

HERALDRY: Escutcheons with the royal arms of England, fols. 5, 13v, 30, etc.; once differenced with a label of three points, fol. 174; escutcheon with the arms of Saint Edmund, fol. 488; banner with the royal arms of England, fol. 5; badge of rose-en-soleil with motto *Dieu et mon droit*, fols. 5, 174, 349v, 391; motto *Honny soit qui mal y pense*, fol. 391

BINDING: London, mid-eighteenth century; brown morocco; the arms of George II gold-stamped on both covers; rebacked

COLLECTION: London, The British Library, Royal Ms. 14 E.v

PROVENANCE: Edward IV, king of England (1442–1483); English royal library, Richmond Palace, in 1535, and Saint James's in 1666; George II, king of England (1683–1760); presented 1757 to the British Museum

R A

One of the secular vernacular texts frequently illustrated during the fifteenth century was a French translation of Giovanni Boccaccio's *De casibus virorum et feminarum illustrium*.[1] Dedicated to the famous bibliophile John, duke of Berry, the second, revised translation was completed in 1409 by the Parisian protohumanist Laurent de Premierfait. Together with an anonymous translation of the *De mulieribus claris*, this work made accessible to French nobles both of Boccaccio's succinct accounts of the fate of great men and women from the past, most notably those from ancient Greece and Rome.

The present volume of *Des cas des nobles hommes et femmes* is by far the most extensively illustrated copy made in Flanders.[2] Although frequently illustrated by French miniaturists from the time of its creation, Premierfait's text appears rarely to have been illustrated by Flemish artists. Despite this fact, the present manuscript shares no direct links in either text or illustrations to the version of the text prepared closest in time and place—the remarkable illustrated edition of the translation printed at Bruges in 1476 by Colard Mansion (cat. no. 72). For example, the latter employs Premierfait's more literal first translation, completed in 1400.[3] Unlike Mansion's edition and most other later manuscripts, the present manuscript also contains the verses by Premierfait in praise of Boccaccio, which first appeared in the copy of the *Des cas* that belonged to Premierfait's fellow scholar Gontier Col.[4] Even in their choice of subjects for the illustrations that open each of the nine books of the *Des cas*, the present manuscript and the printed edition have very little in common.

In the present copy of the *Des cas*, one principal miniaturist, aided by one or possibly two assistants, executed the campaign of seventy-six miniatures. The principal artist contributed all nine large miniatures.[5] In these, he not only painted with a high degree of finish but also revealed a sophisticated interest in the depiction of both interiors and

landscape.[6] *Fortune Appearing to Boccaccio*—which includes both interior and exterior spaces and exemplifies the miniaturist's ability to capture the subtle effects of light on an interior—marks the opening of book 6 (ill. 78). Here, rather than focusing on the symbolically grotesque aspects of Lady Fortune (such as her numerous arms), the miniaturist created a more poetic image for the meeting—a meeting that provided Boccaccio with the inspiration for the second half of his work.

Previously ascribed to the Master of the White Inscriptions,[7] these large miniatures require a new attribution on account of their subtlety of palette, draftsmanship, and composition—all more adept than usually found in images by this master. Numerous qualities of interest and form suggest a closer relationship to the work of the Master of the Getty Froissart.[8] Significant variation in the execution of faces and other details are explicable only if several different artists executed these details. Because assistants worked in a style modeled closely after that of their master and because there is evidence of more than one hand working within individual miniatures, attribution is indeed hazardous throughout the volume. The differing abilities of the contributing miniaturists become most obvious in the small miniatures.[9] Several of these miniatures were not only executed more hastily but also include figures that, in their grotesque angularity and bulk, as well as in the limited

palette employed for them, are closer to the work of the Master of the White Inscriptions. Despite these failings, the miniaturists succeeded in producing varied and sometimes innovative images for an unrelenting succession of gruesome deaths.

As indicated by its heraldry, the present manuscript was illuminated in Flanders for Edward IV. Stylistic links with both the borders and the miniatures of other manuscripts made for Edward in 1479 and 1480 suggest that this volume was produced around the same dates; it thus probably originates from the period in which Edward collected most of his Flemish manuscripts.[10]   S. McK.

Notes

1. Sixty-nine manuscripts are noted in Bozzolo 1973.

2. The only other copies known to me are London, British Library, Add. Ms. 11696, and Paris, Bibliothèque nationale de France, Ms. fr. 132.

3. According to Paris 1975, nos. 99, 117, Mansion's edition was based on a manuscript in the possession of Louis of Gruuthuse (Paris, Bibliothèque nationale, Ms. fr. 132), one of two Flemish manuscript copies of the first translation. The other manuscript (London, British Library, Add. Ms. 11696) was made for Jean de Montferrant (see cat. no. 70).

4. On these verses and Col's manuscript, see Bozzolo 1977: 16–17.

5. Fols. 5, 64, 113v, 174, 233, 291, 349, 391, 450.

6. A particularly fine landscape appears in the miniature *The Execution of Manlius Capitolinus* (fol. 174). A complex and fascinating interior appears in *The Murder of Antyllus* (fol. 349).

7. Durrieu 1921: pl. 66; Winkler 1925: 137, 179.

8. Compare, for example, the grandly dressed figures in the opening presentation miniature (fol. 5) with those in the name manuscript of the Master of the Getty Froissart (cat. no. 79). Compare also the distinctively drawn horses on folio 233 with those in the Getty manuscript, folio 254.

9. These small miniatures seem to have been numbered in a sequence separate from that of the large miniatures. The numbers *30* and *34* are still visible on folios 363v and 280v, respectively. Traces of instructions to the illuminators of these small miniatures are also visible on folios 121v, 256v, 280v, 488, 492v, and 506v. On other numbered sequences of miniatures, see Alexander 1992: 59.

10. For more on the heraldry and decoration of Edward's manuscripts, see McKendrick 1994: 161–63.

79

MASTER OF THE GETTY FROISSART, MASTER OF THE SOANE JOSEPHUS AND ASSISTANT, MASTER OF EDWARD IV, MASTER OF THE COPENHAGEN CAESAR (?), AND MASTER OF THE LONDON WAVRIN (?)

Jean Froissart, *Chroniques*, book 3
Bruges, ca. 1480–83

MANUSCRIPT: 366 folios, 48 × 35 cm (18⅞ × 13¾ in.); justification: 29 × 19.3 cm (11½ × 7⅞ in.); 39 lines of *bastarda* in two columns; 1 three-quarter-page miniature, 24 half-page miniatures, 39 one-column miniatures

BINDING: Fleuron bindery, The Hague, early eighteenth century; gold-tooled green morocco over pasteboard[1]

COLLECTION: Los Angeles, J. Paul Getty Museum, Ms. Ludwig XIII 7 (83.MP.150)

PROVENANCE: Probably Edward IV, king of England (1442–1483); English royal library, Richmond Palace, in 1535, and probably Saint James's in 1666; James de Rothschild (1792–1868); Baron Edmond de Rothschild (1845–1934), Paris; Alexandrine de Rothschild (d. 1965); [H. P. Kraus, New York, by 1974]; to Peter and Irene Ludwig, Aachen; purchased 1983

JPGM and RA

The *Chroniques* of Jean Froissart enjoyed a spectacular revival at the hands of Flemish miniaturists from the late 1460s to the early 1480s.[2] Two complete texts of the *Chroniques*, each in four large folio volumes, were created for the renowned bibliophiles Anthony of Burgundy and Louis of Gruuthuse (for the latter, see cat. no. 71).[3] The first is dated 1468; the second is datable to the mid-1470s. A third complete copy, which entered the Burgundian ducal library sometime before 1487, was produced around 1480; a fourth was first owned by Edward IV's chancellor of the exchequer, Sir Thomas Thwaytes.[4] A further copy of book 4 of the *Chroniques* was made for the chronicler and noble Philippe de Commynes (cat. no. 68).[5] Each of these copies forms a luxury edition of Froissart's text, lavishly decorated and profusely illustrated.

Even among these splendid Flemish manuscripts of Froissart's text, the present manuscript stands out as by far the most profusely illustrated copy of book 3 of the *Chroniques*.[6] Its campaign of sixty-four miniatures, no fewer than twenty-five of which occupy one-third of the text block, greatly exceeds in ambition even its counterpart in the sumptuous set made for Anthony of Burgundy.[7] Even

if one considers only the number and size of illustrations, it is unsurprising that the Getty manuscript has been thought part of the same set as two equally ambitious copies of books 2 and 4 of the *Chroniques*.[8] These two volumes contain, respectively, forty-eight and fifty-four miniatures, a total of forty-one of which also occupy one-third of the text block. Shared codicological features and a plausible shared provenance from the English royal library make the three volumes' belonging to the same set even more likely.[9] The creation of this set would be well explained as part of Edward IV's collecting of Flemish manuscripts around 1480.

The miniaturist responsible for all but five of the large miniatures in the present volume is a remarkable artist. Long identified with the Master of the White Inscriptions,[10] he merits separate classification as the Master of the Getty Froissart. While his work shares some of the characteristics of the other miniaturist, such as gloomy interiors and male faces with full, heavy features, both his draftsmanship and his painting are of a much higher quality. The Master of the Getty Froissart also showed more interest in the depiction of fine costume, light, space, and landscape. His miniature of Charles II of Navarre being burned to death in his bed (ill. 79b) reveals his skill in conveying the drama of such a horrific accident. The Getty Master was also capable of more subtle enhancements of his subjects. In another miniature, which shows the seneschal of Brabant and his army crossing over the River Meuse at Ravenstein and moving into Guelders (ill. 79a), early morning light breaks over the horizon, lighting up patches in the otherwise colorless landscape. The artist not only added atmosphere to his subject but also faithfully reflected Froissart's description of this event as "near the break of day."

Three further miniaturists contributed to the large illustrations. The Master of the Soane Josephus and an assistant painted the opening miniature of Froissart presenting his text, as well as the fifth, sixth, and seventh large miniatures.[11] The Master of Edward IV, possibly still an assistant of the Soane Master at the time, painted the eighth large miniature, showing John of Gaunt receiving the keys of Santiago de Compostela (fol. 122). As for the thirty-nine one-column miniatures, these were executed mainly by a team of two assistants, one of whom may be the Master of the Copenhagen Caesar. As frequently happened in manuscripts of secular vernacular texts, the principal miniaturist also contributed to the cycle of smaller miniatures. In this case the Master of the Getty Froissart painted two such illustrations, one in the middle of the volume and one toward the end (fols. 185, 286). One further small miniature appears to have been contributed by the Master of the London Wavrin (fol. 171). A team of no fewer than seven artists was therefore responsible for the illustration of the Getty Froissart.

The distribution of the illustrations in the present manuscript is remarkably uneven. Most notably, two sections of text, each more than 130 pages long, contain no illustrations whatsoever.[12] These lacunae stand in marked contrast to the evenly distributed miniatures of the Getty Froissart's probable companion volumes, not to say to

deseonfist entre muestam et
la ville de gynue engues dree.
Clappitre. iiij.rr vij.e

T uie petitee
lieuee de gyn
ue siet la vil
le et le chaste
au de muef
tam lequel
est au seigneur de borne lequel
est dee hommee et tenablee
de brabant. Et fut a ce conseil
requis et prie le sire de borne de
par sec barone z chevalliere. et
premierement se par le cōseil
de la ducheffe de brabant z dee
bonnee villee il saccorda a ou
urir sa ville. Le duc de gu
erlee qui se tenoit a nymegue

fut informe veritablement ne
scay parqui que le sire de borne
luroit passaige aux brabanconc
et entreroient en sa terre par la
ville z pont de muestam. Quant
cec nouvellec luy furent venuec
si fut tout penfif z melancolie.
car il veoit quil navoit prefen
tgene affec pour refifter a tou
te la puiffance de brabant ou
bien pouoit auoir se il paffoient
touc quarante mille hommee
que vnc que autrec et eut le
Duc plufeurc imaginatiōc
fur ce pour faruoir et aduifer
comment il fe mantiendroit.
Et finablement tout confide
re il regarda quil mettroit tou
tee fec gene enfemble et femec

79a
MASTER OF THE
GETTY FROISSART
*The Soldiers of Brabant
Entering Ravenstein,*
fol. 318 (detail)

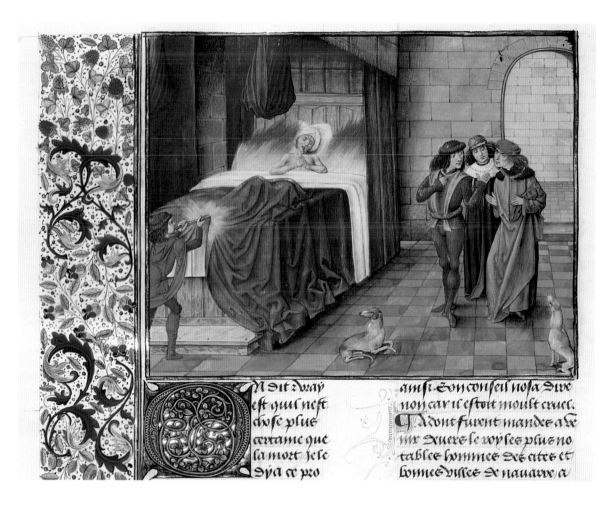

most other illustrated manuscripts of the *Chroniques*. Given that the general distribution of miniatures in the Getty Froissart seems to reflect the deliberate selection of parts of the text to be illustrated, the two lacunae require some explanation. Although one possible explanation is a total disinterest on the part of the volume's planners in these two parts of the text, the unillustrated parts more likely reflect an earlier stage in the genesis of the volume when very few miniatures were going to be included. Since these two sections come at the beginning of each of the two halves of the volume,[13] it is very possible that the scribe copied them first.

S. McK.

Notes

1. Thanks to Jan Storm van Leeuwen for help in identifying the binding and to Philippa Marks for making the contact between Van Leeuwen and the author possible. The tooling is identical to that on the binding of cat. no. 81.

2. See Le Guay 1998.

3. Respectively, Berlin, Staatsbibliothek, Ms. Dep. Breslau 1, vols. 1–4; Paris, Bibliothèque nationale de France, Mss. fr. 2643–46.

4. Paris, Bibliothèque de l'Arsenal, Mss. 5187–90; London, British Library, Royal Mss. 14 D.ii–vi.

5. London, British Library, Harley Mss. 4379, 4380.

6. For an overview of illustrated manuscripts of book 3, see Le Guay 1998: 155–56.

7. Anthony of Burgundy's copy of book 3 contains only one large miniature and thirty-seven one-column miniatures.

8. Books 2 and 4 are, respectively London, British Library, Royal Ms. 18 E.i and Royal Ms. 18 E.ii. For details, see Warner (G.) and Gilson 1921, 2: 314–15.

9. The three manuscripts share text blocks of identical dimensions and number of lines, as well as very similar subsidiary decoration. Given the inclusion of Edward IV's supporters of the lions of March in the border of the opening miniature of book 4, this volume was definitely made for the English royal library. It is most probably to be identified with the "booke called Froissard" for the binding, gilding, and dressing, for which the stationer Piers Bauduyn was paid by Edward in 1480. In 1666 the London book 4 was recorded in the royal library at Saint James's as one of a set of Froissart in three volumes. As one of these volumes was certainly the London book 2, the drawn arms of Hastings in its opening border may not have related to an actual owner, or if they did, Hastings quickly ceded the volume to the royal library. It is, moreover, plausible that the Getty manuscript of book 3 was the third volume of Froissart recorded in 1666. Like another escapee from the royal library last recorded in 1666, the Soane Jose-phus (cat. no. 81), the Getty Froissart appears to have passed to the Netherlands early in the eighteenth century, where it was rebound, presumably for resale.

10. Von Euw and Plotzek 1979–85, 3: 265–66.

11. Comparison with London, Sir John Soane's Museum, Ms. 1, fol. 272v, suggests that the Soane Master painted the miniature on folio 106 working alone and those on folios 9 and 116v working with assistants. The last compares most closely with the final miniature in the Soane Josephus (fol. 305). The miniature on folio 112 was painted by the assistant responsible for the miniature on folios 58 and 116v in the Soane Josephus.

12. There are no miniatures from folios 10 through 79, nor from folios 189 through 253.

13. As stated in note 12, the second lacuna begins at folio 189, a point very close to the midpoint of a volume now comprising 366 folios.

79b

MASTER OF THE
GETTY FROISSART
*The Bed of the King of
Navarre Set on Fire,*
fol. 274v (detail)

MASTER OF THE WHITE INSCRIPTIONS

The Master of the White Inscriptions was named by Paul Durrieu in 1921 after two large manuscripts made for Edward IV of England that contain French translations of Giovanni Boccaccio's *De casibus virorum illustrium* (cat. no. 78) and Benvenuto da Imola's *Romuléon* (London, British Library, Royal Ms. 19 E.v).[1] Of the white inscriptions that form a prominent and distinctive part of the miniatures of both volumes, one includes the date 1480.[2] In 1925 Friedrich Winkler added attributions for miniatures by this illuminator in two more manuscripts of secular texts made for Edward (cat. no. 80; London, British Library, Royal Ms. 18 E.vi), the first of which includes a miniature dated 1479.[3] More recently, in 1994, I expanded the corpus of works by the the Master of the White Inscriptions to include Edward IV's copies of Jean de Courcy's *Chemin de Vaillance* and Raoul de Presle's French translation of Saint Augustine's *Cité de Dieu* (London, British Library, Royal Mss. 14 E.ii, 17 F.iii).[4] At the same time I noted a few miniatures by the Master of the White Inscriptions in two manuscripts of Vincent de Beauvais's *Speculum historiale* in French translation (London, British Library, Royal Ms. 14 E.i)[5] and Jean de Wavrin's *Chroniques d'Angleterre* (London, British Library, Royal Ms. 14 E.iv)[6] that also came to form part of Edward's library. Finally, in 2002, Hanno Wijsman attributed the large opening miniature in a copy of *Le livre des faits de Jacques de Lalaing* (Paris, Bibliothèque nationale de France, Ms. fr. 16830) to the same artist.[7] This volume is the only one noted to date that did not belong to Edward IV.[8] Some of the miniatures previously attributed to the Master of the White Inscriptions, including the most accomplished miniatures in the Getty Froissart (cat. no. 79) and Edward IV's copy of Boccaccio (cat. no. 78),[9] are more credible as the work of a more talented artist, whom I have named the Master of the Getty Froissart. The Master of the White Inscriptions was most likely this artist's follower.

All the miniatures attributed to the Master of the White Inscriptions are remarkable for their spare and forceful simplicity.[10] They repeatedly depict only one subject, and in many cases they do so with such economy of means in terms of setting and figures that the subject is either very easy or very difficult to identify.[11] The master's male figures are drawn in a manner that gives prominence to facial ugliness, physical bulk, and awkwardness of pose and frequently suggests a capacity for violent aggression. His female figures are similarly angular in form but more elegantly shaped; their faces, which show little differentiation, suggest simple passivity. Interior scenes are set in sparsely furnished rooms dominated by bare gray stone walls. Whatever the setting, the palette is dominated by orange, green, and gray or black. Among the white inscriptions that led Durrieu to give this name to the miniaturist is the motto *Tousdis joyeulx*, variants of which occur four times in three manuscripts and may be some form of signature.[12]

All of the works attributed to the Master of the White Inscriptions are datable to a very short period around 1480. The volumes to which he contributed were produced by scribes and border artists engaged in the commercial production of manuscripts of vernacular texts at Bruges. Most frequently this artist was responsible either for the most miniatures in a volume or for the frontispiece. Within these volumes he collaborated with several miniaturists known to have been active in Bruges, such as the Master of Edward IV and the Master of the Getty Froissart.[13] The Master of the White Inscriptions appears to have derived much of his artistic style from these two more talented miniaturists, including aspects of his palette, figure drawing, interiors, and landscapes. The corpus of works thus far attributed to the Master of the White Inscriptions requires some review.

S. McK.

Notes

1. Durrieu 1921a: 61, pls. 65, 66. Elsewhere (McKendrick 1994: 150) I have identified two of the miniatures in the *Romuléon* (fols. 32, 125) as the work of two other artists.

2. London, British Library, Royal Ms. 19 E.v, fol. 367v.

3. Winkler 1925: 137, 179.

4. McKendrick 1994: 163–64. Only the opening miniature of the *Chemin de Vaillance* (McKendrick 1990: pl. 2) is by a different artist. For miniatures by the Master of the White Inscriptions in both these manuscripts, see McKendrick 2003: pls. 61, 62.

5. Vol. 1, fol. 3 (Backhouse 1987: pl. 3).

6. Fols. 81, 98v, 114, 121, 169v, 299.

7. Wijsman 2002: 1641–64.

8. Wijsman (2002: 1645) does, however, argue that this volume was originally intended for Edward's close associate and lord great chamberlain, William Lord Hastings.

9. For the attribution of the Getty miniatures to the Master of the White Inscriptions, see Von Euw and Plotzek 1979–85, 3: 265–66.

10. For other accounts of the style of the Master of the White Inscriptions, see Dogaer 1987a: 125; and Smeyers 1998: 424.

11. Miniatures such as *The Rape and Death of Lucretia* (London, British Library, Royal Ms. 18 E.iv, fol. 71) are easy to identify; difficult to identify are miniatures such as one showing a group of male figures in debate in an interior (London, British Library, Royal Ms. 19 E.v, fol. 238).

12. These variants are *Ainsi va le monde tousdis joyeulx* and *Josne et joyeulx* (London, British Library, Royal Ms. 14 E.v, fols. 313v and 391); *Je suis bien tousdis joieulx* (London, British Library, Royal Ms. 18 E.iii, fol. 24); and *Joye sans fin* (London, British Library, Royal Ms. 18 E.vi, fol. 8). None of these inscriptions relates to the subject of the miniatures, except the one in Royal Ms. 14 E.v, fol. 313v, which serves as a darkly sardonic commentary on a particularly vicious depiction of the murder of Herod. The only other example of such an inscription known to me is *Tous iours ioieuls*, which occurs in a book of hours dated 1480 (cat. no. 36).

13. As noted under cat. no. 80, he also collaborated with at least one Ghent miniaturist, the Master of the Flemish Boethius.

80

MASTER OF THE WHITE INSCRIPTIONS

Valerius Maximus, *Faits et dits mémorables des romains*, translation by Simon de Hesdin and Nicolas de Gonesse of *Facta et dicta memorabilia*, volume 1
Bruges, 1479

MANUSCRIPT: 342 folios, 47.3 × 33 cm (18⅝ × 13 in.); justification: 29.3 × 19.4 cm (11½ × 7⅝ in.); 39 lines of *bastarda* in two columns; 4 three-quarter-page miniatures

HERALDRY: Escutcheons with the royal arms of England, two recumbent and differenced with labels of three and five points, one encircled by the Garter and surmounted by crowned helm with crest of white lion, fols. 24, 133, etc.; banners with the royal arms of England, fols. 24, 133, etc.; badges of rose-en-soleil with motto *Dieu et mon droit*, fols. 24, 133, etc.; motto *Honny soit qui mal y pense*, fol. 24

BINDING: London, mid-eighteenth century; brown morocco; the arms of George II gold-stamped on both covers; rebacked

COLLECTION: London, The British Library, Royal Ms. 18 E.iii

PROVENANCE: Edward IV, king of England (1442–1483); English royal library, Richmond Palace, in 1535, and Saint James's in 1666; George II, king of England (1683–1760); presented 1757 to the British Museum

R A

Together with its companion volume (Royal Ms. 18 E.iv), this manuscript contains the *Facta et dicta memorabilia* of Valerius Maximus in the popular French version that was begun by the Hospitaller Simon de Hesdin (d. 1383) in 1375 and completed by Nicolas de Gonesse by 1401.[1] Unlike most other Flemish illuminated copies of this translation, these volumes are securely dated and have an identifiable patron. In the opening miniature, depicting the translator at work, an inscription on the back wall shows the date 1479. The decorated border accompanying this and the other eight large miniatures includes the arms and devices of Edward IV together with the arms of his two sons, the ill-fated Princes in the Tower.

Eight of the nine miniatures have long been attributed to one miniaturist, the Master of the White Inscriptions.[2] Discernible in several other manuscripts produced for Edward IV, his style is distinguished by a palette in which salmon, green, and gray or black often predominate and by drawing that accentuates the differences between male and female figures by stressing the ungainliness of the former and the gracefulness of the latter. Also characteristic are gloomy interiors with gray stone walls, most of which are bare of any embellishment, except the artist's calling card of white inscriptions, which tend to dominate the picture space and its subject. As exemplified by his illustration for book 3 of Valerius Maximus (ill. 80), the Master of the White Inscriptions was capable of painting arresting and bold images that convey with a simple directness a particular idea or narrative. Always inclined to employ oversize figures, the miniaturist delighted in the opportunity to depict a true giant of a man as representative of force of courage. Both the tiny child trying to spin a top and the pleasant, winding landscape merely accentuate the dark vigor of the giant as he struggles with the roaring lion.

Here, as with other texts containing his work, the Master of the White Inscriptions appears to have developed a campaign of illustrations independent of those previously created for the manuscript at hand. This independence is all the more remarkable given the attention paid to the illustration of Valerius Maximus by contemporary miniaturists in Bruges.[3] Most notably, the Master of the White Inscriptions omitted the two figures of Valerius Maximus and the Emperor Tiberius, which were introduced by previous miniaturists as mediators between the text and the viewer. In a series of bold images, he sought instead to convey directly to the viewer the virtues commended by the text.

S. McK.

Notes

1. For further details of this text and its popularity, see cat. nos. 66, 67, 72, and McKendrick, "Reviving the Past: Illustrated Manuscripts of Secular Vernacular Texts, 1467–1500," this volume.

2. Durrieu 1921a: pl. 65; Winkler 1925: 137, 179. The ninth miniature (18 E.iv, fol. 19) is attributable to the Master of the Flemish Boethius.

3. See McKendrick, "Reviving the Past: Illustrated Manuscripts of Secular Vernacular Texts, 1467–1500," note 11, this volume; and cat. no. 72.

80 (opposite)
MASTER OF THE
WHITE INSCRIPTIONS
Samson and the Lion,
fol. 227

N ce tiers li
ure ya huit
chappitre.
Le premier
est de indole
Le second de
force. Le tiers de patience. Le
quart de ceulx qui vindrent
de petit lieu qui puis furent
puissant et vaillant. Le v.e

de ceulx qui furent extrais de
noblece qui ne lee sieuuirent
pas en oeuure et en bonnee
meurs. Le sixieme des nobles
parens qui prindrent plus
conte subit et autre maniere
Sgouurnemene que la coustu
me du pays nestoit. Le vij.e de
france de soy. Le huitiesme de
constance. Translateur. Indole

MASTER OF THE SOANE JOSEPHUS

The Master of the Soane Josephus is named after a copy of Josephus's *Histories* in French translation that passed into the possession of Edward IV in 1480 (cat. no. 81). Previously considered the work of the Master of Edward IV, the miniatures in this book were first identified by Bodo Brinkmann as the work of another artist.[1] Although Brinkmann has attributed five other manuscripts of secular texts to his Master of the Soane Josephus,[2] little consideration has been given to this miniaturist and his work to date.

As noted by Brinkmann, the Master of the Soane Josephus appears to be the senior partner in collaboration with the Master of Edward IV. Although clearly a less talented artist, the Master of the Soane Josephus was regularly assigned frontispieces and large miniatures within deluxe copies of long historical texts in the late 1470s. Brinkmann noted this pattern in the last volume of Edward IV's *Bible historiale*. It is also apparent in the Getty Froissart (cat. no. 79), to which he contributed the opening miniature; two copies of the *Fleur des histoires* (Paris, Bibliothèque nationale de France, Ms. fr. 296;[3] Copenhagen, Kongelige Bibliotek, Ms. Thott 568 2°);[4] and a copy of the *Trésor des histoires* (London, British Library, Royal Ms. 18 E.v),[5] in which he painted the large miniatures. The Master of the Soane Josephus's collaboration within these volumes with the Master of the Getty Froissart, the Master of the Copenhagen Caesar, the Master of the Harley Froissart, and a follower of Loyset Liédet strongly suggests that he was working in Bruges. A book of hours in Dutch that includes illuminations by the Master of the Soane Josephus (Chicago, University Library, Ms. 347) appears to suggest the same center of production.[6]

Miniatures by the Master of the Soane Josephus and the Master of Edward IV are easily confused since their styles are very similar in many respects. The work of the Master of the Soane Josephus, however, displays several distinctive features. His palette is much brighter and more varied, and paint is applied more fluidly and with fewer visible brushstrokes. Faces are also more chiseled in appearance; a particularly common type is sharp-nosed and fork-bearded. In addition, compositions are more obviously assembled from models, figure groups awkwardly tight and separately conceived, and architecture highly unstable and illogical in structure.   S. McK.

Notes

1. Brinkmann 1987–88: 126, n. 22; Brinkmann 1997: 295.
2. Brinkmann 1997: 399. Of the manuscripts that he lists, I consider one (New York, Morgan Library, Ms. M.214) stylistically unrelated to the Master of the Soane Josephus. On this volume, see the biographies of the Master of Margaret of York and associates, this part. Three manuscripts that Brinkmann lists (cat. nos. 79, 81–83) do indeed include miniatures by the Master of the Soane Josephus. I have not seen his fifth example, one of the Flemish copies of René of Anjou's *Livre des Tournois* (Paris, Bibliothèque nationale de France, Ms. fr. 2693).
3. This volume and its companions (Paris, Bibliothèque nationale, Mss. fr. 297–99) are datable to before 1482, before the death of their first owner, Jean-Louis de Savoie, bishop of Geneva. See Paravicini Bagliani 1990: pl. 31.
4. See Copenhagen 1999: no. 126.
5. The text of this volume is dated 1473. Its border decoration, however, suggests a later dating for the illumination, probably as part of Edward IV's acquisitions in the late 1470s (see McKendrick 2003: pl. 28).
6. See Parshall 1969: 333–37. Parshall and Brinkmann (1997: 300 n. 46, 397) are incorrect in attributing the miniatures in this book to the Master of Edward IV.

81

MASTER OF THE SOANE JOSEPHUS AND ASSISTANTS

Flavius Josephus, *Antiquités judaïques et la guerre des Juifs*, translation of *Antiquitates Judaicae et bellum Judaicum*, books 15–27
Bruges, ca. 1478–80

MANUSCRIPT: i + 353 + v folios, 49.2 × 35 cm (19⅜ × 13¼ in.); justification: 29.3 × 19.5 cm (11½ × 7¼ in.); 39 lines of *bastarda* in two columns; 12 three-quarter-page miniatures

HERALDRY: Escutcheons with achievement of the arms of Louis of Gruuthuse, encircled by collar of the Order of the Golden Fleece and flanked by his bombard device, all overpainted by the arms of England, surmounted by crowned helm and crest of leopard passant and double fleur-de-lis and encircled by the Garter, fols. 11, 150; the arms of England on standard in decorated border, fol. 11; motto *Plus est en vous* overpainted on scroll in decorated border, fol. 150

BINDING: Fleuron bindery, The Hague, early eighteenth century; gold-tooled black morocco[1]

COLLECTION: London, Sir John Soane's Museum, Ms. 1

PROVENANCE: Edward IV, king of England (1442–1483), by 1480; English royal library, Richmond Palace, in 1535, and Saint James's in 1666; Thomas Noel Hill, second baron Berwick (1784–1832), Attingham Hall [his sale, Robins, Attingham Hall, July 30, 1827, lot 152]; to Sir John Soane (1753–1837)

RA

Sometime during the reign of Charles VI of France, an unknown author compiled French translations of *Jewish Antiquities* and *The Jewish War* by Flavius Josephus (b. A.D. 37/38).[2] Combined into one long text in twenty-seven books, these translations transmitted to late medieval

Et commence le quinzies
me liure de Josephus de sainct
entete des Juifz. Et mons
tre ou premier chapitre Com
ment herode occist antigon.

Dant herode eut
prins la princi
paulte de toute
Judee tous ceulx
quil trouua a prince; et fa

Et comment il deposa hir
can de leuesche et fist
mourir aristobole. Inn
ombles il esleua a grans
dignitez a tous ceulx qui
sentoient ou faisoient du
contraire il ne cessoit tous
les jours de mettre a chiefs
tourmens Et sur tous
les autres estoient honou

nobles a detailed account of the history of the Jews from
Creation to Josephus's own time. Whereas the very small
number of surviving manuscripts suggests that few nobles
obtained or read copies of this text, the consistently high
ambitions of their illustrations mark it as one in which
some important bibliophiles and miniaturists of the
fifteenth century took considerable interest.[3]

The present volume is one of only five volumes written
and illustrated in Flanders that preserve the translation of
Josephus. Whereas the other four form two complete texts,
each in two volumes,[4] the Soane manuscript contains only
the second half of the translation. Its narrative therefore
begins in book 15 with Herod the Great's ascent to the
throne of Judaea in 37 B.C. Twelve large miniatures accompanied by full decorated borders mark the openings of
books 15–26.[5]

One principal artist, known from this manuscript as
the Master of the Soane Josephus, worked together with
three assistants on the twelve large miniatures. He alone
appears to have been responsible for five of them.[6] Two
assistants contributed two miniatures each,[7] and another
assistant, probably the Master of Edward IV, assisted the
Master of the Soane Josephus in three others.[8] Typical of
the contribution of the Master of the Soane Josephus is his
opening miniature depicting the drowning of the Has-
monean Aristobulus by the agents of Herod the Great (ill.
81). Within this illustration the miniaturist suggests the outlines of the bodies of the five swimmers under the water
and the ripples that their movements make across the surface of the water. As elsewhere in his work, the attendant
cityscape is packed to bursting with a jumble of unstable
and architecturally varied buildings, onlookers to the central event are gathered in two characteristic huddles, and
the landscape is peppered with stubby, bushlike trees, large
white pebbles, and a strange palmlike tree. Although some
of these elements detract from the emotional impact of
Aristobulus's last desperate struggle in the water before he
drowns, the artist succeeds in revealing through the
onlookers on the right the political intrigue that lay behind
this murder.

The Soane manuscript is probably the earliest of the
three Flemish copies of the Josephus translation.[9] Almost
without doubt it can be identified with the "booke of Josephus" for the "dressing" of which the London stationer
Piers Bauduyn was paid by Edward IV in 1480.[10] The
heraldic and subsidiary decoration is certainly consistent
with such a date, as is the evidence of costume in the miniatures.[11] The manuscript is also best explained as belonging
to Edward's intense period of collecting around 1479. If, as
I have argued elsewhere,[12] the overpainted arms of Louis of
Gruuthuse reflect not actual but intended ownership by
Gruuthuse, the volume need not have been begun much
before 1480.

With the probable intention of replacing the manuscript that he ceded to Edward, Louis of Gruuthuse commissioned another copy of the Josephus translation (Paris,
Bibliothèque nationale, Mss. fr. 11–16). The second volume
of this even grander copy was written at Ghent in 1480 and
the first at Bruges in 1483. Both volumes were opulently
illustrated by the Master of the Flemish Boethius. Thereafter, the son of the bibliophile Anthony of Burgundy—
Philip, lord of Beveren (d. 1498)—commissioned the third
surviving Flemish copy (Paris, Bibliothèque de l'Arsenal,
Mss. 5082–83). Its illustrations were also provided by the
Master of the Flemish Boethius, this time in partnership
with the Master of Edward IV and his assistant the Master
of the Trivial Heads. Comparison of all three campaigns of
illustration reveals them each to be independently derived
from the text.   S. McK.

Notes

1. Thanks to Jan Storm van Leeuwen for help in identifying the
binding and to Philippa Marks for making the contact between Van
Leeuwen and the author possible. The tooling is identical to that on
the binding of cat. no. 79.

2. The earliest recorded copy is that given to the French royal
library by the Dauphin Louis, duke of Guienne, in 1410 (Delisle
1868–81, 3: 155, no. 892). The earliest surviving copy is that acquired by
John, duke of Berry, around 1410 (Meiss 1974: 44, 381).

3. In addition to the present manuscript, I know of only Cologny-
Geneva, Bibliotheca Bodmeriana, Ms. Bodmer 181; Paris, Bibliothèque
de l'Arsenal, Mss. 5082, 5083; Paris, Bibliothèque nationale de France,
Mss. fr. 11–16, 247 + n.a.fr. 21013 and 6446. In addition to the Flemish
illustrations discussed in the present entry, several very fine illustrations were produced by French artists, most notably by Jean Fouquet
(Paris 1993: no. 71). Significant owners of the other copies of Josephus
included John, duke of Berry; John the Fearless; and Philip the Good.

4. Paris, Bibliothèque de l'Arsenal, Mss. 5082–83; Paris, Bibliothèque nationale, Mss. fr. 11–16.

5. Books 26 and 27 are merged into one book in the translation.

6. Fols. 11, 150, 232v, 272v, 305.

7. One assistant was responsible for folios 36v and 256 and the
other for folios 58 and 116v. The former appears also to have been
responsible for the *Joshua* miniature in Edward IV's *Bible historiale*
(London, British Library, Royal Ms. 18 D.ix, fol. 275).

8. Fols. 85, 135v, 193v.

9. It seems likely that it is derived from an earlier Parisian copy of
the type acquired by John, duke of Berry, around 1410.

10. Omont 1891: 4

11. McKendrick 1994: 162.

12. McKendrick 1992: 153–54.

MASTER OF EDWARD IV (A)

The Master of Edward IV was first identified by Friedrich Winkler and named by him as the Master of Edward IV of 1479 after two volumes of a *Bible historiale* produced for Edward IV in 1479 (cat. no. 83).[1] Based on the style of five miniatures in the first of these volumes,[2] Winkler attributed to him a larger corpus of illustrations in seven further manuscripts of vernacular texts. Subsequently, the Master of Edward IV has been credited with the illustration of many other manuscripts, including several books of hours, that range in date from the 1470s to 1500.[3] Bodo Brinkmann's recent listing of works attributed to the Master of Edward IV comprises no fewer than forty-seven manuscripts and twenty separate leaves.[4] Despite increasing awareness of his importance as an illuminator, however, there remains no chronology for his work, no synthetical analysis of his style, and no discussion of his artistic origins and impact.

As first observed by L. M. J. Delaissé,[5] the Master of Edward IV contributed to several large manuscripts of vernacular texts made for Edward IV. Datable to between 1479 and 1482, these manuscripts[6] help define the artist's early career. In the first place, they firmly establish his place of work as Bruges. They also illustrate his close stylistic relationship to and close collaboration with another Bruges illuminator, the Master of the Soane Josephus (see separate biography, this volume, and cat. no. 82). As suggested by Brinkmann,[7] the Master of Edward IV appears to be the junior partner in this association. And yet, although the Master of Edward IV appears to have been considered of insufficient stature to be assigned the illustration of frontispieces in the manuscripts of Edward IV, the many miniatures that he did paint in these manuscripts reveal his manner of painting to be well developed. Within his small miniatures he repeatedly showed a talent for compositional invention and concise narrative. Figures appear in a wide range of poses and are combined skillfully in groups. Their faces are well defined, with full red lips, rouged cheeks, and receding hairlines. Aspects of these figures that led Friedrich Winkler to describe them as "gypsylike"[8] include the men's unkempt and straggly hair and somewhat rough and roguish expressions. The Master of Edward IV consistently applied a relatively narrow palette of salmon, green lake, gray-blue, and a fully saturated azure. These colors were supplemented by brown highlighted in gold to imitate gold cloth; black, gray, and white for brightly shining armor; and white on its own for horses or additional drapery. Scarlet was employed as a secondary color for small details and occasional patches of drapery. Most colors were applied with prominent brushstrokes that add texture and bulk to the forms. Landscapes either recede in atmospheric perspective with a gradual bluing of all features or are blocked off midground by sunken townscapes. They regularly include squat, bushlike green trees; lumpy rock formations; interlocking grassy hillocks; sandy paths strewn with a few large pebbles; mirrorlike water; and structures with high turreted walls of gray stone with blue or brown roofs. Most unusually, single, leafless trees occasionally protrude at forty-five-degree angles from hillsides, rocks, and even buildings. All these features are repeated in his subsequent works.

Many of the manuscripts illuminated by the Master of Edward IV during the 1480s (cat. nos. 95–98) have a more homogeneous appearance;[9] in addition to the miniatures in these manuscripts, the borders and even major illuminated initials appear to have been undertaken by the artist. One particular scribe transcribed several of the manuscripts illuminated by the Master of Edward IV during this period.[10] In the case of one of their most complex projects—an illustrated world chronicle (Saint Petersburg, Russian National Library, Ms. Fr.F.v.IV.12)[11]—so close was the collaboration required between scribe and illuminator that it is credible that this scribe was the Master of Edward IV himself. The miniaturist's fresh and detailed response to a wide range of secular and devotional texts would certainly be well explained if he was also responsible for their transcription. His repeated work for Baudouin II de Lannoy (d. 1501) during this period has been noted[12] but is as yet unstudied.[13] Also unstudied is the Master of Edward IV's reuse in devotional manuscripts of designs devised by other Flemish miniaturists.[14]

The Master of Edward IV continued to collaborate with other Bruges book producers.[15] By the early 1490s he was recognized as one of the very few miniaturists who was capable of producing illustrations for deluxe copies of secular vernacular texts. Thus, he came to illustrate, very late in his career, such texts as Vasco da Lucena's translations of Quintus Curtius's history of Alexander (Geneva, Bibliothèque publique et universitaire, Ms. fr. 76; London, British Library, Royal Ms. 20 C.iii) and Xenophon's *Cyropaedia* (Brussels, Bibliothèque royale, Ms. 11703), both of which had been illustrated by several other commercial illuminators much earlier. He was also chosen to illustrate two of the latest—and, by that date, somewhat antiquarian—copies of the prose romance *Guiron le Courtois* (Oxford, Bodleian Library, Douce Ms. 383; Paris, Bibliothèque nationale de France, Mss. fr. 359–63). During the 1490s, however, the style of the Master of Edward IV began to become more mannered. Even more prominent brushstrokes, heavy modeling, highly irregular forms, and a more exotic palette combine to both animate and disrupt his compositions. Many figures in his miniatures are gray-haired, bearded, and aged regardless of their actual age in the narrative, as in the case of Alexander the Great. Increasingly, work was delegated to less talented assistants, such as the Master of the Trivial Heads.[16] Clearly the career of this talented artist was nearing its end.

One of the aspects of the career of the Master of Edward IV that requires much further investigation is his artistic origins. Central to any such study would have to be his additions to the book of hours recently identified by Marc Gil as having been begun around 1450–55 for Antoine de Crèvecoeur (Leeds, University Library, Ms. 4).[17] Datable to around 1470–75 on the basis of the costume and the style of the accompanying border decoration, the miniatures added to this book of hours appear to foreshadow many of the stylistic characteristics of the miniatures produced by the Master of Edward IV in the manuscripts of Edward IV at the end of the same decade. The master's collaboration with Willem Vrelant on these additions to the Leeds Hours may be particularly significant.[18] In his later career the Master of Edward IV appears to have had access to patterns devised by Vrelant (see cat. no. 97). Moreover, the Master of Edward IV's career matured at the very point that Vrelant's career was coming to an end. One possible explanation is the identification of the Master of Edward IV with one of Vrelant's principal assistants, Adriaen de Raet.[19]

S. McK.

Notes

1. Winkler 1915: 336; Winkler 1925: 137.

2. Winkler (1925: 179) cited as the name works of the Master of Edward IV miniatures on folios 109, 173, 196 (*recte* 195v), 275, and 291v of London, British Library, Royal Ms. 18 D.ix. Brinkmann (1997: 295, n. 23) correctly attributed to the Master of Edward IV all these miniatures, except that on folio 275. For the miniatures by the Master of Edward IV in 18 D.x, see cat. no. 83.

3. Building on Winkler's attributions, Dogaer (1987a: 117) listed fourteen manuscripts. Unfortunately, several of those listed (Vatican City, Vatican Library, Ms. Pal. lat. 1990; Brussels, Bibliothèque royale de Belgique, Ms. 10485; Stuttgart, Württembergische Landesbibliothek, Ms. HB XI 34 fol.; Copenhagen, Kongelige Bibliotek, Ms. Thott 399 fol.) are stylistically unrelated to the work of the Master of Edward IV. Two others (London, British Library, Yates Thompson Ms. 32; The Hague, Koninklijke Bibliotheek, Ms. 133 A 1) are by a follower, the Master of the Trivial Heads. The miniatures Dogaer chose to reproduce (figs. 67–68) are from the London Yates Thompson manuscript.

4. Brinkmann 1997: 397–98. Those listed that I consider stylistically unrelated to the Master of Edward IV include the following: Copenhagen, Kongelige Bibliotek, Mss. Thott 413 fol. and 544 fol. I attribute to the Master of the Soane Josephus (see separate biography, this part): Chicago, University Library, Ms. 347, and some miniatures in Copenhagen, Kongelige Bibliotek, Ms. 568 fol.

5. Brussels 1959: 159, 188. Unfortunately Delaissé never cited any specific manuscripts.

6. I attribute to the Master of Edward IV the following: all the one-column miniatures in London, British Library, Royal Ms. 14 E.i (datable to ca. 1479) and 17 F.ii (dated 1479); the final two miniatures (fols. 200, 269) in 15 E.iii (dated 1482); and the penultimate miniature (fol. 293) in 14 E.iv.

7. Brinkmann 1997: 295.

8. Winkler 1925: 137 ("zigeunerhaft").

9. A notable exception is a copy of the *Miroir de la salvation humaine* (Paris, Bibliothèque nationale de France, Ms. fr. 6275). This manuscript was, however, written much earlier, and its illumination was begun by Jean Le Tavernier probably in the 1450s. The Master of Edward IV merely completed its illumination.

10. For a list of these manuscripts, see cat. no. 95. A further example of this collaboration—Valenciennes, Bibliothèque municipale, Ms. 243—is dated 1492 (n.s.).

11. For color reproductions, see Voronova and Sterligov 1996: pls. 362–73.

12. E.g., in Smeyers 1998: 444. See also cat. nos. 95, 97.

13. This patronage needs to be studied in relation to the Master of Edward IV's likely place of work. The greater independence of the works produced by him during the 1480s would suggest a temporary withdrawal from Bruges to another center. The contemporary patronage of the Master of Edward IV by another member of the Hainaut élite, John II of Oettingen, could support an identification of that center as Hainaut.

14. An obvious example of such reuse is his *Pentecost* in the Blackburn Hours (cat. no. 98, fol. 40v), which depends on the same model first seen in the Berlin Hours of Mary of Burgundy and Maximilian (cat. no. 38) and preserved in the drawing in the Paris, École des Beaux-Arts (cat. no. 26). This compositional source is particularly noteworthy given the Master of Edward IV's general independence of the visual tradition of the Ghent Associates. A less predictable visual connection is that between the *Mass of Saint Gregory* in the Blackburn Hours (cat. no. 98, fol. 166) and, in reverse, Simon Marmion's panel of the same subject (cat. no. 8).

15. In a deluxe copy of Josephus's *Histories* of around 1485–95 (Paris, Bibliothèque de l'Arsenal, Mss. 5082–83), the Master of Edward IV and his assistant the Master of the Trivial Heads collaborated with the Master of the Flemish Boethius (see separate biography, this part).

16. The Master of the Trivial Heads collaborated with the Master of Edward IV on Paris, Bibliothèque de l'Arsenal, Mss. 5082–83, Oxford, Bodleian Library, Douce Ms. 383, and The Hague, Koninklijke Bibliotheek, Ms. 128 C 1. He alone was responsible for London, British Library, Yates Thompson Ms. 32, and The Hague, Koninklijke Bibliotheek, Ms. 133 A 1 (datable after 1486).

17. Arras 2000: no. 31.

18. Vrelant was responsible for *The Mass of Saint Gregory* (fol. 1v). *Pace* Gil (Arras 2000: 87), I consider this miniature to have been added at the same time as the miniatures by the Master of Edward IV.

19. Van Buren (1999: 22–23) recently reconsidered the documented careers of Vrelant's principal assistants, Adriaen de Raet and Betkin Scepens. The Master of Edward IV's career is compatible with de Raet's. In brief, de Raet was registered with the Confraternity of Saint John at Bruges as an apprentice to Vrelant in 1474 and subsequently became a full member of the confraternity. For seven years after Vrelant's death in 1482, de Raet—together with Betkin Scepens—was closely associated in the confraternity records with Vrelant's widow. In 1487 de Raet took on his own first apprentice, and from 1499 onward he assumed successively higher offices within the confraternity, ending up as its governor in 1530. He died in 1534. For these details, see Weale 1864–65a: 301–3.

82

MASTER OF EDWARD IV, MASTER OF THE SOANE
JOSEPHUS, MASTER OF THE VIENNA *CHRONIQUES
D'ANGLETERRE*, MASTER OF THE HARLEY
FROISSART, AND FOLLOWER OF LOYSET LIÉDET

Bible historiale, Tobit to Acts
Bruges, between 1471 and 1479

MANUSCRIPT: iii + 439 + iii folios, 43.5 × 32 cm (17⅛ × 12⅝ in.);
justification: 26.8 × 19.7 cm (10½ × 7¾ in.); 33 lines of *bastarda* in
two columns by J. du Ries; 11 three-quarter-page miniatures, 66 one-
column miniatures

HERALDRY: Escutcheons with the royal arms of England, fols. 18, 31,
etc., the first surmounted by crowned helm and encircled by the
Garter; banner with the royal arms, fol. 18; standard with rose-en-
soleil with motto *Dieu et mon droit*, fol. 18

BINDING: London, mid-eighteenth century; brown morocco; the
arms of George II gold-stamped on both covers

COLLECTION: London, The British Library, Royal Ms. 15 D.i

PROVENANCE: Edward IV, king of England (1442–1483); English royal
library, Richmond Palace, in 1535, and Saint James's in 1666; George II,
king of England (1683–1760); presented 1757 to the British Museum

R A

Together with two companion volumes (see cat. no. 83),
the present manuscript has been described as forming
the most beautiful Bible in French ever made.[1] Its seventy-
seven miniatures, which illustrate a wide range of Old and
New Testament subjects, certainly make it one of the most
profusely illustrated.[2] Moreover, eleven of its illustrations
treat their biblical subjects with a breadth and spaciousness
that distinguish them from any contemporary or earlier
Bible miniatures.

The text illustrated is the concluding part of a French
adaptation of Petrus Comestor's *Historia scholastica* by
Guiart Des Moulins (1251–1312/22). Despite the late date of
the present copy, the version of Des Moulins's popular text
that it preserves is a rare version of the second edition that
retains much of his original work.[3] Des Moulins's text,
which was begun in 1291 and completed in 1295, survives
mostly in later versions that, to varying degrees, complete
his biblical narrative. In the present manuscript the text
begins with the Apocryphal Book of Tobit and ends with
the Acts of the Apostles. In between it encompasses the
Books of Jeremiah, Ezekiel, Daniel, Judith, Esther, and
Maccabees, as well as a Gospel history in which the separate narratives of the four Evangelists are woven into one.

Two artists were responsible for all but two of the sixty-
six one-column miniatures in the present manuscript. One
was a follower of Loyset Liédet and the other possibly the
Master of the Harley Froissart. Although both painted their
subjects in semi-grisaille, the two artists employed this
technique in very different ways. In the case of the second
artist, forms are hastily outlined and modeled over thin
washes of gray, blue, or brown.[4] In the miniatures of the
first, forms are much more sharply defined and more
subtly modeled; color is applied more extensively in counterpoint to the grisaille.[5] The Master of the *Chroniques*

d'Angleterre and the Master of Edward IV, respectively,
painted the two remaining small miniatures: *Saint Paul
Beaten at Philippi* (fol. 425v), the book's final illustration in
color, and *Judas Returning the Pieces of Silver* (fol. 346), a
subtle semi-grisaille.[6]

All but one of the eleven large miniatures—which are
the most prominent feature of the manuscript—were contributed by the Master of the Soane Josephus, together with
the Master of Edward IV.[7] In these miniatures the Master of
the Soane Josephus developed several striking compositions, the basic simplicity of which is enlivened by the bold
application of a lively palette and the introduction of a
range of complicated figure poses. Despite their large size,
all these miniatures focus almost entirely on one episode
each. Additional episodes are relegated to obscure corners
of the miniatures and easily overlooked by the viewer. In
putting together their miniatures, the two miniaturists
drew on a stock of patterns of both individual figures and
groups. Within *The Vision of Zacharias* (fol. 219), the group
of onlookers kneeling outside appear to be derived from a
miniature of the more common subject of Pentecost.
Sources for the impressive *Crucifixion* (ill. 82) include the
engraving of the same subject by the Master IAM of Zwolle
for the two thieves and one of the many versions of the central panel of Rogier van der Weyden's Vienna *Crucifixion*
triptych for the crucified Christ.[8] The only large miniature
not painted by these two miniaturists, *The Death of
Holofernes* (fol. 66v), was contributed by a miniaturist with
a more subdued palette and greater interest in the depiction of space and the play of light over forms. This miniaturist was considered of sufficient ability to contribute
several frontispieces to contemporary manuscripts of secular vernacular texts.[9]

The dating of the miniatures needs careful consideration. At the opening of the table of contents, a colophon by
the scribe Jan Du Ries[10] identifies the place of transcription
as Bruges, the date as 1470, and the patron as Edward IV of
England. Edward's name and titles have, however, clearly
been written over an erasure and were not the name and
title originally written by Du Ries.[11] The description of
Edward as "très victorieux" was wholly inappropriate to
him before his final defeat of the Lancastrians at Tewks-
bury on May 4, 1471, and used in only one other manuscript,
made for him in 1479.[12] Moreover, the two companion volumes that make up the remainder of Edward's *Bible historiale* are dated 1479, a date that conforms with what we now
know to have been his principal period of collecting Flemish illuminated manuscripts. Detailed analysis of the heraldry and border decoration of the present manuscript
confirms that decoration of the volume formed part of
Edward's campaign of collecting around 1479.[13] Analysis of
the costumes in the large miniatures also suggests a date
nearer the end than the beginning of the 1470s.[14] Probably
for lack of an earlier patron with sufficient interest and
wealth, the high ambition of the planners of this copy of the
Bible historiale remained unfulfilled until several years after
the transcription of the text.[15]   S. McK.

Notes

1. Berger 1884: 389.

2. On the most comparable Flemish *Bible historiale*, see Komada 2002: 185–98.

3. On this version, see Komada 2000: 1, chap. 1. According to Komada (2000: 1, chap. 4), the present manuscript reflects a deliberate preference for the historical narrative of this version of Guiart's text.

4. See fols. 36v, 43, 47, 57, 58, 62v, 86v, 93v, 101, 109, 117, 123, 128, 165, 166, 170, 336v, 340v, 342, 348, 348v, 358v, 361, 364v, 368, 370v, 376, 380, 392, 396v, 405v. The same artist was responsible for the one-column semi-grisaille miniatures in London, British Library, Burney Ms. 169, datable between 1468 and 1475, and Vienna, Österreichische National-bibliothek, Ms. 2534, datable to around 1470. In both manuscripts the large miniatures were painted by the Master of the Vienna *Chroniques d'Angleterre*. (For the Vienna one-column miniatures, see Pächt and Thoss 1990: 45, pls. 57–60, 66–68.) He was also responsible for the two-color miniatures in Vatican City, Vatican Library, Ms. Reg. lat. 736, fols. 63, 184, datable between 1468 and 1477 (see Vatican City 1996: 403, figs. 401, 402). The composition of folio 63 in the Vatican manuscript is partly repeated on folio 128 in the present manuscript.

5. See fols. 23, 39v, 41, 134, 138v, 143, 151v, 154, 161v, 178, 182v, 186, 190v, 203, 211, 221, 226, 227v, 229v, 233, 241, 246v, 254v, 263v, 267, 277v, 280v, 286, 290v, 297, 302v, 311, 319. The same artist painted all the one-column, semi-grisaille miniatures in London, British Library, Royal Ms. 18 E.v, in which the large miniatures were also painted by the Master of the Soane Josephus. He also contributed all the surviving one-column semi-grisaille miniatures in a copy of Lefèvre's *Recueil des histoires troyennes* (Geneva, Bibliothèque publique et universitaire, Ms. Comites Latentes 190; ex Sotheby's, London, July 13, 1977, lot 60).

6. Further examples of the abilities of the Master of Edward IV in this medium occur in the companion volume, London, British Library, Royal Ms. 18 D.x, fol. 165, and Copenhagen, Kongelige Bibliotek, Ms. Thott 568 2° (Copenhagen 1999: no. 126).

7. As suggested in the biography of the Master of Edward IV earlier in this part, the Master of the Soane Josephus worked jointly with this talented assistant on several of the large miniatures. The miniatures on folios 91, 119v, 197, and 353 (ill. 82) in particular betray the contribution of the Master of Edward IV.

8. For the engraving (Bartsch 6: 5), see Bartsch 1978–, 8: 199. In the miniature the left-hand thief has been rotated clockwise forty-five degrees. Minor changes include the addition of loincloths to both thieves. A major and iconographically incorrect change is the blindfold on the right-hand thief. The left-hand thief is ultimately derived from the lost *Descent from the Cross* of the Master of Flémalle, as witnessed by the silverpoint drawing in the Fogg Art Museum and triptych copy in the Walker Art Gallery, Liverpool. Christ's head, torso, wound, fluttering loincloth, and legs have more in common with the Rogierian model than with the engraving. The reversal of the direction of the bent knees may suggest a reversed intermediate between panel and miniature.

9. See, for example, the frontispieces to the *Chemin de Vaillance*, the *Histoire d'outremer*, *Grande histoire César*, *Fleur des histoires*, vol. 2 (London, British Library, Royal Mss. 14 E.ii, fol. 1, 15 E.i, fol. 16, 17 F.ii, fol. 9, 18 E.vi, fol. 8).

10. Further manuscripts signed by Du Ries include Copenhagen, Kongelige Bibliotek, Ms. Thott 463 2° (dated 1476); London, British Library, Royal Mss. 14 E.vi, 15 E.ii–iii (dated Bruges 1482).

11. Despite repeated examination under enhanced lighting, the original text remains undecipherable.

12. This other manuscript is London, British Library, Royal Ms. 17 F.ii. See McKendrick 1990: 110.

13. McKendrick 1994: 161–62. With striking consistency the birds found in the margins of folios 18, 76v, 119v, 175, 197, and 353 recur in the margins of three manuscripts illuminated by the Master of the Soane Josephus (Copenhagen, Kongelige Bibliotek, Ms. Thott 568 2°, fol. 102v; Paris, Bibliothèque nationale de France, Mss. fr. 296, fol. 1, and 297, fol. 1) and of one illuminated by one of the miniaturists responsible for the one-column miniatures in the present manuscript (Vatican City, Vatican Library, Ms. Reg. lat. 736, fol. 11v).

14. See in particular the costumes in the miniatures on folios 45, 91, 119v.

15. Given that the present manuscript was once intended as the fourth volume of a set, the ambitions of these planners may have been even greater for this *Bible historiale*. The person named in the original text of du Ries's colophon presumably declined the volume. The arms drawn in under Edward's in the lower margin of folios 18 and 31 probably also relate to this intended owner. *Pace* Komada (2000: 1, chap. 4 §4), they are not decipherable as those of Louis of Gruuthuse. How far the decoration had progressed before the volume was abandoned is difficult to assess. It is possible that only the one-column miniatures had by then been completed. As in the other manuscripts cited in note 4, these miniatures may at first have lacked borders. The one-column miniature painted by the Master of Edward IV was presumably created in a second campaign, the space left on that page having been overlooked in this first campaign.

82

MASTER OF EDWARD
IV AND MASTER OF
THE SOANE JOSEPHUS
The Crucifixion, fol. 353

Ainsi que
ceste toibe
mauldicte
des Juyfz
menoit
Ihesus en son dernier tour
ment au mont de caluaire
pour le cruaffiler a lyffue
de la cite de Jherusalem ilz
rencontrerent ung grant
bon homme nomme symon

le cyreneem qui leur sam
bloit fort et robufte pour
fouftenir et porter ceste croix
Auquel voure voulfift
il ou non Ilz la chargerent
et lui troufferent fur le col
Ceftuy symon eftoit pere de
alixandre et ruffm deux
des difaples nrefeigneur
Et menerent ihefus moult
auellement et Inhumaine

83

MASTER OF EDWARD IV, ASSISTANT OF
MASTER OF THE SOANE JOSEPHUS, MASTER OF
THE HARLEY FROISSART, CIRCLE OF THE MASTER
OF THE LONDON WAVRIN AND OTHERS

Bible historiale, Genesis to Ecclesiasticus
Bruges, 1479

MANUSCRIPT: ii + 319 + i folios and iii + 341 + ii folios, 43 × 31.3 cm
(17 × 12⅜ in.); justification: 27.4 × 19.3 cm (10¼ × 7⅝ in.); 33 lines
of bastarda in two columns; 13 two-column miniatures, 7 one-column
miniatures

HERALDRY: Escutcheons with the royal arms of England, one
surmounted by crown and two differenced by labels of three points,
one with canton on the center point, all Royal Ms. 18 D.ix, fol. 1;
banners and standard with the royal arms of England, Royal Ms. 18
D.ix, fols. 1, 275; badges of rose-en-soleil, partly with motto Dieu et
mon droit, Royal Ms. 18 D.ix, fols. 1, 5, 153, etc.

BINDING: London, mid-eighteenth century; brown morocco; gilt-
lined; gold-tooled spine

COLLECTION: London, The British Library, Royal Mss. 18 D.ix–x

PROVENANCE: Edward IV, king of England (1442–1483); English royal
library, Richmond Palace, in 1535, and Saint James's in 1666; George II,
king of England (1683–1760); presented 1757 to the British Museum

JPGM (Royal Ms. 18 D.ix) and RA (Royal Mss. 18 D.ix–x)

These two volumes form part of the remarkable *Bible
historiale* of Edward IV of England. Their text begins
with Guiart Des Moulins's preface to his French version of
Petrus Comestor's *Historia scholastica* and continues with
their retelling of the Octateuch, the four Books of Kings,
and the Book of Job. The further inclusion of French versions of a full Psalter and the five sapiential books, none of
which is based on the *Historia*, is characteristic of the
extended version of Des Moulins's text known as the *Bible
historiale complétée*.[1] Together with their companion volume (cat. no. 82), which starts with the Book of Tobit and
ends with the Acts of the Apostles, these two volumes form
a satisfactory, if hybrid, biblical set.[2]

The two volumes form a closely related pair. Both were
written by the same scribe in 1479.[3] Their *mise-en-page* and
subsidiary decoration are the same. After allowing for one
large and three one-column illustrations for Genesis, the
scribe settled into a more regular allocation throughout the
volumes, whereby he left spaces for large miniatures at the
beginning of the principal books.[4] Two smaller two-
column spaces were left for additional illustrations of the
Jewish tabernacle.[5] To distinguish these smaller miniatures
from the miniatures marking the main textual divisions,
the decorators of the volume accompanied the latter with
full borders and the former with only one-sided borders. In
contrast to the illustrative campaign of their companion
volume (cat. no. 82), the miniatures of the present two volumes do not attempt to form a continuous visual narrative.

The miniaturist who painted all but two of the large
miniatures marking the main textual divisions is named
after this work as the Master of Edward IV.[6] He also contributed two one-column miniatures, one in semi-grisaille
at the beginning of the Book of Job and the other in full
color at the beginning of the sapiential books (Royal Ms. 18

D.x, fols. 165, 244). In all these miniatures the Master of
Edward IV repeatedly showed his debt to the Master of the
Soane Josephus. As in the work of the latter miniaturist,
high horizons conclude in atmospheric perspective and are
often reached by means of steeply winding rivers. Short,
bushlike trees; lumpy rock formations; and large white
pebbles help define a landscape and the overall composition. Reflections on water and shadows add atmosphere
and a sense of light. In each case, however, the Master of
Edward IV's execution of these artistic formulas was different from that of the Master of the Soane Josephus. In his
more subtle atmospheric perspective, the landscape fades
from a blue-green midground to a misty blue and indistinct
horizon rather than moving quickly from blue-green to a
more sharply defined blue horizon. The same bushy trees
were painted with a looser application of dark and light
tones over a green base and without the Soane Master's
more formulaic horizontal strokes. Forms are generally
defined with a softer touch, and tonal transitions are more
gradual. The Master of Edward IV also employed a subtler
palette and had a keener appreciation of color balance. His
architecture, although similar in its elements, is more stable
and spatially credible.

A fine example of the work of the Master of Edward IV
is the miniature at the beginning of Exodus that depicts the
exposure and recovery of the baby Moses (ill. 83a). In this
miniature the narrative progresses in a simple manner
from the left foreground to the upper right. The two successive scenes are presented in a unified setting but are
divided by a clump of rocks in the middle of the river that
acts as the central hub of the composition. Although the
setting is reminiscent more of the Low Countries than of
Egypt, the fanciful outcrop of rocks dominates the landscape, and differences in costume clearly differentiate
Moses' Jewish mother from Pharaoh's daughter and her
ladies-in-waiting. Another example of this master's work is
the miniature marking the beginning of the fourth Book of
Kings (ill. 83b). In this the narrative progresses from the top
right-hand corner—in which Ahaziah from his sickbed
orders successive captains and their companies of fifty
armed men to fetch the prophet Elijah—down to the foreground. Together with these armed men the narrative then
proceeds to the upper left-hand corner, in which a tiny Elijah summons down fire from heaven upon these men. To
define the successive parts of this narrative, the miniaturist
created four separate but interrelated spaces. The viewer is
led from a closed interior to a more open one, then to an
exterior defined by architecture and finally to an open landscape near the horizon. The illustration of all these Old Testament subjects introduced the Master of Edward IV to a
wide iconography at an early stage in his career. His subsequent development as a miniaturist shows how he built on
this experience and became one of the most versatile miniaturists of his generation, capable of illustrating well a wide
range of texts and subjects (see cat. nos. 82, 84, 95–98).

Two further miniaturists contributed the miniatures of
the Creation (ill. 83c) and Joshua crossing the Jordan (Royal
Ms. 18 D.ix, fol. 275). The first miniaturist was particularly
accomplished in the handling of landscape, and his style is

83a (opposite)
MASTER OF
EDWARD IV
The Finding of Moses,
vol. 1, fol. 109

Es font les
noms des
filz pfrael
qui entriret
en egipte
auec iacob Et y entra chun
auec fa mefnpe Ceft affa
uoir Ruben fymeon leup
Juda pfachar zabulon ben
Jamin dan neptalim Gad
et azer Et furent toutes les

perfonnes qui loes eftorent
yffus de iacob lppp en no
bit et iofeph eftoit en egip
te Quant Joseph fut
mort et fes freres et toute
fa ligmc les filz pfrael au
rent et multiplpcrent et en
foreuent trop et emplierent
la terre Dont y eut ung mau
uaiz rop en Egipte qui Jo
feph ne congnoiffoit Lequel

chofie le filz
achab comme
ca a regner en
famarye fur
yfrael au · vvne an de Iofa
phat roy de iudee, et regna
deux ans / Et fift mal deuät
nreſeigneur et ala en toutes
les mauluaifes voyes achab
et fa mere Iezabel / et ez voyes
Iherobaam qui fift les veaux

dr · Gloſe · dont on lift ou
tiers liure des roys ou cha
pitre de Iherobaam Tepte ·
Et fift pecchier yfrael · et -
feruy achofie baal · et laou
ra / et courrouca nreſeigr
en toutes les choſes õ ſon
pere ſauoit courrouee /·
Quant achab fut -
mort / le peuple de moabne
voult plus payer le truage

in some respects similar to that of the Master of the London Wavrin. Particularly distinctive are the unnaturally tall trees that frame the hovering figure of the Creator and the double horizon formed by successive mountain ranges, the first horizon at a low, strictly perspectival level and the second marking a farther bird's-eye view of the landscape beyond. This artist was also responsible for the two illustrations of the tabernacle (Royal Ms. 18 D.ix, fols. 153, 197v). The second miniaturist is identifiable as one of the assistants of the Master of Soane Josephus in the master's name manuscript (cat. no. 81).[7] The most distinctive aspect of his style is the daring application of a bright palette of green, white, red, pink, and blue.

In addition to these three artists, two or possibly three other miniaturists participated in the painting of the smaller miniatures in the first volume. Despite its poor condition, the opening one-column miniature of Des Moulins at work (Royal Ms. 18 D.ix, fol. 1) can be attributed to the Master of the Harley Froissart or a follower. The three one-column miniatures in Genesis, two two-column miniatures of the tabernacle, and one one-column miniature at the opening of Deuteronomy are less easy to attribute.[8] In the one-column miniatures the figures seem to be by a more able artist than that responsible for the landscape settings. This artist may be the same as that responsible for the miniatures of the tabernacle and the Creation already discussed. The involvement of five or six miniaturists in

only twenty illustrations may be a further reflection of the practical measures required to satisfy quickly Edward's substantial order for Bruges manuscripts around 1479.

S. McK.

Notes

1. Warner and Gilson 1921, 2: 313. Confusingly, Berger (1884: 163) disregarded the present volumes' inclusion of the Psalter and sapiential books, but elsewhere (203, 296) he does mention the Psalter. On the texts, see Komada 2000: 1, chap. 4, sec. 4.

2. The table of contents at the beginning of the first volume of Edward's *Bible historiale* lists only the contents of the three volumes, plus the Apocalypse appears never to have been included. The description of the companion volume (cat. no. 82) as volume 4 is a remnant of earlier plans for an even more ambitious set. The present two volumes are never described in their own text as volumes 1 and 2. Only subsequent designation of these volumes as such has given rise to the suggestion that there was once a volume 3. As early as 1535, only the present three volumes were listed (Carley 2000: H1.31, H1.45–46).

3. That scribe is not Jan du Ries, who copied the companion volume (cat. 82).

4. These large miniatures mark the beginning of Genesis, Exodus, Leviticus, Numbers, Joshua, Judges, Kings 1, Kings 2, Kings 3, Kings 4, and the Psalter. Deuteronomy, Job, and the sapiential books are marked only with a one-column miniature (Royal Mss. 18 D.ix, fol. 241, and 18 D.x, fols. 165, 244).

5. See Royal Ms. 18 D.ix, fols. 153, 197v.

6. These miniatures by the Master of Edward IV are on Royal Mss. 18 D.ix, fols. 109, 173, 195v, 291v, and 18 D.x, fols. 2, 36, 68, 115v, 168.

7. This assistant was responsible for the miniature on folio 36v of London, Sir John Soane's Museum, Ms. 1.

8. Respectively, Royal Mss. 18 D.ix, fols. 12, 56, 84, 153, 197v, 241.

83b (opposite)
MASTER OF EDWARD IV
AND MASTER OF THE
SOANE JOSEPHUS
Ahaziah and Elijah, vol. 2,
fol. 115v

83c (above)
CIRCLE OF THE
MASTER OF THE
LONDON WAVRIN
The Creation of the Animals,
vol. 1, fol. 5 (detail)

Ken William buftard / duk of Normandy had / affembled his armee

pepiff al that euer he couthe make / of ffreuſſh men of Normans of Gaſ / coins of Brutons of Burgynons

84

MASTER OF EDWARD IV AND ASSISTANTS

Prose *Brut* to 1436 (Chronicle of Saint Albans)
England(?) and Bruges, ca. 1480

MANUSCRIPT: i + 258 folios, 43 × 31 cm (17 × 12¼ in.); justification:
25.3 × 19 cm (10 × 7½ in.); 34 lines of *bastarda* in two columns;
19 three-quarter-page miniatures, 51 one-column miniatures

HERALDRY: Escutcheon with unidentified arms, quarterly 1 and 4
argent a fess sable 3 bezants (Thwaites family), 2 and 3 argent a lion
rampant azure armed and langued gules, fol. 1

BINDING: Lamacraft and Lawrence, London, early twentieth century;
brown morocco over wood boards

COLLECTION: London, Lambeth Palace Library, Ms. 6

PROVENANCE: Henry Fitzalan, twelfth earl of Arundel (1512–1580);
John Lumley, baron Lumley (1534?–1609); probably at Lambeth
by 1633

RA

84
MASTER OF
EDWARD IV
The Battle of Hastings,
fol. 109 (detail)

The present manuscript is by far the most opulent and
extensively illustrated copy of the Middle English text
that was second only to the Wycliffite Bible in popularity
during the fifteenth century.[1] Its uniqueness reflects the
aspirations of an as yet unidentified English patron.[2] For the
fulfillment of such aspirations for an English text, however,
it was necessary to turn to Flemish miniaturists. Even more
than the manuscripts produced in the Low Countries for
Edward IV (cat. nos. 66, 74, 75, 78, 81–83, 87), this copy of
the prose *Brut* illustrates both the dependency of late
medieval English culture on the continent and the opportunities that close cultural links provided to the English.

The Master of Edward IV and two assistants were
responsible for all seventy miniatures. The Master himself
contributed all but one of the nineteen large miniatures
and most of the fifty-one small miniatures, sometimes with
the aid of an assistant capable of close imitation of his
master. That same assistant independently painted about
fourteen of the small miniatures.[3] Another assistant painting in a related but different style contributed the remaining large miniature and six of the small miniatures.[4] The
three artists were aided in their work by instructions written in French along the lower edge of the page on which

the miniature was to be painted.[5] Like many other such notes to illuminators, these instructions outline the subject of each miniature in simple terms.

Together the three artists created a continuous narrative that illustrated their text from its opening with the legend of how Brutus, a descendent of the Trojan leader Aeneas, overcame the giants that inhabited Albion, to its conclusion in 1436, shortly after the historical signing of the Treaty of Arras. This visual narrative is unified by the artists' shared use of patterns for both individual figures and groups, as well for characteristic landscape and architectural features, but it never stagnates into exact repetition. The miniature of the Battle of Hastings (ill. 84) presents a battle scene that reworks several of these patterns and contains only very few elements that relate to the historical event as described by the text. Typical of the work of the Master of Edward IV are the archers to the right and left, who frame the composition; a large mound that swells up at its center; tall rocks to the right from behind which emerge various figures; and small, leafless trees that protrude from rocks and even rooftops.

The uncharacteristic *mise-en-page* of the opening page, in which the miniature is no larger than those that succeed it, combines with other unusual features in the layout of the present volume to suggest that the scribe was not regularly involved in the production of manuscripts decorated by Flemish illuminators.[6] Given his linguistic proficiency in English and his particular adaptation of the Flemish *bastarda* script, it seems likely that this scribe was English. The quality of his script suggests that he was a commercial scribe. It is therefore possible that the present manuscript had its text written in England before being sent to the Low Countries to be illuminated.   S. McK.

Notes

1. Matheson (1998: xxi–xxxii) cited 171 located manuscripts. In addition, thirteen printed editions were produced between 1480 and 1528 (Matheson 1998: xxxiii–xxxvi). The text of the present manuscript is a version found in only one other copy (London, British Library, Harley Ms. 53) and is not copied from the first printed edition.

2. The arms added to the lower border of folio 1 have been repeatedly associated with William Purchase, mercer, alderman, and mayor of London (on him, see Thrupp 1989: 362). As described in London, British Library, Harley Ms. 1349, his arms were argent a lion rampant azur over all a fess sable three bezants. Although Purchase is an appropriate owner, there remains a significant discrepancy between his accredited arms and the arms in the present manuscript.

3. Fols. 12, 36v, 49v, 62v, 63v, 83v, 87v, 119v, 154, 160v, 167v, 205, 231, 240.

4. Fols. 20, 28, 29, 37v (large), 66v, 72v, 125.

5. Instructions are legible on folios 10v, 16v, 36v, 66v, 128v, 174, 186v, 195v. Most of these are transcribed in Millar 1925: 78–81. Traces of instructions are also visible on folios 20, 23, 26, 27v, 32, 33, 37v, 52, 62v, 72v, 77, 79, 80v, 81v, 85, 87v, 91v, 97, 105v, 109, 116, 142, 147, 154, 160v, 167v, 177v, 197v, 205, 209, 218, 221v, 231, 233, 243, 246, 251v.

6. Clues to the identity of the scribe may be found in his insertion of "on le dit" within two cadelles in the top lines on folios 137v and 142v. The first appears within the *w* of *wetyng* in the phrase "it was not his will nor his wetyng"; the second appears within the *w* of *wynde*. Together with the repeated inclusion in the cadelles of faces blowing air with puffed-out cheeks, these inscriptions might identify the scribe as William Wynde.

MASTER OF THE FIRST PRAYER BOOK OF MAXIMILIAN (B)

For biography, see part 2

85

MASTER OF THE FIRST PRAYER BOOK OF MAXIMILIAN

Chroniques de Flandres
Ghent, 1477

MANUSCRIPT: 293 folios in two continuously foliated volumes, 41 × 29.5 cm (16⅛ × 11⅝ in.); justification: 25.5 × 7.7–1.8–7.7 cm (10¹/₁₆ × 3–¹¹/₁₆–3 in.); 32 lines of *bastarda* in two columns by David Aubert; 22 miniatures

HERALDRY: Escutcheon with the arms of Margaret of York, fol. 2

INSCRIPTIONS: *Par le commandement et ordonnance de tres haut, tres excellente et tres puissante, ma tres redoubtee princesse Marie, par la grace de Dieu duchesse de Bourgoigne . . . ont ces presentes croniques . . . este apres la translation faicte de latin en cler francois grossees, . . . en l'an de grace mil quatre cens soycante et seze que madite tres redoubtee princesse apres le trespas de feu monseigneur Charles . . . print la saisine de sa conte de Flandres . . . et tost apres en l'an . . . mil quatrecens soycante et dix sept print la tres noble princesse la possession de ses duchie de Brabant et . . . ,* fol. 1v; *margarete d'Angleterre,* fol. 293

BINDING: Jones of Liverpool, early nineteenth century; gold-tooled and blind-stamped red morocco over wood boards; device of the Coke family, an ostrich holding a horseshoe on its beak, on front cover

COLLECTION: Wells-next-the-Sea, Holkham Hall, earl of Leicester, Ms. 659

PROVENANCE: Mary, duchess of Burgundy (1457–1482); gift to Margaret of York, duchess of Burgundy (1446–1503); Count-Duke of Olivarès, seventeenth century; to Gaspar de Guzman, count of Haro; [Augustinians of the Croix-Rousse, Lyons] (cat. 1712, no. 169); to Thomas William Coke, second earl of Leicester (1752–1842)

JPGM and RA

Mary of Burgundy ordered the transcription of this volume of the chronicle of the counts of Flanders in 1476, following its translation from Latin into French. Thus it was begun before her father's disastrous defeat and death at Nancy in January 1477.[1] It was completed after Easter of that year, when Mary actually assumed the title of duchess. She appears to have offered this copy as a present to her stepmother, Margaret of York. Margaret's coat of arms appears in the border of the opening page of the text (fol. 2). The text recounts the story of the counts of Flanders, from the legendary Liederik van Harelbeke through Louis of Mâle (d. 1384). Louis's daughter Margaret was the great-grandmother of Charles the Bold. Thus Margaret of York received her copy of this text just as the County of Flanders passed from her husband, Charles, to her stepdaughter.

The frontispiece shows the Holy Roman Emperor Charlemagne, standing before his palace, presenting the County of Flanders to Liederik, who genuflects before him (ill. 85). This and the other miniatures in this book have a distinctive, limited palette, reminiscent of other of Margaret's books of the mid-1470s (cat. nos. 27–29). The artist,

the Master of the First Prayer Book of Maximilian,[2] treated the figures in gray or subdued hues, dressing a key figure or two in a gold brocade or other colored garments in most miniatures. Sky and terrain were given naturalistic coloring, and other details, such as the horses' trappings, were often colored. Especially typical of this artist are the faces modeled in gray with pink highlights on the tip of the nose, on the chin, above the lips, and to set off the cheekbones. Probably because few patterns were available for the miniatures, an unsurprising circumstance for unusual secular subjects, the Maximilian Master betrayed his awkwardness as a draftsman. The chronicle is the only known extended pictorial cycle in a secular manuscript by the artist and his workshop. It is also his only work for the ducal family and his earliest dated work.   T. K.

Notes

1. A partial transcription of the dedication has been published by many authors: Pächt 1948: 64; Hassall 1970: 14; Barstow 1992: 260, no. 11; Straub 1995: 117. Thanks to Suzanne Reynolds for undertaking a full transcription for me.

2. Kren, in Malibu 1983a: 23, 26; Pächt and Thoss 1990: 101; Arnould, in Cambridge 1993: 149, no. 48.

86

MASTER OF THE FIRST PRAYER BOOK
OF MAXIMILIAN

La Chronique des haulx et nobles princes de Cleves
Probably Ghent, between 1472 and 1481

MANUSCRIPT: iv + 40 + iv folios, 28.4 × 20.9 cm (11³⁄₁₆ × 8¼ in.); justification: 13.2 × 10.5 cm (5⁵⁄₁₆ × 4⅛ in.); 12 lines of *bastarda*; 1 half-page miniature

HERALDRY: Escutcheons with the arms of the dukes of Cleves and their wives, beginning with Elias and Beatrice

BINDING: Gold-tooled red morocco; central medallion with pair of arms under crown (the arms include the eight gold spears of the house of Cleves)

COLLECTION: Munich, Bayerische Staatsbibliothek, Ms. Gall. 19

PROVENANCE: Philip of Cleves, lord of Ravenstein (1459–1527); library of the dukes of Cleves; Wittelsbacher Hofbibliothek

JPGM and RA

I n 1472 Gert van der Schueren wrote a chronicle of the House of Cleves in German (Kleve, Stadtarchiv).[1] It traces the Cleves family tree from the legendary eighth-century Knight of the Swan and his wife, Beatrice, to the then duke, John I. The Munich volume is a French

86

MASTER OF THE
FIRST PRAYER BOOK
OF MAXIMILIAN
The Knight of the Swan,
fol. 1

translation of a manuscript in Dutch containing an excerpt from the text of 1472 that is supplemented by illustrated armorials of family members along with genealogical descriptions (Cleves, Stadtarchiv).[2] The three versions also appear to date before 1481, as the death of John I in that year goes unmentioned in the manuscripts.[3] He was the patron of the original version, and Philip of Cleves, his nephew, is the first recorded owner of this copy of the French version.[4]

This book is also the only copy with a miniature, which shows the arrival of Elias, the Knight of the Swan, at Beatrice's castle in 711 (ill. 86). He has with him a ring, a horn, and a sword, treasures that he would pass to his three sons. Beatrice, dressed in gold, waits by a window of the castle. The miniature shows the refinement and subtlety of tonality most characteristic of miniatures by the Master of the First Prayer Book of Maximilian at the beginning of his career, about 1475–85. The skin tones, with grays in the shadows and light flesh tones for highlights, are characteristic, as is the overall cool blue-gray tone in the sky, the palace, the water, and the reflections of the palace in the water. Elias's curly hair is soft and fine, his eyes deep and penetrating, reflecting a care in painting the figures that is found only in this painter's most accomplished illuminations. The facial type, fine brown hair, and modeling of the face, the reflections on the water, and the cool grays of the architecture call to mind *Saint Louis of France* in the Hours of Charlotte of Bourbon-Montpensier (fig. 66). The two miniatures share nearly identical border motifs, particularly in the bas-de-pages. Although apparently inserted after the book's first campaign, the latter miniature probably dates before Charlotte's death in 1477.[5] Thus the Munich manuscript might also date this early.   T. K.

Notes

1. Cleves 1984: 370, no. D 36. Thanks to Anne Korteweg for sharing with me her observations on the relationships among the three copies.

2. Cleves 1984: 373, no. D 42.

3. Although it is possible that the book was made later by someone who did not know that John had died in 1481 and thus failed to insert the death date, this seems unlikely.

4. Since Philip was only twenty-four in 1481, it is conceivable that this copy was made for his bibliophile father, Adolf, lord of Ravenstein, per the suggestion of Anne Korteweg. Adolf, however, customarily embellished his books with his own elaborate armorials and other heraldic devices.

5. See cat. no. 44.

Figure 66
MASTER OF THE
FIRST PRAYER BOOK
OF MAXIMILIAN
Saint Louis of France.
In the Hours of Charlotte
of Bourbon-Montpensier,
fol. 169v (see cat. no. 44)

MASTER OF THE FLEMISH BOETHIUS

The miniaturist incorrectly identified by Paul Durrieu as Alexander Bening (d. 1519),[1] father of Simon Bening, and subsequently renamed by Friedrich Winkler as the so-called Alexander Bening[2] is now best referred to as Master of the Flemish Boethius.[3] This name derives from an opulent, oversize copy of Boethius's *De consolatione philosophiae* in Latin and Flemish (Paris, Bibliothèque nationale de France, Ms. néerl. 1), written at Ghent in 1492 and possibly the last manuscript commissioned by the Bruges bibliophile Louis of Gruuthuse (1422–1492).[4] The miniatures in this volume present a strong and somewhat idiosyncratic artistic style. Particularly prominent are female figures with long limbs, narrow waists, close-fitting robes, elongated necks, high foreheads, and oval faces that resemble wood carvings. Male figures are similarly elongated but bulkier, with more individualized faces. Although this miniaturist is no longer seriously considered to be Alexander Bening, some aspects of his painting, including his female types, are clearly more closely related to the work of the Ghent Associates and the Master of the First Prayer Book of Maximilian (see separate biographies, part 2), the miniaturist now most frequently identified with Alexander Bening.

The earliest miniatures attributable to the Master of the Flemish Boethius are three copies of a French *Vie du Christ*. The first of these (Kraków, Biblioteka Czartoryskich, Ms. 2919) was written for Guillaume de Ternay in 1478[5] and the second written at Ghent by David Aubert for an unknown patron in 1479 (London, British Library, Royal Ms. 16 G. iii).[6] Although the London miniatures are more developed in style and alternate between grisaille and full color—unlike the Kraków miniatures, which are all in grisaille—the two volumes are remarkably similar in their illustration program,[7] border decoration,[8] and script. In the third copy (Paris, Bibliothèque nationale, Ms. fr. 181), made for Louis of Gruuthuse probably around 1480, the Master of the Flemish Boethius painted the frontispiece and only some of the other grisaille miniatures.[9] During the same period he contributed one miniature to a copy of Valerius Maximus in French translation made for Edward IV in 1479, in which the other miniatures are painted by the Bruges illuminator the Master of the White Inscriptions (cat. no. 80). The Master of the Flemish Boethius also collaborated with other Bruges artists in the illustration of a copy of William of Tyre's *Historia* (cat. no. 87).

During the 1480s he was responsible for a sequence of large, imposing miniatures illustrating secular subjects. For Louis of Gruuthuse and Philip of Burgundy he contributed to the illustration of two copies of the French translation of Josephus's *Histories*.[10] The twenty-seven miniatures in Louis's copy (Paris, Bibliothèque nationale, Ms. fr. 11–16), which was written at Ghent and Bruges in 1480 and 1483,

are entirely the work of the Master of the Flemish Boethius. The same number of miniatures in Philip's copy (Paris, Bibliothèque de l'Arsenal, Mss. 5082–83) are shared between this master and two other miniaturists: the Master of Edward IV and the Master of the Trivial Heads. Also, for Louis of Gruuthuse, the Master of the Flemish Boethius illustrated a copy of Caesar's *Commentaires*, dated 1482 (Paris, Bibliothèque nationale de France, Ms. fr. 38); two hunting treatises, dated 1485 and 1486 (Cambridge, Mass., Houghton Library, Mss. Typ. 129–30);[11] and a copy of Ptolemy, dated 1485 (Paris, Bibliothèque nationale de France, Ms. lat. 4804).[12] Of the manuscripts made for Gruuthuse all were written at Ghent and four signed by Jan Kriekenborch, the scribe also responsible for the Flemish Boethius of 1492. For Philip of Cleves the Master of the Flemish Boethius illustrated a copy of the *Jouvencel* written by Kriekenborch in 1486.[13]

S. McK.

Notes

1. Durrieu 1891: 353–67; 59–69, Durrieu 1921a: pl. 59.

2. Winkler 1925: 117.

3. This name was used by Lemaire and de Schryver (in Bruges 1981: 263) and Wieck (in Cambridge, Mass., 1983: no. 25). Dogaer (1987a: 157–58) retained Winkler's clumsy name.

4. On this manuscript, see Brussels 1973: no. 28; and Bruges 1981: no. 115.

5. See Płonka-Bałus 2002a: 505–19. Thanks to the author for an early copy of this article.

6. Backhouse 1987: 26, pl. 8; McKendrick 2003: pl. 43.

7. Although the London copy contains only nine miniatures and the Kraków copy twelve, the corresponding miniatures are closely related and clearly based on the same models.

8. The border decoration in both manuscripts is similar to that found in two slightly earlier manuscripts copied by David Aubert for Margaret of York (Jena, Thüringer Universitäts- und Landesbibliothek, Ms. gall. fol. 85; cat. no. 43).

9. Bruges 1981: no. 112. A group of miniatures that replicate the Paris miniatures have been exposed as modern copies (Wieck 1981: 151–61).

10. Deutsch 1986: 190–91, pls. 29–139 passim.

11. Cambridge, Mass., 1983: nos. 25–26.

12. The large miniature with a portrait of Gruuthuse in this volume (Bruges 1992: 40) was overpainted by a French illuminator to include a portrait of its second owner, Louis XII.

13. For Philip of Cleves's last volume the miniaturist appears to have reused compositions devised by the Master of Edward IV for Gruuthuse's copy of the *Jouvencel* (Paris, Bibliothèque nationale de France, Ms. fr. 192). It is possible that Philip's copy was a gift commissioned by Gruuthuse.

Comment baudouin filz souâz   sa son coeur toutes enffancees. Il

87

MASTER OF THE FLEMISH BOETHIUS AND
TWO ASSISTANTS, MASTER OF EDWARD IV,
AND ANOTHER ILLUMINATOR

**Livre d'Eracles, continuation to 1232 of William of Tyre's
*Historia rerum in partibus transmarinis gestarum***
Bruges, ca. 1475–80

MANUSCRIPT: i + 495 + i folios, 47 × 34.2 cm (18½ × 13½ in.);
justification: 29.2 × 19.7 cm (11½ × 7¾ in.); 39 lines of *bastarda* in
two columns; 1 three-quarter-page miniature, 17 half-page
miniatures, 36 one-column miniatures

HERALDRY: Escutcheon with the royal arms of England surmounted
by crowned helm and encircled by the Garter, fol. 16; banner with
the royal arms of England, fol. 16; badge of rose-en-soleil with motto
Dieu et mon droit, fol. 16

BINDING: London, mid-eighteenth century; brown morocco; the
arms of George II gold-stamped on both covers; rebacked

COLLECTION: London, The British Library, Royal Ms. 15 E.i

PROVENANCE: Edward IV, king of England (1442–1483); English royal
library, Richmond Palace, in 1535, and Saint James's in 1666; George II,
king of England (1683–1760); presented 1757 to the British Museum

RA

87
MASTER OF THE
FLEMISH BOETHIUS
*The Coronation of Baldwin
III*, fol. 259 (detail)

Under the title *Livre d'Eracles*,[1] this text comprises an
early thirteenth-century continuation of the history
of the Crusades compiled by William of Tyre, archbishop
of Jerusalem (d. 1186). It tells of the rise and fall of the Cru-
sader states in the East, from the launch of the first Crusade
in 1095 and recapture of Jerusalem in 1099 to the loss of the
Holy Cross and fall of Jerusalem to Saladin in 1187. Of the
twenty-two manuscripts of this historical continuation to
1232, most date from before 1300.[2] Sometime in the 1460s
the text was revived in Flanders. The present manuscript is
the last and most ambitious of the four illustrated manuscripts produced there.[3]

Three miniaturists painted most of the fifty-four
miniatures in the manuscript. The Master of the Flemish
Boethius contributed thirteen of these, all but one of which
occur in the first half of the volume and most of which are
large and depict interiors.[4] Typical of his work is the hieratic miniature *The Coronation of Baldwin III* (ill. 87) and the
more poignant miniature *The Death of Godfrey of Bouillon*
(fol. 150v). A second artist was responsible for the remaining thirteen miniatures in the first half of the volume, most
of which are small and depict exteriors.[5] In his miniatures
of battles, sieges, surrenders, and the like, this artist is

particularly adept at the depiction of vast crowds of armed men. His most accomplished work is an additional large miniature, *The Siege of Damascus* (fol. 280v), painted near the beginning of the second half of the volume. An assistant, who clearly modeled his style on that of the Master of the Flemish Boethius, contributed almost all of the remaining miniatures and was thereby almost solely responsible for the illustration of the second half of the volume.[6] The latter's independent work can be found in a *Propriétés des choses* written at Bruges in 1482.[7] In addition to these three artists, a fourth, who was responsible for several frontispieces and individual miniatures, contributed the opening miniature, *Heraclius Returning the True Cross* (fol. 16).[8] The Master of Edward IV painted one small miniature of a pilgrim ship at Damietta (fol. 404v) toward the end of the volume and two at the end of the *Propriété des choses*, primarily illuminated by the assistant to the Master of the Flemish Boethius.[9]

Given its heraldry, likely date of production, and stylistic links with other manuscripts in the old royal collection, the present volume was probably produced for Edward IV. Its historical text fits the profile of Edward's collection.

S. McK.

Notes

1. The name derives from that of the Emperor Heraclius, who returned the True Cross to Jerusalem in A.D. 629.

2. According to Folda (1973: 93–94), fourteen manuscripts date from the thirteenth century, three from ca. 1300, and only one from the fourteenth century.

3. The other Flemish copies are Geneva, Bibliothèque publique et universitaire, Ms. fr. 85; Paris, Bibliothèque nationale de France, Mss. fr. 68, 2629. On the first, which contains miniatures attributed to Simon Marmion, see Geneva 1976: no. 69. The second was made for Louis of Gruuthuse (Bruges 1992: 198, no.62).

4. Fols. 69v, 77, 91, 108v, 137v, 150v, 155v, 170, 185, 192v, 241, 259, 438.

5. Fols. 32v, 47, 51, 56, 74, 85, 98v, 101v, 116, 122, 128v, 134, 162v. This artist also worked with the Master of the Flemish Boethius in Paris, Bibliothèque nationale, Ms. fr. 82.

6. Fols. 177v, 209, 224v, 266, 273v, 293v, 300, 308, 317v, 321v, 330v, 335, 342, 347, 353, 357, 365v, 368v, 375v, 377, 383, 393, 420v, 433v, 450v.

7. London, British Library, Royal Mss. 15 E.ii, fols. 10v, 19v, 60, 77v, 139v; 15 E.iii, fols. 32, 102, 126.

8. See cat. no. 83.

9. London, British Library, Royal Ms. 15 E.iii, fols. 200, 269.

PART 4

CONSOLIDATION AND RENEWAL: MANUSCRIPT PAINTING UNDER THE HAPSBURGS, CIRCA 1485–1510

THOMAS KREN

By 1485 the last of the Burgundian line, Duchess Mary of Burgundy, had been dead for three years, and her widower, the Hapsburg prince Maximilian of Austria (1459–1519) had assumed the role of regent for their son Philip the Handsome (1478–1506). During the reign of duke Charles the Bold (r. 1467–1477) an artistic revolution had taken place, and like many periods of artistic innovation, this one was characterized by the creation of a series of strikingly original works in a brief time span. The Vienna Master of Mary of Burgundy, who first appeared around 1470, was gone from the artistic scene by the end of the 1470s, while the Master of the Houghton Miniatures came and went even more quickly. By the early 1480s the new aesthetic of naturalism in miniature and border propagated by the Vienna Master, the Master of the Houghton Miniatures, Simon Marmion, and others had been codified. The borders with strewn naturalia and white or gold acanthus, all casting shadows on solid-colored grounds, became the hallmark of the new style that defined Flemish manuscript painting for a growing audience. The illuminators' mastery of these pictorially rich borders demonstrated the high level of craftsmanship of the Flemish book industry. By the end of the fifteenth century the new type of border had been adapted in Dutch manuscripts and by such major French illuminators as Jean Bourdichon. By the beginning of the sixteenth century versions of the border could be found in German, Italian, English, and Spanish manuscripts. The new style had triumphed across Europe, inspiring countless imitations, some, like Bourdichon's, dazzling and original, and others, like the many German examples, more modest.

The period 1485 to 1510 also saw several major new developments: the emergence of another artist of genius, the Master of James IV of Scotland; the influential role played by Gerard David as an illuminator; and continuing innovation by Simon Marmion. All three helped to shape the character of the period. The Master of James IV of Scotland pushed the aesthetic of naturalism in a new direction. The older tradition, epitomized by the work of Marmion and the Vienna Master, concentrated on the inserted single-leaf miniature and left it to the borders to unify a two-page opening. The Master of James IV, starting around the turn of the century, painted large miniatures on both leaves in an opening, reducing the role of the text and increasing dramatically the role of pictorial elements. In this way he doubled the length of pictorial cycles in such offices as the Hours of the Virgin and the Hours of the Passion, giving narrative cycles a more vivid, finely detailed character (see cat. no. 109). Eventually he would endeavor to unify the pictorial and narrative space of the border with that of the central miniature (see cat. no. 124). The

GERARD DAVID
Saint Elizabeth of Hungary
(detail, ill. 105a)

Master of James IV's style was carried on by artists trained in his workshop (see cat. no. 138), including the Master of the David Scenes in the Grimani Breviary (see cat. nos. 114–16, 136, 137). The thoroughly engaging Master of the Lübeck Bible, a somewhat mysterious artist who collaborated on several occasions with the Master of James IV and exchanged artistic ideas with him, illuminated manuscripts only occasionally. He painted his finest cycle of miniatures in this period (cat. no. 112).

The case of the Bruges painter David illustrates the ongoing interchange between painters and illuminators and the fluidity of the boundaries between the media. He contributed miniatures to books of widely varying quality and ambition, but the evidence of his manuscript production shows his importance to court patrons (see cat. no. 104), such as Isabella of Castile (see cat. nos. 100, 105), and other families close to the Hapsburg court, such as the Egmonds and Van Bergens (see cat. no. 103).[1] Although his production of illuminations was limited, his impact was lasting, both on contemporaries such as the Master of the First Prayer Book of Maximilian and on the next generation of illuminators, above all Simon Bening.

Simon Marmion, who lived until 1489, is remarkable for his continuous inventiveness throughout his career. During the 1480s his major achievement was a cycle of twenty-four mostly half-page miniatures, all but two of which came to be incorporated in the book of hours called La Flora (cat. no. 93).[2] The cycle was so greatly admired that artists continued to copy its miniatures faithfully, down to details of color, for decades (see cat. no. 105). It also spurred an interest in half-length and three-quarter-length figures on the part of illuminators, among whom the most innovative were the Master of the Munich Annunciation (ill. 90b), the Master of the David Scenes in the Grimani Breviary (ills. 114a, 115a, 116a), and Simon Bening (ills. 146a–d, 156c).

The major heir to the innovations of the Vienna Master and the Master of the Houghton Miniatures was the relatively conservative Master of the First Prayer Book of Maximilian and his prolific workshop. He possessed a large body of pattern designs by these artists or derived from their miniatures and from paintings by Hugo van der Goes. Over the course of the long activity of this workshop, which saw the participation of such innovative figures as the Master of the Munich Annunciation (see cat. no. 90), it expanded its pictorial repertoire by adding patterns based on more recent imagery from Marmion and the followers of Van der Goes (cat. no. 92). The Maximilian Master's highly systematized, pattern-based production, coupled with the hallmark border style, resulted not only in lavish volumes, but also in work of growing uniformity.[3]

The presence of some of the most ambitious pictorial cycles of this era in breviaries (cat. nos. 91, 92, 100, 112) reflects the expanding taste for Flemish manuscript illumination across Europe and in particular on the Iberian Peninsula. Such works were particularly favored by rulers and their retinues—names such as Isabella of Castile, Eleanor of Portugal, and the Carondelet family of courtiers come to mind—and in this respect they were probably following the example of Dukes Philip and Charles, both of whom commissioned lavish breviaries (see cat. no. 10). Flemish artists had achieved such status internationally that rulers across Europe and the nobles closest to them preferred Flemish creations to those of local illuminators. This shift in the locus of patronage seems to have accelerated with the intermarriage of the Burgundian Hapsburg and Spanish ruling families and the eventual move of Hapsburg rule to Spain. These breviaries often had cycles of sixty or more miniatures and, thanks to the nature of their devotional content, fostered a revival of interest in Old Testament themes that would grow steadily in Flemish art during the course of the sixteenth century. Not surprisingly, because of the organization of the breviary around the Psalter, interest in the King David story was particularly nurtured by this development, and a number of distinguished and innovative cycles survive from this period in books of hours (see cat. no. 111) as well as in breviaries (see cat. no. 100).[4]

The decline of Burgundian ducal patronage had a stronger impact on the character of manuscript illumination over the next several decades than the disappearance of the Vienna Master. Archduke Maximilian of Austria would become a great patron of the arts in the tradition of the dukes of Burgundy. Yet ultimately he became an important patron of the printed book, especially following his assumption of the title of emperor in 1493. He returned to Germany and turned to German artists such as Albrecht Dürer and Lucas Cranach to meet the needs of his court.

By the mid-1490s the bibliophile manuscript, especially the secular text, was no longer a central part of Flemish production, the result of a diminishing interest on the part of courtiers and the archduke himself. Nevertheless, lieutenants of the Burgundian realm, such as Louis of Gruuthuse (see cat. nos. 58–60, 62) and Engelbert of Nassau (see cat. nos. 18, 120), commissioned some of their finest manuscripts after the death of Charles the Bold in 1477. Other prominent courtiers—such as Baudouin II de Lannoy (cat. nos. 95, 97), John II of Oettingen and Flobecq (cat. no. 96), and Antoine Rolin (cat. no. 123), all residing in the Hainaut region—also continued the Burgundian court tradition of bibliophile patronage.[5] Despite the increasing focus on devotional books toward the end of the century, one distinguished illuminator of secular texts emerged in this period, the Master of the Prayer Books of around 1500 (cat. nos. 118–21). His wonderfully evocative imagery has strongly shaped our understanding of court pageantry at the end of the century.[6] Another original illuminator who excelled at decorating large-scale bibliophile manuscripts was the Master of Antoine Rolin, a follower of Marmion from Mons (cat. no. 123). Still, more than ever during the period from 1485 to 1510, Flemish manuscript illumination appears to have been a product for export beyond the boundaries of Burgundian Flanders, and it was devotional books, not secular texts, that excited the greatest demand.

Notes

1. The Mayer van den Bergh Breviary (cat. no. 92), which also features superb illuminations by David, was made for an unidentified Portuguese patron but certainly one of elevated rank and imposing wealth.

2. The other two were incorporated rather haphazardly into the Munich Hours (cat. no. 90).

3. Although the Maximilian Master's workshop was the most active in using patterns, this practice was not restricted to his workshop (as the work of some of the Ghent Associates demonstrates; see part 2). A calendar cycle conceived in the workshop of the Master of James IV was copied in at least seven of the most luxurious books of hours and breviaries of the time (including cat. nos. 91, 92, 110, 124, 138; see also cat. no. 91, n.10). Related evidence of standardization is the growing number of calendars that strongly agree in the choice of feasts among books that otherwise come from different workshops (e.g., cat. nos. 90, 110, 124). Perhaps due to the invention of the printing press and the ready availability of printed books of hours (mostly produced in France), the expectation for individualization in manuscripts shifted from the calendar to other textual features. The growing standardization may also result from the possibility that manuscripts came to be produced more often on speculation. The lack of firm evidence of an intended owner even for some of the more lavish manuscripts of the period (e.g., cat. nos. 90, 93, 109, 124) is consistent with this last proposal.

4. Since so many of these cycles belong to manuscripts made for European rulers or their closest officials, they are a fertile subject for further research.

5. Henry VII also acquired some Flemish manuscripts (cat. nos. 119, 121), but his patronage was not on the scale of that of Edward IV. Although he seems to have preferred French manuscripts, Henry VII had the Flemish scribe Quentin Poulet as his librarian at Sheen (see "Biographies of the Scribes," this volume).

6. See Scot McKendrick's essay "Reviving the Past: Illustrated Manuscripts of Secular Vernacular Texts, 1467–1500" (this volume).

MASTER OF THE FIRST PRAYER BOOK OF MAXIMILIAN (C)
For biography, see part 2

88

WORKSHOP OF MASTER OF THE FIRST PRAYER
BOOK OF MAXIMILIAN

Hours of Katharine Bray
Use of Sarum
Probably Ghent, ca. 1490

MANUSCRIPT: ii + 195 folios, 13.4 × 9.3 cm (5¼ × 3⅝ in.); justification:
7.5 × 5 cm (2¹⁵/₁₆ × 1¹⁵/₁₆ in.); 18 lines of *bastarda*; 19 full-page
miniatures

INSCRIPTIONS: *Hac die profecta est ad Deum anima D. Kat[er]ine Bray
op[time?] femine mane septima . . .* and note by Robert Thweng dated
1647 concerning John Thweng, prior of Bridlington, and inscription
of the English College of the Jesuits, fol. 1v; *Pray for the soules of Dame
Cattrayn Bray and of Ion Colett den of Paules*, fol. 104v

BINDING: Purple velvet over wood boards; silver corner pieces
decorated with fleurs-de-lis; central medallion bearing the Jesuit
insignia

COLLECTION: Lancashire, Stonyhurst College, Ms. 60

PROVENANCE: Katharine Bray (d. 1507), wife of Sir Reginald Bray
(d. 1503); Robert Thweng (d. 1642) (?); Library of the English College
of the Jesuits, Liège, before 1794

RA

88
WORKSHOP OF
MASTER OF THE
FIRST PRAYER BOOK
OF MAXIMILIAN
The Man of Sorrows,
fol. 162v

This book was made according to a highly systematized
method of production that helped to turn the new naturalistic style of manuscript illumination into a successful
Flemish luxury commodity for export. Nearly every one of
its miniatures can be linked to an illuminator's pattern,
specifically those patterns employed commonly by the
Master of the First Prayer Book of Maximilian and by
similar artists such as the Ghent Associates, who together
furthered the ideas of the Vienna Master of Mary of
Burgundy, Hugo van der Goes, and others.[1] *The Man of Sorrows* (ill. 88), for example, based ultimately on Van der
Goes's Edinburgh panel *The Trinity*, is derived from a pattern that was especially popular with illuminators between
1475 and 1490.[2] Since the book was made for Sarum use, its
intended owner was certainly English. Katherine Bray (d.
1507), the wife of Sir Reginald Bray (d. 1503), is securely
identified from inscriptions as an owner of the book. She or
her husband may have been its patron, but this is not certain.[3] Sir Reginald was a member of Lady Margaret Beaufort's household. Subsequently, with the accession to the
throne in 1486 of Henry VII, who was Lady Margaret's son,
Sir Reginald's career took off. He became a high court
official and, in the year of his death, a knight of the Order
of the Garter.

Although the book has much in common iconographically and pictorially with the two Hastings Hours (cat. nos.
25, 41), two other Flemish manuscripts produced in the
same circle for English patrons, it is more modest in most
respects. It has many fewer suffrages and more limited illumination, lacking the generous use of expensive pigments
found in the Hastings books.[4] Indeed, while some of the
book's miniatures are painted in full color (fols. 5v, 17v, 42v,
48v, 51v, 53v, 76v, 162v), others are largely in grisaille (fols.
1v, 13v, 104v, 177v), and still others are painted in varying
combinations, with settings largely in grisaille or partially
in color and some figures entirely in grisaille or partially
colored (fols. 9v, 21v, 26v, 31v, 38v, 45v).[5]

The illuminator of the Hours of Katharine Bray, who
probably belonged to the workshop of the Maximilian Master,[6] used five patterns for full compositions and settings
that the latter had employed in the London Hastings
Hours, but he simplified the settings and subtly generalized
other features.[7] The patterns were less carefully adapted to
the format of the miniatures and the figures less well modeled than those in the London Hastings Hours.

The book itself is difficult to date with much precision
and has generally been assigned a date around 1490, based
in part on the presence of the single miniature with a half-
length figure, *Saint John the Baptist*.[8] The half-length format,
though popularized in the 1470s by the painter Van der
Goes, gained wider currency among illuminators during
the 1480s through the example of a cycle of miniatures by
Marmion (see cat. no. 93) that the Maximilian Master may
have had in his possession.   T. K.

Notes

1. Alexander (1989: 312–14) identified several of these patterns.

2. Cf., e.g., Brinkmann 1998: 119, 125–26.

3. Perhaps the book was made for a couple named John and Anne, since its sequence of only four suffrages features both John the Baptist and John the Evangelist, while the single suffrage to a female saint is to Saint Anne. Anne also features prominently in the litany, placed at the head of the virgins, even before Mary Magdalene.

4. The book shares with both of the Hastings Hours a group of secondary devotions also found in other English *horae* of the period (e.g., cat. no. 15): the Fifteen Odes of Saint Bridget (which, despite its rubric to the contrary, in the Bray Hours includes only the first three), the Psalms of the Passion, the Commendation of Souls, and the Psalter of Saint Jerome (Ker 1969–92, 4: 447–49). Its litany also features a selection of distinctive virgins that are also found in the Madrid Hastings Hours: Sitha (perhaps Saint Osith of Essex), Praxedes, Sotheris, Editha, and Affra. It also has several texts lacking in the two Hastings Hours: the Spiritual and Temporal Joys of the Virgin and the Hours of the Holy Spirit. Unfortunately only the month of December remains from its calendar, and the book lacks a miniature to accompany the suffrage for Saint Anne.

5. A number of the draperies in grisaille are tinted with a very pale hue, a red or a blue, and their highlights are executed in yellow, gold, or white.

6. The book was first attributed to the Maximilian Master by Pächt, in London 1953–54: 160, no. 599. The range of facial and figural types seems to stem from the variety of pattern sources rather than from different hands. Yet all the miniatures are painted fairly loosely, and some—including *The Annunciation to the Shepherds*, *Pentecost*, and *David in Prayer* (fols. 17v, 66v, 76v)—are weaker than others.

7. Folios 1v, 5v, 9v, 21v, 31v, corresponding to folios 250v, 73v, 85v, 119v, 131v in the London Hastings Hours. See Alexander 1989: ills. between 310 and 311.

8. Manchester 1976: 30, no. 53; Alexander 1989: 314. If one compares this book with the Glasgow breviary of 1494 (ill. 89), which uses the same composition for its *Annunciation*, the heavier figure types of the breviary indicate that the version in the present volume (fol. 5v) is in all likelihood earlier in date.

89

WORKSHOP OF MASTER OF THE FIRST PRAYER
BOOK OF MAXIMILIAN

Breviary
Use of Rome
Probably Ghent, 1494

MANUSCRIPT: iii + 383 + ii folios, 25 × 16.4 cm (9⅞ × 6½ in.); justification: 17 × 9.4 cm (6¾ × 3¾ in.); 43 lines of *gotica rotunda*; 1 full-page miniature, 9 small miniatures

BINDING: Anthonius van Gavere (d. 1505), Bruges; blind-stamped brown calf over wood boards; remounted

COLLECTION: Glasgow, University Library, Hunter Ms. 25 (S.2.15)

PROVENANCE: In Britain by the seventeenth century; William Hunter, M.D. (1718–1783); bequeathed to Glasgow University

RA

Like a number of the much more luxurious breviaries created during this period (cat. nos. 91, 92, 112), this relatively modest example was made for Franciscan use.[1] It is one of the few manuscripts of this time to be securely dated.[2] Its ten miniatures were illuminated by the workshop of the Master of the First Prayer Book of Maximilian, and like other books produced by this shop, it exploited a familiar body of patterns.[3] The only full-page example is

The Annunciation (ill. 89), now rather faded, which is partially based on an Annunciation that the Maximilian Master had painted more than a decade earlier for the London Hastings Hours (cat. no. 41, fol. 73v).[4] In the present version the position of the upper body is modified so that Gabriel's hand is raised overhead, pointing heavenward.[5] The setting is derived from another Annunciation, the one in the Hours of Engelbert of Nassau (cat. no. 18, fol. 97v), where it appears in mirror image. The fairly robust figures, the plain facial type of the Virgin, and the distinctive profile of Gabriel, with the upper lip slightly flared, recall a Maximilian workshop style that was common around the turn of the century in manuscripts such as the Breviary of Eleanor of Portugal and a book of hours in Munich (cat. nos. 91, 90). Here, however, the execution is less mannered than in those two books.

The inclusion of several types of absolutions in the text prompted Nigel Thorp to suggest that the breviary was made for a confessor.[6] If this is correct, then it was probably made for the confessor to a court patron, for use in the latter's private chapel. The book's original binding, now heavily restored, was by Antonius van Gavere (active ca. 1460–1505), a member of the Bruges confraternity of book producers. The volume appears to have been in England by the seventeenth century.[7]   T.K.

89
WORKSHOP OF
MASTER OF THE
FIRST PRAYER BOOK
OF MAXIMILIAN
The Annunciation,
fol. 7v

Notes

1. The calendar appears to be Franciscan, and certain texts are particularly for Franciscan use, such as the absolutions on folios 229v–230 (Toronto 1987: 189).

2. The date 1494 appears on folio 383. Another dated example is the Carondelet Breviary (cat. no. 112).

3. Another miniature, possibly full page and representing *The Resurrection*, is lacking before folio 85, where the Office for Easter Sunday begins.

4. It seems likely that the bedclothes in the present *Annunciation* were originally red.

5. The pattern for Gabriel had evolved since the creation of the London Hastings miniature because the form of Gabriel in the present manuscript reappears some years later in the *Annunciation* in the Breviary of Eleanor of Portugal (cat. no. 91, fol. 388v).

6. In Toronto 1987: 189.

7. Young and Aitken 1908: 23.

90a
ANONYMOUS
Saint Catherine, fol. 255v

90

WORKSHOP OF MASTER OF THE FIRST PRAYER BOOK OF MAXIMILIAN, INCLUDING MASTER OF THE MUNICH ANNUNCIATION; MASTER OF THE PRAYER BOOKS OF AROUND 1500 AND WORKSHOP; SIMON MARMION; AND ANOTHER ILLUMINATOR

Book of Hours
Use of Rome
Valenciennes, before 1489; Bruges and probably Ghent, ca. 1495–1500

MANUSCRIPT: i + 345 + iii folios, 20 × 13.5 cm (7⅞ × 5⁵⁄₁₆ in.); justification: 9.4 × 6 cm (3¹¹⁄₁₆ × 2⅜ in.); 19 lines of *gotica rotunda*; 28 full-page miniatures, 27 half-page miniatures, 31 quarter-page miniatures, 2 small miniatures, 24 bas-de-page calendar miniatures

BINDING: Early eighteenth century; gold-tooled brown leather over wood boards; silver clasps

COLLECTION: Munich, Bayerische Staatsbibliothek, Ms. Clm. 28345

PROVENANCE: Spanish collection, late sixteenth or early seventeenth century; Hofbibliothek, Munich, nineteenth century; transferred to Nationalmuseum, Munich, 1857; returned 1923 to Bayerische Staatsbibliothek, Munich

JPGM

This complex book of hours contains four lavish pictorial cycles. The volume was illuminated primarily by two major workshops, one led by the Master of the First Prayer Book of Maximilian and the other by the Master of the Prayer Books of around 1500. The book also contains a few miniatures by other artists, including two exceptional half-length miniatures by Simon Marmion, which were resized to fit this manuscript and inserted in unusual locations.[1] The same group of artists also contributed to the illumination of a comparably distinctive and ambitious but earlier book, La Flora (cat. no. 93), and it appears that the two miniatures by Marmion were originally part of the cycle that appears in that book. Although the Munich book and La Flora are distinct in iconography and overall pictorial character in many ways, the skein of correspondences between them is striking: the decorated initials with white acanthus, the relatively narrow carved architectural borders in brown, the strewn full borders with particularly large flowers, the style of the bar borders, the script, features of the layout,[2] and even some uncommon devotional texts.[3] In both books two or more illuminators often collaborated on a single cycle of miniatures.

Besides the two Marmion miniatures from the pictorial cycle found in La Flora, the Munich hours also includes several miniatures that are copies of miniatures by Marmion in La Flora and still others based upon other miniatures (or the patterns for the miniatures) that were executed in La Flora by the Maximilian Master and his workshop.[4] Moreover, the book's contents may have been shuffled when it was rebound in the eighteenth century. The Penitential Psalms and Office of the Dead are out of sequence, the latter preceding the former, while the suffrages, contrary to custom, open with a group of female saints, switch to a long series of male saints, and then revert to the sequence of virgins.[5]

90b
MASTER OF
THE MUNICH
ANNUNCIATION
The Annunciation, fol. 14v

90c
WORKSHOP OF
MASTER OF THE
FIRST PRAYER BOOK
OF MAXIMILIAN
The Arrest of Christ,
fol. 95v

The finest and most original of the four pictorial cycles in the Munich Hours is the calendar. One of the most charming of all Flemish calendars, it was illuminated entirely by the Master of the Prayer Books of around 1500. The twenty-four half-page miniatures depict a great variety of recreation as well as labor, often showing several phases of a particular farming or leisure activity and heightening the sense of continuous narrative. A tall diaphragm arch beneath elaborate tracery patterns frames the large bas-de-page scenes.[6] While the calendar represents the finest work by the Prayer Books Master in this manuscript, he and/or his workshop also painted all of the smaller miniatures, several historiated borders, and several full-page miniatures.[7]

The Hours of the Virgin features a cycle of full-page miniatures of the life of the Virgin, with half-page miniatures opposite them that either illustrate the Virgin's life or are typological in nature. The finest and most distinctive hand from the workshop of the Maximilian Master painted the half-length *Annunciation* (ill. 90b). (Although the Maximilian Master himself and other members of his workshop had collaborated on La Flora, only workshop members contributed to the Munich hours.) In *The Annunciation* the illuminator depicted the broad figure of the archangel Gabriel as if he were just alighting at the side of the Virgin, adding even greater immediacy to the intimate half-length format. Although the pose of the Virgin reflects that of Marmion's figure of Mary in the *Annunciation* in La Flora (fol. 81v), the illuminator nevertheless displayed a largely independent sensibility. The youthful facial type of Gabriel is distinctive—with a long oval face, sweet lips, small nose, and a headful of spit curls—while the Virgin has matronly features. The same facial types appear in the artist's full-page miniatures of the Coronation of the Virgin in the Hours of the Virgin, and of Saint John the Evangelist, Saint Barbara, and Saint Mary Magdalene.[8] These are not the facial types of the Maximilian Master; they are in some ways more distinctive, both smoother and more substantial.[9] I call the painter of these miniatures the Master of the Munich Annunciation. Another member of the workshop of the Maximilian Master painted *The Nativity* and *The Presentation in the Temple* in the Hours of the Virgin. This workshop artist probably also illuminated miniatures in the

Breviary of Eleanor of Portugal (cat. no. 91). His figure types have long spit curls; an extended, sometimes flared upper lip with slight overbite; a high forehead; and a relatively large head. Both artists show to a degree the influence of the facial types of the Prayer Books Master.

In a vein similar to the Hours of the Virgin, the pictorial program of the Hours of the Passion, illustrated by the Passion narrative from the Arrest of Christ to the Entombment, consists of full-page miniatures opposite half-page miniatures. The smaller illustrations again either serve to continue the Christological narrative or have a typological connection to the facing miniature. The style of the full-page Passion miniatures—including *The Arrest of Christ* (ill. 90c), *The Road to Calvary*, *The Flagellation*, and *The Entombment*—is also reminiscent of the Maximilian Master, and they are probably by the same workshop hand as *The Nativity* and *The Presentation in the Temple* in the Hours of the Virgin.[10] There can be little doubt that the prevalence of the half-length or three-quarter-length format in the Munich Hours resulted from the involvement of the Maximilian Master and his workshop in La Flora. Exceptionally within the Passion cycle, the full-page miniature *The Sacrifice of Isaac* by Marmion appears at terce, interrupting the narrative, while a smaller miniature of the same subject appears opposite it. The former must have been inserted at the last minute, probably because of its superb quality.[11] The miniatures painted by Marmion in this volume are among the book's finest.[12]

The largest section of the manuscript, that of the thirty-five suffrages, includes thirty-one quarter-page miniatures and seven full-page miniatures, so that several openings (the suffrages for Saints George, Catherine, and Anthony Abbot) have two miniatures. Additionally, the suffrages for Saint Barbara and Saint Anthony Abbot have historiated borders. The book's most beautiful miniature—the full-page, half-length standing Saint Catherine (ill. 90a)—appears in this cycle. Her face and flowing locks are beautifully modeled in soft light with palpable shadows, the kind of subtlety in modeling that a master of the glazing technique in oil on panel might achieve. The placement of the figure somewhat to the right of center is unusual, and the landscape and her mantle, although beautiful, are a bit more broadly painted than the flesh areas. It is a miniature worthy of closer scrutiny. I cannot identify a painter of the period whose work closely resembles it, and no other illumination by the artist appears in the Munich Hours.[13]

The Munich volume is difficult to date and localize. Marmion (d. 1489) was probably deceased for some years when it was created. Although La Flora is not exactly a twin of this manuscript, they share so many particulars of conception and execution that one is tempted to view them as executed one right after the other. This thesis, however, is offered cautiously, and a somewhat broader dating is prudent. Since the illuminations in the Munich Hours more likely derived inspiration from images in La Flora than vice versa, it is later in date. (Moreover, the miniatures by the Maximilian Master and his workshop in La Flora are striking for not yet having succumbed to the influence of Marmion's half-lengths, while those in the Munich Hours

have.) The calendar has a strong concentration of saints from the diocese of Utrecht, while the litany has a strongly Franciscan character.[14] These features may tell us more about the market for the book than about where it was produced.[15] Some of the book's illuminators are associated with Bruges and others with Ghent.   T. K

Notes

1. Each of the two miniatures was trimmed close to the edge of the image and mounted in a four-sided parchment support, the outer dimensions of which fit those of the Munich Hours.

2. The layout of the Hours of the Passion and the Hours of the Virgin is similar in the two books, each showing at every hour a full-page miniature opposite a half-page miniature. Further, like the Munich Hours, La Flora has a lengthy cycle of suffrages, twenty-six in all (fols. 318v–342v), the majority of which have quarter-page miniatures. Only five have full-page miniatures.

3. Both books feature the dominical prayers for the year and masses for Easter, Pentecost, All Saints, and Palm Sunday, along with, exceptionally, the Gospel reading for Friday of the third week in Lent, the Epistle reading for the third Sunday in Lent, the Gospel reading for Monday after Easter, and the Gospel reading for Friday after the fourth Sunday in Lent. In La Flora these readings appear in the above sequence (fols. 285–302), following the Mass for Palm Sunday (fol. 269–302). In the Munich Hours they are distributed throughout the book (fols. 145–49, 275–79, 155–57, 141–44). See also cat. no. 93, note 1.

4. Copies after La Flora miniatures include *The Annunciation to the Shepherds* (fol. 46v) and *The Preaching of Saint James the Greater* (fol. 264v), both by Marmion in La Flora, and *The Capture of Christ* (fol. 95v), *Ecce Homo* (fol. 108v), *The Deposition* (fol. 125v), *The Road to Calvary* (fol. 112v), and *The Entombment* (fol. 130v), all by the Maximilian Master or his workshop there.

5. The calendar is also out of sequence. June and July appear between September and October, so that folio 9v shows the first half of July but folio 10 shows the second half of August. Folio 7v shows the first half of September, while folio 8 shows the second half of May. Folio 5v shows the first half of May, while folio 6 shows the second half of July. The full-page miniature of the Mass of Saint Gregory (fol. 265) was undoubtedly intended as a verso but appears as a recto.

6. The complete calendar is reproduced in color in Leidinger 1936.

7. In the Munich Hours, the Prayer Books Master painted the historiated border for the suffrage of Saint Anthony (fol. 260) and the full-page miniatures *Saint Anthony* (fol. 259v), *The Virgin and Child with Angels* (fol. 74v), and perhaps *Saint George and the Dragon* (fol. 244v), while his workshop executed the historiated border of the life of Saint Barbara (fol. 253v) and perhaps *The Mass of Saint Gregory* (fol. 265).

8. This artist may also have painted the copies after Marmion's *Annunciation to the Shepherds* and *Preaching of Saint James the Greater* in the Munich Hours. The same facial types and hands, with darkly outlined nails, appear in miniatures of Saint John the Evangelist and of Saint Barbara in the Hours of Isabella of Castile (cat. no. 105). If the last were not painted by the Master of the Munich Annunciation, they were at least based on his designs.

9. It may be that earlier miniatures by this artist appear in the Hours of Louis Quarré (Oxford, Bodleian Library, Ms. Douce 311), where certain miniatures feature a similar treatment of eyes, mouth, and hair (fols. 8v, 16v, 59v, 102v). These figures, however, lack the robustness of those in the Munich Hours.

10. This artist also painted *Pentecost* and *King David*.

11. The full-page miniature of the Raising of Lazarus (fol. 140v) by the workshop of the Maximilian Master is, like the two miniatures by Marmion, set into four-sided parchment supports and also must have been inserted as an afterthought.

12. The second full-page miniature by Marmion, *Christ Taking Leave of His Mother* (fol. 230), is also oddly located, at the end of a devotional section of Marian prayers rather than the beginning, corroboration that it too was inserted as an afterthought.

13. Saint Catherine's distinctive beaded gown, the flared cuffs, and the heavy mantle draped mostly below the waist are clearly variants

of the garment worn by Saint Barbara in the Hours of Isabella of Castile (cat. no. 105, fol. 191v). The latter miniature seems to have been designed and perhaps painted by the Master of the Munich Annunciation.

14. The litany includes Saint Francis, Saint Louis of France, Saint Bernardino of Siena, and Saint Clara. Among the Franciscan saints in the illuminated suffrages are Saint Francis, Saint Clara, and Saint Anthony of Padua. The Munich litany also features Saint Donatian, a figure usually associated with Bruges, although, as Clark (2000: 321) has shown, also linked to Lille, Ghent, and other centers. The calendar of La Flora, which is otherwise quite different in character from that of the Munich hours, features a number of Franciscan feasts.

15. The book displays an extremely high level of agreement with the comparably full calendars in both the Hours of James IV of Scotland (cat. no. 110; 93.68 percent) and the Spinola Hours (cat. no. 124; 92.47 percent), two of the most luxurious books of hours of the sixteenth century.

91

WORKSHOP OF MASTER OF THE FIRST PRAYER BOOK OF MAXIMILIAN AND MASTER OF JAMES IV OF SCOTLAND AND/OR WORKSHOP

Breviary of Eleanor of Portugal
Franciscan use
Probably Ghent, ca. 1500–1510

MANUSCRIPT: i + 590 + ii folios, 23.9 × 17.3 cm (9⁷⁄₁₆ × 6¹³⁄₁₆ in.); justification (pages with text only): 15.4 × 4.5–1.3–4.5 cm (6¹⁄₁₆ × 1¾–½–1¾ in.); 32 lines of *textura* in two columns; justification (pages with text and illuminated border): 14 × 4.2–1–4.2 cm (5½ × 1¹¹⁄₁₆–⁷⁄₁₆–1¹¹⁄₁₆ in.); 32 lines of *textura* in two columns; 25 full-page miniatures, 32 small miniatures, 11 historiated borders, 12 bas-de-page calendar miniatures with additional scenes set into architectural borders

HERALDRY: Escutcheon with the arms of Eleanor of Portugal painted over original armorials on the side of the prie-dieu, her fishing-net device painted over armorials on the front of the prie-dieu, each painted over lozenges, fol. 1v

BINDING: Portugal, seventeenth century; green velvet; central silver-gilt medallions with the coat of arms of Cardinal Rodrigo de Castro de Lemos; brass corner pieces

COLLECTION: New York, The Morgan Library, Ms. M.52

PROVENANCE: Eleanor of Portugal (1454–1525); Cardinal Rodrigo de Castro de Lemos (1523–1600); [Hamburger Frères, Paris]; to J. P. Morgan (1837–1913) in 1905

JPGM

This elaborate Franciscan breviary is roughly similar in the quantity of its illumination to the Franciscan breviary in Antwerp (cat. no. 92).[1] Both became the property of Portuguese patrons early on, and it appears that the present breviary was originally intended for a Portuguese patron as well. The prominence given to Saint Anthony of Padua in the decorative program, including a full-page miniature and a full historiated border devoted to him, is consistent with Portuguese patronage (fols. 411v–412). Saint Anthony of Padua was widely venerated in the early sixteenth century, but he was born in Lisbon and especially honored there. The frontispiece shows Eleanor of Portugal (1458–1525) kneeling in adoration before an altar with a monumental lifelike statue of the Virgin and Child before a carved triptych with Saint John the Baptist, the Salvator Mundi, and Saint Andrew (ill. 91b). Although the miniature

appears to be largely original to the book (but was perhaps moved to the front from another location), Eleanor's armorials and device are painted over an older set,[2] and the head of the queen was painted by a different artist from the rest of the miniature.[3] So she may not have been the book's first intended owner.

The workshop of the Master of the First Prayer Book of Maximilian painted all of the full-page miniatures, six of the historiated borders, and twenty-five of the one-column miniatures. One of these artists seems also to have begun two of the one-column miniatures (fols. 349v, 351), which were then completed by the Master of James IV of Scotland or his workshop.[4] The Maximilian Master workshop miniatures range in quality, probably reflecting the participation of several hands. Some of its best illumination can be found in the smaller miniatures, such as the one-column *Virgin and Child* (fol. 528) and *Saints Simon and Jude* (fol. 530v). More characteristic of the book as a whole is the work of one of the painters of the large miniatures. In many of these the figures are broad and squat with relatively large heads. The facial types are also distinctive. The hoary male type has a high forehead; strong brow; loose, wavy hair; a receding hairline; and vertical creases near the mouth. The upper lip is large, flared, and slightly protruding, and some of the figures, including the men, have long spit curls, perhaps inspired by Marmion's miniatures in La Flora (cat. no. 93).[5] A particularly expressive and original example of this artist's style is *The Calling of Saint Peter and Saint Andrew* (ill. 91c), which also betrays his awkwardness in relating the figures to one another.[6] The same hand appears to have worked in the Munich hours (ill. 90c), where the men have comparable Marmionesque spit curls, also wear baggy tunics with a thin horizontal double stripe, and have a similar upper lip and strong brow.[7] In the breviary the figures are particularly stiff and sometimes cramped within the composition or awkwardly posed, as if the artist was combining imagery from different patterns.[8] Whereas the figures usually have large heads,[9] in some compositions the opposite is true—the heads are surprisingly small—reflecting the hand of another member of the workshop (see *The Ascension of Christ*, fol. 170v). The Master of James IV of Scotland or his workshop painted all the miniatures in the calendar and four historiated borders and ten one-column miniatures (including the two on fols. 349v and 351).[10] The illumination here is not up to his best work.

A striking pictorial feature of the book is the way many pages combine a large miniature with a historiated border that has a unified landscape setting.[11] In *The Crucifixion* (ill. 91a), the landscape is continuous with the border, and in other instances the landscape of the historiated border is continuous *behind* the full-page miniature (see fols. 257v, 398v, 411v). In *The Crucifixion* the aforementioned artist from the workshop of the Maximilian Master compressed the Good and Bad Thieves each into a narrow strip of side border.[12] Although the thieves are not particularly well drawn, the device is still dramatically effective.[13] By reducing the scale of the soldiers playing dice in the separate but contiguous compartment of the bas-de-page, the artist failed to fully integrate them spatially with the larger miniature.

Yet the similarity of their grassy setting to that of *The Crucifixion* and the placement of the vignette with soldiers underneath it still links the two visually. In some of the historiated borders by the Master of James IV of Scotland and his workshop, the landscape setting is continuous behind the two columns of text, even *between* the columns (see fols. 33, 141, 412).

Scholars have dated this manuscript as early as the last years of the fifteenth century and as late as 1520.[14] As Eleanor was a dowager for thirty years, the indications of her ownership help little with the book's dating unless the overpainted shields were originally those of Eleanor and King John II (r. 1481–95), which is not certain.[15] If correct, this would indicate that the book was begun by 1495, and the 1490s would be a plausible dating for the book.[16] Margaret Scott pointed out that the costumes of the upper-class couple by the fountain in the bas-de-page of folio 291, so reminiscent of those in the Harley *Roman de la rose* (cat. no. 120) belong to the 1490s: the man's cap with its turned-up brim, the medium-size lapels, and the narrow gown sleeves. The male in the noble couple in March (fol. 3) has a much larger cap and much wider sleeves, however, pointing to a later date, at the beginning of the new century, so it is likely that the book's execution belongs instead to the first decade of the sixteenth century.[17]   T. K.

Notes

1. A large number of Franciscan feasts appear in this breviary's calendar, including the Stigmatization of Saint Francis (September 17) and the Translations of Saint Francis (May 25), Saint Anthony of Padua (February 15), and Saint Clare (October 2). Saint Francis and Saint Anthony both appear in red (October 4 and August 2). Each of these saints also receives a full-page miniature and a historiated border with scenes from his or her life. Saint Louis of Toulouse also appears in red (August 19), and the Franciscan office for parents of members of the order appears in the calendar on November 26. There are also many Franciscan feasts in the Sanctorale.

2. Originally there was a large lozenge-shaped shield on the front of the prie-dieu and a smaller one on the side. They have been overpainted with the escutcheon of Eleanor of Portugal, bearing her arms and her device of the fishing net. With the generous assistance of Morgan Library conservator Patricia Reyes and curator William Voelkle, I was able to study the miniature with transmitted light.

3. The miniature was certainly begun by one of the illuminators of the breviary itself, as the facial type of the Virgin—with a wide, flat upper lip, and narrower, pouty lower lip—is found in *The Adoration of the Magi* (fol. 61v). Both are doubtless by the same illuminator in the workshop of the Maximilian Master. There are a number of pentimenti in the areas of the headdress at the back of the queen's head, around her hands, her ear, and the proper left side of her face from the eye to the chin. Hard to explain are the white sleeves hanging from Eleanor's arms, which have no relationship to the rest of her costume. The painting of Eleanor, including her face and her finely detailed costume, is more carefully finished than the rest of the miniature and uncharacteristic of the Maximilian Master or his workshop. It may be that a space was left for another artist to complete this figure and that the second artist made a number of changes in the course of painting the figure. A strip of red was also repainted in the altar frontal along the contour of the queen's face.

91a (opposite)
WORKSHOP OF
MASTER OF THE
FIRST PRAYER BOOK
OF MAXIMILIAN
The Crucifixion, fol. 140v

91b (above left)
WORKSHOP OF
MASTER OF THE
FIRST PRAYER BOOK
OF MAXIMILIAN
*Eleanor of Portugal
Adoring the Virgin
and Child*, fol. 1v

91c (above right)
WORKSHOP OF
MASTER OF THE
FIRST PRAYER BOOK
OF MAXIMILIAN
*The Calling of Saint Peter
and Saint Andrew*,
fol. 345v

4. Except as noted here, I agree with the breakdown of the two main styles in the recent description of the manuscript available in the reading room of the Morgan Library.

5. This type is closely anticipated in the half-length *Saint John the Baptist* in the earlier Hours of Katharine Bray by the Maximilian Master workshop (cat. no. 88, fol. 48v).

6. The youthful, bearded, and rather pretty type of Christ shown in this miniature also appears to be characteristic of the style of this illuminator.

7. Cf., e.g., fols. 56v, 61v, 95v, 103v, 328v.

8. The figure of Mauritius in *The Adoration of the Magi* illustrates this awkwardness. He is shown striding toward the Christ child in such a way that his legs have nearly disappeared from view and he seems to float from the knee up (fol. 61v).

9. A striking example is the Saint Catherine, whose head is as wide as her shoulders. These ungainly proportions contrast with those in the Maximilian Master's earlier, more demure interpretations of this popular figure type (e.g., cat. no. 41, fol. 68v; cat. no. 93, fol. 339v).

10. Elizabeth Morrison kindly advised me that iconographically the calendar decorations belong to a larger group of seven calendars that feature wood tracery borders, roundels set into the border depicting saints whose feasts are indicated in red in the text of the calendar (sometimes in color and sometimes in grisaille), and similar compositions for the labors of the month. Additionally, the zodiacal signs are also closely related, and in all seven calendars they appear out of order in exactly the same way (Virgo, Scorpio, Libra, Sagittarius instead of Virgo, Libra, Scorpio, Sagittarius). Because the common artistic link among the books is that the calendars were either by followers of the Master of James IV or appear in manuscripts in which he was active, it is clear that a popular set of calendar miniature patterns was available in the workshop of the Master of James IV. The list of manuscripts includes cat. nos. 91, 92, 109, 110, 124, 138, and the Rothschild Hours (private collection). The cycle in the Morgan breviary is the finest of all of these and the closest in execution to the work of the Master of James IV himself.

11. For the examples on folios 257v and 398v, see New York 1988b: 96, 97, nos. 1052, 1056. Another example by the Maximilian Master (or his workshop) in which the landscape of the miniature continues into the border is the page with *David and Goliath* in the Mayer van den Bergh Breviary (cat. no. 92, fol. 20v; Nieuwdorp and Dekeyzer 1997: 28, pl.).

12. This miniature appears to be by the same hand as *The Calling of Saint Peter and Saint Andrew*.

13. The composition of the miniature itself is based on a pattern that goes back at least to the Hours of Mary of Burgundy and Maximilian (cat. no. 38, fol. 150). The Maximilian Master workshop altered the scene to illustrate the moment when the sky darkened and amended the original pattern with the figures of the thieves.

14. De Winter 1981: 424, n. 20 (ca. 1497); Beck 1933: 266 (between 1515 and 1520). Most scholars have placed it between 1500 and 1510, including Winkler (1964: 175; ca. 1500), Gaspar (1932: 23; early sixteenth century), and De Coo (1978: 168; ca. 1510).

15. The larger of the overpainted shields is lozenge-shaped, suggesting a female rather than a male patron.

16. De Figueiredo (1931: 63) believed that the book could not be later than 1503 because Eleanor is not attired as a Franciscan tertiary; she joined the order in that year.

17. Margaret Scott, correspondence with the author, September 6, 2002 (Department of Manuscripts files, JPGM). It is of course possible that the calendar's illumination is later in date than the rest of the book and that the book's illumination was drawn out over a long period.

92

MASTER OF THE FIRST PRAYER BOOK OF
MAXIMILIAN AND WORKSHOP, MASTER OF
JAMES IV OF SCOTLAND AND WORKSHOP,
GERARD DAVID, AND OTHERS

Leaves from the Mayer van den Bergh Breviary
Use of Rome
Ghent and Bruges, ca. 1500

January–February, fols. 1v–2
The Trinity, fol. 326v
The Annunciation, fol. 427v
The Visitation, fol. 473v
Our Lady of the Snow, fol. 501v
The Birth of the Virgin, fol. 536v
Saint Michael, fol. 552v
The Martyrdom of Ten Thousand, fol. 596v
Saint Catherine, fol. 611v

MANUSCRIPT: vii + 706 + iv folios, 22.3 × 16 cm (8¹³⁄₁₆ × 6⁵⁄₁₆ in.); justification: 13.3 × 9.2 cm (5¼ × 3⅝ in.); 32 lines of *gotica rotunda* in two columns; 29 full-page miniatures, 7 half-page miniatures, 20 small miniatures, 9 historiated borders, 12 calendar pages with bas-de-page calendar miniatures and additional scenes set into architectural borders

BINDING: Temporarily disbound since 1994; previous binding: blind-stamped leather by Charles Weckesser, Brussels, 1932, which replaced an eighteenth-century binding of red velvet

COLLECTION: Antwerp, Museum Mayer van den Bergh, inv. no. 946

PROVENANCE: Manuel I, king of Portugal (1495–1521) (?); Martin Heckscher, Vienna [his sale, Christie's, London, May 4, 1898, lot 280]; [Harding, London]; to Fritz Mayer van den Bergh (d. 1901)

JPGM: Fols. 1v–2, 326v, 473v, 536v, 596v;
RA: Fols. 427v, 501v, 552v, 611v

The Mayer van den Bergh Breviary belongs to the distinguished group of deluxe Flemish manuscripts from the turn of the century.[1] More than a dozen illuminators worked on its roughly eighty miniatures:[2] the Master of the First Prayer Book of Maximilian and his workshop collaborators (ills. 92a, 92f), Gerard David (ills. 92a–c), the Master of James IV of Scotland (ills. 92d, e), and an anonymous panel painter whom Friedrich Winkler identified incorrectly with Jan Provost (ills. 92h, i).[3] The Maximilian Master was the leader of the project. He and his workshop were responsible for nearly three-quarters of the decoration. *The Annunciation* (ill. 92f) represents the high point of his style. Here the monumental figures of Mary and the angel Gabriel, their visages reminiscent of Gerard David's facial types, occupy the immediate foreground. Within the modulated atmospheric light of the church, they radiate their own delicate luminosity.

Besides the Maximilian Master, five members of his workshop contributed to the decoration.[4] Representative of the first of these illuminators is the miniature *Tobias and the Fish* (fol. 41), and representative of the second is *The Resurrection* (fol. 284v). The hand of the third artist is apparent in *The Circumcision* (fol. 182v), while the fourth and fifth appear only in the Sanctorale, painting, respectively, *Saint James* (fol. 489v) and *The Apostles* (fol. 583v).[5] The Maximilian Master and his assistants executed the border decoration around their miniatures, which shows little originality in comparison to that of other Flemish manuscripts of the

hand, the miniatures *Saint Catherine* (ill. 92b) and *The Visitation* (ill. 92c), both attributed to Gerard David, possibly indicate a break in the manufacture of the book. On the basis of a comparison with the panel paintings of Gerard David, Maryan Ainsworth has dated *The Visitation* around 1515.[12] But to my mind such a dating seems late.

The patron or intended owner of the Mayer van den Bergh breviary remains to be identified. José de Figueiredo and many scholars following him have thought that Manuel I, king of Portugal (1495–1521), was the original owner of the codex.[13] The book offers only vague support for this hypothesis, however: the luxuriousness of the manuscript, the added text in Portuguese for the calculation of the date of Easter, the calendar with many saints specific to Portugal, and a proposed dating, around 1500, that falls just within the period of the reign of Manuel I. More important, Manuel's coat of arms, device, and motto are all lacking. Saint Jerome, the king's patron saint, is highlighted in the calendar (September 30), but he is not featured elsewhere in the breviary, a telling omission. The book contains no reference to Manuel's position as Grand Master of the Order of the Templars;[14] nor is there even iconography suitable to a king. The psalters of breviaries made for powerful rulers often feature elaborate David cycles, as in Queen Isabella's breviary (cat. no. 100).[15] Here the psalter is illustrated largely by other Old Testament themes.

The breviary appears to have been written in two phases, the result perhaps of a change in the book's intended owner while it was still in production.[16] The first campaign consisted of the Psalter, the Temporale, and the first part of the Proper of Saints.[17] The only distinctive textual feature in this portion is the rare suffrage and miniature in honor of the Italian saint Felix and his brother (fol. 395v) in the first part of the Proper.[18] Saint Felix was particularly venerated in Florence, so perhaps the book was begun for an Italian patron. The second phase includes the rest of the Proper, the suffrages and special prayers, the calendar, and the table for the calculation of the date of Easter. These sections have a character that is strongly Franciscan (especially the calendar), with many references to the Augustinians as well. Inclusion of saints in the calendar connected to the Franciscan tertiaries (Saints Eleazar [September 27] and Ivo [October 27]) suggests that the second patron was a member of this order. The Easter table written in the vernacular shows that by this juncture the patron was Portuguese.[19] Further, the illuminations by the Master of James IV of Scotland appear only in the second half of the manuscript, probably in connection with the arrival of the new patron. Among these miniatures are *Saint Benedict* (fol. 242v) and *Our Lady of the Snow* (ill. 92e).

Although the illumination of the psalter does not focus primarily on King David, it features the most unusual and surprising iconography in the book. After the openings with scenes from David's youth,[20] especially striking are *Tobias and the Fish* (fol. 41), *Aaron and Moses Ask the Lord to Heal Miriam* (fol. 50v), *Adoration of the Golden Calf* (fol. 58), *Joseph Sold by His Brothers* (fol. 65), and *The Passage through the Red Sea* (fol. 83v). Unlike most Psalter illustration, its miniatures do not depict the opening words of the

period. They decorated both the text pages and the inserted full-page miniatures, giving the breviary a striking visual unity.[6] Only the borders around the illuminations by the Master of James IV and by the anonymous panel painter show a somewhat different aesthetic.[7] Those by the Master of James IV of Scotland and his workshop include *Saint Benedict* (fol. 424v), *Our Lady of the Snow* (ill. 92e), *All Saints* (fol. 562v), *The Martyrdom of Ten Thousand* (ill. 92d), *The Miracle of Saint Anthony of Padua* (fol. 651v), and *The Presentation in the Temple* (fol. 687v).[8]

The dating of the manuscript is problematic. In the older literature invariably the years 1510–15 are given,[9] but more recent research situates the production closer to 1500.[10] On the one hand, the costumes of the figures; the design of the border decoration, which is so characteristic of the Maximilian Master in the 1490s;[11] the spatial settings in the miniatures of the Master of James IV, which belong early in his development; and the absence of Renaissance figural types support such an early dating. On the other

92b

GERARD DAVID
Saint Catherine, fol. 611v

92c

GERARD DAVID
The Visitation, fol. 473v

accompanying psalm. Instead, the particular Old Testament illustrations convey the meaning of the psalm as a whole. The miniatures demonstrate the powerful intervention of the Lord. Despite the novelty of subject matter in the Psalter, which presumes a patron with a strong intellectual background, the iconography derives from an existing tradition. *Tobias and the Fish* and *Joseph Sold by His Brothers* depend directly on glass paintings that are based on drawings attributed to Hugo van der Goes.[21] Although less common, the scene with Miriam, Aaron, and Moses is also a known one. It appears, rather differently modeled, in the *Biblia figurata* (Ghent, Universiteitsbibliotheek, Ms. 10) of Raphaël de Mercatellis, abbot of Saint Bavo's in Ghent and patron of many richly illustrated codices.

In contrast to those in the Psalter, the illustrations in the rest of the manuscript are more traditional. The miniatures in the Temporale—*The Nativity* (fol. 158v), *The Circumcision* (fol. 182v), *The Adoration of the Magi* (fol. 189), *The Resurrection* (fol. 284v), *The Ascension of Christ* (fol. 309v), *The Pentecost* (fol. 318v), *The Trinity* (ill. 92a), and *The Last Supper* (fol. 331v)—depict the most important feast days of the church year. Also, with the exception of those attributed to the Master of James IV of Scotland and the anonymous panel painter, most of the depictions of saints from

the Proper and Common of Saints follow standard iconography. Thus the Mayer van den Bergh breviary lies between tradition and renewal.

B. D.

Notes

This entry is based upon my doctoral thesis defended at the Katholieke Universiteit, Leuven, on September 23, 2002.

1. The components of this breviary include a calendar (fols. 1–7); several lesser texts, including tables for the calculation of the date of Easter (fols. 9–19); the Psalter (fols. 20v–132v); the Temporale (fols. 133–378); the Proper of Saints (fols. 379–582v); the Common of Saints (fols. 583v–618); and some additional devotions (fols. 618–706v).

2. In the literature the attributions are in general vague. For a summary of the problem and references to the older literature, see De Coo 1978: 168–74. Attributions to Simon Bening are put forward in Wescher 1959: 133; Salmi and Mellini 1972: 32; Euw and Plotzek 1979–85, Plotzek 2: 274–75; Dekeyzer et al. 1999: 307–11 (where I, following the traditional view, mistakenly assert that most of the miniatures are by Simon Bening); and Goehring 2000: 214–15.

3. Winkler 1957: 285–89; Brinkmann (1997: 175–76) supported the view of Winkler that *The Birth of the Virgin* (fol. 536v) and *Saint Michael* (fol. 552v) should be attributed to Provost.

4. My stylistic investigations were aided by codicological analysis, pigment analysis, and infrared reflectography. See Dekeyzer et al. 1999: 311–15; Vandenabeele et al. 1999: 169–72; Vandenabeele 2000; and Vandenabeele and Moens 2002.

5. The Maximilian Master presumably illuminated the following miniatures: fols. 20v, 100, 167v, 383v, 395, 427v, 436. 438, 440, 486, 512v,

531, 549, 558, 561v, 575, 581. Work by his workshop collaborators can be found on the following folios: 41, 58, 75v, 83v (Master A); 158v, 189, 284v, 309v, 318v (Master B); 50v, 182v, 387v, 397, 400v, 411v, 451v, 457v (Master C); 583v (Master D); 466v, 489v (Master E). The following folios were presumably created as collaborations: 65 (Master A and an unidentified illuminator); 326v (Gerard David and an unidentified illuminator); 331v (Master B and Gerard David); 590v (Master D and an unidentified illuminator). The miniatures on folios 163, 392, 406, 421, 506v, 520v were created in the artistic circle of the Maximilian Master, but it is difficult to assess precisely who painted them.

6. Perhaps still other illuminators created the historiated borders and the calendar scenes. In light of the restricted format and the stereotypical character of the illumination, however, it is difficult to sort out. In any case two to three hands appear in the calendar. The

Maximilian Master himself was perhaps responsible for the landscape settings for January (ill. 92g), February, March, April, November, and December; they are clearly by a different hand from the other months. For reproductions, see Gaspar 1932; Dekeyzer and De Laet 1997; and Nieuwdorp and Dekeyzer 1997.

7. The miniatures attributed to Gerard David—*The Trinity* (only God the Father; ill. 92a); *The Last Supper* (only Judas; fol. 331v); *The Visitation* (ill. 92c); and *Saint Catherine* (ill. 92b)—form a greater unity with those of the Maximilian Master than with those of the Master of James IV.

8. For the attributions, see Gaspar 1932: 76; and Winkler 1943: 60, n. 5. *The Miracle of Saint Anthony of Padua* was possibly executed in the workshop of the Master of James IV. On the one hand, the style of border decoration on this leaf, characteristic of the inserted miniatures

92d
MASTER OF JAMES IV
OF SCOTLAND
*The Martyrdom of
Ten Thousand*, fol. 596v

92e

MASTER OF JAMES IV
OF SCOTLAND
Our Lady of the Snow,
fol. 501v

of the Master of James IV, makes such an attribution plausible. On the other hand, the miniature itself does not exhibit the painterly style of the Master of James IV, perhaps because in copying a pattern more common to the workshop of the Maximilian Master, he showed greater restraint in his brushwork.

9. See the summary of the literature in De Coo 1978: 168–74.

10. Only partially explained in Goehring 2000: 167.

11. Compare the borders in the Glasgow Breviary of 1494 (cat. no. 89).

12. See the essay by Thomas Kren and Maryan W. Ainsworth, "Illuminators and Painters: Artistic Exchanges and Interrelationships" (this volume).

13. De Figueiredo 1931: 16; taken over and argued further in Gaspar 1932: 77; De Coo 1978: 170–71; and Dekeyzer, in Smeyers and Van der Stock 1996: 55–57.

14. An entry for the feast day of Saint Louis of France, a royal saint especially esteemed by Franciscans, would have been pertinent to the Portuguese king, but it too is lacking.

15. See also the Breviary of Eleanor of Portugal (cat. no. 90) and the Grimani Breviary (cat. no. 126).

16. From the moment of the volume's initial binding, however, the book formed a coherent whole. See Watteeuw 2002: 1610–13.

17. After folio 400v the layout of the small miniatures was altered, without apparent reason. Visually the Proper of Saints falls, although not obviously, into two parts. The change is indicated by the appearance of a new copyist and a new illuminator for the decorated initials.

18. Moreover, the prayer in honor of Saint Felix and his brother appears in the Proper of Saints for the month of December, while the feast day, according to the calendar—and this is more the custom—falls on January 14.

19. In the same years Portuguese patrons acquired other lavish Flemish breviaries (e.g., cat. no. 90).

20. *David Wrestling with the Lion, Jesse Presents His Sons to Samuel, Samuel Anoints David, David Brings His Brothers to Eat, David Battles Goliath and Returns Triumphant to Jerusalem.*

21. See New York 1995: 56–59, 66–67, nos. 7–9, 13–14.

92f
MASTER OF THE
FIRST PRAYER BOOK
OF MAXIMILIAN
The Annunciation,
fol. 427v

92g
MASTER OF THE
FIRST PRAYER BOOK
OF MAXIMILIAN (?)
AND ANOTHER
ILLUMINATOR
January, fol. 1v

92h
ANONYMOUS
Saint Michael, fol. 552v

92i
ANONYMOUS
The Birth of the Virgin,
fol. 536v

SIMON MARMION (C)
For biography, see part 1

93

SIMON MARMION, MASTER OF THE DRESDEN
PRAYER BOOK, MASTER OF THE FIRST PRAYER
BOOK OF MAXIMILIAN AND WORKSHOP, AND
MASTER OF THE PRAYER BOOKS OF AROUND 1500

La Flora (Book of Hours)
Valenciennes, before 1489; Bruges and probably Ghent, before 1498

MANUSCRIPT: 368 folios; 20.4 × 13.4 cm (8¹/₁₆ × 5¼ in.); justification:
8 × 6 cm (3⅛ × 2⅜ in.); 17 lines of *gotica rotunda*; 36 full-page
miniatures, 28 half-page miniatures, 30 small miniatures, 24 bas-de-
page calendar miniatures, 6 historiated borders, 3 historiated initials,
1 full-page coat of arms added by 1498

HERALDRY: Full-page escutcheon with the arms of Charles VIII
surmounted with crown in gilt medallion surmounted by his initial
K crowned, fol. 2v

BINDING: Probably workshop of Angelo Trani, Naples, late
eighteenth or early nineteenth century; gold-tooled green morocco;
the arms of Ferdinand I, king of the Two Sicilies (1751–1825)

COLLECTION: Naples, Biblioteca Nazionale di Napoli, Ms.I.B.51

PROVENANCE: Charles VIII, king of France (1470–1498); Isabella
Farnese (1694–1766); to her son Charles III, king of Spain and (as
Charles VII) king of Naples (1716–1788); to Biblioteca Reale in 1736

JPGM and RA

The innovative character, variety in format, and iconography of its illumination and the complexities of
its codicology make this manuscript, known as La Flora,
among the most important and challenging of its day. It has
an unusual devotional program with images fitting the
devotions in some places only awkwardly, apparently the
result of an endeavor to incorporate a preexisting cycle of
miniatures. The program includes four major pictorial
sequences, one each illustrating the Hours of the Passion
(fols. 21v–58v), the Hours of the Virgin (fols. 81v–149v), a
sequence of masses (fols. 247–306v), and twenty-six suffrages (fols. 318v–342v). The Hours of the Passion illustrates
the Christological narrative from Christ Washing the Feet
of the Disciples to the Entombment, while the Hours of the
Virgin treats the Infancy cycle from the Annunciation to
the Massacre of the Innocents, with an exception that is
noted below. Both cycles feature full-page miniatures on
the left side of the opening opposite half-page miniatures
(e.g. ill. 93a).[1] In the Passion cycle these scenes constitute a
continuous narrative. In the Hours of the Virgin every
other half-page miniature has a typological connection to
the full-page Infancy scene opposite, while the remainder
continue the Infancy story.

The sequence of seven masses is an idiosyncratic section in particular for the special treatment given to the
Mass for Palm Sunday and the Gospel and Epistle readings
for Lent that follow it (fols. 269–302). These texts feature no fewer than three full-page miniatures, five half- or

quarter-page miniatures, and two historiated borders.
These texts, while connected to the Lenten celebration, are
an odd assortment,[2] and the subjects of their full-page
miniatures: *Christ and the Samaritan Woman* (ill. 93b), *The
Trial of Susanna* (fol. 289v), and *The Supper at Emmaus* (fol.
295v) are also uncommon. They rarely appear in books of
hours. The rest of the masses follow the program of other
cycles, featuring full-page miniatures (with two exceptions)
opposite half-page miniatures, yet several of the large
miniatures are out of place.[3]

The sequence of suffrages features five full-page miniatures and twenty quarter-page miniatures. (The suffrage
for Saint Michael lacks a miniature.) It includes two suffrages for Saint Barbara and two for Saint Catherine; a
quarter-page miniature illustrates the first of each, while a
full-page miniature illustrates the second. Other miniatures, such as *The Last Judgment* (at Compline of the Hours
of the Virgin, fol. 143v) within the cycle of the Life of the
Virgin, are eccentrically situated. Thus both the devotional
contents and the iconographic program of La Flora have a
number of odd features.

La Flora features illumination by Simon Marmion, the
Master of the Dresden Prayer Book, the Master of the First
Prayer Book of Maximilian, and the Master of the Prayer
Books of around 1500. These artists did not work on this
manuscript at the same time; the present manuscript has a
character of being pieced together, the product of distinct
campaigns of illumination. For example, all of Marmion's
twenty-two full-page miniatures and five others by the
Maximilian Master were trimmed close to the edge of the
image so that, if they had had decorated borders originally,
these were trimmed away.[4] Each miniature was then
mounted within a four-sided parchment support, the outer
dimensions of which fit those of the current codex. Then
architectural borders were added to each one. Evidently
these miniatures, a total of twenty-seven of La Flora's
thirty-six full-page miniatures, were either recycled from
another manuscript or their presentation was rethought at
an advanced stage in their execution.

The suite of full-page miniatures by Simon Marmion is
the earliest illumination contained in the manuscript. It
constitutes his most distinctive illumination and arguably
his greatest achievement (ills. 93a, b). The miniatures represent a pinnacle in the development of the half-length
composition, which offers a more direct and intimate relationship between subject and beholder than conventional
full-length depictions. Such an image is referred to as a
dramatic close-up.[5] The half-length format is one of the
key innovations in Flemish art of the second half of the
fifteenth century, spurred by the explorations of painters
such as Dieric Bouts and Hugo van der Goes (see cat. no.

93a
SIMON MARMION
The Annunciation to
the Shepherds and
MASTER OF
THE DRESDEN
PRAYER BOOK
The Adoration of the
Shepherds, fols. 120v–121

31). *The Annunciation to the Shepherds* (ill. 93a) epitomizes the expressive half-length. Two shepherds, seen from behind, stand in the immediate foreground up against the frame. The viewer peers over their shoulders to observe the annunciate angel in the sky as they do. *The Death of the Virgin* (fol. 150v) achieves its emotional power from the tightly packed, grief-filled faces of the apostles at the Virgin's bedside. The artist achieves an uncommonly tactile effect in tempera; he uses the thick texture of the fabrics behind the bed to press the figures discreetly toward us.[6] The contrasts among the flesh tones—from the Virgin's deathly pallor, to John's youthful vibrancy, to the darker coloring of the older men—heighten the figures' physical presence.

Eighteen of the miniatures by Marmion are dramatic close-ups (ills. 93a, b). Although he had used the format previously in his work (see cat. nos. 33, 45), this is his most wide-ranging and masterful treatment of it. The miniatures include eight events from the life of the Virgin, from the Annunciation to her death. Many of the other subjects are also typical for books of hours: the Penitent David, the Raising of Lazarus, Pentecost, the Ascension of Christ, the Last Judgment, and scenes from the lives of particular saints.

Yet, as noted earlier, some subjects are much less common in books of hours, especially as full-page miniatures: Christ and the Samaritan Woman, the Supper at Emmaus, *Noli me tangere*, and the Trial of Susanna. Two half-length miniatures by Marmion originally belonged to this series but ended up in a different devotional book altogether (cat. no. 90, fols. 117v, 230). They also represent less common subjects for a book of hours: the Sacrifice of Isaac and Christ Taking Leave of His Mother.[7] The extent of Marmion's series, totaling twenty-four miniatures; its innovative quality; and the unusual, specific character of some of its subject matter make it one of his most distinctive. It was almost certainly intended for a book of hours made for a high-ranking patron whose particular devotional requirements are reflected in the cycle's singular iconography.[8] Marmion died in 1489, and the present codex was likely put together later, ultimately for someone else.

After Marmion's work, the illuminations by the Master of the Dresden Prayer Book are the most sophisticated (ills. 93a, b). This artist painted the half-page miniatures in the Gospel sequences, several half-page miniatures in the Hours of the Virgin, and the quarter-page suffrages, along

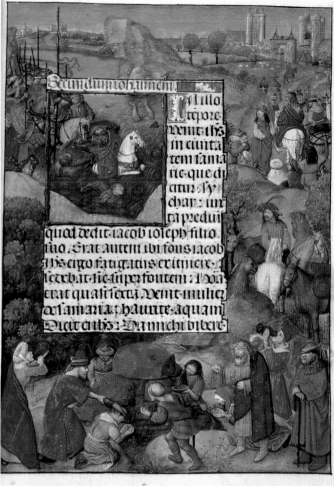

93b

SIMON MARMION
*Christ and the
Samaritan Woman* and
MASTER OF
THE DRESDEN
PRAYER BOOK
*The Crossing of the Red
Sea*, border, fols.
284v–285

with four historiated borders in the sequence of masses (fols. 247, 263, 290, and ill. 93b), which are among his most original illuminations.[9] They brilliantly integrate related narrative events, usually in a single elaborate outdoor setting, seamlessly joining miniature and border.

The Master of the First Prayer Book of Maximilian and his workshop illuminated most of the rest of the book, including the Hours of the Passion, many of the half-page miniatures in the Hours of the Virgin, and several full-page miniatures in the suffrages. The finest miniatures and those most likely by the master himself are a small group of full-page miniatures that meticulously copy well-known models: *Christ Washing the Feet of the Disciples* (fol. 21v), *The Road to Calvary* (fol. 37v), *Saint Catherine of Alexandria* (fol. 339v), *Saint Barbara* (fol. 341v), probably *Saint Anthony Abbot* (fol. 322v), and some of the half-page miniatures in the Hours of the Virgin. They rank among the miniaturist's best work. He also may have painted the full-page *Ecce Homo* (fol. 33v), a composition that is derived from several different patterns. Some full-page miniatures that are also pastiches, such as the curious *Betrayal of Christ* (fol. 28v),[10] are less finely painted and are perhaps by an artist in his workshop. Many of the half-page miniatures in the Passion

cycle are also by this artist. They show sloppy brushwork, internal discrepancies in scale, and stiff, inexpressive figures. A third artist working in the Maximilian Master's style painted the semi-monochrome miniatures of the full-page *Lamentation* (fol. 151), the half-page *Virgin and Child with Musical Angels* (fol. 151), *Christ's Entry into Jerusalem* (fol. 269), and others. The Prayer Books Master painted the twenty-four relatively modest bas-de-page miniatures of the calendar and a number of half-page miniatures in the Hours of the Virgin and one in the Hours of the Holy Spirit.[11] His miniatures have elaborate architectural frames in gold that are strongly reminiscent of those in the calendar.

Bodo Brinkmann has suggested that the Master of the Dresden Prayer Book, who illuminated only text pages in the book, began his work on La Flora as early as the 1480s, when Marmion was still alive.[12] He argued further that the Dresden Master abandoned it before the Maximilian Master took it up again, a decade or more later, and brought it to completion around 1500. Brinkmann shrewdly noted how the Maximilian Master replaced a page elaborately illuminated by the Dresden Master with a fresh page containing the same text and his own illumination.[13] According to Brinkmann, then, the Dresden Master and the Maximilian Master worked on the book in separate and successive campaigns. Did the Maximilian Master acquire both an unfinished book by the Dresden Master and the separate miniature cycle by Marmion and bring them together in order to complete the project? If so, then why did he execute some miniatures that also had to be adapted to the new format? It is more likely that the cycle was Marmion's last, from the end of his life, and that the Maximilian Master acquired it to complete it, only to adapt it to a different book project and subsequently to alter the style of the borders to suit changing tastes. According to this hypothesis, the Dresden Master would have been the Maximilian Master's collaborator on the project rather than being responsible for an earlier stage.[14]

Finally, Brinkmann doubted that the coat of arms could date from the lifetime of Charles VIII (r. 1483–98) because its thick, "perspectival" frame is in a Renaissance style.[15] Yet the identical style of frame, in a square rather than round format, is found around the miniatures of one of Charles's court artists, Jean Bourdichon, in a manuscript he executed shortly after the king's death in 1498.[16] Thus, even if Charles's armorials were painted over an earlier set, it is not difficult to imagine that they date from Charles's lifetime and that the manuscript thus once belonged to him. This makes it probable that they were added to the book by the time of his death, so that the book was completed by 1498, or even a few years earlier.

Finally, whatever the story behind the genesis of La Flora,[17] Marmion's pictorial cycle was influential, inspiring not only copies that are faithful even to peculiarities of color but also many imitations and adaptations. The copies and imitations appear most often in the art of the Master of the First Prayer Book of Maximilian and members of his workshop (see cat nos. 90, 105),[18] but also in miniatures by the Master of the Prayer Books of around 1500,[19] by the Master of the David Scenes (see cat no. 115), and even by Simon Bening.[20] For two decades after Marmion's death, they continued to be an important inspiration in Flemish manuscript illumination.   T. K.

Notes

1. Other devotions illustrated with both a full-page and a half-page miniature include the Hours of the Holy Spirit (fols. 67v–73v), the Mass of the Virgin (fols. 74v–80v), the Advent Office (fols. 150v–158v), the Stabat Mater (fols. 166–167v), Penitential Psalms (fols. 169–187v), Office of the Dead (fols. 189–227v), Psalter of Saint Jerome (fols. 230v–245v), and the Saint Gregory prayer ("O Domine adoro te in cruce . . . "; fols. 307v–311v). The Hours of the Cross are illustrated by a full-page miniature, facing historiated border, and quarter-page miniature. The following are illustrated by half-page or quarter-page illuminations only: "Obsecro te," "O Intemerata," the verses of Saint Bernard, the Seven Words of Christ on the Cross, and the prayer of Saint Thomas Aquinas ("Concede michi misericors . . . ").

2. The three readings are the Gospel reading for the third week of Lent (John 4: 5–42), the Epistle reading for Saturday after the third Sunday in Lent (Daniel 13), and the Gospel reading for Monday after Easter (Luke 24: 13–53). The same texts also appear in the above-mentioned Munich Hours, but in a wholly different arrangement and with more modest decoration, especially within the context of the book as a whole (see cat no. 90, n.3). The last text in the La Flora group deals with the raising of Lazarus, but its illustration deals with the meal

afterward. *The Raising of Lazarus*, also by Marmion, appears elsewhere in the book, at the Office of the Dead (fol. 188v), which is typical for a Flemish manuscript of this period. Thanks to Susan L'Engle for her research on the section of the Masses in La Flora.

3. Notably *The Ascension* (fol. 253v) and *The Virgin and Child and All Saints: The Church Militant* (fol. 262v).

4. The five miniatures by the Maximilian Master are *Christ Washing the Feet of the Disciples* (fol. 21v), *The Betrayal of Christ* (fol. 28v), *Christ Nailed to the Cross* (fol. 41v), *The Deposition* (fol. 44v), and *The Crucifixion* (fol. 59v).

5. On the dramatic close-up, see Ringbom 1984: 193–210.

6. Uncharacteristically for the tempera technique, Marmion here built up chalky layers of pigment to give his textiles this more tactile character. See also the bodice of Elizabeth in *The Visitation* (fol. 103v).

7. On their improvised placement in the manuscript, see under cat. no. 90, which is now in the Bayerische Staatsbibliothek, Munich. Two miniatures by the Maximilian Master in the Munich book, *The Raising of Lazarus* (fol. 140v) and *David in Prayer* (fol. 328v), also are set into four-sided parchment supports. Their place in the original series is difficult to account for since Marmion had already treated both of these subjects in the series.

8. That the patron may have been female is suggested by the prominent miniature devoted to Susanna, a relatively uncommon subject that, as König (1998a: 105–6) has shown, held particular importance for female patrons. A copy of this miniature figures prominently in the Hours of Isabella of Castile. For a fuller discussion, see under cat. no. 105.

9. They include *Daniel and the Punishment of the Elders* (fol. 290); *The Emperor Augustus and the Tiburtine Sibyl, Moses and the Burning Bush,* and *Gideon and the Golden Fleece* (fol. 263); *Moses Striking Water from the Rock* and *The Crossing of the Red Sea* (ill. 93b); and Passion scenes from *The Resurrection* (fol. 247).

10. In this miniature the soldier at the left is copied, down to the details of costume, from the soldier at the left in *The Martyrdom of Saint Thomas Becket* in the London Hastings Hours (cat. no. 41), while the figure with arms raised at the left in *Ecce Homo* is derived from *The Martyrdom of Saint Catherine* in the Voustre Demeure Hours (cat. no. 20).

11. The calendar pages have an elaborate architectural framework that fills the upper two-thirds of the page behind the text block and frames the miniature itself within a wide arch. This format anticipates that of the calendar in the Munich Hours (cat. no. 90), which is more finely proportioned.

12. Brinkmann (1997: 209–10) does not indicate that the Marmion miniatures were necessarily intended originally to go with the book begun by the Dresden Master, so that his conception of the book's genesis is especially complex. His analysis includes a theory (to which I do not subscribe) that the Master of the David Scenes in the Grimani Breviary painted some of the book's decorative borders (see Brinkmann 1997: 201–13).

13. The Dresden Master's leaf is now folio 51 in a book of hours in Poitiers dated 1510 (Bibliothèque municipale, Ms. 57/269; Brinkmann 1997: color pl. 38).

14. Brinkmann's argument is predicated on a hypothetical chronology for the Dresden Master's peregrinations during the 1490s that would remove him from the artistic milieu of the Maximilian Master then. Neither the argument in favor of the former artist's displacement from Bruges, however, nor the notion that he might not continue to work with his Ghent and Bruges associates seems a certainty (see Brinkmann 1997: 209–11, 245–60).

15. Brinkmann 1997: 202.

16. The so-called Hours of Henry VII (London, British Library, Ms. Royal 2 D XL and Add. Ms. 35254, fols. T, U, V; and various private collections) was probably begun for Charles's successor, Louis XII, at the time of the latter's succession (Malibu 1983a: 136–38, no. 21; Paris 1993: 294–96, no. 162).

17. Winkler (1925: 189) believed that the cycle by Marmion was removed from another book. Brinkmann (1997: 206) doubted this.

18. Another example from the workshop of the Maximilian Master is the Hours of Louis Quarré (Oxford, Bodleian Library, Ms. Douce 311; Oxford 1984: 171).

19. Examples include the Hours of Jean de Noval and Jeanne Meyngart (art market: Les Enluminures 1997: 66–69, no. 14), which is dated 1499; the Vienna-Poitiers Hours (Vienna, Österreichische Nationalbibliothek, Ms. 1887, and Poitiers, Bibliothèque municipale, Ms. 57/269; see under cat. no. 138), which is dated 1510, and perhaps the Croÿ-Arenberg Hours (collection of the dukes of Arenberg; Saint Petersburg 1996: 130–33, no. 7), probably from the early sixteenth century.

20. Examples include *The Adoration of the Magi* and *The Presentation in the Temple* in the Stein quadriptych (cat. no. 146).

94

FOLLOWER OF SIMON MARMION AND MASTER OF ANTOINE ROLIN

Book of Hours
Use undetermined
Mons, 1490s (before 1497?)

MANUSCRIPT: i + 116 folios, 17.1 × 11.8 cm (6¾ × 4⅝ in.); justification: 8.7 × 5.9 cm (3⁷⁄₁₆ × 2⁵⁄₁₆ in.); 15 lines of *bastarda*; 12 full-page miniatures

HERALDRY: Escutcheon with unidentified coat of arms, argent a cross sable, in the first quarter a crown or, in the fourth quarter, a hammer sable, fols. 23, 67, possibly added or modified; initials *AM*, fols. 14, 19, 72

INSCRIPTIONS: *Che livre appartient / Wilh' Godefroy escheuin de liege*, fol. 52

BINDING: Flemish, late fifteenth or early sixteenth century; blind-tooled brown calf; rebacked

COLLECTION: Baltimore, Walters Art Museum, Ms. W.194

PROVENANCE: Antoine Rolin (ca. 1424–1497) and Marie d'Ailly (d. 1498), Mons (?); Wilhelmus Godefroy, Liège, and his heir; [Léon Gruel, Paris]; to Henry Walters (1848–1931) between 1895 and 1931

JPGM

This book of hours features a particularly fine cycle of eleven miniatures—some in color, others in grisaille—by the Master of Antoine Rolin.[1] As is typical for this artist, many of his compositions are derived from miniatures by Simon Marmion and show a preoccupation with architecture that frames a narrative or a vista. Like a few of the latter's books, the manuscript lacks decorated borders, a relatively uncommon feature in Flemish manuscript illumination of this time. Nevertheless, the book's most original and beautiful miniature, the half-length *Saint Anthony Abbot* (ill. 94), is probably by another follower of Marmion. The standing hermit looks out at the viewer, his head tilted thoughtfully, his eyelids heavy and sad, his large hands firmly grasping his prayer book. His book projects over the ledge into our space, heightening the unusual immediacy of the viewer's encounter with this pious figure. The miniature may be a subtle rethinking of the popular pattern for the full-length figure of this saint seen in the work of the Master of the First Prayer Book of Maximilian (see cat. no. 93, fol. 322v).[2] The draping of part of the mantle back over the shoulder is similar to the pattern, though treated in a more crinkly fashion, a bit more in the manner

one finds in the illuminations of the Master of Antoine Rolin. Still more striking, the expressive tilt of the head and the muted character of the violet and brown are reminiscent of the illuminations of Marmion, with whom some scholars have associated this miniature.[3]

The manuscript was no doubt made for a man named Antoine. It features a suffrage to Saint Anthony in rhymed couplets, one of two suffrages to the saint, and it is the only one of the sixteen suffrages that is illustrated.[4] The verse suffrage appears to have been inserted, perhaps while the book was still in production.[5] As the first in the sequence, it precedes even the suffrage to Saint John the Baptist. Further, the initials *A* and *M* appear *en lac* in several of the book's decorated initials, the first initial presumably referring to Antoine too. The pair of initials and their form recall the form of joined initials employed by Antoine Rolin (ca. 1424–1497), after whom the illuminator was named, and his spouse, Marie d'Ailly.[6] Antoine, son of the former Burgundian chancellor Nicolas Rolin and *grand bailli* of Hainaut, and Marie, the daughter of Raoul d'Ailly, the vidame of Amiens, also commissioned several major secular works from the Master of Antoine Rolin (see cat. no. 123).[7] They would appear to be logical patrons for this book, yet the book's calendar points strongly to the diocese of Liège, while the Rolins were more closely associated with Hainaut.[8]

T. K.

94
FOLLOWER OF
SIMON MARMION
Saint Anthony Abbot,
fol. 102v

Notes

1. Legaré (1999a: 450) first attributed the miniatures to the Master of Antoine Rolin. The miniatures illustrate the Hours of the Virgin, the Hours of the Cross, the Hours of the Holy Spirit, and the Penitential Psalms. See biography of the artist (this part).

2. In the miniature in La Flora (cat. no. 93, fol. 322v), even the colors are the same; see De Maio 1992: 188.

3. Randall 1997: 385–87; Legaré 1999: 450. The figure's pose is not unlike that of the knight Tondal in the frontispiece of the Getty manuscript (ill. 14a), and the expressive tilt of the head is echoed in one of the onlookers in the frontispiece to the Guy de Thurno manuscript (ill. 13). Still, Marmion rarely invited such direct contact with his protagonists as in the Walters *Saint Anthony*. The physical type with the wide gray beard is closer to the Master of Antoine Rolin, although the latter's characterizations are not as psychologically acute. Nevertheless, even the black cap is a type found often in the latter's work (cf., e.g., Legaré 1991a: 23, 25, 69, 71).

4. The only other devotion that is in verse is the Stabat Mater (fols. 97v–99v).

5. It is on a bifolio, though the format of the miniature fits perfectly with the rest of the book (Randall 1997: 383).

6. For example, they appear in a similar form in *Le Livre des échecs amoureux* (Paris, Bibliothèque nationale de France, Ms. fr. 9197; Legaré 1991: 19, 25, and so on).

7. See the biography of the artist, later in this part.

8. The Liège link is underscored by an early handwritten ex libris (fol. 52) and other notes from a Liège family (fol. i), apparently from the early sixteenth century (Randall 1997: 387).

MASTER OF EDWARD IV (B)
For biography, see part 3

95

MASTER OF EDWARD IV

**Thomas à Kempis, *De imitatione Christi*, books 1–4;
Jean Gerson, *De meditatione cordis***
Bruges, ca. 1481–90

MANUSCRIPT: i + 196 + i folios, 25.1 × 17.5 cm (9⅞ × 6⅞ in.); justification: 15 × 10.3 cm (5⅞ × 4 in.); 21 lines of *bastarda*; 4 half- to three-quarter-page miniatures

HERALDRY: Escutcheon with the arms of Lannoy-Molembaix encircled by collar of the Order of the Golden Fleece, fol. 9; *Otez Lannoy*, fol. 45v

BINDING: Early eighteenth century (before 1720); gold-tooled red morocco over pasteboard

COLLECTION: Vienna, Österreichische Nationalbibliothek, Ms. 1576

PROVENANCE: Baudouin II de Lannoy, lord of Molembaix (d. 1501); Françoise de Barbançon, second wife of Philippe de Lannoy, lord of Molembaix (d. 1543); Georg Willem von Hohendorf [his sale catalogue, Abraham de Hondt, The Hague, 1720, lot 4 in the section; Mss in Quarto; sale did not take place]; purchased 1720 by the Hofbibliothek

R A

Among the more than seven hundred manuscripts that preserve the uniquely influential text known as *De imitatione Christi*,[1] the present manuscript is unusual in its inclusion of four illustrations (most manuscripts of this text have none). These illustrations mark the beginning of each of the four main components of the work.[2] Three of these miniatures illustrate the devotional practices advocated by the last three components of the text.[3] Illustrating the section on how to achieve inner consolation, a well-dressed layperson kneels at prayer within a private chapel, before an open prayer book and a painting of the Crucifixion. At the beginning of the next section, on inner conversation with Christ, the same layperson, kneeling at prayer, has a vision of the wounded Christ (ill. 95). The final miniature illustrates the section on Communion, with the kneeling layperson having the wafer brought directly to him by two angels and Christ himself. Most notably, in each of these miniatures no priest is present, and the layperson is male.

The present manuscript formed part of a collection made for Baudouin II de Lannoy, lord of Molembaix, who under Maximilian became principal maître d'hôtel, knight of the Order of the Golden Fleece (in 1481), and one of his most trusted captains in Hainaut. This collection is distinctive in that it comprises devotional texts by Jean Gerson, Matthew of Kraków, and Jan van Eeckoute.[4] Like the present manuscript, several of these volumes were illuminated by the Master of Edward IV. At least one was also written out by the same scribe and had its initials illuminated by the same hand as in the present manuscript.[5] The Master of Edward IV collaborated again with this scribe and initial

artist in the Blackburn Hours (cat. no. 98), a fragmentary psalter (New York, private collection), a *Vie du Christ* (cat. no. 96), and a World Chronicle (Saint Petersburg, Russian National Library, Ms. Fr.F.v.IV.12). All the illustrations in these manuscripts present their Christian iconography with an immediacy that matches the devotional advice of the text of the present manuscript. Several were produced for Hainaut patrons.   S. McK.

Notes

1. See Delaissé 1956: 87–109. The opening rubric of the present manuscript identifies Thomas à Kempis as the author, and the opening miniature depicts the author as an Augustinian canon.

2. These components appear in a different order in different manuscripts. In the present manuscript the order (employing Delaissé's numbering, based on Thomas à Kempis's autograph manuscript) is I, II, IV, III—one of the most common orders in surviving manuscripts (Delaissé 1956: 92).

3. The opening miniature, which marks the beginning of the whole work, rather than illustrating the first section, merely depicts Thomas à Kempis in his study.

4. These manuscripts include Valenciennes, Bibliothèque municipale, Mss. 209, 210, 230, 240, 243, and Paris, Bibliothèque de l'Arsenal, Mss. 5205, 5206 (see cat. no. 97).

5. Valenciennes, Bibliothèque municipale, Ms. 243 (dated 1492).

95
MASTER OF
EDWARD IV
A Vision of Christ, fol. 150

96

MASTER OF EDWARD IV AND ASSISTANT

Ludolph of Saxony, *Vie du Christ*, translation by Guillaume Le Menand of *Vita Christi*, volumes 1 and 3
Bruges, after 1487

Vie du Christ, volume 1

MANUSCRIPT: ii + A–H + 290 + ii folios, 44.5 × 31.5 cm (17½ × 12⁷⁄₁₆ in.); justification: 30 × 19.6 cm (11¹³⁄₁₆ × 7¹¹⁄₁₆ in.); 38 lines of *bastarda* in two columns; 32 two-column miniatures, 5 one-column miniatures, 1 historiated border

HERALDRY: Escutcheon with the arms of Oettingen of Swabia, surmounted by helm, crest, and mantling, fol. 4; motto *Ou que je soye*, fols. 1, 17v, 31, 77

BINDING: Paris, mid-eighteenth century; red morocco, gilt

COLLECTION: Paris, Bibliothèque nationale de France, Ms. fr. 20096

PROVENANCE: John II, lord of Oettingen and Flobecq (d. 1514); Louis-César de La Baume Le Blanc, duc de La Vallière (1708–1780) [his sale, De Bure, Paris, January 12–May 5, 1784, lot 146, as part of imperfect set of two volumes]; purchased for the Bibliothèque du Roi

R A

Vie du Christ, volume 3

MANUSCRIPT: 249 folios, 46.8 × 33.8 cm (18½ × 13⅜ in.); justification: 28.5 × 19.6 cm (11¼ × 7¾ in.); 38 lines of *bastarda* in two columns; 47 two-column miniatures, 3 one-column miniatures

HERALDRY: Escutcheon with the arms of Oettingen of Swabia surmounted by helm, crest of hound's head, and mantling; linked initials *JY* and monogram *IH*; motto *Ou que je soye*, all fol. 9

BINDING: New York, mid-twentieth century; blind-tooled brown morocco over wood boards

COLLECTION: New York, The Morgan Library, Ms. M.894

PROVENANCE: John II, lord of Oettingen and Flobecq (d. 1514); Peeter Stoffelt, Zeeland, 1638 (?) (signed fol. 236v);[1] Jan Baptista Verdussen III (1698–1773), Antwerp [his sale, Antwerp, July 15, 1776, 4, lot 29]; to Jan Desroches, Brussels [his sale, December 1788, lot 46]; private collection (John Thomas Simes?), London, by 1831; Nathaniel Phillips Simes [his sale, Sotheby's, London, July 9, 1886, lot 1647]; [Bernard Quaritch, *Catalogue 369*, 1886, no. 35692]; B. T. and Philander L. Cable, Rock Island [sale, Sotheby Parke Bernet, New York, November 11–12, 1942, lot 23]; [Harry A. Levinson, New York, *Catalogue 16*, 1943, no. 1]; gift of Mrs. Edgar S. Oppenheimer in memory of her husband, in 1960

J P G M

Together with a companion volume (Paris, Bibliothèque nationale de France, Ms. fr. 20097), the present two volumes preserve one of the longest campaigns of miniatures undertaken to illustrate the late medieval text that, in influence on devotional practice, was second only to *De imitatione Christi*. In so doing, they exemplify both the commitment of a wealthy lay patron to such a devotional text and the ability of Flemish miniaturists to respond to both its narrative and its devotional elements.

The text that the miniatures of the Paris and New York volumes illustrate is a French translation of the *Vita Christi* by the fourteenth-century Carthusian monk Ludolph of Saxony.[2] According to the preface in the Paris volume, this translation was compiled during the reign of Charles VIII of France (r. 1483–98); dedicated to John II, duke of Bourbon (1426–1488); and written by the observant friar Guillaume Le Menand.[3] As a faithful and full translation, this text

nombzent ne le premier ne   non plus acc que par la lou

96a

MASTER OF
EDWARD IV
The Transfiguration,
vol. 3, fol. 22

retains Ludolph's distinctive presentation in tandem with New Testament exegesis and devotional advice. As in Ludolph's Latin text, each episode from the life of Christ is first narrated and explained by reference to Church authorities and then presented as a focus for personal devotion.

An earlier French version of the *Vita Christi* attributed to Jean Mansel attests to the interest in Ludolph's work among the laity during the fifteenth century.[4] The translation contained in the present volumes was printed at Lyons in 1487,[5] very soon after its date of composition, and was quickly reprinted at Lyons in 1494.[6] Manuscripts of this translation are, however, rare. Each of these volumes appears to reflect a preference for deluxe manuscript copies on the part of the grandest of patrons. Like the Paris–New York copy of the translation ascribed to Le Menand, two further copies—one made for Charles VIII of France and the other for Philippa of Guelders, the second wife of René II, duke of Lorraine[7]—are manuscripts of the highest quality and include extensive campaigns of illustration. By way of a compromise, Philip of Cleves acquired a deluxe copy of the 1494 Lyons edition of Le Menand's text, printed on parchment and richly illuminated.[8]

The Master of Edward IV, together with at least one assistant,[9] painted all the miniatures in the Paris–New York

volumes. These miniatures, which generally occupy half of the text block and mark the beginning of a chapter,[10] include a detailed, synoptic narrative of the life of Christ from the birth of his mother to his entry into Jerusalem before the Passion. (The missing fourth volume would have continued this narrative through the Passion and concluded with his descent into Hell.)[11] In addition to this narrative sequence, many miniatures illustrate the subjects of Christ's sermons, most notably his many parables. For these miniatures, the Master of Edward IV created some of his most inventive and original compositions.[12] In both sequences he repeatedly inserts men and women dressed in contemporary fashion as onlookers to events in Christ's life or as part of the audience to Christ's words.[13] These figures are intended to draw contemporary viewers directly into the life and teachings of Christ and to facilitate an experience of these in the manner recommended by Ludolph.

Further illustrations draw out devotional and exegetical strands of the *Vie du Christ*. At the beginning of the Paris volume, the miniaturist illustrated the prefaces of Le Menand and Ludolph with two imposing miniatures (fols. 1, 4). Whereas the first is a conventional presentation miniature,[14] the second includes not only an author portrait of Ludolph but also a programmatic illustration of

male nobles engaged in personal devotion. Within the marginal decoration, which is clearly distinguished by the miniaturist from the worldly space of Ludolph and the nobles by the use of a very restricted range of colors, is the subject of these devotions—a vision of Christ lifted from the tomb by an angel and surrounded by others bearing the instruments of the Passion. Shortly after this page, in the Paris volume, a miniature illustrates a complex passage of exegesis said to be derived from Saint Bernard's sermon on the Annunciation. This miniature (ill. 96b) shows a debate before God between female personifications of, on the one hand, Pity and Peace and, on the other, Truth and Justice. The subject of their debate is whether God should intervene to save man after the Fall, as recommended by Pity and Peace, and the eventual outcome is Christ's Incarnation, Passion, and Resurrection, as subsequently narrated by Ludolph. The miniature of the Transfiguration in the New York volume (ill. 96a), by contrast, illustrates part of the main narrative sequence. Most prominent within this miniature is the yellow flesh of Christ, which is intended to represent the miraculous light on Mount Tabor.

Given that the translation was done in France, probably Lyons, and that no other south Netherlandish copy of his

text has survived, some consideration needs to be given to the circumstances that gave rise to the Paris–New York volumes. In the first place, an initial examination of their texts suggests that they had as their exemplar not a manuscript, but the 1487 Lyons printed edition.[15] Although this printed edition would have been more readily available in the Low Countries than a manuscript, the copying of this text seems likely to have been prompted by an informed patron rather than as a result of enterprise on the part of a bookseller.[16]

Since the text of the Lyons edition was copied unrevised into the Paris–New York volumes, these volumes cannot date from before 1487.[17] The only borders in the Paris–New York volumes (Bibliothèque nationale, Ms. fr. 20096, fol. 4, and Morgan Library, Ms. M.894, fol. 9) are consistent with this dating. Their contrasting styles indicate that the Paris–New York set was compiled during the period in which strewn-flower borders were replacing other types of borders as the standard form in manuscripts of such vernacular texts. This transition occurred sometime in the second half of the 1480s.

The principal heraldic decoration of the Paris–New York *Vie du Christ* indicates that the volumes were made for

John II of Oettingen (d. 1514) after his marriage in 1483 to Isabelle de la Hamaide.[18] As revealed by his ownership of at least four manuscripts of secular vernacular texts produced in the last two decades of the fifteenth century, John was a bibliophile of some note.[19] His residence in Hainaut during this period doubtless provided the opportunity and stimulus for the patronage of books. The Paris–New York volumes also suggest an engagement with contemporary devotional practice.[20]

S. McK.

Notes

1. A note by the same owner, Peeter Stoffelt, signed *P. S. 1630*, appears in Geneva, Bibliothèque publique et universitaire, Ms. fr. 76, another manuscript made for John II of Oettingen.

2. On Ludolph and his *Vita Christi*, see Bodenstedt 1944.

3. According to Masami Okubo (1995), this translation was merely adopted by Le Menand for the printed edition of 1487 and was not his own work. Okubo also considers the dedication to be a promotional fiction. Le Menand falsely claimed to have revised for the 1488 Lyons printing the *Mirouer de la Redempcion de l'umain lignage* of Julien Macho. Thanks to Masami Okubo for help with Le Menand's text.

4. On translations of the *Vita Christi*, see Baier 1977: 160–64. One of the supposed French versions has now been identified as deriving from the *Meditationes Vitae Christi* attributed to Michael of Massa (Geith 1996: 237–49). For a version by Miélot, see cat. no. 97.

5. ISTC il00357600. Printed on July 7, 1487, by Mathias Huss and Jacques Buyer in two parts, with woodcut illustrations. A very rare edition.

6. ISTC il00358000. Printed on March 1, 1493/94, by Mathias Huss in two parts, with woodcut illustrations.

7. Respectively, Glasgow University Library, Mss. Hunter 36–39 (Toronto 1987: no. 60)—which preserves all four parts; and Lyons, Bibliothèque municipale, Ms. 5125, plus former Yates Thompson Ms. 39 (Paris 1993: no. 152)—which preserves only parts one and two.

8. Jena, Thüringer Universitäts- und Landesbibliothek, Mss. El. fols. 83, 84 (Korteweg 1998: 30–31, pl. 31).

9. A weaker hand working in the style of the Master of Edward IV from his patterns but employing a duller palette is discernible in Paris, Bibliothèque nationale de France, Ms. fr. 20096, fols. 13v, 21, 49v, 54v, 70, 177v, 182v, 188v, 196v, 199, 208, 214, 218v, 228, 267v; Ms. fr. 20097,

fols. 6, 17v. Several of these miniatures are the joint work of assistant and master.

10. Exceptions to this pattern are the one-column miniatures set within chapters in Paris, Bibliothèque nationale, Ms. fr. 20096, fols. 13v, 21, 70, 196v, 228; Morgan Library, Ms. M. 894, fols. 35v, 47v, 49v.

11. All previous critics have assumed that this fourth volume was in fact produced. There is, however, no evidence for its existence.

12. E.g., Morgan Library, Ms. M.894, fols. 210 (*The Faithful Awaiting the Second Coming*), 241v (*The Last Judgement Compared to the Separation of the Wheat*).

13. E.g., Paris, Bibliothèque nationale, Ms. fr. 20096, fols. 90, 174v; Ms. fr. 20097, fols. 6, 22, 86, 134v, 192, 197, 214, 218, 228, 294v. Grand contemporary costume is also used for those receiving bread and fish from Christ and those who abandon Christ (Paris, Bibliothèque nationale, Ms. fr. 20097, fols. 158, 180). At the center of the last miniature a grandly dressed figure hesitates as to whether to stay with or abandon Christ; the figure's body is turned away from Christ, but his head is turned toward him.

14. A later version by the Master of Edward IV occurs in John II of Oettingen's copy of the *Cyropédie*, Brussels, Bibliothèque royale, Ms. 11703, fol. 6.

15. Independently, Okubo (1995) reached the same conclusion. She has also demonstrated that the Glasgow and Lyons volumes are dependent, like Vérard's edition, on the 1494 Lyons edition.

16. For similar reasons an assistant of the Master of Edward IV, the Master of the Trivial Heads, illuminated another manuscript (The Hague, Koninklijke Bibliotheek, Ms. 133 A i), the text of which was copied from the 1486 Lyons edition of the *Vie des anciens pères* (Korteweg 1998: 29, 47, pl. 30). See also cat. no. 120.

17. For the same reason, their inclusion of the dedication to John II of Bourbon (d. 1488) does not restrict the dating to before 1488.

18. Lemaire 1993: 244–45. Lemaire's claim (p. 246) that the motto "Ou que je soye" is that of John II of Oettingen awaits independent confirmation. For the moment it is worth noting that while still count of Clermont, John II of Bourbon added to his copy of the *Divine Comedy* the inscription "Mais que je y soie, Clermont" (Surirey de Saint Remy 1944: 67 n. 5).

19. Lemaire 1993: 243–51.

20. John II also owned a profusely illustrated copy of the *Legende dorée* (Cambridge, Fitzwilliam Museum, Ms. 22). I am grateful to Anne-Marie Legaré for drawing this volume to my attention.

97

MASTER OF EDWARD IV

Jean Mansel, *Vie, passion, et vengeance de nostre seigneur Jhesu Christ*, volume 2; Jacob van Gruytrode, *Miroir de l'âme pécheresse*, translation by Jean Miélot of *Speculum aureum animae peccatricis*; and Saint Bonaventure, *Le Soliloque*, translation of *Soliloquium de quattuor mentalibus exercitiis*
Bruges, ca. 1486–93

MANUSCRIPT: i + 104 + i folios, 35.5 × 24.7 cm (14 × 9¼ in.); justification: 22.5 × 15–15.5 cm (8⅞ × 5⅞–6⅛ in.); 31 lines of *bastarda* by Thierion Anseau; 20 half-page miniatures, 1 historiated initial

BINDING: France, eighteenth century; yellow morocco, gilt; doublures of blue morocco, gilt

COLLECTION: Paris, Bibliothèque de l'Arsenal, Ms. 5206

PROVENANCE: Baudouin II de Lannoy, lord of Molembaix (d. 1501); Françoise de Barbançon, widow of Philippe de Lannoy, lord of Molembaix (d. 1543); to Jeanne de Hallewin, in 1559, the year of her marriage to Philippe de Croÿ, duke of Arschot (d. 1595); Charles de Croÿ, duke of Arschot (d. 1612), by 1584 [his sale, Brussels, 1613]; Charles-Adrien Picard, Paris, by 1772 [his sale, Mérigot, Paris, January 31, 1780, lot 55]; to Antoine-René de Voyer d'Argenson, marquess of Paulmy (1722–1787)

RA

One of the manuscripts illuminated by the Master of Edward IV for Baudouin II de Lannoy, this is a profusely illustrated life and Passion of Christ based on the *Vita Christi* of Ludolph of Saxony and is said to be compiled by Jean Mansel of Hesdin. The *Vie du Christ* is followed by two devotional texts, the first on the vanities of corporeal existence and the other on the nobility of the soul.[1] Whereas the Master of Edward IV painted only one miniature at the beginning of the first treatise by Jacob van Gruytrode, he produced four for the second treatise by Saint Bonaventure. These include an opening illustration (ill. 97) in which the miniaturist depicts, in a charming domestic setting, the mystery of the creation of the human soul. In contrast to most of the manuscripts illuminated by the Master of Edward IV, this volume had its text copied by a noncommercial scribe at the request of Lannoy.

In the attempt to reconstruct a *Vie du Christ* for which Willem Vrelant had painted fifty-five miniatures and was paid by Charles the Bold in 1469, critics have proposed that the present manuscript and its companion volume (see fig. 23) were copied after Vrelant's manuscript.[2] Another manuscript that includes the two devotional texts and was transcribed by David Aubert for Philip the Good (Valenciennes, Bibliothèque municipale, Ms. 240) has been identified by these critics as the concluding portion of Vrelant's manuscript. Together with the forty-five miniatures that illustrate the Arsenal *Vie*, the ten miniatures the Valenciennes manuscript preserves would indeed make up the number of miniatures recorded in 1469. The Valenciennes manuscript was copied by Aubert in 1462, however, seven years before Vrelant was paid for his miniatures (an uncommonly long time between the likely date of execution of the miniatures and the date of payment). Even more remarkable is that the five miniatures that illustrate the two

devotional texts in the Valenciennes correspond only in subject to those of the Arsenal manuscript.

Given the Master of Edward IV's early association with Vrelant, it seems more likely that the present manuscript is merely the former artist's version of a cycle of illustrations based on models he had acquired or copied from Vrelant. If Vrelant himself illustrated at least two copies of the *Vita*, one in 1462/63 and the other shortly before 1469, such models would certainly have been necessary. Further use by the Master of Edward IV of the models employed by Vrelant for the 1462 manuscript is attested to by five miniatures that accompany the same texts in another manuscript (Valenciennes, Bibliothèque municipale, Ms. 230). Previously, these miniatures were considered direct copies of those in Aubert's 1462 copy because they were made for Baudouin II de Lannoy, a known later owner of the 1462 manuscript. Closer comparison reveals, especially through his reversal of one of Vrelant's compositions,[3] that the Master of Edward IV probably produced his miniatures based on models, not on finished miniatures. The later Valenciennes manuscript (Ms. 230) appears to have been a supplement to the present manuscript.[4] It differs from the present volume, however, in that the hand responsible for copying the text was more obviously that of a commercial scribe. At present it is impossible to tell which was created first—the Arsenal or the Valenciennes portion of the manuscript.   S. McK.

Notes

1. These three texts are preserved together within the text of volume 4 of Jean Mansel's *Fleur des histoires* (Paris, Bibliothèque nationale, Ms. fr. 739, fols. 504–27). The two devotional texts are also preserved separately in Madrid, Biblioteca Nacional, Ms. Vit. 25-2, fols. 76–138 (dated 1462), and Valenciennes, Bibliothèque municipale, Ms. 240, fols. 211–72.

2. Lieberman 1970: 369–74 and Charron and Gil 1999: 90–95.

3. Compare the corresponding miniatures of the *Calling of Peter and Andrew* (Ms. 230, fol. 102; Ms. 240, fol. 419).

4. The outer measurements of Valenciennes Ms. 230 (37 × 24.5 cm [14⁹⁄₁₆ × 9⅝ in.]), as well as the number of lines to the page (thirty-two), are certainly comparable. The texts in the first half of the Valenciennes Ms. 230 combine with those of the Arsenal volume to replicate what were probably the original contents of Aubert's 1462 manuscript, of which the earlier Valenciennes Ms. 240 once formed the second part.

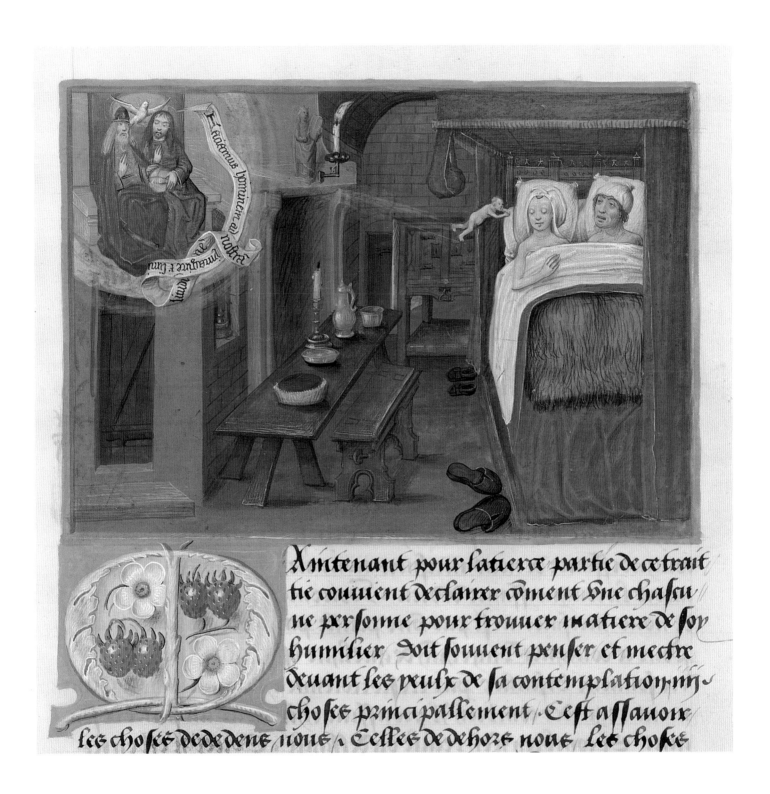

Amtenant pour la tierce partie de ce trait
tie conuient declairer coment hne chascu
ne personne pour trouuer matiere de soy
humilier Doit souuent penser et mectre
deuant les yeulx de sa contemplation iiij
choses principallement Cest assauoir
les choses dededens nous Celles de dehors nous Les chose

97
MASTER OF
EDWARD IV
*The Creation of the
Human Soul*, fol. 174

98

MASTER OF EDWARD IV

Book of Hours
Use of Rome
Bruges, ca. 1480–90

MANUSCRIPT: ii + 207 + i folios, 16 × 11.5 cm (6⅜ × 4½ in.);
justification: 9.2 × 6.2 cm (3⅝ × 2½ in.); 19 lines of *bastarda*;
5 full-page miniatures, 39 three-quarter-page miniatures,
13 historiated borders

BINDING: Flanders(?), late fifteenth century; blind-stamped calf over
wood boards

COLLECTION: Blackburn, Blackburn Museum and Art Gallery, Hart
Ms. 20884

PROVENANCE: Eugène de Noyelles, count of Marles and baron of
Rossignol, mid-seventeenth century; purchased by M. Duval from
secondhand clothes dealer at Saint Omer in 1801; Baron van Zuylen,
Liège [his sale, Sotheby's, London, March 21, 1929, lot 193]; [to Maggs
Bros., London]; to R. Edward Hart; to the City of Blackburn in 1946;
transferred from the Public Library in 1974

JPGM and RA

98a
MASTER OF
EDWARD IV
The Crucifixion and
*The Return of the Cross
by Heraclius*, fols. 33v–34

The Blackburn Hours is the book in which the Master of
Edward IV produced his most innovative campaign of
illustrations and illumination of the most consistently high
quality. Every element of its remarkably homogeneous
decoration appears to have been executed by his hand. The
subjects of numerous miniatures spill over into the accompanying borders, and the distinction between miniature
and border is repeatedly challenged.[1]

The devotional texts of the Blackburn Hours form a
fairly conventional sequence.[2] The placement and principal
subjects of the accompanying miniatures are for the most
part conventional.[3] What is innovative is the treatment of
these subjects. Most noteworthy are the five double-page
spreads at the openings of the Hours of the Cross, the
Hours of the Holy Spirit, the Penitential Psalms, the Office
of the Dead, and a prayer on the Annunciation.[4] In the first
of these double-page spreads (ill. 98a), the miniature on the
left-hand page has the Crucifixion as its subject. The upper
part of the cross breaks out of the miniature space at the top
of the page and thrusts the body of Christ toward the
viewer. In counterpoint to this, the lower marginal scene in
semi-grisaille of Christ carrying the cross overlaps the
frame and foreground of the miniature and spills out of the
border space toward the viewer.[5] Together with the upper

98b
MASTER OF
EDWARD IV
The Virgin and Child,
fol. 180v

border of strewn flowers, these features build up unsettling spatial uncertainties that work with the instability of many of the figures to enhance the impact of this central image of Christ's suffering and God's sacrifice on behalf on humankind. Further complexities and subtleties of meaning and artistic achievement are revealed in the facing right-hand page. Here the unusual miniature of the Emperor Heraclius returning the cross to Jerusalem is distinguished from and marked as secondary to the facing full-color *Crucifixion* by its execution in semi-grisaille. *The Return of the Cross by Heraclius* is intended as an inspirational image of salvation that offsets the pain and degradation inflicted by men on God, as seen in the marginal scene of men playing dice for Christ's robe and on the facing page. This two-page spread is further unified by the inclusion of armed men from the procession preceding Christ carrying the cross in the left-hand margin of the right-hand page and by their rapt gaze upward toward the cross.

In the double-page opening to the Penitential Psalms, the miniature of the Last Judgment spills over the whole border. In the facing miniature, David's prayerful gaze is turned toward the figure of Christ within *The Last Judgment.* In the miniature facing the opening of the Office of the Dead, the resurrected Lazarus and his sister hover between

the viewer's space and that of the divine narrative. In the miniature facing the prayer to the Annunciation, angels crowning the Virgin, the Virgin's left sleeve, the Christ child, and the cushion on which he rests spill out of the window frame into the acanthus and flowers of the border (ill. 98b). A diminutive woman musician in the border adds to the spatial complexity and accentuates the arresting monumentality of the Virgin and Child.

The Blackburn Hours was probably produced in the 1480s; several other manuscripts illuminated by the Master of Edward IV around this time are very closely related to the Blackburn Hours in their script, subsidiary decoration, and miniatures.[6] Of these, the most closely related volume is the Vienna *De imitatione Christi* (cat. no. 95). Although the Blackburn Hours now bears no mark of its first owner,[7] the patronage of these contemporaneous manuscripts suggests that a likely patron was a member of the Hainaut elite.[8] Nothing in the Blackburn Hours is inconsistent with its being intended, like the other volumes, for use by a male owner.[9]   S. McK.

Notes

1. In addition to the five double-page openings discussed in this entry, the relevant miniatures are those on folios 22, 61v, 70v, 74v, 82, 86, 92, and 179.

2. Calendar, Gospel extracts, Passion according to Saint John, prayers, Hours of the Cross, Hours of the Holy Spirit, Hours of the Virgin, Penitential Psalms, Office of the Dead, prayers—including "Obsecro te" and "O intemerata"—and suffrages.

3. The unillustrated calendar may appear unusual for such a lavish book of hours. I know, however, of only one set of calendar miniatures by the Master of Edward IV (Sotheby's, London, June 19, 2001, lot 35). Two subjects that are unusual are *The Return of the Cross by Heraclius* (ill. 98a) and *The Sacraments of Confirmation and Marriage with Saints Peter and Paul* (fol. 41).

4. Fols. 33v–34, 40v–41, 107v–108, 125v–126, and 180v–181.

5. See a similarly treated miniature in Oxford, Bodleian Library, Ms. Douce 381, fol. 160.

6. These other manuscripts include cat. nos. 95 and 97 and Valenciennes, Bibliothèque Municipale, Ms. 230. The Mansel volume (cat. no. 97) is datable to between 1486 and 1493, and the other two volumes are datable to after 1481. The borders, decorated initials, and script of the Blackburn Hours are particularly close to those in an undated psalter now in a New York private collection (Sotheby's, London, June 24, 1986, lot 97). The male costumes depicted on folios 82, 86, 193v, 194v, and 197 in the Blackburn Hours are consistent with such a dating.

7. According to an inscription in pencil on the front flyleaf, the Blackburn Hours did once include a *dedicace et armes.* As in Cambridge, Fitzwilliam Museum, Ms. 108, these arms may, however, have related to the Noyelle family, into whose possession both books of hours passed by the seventeenth century.

8. The principal patron of these other manuscripts was Baudouin II de Lannoy (see cat. no. 95).

9. The prayer "Obsecro te" (fols. 168–71) is for male use. *Pace* Manchester (1976: 31), the female musician on folio 180v (ill. 98b) is unlikely to be a portrait of the original owner. Such a portrait would be unique to my knowledge. Instead the lady seems intended merely to add music to the celebration of Christ's birth.

GERARD DAVID

The little that is known about Gerard David's origins is derived from the epitaph on his tombstone in the Church of Our Lady in Bruges and from a brief account by Antoine Sanderus (1641–44).[1] David was born in the northern Netherlands, near Gouda, in a town called Oudewater. He must have trained there and in the nearby artistic center of Haarlem, for when he moved south to Bruges, he joined the image makers' and saddlers' guild in 1484 as a full-fledged master. His early paintings show that he had assimilated the work of the Haarlem School painters, especially that of Dieric Bouts, who had left Haarlem to establish a workshop in Leuven, perhaps attracting David as a newcomer to the area.

David moved to Bruges during a period of intense political upheaval and insurrection against the efforts of Maximilian I to claim regency over the Burgundian territories following the sudden death of his wife, Mary of Burgundy, in 1482. David's apparently pragmatic dealings during this troubled era with both civic officials and fellow guild members allowed him to advance quickly to positions of leadership and to garner important commissions. In 1488—even as Maximilian was imprisoned at the Craenenburgh house, on the Market Square—David became *tweede vinder*, or second assistant, in the painters' guild. Just seven years later, he was appointed *eerste vinder* (first assistant), a position that he held again beginning in 1498, and in 1501 he was installed as dean of the guild.

During this period David was working on his first important civic commission, *The Justice of Cambyses* (Bruges, Groeningemuseum) for the town hall of Bruges, which he completed in 1498, when he inscribed the date on one of the panels of the diptych. The success of this commission led to a decade of intense activity, as evidenced by the major altarpieces for local and foreign patrons that can be ascribed to David on the basis of style. For Saint Donatian's Church, he produced a diptych with *Canon Bernardinus de Salviatis, with Saints Bernardinus, Martin, and Donatian* (London, National Gallery) and *The Crucifixion* (begun after 1501; Berlin, Gemäldegalerie), as well as *The Virgin and Child with Saints and the Donor Richard de Visch van de Capelle* (commissioned around 1502; London, National Gallery). He enlisted workshop assistance to complete a *Marriage at Cana* (after 1501; Paris, Louvre), possibly destined to hang in the Basilica of the Holy Blood. In the same years (ca. 1502–8) David began a large altarpiece, *The Baptism of Christ* (Bruges, Groeningemuseum), for Jan de Trompes. He also produced his most ambitious work, a multipanel altarpiece for export to the abbey church of San Gerolamo della Cervara, near Santa Margherita Ligure, which, according to an inscription on the now-lost frame, was commissioned in 1506 by Vincenzo Sauli

(Paris, Louvre; New York, Metropolitan Museum; Genoa, Palazzo Bianco).

That David enjoyed social prominence at this time may be inferred by his membership as of 1507 in the prestigious Confraternity of Our Lady of the Dry Tree, a group that included the dukes of Burgundy as honorary members, as well as members of the top echelons of society and the local nobility. Perhaps in an effort to secure and further promote his position, he painted a large and impressive *Virgin among Virgins*, prominently featuring portraits of himself and his wife, Cornelia Cnoop, as donors (fig. 68). According to documents, David presented the work to the Convent of Sion in 1509. It is not known exactly when David married Cornelia, the daughter of Jacob Cnoop the Younger, who held important positions in the goldsmiths' guild, or when their daughter, Barbara, was born.

There are certain indications that David was a savvy businessman, even somewhat opportunistic. His major competitor was Hans Memling, the leading painter in Bruges when David first arrived. Upon Memling's death in 1494, David moved his workshop across the Fleming Bridge and set up his atelier near the property where the older artist had carried out a thriving business. His membership in the Confraternity of Our Lady of the Dry Tree afforded him the opportunity to mingle with the most notable aristocratic and upper-class families of Bruges, many of whom were Italian and Spanish businessmen. His largesse in donating the majestic *Virgin among Virgins* to the Carmelite Convent of Sion in 1509 could not have escaped the notice of the foreign community, including the Hanseatic League, the Catalans, and the Aragonese, who held their religious services at the high altar where the painting was placed. Later on, in 1515, when the opportunities for marketing art in Antwerp had significantly surpassed those in Bruges, David registered with the Antwerp painters' guild in order to be able to take advantage of increased sales. In 1519–20 he was engaged in a legal dispute with a journeyman, Ambrosius Benson, over the ownership of two trunks of workshop drawings and paintings in progress retained by David in escrow for unfulfilled work by Benson. The accounts of the proceedings provide valuable documentation of workshop paraphernalia in the trunks, including patterns for both painting and illumination.[2]

The relationship between the painters' guilds and the illuminators in Bruges in the fifteenth century was sometimes contentious, with the painters usually maintaining control of the illuminators' activities through various rules and regulations. David's own participation in the craft of illumination has always been a matter of speculation.[3] Although his name appears nowhere in the registers or accounts of the book traders' confraternity, his wife paid the confraternity for mortuary debts, a burial cloth, and a mass to be said in David's honor upon his death in 1523.[4] At the very least, this indicates a special relationship between David and the confraternity (and it is noteworthy that the fee was paid to the book traders' confraternity rather than to the image makers' guild). A careful look at David's work indicates that he had a very close relationship with the leading illuminators of the day, exchanging patterns with them for use in both painting and illumination and cooperating on the production of miniatures for lavish books.[5] He worked in a limited way on some of the most prestigious commissions produced in Flanders and always on the premier illuminations of each book (see cat. nos. 99, 100, 103–5).

Although undoubtedly somewhat restricted by the established conventions of the times, David strove to introduce new formal approaches to age-old themes. In particular, he made a close study of humanity—of different types and different expressions. His remarkably fresh and candid sketches from life of heads and hands served as the basis for paintings imbued with a sense of contemporary reality (see cat. no. 106). Likewise, he produced studies after nature in order to portray standard themes within the context of identifiable local settings. His commissions for Italian patrons, a possible trip to northern Italy, and his workshop journeyman from Lombardy, Ambrosius Benson, all afforded opportunities for the rapid assimilation of Italianate influence into his paintings in the early stages of its incorporation into Netherlandish painting. David took innovative measures, developing methods of streamlining production, for example, in order to increase supply and meet the demands of a growing open market. At the same time, he introduced new themes in painting, such as the Virgin and Child with the Milk Soup, which achieved great success.   M. W. A.

Notes

1. Sanderus 1641–44, 2: 154.

2. Bruges State Archives, Anwinsten 3804, Register Schepenkamer, 1518–19, fols. 82v, 83r; Parmentier 1937: 92–93.

3. On the relationship between painters and illuminators, see Catherine Reynolds, "Illuminators and the Painters' Guilds" (this volume). On David as an illuminator, see Weale 1895; Winkler 1913a: 271–80; Winkler 1978; Schöne 1937: 153–81; Parmentier 1942: 9; Boon 1946: 11–12; Van de Walle de Ghelcke 1952: 399–422; Scillia 1975; Kren, in Malibu 1983a: 46; Van Miegroet 1989: 12, 13, 73–89; Ainsworth 1998: 33–44; Krieger 2000; Ainsworth 2003.

4. First published by Weale 1864–65b: 293–94.

5. Ainsworth 2002: 1–25. See also Thomas Kren and Maryan W. Ainsworth, "Illuminators and Painters: Artistic Exchanges and Interrelationships" (this volume); and Ainsworth 2003.

99

GERARD DAVID AND MASTER OF EDWARD IV AND WORKSHOP

Book of Hours
Use of Rome
Bruges, 1486

MANUSCRIPT: 235 folios, 14.6 × 10.3 cm (5¾ × 4¹/₁₆ in.); justification: 8.3 × 5.6 cm (3¼ × 2³/₁₆ in.); 17 lines of *gotica rotunda*; 15 full-page miniatures, 4 small miniatures

INSCRIPTIONS: *Respice finem 1486* on banderole in border, fol. 136v; *Fr. Jo[hann]es Vidal / 21 Mai 1585*, fol. 235

BINDING: Fifteenth century (?); black Mudejar, blind-stamped panels; silver clasp engraved IHV FILI DEI I / LIBERA ME / A PENIS IN / FERNI in border around two plumelike features; full-length depictions of the Virgin and Child and the Visitation on front endpieces

COLLECTION: Biblioteca del Monasterio de San Lorenzo de El Escorial, Vitrinas 12

PROVENANCE: Father Johannes Vidal, sixteenth century (?)

JPGM and RA

Salvator Mundi
Miniature from a Book of Hours

One full-page miniature, trimmed and laid down on thin walnut panel, 9 × 5.4 cm (3½ × 2⅛ in.)

COLLECTION: New York, The Metropolitan Museum of Art, The Robert Lehman Collection, 1975.1.2486

PROVENANCE: Luigi Grassi, Florence (?); [M. and R. Stora, Paris (?)]; Robert Lehman (1891–1969), New York, in 1926

JPGM and RA

99a
GERARD DAVID
The Virgin and Child,
fol. 30v

In the 1930s, following the suggestion of Georges Hulin de Loo, Wolfgang Schöne attributed all of the fifteen full-page miniatures in this 1486 volume, known as the Escorial Hours, to Gerard David.[1] Diane Scillia and Hans van Miegroet whittled down the number in which he participated to three, an opinion that was recently supported by Sandra Hindman.[2] Bodo Brinkmann, however, proposed a more complex and nuanced reading of David's participation that, in our view, is more convincing.[3] While accepting The Virgin and Child (ill. 99a) as entirely by David, he saw all of the other miniatures as painted largely by another hand, whom he identified as the Master of Edward IV.[4] At the same time he argued that David contributed to the completion or repainting of most of these, commonly in the faces and hands, but sometimes offering even more extensive interventions.[5]

Neither The Crucifixion (fol. 17v) nor The Adoration of the Magi (fol. 83v)—the other two miniatures attributed to David by Scillia, Van Miegroet, and Hindman—is uniform in terms of quality and execution, even though they are among the most proficient miniatures in the book. In The Crucifixion, most of the faces are certainly by David, and the modeling of Christ's body betrays attention to anatomy and subtleties of modeling that are at once close to David and divorced from the vocabulary of the Master of Edward IV. In The Adoration, the faces of the kneeling magus, the Virgin, and the lively Christ child are those of David.[6] The broadness in the handling of the drapery, seen in the male figure under the cross in the foreground of The Crucifixion, is much closer to the style of the Master of Edward IV. In this book the Master of Edward IV fashioned some of his compositions, many specific motifs, and occasionally his use of color closely after the Master of the Dresden Prayer Book,[7] and his treatment of the drapery in The Crucifixion is filtered through the example of the Dresden Master.

Some other especially beautiful interventions probably by David are the face and hands of the Virgin in The Visitation (fol. 61v), the faces of Gabriel and the Virgin in The Annunciation (fol. 42v), the face of the wailing mother in the otherwise awkwardly constructed Massacre of the Innocents (fol. 93v), and the faces of the angels in The Virgin and Child with Angels (fol. 175v). Generally striking in these and the remaining miniatures is the considerable difference in the quality of brushwork between the Davidian portions and the rest. Not surprisingly, the book's most beautiful miniature is a fully autograph work by David, the half-length Virgin and Child (see ill. 99a). The mother and baby Jesus are illuminated from the left, as is typical in David's compositions, and as Scillia noted, the Virgin is closely related in pose and facial type to the Virgin in his Nativity (ca. 1485; Budapest, Szépmüvészeti Museum). This Virgin, in turn, is derived from Boutsian types, signaling David's likely early training in the Bouts workshop.[8] Although the sharp features of the heads in Mary and Saint John with the Female Mourners (ca. 1480; Antwerp, Koninklijk Museum voor Schone Kunsten) have given way here to more lifelike rounded forms, David reused from the Antwerp painting a specific hand pose that must have been available as a workshop model. This same pose is taken both by Mary Magdalene to hold her pyxus in the Female Mourners and by the Virgin as she tenderly supports the right foot of the Christ child in the Escorial miniature.[9] The Escorial Virgin and Child, with their somewhat naive-looking expressions, are forerunners of the more evolved and commonly known Davidian types found in the Van Bergen Hours (cat. no. 103, fol. 93) or the diminutive Serra de Alzaga panel of circa 1490 (cat. no. 102).[10]

The Escorial Hours lacks the important full-page miniature that normally accompanies the "Salve sancta facies," which is the book's first devotion. Beginning with Pope Innocent III in 1216 and continuing with his successors, this prayer, recited before a vera icon or Holy Face, was connected with indulgences of increasing lengths of time over the years.[11] Toward the end of the fifteenth century in books of hours made in Bruges, this image was a Holy Face, commonly of the Salvator Mundi type, rather than a vera icon representing just the head of Christ on a sudarium or plain dark background.[12]

Recently a possible candidate for the missing miniature has been identified, namely, the Salvator Mundi in the Robert Lehman Collection (ill. 99b).[13] The painting in tempera on parchment has been trimmed on both sides and at the top and laid down onto a thin walnut board.[14] It is unvarnished, and the tall, narrow format; arched frame; and dimensions of the leaf are closely aligned with those of the Escorial Hours. Furthermore, the details of the handling and execution are those of David's early works. The rather square-shaped head of Christ and his thick fingers are akin to the same features in figures in the Soldiers (Quod Scripsi Scripsi) (ca. 1480; Antwerp, Koninklijk Museum voor Schone Kunsten). Although more elegantly elongated (and unfortunately very abraded), the Christ of the later Transfiguration (ca. 1500; Bruges, Church of Our Lady) shares many similarities with the Lehman Christ: the phys-

99b
GERARD DAVID
Salvator Mundi

iognomy, especially the modeling of the face and the precisely placed highlight at the left corner of the iris of each eye; the treatment of the hair and beard; the modeling of the torso; the pose of the right hand; and the arrangement of the folds of the garment.[15] If this miniature was once part of the Escorial Hours, along with *The Virgin and Child*, it sets a precedent for David's contribution of the most important miniatures to precious books produced in Flemish illumination at this time.

The book's calendar has a very strong Bruges character, which is consistent with the location of the workshops of its two illuminators.[16] The only distinctive saint in the litany is Saint Alexius among monks and hermits. His feast day also appears in the calendar (July 17) but not as a red-letter day.

M. W. A., and T. K.

Notes

1. Hulin de Loo 1931: 39–43; Schöne 1937: 170–74.

2. Scillia 1975: 166–73; Van Miegroet 1989: 326–27, no. 84; Hindman et al. 1997: 90.

3. Brinkmann 1997: 143–48.

4. Brinkmann was correct in suggesting that the traditional attribution to the Master of the Dresden Prayer Book is incorrect. The attribution to the Master of Edward IV, however, deserves closer study. These miniatures seem quite close to his in the hatching of the drapery—for example, in *The Visitation* and *The Crucifixion* (fols. 61v, 17v; Brinkmann 1997: figs. 129, 131)—but the handling is not consistent throughout. Features such as the multicolored aureole that frames *The Coronation of the Virgin* (fol. 107v) are also reminiscent of the Master of Edward IV (fig. 26), but they show less attention to detail. The handling of the settings also seems weaker than that in the art of the Master of Edward IV.

5. In our view David contributed something to all of the full-page miniatures but not to the four small miniatures of the Evangelists (fols. 182, 196v, 208v, 220v).

6. Brinkmann (1997: 144) also proposed that the Bruges painter-illuminator brought form to the Virgin's blue mantle through the addition of gold highlights.

7. *The Pentecost* (fol. 24v), *The Visitation* (fol. 61v), and *The Nativity* (fol. 73v) are copied, down to many details of setting, from miniatures by the Dresden Master in the Nová Říše Hours (cat. no. 36, fols. 32v, 50v, 64v; Brinkmann 1997: 145).

8. See Ainsworth 1998: 93–153 passim.

9. Ainsworth 1998: 97, fig. 93.

10. The Escorial miniature illustrates the Mass of the Virgin ("Introibo ad altare dei," fols. 31–41v).

11. See Ringbom 1984: 23.

12. See Hindman 1997: 89–90. Such images also existed as independent devotional miniatures.

13. Attributed to David by Ainsworth and first published as such by Hindman 1997: 84–92. See also New York 1998: 286–87, no. 74.

14. Peter Klein of the Department of Wood Biology, University of Hamburg, determined that the wood is walnut and noted that, given its type and normal use, it is highly unlikely that it was the original secondary support of the painting (report, May 8, 1996, Sherman Fairchild Paintings Conservation Department files, Metropolitan Museum of Art).

15. Ainsworth 1998: 41, fig. 53.

16. John Plummer found a level of agreement of 84.04 percent with a book of hours, likely also made in Bruges, from the Vrelant shop in the Walters Art Museum (W.197; in Randall 1997: 295–98, no. 259).

100

MASTER OF THE DRESDEN PRAYER BOOK, GERARD DAVID, MASTER OF JAMES IV OF SCOTLAND, AND OTHERS

Breviary of Isabella of Castile
Dominican use
Bruges and probably Ghent, late 1480s and before 1497

MANUSCRIPT: ii + 523 + i folios, 23.2 × 15.9 cm (9⅛ × 6¼ in.); justification: 13.4 × 9.6 cm (5¼ × 3¹¹⁄₁₆ in.); 34 lines of *gotica rotunda* in two columns; 1 full-page miniature, 1 full-page armorial, 41 half-page miniatures, 98 one-column miniatures, 7 historiated initials, 12 historiated calendar borders; there were 4 half-page miniatures, and 4 one-column miniatures added, Spain(?), ca. 1500; 1 half-page miniature, 3 one-column miniatures added, England, nineteenth century

HERALDRY: Full-page armorial composed of large escutcheon with the arms of Aragon and Castile as combined by Ferdinand and Isabella of Spain, including pomegranate badge, surmounted by crown and large eagle; two smaller escutcheons with the arms of Juan of Castile impaling those of Margaret of Austria and the arms of Philip the Handsome impaling those of Joanna of Castile, the latter escutcheon surmounted by archducal coronet, all fol. 436v; escutcheon with the arms of de Rojas, fol. 437

BINDING: Early nineteenth century; dark brown morocco, blind-tooled Spanish Mudejar-style panels of fifteenth-century binding remounted on front and back boards

COLLECTION: London, The British Library, Add. Ms. 18851

PROVENANCE: Francisco de Rojas; presented to Isabella, queen of Castile (1451–1504), probably in 1497; John Dent (d. 1826), by 1817 [his sale, Evans, London, March 29–May 6, 1827, lot 484]; to Philip Hurd [his sale, Evans, London, March 29, 1832, lot 484]; to Sir John Soane (1753–1837); to Sir John Tobin (d. 1851), Liverpool; by descent to Rev. John Tobin, Liscard, Cheshire; [to William Boone, London, in 1852]; purchased 1852

JPGM and RA

This Dominican breviary, with spaces for 172 miniatures,[1] was conceived as one of the most lavish of all Flemish breviaries.[2] Its first and primary illuminator, the Master of the Dresden Prayer Book, was responsible for its single full-page miniature, thirty-two half-page miniatures, forty-eight one-column miniatures, and seven historiated initials. All but one of these illuminations belong to the first three-quarters of the book, from the Temporale through the Psalter and into the Sanctorale (through the feast of Saint Vincent Ferrer; fols. 8v–358). Gerard David painted three of the most important half-page miniatures within these sections—*The Nativity* (ill. 100a), *The Adoration of the Magi* (ill. 100b), and *Saint Barbara*—while one other, *Saint John on Patmos*, was illuminated by a still unidentified artist. An associate of the Master of the Dresden Prayer Book illuminated the calendar with fully historiated borders (fols. 1v–7) and was also responsible for some of the book's borders.[3] The decorated borders include a distinctive combination of the modern illusionistic borders of strewn flowers, acanthus, and entwined branches on solid grounds, and the older type of blue and gold acanthus with flowers, insects, and birds on plain grounds, along with a variant of this, in gray and black on plain grounds.

Leaving a dozen spaces for miniatures blank after folio 358, the Master of James IV of Scotland conducted a second

100a

GERARD DAVID

The Nativity, fol. 29

campaign of illumination, painting three half-page miniatures (see fig. 25) and forty-five one-column miniatures in
the remainder of the Sanctorale (fols. 404v–495v). Their
quality is superb, and they are enlivened by a rich palette;
in the miniature of the seated bishop Saint Apollinaris, for
example, there is lime green, orange, and violet, the last
two combined in a radiant *couleur changeant* effect. In this
section, only illusionistic borders appear. The book was
likely incomplete when it left Flanders for Spain at the end
of the fifteenth century. Around this time a clumsy painter
executed eight miniatures between folios 363v and 399, six
of which were painted on separate pieces of parchment and
pasted in.[4] Four others, including one of the two-column
miniatures, were painted in the nineteenth century, after
the book had arrived in England.

The breviary represents the largest, most demanding
commission awarded the Master of the Dresden Prayer
Book. His miniatures include a wealth of uncommon subject matter. The Temporale features both a rare (for a breviary) group of scenes of Christ's miracles and an unusual
opening with the full-page miniature, *The Sibyls Foretelling
the Coming of Christ,* opposite a half-page miniature. The
latter shows David on his deathbed, where he meditates
on the construction of the first altar of the Temple at
Jerusalem. The Psalter features a mixture of Old Testament
themes of destruction and a variety of scenes of music in
the Temple. Even the Sanctorale, whose subject matter is
often more conventional, is striking for the freshness of
its Old Testament themes, Solomon Instructing His Son
and the Tribulations of Job as well as the dramatic Gospel

parable of Dives and Lazarus. For iconographic invention the work of the Master of the Dresden Prayer Book in the Isabella breviary had few equals in its time. The conception behind its pictorial program merits greater attention.[5]

Bodo Brinkmann, in a revealing observation, noted that the book has traditionally been dated to the 1490s based on the identification of Isabella of Castile as its first owner, but the style of some of its decorated borders was likely out of fashion before then.[6] The Master of the Dresden Prayer Book himself combined the older and newer border styles in a series of books dating between the mid-1470s (see cat. no. 44) and 1482, but the older style almost certainly disappeared by the end of the 1480s. As a result, Brinkmann proposed that the campaign of the Master of the Dresden Prayer Book be dated to that decade. Since some of David's miniatures appear to belong to the first campaign, this phase probably dates after 1484, when he first joined the painter's guild in Bruges.[7] The campaign by the Master of James IV of Scotland, showing a fully mature style, surely postdates his work in the Manchester breviary (cat. no. 108), which is dated 1487, probably by a number of years. It may well belong to the 1490s and would have been completed no later than 1497, when the book was likely in the hands of Queen Isabella herself.

The three miniatures by David fall into two groups, with The Nativity and The Adoration of the Magi corroborating the dating of the book's first campaign to the second half of the 1480s.[8] Both miniatures owe a debt to paintings by Hugo van der Goes, the former in general to elements of his Portinari Altarpiece and the latter to a presumably lost Adoration of the Magi that David copied in a large painting of around 1500–1505 (Munich, Alte Pinakothek). The Nativity miniature relates to several painted versions in which David explored some of the motifs.[9] In its intimate setting, showing a receding diagonal wall on the left that meets a back wall parallel to the picture plane, and in the curious shepherds who eagerly peer in through the side opening of the left wall, the miniature resembles a Nativity that the Maximilian Master painted in the London Hastings Hours (cat. no. 41, fol. 106v).[10] It is likewise possible that David's introduction to the Van der Goes composition employed for his Adoration of the Magi may have come through drawings made available by the Maximilian Master, whose patterns were a source for both David's paintings and his illuminations.[11]

The third miniature by David, Saint Barbara (fol. 297), is demonstrably from the breviary's second campaign. The angle of the head, the manner of the application of highlights to the hair, the delicate features of the face, and the carefully posed hands with their finely articulated bony structure are found in David's sketchbook drawings, such as Four Girls' Heads and Two Hands (cat. no. 106).[12] Diane Scillia noted the similarity of the figure of Saint Barbara to that of the seated Virgin in the Sedano Triptych of circa 1490.[13] The configuration of the drapery folds is not identical but is an extremely close version in reverse, and it follows a pattern that was repeatedly used in David's workshop even after about 1510, when it served for the Virgin's drapery in The Virgin and Child with Two Angels (Phila-

delphia Museum of Art).[14] The delicately painted plants and grasses around the saint as well as the tower are seamlessly joined with the figure and appear to have been painted by the same hand, but the background landscape is not by David.[15]

Considered by Friedrich Winkler and others to be a fourth miniature by David,[16] an attribution retained to this day by several scholars,[17] Saint John on Patmos, with its lush island setting, is closer to the work of such manuscript illuminators as the Master of James IV of Scotland and the Master of the Lübeck Bible. Although these artists painted more broadly, with less crisp contours, their work shows a similar interest in atmospheric effects with a painterly handling of the sky. A similar, though not identical handling of the wavelets in the water, which is dense with reflections, also appears in the work of the Master of James IV.[18] It probably belongs to the second campaign.

The choice of David and the remarkable painter of Saint John on Patmos to create only these miniatures, two of them within the book's initial campaign, probably reflects the preference of the book's original patron. The Nativity and The Adoration of the Magi illustrate a breviary's most hallowed feasts, while Saint Barbara and Saint John likely enjoyed the patron's particular veneration.[19] Since both rank with the most popular saints of that time, however, they offer little ground for speculation on the patron's identity.

The original intended owner of the book is uncertain, particularly if, as appears likely, the project was begun in the 1480s. In or shortly before 1497 the book was presented by the Spanish ambassador Francisco de Rojas, whose arms were added over a fully painted illusionistic border on folio 437, to Isabella of Castile (1451–1504), queen of Castile and consort of Ferdinand, king of Aragon and Sicily. Her arms were added on the page opposite those of Rojas in a display that also featured the arms of the children of Isabella and Ferdinand, Juan of Austria and Joanna of Castile, united with those of their new spouses, Margaret of Austria and Philip the Handsome. The double wedding took place by proxy in November 1495 in Flanders, with Rojas standing in for the young Spanish prince and princess. Rojas's presentation of the magnificent book to his queen was perhaps intended to commemorate this august event. Without offering any occasion or reason, an inscription added in the margin of folio 437 documents Rojas's presentation of the book.[20]

Who initially commissioned such an elaborate book? The three most ambitious Flemish breviaries ordered in the preceding decades were begun for Philip the Good and Charles the Bold (cat. no. 10). Most of the subsequent breviaries produced by Flemish illuminators ended up in the hands of individuals at the pinnacle of the ruling class, the Namur breviary (cat. no. 112), with a member of the Carondelet family (Jean Carondelet was Maximilian's chancellor); the Morgan breviary (cat. no. 91), with Eleanor, queen of Portugal; the Antwerp breviary (cat. no. 92), perhaps with Manuel of Portugal; and the Venice breviary (cat. no. 126), with Cardinal Domenico Grimani. Remarkably, however, none offers sure evidence of the identity of its original patron, and the circumstances of the creation of these books remain mysterious. Brinkmann's suggestion that the Isabella breviary may have been commissioned by Maximilian I for Isabella is consistent with this pattern, but the book offers no other clues to support his thesis. The evidence that it was intended for a Spaniard, long mooted in the literature, is not secure.   T. K. and M. W. A.

Notes

1. This total includes a space for a miniature inside the initial *A* on folio 297v that was never executed and the one full-page miniature (fol. 8v). It does not include the full-page coat of arms (fol. 436v), which was added when Francisco de Rojas gave the book to Queen Isabella. Since his arms and the dedicatory inscription from his hand on the facing page were added over a fully painted border, the coat of arms must have been added around the same time, i.e., after the first two campaigns were completed.

2. Some of the breviary's iconography reflects the Dominican use, such as *The Miracle of Saint Thomas Aquinas*, a large miniature (fol. 348). Other Dominican feasts are illustrated, including the Translation of Saint Thomas Aquinas, Saint Dominic, and Saint Vincent Ferrer.

3. Brinkmann (1997: 135) rightly disputed Kren's attribution of these borders to the Dresden Master himself (Malibu 1983: 41).

4. The book was bound in Spain, not in Flanders. It seems likely that the miniatures that are pasted in were supplied after the book was bound, though certainly not long afterward.

5. McKinnon (1984: 29–49) made a compelling case that Nicholas of Lyra's influential commentary on the Psalms influenced the breviary's Psalter iconography. Significantly, the closest parallels in the choice of subject matter for this book do not belong to the other leading Flemish examples of this time, such as the Brussels breviary of Philip the Good or breviaries in the exhibition (cat. nos. 91, 92, 112, 126). Closer in the emphasis on certain Old Testament themes, especially those involving specific episodes from the life of David (along with his musical activities), are the two elaborate Franciscan breviaries made for René II of Lorraine during the 1490s. One, dated around 1493, is a breviary (Paris, Bibliothèque de l'Arsenal, Ms. 601, and Musée du Petit Palais, Ms. 42), while the other, dated 1492–93, is a diurnal and breviary (Paris, Bibliothèque nationale de France, Ms. lat. 10491). See Leroquais 1934, 2: 345–47; 3: 216–21, 436–40. Note that, like the frontispiece of the Isabella breviary, the diurnal features the prophesying Sibyls. The ducal illuminator Georges Trubert illustrated both of René's manuscripts. See Reynaud, in Paris 1993: 378–83, nos. 215, 216.

6. Brinkmann 1997: 134–39; a similar observation was put forth by Consuelo Dutschke in a 1984 response (Department of Manuscripts files, JPGM) to the Getty exhibition catalogue (Malibu 1983).

7. Brinkmann 1997: 140.

8. Scillia (1975: 191) attributed the *Adoration* and *The Nativity* to an assistant of David, except for the figure of Joseph in *The Nativity*, which she ascribed to David himself; Krieger 2000: 227.

9. Ainsworth 1998: 102–16.

10. Turner 1983: pl. 106b.

11. See Ainsworth 2003.

12. The lighting of the figure of Saint Barbara from the left and the system of shading along the proper left side of her head and nose and at her chin are characteristic of David's works of 1490–1510 as found in his drawings and in the underdrawings of his paintings. For examples, see Ainsworth 1998: figs. 7, 14, 15, 17–19, 22, 26, 27, 35, 37, 65, 66, and passim.

13. Scillia 1975: 192.

14. Ainsworth 1998: 290–94. The extremely fine parallel hatching used to model the draperies in David's underdrawings for panel paintings also appears in the folds of Saint Barbara's blue cloak. Gold highlights in short parallel strokes like stitching go across the peak of the folds in order to create a shimmering effect.

15. Scillia (1975: 192) first pointed out that the miniature's landscape is by another artist; she thought he was perhaps from Marmion's circle.

16. Winkler 1913a: 276–77; and Van Miegroet 1989: 327–28, no. 85.

17. Most recently Brinkmann (1997: 135–38) and also Scillia 1975: 193. See Brinkmann 1997: 137 for a summary of recent attributions of this miniature.

18. For example, the water in *The Appearance of Christ to Saint Julian* in the Spinola Hours (cat. no. 124, fol. 256v). On this, see also Kren, in Malibu 1983a: 46, 48, n. 34.

19. See, for example, the discussion of the Saint Elizabeth miniature in the Hours of Isabella of Castile (cat. no. 105).

20. Scholars have questioned the authenticity of this inscription (e.g., Lázaro 1928: 12–26). Consuelo Dutschke, in unpublished correspondence with Thomas Kren of 1984 (Department of Manuscripts files, JPGM), raised concern about the inscription on the basis of the script, the use of terms such as "Dive" for Isabella, considered more appropriate for a saint than for a ruler, and the spelling of "Siscilie." Backhouse (1993b: 24–28) has argued strongly for its authenticity. See also Brinkmann 1997: 131–33.

IOI

GERARD DAVID

Diptych with *The Virgin and Child with Angels* and *Christ Taking Leave of His Mother*

Bruges, ca. 1490–95

Oil on wood panel, 11.5 × 8 cm (4½ × 3⅛ in.) and 11.5 × 7 cm (4½ × 2¼ in.)

COLLECTION: Basel, Öffentliche Kunstsammlung

PROVENANCE: Max van Gelder, Uccle; his bequest, 1958

RA

This is one of three extant diptychs produced by Gerard David between about 1490 and 1510.[1] The others are in the Alte Pinakothek, Munich (fig. 67), and divided between Upton House in Warwickshire and the Metropolitan Museum of Art, New York.[2] These diminutive diptychs were created as counterparts to books of devotional literature that inspired their imagery. Not found in the Gospels, but based on the *Meditations on the Life of Christ* by the Franciscan friar known as the Pseudo-Bonaventure, the themes of the Virgin and Child, and Christ Taking Leave of His Mother invite the viewer to contemplate the beginning and end of Christ's earthly existence. On the left wing, the Virgin tenderly embraces the Christ child, offering him a pear, while two angels play the lute and the viol.[3] Chapter 72 of the *Meditations* is the source for the right wing. It describes a supper attended by Christ at the house of Mary and

Martha in the presence of Mary Magdalene and his mother. There, as he takes his leave, Christ addresses the Virgin: "Most beloved Mother . . . the time of redemption is coming. Now all things said of me will be fulfilled, and they will do to me what they wish."[4] In these two paintings the Virgin Mary, especially venerated by the Franciscans, provides an exemplar of compassion and empathy for the devotee, who vicariously experiences her joys and sorrows.

The subject of Christ's leave-taking is relatively rare in Flemish panel painting and manuscript illumination.[5] In this regard, it is worth noting that one of the two full-page miniatures of half-length figures by Simon Marmion in a book of hours in Munich represents Christ Taking Leave of His Mother (cat. no. 90, fol. 230).[6] As Thomas Kren has pointed out, this tipped-in illumination oddly concludes a devotional section instead of beginning it, indicating perhaps that it was inserted as an afterthought. This is all the more interesting as the litany of the Munich Hours has a Franciscan character.[7] It would seem that the infrequently depicted theme of Christ Taking Leave of His Mother was specifically connected to Franciscan devotional practices. The mendicant communities were well established in Flanders, the Franciscans being the first to found a monastery in Bruges. Perhaps these small devotional diptychs and their distinctive imagery were the result of demand from the Franciscan community, many of whose members were wealthy foreigners.[8]

IOI

GERARD DAVID
The Virgin and Child with Angels and *Christ Taking Leave of His Mother*

Although finely executed in oil, the Basel diptych is handled with the precision of a miniaturist, recalling David's association with manuscript illumination.[9] In format as well, David's paintings find a parallel in illuminated books from the end of the fifteenth century that favored half-length or three-quarter-length figures in dramatic close-up. This convention is evident especially in books associated with the workshop of the Master of the First Prayer Book of Maximilian, with which David apparently had close contact.[10] Key examples include the previously-mentioned Munich book of hours (before 1489 and ca. 1495–1500) and La Flora (before 1489 and before 1498; cat. no. 93). These two books are notable because portions of an original cycle of twenty-four dramatic close-up miniatures, which are considered among Marmion's most influential creations in the half-length format, were inserted into both.[11]

M. W. A.

Notes

1. See Ainsworth 1998: 272–76.

2. See New York 1998: 289–90, no. 76.

3. These were known as *bas* instruments, having a soft, silvery timbre, and were often played as the accompaniment to liturgy. See Bowles 1954; Bowles 1983; Strohm 1985: 81–82.

4. Ragusa and Green 1961: 308–9.

5. David treated the theme one other time in a large-scale painting (Dublin, National Gallery of Ireland). See Vogelaar 1987: 22–24, no. 13; Van Miegroet 1989: 283, no. 12.

6. The Marmion and David examples relate in terms of the half-length poses of Christ and the Virgin, who face each other. David's Christ, however, raises his right hand in a gesture of farewell and blessing, and the painter exchanged Marmion's interior setting with a landscape view for a gold background.

7. See the discussion by Thomas Kren in cat. no. 90.

8. See Martens (M.) 1992: 305–14.

9. Conway 1916: 309; Conway 1921: 288; Boon 1946: 49.

10. For the close working relationship between Gerard David and the Maximilian Master, see Thomas Kren and Maryan W. Ainsworth, "Illuminators and Painters: Artistic Exchanges and Interrelationships" (this volume), and Ainsworth 2003.

11. For further discussion of this issue, see cat. nos. 90 and 93.

Figure 67
GERARD DAVID
Diptych with *The Virgin and Child* and *Christ Taking Leave of His Mother*, ca. 1490–95. Oil on panel, each 9.7 × 7.5 cm (3³⁄₁₆ × 2¹⁵⁄₁₆ in.). Alte Pinakothek, Munich, Inventory nos. 1080 and 1079

Ridderbos have noted, the link of these prayers of indulgence with the image of the Virgin of the Sun was not uncommon by 1500 in Flemish, Lower Rhenish, and German devotional books.[4] The Serra de Alzaga *Virgin and Child* is mounted in its original thin metal frame with a loop at the top allowing it to be hung in a convenient location for the recitation of daily devotions. David's remarkable quality of execution and subtlety of expression in this example distinguish the painting from the many devotional images of this type that were mass-produced in the late fifteenth and early sixteenth centuries in northern Europe.[5]   M. W. A.

Notes

1. See Ainsworth 1998: 272–76.
2. Conway 1916: 309; Conway 1921: 288; Boon 1946: 49.
3. See Ainsworth, in New York 1993–95: 1–7.
4. See Smeyers 1994: 286; Ridderbos, in Amsterdam 1994: 151–56.
5. Honée, in Amsterdam 1994: 163, fig. 75.

102

GERARD DAVID

The Virgin and Child
Bruges, ca. 1490

Oil on wood panel, 9 × 7 cm (3½ × 2¾ in.)

COLLECTION: Valencia, Serra de Alzaga Collection

PROVENANCE: Acquired 1975

JPGM

Between about 1490 and 1510 Gerard David and his workshop specialized in small, independent panels of the Virgin and Child and diptychs of the Virgin and Child joined with Christ Taking Leave of His Mother (see, for example, cat. no. 101 and fig. 67).[1] Their diminutive size and detailed execution suggest the craftsmanship of a miniaturist, and for some scholars this has been the most compelling argument that David was indeed involved in manuscript illumination.[2]

David employed the Eleousa type of Virgin and Child in painting and illumination alike (see cat. no. 103) and presented it in identical fashion, with a gold background in the style of Byzantine icons. The repetition of this specific motif of the Virgin and Child ensured the transference of the spiritual value associated with the cult image from which it is derived, namely, the Cambrai Madonna, an icon that was especially noted for its perceived ability to perform miracles.[3]

The further association by late-fifteenth-century viewers of the Serra de Alzaga *Virgin and Child* (ill. 102) with indulgenced images of the Virgin of the Sun (cat. no. 103) may well have been automatic. The identical type in the Hours of Margaretha van Bergen (cat. no. 103) offers the promise of indulgence from Pope Sixtus IV in a text directly beneath the image. As Maurits Smeyers and Bernhard

103

GERARD DAVID, CIRCLE OF MASTER OF JAMES IV OF SCOTLAND, AND ANOTHER ILLUMINATOR

Hours of Margaretha van Bergen
Use of Windesheim
Bruges, probably shortly before 1500

MANUSCRIPT: iii + 120 iii + folios, 15.3 × 11.4 cm (6 × 4½ in.); justification: 10.3 × 7 cm (4¹⁄₁₆ × 2¾ in.); 20 lines of *textualis*; 1 full-page miniature, 6 large miniatures, 26 small miniatures, and one full-page armorial

HERALDRY: Escutcheon with the arms of Margaretha van Bergen, fol. iv

BINDING: Flemish, seventeenth century; gold-tooled red morocco; blue silk endleaves; gilt edges

COLLECTION: San Marino, The Huntington Library, HM 1131

PROVENANCE: Margaretha van Bergen; Ambroise Firmin-Didot (1790–1876) [his sale, Hôtel Drouot, Paris, June 12, 1882, lot 18]; to Baron de Beurnonville; William K. Bixby (1858–1931), Saint Louis; [George D. Smith, New York]; to Henry E. Huntington (1850–1927) in August 1918

JPGM

This book of hours is distinctive among Flemish prayer books of its time in several ways. The use of the Hours of the Virgin is for Windesheim, the congregation that followed the Devotio Moderna.[1] Moreover, the book's script resembles that of other manuscripts associated with Windesheim (cat. nos. 24, 39, 108). Its calendar is closely related to a group of calendars for Utrecht, and unlike most other Flemish books of hours of the time, it has only one full-page miniature, *The Last Judgment* (which illustrates the Office of the Dead), despite its program of thirty-three miniatures. Indeed, only six others, at half-page, are large. They illustrate the Hours of the Cross, the Hours of the Virgin, the Penitential Psalms, the Office of the Dead, the ubiquitous prayer "Adoro te in cruce," and a less common indulgence prayer, "Ave sanctissima mater Maria dei regina celi." At the same time, the book has three full pictorial

102
GERARD DAVID
The Virgin and Child

appeared in great profusion as painted and printed book illustrations, independent prints, small panel paintings, and sculptures.[3] The specific type of the Virgin and Child in the Hours of Margaretha van Bergen is a descendant of Byzantine icons that became known in the Burgundian Netherlands both in originals collected by the dukes of Burgundy and through Italian Duecento and Trecento versions. Because certain of these icons, such as the Cambrai Madonna or Nôtre-Dame de Grâce (Siena, ca. 1340), were believed to have been painted by Saint Luke himself and invested with the ability to perform miracles, they provided ideal models for the revered images to be associated with prayers of indulgence. Around 1455–60 Dieric Bouts and his workshop produced a variant of Nôtre-Dame de Grâce in multiple examples,[4] which in turn provided the model for Gerard David's own version a generation later. David and his workshop specialized in paintings of this type of the Virgin and Child from about 1490 to 1510, made as single devotional panels (see cat. no. 102); in diptych form, along with *Christ Taking Leave of His Mother* (see cat. no. 101, fig. 67),[5] and as miniatures.

The intimate stylistic relationship of *The Virgin and Child* with David's diminutive panels supports an attribution to him.[6] The somewhat broader forehead, more accentuated part in the hair, and more elongated face of the Virgin in the miniature than in the Serra de Alzaga panel suggest the closer connection of the former to Bouts's model and its earlier date.[7] In terms of execution, the Virgin's hands show the repeated parallel lines in brown across the knuckles, the curved parallel strokes suggesting the volume of the back of the hand, and the long strokes for shading at the lower side of the hand that are typical of David's manner. The short stippling and disengaged strokes in pinkish and brown tones used to model the faces are also found in David's earlier *Virgin and Child* in the 1486 Escorial Hours (ill. 99a). From the details of the coat of arms on folio 1v, we know that the Hours of Margaretha van Bergen must have been made before 1500, that is, at precisely the time when David was engaged in producing panels depicting this type of the Virgin and Child.[8]

Two other artists shared responsibility for the remaining miniatures. The better of the two, who was from the circle of the Master of James IV of Scotland, painted *David and Nathan* and *The Raising of Lazarus*, among the book's finer miniatures, and he painted twenty-seven others, perhaps with the aid of assistants. His work closely resembles the miniatures of the better illuminator in a book of hours in the Morgan Library, New York (M.74), which offers other parallels to the Van Bergen Hours. It is written in a similar (though not identical) *textualis* and has a closely related though fuller calendar for the use of Rome that is also connected to Utrecht. The two calendars agree 90.39 percent.[9] The Hours of the Virgin in the Morgan Hours is for the use of Rome, but its Office of the Dead is for the use of Windesheim/Utrecht.[10] The third hand in the Van Bergen hours is related to the second but, in our view, distinct. This artist, who favored lighter tonalities, painted *The Last Judgment*, *The Annunciation to the Shepherds*, and *The Massacre of the Innocents*.[11]

cycles composed of smaller miniatures: the Passion of Christ, the Life of the Virgin, and the saints.

The book has only a single miniature of superb quality, *The Virgin and Child* (ill. 103), a work that has been largely overlooked in the literature. The illumination is labeled at the bottom of the page MARIA · MATER · [DEI] and is distinguished from the rest of the book both visually and textually. The rubric directly under the illumination refers to an indulgence of eleven thousand years attached to the image of "Maria in Sole" (the Virgin of the Sun) for those who would recite the prayer beneath, which begins "Ave sanctissima maria mater dei regina celi porta paradisi."[2] The indulgence is offered by Pope Sixtus IV, who is shown kneeling in adoration in the border at the right.

The guarantee of indulgences that would cancel penance required for the expiation of sins was an especially popular notion in the last two decades of the fifteenth century. This created a demand for the production of devotional images associated with indulged prayers that

Margaretha van Bergen was the daughter of Cornelis van Bergen, lord of Grevenbroeck and of Zevenbergen. Cornelis was an army captain under Maximilian of Austria, who may also have been a patron of Gerard David (see cat. no. 104). His service to the court earned him induction into the Order of the Golden Fleece in 1501.[12] Margaretha married Floris von Egmond (1469–1539), count of Buren and Leerdam, territories just south of Utrecht. Egmond served Maximilian as lieutenant stadtholder of Holland, Zeeland, Guelders, and West Friesland. He became a knight of the Golden Fleece in 1505.   M. W. A. and T. K.

Notes

1. Dutschke et al. 1989, 2: 437
2. See Ringbom 1962: 326–30. Pope Sixtus IV supported the theological doctrine of the Immaculate Conception, and in 1476 he initiated an Office for the Feast of the Immaculate Conception, offering indulgences to those who celebrated it.
3. Smeyers 1994: 271–99.
4. Ainsworth, in New York 1993–95: 1–19. The primary version is in the Metropolitan Museum of Art, New York; workshop copies are in the California Palace of the Legion of Honor, San Francisco, and the Museo Nazionale del Bargello, Florence.
5. See Ainsworth 1998: 272–76.
6. The connection with David was first suggested by Dutschke (in Dutschke et al. 1989, 2: 439).
7. See Ainsworth 1993: 2–3, figs. 1–3.
8. Dutschke et al. 1989, 2: 440.
9. John Plummer, analysis of the calendars (Department of Manuscripts files, JPGM).
10. The compositions in the two books that are most closely related include *The Nativity*, *The Mass of Saint Gregory*, and *The Raising of Lazarus*. We are grateful to Gregory Clark for drawing our attention to the Morgan volume's textual links to the Van Bergen Hours. The use of the Office of the Dead in the Van Bergen Hours is still undetermined but different from that of the Morgan volume.
11. Despite the connection of most of the miniatures to the circle of the Master of James IV of Scotland, a number are based on patterns that were available in the workshop of the Master of the First Prayer Book of Maximilian, such as *The Annunciation*, *The Massacre of the Innocents*, and probably *The Last Judgment*.
12. Cornelis belonged to the prominent Glymes (Berghes) family of Bergen-op-Zoom. His older brother Henri de Berghes was chancellor of the Golden Fleece from 1493 to 1502, and another brother, Jean, was also a knight of the order. See also under cat. no. 168.

104

GERARD DAVID

Johannes Michael Nagonius, *Encomia* for Maximilian
Bruges, between 1493 and 1504

MANUSCRIPT: 90 folios, 24 × 16.5 cm (9⁷⁄₁₆ × 6½ in.); justification: 14.2 × 9.7 cm (5⁹⁄₁₆ × 3¹³⁄₁₆ in.); 19 lines of *textura* and *humanistica cursiva*; 1 full-page miniature

BINDING: Vienna, nineteenth century; pasteboard

COLLECTION: Vienna, Österreichische Nationalbibliothek, Ms. 12750

PROVENANCE: Presumably Emperor Maximilian I (1459–1519); acquired 1848 by Hofbibliothek

JPGM

Although elected king of the Romans in 1486, Maximilian did not become Holy Roman Emperor until 1493, after the death of his father, Frederick III. This clearly propagandistic text argues in favor of his elevation to emperor in a codex consisting of three books of panegyric poems. The *Encomia* was written by Johannes Michael Nagonius, an Italian poet who had been called into service to pen similar texts for Louis XII, Ercole d'Este, Pope Julius II, and Wladislaus II of Bohemia and Hungary.[1] Toward the end of book 3 there is an epigram to Philip the Handsome, son of Maximilian, who was crowned in 1504 as king of Castile.

The book's only miniature (ill. 104) is set within a border of flowers (rose, columbine, carnation, and lily) and thin golden rays that emanate from the central image. Labeled with the legend *Sic ego cesar maximus orbis herus* [Therefore I am the emperor of the known world], it shows an idealized, youthful Maximilian (without his hereditary prognathism) dressed as emperor. He wears his imperial crown, armor,[2] and an ermine-lined cloak secured by a gold chain on which a Medusa head hangs, and he carries the attributes of his office: the sword of justice and the imperial orb. Maximilian sits on a marble throne, before a gold brocade cloth of honor, and beneath a green canopy (held open by two eagles of the Habsburg coat of arms come to life) with the letters · S · P · Q · R · [Senatus Populusque Romanum], denoting his claim to the Holy Roman Empire.[3] Allegorical references to his personal virtues are perhaps found in the four partially hidden bas reliefs on the throne. They appear to depict two biblical scenes above: Adam and Eve at the left and the two driven from the Garden of Eden at the right, possibly a reference to just judgment. Below this are two mythological scenes: Hercules and Deianeira or Ceres and Triptolemus at the left and a sleeping Venus with Cupid at the right. The specific meaning of this juxtaposition of images is yet to be determined, but it is worth recalling that the aldermen's chambers in Flemish town halls were decorated with depictions of justice and judgment from the Bible and classical antiquity. Indeed, the same bas relief shown at the lower left of Maximilian's throne in the miniature appears as a medallion on the back wall in Gerard David's 1498 *Justice of Cambyses* panel *The Arrest of Sisamnes*, which was made for the aldermen's chambers in the Bruges town hall.[4]

104
GERARD DAVID
Maximilian as Emperor,
fol. 4v

The miniature of Maximilian was first attributed to the Master of James IV of Scotland by Friedrich Winkler, subsequently to the Master of the First Prayer Book of Maximilian by Anne van Buren, and then to Gerard Horenbout by Winkler and Georges Dogaer. Following Otto Pächt, Dagmar Thoss suggested the close proximity to David's style, an attribution that was also supported by Hans van Miegroet.[5] The placement of the throne on the perspectivally receding tile floor as well as the repeated use of the medallion are related to the artist's *Justice of Cambyses* panels of 1498. Particularly close to David, however, are the details of the execution and handling of the finely articulated facial features and the hands of Maximilian. The head

is illuminated from the left, which was David's habitual practice. Furthermore, the system of curved, parallel hatching for the modeling in the shaded part of the face at the right and the short, diagonal strokes along the side of the nose are features readily recognized in David's metalpoint drawings of heads (see cat. no. 106) and found in the underdrawings of his paintings.[6] The almond-shaped eyes are a feature that appears in the drawings for paintings dating from about 1500 on.[7] The hands of figures are always a key part of the expressive mode of David's works. Here, he carefully selected the poses of the two hands to convey meaning at a glance, calling attention to them by accentuating their form, in particular their skeletal structure. The hand that holds the sword is reflected in Maximilian's armor, reinforcing the dual concepts of justice and power.

The circumstances of the commission of the Nagonius manuscript are not known. Eva Irblich proposed that the text may have been composed in Italy and then sent north, where three additional poems and the miniature were added.[8] The localization of the illumination of the Nagonius manuscript to Bruges has interesting political connections.[9] On January 31, 1488, the citizens of Bruges revolted against Maximilian in his efforts to claim his authority over the Burgundian Netherlands after the death of his wife, the duchess Mary of Burgundy. They seized Maximilian when he entered the city accompanied by two hundred German soldiers, and he was imprisoned in the Craenenburg house and subsequently in the mansion of Jean de Gros.[10] Ultimately rescued by Frederick III and his German troops, Maximilian prevailed until his son Philip the Handsome became archduke of the Burgundian Netherlands in 1494.

Was this manuscript and its illumination commissioned by some well-placed pro-Maximilian nobleman in Bruges as appeasement for the trials and tribulations of the ruler in that city, or was it offered by Philip in recognition of his father's rightful claim as Holy Roman Emperor? The possibility that it was ordered by Maximilian in an effort at self-promotion must not be discounted. The death of Nagonius in 1505 provides a terminus ad quem for the book, which, based on the style of the illumination and historical information, was probably produced between 1493 and 1504.

M. W. A.

Notes

1. Wormald 1951: 118–19.

2. This is a generalized rendering of Maximilian's armor as it is also known in Bernhard Strigel's painted portrait of him (ca. 1507/8; Vienna, Kunsthistorisches Museum, inv. 4403) and Hans Burgkmair's chiaroscuro woodcut of 1508 or design for a monument of 1510 (Vienna, Graphische Sammlung Albertina). I am grateful to Don LaRocca, Department of Arms and Armor, Metropolitan Museum of Art, for discussions concerning this matter.

3. Such a representation further alludes to Maximilian's succession to the throne of the ancient imperial Caesars. This motif, originating from models of Asiatic monarchs of antiquity and late antique and Byzantine examples, represented the ceremonial concealment of the monarchs from their subjects (Eberlein 1983: 61–66).

4. The identification of the scene in the Justice panels as Ceres and Triptolemus or Hercules and Deianeira has likewise not been solved definitively (see Van Miegroet 1989: 160; Van der Velden 1995: 40–62).

5. For opinions, see Van Miegroet 1989: 328–29, no. 87.

6. See the discussion in Ainsworth 1998: 9–31 and passim.

7. See, for example, cat. no. 106.

8. In Innsbruck 1992: 284.

9. In fact, Maximilian had previously commissioned a Flemish prayer book illuminated by the Master of the First Prayer Book of Maximilian around 1486, in which he appears in all of his regalia, kneeling before Saint Sebastian (Vienna, Österreichische Nationalbibliothek, Ms. Vindob. 1907, fol. 61v).

10. Weale (1895: 8) reported that David was paid £2 10s to paint the wrought-iron gratings installed over the windows of Maximilian's temporary prison in the de Gros mansion but did not provide documentation for his assertion.

105

MASTER OF THE FIRST PRAYER BOOK OF
MAXIMILIAN AND WORKSHOP, MASTER OF THE
PRAYER BOOKS OF AROUND 1500 AND WORKSHOP,
GERARD DAVID, MASTER OF JAMES IV OF
SCOTLAND, AND ANOTHER ILLUMINATOR

Hours of Isabella of Castile

Bruges and probably Ghent, beginning of sixteenth century
(before 1504)

MANUSCRIPT: 279 folios, 22.6 × 15.2 cm (8¹⁵⁄₁₆ × 6 in.); justification:
10.7 × 7.1 cm (4³⁄₁₆ × 2¾ in.); 17 lines of *gotica rotunda*; 40 full-page
miniatures, 10 half-page miniatures, 24 calendar roundels

HERALDRY: Full-page armorial composed of escutcheon with the
arms of Queen Isabella of Castile, with Castile in first and fourth
quarters, surmounted by the royal crown and protected by the eagle
of Saint John; above yoke, emblem of Isabella and arrows and
emblem of Ferdinand; below, motto *Tanto Monta sub umbra Alaru[m]
tuaru[m] protege nos*, fol. 1v; shields and banners below clerestory of
choir, fol. 219v: A. lozenges quartered 1 and 4 azure, 2 and 3 or
(difficult to read but likely identical to D); B. pendant gules with
initials *HR en lac*; C. mail with or bendy sinister gules; D. large
standard quartered 1 and 4 azure a chevron or, three bezants or, 2
and 3 argent a bend sable within chief a lion sable, in base 3 roundels
sable; E. standard with gules a lion or

BINDING: Modern; brown calf

COLLECTION: Cleveland, The Cleveland Museum of Art, 1963.256

PROVENANCE: Flemish noblewoman (?); to Isabella, queen of Castile
(1451–1504); Anselm Solomon von Rothschild (1803–1874); to Baron
Edmond de Rothschild; acquired 1963

JPGM

The Hours of Queen Isabella of Castile is one of the finer commissions of the Master of the First Prayer Book of Maximilian. He and his workshop executed thirty-one full-page miniatures, all ten of the half-page miniatures, and the twenty-four roundels in the calendar,[1] more than 80 percent of the book's narrative decoration. Several other artists participated in its execution. Gerard David painted *Saint Elizabeth of Hungary* (ill. 105a), while the Master of James IV of Scotland executed *Saint Roch* (fol. 181v) and *The Mass for the Virgin* (fol. 87v). The Master of the Prayer Books of around 1500 painted *The Procession of the Eucharist* (fol. 43v), and perhaps he or an assistant painted *The Ecstasy of Mary Magdalene* (fol. 193v), *The Pentecost* (fol. 31v), and *The Visitation* (fol. 115v).[2] A fifth artist painted *Saint Anthony of Padua and the Miracle of the Host* (fig. 20) and *Saint Bernard's Vision of the Virgin and Child* (fol. 267v).

The decorative program of the Isabella Hours is extensive but relatively standard. It includes a full-page miniature for each of the offices for the days of the week and half-page miniatures at each hour of the Friday Hours of the Passion. The only rare subject among the fifteen illuminated suffrages, each also with a full-page miniature, is Susanna, whose suffrage is illustrated with unusual iconography (ill. 105b). A handful of openings feature a full-page miniature facing a half-page miniature: Vespers of the Hours of the Cross, the Penitential Psalms, and the Office of the Dead.

Well over half of the miniatures painted by the Maximilian Master copy or adapt patterns he had been using for

several decades.[3] Several copy designs by or from the circle of the Vienna Master of Mary of Burgundy, and four copy, down to details of color, miniatures from Simon Marmion's celebrated pictorial cycle incorporated into La Flora (cat. no. 93).

One of the most exquisitely rendered miniatures of the book is *Saint Elizabeth of Hungary*.[4] Unlike the somewhat earlier *Saint Barbara* in the Breviary of Isabella of Castile (cat. no. 100), where David's contribution was restricted to the figure and foreground, *Saint Elizabeth of Hungary* is

entirely by him.[5] The pose of Elizabeth's head and the sensitively rendered features of her face are practically identical to those of the virgin at the far right edge in the Morgan *Virgin among Virgins* of about 1505–10 (cat. no. 107). The head at the right side of a delicate silverpoint study from life of three female heads (ca. 1500–1505; Kraków, Czartoryski Museum) likely served as a model for both miniatures,[6] as well as for some of David's panel paintings, namely, for the figure of Saint Elizabeth in the right wing of David's Baptism triptych (1502–8, Bruges, Groningemuseum).[7]

105b
MASTER OF THE
FIRST PRAYER BOOK
OF MAXIMILIAN
The Trial of Susanna,
fol. 195v

The sympathetic approach to the beggar is paralleled in a kindred fellow in David's *Canon Bernardijn Salviati and Three Saints* (probably commissioned in 1501; London, National Gallery), which formed the left half of a diptych with a *Crucifixion* (Berlin, Staatliche Museen).[8] Moreover, the London panel and the Saint Elizabeth miniature share comparable landscape features: paired trees that are similar in their form and structure,[9] the well-worn path strewn at its edges with pebbles, and overlapping green hills with shrubs that turn into a rich ultramarine blue in the distance. The London-Berlin diptych, as well as the Baptism triptych, exhibits a somewhat overcast sky, blending dark, streaky clouds with lighter, more luminous ones, just as in the Saint Elizabeth miniature. This interrelated group of miniatures and panel paintings points to a date around 1500 for the Saint Elizabeth miniature.

Saint Anthony of Padua and the Miracle of the Host and *Saint Bernard's Vision of the Virgin and Child* are Davidian but not by David. The first is a mirror image and more open variation of the tightly and awkwardly cropped composition in a painting by David of around 1505 in the Toledo Museum of Art (see fig. 21).[10] The pattern for these two miniatures was probably created by David, but the miniatures themselves were carried out by another artist, perhaps one trained in his workshop.[11]

The book contains the arms of Isabella displayed prominently as a frontispiece (fol. 1v). They appear to be by a Flemish artist and roughly contemporaneous with the book's origins. But the history of the book's early ownership is not entirely clear. The fact that David was selected to paint the miniature *Saint Elizabeth of Hungary* may reflect special veneration for this saint on the part of the book's patron or intended owner. Since the Spanish queen is the namesake of the saint, this seems likely. David's contributions to books of hours are distinctive, as they tend to comprise at best a handful of miniatures and often only one of particular significance within the program. Still, as is true of the Isabella Breviary (cat. no. 100), none of the liturgical indications within the calendar, litany, Hours of the Virgin, or Office of the Dead in the Hours of Isabella points to an intended Spanish user.[12] Moreover, as Patrick de Winter has pointed out, the elaborate arms represented on banners and lozenges in the miniature of the Mass for the Dead might be the arms of the book's original patron, also likely a woman,[13] who commissioned the book either for her own use, for presentation to Isabella, or perhaps initially for herself, but ultimately for Isabella. (Isabella's breviary contains both her arms and those of Francisco de Rojas, who presented that manuscript to her.) The banner with the initials *H* and *R en lac* suggests that the patron's first initial may have been an *R*. Whether or not it was true at the outset, by the time David was on board for this project, it seems likely that the book was intended for Isabella.

The presence of the illustrated suffrage for "Saint" Susanna, the Old Testament heroine, lends support to the suggestion that the book was intended for Isabella from an early stage (fig. 105b). It is noteworthy for two reasons. Another rare suffrage of Susanna with a full-page miniature appeared a decade earlier in the Hours of Mary of Burgundy and Maximilian (cat. no. 38, fol. 340v), in an opening with both the arms of Maximilian and the initials of the couple twice. A miniature of the saint also shows up on a leaf with the arms of Margaret of York added to a book of hours (fol. 231) originally made for her spouse or his father before her marriage.[14] In the latter two *horae* the theme of Susanna's tribulations in the suffrage is aptly illustrated by *Susanna and the Elders*, but this theme is even more pointedly illustrated in the present manuscript, which features instead *The Trial of Susanna* (ill. 105b).[15] Most of the rare examples of such illustrated suffrages appear in books intended for female owners,[16] and they would be especially appropriate to lives as turbulent as Mary's, Margaret's, and Isabella's. Are the presence of this suffrage and the distinctiveness of its illustration evidence that the book was intended for an owner of the rank of queen? The lack of any liturgical connections to Isabella's domains is grounds for skepticism but not rejection of the thesis. Isabella took as her confessor Cardinal Francisco Cisneros de Ximenas, a Franciscan, around 1498, and her book of hours shows some bias toward saints of the Franciscan order.[17] It is possible that a Flemish courtier of the queen (or of her daughter Joanna) in Flanders commissioned the book for her, but it is clear that the book was intended for Isabella from an early moment in its creation.

The calendar and litany are broadly Flemish and northern French.[18] The only artist whose work provides a strong basis for dating within Isabella's hours is the well-documented Gerard David, whose *Saint Elizabeth* is datable to around 1500–1505 on stylistic grounds. Since these parameters fall for the most part within the queen's lifetime, the book was perhaps under way as early as the turn of the century.

T. K. and M. W. A.

Notes

1. The calendar roundels have often been attributed to the Master of the Dresden Prayer Book (De Winter 1981: 343, 348, 349), but they are merely based on patterns or designs that he made during the 1480s (as suggested by some of the fashions, e.g., fol. 5; cf. cat. nos. 32, 33). Brinkmann (1997: 15, n. 32) also rejected the attribution of the calendar medallions to the Dresden Master.

2. It is clear that the four miniatures are not all by the same hand, and each calls to mind the Prayer Books Master in different ways. *The Visitation*, or the pattern upon which it is based, is copied in the Evora Altarpiece in Portugal.

3. Nine of the patterns were employed nearly two decades earlier in the London Hastings Hours (cat. no. 41), and another eight, including six of the Passion cycle, in the Hours of Mary of Burgundy and Maximilian (cat. no. 38).

4. While De Winter (1981: 417–20), and Van Miegroet (1989: 88), attributed the illumination to Horenbout, Scillia (1975: 228–31) was the first to identify the hand of Gerard David. Her opinion has more recently been supported by Krieger (2000: 215–33).

5. This includes the architecture at the right of the miniature, which is very similar in its forms, coloring, and details of execution to the tower in the Saint Barbara miniature.

6. See Ainsworth 1998: 13–14, fig. 15.

7. Illustrated in Ainsworth 1998: 225, fig. 213.

8. For discussion and illustrations, see Campbell 1998: 122–33.

9. Indeed, the motif of the paired trees was a favorite of David's, found not only in many of his paintings but also in a surviving metal-point study of a tree and a man's head (Hamburger Kunsthalle). See Ainsworth 1998: 31–33, fig. 38.

10. De Winter 1981: 401 (fig. 125), 418. On the relationship between this miniature and this painting, see also Kren and Ainsworth, "Illuminators and Painters: Artistic Exchanges and Interrelationships" (this volume).

11. This is also suggested by the flesh tones in the faces, which are more fully blended than those in other miniatures in the book and than is usually seen in illuminations.

12. The following petition in the litany might be deemed appropriate to Isabella, but it is not uncommon: "Ut regib[us] et principibus [Christ]ia/ nis pacem et veram Concordia[m] do/nare digneris Ter/ Ut cuncto populo [Christ]iano pa/cem et vnitate[m] largire digneris Tr." A Flemish book of hours made for Juana Enriquez, Isabella's mother-in-law, is noteworthy for its wealth of Spanish saints in the calendar and the litany (Madrid, Biblioteca de Palacio; Clark 1997: 70). The script of Isabella's breviary has often been called Spanish, but similar rounded Gothic script is also found in books for northern European patrons, such as the book of hours made for the use of a cleric at Saint Peter's, Blandin, in Ghent (cat. no. 40).

13. De Winter 1981: 347–50. It is common in Flemish books of this period for the arms of the owner to appear in miniatures of the Mass for the Dead, as, for example, in the London Hours of William Lord Hastings (cat. no. 41, fol. 184v). De Winter believed that the arms in Isabella's hours might be the arms of a woman of the Nassau or Cleves families. Faustino Menéndez Pidal de Navascués kindly pointed out in correspondence of January 8, 2002 (Department of Manuscripts files, JPGM), that the pendant gules with lion rampant or, while found throughout Europe, appears in the arms of the Burgos families Ruiz de la Mota and Gonel. Following his argument, many families of Burgos had commercial and matrimonial ties with Flanders. Thus, one possibility is that the original patron was a Flemish woman married to a Spanish man, with the banner referring to him (cf., e.g., Menéndez Pidal de Navascués 1996: 73, 75–76, 80, 82, 117, 131, 179, 188). Thanks to Menéndez Pidal de Navascués for sharing his ideas.

14. See König 1998a: 105–6, on the Berlin miniature and its suffrage, and Farquhar 1976: 92, fig. 73, on Margaret's hours.

15. This miniature is a faithful copy, down to the colors, of Marmion's novel miniature in the Naples Hours (cat. no. 93, fol. 289v), which, however, illustrates a lesson from the book of Daniel in an Office for Palm Sunday.

16. A notable exception is the very lavish Hours of Louis de Laval, with more than one hundred full-page miniatures (Paris, Bibliothèque nationale de France, Ms. lat. 970; Paris 1993: 328–32, no. 179).

17. The connection to the Franciscan order is suggested by the appearance of Bernardino of Siena (May 20), Clare (August 12), Francis himself (October 4), and the aforementioned Elizabeth of Hungary (November 18), a Franciscan tertiary, in both the calendar and the litany, although not as red-letter feasts in the calendar. Saint Anthony of Padua, a Franciscan friar, appears among the suffrages, with a full-page miniature. Saint Louis of Toulouse, also a Franciscan, appears only in the litany.

18. It follows Plummer's model for a Bruges calendar (in Baltimore 1988: 153–56) but lacks key saints associated with Bruges or Ghent, such as Donatian, Basil, and Bavo. The saints in red are largely those from the Roman calendar. Among the saints venerated in Flanders or northern France are Adrian (March 4), Gertrude (March 17), Quentin (May 31), Quirin (April 30), Erasmus (June 3), Eligius (June 25 and December 1), Egidius (September 1), Bertin (September 4), Lambert (September 17), Hubert (November 3), Catherine (November 25), and Barbara (December 4).

106

GERARD DAVID

Four Girls' Heads and Two Hands
Bruges, ca. 1505

Metalpoint on white prepared paper, 8.9 × 9.7 cm (3½ × 3¹³⁄₁₆ in.)

COLLECTION: Paris, Musée du Louvre, Cabinet des dessins, R.F. 3812

PROVENANCE: Philipp Dräxler von Caris, Vienna; Josef C. von Klinkosch (d. 1888), Vienna, in 1874 [his sale, C. J. Wawra, Vienna, April 15, 1889, lot 468 (as Hans Holbein the Younger)]; Freiherr A. von Lanna, Prague [his sale, H. G. Gutekunst, Stuttgart, May 6–10, 1910, lot 199]; acquired 1910

JPGM

This startlingly fresh rendering of the heads of four girls, along with studies of two hands, was most likely part of one of Gerard David's sketchbooks in which he recorded the likenesses of male and female figures after life.¹ At least six other extant sheets share the same technique of metalpoint on prepared paper on the recto with preliminary black chalk sketches on unprepared paper on the verso, carry numbers in a contemporary hand in pen and brown ink, and show similar areas of damage at the lower edge of each folio. The present sheet was cut at the bottom, most likely to excise this damaged portion, which is partially visible at the extreme lower middle edge.

David was a master of nuanced expression, a characteristic of both his paintings and his illuminations that imbued them with a sense of immediacy not often encountered in the works of contemporaries. His female and male figures are not simply types repeated over and again, but are modeled after living persons whom David knew or encountered in his daily life. He economically used every bit of the sheet, sometimes, as here, studying the same head in two different positions and adding sketches of a left and a right

hand as well. The images that he captured range from impromptu jottings recording pose and demeanor to more fully worked up heads for which he had a particular purpose in mind.

This sheet exemplifies the duality of purpose of David's drawings for both paintings and illuminations. In a general sense, the variety of poses encountered in the drawing is preparatory for the myriad head types and positions encountered in the *Virgin among Virgins* that David donated to the Convent of Sion in 1509 (fig. 68). The angles of the heads of Saint Godelieve, Saint Cecelia, and the two saints flanking the throne of the Virgin are similar to those of the present drawing, their expressions of concentration lending a powerful impression of introspection to the gathering, each saint inhabiting her own isolated, meditative world.

A close look at the modeling of the heads in the drawing shows a different scheme of illumination than is evident in the Rouen painting, however, and indicates the more direct relationship of the drawing to the earlier (ca. 1505) manuscript leaf of the same subject in the Morgan Library (cat. no. 107). The two saints directly behind the Virgin in the Morgan leaf—one looking down, and the other with her head turned to the right—show the same system of lighting as parallel heads in the present sheet. David handled the metalpoint freely, caressing the sides of the faces with slightly angled strokes to suggest their volume as well as their illumination. The subtlety of his execution allowed him to focus on certain forms (for example, the direction of the eyes, in order to convey emotion and meaning), while leaving others unresolved (such as the lower lids of eyes). David let forms blend into one another rather than making sharp demarcations and contours for facial features. The result is an impression of fleeting form and a true-life sense of movement and changing light effects.

An equally significant part of David's expressive mode was the importance he invested in hand gestures. As the drawing shows, this involved an understanding of the bony structure of the hand and changes of position and pose. The lower left-hand corner of the Morgan leaf is a veritable ballet of hand gestures that enfold and directly engage the Christ child, playfully diverting his interest in a flower or a piece of fruit. Such an accomplished diversity and arrangement of hand gestures could not have been achieved without preparatory drawings such as the present example, which explores the model for the proper left hand of the Virgin at the lower edge of the sheet.   M. W. A.

Note

1. For further discussion of David's sketchbook and related drawings, see Ainsworth 1998: 7–26.

Figure 68
GERARD DAVID
The Virgin among Virgins,
1509. Oil on panel, 118 ×
212 cm (46½ × 83½ in.).
Rouen, Musée des
Beaux-Arts, Inv. D.803.4

107

GERARD DAVID AND ANOTHER ILLUMINATOR

The Virgin among Virgins
Miniature from a Devotional Book
Bruges, ca. 1505–10

One full-page miniature, 18 × 13.4 cm (7⅛ × 5¼ in.); image:
16.5 × 11.5 cm (6½ × 4½ in.); back: blank

COLLECTION: New York, The Morgan Library, Ms. M.659

PROVENANCE: Frederick Locker-Lampson (1821–1895), by 1886;
purchased by J. P. Morgan Jr. (1867–1943) by 1926

JPGM and RA

A more usual subject of panel painting, the Virgin among Virgins did not often appear in books of hours or breviaries, where the more common depiction was the Holy Virgins alone.[1] When the theme did appear, as in the case of folio 719v of the Grimani Breviary (cat. no. 126), it generally followed a composition derived from Hugo van der Goes, wherein the Virgin and Child are surrounded by five female saints in an enclosed garden. In David's miniature (ill. 107) the richly attired virgins crowded on the foreground plane are not identified individually by their attributes. Their collective purpose is to honor the Virgin and Child: one offers the Christ child a white rose, another presents a piece of fruit, and a third touches rose petals in her basket. The emphasis on the gathering and presentation of flowers and fruit relates to the imagery of the *Song of Songs*, and to the preparations made previous to the marriage consummation of the Bride and Bridegroom, a metaphor for the union of God with the human soul.[2] An inscription on the neckline of Mary's dress can be partially read as H RA P S[?]: O MARIA; it perhaps refers to the opening words of a prayer or hymn sung to the Virgin.

The virgins congregate before a grand Gothic house whose detailed depiction suggests that it represents a specific site.[3] The same building—as well as the wall, gate, and identical town at the upper left in the background—appears in at least four other miniatures. Three of these are in books of hours,[4] and one is the centerpiece of *The Virgin and Child with Saints Catherine and Barbara* (see fig. 9), a triptych on parchment that is attributed to Simon Bening and his workshop.[5] As all of these examples are associated with Bening, there must have been a workshop pattern of this background scene that was derived from David's illumination and thereafter used for varied purposes.

It is not possible to establish the commission of this work from the scanty indications of either the location or the religious order of the women depicted. The nuns advancing from the city in the background wear gray robes and black headdresses. Could these be the Gray Sisters of Elizabeth or the Observants of the Poor Clares, who were among the Third Orders of Saint Francis that were established at Bruges?[6] If so, this miniature may have illustrated a book associated with one of these orders.

Although not unanimously accepted as by David,[7] this miniature has continued to be linked with his name since first attributed to him in 1960.[8] While the background of

Figure 69
GERARD DAVID
Head of a Girl,
ca. 1505–10. Brush and
black ink over black
chalk with some white
heightening on paper,
14.2 × 10.2 cm
(5⁹⁄₁₆ × 4 in.).
Hamburg, Kunsthalle,
Kupferstichkabinett,
inv. no. 21575 recto

the illumination, with its looser brushwork and muted color sense, appears to be by another hand, the foreground figures were certainly painted by David. Indeed, they are specifically related to *The Virgin among Virgins* (fig. 68), a large panel painting that David donated to the Carmelite Convent of Sion in 1509, particularly in regard to the tightly compressed arrangement of distinctly varied female types, who are attired similarly to those in the illumination. Also closely connected are four sheets of head studies that David made in preparation for both paintings and illuminations. *Four Girls' Heads and Two Hands* (ill. 106), *Three Female Heads* (Kraków, Czartoryski Museum), *Seated Girl with a Flowered Background* (Paris, Musée du Louvre), and *Head of a Girl* (fig. 69) all show poses and diverse expressions that can be linked to certain heads in the Morgan miniature.⁹ Studied from life, these heads imbue the miniature with a striking sense of verisimilitude.

In terms of execution, a comparison of the Hamburg *Head of a Girl* with the head of the Virgin Mary in the miniature reveals David's consistency of handling in both drawing and illumination, providing the most convincing argument for the attribution of the illumination to David himself. In addition to the similar physiognomy and treatment of the head, specific details of David's execution with the brush are identical. Instead of the metalpoint of the other drawings, David employed point of the brush and

black ink in the Hamburg sheet in order to study chiaroscuro effects in the modeling of the head. He used lightly feathered, angled strokes in even parallel hatching along the side of the face at the right in both drawing and illumination to simultaneously suggest volume and shading. Longer, more vertically arranged parallel hatching models the sides of the two faces at the left in half shadow. As the Hamburg drawing specifically studies chiaroscuro effects that David favored in his paintings after about 1505,¹⁰ both the drawing and the illumination must date to around 1505–10.¹¹

M. W. A.

Notes

I am grateful to Dominique Vanwijnsberghe and Christina Ceulemans for information regarding religious orders in Flanders.

1. For example, the assembled virgins in the Grimani Breviary (fol. 432v) follow a pattern similar to that of the Morgan leaf in their tight arrangement in the foreground of the miniature, taking up only two-thirds of the space, with the remaining third given over to a gold ground. Although the Morgan miniature has sometimes been considered an independent work, its ragged edges indicate that it was cut from a larger sheet. Books of considerable size that could have accommodated such a large-scale illumination have survived; indeed, the Grimani Breviary includes full-page miniatures of similar size and with a nearly identical painted gold frame. No book is known, however, that is lacking a page of the size and subject matter of the Morgan leaf.

2. For a thorough discussion of this imagery, see Falkenburg 1994: 52 and passim.

3. Paintings produced in Bruges and in Brussels during this period often show identifiable local architectural sites in the backgrounds. For a discussion of this phenomenon, see Harbison 1995: 21–34.

4. One is in the Walters Art Museum, Baltimore (W.426, fol. 60) and another in the Morgan Library (M. 451, fol. 69v); a third is in the Hennessy Hours (cat. no. 150, fol. 175v). Thanks to Thomas Kren for calling my attention to the latter two examples.

5. Illustrated and discussed in Bruges 1998: 166, no. 71.

6. Martens (M.) 1992: 305–6.

7. Scillia maintained doubts and did not include the Morgan illumination in her 1975 dissertation.

8. Detroit 1960: 399, no. 212; Kren (in Malibu 1983: 47) suggested David or workshop and now believes the work to be autograph; Van Miegroet (1989: 83, 328, no. 86) and Ainsworth (1998: 13, 20–21, 23; New York 1998: 277–78) affirmed the attribution to David himself.

9. For illustrations and further discussion, see Ainsworth 1998: 17–25, figs. 14–16, 22, 26.

10. For example, the Cervara Altarpiece, *The Virgin and Child with Saints and a Donor, The Virgin among Virgins*, the Metropolitan Museum of Art *Rest on the Flight into Egypt, The Virgin and Child with Four Angels*, and *The Virgin and Child in a Landscape*. For illustrations, see Van Miegroet 1989: figs. 191, 204, 213, 234, 239, 244.

11. The Morgan leaf has been dated to the 1490s in the past (Van Miegroet 1989: 328, no. 86).

MASTER OF JAMES IV OF SCOTLAND (A)

The finest illuminator of the generation between the Vienna Master of Mary of Burgundy (act. ca. 1470–80) and Simon Bening (1483/4–1561) is the Master of James IV of Scotland. He takes his name from the magnificent full-page dedication miniature he painted showing King James, accompanied by Saint Andrew, in prayer in a book of hours in Vienna (ill. 110a). Like the Master of the Dresden Prayer Book before him and Bening after, he enjoyed an exceptionally long career. A breviary in Manchester (cat. no. 108), the only example of his youthful style, is dated 1487, while the calendar and frontispiece portraits in the Holford Hours of 1526 (ill. 127) are his latest miniatures. Unfortunately for our understanding of his development, very few of the books produced in between can be dated with much precision. (A miniature in the style of the Master of James IV that serves as the frontispiece to the register of the woodcutters' guild in Ghent is dated 1510.)[1]

Although this illuminator's activity was first defined by Friedrich Winkler eighty years ago, his importance was much less obvious then than it is today.[2] Our knowledge of this artist's production has grown exponentially since then. Such major works as the Spinola Hours (cat. no. 124), the Rothschild Book of Hours (private collection),[3] and the two leaves in the Metropolitan Museum of Art (cat. no. 125) were unknown to Winkler, as were the three aforementioned dated works and the Chantilly *Speculum humanae salvationis* (Musée Condé, Ms. franc. 1363),[4] the last being largely workshop. Others, such as the Vatican Hours (cat. no. 111), were little studied, and one major work, the prayer book for a member of the Portuguese royal family in the Museu Nacional de Arte Antiga in Lisbon (Ms. 13), long attributed to Simon Bening, is here attributed to the Master of James IV and his workshop for the first time. It is a brilliant example of his late manner.[5]

Despite building upon the innovations of the Vienna Master of Mary of Burgundy and others of the previous generation, the Master of James IV was stylistically wholly independent of them. His types are robust, fleshy, and unidealized. His handling is remarkably free and spontaneous—painterly in the classical sense of the term.[6] His brushwork and his ruddy handling of flesh look ahead to Peter Paul Rubens rather than back to any earlier Flemish painter or illuminator. His colorful landscapes eschew the interest in atmosphere of the Vienna Master in favor of the play of light. He was a poet of light and color who favored saturated hues, especially blues and reds, but often displayed the variety (and effects) of the rainbow. He used light in diverse ways: to define spatial depth, to reveal texture, and to focus a narrative.

One of the artist's key innovations resides in his conception of the illuminated two-page opening (see cat. nos. 109, 124). In several of his books he reduced the space for text to a minimum, sometimes eliminating it altogether (e.g., cat. no. 126, fols. 138v, 139), with one large miniature facing another. In the Spinola Hours he carried this development to an enchanting extreme, incorporating the border area into the pictorial space of the central miniature, often without eliminating the architectural moldings that demarcate the traditional divisions within the page. In several instances he exploited the proximity of border and miniature in a clever way, showing the interior of a building in the miniature and its exterior in the border. In the celebrated Office of the Dead miniature from this book (ill. 124b), he even managed to depict in the bas-de-page the crypt of the church whose choir and exterior are shown in the compartments for the miniature and lateral border, respectively. This development also has a narrative logic, by uniting in physically contiguous spaces successive, simultaneous, or otherwise interrelated incidents of a larger narrative. Finally, by showing scenes from the same narrative on facing pages, the artist increased the length of the continuous narrative (as, for example, in the fourteen-episode Passion cycle of a book of hours in London [cat. no. 109]), marking the beginning of a trend in Flemish illumination that would continue well into the sixteenth century.

The Master of James IV also took up the new illusionism of Flemish manuscript borders that began in the 1470s and pushed the envelope, exploring the possibilities of trompe l'oeil. The Spinola Hours again contains some of his most remarkable inventions, including, memorably, the incipit of a devotion written on a painted piece of parchment that appears pinned to the three-dimensional space of the miniature, one spatial illusion painted on top of (or literally into) another (cat. no. 124, fols. 10v–11). In this way the devotion itself becomes a component of the image.

The origins of the Master of James IV's style are not entirely clear, although, like other illuminators of this time, he used motifs and compositions from Hugo van der Goes and Joos van Ghent. He collaborated fairly early in his career with the still mysterious illuminator/book illustrator called the Master of the Lübeck Bible (see cat. nos. 112, 113), who may have contributed to the formation of his style. The latter's influence is still apparent at the turn of the century in the Vatican Hours (cat. no. 111). The Master of James IV had the more wide-ranging career as an illuminator, however, and contributed to shaping the next two generations of illuminators, including the Master of the David Scenes in the Grimani Breviary, the Master of the Soane Hours, and Simon Bening. The activity of the

Master of James IV is difficult to localize, although one might well expect a local master or workshop to be responsible for the Ghent guild register mentioned above. His only surviving portraits, which show that he was also a master of painting in oil on panel, represent the prominent Ghent citizen Lievin van Pottelsberghe and his wife, Livina de Steelant (see fig. 14).[7] The artist collaborated with illuminators from Bruges, such as the Master of the Dresden Prayer Book and Gerard David, but worked even more often with the Master of First Prayer Book of Maximilian, whose artistic roots were in Ghent. Georges Hulin de Loo and many scholars following him have identified the Master of James IV of Scotland with Gerard Horenbout.[8]   T. K.

Notes

1. Casier and Bergmans 1921: 91–92, fig. 261. Unfortunately I know the miniature only through a digital image kindly provided by the Archives of the City of Ghent, the book's owner. Thanks to Elizabeth Morrison for bringing this manuscript to my attention.

2. Winkler 1925: 127.

3. Trenkler 1979; sale, Christie's, London, July 9, 1999, lot 102. The manuscript has long been called a prayer book but is in fact a book of hours.

4. Kessler 1977; Vergne 1995: 135, 210, 244, 245.

5. This is the so-called Hours of Queen Catherine. See Santos 1932: 26–27, pl. 33; and Lisbon 1992: 159, no. 19. One other important overlooked example of this artist's work (Vienna, Österreichische Nationalbibliothek, Ms. ser. n. 2625) will be published by Dagmar Thoss in the third installment of the catalogue of Flemish manuscripts in the Österreichische Nationalbibliothek.

6. This is illustrated by considering the copy of *The Road to Calvary* from the illuminator's workshop (cat. no. 109, fol. 28v) after that by the Vienna Master of Mary of Burgundy and his workshop in the eponymous hours (cat. no. 19). See Malibu 1983a: 64, figs. 8a, 8b.

7. Martens (M.) 2000.

8. This notion is discussed in the biography of Horenbout in part 5, this volume.

108

MASTER OF JAMES IV OF SCOTLAND

Breviary
Use of Windesheim
Probably Ghent, 1487

MANUSCRIPT: i + 265 + ii folios, 17.9 × 12 cm (7¹⁄₁₆ × 4¼ in.); justification: 11.3 × 3.3–0.7–3.8 cm (4⁷⁄₁₆ × 1⁵⁄₁₆–¼–1⁷⁄₁₆ in.); 22 lines of *hybrida* in two columns; 12 two-column miniatures, 18 one-column miniatures

HERALDRY: Escutcheon with unidentified coat of arms, azure a scourge or and 3 clous argent, and *Nostri Officii*, fol. 213; row of fleurs-de-lis alternating with crowns, fol. 241v; initials *JG en lac*, fols. 107, 118, 146, etc.

BINDING: Modern; red velvet

COLLECTION: Manchester, The John Rylands University Library, Ms. 39

PROVENANCE: Unidentified Augustinian canon with the initials *JG*; James Ludovic Lindsay, twenty-sixth earl of Crawford and ninth earl of Balcarres (1847–1913) (Bibliotheca Lindesiana, Ms. 39); to the John Rylands Library in 1901.

R A

The Meeting of Abraham and Melchizedek
Leaf from a breviary

One leaf, 15.3 × 10.8 cm (6 × 4¼ in.); justification: 11.5 × 3.6–0.7–3.6 cm (4½ × 1⅜–¼–1⅜ in.); 22 lines of *hybrida* in two columns; 1 two-column miniature

COLLECTION: New York, The Morgan Library, Ms. M 1046

PROVENANCE: Mr. and Mrs. Percy S. Straus by 1937; Mrs. Donald B. Straus; her bequest, 1983

JPGM

The miniatures in this lush breviary are among the earliest works by the Master of James IV of Scotland.[1] A number of stylistic and compositional elements—a rich palette; faces with big, clearly defined eyes; figures and action placed in the foreground; processions of densely placed figures; and an inherent narrative quality—prefigure the mature style of the artist. In *All Saints* (fol. 206), for example, an expansive, painterly, and atmospheric landscape filled with saints suggests the epic compositions found in the artist's later work. The breviary's *Assumption of the Virgin* (ill. 108a) closely anticipates the masterful composition in the Spinola Hours (cat. no. 124, fol. 148v), where angels lift the Virgin above her grave containing three Eucharistic wafers, an unusual iconography. In the book of hours, however, the artist extended the pictorial field into the border and added supplemental narratives, such as the scene of Thomas receiving Mary's girdle.

This breviary was highly personalized for its original owner, an Augustinian canon, who is depicted twice in the book.[2] In a two-column miniature prefacing the Common of Saints (fol. 213), John the Evangelist presents him to an assembly of saints featuring John the Baptist in the central position. The emphasis placed on these saints and the linked initials *JG* appearing throughout the manuscript indicate that the owner's Christian name was a form of John. In another two-column miniature the patron, recognizable as a canon by his black amice, kneels in devotion before a large figure of Saint Barbara that dominates the

108a

MASTER OF JAMES IV
OF SCOTLAND
*The Assumption of the
Virgin,* fol. 191

108b

MASTER OF JAMES IV
OF SCOTLAND
*The Meeting of Abraham
and Melchizedek*

miniature for her feast. Barbara also figures among the saints in the miniature introducing the Sanctorale. It is probable that the canon was associated with an Augustinian house devoted to Barbara, such as the Windesheim Sister house of Barberendal in Tienen, near Leuven. A connection with a Windesheim congregation is supported by the liturgical use of the manuscript's Office of the Dead. If the canon were associated with Barberendal, he perhaps was its rector, but attempts to match a name with the initials *JG* have been unsuccessful.[3]

The manuscript has folios bound out of sequence, and others are lacking altogether.[4] A leaf now in the Morgan Library, New York (ill. 108b), shares several elements—including the artist, the number of text lines, and the size of the text block—confirming its origin in the breviary.[5] It originally prefaced the Office of Corpus Christi and depicts the meeting of Abraham and Melchizedek, a fitting but relatively uncommon subject for the office.[6] Melchizedek, a king and high priest, offers Abraham wine and bread, types for the Eucharistic elements (Gen. 14:18–24). This subject also prefaces the Office of Corpus Christi in another breviary for the Windesheim congregation, which was painted around 1500 by an artist in the circle of the Master of James IV.[7] The Master of James IV himself repeated the theme again later in his career in the border surrounding the same

office in the Spinola Hours (fol. 49). In each of these, Melchizedek wears comparable ceremonial vestments.

R. G.

Notes

1. The date 1487, written beside two circular diagrams—"Ad inveniendum aureum numerum" and "Ad inveniendum literam dominicalem"—likely signals the year of production. The manuscript lacks its calendar.

2. The patron appears in miniatures on folios 150 and 213. Saint Augustine appears first among the confessors in the litany and in a two-column miniature prefacing his feast on folio 194.

3. Johannes Ghisens was rector in the 1460s but died before the manuscript's production. Johannes Gilemannus, the famous hagiographer of Windesheim, died at Rooclooster in 1487, the date of the manuscript's production.

4. James 1921: 97–102.

5. The dimensions for the leaf published in New York 1974 are incorrect. The actual justification is 11.5 × 3.6–0.7–3.6 cm (4½ × 1⅛–¼–1⅜ in.). Initially this seems not to match that of the breviary; the width of the breviary's columns, however, varies within the overall text block. At times, the right column is slightly larger than the left, and at others the columns are of equal size, matching those of the leaf.

6. The leaf apparently preceded folio 125, which contains incomplete text for the Office of Corpus Christi. It would not have immediately followed folio 124, a singleton bound out of order, because that folio includes Advent anthems and should be bound earlier in the manuscript.

7. König 1998b: 452–63.

109

MASTER OF JAMES IV OF SCOTLAND AND
WORKSHOP AND WORKSHOP OF MASTER OF THE
FIRST PRAYER BOOK OF MAXIMILIAN

Book of Hours
Use of Rome
Probably Ghent, ca. 1500

MANUSCRIPT: ii + 237 + ii folios, 23.7 × 15.2 cm (9⁵⁄₁₆ × 6 in.);
justification: 10.5 × 7.2 cm (4⅛ × 2¹³⁄₁₆ in.); 16 lines of *textura*; 75 full-
page or large miniatures, 12 bas-de-page calendar miniatures with
additional scenes set into architectural borders

HERALDRY: Lozenges with unidentified coat of arms argent a chevron
azure, fol. 159

BINDING: Probably continental Europe, eighteenth century; gold-
tooled brown leather

COLLECTION: London, The British Library, Add. Ms. 35313

PROVENANCE: Baron Ferdinand de Rothschild (1839–1898); his
bequest to the British Museum, 1898

JPGM and RA

109a
MASTER OF JAMES IV
OF SCOTLAND
OR WORKSHOP
*The Presentation in
the Temple* and *The
Presentation of Samuel*,
fols. 106v–107

Two elaborate pictorial cycles, one for the Hours of the
Cross and another for the Hours of the Virgin, form
the innovative heart of the extensive illumination of this
manuscript. Both were executed by the Master of James IV
of Scotland and his workshop, and both appear in the first
half of the book. The Hours of the Cross features fourteen
paired miniatures that relate the narrative of Christ's Passion, from the Entry into Jerusalem to the Entombment.
The Hours of the Virgin contains eight pairs of miniatures.
In all but two cases, an episode from the Life of the Virgin,
beginning with the Annunciation and ending with the
Coronation of the Virgin (ill. 109b), is placed opposite a
typologically related Old Testament subject (ill. 109a).[1]

The two sequences in the present book of hours contain the volume's finest painting. They are important historically as evidence of the artist's emerging interest in
reducing the amount of text space in each opening to a
minimum—as little as two lines on the right-hand page
with a full-page miniature opposite—so that the openings
themselves are remarkably close to being fully illuminated.[2] Matching borders, either of the strewn type or of
the carved Gothic frame type, further strengthen each
opening's impression of visual unity.

109b
WORKSHOP OF
MASTER OF JAMES IV
OF SCOTLAND
*The Coronation of
the Virgin*, fol. 120

The Master of James IV of Scotland and his workshop provided thirty-eight of the miniatures, and the workshop perhaps also illuminated the elaborate calendar, with its twelve bas-de-pages plus vignettes illustrating the red-letter days within each page's architectural frame.[3] The workshop of the Maximilian Master provided thirty-seven miniatures, twenty-four of them half-page miniatures in the suffrages, the majority based on existing patterns.[4] Despite the novelty of a portion of the decorative program and its importance for the development of the style of the Master of James IV, overall the book's illumination is uneven and, in the cycle of the suffrages, often weak.[5] The participation of these two workshops suggests that the book was probably illuminated in Ghent.

The presence of the martyrs Saint Emeterius and Saint Celidonius; the confessors Saint Ildefonsus, Saint Isidore, and Saint Adelelmus; and the virgin Saint Marina in the litany indicates that the book was made for a patron from Spain.[6] The Office of the Dead features a rare copy of the unusual miniature from the Berlin Hours of Mary of Burgundy that shows Mary as one of the Three Living Menaced by Death (cat. no. 38, fol. 220v). This may indicate that the book was made for a woman, since it is unusual to depict a woman as one of the three living, or that it was made for someone one who held dear the memory of the late Burgundian duchess.[7]   T. K.

Notes
1. The two exceptions are terce and compline, where two scenes from the life of the Virgin illustrate the opening. In a number of cases, the miniatures from the present manuscript seem to have been literally copied into the Soane Hours. See Millar 1914–20: 96–101, 103–4, and under cat. no. 138.

2. A comparable two-page opening by this artist or his workshop illustrates the Hours of the Holy Spirit (the one decorated opening for this text) and the Office of the Dead.

3. The calendar is based closely on a set of patterns used in other manuscripts in this exhibition (cat. nos. 91, 92, 110, 124, 138), which are discussed in cat. no. 91 and in the Rothschild Hours (private collection; Trenkler 1979: fols. 1v–7). This particular calendar agrees with the Rothschild Hours in nearly all details of the bas-de-page; the architectural framework, with its monochrome scenes of the red-letter days; and the treatment of the zodiacal signs. They differ dramatically only in the liturgical content. The British Library hours has a full calendar, while the Rothschild one is relatively sparse.

4. Winkler (1925: 127, 128) and subsequently Kren (in Malibu 1983a: 66–68) attributed these miniatures to the Master of the Hortulus Animae—an artistic personality whose oeuvre subsequent scholars have distributed among other artists, including the Maximilian Master—or his assistants. See the biography of the Master of the First Prayer Book of Maximilian (part 2, this volume).

5. Over the years it has become clear to me that the quality of this book's illumination in the style of the Master of James IV is well below his best and may be largely workshop. The miniatures that most likely show his hand—*The Visitation* and *Sarah and Tobias Welcomed by Anna* (fols. 76v–77; Smeyers 1998: 442)—have suffered from fading. With regard to the miniatures related to the Maximilian Master, it seems to be characteristic of the manuscripts to which he contributed that the cycle of suffrages, usually pattern-based half-page miniatures, do not match the quality of the rest of the book. These cycles are often painted by several hands (cf., e.g., cat. no. 90). The cycle in the present manuscript is lower in quality than the otherwise quite similar cycles in the Rothschild Hours or other books in the exhibition (cat. nos. 92, 105, 124).

6. The calendar, however, which is full, contains few feasts for Spanish saints and none as red-letter days. It is largely Flemish, with Saints Remi and Bavo (October 1), Saint Donatian (October 14), and Saint Gilles (December 1) as special feasts. A less common special feast is the Translation of Saint Thomas the Apostle, on July 3, which nevertheless is celebrated in many dioceses.

7. Backhouse (1985: 18–20) suggested that the book was made for Mary's daughter, Margaret of Austria, an interesting theory since she inherited the Berlin book of hours from her mother (see also Smeyers 1998: 441–42). Another possible first owner is Joanna of Castile, who married Mary's son Philip the Handsome. Joanna, at least, was Spanish (Kren, in Malibu 1983a: 68). Perhaps Margaret had the book made for Joanna.

110

MASTER OF JAMES IV OF SCOTLAND AND OTHERS

Hours of James IV of Scotland
Use of Rome
Probably Ghent, ca. 1502–3

MANUSCRIPT: ii + 248 + ii folios, 20 × 14 cm (7⅞ × 5½ in.); justification: 12–12.7 × 7.5–8.3 cm (4¾–5 × 2¹¹⁄₁₆–3¼ in.); 20 lines of *bastarda* by the Thin Descender Scribe; 19 full-page miniatures, 46 small miniatures, 2 historiated initials, 9 historiated borders, 12 half-page calendar miniatures with additional scenes set into architectural borders

HERALDRY: Full-page armorial composed of escutcheon with the arms of James IV of Scotland encircled by collar of the Order of the Golden Fleece, surmounted by crowned helm and lion, supported by unicorns; escutcheon with the arms of James IV, fols. 24v, 109v, 141v; escutcheon with the arms of Margaret Tudor, fols. 14v, 243v; initials *IM en lac*, fols. 14v, 183v, 243v; motto of James IV *In my defens*, fols. 24v, 189v; motto of James IV *God us defend*, fol. 243v

INSCRIPTIONS: *Madame I pray your grace / Remember on me when ye / loke upon thys boke / Your lofing syster / Margaret*, fol. 188

BINDING: Austria, 1978; stamped leather

COLLECTION: Vienna, Österreichische Nationalbibliothek, Ms. 1897

PROVENANCE: James IV, king of Scotland (1472–1513), and Margaret Tudor (1489–1541); to Mary Tudor (1495/96–1533); Emperor Leopold I (1653–1705); Hapsburg Court Library

JPGM

This manuscript is most widely known for its full-page portrait of the Scottish king James IV, the exceptional quality of which led Friedrich Winkler to identify the artist as the Master of James IV of Scotland.[1] The sumptuous manuscript contains an additional eighteen full-page illuminations, an unusual series of uninhabited landscapes in the calendar, and a quarter border for every text page.[2] Despite moments of brilliance, however, the manuscript in its entirety presents a rather odd picture of heterogeneity, mostly due to the large number of artists who contributed miniatures, many of them of inferior quality.

The two full-page portraits of the king and queen represent the greatest painting in the book, although by different artists (ills. 110a, 110b). Both portraits are linked iconographically to the panel paintings of James III and his wife, Margaret of Denmark, that Edward Bonikel of Edinburgh commissioned from Hugo van der Goes (Trinity College, Edinburgh). Since it is clear that detailed drawings of the couple's coats of arms—as well as other information, such as their mottoes—must have been taken to Flanders as part of the commission for the manuscript, it is probable that drawings of the altarpiece were also taken at the same time.[3] The quotation of the Van der Goes panels in this Flemish book of hours may have been a flattering allusion both to the Scottish Stuart dynasty and to that ruling family's continued appreciation of the work of Flemish artists.

The portrait of the king is one of only two illuminations in the book by the Master of James IV.[4] The sheer size of the miniature—a full page without borders—and details such as the hoary face of Saint James and the painterly modeling of cloth throughout the miniature rank it among the Master of James IV's finest and most ambitious works. The portrait of the queen, Margaret Tudor, is

110a
MASTER OF JAMES IV
OF SCOTLAND
James IV in Prayer,
fol. 24v

painted in a much softer, delicate technique quite different from the vigorous energy that characterizes the James IV miniature.[5] Although the artist has not been identified and this miniature represents his sole contribution to the manuscript, the influence of Van der Goes is evident, especially in the treatment of the Virgin and Child.[6] The pale, clear faces of the two women and the pastel palette recall the best work of the Master of the First Prayer Book of Maximilian, but without any of the heavy awkwardness that often characterizes his miniatures.[7]

The miniatures that accompany the calendar are remarkable for their atmospheric quality and their exclusion of figures in the landscape. They have an ancestor in the calendar miniatures of the Voustre Demeure Hours (cat. no. 20 and fig. 30), which are composed largely of landscapes inhabited by barely visible figures, but the text of the calendar in the Hours of James IV is most closely related to that found in the Spinola Hours (cat. no. 124).[8] The calendars of both the Hours of James IV and the Spinola Hours, perhaps illuminated by the same follower of the Master

of James IV, are characterized by craggy hills, the use of a distinctive brownish green for the ground cover, and distant backgrounds whose buildings and trees are done almost entirely in blue. The entries in the texts of the two calendars agree 92.62 percent, suggesting a very close connection between the two manuscripts.[9] Despite their novelty and individual beauty, the landscapes in the Hours of James IV are almost totally uniform, unlike the landscapes in the Voustre Demeure Hours, which change according to the seasons.

A large number of artists completed the rest of the miniatures in the manuscript. The illuminations can be grouped as follows: the four Evangelist portraits and some of the male saints in the suffrages, most of the female saints and a number of historiated borders, and the series of narrative Passion images in unusual four-part miniatures that accompany a long cycle of Passion texts. The full-page miniatures of the Hours of the Virgin are the work of several additional artists: *The Annunciation*, *The Visitation*, and *The Dream of Joseph* form a set; the miniatures *The*

Notes

1. Winkler 1925: 205.

2. The elegant and somewhat spiky script of the text can be identified in a number of other manuscripts (see cat. no. 137).

3. The *Légende de Saint Adrien* (cat. no. 42) from before 1483 contains an image of the king and queen of France (ill. 42) related to these Van der Goes portraits, raising questions about whether drawings of the panels were available in Flanders. It seems highly improbable, however, that both artists working on the Hours of James IV chose these specific compositions for their portraits of James IV and his wife without knowing the Trinity College panels.

4. The second is *The Flight into Egypt* (fol. 104v), which is similar in composition to the same subject by the Master of James IV found in the Spinola Hours (cat. no. 124, fol. 140v). The miniature of James IV currently stands near the front of the book, opposite the Devotions to Saint Bridget, but the manuscript has been rebound, and its original placement remains a question.

5. The portrait of a queen at prayer (cat. no. 91, fol. 1v), perhaps Eleanor of Portugal, bears striking compositional similarities to this miniature, indicating that the pattern was available to artists in the circle of the Master of James IV of Scotland. The miniature of Margaret appears at the very end of the book, facing the "Obsecro te." While this appears to be an appropriate placement for the miniature, it is clear that the folios at the end of the book were bound in the incorrect order during a rebinding, confusing the issue (Unterkircher 1987: 18).

6. This composition does not exactly match any known Van der Goes painting, but the oddly turned foot of Christ and crossed hands of the Virgin can be seen in a Van der Goes *Virgin and Child* (Brussels, Musées royaux des Beaux-Arts de Belgique). Lorne Campbell (in Thompson and Campbell (C.) 1974: 47) has suggested that the missing central panel of the Trinity College triptych could have been similar to one now in the Cathedral of Moulins depicting the Virgin of the Immaculate Conception. It is possible, therefore, that the artist derived his inspiration from the missing central panel of the Trinity triptych.

7. A number of miniatures by the Maximilian Master in the Grimani Breviary (cat. no. 126) offer favorable comparisons, such as *The Visitation* (fol. 610v) and *The Coronation of the Virgin* (fol. 684), but none of them has the delicacy of touch that infuses the Margaret miniature.

8. The calendar is actually one of seven related calendars (see cat. no. 91), but the Hours of James IV is the only manuscript in the group that has pure landscapes instead of labors of the month, and it is also the only calendar in which each month occupies two pages instead of one.

9. John Plummer provided these statistics (Department of Manuscripts files, JPGM).

10. Despite the fact that they are by more than one artist, the *Annunciation, Visitation, Presentation,* and *David in Prayer* miniatures appear to be color copies from the same source, the Hours of Engelbert of Nassau (cat. no. 18).

11. Macfarlane (1960: 5) established that the book belonged to Margaret by pointing out her signature on folio 188 presenting the book to her sister. The manuscript must have been commissioned by James IV, not only because of the inclusion in it of numerous references only available at the Scottish court but also because the manuscript's decorative scheme mirrors that of the Scottish marriage contract (London, Public Record Office, E39/81).

12. A full-page representation of their heraldry appears on folio 14v, including both their mottoes and both their coats of arms, along with intertwined initials and the thistle and daisy. Other heraldic symbols can be found on folios 9, 21, 109v, 141v, 183v, and 189v.

13. Unterkircher (1967: 246) was the first to propose that the wedding may have provided an impetus to finish the manuscript hurriedly. There is evidence to suggest that perhaps the text at least was written prior to the commission, such as the fact that there is no suffrage addressed to James. The page for the suffrage of Saint Margaret, however, was personalized in the border by the addition of daisies and thistles.

Circumcision and *The Presentation*, another; and the half-length *Nativity* and *Adoration of the Magi*, a third.[10] The variation in format and style among the miniatures gives the manuscript a makeshift quality.

The manuscript must have been commissioned sometime between the marriage of James and Margaret in 1503 and James's death in 1513. It is probable, however, that James commissioned the manuscript as a wedding present for the young Margaret Tudor.[11] The dynastic marriage was meant to ensure a lasting peace between Scotland and England, and this book may have been a part of the opulent welcome Margaret received upon her arrival for the festivities, for which James had procured many Flemish goods. A number of miniatures in the Hours of the Virgin emphasize the role of Joseph, including the extremely rare depiction of the Dream of Joseph (fol. 82v). It is possible that the pairing of Joseph and Mary was intended to serve as a *beau ideal* for the young Margaret Tudor of her own relationship with her new husband. The presence of heraldic references throughout the manuscript, moreover, indicates that the portraits of the king and queen were not simply added at the end in an attempt to personalize the manuscript.[12] The absence of any texts specifically related to the couple and the involvement of many contributing artists, however, raise the possibility that the manuscript was already written and partially completed when the project was taken over for James IV, perhaps to meet the deadline imposed by the wedding.[13]   E. M.

110b
ANONYMOUS
Margaret Tudor in Prayer,
fol. 243v

III

MASTER OF JAMES IV OF SCOTLAND, WORKSHOP
OF MASTER OF THE FIRST PRAYER BOOK OF
MAXIMILIAN, AND OTHERS

Book of Hours
Use of Rome
Probably Ghent, ca. 1500

MANUSCRIPT: 231 folios, 20.2 × 14.4 cm (8 × 5⅝ in.); justification:
11.2 × 8.4 cm (4⅛ × 3³⁄₁₆ in.); 22 lines of *textura*; 19 full-page
miniatures, 8 quarter-page miniatures, 12 small calendar miniatures

BINDING: Blind-stamped brown leather; missing clasp

COLLECTION: Vatican City, Biblioteca Apostolica Vaticana, Vat.
lat. 3770

PROVENANCE: Jean de Pallant (ca. 1480–ca. 1540) and Anna van
Culenborgh

RA

IIIa
MASTER OF JAMES IV
OF SCOTLAND
The Last Judgment, vol. 1,
fol. 222v

Comprising more than 560 leaves, this book of hours, now divided into three volumes (vols. 2, 3 are Vat. lat. 3769, 3768), contains the most extensive pictorial cycle by the Master of James IV of Scotland. In devotional terms it is complex. It is properly a psalter-hours, a type that is more common both to French illumination and to an earlier era, containing the complete Psalter following the calendar (see also cat. no. 136). It also has a selection of miscellaneous prayers, including a remarkable fifty-three suffrages. Although the Offices for the Days of the Week are not an unusual feature of the more luxurious books of hours of this era (e.g., cat. nos. 38, 44, 105, 124), the particular offices chosen here—especially the Sunday Hours of the Guardian Angel, the Monday Hours of Eternal Wisdom, and the Wednesday Hours of the Mercy of the Lord—are uncommon.

The book's program of decoration is extensive even within the context of the extravagantly illuminated Flemish books of hours and breviaries of this time. The Psalter has a cycle of eight full-page miniatures. Each of the fifty-three suffrages has a quarter-page miniature. Seven of the nine accessory prayers also have a quarter-page miniature, while one has a full-page miniature. The latter is a particularly splendid composition, showing a nobleman offering confession to a priest while a noblewoman, her back to the viewer, kneels in prayer (ill. 111b).[1] This proliferation of imagery makes the book's decorative program unusual in a number of ways. In the offices for the seven days of the week, there is a full-page miniature at the beginning of each office, a typical arrangement. And, exceptionally, an extra full-page miniature illustrates a prayer that appears with the Wednesday office, while the Thursday office is further illustrated with a full-page miniature of Saint John on Patmos and a cycle of six quarter-page Passion miniatures accompanying the Evangelist's narrative of the Passion. Equally rare is the series of illustrations for the Office of the Dead, with full-page miniatures at each of its three hours. Even the litany, which is generally not illuminated, has a quarter-page miniature.

The identity of the book's patron, who was probably male, is unclear, although broad clues abound. Most intriguing is the David cycle that is placed toward the front of the book. The distinctive cycle traces David's exploits in the lifetime of Saul, including his betrothal to Saul's daughter Michal—an unusual subject—and his coronation as Saul's successor as king of Judea (ill. 111d). It underscores the young David's valor and his martial exploits, including no fewer than four scenes linked to his encounter with Goliath.[2] David cycles grew increasingly popular in both Flemish and French manuscripts at the end of the fifteenth century and appear both in breviaries, which are organized around the Psalter, and in books of hours, which are not.[3] Since rulers of this time strongly identified with David,[4] the presence of this cycle may indicate that the book was made for someone powerful at the Hapsburg court in Germany. A number of texts, including the Hours of Eternal Wisdom and Hours of the Mercy of the Lord, are characteristic of Dutch books of hours, although Dutch *horae* are usually made for Utrecht/Windesheim use, which this book is not.[5] Bodo Brinkmann pointed out that the use of the term

IIIb

MASTER OF JAMES IV
OF SCOTLAND
A Man Confessing, vol. 3,
fol. 51v

IIIc

MASTER OF JAMES IV
OF SCOTLAND
The Resurrection, vol. 2,
fol. 178v

cursus in the rubrics for *office* is more typically German, and a Rhenish patron is suggested by some of the saints in the suffrages: Saint Lambert (Liège), Saint Quirinus (Neuss), The Three Kings (Cologne), Charlemagne (Aachen), and Saint Florent (Strasbourg). The armorials in the deathbed scene and the *Mass for the Dead* are painted over an earlier set, neither of which has been identified with certainty.[6]

The Master of James IV of Scotland was responsible for most of the book's illumination, including nearly all of the full-page miniatures and many of the smaller miniatures. Among them is a group of half-length miniatures in the Hours of the Virgin that represents a fresh take on Marmion's cycle from the La Flora Hours (cat. no. 93). The brilliantly colored *Last Judgment* (ill. IIIa) shows the artist's ability to focus on the personal in the midst of an epic theme as the angel guides the souls of the saved to heaven.

The Master of James IV's miniatures show stylistic features that are distinctive even for his illuminations, such as the exceptionally full and silky beards on many of the Old Testament figures (vol. 1, fols. 25v, 47v, and ill. IIId). They recall figures in the Poortakker Triptych in Ghent, including Salomé at the left in the central panel (fig. 70). The triptych is a little-studied work signed *Gerardus* and associated by Georges Hulin de Loo with Gerard Horen-

bout.[7] The wide, low hats, some with floppy brims, worn by the men in the manuscript also bring the triptych to mind. An artist from the workshop of the Maximilian Master was responsible for the calendar, the full-page *Adoration of the Magi*, and a number of the smaller miniatures (e.g., vol. 2, fols. 77, 91).[8] Although the book has generally been dated to the second decade of the sixteenth century, the particulars of costume suggest that it could date much earlier. Margaret Scott pointed out a number of elements of costume that may date as early as the late 1490s.[9]   T. K.

Notes

1. It illustrates the prayer "Heu michi infelix anima. . . ."

2. Thanks to Kristen Collins for her research on the subject matter of this cycle. One other rare subject (fol. 47v), which shows Goliath's armor being displayed after battle, appears to be extra-biblical. I know of no other example of it.

3. In the Hours of Philip of Cleves from the late fifteenth century (Vienna, Österreichische Nationalbibliothek, Ms. s.n. 13239), the Penitential Psalms has a cycle of seven scenes from the life of David (Pächt and Thoss 1990: 94–95, figs. 182–87). See also cat. no. 100.

4. One ruler of this period who favored books with elaborate David iconography was Duke René II of Lorraine, who acquired two elaborate Franciscan breviaries during the 1490s (Paris, Bibliothèque de l'Arsenal, Ms. 601, and Musée du Petit Palais, Ms. 42; Paris, Bibliothèque nationale de France, Ms. lat. 10491). See Paris 1993: 378–83, nos. 215, 216.

5. Cologne 1992: 288.

6. Brinkmann (in Cologne 1992: 287) summarized the history of these identifications.

7. Hulin de Loo 1939a: 20, figs. 12–15, esp. fig. 14.

8. Brinkmann (in Cologne 1992: 286) indicated that Simon Bening may have painted some of the smaller miniatures, but I have not been able to confirm this. I was unable to examine Vat. lat. 3768, which was in restoration at the time of my visit to the Vatican library.

9. In correspondence of October 8, 2002 (Department of Manuscripts files, JPGM), Margaret Scott suggested parallels for the costume of the kneeling male supplicant in folio 51v in two paintings from the 1490s: the portrait of Pierre de Bourbon by the Master of Moulins (Paris, Musée du Louvre) and the panel *Saint Giles and the King of France* (London, National Gallery). A similar bulkiness to the men's attire is found in Pierre Louis de Valtan's *Commentary on the Apostles' Creed*, datable before 1498 (British Library, Add. Ms. 35320, e.g., fol. 2v; Malibu 1983a: 173, fig. 22g).

Figure 70
GERARD HORENBOUT (?)
The Family of Saint Anne
(Poortakker Triptych).
Oil on panel, left panel,
87.3 × 39.1 cm (34⅛ ×
15⅛ in.); central panel, 87.4
× 92.5 cm (34⁷⁄₁₆ × 36⁷⁄₁₆ in.);
right panel, 87.4 × 39.2 cm
(34⁷⁄₁₆ × 15⁷⁄₁₆ in.). Ghent,
Museum voor Schone
Kunsten

111d
MASTER OF JAMES IV
OF SCOTLAND
Coronation of David,
vol. 1, fol. 95v

MASTER OF THE LÜBECK BIBLE

The Master of the Lübeck Bible takes his name from the celebrated series of woodcuts he designed for a Bible printed by Stephan Arndes at Lübeck in 1494.[1] Although this artist was long known only as a woodcut designer, the marked eccentricities of his style have allowed scholars to identify a number of manuscript illuminations by him as well.[2] His works in both media are characterized by energetic compositions filled with a sense of movement; figures appearing in odd, almost contorted positions; and distinctive facial types, including women with large, domed foreheads and older men with heavy jowls.

The Master of the Lübeck Bible designed woodcuts for at least two other incunabula, one a 1489 *Dance of Death* also printed in Lübeck, and the other a copy of Terence's works printed in Lyons in 1493.[3] Fedja Anzelewsky made the crucial link between the style of the artist's woodcuts and an illumination in the Kupferstichkabinett, Berlin (cat. no. 113 [Berlin, Kupferstichkabinett, no. 667]).[4] Bodo Brinkmann then extended the known illuminated oeuvre of the artist to include a number of miniatures from the same series as the Berlin piece identified by Anzelewsky (see cat. no. 113), some contributions to the Spinola Hours (cat. no. 124), two miniatures cut from a book of hours,[5] and possibly a few illuminations in a manuscript in Cambridge (Fitzwilliam Museum, Ms. 1058-1975).[6] All of these together make up only a relatively small number of illuminations. The Carondelet Breviary (cat. no. 112), dated 1489, contains not only his earliest known work in illumination but also his most extensive series of illuminations.[7]

Illuminations by the Master of the Lübeck Bible can often be easily spotted due to an almost frenetic sense of energy and a consistent sense of distortion in the figures and their settings. Figures often seem to stagger rather than walk, with one foot placed far out in front of the other. Faces appear with features that are either somehow squashed or unnaturally elongated, with the head tilted back at an angle. Dramatic foreshortening and strangely telescoped perspective frequently are an integral part of his compositions. The closest stylistic parallels to the work of the Master of the Lübeck Bible can be found in the work of the Master of James IV of Scotland. Both feature figures modeled vigorously, with a consistent emphasis on physical actions. The illuminations of the Master of the Lübeck Bible are overall more matte in finish, however, than the work of the Master of James IV, who used more lustrous colors. In addition, the technique of the Master of the Lübeck Bible is less polished, with a visible sketchiness to his miniatures. There are nevertheless enough similarities between the two artists that it is not always easy to distinguish which illumination should be attributed to which artist in manuscripts to which they both contributed, especially in the case of the Carondelet Breviary. Because so few manuscripts by either artist can be dated as early as around 1490, it is difficult to determine which way the lines of influence were flowing. It is tempting to suggest, however, that the Master of James IV had not yet fully developed his artistic personality at this point and that close collaboration with the Master of the Lübeck Bible resulted in a strongly parallel style.

Localizing the Master of the Lübeck Bible has proved difficult, as is the case for many other artists of the period. His woodcut designs appear in books produced in Germany and France, yet some of them seem to be strongly Italianate in flavor.[8] The manuscripts in which he worked, meanwhile, point to Flanders and perhaps Spain (see cat. nos. 112, 113). The wide-ranging evidence notwithstanding, it is most probable that this artist was Flemish or at least trained in Flanders and that the far-flung places associated with his work are simply further confirmation of the international appeal of Flemish artists. His close association with the Master of James IV at key intervals in his career—around 1490 and then again, decades later, in the Spinola Hours—suggests that he may have been based in Ghent.

E. M.

Notes
1. Goldschmidt (1901: 59) attempted to link the Master of the Lübeck Bible with the Lübeck painter Bernt Notke, but Friedländer (1923b: 10) rightly argued that the artist was in fact more likely Flemish.

2. It is possible that the Master of the Lübeck Bible turned his talents to the medium of painting as well. A painting of Saint Peter (sold, Sotheby's, London, April 6, 1977, lot 46) shows several stylistic similarities to this artist's work, most strikingly in the treatment of the head, seen at three-quarters angle, tilted back and slightly elongated.

3. Friedländer 1923b: 11; Kristeller 1905: 112.

4. Anzelewsky 1964.

5. Sotheby's, December 10, 1973, lots 24, 25.

6. Brinkmann 1987–88; Brinkmann 1992b: 208. I follow Brinkmann in thinking that the Fitzwilliam images should be ascribed only tentatively to this artist.

7. Brinkmann (1987–88: 151 n.) attributed the Carondelet Breviary to the circle of the Master of the Lübeck Bible. Here it is firmly attributed to the artist himself.

8. Friedländer (1923b: 10) posited that the artist studied in Italy.

112

MASTER OF THE LÜBECK BIBLE, MASTER
OF JAMES IV OF SCOTLAND, AND WORKSHOP
OF MASTER OF THE FIRST PRAYER BOOK OF
MAXIMILIAN

Carondelet Breviary
Franciscan use
Namur, 1489, and probably Ghent, early 1490s

MANUSCRIPT: iii + 606 + i folios, 28 × 22 cm (11 × 8¹¹⁄₁₆ in.);
justification: 17.2–17.6 × 12.2–12.5 cm (6¾–6¹⁵⁄₁₆ × 4¹³⁄₁₆–4⅞ in.);
29 lines of *bastarda* in two columns; 1 full-page miniature, 8 two-
column miniatures, 48 one-column miniatures

HERALDRY: Escutcheon with Carondelet arms, fols. 8, 417v; motto
(of Jean Carondelet?) ГNOTHI SE AUTON, fol. 8; COGNOSCE TE IPSUM,
fols. 33, 417v

INSCRIPTIONS: *Incipit ordo breviarii s[e]c[un]d[u]m cursum s[an]c[t]e
Romane ecclesie Sabbato d[omi]nice p[r]ime adve[n]tus d[omi]ni ad vespers
Capit[u]l[u]m: 1487,* fol 8v; *In nomi[n]e d[o]m[inus] nostri ih[es]u christi
incipit officiu[m] psalmiste secundu[m] modum Romane ecclesie 1488,* fol.
254; *Deo gratias .1489. littera d[om]inicali d. aureo numero viij finit
namurci,* fol. 582

BINDING: Ludovicus Bloc, Bruges, late fifteenth century; stamped
leather over wood boards, stamped with zoomorphic pattern

COLLECTION: Berlin, Staatsbibliothek zu Berlin, Ms. theol. lat. fol. 285

PROVENANCE: Member of the Carondelet family, late fifteenth
century; Friedrich Heinrich Jacobi (1743–1819); acquired 1820

JPGM

The Master of the Lübeck Bible, whose illuminations
are relatively rare, executed most of the miniatures in
this Franciscan breviary. Six two-column miniatures and
the majority of the forty-eight one-column miniatures constitute his most extensive known contribution to a manuscript. The Master of James IV of Scotland, at this date (ca.
1490) a relatively young artist, contributed a number of the
one-column miniatures. The workshop of the Master of the
First Prayer Book of Maximilian, painted the most important miniatures in this breviary. The only full-page miniature, *The Israelites Beseeching God,* is an unusual subject that
appears in another ambitious breviary for Franciscan use,
the Grimani Breviary (cat. no. 126, fol. 14v). The two-
column *Ecstasy of Saint Francis* in the present breviary is the
only large miniature devoted to a saint. The workshop of
the Maximilian Master contributed one other two-column
miniature and ten one-column miniatures to the volume.

The miniatures by the Master of the Lübeck Bible are
startling in their originality and liveliness. The one-column
illuminations depict individual saints, while the two-
column miniatures are devoted to major Church feasts.
Examples such as *The Pentecost* (ill. 12) show the pronounced eccentricities of his style, including figures whose
heads are tilted back, unnaturally elongated, and sunk
below the shoulders. A sense of energy pervades the entire
miniature due to the arrangement of the apostles in a sinu-
ous line, the rhythm of their drapery, and the exaggerated
spatial recession. The whole room looks slightly askew. In
The Beheading of a Martyr (fol. 354v), the remarkable abilities
of this artist in rendering movement can be seen in the
stance of the executioner as he shifts his entire weight to his

right foot and swings his sword far behind him to deliver
the fatal blow.

The Master of James IV illuminated *The Confessor Saints*
(fol. 365), where the facial types—with their fleshy jowls,
rounded eye sockets, and clearly defined eyelid creases—
are unmistakably his, in contrast to those of the Master of
the Lübeck Bible, which often have a thinner aspect, with
eyes indicated by a simple black dot attached to the upper
eyelid.[1] The figures are also more solid than those of the
Master of the Lübeck Bible often are, and they are tightly
grouped in typical Master of James IV fashion. In other
cases the dividing line between the two artists is less clear.[2]
In the *Beheading of a Female Saint* (fol. 368), the exaggerated
leaning pose and striped tights of the executioner seem to
indicate that the miniature is by the Master of the Lübeck
Bible, yet the young men witnessing the event to the left
are such classic Master of James IV types that they seem to
have strolled in from one of his miniatures. Although the
two artists may have collaborated on some illuminations in
this breviary, it is more likely that the breviary represents a
point in their careers when they worked particularly closely
and each influenced the other's style.

The Israelites Beseeching God, from the workshop of the
Maximilian Master, is undeniably ambitious. The figures
are distinctive for their oddly short stature, large heads,
small feet, and above all their expressive, oversized hands.
These features—along with the profiles of some of the
figures, with their prominent noses and jaws with a distinct
overbite—and the abnormally large sleeve of the central
figure link them to the large miniatures by a member of the
Maximilian Master's workshop in the Breviary of Eleanor
of Portugal (cat. no. 91). As is apparent in those compositions, there is an awkwardness in the relationship of parts
of the illumination to one another, as if the artist were combining portions of different patterns with some difficulty.

At the beginning of the manuscript (fol. 8), the date
1487 is mentioned, and on folio 254 the date 1488 appears.
These dates probably refer to the printing dates of the
incunabula from which various parts of the manuscript
were copied.[3] The explicit on folio 582, however, does most
likely indicate the year and location in which the manuscript was copied. The text was completed in Namur in
1489, so that the manuscript may then have been sent on
to Ghent to be illuminated.[4] The coat of arms found in the
border facing the frontispiece miniature has been identified
as that of the Carondelet family. Jean Carondelet (d. 1501),
the chancellor of Burgundy under the regent Maximilian of
Austria, was the sort of powerful courtier who could have
acquired such a lavish breviary.[5]   E. M. and T. K.

Notes

1. The figure of Saint Dominic kneeling at the front of the group is particularly familiar, for it is closely related to the depiction of that saint in the Spinola Hours (cat. no. 124, fol. 260v). Even the small dog and fanciful demon in front of him find their counterparts in the Spinola image.

2. Although the Master of James IV seems also to have been wholly responsible for other miniatures—such as those on folios 358, 474, and 546—there are a number where the characteristics of his hand occur side by side with those of the Master of the Lübeck Bible, such as on folios 358 and 495, making it more difficult to attribute the illumination.

3. Thanks to Barbara Haggh-Huglo for her information regarding the fact that the wording of these rubrics implies that they are referring the reader to the printed source from which the text was copied.

4. Margaret Scott has indicated that the elaborate feathered hats, striped stockings, and clunky shoes are consistent with a dating for the illumination in the early 1490s (correspondence with Thomas Kren, March 6, 2002, Department of Manuscripts files, JPGM). Although the illuminators of this book are associated with Ghent, it was bound in Bruges by Ludovicus Bloc.

5. Fourez 1948: 13. We have been unable to confirm that the motto, which appears in the border in Latin and Greek, is indeed that of Jean Carondelet.

113

MASTER OF THE LÜBECK BIBLE AND OTHERS

Leaves Probably from a Devotional Book
Ghent or Bruges, ca. 1500–1510

Saints Apollonia, Agatha, Cecilia, and Ursula
One leaf, 22.9 × 15.9 cm (9 × 6¼ in.); 1 full-page miniature;
back: blank

COLLECTION: Berlin, Staatliche Museen zu Berlin,
Kupferstichkabinett, KdZ 641

PROVENANCE: Karl Ferdinand Friedrich von Nagler (1770–1846);
to Kupferstichkabinett in 1835

JPGM and RA

Scenes from the Life of the Virgin
One leaf, 23 × 16 cm (9¹⁄₁₆ × 5⁵⁄₁₆ in.); 1 full-page miniature;
back: blank

COLLECTION: Berlin, Staatliche Museen zu Berlin,
Kupferstichkabinett, KdZ 667

PROVENANCE: Acquired by 1925

JPGM and RA

***Saints Anne, Mary the Mother of James, Mary Salome,
and Helena***
One leaf, 22.5 × 15.5 cm (8⅞ × 6⅛ in.); 1 full-page miniature;
back: blank

COLLECTION: New York, The Morgan Library, Ms. G.46

PROVENANCE: Col. H. G. Sotheby of Ecton Hall [his sale, Sotheby's,
London, July 24, 1924, lot 153]; [Maggs Brothers, London]; C. Peter
Jones [his sale, Sotheby's, London, July 8, 1957, lot 61]; bought by
Maggs Brothers, London, for William S. Glazier (1907–1962);
deposited by the Trustees of the William S. Glazier Collection in
1963; gift of the Trustees of the William S. Glazier Collection in 1984

JPGM

Saints Catherine, Clare, Agnes, and Barbara
One leaf, 22.5 × 15.3 cm (8⅞ × 6 in.); 1 full-page miniature;
back: blank

COLLECTION: Cambridge, Fitzwilliam Museum, Ms. Marlay Cuttings
Sp. 5

PROVENANCE: Possibly Celotti and/or Rogers collections;
Thomas Miller Whitehead; Charles Brinsley Marlay (1831–1912);
his bequest, 1912

RA

These leaves, each featuring four distinct compartments, come from a larger series of twelve detached
miniatures of the same format.[1] Seven of the leaves show
four male or female saints, each of the four in a separate
quadrant of the miniature, surrounded by an illusionistic
border. Four more are also divided into four quadrants but
show scenes from the life of the Virgin and the Passion.[2]
The repetition of certain details and the similar dimensions
firmly link all twelve leaves together as a set.[3] Although the
leaves are related stylistically to the work of the Master of
the Lübeck Bible, there is a great variety in quality among
them, and the master himself probably painted only two of
them (Berlin, Kupferstichkabinett, KdZ 667, and Cambridge, Fitzwilliam Museum, Marlay Cutting Sp. 3).

The best of the leaves is the example in Berlin attributed to the Master of the Lübeck Bible (ill. 113a), which
depicts events from the life of the Virgin. The architectural

113b
WORKSHOP OF
MASTER OF THE
LÜBECK BIBLE
*Saints Anne, Mary the
Mother of James, Mary
Salome, and Helena*

113c
WORKSHOP OF
MASTER OF THE
LÜBECK BIBLE
*Saints Catherine, Clare,
Agnes, and Barbara*

framework, which in most of the other miniatures is simply
a border device used to divide the illumination into four
compartments, is here treated as a physical structure,
almost like a stage set for the individual scenes (see also ill.
113b). In the bottom half of *Scenes from the Life of the Virgin*,
narratives taking place in the interior rooms spill into the
foreground courtyard. Overhead, the donkey walks out
onto the thin lip of the cornice while King Herod casually
leans against a pillar, the woman clutching a child to the left
of his feet seemingly rising from nowhere. This daring
treatment of space is akin to the distorted perspective often
seen in the Carondelet Breviary (cat. no. 112) and shares an
affinity with the illusionistic ploys used by the Master of
James IV of Scotland in the Spinola Hours (cat. no. 124).
The figure types are entirely those of the Master of the
Lübeck Bible, especially that of Herod, with his elongated
head, finely painted beard, and the ambitious foreshortening of his arm.

One of the best preserved of the leaves depicting female
saints is the example in the Morgan Library, New York (ill.
113b). The women have a curious head shape characterized
by a broad forehead, wide-set eyes, fleshy cheeks, and a
weak jawline, along with large bodies and very small hands.
This type appears in all the leaves with female saints (ills.
113c, 113d, and Cambridge, Fitzwilliam Museum, Marlay

Cutting Sp. 4). The figure of the Virgin from *The Coronation
of the Virgin* by the Master of the Lübeck Bible in the Spinola Hours (fol. 153v) shares some of these characteristics,
yet these leaves should probably not be ascribed to his
hand; they are more likely productions of an artist in his
workshop. Among the leaves dedicated to male saints, a
leaf formerly in the Cardon collection can be grouped
together with the leaves containing female saints. In one of
the other leaves with male saints (Cambridge, Fitzwilliam
Museum, Marlay Cutting Sp. 3), however, the corpulent
face of Saint Philip, the carefully delineated beard of Saint
Andrew, and the awkward, extended fingers of Saint
Bartholomew's hands are all characteristic of the work
of the master himself.[4] The remaining leaves are in such
poor condition that it is difficult to group them with
any certainty.

While it is possible that the leaves were originally
intended as separate objects to be mounted like paintings,[5]
their number and size lend more credence to the theory
that they came from some sort of devotional book. The
numerous saints could correspond to an illustrated litany
or even a visual set of suffrages from an unorthodox book
of hours. Bodo Brinkmann has pointed out that one of the
leaves contains scenes from the infancy of Christ that
match the traditional subjects of illustration for lauds,

prime, sext, and none for the Hours of the Virgin in a book of hours.[6] The leaf discussed previously (Berlin, Kupferstichkabinett, KdZ 667), however, shows four subsequent scenes from the life of the Virgin, which would be too many for the remaining two hours of vespers and compline. The closest precedent for these leaves is, surprisingly, a devotional book illuminated in Hungary in the fourteenth century.[7] It is an anomaly for its time, featuring unconventional four-part miniatures concerning both saints and the life of Christ, with no other text except labels at the top. It is possible that, as with the Hungarian manuscript, the leaves do not correspond to any particular type of book of the period precisely because they were part of a unique creation.

Another mystery surrounding these leaves is their place of origin. Many of the saints who appear in the sheets are decidedly unusual, including Saints Mary of Egypt, Mary Salome, Ildefonse, Theodora, and Thais of Alexandria. A number of these saints have Spanish connections, and the accompanying labels are written in a Spanish display script. These clues have led scholars to wonder whether the leaves could have been illuminated in Spain. The Spanish vogue for Flemish illumination suggests, however, that the leaves were more likely illuminated in Flanders for a Spanish patron.[8]

E. M.

Notes

1. Brinkmann (1987–88: 152–60) grouped the twelve together in an article discussing the work of the Master of the Lübeck Bible. In addition to the four here, three others are in Cambridge, Fitzwilliam Museum, Marlay Cuttings 2–4; three came up for sale at Sotheby's, December 11, 1972, lots 10–12; and two were in the Cardon collection, Brussels.

2. Winkler (1925: 159) described the twelfth leaf, one of two from the Cardon collection, as representing a single scene, the Crucifixion, instead of four, but he nonetheless tied it to the leaf depicting four male saints.

3. Brinkmann 1987–88: 151–60.

4. Arnould (in Cambridge 1993: 86) pointed out that a second artist must have been responsible for the border of this miniature, as the iconography of one of the accompanying roundels does not match the main subject.

5. Brinkmann (1987–88: 152) noted that the borders around the miniatures are symmetrical, which would be unusual in a book format.

6. Sotheby's, December 11, 1972, lot 10. The subjects are the Visitation, the Nativity, the Adoration of the Magi, and the Presentation in the Temple (Brinkmann 1987–88: 160).

7. Thanks to Susan L'Engle for bringing this book to my attention. The manuscript is now divided between the Morgan Library, New York (Mss. M.360, M.360c), and the Vatican Library (Ms. Vat. lat. 8541).

8. The Carondelet Breviary had a similar history, as it was written in Namur and then likely sent to Ghent for illumination. The leaves could also have been written by a Spanish scribe living in a Flemish town.

113d
WORKSHOP OF
MASTER OF THE
LÜBECK BIBLE
Saints Apollonia, Agatha,
Cecilia, and Ursula

MASTER OF THE DAVID SCENES IN THE GRIMANI BREVIARY (A)

Otto Pächt first identified the Master of the David Scenes in the Grimani Breviary as a distinct artistic personality in 1966, basing his somewhat unwieldy name on a cohesive series of lively illuminations illustrating the life of David in the famous breviary now in Venice (cat. no. 126).[1] In these miniatures depicting rarely illustrated scenes from the life of David, large figures dressed in brightly colored, fashionable attire gesticulate theatrically in crowded scenes, with the primary action taking place close to the picture plane (see fig. 71). The wide-set eyes and carefully curled hair of the men and the oval, almost chinless faces of the women — with figures of both sexes often characterized by blank, expressionless stares — are easily recognizable. Although the Master of the David Scenes was not mentioned by Friedrich Winkler, Paul Durrieu, or Georges Dogaer, he has recently begun to garner more attention as an original and prolific illuminator.[2]

Nothing definitive is known about the training of the Master of the David Scenes, but his precise draftsmanship and the occasional appearance of fine half-length portraits in his work have led some scholars to posit that he was trained in the workshop of a panel painter.[3] His mature work, however, is characterized by the bright palette, sturdy body forms, and narrative flair and invention associated with the work of the Master of James IV, and it is possible that the Master of the David Scenes was the latter's most successful student. The Master of the David Scenes was greatly influenced by the Master of James IV's compositional style,[4] but whereas the figures of the latter artist have a graceful sense of movement through space, those of the former are frozen midaction. The work of the Master of the David Scenes is also characterized by less fluid brushwork and more generic landscapes than the illuminations of his probable teacher.

The early work of the Master of the David Scenes consists almost entirely of small private devotional books in which traditional subjects in stock compositions are often repeated with little variation.[5] The frequent collaboration on these works with the same set of assistants attests to the existence of a prolific workshop operated by the Master of the David Scenes as early as the 1490s.[6] A softness of color and shape characterizes these early works, a vagueness that seems pervasive. The small, pliable figures tentatively inhabit largely undefined spaces, whether interior or exterior. The faces often have a sentimental sweetness to them, yet they already possess the vacant eyes and unfixed gazes that are one of the hallmarks of the artist's oeuvre.[7] Most of these devotional books produced between 1490 and 1505 contain only standard texts and traditional iconography,

making the much more lavish and individualized Hours of Joanna of Castile (cat. no. 114) stand out among his early works as undeniably the highest in quality and the most ambitious.

It was through the books produced during the early part of his career that the Master of the David Scenes, in collaboration with his workshop, popularized a new type of border featuring architectural elements combined into fantastical edifices.[8] Although the borders are more predominant in early books of hours dating to the years around 1500, they never disappeared from the work of the Master of the David Scenes, becoming increasingly three-dimensional in their depiction of space in later manuscripts such as the Ince-Blundell Hours (cat. no. 115) and a book of hours in Oxford (cat. no. 137).

In the years approaching 1510 the Master of the David Scenes attained a more mature style, distinguished by a greater attention to naturalistic detail and increasingly distinct contours, which impart a cleaner, more linear quality to all his work. In manuscripts of this period such as the so-called Brukenthal Breviary, a book of hours in Brussels, and one in Vienna,[9] the stocky figures have more weight; no longer lost within their settings, they dominate the space.[10] It was during this phase of his career that the Master of the David Scenes discovered his penchant for colorful narratives such as the remarkable deathbed scene in the Brukenthal manuscript, in which Death crouches at the foot of the bed while a horrifying devil eagerly waits to take the terrified man to hell. Although the narratives are often full of action, the figures still appear stilted and wooden. The flat, angular faces, sometimes with sunken cheeks and well-defined, round eyes, are impassive and detached.

By the middle of the 1510s the Master of the David Scenes was at the peak of his career, painting miniatures characterized by the frequent inclusion of completely original iconography, a fascination with contemporary costume, a greater psychological complexity in the interaction of the figures, and a pleasing rounded suppleness in their muscular bodies. Manuscripts from this period include his contributions to the Grimani Breviary (cat. no. 126), the Copenhagen Hours (cat. no. 136), the Oxford Hours (cat. no. 137), and one of the few secular works associated with the artist, which is dated 1514 (Paris, Bibliothèque nationale de France, Ms. fr. 19059).[11] The large, lavishly dressed figures stride confidently through intricate contemporary interiors or enact their stories amid throngs of people in front of carefully painted cityscapes. These more dramatic compositions often relate unusual Old Testament stories or vivid contemporary narratives, making the Master of the David Scenes one of the most interesting storytellers of his age. Sometimes a single figure tosses a knowing look out of the picture directly at the viewer, helping to draw us into the narrative.

The few pieces of evidence for localizing the Master of the David Scenes and his workshop mostly point to Bruges as the center for his activities. Three manuscripts containing his work or that of his workshop were bound in Bruges,[12] and a number of manuscripts produced by his workshop have ties to Italian families with business connections in the city.[13] The Imhof Prayer Book (cat. no. 139), however, to which he contributed a single miniature, was illuminated in 1511, when Simon Bening was still living in Ghent, and Brinkmann has suggested that the two manuscripts by the Master of the David Scenes in Oxford (Douce 256 and cat. no. 137) can be ascribed to the Ghent tradition.[14] The artist's strongest links, both stylistic and physical, are to the workshop of the Master of James IV. Two of the few manuscripts showing evidence of his collaboration with artists outside his own workshop contain the work of the Master of James IV, an artist who has also proved problematic to localize, or of his followers.[15]

Manuscripts illuminated by the Master of the David Scenes were produced for some of the highest-ranking members of courts across Europe, including Cardinal Domenico Grimani (see cat. no. 126), Joanna of Castile (see cat. no. 114), Maximilian I or Henry VIII,[16] possibly Pope Alexander VI,[17] and Frederick the Wise, elector of Saxony.[18] At least one manuscript, however, is known to have been made for members of the bourgeoisie: a "Monsieur de Flagy."[19] Almost all of the known works by the artist are either prayer books or books of hours.[20] Judging from the relatively large number of surviving manuscripts by his hand dating from about 1490 to 1520, the Master of the David Scenes—with his stylishly dressed figures, aptitude for narrative innovation, and bright, dynamic compositions—was an artist with wide appeal.   E. M.

Notes

1. Pacht and Alexander 1966–73, I: 30; Oxford 1895–1953, I: 30. The Grimani Breviary miniatures by the Master of the David Scenes include folios 288v, 310v, 321v, 337v, 348v, 357v, and probably also 286v.

2. Brinkmann (1992c) in particular has done much to delineate his contributions.

3. Dagmar Thoss (in Leuven 1999: 55) proposed that the Master of the David Scenes may have been trained by Hans Memling. The few half-lengths in his oeuvre owe their inspiration to the works of Simon Marmion; see the examples in the Hours of Joanna of Castile (cat. no. 114, fol. 411v) and a book of hours in Paris (Musée du Petit Palais, Ms. Dutuit, fol. 197v) and the large groups in the Ince-Blundell Hours (cat. no. 115) and the Ware Hours (cat. no. 116). There are also two probably early works by the artist that may show the influence of Marmion in their soft colors and fine draftsmanship: London, British Library, Add. Ms. 32388, and London, Wallace Collection, M.319.

4. Although many of the mature illuminations of the Master of the David Scenes have a strong resemblance to the kinds of compositions found in the work of the Master of James IV, there is almost no overlap in terms of exact copies.

5. For example, almost half of the compositions in a book of hours in the Vatican Library (Cod. Vat. lat. 10293) can also be found in the hours produced for Joanna of Castile (cat. no. 114). Many more instances of the reuse of compositions can be found in Brinkmann 1992c.

6. To the list of early works compiled by Brinkmann (1992c: 179–82) can be added a small book of hours sold on March 29, 1985, by the Hôtel Drouot, Paris, lot 28.

7. These characteristics can be seen even in the best of the works produced by the Master of the David Scenes and his workshop in these years, such as Milan, Biblioteca Ambrosiana, Ms. S.P.II, 189; Brussels, Bibliothèque royale de Belgique, Ms. IV.237; and the Hours of Joanna of Castile.

8. Kren (1974 and in Malibu 1983: 59–60) first recognized the grouping and traced how patterns for these borders were used in a large number of books. Brinkmann (1992c) added to the list of manuscripts in which the borders are found and tied the propagation of the borders more closely to the workshop of the Master of the David Scenes. A second type of border decoration recently identified with the workshop of the Master of the David Scenes by As-Vijvers (1999: 250; 2002) enjoyed a much less widespread popularity. These text page borders, which she terms *Einzelmotive*, are composed of single examples of flowers, small animals, and insects, each painted directly onto the parchment of the three outer borders.

9. Sibiu, Romania, Museu Brukenthal; Brussels, Bibliothèque royale, Ms. IV.480; and Vienna, Österreichische Nationalbibliothek, Ms. 1887. The last manuscript has a missing portion that can now be found as Poitiers, Médiathèque François Mitterand, Ms. 57/269. That portion, dated in a border to 1510, contains a miniature that Brinkmann (1997: 207–9) persuasively argued was originally intended for La Flora (cat. no. 93). The Vienna section, meanwhile, contains a number of copies of La Flora half-lengths by the Master of the Prayer Books of around 1500. Since the suite of related images in the Vienna manuscript was likely done directly from La Flora, the Master of the David Scenes could well have seen them at that time. This sequence of events would help to explain the appearance of a series of half-lengths related to La Flora in the Ince-Blundell Hours and the Ware Hours in the years around 1510.

10. The following can also be placed within this period: Berlin, Kupferstichkabinett, KdZ 668; ex Durrieu Book of Hours, Sotheby's, June 20, 1995, lot 109; and a single miniature in the Imhof Prayer Book (cat. no. 139), which is dated 1511. The Manderscheid Hours (Renate König collection), four miniatures in Altenburg (Staatliches Lindenau Museum, inv. 185–88), and a series of miniatures in London (British Library, Ms. Harley 2924; brought to my attention by Janet Backhouse and Scot McKendrick) also contain work by the Master of the David Scenes, but have never been viewed by the author.

11. Another secular work can be assigned to these years: Vienna, Österreichische Nationalbibliothek, Ms. 2579. A book of hours in Oxford, Bodleian, Ms. Douce 256, probably painted between 1510 and 1515, and a prayer book in Berlin (Staatsbibliothek, Ms. germ oct. 672), which I have never seen, may have been painted in the same years. A second book of hours with Mannerist images contains a single image by the Master of the David Scenes: Vienna, Österreichische Nationalbibliothek, Ms. 1875, fol. 184v.

12. Two—Baltimore, Walters Art Museum, M.428, and Detroit Institute of Arts, inv. 63.146—are early workshop productions, and the third is a manuscript whose sole illuminator is the Master of the David Scenes (Renate König collection; Cologne 2002: 372–87, no. 24). All three were bound by Ludovicus Bloc, who was active in Bruges from 1484 to 1526.

13. Brinkmann (1992c: 100–102) noted that one of the members of the workshop of the Master of the David Scenes had ties to Bruges. As-Vijvers (2002: 409) also argued for a Bruges localization of the artist and his workshop, discussing the Italian merchants who bought his manuscripts.

14. Brinkmann 1992c: 102–4.

15. The Grimani Breviary and Vienna, Österreichische Nationalbibliothek, Ms. 1887; Poitiers, Médiathèque François Mitterand, Ms. 57/269.

16. The coats of arms of both appear in Jena, Thüringer Universitäts- und Landesbibliothek, Ms. 4 (Leuven 1999: 90).

17. The arms that appear in Brussels, Bibliothèque royale, Ms. IV.480, are very close to those of Pope Alexander VI. It is possible that the artist misunderstood the instructions about the heraldry or, more

likely, that the manuscript was intended as a gift for one of the pope's natural children.

18. Jena, Thüringer Universitäts- und Landesbibliothek, Ms. 5 (Leuven 1999: 95).

19. An explicit by the scribe Jehan Coppre de Varromgnes (Paris, Bibliothèque nationale de France, Ms. fr. 19059) names Monsieur de Flagy as well as the date 1514.

20. Three secular manuscripts can be ascribed to the Master of the David Scenes: a collection of philosophical works (Paris, Bibliothèque nationale, Ms. fr. 19059); a collection of historical and moral treatises (Vienna, Österreichische Nationalbibliothek, Ms. 2579); and Petrarch's commentary on the seven Penitential Psalms (Renate König collection).

114

MASTER OF THE DAVID SCENES IN THE GRIMANI BREVIARY AND WORKSHOP

Hours of Joanna of Castile
Use of Rome
Bruges or Ghent, between 1496 and 1506

MANUSCRIPT: v + 422 + iii folios, 10.7 × 7.7 cm (4³/₁₆ × 3 in.); justification: 5.5 × 3.8 cm (2⅛ × 1⁹/₁₆ in.); 14 lines of *gotica rotunda*; 28 full-page miniatures, 20 three-quarter-page miniatures, 7 small miniatures, 4 historiated borders, 24 historiated calendar borders

HERALDRY: Escutcheon with the arms of Joanna of Castile; escutcheon with the arms of Philip the Handsome, surmounted by archducal coronet; mottoes *Qui vouldra* and *je le veus*; linked initials *PI en lac*, all fol. 26

BINDING: Seventeenth century (?); red velvet; chased silver-gilt corner pieces and clasp

COLLECTION: London, The British Library, Add. Ms. 18852

PROVENANCE: The Infanta Joanna of Castile (1479–1555); Philip A. Hanrott [his sale, Evans, London, August 5–17, 1833, lot 2555]; [to Evans, London]; Sir John Tobin, Liverpool; Rev. John Tobin, Liscard, Cheshire; [William Boone, London]; purchased 1852 by The British Museum

JPGM and RA

This luxurious manuscript by the Master of the David Scenes in the Grimani Breviary is remarkable not only because it is one of his few known royal commissions but also because it is the most personalized in text and image of all his early manuscripts. Joanna of Castile, daughter of Queen Isabella of Castile and King Ferdinand of Aragon, married Philip the Handsome, son of the Holy Roman Emperor Maximilian of Austria, and Mary of Burgundy, in 1496. Because both her arms and those of her husband appear in a border of the manuscript, the book must have been commissioned between the time of her marriage and the death of her husband in 1506.[1] The manuscript contains a number of texts not usually found in books of hours, including an entire series of catechismal texts that might have been judged appropriate for a young wife; an exceedingly rare Office of a Guardian Angel, accompanied by a portrait of Joanna; three elaborate series of texts and illuminations for the Passion of Christ;[2] and an uncommon prayer to the Virgin, accompanied by a second portrait of the archduchess (ill. 114a).

The short texts concerning the fundamental elements of the faith form the first section of the manuscript after the calendar.[3] A full-page miniature of the Temptation of Adam and Eve (ill. 114b), in which the artist has cleverly used the architectural border for narrative ends, prefaces the entire set. A smaller miniature opposite it depicts the rare subject of the *speculum consciencie*, a skull reflected in a mirror. As James Marrow has discussed, this miniature is unusual in that it depicts the reflection in the mirror from the standpoint of the viewer, forcing the viewer to contemplate her own mortality.[4] Since each of the individual precepts of the faith named in the text is followed by a short explanation of how it relates to human sin, the paired miniatures served as a warning to Joanna of the necessity of constant vigilance in a world where sin is an inherent part of human nature, preparing the soul for a death that might come at any time.

The first of the portraits of Joanna occurs directly after the catechismal texts, introducing the Office of the Guardian Angel. Surrounded by a border containing the arms, mottoes, and initials of the archduchess and her husband, Joanna is presented by her guardian angel and John the Baptist to Saint Michael in the full-page miniature opposite (fols. 25v–26). The second portrait of Joanna is found after the Hours of the Virgin and the Office of the Virgin for Advent, accompanying a prayer to the Virgin that Joanna must have specifically requested be included (see ill. 114a).[5] In both, her large forehead, thin face, and pointed chin agree well with the portrait of her by Juan de Flandes presumably painted on the occasion of her engagement (Vienna, Kunsthistorisches Museum, inv. 3873).

Specific imagery included in the book is likely to have had personal meaning for Joanna. Susie Nash has posited that the well-known Virgin and Child in Joanna's hours (ill. 114a), which is after a composition by Rogier van der Weyden, was copied by the Master of the David Scenes from a painting in Joanna's collection.[6] As Joanna is known to have had an interest in Flemish painting and she is depicted on the opposite page in prayer before the image, which is framed without a border, Nash's interpretation is plausible. On folio 177, prefacing the Mass of the Virgin, is a full-page Hodegetria Virgin and Child. The position of the Virgin's right hand, her dark blue robe and head covering, and the star on her shoulder are all classic elements of the Hodegetria type.[7] The iconography does not recur in any of the known manuscripts by the Master of the David Scenes, nor is it common in Flemish prayer books of the period.[8] One wonders whether this miniature was perhaps a copy of the Byzantine icon described in an inventory of Joanna's goods.[9]

A number of the miniatures in the Hours of the Virgin as well as the three Passion cycles are standard productions found with little variation in other Master of the David Scenes manuscripts. These miniatures all show characteristics of the early style of the Master of the David Scenes: small, sturdy figures set close to the picture plane; simple interiors and landscapes; and faces with broad foreheads, wide-set eyes, and rather expressionless features. The weak quality and uninspired painting of some of the smaller pattern-based miniatures suggest that the Master of the David Scenes may have employed assistants to help finish the lavish book. Two of the suffrages are such close copies

of illuminations from the Huth Hours (cat. no. 33) that it is probable that the Master of the David Scenes had access to that manuscript.[10]

Besides the usual strewn-flower border, a type of border associated especially with the workshop of the Master of the David Scenes appears throughout the manuscript. It is a novel variation on the concept of a spatial border, composed of architectural elements designed to create the impression of a shallow space into which the text block or miniature is set.[11]

E. M.

Notes

1. In an inventory of Joanna's belongings of 1545, the manuscript is described in detail: "otro libro chiquito de paramino de mano mediano de muchas ystorias e yluminaciones la primera ystoria es de como pecaron adan y heba y fueron hechados de parayso comiença especulum conçiencia e tiene las coberturas de terciopelo carmesi altibaxo aforrado en çeti carmesi cayrelado de oro e uvas rrosicas de oro por escudos con cada dos asicas e una çinta con que se cierra" (Ferrandis 1943: 222–23). Thanks to Mari-Tere Alvarez for suggesting that I look in Joanna's inventory.

2. The first series accompanies five short prayers on specific events from the life of Christ, the first two illuminated with full-page miniatures and the following three with three-quarter-page miniatures. The second and third sequences illustrate the Hours of the Passion and the Office of the Passion. The Hours of the Passion is illustrated with three-quarter-page miniatures throughout, while the

Office would have begun with a full-page miniature (now missing) facing a three-quarter-page miniature, with the rest of the hours accompanied by smaller miniatures. Interestingly, the manuscript contains only seven suffrages, a relatively small number for a manuscript of this complexity.

3. These include the Ten Commandments, the Seven Mortal Sins, the Articles of the Faith, the Five Senses, the Seven Acts of Mercy, the Theological Virtues, the Cardinal Virtues, the Seven Gifts of the Holy Spirit, and the Sacraments.

4. Marrow 1983a: 161.

5. This prayer is not found among the manuscripts catalogued by Leroquais (1927). The rubric reads: "Oratio devota de b[ea]ta virgine maria vers," and the incipit is: "Dignare me laudare te virgo sacrata da michi."

6. Nash 1995: 437. The theory was later supported by Stroo and Syfer-d'Olne (1996: 170), who traced a number of copies of the painting and concluded that it was a popular composition that may well have been represented in the collection of the archduchess.

7. The unusual coloring of Christ's clothing—lavender and red—and the green lining and red edging of the Virgin's mantle are also elements seen in Byzantine Hodegetria icons.

8. The composition recurs in a Dutch book of hours, the Van Hooff Hours (Amsterdam, Vreijeuniversiteit, Ms. XV 05502), where the accompanying prayer states that the original icon was painted by Saint Luke and hung in the Church of Santa Maria Maggiore in Rome. Thanks to Maryan W. Ainsworth, Bodo Brinkmann, and Anne Margreet As-Vijvers for bringing this image to my attention.

9. In the 1545 inventory of Joanna's goods, there is a mention of a Byzantine painting of the Virgin and Child in her possession: "otro

114a

MASTER OF THE DAVID SCENES IN THE GRIMANI BREVIARY
The Virgin and Child and *Joanna of Castile in Prayer,* fols. 287v–288

114b
MASTER OF THE
DAVID SCENES IN THE
GRIMANI BREVIARY
Adam and Eve, fol. 14v

rretablo griego de nuestra señora con su hijo en los braços" (Ferrandis 1943: 231).

10. The Master of the David Scenes took great pains to copy carefully the half-length of Saint James on folio 411v from the Huth Hours with only limited evidence of the interpolation his own style, seen mostly in the deep-set eyes and blank stares of the faces. The Saint George on folio 413v, however, shows a number of departures from the original, in both composition and color.

11. The style of border was first identified by Kren (1974), with a summary in Malibu 1983a. The text pages in the manuscript are decorated with individual objects painted directly onto the parchment; see As-Vijvers 1999: 250. It is interesting that this type of border occurs in the Copenhagen Hours (cat. no. 136), which also contains the unusual series of catechismal texts.

115

MASTER OF THE DAVID SCENES IN THE GRIMANI BREVIARY AND WORKSHOP

Ince-Blundell Hours
Use of Rome
Bruges or Ghent, ca. 1510

MANUSCRIPT: 244 folios, 12 × 8.5 cm (4¼ × 3⁵⁄₁₆ in.); justification: 5.8 × 4.1 cm (2¼ × 1⅝ in.); 15 lines of *gotica rotunda*; 18 full-page miniatures, 27 small miniatures, 1 historiated initial, 24 historiated calendar borders

HERALDRY: Escutcheon with unidentified arms or a three pales sable (possibly Negrone or Alliata family), fols. 16v, 30, 96, etc.

BINDING: Seventeenth or eighteenth century; French maroon gilt leather over pasteboard; HORAE BEATE VIRGINIS on spine

COLLECTION: Ramsen, Heribert Tenschert

PROVENANCE: Female member of the Agliata or Alliata family of Pisa and Sicily, or the Negrone family of Genoa; perhaps acquired by Charles Blundell (d. 1837) or by Thomas Weld, Lulworth Castle (1750–1810); Thomas Weld-Blundell, Ince-Blundell Hall, by twentieth century; [sale, Christie's, London, November 23, 1998, lot. 11]; Collection Heribert Tenschert, Ramsen

JPGM and RA

This recently discovered manuscript contains the most extensive series of half-length miniatures in the oeuvre of the Master of the David Scenes in the Grimani Breviary.[1] Every major text—except for the Hours of the Cross, the Gospel sequences, and the suffrages—is illuminated with a half-length miniature or a sequence of them, giving the book a sense of visual unity.[2] In the Hours of the Virgin the half-lengths are all divided into two evenly weighted halves, with six of the eight miniatures limited to two large figures. Moreover, the opening of each hour is marked by matched facing full borders, carefully alternating between strewn-flower borders and architectural borders.

Here, as in his other works, the Master of the David Scenes was influenced by the half-lengths by Simon Marmion, especially those in La Flora (cat. no. 93).[3] The compositions in the Ince-Blundell Hours are not slavish copies of Marmion's work, however, but inventive interpretations of them. The beautifully painted miniature of David in Prayer (fol. 166v), for instance, shows David from an entirely different angle than the miniature in La Flora, but the similarity in details of his costume indicates a relationship between the two. David's face, with its network of fine wrinkles etched around the eyes, shows how suffering and worry have prematurely aged him, particularly appropriate for the opening of the Penitential Psalms.

In two openings the patroness is shown kneeling at her prie-dieu opposite half-length miniatures (ills. 115a, 115b), with her coat of arms displayed prominently below.[4] The format of the portraits is familiar from the Hours of Joanna of Castile (cat. no. 114), but the technique in Ince-Blundell argues for a later date. In the portraits of Joanna, her evenly lit oval face has an unfixed gaze, and her long, thin hands are virtually undelineated. The patroness of the Ince-Blundell Hours, by contrast, seems to look across the page at *The Lamentation*, in one case, or down at an illuminated prayer book, in the other. The light falls on her face from

the front in both miniatures, indicated by the pattern of shadows across her cheeks and the back of her neck, while her hands are well defined by a series of fine pen strokes.

This greater interest in expression and delineation of the human form appears as well in many other miniatures of the Ince-Blundell Hours, indicating an overall maturity of style. The figures in the Ince-Blundell Hours, however, are not quite as fully developed as those in the late illumination of the Master of the David Scenes, nor do the miniatures evidence the interest in lavish contemporary costumes[5] and original narrative that characterizes his work in such manuscripts as the Grimani Breviary (cat. no. 126), dated around 1515. A dating of around 1510 for the Ince-Blundell Hours therefore seems most likely.

Although the exact identity of the patroness has not been established, it has been thought she was Italian, based on her Italianate dress and hair arrangement and the rounded Gothic script of the manuscript.[6] Two Italian families of the time used the coat of arms found in the manuscript: the Alliata family of Pisa and Sicily and the Negrone family of Genoa.[7] The fact that the coat of arms is repeated on the page devoted to Mary Magdalene's suffrage and that Mary Magdalene plays a prominent role in *The Lamentation* (fol. 29v) opposite one of the portraits could indicate that the name of the patroness was Maria or Maria Maddalena.[8] It was evidently by her particular request that the only two

unusual texts in the manuscript were included, both prayers accompanying the portraits discussed above. One is a prayer to the blessed Virgin, facing *The Virgin and Child*,[9] and the other is directed toward both Mary and John,[10] appropriately facing the half-length *Lamentation*.   E. M.

Notes

1. The Ince-Blundell Hours is much more elaborate than the only other known manuscript to contain numerous half-lengths by the Master of the David Scenes (cat. no. 116).

2. The workshop of the Master of the David Scenes contributed the calendar series and may have been responsible for some of the smaller miniatures elsewhere in the book as well.

3. The Pentecost miniature (fol. 32v) is closely related to the same subject by Marmion in the Huth Hours (cat. no. 33), and *The Coronation of the Virgin* (fol. 129v), while not as close, shows certain affinities in terms of composition and color with *The Crowned Virgin* in the Huth Hours. A number of the half-lengths in the Hours of the Virgin found in Ince-Blundell are distantly related to those in La Flora.

4. The miniature of the Virgin and Child opposite one of the portraits (fol. 141v) indicates the influence of contemporary panel painters such as Gerard David. A manuscript containing closely related Virgin and Child by the Master of the David Scenes, surrounded by a distinctive jeweled border similar to one in the Ince-Blundell Hours, was sold at Hôtel Drouot on March 29, 1985.

5. A notable exception is the depiction of the patroness herself.

6. Margaret Scott's studies confirm that the tight, round ponytail of blonde hair, large linen sleeves, velvet bodice, and high-waisted belt worn by the patroness in the miniatures of the Ince-Blundell Hours

115a

MASTER OF THE DAVID SCENES IN THE GRIMANI BREVIARY
The Lamentation and *The Patroness in Prayer*, fols. 29v–30

correspond to Netherlandish representations of Italian costume, particularly Genoese fashion (correspondence with the author, March 12, 2002, Department of Manuscripts files, JPGM). The identification with the Negrone family of Genoa might possibly be preferred on this basis.

7. In a manuscript by the Master of the David Scenes now in Brussels (Bibliothèque royale de Belgique, Ms. IV 480), the arms of the Borgia family are impaled by arms matching the ones in the Ince-Blundell Hours. The coat of arms is crowned by a papal tiara. Either the arms of the Borgia family were simply misunderstood (six horizontal stripes of black and gold), or the manuscript was a wedding gift for a natural daughter of the pope and a member of the Alliata or Negrone family. Given the connection between the Master of the David Scenes and this family, the latter seems more likely.

8. These theories were originally proposed by Kay Sutton in the London Christie's catalogue of November 23, 1998.

9. The rubric for this prayer is "Devotissima oratio ad beatam virginem Mariam," and the incipit is "O domina glorie O fons pietatis et misericordie O sanctitatis libertas" (fol. 142). The prayer was not found in any of the manuscripts catalogued by Leroquais (1927).

10. This prayer has the rubric "De compassione virgi[ni]s et matris marie et mutua com[m]endatione ei[us] iohan[n]is" and an incipit of "O Domine ih[es]u xp[ist]e filii dei vivi qui a fideli discipulo tuo" (fol. 30). This prayer is also not among those catalogued by Leroquais (1927).

115b

MASTER OF THE
DAVID SCENES IN THE
GRIMANI BREVIARY
The Virgin and Child and
The Patroness in Prayer,
fols. 141v–142

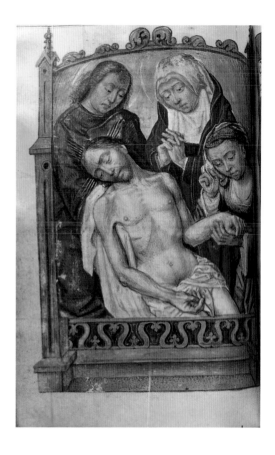

116

MASTER OF THE DAVID SCENES IN THE GRIMANI BREVIARY AND ANOTHER ILLUMINATOR

Book of Hours
Use of Rome
Bruges or Ghent, ca. 1510

MANUSCRIPT: i + 303 + i folios; 8.8 × 6.2 cm (3⁷⁄₁₆ × 2⁷⁄₁₆ in.);
justification: 5.3 × 3.3 cm (2¹⁄₁₆ × 1⅜ in.); 15 lines of *gotica rotunda*;
10 full-page miniatures, 13 historiated initials, 12 small calendar
miniatures with additional scenes set into architectural borders

BINDING: Nineteenth century

COLLECTION: Ware, Saint Edmund's College

PROVENANCE: Unidentified man named Thomas, ca. 1510; Sir Kenelm
Digby (1603–1665) (?)

R A

This diminutive and almost unknown book of hours features a series of full-page inserted miniatures, all in the
half-length format, by the Master of the David Scenes in the
Grimani Breviary.[1] The calendar illuminations and the
smaller miniatures are by a different hand, related to an
artist in the circle of the Master of James IV who collaborated with the Master of the David Scenes on a book of
hours now divided between Vienna and Poitiers.[2] In the
case of the Hours of the Virgin, a full-page *Annunciation*
(fol. 55v) by the Master of the David Scenes accompanies
matins, while seven of the smaller miniatures mark the
other hours.

The Ware manuscript's full-page miniatures are all
based on compositions found in the Ince-Blundell Hours
(cat. no. 115), although the Master of the David Scenes often

altered his models to accommodate a new purpose.[3] *The
Patron in Prayer* (ill. 116a) accompanies a prayer to the Virgin
that gives the patron's name, Thomas.[4] He is sensitively
portrayed with a chiseled chin, fine lips, and a lock of hair
curling over his forehead. The accompanying figures of the
Virgin and Child, meanwhile, were copied from *The Adoration of the Magi* in the Ince-Blundell Hours (fol. 101v), including details such as the folds of the drapery. Two of the other
illuminations in the Ware Hours were loosely based on full-
length compositions from the Ince-Blundell Hours but
refashioned into half-lengths.[5] Thus, the Master of the
David Scenes ensured that every one of the full-page miniatures in the Ware Hours appeared in a consistent format,
lending a sense of unity to the manuscript.

In the Ware *Lamentation* (ill. 116b), only the positions
of the women's hands and the background differ from the
depiction of the same subject in the Ince-Blundell Hours
(ill. 115a). The figures in each feature the unexpressive facial
types so characteristic of the work of the Master of the
David Scenes, and the deathly pale body of Christ is rendered similarly by delicate pen strokes in shades of gray.[6]
Because the two manuscripts are so closely related, it seems
probable that they are nearly contemporaneous.[7] Although
it is not clear whether the Master of the David Scenes
worked in Ghent or Bruges, the entries in the Ware Hours'
calendar correspond almost exactly to those of a manuscript written in Bruges around 1500 (London, The British
Library, Egerton Ms. 1147).[8]   E. M.

116a
MASTER OF THE
DAVID SCENES IN THE
GRIMANI BREVIARY
The Patron in Prayer,
fol. 180v

116b
MASTER OF THE
DAVID SCENES IN THE
GRIMANI BREVIARY
The Lamentation,
fol. 225v

Notes

1. Ker (1969–92, 4: 554–56) includes this manuscript as no. 333 in Saint Edmund's College, but that shelf mark is unknown at the college today. The catalogue for the large exhibition held at the South Kensington Museum in 1862 (London 1862: 583, no. 6829) links the manuscript stylistically to the Hours of Joanna of Castile (cat. no. 114). Thanks to Scot McKendrick for bringing this manuscript to my attention and Peter Kidd for providing study photographs of it.

2. Vienna, Österreichische Nationalbibliothek, Ms. 1887, and Poitiers, Médiathèque François Mitterand, Ms. 57/269. The style of the small Ware Hours miniatures, especially the shape of the faces and the way they are built up with lighter highlights over a darker ground, recalls miniatures such as folios 28, 80, 83, and 86 in the Poitiers manuscript and folios 21 and 59 in the Vienna portion.

3. The Ware Hours features a sixteenth-century foliation that indicates that the manuscript was rebound at some point in its history and the texts reordered. It may be coincidental that the new sequence of images corresponds to the order of the same compositions' appearance the Ince-Blundell Hours, but it is intriguing nonetheless.

4. Leroquais (1927, 2: 278) recorded the prayer, which begins, "O sanctissima, o dulcissima, o piissima," in one fifteenth-century French book of hours.

5. *The Crucifixion* (fol. 16v) and *The Agony in the Garden* (fol. 210v) from the Ware Hours correspond to folios 24v and 19v, respectively, in the Ince-Blundell Hours.

6. Although the artist often used a series of dark parallel lines to indicate shadows, a technique not seen elsewhere in his work, this is likely a result of the very small size of the miniatures, even smaller than their counterparts in the Ince-Blundell Hours.

7. Unlike the Ince-Blundell Hours, however, the Ware manuscript features *Einzelmotiv* borders (see cat. nos. 114, 136).

8. Egerton Ms. 1147 was begun by the Master of the Dresden Prayer Book and finished by either Simon Bening or a member of his workshop. John Plummer indicated that although the July calendar page of Egerton Ms. 1147 is missing, the correlation between its calendar and that of the Ware Hours is otherwise exact, except for four entries (unpublished report, Department of Manuscripts files, JPGM). The calendar also shares a large number of entries with other books connected to Bruges, including Baltimore, Walters Art Museum, Mss. W.438 and W.190. The litany is closest to Vienna, Österreichische Nationalbibliothek, Ms. 1858.

MASTER OF THE DRESDEN PRAYER BOOK (C)

For biography, see part 2

117

MASTER OF THE DRESDEN PRAYER BOOK

Book of Hours
Use of Rome
Bruges, ca. 1495

MANUSCRIPT: iv + 68 folios, 15.1 × 11.1 cm (5¹⁵⁄₁₆ × 4⅜ in.); justification: 7.4 × 4.8 cm (2⅞ × 1⅞ in.); 14 lines of *bastarda*; 16 large miniatures, 28 small miniatures, 30 historiated initials, 66 border roundels

HERALDRY: Achievement of the arms of Philip the Handsome, fol. iv; escutcheon with the arms of Joanna of Castile, fol. 2; both nineteenth century, added ca. 1840

INSCRIPTIONS: Erased inscription, fol. 4

BINDING: Bifolia were cut at gutter, and leaves are now mounted on guards; former binding: early nineteenth century; purple velvet; covers edged with filigree work and studded with four agates and one coral cameo; filigree work at head and foot of spine; two filigree clasps

COLLECTION: London, The British Library, Add. Ms. 17280

PROVENANCE: Col. Theubert [his anonymous sale, Phillips, London, July 19, 1842, lot 54, bought in]; sold privately to William Knight, F.S.A., in 1842 [his sale, Sotheby's, London, August 2, 1847, lot 728]; [to Thomas Rodd, London]; purchased January 1848 from Rodd by the British Museum

JPGM and RA

The calendar roundels that the Master of the Dresden Prayer Book executed in earlier books of hours (cat. nos. 32, 33) demonstrate his inventive use of narrative within the new style of borders with naturalistically colored flowers and nonnaturalistically colored acanthus on solid-colored grounds, the so-called strewn-pattern borders. Here the artist adapted the border roundel to the devotional openings, perhaps inspired by the example of his teacher the Master of Anthony of Burgundy.[1] Fourteen two-page openings (out of seventeen originally) show on the left side a large miniature with a full border featuring a historiated roundel in the left margin and another in the lower border.[2] On the facing page a five-line initial is historiated, and the full border contains two more narrative roundels. This type of opening appears for every major text, including all eight Hours of the Virgin as well as the Penitential Psalms, the Office of the Dead, and each of the offices for the days of the week. In sum, each of these openings features six interconnected miniatures. The five smaller illuminations either expand the narrative of the miniature, often adding incident, or they relate to it typologically or symbolically.

In each border roundel at the opening of the Office of the Dead, Death approaches a single individual, a man or a woman representing a different social station, creating a loose dance of death across the pages (ill. 117a). They complement both the main miniature, which shows a

II7a

MASTER OF
THE DRESDEN
PRAYER BOOK
Vigil for the Dead,
fols. 280v–281

death vigil with a churchyard burial viewed through the chapel window, and the historiated initial, which shows Saint Michael protecting a soul from demons. The opening for the Monday Hours of the Dead, part of an illuminated sequence of offices for the days of the week, features at the left *Judas Maccabeus Presenting the Silver in the Temple*, surrounded by roundels with varying roles (ill. 117b). The silver is Judas Maccabeus's sacrifice for the sins of the dead, a rare but appropriate theme for this office.[3] The border roundel on the miniature's left shows a young noble attacked by soldiers and Death, also an unusual theme but a variation on popular ones that remind the devout of death's unpredictability and inevitability. Below the miniature appears Elias Raising the Son of the Widow of Sarepta, an Old Testament prefiguration of the Raising of Lazarus. The latter is the subject of the historiated initial on the facing page, so they share the theme of resurrection. In the margins on the right are the Last Judgment and the mouth of hell. Drawing imagery from the Old and New Testaments and moralizing themes about death, the opening touches upon life's brevity and themes of sin, judgment, resurrection, and punishment as well as the New Testament fulfillment of the prophecy of the Old Testament.[4]

Following the popular convention of Flemish painters and illuminators, the Master of the Dresden Prayer Book introduced a secondary scene into a contiguous space within the large miniatures. Christ is shown washing the

feet of the Apostles in a small chamber behind the long hall showing the Last Supper (fol. 96v). In *Vigil for the Dead* (ill. 117a) we view the burial scene through the window situated above the tomb of the dead in a chapel where a couple of monks maintain their sleepy watch. The miniature exploits the window motif used for narrative ends in the Vienna Hours of Mary of Burgundy (fig.65), but here the mood is less formal and more intimate. Not normally admired for light effects, the Dresden Master showed an unusual concern with the expressive play of light in the nocturnal *Capture of Christ* (fol. 110v) and in the interiors. The artist could sometimes be sloppy or hasty in his execution, but in this book he demonstrated a mastery of all details. The execution of decorative borders and miniatures in the manuscript is so consistent that it appears that all were illuminated by the master himself.

The book seems to have been made for a patron with strong connections to Évreux, as suggested by the appearance in the litany of Saints Taurinus, Aquilinus, and Gaudus, all associated with this Norman town. The Master of the Dresden Prayer Book had previously enjoyed significant patronage from the Norman nobility (see cat. no. 48). The book has a curious calendar, ruled like the rest of the book but written in a different hand and very sparse.[5] The appearance of Saint Claude of Besançon on June 6 and Saint Denis on October 9, both in gold, confirms that the book was made for a Frenchman. Claude appears again, along with Maurice, among the twenty-nine illuminated suffrages. The sophisticated iconography indicates that the book was intended for a high-ranking patron, perhaps for use in a private chapel. Bodo Brinkmann has dated the manuscript to around 1495 on stylistic grounds, a hypothesis corroborated by Margaret Scott on the basis of costume.[6]

The frontispiece diptych with portraits of Philip the Handsome and Joanna of Castile, after whom this book was called for many years, is a nineteenth-century fake.[7]

T. K.

Notes

1. Perhaps specifically after the famous Black Prayer Book (Vienna, Österreichische Nationalbibliothek, Ms. 1856; cf. Backhouse 1993–94: 49). The two books have completely different iconographic programs, however, not only in the roundels but also in the miniatures. The Vienna Hours is traditionally attributed to the Master of Anthony of Burgundy. Thoss (in Jenni and Thoss 1982; and Pächt and Thoss 1990: 34) accepted the broad grouping with the Master of Anthony of Burgundy but considered the Black Prayer Book to be by a different illuminator. The tradition of historiated border vignettes was developed in the fifteenth century, especially in France.

2. Missing are the full-page miniatures for the Hours of the Holy Spirit for Tuesday (before fol. 61), Matins of the Hours of the Virgin (before fol. 146), and the Penitential Psalms (before fol. 251).

3. Although the subject (2 Maccabees 12:43–45) is not alluded to in the abbreviated office contained in this book of hours, it does appear in various incarnations of the full Office of the Dead (see Ottosen 1993: 63–64; Dickinson 1861–83, col. 862). Thanks to Scot McKendrick for assistance with identifying this subject and its liturgical source. Susan L'Engle contributed research for this entry.

4. Taken together with various, mostly smaller illustrations for the Gospel extracts, Marian prayers, verses of Saint Bernard, and the twenty-seven suffrages, the book includes 140 images altogether. Allowing for the three pages with full-page miniatures and two historiated roundels each that are missing, there would have originally been nineteen large miniatures and seventy-two historiated roundels, for a total of 149 images.

5. Although the book is written in brown ink with red rubrics, its calendar is written in blue with special feasts in gold. There are only three entries for March, two for April, and five for October, an indication that the calendar may not have been completed.

6. Brinkmann 1997: 279; Margaret Scott, correspondence with the author, March 4, 2002, Department of Manuscript files, JPGM.

7. Backhouse 1993–94: 49–54.

117b

MASTER OF
THE DRESDEN
PRAYER BOOK
*Judas Maccabeus
Presenting the Silver in
the Temple*, fol. 43v

MASTER OF THE PRAYER BOOKS OF AROUND 1500

The Master of the Prayer Books of around 1500 was named by Friedrich Winkler after a group of roughly contemporaneous devotional manuscripts.[1] Foremost among Winkler's early attributions was a book of hours first owned by Margaret of Austria (Vienna, Österreichische Nationalbibliothek, Ms. 1862), the illustrations of which are remarkably homogeneous in style and appear largely to be the work of one miniaturist.[2] Winkler ascribed to his master miniatures in two other books of hours (Berlin, Kupferstichkabinett, Ms. 78 B 15, and Vienna, Österreichische Nationalbibliothek, Ms. 1887) and two detached miniatures of the Virgin and Child and of the Raising of Lazarus (Berlin, Kupferstichkabinett, KdZ 640, 1761). He also noted as one of the most extensive works of this miniaturist ninety-two miniatures in a late copy of the *Roman de la rose* (cat. no. 120). Subsequently, both Winkler and other critics have expanded the list of attributions to the Master of the Prayer Books of around 1500. Most notably, Winkler identified further imaginative contributions by this artist to illustrated copies of Monstrelet's *Chroniques* (Leiden, Universiteitsbibliotheek, Ms. Voss. GG. F.2) and the poetic works of Virgil (cat. no. 118).[3] Otto Pächt recognized the miniaturist's hand in copies of Vasco da Lucena's translation of Quintus Curtius (Geneva, Bibliothèque publique et universitaire, Ms. fr. 75) and the poems of Charles d'Orléans (cat. no. 119).[4]

Although the Prayer Books Master is now credited with a large corpus of works,[5] the chronology and interrelationships of these works remain largely unstudied.[6] Several different levels of artistic achievement have been noted among the works that form this corpus, but these differences remain to be collated and explained. Repeated patronage by Engelbert of Nassau and Henry VII has also been noted[7] but has so far been given little detailed consideration, despite the fact that the works created by the Prayer Books Master for these two patrons constitute by far the most fascinating and high-quality manuscripts in the collections of these patrons. His particular talent as an illustrator of the daily lives of both the upper and the lower classes within contemporary society has again been repeatedly noted but has not yet been given due credit within the overall development of Flemish art. Whereas Winkler believed that the Prayer Books Master was a pupil of the Master of the Dresden Prayer Book, more recent critics have proposed that a sequence of miniatures added to a book of hours made for Philip the Good (The Hague, Rijksmuseum Meermanno-Westreenianum, Ms. 10 F 12) is evidence of an independent early career.[8]

What is clear is that in the last decade of the fifteenth century the Prayer Books Master established himself as one of the very few miniaturists in the southern Netherlands who could produce illustrations for a deluxe manuscript of a secular text that equaled in imagination and artistic accomplishment works from the two previous decades. Indeed, despite his name, this miniaturist's major achievements lie in the field of secular imagery and in such depictions of courtly life and rural activities as *The Garden of Pleasure* (cat. no. 120, fol. 12v) and the opening miniature to Virgil's *Georgics* (ill. 118b), respectively. These secular works reveal him as an artist responsive to a wide range of subjects and capable of the novelty of invention in the absence of a visual tradition. Much more conventional are several high-quality devotional books that he and a team of assistants produced, at least two of these (Berlin, Kupferstichkabinett, Ms. 78 B 15, and Brussels, Bibliothèque royale, Ms. IV 280) written by the same scribe and decorated by the same subsidiary illuminator.[9] Similar in kind are smaller contributions to some of the most luxurious devotional books created by Flemish miniaturists between 1490 and 1515, including the Hours of Isabella of Castile (cat. no. 105), the Spinola Hours (cat. no. 124), and the Rothschild Book of Hours (private collection). Also within devotional books, however—most notably in the Munich Hours (cat. no. 90)—he created imaginative cycles of calendar illustrations that reveal both a knowledge of the work of the Master of the Dresden Prayer Book and a sympathy for the daily labors of ordinary people.[10] He also painted several charming miniatures of the Nativity in which he depicts the simple amazement and joy of the shepherds who learn of the birth of and then see the infant Christ.[11] These Nativity miniatures owe their origins at least in part to the Maximilian Master, with whom the Prayer Books Master collaborated on several manuscripts. In two further books of hours (Vienna, Österreichische Nationalbibliothek, Ms. 1887, and London, British Library, Egerton Ms. 1149), a series of half-length miniatures by the Prayer Books Master demonstrate a knowledge of the work of Simon Marmion. Cumulative evidence suggests that the Master of the Prayer Books of around 1500 worked in Bruges.   S. McK.

Notes

1. Winkler 1915: 334–42.

2. Thoss 1987: no. 69. The only large miniature not by the master is reproduced in Brussels 1987a: no. 37.

3. Winkler 1925: 129, 175, 179, 187.

4. Geneva 1976: no. 74; London 1953–54: no. 615.

5. See Dogaer 1987a: 159–60.

6. An exception is De Kesel 1992: 182–202.

7. Korteweg 1998: 21–22; Meale 1989: 205.

8. Schatborn 1970: 45–48.

9. Another devotional volume illuminated by the Master is the Hours of Juan Rodriguez de Fonseca (Saragossa, Biblioteca del Real Seminario Sacerdotal de San Carlos, inv. 6209).

10. See also the La Flora Hours (cat. no. 93) and Sotheby's, London, June 19, 1990, lot 40.

11. E.g., in the Spinola Hours (cat. no. 124, fol. 125v) and in the Rothschild Hours (private collection, fol. 108v).

118

MASTER OF THE PRAYER BOOKS OF AROUND 1500 AND MASTER OF FITZWILLIAM 268

Virgil, *Eclogae*, *Georgica*, and *Aeneis*
Bruges, 1473 and ca. 1490

MANUSCRIPT: i + 256 folios, 35.3 × 25 cm (13⅞ × 9⅞ in.); justification (text and commentary): 28.7 × 20.2 cm (11⁵⁄₁₆ × 8 in.); justification (text only): 15.3 × 13.2 cm (6 × 5³⁄₁₆ in.); 15 lines of *humanistica* (text) and 84 lines of *gotica rotunda* (commentary); 2 full-page miniatures, 1 small miniature

HERALDRY: Monogram *JC* in decorated initial, fol. 9; escutcheon with the arms of the Crabbe family overpainted by those of the De Baenst family of Bruges, fol. 9v

BINDING: Possibly Anthonius van Gavere (d. 1505), Bruges; blind-stamped brown calf over wood boards; five metalwork bosses on each cover; remains of two clasps

COLLECTION: Wells-next-the-Sea, Holkham Hall, earl of Leicester, Ms. 311, vol. 1

PROVENANCE: Jan Crabbe (d. 1488), abbot of the Abbey of Ter Duinen, near Bruges; Paul de Baenst, Bruges, by late fifteenth century; Thomas William Coke, second earl of Leicester (1752–1842), in 1818

J P G M and R A

The present volume and its companion (Ms. 311, vol. 2) form one the most elegant manuscripts of a classical text produced in northern Europe during the fifteenth century. They also constitute one of the most handsome illustrated copies of three verse works universally accepted as by the Roman poet Publius Vergilius Maro (more commonly known as Virgil; 70–19 B.C.).[1] As such they offer an important reflection of the revival of interest, on the part of the wealthy elite of the Low Countries, in these landmarks in Western literature.[2]

The texts that form the core of the Holkham Virgil are the *Eclogae* (*Eclogues*), ten short pastoral poems; the *Georgica* (*Georgics*), a much longer didactic poem in four books on farming; and the *Aeneis* (*Aeneid*), an epic in twelve books describing the quest of the Trojan hero Aeneas to found a new home in Italy. Appended to the *Aeneid* is a sequel written by Maffeo Veggio (1407–1458). The *Eclogues*, the *Georgics*, and the *Aeneid* are each accompanied by a commentary of the fourth-century grammarian Servius; the

Aeneid is also accompanied by the commentary of Servius's predecessor, Aelius Donatus. Preceding all the texts is a glossary by the ninth-century Mico of Saint Requier.[3] The transcription of the commentary of Donatus on book 5 of the *Aeneid* was completed on March 7, 1473, and that on book 6 on March 24. Although the script is modeled on those employed by Italian scribes in contemporary humanistic manuscripts and the dating formula used by one of the scribes of the volume suggests that he was of Italian origin, the Holkham Virgil is now generally accepted as one of a group of manuscripts produced in Bruges, possibly under the direction of an Italian.[4] All these manuscripts contain humanistic texts and were produced in the 1470s for Jan Crabbe (d. 1488), abbot of the wealthy Cistercian Abbey of Ter Duinen, beside Koksijde-Bad in West Flanders.[5]

When made for Jan Crabbe in 1473, the present manuscript was decorated relatively modestly. Besides illuminated initials—one of which (fol. 9) included the initials of Crabbe, and another (fol. 9v) his arms—the principal decoration was formed by small panels of border decoration painted above and below the opening of each part within the *Eclogues*, the *Georgics*, and the *Aeneid*. In addition to this, only one small miniature was painted in a space reserved for such an illustration at the opening of the *Eclogues* (fol. 9). This miniature, which depicts the two herdsmen Tityrus and Meliboeus, is a mere visual translation of the opening lines of the first poem. Its style is consistent with the date of the transcription of the text, is clearly close to that of the Master of Margaret of York,[6] and has been most persuasively attributed to the Master of Fitzwilliam 268.[7] Soon after this decoration was completed, the manuscript was bound in two volumes.

Only much later did the two full-page miniatures for which the Holkham Virgil is rightly celebrated come to form part of the present volume. Painted on two independent parchment leaves that are slightly smaller and thicker than the other leaves in the manuscript, these illustrations were skillfully inserted into the bound volume, facing the openings of the *Georgics* and the *Aeneid*.[8] Much more than the miniature at the beginning of the *Eclogues*, these two miniatures reflect a detailed and subtle understanding of the texts they illustrate. The first offers a visual summary of the principal topics of the *Georgics*. Moving from foreground to background through one unified space, the miniaturist depicts in succession the subjects of books 1 through 4 (ill. 118b). Thus, he moves from plowing and sowing (book 1) to tending trees and vines (book 2); rearing horses, cattle, sheep, and goats (book 3); and finally beekeeping (book 4). In his depiction of beekeeping, the miniaturist also illustrated the short passage of Virgil's text (*Georgics* 4:64) in which he tells how bees can be attracted to a hive with cymbals. The miniature at the opening the *Aeneid* is similar in its unified presentation of a series of episodes that start in the lower left-hand corner of the miniature and end in the upper right-hand corner. Its narrative is, however, even subtler than that of the *Georgics* miniature;[9] it summarizes key themes of the *Aeneid* in its movement from images of destruction (Troy) to images of construction (Carthage) and in its succinct presentation of

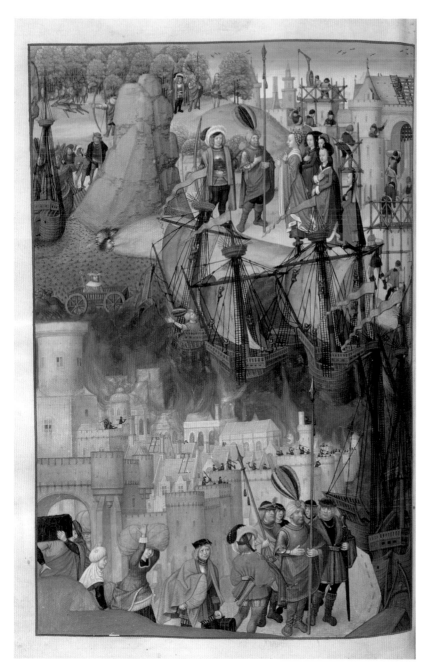

the threat to Aeneas's mission to found a new Troy in Italy (ill. 118a).[10]

The sympathetic response to a complex secular text observed in these two inserted miniatures is a distinctive characteristic of the best work of the Master of the Prayer Books of around 1500. Given, therefore, the presence of all the other hallmarks of the style of this miniaturist in both of the Holkham miniatures,[11] there seems little reason to doubt an attribution to him.[12] On the basis of the costume and the lack of any other such opulent commission from Crabbe, it seems most likely that the *Georgics* and *Aeneid* miniatures were not painted for Crabbe. Instead they were probably added after his death in 1488 for the manuscript's next owner, a member of the wealthy De Baenst family of Bruges.

S. McK.

Notes

1. On illustrated manuscripts of Virgil, see Courcelle 1984, 2.

2. Other illustrated Flemish manuscripts of Virgil's works are Edinburgh, University Library, Ms. 195; Ghent, Universiteitsbibliotheek, Ms. 9; and The Hague, Koninklijke Bibliotheek, Ms. 76 E 21.

3. The selection of texts found in the Holkham Virgil suggests that it was based on two manuscript exemplars, one of Italian humanistic origin and the other of Carolingian origin. Although by 1473 Virgil's text had been printed in no fewer than twelve editions—the first appearing in 1469—the Holkham Virgil does not appear to have been copied from any of these editions.

4. See especially Geirnaert 1992: 178–79. In a talk presented in Brussels in November 2002, "An Italian Scribe at Bruges in the Second Half of the XVth Century: Francesco Florio," Gilbert Tournoy identified the scribe of this volume as Francesco Florio.

5. Bruges 1981: 176–94; Bruges 2002: 183, n. 77.

6. One of the herdsmen, his dog, and the sheep are based on patterns very close to those used by the Master of Margaret of York in Louis of Gruuthuse's copy of Valerius Maximus (Paris, Bibliothèque nationale de France, Ms. fr. 288, fol. 174).

7. Brinkmann 1997: 168.

8. Each of these two leaves is glued to the verso of the preceding leaf by means of a conjoint stub. Because the leaves were not part of the volume when it was bound, their edges are neither gilt nor tooled like the rest of the leaves in the volume.

9. For a full analysis of the *Aeneid* miniature, see Courcelle 1984, 2: 250–52.

10. Instead of showing Aeneas's passage from Troy to Italy, the miniaturist shows his passage to Carthage. Here, in the person of Dido and her rising city, Aeneas faces the most human challenge to his divinely ordained mission. In this light the miniature is essentially an illustration of *Aeneid* 1:437, "o fortunati, quorum iam moenia surgunt."

11. These hallmarks include the delight in extravagant costume and complex compositions, disinterest in facial characterization except when distinguishing low social types, and employment of a somewhat cool but wide-ranging palette.

12. *Pace* Geirnaert (in Bruges 1981: no. 87 and Bruges 2002: 183, n. 77).

118a (above)
MASTER OF THE
PRAYER BOOKS OF
AROUND 1500
Scenes from the Aeneid,
fol. 122v

118b (opposite)
MASTER OF THE
PRAYER BOOKS OF
AROUND 1500
Scenes from the Georgics,
fol. 41v

119

MASTER OF THE PRAYER BOOKS OF AROUND 1500 AND THE MASTER OF THE TOWER OF LONDON

**Charles d'Orléans, *Poèmes*; Pseudo-Héloise, *Art d'Amour*;
Les Demandes d'amours; and *Livre sur le gouvernement d'un prince***
Bruges, ca. 1483 and ca. 1490

MANUSCRIPT: ii + 248 + ii folios, 37 × 26.5 cm (14½ × 10½ in.);
justification: 22 × 15.5 cm (8¼ × 6⅛ in.); 22 lines of *bastarda*;
5 three-quarter-page miniatures, 1 half-page miniature

HERALDRY: Escutcheon with the arms of Saint Edward the Confessor;
escutcheon with the arms of Saint George; escutcheon with the arms
of Elizabeth of York, surmounted by crown; escutcheon with the
arms of England, surmounted by crown; escutcheon with the arms
of England, differenced with label of three points and again
surmounted by coronet; badge of rose-en-soleil; red rose supported
by white greyhound and red dragon between red and white roses;
motto *La plus eure*, all fol. 1; motto *Dieu et mon droit*, fols. 1, 137, etc.;
escutcheon with the royal arms of England surmounted by ermine
cap and crown, supported by two white lions, fol. 73; red rose badge
supported by white greyhound and red dragon; ostrich feather with
Ic dene; portcullis surmounted by crown; red and white roses, all
fols. 89, 137, etc.

BINDING: London, mid-eighteenth century; brown morocco; the
arms of George II gold-stamped on both covers

COLLECTION: London, The British Library, Royal Ms. 16 F.ii

PROVENANCE: Edward IV, king of England (1442–1483); English royal
library, Richmond Palace, in 1535, and Saint James's in 1666; George II,
king of England (1683–1760); presented 1757 to the British Museum

JPGM and RA

O
ne of the most intriguing volumes produced for the
English royal library in the last quarter of the
fifteenth century is the collection of texts in French verse
and prose in the present manuscript. In this manuscript all
but the last text[1] are either lyric verses or concerned with
love;[2] as such most of the texts are totally different in character from the histories and advisory texts found in other
Flemish manuscripts made for the royal library. The manuscript also includes three unparalleled miniatures illustrating poems written by Charles, duke of Orléans (1394–1465),
during his captivity in England. Flemish miniaturists very
rarely illustrated lyric poetry of the fifteenth century.
Moreover, no other miniaturist of any origin illustrated the
verses of Charles d'Orléans so lavishly, and by the time the
present manuscript was made, Charles d'Orléans's verses
had largely been forgotten, even in France.

Of the six miniatures contained in the present manuscript, four are now generally accepted as the work of
the Master of the Prayer Books of around 1500.[3] The first
of these miniatures (ill. 119a), which illustrates Charles
d'Orléans's poem on Paris with a topographical view of the
city, displays many of the hallmarks of the artist's style. The
second, at the opening of the "Demandes d'amours" (fol.
188), depicts youthful outdoor courting reminiscent of the
master's miniatures in the Harley *Roman de la rose* (cat. no.
120). The third and fourth, at the beginnings of Héloise's
Art d'Amour and the instructional text *Grace entière* (ill. 119b
and fol. 210v), employ a model interior and figure types
used elsewhere by the master.[4] Together with the illustrations of a copy of the *Imaginacion de la vraie noblesse* dated

1496 (cat. no. 121), these four miniatures form a group of
works painted by the master for Henry VII.[5] As has often
been proposed,[6] it seems likely that these miniatures were
all produced under the direction of Quentin Poulet, scribe
of the *Imaginacion* and librarian of Henry VII since 1492.[7]
The border decoration accompanying the four miniatures
in the present manuscript and the costumes of the figures
in the miniatures are certainly consistent with a dating in
the 1490s.[8]

The origins of the first two miniatures in the volume
that illustrate the poems of Charles d'Orléans are more
difficult to determine. Remarkably, the many critics who
have studied the second of these miniatures—*Charles
d'Orléans in the Tower of London* (fol. 73), one of the most
famous medieval views of a major English building—have
been unable to make a convincing attribution to a particular artist. Its topographical accuracy suggests an artist with
firsthand knowledge of the tower and other London landmarks. Its style, however, is not typical of contemporary
English miniaturists. What is more, the style of painting
seen in the tower miniature and the opening miniature of
the young prince introduced to the court of Love (fol. 1), as
well as in both their borders, is unlike that of any known
Flemish illuminator, for the two miniatures and borders
merely reflect an awareness of Flemish models.[9] The acanthus in the border accompanying the tower miniature is,
moreover, closer in style to Dutch examples.[10]

Several previous critics have interpreted the present
manuscript as a cornerstone of the revival of court culture
in England under Henry VII.[11] The distinctive collection of
verses and treatises in this manuscript has also been repeatedly interpreted as tailored to the needs of Prince Arthur as
he awaited his wedding to Catherine of Aragon and was
prepared for rule.[12] Part of the collection of verses by
Charles d'Orléans certainly reflects the emotions roused by
separation from a loved one. The three treatises concern
love and kingship. If, however, such claims are to be maintained for the volume, it is necessary to address the revisionist argument of Janet Backhouse that the manuscript
was begun as a gift for Edward IV, abandoned on his death
in 1483, and only much later revised and completed for
Henry VII.[13] According to this view, the two different styles
of the miniatures reflect two distinct campaigns undertaken successively in the 1480s and 1490s. Within the second
campaign the Prayer Books Master painted the final miniature illustrating the verses of Charles d'Orléans in a space
left unfilled by the earlier campaign. The three remaining
miniatures were produced on new leaves on which the text
was recopied, possibly by Poulet himself.[14] The last of these
three new leaves includes the opening of *Grace entière*, in
which the setting of the text was altered by the scribe from
1347 to 1500.[15]

Until a full reexamination of this manuscript is undertaken, it is worth making a few observations. In the first
place, the selection of texts contained in the manuscript is
as intended by its first planners.[16] If, therefore, it is accepted
that the manuscript was conceived as a gift to Edward IV,[17]
some further consideration needs to be given to the implications for the reading of and interest in lyric verses and

119a (opposite)
MASTER OF THE
PRAYER BOOKS OF
AROUND 1500
*Paris under the Protection
of the Virgin and Christ,*
fol. 89

Rance iadis on te souloit
nommer
En tous pays le tresor de
noblesse
Ar vng chascun pouoit en toy trouuer
Onte honneur loyaulte gentillesse.

119b
MASTER OF THE
PRAYER BOOKS OF
AROUND 1500
Héloise Instructs Her Pupil,
fol. 137

amatory texts at the English royal court. Second, since the subsidiary illumination was originally planned on an extremely lavish scale—parts still include both silver and gold—the gift clearly had a wealthy sponsor. With this in mind, future research might reconsider the prominence of London and such landmarks as the Old Custom House in the miniature of Charles d'Orléans in the tower. It has often been remarked that Charles was in fact never held in the tower. Instead of explaining this setting as an appropriate, if factually incorrect, prison for Charles, future critics might consider whether the London setting of this most unusual miniature is significant. One possibility is that the setting reflects the origin of the volume's sponsor, possibly a merchant or other wealthy burgher of London.   S. McK.

Notes

1. On this text, see Hobbs 1989: 49–62.

2. For these texts, see Fox 1973 and Brook 1993.

3. The attribution was first made by Pächt, in London 1953–54: no. 615.

4. Compare, for example, *Héloise Instructing Abelard* (fol. 137) with *Saint Anne Instructing the Virgin* (Brussels, Bibliothèque royale de Belgique, Ms. IV.280, fol. 229v).

5. Other related works include a mutilated copy of *Perceforest* (London, British Library, Royal Mss. 19 E.ii–iii; McKendrick 2003: pl. 92) and a book of hours presented by Henry VII to his daughter Margaret in 1503, now at Chatsworth (Backhouse 1995: 183–84).

6. First proposed in Kipling 1977: 42–46.

7. See the biography of Quentin Poulet in this volume.

8. Compare, for example, the border decoration of two volumes illustrated by the Master of Edward IV around 1490 (Vienna, Österreichische Nationalbibliothek, Ms. 2546, and Geneva, Bibliothèque publique et universitaire, Ms. fr. 76).

9. For a Flemish border close to the presumed model of the tower miniature border, see Smeyers 1998: 445, fig. 38.

10. Compare, for example, the acanthus in two Dutch devotional books dating from 1496 and 1485 or shortly afterward (Moscow 1990: nos. 83, 94). Future research might consider whether the first two miniatures in the present manuscript were produced in London by one of the Dutch artists who are known to have worked there toward the end of the fifteenth century.

11. For example, Kipling 1977: 42–43; Kipling 1981: 127; Strong, in London 1983: no. 1.

12. Fox 1973: xvi–xxiii; Hobbs 1989: 53–54; Brook 1993: 1–3.

13. Backhouse 1987: 36–38; Backhouse 1995: 175–76; Backhouse 2000: 158–59.

14. Backhouse 1995: 176.

15. For the original opening lines, see Genet 1977: 210.

16. Although the subsidiary illumination of the second, third, and fourth texts differs markedly from that of the first text, it was originally planned to be the same. Close inspection of this subsidiary decoration has revealed that minor initials similar to those of the first text were sketched in also for the later texts. On folio 245 illuminated line fillers identical to those employed in the first text (fols. 1–16v, 73–80v, 95v, 97–104v) have been erased.

17. Given the position of their tails in the escutcheon on fol. 73, the lion supporters (fol. 73) are not, strictly speaking, the supporters of Edward IV's arms, the lions of March. It is, however, difficult to offer an explanation of the roses-en-soleil on the opening page (fol. 1) other than in a Yorkist context. The only other Yorkist monarch of the period apart from Edward IV, Richard III, had boars as the supporters for his arms.

120

MASTER OF THE PRAYER BOOKS OF AROUND 1500

Guillaume de Lorris and Jean de Meun, *Le Roman de la rose*
Bruges, ca. 1490–1500

MANUSCRIPT: ii + 186 + ii folios, 39.4 × 29.2 cm (15½ × 11½ in.);
justification: 26 × 19.5 cm (10¼ × 7⅝ in.); 34 lines of *bastarda* in two
columns; 4 three-quarter-page miniatures, 88 one-column miniatures

HERALDRY: Escutcheon with the partially overpainted arms of Nassau
quartering those of Vianden, surmounted by helm with mantling of
azure and or and crest of two raised wings of peacock feathers,
encircled by collar of the Order of the Golden Fleece, fol. 7

BINDING: London, ca. 1900; gold-tooled green morocco; fragments
of early-eighteenth-century gold-tooled red morocco spine, bearing
device of three interlaced crescents and monogram *DDLLM* encircled
by collars of the Orders of Saint Michael and the Holy Spirit and
surmounted by ducal coronet, pasted on fol. 1

COLLECTION: London, The British Library, Harley Ms. 4425

PROVENANCE: Engelbert II, count of Nassau and Vianden (1451–1504);
Jean Antoine II de Mesmes, count of Avaux and Brie-Comte-Robert
(1661–1723); Valentin Esprit Fléchier, bishop of Nîmes (d. 1710) [his
sale, London, January 25, 1726, lot 67]; to Edward Harley, second earl
of Oxford (1689–1741); Margaret, duchess of Portland (1715–1785);
purchased 1753 by the British Museum

R A

The survival of around three hundred manuscripts of
the *Roman de la rose* is testimony to the text's immense
popularity among medieval readers. The large proportion
of deluxe illustrated copies also reveals the extent to which
the nobility favored the *Roman*.[1] Of all these illustrated
copies, none is more splendid than the present copy from
the Harleian library, with its four large and eighty-eight
small miniatures. Made toward the end of the fifteenth century by Flemish book producers, this manuscript is a truly
exceptional work. For, although the *Roman* was well
known within court circles in the Low Countries, it was
very rarely illustrated by Flemish miniaturists.[2]

Comprising around twenty thousand octosyllabic lines
of French verse, the *Roman de la rose* narrates the dream of
a young lover, in which the long quest he has undertaken
ends when he breaches the castle of Jealousy and obtains
the much longed-for rose. As is now well established, the
Roman is a composite of two texts composed by different
authors at least forty years apart. The second and much
longer part, produced by the French writer Jean de Meun
sometime between 1269 and 1278, was appended to a preexisting text of four thousand lines. This earlier text—originally attributed to Guillaume de Lorris (although this is
now disputed)—is significantly different in character from
its sequel. Whereas Jean de Meun's text is didactic, scholarly, pessimistic, and clerically misogynistic, the first fifth of
the *Roman* is lyrical, courtly, and redolent of the world of
romance. Most notably, the earlier text concluded with the
lover barred from the object of his love—the rose. If, as
seems likely, this was the earlier author's intended conclusion to his work, his theme—the pain and delight of
unfulfilled desire—could hardly be more different than
that of Jean de Meun, for whom the fulfillment of desire
was an achievable and necessary evil.

The text of the Harley *Roman de la rose* was, like those
of several contemporary manuscripts, copied from a
printed edition. As in the case of some other Bruges manuscripts (see cat. no. 96),[3] the textual model was an edition
printed in Lyons.[4] The use of this edition issued by Guillaume Le Roy probably in 1487 establishes the date after
which the present manuscript must have been produced; it
also raises more interesting questions. Why, for example,
was a manuscript exemplar not employed? Although very
few manuscripts of the *Roman* were produced during the
second half of the fifteenth century in the Low Countries,
several earlier manuscripts are known to have been in circulation. Was it, therefore, the availability of the printed
edition that prompted the production of the manuscript?

Although more research needs to be done on the
impact of printed editions on Flemish manuscript production, the text for this manuscript seems likely to have been
chosen by the book's patron, Engelbert II, count of Nassau
and Vianden (1451–1504). Engelbert is well known as an
important bibliophile of his time.[5] By the date that the
Harley *Roman de la rose* was being produced, however, very
few nobles appeared to want new deluxe manuscripts of
secular texts, and speculative production had dramatically
declined. Engelbert's acquisition of the present manuscript
was therefore a more considered act than that of bibliophiles in the 1470s and first half of the 1480s.

The producers that Engelbert chose to make his copy
of the *Roman de la rose* were also ones with whom he had
a more extended relationship. The scribe of the present
manuscript can be identified as the one also responsible for
Engelbert's copy of Monstrelet's *Chronique* (Leiden, Universiteitsbibliotheek, Ms. Voss. GG F.2). The miniaturist
responsible for the Harley volume, long identified as the
Master of the Prayer Books of around 1500,[6] illustrated
for Engelbert not only his Monstrelet but also a fine copy
of Vasco da Lucena's *Cyropédie* (Geneva, Bibliothèque
publique et universitaire, Ms. fr. 75).[7] The borders of all
three manuscripts are very similar in style and may be the
work of the same illuminator.

In the Harley manuscript, although the scribe followed
his printed exemplar when planning the number and distribution of illustrations, the miniaturist created illustrations
that rely on the verse titles of the printed source but not on
its illustrations.[8] In so doing, the miniaturist responded
most imaginatively to the courtly and poetic aspects of the
text. He dressed the principal characters in the extravagant
costume fashionable in the highest circles of contemporary
society.[9] His favored settings are idealized gardens and lush
green landscapes, from which handsome trees reach into
open skies populated only by wheeling birds. The most
lavish treatment is reserved for the first part of the text and
its courtly tale of unfulfilled love. In four large miniatures
that illustrate the first part of the *Roman*, the artist follows
the original narrative from the point when the lover's
dream begins (fol. 7) to when he is barred from reaching the
rose in the castle of Jealousy (fol. 39). Between these two
events, the lover is shown entering the garden of Pleasure
(fol. 12v) and being invited to join the dance there, led by
Sir Mirth (ill. 120).   S. McK.

Notes

1. Meredith McMunn, who is preparing a catalogue of all illustrated manuscripts of the *Roman de la rose*, has identified around two hundred copies that were, or were intended to be, illustrated.

2. Of the two other manuscripts of the *Roman de la rose* attributed by Winkler (1925: 33, 194, 207) to much earlier Flemish miniaturists, one (Vienna, Österreichische Nationalbibliothek, Ms. 2568) has recently been attributed to a Lyons miniaturist (Paris 1992: 199–201). Four surviving copies of the *Roman* from the Burgundian ducal library (Brussels 1967a: nos. 89–92) all date from the fourteenth century.

3. A further example is The Hague, Koninklijke Bibliotheek, Ms. 133 A i, the text of which is copied from a Lyons edition of 1486 (Korteweg 1998: 47, no. 30).

4. Bourdillon 1906: 12, 149.

5. Korteweg 1998: 17–22.

6. An identification first made by Winkler (1915: 339).

7. Geneva 1976: no. 74; also Gallet-Guerne 1974: 166–67, pls. 28–32. On the basis of photographs, I suspect that the scribe of the Geneva *Cyropédie* is also the same as that of the Harley *Roman*.

8. On the ninety-two woodcuts that illustrate the Lyons edition and the verse titles it includes, see Bourdillon 1906: 97–143.

9. On this costume, see Madou 1981: 111–22.

121

MASTER OF THE PRAYER BOOKS OF AROUND 1500

Jean de Lannoy (?), *Imaginacion de la vraie noblesse*
London, 1496, and Bruges, ca. 1496–97

MANUSCRIPT: ii + 97 + i folios, 31.2 × 21.5 cm (12¼ × 8½ in.); justification: 19 × 13.5 cm (7½ × 5¼ in.); 25 lines of *bastarda* by Quentin Poulet; 6 three-quarter-page miniatures, 1 historiated initial

HERALDRY: Escutcheon with the royal arms of England, surmounted by crown, fol. 3

BINDING: London, mid-eighteenth century; brown morocco; the arms of George II gold-stamped on both covers

COLLECTION: London, The British Library, Royal Ms. 19 C.viii

PROVENANCE: Henry VII, king of England (1457–1509); English royal library, Richmond Palace, in 1535, and Saint James's in 1666; George II, king of England (1683–1760); presented 1757 to the British Museum

JPGM and RA

The present manuscript of the *Imaginacion de la vraie noblesse* provides an important point of reference within the career of the Master of the Prayer Books of around 1500. As noted in the closing colophon, the text was completed on June 30, 1496. The volume's seven miniatures were probably executed soon after that date.

The context in which the manuscript was produced requires some explanation, for in 1496 its text was copied not in the Low Countries, but at the English royal palace of Sheen. Quentin Poulet, the person responsible for the text's transcription, was a scribe from Lille who had registered as an apprentice in the book producer's confraternity in Bruges in 1477–78.[1] By 1492, however, Poulet had been appointed keeper of the library of Henry VII. Among the payments made to Poulet from Henry VII's chamber, two large sums, paid on July 26, 1497, have been proposed as marking the completion of the present volume.[2]

Poulet's manuscript of 1496 was once considered key early evidence of the Tudors' revival of English court culture and the patronage of resident continental artists in England.[3] More recently, however, that revival has been shown to have begun during the reign of Edward IV (r. 1461–83), most notably through the collection of deluxe Flemish illuminated manuscripts by both him and other prominent members of his court. It is also now recognized that Henry VII (r. 1485–1509) was more interested in deluxe printed books from France than in Flemish illuminated manuscripts and that the present manuscript and Henry's copy of the poems of Charles d'Orléans (cat. no. 119) are exceptional within his patronage of books.[4] Moreover, there is no conclusive evidence that the miniaturists responsible for the illustrations of Henry's manuscripts migrated to England to undertake this work. The picture of the present manuscript as the product of a royal scriptorium of scribes and illuminators headed by Poulet and located first at Sheen and later at Richmond has therefore largely been exposed as illusory.

The present manuscript, however, still supports the claim that Poulet was an arbiter of continental taste for the English royal court. The manuscript's inclusion of what is elsewhere known as the *Enseignement de la vraie noblesse*—a text copied for only one other English noble, Richard Neville, earl of Warwick, much earlier, in 1464[5]—is best explained as the choice of the royal librarian. Poulet's origins in Lille certainly help explain why a text generally attributed to a member of the Lannoy family of Flanders[6] and describing a pilgrimage made from Lille in 1440 should find favor in England in the 1490s. Poulet's addition of a preface addressed to Henry VII, change of the work's title to *Imaginacion de la vraie noblesse*, and ascription to himself of its authorship also suggest that he was shaping the text to his advantage. Constituting a sequence of recommendations for noble conduct, the *Imaginacion* may well have appeared to offer a welcome addition to the education of the ten-year-old heir to the throne, Prince Arthur.

To gain further favor from the king, Poulet turned to one of the most inventive Bruges illuminators of secular texts available to him to undertake the illustration of the *Imaginacion*—the Master of the Prayer Books of around 1500. Whether he also provided guidance for the illustrations is unknown. What is certain is that the miniatures present the key parts of the text with remarkable clarity. Most notably, the two central characters—Lady Imagination and the young *lillois* knight to whom Imagination offers the advice—are clearly distinguished for the viewer. In each miniature in which they appear, they wear exactly the same costumes, and in three of these miniatures (ills. 121a, 121b, and fol. 32v) the knight assumes an identical pose. The setting of their conversation on a hill overlooking the town of Halle in Brabant, the destination of the knight's pilgrimage, is established in the opening miniature (ill. 121a).[7] Although subtly varied by the miniaturist in subsequent miniatures, the setting remains recognizably the same throughout. Yet there is also room for more complex imagery. At the opening of book 5, for example (fol. 41), the miniature illustrates within the same pictorial space as the two main characters three aspects of the advice offered to the knight to be conveyed to the nobility. First we see the illustration of Lady Imagination's warning about malicious

and imprudent counselors who threaten the good judgment of a prince. We also see archers and a carter; the former's skill in focusing on a target and the latter's dogged determination to reach his destination are offered by Imagination as paradigms of single-mindedness for the prince who wishes to withstand such threats.   S. McK.

Notes

1. See the biography of Quentin Poulet in Richard Gay, "Selected Scribe Biographies" (this volume).

2. Kipling 1977: 43, n. 10; Backhouse 1987: 35. Poulet received £23 sterling for "a boke," together with a reward of 10 marks.

3. Kipling 1977: 41–46; Kipling 1981: 121–28.

4. Backhouse 1987: 33–39; Backhouse 1995: 175–76, 179, 187.

5. Warwick's copy is Geneva, Bibliothèque publique et universitaire, Ms. fr. 166. Four other copies belonged to Philip the Good (Brussels, Bibliothèque royale, Ms. 11047), the Croÿ and Lannoy families (Brussels, Bibliothèque royale de Belgique, Ms. 10314; London, British Library, Add. Ms. 15469), and Philip II, duke of Savoy (Brussels, Bibliothèque royale, Ms. 11049).

6. On the authorship of the *Enseignement*, see Doutrepont 1909: 317–18. Livia Visser-Fuchs is preparing a study of this text.

7. Close compositional similarities between this miniature and an earlier miniature of the same subject from the circle of Willem Vrelant (Geneva, Bibliothèque publique et universitaire, Ms. fr. 166, fol. 2) suggest that the earlier miniature or its model forms the starting point for the sequence of illustrations depicting the knight and Imagination in the present manuscript.

121a (opposite)
MASTER OF THE
PRAYER BOOKS OF
AROUND 1500
A Knight in Prayer Before Lady Imagination, fol. 3

121b (above)
MASTER OF THE
PRAYER BOOKS OF
AROUND 1500
Archers and a Carter as Models for a Prince, fol. 41

122

MASTER OF THE PRAYER BOOKS OF AROUND 1500 (?) AND OTHERS

Statutes and Armorial of the Order of the Golden Fleece
Bruges(?), 1481–91, with additions to 1556

MANUSCRIPT: 123 folios, 23.9 × 17.6 cm (9⅜ × 7 in.); justification: 16.9 × 12.1 cm (6⅝ × 4¾ in.); mostly 26–27 lines of *bastarda*; 6 full-page portraits, 1 three-quarter-page miniature, 6 full-page and numerous small heraldic panels

BINDING: Flanders, mid-sixteenth century; red velvet over wood boards

COLLECTION: Waddesdon Manor, Ms. 17

PROVENANCE: Baron Edmond de Rothschild (1845–1934), Paris (his Ms. 86); James A. de Rothschild (1878–1957); The National Trust

R A

The Waddesdon volume is one of only five deluxe copies of the combined texts of the statutes and armorial of the Order of the Golden Fleece. Like the London manuscript of the same texts (cat. no. 76), the present manuscript commemorates successive patrons of the order in a series of full-length portraits at the beginning of accounts of the first chapter meetings over which they presided. The Waddesdon portraits, which were begun sometime between 1481 and 1491,[1] probably shortly after the production of the London statutes and armorial, develop further the models first seen in the earliest of the five deluxe copies, the one made for Charles the Bold in 1473 (The Hague, Koninklijke Bibliotheek, Ms. 76 E 10). Unlike the London manuscript, the Waddesdon statutes and armorial did not remain frozen in time but underwent several revisions, most notably around sixty years after it was begun. Within these later additions, the portraits reflect further developments in official portraiture.

During the first illustrative campaign, the opening of the statutes was marked with a depiction of a chapter meeting of the order that is based on the same updated model first employed in the London statutes and armorial.[2] Also undertaken then to illustrate the armorial were portraits of the first three patrons of the order and depictions of the arms of those elected as members of the order at the chapter meetings, up to and including that held at Bois-le-Duc in 1481. Whereas an assistant painted the chapter miniature, in which the faces of the members of the order are uniformly weak, a more talented miniaturist contributed to the three portraits.[3] Despite some pigment loss, particularly on the flesh of the figure, the portrait of Maximilian is the most impressive of these portraits (ill. 122). It also comes closest to the style of the Master of the Prayer Books of around 1500. Within the hieratic formula of the full-length portrait, the artist successfully introduced several incidental details, as well as a spaciousness and specificity of place, and anticipated subsequent adaptations of the formula as exemplified by the remaining portraits in the volume. None of the first three portraits, however, is based even at second hand on the individual features of the patrons of the order.[4]

Within the second, much later campaign of illustration, a third artist contributed portraits of Philip the Handsome

122

MASTER OF THE
PRAYER BOOKS OF
AROUND 1500 (?)
Maximilian I, fol. 58v

and Charles V. Philip's portrait was inserted at the beginning of an account of the chapter meeting at Mechelen
that was itself added to the core text of the armorial shortly
after the meeting took place in 1491. The portrait of
Charles V falls in the middle of a major textual addition
made to the volume shortly after 1545 that includes
accounts of all the chapter meetings from 1500 to 1545.
These two portraits are entirely different in conception
from the three earlier portraits and appear to have been
executed by an imitator of Simon Bening. The bodies of the
figures, including the position of the arms and the fall and
detailing of the drapery, are based on the corresponding
portraits in a deluxe copy of the armorial illuminated by
Bening around 1540 (Madrid, Instituto de Valencia de Don
Juan, Ms. 26 I.27).[5] The Renaissance architectural frames
and detailed landscapes in the Waddesdon volume

more loosely related to the Madrid portraits.[6] Unlike the
earlier portraits in the Waddesdon volume, the portraits of
Charles V and Philip the Handsome are ultimately based
on direct observation of their facial features.[7] As in other
copies of the armorial made in the middle of the sixteenth
century,[8] full-page depictions of the arms of the patrons of
the order were inserted opposite all the portraits, both old
and new, in the Waddesdon volume.

The final additions to the Waddesdon statutes and
armorial were made shortly after 1556, when Philip II
presided over his first chapter meeting. To accompany the
account of this chapter meeting, a further artist painted
a full-length portrait of Philip and a full-page depiction of
his arms. This artist contributed to another copy of the
armorial an almost identical portrait bearing the date 1556.[9]
The figures and landscapes in both portraits are again based

on those devised by Bening. In the case of the frame in both miniatures, however, it was transformed into a barrel-vaulted arch whose entablature is supported by flanking terms.[10]

S. McK.

Notes

1. *Pace* Delaissé (in Delaissé, Marrow, and De Wit 1977: 363–65), who argued that the portraits were added after 1491. I consider the account of the 1491 chapter meeting an afterthought to the core manuscript and one that thereby lacked a portrait until after 1545. Delaissé's explanation fails to take account of the identical frames on both the portraits and the depictions of arms of the members of the order up to and including the chapter meeting of 1481. His explanation also places too late a dating on the border accompanying the miniature of a chapter meeting of the order (fol. 5). The borders closest in style to this one (see cat. no. 38; also Smeyers 1998: 451, fig. 52) date from the first half of the 1480s, and certainly not the 1490s, by which point strewn-pattern borders were well established.

2. On this updating, see cat. no. 76.

3. The chapter miniature and the portraits reflect similar preferences for heavily patterned surfaces and elaborate detailing of incidental features. Comparison with the chapter miniature in the London volume reveals that the heavily patterned gold cloth hangings and griffin supporters on the throne in the Waddesdon volume are the Waddesdon artist's own additions to the shared model. The exact repetition of these griffins in the Waddesdon portrait of Maximilian (fol. 58v) suggests that the artist of the chapter miniature also contributed to the portraits. Several much more accomplished features of these portraits, in particular the faces of the patrons, are, however, clearly not the work of the same artist.

4. In outline, the body of Maximilian in the Waddesdon portrait is clearly based on the same model as the London portrait (cat. no. 76, ill 76a). The head, however, is very different and appears unrelated to other portraits of Maximilian.

5. For the Madrid portraits, see the facsimile *Insigne Orden del Toison de Oro* (Valencia 1999a). According to a document dated 1538 (n.s.), Bening was paid for contributing portraits and arms to the armorial of the order's chancellor, Philippe Nigri (Pinchart 1860–81, I: 103–4; Onghena 1968: 190). This armorial has been incorrectly identified with the Madrid volume, and also with Brussels, Bibliothèque royale de Belgique, Ms. IV 84. The Madrid portraits do, however, seem to have been painted by Simon Bening. For a different view, see the biography of Simon Bening (part 5, this volume).

6. These landscapes are clearly similar in kind, if not in detail. Close comparisons within the oeuvre of Bening include the landscape in the Louvre *Portrait of a Man* (cat. no. 153). The first five portraits in another armorial and statutes dating from around 1550 (Brussels, Bibliothèque royale, Fonds Solvay IX 93 LP) include frames and landscapes that are almost identical to the five corresponding Madrid portraits (Onghena 1968: 187–215). In a documented appraisal of an armorial of the order produced by the painter Jan van Battele in 1550, the frames and landscapes were termed "paysaiges, machonnaiges, chyrat et anticquaiges" (Pinchart 1860–81, 3: 213; Onghena 1968: 211). As shown by Onghena, the Solvay armorial cannot be identified with the documented volume illuminated by Jan van Battele in 1550.

7. The facial features of the Waddesdon portraits are derived from the same models employed for the Solvay portraits. On the visual sources for the Solvay portraits, see Onghena 1968: 197.

8. For documented examples from 1536, 1538, and 1550, see Pinchart 1860–81, I: 103–4, 244–45, 3: 212–15.

9. Brussels, Bibliothèque royale, Fonds Solvay IX 93 LP, fol. 93v (see Brussels 1958: pl. 14).

10. Onghena (1968: 200) described the corresponding Solvay portrait cited in note 9 as having been painted by "een meer decoratief schilder die onder invloed stond van de Antwerpse groteskenstijl."

MASTER OF ANTOINE ROLIN

The Master of Antoine Rolin was first identified by Otto Pächt in 1953 as the principal miniaturist responsible for the illustration of a lavish copy of *Le Livre des échecs amoureux* (Paris, Bibliothèque nationale de France, Ms. fr. 9197) and two copies of the *Chroniques de Hainaut* (Oxford, Bodleian Library, Mss. Douce 205 and Holkham misc. 50–53).[1] Of these manuscripts two were made for Antoine Rolin (d. 1497), grand bailiff of the county of Hainaut, and his wife, Marie d'Ailly, and the third for a member of the Berlaymont family of Hainaut. One of the volumes of the *Chroniques de Hainaut* is dated 1490. Pächt later attributed to the master and assistants an extensive campaign of illustrations in a copy of Guillaume Digulleville's *Pèlerinage de vie humaine* (Geneva, Bibliothèque publique et universitaire, Ms. fr. 182).[2] More recently, Anne-Marie Legaré has greatly increased our knowledge of the Master of Antoine Rolin. In a series of studies[3] she has convincingly identified the miniaturist's center of artistic activity as the county of Hainaut[4] and also demonstrated his debt to his more famous predecessor in that region, Simon Marmion (d. 1489). Most notable among her attributions to the Master of Antoine Rolin are more than 120 miniatures in a late copy of Raoul Lefèvre's *Recueil des histoires troyennes* (cat. no. 123) and 11 highly innovative miniatures in the unique copy of the *Allégorie de l'homme raisonable et de l'entendement humain* (Paris, Bibliothèque nationale de France, Ms. fr. 12550). The first was begun in 1495 for Antoine Rolin; the second was produced around 1500–1510 and was subsequently owned by Margaret of Austria. Legaré has also added to the corpus of the Master of Antoine Rolin a large number of devotional manuscripts. These manuscripts range widely in their quality of decoration, but include such opulent works as the Boussu Hours (Paris, Bibliothèque de l'Arsenal, Ms. 1185), which was made shortly after 1490 for Isabelle de Lalaing, the widow of Pierre de Hennin de Boussu. All the works thus far attributed to the Master of Antoine Rolin were produced between 1490 and 1520.

Legaré has recounted in detail the stylistic traits of the Master of Antoine Rolin.[5] Many of these traits reflect a formulaic approach to the depiction of landscape, interiors, and figures. Some—such as the pale blue skies with darker blue striations—constitute a hallmark of his work; most were easily imitated by assistants or associates. In addition to these stylistic traits, Legaré has highlighted the striking originality of many of the images created by the Master of Antoine Rolin, as well as their faithfulness to the texts they illustrate. She also noted within the miniatures he painted in devotional manuscripts a marked dependence on compositions devised by Marmion, especially those in the Huth Hours (cat. no. 33). Although generally conventional in his *mise-en-page*, the master was capable of innovation in his treatment of miniatures and border spaces, sometimes allowing the narrative to spill over into the borders and thus blur the distinction between the two spaces.[6] Several works reveal an uncommon desire to unify miniature and border and also facing pages.

S. McK.

Notes

1. London 1953–54: nos. 612–14.

2. Geneva 1976: no. 75.

3. Legaré 1990: 314–44; Legaré, Tesson, and Roy 1991: 80–94; Legaré 1992: 209–22; Legaré 1996: 201–24; Legaré 2002: 65–124.

4. In her earlier studies Legaré argued for Mons, the administrative capital of the county of Hainaut, as the Master of Antoine Rolin's center of production. More recently (Legaré 1996, Legaré 2002) she has defined his place of work as nearby Valenciennes, the economic capital of Hainaut and former place of work of Simon Marmion.

5. Legaré 1992: 211–12.

6. E.g., Geneva, Bibliothèque publique et universitaire, Ms. fr. 182.

123

MASTER OF ANTOINE ROLIN AND ASSISTANTS

Raoul Lefèvre, *Recueil des histoires troyennes*
Mons and Valenciennes (?), 1495–96

MANUSCRIPT: iv + 293 folios, 38.2 × 27 cm (15 × 10⅝ in.); justification: 25.8 × 17.8 cm (10³⁄₁₆ × 7⁷⁄₁₆ in.); 36 lines of *bastarda* in two columns by Pierre Gousset; 3 full-page miniatures, 111 half-page miniatures, 6 one-column miniatures

HERALDRY: Escutcheon with the partly erased arms of Rolin, in miniature, fol. 14; linked initials *AM*, in miniature, fol. 11v, and in initials, fols. 2, 26v, 33, etc.; escutcheons with the arms of Rolin overpainted by those of Oettingen of Swabia, fols. ii, 119, 207; escutcheon with the arms of Oettingen of Swabia surmounted by helm and mantling, fol. 293; initials *IH* (?), fols. 118bv, 118dv, 207

BINDING: Paris, late eighteenth century; green morocco; gold-tooled spine

COLLECTION: Paris, Bibliothèque nationale de France, Ms. fr. 22552

PROVENANCE: Antoine Rolin (d. 1497) and Marie d'Ailly (d. 1498), Mons; John II, lord of Oettingen and Flobecq (d. 1514); Louis-Jean Gaignat (1697–1768) [his sale, De Bure, Paris, April 10, 1769, lot 2339]; Louis-César de La Baume Le Blanc, duc de la Vallière (1708–1780) [his sale, De Bure, Paris, January 12–May 5, 1784, lot 4087]; purchased for the Bibliothèque du Roi

RA

123
MASTER OF
ANTOINE ROLIN
Danaë Sent into Exile,
fol. 64v

The present manuscript is crucial for both the reconstruction of the oeuvre of the Master of Antoine Rolin and the history of late medieval reception of the stories of the Greek hero Hercules and the city of Troy. The manuscript's colophon naming Pierre Gousset as the scribe suggests that the miniaturist worked in Mons, in Hainaut, in close proximity to his principal patron, the grand bailiff of Hainaut, Antoine Rolin.[1] The campaign in this manuscript of 122 miniatures forms one of the most extensive cycles of illustrations of the story of Troy.

The text contained in Gousset's manuscript forms the most comprehensive and popular version of the story of Troy produced in the Middle Ages.[2] Compiled around 1464 as a sequel to Raoul Lefèvre's earlier *Histoire de Jason* (see cat. no. 59), his *Recueil des histoires troyennes* relates in three books how Troy was destroyed first by Jupiter, then by Hercules, by Jason and the Argonauts, and finally by the Greeks seeking the return of Helen, wife of Menelaus. Its narrative stretches from the beginnings of the struggle between the god Saturn and his son Jupiter to the grisly deaths of the Greek leaders after their return from the Trojan War. Whereas the first two books are Lefèvre's own work, the third is an earlier French version of the late thirteenth-century *Historia destructionis Troiae* of Guido delle Colonne. A dedication to Philip the Good, duke of Burgundy, appears swiftly to have secured popularity for the *Recueil* at the Burgundian court. By the time Gousset had copied his text, the *Recueil* had also become one of the most popular vernacular texts in western Europe. In addition to the twenty-four other manuscripts of the *Recueil* that survive, no fewer than five printed editions were produced before 1500. In 1473/74 an English translation by William Caxton became the first English text to be printed. Printings of a translation into Dutch from 1485 onward further increased the readership of the *Recueil*.

The Master of Antoine Rolin was responsible for almost all the miniatures in the present manuscript of the *Recueil*. Within this long campaign he maintained a remarkable consistency of finish, and only in four of the six one-column miniatures is the hand of an assistant clearly discernible.[3] Typical of the master's spacious, colorful, and contemporary settings for the distant events of his text is the miniature of Danaë sent into exile (ill. 123). The campaign is notable for the large scale of most of the miniatures, and in particular for the three full-page miniatures of Hercules' fleet attacking Troy, the rebuilding of Troy, and the fall of Troy. Inspiration for these three unusual miniatures may lie in the cycle of three full-page miniatures devised to illustrate another version of delle Colonne's *Historia* and copied into at least two Parisian manuscripts at the beginning of the century.[4] The spectacular revival of the *Recueil* in the present manuscript may therefore reflect not only the creative inspiration of the Master of Antoine Rolin but also emulation of a much earlier model. Such emulation was an important influence on the illustration of secular vernacular texts in the final decade of the fifteenth century. Like Jean Colombe in the expansive illustrations he painted in a contemporary manuscript of a French translation of the *Historia*,[5] the Master of Antoine Rolin also created his cycle of miniatures at a time when monumental depictions of the story of Troy in tapestry were well developed.[6]

Although some confusion has recently arisen concerning the patronage of the present manuscript,[7] the full evidence it presents shows that it was originally intended for Antoine Rolin and his wife, Marie d'Ailly. The initials *AM* not only occur repeatedly within the volume's illuminated initials and full illuminated borders[8] but are also painted within one miniature toward the beginning of the volume.[9] Traces of the Rolin arms are also visible beneath those of Oettingen in the lower borders of two miniatures, as well as on their own within another miniature near the beginning of the volume.[10] The subsequent addition of the Oettingen arms to the volume almost certainly reflects a change in the intended owner, probably after the death of Antoine Rolin on September 4, 1497.[11] As one of the other most active bibliophiles in Hainaut, John II of Oettingen[12] may easily have been persuaded to order the completion of the ambitious manuscript originally undertaken for Antoine Rolin.

S. McK.

Notes

1. Legaré, Tesson, and Roy 1991: 86–87; Legaré 1992: 217.
2. For more on the *Recueil*, see Aeschbach 1987.
3. Legaré 1992: 219.
4. On the Parisian miniatures, see Avril 1969: 300–314. In general, see Buchthal 1971.
5. Paris, Bibliothèque nationale de France, Ms. n.a. fr. 24920 (Paris 1993: no. 186).
6. For the tapestries, see McKendrick 1991: 43–82.
7. Lemaire 1993: 246.
8. The initials are on folios 2, 26v, 33, 43, 56v, 66v, 77v, 80, 85, 126v, 138, 144, 149, 158, 165v, 177v, 228, 244v, 258, 262v, 268, 275; the borders on folios 1, 119, 207. The identical form of the *M* on folio 85 suggests that the letters that Lemaire (1993: 246) read as *AH* are actually a repetition of *AM*. In general, see De Vaivre 1999: 56–58.
9. Within the spandrels at the center of the upper portion of the miniature on folio 11v.
10. Traces of blue pigment from the Rolin arms are visible at the edges of the escutcheon bearing the Oettingen arms on folios 119, 207; traces of an escutcheon of azure three keys or (Rolin) are on folio 14.
11. The Oettingen arms—painted with pigments different from those used in the initials, border decoration, and miniatures—occur on folios ii, 119, 207, 293. A monogram formed from knotty branches appears twice in the border decoration of folio 270, once in an initial at the beginning of the table of contents of book 2, and again in a full-page illumination at the end of the same table (Legaré, Tesson, and Roy 1991: 84, fig. 13). *Pace* Lemaire (1993: 246), this monogram is not *HI* or *HJ* and does not relate to the Oettingen couple. Another full-page illumination with the monogram occurs in Antoine Rolin's *Chroniques de Hainaut* (Oxford, Bodleian Library, Douce Ms. 205, fol. 3v).
12. On Oettingen, see Lemaire 1993.

PART 5

NEW DIRECTIONS IN MANUSCRIPT PAINTING,
CIRCA 1510–1561

THOMAS KREN

A variety of fresh artistic concerns began to shape the course of Flemish manuscript painting around 1510 and continued to do so for the next five decades. Around this time began the second half of the career in Flanders of the Master of James IV of Scotland and the known career of Simon Bening.[1] These two artists were the greatest Flemish illuminators of the sixteenth century. The new developments include a more integrated relationship between border and text, the evolution of landscape, the elaboration of narrative cycles, the growing influence of Mannerism, and the emergence of portraiture as a genre. Such ongoing innovation contributed to the continuing popularity of Flemish manuscript painting in Europe.

The greatest achievements of the Master of James IV of Scotland—the magisterial Spinola Hours (cat. no. 124), the Grimani Breviary (cat. no. 126), the prayer book for a member of the Portuguese royal family (Lisbon, Museu Nacional de Arte Antiga, Ms. 13), and two leaves from a book of hours (cat. no. 125)—belong to the period from 1510 to 1525.[2] In the Spinola Hours the artist explores both the illusionistic possibilities of the border and the relationship between text and image. A distinct but certainly equal achievement is his contribution to the Grimani Breviary, also notable for the integration of text with image, and also for the artist's reformulation of a great artwork from another era, the calendar miniatures of the *Très Riches Heures* (Chantilly, Musée Condé). In the breviary's calendar the Master of James IV transformed the courtly and refined art of the Limbourg brothers (and the broader style of Jean Colombe) into something more vigorous, full-blooded, and earthy. This cycle is one of his exceptional accomplishments as a landscape painter.

Significantly the Grimani calendar served in turn as an important model for the calendar cycles executed by Simon Bening in the 1530s and 1540s, although Bening drew upon the individual figures, types, and figural groupings primarily as models and points of departure. He took over elements of landscape from the Grimani Breviary, as in the famous village snow scene (fol. 2v; see also cat. no. 154, fol. 2v, and cat. no. 150, fol. 1v) or the foreground of the grape harvest scene (fol. 9v; see also cat. no. 150, fol. 10v), but then he rethought the setting, opening it up, enhancing the quality of spatial recession, and heightening the atmospheric effects. Drawn to calendar subject matter even before he had become familiar with the calendar of the Grimani Breviary (see cat. no. 140), he carried much further the burgeoning explorations of landscape illumination undertaken earlier by the Master of the Dresden Prayer Book (cat. nos. 20, 32, 33, and fig. 30) and the Master of the Prayer Books of around 1500 (cat. nos. 90, 118). Bening's gifts as a

SIMON BENING
Bathsheba, mid-1530s
(detail, ill. 150c)

colorist, his keen powers of observation, and his profound grasp of the means for conveying continuous spatial recession make his achievement as a painter of landscape singular in this period. Moreover, Bening's art demonstrates the startling originality that the best illuminators brought to the workshop tradition of copying older models. He drew inspiration from the Grimani calendar over and over again for a quarter century, always locating fresh ideas within its miniatures and consistently taking them in new directions.

The greatest manuscripts of the period—such as the Grimani Breviary, the Spinola Hours, and the Prayer Book of Albrecht of Brandenburg (cat. no. 145)—show that illumination for devotional purposes was substantially an art of narrative. Pictorial cycles of eight or more images in continuous narrative are a basic feature of most books of hours, especially in the Hours of the Virgin. Even before 1510 the Master of James IV of Scotland had begun by exploring narratives of greater lengths, often featuring two large miniatures in the opening of a cycle, increasing the number of miniatures in a cycle to fourteen or even sixteen (see cat. no. 109). In the Spinola Hours he introduced sophisticated new ways of spatially unifying miniature and border, helping to integrate the separate compartments of the page with the narrative sequence. It was not new for illuminators to include multiple events in the same setting, but the Master of James IV fashioned an eloquent visual language for accomplishing this in the Spinola Hours.

Subsequently Simon Bening—in works such as the Brandenburg Prayer Book, a manuscript whose forty-one miniatures are organized in a mostly continuous narrative around the life of Christ—pushed the narrative cycle to an extreme. The scenes in the miniatures are lent even greater unity and a sense of forward motion by the quality of lighting, especially in the Passion sequence, in which many images are shown as nocturnal. Flickering torchlight and other internal lighting sources heighten the drama, while Bening's sympathetic characterization of Christ, underscoring his humanity, gives the events greater immediacy. The ultimate expression of the genre of the extended narrative appears in the Stein Quadriptych (cat. no. 146), in which sixty-four largely close-up scenes recount so many specific moments of the Passion that their visualization appears at times to be continuous, a conception that has been called protocinematic by modern critics.[3]

By the second decade of the sixteenth century, the Italian High Renaissance was having a significant impact on Flemish art, in particular on painters based in Antwerp and Brussels: Jan Gossaert, Bernard van Orley, Joos van Cleve, and others. The results of this were felt less immediately in manuscript illumination than in panel painting, but during the 1520s a style that incorporated some of the dramatic gestures and elongated figures of the Mannerist painters crept into illumination, especially in the work of the Master of Charles V, the Master of Cardinal Wolsey, and their circles (cat. nos. 166–70). During the 1530s High Renaissance models also began to play a role in Simon Bening's work (see cat. nos. 148, 150, 154), but he largely avoided the formal exaggerations that are characteristic of many northern painters inspired by Italian art. Indeed Bening, much in the spirit of Gerard David, continued in many ways the tradition of naturalism of fifteenth-century Flemish painting, while exploring with a fresh eye the possibilities of narrative, landscape, and portraiture.

It is often noted that the children of Gerard Horenbout (the Master of James IV of Scotland?), Lucas and Susanna, along with Simon Bening's daughter Levina Teerlinc, were instrumental in developing the new art of the portrait miniature in England. Lucas and Susanna left for England in the 1520s (as did Gerard), while Levina was in England by 1545. Yet independent portraits started to appear as frontispieces in Flemish manuscripts as early as 1526 (see ill. 127).[4] They probably became fairly common in devotional books over the next few years (see cat. no. 168). Outside of books, several such illuminated portraits by Simon Bening survive, among which one pair (cat. no. 149) may date as early as 1531, and he seems to have continued to paint them throughout his career (see cat. nos. 153, 161). Since the chronology of the earliest portrait miniatures in Flanders and England is obscured by the loss of many images and a lack of securely datable works, it is difficult to determine the role of the parents in this new development. They may have not only taught their children the technique of illumination on parchment but also shared ideas about the conception of the formal portrait. Although Gerard Horenbout moved to England by 1528 and lived there for the rest of his life, more than a decade, few of the illuminations he produced there (see cat. no. 130), or works by other artists closely related to his style (see cat. no. 131), have survived. The export of Flemish masters (as opposed to just their books) is a significant indicator of the triumph of Flemish manuscript illumination in Europe; yet it also contributed to a shrinking population of first-rate illuminators in Flanders.

The dominion of Flemish manuscript painting in Europe, already well evident by 1510, was made complete during this period. Few of the major Flemish manuscripts of this era show evidence of having been created for Flemish patrons. True, such patrons did not disappear altogether, and the additions to the Sforza Hours commissioned by the bibliophile Margaret of Austria, regent of the Netherlands and daughter of Mary of Burgundy, rank with the major achievements of the second decade of the sixteenth century. Margaret's name has also been connected to other major books (see cat. no. 124). Still, most of the patronage of Flemish manuscripts of this time came from Spain and Portugal, and to a lesser extent Italy, Germany, and England. With the exception of the last, these were largely Hapsburg domains or areas politically allied with the dynasty. The market for Flemish manuscripts therefore encompassed a great expanse of western Europe. Moreover, in these years the major critical appreciation of Flemish illumination came from southern Europe. Marcantonio Michiel's praise for Cardinal Grimani's recently purchased Flemish breviary shows that Italian Renaissance observers admired the Flemish illuminators' powers of observation along with their directness.[5] Whereas the praise for Flemish illuminators such as Simon Marmion came largely from critics attached to the Burgundian court, which also provided Marmion's patronage, Simon Bening earned acclaim from Portuguese humanists and critics—first, in 1530, as the best illuminator in Europe, and then, in 1548, as one of the five best in Europe.[6] At the same time, despite Bening's continued success abroad, the seeds of decline for Flemish illumination had been sown long before, with the advent of the printing press during the 1450s. While Flemish illumination had continued to flourish for nearly one hundred years, by 1548, when Bening was still in his prime, the production of significant Flemish illuminated manuscripts was rapidly diminishing and no major new talent was emerging on the scene. Within a decade the great era of Flemish manuscript illumination would finally come to a close.

Notes

1. Bening was already twenty-six or twenty-seven years old by 1510, but no work by him from before this time has been securely identified.

2. Among these four examples only the breviary can be securely dated to the period 1510–20. The others are likely to belong to this period on the basis of internal evidence and stylistic considerations.

3. E.g., Kupfer-Tarasulo 1979a: 289.

4. By independent I mean a half-length portrait that shows only the sitter, as opposed to the traditional format depicting the subject of the portrait kneeling in adoration of the Virgin, Christ, or a saint (e.g., ill. 110a).

5. Quoted in Salmi and Mellini 1972: 263 (see cat. no. 126).

6. See cat. nos. 147, 150 and the biography of Bening (this part).

MASTER OF JAMES IV OF SCOTLAND (B)
For biography, see part 4

124

MASTER OF JAMES IV OF SCOTLAND, WORKSHOP
OF MASTER OF THE FIRST PRAYER BOOK OF
MAXIMILIAN, MASTER OF THE DRESDEN PRAYER
BOOK, MASTER OF THE LÜBECK BIBLE, AND
MASTER OF THE PRAYER BOOKS OF AROUND 1500

Spinola Hours
Use of Rome
Bruges and Ghent, ca. 1510–20

MANUSCRIPT: 312 folios, 23.2 × 16.6 cm (9⅛ × 6⁹⁄₁₆ in.); justification:
10.9 × 7.4 cm (4⁵⁄₁₆ × 2¹⁵⁄₁₆ in.); 17 lines of *gotica rotunda*; 1 full-page
miniature, 70 three-quarter-page miniatures, 63 historiated borders,
12 bas-de-page calendar miniatures with additional scenes set into
architectural borders

HERALDRY: Escutcheons, banners, and standards with unidentified
arms, azure cross ancrée or, fol. 185

BINDING: Genoa, eighteenth century; red morocco over pasteboard;
the arms of the Spinola family gold-tooled on both covers

COLLECTION: Los Angeles, J. Paul Getty Museum, Ms. Ludwig IX 18
(83.ML.114)

PROVENANCE: Spinola family, Genoa, eighteenth century; [sale,
Sotheby's, London, July 5, 1976, lot 68]; to Peter and Irene Ludwig,
Aachen; acquired 1983

JPGM and RA

The Spinola Hours is the most pictorially ambitious and
original sixteenth-century Flemish manuscript. Considering the scope and complexity of the book, with contributions by a number of the greatest artists of the day—
including the Master of James IV of Scotland, the Master of
the Dresden Prayer Book, the Master of the First Prayer
Book of Maximilian, the Master of the Lübeck Bible, and
the Master of the Prayer Books of around 1500—uncommonly careful attention went into ensuring a uniformity of
vision.[1] It is set apart from other manuscripts of its period
by the inventive way text is incorporated into the image
and by the novel integration of miniature and border. This
distinction is most clearly seen in the contributions of the
Master of James IV, who may have served as overseer for
the book's production. The Weekday Hours found at the
beginning of the manuscript, whose fourteen illuminations
in facing pairs are entirely by the hand of the Master of
James IV, represents a testament to the exploration of the
limits of illusionism and sets the tone for the rest of the
manuscript.[2] Additionally, the artist illuminated five openings in the Hours of the Virgin, the book's second major
cycle, which also features paired miniatures cleverly linked
to their borders.[3] Only the extensive series of suffrages at
the end of the manuscript, illuminated entirely by half-page
miniatures, departs from this spirit of originality.[4]

The illuminations by the Master of James IV for compline of the Hours of the Virgin (fols. 148v–149) are among

his most accomplished and atmospheric works. In each, the
border and miniature are treated as one continuous space,
with the text panel seemingly placed before, and partially
blocking, the vista. This idea is further developed in the
two images for the Wednesday Hours of All Saints, in
which the facing miniatures are joined as a single space,
with male saints on folio 39v and females on folio 40, all
turned toward a central altar upon which stands the Lamb
of God. The illuminations for the Friday Hours of the Cross
(fols. 56v–57) are treated as individual full-page miniatures
with, again, the text panel partly blocking the view, except
here the artist insisted on the physicality of the text panels
by treating them as separate material objects; attached by
hinges to narrow frames around the miniatures, they seem
to have been swung in front of the miniatures. The interaction between illusion and reality is at its most playful in
the images for the Sunday Hours of the Trinity (fols.
10v–11), where each text panel is "pinned" at once to the flat
surface of the page and to the seemingly expansive space
beyond. In the illumination for matins of the Hours of the
Virgin (ill. 124a), *The Annunciation* provides a glimpse of the
interior of a building, whose exterior can be seen in the border, providing a sort of X-ray vision.

What is remarkable about the Master of James IV's
innovative treatment of the miniatures and borders
throughout the Spinola Hours is that he used this wide
variety of treatments to delight and surprise the viewer
without sacrificing the strong narrative element that characterizes his work in other manuscripts. In the opening for
the *Mass for the Dead*, a series of images about death are
formed into a complex narrative through the clever use of
the miniatures and borders of both pages (ill. 124b), from
death itself in the lower left border, to mourning in the
main miniature, to the celebration of the Mass for the Dead
in the church across the page, and finally, to eternal rest in
the church's crypt below. In both pages the Master of James
IV provided interior and exterior views of the buildings and
used those distinctions to help tell the story. It seems likely
that he did not invent these new types of borders, but
rather that he took the concept to its aesthetic extreme to
achieve the most interesting and complex results.[5]

The Master of the Dresden Prayer Book painted the
openings for lauds and prime of the Hours of the Virgin,
each with a miniature and historiated border similar to
those of the Master of James IV. For prime (fols. 119v–120),
the buildings seen in the miniature *Christ before Caiaphas*
seem at first glance to line up with the structures seen at the
top of the historiated border, but closer examination
reveals this to be an optical trick. These contributions by
the Dresden Master represent some of the best work of his
later years, with passages such as the scene of the Mocking
of Christ in the border surrounding *Christ before Caiaphas*

124a

MASTER OF JAMES IV
OF SCOTLAND
The Annunciation and
*Gideon and the Golden
Fleece*, fols. 92v–93

standing out for their strong narrative sense and the easy, naturalistic movements of the figures. The one pair of miniatures by the Prayer Books Master, for terce of the Hours of the Virgin (fols. 125v–126), also echoes the example set by the other illuminations in the cycle. The landscape of *The Adoration of the Shepherds* is continuous with the landscape in the border, but only on one side.

The Master of the Lübeck Bible painted *The Coronation of the Virgin* (fol. 153v), *David in Prayer* (fol. 166), and *The Assumption of the Virgin* (fol. 247v), along with four historiated borders (fols. 83v, 84, 153v, 166) and a few suffrages.[6] The miniature for the suffrage of Saint Nicholas (fol. 261v) is one of his most successful, especially the figure of the saint himself, with the beautifully rendered folds of his crimson velvet robe set off by the luminous lime green lining and his bright pink gloves. In the opening for the Gospel extract of Saint John (fols. 83v–84), the two facing historiated borders do not interact spatially or conceptually with the main miniature, as is seen elsewhere in the manuscript, but are purposefully set apart by their whitewashed tonality.[7] The figures of the Master of the Lübeck Bible are

smaller in comparison to those found in the work of the book's other artists and are placed in groups within a vast space. They retain a sense of liveliness, however, through their eager expressions and the comparatively loose technique in which they are painted.

The large number of miniatures in the Spinola Hours by the workshop of the Master of the First Prayer Book of Maximilian, which are all based on familiar patterns, fall into two broad categories. The miniatures in the first group show a refinement that is characteristic of the work of the master himself, but they exhibit none of the gray undertones often found in his illuminations. The *Salvator Mundi* (fol. 9), *The Virgin and Child* (fol. 239v), *Saint Michael* (fol. 248v), and many of the images of female saints are by this hand, linked by a pink tonality in the skin and large, broad heads.[8] The second group, characterized by swarthier types and more expression in the delineation of faces, is much larger and includes the Evangelist portraits, the rest of the male saints, *The Last Judgment* (fol. 165v), and *Saint John the Baptist Preaching* (fol. 276v), as well as the illustrations to various accessory texts. It is possible that the miniatures

in this group are all by the same hand, as there is a consistent level of care in their high finish, as well as a curious awkwardness in the joining together of various parts of the miniatures. Overall, however, a great variety is apparent in the way that the miniatures are painted, which, combined with the fact that the miniatures are all pattern-based, makes it difficult to decide where one hand from the workshop ends and another may begin.

Like many of the grandest productions of the early sixteenth century, the Spinola Hours contains little information to help identify the patron. The *Office of the Dead* illumination (ill. 124b) does contain multiple examples of an escutcheon with a gold cross on a blue field, but those arms remain unidentified and may simply serve as a generic stand-in.[9] The Spinola Hours has been associated with Margaret of Austria based on circumstantial evidence. It has always been assumed that Gerard Horenbout, who served as court artist from 1515, must have illuminated more than the Sforza Hours (cat. no. 129) for her, and as he has been identified with the Master of James IV, the lavish Spinola Hours is considered a likely candidate as a commis-

sion of hers. In addition, the eighteenth-century binding of the Spinola Hours is red morocco gold-tooled with the Spinola family arms, matching the binding of the *Très Riches Heures*, which many scholars believe once belonged to Margaret of Austria.[10] Although the identification of Horenbout with the Master of James IV seems increasingly likely, the *Très Riches Heures* is linked to Margaret only circumstantially.[11] In all, the identification of Margaret as the patron seems possible but uncertain.

Determining the date and place of origin of the Spinola Hours is equally difficult due to a lack of concrete evidence. Little information is revealed by an examination of the manuscript's contents; the only unusual text is the prayer of Pope Leo (fol. 290v).[12] Although perhaps not much should be concluded from its presence, if it was included in tribute to Pope Leo X (1475–1521), it would provide a terminus post quem for the manuscript of 1513, when he became pope. An argument based on the artists involved is the only way to shed light on the question. The Dresden Master probably began his career in the late 1460s, so even supposing that he remained active well into his seventies, a date much beyond 1520 seems unlikely. The Master of James IV exhibited his fully developed artistic style during the 1490s (cf. cat. no. 100). His interest, however, in playfully incorporating text into image and integrating miniature and border seems to have emerged later in his career in manuscripts such as the Grimani Breviary (cat. no. 126) and a book of hours made for a member of the Portuguese royal family (Lisbon, Museu Nacional de Arte Antiga, Ms. 13), which would suggest a date in the decade between 1510 and 1520.[13] None of the artists who participated in the illumination of the manuscript has been firmly placed in either Ghent or Bruges, and given the complexity and expense of the project, it is possible that the manuscript traveled from one city to the other in the course of its completion.

E. M. and T. K.

Notes

1. There is only one full-page miniature in the manuscript, *Saint John the Baptist Preaching* (fol. 276v), which is blank on its recto and was tipped in. All other pages with miniatures contain text. The first three-quarters of the Spinola Hours is remarkably consistent in its codicology, but toward the end of the book more anomalies appear in the gatherings. A full border surrounds all text pages, but in the last quarter of the book inconsistencies in border sizes are also present.

2. The Vatican Hours (cat. no. 111) also has a series of weekday offices, but each office is marked by a single full-page illumination, not a pair, as in the Spinola Hours.

3. The Master of James IV painted the illuminations for matins, sext, none, vespers, and compline. The uneven mixing of narrative and typological scenes in the Hours of the Virgin, as seen in the Spinola Hours, is not uncommon in sixteenth-century manuscripts (see cat. nos. 33, 93, 109, 138).

4. The Master of James IV also contributed some miniatures to the suffrages (fols. 256v, 257v, 259v, 260v, 262v, 263v,).

5. Brinkmann (1997: 327) noted that Jean Fouquet had already integrated the traditional border space into a full-page miniature in the Hours of Étienne Chevalier (Chantilly, Musée Condé). Both Marmion (see cat. no. 10) and the Master of the Dresden Prayer Book (see cat. no. 93, fols. 285, 290) had also experimented with the miniature-border relationship.

6. The Master of the Lübeck Bible painted folios 258v, 261v, and 272v.

7. It is interesting that in terms of border treatments there is no possibility of confusing the work of the Master of the Lübeck Bible and the Master of James IV, yet in the suffrages the distinctions between the two are not as clear (see also cat. no. 112).

8. The sequence of female saints includes folios 264v, 265v, 266v, and 269v. Folios 267v and 268v, although they exhibit a different palette and a slightly different painting technique, are also likely by this artist.

9. Christiane van den Bergen-Pantens, who kindly researched the arms, suggested that they could be those of the Boussoit family from Hainaut, although their arms feature a gold cross *ancrée* on a field of silver, not blue.

10. Euw and Plotzek 1979–85, 2: 261–62; Brinkmann 1997: 328–29. The armorial on the front of the *Très Riches Heures* has been replaced with the arms of the Serra family but is otherwise almost identical to the Spinola Hours binding.

11. Dagmar Eichberger has kindly indicated to us that the descriptions in Margaret of Austria's catalogue are so general that the identification of the *Très Riches Heures* as an item is by no means firm.

12. The calendar of the Spinola Hours agrees closely with two other ambitious Flemish manuscripts of the same era, cat. nos. 90 and 110, at 96.21% and 95.20%, respectively. This probably reflects the increasing standardization of Flemish calendars at this time.

13. In the miniature *Saint John on Patmos* in the Da Costa Hours (cat. no. 140, fol. 111v), which also belongs to this decade, Simon Bening integrated the space of miniature and border in a manner comparable to the approach seen in the Spinola Hours. The Lisbon manuscript, the so-called Hours of Catherine of Portugal, has traditionally been attributed to Bening (Santos 1930: 26–27) but is instead by the Master of James IV.

125

MASTER OF JAMES IV OF SCOTLAND

Miniatures from a Devotional Book
Probably Ghent, ca. 1515–25

The Adoration of the Magi
One full-page miniature with historiated border, 17 × 12.5 cm
(6¹¹⁄₁₆ × 4⅞ in.); recto: blank

Saint John the Baptist
One full-page miniature with historiated border, 17 × 12.6 cm
(6¹¹⁄₁₆ × 4¹⁵⁄₁₆ in.); recto: blank

COLLECTION: New York, The Metropolitan Museum of Art,
Department of Medieval Art and the Cloisters, 48.149.15, 48.149.16

PROVENANCE: Bequest of George D. Pratt, 1935

JPGM and RA

Judging from the extremely high quality and relatively
large size of these two miniatures by the Master of James
IV of Scotland, the devotional book to which they once
belonged may have rivaled the greatest manuscripts of the
period. The miniatures are most closely related in conception to those by the Master of James IV in the Spinola
Hours (cat. no. 124), manifesting a similar playfulness in the
interaction between border and miniature.[1] In the Spinola
Hours the Master of James IV sometimes treated the miniature and the border as one continuous space, with a frame
seemingly set in front of the scene. These miniatures take
that concept one step farther. In both leaves, only the background landscape is continuous between miniature and
border, while the foreground of each miniature occurs in a
separate space, leaving the bottom half of the border to be
filled by narrative scenes.[2] The resultant effect of simultaneous continuity and discontinuity is remarkable.

The leaves, moreover, represent some of the finest
painting of the artist's oeuvre. The use of color, always a
strong component of the work of the Master of James IV, is

125a
MASTER OF JAMES IV
OF SCOTLAND
Saint John the Baptist

125b
MASTER OF JAMES IV
OF SCOTLAND
The Adoration of the Magi

105, fol. 181v), providing a precedent for this case. Like many of the manuscripts to which the Master of James IV contributed miniatures, the one to which the leaves belonged most likely contained the work of a number of artists. The compositional and stylistic links between the leaves and the Spinola Hours indicate that the two works were probably created around the same date,[4] but the greater level of sophistication in the spatial relationship between miniature and border in the leaves and the refinement of the painting technique perhaps argue for an even later date.[5]   E. M.

Notes

1. Compositionally the Adoration of the Magi in the Metropolitan leaf is very similar to the same subject in the Spinola Hours (fol. 130v).

2. In the case of the Adoration of the Magi leaf, although the bottom half of the border is not continuous with the scene in the main miniature, the line of the sloping roofs of the flanking buildings in the border lines up with elements in the miniature: on the left, the cloak of the standing Magus and, on the right, the hanging red drapery.

3. Both miniatures are blank on the recto, indicating that they would have been tipped-in full-page miniatures. It is possible but unlikely that the manuscript was a breviary, as it would be fairly unusual for a breviary of the period to feature tipped-in miniatures.

4. Wisse (2002) was the first to publish the Metropolitan miniatures, stylistically linking them to the Spinola Hours. Based on a stylistic comparison of the leaves to the Sforza Hours (cat. no. 129), he further argued that the leaves should be regarded as the work of Gerard Horenbout.

5. The miniature of Saint John the Baptist appears to have been copied in the Soane Hours (cat. no. 138, fol. 109v) which is dated to no earlier than 1512, and it may date considerably later.

here even more highly developed, seen in passages such as the bright orange cloth beneath the Virgin shadowed with a brilliant blue. The Master of James IV also varied his painting technique according to purpose; the delicate white skin of the Virgin is rendered in fine brushstrokes that create an alabaster finish, while the face of Saint John is modeled with tiny dots of color to give him a weathered look.

The manuscript from which the miniatures were taken was likely a lavish book of hours featuring numerous full-page miniatures. The appearance of *The Adoration of the Magi* as a full-page miniature is not surprising, as it no doubt was part of the cycle for the Hours of the Virgin, a text that often received a series of tipped-in miniatures.[3] Less common for a full-page miniature without text is the subject of Saint John the Baptist, because the suffrages section of a book of hours to which it probably belonged did not often receive full-page miniatures in the oeuvre of the Master of James IV. The artist had, however, provided two full-page illuminations for the Hours of Isabella of Castile, including an image of Saint Roch for the suffrages (cat. no.

126

MASTER OF JAMES IV OF SCOTLAND, ALEXANDER
BENING (MASTER OF THE FIRST PRAYER BOOK OF
MAXIMILIAN?), MASTER OF THE DAVID SCENES IN
THE GRIMANI BREVIARY, SIMON BENING, AND
GERARD DAVID

Breviary of Cardinal Domenico Grimani
Franciscan use
Ghent and Bruges, ca. 1515–20

MANUSCRIPT: 832 folios, 28 × 19.5 cm (11 × 7¹¹⁄₁₆ in.); justification:
15.5 × 11.5 cm (6⅛ × 4½ in.); 31 lines of *gotica rotunda* in two columns;
50 full-page miniatures, 18 large miniatures, 18 small miniatures,
numerous historiated borders, 12 full-page calendar miniatures,
12 bas-de-page calendar miniatures

HERALDRY: Escutcheon with the arms of Antonio Siciliano, fol. 81

BINDING: Italy, sixteenth century (?); crimson velvet; silver-gilt covers,
framed by relief border decorated with running vine stem and four
roundels; inner rectangle of each cover has corner roundels and a
large central portrait medallion, with a small inscribed plate above
it and the Grimani arms below (front cover: portrait of Cardinal
Domenico Grimani; *Dominici cardinalis Grimani ob singularem erga
patriam pietatem nunus ex testamento patriae relictum*; back cover:
portrait of Doge Antonio Grimani; *Quod munus Antonius princeps
et pater cum ad superos esset revocatus, approbavit*)

COLLECTION: Venice, Biblioteca Nazionale Marciana, Ms. Lat. I, 99
(2138)

PROVENANCE: Antonio Siciliano; Cardinal Domenico Grimani
(1461–1523), Rome or Venice, 1520; by bequest to his nephew, Marino
Grimani; bequeathed to the Signoria of Venice, but kept by his
brother Giovanni Grimani until his death in 1594; to the Treasury
of San Marco; by decree from the Municipality of Venice to the
Biblioteca Nazionale Marciana, October 4, 1797

[NOT EXHIBITED]

The Grimani Breviary is the most elaborate and arguably the greatest work in the history of Flemish manuscript illumination. Purchased by Cardinal Domenico
Grimani by 1520 for the enormous sum of five hundred
ducats,[1] it brought together the leading illuminators of the
time, including the Master of James IV of Scotland (probably Gerard Horenbout), Alexander Bening (the Master of
the First Prayer Book of Maximilian?), the Master of the
David Scenes in the Grimani Breviary, Simon Bening, and
Gerard David. More important, each of these artists created for this manuscript some of his most exquisite and
original miniatures.

Historically the Grimani Breviary has been the starting
point for the study of Flemish manuscript illumination
after 1470, yet the countless related manuscripts with which
scholars have compared it generally have received closer
scrutiny. The book's illumination itself has not been the
subject of systematic examination since Giulio Coggiola's
study at the start of the twentieth century.[2] A return to the
study of this book's decoration and its place in the history
of Flemish manuscript painting is overdue. In many miniatures the quality of execution is so refined that it surpasses
the known work of those illuminators usually associated
with the book. This often makes issues of attribution surprisingly problematic. Indeed, the two-day examination of
the manuscript by Maryan W. Ainsworth and Thomas
Kren proved woefully inadequate to the task of sorting
out all of the stylistic and technical issues that the book
raises. Nevertheless, the visit underscored the need for a
more systematic study of the breviary's illumination. As a
result, these comments on the work of the manuscript's
artists—in particular, Alexander Bening, Simon Bening,
and Gerard David—should be seen largely as suggestions
for further research.

The Grimani Breviary represents a pinnacle in the
achievement of the Master of James IV of Scotland, whose
miniatures are among the easiest to distinguish as a group.[3]
His contributions include one of only two openings with
two full-page miniatures. It is a focus of the book, featuring
on the left a nocturnal *Crucifixion* and on the right *Moses
and the Brazen Serpent* (ill. 126a), its Old Testament prefiguration. The miniatures are more richly detailed and
nuanced in their brushwork and use of color than any of his
previous works.[4] Moreover, each is enshrined in a simulated carved wooden frame dense with reliefs illustrating
the Passion of Christ, reading continuously from left to
right across the opening. Although the inclusion of subsidiary narration in a simulated carved frame was a convention of Flemish manuscript illumination at this time,
the frame had never before taken this monumental form.
Most of the flamboyant Gothicizing details that Flemish
illuminators, including the Master of James IV, favored for
the frames of miniatures have been subjugated here to a
cleaner profile and a more restrained design. While the
Master of James IV and his workshop aggressively developed the role of illumination within the two-page opening
(see cat. nos. 109, 124, 138), this is a relatively rare instance of
such an opening without any text.

The single surviving critical comment about the manuscript from the lifetime of the Master of James IV shows
that his earthy naturalism enjoyed international appeal.
Marcantonio Michiel, who viewed the breviary in Cardinal
Domenico Grimani's Venetian palace in 1521, marveled at
the quality of observation in the vignette in *February* (fol.
2v), which shows a child urinating in the snow, turning it
yellow.[5] The remark sheds light on Italian critical appreciation of the naturalism of the northern artists. The contribution of the Master of James IV extends, however, beyond
the abundance of evocative, closely observed details. He
also heightened the importance of calendar illumination in
devotional books, both by selecting the influential full-page
format for the illustration of each month and by turning to
older, more exotic models to renew its iconography.

The Master of James IV breathed life into landscape
painting in the Grimani Breviary through the spontaneity
of his handling and his reformulation of the hundred-year-
old calendar illuminations by the Limbourg brothers in the
Très Riches Heures of the duke of Berry (Chantilly, Musée
Condé).[6] The Master of James IV did not just copy from his
French model the symbolic agricultural labors and aristocratic leisure activities, but he also reconsidered figural
groupings, creating a new set of models for Flemish illuminators.[7] He developed a richer aerial perspective, capturing
the frisson in the interaction of daylight and atmosphere
that sets his work apart.[8] Some of the most beautiful passages in the calendar occur in the marginal scenes opposite

MASTER OF JAMES IV
OF SCOTLAND
The Crucifixion and *Moses
and the Brazen Serpent,*
fols. 138v–139

the large miniatures, among which the nocturnes are note-worthy. This illuminator's treatment of landscape distinguishes him from his great contemporary, the painter and landscape specialist Joachim Patinir, while his lasting influence can be seen in the landscapes of Simon Bening and of Pieter Bruegel the Elder.

Michiel identified one of the artists of the breviary as "Girardo da Guant," whom Joseph Destrée considered to be the Ghent painter and illuminator Gerard Horenbout.[9] Later scholars, including Georges Hulin de Loo and Friedrich Winkler, agreed that Horenbout was Girardo da Guant and, moreover, identified him as the painter of those miniatures in the breviary currently attributed to the Master of James IV of Scotland.[10]

A follower of the Master of James IV illuminated the miniatures that accompany the Psalter portion of the breviary, and the extent of his participation is also clear. The Master of the David Scenes in the Grimani Breviary is named for the unusual and vivid iconography of this cycle. Only one miniature in the series of eight is by a different hand; it belongs to the Maximilian Master group (fol. 289). Five of the remaining miniatures focus on the life of David (fig. 71),[11] including several obscure episodes, such as the moving of the Ark of the Covenant (fol. 348v) and David and his people praising God (fol. 357v).[12] There is an emphasis on courtly display and ceremony in these miniatures,

seen especially in the colorful and elaborate clothing worn by the figures and their exaggerated gestures of acceptance, recognition, or deference. The miniature that begins the entire series is, surprisingly, not from the life of David. It is *The Temptation of Adam and Eve* (fol. 286v), an unusual choice as frontispiece to the Psalter, although it is a subject that the Master of the David Scenes treated in other manuscripts.[13] A second illumination also falls out of the sequence of David imagery, as it depicts scenes from the Passion of Christ (fol. 337v). It illustrates Psalm 22, which begins with the anguished cry often associated with the Passion: "My God, my God, why have you forsaken me?" The Master of the David Scenes contributed miniatures only to the breviary's Psalter,[14] and they are among his best work due to their close attention to texture and detail, lively evocation of courtly splendor, and strong sense of narrative.

A remarkable feature of the Grimani Breviary is the inclusion of what appears to be an illuminator's signature. In 1977 Erik Drigsdahl published a brief article, little noticed in the subsequent literature, that analyzed an inscription in a bar border on a text page of the breviary (fol. 339v): A·BE·NI·71. Drigsdahl interpreted this as an abbreviated signature of Alexander Bening followed by his age. While the birth date of Alexander Bening is unknown, an age of seventy-one at this time would be consistent with

feature of these works is the modeling, which is fuller than one finds in the Maximilian Master's other works, with more blended brushstrokes and richer coloring in the flesh. This is seen, for example, in the face and hands of Saint John the Evangelist or in the male figures around Solomon and at the Circumcision.[19] This illuminator also employed more varied types than are typically found in the work of the Maximilian Master (see, for example, cat. nos. 90–92). Faces such as those of the two fleshy middle-aged males behind Simeon in *The Circumcision* are uncharacteristic of him, as are the foreshortened, twisting postures of the poisoned men in the John the Evangelist miniature. The heads in these miniatures also show a depth of psychological expressiveness that the miniatures by the Maximilian Master workshop rarely approach. Thus it is possible that these miniatures are not the work of the Maximilian Master or, alternatively, that most of what is ascribed to the master in other manuscripts is merely workshop production. If the latter is true, the Grimani Breviary represents a rare example of this long-lived illuminator actually wielding the brush.

A relatively small number of miniatures show the facial types employed by Alexander Bening's son Simon. They include the pretty young women with small but full lips and contemplative air of many figures found in *The Miracle of Saint Anthony of Padua* (fol. 579v), *The Church Militant: All Saints* (fol. 788v), *The Virgin and Child with Five Female Saints* (fol. 719v), *Mystic Attributes of the Virgin* (fol. 830), and most of *The Holy Virgins* (fol. 432v). At the same time, as in the work ascribed to the Maximilian Master above, the brushwork is tighter and the surfaces even more polished than one finds normally within the oeuvre of this accomplished illuminator.[20]

The contribution of Gerard David to the Grimani Breviary is noteworthy but has remained largely unrecognized. One illumination that can be assigned in its entirety to David is the remarkable *Mary Magdalene Penitent* (ill. 126b), which has long been ascribed to Simon Bening. The landscape setting is arguably the most naturally conceived of the book, balancing a far view to the horizon beyond the mountains and sea with a detailed description of plant and animal life on a rocky hillside near a tranquil stream in the foreground. Such bucolic passages studied directly from nature may be found in David's drawings and panel paintings after about 1500.[21] The successful integration of the figure of Mary Magdalene within rather than before the landscape parallels David's achievement in *The Rest on the Flight into Egypt* (New York, Metropolitan Museum of Art) of around 1510–15.[22] The configuration of folds in the Magdalene's draperies, the specific manner of modeling with gold parallel hatching, and the technique for providing zones of shading in the flesh are characteristic of David's approach in paintings of around 1505–15.

David often worked collaboratively on individual miniatures (see cat. nos. 92, 99, 100), and the breviary appears to contain miniatures of this type. *Saint Barbara* (fol. 828v) and *The Holy Virgins* (fol. 432v) are particularly Davidian, but only the exquisitely rendered Saint Catherine and Saint Barbara in the foreground of the latter are by

what is known of his life.[15] Several of the large miniatures following the leaf with the signature appear to belong to a group of miniatures that have been connected to the Master of the First Prayer Book of Maximilian (fols. 401, 407v, 422v).[16] Thus the Grimani Breviary presents evidence for the association of the name of Alexander Bening, the Ghent illuminator, with the Maximilian Master.[17]

Complicating any identification of Bening with the Maximilian Master is the problematic nature of the group of illuminations that are associated with the latter, the largest group that can be related to a single artist. These miniatures can be linked with one another first and foremost by their dependence on the body of illuminators' patterns invented by the Vienna Master of Mary of Burgundy, Hugo van der Goes, and others, mostly during the 1470s. They continued to be used and reused for four decades by many artists, but most consistently by the Maximilian Master and his workshop. The finest of these miniatures include *Saint John the Evangelist and the Poison Cup* (fol. 52), *The Circumcision* (fol. 67v), *The Queen of Sheba before Solomon* (fol. 75), *Saint Peter Offering a Papal Blessing* (fol. 602v), and *The Disputation of Saint Catherine* (fol. 824v).[18] The striking

him.[23] Likewise, David's contribution to another miniature may also have been limited, namely to the heads and hands in *The Trinity* (fol. 213v), which show the painter's characteristically solemn yet emotionally affecting facial types and highly articulated hand poses. *The Adoration of the Magi* presents certain small adaptations in composition and figures from its predecessor by David in the Isabella Breviary (ill. 100b) and follows closely the poses and nearly exactly the drapery patterns of the two kneeling kings and the Virgin in the foreground. Several faces are extremely sensitively rendered in the manner of David, but the Christ child is more awkward looking, leading to uncertainty about the attribution. Several other miniatures in the breviary illustrate the fluid exchange of patterns between the Maximilian Master and David and between Simon Bening and David. In these miniatures David's participation is limited or difficult to establish because the merging of their characteristic traits is so complete. They include *The Resurrection* (fol. 162v), *The Pentecost* (fol. 205v), *The Transfiguration* (fol. 660v), and *The Miracle of Saint Anthony of Padua* (fol. 579v).[24]

Finally, with regard to the book's origins, did Cardinal Domenico Grimani commission this volume, with its nearly one hundred miniatures? The arms of Antonio Siciliano, chamberlain and equerry of Massimiliano Sforza, duke of Milan, appear inconspicuously in the bar border of a text page (fol. 81). Michiel reported that Siciliano sold the book to Cardinal Grimani, and nothing about it reflects Grimani personally, save the extraordinary binding, which was undoubtedly added in Italy. Little else is known about Siciliano except that he commissioned from Jan Gossaert a remarkable diptych (Rome, Galleria Doria Pamphili) and that he was at the court of Margaret of Austria in 1513, where the *Très Riches Heures* of the duke of Berry may have been located at this time.[25] Still, some critics have wondered whether Siciliano was the original patron.[26] On the one hand, the book displays a striking lack of individualization, starting with the self-effacing placement of Siciliano's secular armorials themselves. On the other hand, evidence of the commissioner of other lavish Flemish breviaries in this period is often ambiguous or lacking altogether (see cat. nos. 91, 92, 100). This has prompted some critics to suggest that such books were produced for the open market.[27] Did Siciliano himself purchase the book when it was already well under way? Might he also have had the expectation that he could resell it quickly to Grimani (or an Italian collector like him) at a handsome profit?[28] To fully ascertain the place of this book in the larger history of Flemish manuscript illumination, these questions and those noted earlier concerning its artistic genesis will need to be explored more fully.   T. K., M. W. A., and E. M.

Notes

1. Cardinal Grimani (1461–1523) also owned paintings ascribed to Hans Memling, Hieronymus Bosch, and Joachim Patinir. He made special provisions for the Grimani Breviary in his will (Salmi and Mellini 1972: 263).

2. Coggiola 1908; see also Winkler 1925: 201. Grote (1973: 35–90) looked more closely at the iconography than at the style of the miniatures and questions of attribution.

3. Besides the miniatures mentioned in this entry, others include *The Nativity* (fol. 43v), *The Tower of Babel* (fol. 206), and *The Death Vigil* (fol. 449v); Salmi and Mellini 1972: pls. 27, 41, 57.

4. Compare, for example, the finely painted, though less monumental version of *The Brazen Serpent* in the Spinola Hours (cat. no. 124, fol. 57). (Nevertheless, certain of the Master of James IV's miniatures in the breviary are fairly broadly painted, notably the much-lauded *Nativity* [fol. 43v].) The second two-page opening without text is found at the end of the manuscript on a bifolium unconnected to any text (fols. 829v–830).

5. "Lodansi in esso sopratutto li 12 mesi, et tralli altri il febbraro, ove uno fanciullo orinando nella neve, la fa gialla et il paese ivi è tutto nevoso et giacciato" (Frimmel 1888: 104; Salmi and Mellini 1972: 263).

6. The Master of James IV and his workshop would draw upon the Grimani calendar repeatedly (see cat. no. 127 and the Lisbon prayer book [Museu Nacional de Arte Antiga, Ms. 13]).

7. See cat. nos. 150, 154, 155, 159; Kren, in Kren and Rathofer 1988: 248–50, 256, 258–60.

8. In this respect the illuminator surpassed even his achievements in the calendar in *The Tower of Babel* (fol. 206), with its ethereal handling of atmosphere and light to meld foreground, middle ground, and far distance.

9. Destrée 1894a: 510, although he assigned to Horenbout miniatures other than those that we assign to the Master of James IV of Scotland today.

10. See the biography of Gerard Horenbout (this part). Michiel was writing when Horenbout was still alive and at the height of his success, yet his credibility is undermined by his identifications of other artists in the breviary: "Livieno da Anversa," probably the painter-illuminator Lieven van Lathem, and "Zuan Memelin," better known as Hans Memling. They died in 1493 and 1494, respectively, or roughly two decades before the book was illuminated. In addition, Michiel disconcertingly failed to note the participation of Gerard David, certainly the most distinguished Flemish painter of the older generation, who was still alive, and of Alexander Bening, whose signature appears in the book (see below).

11. See cat. no. 138 for a discussion of other David sequences from the period.

12. A similar subject by the Master of the David Scenes relating to the ark appears in a book of hours (cat. no. 137, fol. 51).

13. The lush, parklike setting is unusually detailed, and the bodies are modeled more fully compared with some of his other versions of the subject (see ill. 114a; cat. no. 137, fol. 36; and the so-called Brukenthal Breviary [Sibiu, Romania, Museu Brukenthal]).

14. Although the psalms are given sequential numbers in the rubrics, they are actually arranged according to the ferial secular Psalter by the days of the week (see Harper 1991: 258).

15. Drigsdahl 1977; Alexander's acceptance into the Ghent painters' guild in 1469 suggests that he was in his early to mid-twenties at the time. Most authorities place the Grimani Breviary around 1515, though a date between 1515 and 1520, when it is mentioned in Grimani's will, is also possible. If the book was completed in 1515, then Alexander would have been born in 1444 or 1445 and entered the guild at twenty-five. If the book was completed a bit later, then he would have been a bit younger when he entered the guild.

16. Salmi and Mellini 1972: pls. 53–55.

17. On this issue, see the biography of the Master of the First Prayer Book of Maximilian (part 2, this volume).

18. Salmi and Mellini 1972: pls. 30, 31, 33, 72, 106. Within the group that we associate loosely with the Maximilian Master is another where the figures are less expressive and not always as finely modeled, e.g., *The Israelites Beseeching the Lord* (fol. 14v), *Jacob Sending Joseph in Search of His Brother* (fol. 15), *Saint John on Patmos* (fol. 51v), and *The Resurrection* (fol. 162v) (Salmi and Mellini 1972: pls. 25, 26, 29, 36).

19. Independently Erik Drigsdahl (in a lecture delivered in Brussels, November 2002) and Ainsworth (2003) suggested that two male figures standing near Solomon (on fol. 75) are portraits of Simon and Alexander Bening.

20. Winkler (1925: 201–2), while acknowledging that the book needed more systematic study, proposed that Simon Bening was the lead artist for the project. This is doubtful, but the book deserves to be

studied more closely in relationship to other relatively early works by the artist, such as the Da Costa Hours (cat. no. 140) and the Imhof Prayer Book (cat. no. 139).

21. On David's landscapes, see Ainsworth 1998: 207–55; for his drawings, see Ainsworth 1998: figs. 38, 40. Especially helpful for comparison are *Saint Jerome* (Frankfurt, Städelsches Kunstinstitut), the Baptism Triptych (Bruges, Groeningemuseum), and *The Rest on the Flight into Egypt* (New York, Metropolitan Museum of Art).

22. The pose of Mary Magdalene's upper torso mimics that in the miniature of Saint Barbara, yet Mary's cloak falls gently open to reveal subtly modulated tones describing soft flesh.

23. The remaining female saints are less subtle in details of handling and execution than those in David's contemporary illuminations, such as Saint Catherine in the Mayer van den Bergh Breviary or the female saints in *The Virgin among Virgins* (cat. nos. 92, 107). They appear closer to Simon Bening's types.

24. See Ainsworth 2003 for the relationship between Simon Bening's patterns and David's illuminations.

25. Gossaert exercised some influence on the depiction of architecture in the book. The inscription COSART in the miniature *The Disputation of Saint Barbara* has been linked to him, even though he did not illuminate this miniature.

26. Many have proposed that Margaret of Austria herself was the first patron (e.g., Destrée 1894a: 512; Brinkmann 1997: 133, 328, n. 53).

27. Grote 1973: 39.

28. One feature that might be pertinent to this discussion is the subtly Italianate character of *The Crucifixion*. Several of the equestrian figures to the right under the cross recall medals by Pisanello. Also, Grote (1973: 56) remarked that the treatment of the Good Thief and the Bad Thief more closely follows Italian conventions. Susan L'Engle contributed research to this entry.

127

MASTER OF JAMES IV OF SCOTLAND AND WORKSHOP AND SIMON BENING

Holford Hours
Use of Rome
Bruges and probably Ghent, 1526

MANUSCRIPT: 191 + iii folios, 19.5 × 13.0 cm (7¹¹⁄₁₆ × 5⅛ in.); justification: 10.5 × 6.6 cm (4⅛ × 2⁹⁄₁₆ in.); 20 lines of *bastarda*; 13 full-page miniatures, 32 small miniatures, 2 historiated borders, 36 small calendar miniatures; 1 small bas-de-page miniature added, seventeenth century, fol. 127v

HERALDRY: Full-page armorial composed of escutcheon with unidentified arms (argent three pellets) surmounted by helm, wreath, crest of wings charged argent three pellets, and mantling of sable doubled argent, fol. 1 initials *AM* [or *MM*], fol. 24v; Burgundian badge of briquet on two crossed boughs supported by griffin and lion, fol. 48

INSCRIPTIONS: ACTV[M]DECIMA IVNI Å XXVI, fol. 2

BINDING: Modern; original stamped binding replaced by Gordon and Forster after 1816 with a green velvet binding that was replaced by red velvet by 1932

COLLECTION: Lisbon, Museu Calouste Gulbenkian, Ms. LA 210

PROVENANCE: Unidentified male patron pictured on fol. 1; a charitable institution, England; [John and Arthur Arch, London]; [Longman, Hurst, and Co., London (cat. 1816, no. 6284)]; [Gordon and Forster, London]; Sir Robert Stayner Holford (1808–1892); Sir George L. Holford (1860–1926); A. Chester Beatty (1875–1968) [his sale, Sotheby's, London, June 7, 1932, lot 31]; [to Rosenthal, Munich]; to Calouste Gulbenkian (1869–1955)

JPGM

Although this book of hours has a distinguished provenance and was greatly admired by nineteenth-century connoisseurs, it has barely been studied until now.[1] The volume is important for a number of reasons. It is inscribed with a date—June 10, 1526 (fol. 2)—a rare occurrence in a book of hours.[2] Its frontispiece features a diptych with, on the left, a portrait of the volume's male patron in half-length and, on the right, his armorials (ill. 127). This is the earliest Flemish portrait in a manuscript of a devotional book's patron unaccompanied by any devotional figure. The book is also the last dated work by the painter of the portrait, the Master of James IV of Scotland, whose earliest dated work (cat. no. 108) was created nearly forty years earlier. Finally the book represents a rare example of a collaboration between the two leading illuminators of that time: the Master of James IV and Simon Bening.[3]

The Master of James IV and his workshop contributed illumination only to the front of the book. Their work includes the aforementioned portrait, the decoration of the table for calculating the date of Easter (fols. 2–2v), the elaborate decoration of the calendar (fols. 3–14v), a full-length portrait of the patron in prayer before an altar in a church chapel (fol. 15v), and probably the patron's armorials. Although the frontispiece portrait is water-damaged, the sitter is vividly characterized by his genial expression and wide-eyed gaze. His very full mantle lends his form an imposing presence, while his tight grasp of his glove adds an element of tension to the image. The pose and half-length type owe something to Joos van Cleve's *Portrait of a Man* from 1520 (Florence, Galleria degli Uffizi), but the figure's stately breadth and the plain background look forward to portraits ascribed to Hans Holbein the Younger, such as *Henry Wyatt* (Paris, Musée du Louvre).[4]

In his full-length portrait, the patron is depicted kneeling at an altar before a looming vision of the Trinity. This composition fits a type especially favored by the Master of James IV. It shows a nobleman engaged in an act of devotion in a church (see, for example, ill. 110a and the prayer book in Lisbon [Museu Nacional de Arte Antiga, Ms. 13, fol. 48v]).

The book's calendar is ambitious in the spirit of the artist's historic calendar for the Grimani Breviary (cat. no. 126, fols. 1v–13), although it depends more on the breviary's openwork treatment of the tracery in the borders and the continuity of setting between compartments than on its individual motifs and compositions.[5] Each opening features the second half of one month and the beginning of the next, with a bas-de-page scene that extends into the lateral margins on both pages, and a large miniature at the top of the recto in each opening. The calendar's subject matter largely concerns the traditional labors of the months. Particular agricultural activities sometimes are narrated sequentially over two or three miniatures, and hunting is a recurring theme (fols. 3v, 6v, 7v, 8v, 11v, 14v). In these miniatures the characteristic loose brushwork of the Master of James VI is particularly delicate, and the landscapes' atmospheric effects are subtle.

The remainder of the book's miniatures are by Simon Bening, among which the full-page ones are excellent. Although they are all based on familiar patterns, Bening reinvigorated his models repeatedly through the quality

of the protagonists' psychological interaction.[6] He also brought a fresh resonance to the compositions by developing interior or landscape settings to frame the narrative or echo the rhythms of the composition. The book appears to have been illuminated within a few years of the Prayer Book of Albrecht of Brandenburg (cat. no. 145), and the two feature a nearly identical version of *The Adoration of the Magi* (fols. 47v and 36v, respectively). These sister paintings include the same compositions and facial types, along with similar color and patterning.

The armorials of the book remain to be securely identified. Related armorials were held by the Swabian family Rein[7] and the Bruges family Kokelaere,[8] but neither corresponds in all details to those depicted. At none in the Hours of the Virgin, the bas-de-page features the Burgundian badge of a briquet on two crossed boughs flanked by a griffin and a lion (fol. 48), symbols that were taken up by Charles V[9] and evidence that the book's armorials belong to a Hapsburg subject, who was perhaps also a courtier.[10] In this context a striking feature of the book is its Burgundian-style *bastarda* script, which by this relatively late date had become less common in such luxurious Flemish illuminated manuscripts.   T. K.

Notes

1. Notably Dibdin (1817, 1: 168–71) and Waagen (1854–57, 2: 214–15).

2. The date appears in the table for calculating the date of Easter. Scot McKendrick kindly suggested that this painted (rather than written) inscription should be read as "Executed tenth June [15] 26." It probably refers to the book as a whole rather than the Easter table itself. It is more likely that the inscription written in ink below it (*Iniciu[m] ap[ri]lis . . .*), which is overwritten in the second line, refers to the table.

3. Another example of their collaboration is found in the Grimani Breviary (cat. no. 126) about a decade earlier.

4. Friedländer 1967–76, 9, pt. 1: 72, pl. 125; Salvini, in Grohn 1971: 97.

5. For example, the calendar of the Lisbon prayer book.

6. They include patterns designed by both the Vienna Master of Mary of Burgundy and the Master of the Houghton Miniatures.

7. London 1908: 82. The Rein family arms are argent three tourteaux sable (Rietstap 1972, 2: 544, pl. 141).

8. The Kokelaere arms are azure three besants argent (Rietstap 1972, 1: 460, pl. 124). I am grateful to Patricia Stirnemann for this suggestion.

9. The Burgundian flint and briquet intersected by the cross of Saint Andrew appears with the emperor's motto PLUS OUTRE in the bas-de-page of a suffrage for the Burgundian patron Saint Andrew in a book of hours made for Charles V (cat. no. 167, fol. 60v; see also ill. 167a).

10. In the border of folio 24v, a pair of initials appear, AM or MM. The border frames a miniature of the Annunciation. Another identity that has been proposed for the coat of arms is the Aloy family of Namur (see A. Chester Beatty sale, London, Sotheby's, June 7, 1932, lot 53).

127
MASTER OF JAMES IV
OF SCOTLAND
Portrait of a Man and
A Coat of Arms,
fols. i verso–1

128

MASTER OF JAMES IV OF SCOTLAND AND WORKSHOP

Book of Hours
Use of Rome
Probably Ghent, mid- to late 1520s

MANUSCRIPT: iii + 246 + iii folios, 13.2 × 9.8 cm (5⁵⁄₁₆ × 3⁷⁄₈ in.);
justification: 8.1 × 5.6 cm (3³⁄₁₆ × 2³⁄₁₆ in.); 15 lines of *gotica rotunda*;
4 half-column miniatures, 19 historiated initials, 17 historiated borders

BINDING: Robert Steel, London, late seventeenth century; gold-tooled
red morocco[1]

COLLECTION: Chatsworth, duke of Devonshire

PROVENANCE: In England by late seventeenth century; Spencer
Compton, eighth duke of Devonshire (1833–1911) (his bookplate)

RA

This book of hours, which now appears relatively austere, was probably conceived on a more lavish scale.
Although it lacks its calendar and any full-page miniatures,
the present state of the book's illumination suggests that a
substantial program of full-page miniatures was planned
but never executed or, alternatively, that they have been
lost. A historiated initial of Gideon in prayer, for example,
at matins of the Hours of the Virgin (fol. 1), suggests that

this opening originally had a full-page miniature of the
Annunciation. The Gideon narrative is commonly paired
with the Annunciation as its Old Testament antecedent.
Typically in Flemish *horae*, an Annunciation at matins
would be the first miniature in a cycle of the life of the Virgin. Such a cycle would have included seven more full-page
miniatures. The combination of historiated initial and historiated border with a full-page miniature would have created a very rich effect at these openings.[2] As many as
nineteen full-page miniatures may have been conceived for
the book as a whole.[3] Because one of the book's historiated
borders, that for none of the Hours of the Virgin, was never
finished, and because the calendar is often the last part of a
book to be written, on balance it seems more likely that the
book, including some of its illumination, was never completed.

The volume's one unusual devotional feature is the
inclusion of accounts of the Passion of Christ from each of
the four Gospels: those of Saints Matthew, Mark, Luke, and
John. Typically, if the Passion is recounted at all, a book of
hours would include the version of just one Evangelist,
usually Saint John (see also cat. no. 140). Each of the four
Passion narratives in this manuscript has a historiated initial and a historiated border. It is not certain, but it seems
likely that each of these, too, would have had a full-page
illustration depicting Passion events, since three of the four
accompanying historiated initials already include author
portraits and some of the borders depict lesser Passion incidents. Among the finest of the openings is that for Saint
Luke, where the border depicts carpenters building the
cross for the crucifixion of Christ (ill. 128).

Previously classified as in the style of Simon Bening,[4]
the manuscript is instead a good example of the painterly
illumination of the Master of James IV of Scotland and his
workshop. Both the figure type of Saint Luke in the initial
of his Passion narrative (ill. 128) and the heavy jowls of
Pilate on the right side of the border are typical of this
artist. At the same time the script and the colorful line
endings and initials recall closely the corresponding features in some books illuminated by Bening in the late 1520s
(especially cat. no. 143). This suggests that the work is a relatively late example by the Master of James IV, probably
dating to the mid- to late 1520s.   T. K.

Notes

1. Thanks to Philippa Marks for the description of the binding.
2. Especially striking might have been the opening for the Penitential Psalms (fol. 92), where the initial shows David and Goliath and
the historiated border shows other incidents of David's youthful valor,
with scenes of him wrestling the bear and the lion.
3. If the calendar had full-page miniatures, or if the book originally
had suffrages, there were possibly even more full-page miniatures.
4. Manchester 1976: 31, no. 56.

GERARD HORENBOUT

Perhaps born in Ghent during the 1460s, Gerard Horenbout became a master in that city's painters' guild in 1487.[1] He may have trained with Lieven de Stoevere (fl. 1463), who was the only painter among the five artists to sponsor his guild membership.[2] In Ghent, Horenbout led a productive workshop. In 1498 he hired a journeyman, Hannekin van den Dijcke, and in 1502 he accepted an apprentice illuminator, Heinric Heinricxzone. His workshop almost certainly included at least three of his children: Lucas, Susanna, and another son.[3] By 1503 Horenbout owned a house in the Drabstraat with an unusual painted facade, presumably by the artist. He was also part owner of a Ghent property called "The Orchard," which he sold in 1517.

In April 1515 Horenbout was appointed court painter and valet de chambre to Margaret of Austria, daughter of Maximilian I and regent of the Netherlands, with wages and pension of forty livres. With this post he was granted permission to live in the city of his choice but was required to come without delay or excuse when summoned to Margaret's court. Horenbout later claimed that his pension was never paid, and the account was settled in 1519. He may have served as host to Albrecht Dürer when Dürer visited Ghent in April 1520, and they definitely met in Antwerp in May 1521, when the German artist bought a miniature of Christ by Horenbout's daughter, Susanna. Horenbout continued to work for Margaret of Austria until at least 1522, when she purchased from him a portrait of Christian II of Denmark. There are no surviving documents of his activity between 1522 and 1528. By at least 1528 and through 1531 or later he was in England working for Henry VIII.[4] It has been suggested that the family relocated to participate in a royal workshop of illuminators, but the existence of such a workshop has recently been challenged.[5] Horenbout probably died in 1540 or 1541, when his heirs are recorded as paying duty on his property in Ghent.

Horenbout's prolific workshop produced varied commissions. In 1508 and 1509 it executed ten cartoons for large tapestries commissioned for the church of Saint Pharahildis by the Confraternity of Saint Barbara. The next year he prepared a map of Ghent and its environs for the town. Collaborating with the nuns of Galilee in Ghent, Horenbout produced a *jardinet*, a garden composed of embroidered silk flowers and trees and including figures of the Holy Family. The ensemble was described in the 1524 inventory of Margaret of Austria's collection. Records indicate that for Margaret he also produced books of hours, and he completed the well-documented Milanese Hours of Bona Sforza (cat. no. 129), for which he received payment in 1520. This masterwork is a key document in the history of illumination, yet it is perplexing. There is no other manuscript illumination produced in Flanders in precisely the same style as Horenbout's contribution to the Sforza Hours. Nevertheless an example of the same style of illumination appears in a manuscript produced in England, where Horenbout eventually settled (ills. 130a, 130b).

Carel van Mander, writing in 1604, described in detail two paintings in Ghent by Horenbout.[6] One is a set of wings for an altarpiece commissioned by Lieven Huguenois, abbot of Saint Bavo, which was placed to the left of the choir in the Church of Saint John. They depicted the Flagellation and the Descent from the Cross. The second is a two-sided round panel with a seated Christ wearing the crown of thorns on one side and the Virgin surrounded by angels seated with the Christ child on the other. All of these works are untraced today. Lorne Campbell and Susan Foister have stressed that, with four known exceptions, contemporary documents refer to Horenbout exclusively as a painter.[7] Yet Lodovico Guicciardini, writing about twenty years after Horenbout's death, described him as "Gherardo eccellentissimo nell'alluminare."[8]

Georges Hulin de Loo, Friedrich Winkler, Robert G. Calkins, and others have identified Horenbout as the prolific Master of James IV of Scotland, one of the illuminators of the Grimani Breviary (cat. no. 126).[9] This is based largely on Marcantonio Michiel's identification in 1521 of Girardo da Guant (Gerard of Ghent) as one of the breviary's illuminators, even though the other artists he named as responsible, Hans Memling and Lieven van Lathem, were deceased when the manuscript was executed.[10] According to the reasoning of the above-named specialists, Horenbout probably adapted his painterly style to the more linear, restrained Italian style of the original book. Some scholars have gone further, hypothesizing that Margaret of Austria inherited from her husband, Philibert of Savoy, the *Très Riches Heures* of the duke of Berry (Chantilly, Musée Condé), the key pictorial source for the Master of James IV's miniatures in the Grimani Breviary. Since Horenbout became Margaret's court painter around the time the Grimani was painted, he would have been ideally positioned to have access to it.[11]

Other circumstantial evidence supports the identification of Horenbout with the Master of James IV. The earliest and latest dated works of the Master of James IV belong to 1487 and 1526, respectively, and this is compatible with what is known of Horenbout's extended activity in Ghent. The evidence that the Master of James IV may have worked in Ghent also supports the identification. The Master of James IV was, moreover, also a painter, as is the case with Horenbout, and both painted portraits. The art of the Master of James IV was acquired by the same circle of lofty patrons, the ruling houses of Europe, especially those connected to the Hapsburgs. He executed miniatures for both the breviary and hours acquired by Queen Isabella of Castile (cat. nos. 100, 105), for the Hours of James IV of Scotland (cat. no. 110), and much later, for a prayer book for a member of the Portuguese royal family (Lisbon, Museu Nacional de Arte Antiga, Ms. 13). One of his portrait subjects, Lieven van Pottelsberghe, served at the court as receiver general under Emperor Charles V.

The stylistic links between the Sforza Hours, Horenbout's only surviving documented manuscript, and the work of the Master of James IV are less obvious but still discernible. The Sforza Hours offers many echoes of the latter's illuminations. Jacob Wisse has argued for a similarity in painting technique, color, and modeling between the Master of James IV's *Adoration of the Magi* in New York (ill. 125b) and Horenbout's Sforza miniature of this subject.[12] For example, in these two miniatures the Virgin's blue mantle is set off against a gold blanket, with both modeled in blue highlights. Teal, one of the colors favored by the Master of James IV, shows up a number of times in the Sforza Flemish miniatures. The facial types of God the Father and Christ in the Sforza *Coronation of the Virgin* bear a strong family resemblance to those of the three members of the Trinity in the miniature of that subject in the Spinola Hours (cat. no. 124, fol. 10v), although the brushwork is tighter and more blended in the former. Moreover, a fleshy older male figure with large jowls, a staple of the vocabulary of the Master of James IV, appears in the Sforza *Crucifixion of Saint Andrew*. Horenbout even incorporated the incipit within the pictorial space of the image in a Sforza miniature (cat. no. 129, fol. 133v), much as the Master of James IV did in an image in the Spinola Hours (cat. no. 124, fol. 8v).[13] Finally, in the Sforza *Virgin and Child with Musical Angels*, the round-topped throne closely resembles that of Saint Anne in the Poortakker Triptych (fig. 70), an early painting in the style of the Master of James IV that is signed *Gerardus*.[14] While the identification of Horenbout with the Master of James IV seems likely and has been widely accepted, in stylistic terms the connection is subtle rather than readily apparent.[15]   T. K. and R. G.

Notes

1. The documentary evidence on Horenbout's life is examined in Campbell and Foister 1986: 719–21, to which we are indebted.

2. Brinkmann, in DOA 1996, 14: 759.

3. Campbell and Foister 1986: 721.

4. The records before October 1528 and after April 1531 have not survived; see Campbell and Foister 1986: 720. Paget (1959: 400) posited that the Horenbout family was Lutheran and emigrated seeking religious tolerance.

5. See the biography of Lucas Horenbout (this part), note 2.

6. Van Mander 1604: fol. 204v.

7. In 1520, 1521, and 1522 Horenbout was called "paintre et illumyneur," and Dürer referred to him as "maister Gerhart, jlluminist" (Campbell and Foister 1986: 721).

8. Guicciardini 1588: 128.

9. Hulin de Loo 1939a; Winkler 1943; Calkins 1998.

10. Quoted in Salmi and Mellini 1972: 263.

11. Margaret undoubtedly acquired the Hours of Bona Sforza through her brief marriage to Philibert. None of the entries in the extensive inventories of Margaret's holdings can, however, be securely

identified with the *Très Riches Heures*, according to information kindly provided by Dagmar Eichberger; see Eichberger 2002.

12. Wisse 2002: 1676.

13. The Master of James IV did this often in the Spinola Hours. In the Sforza miniature, putti carry a banderole with the incipit. In the Spinola *Last Judgment* (fol. 165v), which is by the Maximilian Master workshop, angels carry the incipit on a banderole.

14. Hulin de Loo 1939a: 20–21.

15. Brinkmann is one of the skeptics on the matter (in Evans and Brinkmann 1995: 130–36, 581–86).

129

GERARD HORENBOUT AND GIOVANNI PIETRO BIRAGO

Leaves from the Hours of Bona Sforza
Milan, ca. 1490, and Ghent, ca. 1517–21

Saint Mark in His Study, fol. 10v
Christ Nailed to the Cross, fol. 12v
The Annunciation, fol. 41
The Visitation, fol. 61
The Nativity, fol. 82v
The Annunciation to the Shepherds, fol. 91
The Adoration of the Magi, fol. 97
The Presentation in the Temple, fol. 104v
The Flight into Egypt, fol. 111
The Coronation of the Virgin, fol. 124
The Virgin and Child, fol. 133v
The Entry into Jerusalem, fol. 136v
The Virgin and Child Enthroned, fol. 177v
Saint Andrew, fol. 189v
David in Prayer, fol. 212v
The Raising of Lazarus, fol. 257v

MANUSCRIPT: 348 + i folios in four continuously foliated volumes, each 13.1 × 9.3 cm (5⅛ × 3⅝ in.); justification: 6.4 × 4.9 cm (2½ × 1⅞ in.); 11 lines of *gotica rotunda*; replacement text by Etienne de Lale, 1517; 63 full-page miniatures, 1 half-page miniature, 139 text pages with decorated borders, most with figured vignettes

HERALDRY: *Diva Bona*, fols. 66v, 79, 122; *Bona Duc[issa]*, fol. 210v; *BM*, fol. 56, 88v; *Sola fata, solum Deum sequor* with phoenix, fol. 93; medallion of Charles V, in border, fol. 213

BINDING: London(?), ca. 1896; dark red morocco; bifolia were cut into leaves and tipped into four volumes; former binding (kept separately): Spain, nineteenth-century red velvet (faded to orange) over wood boards with two metal clasps

COLLECTION: London, The British Library, Add. Ms. 34294

PROVENANCE: Bona Sforza, d. 1503; Philibert II, duke of Savoy (d. 1504), ca. 1503; his wife, Margaret of Austria (1480–1530), by 1517; possibly to Emperor Charles V (1500–1558), ca. 1521; in Spain by ca. 1600; a Spanish noble by 1871; to Sir J. C. Robinson, 1871; John Malcolm of Poltalloch, ca. 1871; presented 1893 to the British Museum

JPGM and RA: Fols. 10v, 61, 82v, 91, 104v, 124, 133v, 136v;
RA only: Fols. 12v, 41, 97, 111, 177v, 189v, 212v, 257v

This manuscript, one of the grandest of all Italian books of hours, has an exceptionally colorful history. The Milanese illuminator and priest Giovanni Pietro Birago mentioned in a letter that a portion of a book of hours that Bona Sforza, duchess of Milan, had commissioned from him was stolen by Fra Gian Jacopo, a friar from the convent of San Marco. The thief went to prison.[1] Only in the last century have any of the stolen portions come to light.[2] The purloined pages included the book's calendar and the

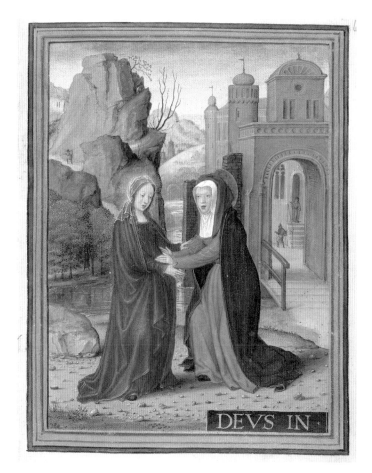

129a
GERARD HORENBOUT
The Visitation, fol. 61

129b
GERARD HORENBOUT
The Nativity, fol. 82v

Hours of the Virgin, both of which had been richly illuminated. After her husband's death Bona returned to Savoy, where she died in 1503. The incomplete book then passed into the hands of her nephew, Philibert, duke of Savoy, who died the following year. Two years later Margaret of Austria, his widow, took the book with her when she returned to the north to serve as regent of the Netherlands on behalf of her nephew, the future emperor Charles V.

In 1517 Margaret hired the scribe Etienne de Lale to complete the text, and within the next two years she engaged her court painter, Gerard Horenbout, to provide sixteen full-page miniatures along with two borders. These include a full cycle of the life of the Virgin and miniatures in the suffrages and at major divisions such as the Penitential Psalms and the Office of the Dead. He depicted Elizabeth in *The Visitation* (ill 129a) with the facial features of Margaret, while her nephew, Charles V, is depicted in a medallion in one of the borders (fol. 213). The dates 1519 and 1520 appear on leaves that Horenbout illuminated (ill. 29c and fol. 213), and he received payment for his work in 1520, including payments to a Brussels scribe for writing some folios.[3] The book is next recorded in Spain in the nineteenth century. This extraordinary volume may have ended up there because Margaret intended it as a present for her nephew,[4] or perhaps Charles inherited it at her death.[5]

The sixteen miniatures added to the Italian book by Horenbout are among the most beautiful in sixteenth-century Flemish illumination, the work of an artist of the first rank. *The Nativity* (ill. 129b) infuses the Flemish genre of the nocturne with a new poetry and subtlety. The soft, warm light emanating from the Christ child himself reveals the cherubic faces of the adoring angels in delicate patterns reflecting their movement, leaving some faces in full or partial shadow, while piercing the thin yellow robe of the angel overhead. Here Horenbout seems to have studied the art of Joos van Cleve, although he avoided the contorted figural movement and the exaggerated figural proportions of Antwerp Mannerist painting of this period. Many of the miniatures are based on the time-honored patterns of late-fifteenth-century Flemish illumination, but Horenbout often gave them new meaning and freshness. An example is *David in Prayer* (fol. 212v), where the pattern, showing David's radically twisting posture, his hands directed nearly 180 degrees away from the his gaze, was copied in mirror image.[6] This inventive copy succeeds better than earlier illuminators' copies, due to the finely elaborated, more fully spatial setting of his devotion. The aedicula, drawn in perspective and inspired by a northern notion of Italian Renaissance architecture, frames an elaborately detailed scene of the palace and a grand courtyard. Another example is *The Adoration of the Magi* (fol. 97), where such qualities as the splendor and originality of the costume of Mauritius and the monumentality and classicizing architecture of the manger give this composition a new

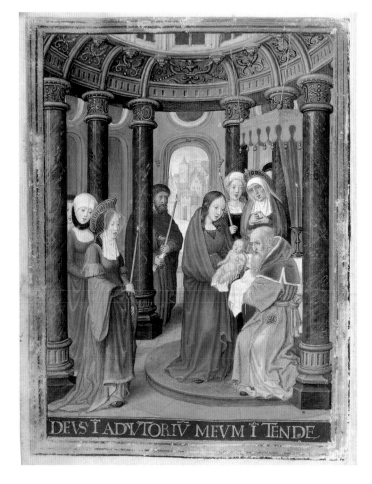

magnificence. By contrast, *The Raising of Lazarus* (fol. 257v), which is based particularly closely on a pattern, is relatively little altered, and not especially Italianate.[7]

Even though not all of Horenbout's miniatures owe a debt to Birago, there is nothing in Flemish art, and especially book illumination, quite like those that do.[8] He paid tribute to the Italian Renaissance style of Birago in small but distinct ways, such as by adapting the brightly colored pebbles with which the Italian master often strewed the foreground or by giving the angels the flowing golden locks and bunched-up sleeves of Birago's figures. Sometimes, as in *Saint Mark*, the Italianate elements are largely a veneer grafted onto the architecture (ill. 129c). But whereas contemporary Flemish painters were looking at High Renaissance models, the Birago miniatures offered a quattrocento inspiration. If Gerard Horenbout is the Master of James IV of Scotland, the finest Flemish illuminator of Horenbout's generation, as seems likely, then clearly Horenbout adapted a free, painterly style to a quattrocento aesthetic. The crispness of the contours, the use of large areas of strong color, and the emphasis on the foreground all reflect this response.[9]

Finally, even though the style of the sixteen Flemish miniatures is fairly homogeneous, subtle differences in execution are apparent in the scenes from the Life of the Virgin and in the two miniatures of the Virgin and Child with angels in heaven (fols. 133v, 177v). Since Gerard Horenbout's children, Lucas and Susanna, must have learned their art from their father in the same years, it is possible that one, the other, or both collaborated with him on this cycle of miniatures.[10] It was only a year after the book's completion that the great German painter Albrecht Dürer expressed admiration for Susanna's illumination and purchased a miniature by her.   T. K.

Notes

1. Warner (G.) 1894: viii–ix; Evans 1992: 8–9.
2. They include miniatures for *May* (London, British Library, Add. Ms. 62997), *October* (New York, Bernard Breslauer collection), and *The Adoration of the Kings* (London, British Library, Add. Ms. 54722). See Evans and Brinkmann 1995: 475, 476, 477, or Evans 1992: 6, 20.
3. Campbell and Foister 1986: 720.
4. Evans, in Malibu 1983a: 114; see also Warner (G.) 1894: x.
5. The book's picaresque history does not end here. The connoisseur J. C. Robinson, who acquired the book in Spain, recounted a further incident of theft while the book was about to change hands in Madrid in 1871 (in Evans 1992: 7–8).
6. An example is in the Munich Hours (cat. no. 90, fol. 328v; Evans and Brinkmann 1995: 427). Others are in the London Hastings Hours (cat. no. 41, fol. 150v), the Hours of Philip of Cleves (Brussels, Bibliothèque royale de Belgique, Ms. IV 40, fol. 109v), and a book of hours made for a cleric (Kraków, Biblioteka Czartoryskich, Ms. 3025, p. 418).
7. On this pattern, see under cat. no. 162.
8. But compare especially the miniatures added to an English manuscript (ills. 130a, 130b).
9. For further discussion of the topic, see also the biography of Gerard Horenbout (this part), note 13.
10. Kren, in Malibu 1983a: 121; and Backhouse 1997b: 16.

129c (opposite, top left)
GERARD HORENBOUT
Saint Mark in His Study,
fol. 10v

129d (opposite, top right)
GERARD HORENBOUT
The Annunciation to the Shepherds, fol. 91

129e (opposite, bottom left)
GERARD HORENBOUT
The Presentation in the Temple, fol. 104v

129f (opposite, bottom right)
GERARD HORENBOUT
The Coronation of the Virgin, fol. 124

130a (above right)
GERARD HORENBOUT
Lydgate and the Pilgrims Departing from Canterbury, fol. 148

130

GERARD HORENBOUT, ANOTHER FLEMISH ILLUMINATOR, AND TWO ENGLISH ILLUMINATORS

Guido delle Colonne, *Troy Book*, translation by John Lydgate of *Historia Troiana*; *Siege of Thebes*, translation by John Lydgate of *Roman de Thèbes*; John Lydgate, *Testament of John Lydgate*; and other texts partly relating to the Percy family
London(?), ca. 1455–62, ca. 1490, ca. 1516–23, and ca. 1530

MANUSCRIPT: i + 212 folios, 39.5 × 28.8 cm (15½ × 11⅜ in.); justification: 28.2 × 19.8 cm (11⅛ × 7¾ in.); 50 lines of *bastarda anglicana* and *bastarda* in two columns; 25 one-column miniatures

HERALDRY: Escutcheons with the arms of Herbert and Devereux, fol. 6; mottoes *E las sy longuement* and *De toute*, fol. 6; escutcheon with the quartered arms of Percy and Lucy, flanked by initials *HP*, accompanied by badges of crescent and shackle-bolt, and encircled by the Garter, fol. 162

BINDING: London, mid-eighteenth century; brown morocco; the arms of George II gold-stamped on both covers; rebacked

COLLECTION: London, The British Library, Royal Ms. 18 D.ii

PROVENANCE: Begun for Sir William Herbert, earl of Pembroke (d. 1469), and his wife, Anne Devereux, probably for presentation to Edward IV, king of England (1442–1483); Henry Percy, fourth earl of Northumberland (1446–1489), and his wife, Maud Herbert (d. 1485); Henry Algernon Percy, fifth earl of Northumberland (1478–1527); Henry Fitzalan, earl of Arundel (1512–1580); John Lumley, baron Lumley (1534?–1609); English royal library at Saint James's in 1666; George II, king of England (1683–1760); presented 1757 to the British Museum

RA

This English manuscript, which contains writings of John Lydgate, the court poet of Henry V, was written and illuminated in several stages. The original portion consists of the *Troy Book*, Lydgate's English translation of Guido delle Colonne's *Historia destructionis Troiae*, and the *Siege of Thebes*, Lydgate's English version of the prose *Roman de Thèbes*. This portion of the manuscript was probably transcribed for Sir William Herbert and his wife, Anne Devereux, to present to the king, either Henry VI or Edward IV, before 1462.[1] Around this time, only some of

130b

GERARD HORENBOUT
Saint Michael and the
Demons, fol. 161v

Sforza *Annunciation to the Shepherds* (ill. 129d). Both have faces that are more white than flesh-colored; frizzy, bronze-colored hair; and large green wings with patches of yellow on the underside and red at the ends. These two Lydgate miniatures are thus the only other fully painted miniatures that are certainly by the documented Horenbout of the Sforza Hours.

The second artist of the third campaign painted the remaining fifteen miniatures in the *Troy Book* and the *Siege of Thebes*. This style may be loosely described as "Flemish"; the miniatures are colorful, are carefully drawn, and show considerable attention to court costume and ceremony. Janet Backhouse suggested that this hand might be that of Susanna Horenbout, but the only basis for the attribution is the possible artistic presence of another Horenbout in the manuscript. No work by Susanna Horenbout has been securely identified. Moreover, the second style of the final campaign of illumination does not particularly reflect the aesthetic of the two Horenbout miniatures.[5]

Backhouse dated these miniatures to around 1525, although it is uncertain that Gerard Horenbout had arrived in England by this date.[6] Thus, their date of execution belongs later in the decade.[7]   T. K.

Notes

1. K. Scott (1996, 2: 282–84) gives an account of the book's history and illumination in the fifteenth century.

2. For another manuscript for the Percy family written by the same scribe after 1519, see Parkes 1969: 15.

3. Dickens 1955.

4. Backhouse (1997a: 229) first observed that the Saint Michael miniature "is very close in style to the Horenbout miniatures in the Hours of Bona Sforza."

5. Backhouse 1997a: 229. Croft-Murray (1956: 123, pls. 23, 24) speculated that these miniatures might be "associated" with Lambert Barnard, the court painter of Robert Sherborne, bishop of Chichester.

6. Backhouse 1997a: 229.

7. Margaret Scott indicated that many of the costumes in the miniatures by the second artist of the third campaign are datable to around 1530 (correspondence with the author, January 12, 2003, Department of Manuscripts files, JPGM).

the spaces provided for miniatures were filled; additional miniatures were furnished later in the fifteenth century (fols. 74, 75, 82v). Between 1516 and 1523 a verse chronicle of the Percy family (fols. 186–95), to whom the manuscript had descended from the Herberts, was added. Other additions (fols. 195v–210) then included didactic poems transcribed from the walls and ceilings of Percy homes[2] and a full-page drawing featuring the Tudor-Percy emblem (fol. 200).[3] Toward the end of the 1520s a final campaign of seventeen miniatures completed the cycle begun in the mid-fifteenth century.

The principal concern here is with this last campaign of illumination, which was carried out by two artists. *Lydgate and the Pilgrims Departing from Canterbury* (ill. 130a) and *Saint Michael and the Demons* (ill. 130b), the finest of these miniatures, are, in my view, by the painter of the Flemish miniatures in the Sforza Hours (cat. no. 129), Gerard Horenbout.[4] The congruence in style and technique is most evident between the Canterbury miniature and the Sforza *Christ Nailed to the Cross* (fol. 12v), especially in the drawing, modeling, and coloring of the heads of the white horses, the donkey, and their trappings. Other close similarities are apparent in the facial types of the men, with their large noses; small, round mouths; full, ruddy flesh; and lined faces. Moreover, the Canterbury miniature features a road liberally strewn with small oval stones, of the type that Horenbout adapted from Giovanni Pietro Birago in Sforza miniatures such as *The Visitation* (ill. 129a) and *The Flight into Egypt* (fol. 111). The face of the archangel Michael in the Lydgate volume is identical to that of the angel in the

131

GERARD, LUCAS, OR SUSANNA HORENBOUT (?)

Letters Patent of Henry VIII for Cardinal College, Oxford
England, May 5, 1526

Two membranes, 68 × 108 cm (26¼ × 42½ in); English chancery hand; 1 historiated initial

HERALDRY: The arms of England crowned, encircled by the Garter, and supported by Tudor dragon and lion; devices of pomegranate and crowned Tudor rose; Beaufort badge of castle with portcullis, crowned; First Great Seal of Henry VIII attached with green, white, and silver silk thread

COLLECTION: Kew, The Public Record Office, E 24/6/1

PROVENANCE: Cardinal Thomas Wolsey (ca. 1475–1530); Treasury of the Receipt of the Exchequer

R A

In 1524 the leading statesman and churchman in England, Cardinal Thomas Wolsey, obtained authority from Pope

131
GERARD, LUCAS,
OR SUSANNA
HORENBOUT (?)
Initial H: Henry VIII

Clement VII to convert the priory of Saint Frideswide at Oxford into Cardinal College.[1] Together with a foundation at Wolsey's hometown of Ipswich, that college formed part of an ambitious program of cultural and religious patronage intended to secure for Wolsey glory both within and after his lifetime. It also formed part of an attempt to reform the Church in England.[2] Careful and detailed preparations for these twin foundations required the securing of legal authority from Henry VIII for a range of privileges and benefits. Among many documents that formalized that authority,[3] the present patent letter confirming all the possessions granted by the king to the college[4] is a key piece in any discussion of the work of the Horenbout family.

The full-length portrait of Henry VIII that is contained within the opening initial of the present patent letter is particularly distinctive, for it successfully presents both a ruler dominating his setting with a most imposing presence and a person with individual characteristics. As such, it is the earliest of a sequence of portraits of the king produced in documents intended both for the king and for Wolsey that reflect a significant change that took place in how English monarchs were officially portrayed—in essence the transformation from medieval king to Renaissance prince. Since the timing of that change coincides with the first record, dated 1525, of the Flemish artist Lucas Horenbout's being in

Henry's service, both the change as a whole and the present portrait have been explained as a product of the migration to England of Lucas and his family.[5] Wolsey's advanced taste for Italianate Renaissance styles may also have been a significant factor in this important development in official portraiture.[6]

Although the present portrait of Henry VIII has been considered close to the style of Hans Holbein,[7] several features suggest a closer relationship to the work of the Horenbouts. The means by which the artist suggests space around the figure is certainly similar to those employed by the Master of James IV of Scotland in comparable seated figures in the Breviary of Isabella of Castile (cat. no. 100).[8] (Gerard Horenbout has been identified with the Master of James IV.) The treatment of Henry's eyes and nose also finds parallels in the work of the Master of James IV. As for the mannered folds of Henry's robes, these seem to have more in common with the drapery seen in the work of the Milanese miniaturist Giovanni Pietro Birago than with contemporary Flemish work. The easiest explanation of such a link is of course the documented completion by Gerard Horenbout of Birago's work in the Hours of Bona Sforza (cat. no. 129). There are no documented works of either Lucas or Susanna Horenbout with which to make a comparison.

S. McK.

Notes

1. On this college, refounded in 1546 by Henry VIII as Christ Church, see Newman 1991: 103–15.

2. Gwyn 1990: 341–53.

3. Auerbach (1954b: 39–40) noted around seventy patents within the documents of the series E 24 at the Public Record Office.

4. Brewer 1862–1932, 4, pt. 1: no. 2152.

5. The subsequent use of this new royal portrait in the Golden "Bulla" of 1527 (Strong, in London 1991a: V.35), as the initial portrait in Francis I's copy of the Treaty of Windsor of 1532 (Strong 1991: V.38), and in Henry's third Great Seal of 1542 (Thurley 1993: fig. 321b) also coincides with the Horenbouts' continuing service under Henry. The "Gerarde" mentioned in payments for the Wolsey patents is, however, no longer accepted as Gerard Horenbout (Campbell and Foister 1986: 721).

6. Just as this taste of Wolsey's appears to have been fed and satisfied by Flemish or French interpretations of Italian Renaissance forms, so the introduction of this new type of royal portrait may well have as its immediate models Renaissance images of the king of France and the Hapsburg emperor. On the king of France, see Scheller 1983.

7. Auerbach 1954b: 44.

8. E.g., *Saint Apollinaris* and *Saint Anne Teaching the Virgin* (fols. 411v, 414). Compare also the upper body and hands of *Saint Edward the Confessor* (fol. 472v).

LUCAS HORENBOUT

Son of the illuminator Gerard Horenbout, Lucas Horenbout (d. 1544) served as court painter to Henry VIII for nearly twenty years. He immigrated to England from Ghent in the 1520s, as did his father—who is documented in the king's service between 1528 and 1531—and his sister, Susanna, who was also an illuminator.[1] It has been assumed that the family relocated to work in the royal workshop as illuminators, but the existence of a royal atelier of illuminators is questionable.[2] Likely trained by his father in Ghent, Lucas Horenbout may have contributed to the Sforza Hours (cat. no. 129).[3] The first mention of him in England appears in English royal accounts of September 1525. The description of him there as "pictor maker" suggests that he worked in a variety of media.[4] By 1531 he was appointed king's painter, and on June 22, 1534, the post was conferred on him for life. On that day he became a denizen (a citizen of foreign origin), was granted a tenement in Charing Cross, and was permitted to hire four foreign journeymen.[5] He died in London in 1544 and was buried at Saint Martin in the Fields, survived by his wife, Margaret, and daughter, Jacquemine.

No signed or authenticated work by Lucas Horenbout has survived, but other evidence suggests the types of projects he undertook for the king. Carel van Mander mentioned that a Lucas, who is generally accepted to be Lucas Horenbout, introduced Hans Holbein to the art of illumination.[6] The king employed both artists, and Horenbout was paid slightly more per year, an indication of his comparative value to the monarch (thirty-three pounds, six shillings to Holbein's thirty pounds).[7] In 1547 his widow received payment of sixty shillings from Catherine Parr, the sixth and last queen of Henry VIII. The payment was for portraits of the king and queen, presumably painted by Lucas.[8] Further documentary evidence suggests that he also designed woodcuts and painted props for revels.[9] It is widely assumed that he was responsible for the first portrait miniatures produced in England. The earliest surviving examples date shortly after he arrived at court and are painted in the technique of an illuminator, with physical characteristics defined by carefully built up, minute brushstrokes over opaque colors. Given his background as an illuminator and his status as the king's painter, it seems plausible that Lucas Horenbout was indeed responsible for the earliest portrait miniatures in England, those of Henry VIII, his wives, and his courtiers. Twenty-three portrait miniatures have been attributed to him (cat. nos. 133, 134), along with legal documents (see cat. nos. 131, 135), manuscripts, and—tenuously—a few paintings.[10] Because these works—apart from the portrait miniatures—do not form a cohesive stylistic group, further study of his proposed oeuvre is needed.   R. G.

132 (opposite)
LUCAS OR SUSANNA
HORENBOUT (?)
Saint Luke, fol. 4

Notes

1. The documentary evidence on the Horenbout family is examined in Campbell and Foister 1986. Lucas is documented in England by 1525, Gerard by 1528. It is possible that Gerard was in England earlier than 1528, since the relevant accounts have been lost; see Campbell and Foister 1986: 720.

2. Strong (1983: 12–13) described such a workshop, as did Murdoch et al. (1981: 28). As Campbell and Foister (1986: 722) noted, payments to scribes and binders abound in the royal accounts, but only one illuminator, Richard James, is mentioned. The employment of a team of illuminators by the king is therefore questionable.

3. Kren (in Malibu 1983a: 121) suggested that Lucas or Susanna may have painted miniatures of the Virgin and Child with angels in the Sforza Hours, fols. 133v and 177v. See also Backhouse 1997b: 16.

4. Campbell and Foister 1986: 721–22.

5. Campbell and Foister 1986: 722.

6. Van Mander 1604: fol. 222v.

7. In 1544 Henry VIII stated, "For a long time I have been acquainted not only by reports from others but also from personal knowledge with the science and experience in the pictorial art of Lucas Horenbolte" (Auerbach 1954b: 50).

8. The large amount paid suggests the portraits were large scale and not portrait miniatures (Reynolds [G.] 1999: 45).

9. Campbell and Foister 1986: 723–24.

10. On the portrait miniatures, see Strong 1983: 189–90; on the legal documents, Auerbach 1954b: 51; and Coombs 1998: 19; on the manuscripts, Murdoch et al. 1981: 30; and on the paintings, Paget 1959: 396–402; London 1983: 43–44, nos. 23–24; and Strong 1983: 42–44, who linked Lucas Horenbout to the Cast Shadow Workshop.

132

LUCAS OR SUSANNA HORENBOUT (?)

Acts of the Apostles and the Apocalypse
England, between 1528 and 1533

MANUSCRIPT: 307 + i folios, 45.5 × 33 cm (18 × 13 in.); justification: 34.5 × 31.8 cm (13⅝ × 12½ in.); 12 and 24 lines of *humanistica* in two columns attributed to Pieter Meghen; 2 large miniatures

HERALDRY: The arms of England crowned and supported by Tudor dragon and greyhound, fol. 4; devices of red and white rose-en-soleil and fleur-de-lis, fol. 4; crowned red and white rose, fol. 168; portcullis and linked initials *HK* on grounds parted per pale vert and argent, fol. 4

BINDING: Joseph Pomfrett, ca. 1712; red morocco; the arms of James Cecil, fifth earl of Salisbury, gold-stamped on both covers

COLLECTION: Hatfield House, marquess of Salisbury, Cecil Papers Ms. 324

PROVENANCE: Henry VIII, king of England (1491–1547), and Catherine of Aragon (1485–1536); probably William Cecil, lord Burghley (d. 1598), and Robert Cecil, first earl of Salisbury (d. 1612); at Hatfield by 1712

R A

This manuscript contains the finest examples of Flemish manuscript illumination acquired by Henry VIII. The book's biblical texts are the Acts of the Apostles and the Apocalypse, with the Vulgate and Erasmus's Latin

translation of his new Greek edition written in parallel columns. Pieter Meghen, who served as writer of the king's books from 1530 until 1540, wrote the stately humanist script. The book was probably executed between 1528 and 1533, possibly as the final volume of a set of four volumes of New Testament texts begun by Meghen as early as 1506 for John Colet (d. 1519), the dean of Saint Paul's.[1] The others are the Gospels of Saint Matthew and Saint Mark of 1509 (Cambridge, University Library, Ms. Dd.vii.3), the Gospels of Saint John and Saint Luke of 1509, and the Epistles of 1506 (London, British Library, Royal Ms. 1 E.v, vols. 1 and 2).

The volume contains only two miniatures. The first and finest, showing Saint Luke in his study (ill. 132), marks the opening of Acts. This miniature is one of the few surviving in an English manuscript that echoes the style of Gerard Horenbout, the Flemish painter who came to England to enter the king's service by 1528.[2] For example, the large area of turquoise in the foreground, with the numerous accents of saturated reds and blues, is among the miniature's most striking features. These colors also play a strong role in *Saint Mark in His Study* in the Sforza Hours (ill. 129c), Horenbout's only documented work. Both miniatures include architecture and furnishings that incorporate a veneer of classical decorative motifs. As the facial type of Saint Luke finds no correspondence in Horenbout's Sforza miniatures, it is possible that this miniature is by one of his children, Lucas or Susanna, the only illuminators in England at the time who were likely trained by Gerard. Other important stylistic features of this composition— such as the broad curtain, the bench in the foreground, the cluttered shelves, and the descending steps—were inspired by Dürer prints depicting Saint Jerome in his study.[3] Flemish illuminators routinely used German print sources in these years.

The second miniature, showing Saint John on the island of Patmos, opens the Apocalypse.[4] It is an entirely different type of scene, equally idiosyncratic and decorative in the use of color, but with a lush outdoor landscape. John wears a pink robe with gold highlights. Although the handling of the two miniatures in the manuscript seems dissimilar, they may be related. The foliage glimpsed through the window of Saint Luke's study is not so different from what one sees behind Saint John. Nevertheless, in comparison with the first miniature, the style of this one has less to do with the art of Horenbout (and, for that matter, that of his doppelgänger, the Master of James IV of Scotland).

J. B. Trapp dated the book after 1528, when Meghen was working for Cardinal Wolsey and Nikolaus Kratzer, but before 1533.[5] He believed that it was written for presentation to Henry VIII.   T. K.

Notes

1. Brown (A.) 1984: 360–61, 370–71.

2. The study of Murdoch et al. (1981: 28–29) on the English miniature identifies this work as Flemish, dating it to around 1509, more than a decade before the arrival of Lucas Horenbout in London.

3. Specifically the woodcut of 1511 (B.114) and the engraving of 1514 (B.60).

4. Gibaud 1982: 532.

5. Trapp 1983: 24; followed by Brown (A.) 1984: 361.

133
LUCAS HORENBOUT (?)
Portrait of Henry VIII

133

LUCAS HORENBOUT (?)

Portrait of Henry VIII

England, ca. 1525–27

Parchment laid on card, 4.7 cm (1⅞ in.) diameter

COLLECTION: Windsor Castle, inv. RCIN.420640

PROVENANCE: Theophilus Howard, second earl of Suffolk (1584–1640); to Charles I, king of Great Britain and Ireland (1600–1649); possibly recovered at the Restoration; presumably by descent and inheritance through the English royal houses

RA

One of the earliest portrait miniatures produced in England, this image depicts Henry VIII at approximately thirty-five years of age.[1] The bearded king is shown in his prime, wearing a black cap with gold ornaments, a tunic of pale green brocade, a white shirt with black embroidery, and a fur-trimmed cloak. The work, perhaps painted from life,[2] is one of seven portrait miniatures of the king attributed to Lucas Horenbout.[3] Each depicts the king in a slightly different costume but follows the standard conventions for the portrait miniature, presenting the sitter at bust length, usually in three-quarter profile, against a blue background with a gold edge.

The theory that the origin of the portrait miniature can be found in Flemish manuscript illumination is evidenced by a shared artistic technique and attention to nearly microscopic detail.[4] The brow and nose of the king are modeled with tiny strokes of gray over opaque pink, his cheeks defined by minute hatches of red paint. Moreover, his hair is built up of tiny strokes over opaque color. A similar technique is found in manuscripts illuminated by Gerard Horenbout (see cat. no. 129); in others by the Master of James IV of Scotland, who was probably Gerard Horenbout (see cat. no. 124); and in the works of other Flemish artists of a generation earlier. Further evidence is found in the rectangular portrait miniature of Henry VIII attributed to Lucas Horenbout in the Fitzwilliam Museum (Cambridge, Fitzwilliam Museum, inv. PD 19–1949).[5] Angels in the spandrels surrounding the portrait are particularly close in technique to those appearing in the borders in numerous Flemish books of hours (see cat. no. 162, fol. 8v), visually linking the portrait miniature as an art form to Flemish illumination.[6] Moreover, the numerous copies of the portrait miniatures depicting the king, including this one, show the popularity of the art form at the Tudor court.

R. G.

Notes

1. G. Reynolds (1999: 47) discussed the age of the king. The portrait's inscription can be interpreted to mean the king "was entering his 35th year or had attained the age of 35." Starkey (in London 1991a: 91) noted that the portrait dates either to 1527, when Henry sent a miniature of himself to France, or to 1525, when he exchanged miniatures with Princess Mary, who was departing for Ludlow.

2. Reynolds 1999: 47; Murdoch et al. 1981: 32.

3. The others are Cambridge, Fitzwilliam Museum, inv. PD 19–1949; Paris, Musée du Louvre, inv. RF. 44315 (cat. no. 134); Windsor, Royal Collection, inv. RCIN 420010; one in the Buccleuch collection; unidentified private collection (see Strong 1983: 37, fig. 23; 190, no. 18); and the Netherlands, Collection V. de S. (see Strong 1983: 189–90).

4. On the development of the portrait miniature, see Backhouse 1989: 1–17.

5. Its inscription reads H R / VIII and A𝞼/ XXXV. Reynolds (1999:47) logically argued that it was not unusual for the king to be both bearded and clean shaven within in a single year.

6. Murdoch et al. 1981: 3; Coombs 1998: 16.

134

LUCAS HORENBOUT (?)

Portrait of Henry VIII

England, ca. 1525–27

Parchment laid on card, 5.6 cm (2³⁄₁₆ in.) diameter

COLLECTION: Paris, Musée du Louvre, RF. 44315

PROVENANCE: Private collection, France [Paris, Drouot, November 18, 1994, lot 52]; to Société des Amis du Louvre; its gift, 1994

JPGM

Among the twenty-three portrait miniatures attributed to Lucas Horenbout, this image is one of seven portraying Henry VIII.[1] Although lacking an inscription, it is closely related to a portrait miniature in the British royal collection (cat. no. 133) and surely dates to the same period—around 1525–27. Both portraits show the king bearded, richly dressed in brocade and fur, in three-quarter profile against a blue background edged in gold. Similar treatment of facial features—including wide-set eyes, rosy cheeks, and a rosebud mouth—and forms defined by brushwork of red and gray hatch marks over opaque pink, as well as a diffuse light that softens edges, demonstrate that the portraits are by the same hand.

The backgrounds in these miniatures—blue edged in gold—echo those of portrait medallions depicting contemporary and historical figures in a three-volume set of *Les Commentaires de la guerre gallique*, dating to 1519–20 (see London, British Library, Harley Ms. 6205, vol. 1, fol. 3). The medallions in the first volume are attributed to Godefroy le Batave, who was trained in Antwerp, while others in the second volume are by Jean Clouet, a Flemish artist working for the French court.[2] Such medallions (see cat. no. 135)—in which the subjects appear in three-quarter view or profile—may be precursors of the independent portrait miniature.[3]

In 1526 Henry VIII received as gifts from Francis I, king of France—delivered by Marguerite, madame d'Alençon—lockets with portrait miniatures of Francis I and his two sons. About this time, Henry likewise sent small portraits, likely portrait miniatures, to the French king; these portraits were of himself, Catherine of Aragon, and Princess Mary. Thus, it is possible that the English portrait miniature was a diplomatic response to French generosity. The uncertain chronology of these exchanges, however, does not allow for a conclusive interpretation of the events.[4] Katherine Coombs has noted that too much evidence has been lost to attribute the origins of the portrait miniature to a single country or artist.[5] In any event, given the Flemish origins of both Horenbout and Clouet, as well as Godefroy's training in Antwerp, it is likely that the portrait miniature as an art form is ultimately derived from the Flemish manuscript tradition.

R. G.

Notes

1. See Strong 1983: 189–90, for a list of all of the miniatures by Horenbout.

2. Volume 2 is Paris, Bibliothèque nationale de France, Ms. 13429; volume 3 is Chantilly, Musée Condé, Ms. 764. On these volumes, see Backhouse 1989: 5–6; and Coombs 1998: 17–18.

3. On the development of the portrait miniature, see Backhouse 1989: 1–17.

4. Reynolds (G.) 1999: 47.

5. Coombs 1998: 18. See also Backhouse 1989: 16–17.

135

LUCAS HORENBOUT (?)

Letters Patent of Henry VIII to Thomas Forster
England, between April 28, 1524, and February 8, 1528

One membrane, 33 × 61 cm (13 × 24 in.); 30 lines of English
chancery hand; 1 historiated initial

HERALDRY: Beaufort badges of portcullis; pomegranate badges of
Catherine of Aragon; Tudor roses; First Great Seal of Henry VIII
attached with green, white, and gold silk thread

COLLECTION: Private collection; on loan to the Victoria and Albert
Museum, London

PROVENANCE: [sale, Sotheby's, London, July 11, 1983, lot 25]; private
collection

RA

135
LUCAS HORENBOUT (?)
Letters Patent of
Henry VIII to
Thomas Forster, with
Portrait of Henry VIII
(and detail of portrait)

Ever since it came to light twenty years ago, the present
document has been recognized as a vital piece of evidence for the history of portrait miniatures in England.
Unlike all other surviving portrait miniatures of Henry
VIII, the bust portrait contained within the opening initial
of the patent letter to Thomas Forster has a clear context.[1]
In the first place the portrait is securely datable to between
Henry's grant to Forster on April 28, 1524, and Forster's
death on February 8, 1528.[2] Second, the person for whom it
was undertaken, Thomas Forster, is identifiable as comp-
troller of the king's works.[3] Third, the portrait is painted
within a larger scheme of decoration that has clear connections to contemporaneous Flemish manuscript illumination. Indeed, the dominance in the border and initial of
the most advanced European decorative styles, including
grotesque work, suggests the hand of a Flemish artist of
considerable sophistication. All of these contexts are compatible with an attribution to a member of the Horenbout
family, particularly to Lucas Horenbout.

This bust portrait painted at the opening of Forster's
patent is a variant of the bearded portrait of Henry VIII preserved in two independent miniatures (cat. nos. 133, 134),
both of which have been attributed to Lucas Horenbout.
The inscription recording Henry's age in the first of these
portraits has been interpreted as providing a dating for that
portrait of 1525–26 or 1526–27.[4] Together with three other
miniature portraits showing a beardless Henry VIII, the
two independent portraits of the bearded Henry form the
earliest detached portrait miniatures known to have been
painted in England. Since it is possible that the portrait
in the initial was added to the present document at a similar date, it is not certain that it constitutes the model on
which the two other bearded portraits were based or that
the conception of the initial portrait preceded that of the
detached portraits.   S. McK.

Notes

1. For a summary of the text, see Brewer 1862–1932, 4, pt. 1: no. 297 (28).

2. The prominent inclusion in the accompanying border decoration of the pomegranate badge of Henry's wife Catherine of Aragon also suggests a dating before 1528.

3. Campbell and Foister 1986: 722, n. 41.

4. The inscription can be read as either "in his 35th year" (June 28, 1525–June 28, 1526) or "aged 35" (June 28, 1526–June 28, 1527).

136a
MASTER OF THE
DAVID SCENES IN THE
GRIMANI BREVIARY
Joseph and Potiphar's Wife,
fol. 26

MASTER OF THE DAVID SCENES IN THE GRIMANI BREVIARY (B)

For biography, see part 4

136

MASTER OF THE DAVID SCENES IN
THE GRIMANI BREVIARY

Prayer Book
Use of Rome
Bruges or Ghent, ca. 1515–20

MANUSCRIPT: ii + 319 + ii folios, 20.5 × 13.8 cm (8⅛ × 5⁷⁄₁₆ in.); justification: 12 × 7.5 cm (4¾ × 2¹⁵⁄₁₆ in.); 21 lines of *gotica rotunda*; 18 three-quarter-page miniatures, 24 bas-de-page calendar miniatures with additional scenes set into architectural borders

BINDING: Gold-tooled red leather over wood boards; gold clasps in form of sea creatures

COLLECTION: Copenhagen, Det Kongelige Bibliotek, Gl. Kgl. Saml. 1605, 4°

PROVENANCE: Rosenborg Castle, Copenhagen; Royal Library, 1781

JPGM

Once a lavish prayer book, this incomplete manuscript is nevertheless of considerable interest because it contains a series of teaching texts illuminated with original iconography by the Master of the David Scenes in the Grimani Breviary. The manuscript is certainly missing a large number of full-page illuminations, but an Hours of the Virgin as well as some suffrages may also have once been included in the volume.[1] At the beginning of the manuscript is a set of texts connected with the catechism: the Ten Commandments, the Seven Deadly Sins, the Seven Acts of Charity, and the Seven Sacraments, among others. These texts are not usually found in books of hours, and the illuminations that accompany them are inventive. In the image for the deadly sin of lust, a foppishly dressed Joseph, in pink tights, hurriedly flees from the bed of Potiphar's wife (ill. 136a).[2] The garment she snatches off him as he runs, a detail described in Genesis, helps the reader to identify the story. For the sin of anger, the artist turned instead to the world around him for inspiration, depicting four men fighting over the winnings in a game of cards (ill. 136b).

The style of the miniatures in this manuscript is closely related to the artist's work in the Grimani Breviary (cat. no. 126), suggesting a similar dating for this manuscript of around 1515. The artist's fondness for lively figures dressed at the height of fashion is evident in both manuscripts, with men wearing black round-toed shoes with a thin strap and women with the back of the skirt brought up to the waist to reveal the fur lining.[3] A palette of rich blues, yellows, and reds—enlivened with flashes of hot pink, striped fabrics, and spotted furs—is also apparent in both. The figures, moreover, occupy the space in a similar way, with the fairly large, sturdy forms enacting the scene at the front of the picture plane. In addition, the images in both books attest to a partiality for Old Testament narratives full of action.

The Psalter of the Copenhagen manuscript was divided into fifteen sections, each of which originally began with a full-page miniature, all of which are now missing. The series would likely have focused on the life of David, much like the sequence of narratives in the Grimani Breviary after which the artist is named.[4]

The manuscript is unusual for its inclusion of the cate-chismal texts discussed above, the Psalter of Saint Augus-tine, and a full copy of all 150 psalms, raising questions about the original function of the book. It is not known for whom the manuscript was made, but within the series of suffrages is an illumination accompanying a prayer to a guardian angel. The young boy dressed in fur-trimmed robes who kneels at a prie-dieu with a prayer book open before him was likely the original owner of the manuscript. The presence of catechismal texts and the full Psalter there-fore becomes clear; the book was intended in part to teach the precepts of the faith. A number of these short texts can also be found in the Hours of Joanna of Castile (cat. no. 114). Although the texts there are not illuminated, other minia-tures in that manuscript are also by the Master of the David Scenes. The two manuscripts are also linked by the fact that the text pages are all decorated with small objects, such as birds and flowers, set directly on the parchment in the three outer borders, an unusual feature seen in a number of man-uscripts by this workshop.[5]

E. M.

Figure 71
MASTER OF THE
DAVID SCENES IN THE
GRIMANI BREVIARY
*The Return of David with
the Head of Goliath.* In
the Breviary of Cardinal
Domenico Grimani, fol.
288v (see cat. no. 126)

136b
MASTER OF THE
DAVID SCENES IN THE
GRIMANI BREVIARY
Men Gambling, fol. 27

Notes
1. The texts remaining in the book include a calendar, the Psalter of Saint Augustine, a number of catechismal texts, a small group of suffrages, all 150 psalms, the Canticle of Isaiah, the Seven Penitential Psalms, a litany, a few lections, and the Office of the Dead. While the manuscript might have been a psalter, it is more likely that it was a psalter-hours and that the Hours of the Virgin was removed along with its illuminations at the same time that the full-page illuminations originally illustrating the psalms, the canticum, the Penitential Psalms, and the Office of the Dead were removed. Although the calendar has scenes set in architectural borders, it does not belong to the group of calendars discussed with the Breviary of Eleanor of Portugal (cat. no. 91).

2. A painted glass roundel with similar iconography was painted around 1490–1500 by the Master of the Joseph Sequence (Munich, Bay-erische Staatsgemäldesammlungen, Alte Pinakothek), but it is part of a series concerning biblical dream interpretation. I know of only one other series of painted images from around this time devoted to the Seven Deadly Sins: the famous tabletop by Hieronymus Bosch now in Madrid. Like the series in the Copenhagen manuscript, it incor-porates scenes from daily life, but its compositions are unrelated. Several tapestry cycles do have the Deadly Sins as their subject (see Campbell 2002).

3. Margaret Scott (correspondence with the author, March 11, 2002) has suggested a dating of around 1515–20 for the manuscript based on these costumes, including the base coats and shoes of the men and the headdresses with French hoods, square necklines, and turned-back sleeves of the women.

4. The codicology of the manuscript indicates that fifteen full-page illuminations would have divided the Psalter portion of the book into sections of ten psalms each. The illuminations in the Grimani Breviary follow the more common liturgical eight-part division.

5. As-Vijvers (2002) made a study of the group of manuscripts fea-turing this decorative scheme, which she has termed *Einzelmotiv.*

137

MASTER OF THE DAVID SCENES IN
THE GRIMANI BREVIARY

Book of Hours
Use of Rome
Bruges or Ghent, ca. 1515–20

MANUSCRIPT: i + 173 + iii folios, 20.4 × 13.7 cm (8¹⁄₁₆ × 5⅜ in.);
justification: 10.7 × 7.1 cm (4³⁄₁₆ × 2¾ in.); 18 lines of *bastarda*;
3 full-page miniatures, 41 three-quarter-page miniatures, 1 small
miniature, 2 historiated initials, 24 historiated borders

INSCRIPTIONS: *Formerly belonging to Marie de Medici Queen of France
who left it at Cologne whence it came into possession of Fockem [sic].
Supposed to have been illuminated by Hans Memling*, nineteenth-century
hand, inside front cover

BINDING: Red velvet over wood boards; embroidered with flowers
and birds in colored silk and metal thread

COLLECTION: Oxford, Bodleian Library, Ms. Douce 112

PROVENANCE: Marie de Medici (1573–1642) (?), seventeenth century;
H. Fochem, rector of the Church of Saint Ursula in Cologne, by 1813;
Francis Douce (1757–1834); his bequest, 1834

JPGM

137a
MASTER OF THE
DAVID SCENES IN THE
GRIMANI BREVIARY
Pentecost, fol. 10v

The Master of the David Scenes in the Grimani Breviary
indulged to the fullest his penchant for innovative iconography in this lavish book of hours. Although the book
contains no unusual texts, it is one of the most densely illuminated manuscripts by the artist, including forty-one
three-quarter-page miniatures, and three full-page miniatures.[1] It was originally illustrated with at least eleven more
full-page miniatures, now missing.[2] In addition, although
the artist occasionally included historiated borders in his
other manuscripts, he never utilized them as regularly or
imaginatively as in this book. Often featuring unusual iconography, these borders help to elaborate and comment
upon the narratives of the main miniatures.

At the beginning of the prayer to the Holy Face is a
miniature of the Salvator Mundi, the subject that traditionally illustrates this text. The two facing historiated borders,
however, feature rarely seen narratives drawn from the
Golden Legend that are related iconographically to the main
miniature. In the border surrounding the Salvator Mundi,
different moments from the story of the sudarium occur in
clockwise order. The scenes show how Veronica healed the
sick emperor Tiberius with the cloth imprinted with the
image of Christ's face. The facing border shows a single
scene of Titus and Vespasian razing the city of Jerusalem as
punishment to the Jews.[3] Like the Master of James IV in
manuscripts such as the Spinola Hours (cat. no. 124), the
Master of the David Scenes in this manuscript utilized the
border space in two different ways: on the one hand, to
structure a chronological narrative and, on the other, to
create an illusionistic vista, as if one could lift up the text
block and see the rest of the image beneath.[4] Each opening
for the Hours of the Virgin would have originally had a full-
page miniature (all now missing) facing a recto composed
of a typologically related three-quarter-page miniature and
historiated border,[5] and many of the suffrages also have
borders containing scenes from the lives of the saints (see
ill. 137b).

The three extant full-page miniatures are presented in
a manner that recalls Flemish panel paintings of the period.
The image of the Virgin and Child that accompanies the
Mass of the Virgin (fol. 16v) is closely related to a painting
by the workshop of Gerard David now in the Lazaro-
Galdiano Museum in Madrid. The exact correspondences
between the two, including details such as the folds of the
Virgin's head cloth and the identical position of the Christ
child, indicate that both were based on a David composition.[6] The two other full-page miniatures in the manuscript, *The Agony in the Garden* (fol. 27v) and *Pentecost* (ill.
137a), are more closely related to iconography traditionally
found in manuscripts,[7] but both are prominent within the
illumination scheme of the manuscript because of their
sense of monumentality and the individualized treatment
of the figures. The absence of a border and the presence of
an illusionistically painted wooden frame in all three miniatures heighten the sense that the illuminations were meant
to evoke contemporary devotional paintings.

There are no unusual texts in the book except for a
prayer to the Holy Sacrament, which is illustrated by an

Notes

1. Among the manuscripts in which the Master of the David Scenes was the primary artist, only the so-called Brukenthal Breviary (Sibiu, Romania, Museu Brukenthal), with a total of ninety-two miniatures, is more heavily illuminated than this manuscript. Like this book, the breviary contains an unusual number of illustrated suffrages.

2. In addition to the eight miniatures missing from the Hours of the Virgin, the full-page miniatures that would have opened the Hours of the Cross, the Hours of the Virgin for Advent, and the Office of the Dead have also been removed. Additionally, the manuscript is missing its calendar, making it difficult to localize.

3. According to the *Golden Legend*'s account of the life of Saint James, Vespasian, governor of Galatia under Tiberius, was also sick, but he was healed simply by proclaiming his faith in Jesus to heal him. The story occurs just before the description of the siege of Jerusalem (depicted on the facing page of this opening), and one of the figures in the border of the Veronica story wears a pilgrim's badge (associated with Saint James), so it is possible that the similarities between the stories of the two sick men led the artist to pair the Veronica story with the razing of Jerusalem.

4. As in the Spinola Hours, certain figures are repeated to add to the sense of an unfolding story. In this case, the young man in red tights appears twice, as do the messenger and the emperor.

5. The beginning of lauds (fol. 51), for example, depicts the rarely illustrated Old Testament story of King David's servants placing the Ark of the Covenant temporarily in the house of Obededom. The surrounding border shows the birth of John the Baptist, while the facing scene would no doubt have shown the Visitation. The Virgin Mary had stayed with Elizabeth for the three months following the Visitation until the birth of John the Baptist, just as the ark rested in the home of Obededom for three months before its removal to Jerusalem.

6. According to Maryan W. Ainsworth (correspondence with the author, December 5, 2001), the Lazaro-Galdiano Virgin and Child is probably by a close follower of David. The motif ultimately comes from Rogier van der Weyden, but she suspects that there was an "original" by David as well.

7. The composition of *The Agony in the Garden* is based on a generic pattern repeated in innumerable manuscripts, while *Pentecost* is most closely related to Pentecost scenes in manuscripts by the Master of James IV, including a book of hours in the British Library (cat. no. 109, fol. 33v).

8. MacFarlane (1960: 16) attributed four other manuscripts to this scribe, including the Hours of James IV of Scotland (cat. no. 110). Brinkmann (1997: 323) identified a set of six manuscripts containing the scribe's work, including the Prayer Book of Charles V (Vienna, Österreichische Nationalbibliothek, Ms. 1859). Only the present manuscript and one in Berlin (Kupferstichkabinett, Ms. 78 B 15) appear in both lists.

9. Margaret Scott (correspondence with the author, March 11, 2002) has found that the fashions in the manuscripts draw on elements dating to the late 1510s. The women wear the same dark looped-up fur on their trains seen in the Copenhagen manuscript (cat. no. 136), and the headdresses with gold undercaps seen beneath black hoods were popular after around 1515. The pillbox hats with turned-up brims of the men are seen until the end of the 1510s.

image of a woman taking Communion (fol. 21). Since a woman is also depicted in the miniature for the suffrage to a guardian angel (fol. 147v), and again kneeling next to a man as the Host is raised in the historiated border for the Mass of the Virgin (fol. 17), it seems likely that a woman with a special devotion to the Host was the original owner. The manuscript's scribe was a prolific and highly regarded craftsman, judging from the number and caliber of manuscripts that he was commissioned to copy.[8] The costumes depicted in the manuscript are reminiscent of those found in the Grimani Breviary of around 1515 (cat. no. 126),[9] but the intricate narrative relationships among the series of illuminations for each major opening and the developed style of the full-page miniatures perhaps argue for date as late as 1520.   E. M.

137b

MASTER OF THE
DAVID SCENES IN THE
GRIMANI BREVIARY
Saint James the Greater,
fol. 151

MASTER OF THE SOANE HOURS

Since the time of Friedrich Winkler, the cohesive group of miniatures that dominates the Soane Hours (cat. no. 138) has been recognized as the work of a close imitator of the Master of James IV.[1] The strong stylistic links between the artist of the Soane Hours, here introduced as the Master of the Soane Hours, and the Master of James IV make it probable that the former was a talented member of the workshop of the Master of James IV. Although the artist is known only from his work in the Soane Hours, the most skillfully painted images of that manuscript and the unusually complex and original narratives that appear there betray an artist of sensitivity and acute observational powers.

The bright colors—including orange, magenta, lavender, and a vibrant teal—and stocky, stalwart male figures with prominent noses and deep-set eyes are seen in the work of both the Master of James IV and the Soane Master. There is less variety and individualization, however, in the often ungainly figures of the Soane Master, and his coloring sometimes seems almost gaudy in comparison with that of the Master of James IV. The spaces inhabited by the figures are also similarly conceived in the work of the two artists, the action usually taking place close to the picture plane, with the figures looming large in the landscape. In the illuminations of the Master of James IV, however, the landscape is often cleverly utilized to carry on the narrative, whereas in the work of the Soane Master, the landscape is simply a backdrop. The affiliation between the Master of James IV and the Master of the Soane Hours is perhaps most clearly seen in the latter artist's reliance on copying the former's compositions. In the Soane Hours no fewer than twenty-five miniatures can be directly linked to illuminations from the workshop of the Master of James IV. The occasional copying of such details as colors suggests the existence of a set of color models available in the workshop.

Although the work of the Soane Master often seems to pale in comparison with that of the Master of James IV, there are passages of great beauty in his illuminations in the Soane Hours. The artist's mastery of the human form can be seen in illuminations such as the Salvator Mundi (fol. 9v), especially in Christ's slender fingers raised in blessing and gently grasping the orb, along with the oval face with wide-set, hooded eyes and long, delicate nose. The Soane Master was also interested in depicting unusual Old Testament narratives in which the figures are often delineated with great psychological acuity, such as the pair of illuminations depicting David's grief over the death of his son (ill. 138). Other examples from the Soane Hours, in addition to the series devoted to the life of David, include God revealing the stars of the Pleiades to Job (fol. 32) and the story of Elisha miraculously cleansing the water of Jericho (fol. 34). Although it is possible that all these images are copied from lost compositions by the Master of James IV, they are nonetheless an important record of the kind of original biblical iconography generated by the Master of James IV and his followers.

Although no other works by the Master of the Soane Hours have been definitively identified, there is a close affinity between his illuminations and the style of another follower of the Master of James IV, whose work can be found in a manuscript now divided between Vienna (Österreichische Nationalbibliothek, Ms. 1887) and Poitiers (Médiathèque François Mitterand, Ms. 57/269).[2] The treatment of the faces in this artist's work calls to mind the technique of the Master of James IV, but his figures are bulkier and stiffer, closer to those of the Soane Master. Another distinctive feature shared by these two followers of the Master of James IV is a tendency toward slope-shouldered figures whose arms seem to attach to their bodies well below the shoulder line. Because it is thought that the Master of James IV was probably based in Ghent (see the biography of the Master of James IV, part 4, this volume), it is likely that his workshop and followers worked there as well.　　　E. M.

Notes

1. Winkler (1943: 60), who did not make a distinction between the Master of James IV and Horenbout, identified them as weak executions by Horenbout's workshop, while Dogaer (1987a: 166) thought that they could perhaps be by Horenbout himself. Most recently, Brinkmann (1997: 179–81) attributed them to the Master of the David Scenes in the Grimani Breviary, a theory to which I do not subscribe.

2. The texts appearing in the Vienna manuscript, including a calendar and an Hours of the Virgin, are precisely the texts missing from the Poitiers manuscript. The identical measurements, borders, initials, and script allow an identification of these two fragmentary manuscripts as once having formed a whole.

138

**MASTER OF THE SOANE HOURS
AND ANOTHER ARTIST**

Soane Hours
Use of Rome
Ghent or Bruges, after 1512

MANUSCRIPT: i + 179 + iii folios, 20.9 × 14.2 cm (8¼ × 5⁹⁄₁₆ in.);
justification: 10.5 × 7 cm (4⅛ × 2¾ in.); 18 lines of *gotica rotunda*;
62 three-quarter-page miniatures, 16 half-page miniatures,
12 bas-de-page calendar miniatures with additional scenes set
into architectural borders

INSCRIPTIONS: Notes in German and Latin concerning gift of
manuscript from Wolfgang Wilhelm to Johanna, wife of Fernando
of Aragon, fols. i verso–1; inscription concerning Knight sale, fol. 1v;
"fr. Bone de Medina," back flyleaf

BINDING: Eighteenth century (?); red velvet

COLLECTION: London, Sir John Soane's Museum, Ms. 4

PROVENANCE: Wolfgang Wilhelm (1578–1653), his gift to Johanna,
wife of Fernando of Aragon (d. 1592); Edward Knight; to Richard, first
duke of Buckingham (1776–1839), May 10, 1821; to Sir John Soane
(1753–1837), September 1833

RA

This book of hours is distinctive for the facing three-quarter-page miniatures with innovative subject matter that demarcate each division of its four major cycles: the Hours of the Cross, the Hours of the Holy Spirit, the Hours of the Virgin, and the Penitential Psalms. The majority of these miniatures are by an artist heavily influenced by the Master of James IV of Scotland, here presented as the Master of the Soane Hours.[1] Because all the miniatures are integral to the manuscript, and because miniatures by the Soane Master sometimes appear opposite illuminations by another artist, the book must have been carefully planned from the beginning.[2] Each of the illuminations appears in exactly the same three-quarter-page format throughout the book, and the borders for every opening are matched with a consistency uncommon in manuscripts of the period.

Two of the cycles, that for the Hours of the Holy Spirit and that for the Penitential Psalms, contain examples of iconography that are exceedingly rare in books of hours. The sequence for the Hours of the Holy Spirit, comprising fourteen miniatures, begins with a typical pairing of Pentecost and the Tower of Babel (fols. 25v–26) but quickly moves into unfamiliar typological territory. The most unusual, perhaps, is the pairing of the Dream of the Seven Fat and Seven Lean Cows (Genesis 40) and Job's Vision of the Pleiades (Job 38), subjects rarely depicted in manuscript illumination (fols. 31v–32). Although these are both Old Testament scenes and there are two other pairings that also break the pattern, it seems that the general intent was a typological sequence.[3] It also seems likely that this cycle is related to the theme of the Seven Gifts of the Holy Spirit, an uncommon but not completely unknown theme for the Hours of the Holy Spirit.[4] That these were unusual representations is implied by the inclusion of strips of text beneath each illumination indicating the corresponding biblical passage, helping the reader to identify the story in

the image. These aids were not thought necessary elsewhere in the book.[5]

The fourteen illuminations accompanying the Penitential Psalms represent some of the best painting in this manuscript, with unusual subjects, complex narratives, and beautifully handled landscapes. The stories are all taken from 2 Samuel, which tells of the time of greatest upheaval in David's life. During that period he committed the actions he would most repent, including his affair with Bathsheba and the rebellion that ended in death for his son Absalom. In one of the sets of paired images (ill. 138), three women in an interior attend to the tiny corpse of David's son, struck dead for his father's adulterous sin. Two of the women gently lay the body in a wooden box, while the third woman holds a cloth to her face, overcome with grief. In the facing image, David appears absorbed in private prayer and remorse, left completely alone to contemplate his wrongful actions. The muted blues and greens of the surrounding borders perfectly complement the subdued tone and rich reds of the miniatures. Although the illuminations capture particular moments in David's life, the sense that they concern the theme of penitence is never lost, for the artist incorporated an image of David earnestly praying in either the foreground or background of one illumination in every opening.

The Master of the Soane Hours was responsible for most of the miniatures in the manuscript, and his best illuminations approach the quality of the work of the Master of James IV of Scotland. In *The Virgin and Child with Angels* (fol. 40), the fluid movements of the baby Christ as he reaches for his mother and the beautifully painted drapery of the angel to the right evidence the work of a skilled artist. Many of the other miniatures are populated by stout, active figures with expressive faces and vigorous gestures, closely based on those by the Master of James IV. The loose brushwork, vivid colors, and atmospheric landscapes that characterize the miniatures were all also successfully adopted by this artist from the Master of James IV. A small group of illuminations in the manuscript, also within the stylistic sphere of the Master of James IV, are not as well executed.[6]

A large number of miniatures in the manuscript can be associated with specific compositions in a wide range of manuscripts painted by the Master of James IV over the course of his career, forming a virtual compendium of copies. About half of the miniatures for the Hours of the Cross and the Hours of the Virgin rely on compositions that can also be found in a book of hours in the British Library, London (cat. no. 109). Other miniatures in the Soane Hours can be related to illuminations found in the Spinola Hours (cat. no. 124); a book of hours at the Vatican (cat. no. 111); a leaf in the Metropolitan Museum of Art, New York (ill. 125a); a breviary in Berlin (cat. no. 112); and a *Miroir de humaine salvation* in Chantilly, all by the Master of James IV or his workshop.[7] This evidence points to the likelihood of an extensive set of color patterns in the workshop of the Master of James IV.

The manuscript contains an equal quantity of miniatures that seem wholly new. It is impossible to know whether these images are based on lost Master of James IV

138
MASTER OF THE
SOANE HOURS
Death of David's Son
and *David in Prayer*,
fols. 125v–126

models; if they are, the sheer number of unusual scenes found in the manuscript would indicate a large corpus of Master of James IV imagery that has been lost. Especially intriguing is the case of the sequence of scenes devoted to the life of David. The Soane Hours is one of a group of manuscripts clustered around the Master of James IV and his workshop that all contain extensive narrative cycles concerning David, although the individual subjects are almost never repeated.[8]

A second, less skilled workshop also active in the manuscript was limited to copying miniatures from the Huth Hours (cat. no. 33).[9] Because the copies that appear in the Soane Hours were taken from compositions in the Huth Hours by both Simon Marmion and the Master of the Houghton Miniatures, and because copies after the Huth Hours are so rare, it is probable that the artist or artists were working directly from the manuscript itself rather than copying from models. The inclusion of specific compositions from the Huth Hours may indicate that the patron knew of it and encouraged the incorporation of images from it into the Soane Hours.

The dating of this manuscript and its patronage are problematic. A date around 1500 has traditionally been proposed for the manuscript, based on the supposition that the book of hours in London (cat. no. 109) is an early work by the Master of James IV and that this manuscript was made soon after. Research by Kurt Köster on the pilgrims' badges in the borders confirms that the manuscript must date later than 1512.[10] As seen above, moreover, compositions from a wide range of Master of James IV manuscripts appear in the Soane Hours, including some that are perhaps as late as 1525,[11] which may argue for a even later date. Information about the original patron is even scarcer, for the earliest known provenance is from the early seventeenth century. The texts of the manuscript are those found in most books of hours, although the exceptional illumination in the Hours of the Holy Spirit may indicate a special devotion to the Holy Spirit. The calendar provides few clues beyond a tenuous connection to Antwerp, while the litany is unusually close in content to one found in a book of hours printed in Paris in 1490.[12]

E. M.

Notes

1. Brinkmann (1997: 179–81) has argued that all the miniatures in the manuscript are by the Master of the David Scenes. I would disagree.

2. There are no singletons in the manuscript; all pages with miniatures have text on both their recto and verso.

3. This uneven pattern of combining narrative and typological scenes is true of the cycles for the Hours of the Virgin in the British Library manuscript (cat. no. 109), the Spinola Hours (cat. no. 124), the Huth Hours (cat. no. 33), and La Flora (cat. no. 93).

4. The Hours of Catherine of Cleves (New York, the Morgan Library, Ms. M.917, M.945) contains a sequence for the Hours of the Holy Spirit relating to the Seven Gifts, but the illuminations feature mostly contemporary scenes, not biblical stories.

5. Each of these short texts begins with the phrase, "Gratia sancti spiritus figuratur," which suggests that these were indeed meant to be typological representations of the Seven Gifts. The references to particular biblical passages also indicate that this sequence is related to an unidentified text on the subject of the Seven Gifts.

6. These miniatures include those in the calendar, related closely to the calendar in the Mayer van den Bergh Breviary (cat. no. 92), and those on folios 11v, 12, 15v, 16, 17v, 27v, 28, 29v, 30, 35v, 36, 78v, 79, 106, and possibly 37v. It is difficult to say whether these are simply weaker works by the same artist, or those of a less skilled colleague.

7. The miniatures in the Soane Hours that repeat subjects found in *Le Miroir de humaine salvation* (Chantilly, Musée Condé, Ms. 139) are not identical to their counterparts in that manuscript but rather show an overall strong resemblance in terms of the iconography. They are often reversed versions of those found in the *Miroir* manuscript (fols. 28, 75, 83), indicating reliance on models available in the workshop of the Master of James IV.

8. Besides the Soane Hours, full David sequences by the Master of James IV or his followers appear in the Grimani Breviary (cat. no. 126), the Vatican Hours (cat. no. 111), and the Breviary of Eleanor of Portugal (cat. no. 91). Another cycle, by the Master of the Dresden Prayer Book, appears in the Hours of Philip of Cleves (Vienna, Österreichische Nationalbibliothek, Ms. s.n. 13239).

9. The seven images that copy compositions in the Huth Hours are on folios 18, 65v, 113v, 115v, 116v, 117v, and 118v. *The Annunciation*, which may copy a lost *Annunciation* in the Huth Hours, is on folio 50. That composition can also be found in a manuscript in Vienna (Österreichische Nationalbibliothek, Ms. 1862, fol. 26v). On the copies, see Brinkmann 1997: 177–79.

10. Köster 1965: 473. Margaret Scott has confirmed a dating of at least after 1505 based on the various fashions that the figures wear in the manuscript, including hats with turned-up brims and chemises with bulky sleeves (correspondence with the author, March 11, 2002). Many of the figures also wear base coats, seen commonly in the 1510s.

11. The composition of the miniature for the suffrage to Saint John (fol. 109v) is based on a composition by the Master of James IV seen in a leaf from the Metropolitan Museum of Art (cat. no. 125).

12. John Plummer has placed the Soane manuscript calendar broadly with Antwerp calendars because of the appearance of Rumold (July 1), but it also contains a few local feasts associated with Utrecht, such as Theodosia (April 3), Firminus (April 6), Bonifacius (June 5), Fausta (September 20), and Remigius (October 1). The Parisian book of hours was printed by Vérard on August 20, 1490. He has also determined that the petitions at the end of the litany, as well as the prayers that follow the readings, are virtually identical in the Vérard printed book and the Soane Hours (2002, Department of Manuscripts files, JPGM).

SIMON BENING

In 1558, in an inscribed self-portrait (cat. no. 161), Simon Bening gave his age as seventy-five, indicating that he was born in 1483 or 1484. The inscription also states that he was the son of Alexander (or Sanders), the Ghent illuminator. Simon Bening was presumably born in Ghent.[1] His mother was Catherine de Goes, who is generally thought to have been a sister or niece of the painter Hugo van der Goes. In 1500 Bening registered his illuminator's mark at the painters' hall in Bruges, evidence that he was already participating in the book trade and, moreover, doing so beyond the boundaries of his hometown.[2] His earliest dated work, however, the Imhof Prayer Book (cat. no. 139), belongs to 1511, more than a decade later. Bening joined the confraternity of the book trade in Bruges in 1508 and is recorded as visiting the city in 1512 and 1516.[3] From 1516 he made regular annual payments to the confraternity. In 1516 his dues were paid by Antonius van Damme, a Bruges scribe, who appears to have been a lifelong friend and collaborator of the artist.

Significantly the Imhof Prayer Book was written in Antwerp, and Bening visited there on family business in 1514, 1516, and 1517. Damião de Góis, then based in Antwerp, was the artist's contact for two major commissions in the early 1530s (cat. nos. 147 and perhaps 150). Thus, from early in his career, Bening's activity as an illuminator involved him directly not only with his hometown of Ghent, a center of illumination, but also with nearby cities in Flanders and Brabant that were important artistic centers. Bening became a citizen of Bruges in 1519, apparently settling there at or around the time of his father's death in Ghent that year. In 1522 he made the gift of a large *Crucifixion*, presumably by his own hand, for his Bruges confraternity's missal.[4] In 1524, 1536, and 1546 he served as dean of the confraternity. By his first wife, Katherine Scroo, he had five daughters, one of whom, Levina Teerlinc, became a successful artist in England. Katherine died in 1542, and one of his daughters died the following year. Bening then married Jane Tancre, who died in 1555. They had no children.

Documentary evidence gives us a clear picture of the character of Bening's patronage and offers the basis for defining his style. In 1530 the *magistrat* of the city of Dixmude paid him for a *Crucifixion* to illustrate the Canon of the Mass in a missal that was written by Pierre Escaillet, countertenor of the church of Saint Nicholas in Dixmude.[5] The work was destroyed in World War I but is recorded in photographs.[6] Also in 1530, as noted above, the Portuguese diplomat, courtier, and humanist Góis, on behalf of the Infante Dom Fernando of Portugal, engaged Bening to illuminate a monumental genealogy (cat. no. 147). Góis also commissioned from him a book of hours that he gave to Queen Catherine of Portugal in 1544 (perhaps cat. no. 150).

In 1537 the Hapsburg accounts show payment to Bening for the illumination of a book of the statutes of the Golden Fleece (Madrid, Instituto de Don Juan de Valencia). In 1539 and 1540 Mencía de Mendoza, the widow of Charles V's chamberlain Henry III of Nassau, commissioned miniatures for a book of hours and another manuscript from Bening, but they have not been identified.[7] Finally, an illuminated monogram in the Prayer Book of Albrecht of Brandenburg (cat. no. 145, fol. 336) has often been interpreted as belonging to Bening.

The Dixmude *Crucifixion*, the Portuguese genealogy, the statutes of the Golden Fleece, and the Prayer Book of Albrecht of Brandenburg have remarkably consistent artistic features. They represent a decade of Bening's activity when his art was in full bloom and present a clear picture of his artistic style. Their features include sweet, round-faced women with rosebud lips; a humane and tenderly sympathetic conception of the adult Christ; solid figure types; and saturated colors dominated by strong reds and blues that are used expressively. Other qualities include the modeling of form in light and dark tones of the same color; the predilection for nocturnal subjects; the flecklike brushwork, evident especially in the treatment of outdoor settings in works after 1530; and a gift for representing atmospheric, deep-set landscapes. These commissions also reveal Bening as exceptionally creative in his employment of an extensive body of illuminators' workshop patterns.

Bening must have served his apprenticeship as a teenager, and he probably studied with his father, Alexander, who is sometimes identified with the Master of the First Prayer Book of Maximilian (see cat. no. 126). The Maximilian Master drew extensively upon the aforementioned body of illuminators' patterns, which had emerged already during the 1470s and early 1480s. Simon may have inherited this group of patterns, as he used them over and over again for miniatures throughout his career. Simon's early work shows a debt to the Bruges illuminator called the Master of the Prayer Books of around 1500, in figure types and the treatment of calendars. The Bruges painter and illuminator Gerard David had a strong influence on his art, also providing inspiration for figure types and sources for compositions. Later in his career the landscapes of the Antwerp painter Joachim Patinir shaped his approach to the construction of space and his conception of deep vistas.

The art of no other Flemish illuminator so fully epitomizes the triumph of Flemish manuscript painting in Europe and its enduring eminence as a court art. If one takes into account the undocumented works—that is, those with miniatures generally accepted as by Bening or his shop—his patrons encompass the Hapsburg imperial family (see cat. nos. 151, 156) and the great and wealthy across Europe, above all those within the Hapsburg realms and their sphere of influence. These include, besides Damião de Góis and Cardinal Albrecht of Brandenburg, the Portuguese noble family Sá (see cat. no. 140); the great Spanish family Enriquez y Ribera;[8] probably Alonso de Idiaquez (see cat. no. 154), who was a member of the court secretariat of Emperor Charles V; and possibly Henry III of Nassau (see cat. no. 149). Included among the commissions mentioned thus far are many of Bening's most extravagant and important works. In sum he enjoyed a long career and exalted patronage, not unlike that of his forebear Simon Marmion, whose artistic activity also flourished due to ongoing support of a ruling household and ranking courtiers.

Given the wide circle of Bening's prominent patrons, it is not surprising that his critical reputation was spread across Europe. Góis called him "the greatest master of the art of illumination in all of Europe,"[9] while Francesco de Holanda (1517–1584)—the Portuguese artist, humanist, and courtier—named him as one of the five greatest illuminators of Holanda's time, a weighty compliment from a staunch partisan of the Italian Renaissance.[10] Holanda also praised him as "among the Flemish the most pleasing colorist who best painted trees and far distances."[11] His reputation lived on after his death, earning him praise from Italian historians and critics such as Lodovico Guicciardini and Giorgio Vasari[12] and from Flemish historians such as Denis Harduyn and Antoine Sanderus.[13] Harduyn, significantly, described him as a master of illumination *and* of the oil medium.[14]

Simon Bening was the last great Flemish illuminator and the last exponent of the style of Flemish manuscript illumination that first emerged in the 1470s. By 1558, the time of his final dated work (cat. no. 161), the tradition of Flemish manuscript illumination had ceased to be important. While his own art was widely copied and imitated at the height of his career in the 1520s, he continued until the end of his career to be an influence on such eminent painters as Pieter Bruegel the Elder (cat. no. 165). Although Bening was unable to foster a new generation of illuminators, Sanderus reported that Bening's daughter Levina Teerlinc earned renown as a miniaturist and painter. Having moved to England, she probably turned to the art of the portrait miniature.[15]   T. K.

Notes

1. Weale (1864–65a: 307) suggested that he was a native of Antwerp but offered no evidence of this.

2. Destrée 1923: 12. He identified his source inaccurately, however, as Weale 1864–65a: 306.

3. Weale 1864–65a: 307.

4. Weale 1864–65a: 311.

5. Weale 1872–73a: 118–19.

6. Destrée 1923: 64–65, pl. 11.

7. Steppe 1969: 501–4.

8. Testa 1991: 89.

9. Weale 1864–65a: 311.

10. The others include the Italians Giulio Clovio, Vincenzo Raimondi, Attavanti degli Attavante, and his father, António de Holanda (see cat. no. 147); Holanda 1930: 284–86.

11. Holanda 1930: 286.

12. Guicciardini 1588: 143; Vasari 1927, 4: 254.

13. Ainsworth 2002: 1–2.

14. Cited by Destrée 1923: 13.

15. Sanderus 1641–44, 2: 175.

139

SIMON BENING AND MASTER OF THE DAVID SCENES IN THE GRIMANI BREVIARY

Imhof Prayer Book
Ghent and Antwerp, 1511

MANUSCRIPT: 329 folios + 11 flyleaves, 9 × 6.2 cm (3½ × 2⁷⁄₁₆ in.); justification: 4.1 × 3.6 cm (1⁹⁄₁₆ × 1⅛ in.); 13 lines of *bastarda*; 11 full-page miniatures, 8 small miniatures, 15 very small miniatures, 12 calendar miniatures, 17 illuminated or historiated borders

HERALDRY: The arms of the Imhof family, erased, fol. 25

INSCRIPTIONS: *Scriptus et finitus est liber iste in opido mercuriali Hantw[er]pia, Anno 1511°*, fol. 334v

BINDING: Sixteenth century; red velvet over wood boards; gilt and goffered edges; pierced silver clasp and catch in floral design; later colored and tasseled silk bookmarkers

COLLECTION: Private collection

PROVENANCE: Hans V Imhof (1461–1522) (?), Nuremberg; Herman Hendrik Beels, van Heemstede (1827–1916), by descent; [sale, Sotheby's, London, June 21, 1988, lot 107]; private collection

JPGM

This diminutive prayer book of 1511 contains the earliest dated illumination by Simon Bening. Bening was twenty-seven or twenty-eight years old by this date, and the volume shows the art of a fully formed illuminator. Its pages announce many of the features of his art for the next half century: a jewel-like richness of color; reliance on a body of illuminators' patterns,[1] many of which date back to the 1470s; and a subtlety of psychological expression, showing passion, intelligence, and often an introspective quality. In addition, Bening's predilection for virtuoso depictions of vast terrain within a constricted format is anticipated in miniatures such as *The Ecstasy of Saint Francis* (ill. 139) and *The Agony in the Garden* (fol. 27v). The book is striking for the extremely high quality of the borders, apparently also by Bening, and for the delicate way in which the colors of the borders find their complement in the miniatures. One of the more unusual borders is that opposite *The Mass of Saint Gregory* (fol. 127v), where the

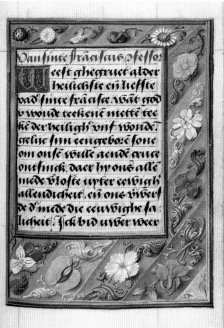

artist omitted the usual colored ground from the border so that the flowers cast their shadows on the bare parchment. Other examples of his early activity, such as the Da Costa Hours (cat. no. 140) and the Ghistelles Prayer Book (cat. no. 141), do not display as consistently the high level of finish of this book's illuminations.

Christopher de Hamel convincingly proposed that the effaced arms on folio 25 are those of the prominent Imhof family of Nuremberg, and that the intended owner was Hans V Imhof (1461–1522).[2] Of the book's eleven full-page miniatures, two are devoted to Saint John the Evangelist and Saint John the Baptist, respectively; both are name saints for Hans. The miniature showing the former, the author of the Gospel lesson, is the first in the book. The Imhof Prayer Book also includes illustrated suffrages for Saints Sebald and Lawrence, the name saints of Nuremberg's most important churches. The Imhof family had their burial site in the Sebalduskirche.

The Imhof family obtained its tremendous wealth from the spice trade, having offices from Linz to Lisbon, including such locations as Venice, Naples, Amsterdam, and Antwerp, where this book was written.[3] Hans V had headed the firm for many years at the time of his death. The Imhof family were important art patrons in Nuremberg, and Hans V was a friend of the city's renowned artist Albrecht Dürer, the sculptor Adam Kraft, and the humanist Willibald Pirckheimer. He was one of several Germans who sought out Bening for luxurious devotional books during the second decade of the sixteenth century. Another such patron was Melchior Pfinzing, provost of the same Sebalduskirche and a secretary to Emperor Maximilian I (Stockholm, Kungliga Biblioteket, Ms. A 227, and Kassel, Landesbibliothek, Ms. math. et art. 50).[4] Also during the second decade of the sixteenth century, an unidentified German patron commissioned a book of hours from

Bening written in a similar *bastarda* and of roughly the same dimensions as the Imhof Prayer Book.[5]

The Baptism of Christ (fol. 297v) was painted by the Master of the David Scenes in the Grimani Breviary. It is a rare firmly dated miniature in this painter's oeuvre.[6]

Finally, although the book's scribe has not been identified, one scribe active in Antwerp in 1511, Petrus Alamire, hailed from Nuremberg. Moreover, his original family name was not Alamire, but Imhof. A highly respected scribe, he was employed at the court of the young Archduke Charles from 1508.[7] One cannot help but wonder if Alamire might have been the scribe of this book. T. K.

Notes

1. Lieftinck (1957: 17–25) identified some of the patterns.

2. Sale catalogue, Sotheby's, London, June 21, 1988, lots 106–8.

3. The book's colophon indicates that it was written, not in Ghent, where Simon was probably living at that time, but "in opido mercuriali Hantw[er]pia" (fol. 334v), perhaps a reference to Antwerp as a commercial center. The German business community had a large presence there. Christina Nielsen contributed research on the patronage of the Imhof family to this entry.

4. Testa 1992b: 58. For an important example of German patronage from the 1520s, see the Brandenburg Prayer Book (cat. no. 145). See also Leesti 1991.

5. Walters Art Museum, W.426, 8.5 × 7 cm (3⅜ × 2¾ in.); Randall 1997: 521–31, esp. 530–31, no. 296.

6. See the biography of the artist (part 4, this volume).

7. Eugeen Schreurs, in Leuven 1999: 15–17.

140

SIMON BENING AND CIRCLE OF THE MASTER OF THE PRAYER BOOKS OF AROUND 1500

Da Costa Hours
Use of Rome
Ghent, ca. 1515

MANUSCRIPT: 388 folios in two continuously foliated volumes, 17.2 × 12.7 cm (6¾ × 5 in.); justification: 9.7 × 7 cm (3¹³⁄₁₆ × 2¾ in.); 17 lines of *textura*; 67 full-page miniatures, 14 small miniatures, 16 historiated borders, 12 full-page calendar miniatures, 12 zodiacal vignettes

HERALDRY: The arms of the Sá family overpainted by those of Da Costa, fol. 1v; the arms of Don Alvaro da Costa, flyleaf

BINDING: Deborah Evetts, New York City, 1983; dark green oasis morocco; former binding: green velvet, silver clasps, and in one volume.

COLLECTION: New York, The Morgan Library, Ms. M.399

PROVENANCE: Probably made for a member of the Portuguese Sá family, possibly João Rodrigues de Sá; Don Alvaro da Costa, chamberlain of Manuel I of Portugal, ca. 1520; to the duque de Mesquitela, by descent through the late nineteenth century; [Bernard Quaritch, London]; to George C. Thomas, Philadelphia, in 1905; to his heirs; to J. P. Morgan (1837–1913), in 1910

JPGM

140a
SIMON BENING
December, fol. 13v

140b
SIMON BENING
The Martyrdom of Saint Ursula and the Eleven Thousand Virgins,
fol. 338v

This book of hours is the most ambitious of Simon Bening's early career and one of the most elaborate he ever created, with more than one hundred miniatures and historiated borders, the vast majority executed by Bening

himself. The book's celebrated calendar cycle may be the earliest in Flemish illumination to feature full-page miniatures without borders.[1] The book's miniatures also encompass two Passion cycles, a life of the Virgin cycle, a cycle of thirty-six full-page miniatures for the suffrages, and two cycles of full-page miniatures of the four Evangelists.

The new format of the calendar elevates its pictorial importance to equal that of the illustrations of the devotional section. Indeed, all but a handful of the full-page miniatures outside the calendar have full decorated or historiated borders, so that by comparison the illustrations of the calendar are actually physically larger than the rest. Moreover, they are so original and accomplished that Bening must have intended them as a focus of the book.

The calendar miniatures represent the culmination of a period of intensive exploration of landscape in Flemish calendar miniatures that extends from the Master of the Dresden Prayer Book (see fig. 30 and cat. nos. 20, 32, 33)—who painted the first Flemish cycle of full-page calendar miniatures, albeit with full borders (Dresden, Sächsische Landesbibliothek, Ms. A 311)[2]—to the Master of the Prayer Books of around 1500 (see cat. nos. 90, 93). These artists increased the range and variety of subjects illustrating the months, not only including more leisure activities but also conveying a precise sense of the time of year, its particular weather conditions, and atmosphere. In the Da Costa Hours the iconography of the calendar is largely conventional, but

Bening's treatment of the settings makes the personality of the months come sharply to the fore. He shows here the expressive force of a single well-chosen, subtly modulated color. The *December* miniature (ill. 140a) shows how brilliant sunlight plays across a fresh layer of snow. At the same time the snow's cool whiteness conveys the chill of winter while also unifying the composition tonally. In *June* (fol. 7v), the brilliant greens suggest the freshness and vitality of a spring day. Bening was also enamored of the pictorial effects of firelight for much of his career. In *January* (fol. 2v), set indoors, the male head of household warms his hands by the roaring fire, while the light from the tall hearth begins to melt the chill of the room. Finally, even though this is Bening's first full-page calendar landscape series, its treatment of spatial recession is still relatively circumscribed. The emphasis is, for the most part, on the foreground and middle ground.[3]

Especially noteworthy among the miniatures outside the calendar are two other full-page miniatures without borders: *The Martyrdom of Saint Ursula and the Eleven Thousand Virgins* (ill. 140b) and the nocturnal *Nativity* (fol. 151v). The Saint Ursula miniature shows the martyrdom of the eleven thousand virgins with the Huns' attack on their boats at Cologne, a subject also treated in the Saint Ursula shrine by the Bruges painter Hans Memling (Bruges, Saint John's Hospital).[4] But Bening's composition is much more spacious and open than Memling's, with a strong suggestion of the airy and poetic "far distances" for which Bening would become famous much later in his career. The splendid Gospel illustration showing Saint John on Patmos (fol. 111v) depicts the pictorial space of the historiated border as largely continuous with that of the miniature, thereby expanding the scope of the landscape. This is a relatively recent innovation (see cat. nos. 124, 125). One of the two Evangelist cycles shows the authors writing their Gospels, while the other represents them, less typically, as standing figures in a landscape.[5]

The Da Costa Hours contains several miniatures that are clearly not by Bening in the life of the Virgin cycle, including *The Visitation* (fol. 140v), *The Annunciation to the Shepherds* (fol. 157v), and *The Presentation in the Temple* (fol. 166v), along with their borders and the borders to the miniatures on folios 167, 170v, and 176v. Their style is closer to that of the Prayer Books Master, but these illuminations appear not to be by him either.

In terms of its devotional texts, the book is no less ambitious and complex than its decorative program. Besides the Hours of the Virgin and other standard features, it includes the Hours of the Passion and the Office of the Five Wounds of Christ, followed by the four Evangelists' accounts of the Passion, the Hours of the Compassion of the Virgin, and the Fifteen Os of Saint Bridget. Following the extensive cycle of suffrages are the Sunday Hours of the Trinity, the Hours of the Conception of the Virgin, and fifteen prayers to the Wounds of Christ.

A splendid heraldic frontispiece with the arms of Don Alvaro da Costa (d. 1535), the chamberlain of King Manuel I, opens the book (fol. 1v). It is so well painted that it could be by Bening himself. The armorials are displayed in an aedicula enlivened with swags and putti. The Da Costa shield is painted over another coat of arms, chequy argent and azure, which appears to be that of the Portuguese Sá family, possibly those of João Rodrigues de Sá.[6] The manuscript was therefore likely begun for him or for another member of the Sá family, but it was soon acquired by Don Alvaro da Costa, perhaps even as it was being finished.[7] The work has generally been dated to the middle of the second decade of the sixteenth century.[8]   T. K.

Notes

1. The calendar of the Grimani Breviary (cat. no. 126) also features full-page miniatures without borders and was painted at roughly the same time.

2. Brinkmann 1997: figs. 1–10.

3. An exception to this is the vista from a precipice in *February* (fol. 2v).

4. Friedländer 1967–76, 6, pt. 1: pl. 24.

5. The second cycle of Evangelist miniatures illustrates their suffrages (fols. 121v–128v), which is separate from the larger cycle of suffrages (fols. 271v–340). The suffrages for the Evangelists immediately follow the Gospel lessons (fols. 111v–120v). The total number of suffrages illustrated by full-page miniatures is forty.

6. The book's owner probably had Franciscan connections, given the prominence in the suffrages of Franciscan saints, including Saint Francis, Saint Anthony of Padua, Saint Bernardino of Siena, and the Eleven Thousand Virgins, who are associated with Saint Ursula. All but Saint Anthony of Padua also figure in the calendar, and Saint Clare, another Franciscan, also appears there. The suffrages, moreover, feature the rare Saint Berard, who was important to the Franciscans, while the Hours of the Conception of the Virgin celebrates a Marian event particularly venerated by the Franciscans.

7. A distinctive feature of the calendar is that it resembles closely that in a book of hours made for a great German patron, Cardinal Albrecht of Brandenburg (private collection). John Plummer has identified a level of agreement between the two at 88 percent (report in Department of Manuscripts files, JPGM). A few saints associated with German-speaking areas or the north Netherlands are Erhard (January 8), Zoe (July 5) Affre (August 6), Zacchaei (August 23), Maternus (September 13), the Eleven Thousand Virgins (October 21), and Joachim (December 9), although none is a red-letter day. The Da Costa Hours has been described on occasion as of Strassburg use, but I find this notion unconvincing. It appears to be based on the book's purported relationship to an edition of the *Hortulus animae* printed in Strasbourg in 1498 (see Morgan Library files; the Strasbourg use has been cited by Randall [1997: 518]). Susan L'Engle has explored the relationship between the texts of the Da Costa Hours and the printed edition of the *Hortulus* and found it minimal and of no consequence (report in Department of Manuscripts files, JPGM).

8. Jethro Hurt was the first to identify the Sá arms. He apparently also dated the book to around 1517/18, according to Marrow (1984: 455).

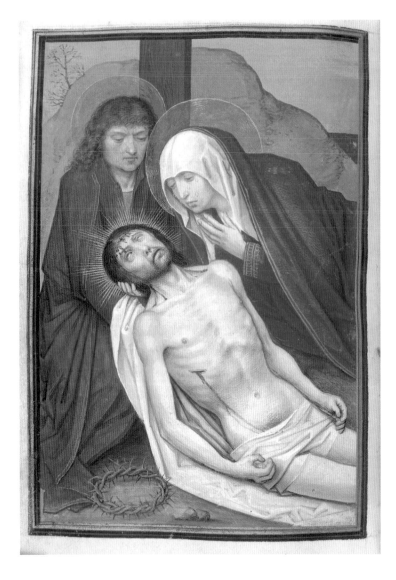

141

SIMON BENING AND WORKSHOP

Prayer Book of Joanna of Ghistelles
Ghent, probably ca. 1516

MANUSCRIPT: iii + 220 + iii folios, 15.3 × 10.8 cm (6 × 4¼ in.);
justification: 9.5 × 6.6 cm (3¾ × 2⁹⁄₁₆ in.); 16 lines of *textura*;
22 full-page miniatures

INSCRIPTIONS: *A B J Flament I.V.L. H[a]nno-Perwa[nu?]s 1803*, front
pastedown; *Sum Antᵒ Bernardo / Josepho Flament I.V.L. in / Peruwelz
Depart. Jemmap. / manenti*, back pastedown

BINDING: Ludovicus Bloc (d. 1529); blind-stamped leather over wood
boards; stamped *Ob lavdem xpristi librvm hvnc recte ligavi Ludovicus Bloc*

COLLECTION: London, The British Library, Egerton Ms. 2125

PROVENANCE: Joanna of Ghistelles, abbess of Messines (d. 1561);
probably Abbey of Messines (suppressed 1776); Antonius Bernardus
Flament, Peruwelz, Hainaut, by 1803; M. Deltil, Peruwelz; Carlo
Ferrario (1833–1907); purchased 1870

RA

Simon Bening and his workshop were responsible for all
twenty-two miniatures in this collection of prayers in
Latin, Dutch, and French that is accompanied by services
for the dead, the Penitential Psalms, suffrages, and other
devotions.[1] Internal evidence offers clues to the identity of
the book's original owner. The grading of the calendar suggests that it was made for a member of the Benedictine
order. A full-page miniature (fol. 206v) and a suffrage are
devoted to Saint Benedict, the founder of the order. Further, an entry in the calendar on January 8 commemorates
Adela, the founder of the Benedictine Abbey of Messines
(Mesen), and the widow of Baudouin, count of Flanders.
The book meanwhile also includes an office for Saint
Godeleva of Ghistelles, who was the special protector of
the Ghistelles family. A section containing devotions written in French that was likely added very soon after the
book's completion (fols. 218–221v)[2] indicates that the book
was then in use at the Abbey of Messines, which is near
Ypres. These devotions include instructions for the abbess.
Taken together, this diverse evidence suggests that the
book was created for Joanna of Ghistelles, a member of an
old Flemish noble family, who in 1516, at the age of seventeen, was elevated to the office of abbess. It was likely a
present to her, and she probably ordered the additional
devotions after receiving the book.

The volume is representative of Bening's more routine
work of the second decade of the sixteenth century, with
many miniatures based on the patterns that originated during the late 1470s and early 1480s, including the touching
Lamentation (ill. 141).[3] The suffrages—the largest single section of the book, with more than forty-five devotions—has
fourteen full-page miniatures, among which *Saint Adrian*
(fol. 200v), *Saint Benedict*, and *Saint Mary Magdalene* (fol.
215v) are particularly beautiful. The relatively broad brushwork, the figure proportions, and the handling of landscape, which emphasizes the foreground, recall features of
the Da Costa Hours (cat. no. 140), Bening's most ambitious
early work.[4] It was most likely commissioned around the
time that Joanna of Ghistelles took charge of the abbey
in 1516.[5]

T. K.

Notes

1. A number of the prayers in Latin are rhymed (fols. 147–150v,
158–159v). A devotion on the Last Supper is in Dutch (fols. 143–143v).

2. These pages appear to be written by a different hand from the
rest of the book, and their decorated initials were not executed.

3. The earliest version of this composition may be that inserted
belatedly in the Bourbon-Montpensier Hours (cat. no. 44, fol. 146v).

4. The book's exquisite original binding by the Bruges craftsman
Ludovicus Bloc ensures that it was executed no later than 1529, the
date of Bloc's death.

5. Testa (1986: 47) dated the book to the late 1520s on the basis of
similarities to the Brandenburg Prayer Book (cat. no. 145).

141
SIMON BENING
The Lamentation,
fol. 154v

142

ATTRIBUTED TO SIMON BENING

The Virgin and Child
Bruges, ca. 1520–25

Oil on oak panel; painted surface: 24.4 × 21 cm (9⅝ × 8¼ in.); panel: 25.4 × 21.5 cm (10 × 8½ in.), with added strip of 1 cm (⅜ in.) at top

COLLECTION: New York, The Metropolitan Museum of Art, The Friedsam Collection, Bequest of Michael Friedsam, 1931, 32.100.53

PROVENANCE: Claramonte family, counts of La Bisbal, Madrid; R. Traumann, Madrid, until 1914; [Agnew, London, 1914–16]; [Duveen, New York, 1916–18]; Michael Friedsam, New York, 1918–31; his bequest, 1931

JPGM

142
ATTRIBUTED TO
SIMON BENING
The Virgin and Child

Figure 72
GERARD DAVID
The Rest on the Flight into Egypt, ca. 1510–15. Oil on oak, 50.8 × 43.2 cm (20 × 17 in.). The Metropolitan Museum of Art, The Jules Bache Collection, 1949 (49.7.21)

The Bruges historian Denis Harduyn indicated in the sixteenth century that Simon Bening was active as a panel painter, yet this aspect of his production is little known today.[1] *The Virgin and Child*, however, supports Harduyn's contention. It is derived from the full-length figures in Gerard David's *Rest on the Flight into Egypt* (fig. 72) of about 1510–15. In a shift from the context and meaning of David's example, the painting presents the model of a

nurturing mother rather than an episode from a biblical narrative. The artist has omitted the customary fillet and veil adorning the Virgin's head; the figures of Joseph, Mary, and the Christ child en route in the background; and all other references to the theme of the Rest on the Flight into Egypt. Instead, a mother tenderly holds her child, nursing him, as he grasps a spoon in his right hand and, temporarily distracted, turns toward the viewer. The two sit on a stone ledge covered with mint and violet plants, before a bucolic landscape with a meandering river and cottage.

For some time this painting has been recognized as the work of a close follower of Gerard David. Certain aspects of it differ from David's characteristic late manner: the rounder, fuller face of the Virgin and the stylized facial features (crescent-shaped slits for eyes; a prominent ovoid chin; thin, short eyebrows), the denser buildup of paint for the flesh tones, the lack of chiaroscuro treatment for the modeling of the face, the formulaic brushwork in the golden highlights of the hair, and the more generalized treatment of the hands. Different pigments are substituted for David's customary combinations of ultramarine and azurite in the Virgin's robe and cloak, lending this Virgin's robe a more purplish brown hue. Moreover, the arrangement of the landscape features is untypical of David but highly representative of that found in the works of his close follower Simon Bening, the great innovator of landscape portrayal in Flemish miniatures of the early sixteenth century.

Typical of Bening's early landscapes is the patternlike treatment of the foreground plants and a leap to distant views of mountains, trees, and rivers. The *Saint Bartholomew* miniature in a book of hours from the second decade of the sixteenth century (Kassel, Landesbibliothek, Ms. math. et art. 50, fol. 3) shows gray, rocky masses closing off the composition at the left, a small house or castle nestled in the trees near a meandering river in the middle distance at the right, and beyond, a pale blue distant horizon of rolling hills or mountain peaks, as in *The Virgin and Child*. The *Saint Jerome* painted on parchment mounted on panel in the Musée du Louvre, Paris, is filled with such naturalistic anecdotal details, and like the present painting, features Bening's lush, full trees grouped together with three equidistant trunks and discrete round clusters of leafy branches evenly dotted with highlights. Another type of tree with spiky branches pointing toward the sky is likewise found both in the present panel and in the *Saint Jerome* miniature. One need only consult Bening's calendar cycles to discover charming genre motifs—such as the tiny figures by a country house occupied with their daily chores in the *June* miniature of the Da Costa Hours (cat. no. 140, fol. 7v)—that likewise appear in *The Virgin and Child*.

Bening was greatly influenced by David, and a number of Bening's miniatures from his mature phase (notably from about 1515 on and especially after 1519, when he permanently settled in Bruges) show this debt to David's works.[2] This is especially true of Bening's figure types, in particular of the Virgin and Child. Closely comparable to the treatment of the Virgin and Child in the present painting are, among others, a single mounted leaf in the Museum voor Schone Kunsten, Ghent, and the central panel of the triptych on parchment *The Virgin and Child with Saints Catherine and Barbara* (see fig. 9), both illuminations of the 1520s and 1530s. During this time and into the 1540s Bening increasingly made independent miniatures on parchment, both portraits and devotional subjects (cat. nos. 149, 157, 158), that were mounted on wood and functioned as panel paintings.[3] This intermediate stage between illumination and panel painting may well have led to his practice in the latter art.

The provenance of *The Virgin and Child* includes Spain, where Simon Bening had many patrons, not the least of whom was Mencía de Mendoza. A work such as this—with figures in the style of Bruges's leading panel painter, Gerard David, and a landscape of the type that Bening made famous in illuminated books—would have greatly appealed to Spanish clients.   M. W. A.

Notes

1. Sanderus 1725, 2: 175; Van Arenbergh 1880–83: cols. 714–17; Ainsworth 2002: 1–2.

2. For further discussion of this issue, see Ainsworth 2002: 1–25.

3. See Thomas Kren and Maryan W. Ainsworth, "Illuminators and Painters: Artistic Exchanges and Interrelationships" (this volume).

143

SIMON BENING

Arundel Hours
Bruges, probably late 1520s

MANUSCRIPT: vi + 85 + vi folios, 13.9 × 10 cm (5⁷⁄₁₆ × 3¹¹⁄₁₆ in.); justification: 10.6 × 7 cm (4¹⁄₁₆ × 2¼ in.); 15 lines of *gotica rotunda*; 8 full-page miniatures, 3 historiated borders

INSCRIPTIONS: *D. Fellippa de Norae*, fol. i

BINDING: England, eighteenth century (?); mottled brown morocco

COLLECTION: Arundel Castle, duke of Norfolk

PROVENANCE: Cardinal Philip of Norfolk (1629–1694); Henry Fitzalan-Howard, fifteenth duke of Norfolk (1847–1917); by descent to the current duke of Norfolk

R A

This manuscript is an incomplete book of hours that is missing nearly all of its devotions. All that remains is the Hours of the Virgin, the book's core text, and the Advent Office of the Virgin. The former is illustrated with a cycle of full-page miniatures of the life of the Virgin, commencing with *The Annunciation* (ill. 143). An unusual subject in this cycle is *Christ Child Teaching in the Temple* at the hour of sext (fol. 49v).[1] Although not an example of Simon Bening's art at its very best, the work features his characteristic figure types, composition, and color. Nearly all of the miniatures are based on fifteenth-century patterns, including the work of not only the Vienna Master of Mary of Burgundy (e.g., fol. 23) but also Martin Schongauer. One of the more distinctive miniatures, *The Rest on the Flight into Egypt* (fol. 55v), features a Virgin and Child in three-quarter

143
SIMON BENING
The Annunciation, fol. 1v

length that is based on a painting by Gerard David, while the background of the miniature is derived from a print by Schongauer.[2]

On the basis of the dimensions and stylistic similarities, Judith Testa has plausibly argued that four full-page miniatures of the Evangelists now in the Brooklyn Museum originally belonged to this book.[3] Yet, since the Arundel volume lacks even the Gospel extracts that these subjects would customarily illustrate, her hypothesis is difficult to prove. The Brooklyn leaves are dated 1521, and the Arundel Hours may have been illuminated in the 1520s, although quite possibly later in the decade. In certain historiated borders (for example, fols. 23, 56), the brushwork is a bit more broken up and "flecklike," in keeping with a stylistic development that was under way closer to 1530 (see cat. no. 148).

The book's script, with its distinctive display capitals in the incipit lines, is related to the script in Bening's Munich-Montserrat Hours (cat. no. 154) and in a book of hours by the Master of James IV of Scotland and his workshop (cat. no. 128).   T. K.

Notes

1. Testa (1994: 419) noted that the subject is out of sequence, coming before *The Rest on the Flight into Egypt* at none. Yet the error must have been made at the time of the book's production because *The Rest on the Flight* belongs at none. Its historiated border shows the related episode of the Flight into Egypt.

2. David's *Virgin and Child in a Landscape* (Rotterdam, Museum Boijmans Van Beuningen), see Testa 1994: 421.

3. Testa 1994: 424–26.

144

SIMON BENING

Leaves from a Rosary Psalter
Bruges, 1520s

The Presentation in the Temple
One leaf, 10 × 8 cm (3¹⁵/₁₆ × 3⅛ in.), 1 full-page miniature; justification: 8.7 × 5.8 cm (3⁷/₁₆ × 2¼ in.); verso: 16 lines of *gotica rotunda, O Virgen ta[n] ensalçada q[ue] te viste virge[n] y madre . . .*

The Ascension
One leaf, 10 × 8 cm (3¹⁵/₁₆ × 3⅛ in.), 1 full-page miniature; justification: 8.7 × 5.8 cm (3⁷/₁₆ × 2¼ in.); verso: 16 lines of *gotica rotunda, O Reyna y señora mia madre de dios q[ue] la grandeza de tus dolores . . .*

COLLECTION: Cambridge, Fitzwilliam Museum, Ms. 257a, 257b

PROVENANCE: Henry Yates Thompson (1838–1928); his gift, 1895

R A

Marian devotion and the use of the rosary were prominent aspects of Catholic spirituality in sixteenth-century Spain. The Fitzwilliam Museum's *Presentation in the Temple* and *The Ascension*, each with text on the reverse, belonged to a rosary psalter, a collection of fifteen short devotions organized around each of the Fifteen Mysteries of the Virgin. Both illuminations have a complete prayer in Spanish on the reverse, evidence that the cycle itself was created for a Spanish patron.[1] Each prayer is followed by indications for reciting one Paternoster and ten Ave Marias.[2] The original psalter had sixteen leaves, each with a miniature. (The sixteenth miniature, representing the empty cross, lacks a devotional text on the reverse but is inscribed SPALTERIUM CRUCIS.) Twelve, including *The Empty Cross*, are in the Boston Public Library and two, *The Agony in the Garden* and *The Crucifixion*, are untraced.[3] All

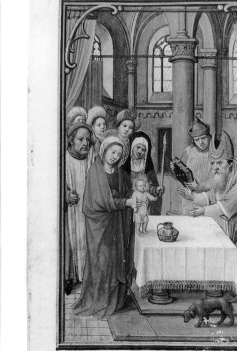

144a
SIMON BENING
The Ascension

144b
SIMON BENING
The Presentation in the Temple

the surviving miniatures from this rosary psalter are finely painted works by Simon Bening, probably belonging to the 1520s, the period of such related works as the Brandenburg Prayer Book (cat. no. 145). The original volume must have been very thin, even thinner than Bening's later rosarium in Dublin (cat. no. 156), a collection of Marian devotions that was likewise produced for a Spanish-speaking patron.[4]

Another rosary psalter in Spanish, with the same devotions for the most part and similar iconography, was produced by Bening's workshop in 1545 for a member of the noble Acuña family (private collection).[5]　　　T. K.

Notes

1. All but two of the fourteen surviving miniatures from this book have on the reverse a complete prayer in Latin or Spanish.

2. The prayers were sixteen to eighteen lines long. Kupfer-Tarasulo (1979b: 222) gives an excellent account of the book.

3. See Kupfer-Tarasulo 1979b: 212–13.

4. The National Gallery, Washington, D.C., owns a miniature of the Resurrection by Simon Bening that is comparable in size to the Boston/Cambridge cycle and also has eighteen lines of text in Spanish on the back. The text is difficult to read today, but perhaps the leaf is derived from another rosary psalter of the type under discussion here, since this subject is already represented among the Boston Public Library leaves (Washington 1975: 190–91, no. 49).

5. König 1991: 530–45; Sotheby's, London, July 6, 2000, lot 57.

145

SIMON BENING

Prayer Book of Cardinal Albrecht of Brandenburg

Bruges, ca. 1525–30

MANUSCRIPT: iii + 337 + iii folios, 16.8 × 11.5 cm (6⅝ × 4½ in.); justification: 10.1 × 6.3 cm (4 × 2½ in.); 19 lines of *gotica rotunda*; 41 full-page miniatures, 35 historiated borders, 1 full-page coat of arms

HERALDRY: Full-page escutcheon with the arms of Cardinal Albrecht of Brandenburg surmounted by cardinal's hat and cross, with bishop's crosier and sword crossed behind escutcheon, fol. 1v

INSCRIPTIONS: Monogram *SB* in border, fol. 336

BINDING: Netherlands(?), nineteenth century; red velvet over wood boards; early-sixteenth-century chased silver-gilt mounts and clasps, possibly original

COLLECTION: Los Angeles, J. Paul Getty Museum, Ms. Ludwig IX 19 (83.ML.115)

PROVENANCE: Cardinal Albrecht of Brandenburg (1490–1545); presumably acquired by Elector Lothar Franz von Schönborn (1655–1729), founder of the Schönborn'sche Bibliothek, Schloss Gaibach, Pommersfelden; Anselm Solomon von Rothschild (1803–1874), Vienna, by 1869; Martin Bodmer (1899–1971); [H. P. Kraus, New York, in 1956]; to Peter and Irene Ludwig, Aachen, 1960; acquired 1983

JPGM and RA

The Prayer Book of Albrecht of Brandenburg is universally recognized as one of Simon Bening's masterpieces.[1] Belonging to an era when Passion subject matter was a preoccupation of northern European artists, this work offers one of the most moving and compassionate depictions of Christ's suffering and death. Its text consists of a series of meditations on the life of Christ and his Passion arranged roughly in sequence. While illuminated devotional books usually contain short cycles of narrative images, the Brandenburg Prayer Book was conceived with a nearly continuous cycle of forty-two miniatures.[2] At this length it may be unprecedented in Flemish illumination up to this time.[3] The program is derived in part from the text, a series of meditations on the life and Passion of Christ in German that was copied from an illustrated prayer book first printed in Augsburg in 1521.[4] The printed book was illustrated with a cycle of thirty-five woodcuts designed by the Petrarca Master, a follower of Albrecht Dürer. The choice of subjects in the Brandenburg Prayer Book largely follows that of the Augsburg publication. The Christological narrative begins with *The Annunciation* (fol. 13v) and concludes with *The Entombment* (ill. 145a), with images outside the story, *The Creation of Eve* (fol. 7v) and *The Adoration of the Five Wounds of Christ* (fol. 335v), as bookends.[5] A few iconic images—including *The Man of Sorrows* (fol. 202v), *The Worship of the Inscribed Tablet from the Cross* (fol. 235v), and *The Seven Sorrows of the Virgin* (fol. 251v)—interrupt the flow of the Passion tale. Thirty-three of the borders opposite the full-page miniatures are historiated with complementary biblical scenes, some related typologically. Two others have extrabiblical subjects.

Despite the subject matter shared between printed book and manuscript, Bening did not use the Petrarca Master's illustrations as models. Instead he drew heavily on the body of Flemish patterns at his disposal and from German printmakers such as Dürer and Martin Schongauer.[6] But he adapted each miniature, visually and psychologically, so that the series works together dramatically. Above all, he deepened and enriched the characterization of Christ with each new incident in the story. For example, *The Entombment* (ill. 145a) is a reasonably faithful copy of Schongauer's masterful engraving of this subject. Yet through the use of color and the manipulation of light, and by introducing framing arches, Bening draws the viewer closer to the fragile beauty and humanity of Christ. His images convey Christ's joy and humility, anger and surprise, physical pain and exhaustion. Bening further enhanced this emotional expressiveness by means of haunting nocturnal settings, both interior and exterior, many lit only by torchlight. *The Denial of Saint Peter* (ill. 145b) is especially touching in this respect, the light from the courtyard fire revealing Peter's face as he denies Christ for a third time. In its intense drama, powerful atmosphere, and accumulation of incident, the pictorial storytelling in the Brandenburg Prayer Book assumes an epic quality.

The place of the manuscript in the holdings of Cardinal Albrecht of Brandenburg, archbishop and elector of Mainz, is an intriguing one. A few years earlier he had acquired an even more lavish devotional work from Bening, a large book of hours that the illuminator executed with his workshop.[7] His acquaintance with Bening's art may have stemmed from his contacts with such individuals as Melchior Pfinzing, provost of Saint Alban's at Mainz and secretary to Maximilian I, who previously had acquired an elaborate book of hours by Bening.[8] Brandenburg was a voracious collector of art and relics and a patron of Dürer, Lucas Cranach, Matthias Grünewald, and the Nuremberg

sculptor Peter Vischer. He endowed the collegiate church of Saints Maurice and Mary Magdalene at the Moritzburg, Halle, where he kept his religious art and relics.

Cardinal Albrecht's esteem for Bening is further evidenced by the work of a group of German artists at his court who copied and imitated Bening's miniatures, including those from the Brandenburg Prayer Book. One of these artists was the German illuminator Nikolaus Glockendon, a favorite of Brandenburg. In 1534, the year of his death, Glockendon copied in a prayer book most of the manuscript's miniatures, generally closely, and adapted many of the historiated borders, the latter often in reverse (Modena, Biblioteca Estense, Ms. α.U.6.7).[9] Nikolaus's son, Gabriel Glockendon, also used the Bening prayer book as a source for a Passion prayer book of 1537 (Vienna, Österreichische Nationalbibliothek, Ms. 1847).[10] The Brandenburg Prayer Book shows the high esteem for Flemish manuscripts in Europe in the sixteenth century and the powerful influence Flemish manuscript illumination exercised on illuminators outside Flanders. Like many great works of art, it cast a spell even in the artist's own day.

Since the charges on Brandenburg's armorials (shown in folio 1v) changed in 1530, the book must date before then; the second half of the 1520s is generally accepted.[11]   T. K.

145a
SIMON BENING
The Entombment,
fol. 328v

145b
SIMON BENING
The Denial of Saint Peter,
fol. 123v

Notes

1. The apparent monogram on fol. 336, *SB,* also makes it the artist's only signed work.

2. One of the original forty-two, *The Massacre of the Innocents,* is missing today from before folio 51.

3. The Stein Quadriptych (cat. no. 146) is a bit later in date, perhaps an immediate consequence of Bening's success with this cycle.

4. *Gebet und betrachtungen des Lebens des mitlers gottes und des mentschen unsers herrens Jesu Christi,* published by Sigmund Grimm and Marx Wyrsung. See Steinmann 1964: 139ff.

5. This cycle contains some of the most beautiful of Bening's renderings of particular subjects, including *The Annunciation, Christ Led from the Garden of Eden* (fol. 107v), *Christ before Annas* (fol. 119v), *The Denial of Saint Peter* (fol. 123v), *Christ before Pilate* (fol. 128v), *Pilate Washing His Hands* (fol. 173v), and a nocturnal *Crucifixion* (fol. 178v).

6. See especially Biermann 1975: 77–86, 101–2; Plotzek, in Euw and Plotzek 1979–85, 2: 302–11.

7. Sotheby's, London, June 19, 2001, lot 36; see 68–70 for bibliography.

8. Pfinzing was also provost of the Sebalduskirche in Nuremberg. The manuscript is Stockholm, Kungliga Biblioteket, Ms. A 227, and Kassel, Landesbibliothek, Ms. math. et art. 50; see Testa 1992b. Christina Nielsen contributed research on Brandenburg as a patron.

9. Biermann 1975: 198–204; Modena 1997.

10. Biermann 1975: 205–9.

11. Plotzek, in Euw and Plotzek 1979–85, 3: 286; Testa 1986: 46; Kren, in Kren and Rathofer 1988: 220.

146

SIMON BENING AND WORKSHOP

Stein Quadriptych
Bruges, probably late 1520s or later

Parchment mounted on paper affixed to four wood boards, with four modern gilt molded frames, 35.5 × 29 cm (14 × 11⁷⁄₁₆ in.); 64 miniatures, each 6.8 × 5.2 cm (2¹¹⁄₁₆ × 2¹⁄₁₆ in.)

COLLECTION: Baltimore, Walters Art Museum, W.442

PROVENANCE: Charles Stein, Paris [his sale, Galerie Georges Petit, Paris, May 10, 1886, lot 241]; to Bourgeois; in Spain(?) after 1888; purchased by Henry Walters (1848–1931) between 1895 and ca. 1911

JPGM

The Stein Quadriptych features sixty-four miniatures that tell the story of the lives of the Virgin and Christ from Joachim and Anne at the Golden Gate to the Last Judgment. The individual miniatures, at 6.8 by 5.2 centimeters (2¹¹⁄₁₆ × 2¹⁄₁₆ in.), are not Bening's smallest, but they are modest in size.[1] They are currently organized in four panels of sixteen miniatures and have been so arranged since they were first uncovered in the late nineteenth century. Inevitably, given the unusual format of the piece, especially for a manuscript illuminator, scholars have wondered whether this series was originally conceived as an altarpiece or for a book.[2] It is difficult to be sure, but it seems very likely that the epic cycle of miniatures was intended to be shown in something like its present form. Michelle Brown has discovered a fourteenth-century cycle from Dalmatia, also in tempera on parchment but with fewer images, which was mounted in a manner similar to the arrangement of the quadriptych.[3] Furthermore a number of Flemish altarpieces in oil on panel featuring several dozen scenes from the life of Christ were made before this time. One such work, thought to have originated in Bruges, features a central panel with sixteen miniatures, and on its wings four more miniatures each. It tells the story of the lives of Christ and the Virgin from the Annunciation to the Death of the Virgin semicontinuously, with, in the central panel, two parallel and overlapping sequences of Passion scenes.[4] Bening's quadriptych is still more elaborate and may represent an ambitious variation on this format.[5]

Bening's interest in creating devotional art wholly independent of text, evidenced by the handful of triptychs illuminated by him and/or his workshop, may have impelled him to consider presenting an elaborate cycle of single-leaf miniatures in this way. Moreover, it may also be the case that, having succeeded powerfully in the Brandenburg Prayer Book (cat. no. 145) with a cycle of forty-two miniatures of the life of Christ presented in a relatively continuous narrative, Bening saw the longer cycle of the Stein Quadriptych as a next step. In the altarpiece he undertook

146 (above and opposite)
SIMON BENING
AND WORKSHOP
Scenes from the life of
Christ and the Virgin

an even more continuous narrative, integrating iconic images into the flow of the story. In addition, by shifting to the close-up, he strengthened the focus on suffering and emotion that was so effective in the prayer book.

Ultimately, in the quadriptych Bening devised one of his most original artistic conceptions. Not only did he exploit the close-up for dramatic effect, but he also heightened the immediacy of the story by knitting together successive narrative moments visually, sparking the sensation of minute-by-minute storytelling. Certain subjects traditionally treated in a single image—such the Agony in the Garden, the Road to Calvary, and Christ on the Cross—are each narrated in a series of closely interrelated miniatures, evoking a sense of the moment and drawing the viewer closer to the event. For example, the sequence from the Deposition to the Entombment is told in four consecutive miniatures, but through the subtly altered placements of Christ's body, these miniatures suggest the continuous motion of his corpse from the cross to the grave.[6] The close-up had been used extensively in manuscript illumination for several generations, but rarely so systematically, so tightly focused, and without the many compositional linkages between individual miniatures that Bening introduced here.[7]

For all of the work's quality of invention, however, some of the miniatures do not measure up to Bening's best and were painted either in haste or with the help of assistants.[8] The awkward *Nativity* is an example. Even in the earliest known devotional miniatures of comparable size, such as those of the Imhof Prayer Book (cat. no. 139), Bening painted with greater refinement than in some of the images in the Stein cycle.[9] The occasional awkwardness is perhaps a result of the density of figures demanded by the close-up format and limited dimensions. These weaknesses, however, do not impair significantly the work's overall impact and novelty. Indeed, even if one holds to the view that they were never intended to form an altarpiece, the miniatures show Bening refreshing the art of devotional narrative.

Most scholars assign this work to the 1520s, although the unusual extreme close-up format makes it difficult to date precisely.[10] If my hypothesis that the work grew out of the Brandenburg Prayer Book is correct, a date in the late 1520s (or even somewhat later) may be possible. Marcia Kupfer-Tarasulo argued that the work may have been made for Cardinal Albrecht of Brandenburg on the basis of its various links to German artistic traditions.[11]   T. K.

Notes

1. See the entry on the book of hours in the Morgan Library (cat. no. 148), note 1.

2. Winkler (1925: 140; 1962: 12) thought that they were derived from a book of hours. Kupfer-Tarasulo (1979a: 275–80) summarized the various arguments for and against the quadriptych format. See also Catherine Reynolds, "Illuminators and the Painters' Guilds" (this volume). It is unlikely that finely painted small sheets of parchment were ever intended to be loose; they would have been too fragile to survive under such conditions.

3. London, British Library. Thanks to Michelle Brown for allowing me to cite her discovery, which she will publish soon.

4. Recently on the art market; see Bruges 1994: 233–36, no. 90, as "Bruges, early sixteenth century." The wings each have a continuous narrative from the beginning and the end of the story; see also the multiple scenes in the single-panel altarpiece with the *Fifteen Mysteries and the Virgin of the Rosary* attributed to Goswijn van der Weyden (New York 1998: 347–49). The four scenes from the Passion by a follower of Bernard van Orley in the Metropolitan Museum of Art, New York, may have originally contained more scenes (New York 1998: 344–46).

5. In the current arrangement in the quadriptych, a number of miniatures are out of sequence—including *Christ's Farewell Address to the Disciples, Christ in the River Cedron, Noli me tangere,* and *Christ's Appearance before the Virgin*—perhaps the result of a modern remounting (Kupfer-Tarasulo 1979a: 281–84). It should be noted, however, that in the painted altarpiece of twenty-four scenes mentioned above, where all the scenes are in their original positions, some are out of sequence (Smeyers 1997c: 190–94). Their arrangement remains to be properly explained. See also Kupfer-Tarasulo 1979a: 274–98.

6. The Boston rosary psalter (see cat. no. 144) is often compared with the Stein Quadriptych, but the two works differ in a number of respects. The former originally had only sixteen miniatures, its scenes are full-length, and they have text on the reverse (see Kupfer-Tarasulo 1979b: 209–26). Moreover, the compositions are not, as in the Stein Quadriptych, visually integrated.

7. Kupfer-Tarasulo 1979a: 280, 296–98.

8. Some scholars have accepted the series as entirely by Bening himself (Kupfer-Tarasulo 1979a: 275; Testa 1986: 56), but Winkler (1925: 197) called it "wohl typisches Werkstatterzeugnis." Randall (1997: 539, 547) ascribed the work to "Simon Bening and one or more associates"; see also Kren, in Bruges 1998: 101, no. 70.

9. Dated 1511, the large miniatures in the Imhof Prayer Book, all full-length compositions, are on leaves measuring 9 by 6.8 centimeters ($3^{9}/_{16} \times 2^{11}/_{16}$ in.).

10. Biermann 1975: 103–4, as ca. 1525; Kupfer-Tarasulo 1997a: 275, as ca. 1525; Kren, in Kren and Rathofer 1988: 218–19, as ca. 1525–30; Randall 1997: 539, 547, as ca. 1525–30.

11. Kupfer-Tarasulo 1979a: 293–95; see also Randall 1997: 546–47.

147a (opposite)
SIMON BENING
AND ANTÓNIO DE
HOLANDA
*Genealogical Tree of the
Kings of Aragon,* fol. 4

147

SIMON BENING AND ANTÓNIO DE HOLANDA

Leaves from the Genealogy of the Royal Houses of Spain and Portugal
Lisbon and Bruges, ca. 1530–34

Genealogical Tree of Magog, fol. 2
Genealogical Tree of the Kings of Aragon, fol. 4
Genealogical Tree of the Kings of Aragon, fol. 5
Genealogical Tree of the Kings of Aragon, fol. 5*
Genealogical Tree of John, Duke of Lancaster, fol. 10
Genealogical Tree of the Kings of England and Castile, fol. 11

Six detached leaves, each 58 × 43 cm (23 × 17 in.); 4 large miniatures, 1 large miniature drawn but not painted, 5 historiated borders

COLLECTION: London, The British Library, Add. Ms. 12531

PROVENANCE: Commissioned by the Infante Dom Fernando of Portugal (1507–1534), but unfinished at his death; to his widow, Dona Infanta Guimar Coutinho, countess of Marialva and Loulé; probably to her mother Dona Brites de Meneses; probably to Infante Dom Luis, brother of Dom Fernando; eleven leaves (fols. 1–11) acquired in Lisbon by Newton Scott (or Smith?) in 1842; subsequently sold to the British Museum; two leaves (fols. 5*, 9*), Baron Hortega, Madrid; to the British Museum in 1868

JPGM: Fols. 4, 5, 5*, 11; RA: Fols. 2, 4, 5, 5*, 10, 11

This extraordinarily large and politically weighted royal genealogy attests to the tremendous prestige enjoyed by Flemish illumination at the European courts in the first half of the sixteenth century. The close intermarriage of the Portuguese crown with the family of the Hapsburg emperor—King John III of Portugal married the emperor Charles V's sister Catherine, while Charles married John's sister Isabella, both in 1524—underscores Portuguese dynastic ambitions. The Portuguese claim to the entire peninsula is generously supported in the volume.[1] Although the book was never completed, its creation is unusually well documented. Damião de Góis (1501–1573)—a diplomat and humanist and the secretary to Indiahouse, the Portuguese trade mission in Antwerp, from 1523—related the complex circumstances behind the conception and execution of the genealogy.[2] He stated that during his Antwerp sojourn in the service of King John III, the king's brother Dom Fernando

> ordered me to find whatever chronicles I could, either manuscript or printed, in whatever language, so I ordered them all. And to compose a chronicle of the kings of Hispanha since the time of Noah and thereafter, I paid a great deal to learned men: salaries, pensions, and other favors. I ordered a drawing of the tree and trunk of this line since the time of Noah to King Manuel I, his father. [Dom Fernando] ordered it illuminated for himself by the principal master of this art in all of Europe, by name of Simon of Bruges in Flanders. For this tree and other things I spent a great deal of money.[3]

The drawings were supplied by António de Holanda,[4] as indicated by the notations of his son Francesco, the artist and humanist, in the latter's copy of Vasari.[5] The project was under way in 1530 because Góis wrote to Dom Fernando on August 15 of that year with a progress report, informing him that the aforementioned Simon of Bruges,

147b

SIMON BENING
AND ANTÓNIO DE
HOLANDA
*Genealogical Tree of the
Kings of Aragon*, fol. 5

who was certainly Simon Bening, was disappointed because only a single drawing had arrived.[6] Bening expected the project to take up to two years, and he had finished all other projects so that he could concentrate on this one. He had hoped to receive as many as four drawings by then.[7] In 1539, five years after the project was interrupted by the death of Dom Fernando, António still had not been paid for his work. Ultimately Bening had illuminated only five leaves of the surviving thirteen (ills. 147a–c, fols. 2, 10). Holanda colored another seven of his drawings (fols. 1, 3, 6, 7, 8, 9, 9★), while the illumination of one of the drawings was never begun (ill. 147d).

Simon Bening illuminated the border of the first surviving leaf to feature the actual ancestral tree (fol. 2).[8] It shows the tree of Magog with the legendary ancestors of the kings of Hungary. Góis tells us that the book begins with the time of Noah; Magog was Noah's grandson. Bening also illuminated the three leaves representing the entwined lines of Navarre and Aragon (ills. 147a–c), and the first of the two tables illustrating the line of John of Gaunt, duke of Lancaster (d. 1399; fol. 10). The latter's descendants included rulers of Burgundy, Germany, Portugal, and Castile. Among those depicted at the far right are Charles the Bold and Maximilian I. António de Holanda illuminated the prologue, the trees for the rulers of Leon and Castile, and those of the monarchs of Portugal. It is clear that some of the trees are lacking, such as those for the Hungarian line, for the ancestors of Manuel I, and for the ancestors of Dom Fernando through his mother's line. They were perhaps never completed or were simply lost over the years.[9] Martim de Albuquerque and João Paolo de Abreu e Lima have argued that the conventional sequence followed by most scholars over the years is incorrect and that the tree of Count Dom Henrique (fol. 6), now seventh in the sequence, belongs earlier, to the lines connected to the kings of Hungary.[10]

The second of the tables linked to John of Gaunt, showing the tree of the kings of England and Castile (ill. 147d), is one that was drawn but never illuminated. This exquisite drawing, partially damaged by water, demonstrates Holanda's considerable gifts as a draftsman, which surpassed his abilities as an illuminator. The figures are modeled in short, closely placed parallel strokes and crosshatchings. The refined technique gives the materials a velvety quality and provided Bening with a crisp, fully elaborated design to paint. This drawing suggests that Bening followed Holanda's other designs closely, as indicated by the similar poses and figural arrangements of the five leaves he completed, but Bening left his mark on them nevertheless, in the liveliness of expression and in the treatment of light and shadow, the flesh tones, the facial types, and the costly brocades.   T.K.

Notes

1. The present genealogy is not without precedent. The Flemish tapestry artist Pieter Coecke van Aelst provided designs for a tapestry of the genealogy of the Portuguese kings in 1511. Campbell 2002: 139.

2. Góis 1566, 2: 65

3. Góis 1566, 2: 65. Barbara Anderson kindly provided the translation of this passage.

4. Holanda (ca. 1480–1557) was born in the Netherlands and arrived in Portugal in about 1500. He quickly entered the royal service, participating in the workshop of the royal archives, illuminating the *Leitura nova* (Lisbon, Arquivo Nacional) and various chronicles. He enjoyed commissions from the crown throughout his career, including a book of hours for King Manuel I (perhaps Lisbon, Museu Nacional de Arte Antiga, Ms. 14; Markl 1983), a breviary for Queen Eleanor, and, between 1541 and 1555, various projects for Queen Catherine. Also trained as a heraldist, he further served the court from 1517 as pursuivant at arms. See Deswarte, in DOA 1996, 14: 658, 659. In 1534 he signed another genealogy, more modest than the present one, that he illuminated for Dom Manuel Pereira, third count of Fiera (Lisbon, Biblioteca Nacional).

5. Albuquerque and Abreu e Lima 1984: 67.

6. Destrée 1923: 24–25, 89; see also Santos 1930: 26–27; Albuquerque and Abreu e Lima 1984: 71, where portions of the letter are quoted.

7. Destrée 1923: 24–25.

8. The two large columns set aside for its text were never written.

9. Malibu 1983a: 70; Albuquerque and Abreu e Lima 1984: 50, 60. The thirteen leaves now in the British Library entered the British Museum in two separate batches from distinct sources. The two leaves that came later (fols. 5*, 9*) had the upper portion of the leaves cut out so that the upper edges are now formed by the elaborate frames of the miniatures (ill. 147c). For discussion of the arrangement of the leaves and their content, see Figanière 1853: 271–76, Kaemmerer and Ströhl 1903, 1: 5–9; Aguiar 1962: chap. 4; Kren, in Malibu 1983a: 69–76; Albuquerque and Abreu e Lima 1984: 50–66.

10. Albuquerque and Abreu e Lima (1984: 52–55) also discuss the historiography of this matter.

147c
SIMON BENING
AND ANTÓNIO DE
HOLANDA
*Genealogical Tree of the
Kings of Aragon*, fol. 5*

147d
ANTÓNIO DE
HOLANDA
*Genealogical Tree of the
Kings of England and
Castile*, fol. 11

148

SIMON BENING

Book of Hours
Use of Rome
Bruges, 1531

MANUSCRIPT: 129 folios, 7.4 × 5.6 cm (2⅞ × 2³⁄₁₆ in.); justification: 4.8 × 3.3 cm (1⅞ × 1⁵⁄₁₆ in.); 20 lines of *gotica rotunda* by Antonius van Damme; 32 full-page miniatures, 12 calendar miniatures

INSCRIPTIONS: *Author ac scriptor hui[us] operis presentis nomen est ei antonius van damme morans in trahes brugis an[n]o 1531*, fols. 128v–129

BINDING: Eighteenth century; red velvet; black fleur-de-lis doublures, with cross and initials *J.H.S.*; silver filigree chemise in red morocco case, lettered *Horae-Bruges-1531*

COLLECTION: New York, The Morgan Library, Ms. M.451

PROVENANCE: John Strange [his sale, Sotheby's, London, March 16, 1801, lot 720]; to Cummings; marquess of Blandford [his sale, R. H. Evans, London, Thursday, June 24, 1819, lot 2822]; to Jarman; Philip Augustus Hanrott (?); William Beckford (1760–1844), Fonthill Abbey; D. Morgand (his inventory number 17610); Leboeuf de Montgermont (cat. 1914, VII, no. 37); [Edouard Rahir]; to J. P. Morgan (1837–1913), July 1911

JPGM and RA

S imon Bening's devotional subject matter appeared in works of every type and dimension, from freestanding altarpieces on parchment (cat. nos. 146, 157) to large breviaries (cat. no. 126) to tiny devotional manuscripts. This book of hours belongs to the last category, although, at a little under three inches tall, it is still far from the smallest book that he illuminated.[1] Despite the restricted format, the volume is embellished with several cycles of full-page miniatures, including scenes from the Life of the Virgin and eighteen depictions of saints in the suffrages. There is also a cycle of small miniatures in the calendar.

The quality of the book's best miniatures is superb and notable for masterful effects of color. They include *Saint*

148a
SIMON BENING
Saint Bernard Bearing Christ from the Cross, fol. 118

148b
SIMON BENING
Saint Mary Magdalene, fol. 125v

Bernard Bearing Christ from the Cross (ill. 148a), *Saint Mary Magdalene* (ill. 148b), *The Virgin and Child* (fol. 97v), *Saint Michael and the Demons* (fol. 103v), *Saint Catherine* (fol. 126v), *Saint Athanasius* (fol. 93v), and *Saint John the Evangelist* (fol. 107v). The miniatures are also important in Bening's artistic development as the earliest dated examples of the technique of brushwork characteristic of his last thirty years. Here he employs the flecklike dabs of paint, evident especially in the handling of landscape, that he came to use to great effect over the next two decades, in his calendar cycles (cat. nos. 150, 154, 159) and elsewhere (cat. no. 156). In such miniatures as *Saint Athanasius*—which shows the saint standing in a verdant, richly detailed riverside setting—or *The Penitent Saint Jerome* (fol. 115v), set before a colorful wooded area, the brushwork gives the whole a velvety texture and a more atmospheric character.

During the 1530s Bening showed a reliance on models from the Italian High Renaissance (e.g., cat. nos. 150, 154), known to him mostly through prints and other reproductions.[2] In the Morgan Hours this is evident in the frank nudity of Saint Mary Magdalene, who stands before the viewer in a gentle contrapposta, draped only in a diaphanous pink mantle, with her breasts exposed. Here the lush vegetation that covers the entrance to the cave helps to set off the figure's pale flesh in strong relief. Another example can be found in the depiction of Saint John the Baptist (fol. 106v), who moves toward us yet points over his shoulder in a Leonardesque gesture.

Liturgically the book has several Franciscan features. Its calendar agrees 93 percent with the strongly Franciscan calendar of the Hennessy Hours.[3] The calendar is a sparser version of the Franciscan calendars that appear in Flemish breviaries of the late fifteenth and early sixteenth centuries (cat. nos. 89, 91, 126).[4] The book also includes the uncommon Office of the Conception of the Virgin, which is connected to Franciscan use,[5] and in the litany three rare saints—Accursius, Adjutus, and Otto—who were among those sent by Saint Francis to Morocco to evangelize the Moors. They were canonized only in 1481. Perhaps the book was made for a member of the Franciscan Tertiaries, who counted kings, queens, and other ranking nobles among their number. Finally, the book is noteworthy for being signed by the Bruges scribe Antonius van Damme, a friend and collaborator of Bening for more than three decades.   T. K.

Notes

1. Even smaller is a book of hours sold recently in London (Christie's, July 9, 2001, lot 35; 5.9 × 4.2 cm [2⁵⁄₁₆ × 1⅝ in.]). Not much larger is another book of hours in the Morgan Library, M.307 (7.5 × 5.6 cm [2¹⁵⁄₁₆ × 2³⁄₁₆ in.]). The largest of Bening's triptychs, *The Penitent Saint Jerome* (fig. 15), is more than fifteen inches tall.

2. See also the entry for the Munich-Montserrat Hours (cat. no. 154) and Kren and Rathofer 1988: 302–4.

3. Data from the computer analysis provided by John Plummer (2002, Department of Manuscripts files, JPGM), to whom I also owe the analysis of the litany.

4. Another intriguing aspect of the relationship between the Morgan Hours and the Hennessy Hours is a shared background—that is, the design for landscape and architecture—in miniatures with different subjects (fols. 69v and 175v, respectively; Destrée 1923: 47). Further to this, an example of the same background design appears much earlier in Gerard David's *Virgin among Virgins* (cat. no. 107) and in a triptych by Bening and his workshop (fig. 9). Might the building and site be identifiable?

5. The Franciscans in particular observed the feast of the Conception of the Virgin (December 8).

149

SIMON BENING

Two Portraits
Bruges, probably 1531

Portrait of Henry III, Count of Nassau
Tempera on parchment mounted on oak panel, 8.4 × 5.5 cm (3⁵⁄₁₆ × 2⅛ in.)

INSCRIPTIONS: HE[N]RIC[US]. CO. NASSAVIAE. MAR. ZENETAE.

COLLECTION: Berlin, Staatliche Museen zu Berlin, Gemäldegalerie, cat. no. M.513

PROVENANCE: Willem, count of Nassau-Dillenberg (?), from 1531; presumably transferred from the Kunstkammer after 1838

JPGM

Portrait of Mencía de Mendoza
Tempera on parchment mounted on oak panel, 8.4 × 6 cm (3⁵⁄₁₆ × 2⅜ in.)

INSCRIPTIONS: MENCIA MENDOCA. MAR. ZENETAE.

COLLECTION: Berlin, Staatliche Museen zu Berlin, Gemäldegalerie, cat. no. M.514

PROVENANCE: Willem, count of Nassau-Dillenberg (?), from 1531; presumably transferred from the Kunstkammer after 1838

JPGM

These pendant illuminated portraits are identifiable by their inscriptions as depictions of Henry III, count of Nassau and marquess of Zenete (1483–1538), and his spouse, Mencía de Mendoza, marchioness of Zenete (1508–1554). Henry, chamberlain to Charles V and one of the most powerful figures in the Hapsburg empire, was the nephew of the great bibliophile and courtier Engelbert of Nassau. Henry owned a celebrated art collection that featured among its treasures Bosch's *Garden of Earthly Delights*

149a
SIMON BENING
Portrait of Henry III,
Count of Nassau

149b
SIMON BENING
Portrait of Mencía
de Mendoza

(Madrid, Museo del Prado). Mencía de Mendoza, who married Henry in 1524, was the wealthiest woman in Spain and herself a voracious collector. Among the Netherlandish artists in her employ were Jan Gossaert, Jan Vermeyen, Bernard van Orley, Maarten van Heemskerck, and Simon Bening. The inscribed portraits of Henry and Mencía on parchment, here attributed to Bening, are probably derived from two lost portraits in oil by Gossaert that are documented in copies and variants in oil.[1]

The Berlin miniature portrait of Henry appears to be closest to the copy that was in the Gotisches Haus, Wörlitz a century ago. It has a similar plain background and tight cropping.[2] It differs mainly in the detail of the sitter's embroidered white shirt in the painting. The same embroidered white shirt appears in other copies in the collection of Condé de Revilla Gigedo, Madrid, and in the Museu Nacional d'Art de Catalunya, Barcelona, so the illuminator may have made some alterations from Gossaert's model. Like Gossaert's portrait of Henry, his portrait of Mencía is lost, but his execution of the textures of the sitter's extraordinary costume—the velvet, satin, feathers, and pearls, here rendered meticulously in tempera—must have been a tour de force in the lustrous oil medium. The artist perhaps intended to portray her, so attired, as the Magdalene, an interpretation confirmed by the unguent jar she held in her hand. Two versions in oil survive that show different elements of costume that correspond to the miniature. The version in Chantilly, most recently attributed tentatively and unconvincingly to Joos van Cleve, shows similar sleeves, hands, and facial features, but a different bodice, hat, and jewelry.[3] The other, in an unknown location, resembles the Berlin portrait in the hat, jewelry, and cut of the bodice but omits the hands and introduces a brocade in the bodice.[4] Like the miniature, both of these paintings seem to be derived from a lost original by Gossaert.

Adolf Staring thought that the Berlin miniature reflected the second version in oil of the Mencía portrait (i.e., the one from the unknown location) most closely.[5] If that is correct, then Bening likely also altered certain features of the dress here, such as the velvet bodice. Among the versions that survive, only Bening's fully conveys the youth of Mencía, who was no older than twenty-two or twenty-three when Gossaert painted the original. (Gossaert must have also flattered her by showing her somewhat more finely proportioned than contemporary accounts indicate.) It seems likely that Gossaert's originals date to the last years of his life. Henry and Mencía arrived back in the north only in 1530, after six years in Spain, and Gossaert died two years later, in the early autumn of 1532. He must have executed the original portraits in the interval.

Previously catalogued as either by Van Orley or an anonymous Netherlandish artist,[6] the two miniature portraits may confidently be ascribed to Simon Bening. Characteristics of this illuminator's art found in the pair are the distinctive brushwork seen in Henry's beard and Mencía's hair, the fictive moldings that frame the illuminations, and the format for the inscriptions, which also appears in his signed self-portrait of 1558 (cat. no. 161).[7] It may have been through the execution of these portraits that Bening learned from Gossaert the conventions of showing the sitter's hands with lightly curled fingers and with a clenched fist clasping neatly folded gloves.

Staring suggested that the two portrait miniatures might be the companion portraits given by Henry to his brother Willem of Nassau-Dillenberg in November 1531: "two very small paintings of Nassau and his wife."[8] This is plausible. The miniature portraits would thus date not long after the completion of Gossaert's original portraits. The count would have known Bening's work thanks to the illuminator's popularity in the court circle.[9] If Staring's assertion is correct, the diminutive pair may be dated precisely to 1531. They may thus also be counted among the earliest surviving independent portrait miniatures produced in Flanders.

T. K.

Notes

1. Dessau, Gemäldegalerie (see Staring 1952: 146, ill. as "Vermeyen?"), and Madrid, collection Conde de Revilla Gigedo (Bruges 1965: 227, no. 41, ill. 226, as "after Gossaert"). Friedländer (1924–37, 8: 160, no. 55) also mentioned a version in a museum in Mexico but gave no further details.

2. Bruges 1908: 54, no. 28, pl. 26, as by Joos van Cleve. Benesch (1929: 209) attributed this painting to Vermeyen.

3. Musée Condé; see Friedländer 1967–76, 9, pt. 1: 71, no. 109b, pl. 116.

4. On the version that came onto the art market in Paris in 1913, see Friedländer 1967–76, 9, pt. 1: 71, no. 109a, pl. 116.

5. Staring 1952: 151–52.

6. Bruges 1908: 54, under no. 28, as "pourrait très bien être l'oeuvre de Barend van Orley"; Berlin 1996, as "Netherlandish, ca. 1550," and Toledo 2000: no. 184, as "Anonymous Flemish."

7. Even the dimensions of these two miniatures are remarkably close to the *Self-Portrait* by Bening (cat. no. 161) and its copy in the Lehman Collection (Metropolitan Museum of Art, New York; 8.5 × 5.7 cm [3³⁄₁₆ × 2¼ in.]). Staring (1952: 155) remarked that the miniaturist shows "een bekwamheid gelijk aan de van Simon Bening."

8. "Twee kleyne schilderikens Gen. Van Nassau en zijn gemaal" (Staring 1952: 147– 49).

9. Between 1539 and 1542, following Mencía's husband's death and her return to Spain, she engaged Bening's services for a series of miniatures in two books. It is unlikely that the two portraits belonged to either of these commissions, even though Steppe (1969: 493) thought that the first series of six miniatures was "probablement des petits portraits." The presence of identifying inscriptions on the Berlin miniatures makes it unlikely that they were conceived for a book, and one document states specifically: "que haga master Ximon las *ystorias* del libro, por XL pl. la pieca" (Steppe 1969: 502).

150

SIMON BENING

Leaves from the Hennessy Hours
Use of Rome
Bruges, mid-1530s

January, fol. 1v	*November,* fols. 11v–12
February, fol. 2v	*Saint John on Patmos,* fol. 14v
April, fol. 4v	*Saint Matthew,* fol. 20v
May, fol. 5v	*The Agony in the Garden,* fol. 26v
June, fol. 6v	*The Crucifixion,* fol. 96v
July, fol. 7v	*Bathsheba,* fol. 143v
September, fol. 9v	

MANUSCRIPT: ii + 190 + iii detached leaves, mounted and bound,
11.7 × 8.7 cm (4⅝ × 3⁷⁄₁₆ in.); justification: 7.8 × 6 cm (3¹⁄₁₆ × 2⅜ in.);
13 lines of *gotica rotunda*; 15 full-page miniatures, 8 bas-de-page
miniatures, 2 small miniatures, 12 full-page calendar miniatures and
historiated borders; 2 miniatures added, sixteenth century

INSCRIPTIONS: . . . *[Cr]eio que mereço ser condenada. / Por yso Snor. tenho
neçessidade d[e] mi socorrer avossa misericordia a mayor que toda* . . . ,
sixteenth- or early seventeenth-century hand, fol. 185

BINDING: Temporarily disbound; former binding: Deflinnes atelier,
Tournai, late eighteenth century; gold-tooled red morocco

COLLECTION: Brussels, Bibliothèque royale de Belgique, Ms. II 158

PROVENANCE: Damião de Góis (?); to Queen Catherine
of Portugal (?); Pierre d'Hennessy (d. 1852), Oostende; to
his widow; purchased 1874

JPGM

150a
SIMON BENING
February, fol. 2v

This magnificent book is one of Bening's major works
from the 1530s and one of his supreme achievements as
a painter of landscape, especially as witnessed by the book's
calendar of full-page miniatures with facing historiated
borders. Like the Golf Book (cat. no. 155), to which it
bears more than a passing resemblance, the Hennessy
Hours has been cut up into single leaves that are now all
mounted in a scrapbook. What survives of the original
Hennessy volume is more substantial, however, including
the complete calendar, the Hours of the Virgin, the Penitential Psalms, the litany, a suffrage, and several prayers.
Lacking is the Office of the Dead, and it is likely that other
prayers and suffrages were originally included in a book
with such lavish illumination.

The calendar is the book's most original feature,
notably for such unprecedented scenes as that for February
(ill. 150a), where riders stop by a stream to let their horses
drink, and that for April (ill. 150e), a lively falconing scene.
In the February miniature Bening created a coherent, continuous, deep spatial recession by dramatically varying the
topographical features from low mound to steep, rocky
hillside to sunken valley. He used the barren trees to establish the rhythm of movement from the foreground into the
middle distance and to add texture and variety. In the scene
for April, hunters race across an open field outside a town
in a landscape of beguiling simplicity and openness. These
vistas are joined by vivid urban views, such as those for May
and June (ill. 150f). An intriguing programmatic feature of
the calendar is the emphasis given to aristocratic activities,
especially leisure pastimes, instead of the traditional
monthly labors. Bening has expanded the vocabulary of the
calendar activities to shift the focus to male leisure. Besides
traditional scenes of falconing (*April*) and courting (*May*),
other scenes involve hunters or hunting (*July* and *December*), a joust in a public square (*June*), a contest of courtly
crossbowmen (*November* [ill. 150b]), and cavaliers resting
(*February*). But even the gardening scene for March, a traditional labor of the month, shows the elegantly attired lord
of the manor directing the workers' efforts. Due to the
wealth of contemporaneous costumes and activities, the
Hennessy calendar broadly evokes aspects of aristocratic
life in Flanders. The emphasis on noble pastimes is ultimately derived from the calendar of the *Très Riches Heures*
of John, duke of Berry (Chantilly, Musée Condé), with its
sequence of portraits of ducal and royal palaces and its varied depictions of the leisure of the gentry.[1]

The remainder of the book is noteworthy for Bening's
reliance on High Renaissance pictorial sources for the
figures, including the evangelist portraits (e.g., ill. 150d) and
Bathsheba in diaphanous dress (ill. 150c), all derived, often
loosely, from engravings after Raphael and Michelangelo.[2]
Although this is not the only book in which Bening used
such models (see cat. nos. 148, 154), they are more pervasive
here than elsewhere in his work. The artist adapted his
sources rather than copying them, reinventing the heroic
Italianate figure types to fit his settings and taste.[3] The
highly energized figure of the inspired Saint John on Patmos (ill. 150d) illustrates this quality well. Bening integrated
the lively new figure type into the picturesque landscape
without allowing either to dominate.

The Passion cycle that illustrates the Hours of the Virgin, which is not unusual in itself, features a distinctive program of historiated borders facing these miniatures. They show episodes from the ministry of Christ. The theme of preaching is perhaps linked to the patron's Franciscan spirituality. The manuscript's calendar is notable for resembling, in less exhaustive form, the Franciscan calendars found in a number of Flemish breviaries (see cat. nos. 89, 91, 112, 126).[4] I previously argued loosely on the basis of Bening's landscape style that the Hennessy Hours belongs to the early 1530s. Margaret Scott, however, has suggested that the numerous examples of period costume in the calendar point to a slightly later date, the mid-1530s.[5]

Many years ago Jethro Hurt noted an inscription in the book written by a Portuguese woman in the late sixteenth or early seventeenth century. It is the earliest clue to the book's history of ownership.[6] Elsewhere, Damião de Góis wrote that in 1544 he gave a book of hours illuminated by Simon Bening to Queen Catherine of Portugal.[7] Might the Hennessy Hours be that book?[8] It appears to have been illuminated by the mid-1530s, that is, not long after Góis was in regular contact with Bening regarding the ambitious, aborted commission for a genealogy of the Infante Dom Fernando of Portugal (cat. no. 147). The masculine character of the calendar iconography of the Hennessy Hours indicates that it was originally created for a male

patron. The unusual preponderance of pictorial sources that Bening drew from High Renaissance art may reflect the illuminator's desire to suit a patron with strong humanist interests, such as Góis.[9] Góis himself owned paintings by Quentin Massys, an artist enamored of Italian High Renaissance art, and by Hieronymus Bosch.[10] Finally, the Portuguese illuminator-humanist Francesco de Holanda's oft-quoted praise for Bening as an illuminator, published in 1548—"among the Flemish the most pleasing colorist who best painted trees and far distances"[11]—would make particular sense were he familiar with this book. The remark was published not long after the arrival of the queen's newly presented Flemish book of hours at the Portuguese court four years earlier. At that time Holanda was residing in the royal household, and his father António provided a valuation for the book Góis presented to the queen.[12] All of this is circumstantial evidence—not proof that Góis was the book's patron—but it makes him a logical candidate for this role.[13]

T. K.

Notes

1. The Hennessy Hours is the first of the series of calendar cycles by Bening (see cat. nos. 154, 155, 159) that takes the calendar of the Grimani Breviary as their point of departure. Some miniatures, such as *January* and *December*, follow the Grimani model quite closely, including details of setting. Yet the iconography of the Hennessy calendar appears more coherent and subtly specific than that of the Grimani calendar, and the landscape settings are largely rethought.

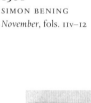

150b

SIMON BENING

November, fols. 11v–12

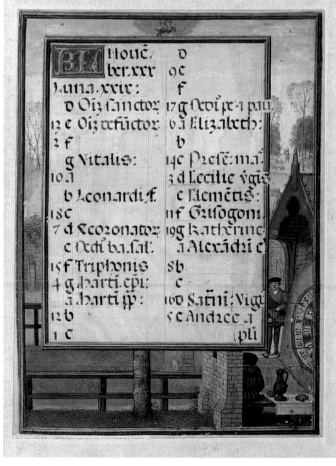

150c (above left)
SIMON BENING
Bathsheba, fol. 143v

150d (above right)
SIMON BENING
Saint John on Patmos,
fol. 14v

150e (near right)
SIMON BENING
April, fol. 4v

150f (far right)
SIMON BENING
June, fol. 6v

2. Testa (2000: 109, 116–19, figs. 1, 13–19) illustrated a number of possible sources for these images. Bathsheba, illustrating the Penitential Psalms, is a subject much more common in French than in Flemish manuscript illumination of the time.

3. Bening was also strongly influenced by the work of other Flemish artists shaped by the Italian Renaissance, above all Jan Gossaert, whose Malvagna Triptych (Palermo, Galleria Nazionale) he quoted repeatedly, largely in architectural motifs and mostly in the borders (Howard 1964: 187–92). See also under cat. nos. 149, 153.

4. John Plummer's analysis reports agreements of 96.31 percent, 94 percent, 93.08 percent, and 96.77 percent, respectively (report, Department of Manuscripts files, JPGM).

5. Kren, in Kren and Rathofer 1988: 247; Margaret Scott, correspondence with the author, March 12, 2002.

6. Hurt 1973: 43–46.

7. Destrée 1923: 26. The book is mentioned during the course of the trial following Góis's imprisonment in 1570.

8. Kren 1998: 231, n. 48.

9. It was during the early 1530s that Góis shifted his focus from the diplomatic life to that of a humanist intellectual, including study in Italy between 1534 and 1538 (Hirsch 1967: 64–114).

10. Hirsch 1967: 46–48.

11. "Entre os framengos foi o mais gracioso coloridor e que melhor lavrou as arvores e os longes" (Holanda 1930: 286).

12. Deswarte, in DOA 1996, 14: 659.

13. I am unable to document a direct connection between Góis and the Franciscans, per the book's calendar, but the Portuguese elite often had strong connections to the Franciscans (see cat. nos. 91, 92).

151

SIMON BENING AND TWO IBERIAN ILLUMINATORS

Hours of Isabella of Portugal
Use of Rome
Bruges and Toledo or environs, 1530s

MANUSCRIPT: iv + 136 + iii, 16.7 × 11 cm (6%₁₆ × 4⅝₁₆ in.); justification: 12.5 × 7.5 cm (4⅞ × 2¹⁵⁄₁₆ in.); 24 lines of *gotica rotunda*, with illuminated folios having 17 lines of *gotica rotunda* on recto and 6 lines of *humanistica* below miniatures on verso; 2 half-page miniatures, 15 small miniatures on parchment mounted on larger sheets of parchment

HERALDRY: Escutcheon with the arms of Charles V and Isabella of Portugal, impaled, fols. 10v, 48v (partly erased)

BINDING: Nicolas-Denis Derôme (Derôme le Jeune), Paris, eighteenth century; green morocco with gold dentelle tooling; pink silk doublures and endleaves; rust on first and last parchment flyleaves from clasps of former binding; gilt edges

COLLECTION: San Marino, The Huntington Library, HM 1162

PROVENANCE: Emperor Charles V (1500–1558) and Isabella of Portugal; Count Justin MacCarthy-Reagh (1744–1811), Toulouse [his sale, De Bure, Paris, January 27–May 6, 1817, lot 396]; William Beckford (1759–1844), Fonthill Abbey; to his son-in-law, Alexander Hamilton, tenth duke of Hamilton (1767–1852); to the Prussian state in 1882 [sale, Sotheby's, London, May 23, 1889, lot 32]; to Trübner; [Jacques Rosenthal, Munich, *Catalogue 27*, no. 31;] William K. Bixby (1857–1931); Henry E. Huntington (1850–1927), possibly August 1918

JPGM

___

Simon Bening usually illuminated manuscripts that were written and produced largely in Flanders, yet there are intriguing exceptions to this pattern. Between 1530 and 1534 Bening illuminated in Bruges the grand genealogy of the Infante Dom Fernando of Portugal, the miniatures of which António de Holanda, a court illuminator in Portugal, drew for him to color (cat. no. 147). In a similar vein this book of hours was written in the area of Toledo, Spain, for Isabella of Portugal, consort of the emperor Charles V and Fernando's sister.[1] The exquisite suite of fifteen miniatures of the life of the Virgin that Bening sent to Spain, mostly based on workshop patterns,[2] were, however, pasted onto leaves in Spain that were then illuminated further. In other words, these miniatures are not the typical singletons inserted opposite appropriate text pages, but rather very small miniatures that are mounted in the upper halves of text pages. Indeed, Bening's miniatures are considerably smaller than the half pages they occupy, so that a second artist, who was presumably Spanish, painted a substantial border around each of them. Most of these borders are decorative, consisting of gold acanthus on colored grounds, but some feature landscapes (fols. 34v, 86v [ill. 151], 111v). A few of the latter extend the space of the landscapes in Bening's miniatures (fols. 98v, 151v). Thus, his illuminations were adapted to a physically larger volume.

The miniature *The Mocking of Christ* (ill. 151) is noteworthy for the lucidity of its crowded composition, for its sympathetic depiction of Christ, and for the individualized physiognomies of each of the animated protagonists. Bening's ability to maintain his expressive means within one of the smallest formats in which he ever worked is remarkable. It may be the case, however, that his cycle of minia-

Non est ei species neq3 decor
& vidimus eũ & non erat as
pectus & desiderauimus de
spectũ & nouissimum viro
rum: virum dolorum & ‹
scientem infirmitatem. ‹ ‹

151
SIMON BENING
AND AN IBERIAN
ILLUMINATOR
The Mocking of Christ,
fol. 86v

The arms of Isabella appear below a frontispiece miniature of a half-length *Christ Blessing* (fol. 10v) that is presumably, like the book's borders, painted by an Iberian artist.[3]
The style and colors are loosely related to the half-length
frontispiece of Christ in the Beatty Rosarium (cat. no. 156),
although a more skillful illuminator painted the Dublin
miniature. The incipit pages in Isabella's hours are striking
not only for their collaborative illuminations but also
because the lower half generally features script in gold written on grounds of deep burgundy or slate blue. Perhaps the
burgundy was intended to refer to the imperial status of the
book's owner. Bening's Beatty Rosarium—which was
made either for Isabella's spouse, the emperor, or for her
son, the future king of Spain—also contains colored leaves.
There some text pages are entirely purple, and others are
painted purple in the margins.

Isabella of Portugal married Charles V in 1526 and died
in 1539. Judith Anne Testa proposed a date for Bening's
miniatures of around 1530,[4] but the rich, dark colors, especially reds and blues, may indicate a somewhat later date.

T. K.

Notes

1. Another book of hours, formerly in the Doheny collection, was
written for Isabella of Portugal by the same scribe (Christie's, London,
December 2, 1987, lot 175).

2. These included not only his designs but also some by Martin
Schongauer and by older illuminators.

3. A second coat of arms, partially effaced but very likely also
Isabella's, appears in the bas-de-page of the leaf with *The Visitation* (fol.
48v), an appropriate location for the armorials of a female patron.

4. Testa 1986: 48.

tures was not originally intended for this book since they
are to a degree arranged unconventionally. Bening provided fifteen miniatures that trace a fairly continuous
narrative from *The Annunciation* (fol. 34v) through *The
Ascension of Christ* (fol. 151v) and *The Coronation of the Virgin*
(fol. 93v), but they are sometimes inserted in the book in
surprising ways. The Hours of the Virgin commences with
the customary Infancy cycle, beginning conventionally at
matins with *The Annunciation*. Yet at none the decorative
program shifts to a Passion cycle starting with *The Agony in
the Garden*. The Passion cycle continues in the Penitential
Psalms with *The Road to Calvary*, an incongruous illustration for this devotion, and then, in the Gradual Psalms,
with *The Resurrection*. Perhaps Bening's series of miniatures
was recycled from another book rather than designed for
this one, or alternatively, the devotional concept for the
book may have changed by the time his miniatures arrived.

engraver's design dramatically on the left side and below, turning a full-length composition into a three-quarter-length format.[2] As a result, the composition is more strongly focused on the downcast face of the jostled and pummeled Christ, while the setting is more claustrophobic. Bening created an even more tightly cropped version of the Schongauer print in the Stein Quadriptych (cat. no. 146).

Christ before Annas is difficult to date precisely; the relatively muted colors suggest that it might date later than 1530.

T. K.

Notes

1. Ralph Bankes acquired this leaf as a single miniature in the mid-seventeenth century. This bears witness to the early point at which collectors came to prize Bening's miniatures, even those originally produced for books, as individual paintings.

2. Schongauer was a favorite source for Passion subject matter for sixteenth-century Flemish illuminators. On Schongauer as a source for Bening, see Kupfer-Tarasulo 1979a: 281, 290–96.

153

SIMON BENING

Portrait of a Man

Bruges, ca. 1535–40

Tempera on parchment, 9 × 7 cm (3½ × 2¾ in.)

INSCRIPTIONS: . . . *ce portrait rapporté d'Allemagne en 1853 / appartenait au D^cur du Musée de Stuttgart* . . . , note taped to back of frame

COLLECTION: Paris, Musée du Louvre, RF. 3.925

PROVENANCE: Johann Peter Weyer (1794–1864), Cologne, 1852; Charles Sauvageot, by 1856 (Sauzay 1861: no. 1064); acquired with his collection in 1856

JPGM

152

SIMON BENING

Christ before Annas

Miniature, probably from a devotional book

Bruges, between ca. 1530 and 1550

One full-page miniature; 12.2 × 9 cm (4¹³⁄₁₆ × 3½ in.)

COLLECTION: Wimborn, Kingston Lacy, KLA/D/3

PROVENANCE: Ralph Bankes, by 1659; by descent[1]

RA

Passion iconography was an important theme in northern European art in the first half of the sixteenth century, and Simon Bening was a key exponent of the trend. From the 1520s on, illuminated Passion cycles were a favored theme in his art. He often used the Passion of Christ rather than the Life of the Virgin to illustrate the Hours of the Virgin (see cat. nos. 150, 155) in books of hours. He also presented the Passion cycle at unusual length on several occasions (see cat. nos. 145, 146, 156) and in unusual formats (see cat. no. 146). In this little-known miniature, soldiers and Pharisees press into the crowded chamber of Annas, where Christ is presented to him. The composition is based on Martin Schongauer's engraving of this subject from his Passion series (B.45), but Bening cropped the

This representation of a handsome middle-aged man is the finest among the small group of surviving portraits Simon Bening executed in tempera on parchment (see cat. nos. 149, 161). It shows an elegantly dressed, probably middle-class sitter, wearing a high ruffled collar and what appears to be a black satin doublet, a black velvet gown, and a black cloak.[1] The sitter engages us directly by both his glance and the gesture of the upturned index finger of his proper right hand. A similar gesture was popular in Flemish portrait paintings of the 1530s by Joos van Cleve, Jan Vermeyen, and Jan van Scorel,[2] calling to mind most closely the portraits of Jan Gossaert. The pose, gaze, and cropping are similar to those in Gossaert's *Portrait of a Grand Commander of the Order of Santiago* (cat. no. 163), as is the gesturing hand, touching the fictive frame. In a comparable manner it extends into the viewer's realm. The piece of paper (or parchment?) curled tightly in the hand of Bening's sitter also echoes a gesture often found in Gossaert's paintings and in Bening's copy of Gossaert's *Portrait of Henry III, Count of Nassau* (ill. 149a), where the sitter holds folded gloves in a similar manner. Bening's painting of black on black on black, with each layer of costume representing a different textile, is exquisitely differentiated, showing the

152
SIMON BENING
Christ before Annas

Notes

1. Margaret Scott argued that the lack of ornament on the costume suggests his bourgeois status (correspondence with the author, March 12, 2002, Department of Manuscripts files, JPGM).

2. See Scailliérez 1992: 27, nn. 37–38, 29, n. 39, for examples.

3. Scailliérez 1992: 27. The catalogue of the Sauvageot collection (Sauzay 1861, no. 1064) indicated that the painting was inscribed with a date of 1525, which subsequent scholars have accepted. No trace of it remains, however, and following Scailliérez, this date seems unrealistic for the reasons given in the text. Richard Gay contributed research on costume dating to this entry.

4. The technique, coloring, and ordering of landscape elements are particularly similar to the backgrounds of the full-length portrait miniatures in the documented copy of the statutes of the Golden Fleece dated 1537 (Madrid, Instituto de Valencia de Don Juan; Madrid 1999: fols. 78v, 102v; Hulin de Loo 1925: 104–5). See also cat. no. 122.

5. *Young Man of the Wedigh Family*, New York, Metropolitan Museum of Art (Roberts 1979: 67, no. 56).

6. See the copy in the collection of Conde de Revilla Gigedo in Madrid (Bruges 1965: 227, no. 41, ill. on 226). Lobelle-Caluwé (in Bruges 1998: 104, no. 74) felt that the costume points to a date of circa 1540. Margaret Scott disagrees with the dating given here primarily on the basis of the closed-up character of the gown across the chest, a feature more characteristic of male fashion during the 1550s (correspondence with the author, July 2, 2002, and July 4, 2002, Department of Manuscripts files, JPGM). In the 1530s men usually had an inner garment such as a doublet that was more open across the chest and tended not to close the inner garment toward the base of the throat. I am not convinced by this argument. Hindman (in Hindman et al. 1997: 117) also preferred the much later dating.

7. Wescher 1946: 208. He was also the first to attribute the miniature to Bening.

8. Scailliérez 1992: 27–28.

9. Although the provenance goes back only to the nineteenth century, the earliest record of it is in a German collection. In the Sauzay catalogue of 1861 (no. 1064), the sitter was identified as Rotscholtz, with the castle of Hartburg in the background.

finesse of the emerging genre of the independent portrait miniature (see cat. nos. 133, 134).

An original feature of the portrait is the hilly landscape behind the sitter, which shows at the far left a château along a river or lake, perhaps the subject's estate. Portraits by the Bruges panel painter Hans Memling offer earlier examples of the full landscape background, though Bening's conception is more lush, atmospheric, and complex. Panel painters of the time rarely provided such a full landscape background in their portraits.

The style of costume and painted landscape corroborate the dating Cécile Scailliérez proposed for the miniature, ca. 1535–40.[3] Bening's technique of minute points of color to evoke a dense atmosphere, lending a fine, feathery texture to the surface, reached its fullest flowering in the 1530s.[4] Although Bening continued to practice his new landscape technique into the next decade, similar elements of costume including the high ruffled collar and flat beret appear in a Holbein portrait as early as 1532.[5] The haircut, which reveals more of the ear, is found in copies of the lost Gossaert portrait of Henry of Nassau painted at the same time or a bit earlier (ill. 149a).[6]

Paul Wescher proposed that the subject of the portrait is Bening himself.[7] Scailliérez identified the sheet held by the sitter as illuminators' parchment and considered the landscape element appropriate to Bening's reputation for this speciality.[8] Although this hypothesis is attractive, the only visual basis for such a conclusion is the late *Self-Portrait* (cat. no. 161), which shows a frail and diminished seventy-five-year-old. While the Louvre sheet might represent the same person, this is not self-evident. The present miniature was once in a German collection.[9] Could the sitter be one of Bening's German patrons?

T. K.

153
SIMON BENING
Portrait of a Man

154

SIMON BENING

Munich-Montserrat Hours
Use of Rome
Bruges, ca. 1535–40

MANUSCRIPT: 404 pages, 14 × 10.3 cm (5½ × 4¹/₁₆ in.); justification: ca. 8.9 × 6.1 cm (ca. 3½ × 2⅜ in.); 16 lines of *gotica rotunda*; 20 small miniatures, 5 historiated initials, 8 historiated borders

INSCRIPTIONS: *En 29 de henero de 1578 años. Yo frai Augustin de Orbaneja prior del Convento de Sanctelmo de la orden de los predic. por comision y mandato del muy ille. Sr. Don Pedro de los Llamos, inquisi.or de Calahorra y su distrito vi estas horas y hallo no tener herror ni cosa contra la fe: y las enmiendas que llenan en la margen son de falta en latinidad; y asi me parece que se puede rezar por ellas, en fe de lo qual lo firme F. Augustin de orvaneja*, p. 354

BINDING: Spain, nineteenth century; gold-tooled red morocco; marbled doublures; DEVOCIONAR LATINO on spine

COLLECTION: Montserrat, Montserrat Abbey, Ms. 53

PROVENANCE: Possibly Alonso de Idiaquez (d. 1547); in San Sebastián, 1578; to Montserrat Abbey in 1858

JPGM

154a
SIMON BENING
February, Munich,
fols. 3v–4

Calendar and Other Miniatures from the
Munich-Montserrat Hours

MANUSCRIPT: ii + 30 [+ i?] folios, 14 × 10.3 cm (5½ × 4¹/₁₆ in.); calendar justification: ca. 9 × 6.4 cm (ca. 3½ × 2½ in.); 17 lines of *gotica rotunda* in two columns; 14 full-page miniatures, 12 historiated borders; added prayers, late sixteenth or early seventeenth century, fols. 16–30

BINDING: Purple velvet; silver corner bosses, central medallions, and clasps

COLLECTION: Munich, Bayerische Staatsbibliothek, Ms. Lat. 23638

PROVENANCE: Possibly Alonso de Idiaquez (d. 1547); probably Joseph Werner, Bern, ca. 1660; to Ferdinand Maria, elector of Bavaria (1636–1679)

JPGM

Leaves from the Munich-Montserrat Hours
The Mass of Saint Gregory
The Martyrdom of Saint Sebastian

Two leaves, each 13.7 × 10.1 cm (5⅜ × 3¹⁵/₁₆ in); justification: 8.9 × 6.4 cm (3½ × 2½ in.); 16 lines of *gotica rotunda*; 2 full-page miniatures

COLLECTION: Los Angeles, J. Paul Getty Museum, Ms. 3 (84.ML.83)

PROVENANCE: Possibly Alonso de Idiaquez (d. 1547); private collection, England [Sotheby's, London, July 3, 1984, lot 25]; acquired 1984

JPGM and RA

Although twelve to fifteen of this book's original complement of full-page miniatures are still untraced, its known illumination has a distinctive pictorial character that focuses on landscape settings.[1] It originally featured three extensive pictorial cycles: the calendar, the Hours of the Virgin, and the suffrages. The calendar cycle, one of Bening's finest, features a dozen full-page miniatures with an equal number of facing historiated borders. In *February* (ill. 154a) and *May* the pictorial space of the full-page miniature is continuous with the facing border, creating horizontal compositions that give the landscape settings an alluring breadth. One of the earliest known representations of a stormy day, the evocative *February* anticipates the early paintings of Pieter Bruegel the Elder in the elevated foreground and, below and beyond, the dramatic sweep of sea and distant terrain.[2] In *May*, Bening captured the dewy atmosphere that hangs like a diaphanous veil over the countryside on a spring day. Besides depicting variegated settings and diverse, acutely observed atmospheric conditions, he transformed and updated the traditional iconography associated with the months. This cycle presents image after highly detailed image of a prosperous and vibrant civilization, a flattering portrait of Flanders.

None of the eight full-page miniatures that originally illustrated the Hours of the Virgin in the Montserrat codex has been identified with certainty. There is evidence to suggest that they featured an unusual cycle of Old Testament themes, from the Creation of Eve through the Flood and probably beyond.[3] In this reconstruction, *The Creation of Eve* would have illustrated matins of the Hours of the Virgin, a subject perfectly complemented by the surviving historiated border with the Expulsion from the Garden and the initial with the Temptation of Adam and Eve.[4] Bening's miniature *The Flood* (ill. 154d), whose subject is extremely rare but not unknown in books of hours, would come further in the cycle, probably around sext.[5] If this hypothesis is correct, then the Hours of the Virgin cycle would be distinguished not only as one of great novelty but also as one that developed the landscape leitmotif in new directions. *The Creation of Eve* presents an incomparably lush and idyllic conception of a garden. *The Flood* focuses on the meteorological cataclysm itself, arguably completing the artist's dogged exploration not only of topography but also of every type of weather condition.

Twenty-one of the miniatures in the suffrages are small, no more than seven lines high, but they continue the landscape theme. The saints, usually the standard single standing figure shown frontally, are all placed outdoors, sometimes before breathtaking vistas. The one large miniature in this cycle, *The Martyrdom of Saint Sebastian* (ill. 154c), is full page. Although the figures are based on familiar patterns, Bening rethought the setting. He situated the drama

154b
SIMON BENING
Christ at the Boat of Simon Peter, Montserrat, p. 403

154c
SIMON BENING
The Martyrdom of Saint Sebastian, Los Angeles, leaf 2v

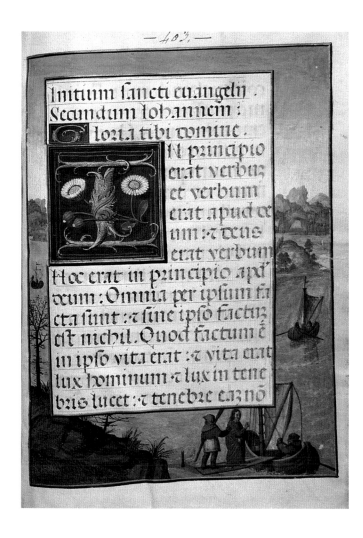

on behalf of the Inquisition in 1578. Father Augustine was then the prior of the Monastery of San Telmo in the northern Spanish coastal town of San Sebastián. Since many of Bening's patrons were Spanish and Portuguese, especially in these years, it seems quite possible that the importance given here to Saint Sebastian reflects a connection to the town named for him. As it happens, Alonso de Idiaquez (d. 1547), the founder of San Telmo, was also a member of the court secretariat of Charles V, and he made several trips to Flanders on the emperor's behalf during the early 1530s and again in 1541. The Munich-Montserrat Hours probably belongs to the second half of the 1530s, hence during the period when Idiaquez's contact with the region was most intimate.[6] Tremendously wealthy, he had a large palace in the center of San Sebastián, and he was buried in the monastery of San Telmo, now a museum, where his tomb still stands. He comes precisely from the inner circle of Hapsburg courtiers and wealthy, high-ranking Spanish nobles that formed the backbone of Bening's elite market.

The Munich-Montserrat Hours represents a summa of Simon Bening's consuming interest in landscape during the 1530s, an interest that encompassed not only all earthly terrains, from mountains to plains and from seas to streams, but also the most varied atmospheric, temporal, and lighting conditions. Here even the historiated borders complement the landscape theme,[7] which is developed not only in the calendar but also through most of the full-page miniatures. Moreover, if we are correct that the book's patron was a powerful Spaniard, and this seems highly probable, then the meaning of the calendar's dense, detailed, and largely original iconography merits reflection. To such a Spanish patron from the ruling class, with a deep and abiding admiration for Flemish art and culture, the calendar miniatures would assume the role of a series of visual reminders of Flanders—of a cultivated, fertile, and industrious land. For a Hapsburg courtier it would also have served as an exquisite, idealized representation of one of the territorial jewels in the Hapsburg crown.   T. K.

Notes

1. The calendar and two full-page miniatures are in Munich. Two other full-page miniatures are in Los Angeles, and the remainder of the text is in Montserrat. See Kren 1998 for a reconstruction of the manuscript. One full-page miniature not included in the exhibition, *The Betrayal of Christ* (New York, Breslauer collection), probably illustrated the Passion according to Saint John.

2. Kren and Rathofer 1988: 259, 280–81.

3. For historical precedents for such a cycle, see Kren 1998: 212–13.

4. Bening sometimes used *The Creation of Eve* to illustrate the prayer "Conditor celi."

5. *The Flood* is based on a woodcut ascribed to Jan van Scorel in the style of Titian (see Kren, in Kren and Rathofer 1988: 303, fig. 46). The Hours of the Virgin contains only one other historiated border, with the New Testament subject of Joseph and Mary at the Inn (p. 97) for prime, so there are no signposts to help us situate this miniature.

6. Kren 1998: 209. Margaret Scott advised me that such a dating is consistent with the particulars of costume (correspondence with the author, March 12, 2002, Department of Manuscripts files, JPGM).

7. The historiated border that accompanies the Gospel extract for Saint John shows Christ at the boat of Simon Peter before a sweeping seascape (ill. 154b).

on a hilltop with a deep valley beyond as well as far distant mountains. The components of this monumental setting are knit together by a limpid atmosphere.

Not all of the book's miniatures feature a distinctive landscape, but most of the surviving ones do. And while other books of hours, notably the Hennessy Hours (cat. no. 150), also feature bold explorations of landscape, none shows Bening working as freely and with such a remarkable range of inventiveness as this manuscript does. The book not only indicates the basis for the artist's reputation in his own lifetime as a painter of landscape, but it also illustrates how much further Bening went than those artists who inspired him: the Master of the Prayer Books of around 1500 (see cat. no. 118), the Master of James IV of Scotland (see cat. nos. 124–26), and Joachim Patinir. It also illustrates the degree to which he surpassed his contemporaries, especially Herri met de Bles and Cornelis Massys (see cat. no. 164).

One of the two Getty miniatures, *The Martyrdom of Saint Sebastian*, provides a clue to the identity of the book's patron. It indicates, at least, that this saint, who was beloved by the Holy Roman Emperor Maximilian (d. 1519) and by knights of the Hapsburg realm, held personal interest for the patron. The nature of this interest is suggested indirectly by an inscription written at the back of the book that documents its review by Father Augustine of Orbaneja

154d
SIMON BENING
The Flood, Munich, fol. 15

155

SIMON BENING AND WORKSHOP

Golf Book (Book of Hours)
Use of Rome
Bruges, probably early 1540s

MANUSCRIPT: 30 detached leaves, mounted and bound, 11.2 × 8 cm
(4⅜ × 3⅛ in.); justification: 8.3 × 5.8 cm (3¼ × 2¼ in.); 12 lines of
gotica rotunda; 9 full-page miniatures with bas-de-page or historiated
borders, 8 other borders with narrative vignettes, 12 full-page
calendar miniatures, 12 historiated calendar borders

BINDING: England, 1927; blue crushed morocco; former binding
(stored separately): Germany, ca. 1800; purple velvet with silver
metalwork and crystal

COLLECTION: London, The British Library, Add. Ms. 24098

PROVENANCE: Baron Ernest von Pöllnitz of Schloss Babenwohl,
Bregenz; purchased 1861

R A

This famous but little-studied group of leaves cut from
a book of hours represents only a small portion of
the original manuscript. Surviving is the complete calendar, the two-page openings for the Hours of the Virgin, and
a full-page miniature depicting a standing bishop, perhaps
Saint Boniface of Lausanne (fol. 1).[1] The calendar and hours
each has a complete cycle of full-page miniatures, but
the text beyond the incipit pages for each of the Marian
hours and the accompanying text for *Saint Boniface of
Lausanne*, probably a suffrage for the saint, are lacking. In
addition to the image of Saint Boniface, the finest miniatures belong to a Passion cycle, from *The Agony in the*

Garden (fol. 2v) to *The Entombment* (fol. 16v), illustrating the
Hours of the Virgin. *Saint Boniface* is set in a lush country
landscape and framed with a three-sided border of a boar
hunt in the woods. Bening himself painted this and many
of the other miniatures, among which the most beautiful
are *The Agony in the Garden*, *The Crown of Thorns* (fol. 8v),
Christ Led before Pilate (fol. 6v), and *Christ Nailed to the
Cross* (ill. 155). In the bas-de-pages of these miniatures in the
Hours of the Virgin, one finds related scenes from the Passion that are close in sequence, such as the soldiers casting
lots for Christ's robe beneath *Christ Nailed to the Cross*. The
borders are composed of painted frames of carved tracery
that appear in the facing pages as well, but with smaller
scenes that are painted in monochrome. The latter are
typologically linked to the large miniature opposite, such as
Jael and Sisera in the border facing *Christ Nailed to the Cross*.

The subjects of the miniatures in the elaborate program of Passion scenes are identical to those in the Hennessy Hours. In addition, although the compositions of the
large miniatures are generally dissimilar, those in the bas-
de-pages are virtually the same for the complete cycle.[2]
In the large Passion miniatures of the Golf Book Bening
situated the figures closer to the front of the image than in
the Hennessy Hours and focused more strongly on the
emotional content, while in the latter he gave greater attention to setting and atmosphere.

It is the book's calendar, painted entirely by the Bening
workshop and rather dryly derived from existing workshop
patterns, that gives the book both its reputation and its
name. The latter is derived from the round of golf being
played by children in the bas-de-page of the page devoted to
September (fol. 27). The compositions for most of the calendar's full-page miniatures appear to be copied after more
elaborately detailed works by Bening's own hand in the
Hennessy Hours and the Munich-Montserrat Hours (cat.
nos. 150, 154).[3] With a few notable exceptions the calendar
eschews the ambitious spatial recessions that are so characteristic of the aforementioned cycles. Like the rest of the
book, the full-page miniatures of the calendar have simulated carved frames with, in the bas-de-pages, illustrations
of children's games in *camaïeu d'or*, grisaille, or brown
against colored backgrounds of red, blue, or brown, following an iconography common to Flemish manuscripts
that goes back close to half a century (see cat. nos. 91, 92,
124).[4] Charmingly a few bas-de-pages on the facing text
pages feature continuations of the same children's games in
matching monochrome (e.g., fols. 19, 20). Yet most of the
bas-de-page scenes below the calendar's texts represent in
full color the traditional iconography of the labors and
leisure activities of the months.

The only strong clue to the manuscript's ownership is
the rare miniature of Saint Boniface of Lausanne (d. 1265)
with the attribute of the statuette of the Virgin and Child
on the open book. He was in fact not a saint and was
beatified only in the eighteenth century.[5] Probably around
1800 the miniature was mounted at the front of a scrapbook
with the other leaves of the book. Thus it comes even
before the calendar, which normally would open such
a devotional book. This transposition suggests that this

regional saint may still have had some importance for its owner then. The British Museum purchased the book from a nobleman residing near Bregenz, at the eastern end of Lake Constance. Perhaps, then, the book was originally intended for a German or Swiss patron with a connection to Lausanne and it remained within the wider region over the centuries.

The book is difficult to date. The costumes appear to a degree to be simplified, derivative versions of the costumes in the Hennessy Hours and the Munich-Montserrat Hours, yet they are not always merely copied either. The Golf Book is thus likely a bit later than the Munich-Montserrat Hours.[6]   T. K.

Notes

1. London 1884–94, 2: pls. 135, 136. Roeder (1955: 336) confirmed that the attributes of Saint Boniface are an image of the Virgin and Child on a book.

2. The figures of the bas-de-page in the Hennessy Hours are in grisaille or brown monochrome against muted backgrounds. The large miniatures of the Agony in the Garden in the two books are based in part on the same pattern.

3. After the Munich-Montserrat Hours are the corresponding miniatures in the Golf Book for January, March (foreground figures only), April (figures at foreground right only), September, November, and loosely, October, while the February miniature in the Golf Book is closely based on the December miniature in the other. After the Hennessy Hours are the miniatures in the Golf Book for May, June (middle ground only), July, and August.

4. Hindman 1981: 455–58, 473–75.

5. Weale (in London 1884–94, 2: pls. 135, 136) believed that Saint Boniface of Lausanne's relics were preserved in the church of Notre-Dame in Bruges, but the relics there are rather those of the more widely venerated Saint Boniface who is associated with the evangelization of Germany and lived in the eighth century. See also *Bibliotheca Sanctorum* 1961–70, 3: 319.

6. Margaret Scott believes that the Golf Book is relatively close in date to the Munich-Montserrat Hours, and possibly a bit earlier, because the men in the latter are bearded and those in the former are not (correspondence with the author, November 25, 2002, and December 3, 2002, Department of Manuscripts files, JPGM).

156

SIMON BENING AND ANOTHER ILLUMINATOR

Leaves from the Beatty Rosarium
Bruges, ca. 1540–45

The Baptism of Christ, fol. 24v
The Lamentation, fol. 40
The Virgin and Child, fol. 44v

MANUSCRIPT: iii + 42 + ii folios, 12.4 × 8.4 cm (4⅞ × 3⁵⁄₁₆ in.); fol. 1: 10.9 × 8.4 cm (4¼ × 3⁵⁄₁₆ in.); justification: 9.6 × 6.7 cm (3¾ × 2⅝ in.); 16 lines of *gotica rotunda*; 33 full-page miniatures

INSCRIPTIONS: *Cornilis Ulfeldt a eu ce livre lequel autrefois a appartenu au Roy D'espagne Phillip II, astheure le dict livre a esté donné par le soubisigné à son Excellence Mons. Le Compte Vrangel, General Gouverneur en Pomeranie 1652 Cornilis Ulfeldt Grand Maistre du Royaume de Danemarc,* fol. ii; *Vom Feldherrn Wrangel kam dies Gebetbuch an seine Tochter vermählt mit dem letzten Putbus Waldemarscher Linie, und wurde seit der Zeit als ein seltenes Kunstwerk in der Familie aufbewart. Es soll der beste damalige Mahler daran gearbeitet haben und es wird dem Pietro de la Mare zugeschrieben,* fol. iii

BINDING: Spain, sixteenth century; elaborately gold-tooled morocco; *IHS* in center of both covers; Bening miniatures (i.e., all but one of the miniatures) excised and mounted separately

COLLECTION: Dublin, Chester Beatty Library, Ms. W. 99

PROVENANCE: Possibly Emperor Charles V (1500–1558); his son, Philip II, king of Spain and (as Philip I) king of Portugal (1527–1598); Corfits Ulfeldt (1610–1664); his gift to Carl Gustav Wrangel (1613–1676), in 1652; to the Putbus family by his daughter's marriage to Prince Ernst Ludwig von Putbus in 1658 and by descent until at least 1837; A. Chester Beatty (1875–1968), by December 1926

R A

The rosarium is a collection of Marian devotions. This volume opens with a prayer to God the Father and all saints that is followed by short prayers in a sequence based on the life of the Virgin that culminates in events from the Passion of Christ (ills. 156a–c). The initial Marian prayer is illustrated by the first of Simon Bening's miniatures, which shows the symbols of the Virgin's Immaculate Conception (fol. 12v). Thirty miniatures then unfold a continuous narrative from the birth of the Virgin to Pentecost. Thus, fittingly for such a devotional volume dedicated to the mother of Jesus, Bening's miniatures belong to a genre that he made a specialty, the extended, continuous Christological narrative (cat. nos. 144–46).[1]

As was typical for the artist, Bening drew upon models from the late-fifteenth-century Flemish tradition of illumination and from Gerard David, but here the range of sources is exceptionally broad, including other Flemish painters, such as the Master of 1499 and Joachim Patinir, and German printmakers such as Martin Schongauer and Albrecht Dürer.[2] The regal but compassionate *Virgin and Child* that concludes the book (ill. 156c) is a luminous copy in half-length of *The Virgin in the Church* by the Master of 1499 (Antwerp, Koninklijk Museum voor Schone Kunsten), itself a copy after Jan van Eyck. *The Baptism of Christ* (ill. 156a) takes its main figures from David (Bruges, Groeningemuseum), but its memorable riverscape was imaginatively drawn from a painting of this subject by Patinir (Vienna, Kunsthistorisches Museum). Bening probably fashioned *The Lamentation* (ill. 156b) from several Flemish illuminators' patterns for this subject.[3] Despite its diverse sources, the rosarium's pictorial cycle displays a remarkable visual unity, even in comparison with Bening's other works, in terms of the consistency of the warm palette; the distinctive treatment of the landscape, with its velvety brushwork and lushness; and the spatial complexity and atmospheric character of the interiors. The elimination of the traditional Flemish decorative borders on both miniature and text pages heightens the focus on the powerful narrative depicted.

An unusual feature of the book is the painted purple margins of the pages. Brief texts at the front and the back of the book, which may have been added shortly after its completion, are on purple leaves, one of them written in gold, so that the book as a whole imparts a regal impression. Indeed purple was used in books made for imperial patrons in late antique and Carolingian times and in at least one manuscript illuminated for Charles the Bold, duke of Burgundy, in the fifteenth century. Charles lost a small prayer book, luxuriously illuminated with gold calligraphy on purple parchment, to the Swiss in battle.[4] In the sixteenth century Isabella of Portugal, consort of Emperor Charles V, owned a book of hours with miniatures by Bening that has pages of deep burgundy written in gold (cat. no. 151). Since the rosarium's dedicatory preface is in Spanish (fol. 1) and a later inscription identifies Philip II (1527–1598) of Spain, son of Charles and Isabella, as a former owner, either he or Charles was likely the book's intended owner, the appropriate patrons from the imperial family.[5]

Although the book was cut up into separate leaves in the modern era, the rosarium may be the latest relatively complete commission to survive from the hand of the artist. The miniatures represent the culmination of Bening's

156b
SIMON BENING
The Lamentation, fol. 40

156c
SIMON BENING
The Virgin and Child,
fol. 44v

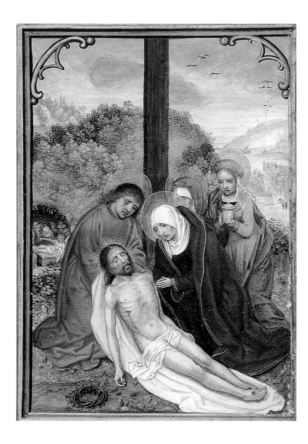

development in landscape construction and his handling of the brush, indicating that they are datable as late as the Munich-Montserrat Hours (cat. no. 154), and probably later. Yet the book was not executed after 1545, the date of the Acuña Rosary Psalter (private collection), illuminated in Bening's workshop, which includes several miniatures based on those in the Beatty Rosarium.[6] The rosarium was probably not painted much before that manuscript and thus belongs to the first half of the 1540s.   T. K.

Notes

1. A thirty-third miniature, showing Christ in profile, was added by another artist, probably in Spain when the book's short preface was added. See Testa 1986: 111–12.

2. For an account of many of these sources, see Testa 1986: 113–78.

3. Esp. cat. no. 25, fol. 59v, and cat. no. 44, fol. 146v.

4. Deuchler 1963: 349, no. 316. See also de Schryver 1999: 51–52. The book is untraced today.

5. Testa (1986: 29) suggested that the first owner was likely Charles V on the basis of an earlier dating for the book.

6. Formerly Amsterdam, Bibliotheca Philosophica Hermetica (König 1991: 530–45, no. 34), and Sotheby's, London, July 6, 2000, lot 57.

157

SIMON BENING

The Virgin and Child with Musical Angels
Bruges, 1540s or later

Parchment glued to thin wood panels; central panel: 16.2 × 12 cm (6⅜ × 4¾ in.); each wing: 16.3 × 4.8 cm (6⁷⁄₁₆ × 1¹³⁄₁₆ in.)

COLLECTION: Private collection

PROVENANCE: [Artemis, London]

JPGM and RA

This very small, unpublished triptych is painted in tempera on parchment. It shows the Virgin and Child seated, flanked by angel musicians, in an enclosed garden.[1] The garden is set within a walled yard, perhaps a cloister, with an imposing Late Gothic house to the left at the wall. The left wing shows *The Nativity*, while the right wing shows *The Christ Child Teaching the Doctors*. The subject of Christ's teaching became popular in Flemish manuscript illumination at the beginning of the sixteenth century. In this scene the doctors line both sides of an aisle that features Christ at the apex while his parents appear at the upper left.[2]

The handling of the landscape behind the Virgin shows attention to the details of individual plants and blades of

grass. The brushwork, which gives the trees and fields a particular lushness, invites comparison with the miniatures for June in the Munich-Montserrat Hours (cat. no. 154, fol. 7v) and in the London cycle (ill. 159b). This suggests that the triptych may date after 1540.[3]

This work is a superb example (and one of the smallest) within the short-lived genre of the illuminated triptych on parchment, which are among the most fragile and personal of private devotional objects. Although few survive, they appear to have enjoyed a vogue in the second quarter of the sixteenth century, and Simon Bening was their major exponent. His most beautiful and imposing parchment triptych, at more than fifteen inches tall, is *The Penitent Saint Jerome* (see fig. 15).[4] Another, executed with his workshop, is in the Houston Museum of Fine Arts (see fig. 9).[5]   T. K.

Notes

1. The angels are derived from a pattern for a similar composition that goes back to the late fifteenth century (cf., e.g., cat. no. 88, fol. 45v, and cat. no. 105, fol. 80v). See De Winter 1981: 374–75.

2. The same composition appears in the Boston rosary psalter of the 1520s (see cat. no. 144). Bening also employed a pattern for this subject in an asymmetrical composition derived from Simon Marmion's miniature *The Trial of Susanna* in the La Flora Hours (cat. no. 93, fol. 289v). See also the Hours of James IV (cat. no. 110, fol. 109v); the Croÿ Hours (Vienna, Österreichische Nationalbibliothek, Ms. 1858, fol. 55); and the versions by Bening (cat. no. 143, fol. 49v, and cat. no. 156, fol. 24).

3. The coloring is consistent with the miniatures of the Beatty Rosarium from the early 1540s, and the *Nativity* particularly recalls features of the same subject in that manuscript (cat. no. 156, fol. 18v).

4. Scailliérez 1992: 20–21.

5. Bruges 1998: 102, no. 71; another small Flemish triptych on parchment, with *The Seven Joys of the Virgin and Saint Bernard and Saint Ildefonsus* (private collection) has been ascribed to the circle of Bening and is of the period (Louf 1992; Bruges 1998: 99–100, no. 69). Two diminutive altar wings on parchment with *The Preaching of John the Baptist* and *The Baptism of Christ*, probably from the circle of Bening, are in the Groeningemuseum, Bruges (inv. 211; Bruges 1998: 99, no. 68).

158

SIMON BENING

The Virgin and Child with Angels
Bruges, 1540s

Parchment mounted on wood panel and varnished; parchment: 31.5 × 22.1 cm (12⅜ × 8¹¹⁄₁₆ in.); panel: 32.1 × 22.5 cm (12⅝ × 8⅞ in.)

COLLECTION: London, Victoria and Albert Museum, inv. E 635–1998

PROVENANCE: Sir Harold Wernher, Luton Hoo, acquired in 1946; accepted in lieu of inheritance tax by the British Government and allocated to the Victoria and Albert Museum in 1998

R A

This *Virgin and Child* is one of Bening's largest paintings on parchment (ill. 158), and it was likely intended as an independent work.[1] The composition shows the Virgin and Child in the immediate foreground seated on elevated terrain and accompanied by enthusiastic music-making putti.[2] Beyond the Virgin extends a landscape that features in the middle distance a palace and its grounds, including a fountain, a fenced garden, and various outbuildings. While a peasant fells a tree at left, putti appear by the fountain and angels near the palace, giving the terrestrial setting a celestial air. A forested landscape beyond leads the eye over rugged terrain to the horizon. The landscape has the jagged, rocky outcroppings that are characteristic of the work of Joachim Patinir and Herri met de Bles but less common in Bening's own miniatures. The features of the middle ground are noteworthy, especially the majestic palace and its subordinate structures, the depiction of which has the character of a portrait of an estate.[3] Perhaps the painting was commissioned by the lord of the estate that is represented here.[4]

The work is also striking for the artist's extensive quotations from Jan Gossaert's Malvagna Triptych (Palermo, Galleria Nazionale), including the groups of musical angels beside the Virgin and the fountain behind her to the left. Bening drew upon Gossaert's art repeatedly during the 1530s (cf. cat. nos. 149, 153) and quoted the Malvagna Triptych elsewhere (cat. no. 150). It was at the beginning of the 1530s that the great Spanish patron Mencía de Mendoza employed Gossaert as her court artist, at a time when she and her spouse, Henry III of Nassau, the chamberlain of Charles V, also engaged Bening's services (cat. no. 149). Yet in the handling of space, with the elevated foreground and elaborately constructed recession, the work recalls most closely Bening's late cycle of London calendar miniatures (cat. no. 159). Therefore the painting, difficult to date very precisely, might be as late as the end of the 1540s.   T. K.

157
SIMON BENING
*The Virgin and Child
with Musical Angels*

Notes

1. The Escorial triptych with *The Penitent Saint Jerome* (see fig. 15) is larger, as is the genealogy of Dom Fernando (cat. no. 147).

2. The figures of the Virgin and Child are based on a workshop pattern also copied in a book of hours from the Bening workshop in Rouen (Bibliothèque municipale, Ms. Leber 142, fol. 151).

3. In the articulation of the windows and their bays, this palace compares closely to the much smaller, yet still imposing building in the *April* miniature from another cycle of calendar miniatures by Bening (ill. 159d).

4. See also the entry for the Morgan *Virgin among Virgins* (cat. no. 107), where the architecture in the background may have played a similar role.

158

SIMON BENING
*The Virgin and Child
with Angels*

159

SIMON BENING

Leaves Apparently from a Calendar
Bruges, probably late 1540s or early 1550s

March, recto; *December,* verso
June, recto; *July,* verso

Two leaves, each 15.2 × 10.2 cm (6 × 4 in.); 4 full-page miniatures

COLLECTION: London, The British Library, Add. Ms. 18855, fols.
108–9

PROVENANCE: Sir John Tobin, Liverpool; Rev. John Tobin, Liscard,
Cheshire; [William Boone]; to the British Museum in 1852

JPGM and RA

April, recto; *May,* verso
August or *September,* recto; *September* or *October,* verso

Two leaves, each 14 × 9.5 cm (5½ × 3¾ in.); 4 full-page miniatures

COLLECTION: London, Victoria and Albert Museum, Salting Ms. 2538
(inv. E. 4575-1910), Salting Ms. 2600 (inv. E. 4576-1910)

PROVENANCE: Salting Ms. 2538: Hollingworth Magniac, Colworth, by
1861 [his sale, Christie's, London, July 2, 1892, lot 193]; George Salting
(1839–1909), by 1908; his bequest, 1910. Salting Ms. 2600: W. Maskell
by 1861; Frederick Locker-Lampson (1821–1895), Rowfant, Sussex,
by 1886; George Salting (1839–1909); his bequest, 1910

RA

159a
SIMON BENING
December

159b
SIMON BENING
June

The eight miniatures of this incomplete calendar cycle are distinctive in several ways.[1] The four leaves are painted on both sides, so they do not lend themselves to a conventional layout for a Flemish calendar with full-page miniatures. The leaves are also the largest among the surviving cycles of calendar miniatures by Simon Bening (see cat. nos. 140, 150, 154) and his workshop (see cat. no. 155). In their sweeping treatment of spatial recession, they are undoubtedly also the most ambitious miniatures among Bening's calendar scenes and the most dramatic (ill. 159b and Add. 18855, fol. 109v). Yet their figures, like those in his other cycles, are based on workshop models, some ultimately derived from the Grimani Breviary (cat. no. 126 and fig. 31). In this cycle it is nearly always the landscape itself, or a significant portion of it, that the artist has chosen to take a step further.

The use of these workshop patterns results in subjects that are typically Flemish, and the figural compositions are largely familiar from Bening's earlier work.[2] The planting of a garden (ill. 159c) is a common theme for March, and the composition here is related to a miniature in the Golf Book (cat. no. 155, fol. 20v). The subject of lovers relaxing in a garden (ill. 159d), typical for April, recalls the composition in the Munich-Montserrat Hours (cat. no. 154, fol. 5v), except

159c
SIMON BENING
March

159d
SIMON BENING
April

it is in a more rural setting. An image of noble music makers on a boat passing through a city, typical iconography for May, relates to an earlier composition in the Hennessy Hours (cat. no. 150, fol. 5v). The sheep-shearing scene (ill. 159b), appropriate for June, follows the pattern for the foreground figures and sheep seen in the Munich-Montserrat Hours (fol. 7v), but the landscape is transformed into the worldview type associated with Joachim Patinir (fig. 29). The elegant depiction of haymaking, typical for July, set on a gentle slope, is a close cousin of the July miniature in the Munich-Montserrat Hours (fol. 8v), but the foreground is more elevated and the horizon deeper. Compared with the miniature for August in the Hennessy Hours (fol. 8v), to which the grain harvest scene here is closely related, the latter is more open and monumental. The setting for the Hennessy's sowing scene for September (fol. 9v) closely anticipates the plowing scene here. The lovely *December* (ill. 159a) presents a late autumn day. The figures and landscape concept are descended directly from the Grimani Breviary (fol. 12v). The same composition appears in the Hennessy Hours, but it is less atmospheric.

While these subjects and compositions belong to the tradition of calendars for devotional books, the conventional layout of Flemish calendar cycles features the full-page miniature on the left and the text for the particular month on the right. In this arrangement the miniatures reside on versos and texts on rectos. It would be unusual but not impossible for these sheets to be inserted as singletons between the appropriate texts for the respective months. However the miniatures on one leaf, which appear to represent *March* and *December*, do not correspond to any known sequence of iconography for the months. Since by 1550 the demand for high-quality illuminated books of hours had declined radically, it is possible that these works were commissioned for another type of book. There is reason to doubt that they were intended for a finished deluxe prayer book.

Although I have dated the cycle previously to around 1540 or the early 1540s,[3] Margaret Scott has suggested on the basis of the costumes that they date closer to the very end of that decade.[4] This would place them among the latest miniatures from Bening's long career, except for the *Self-Portrait* of 1558 (cat. no. 161) and perhaps some other illuminations (cat. nos. 158, 160). Little else by Bening from this late date appears to have survived.[5]   T. K.

Notes

1. The provenance for the leaves goes back only to the mid-nineteenth century, when the leaves were already divided among three separate collections. The fact that all four were in England then indicates that they may have been separated not long before.

2. Both the Hennessy and Munich-Montserrat Hours (cat. nos. 150, 154) also feature more idiosyncratic themes than are found here.

3. Malibu 1983a: 79, 81; Kren and Rathofer 1988: 255.

4. Scott indicated that the shoes, the early form of the trunk hose, and the neckline of the jerkin in the men's clothes, especially as seen in the April miniature, point to a date around 1550 (correspondence with the author, March 12, 2002, Department of Manuscripts files, JPGM). Hindman (in Hindman et al. 1997: 117) has suggested that the cycle dates as late as 1560.

5. There is a rosary prayer book dated 1545 from Bening's workshop (König 1991: 530–45, no. 34).

160

SIMON BENING

Calendar Miniatures from a Book of Hours
Bruges, ca. 1550

Villagers on Their Way to Church, recto
Gathering Twigs, verso

Two bas-de-page miniatures, each 5.6 × 9.6 cm (2³⁄₁₆ × 3¾ in.)

COLLECTION: Los Angeles, J. Paul Getty Museum, Ms. 50 (93.MS.19)

PROVENANCE: Belgium, private collection, ca. 1900; [sale, Phillip's, London, December 7, 1992, lot 9]; [to Sam Fogg Rare Books and Manuscripts, London]; acquired 1993

R A

The small miniatures on either side of this cutting are the bas-de-page portions of successive calendar pages. *Villagers on Their Way to Church* shows a bourgeois family with a brood of children walking to church along a village path on a winter's day. The church's door opens on a brightly lit interior where a religious celebration involving countless candles is under way. It is the winter feast of the Purification of the Virgin, popularly known as Candlemas (February 2).[1] The miniature thus illustrates the month of February.[2] *Gathering Twigs* (ill. 160), on the verso, shows peasants chopping and bundling wood from trees they have pruned, a traditional winter labor that illustrates March.[3]

Both miniatures show the opportunity to explore landscape that calendar decoration afforded Bening throughout his career. In the village scene his interest resides as much in the vista of the low rolling hills, expressive golden light, and atmospheric haze as in the human events of the foreground. The horizon settles an impressive distance beyond the churchyard. In a similar manner a panorama unfolds behind the gatherers of branches and twigs. A river winds behind them and frames the central terrain, a lightly wooded, cultivated area. The barren trees and muted tonalities convey the chill of a winter's day. Human activity pervades the space in both miniatures—on the water, on footpaths, and inside the buildings.

Christian Vöhringer considered *Gathering Twigs* to be one of Bening's most advanced landscapes and thus proposed a dating after 1550.[4] Although the work is difficult to date precisely, Vöhringer's suggestion is plausible.　T. K.

Notes

1. Vöhringer 2002: 73–74.
2. The same subject illustrates the month of February (fol. 2) in a book of hours by Bening offered at Christie's, London, July 9, 2001, lot 35.
3. E.g., cat. no. 150, fol. 3; cat. no. 140, fol. 3v; cat. no. 124, fol. 2.
4. Vöhringer 2002: 56.

161

SIMON BENING

Self-Portrait
Bruges, 1558

Tempera on parchment, 8.6 × 5.9 cm (3⅜ × 2⁵⁄₁₆ in.)

INSCRIPTIONS: SIMO[N] BINNIK ALEXANDRI / F[ILIVS] SEIPSV[M] PI[N]GEBAT AN[N]O AETATIS 75 / 1558

COLLECTION: London, Victoria and Albert Museum, inv. P 159-1910

PROVENANCE: George Salting (1839–1909); his bequest, 1910

R A

This self-portrait by Simon Bening, identified by the inscription at the bottom, is remarkable in several ways. It offers an unflinching portrait of a man who, at the age of seventy-five, was both elderly and frail. The heaviness of the brow, the lines in the forehead and under the eyes, and the downward curve—one might say droop—of the mouth offer a frank record of a long life and a suggestion of infirmity. Although a bit stiff, his hands are fleshy and strong, the real and still vigorous instruments of his artistic practice. Bening portrayed himself at his easel beside a window, a sketch of the Virgin and Child on the parchment before him. He paused from his work to sit for this portrait, removing his glasses.

The inscription at the bottom recalls closely the style and format of the inscriptions below the artist's portrait miniatures of Henry III of Nassau and of Mencía de Mendoza (cat. no. 149), which are very nearly of the same dimensions. All three belong to the new genre of small independent portraits, perhaps fostered by Bening himself. Probably due to their physical delicacy, such portraits have had a poor survival rate. In Frans Francken's *Collector's Gallery,* dated 1619, this self-portrait, or more likely the copy in the Lehman Collection,[1] is displayed prominently on a table featuring a sketchbook, an array of metals, exotic seashells, and small oil paintings. It is shown mounted on a black board, unframed. Under such conditions it is likely that similar portraits on parchment were frequently lost or destroyed.

The evidence of the Lehman copy of the *Self-Portrait,* along with the depiction of it (or another replica) in the foreground of the Francken painting (with its identifying inscription intact), suggests that Bening continued to enjoy a strong reputation until the end of his life and for several generations thereafter. This seems to have been so even though the demand for manuscript illumination had greatly diminished by the middle of the sixteenth century. At the same time it is indicative of the changes in the artistic landscape that the only securely identified work from his last years is a miniature portrait, an independent work.

Bening's own professional pride is evidenced by the references to his trade in the miniature. As Sandra Hindman has pointed out, the subject of the Virgin and Child allies the illuminator with Saint Luke, patron of painters and of the Bruges confraternity of the book trade, who famously painted her and the infant Jesus. Devotional subject matter stood at the center of the activity of both painters and illuminators. In the miniature's inscription Bening took pains to identify himself as the "son of Alexander,"[2] his distinguished forebear in the art of illumination. The self-portrait may reflect a desire to assert the importance of the illuminator—or perhaps even the painter-illuminator. Bening may have felt the changes in the market for illumination keenly in the final years of a very long and highly successful career. Whether this view is sustainable or not, the miniature gains poignancy from the historical reality.   T. K.

Notes

1. Kren 1999: 233. See Hindman (in Hindman et al. 1997: 113–14) on the small differences in motif between the two versions. The Francken painting is illustrated in Hindman et al. 1997: 114, fig. 14.2.

2. Hindman et al. 1997: 115.

162

ANONYMOUS

Book of Hours
Use of Rome
Bruges, ca. 1510–20

MANUSCRIPT: 89 folios, 16 × 10.5 cm (6⁵⁄₁₆ × 4⅛ in.); justification: 10.5 × 6.9 cm (4⅛ × 2¹¹⁄₁₆ in.); 27 lines of *bastarda*; 6 full-page miniatures, 6 small miniatures, 14 historiated borders

BINDING: Nineteenth century; red velvet

COLLECTION: London, The British Library, Add. Ms. 35314

PROVENANCE: [William Boone, London]; Baron Ferdinand de Rothschild (1839–1898); his bequest, 1898

JPGM and RA

161
SIMON BENING
Self-Portrait

This relatively modest but lovely book of hours defies easy categorization. Its style of illumination is at once familiar and singular. The book, now in the British Library, shows links to the art of both Simon Bening and Gerard Horenbout. In style and iconography, however, it is related most closely to another book of hours, the Croÿ Hours (Vienna, Österreichische Nationalbibliothek, Ms. 1858), whose main illuminator is also difficult to categorize.[1] The distinctive *Raising of Lazarus* in the present book (fol. 53v) appears to copy in all details, including color and even the patchy character of the grassy cemetery, the Lazarus miniature in the Croÿ Hours (fol. 126v).[2] The illuminator of the British Library hours introduced to the stone surface of the church indications of weathering—patches of yellowing and other discoloration—that are lacking in the Croÿ version, probably a sign that the two artists are not one and the same.[3]

The main illuminator of the Croÿ Hours, who painted its Lazarus miniature, has been erroneously identified as Simon Bening. Although the facial types in both the British Library volume and the Croÿ Hours are different from those employed by Bening, the use of color and the tight brushwork in both books owe something to him. The treatment of *The Seven Sorrows of the Virgin* (fol. 72v) in the British Library manuscript, so comparable in color and composition to Bening's version of 1511 (cat. no. 139, fol. 290v), shows the close similarities between the two artists as well as their differences. In the British Library book the face of the sorrowful Virgin is paler and more angular, while Bening's Virgin has fuller coloring and more delicate features. The two artists also closely followed the same pattern in their depictions of the Nativity (ill. 162b; cat. no. 140, fol. 151v), but Bening was more ambitious and original, treating the subject as a poetic nocturne.

The illuminator of the British Library hours also copied parts of a miniature by another artist in the Croÿ Hours. The angel Gabriel and the Virgin Annunciate (fol. 12v) are closely based on Gerard David's *Annunciation* in the Croÿ Hours (fol. 38v).[4] David's copyist, however, introduced to the setting architectural elements more reminiscent of the Master of James IV of Scotland and his followers.[5] A notable feature of the artist of the British Library hours is his penchant for elegant architectural backgrounds, as seen in the courtly, up-to-date chamber of the Virgin Annunciate or the imposing rose-colored palace of King David in the *Bathsheba* miniature (ill. 162a). He also offers striking effects of color, such as the *couleur changeant* of Bathsheba's gown, where the fabric is gold and the shadows blue. A group of scholars of the English portrait miniature have frequently cited his technique in relationship to that of the earliest portrait miniatures painted in England.[6] Following Friedrich Winkler,[7] these scholars have associated the illuminations of the British Library hours with Gerard Horenbout (whom Winkler identified as the Master of James IV of Scotland) or his son Lucas. The changes I have noted, such as the interior introduced in *The Annunciation* and the placement of the architectural backdrop in the Bathsheba miniature, are reminiscent of works by both Gerard Horenbout and the Master of James IV.[8] In the end, however, the

use of color and the tight brushwork in both the British Library book and the Croÿ Hours owe more to Bening than to the Master of James IV, but the British Library artist is even more similar to the shadowy main illuminator of the Croÿ Hours. The British Library and Croÿ volumes also show similarities in the types of strewn-flower and architectural borders used.

Finally, another idiosyncratic feature of the British Library book is that its Hours of the Virgin is illustrated by only two miniatures, both full-page.[9] They are *The Annunciation* at matins and *The Nativity* at prime (ill. 162b). This is unlike most Flemish books of hours.

The book is probably datable to the second decade of the sixteenth century, a bit later than Simon Bening's Imhof Prayer Book of 1511 and the Croÿ Hours, which was perhaps executed around 1505–10.[10] The book's calendar recalls books of hours written in Bruges.[11]   T. K.

Notes

1. Mazal and Thoss 1993.

2. The Croÿ Lazarus miniature goes back to an older pattern. A miniature based on the older pattern appears in the Hours of Isabella of Castile (cat. no. 105, fol. 220; De Winter 1981: 411, fig. 147), while a roughly contemporaneous version, by Simon Bening, appears in the Da Costa Hours (cat. no. 140, fol. 226v). Gerard Horenbout undertook a further sophisticated rethinking of the second version of the pattern (as copied in the Croÿ Hours and the present volume) in the Sforza Hours (cat. no. 129, fol. 257v).

3. Winkler (1925: 178) believed that they were the same artist, perhaps from the workshop of the Master of the *Hortulus animae*. (The works formerly attributed to this master have, however, since been reassigned to other illuminators.) Winkler considered the style similar to that of the Master of James IV.

4. David himself based his interpretation on an older pattern. See the London Hastings Hours (cat. no. 41, fol. 73v) for the earliest version of this pattern.

5. For example, the setting of *Pentecost* in a book of hours by the Master of the David Scenes in the Grimani Breviary (ill. 137a).

6. Colding 1953: 64–65, and especially Strong, in Murdoch et al. 1981: 3–4, 30.

7. Winkler 1925: 178.

8. Compare, for example, the interior in the *Pentecost* by the Master of James IV in the Croÿ Hours or in the Spinola Hours (cat. no. 124, fol. 31v) and *The Raising of Lazarus* in the Sforza Hours (cat. no. 129, fol. 257v).

9. According to Brinkmann (1997: 378), this is more characteristic of French manuscripts of the period, as is the script, so that the book was perhaps produced in France. None of the liturgical features of either the calendar or the litany, however, points strongly to a French owner or a French center of production.

10. Maryan W. Ainsworth (2003) assigned the Croÿ Hours this dating on the basis of the execution of David's miniature of the *Head of Christ* (fol. 14v). Mazal and Thoss (1993: 89–90) dated the book a bit later, to the second decade of the sixteenth century. The British Library volume has been dated as early as the end of the fifteenth century and as late as about 1525–30.

11. The calendar shows strong similarities to the Bourbon-Montpensier Hours (cat. no. 44; 93 percent), to the Escorial Hours (cat. no. 99; 91.47 percent), and to a book of hours from the Vrelant circle (Baltimore, Walters Art Museum, Ms. W. 179; Randall 1997: 295–98, no. 259; 91.47 percent).

162a
ANONYMOUS
Bathsheba, fol. 43v

162b
ANONYMOUS
The Nativity, fol. 25v

JAN GOSSAERT

Often known as "Mabuse"—after his native town of Maubeuge, in the Burgundian province of Hainaut—Jan Gossaert was probably born around 1478. Nothing is known of his early training, although certain scholars have suggested that he may have studied in Bruges, perhaps with Gerard David.[1] Gossaert was probably the Jennyn van Hennegouwe (John of Hainaut) who registered as a master in the Guild of Saint Luke in Antwerp in 1503. Unfortunately no painting can be securely connected with this early Antwerp phase.

Gossaert's visit to Rome in 1508 marked a watershed in his career. In October of that year, Philip of Burgundy, an illegitimate son of Philip the Good, undertook a diplomatic mission to Pope Julius II. Gossaert not only visited Rome, where he made a series of drawings after antique sculpture, but also made stops in Trento, Verona, Mantua, and Florence. Exposure to the art of Italy profoundly altered his vision, and his subsequent work demonstrates a sustained effort to develop a fully Italianate style.

After returning from Rome in 1509, Gossaert remained in Philip's service. When the prince moved to Suytburg (Souburg) in late 1515, he involved Gossaert and Jacopo de' Barbari in his plan to decorate his Italian-style palace with figures from classical mythology. It was thus that Gossaert came to paint life-size secular nudes, a subject unprecedented in Flemish art. The 1516 panel painting *Neptune and Amphitrite* (Berlin, Gemäldegalerie), with Gossaert's latinized signature, was perhaps made for Philip's castle.

In 1517 Philip became bishop of Utrecht, and the artist may have accompanied his patron there. In 1523 Gossaert entered the service of Philip's half brother Adolph of Burgundy. Gossaert continued to receive commissions from important private patrons, including Jean Carondelet, chancellor of Flanders, and King Christian II of Denmark. For these, Gossaert painted portraits that served to attract further patronage, such as that of Emperor Charles V and Margaret of Austria. His portraits of Charles of Burgundy (ca. 1525; Berlin, Staatliche Museen), Eleanor of Austria (ca. 1525; H. A. Wetzlar Collection, Amsterdam), and Jean Carondelet (1517; Musée du Louvre, Paris) reveal his acute observation of character.

Gossaert's final years were primarily spent serving the Spanish patron and art collector Mencía de Mendoza. In all likelihood he executed a series of portraits for her collection (see cat. no. 149). The series seems to have been cut short by Gossaert's death on October 13, 1532.   M.-T. A.

Note

1. See Weisz 1913; Winkler 1921a: 14; and von der Osten 1961: 458, 460–62.

163

JAN GOSSAERT

Portrait of a Grand Commander of the Order of Santiago
Antwerp, ca. 1530–32

Oil on wood panel, 43.8 × 33.7 cm (17¼ × 13¼ in.)

COLLECTION: Los Angeles, J. Paul Getty Museum, 88.PB.43

PROVENANCE: Prof. Odilon Lannelongue (d. 1911), Castéra-Verduzan; to Musée Lannelongue, 1911–86; to heirs of Odilon Lannelongue in 1986 [their sale, Briscadieu, Auch-en-Gascogne, December 7, 1986, lot 108]; [Edward Speelman, London]; acquired 1988

JPGM

In this portrait Jan Gossaert depicted a grand commander of the chivalric Order of Santiago, as indicated by the red *flory-fitchy* cross of the order and the suspended jeweled gold cockleshell. The sitter has been identified as Francisco de los Cobos, grand commander of León, who was in the Netherlands during the last two years of Gossaert's life, when the portrait was probably executed.[1] This identification is based primarily on the resemblance between the painting's cockleshell and that depicted in Cobos's portrait medal (Madrid, Museo del Prado, inv. O-1112).[2]

Nevertheless, another possible subject for the portrait—Juan de Zúñiga—has come to light.[3] This painting may once have belonged to Mencía de Mendoza, who employed Gossaert, Bernard van Orley, and Simon Bening.[4] Mencía's household inventory records an extensive portrait collection in the library of her castle in Ayora, Spain, which included "a painting of the Grand Commander of Castile, Juan de Zúñiga [which] measures ½ vara and ¼ palmo by ½ vara minus 2 fingers" (equal to the modern-day measurement 50.8 × 41.3 cm [20 × 16¼ in.]). This corresponds with the Getty portrait measurements, assuming that there was a frame about 1½ inches wide all the way around.[5]

A later inventory seems to describe the Getty portrait again: "Item, a portrait of the Grand Commander for Castile dressed in black, painted with a green backdrop on panel with a cross of Santiago on the chest."[6] (It is worth noting that Gossaert did not often employ green backdrops, as he did in the Getty portrait.) Juan de Zúñiga y Avellaneda, governor and chamberlain to Philip II, was—like Cobos—a grand commander for the order and accompanied Charles V in the Netherlands from late 1530 through mid-1532. Further, Zúñiga sat for a portrait while in the Netherlands; thus, he too could have sat for Gossaert.[7] All of this points to the possibility that the Getty portrait by Gossaert may be identical to the portrait of Zúñiga described in the collection inventories of the great Renaissance patron Mencía de Mendoza.

163
JAN GOSSAERT
*Portrait of a Grand
Commander of the Order
of Santiago*

Gossaert's acute observation of form, facility in rendering surface textures, and psychological insight endow the
sitter with intense physical presence. The elegant, lively
treatment of the hands animates the stiff pose. These
aspects of Gossaert's art profoundly influenced the portraits subsequently executed by other artists—including
Van Orley and Bening—for Mendoza's portrait collection.

M.-T. A.

Notes

1. Los Angeles 1989: 123, no. 30; the identification of the sitter as
Cobos was initially based on research by Víctor Franco de Baux.

2. Toledo 2001: 388.

3. A longer essay by the author on this subject is in progress as of
this writing.

4. Much of what we know to date concerning Gossaert has
stemmed from published correspondence between him and Mencía
de Mendoza. See March 1949: 219–21.

5. This seems to be a standard-size frame in this collection. Most
inventories include the frame in their measurements. Among Gossaert's accepted portraits, none of the others matches the measurements given in the inventories.

6. Inventory of the goods, Duchess of Calabria, 1554, Archivo del
Palau, bundle no. 122. Note that artists' names are generally not listed
in inventories.

7. In 1529 Charles V and his court set sail from Barcelona for his
imperial coronation in Bologna. By November 1530 Charles V and his
court (including both Cobos and Zúñiga) were in Flanders, where
they remained until, at the very least, July 1532. Much of 1531 was spent
in Brussels. By 1533 they were back in Spain. A 1548 document mentions a portrait of himself that Zúñiga had commissioned while he
was in Flanders with Charles V (see March 1949: 219–21).

CORNELIS MASSYS

Cornelis Massys, the son of the famous Antwerp painter Quentin Massys, was probably born around 1510, shortly after the birth of his elder brother Jan, who would also become a well-known painter. In the year following Quentin's death in 1530, Cornelis was registered as a master in the Guild of Saint Luke in Antwerp, although he subsequently disappeared from guild records. By 1538 Cornelis Massys had learned the art of engraving, producing works deeply influenced by Italian Renaissance motifs and forms.[1] More than 150 engravings by this artist survive, featuring not only religious subjects but also numerous genre scenes, including *Four Blind Men*, which served as the source for Pieter Bruegel the Elder's celebrated *Parable of the Blind Leading the Blind*.[2] In 1544, when Massys was exiled from Brabant, he may have sought refuge in England, and he later traveled to Germany and Italy. Archival evidence indicates that he died sometime between April 1556 and January 1557.[3]

Massys was known primarily as an engraver until art historians at the beginning of the twentieth century began to focus on his contributions to the art of landscape painting.[4] The seven surviving landscapes bearing his mark, four of which are dated, have provided the basis for attributing other paintings to the artist.[5] His earliest dated painting, from 1538, is characterized by clumsy figures and a landscape treatment that—with its jagged, rocky outcroppings and high vantage point—was indebted to Joachim Patinir. By 1543, when he painted *Mary and Joseph at the Inn* (ill. 164), Massys had rejected Patinir's grandiose style for one far more realistic and immediate in feel. Although not all of his later landscapes maintained this quality, he did continue to produce works that were more naturalistic in their approach, often fusing soft colors with a sense of intimacy. The paintings from late in his career became more ambitiously panoramic, with a flair for integrating figures and landscape. Massys is also celebrated for a series of landscape sketches he executed,[6] among the earliest of their kind known in the Netherlands. Their rejection of historical narrative in favor of landscape elements represents a significant move toward the depiction of pure landscape.[7]   E. M.

Notes

1. Friedländer 1924–37, 13: 21.

2. Van der Stock (1985) argued that Massys's work paved the way for the extraordinary developments in Antwerp printmaking under Hieronymus Cock.

3. Van der Stock 1984: 119.

4. Dunbar (1974–80: 97) traced the history of the shift in interest from Massys the engraver to Massys the painter.

5. The seven signed paintings are *The Return of the Prodigal Son* (1538, Amsterdam, Rijksmuseum); *Mary and Joseph at the Inn* (cat. no. 164); *Saint Jerome in a Landscape* (1547, Antwerp, Koninklijk Museum voor Schone Kunsten); *Landscape with Singing Figures* (1556, Amsterdam, formerly de Boer Foundation); *Christ Carrying the Cross* (Prague, Narodni Galerie); *Landscape with Hunting Scenes* (Dessau, Staatliche Galerie); and *The Burning of Sodom* (present location unknown). Dunbar (1974–80: 107–13) attributed a few more paintings to him based on style. Van der Stock (1983) provided a revised list.

6. These drawings, a number of which are signed, mostly date to the 1540s (Zwollo 1965; Dunbar 1979).

7. Washington 1986a: 222–23.

164

CORNELIS MASSYS

Mary and Joseph at the Inn
Antwerp, 1543

Oil on oak panel, 27 × 38 cm (10⅝ × 15 in.)

INSCRIPTIONS: *CME 1543*, lower right

COLLECTION: Berlin, Staatliche Museen zu Berlin, Gemäldegalerie, no. 675

PROVENANCE: Solly Collection; acquired 1821

JPGM

Capturing a sense of midwinter with its threatening sky, leafless trees, and brown tonalities, this painting offers an intimate look at village life.[1] At first glance, the figures disporting themselves in the foreground capture the attention, but the eye is slowly drawn to the large inn where Mary and Joseph seek refuge. The emphasis on the foreground and the mixture of contemporary and religious subjects set this work apart from the older landscape tradition, represented by Joachim Patinir and Herri met de Bles, where the view of the distance plays a stronger role. In Massys's carefully observed view of village life, the forces of nature dominate the cadences of human activities.

The rustic theme finds its closest parallel in calendar miniatures, which depict precisely the changing conditions of the seasons. The calendars produced by Simon Bening—for example, the February opening in the Munich-Montserrat calendar (ill. 154a)—not only exhibit closely observed seasonal conditions, such as an approaching winter storm, but also, like the Massys painting, present the scene's action in the nearest plane of the foreground at the lowest edge of the composition (see ills. 140a, 159a–d).

Since the subject of Mary and Joseph's arrival in Bethlehem is quite rare in panel painting of the period, it is likely that Massys turned to manuscript illumination for his inspiration. A similar arrangement of the figures of

the innkeeper, Joseph, Mary, and the donkey—from
right to left—appears in the borders of at least eight Flemish devotional books dating from the 1480s through the
1520s (see cat. no. 21).² The architectural features of
the thatched-roofed inn are also broadly reminiscent of
these illuminations.   R. G.

Notes
1. Massys's landscape style is discussed in Dunbar 1974–80.

2. A sixteenth-century example (see fig. 51) by the workshop of the
Master of James IV of Scotland is in the Chatsworth Hours (fig. 51). For
more on this iconography in manuscripts, see cat. no. 21. *The Arrival in
Bethlehem*, a panel attributed to Master LC depicting the same subject,
is roughly contemporaneous with the Massys panel (New York, Metropolitan Museum of Art, Rogers Fund, 1916 16.69); see New York
1998: 270. Two other panels of the subject, which have been question-
ably attributed to Cornelis's brother Jan, have later dates: 1558
(Antwerp, Koninklijk Museum voor Schone Kunsten, inv. no. 251) and
1562 (private collection). The Massys panel may have directly
influenced the emphasis on the foreground and the handling of the
trees in the latter. See Buijnsters-Smets 1995: 223–25.

164

CORNELIS MASSYS
*Mary and Joseph at
the Inn*

PIETER BRUEGEL THE ELDER

Our principal sources on the painter and drafts-man Pieter Bruegel the Elder (ca. 1525–1569) are a handful of documents and a biography by Carel van Mander printed in 1604, thirty-five years after Bruegel's death.[1] Probably born in Breda,[2] he trained in Antwerp, perhaps under Pieter Coecke van Aelst, who was the court painter of Charles V.[3] This apprenticeship is not supported on stylistic grounds, but Bruegel was demon-strably influenced by Coecke van Aelst's brother-in-law Jan van Amstel (the Brunswick Monogrammist).[4] Bruegel was in Antwerp by 1551, when his name was recorded among the masters in the Guild of Saint Luke.[5] Soon after entering the guild, he traveled through France, Italy, and Sicily, where he sketched landscapes. He met the celebrated illu-minator Giulio Clovio in Rome around 1553 and collabo-rated with him on a miniature for which Bruegel most likely provided the landscape.[6] Bruegel had returned to Antwerp by 1555, when the publisher Hieronymus Cock began issuing engravings after Bruegel's drawings, includ-ing a set of twelve so-called *Large Landscapes*. Because of their wide dissemination, Bruegel was known primarily as a draftsman during his lifetime. In 1563 he married Coecke van Aelst's daughter Maria in Brussels, where he died on September 9, 1569.

Bruegel's work is often moralizing in nature and at times exhibits indebtedness to Hieronymus Bosch (d. 1516). Indeed, by the late sixteenth century Bruegel was widely known as the second Bosch.[7] Cock published engravings after Bruegel's drawings under Bosch's name—for instance, *Big Fish Eat the Little Fish*, dated 1556.[8] Enigmatic Boschian imagery full of hybrids and demons appears in Bruegel's paintings from the early 1560s, such as *The Fall of the Rebel Angels*, *Dulle Griet*, and *The Triumph of Death*.

Bruegel often fashioned his compositions with a high vantage point, which was perhaps influenced not only by Joachim Patinir but also by Bruegel's humanist friend the cartographer Abraham Ortelius, who was royal geogra-pher to Philip II and who in 1570 produced the first modern atlas.[9] Bruegel's townscapes—such as *Netherlandish Proverbs* (1559), *Children's Games* (ca. 1560), and *Battle between Carnival and Lent* (1559?)—are densely populated with his preferred subjects, rugged peasants at work and play. In 1565 he produced a painted series of months for Niclaes Jonghelinck, a royal official and banker in Antwerp. The five surviving landscapes from this series show that Bruegel imbued the worldview landscape popularized by Patinir with a new monumentality and consistent perspec-tive. They exemplify a careful observation of nature and a mastery of both color and texture that create distinc-tive atmospheric conditions for each month—effects previously achieved largely within the tradition of manu-script illumination.

In addition to Jonghelinck, who owned sixteen of his paintings, Bruegel's patrons included Cardinal de Gran-vella, Giulio Clovio, and Hans Franckert (a German mer-chant). The city of Brussels commissioned paintings commemorating the 1565 completion of the Brussels-Antwerp Canal.[10] His sophisticated and scholarly clientele and his friendships with men such as Ortelius suggest that Bruegel moved comfortably among the urban elite and their lively humanist culture. Indeed, recent scholarship has largely disproved the notion of Bruegel the peasant, which was introduced by Van Mander.[11]   R. G.

Notes

1. Van Mander 1604: fols. 233–34. On the documentary evidence, see Marijnissen and Seidel 1971: 13–17.

2. Scholars have debated Bruegel's birthplace. See Guicciardini 1588: 130; Van Mander 1604: fol. 233; Bastelaer and Hulin de Loo 1907: 144–45, n. 2.

3. Van Mander (1604: fol. 233) asserted that Bruegel studied with Coecke van Aelst. Bruegel's name does not appear among those of Coecke van Aelst's pupils registered with the Antwerp guild; see Gibson 1977: 15.

4. See Gibson 1977: 128–29; and Wied, in DOA 1996, 4: 896.

5. Friedländer 1967–76, 14: 13.

6. The miniature, along with paintings by Bruegel, is mentioned in the 1577 inventory of Clovio's property: "Un quadretto di miniatura la metà a fatto per mano sua et altra da Mº Pietro Brugole" (Gross-mann 1966: 16). Clovio's paintings by Bruegel included a *View of Lyons*, a *Tower of Babel* on ivory, and a tree study on linen—none of which survives. Although this attribution is not generally accepted, Tolnay (1965: 110) ascribed to Bruegel a border miniature, *Stormy Harbor with Many Boats* (Towneley Lectionary, New York Public Library, Ms. 91, fol. 23). Miniatures in the Clovio manuscript in Sir John Soane's Museum and in the Farnese Hours in the Morgan Library have also been attributed to Bruegel, but these attributions are generally not accepted. See Royalton-Kisch, in New York 2001: 23, 37, n. 47; and Tolnay 1980, which contains additional bibliography.

7. Dominicus Lampsonius wrote in 1572: "Who is this new Hieronymus Bosch, reborn to the world?" (Grossmann 1966: 9). See also Guicciardini 1588: 130.

8. On the drawing and engraving, see New York 2001: 140–42.

9. Grossmann 1966: 13. On Ortelius and Bruegel, see Muylle 1981.

10. Van Mander 1604: fol. 233v. Bruegel died before the paintings were completed.

11. For example, see Meadow's introduction to De Jong et al. 1997.

165

PIETER BRUEGEL THE ELDER

Landscape with a Magpie on the Gallows
Brussels, 1568

Oil on wood panel, 45.9 × 50.8 cm (18¹⁄₁₆ × 20 in.)

INSCRIPTIONS: BRVEGEL 1568, lower right

COLLECTION: Darmstadt, Hessisches Landesmuseum, inv. no. GK 165

PROVENANCE: Maria Coecke van Aelst Bruegel; Georg Wilhelm Issel (1785–1870); purchased 1865

JPGM and RA

165
PIETER BRUEGEL
THE ELDER
*Landscape with a Magpie
on the Gallows*

This beautiful landscape is one of the smallest, and perhaps the last produced, by Pieter Bruegel. Framed between trees high upon a hillside, a broad plain unfolds below toward a distant horizon. Surrounded by a green landscape tinged in brown, suggestive of a late summer's day, a magpie perches on the crossbeam of a gallows that looms dauntingly at the center of the composition. At left, peasants dance in the merriment of a kermis that continues in the village down the hillside, and to the right a cross and water mill are visible over the hill. The genius of this carefully observed and detailed study of the natural world resides in the marriage of close-up and distant views, in the richly varied textures of the setting, and in the delicacy of the effects of light.

Unlike the panoramic landscapes of Joachim Patinir (ca. 1485–1524), which lack a consistent sense of spatial recession, Bruegel's atmospheric landscape gracefully extends to the distant horizon, where details blur and colors fade, creating a harmoniously smooth progression of space. The measured spatial recession, level of detail, and seasonal atmospheric conditions seen in *Landscape with a Magpie on the Gallows* compare most closely to manuscript calendar cycles such as those by Simon Bening (cat. nos. 150, 154, 159).[1] In this work, Bruegel, like Bening, painted with fine points of color that are seen, for example, in the flecklike strokes reproducing the effects of light and shadow dancing on foliage (see ill. 159a). A miniature by Bening, produced in the late 1540s or early 1550s (ill. 159b), depicting the month of June, shares a common spatial construction with Bruegel's painting: at the lower left, a triangular hill anchors the foreground while trees and houses fill the descent to a wide river valley that extends to the horizon.

Bruegel's familiarity with the art of illuminators is well documented. Not only is he known to have collaborated on a miniature with Giulio Clovio, but his mother-in-law, Mayken Verhulst (ca. 1520–1600), was also a well-regarded miniaturist whom Lodovico Guicciardini considered one of the four finest female painters in the Netherlands.[2] Such evidence suggests that Bruegel was well aware of the Flemish manuscript tradition. The miniature-like quality of this painting, with its close attention to detail, confirms visual evidence suggesting that he looked to the art of manuscript illumination for inspiration.

Carel van Mander, writing in 1604, mentioned that Bruegel had bequeathed the painting to his widow and explained that "by the magpie he meant the gossips whom he delivered to the gallows."[3] Common Flemish expressions—such as "to chatter like a magpie," "as garrulous as a magpie," and "to talk someone to the gallows"—suggest some veracity in Van Mander's comment.[4] The painting has been variously interpreted as alluding to nature's indifference to human folly,[5] the unrelenting courage of Bruegel's homeland in the face of war and devastation,[6] the defiance of political domination and the ability to live in the face of despotism,[7] and the oppression of the Church by civil justice, or vice versa.[8] Recently it has been argued that the painting may have encouraged "viewers to consider questions of order and authority, and the dangers that arose when these were compromised."[9] Regardless of its allegorical interpretation, the landscape remains a tour de force in the history of painting.   R. G.

Notes

1. Bruegel's connection with manuscript illumination has been discussed, notably by Tolnay (1934: 125); Kren (in Malibu 1983a: 7; and in Kren and Rathofer 1988: 205, 206, 253, 256, 259, 263, 278); Buchanan (1990: 543–50), who compares Bruegel's work with that of Simon Bening; and Royalton-Kisch (in New York 2001: 22–23). See also Vöhringer 2002.

2. For his collaboration with Clovio, see Grossmann 1966: 16. For Verhulst, see, among several early editions, Guicciardini 1588: 131. Genaille (1988: 138) suggested that Verhulst introduced Bruegel to miniature painting and that Bruegel knew early in his career the breviaries produced in Bening's workshop. According to Van Mander (1604: fol. 234), after Bruegel's death Verhulst taught Bruegel's son Jan to paint watercolors. No works by Verhulst have been identified.

3. Van Mander 1604: fols. 233v–234. Translation from Marijnissen and Seidel 1971: 314.

4. Wied 1994: 35. The dancing peasants and the man defecating in the lower left corner likewise suggest Dutch proverbial sayings: "to dance to the gallows" and "shitting on the gallows." These themes also appear in Bruegel's *Netherlandish Proverbs* (Berlin, Staatliche Museen). Scholarship on the proverbs is extensive; see, for example, Meadow 2002, which includes additional bibliography.

5. Genaille 1980: 151.

6. Gibson 1991: 45–46.

7. Michel 1931: 65.

8. Wied 1994: 35.

9. Kavaler 1999: 258. I am indebted to Kavaler's overview of interpretations of the painting.

MASTER OF CHARLES V AND CIRCLE

Friedrich Winkler originally named the Master of Charles V to identify the artist who illuminated the Prayer Book of Charles V between 1516 and 1519 (Vienna, Österreichische Nationalbibliothek, Ms. 1859); he then attributed six other manuscripts to this master's hand.[1] Georges Dogaer later grouped fourteen manuscripts under the rubric "Master of Charles V (School)," including some of the same ones as Winkler.[2] Because almost all of these manuscripts are linked codicologically or iconographically rather than stylistically, defining the artist and his circle has proved problematic. In the 1987 exhibition catalogue of Flemish manuscripts in Vienna, Dagmar Thoss declined to attribute any manuscripts to the Master of Charles V, including the Prayer Book of Charles V itself.[3]

If one uses the name manuscript as the basis for characterizing the Master of Charles V as an artistic identity, his work appears most closely related to that of Simon Bening (see fig. 73).[4] Comparable in the illuminations of both artists are sturdy, compact figures that are impressively sculptural in their conception, both in terms of their musculature and in the delineation of their drapery. Unlike Bening's varied palette of saturated colors, however, the colors used by the Master of Charles V are largely pastels or muted blues and reds, which create an overall softer effect. The Master of Charles V was also much more limited than Bening in his conception of space: interiors in his work are simple backdrops, while his exteriors are composed of abbreviated landscapes. In addition, the Master of Charles V occasionally incorporated some elements of Mannerism into his miniatures, such as fluttering pieces of drapery and exaggerated hand gestures, aspects that would play a larger role in the work of later artists in his circle.

A secondary stylistic feature that links many of the manuscripts attributed to the Master of Charles V or his circle is the use of frames composed of a mixture of Gothic and Renaissance decorative elements. The frames, evoking carved wooden altarpieces, have elaborate finials and architectural elements that are set against the bare parchment, making them seem almost as if they were floating on the page.[5] These distinctive frames, which surround every miniature in the name manuscript of the Master of Charles V, have largely provided the basis for attributing other works to the circle of the Master of Charles V.[6] Because the frames share aspects of the architectural fantasies of Bernard van Orley,[7] and because a number of the manuscripts associated with the Master of Charles V were made for patrons at the Hapsburg court, it is likely that Brussels or Mechelen was the center of activity for the artist and his circle.[8]

One of the most important artists in the circle of the Master of Charles V is the illuminator of another prayer book made for Charles V, now in the Morgan Library, New York (cat. no. 166), here named the Master of Morgan M.491.[9] The name manuscript of the Master of Charles V and this later prayer book, dated 1533 by a scribe from Brussels, are similar in terms of their secondary decoration and codicology. The Master of Morgan M.491 sometimes also utilized the compositions of the Master of Charles V, but the former is far more Mannerist in his approach. The figures are taller and more willowy than those of the Master of Charles V, and their draperies attest to a greater interest in surface pattern than in the articulation of the bodies beneath. The Master of Morgan M.491 also devoted more attention to the landscapes of his miniatures, which are atmospheric and dramatic in comparison to the rather bland, stilted backdrops of the Master of Charles V (ill. 166a). The work of the Master of Morgan M.491 can also be seen in books of hours in the Koninklijke Bibliotheek, The Hague (Ms. 133 D II); the British Library, London (Add. Ms. 35218); and the Österreichische Nationalbibliothek (Ms. 1875).[10] A miniature of the Coronation of the Virgin, based on a composition by the Master of Charles V seen in the name manuscript, is almost identical in three of these manuscripts.[11] Illuminations by the Master of Morgan M.491 in all four of the manuscripts share the particular technique of indicating folds in cloth by means of a series of dark, horizontal parallel brushstrokes.

A second artist in the circle of the Master of Charles V is defined by his work in a third prayer book made for Charles V, also in the Morgan Library (cat. no. 167); he is here referred to as the Master of Morgan M.696.[12] The manuscript was illuminated sometime after 1547, almost three decades after the Prayer Book of Charles V, yet it features the same format, many of the same texts, the illusionistic architectural frames, and a number of the same compositions. The Master of Morgan M.696, whose agitated brushwork and use of flowing draperies relate his style to the Mannerism of the Master of Morgan M.491, at the same time also evidences a return to the interest in bodily form that characterized the work of the Master of Charles V, seen in the impressive musculature of some figures and the more stolid presence of others. This artist was also probably responsible for a series of half-lengths in the manuscript showing the strong influence of the Antwerp Mannerist Joos van Cleve, especially in their compositional construction (ill. 167b).

Of the other manuscripts associated with the Master of Charles V, only a few show the direct influence of his style;[13] the others use the vocabulary of the architectural frames and are painted in a Mannerist style more closely related to the illuminations of the Master of Morgan M.491 and the Master of Morgan M.696.   E. M.

Notes

1. Winkler 1925: 151. The seven works are the Prayer Book of Charles V (Vienna, Österreichische Nationalbibliothek, Ms. 1859); the Prayer Book of Archduke Ferdinand (Vienna, Österreichische Nationalbibliothek, Ms. s.n. 2624); two prayer books (Munich, J. Rosenthal; Brussels, Bibliothèque royale de Belgique, Ms. II 668); the Hours of Bona Sforza (cat. no. 129; now identified as a documented work by Horenbout); *Virgin and Child with Saint Anne* (Berlin, Dr. Grabowsky), and the Arenberg Missal (cat. no. 170). The last two were tentatively ascribed to him.

2. Dogaer 1987a: 169–70. Dogaer's list does not include the Hours of Bona Sforza or the two private collection works mentioned by Winkler.

3. Thoss 1987: 133–34.

4. Other manuscripts with miniatures likely by the hand of the Master of Charles V include a book of hours made for Archduke Ferdinand, the brother of Charles V (Vienna, Österreichische Nationalbibliothek, Ms. s.n. 2624); a book of hours in Brussels (Bibliothèque royale de Belgique, Ms. II 668); and the Capricorn Hours (Sotheby's, London, July 6, 2000). The last is a manuscript containing work by Bening as well, which provides another link between the two artists.

5. An early precursor of this frame, much heavier in conception, can be found around a miniature by Bening in the Rothschild Book of Hours (private collection, fol. 245v).

6. Manuscripts containing these borders include Brussels, Bibliothèque royale, Mss. II 668, IV 415, 10895; London, British Library, Mss. Add. 25693, Add. 35218; New York, Morgan Library, Mss. M.491, M.696; Vienna, Archives of the Golden Fleece, Ms. 10; and Vienna, Österreichische Nationalbibliothek, Ms. 1859, Ms. s.n. 2624. Dogaer (1987a: 170) attributed a number of these to the school of the Master of Charles V.

7. The rather minimalist tall structures seen in a diptych by Van Orley in the National Gallery in Washington, D.C., or the more ornate ones seen in the Altarpiece of the Legends of Saints Thomas and Matthew (Vienna, Kunsthistorisches Museum; Friedländer 1927–34, 8: pls. 88, 72) contain forms very similar to those found in the frames associated with the Master of Charles V and his circle.

8. Winkler (1925: 151) was the first to suggest this possibility, later supported by Dogaer (1987a: 169). In addition to the manuscripts made for Charles V, a book of hours illuminated by the Master of Charles V and assistants was made for the emperor's brother, Archduke Ferdinand (Vienna, Österreichische Nationalbibliothek, Ms. s.n. 2624). The scribe of a later prayer book illuminated by artists in the circle of the Master of Charles V identified himself as "Gratianus of Brussels" (cat. no. 166, fol. 18v), providing further evidence for a Brussels localization for the circle of the Master of Charles V.

9. There are two artists active in Morgan Library, Ms. M.491. Although the artist named the Master of Morgan M.491 was responsible for less of the illumination than the second artist in the book, his work is considerably higher in quality. For a discussion of the second artist, see cat. no. 166.

10. The Hague and Vienna manuscripts have the more traditional strewn-flower borders, while the London manuscript features the distinctive architectural frames around its miniatures.

11. The Coronation of the Virgin appears on folio 128 of the Prayer Book of Charles V, and in the others as follows: New York, Morgan Library, M. 491, fol. 172; Antwerp, Koninklijke Bibliotheek, Ms. 133 D II, fol. 61v; and London, British Library, Add. Ms. 35218, fol. 77v.

12. For a discussion of the group of miniatures in this manuscript that are probably by a less capable follower of the Master of Morgan M.696, see cat. no. 167.

13. A devotional manuscript in London (British Library, Add. Ms. 25693) and a prayer book at Oxford (Bodleian Library, Canon. Liturg. 148) have miniatures showing the stocky figures and soft coloring seen in work of the Master of Charles V, but the architectural frames are less carefully sculpted than those in the name manuscript, and the figures are more rounded and less articulated; both manuscripts are probably by a follower of the Master of Charles V.

166

MASTER OF MORGAN M.491 AND CIRCLE OF MASTER OF CHARLES V

Book of Hours
Use of Rome
Brussels, 1533

MANUSCRIPT: 271 + i folios, 14.1 × 8.2 cm (5⁹⁄₁₆ × 3¼ in.); justification: 10.7 × 5.2 cm (4³⁄₁₆ × 2¹⁄₁₆ in.); 26 lines of *hybrida* by F. Gratianus; 82 half-page miniatures, 4 calendar tables

HERALDRY: Escutcheon with the arms of Charles V surrounded by collar of the Order of the Golden Fleece, fols. 19, 54; motto *Plus Outre*, fols. 19, 130; escutcheon with the arms of his chaplain, a member of the Pot family (?) (quartered, 1 and 4, azure three six-pointed estoiles argent; 2 and 3 or a fess azure, in chief a label of five points sable), fol. 35v

INSCRIPTIONS: *Hunc librum antiquitate . . . dono . . .* , fol. 5v; *F. Gratianus Brux: Cap: haec scripsit*, fol. 266v

BINDING: Sixteenth century; brown calf; painted arms of Emperor Charles V, badly rubbed; lettering *Liber Precum / Caroli Quinti / Imperatoris / Anno [1533?]*, nearly obliterated; in brown morocco case

COLLECTION: New York, The Morgan Library, Ms. M.491

PROVENANCE: Emperor Charles V (1500–1558); to his chaplain, a member of the Pot family; Sir Francis B. Palmer, 1908; Jacques Seligmann, Paris; to J. P. Morgan (1837–1913) in 1912

JPGM and RA

166a (opposite)
MASTER OF MORGAN
M.491
Saint Anthony, fol. 59v

166b
ANONYMOUS
Portrait of a Cleric and
CIRCLE OF MASTER
OF CHARLES V
*The Virgin and Child
Enthroned*, fols. 35v–36

This book of hours, dated 1533, is one of four similar prayer books made for Emperor Charles V between about 1516 and 1540. The most distinctive elements of these small books are their unusually vertical format, their similar texts, and—for three of the four—the frames infused with Italianate motifs that appear on each page with a miniature.[1] Of the four prayer books, the two that seem most closely related textually are this manuscript and the Prayer Book of Charles V (Vienna, Österreichische National-albibliothek, Ms. 1859).[2] The two books contain almost identical texts, and for the most part, the texts occur in the same sequence in both manuscripts. Indeed, it is probable that the present volume was copied directly from the earlier Vienna prayer book. Despite the close textual correspondence, however, the iconography of the miniatures illustrating these texts is predominantly unrelated. Nearly all of the miniatures of this book repeat the subjects of those of the Vienna manuscript, yet only eleven of its eighty-two half-page miniatures can be said to follow closely the compositions of the Vienna miniatures.[3]

Although both this manuscript and the Prayer Book of Charles V in Vienna have been ascribed to the circle of the Master of Charles V,[4] only the most general stylistic simi-larity links them. The Vienna miniatures, all by the Master of Charles V, are largely indebted to the work of Simon Bening; this is evident both in the compositional format and in the articulation of the figures, with their large, round heads and relatively small hands (fig. 73). These features are also seen in the miniatures of the present volume, but they are even further removed from Bening, being more dra-matic and mannered in their presentation and, at the same time, characterized by a marked sacrifice in the quality of the drawing.

The work of the first of the two artists active in this book is more closely related in style to the Vienna minia-tures, mostly because he is the more staid and less flamboy-ant artist of the two. This artist was responsible for the majority of the illumination in the volume, and his work is recognizable from figures with sketchy features and extremely small, ineffectual hands, painted rapidly and carelessly. These features can be seen in *The Virgin and Child Enthroned* (ill. 166b) and other miniatures,[5] including the nocturnal miniature of the Arrest of Christ (fol. 110), which combines the kind of theatrical scene prized by the artist with a series of figures who have unarticulated faces and weak anatomy.[6]

Figure 73
MASTER OF
CHARLES V
Mary Magdalene. In
the Prayer Book of
Charles V, 15.3 × 8.2 cm
(6 × 3¼ in.). Vienna,
Österreichische
Nationalbibliothek,
Ms. 1859, fol. 241

The second artist, the more skilled of the two, is introduced here as the Master of Morgan M.491. He is even more Mannerist in his approach than the first artist discussed, painting figures with long, blowing curls; sharp features; and billowing drapery—seen, for example, in the angel in the portrait of Charles V (fol. 54v).[7] One of the hallmarks of his style is a tendency to indicate shadows by short horizontal strokes of a dark color in parallel series. His most accomplished work in the manuscript is the wonderfully painted miniature of Saint Anthony (ill. 166a).[8] The saint is reading a book, a seemingly quiet task, yet there is a strong sense of movement to the right that indicates his engagement with the text, implied by such subtle elements as the turn of his foot, the expression on his face, and the position of his hands. The deep vista seen in the background shows the influence of the work of Joachim Patinir, especially the way the landscape is dramatized through the inclusion of a single, prominent rocky outcropping in the middle distance.

The present manuscript is dated 1533 on folio 18v, and the scribe Gratianus of Brussels is named on folio 266v. The imperial arms and motto appear twice each in the manuscript, and a portrait of Charles V in prayer with his guardian angel appears on folio 54v. This portrait, painted by the better of the two artists described here, is loosely related to the earlier portrait of him in the Vienna manu-

script and would seem, as that portrait does, to indicate patronage. A second portrait appears in the present manuscript, however, and has traditionally been assumed to be a likeness of the chaplain of Charles V (ill. 166b), perhaps a member of the Pot family.[9] The portrait is oddly placed and is stylistically distinct from anything else in the manuscript.[10] It is possible that the portrait was an afterthought or was even added later if Charles gave the manuscript as a gift to his chaplain.[11]

E. M.

Notes

1. All four prayer books have heraldry and portraits of the emperor that indicate they were either made for Charles V, or at his behest as gifts. The earlier three are Vienna, Österreichische Nationalbibliothek, Ms. 1859, between 1516 and 1519; the present volume, dated 1533; and Vienna, Österreichische Nationalbibliothek, Ms. s.n. 13521, after 1537. A second volume in the Morgan Library (cat. no. 167) was made after 1547. Österreichische Nationalbibliothek, Ms. s.n. 13521 lacks the illusionistic architectural frames, is written in a humanistic hand, and its miniatures are in grisaille, but it shares the same texts and the same format as the other three manuscripts.

2. For a full facsimile of the Vienna manuscript, see Liechtenstein 1976.

3. Two of the miniatures, the ones for vespers of the Hours of the Virgin (fol. 167) and for the Rosary of the Virgin (fol. 233v), have entirely different subjects from their counterparts in the Vienna manuscript. Another thirty-seven miniatures have compositions not related to the Vienna miniatures; twenty-three have compositions close, but not identical, to the Vienna miniatures; and the remainder have no correspondents at all in the Vienna manuscript.

4. Dogaer 1987a: 170; Voelkle and Passela 1980: 27.

5. This artist painted all of the miniatures for the excerpts from the Gospels, the Hours of the Passion, the Hours of the Cross, the Hours of the Virgin, and most of the supplemental prayers.

6. This miniature is closely related to its counterpart in the Vienna manuscript (fol. 61v), but the Vienna artist's daylight version, though of a higher quality, is less striking than the miniature in the present volume, where the scene is recast in darkness.

7. This artist was given much less of the book to illuminate. He was active primarily at the beginning of the manuscript—illuminating folios 23v, 45v, 49, 50v, and 54v, as well as the first set of suffrages and the Gospel sequences—and at the very end, where he illuminated the remainder of the suffrages, except for the series between folios 249 and 260.

8. The same subject can be seen in the Vienna manuscript (fol. 233v), but although the two compositions are related, the Vienna miniature lacks the sense of drama and vitality that makes the miniature in the present volume so appealing.

9. The identification of the chaplain as a member of the Pot family is found in the notes on the manuscript held at the Morgan Library. Only the upper right quadrant of the coat of arms in the miniature is legible. The description given by Rietstap (1972, 2: 474) of the arms of the Pot de Rhodes family does not precisely match the coat of arms that appears in the manuscript, as the label in the manuscript is blue and Rietstap describes the Pot arms with a label gules.

10. The portrait appears below the end of a text on folio 35v with a simple rectangular frame instead of the more elaborate frames found in the rest of the manuscript. In addition, the man in the portrait does not even seem to look at the facing image of the Virgin and Child. The portrait interrupts the flow of the prayers, and the austerity of its style, with a heavy emphasis on linear strokes, is quite different from the Mannerist style of the rest of the miniatures in the manuscript.

11. The manuscript was probably tampered with after its creation, for an entire series of texts appears out of order, including a number of the suffrages. Because this manuscript was probably copied directly from the Vienna manuscript, it is possible to use the latter to reconstruct the correct order of texts, but the prayer opposite the portrait of the chaplain is unfortunately one of the few texts not present in the Vienna manuscript.

167a
MASTER OF MORGAN
M.696
Charles V in Prayer,
fol. 56

167

MASTER OF MORGAN M.696 AND ASSISTANT (?)

Book of Hours
Use of Rome
Brussels or Mechelen, after 1547

MANUSCRIPT: i + 288 folios, 16.5 × 9.3 cm (6½ × 3⅝ in.); justification:
11.5 × 6.1 cm (4½ × 2⅜ in.); 21 lines of *bastarda*; 30 half-page
miniatures, 7 small miniatures; 1 pen drawing added by Spanish artist,
eighteenth century

HERALDRY: The arms of Charles V surrounded by collar of the Order
of the Golden Fleece, fols. 3, 56, 73v, 254v, etc.; motto *plus outre,*
fol. 73v, etc.

INSCRIPTIONS: *Son senor Mar de Gaztelu secretario del rey don Felipe
secundo de este nombre y de la senora dona Leonoy de Ecasu muoer 1576 El
escrito antecedente dice son estas Horas del Martin de Gaztelu secretario del
rey Phelipe II de este nombre y de la senora dona Leonor de Ecasu Muoer
L'sta en poder des E'xmo Senor Conde de Sartago des de elano 1734,* fol. 1

BINDING: Spain, eighteenth century; red velvet over wood boards;
marks of two clasps

COLLECTION: New York, The Morgan Library, Ms. M.696

PROVENANCE: Emperor Charles V (1500–1558); Martin de Gaztelu,
secretary of Charles V and Philip II, by 1576; Cristobal Fernandez de
Cordoba y Alagón, 1734; Don Marcial Lorbís de Aragon y Sadaba,
province of Zaragoza, 1881; Edgar Gutmann, Berlin, 1921; [K. W.
Bachstitz Gallery, The Hague, 1924]; C. Romer-Williams, 1925; to J. P.
Morgan (1867–1943) in 1925

JPGM and RA

This prayer book is the last in a series of four made for
Emperor Charles V.[1] Like its predecessors, it features a
narrow vertical format and Italianate architectural frames
around its miniatures. The close correspondences between
the text of this manuscript and two of the other prayer
books made for the emperor—one in Vienna, called the
Prayer Book of Charles V (Österreichische Nationalbibliothek, Ms. 1859) and the other also in the Morgan Library
(cat. no. 166)—indicate that the scribe of the present volume was very likely copying directly from one of these two
earlier manuscripts.[2] Despite the textual similarities, however, the iconographic scheme in the present manuscript is
quite distinct from those of the previous two. Instead of the
more than seventy-five miniatures decorating the 1516–19
and 1533 manuscripts, this prayer book features fewer than
forty; the Hours of the Cross, the Hours of the Holy Spirit,
and the Hours of the Virgin—which had each received
multiple miniatures in the two other manuscripts—are
illuminated only at matins in this volume. In addition, in
their iconography, the miniatures in this manuscript are
almost wholly unrelated to those of any of the other prayer
books produced for Charles V.[3]

The leading artist of the manuscript is introduced here
as the Master of Morgan M.696. He was fully Mannerist in
his approach, as is especially evident in the broken, stippled
brushwork that characterizes his miniatures. In the illumination of Charles V in prayer, the emperor is accompanied
by his guardian angel (ill. 167a), who has flowing locks, a
swaying posture, and exaggeratedly complex tucks in his
robe. The wall in the background—a simple, flat surface in
the corresponding miniature in the earlier Morgan volume
(cat. no. 166, fol. 54v)—here comes alive with hundreds of

What distinguishes this manuscript among the prayer books made for Charles V is the inclusion of a series of portraits of Charles's family, as well as a number of half-lengths deeply influenced by the work of Joos van Cleve. The portraits appearing at the end of the book—including those of Charles's son (Philip II), his two sisters, and his grandfather (Maximilian)[5]—are by an artist whose work is characterized by large heads, flat drapery, and a somewhat archaizing style in comparison with the Mannerist miniatures. The half-lengths of Saint Andrew (fol. 60v) and *The Virgin and Child* (ill. 167b)—along with the portrait of Margaret of Parma, the emperor's illegitimate daughter, as Saint Barbara (fol. 63)—are probably the work of the Master of Morgan M.696; they exhibit the same stippled brushwork and a similar interest in anatomy. The portrait of Margaret bears a striking resemblance to Joos van Cleve's portraits of Eleanor of France (e.g., Hampton Court, Royal Collections). The half-length *Virgin and Child* is likewise based on Van Cleve models, seen in elements such as the diaphanous veil piled in elaborate folds on the Virgin's head and her long, slightly bent fingers supporting the Christ child.[6] It is clear that the illuminator was trying to capture, if rather clumsily, Van Cleve's style, including the broad shoulders, full faces, and elegant hands of his female figures.

The similarities between this manuscript and the Prayer Book of Charles V in terms of layout and text have led scholars to ascribe it to the Master of Charles V, despite the fact that it was made more than thirty years later and exhibits a markedly different style.[7] By the late 1540s, when he ordered this manuscript, Charles V was beset by financial and political troubles, as well as ill health, which eventually led to his retirement to a monastery in 1556, accompanied by his secretary Martin de Gaztelu, to whom this manuscript was bequeathed on the emperor's death. This last prayer book—full of portraits of the emperor's family, including his sisters, his son, his illegitimate daughter, and his grandfather—was the most personal version of a text he had become familiar with over the course of thirty years. Perhaps it served as a source of solace during the difficult last decade of his life.   E. M.

dizzying small brushstrokes. The most skillful miniatures by the Master of Morgan M.696 include the dynamic *God the Father*, which illustrates the Paternoster (fol. 16), and *Christ with the Instruments of the Passion* (fol. 37v), where the body of Christ is delineated in a sculptural way through the use of tiny individual dabs of darker paint over the flesh tones to indicate the curvature of the muscles.[4] A second, less distinguished group of miniatures in the book may be by the same artist, but their overblown Mannerist quality indicates that they were more likely painted by a less capable colleague. These miniatures—such as *The Christ Child* on folio 41 and the series running from the Gospel sequences through the Hours of the Cross (fols. 69–123)— have figures of a cloying sweetness, with animated hands, eager expressions, and slimmer proportions.

Notes

1. For a discussion of all four prayer books, see cat. no. 166, note 1.

2. The present volume does not include a few of the texts found in the previous manuscripts, such as the Athanasian Creed and the Office of the Virgin for Advent, as well as a large number of suffrages, but interestingly it introduces the Penitential Psalms, which are absent in the previous two manuscripts. The order of texts here is much closer to that in the other Morgan volume than to that of the Vienna manuscript, making it the likely source from which this volume was copied.

3. Only the miniatures depicting God the Father (fol. 16), Saint Anthony (fol. 62), the Arrest of Christ (fol. 109v), the Raising of Lazarus (fol. 213), and the Trinity (fol. 254v) repeat the compositions found in the earlier Morgan volume and the Vienna prayer book; all of the others represent the same subjects with different compositions.

167b

MASTER OF MORGAN
M.696 (?)
The Virgin and Child,
fol. 48

4. This artist was also responsible for the miniatures of Saints Catherine (fol. 64), Anne (fol. 65), and Apollonia (fol. 66v).

5. A note in the files on this manuscript at the Morgan Library indicates that the portraits of members of the emperor's family are copied from paintings known to be in the possession of his two sisters, Queen Mary of Hungary and Queen Eleanor of France, but gives no supporting evidence.

6. See Friedländer 1967–76, 9, pt. 1: pls. 65, 69.

7. Voelkle and Passela 1980: 41; Wieck 1997: 18, 108. Wieck indicated that the Master of Charles V is more likely a workshop rather than a single individual.

168

CIRCLE OF MASTER OF CHARLES V

Prayer Book of Antoine de Berghes
Probably Antwerp, ca. 1530

MANUSCRIPT: 116 folios, 15.8 × 11.2 cm (6¹⁄₁₆ × 4⅜ in.); justification: 9 × 6 cm (3½ × 2⅜ in.); 16 lines of *bastarda*; 1 full-page miniature, 32 three-quarter-page miniatures

HERALDRY: The arms of Antoine de Berghes and his wife, fols. 9v, 22v, 106; motto A MON PLAISIR TOUIOURS SERAY, fols. 9v, 22v, 106

BINDING: Red velvet over wood boards; pierced silver-gilt corner pieces and clasps, the latter in the form of an *A*

COLLECTION: Alnwick Castle, duke of Northumberland, Ms. 499

PROVENANCE: Antoine de Berghes

J P G M and R A

This prayer book contains a remarkable number of depictions of its politically well-connected owner, Antoine de Berghes (1500–1541), along with numerous representations of his coat of arms and that of his wife, Jacqueline de Croÿ. Four of the images of Berghes show him in an attitude of prayer (fols. 52v, 53v, 100, 101), but the striking full-page portrayal that opens the book follows in the well-established tradition of secular portraiture (ill. 168). The portraits that Jan Gossaert produced in the second half of

168
CIRCLE OF MASTER
OF CHARLES V
Portrait of Antoine de Berghes, fol. 9v–10

the 1520s present the closest parallels to this depiction of Berghes. Like many of Gossaert's sitters, the splendidly dressed patron is set against a simple, flat backdrop, turned slightly, with his fingers bent at odd angles as he grips his prayer book. The finely painted features convey a sense of both watchfulness and self-confidence.[1] Around 1525 Gossaert was commissioned to paint a portrait of Berghes's sister Anna, the wife of Adolph of Burgundy (formerly Lehman Collection, New York).[2] It is possible, then, that Berghes saw his sister's portrait and asked that the style be emulated in a portrait for his book or that the illuminator copied a now-lost portrait of him by Gossaert.

The remainder of the illuminations in the manuscript are painted in a style reminiscent of the Master of Charles V. Although the colors tend to be much more brilliant than those found in this artist's miniatures, the supple figures, rounded faces, and simplistic backgrounds all recall the illuminations of the Prayer Book of Charles V (Vienna, Österreichische Nationalbibliothek, Ms. 1859).[3] The variation in quality among the miniatures in the present manuscript— ranging from the rather perfunctory (*Christ Being Stripped of His Robes*, fol. 33, and *The Road to Calvary*, fol. 34) to the more accomplished (*The Temptation of Saint Anthony*, fol. 48, and *Saint Catherine*, fol. 49)—indicates that the book may have been painted by more than one artist.[4]

A member of the powerful Glymes family, Berghes was the marquess of Bergen-op-Zoom (Berghes, in French), located just north of Antwerp, the city most clearly reflected in the manuscript's calendar entries.[5] Antoine de Berghes's grandfather Jean served as *chambellan* at the Burgundian court under Philip the Good; his uncle Henry was named chancellor of the Order of the Golden Fleece; and his father, also named Jean, became one of the most valued counselors of Maximilian of Austria. In 1521 Antoine's father cemented the Glymeses' position at court by marrying Antoine to a cousin of Guillaume de Croÿ-Chièvres, the

family's only serious rival.[6] Antoine himself went on to become privy counsel to Emperor Charles V. Because the arms of Jacqueline de Croÿ appear in the manuscript, but the collar of the Order of the Golden Fleece (which Berghes received in 1531) does not surround his own arms, it is possible to date the manuscript between 1521 and 1531. The style of the miniatures and the portrait strongly suggests a date in the second half of that period.

E. M.

Notes

1. Several characteristics of Gossaert's portraits after about 1525 were noted by Herzog (1969: 135), including the use of a neutral background and facial expressions and finger positions suggesting tension (see e.g., Gossaert's portrait of a man, Brussels, Musées royaux des Beaux-Arts de Belgique, inv. no. 4740).

2. Van Mander (1604: 225v) stated that Gossaert was employed at the court of Adolph of Burgundy for a few years. Besides the portrait of Antoine de Berghes's sister, Gossaert also painted a portrait of a girl thought to be Jacqueline de Berghes (London, National Gallery, inv. 2211), the daughter of Antoine's sister Anna.

3. During Antoine's time as privy councillor to Charles V, he could easily have come into contact with the illuminators working for Charles V.

4. Because the artist of the book's opening portrait (fol. 9v) was consciously following the style of Gossaert, it is difficult to determine whether he was also responsible for any of the other illuminations in the book.

5. John Plummer specified that the strong Dutch component of the calendar suggests a connection with Holland, but the lack of many distinctive Dutch feasts indicates that the patron was not from Holland itself (report, Department of Manuscripts files, JPGM). Plummer suggested that Antwerp is the most likely candidate for the location where the book was written. Although the Alnwick manuscript's calendar has far fewer entries than the Hours of James IV of Scotland (see cat. no. 110) and the Spinola Hours (cat. no. 124), the large degree of correspondence between them (94.17 percent and 91.92 percent, respectively) indicates the increasing standardization of calendars during the sixteenth century.

6. Cools (2001) traced the importance of the various members of the Glymes family, as well as following their fortunes at court.

MASTER OF CARDINAL WOLSEY

The Master of Cardinal Wolsey, introduced here, is named after the patron of two impressive liturgical books now in Oxford (cat. no. 169): a Gospel-lectionary (Magdalen College, Ms. Lat. 223) and an epistle-lectionary (Christ Church College, Ms. 101). These two manuscripts have usually been attributed to a member of the Horenbout family, most often Gerard Horenbout, probably because Wolsey was once thought to have been a patron of his work.[1] Scholars have based this supposition more on historical circumstance than on a comparison of the miniatures with Horenbout's oeuvre.[2] The miniatures in fact have little in common with any of the works associated with either Gerard Horenbout or the Master of James IV of Scotland, who has been identified with Horenbout.

The atmospheric landscapes, naturalistic modeling of the figures, and strewn-flower borders link the manuscripts' miniatures to illumination being produced in Ghent and Bruges at the time, yet they are also permeated by Mannerist elements, seen in the excessively dramatic hand gestures, the agitated brushwork, and the muscular putti in the borders. This dichotomy of styles can be seen most clearly in the Wolsey Master's two main methods of delineating drapery, often present in the same miniature. In the Saint Andrew miniature of the Christ Church manuscript (fol. 1), the folds of the saint's cloak are indicated by large, clearly defined areas outlined in shell gold and then filled in with parallel strokes of the same, a version of a conventional Flemish technique. The drapery of the bystanders, by contrast, is full of nervous worrying, conveyed by short, uneven strokes of a darker wash or a contrasting color and occasionally heightened by dots and dashes of black. The two aspects of the Wolsey Master's style are largely juxtaposed rather than blended, sometimes resulting in awkward contrasts.[3]

The Wolsey Master's faces are characterized by small features concentrated toward the center of the face, leaving the foreheads and chins unusually large. The men tend to have double-pronged beards extending from rosebud lips, while the women often have fleshy oval faces, giving them a slightly bovine quality. Their hands frequently have overextended thumbs and crooked pinkies, while the bare feet of the men sometimes have a short big toe that unnaturally crosses over the longer second toe. These figures interact in crowded compositions full of tension, leaning in with imploring faces or gesturing theatrically toward the center of the action.

Although no other manuscripts can be attributed to the Wolsey Master, he had a skilled associate whose work is known in two manuscripts.[4] This artist, who illuminated the Arenberg Missal (cat. no. 170), was also responsible for four illuminations in a book of hours (Ramsen, Switzerland, Heribert Tenschert collection, catalogue 20, 1987, no.

25). He has previously been identified as the Master of Charles V, but his ties to the Wolsey Master are much closer. Both the Wolsey Master and his associate shared an interest in the complex spatial arrangements and dramatic narratives of Albrecht Dürer's woodcuts, employing a number of his compositions in their work. There are also other compositions shared within the workshop that appear in the illuminations of both (see cat. no. 170). The two artists, moreover, utilized the same facial type, as well as a similar manner of treating drapery by filling in geometric sections of the fabric with parallel lines of gold as discussed above. The work of the associate displays none of the agitated brushwork seen in the illuminations of the Wolsey Master, suggesting that the latter artist was more steeped in Mannerist influences. The Wolsey Master was also much more interested in indicating the musculature beneath the drapery of his figures and in using hand gestures to tell a story or convey emotion. The studied contrast between bright and pastel colors used to such advantage by the Wolsey Master is also absent from the work of his associate, who limited himself to cool colors. Lastly, the work of the associate of the Wolsey Master is in general less agitated and detailed, with softer, sweeter faces and more curvilinear, sweeping drapery.

The known works of these two artists all likely date to the decade 1520–30 and incorporate the traditional Flemish borders. The quotations from Antwerp Mannerist works found in the illuminations of the associate of the Wolsey Master and the Mannerist tendencies of the Wolsey Master himself, however, suggest that the artists may have trained in Antwerp or that their workshop was located in that city. Their compositions, moreover, reveal a familiarity with the panel painting motifs of the Antwerp Mannerists Joos van Cleve and Joachim Patinir. E. M.

Notes

1. In 1528 or 1529 a certain "Gerarde" was paid for working on a patent for Wolsey's foundation of Cardinal College at Oxford (Auerbach 1954b: 45). Because Wolsey's two liturgical books were probably also commissioned for Cardinal College, Pächt (in London 1953–54: nos. 623, 624) linked them as well to the Horenbout family. Campbell and Foister (1986: 721), however, have cast serious doubt on the theory that Horenbout ever worked for Wolsey.

2. The following all attribute the manuscripts to a member of the Horenbout family: Paget 1959: 400–401; Hardie 1984: 81; Alexander and Temple 1985: 83; Dogaer 1987a: 166.

3. For instance, in one miniature the artist randomly placed a broken Italianate column on a wall (Magdalen College, Ms. Lat. 223, fol. 7), and in another the artist took a common pattern such as the Nativity and crowded it with gesticulating angels, creating an unwieldy composition (Christ Church College, Ms. 101, fol. 4v).

4. A manuscript in a private collection (Günther 1995: no. 27) contains illumination closely related to the work of the Wolsey Master and his associate. Based on the reproductions, the illuminations do not appear to be by the hand of either artist, but the compositions and certain stylistic elements correspond to aspects of their work.

169

MASTER OF CARDINAL WOLSEY

Pair of Lectionaries
England, 1528, and probably Antwerp, 1529–30

Epistle-lectionary

MANUSCRIPT: iii + 45 + vii folios, 41 × 29.3 cm (16⅛ × 11½ in.); justification: 25.5 × 18.2 cm (10¹⁄₁₆ × 7³⁄₁₆ in.); 18 lines of *humanistica* by Pieter Meghen; 19 half-column miniatures, 1 historiated border

HERALDRY: Escutcheon with the arms of Wolsey surmounted by cardinal's hat, sometimes impaling those of the see of York, fols. 15, 35v, 40, etc.; escutcheon with the royal arms of England encircled by the Garter and supported by crowned lion and griffin, fol. 20; initials T and C, fols. 32, 43; motto *Dominus mihi adiutor*, fols. 15, 20, 23, etc.; motto *Dieu et mon droit*, fol. 20; devices of crossed keys with crown, lion and crown, and double columns, fols. 23, 34v, 35v, etc.

BINDING: Eddington Bindery, England, 1981

COLLECTION: Oxford, Christ Church, Ms. 101

PROVENANCE: Cardinal Thomas Wolsey (ca. 1475–1530); acquired by 1654

JPGM and RA

Gospel-lectionary

MANUSCRIPT: ii + 48 + i folios, 40.5 × 30 cm (16 × 11¾ in.); justification: 26.4 × 18 cm (10⅜ × 7⅛ in.); 18 lines of *humanistica* by Pieter Meghen; 19 half-column miniatures, 1 historiated border

HERALDRY: Escutcheon with the arms of Wolsey surmounted by cardinal's hat, sometimes encircled by the Garter and/or impaling the arms of the see of York or those of Winchester, fols. 3, 7, 12, etc.; initials T and W, fol. 12; motto *Dominus mihi adiutor*, fols. 3, 7, 43, etc.; motto *Honi soit qui mal y pensee*, fol. 3; devices of crossed keys surmounted by crown, lion and crown, and double columns, fols. 3, 7, 12, etc.

BINDING: England, mid-sixteenth century; brown calf; the arms of Henry VIII gold-stamped on both covers

COLLECTION: Oxford, Magdalen College, Ms. lat. 223

PROVENANCE: Cardinal Thomas Wolsey (ca. 1475–1530); Henry VIII, king of England (1491–1547) (?); bishop of Winchester, by 1556; Samuel Chappington, late sixteenth or early seventeenth century; given by John Lant in 1614

JPGM

These two impressive liturgical books were commissioned as a pair by Cardinal Wolsey (ca. 1475–1530), personal chaplain to Henry VIII and lord chancellor of England. Both manuscripts contain only texts for high feast days and the feast days of English saints, particularly those saints associated with Wolsey's offices and foundations.[1] Wolsey spared no expense on the two manuscripts, commissioning Pieter Meghen, who later became scribe to Henry VIII, to write out the text, and then engaging a Flemish artist for the thirty-eight miniatures. These miniatures have long been mistakenly attributed to Gerard Horenbout,[2] but they are by a heretofore unnamed Flemish artist to be called the Master of Cardinal Wolsey. Although it is possible that the Wolsey Master was working in England, it is more likely that the manuscripts were written in England and then illuminated in Flanders.[3] Wolsey's collection of Flemish tapestries was famous; his taste for Flemish art, a reflection of the active patronage of Flemish illumination and textiles at the Tudor court, no doubt served as a sign of his wealth and power.[4]

The work of the Wolsey Master in the two manuscripts is characterized by traditional Flemish painting techniques combined with a Mannerist sensibility. The sophisticated miniature *The Israelites Collecting Manna from Heaven* in the Christ Church manuscript (ill. 169a)—with its soft colors, distant vista, and carefully observed and fashionably dressed figures—exemplifies the artist's Flemish training. *The Last Supper* (ill. 169b) from the Magdalen manuscript, at the other extreme, is a crowded, busy scene whose narrative is told through a complex series of exaggerated hand gestures. The composition is copied very closely from a woodcut by Albrecht Dürer, whose prints served as the source for other images in the two manuscripts.[5] The Wolsey Master's method of delineating drapery in this miniature—with tiny, fussy lines of a deeper tone occasionally accompanied by black to indicate folds—contributes to the sense of restless movement. The artist faced a challenge in illuminating two manuscripts containing texts for the same feast days and clearly meant to be used in tandem on those days. Although several miniatures are consequently very similar in the two manuscripts, it is clear the artist made an effort to vary most of the compositions—for example, in the case of their respective opening miniatures for the feast of Saint Andrew. In the Magdalen manuscript, a monumental Andrew stands alone in front of a serene landscape, while in the more narrative version in the Christ Church manuscript, he is being crucified in the midst of a sympathetic crowd.

Wolsey's personal emblems, mottoes, or arms appear in profusion on every illuminated page of the two manuscripts, and their presence helps to establish the chronological sequence of the manuscripts' creation. In the Christ Church epistle-lectionary, the date 1528 appears in the margin on folio 32. The illumination of the Magdalen Gospel-lectionary must date to the following year because the arms of Winchester appear among Wolsey's other heraldry, and he did not obtain that bishopric until April 6, 1529.[6] The years 1528 and 1529 were tumultuous ones for Wolsey, for he was deeply entangled in a series of court intrigues involving Anne Boleyn and Henry VIII's proposed divorce from Catherine of Aragon, soon after to result in Wolsey's downfall. His fall from grace was accompanied by strenuous efforts on his part to save his personal foundation of Cardinal College, Oxford (see cat. no. 131), for which these two manuscripts were almost certainly commissioned. The arms of Henry VIII appear in the Christ Church manuscript on folio 20 alongside those of Wolsey, perhaps an expression of Wolsey's hopes even as late as 1528 to maintain his position at court and save Cardinal College. By 1529, when the Magdalen manuscript was illuminated, however, Wolsey's downfall seemed all but certain, and significantly, the royal arms are absent from this manuscript.[7]

The size of the manuscripts, the richness of the decoration, the selectiveness of the texts, and the abundance of references to the patron all indicate that the manuscripts were presentation copies intended to memorialize Wolsey's foundation of Cardinal College. Wolsey's foundation at Oxford was as much a chance to display his wealth

169a (opposite)
MASTER OF
CARDINAL WOLSEY
*The Israelites Collecting
Manna from Heaven,*
epistle-lectionary, fol. 31

In fest-o corporis CHRISTI.
Lectio eple beati Pauli, apli. ad Co
rinthios. .I. ad Corinth .XI.

FRATRES.

Ego eni
accepi a
domino,
quod et
tradidi
vobis:

quoniam dominus I E
S V S, in qua nocte tra
debatur, accepit panem et gra
tias agens, fregit et dixit. Ac
cipite et manducate, hoc est cor

mea vére eft cibus : et

Notes

1. The dioceses and foundations with which Wolsey was associated during various stages of his career are particularly well represented: Saint Andrew for the diocese of Bath and Wells, Saint Cuthbert for Durham, Saint Hugh for Lincoln, and Saint William for York. Saint Frediswide, who also appears, was the patron saint of Oxford and subsequently became particularly associated with Cardinal College, which Wolsey founded.

2. As early as the 1953–54 Royal Academy exhibition, both manuscripts were attributed to a "member of the Horenbouts family" (London 1953–54: 166). Although Auerbach (1954b: 42–45) proposed around the same time that the "Gerarde" recorded as the recipient of payment for the decoration of Wolsey's patents might be Gerard Horenbout, Campbell and Foister (1986: 721) doubted that this was true. It seems then that tenuous links between artist and patron provided the only basis for attributing the illumination of the Oxford manuscripts to Horenbout, rather than an examination of the style of the miniatures. Paget (1959: 401) also claimed to see the signature of a "Gherart" in the miniature of the Nativity in the Christ Church manuscript. Nancy Bell, conservator of manuscripts, Oxford, has examined the miniature under microscope and does not see any evidence of a signature.

3. In June 1516 Meghen himself was known to have carried letters from Wolsey to Erasmus on the continent (Trapp, in Beitenholz and Deutscher 1985–87, 2: 421). It is thus possible that he was the courier in 1528–29 for taking the manuscripts he wrote to Flanders. An earlier example of exactly this process is the creation of a copy of the *Imaginacion de la vraie noblesse* (cat. no. 121) made for Henry VII, which was written at the palace of Sheen in 1496 and illuminated in Bruges around 1496–97.

4. Gunn and Lindley (1991: 30–50) discussed at length Wolsey's vast expenditures on artistic endeavors—especially plate, hangings, and architecture—as an effort to display his wealth and authority.

5. Hardie (1982: 80, 84) recognized Dürer woodcuts as the source for some of the miniatures. In the Christ Church epistle-lectionary, *Christ Appearing to His Mother* (fol. 15), *The Ascension* (fol. 20), and *Pentecost* (fol. 23) are taken from Dürer woodcuts of the Small Passion cycle. In the Magdalen Gospel-lectionary, *The Last Supper* is a copy of a woodcut from the Great Passion series, and *The Resurrection* (fol. 19) appears to be a variation on a composition from the same.

6. A note written on the inside back cover of the Magdalen manuscript remarks that the writing out of the text probably predated its illumination, as the festival of Saint Swithun, a saint associated with Winchester, does not appear in the text.

7. Carley (2000: 267) hypothesized that a Gospel-lectionary and epistle-lectionary described in Henry VIII's library with matching silver gilt bindings were the Wolsey manuscripts. Nothing is known of the original binding of the Christ Church manuscript, as it was rebound in 1981 and the previous binding was discarded, but the Magdalen manuscript has a sixteenth-century leather binding with the royal stamp. The time period in which the illumination must have been done is quite short (between April 6, 1529, the date of Wolsey's accession to Winchester, and October 30, 1529, the date of the seizure of all his lands and goods). Thus, Nancy Bell (conversation with the author, January 2002) has theorized that perhaps the binding of the Magdalen book was never completed by Wolsey but was instead completed after Henry VIII had confiscated Wolsey's goods, making the current binding with the royal stamp the original.

8. In 1441 Henry VI had founded King's College, Oxford; in 1448 William Waynflete, bishop of Winchester, founded Magdalen College, Oxford; and in 1517 Richard Fox, bishop of Winchester, founded Corpus Christi College. Wolsey's foundation outstripped all of them in size and magnificence, and even the very name, Cardinal College, was a reference to himself.

and power as it was an expression of personal piety.[8] Although his friendship with Erasmus and his efforts to engage lecturers of the highest caliber for the college show a sincere interest in the new humanist approach to studies, he was at the same time deeply aware of the unease in the Catholic Church fostered by the spread of Lutheranism on the continent and its reflection in humanist intellectual circles in England. In this context it is suggestive that, although Wolsey ordered numerous copies of classical works from Rome and Venice for his new foundation, the only known illuminated manuscripts he commissioned for Cardinal College were two liturgical books full of his personal mottoes and allusions to his various Church offices. These books were designed for use exclusively at the college's religious services, which Wolsey no doubt planned to be a constant source of intercessory prayers on his behalf after his death.   E. M.

169b

MASTER OF
CARDINAL WOLSEY
The Last Supper,
Gospel-lectionary, fol. 36

T C
I
IN DIE

Bo dıvınıs

ILLIS.

Ego ıoannes
vıdı cıuıtate
sanctam hıe
rusalem nouam descendentem de
celo a D E o paratam: sicut
sponsam ornatam vıro suo. Et
audıuı vocem magnam de thro
no: dıcentem. Ecce tabernaculum
D E I cum homınıbus:
et habıtabıt cum eıs. Et ıpsı po
pulus eıus erunt: et ıpe D E
v S cum eıs, erıt eorum

MINVS · MIHI · ADVITOR
DO
DOMINVS · MIHI
AIVITOR

169c
MASTER OF
CARDINAL WOLSEY
Christ and Zacchaeus,
Gospel-lectionary, fol. 45

170

ASSOCIATE OF MASTER OF CARDINAL WOLSEY

Arenberg Missal
Cistercian use
Probably Antwerp, shortly after 1524

MANUSCRIPT: 108 + i folios, 43.9 × 31.2 cm (17⁵/₁₆ × 12⁵/₁₆ in.); justification: 29.6 × 18.1 cm (11¹¹/₁₆ × 7⅛ in.); 24 lines of *textura* in two columns (18 lines in two columns in the Canon of the Mass) by Francis Weert; 1 full-page miniature, 20 one-column miniatures

HERALDRY: Escutcheon with the arms of Marcus Cruyt, fol. 68v

BINDING: Red-stained leather over wood boards; clasps and catches replaced

COLLECTION: Private collection

PROVENANCE: Marcus Cruyt, abbot of Saint-Bernard-sur-l'Escaut (d. 1536); to the Abbey of Saint Bernard, until at least 1745; bought by Prince Auguste d'Arenberg (1753–1833) or Duke Englebert-Auguste d'Arenberg (1824–1875) (Ms. 53 at the Palais d'Egmont, Brussels); to German family, early 1950s; [sale, Sotheby's, London, December 11, 1984, lot 55]; [to Pierre Berès]; to Jaime Ortiz-Patiño [his sale, Sotheby's, London, April, 21, 1998, lot 186]

JPGM and RA

This impressive missal was made for Marcus Cruyt, abbot of Saint-Bernard-sur-l'Escaut from 1518 to 1536 and imperial ambassador to Denmark. Cruyt was a well-known art patron. A now-lost portrait of him by Quentin Massys, a panel in which he appears as the donor (Philadelphia, J. G. Johnson Collection, inv. 384a), and three surviving stained-glass windows he commissioned all attest to his interest in the arts. This missal, one of three manuscripts known to have been made for him,[1] contains not only twenty one-column miniatures illustrating the major feasts of the Church year but also a full-page miniature whose ambitious scope and composition clearly relate it to contemporary panel painting (ill. 170a).

The very large and beautiful illumination of the Crucifixion is formed from components taken from a wide variety of sources, blended seamlessly into a new whole. The figure of Mary Magdalene clutching the cross was copied from a Dürer print of the Crucifixion from around 1500–1504. The Virgin Mary and Saint John to either side seem to be related to similar figures found in paintings of the Crucifixion by Joos van Cleve (e.g., Boston, Museum of Fine Arts, no. 107). Variants of the complex architecture representing Jerusalem seen in the landscape background (ill. 170b), meanwhile, can be found in numerous other Antwerp Mannerist works of the period (see cat. nos. 171, 172). This is the only known manuscript image to incorporate the pattern. Although none of the known versions is identical to any other, the buildings as they appear in the Arenberg Missal seem to be closest to those in a drawing in Berlin, previously attributed to Bles (cat. no. 171). Significantly, the version in the miniature predates the earliest activity of Bles by some years.[2] A second drawing, by an artist in the circle of Pieter Coecke van Aelst, provides evidence that the type of Crucifixion found in the Arenberg Missal, featuring Mary Magdalene at the foot of the cross with the Virgin to the left and John to the right, was associated with this architectural motif (fig. 74).[3] The fact that the artist of the miniature, in forming the whole, so suc-

cessfully integrated elements from a variety of sources indicates a familiarity with the work of the Antwerp Mannerists and a desire to treat this miniature, the most important of a missal, with the spatial grandeur of an independent panel painting.

The artist of the manuscript, previously identified by Friedrich Winkler as the Master of Charles V,[4] must instead be identified as an associate of the Master of Cardinal Wolsey. A number of compositions in the Arenberg Missal are directly related to those found in the Magdalen Gospel-lectionary and the Christ Church epistle-lectionary (cat. no. 169) by the Wolsey Master. The miniatures for Saints Peter and Paul, with the two men seated on a bench before a semicircular construction, and for All Saints, with the disembodied head of Christ floating in clouds above a group of saints below are virtually indentical in all three manuscripts.[5] Both the Wolsey Master and the artist of the Arenberg Missal, moreover, shared a fondness for compositions created by Albrecht Dürer. In the Arenberg Missal, *The Resurrection*, *The Entry into Jerusalem*, and *The Last Supper*, as well as parts of *The Crucifixion* and *The Birth of Saint John*, were all taken from woodcuts by Dürer. Although it is clear that the artist of the Arenberg Missal must have been a close associate of the Wolsey Master—especially when one compares details such as the close-set, small facial features and high foreheads of the figures—this artist is neither as Mannerist, nor quite as sophisticated, as the Wolsey Master. His landscapes, with the notable exception of that of the Crucifixion miniature, lack the drama and subtlety of those of the Wolsey Master, and he tends to use broad strokes of color as a modeling tool, rather than relying on line. All of these features give his miniatures more softness and less definition than those of the Wolsey Master.

The figure of Marcus Cruyt praying in a corner of the border of *The Crucifixion*, along with his coat of arms, also appears in a personal prayer book made for Cruyt (Bornem, Sint-Bernardusabdij, Ms. 9). The inclusion in both books of a version of the *Virgo lactans* copied from a 1524 engraving by Antwerp artist Dirk Jacobsz Vellert provides a terminus post quem for the Arenberg Missal. The Sint-Bernardusabdij in Bornem (ultimately the successor to Cruyt's abbey of Saint-Bernard-sur-l'Escaut) also has records dating from around 1524 that indicate two payments to the scribe Francis Weert, who is likely the scribe of the Arenberg Missal.[6] It is thus possible to suggest a date shortly after 1524 for the manuscript.   E. M.

Notes

1. Cruyt's personal prayer book is discussed below. The third manuscript was a gradual, whose leaves can be found in Brussels (Bibliothèque royale de Belgique, Ms. II 3633), in Cambridge (Fitzwilliam Museum, Marlay Cuttings Fl 1–4), in private collections in Germany and New York, and perhaps in Paris (Musée Marmottan, Wildenstein Collection, no. 227).

2. See cat. no. 171 for a discussion of the relative dating of the pieces incorporating this motif.

3. Because this was a Crucifixion type popular in Flemish panel painting and because this group of architectural elements is known to have been popular, it is possible that there is a lost painting joining together these elements from which the artist drew inspiration.

170a
ASSOCIATE OF
MASTER OF
CARDINAL WOLSEY
The Crucifixion, fol. 68v

170b

ASSOCIATE OF
MASTER OF
CARDINAL WOLSEY
The Crucifixion, fol. 68v
(detail of ill. 170a)

Figure 74

CIRCLE OF PIETER
COECKE VAN AELST
The Crucifixion (detail
of ill. 172)

4. Winkler 1925: 151, 168. Winkler originally hesitated between Simon Bening and the Master of Charles V, but he later ascribed it to the Master of Charles V in an unpublished study (cited in sale cat., Sotheby's, London, April 21, 1998, lot 186), an attribution that has been followed ever since.

5. Variants on a number of other compositions are also present. The unusual subject of Manna from Heaven occurs in both the Christ Church manuscript and the Arenberg Missal, while *The Birth of the Virgin* in the two Oxford manuscripts and *The Birth of John the Baptist* in the Arenberg Missal are all variants on the same composition.

6. Bornem, Archief van de Abdij, Ms. 228, 52, and Ms. 229, 7–8 (see Louvain 1990: 462). A manuscript sold at Sotheby's, London, July 3, 1984, lot 53, is signed by Francis Weert, and although only one page is reproduced, a number of the paleographical elements of that script also appear in the Arenberg Missal. Weert was also the scribe of Cruyt's personal prayer book (Bornem, Sint-Bernardusabdij, Ms. 9).

171

ANONYMOUS

View of Jerusalem
Probably Antwerp, probably 1520s

Black ink on paper, 17.8 × 27.3 cm (7 1/16 × 10 13/16 in.)

COLLECTION: Berlin, Staatliche Museen zu Berlin,
Kupferstichkabinett, KdZ 5525

PROVENANCE: Adolf von Beckerath (1834–1915); acquired 1902

JPGM and RA

The complex architectural elements forming a distant
walled city in this drawing also appear in numerous
other Flemish works of the first half of the sixteenth
century. To the left of center is a double-towered gate
connected at the top by an arch. A multitiered circular
building appears just behind, identifiable as the Temple of
Jerusalem. The walls of the city then slope upward in a long
line to the right, punctuated by a simple round tower, a second round tower half crenellated at the top, and a composite tower. The last is easily recognizable because of its
idiosyncratic elongated buttress extending down from two
arches. A city gate to the far right is the last element of the
line of structures. The popularity of this architectural backdrop is attested to by the appearance of fairly close varia-

tions of it in the works of at least five artists, in different
media and accompanying a wide variety of subject matter.

The motif probably originated in the early 1520s, for
variations of the architectural scheme appear in the background of two paintings from that decade—*Lot and His
Daughters* (Detroit Institute of Arts, inv. 25.65) and a triptych of the Crucifixion (Amsterdam, Rijksmuseum, inv. A-
1598)—both likely by the same artist.[1] The backdrop
appears again in at least two paintings by Pieter Coecke van
Aelst, both probably dating to after 1530,[2] as well as in a
drawing by an artist in his circle (cat. no. 172) and in a painting by an unknown Flemish artist.[3] The motif is also found
in a painting of the Way to Calvary by Herri met de Bles
from around 1535–36 (Princeton University Art Museum,
inv. 50-1) and in a sketchbook drawing (Berlin, Kupferstichkabinett, inv. 79 C 2, fols. 31, 32).

Robert Koch has argued that both the sketchbook
drawing and the drawing discussed here were studies for
the Bles painting, while Holm Bevers asserted that both
drawings copy a Bles painting.[4] The infrared reflectography
done on the Princeton painting indicates that the sketchbook drawing was likely done as a preparatory study for the
painting. The difference in technique between the sketchbook drawing and the drawing under consideration here,
however, as well as the absence of figures in the single-sheet

drawing, raises questions about the sheet's relationship to the painting.[5] Complicating matters is the fact that no drawings survive that are securely attributed to Bles.

Although the horizontal format and landscape elements seen to the right and left in the single-sheet drawing indicate that it was a study for (or a *ricordo* after) a painting, the particular arrangement of the architectural elements closely links it to the background of a miniature of the Crucifixion in the Arenberg Missal (ill. 170a). They both have the same general disposition, as seen in all the works discussed above, but there are a number of individual correspondences that relate these two more closely to each other than to any of the other works. In both, a short curving wall surmounted by a few buildings forms a loop around a small open area just behind the double-towered city gate at the center of the composition.[6] In addition, a second wall in the distant background of both is bisected by a round tower and intersects the multitiered temple at the third level. The hilltop castle to the left of the temple is similar in both as well.[7] Although there is not enough evidence to posit a direct relationship between the drawing and the illumination, it is plausible to suggest that both may be related to a painting done before 1524, the approximate date of the manuscript. Julius Held originally surmised the existence of a lost painting by Jan Wellens de Cock incorporating the architectural motif.[8] That hypothesis was abandoned upon the rediscovery of the 1535–36 Princeton Bles, but the new information provided by the probable early date of the Arenberg Missal and the correspondences between its Crucifixion miniature and the drawing under discussion suggest that the possibility of the appearance of the motif in an influential painting from the early 1520s deserves reconsideration.   E. M. and T. K.

Notes

1. These paintings have traditionally been attributed to Jan Wellens de Cock (Friedländer 1967–76, 11: 37–43; Held 1933: 276–82). Gibson (1969: 188) and Filedt Kok (1996: 350–52), however, have questioned the existence of this artist. It is in any case generally agreed that both paintings are by the same artist and that they date to around 1520–30.

2. *Saint Luke Painting the Virgin* (Nîmes, Musée des Beaux-Arts) and *The Way to Calvary* (Basel, Öffentliche Kunstsammlung).

3. This painting of the Crucifixion was formerly in a Berlin private collection and was reproduced by Held (1933: 282) and Koch (1998: 17).

4. Koch 1998: 16–18; Bevers 1998: 46–48. Bevers proposed that the drawings are either *ricordi* done from the underdrawing of the Princeton painting before it was finished or from a second, now-lost Bles painting. Although the number of correspondences between other drawings in the latter portion of the album and Bles paintings supports the theory that the sketchbook was used in the Bles workshop from about 1535 to 1543, Bevers (1998: 39) pointed out that the watermark on the paper for the earlier portion of the sketchbook most closely matches a watermark from The Hague dated 1524, the very year that other evidence points to as the date of the Arenberg Missal (see cat. no. 170). It is possible therefore that the drawing in the sketchbook was done around the same time as the miniature and is not a product of the Bles workshop.

5. Muller (1998: 28–32) made a number of convincing comparisons between the underdrawing of the painting and the sketchbook drawing, but most of these correspondences relate to the foreground procession. An analysis of the infrared reflectography done on the painting indicates that the landscape and architectural elements are much less fully developed in the underdrawing than in the final work, revealing few clues as to the possible role of the single-sheet drawing, in which the figural procession is absent.

6. This detail is also found in the sketchbook drawing, but the disposition of buildings around the wall is closer between the single sheet and the illumination than either is to the sketchbook. The curving wall is not found in any of the aforementioned paintings, including the Princeton Bles.

7. This combination of details occurs only in the illumination and the single-sheet drawing.

8. Held 1933: 278–83.

PIETER COECKE VAN AELST

Pieter Coecke van Aelst, son of the deputy mayor of Aelst, was born on August 2, 1502. His first wife was Anna van Dornicke (d. 1529), the daughter of Jan Martens, an Antwerp painter who may have taken Coecke van Aelst as an apprentice.[1] Carel van Mander stated that Coecke van Aelst studied with Bernard van Orley, which, although not substantiated by any documents, seems possible given the stylistic links between the two artists.[2] Coecke van Aelst's second wife was Mayken Verhulst, an illuminator.[3] In 1563 one of their daughters, Maria, married Pieter Bruegel the Elder, whom Van Mander stated was an apprentice of Coecke van Aelst, although this idea has largely been rejected.[4] In 1527 Coecke van Aelst is recorded as a master in the Antwerp Guild of Saint Luke, and by 1529 he was accepting students into what would, over the course of his career, become a large workshop (see cat. no. 172). According to Van Mander, Coecke van Aelst visited Rome to study its sculpture and architecture,[5] and in 1533–34 the artist traveled to Constantinople, where he prepared drawings that would be made into woodcuts and published posthumously.[6] In 1537 he was named dean of the Guild of Saint Luke in Antwerp. He moved to Brussels in 1546 and was painter to Emperor Charles V by 1550. Coecke van Aelst died on December 6 of that year.

Coecke van Aelst was among the most versatile artists of his time, producing not only paintings and drawings but also designs for tapestries, stained glass, and woodcuts, as well as establishing himself as a sculptor, an architect, and even as a successful translator. Coecke van Aelst may have introduced the art of painting tapestry cartoons to Antwerp[7] and is known to have executed a number of works for churches, including stained glass and altarpieces.[8] He designed and published woodcuts for a commemorative book celebrating the official entry of Philip of Spain into Antwerp in 1549.[9] He also created designs for a massive sculpture known as the *Giant of Antwerp*,[10] and Van Mander credits him with helping to revive the art of architecture in Flanders.[11] A facility with languages enabled him to undertake translations of the architectural writings of both Vitruvius and Sebastiano Serlio.[12] Although all of these activities undoubtedly absorbed much of his time, Coecke van Aelst was still a prolific painter. His works—with their extravagant decorations, overdressed figures, and crowded compositions—show the influence of Bernard van Orley and Jan Gossaert. His painting style proved so popular that it was widely copied, both in his own workshop and by later artists.   E. M.

Notes

1. Florence 1980–81: 76.

2. Van Mander 1604: 218. Boon (in Florence 1980: 76) posited that if Coecke van Aelst studied with Van Orley, it was probably in Brussels between 1527 and 1533.

3. Lodovico Guicciardini ranked Verhulst among the four greatest female painters of her time (Marlier 1966: 21–22).

4. See biography of Pieter Bruegel the Elder (this part).

5. Coecke van Aelst probably undertook his trip to Rome before he entered the painters' guild in 1527 (Washington 1986a: 114).

6. The woodcuts were published under the direction of his wife in 1553 as *Moeurs et fachon de faire de Turcz* (Marlier 1966: 55–74). Along with a few drawings bearing his signature, they provide the stylistic basis for other attributions to the artist, as no signed panel paintings survive (Friedländer 1924–37, 12: 33–34).

7. The Antwerp archives indicate payment to Coecke van Aelst for having brought a new industry to Antwerp, interpreted by Marlier (1966: 44–45) as the painting of tapestry cartoons. Recent opinion is divided (Campbell 2002: 384).

8. Marlier 1966: 353–75.

9. Marlier 1966: 386–90.

10. The giant, preceded by twelve horses, was a massive emblem of the port of Schelde (Friedländer 1924–37, 12: 33).

11. Van Mander 1604: 218.

12. In 1539 he translated Vitruvius's *De architectura* into Flemish, and starting in the same year, he translated Sebastiano Serlio's architectural treatises into Flemish. He later translated Serlio's treatises into German and French (Marlier 1966: 379–83).

172

CIRCLE OF PIETER COECKE VAN AELST

The Crucifixion
Antwerp, 1536

Gray and brown ink and gray wash on paper, 27.1 × 19 cm
(10¹⁵⁄₁₆ × 7½ in.)

COLLECTION: Berlin, Staatliche Museen zu Berlin,
Kupferstichkabinett, KdZ 13280

PROVENANCE: Adolf von Beckerath (1834–1915); acquired 1902

JPGM and RA

The view of the walled city of Jerusalem seen in the background of this 1536 drawing was evidently favored by Pieter Coecke van Aelst, for it reappears in at least two of his paintings. In the first, *Saint Luke Painting the Virgin* (Nîmes, Musée des Beaux-Arts), an abbreviated version of the architectural elements appears.[1] In a second rendering, *The Way to Calvary* (Basel, Öffentliche Kunstsammlung), they can be found in mirror reverse, indicating that the motif existed as a pattern in Coecke van Aelst's workshop.

The same line of buildings is also employed as a backdrop to the subject of the Way to Calvary in a painting by Herri met de Bles (see cat. no. 171), while its appearance with the Crucifixion in the foreground, as in this drawing, echoes an earlier composition found in the Arenberg Missal (ill. 170b). The disposition of the figures of the Virgin, Mary Magdalene, and Saint John is very similar in both the present drawing and the illumination (ill. 170a). The correspondences between the architectural elements of both, although not exact, indicate that the two artists were at least working from models derived from a common source. Since the illumination can be dated to around 1524, while the drawing dates from 1536, it is clear that the association of this specific Crucifixion type with this architectural pattern existed for more than a decade and may argue for the existence of a painting that incorporated both, from which the two works ultimately descend.   E. M.

Note

1. The inexplicable appearance of tents and artillery before the city walls in this painting, not found in other representations of this subject, might suggest that the backdrop was taken in its entirety from yet another composition, whose subject matter could explain their inclusion.

ladius et fustibus
comprehendistis me
cotidie apud vos eram
in templo docens et non
me tenuistis et ecce fla
gellatum ducatis ad
crucifigendum. Versus
istius quidem ho
minis vadit sicut scri
ptum est et de illo ve
autem homini illi per
quem tradetur ad cru
cifigendum.

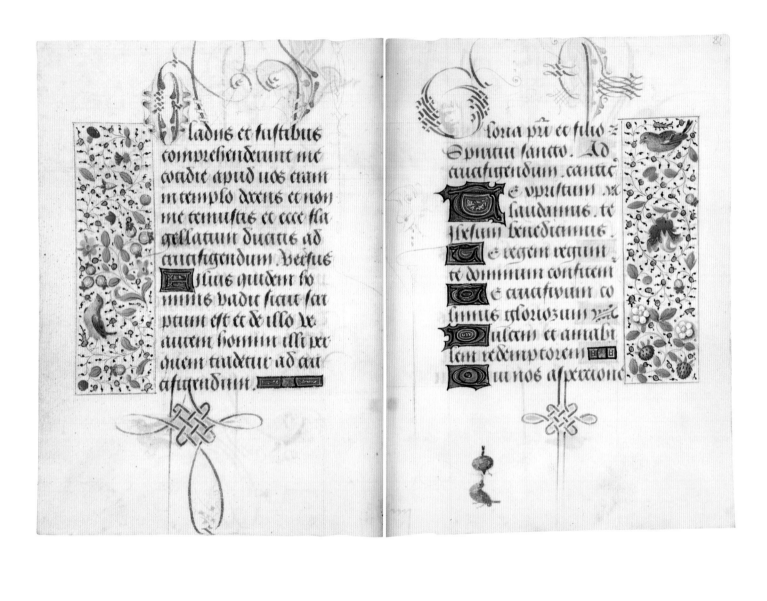

Gloria patri et filio
Spiritui sancto. Ad
crucifigendum. cante
te christum
laudamus. te
Jhesum benedicimus.
te regem regum
te dominum confitem
te crucifixum co
fitemur gloriosum
dulcem et amabi
lem redemptorem
in nos affectione

APPENDIX
THE SCRIBES

Scot McKendrick

Some manuscripts, together with related contemporary documentation, provide crucial information about the circumstances in which manuscripts were produced in the southern Netherlands during the late medieval period and early Renaissance. What follows here—a summary of the careers of a few scribes active during these periods—is based on the surviving evidence that relates to manuscripts included in this volume. Yet much remains unknown about the individuals who transcribed the texts of the vast majority of Flemish manuscripts. Few manuscripts include the scribe's name, and few allow secure identification of the scribe through comparison with signed manuscripts or through independent documentation. Some scholars of the period have made important progress in this area. In general, however, palaeographers have not studied the scripts and scribes of late medieval and early Renaissance Flemish manuscripts with the same intensity that they have treated earlier periods and contemporary Italian humanistic manuscripts; most art historians appear to consider script and scribes of little relevance to their interests.

The present dearth of knowledge about the scribes of Flemish manuscripts is also a reflection of several important factors that pertained within the southern Low Countries during the late Middle Ages and early Renaissance. First, a high level of literacy within the region enabled many people to act as scribes. Second, acting as a scribe required much less investment of money, skill, and time than many other crafts; as a result the activity was open to a wide range of people. Many scribes were women; some were also engaged in different professions or crafts. Although most scribes active during this period worked for money, some did so within the context of a religious life and thus continued the medieval tradition of monastic book production. Even in the case of the deluxe manuscripts presented in this volume, many people of the period would have been capable of writing the text. A further obstacle facing any modern scholar who wishes to identify the work of a particular scribe is the strict adherence of most Flemish scribes to a limited number of types of script, the conventions of which did not encourage the incorporation of personal traits. Also, two or more scribes collaborating on the transcription of a single book would seek to present a text that was uniform in appearance.

The scribes of the devotional manuscripts in this volume employed mainly the categories of script that we call here *bastarda*, *textura*, and *gotica rotunda*. The choice of script depended on several factors. One of these was the status of the manuscript. Strict application of the hierarchy of scripts would ensure that the most lavish manuscripts were written in the highest grade of script. Another factor was the price a patron was willing to pay. Some scripts required more time to execute than others and, as a consequence, incurred higher costs. A final factor was the personal preference of a patron. Of importance here was the degree of influence exerted on a patron by tradition, fashion, and national origin. In contrast, scribes who worked on manuscripts of secular vernacular texts and manuscripts without a devotional or liturgical purpose almost exclusively used *bastarda*, a script lower in grade than *textura* or *gotica rotunda*. Although script is the very element that both defines *manuscript* (literally, "written by hand") and distinguishes such a work from other craft objects, script remains the most understudied aspect of late medieval Flemish manuscripts.

NICOLAS SPIERINC
Decorated text pages,
fols. 80v–81 (cat. no. 16)

SELECTED SCRIBE BIOGRAPHIES

RICHARD GAY

PATOUL' AGILSON (act. ca. 1477–83)

Along the lower right edge of the final text page in *Légende de Saint Adrien* (cat. no. 42, fol. 16v) appears the abbreviated and slightly cropped signature of Patoul' Agilson.[1] Since the work of Otto Pächt in 1948 (or perhaps even earlier), this signature has been understood to be that of the book's scribe.[2] Notable characteristics of the script are the occasional blocky foot on the first letter of a word and the diagonal slant upward to the right of the uppermost portion of the lowercase *d*. The regularity and finesse of the letterforms indicate the hand of a professional scribe. G. I. Lieftinck notes that the script has a French character.[3] No other manuscripts by Agilson are known.

DAVID AUBERT (act. 1449–79)

Known through his numerous inscriptions and from archival evidence, David Aubert is one of the most studied Flemish scribes of the third quarter of the fifteenth century. His father, Jean, was a financial officer for three Burgundian dukes, Philip the Bold, John the Fearless, and Philip the Good; his brother, also named Jean, served as a ducal functionary and as provost of Mons (1467–1481). Because of his family's wealth and close connections to the Burgundian court, David was well positioned when he began his career.[4]

Possibly born in Dijon, Lille, or Hesdin, Aubert was by 1453 working in the fiscal administration of Philip the Good, a position he acquired through his brother's support.[5] His career as a scribe is well documented from 1458 onward, when he was in the service of the duke's counselor and chamberlain, Jean V of Créquy, for whom he began the compilation of the *Chroniques et conquests de Charlemaine* (Brussels, Bibliothèque royale de Belgique, Ms. 9066–68), illuminated by Jean Le Tavernier. Aubert completed this commission for the manuscript's new owner, Philip, whose service he entered in 1459. The years working for the duke were his most productive; nearly half of his work that today has a known provenance was in the duke's library. The archive of 1463–64 records payment to Aubert as "escrivain de monseigneur le duc, pour avoir fait ystorier et relier" for a copy of *Le Gouvernment du josne prince*. This entry shows that Aubert not only functioned as the duke's scribe (although not necessarily of this book) but also coordinated other aspects of book production.[6] In 1469, two years after the duke's death, payments indicate that Aubert and others conducted a partial inventory of the ducal library.[7] Aubert was not, however, retained as *escrivain* by the duke's son and successor, Charles the Bold (r. 1467–77).

Between 1464 and around 1470 Aubert produced three manuscripts for Louis of Gruuthuse (1422–1492), to which Lieven van Lathem contributed miniatures (cat. nos. 58–60), and another manuscript, which Dreux Jean or his workshop illuminated (cat. no. 50) for an unidentified patron. In 1467, the year of Philip's death, Aubert produced for Guillaume Bourgeois a copy of Jacques Legrand's *Livre des bonnes moeurs*, illuminated by Willem Vrelant (Vatican City, Biblioteca Apostolica, Ms. Pal. lat. 1995); this manuscript may have been intended as a gift to Anthony of Burgundy.[8] Anthony, for whom Aubert had transcribed a Gilles de Trazegnies text in 1463 (Dülmen, Collection du duc de Croÿ, Ms. 50), became the scribe's primary client during the period following Philip's death. Between 1468 and 1469 Aubert produced four volumes of Jean Froissart's *Chroniques* (Berlin, Staatsbibliothek, Dep. Breslau 1) for Anthony, with miniatures by Loyset Liédet, and a *Roముléon* (Brussels, Bibliothèque royale, Ms. 9055). Liédet illuminated at least sixteen manuscripts transcribed by Aubert and destined for Philip the Good or his son Anthony of Burgundy (e.g., cat. no. 55).

In 1475 Aubert was employed by Charles the Bold's wife, Margaret of York. He produced, at times with the help of assistants, at least eight manuscripts for her, including an Apocalypse (cat. no. 27), *La Vision de l'âme de Guy de Thurno* and *Les Visions du chevalier Tondal* (cat. nos. 13, 14), *Somme le roi* (Brussels, Bibliothèque royale, Ms. 9106), and *Consolation de philosophie* (Jena, Universitätsbibliothek, Ms. El .fol. 85). Also from this period is a compilation of moral writings for Margaret of York (cat. no. 29) illuminated by the Master of the Moral Treatises, as well as a compilation of devotional texts (cat. no. 43) and a *Chroniques de Flandres* (cat. no. 85), both associated with the hand of the Master of the First Prayer Book of Maximilian.

Thirty-six signed and dated Aubert manuscripts survive, along with seven other signed examples and an additional twenty-seven dated books attributed to his hand.[9] The large number of manuscripts produced and the phrase "manu proprio" in four inscriptions suggest that Aubert may have frequently employed assistants, particularly between 1468 and 1475. The inscriptions also indicate that the scribe (and his assistants) traveled with the ducal household, following them to Brussels, Hesdin, Bruges, and Ghent.[10] Moreover, prologues in manuscripts he produced demonstrate that Aubert worked not only as a scribe but also as an editor and a compiler.[11] His role as translator of texts from Latin into French, however, remains debatable. The variety of roles he played—which still needs clarification—

the artists with whom he is associated, and a wealth of historical documentation make Aubert pivotal to our understanding of book production at the Burgundian court.

ANTONIUS VAN DAMME (act. 1495–ca. 1545)

This Bruges scribe is known today for his close association with the illuminator Simon Bening. The earliest record of Van Damme appears in 1495 in the registry of the Guild of Saint Luke, Bruges. It documents Van Damme's relationship with Bening, noting receipt from Van Damme of the illuminator's dues in 1516, while Bening was living in Ghent.[12]

Two manuscripts signed and dated by the scribe survive, and Bening or his workshop illuminated both of them. The earliest, copied in Bruges, is a tiny book of hours dated 1531 (cat. no. 148).[13] The book's *gotica rotunda* exhibits a remarkable regularity in form with blockish, evenly spaced letters. In 1545 Van Damme signed and dated a rosary psalter (private collection),[14] which is also written in *gotica rotunda* and mentions the scribe as living in Bruges on the Street of the Sombreros behind the Augustinian monastery.[15] Moreover, the accounts of Mencía de Mendoza record payment to both Van Damme and Bening in June 1539, implying that the two collaborated on a now-lost manuscript.[16] This payment, the two manuscripts, and the aforementioned guild record document a thirty-year working relationship between scribe and artist.

Given that relationship, it seems likely that Van Damme wrote other manuscripts painted by the artist; differences in the script among his documented manuscripts and the goal of uniformity in scribal practice make it difficult to attribute other manuscripts to him with certainty. Both the Imhof Prayer Book (cat. no. 139) and the Boston rosary psalter (see cat. no. 144) have been assigned to his hand, but without wide acceptance.[17] The script of the 1531 book of hours most closely resembles that found in the Munich-Montserrat Hours (cat. no. 154), where variants perhaps can be explained by the difference in script size.

In addition to Mencía de Mendoza (ill. 149b), Van Damme had other Spanish patrons. The 1545 rosary psalter—written in Spanish, Latin, and Portuguese—was intended for a member of the Spanish Acuña family. It is notable then that Van Damme's script at times resembles that of Spanish scribes, as it does in the rosary psalter of 1545.

JAN DU QUESNE (act. late 1460s–ca. 1479)

Residing in Lille, Du Quesne worked as a translator and scribe specializing in vernacular and secular texts. Letterforms in his attractive *bastarda* suggest that in the late 1460s he trained with David Aubert, who was employed by the Burgundian dukes.[18] At least ten manuscripts by Du Quesne survive, some of which were owned by Margaret of York and Charles the Bold, as well as by members of the Burgundian court, such as Anthony of Burgundy and Louis of Gruuthuse.

The earliest surviving manuscript by Du Quesne is perhaps a two-volume *Cité de Dieu,* dated 1466, that was owned by Anthony of Burgundy (Turin, Biblioteca Nazionale, Ms. L I 6, and Turin, Archivio di Stato, Ms. B III 12 J). By 1469 Du Quesne was working for Charles the Bold, receiving payment for copying the duke's household ordinances.[19] Between 1468 and 1475 Du Quesne transcribed two copies of Vasco da Lucena's French translation of *Historia Alexandri magni*—one illuminated by the Master of the *Jardin de vertueuse consolation* and an assistant (cat. no. 63), and the other now in the British Library (London, British Library, Royal Ms. 17 F.i). The scribe also signed copies of *Roman de Jean d'Avesnes* (Paris, Bibliothèque de l'Arsenal, Ms. 5208) and *Fortresse de la foi* (London, British Library, Royal Mss. 17 F.vi–vii). He transcribed two copies of Brunetto Latini's *Trésor,* an encyclopedia in prose covering both sacred and profane topics—one owned by Margaret of York (Saint-Quentin, Bibliothèque municipale, Ms. 109) and another by Louis of Gruuthuse (Paris, Bibliothèque national de France, Ms. fr. 191). His work also includes a *Bulla aurea* of Emperor Charles IV in French (Oxford, Bodleian Library, Ms. Rawl. C.29).[20]

Copies of Julius Caesar's *Commentarii* attest to Du Quesne's activity as translator and compiler.[21] In 1473 or 1474, he translated Caesar's text, augmenting it with interjections and supplemental chapters compiled from other literary sources and dedicating the work to Charles the Bold. One copy, which was transcribed by Du Quesne and is now in the British Library, contains early miniatures by the Master of the London Wavrin (cat. no. 74). A second copy, written out by the scribe in 1478/79, making it his latest known work, includes *Cronique habregie,* a synopsis of historical events from the time of Caesar to the present compiled by Du Quesne (ex Longleat, Marquess of Bath, Botfield Ms. 2 [Christie's, London, June 13, 2002, lot 2]). A third copy of Caesar's text may also have been transcribed by Du Quesne (Copenhagen, Det Kongelige Bibliotek, Ms. Thott 544 2°).[22]

YVONNET LE JEUNE (act. 1468–1470)

The accounts of the Burgundian dukes record the only known activity of this *clerc.*[23] In July 1468 he received payment for having written *La Vengance de nostre seigneur Jhésu-Crist* (Chatsworth, Duke of Devonshire, Ms. 7310) and a *Bible moralisée.* The table of contents in the Chatsworth manuscript records the date 1465, which suggests the book was intended for Philip the Good, who died in 1467.[24] For Charles the Bold, Le Jeune produced a copy of Vasco da Lucena's French translation of Quintus Curtius Rufus's *Historia Alexandri magni,* for which the scribe was paid in January 1470 (cat. no. 54). His work for the dukes suggests that Le Jeune was perhaps a court official, like Aubert, and therefore might have been peripatetic.[44]

Le Jeune seems to have had an association with the illuminator Loyset Liédet. Both the *Vengance* and Alexander manuscripts contain miniatures by Liédet, and the accounts of July 1468 record payment not only to the scribe for his work but also to Liédet for twenty *histoires* in a *Bible moralisée*. Since Liédet is documented as living in Bruges between 1469 and 1478, it seems plausible that the scribe resided in that city as well.

PIETER MEGHEN (1466/67–1540)

Born in Brabant, Pieter Meghen described himself in colophons as "of 's-Hertogenbosch in the diocese of Liège." He may be the same Petrus de Meghen from that district who matriculated at the University of Louvain on June 15, 1497. Regardless, this scribe is well documented not only by his own inscriptions but also in the letters of Erasmus and in the accounts of Henry VIII of England. Indeed, between 1511 and 1519 Meghen served as courier for Erasmus, who at times called him "Cyclops" because he lacked an eye. Beginning March 25, 1530, he was in England as writer of the king's books, a post he held for the final ten years of his life. Attributed to Meghen is a manuscript at Hatfield House containing the Acts of the Apostles and the Apocalypse that was produced for the king between 1528 and 1533 (cat. no. 132). The manuscript contains the Vulgate text, another Latin translation by Erasmus, and two miniatures by Flemish illuminators.

Scholars associate nearly thirty manuscripts with Meghen, all in Latin, with the overwhelming majority written in *humanistica*.[26] Textual analysis shows that he usually copied his texts from printed editions.[27] His early manuscripts are smaller than his later ones, and his script became heavier and bulkier around 1517.[28] His earliest and most consistent patrons include the English humanists John Colet (dean of Saint Paul's, London) and Christopher Urswick. For the latter, he copied in 1503 Cicero's *De officiis*, which is the scribe's earliest dated work (Rouen, Bibliothèque municipale, Ms. 929 [0.41]). In the late 1520s he produced for Cardinal Thomas Wolsey a pair of lectionaries illuminated by a Flemish artist, newly named in this volume the Master of Cardinal Wolsey (cat. no. 169). At least eight additional manuscripts produced by Meghen were illuminated by Flemish artists.[29]

The scribe traveled regularly as a courier between the Low Countries and England, delivering books and letters between Erasmus and his colleagues. He may have delivered a *Novum instrumentum* from Erasmus to Pope Leo X in Rome in 1516.[30] It was Meghen who in 1517 transported to Thomas More in Calais a diptych by Quentin Massys portraying Erasmus and the Antwerp humanist Pieter Gillis. It appears that these journeys stopped in 1519, the year Erasmus last mentioned the scribe. Meghen was actively working in his later years, as evidenced by a manuscript containing Nikolaus Kratzer's *Canones horoptri baculi* (Oxford, Bodleian Library, Ms. Lat. misc. f 51). According to J. B. Trapp, Meghen transcribed this text in 1537 at the age of seventy.[31]

QUENTIN POULET (act. 1472–1506)

Born in Lille, Poulet was in Bruges in 1477/78, when his name appears on a list of apprentices registered with the Confraternity of Saint John.[32] This record led some scholars to conclude that Poulet trained as an illuminator.[33] Since the confraternity included members not associated with the book trade,[34] it is possible that Poulet was never an illuminator. Moreover, no evidence of his working as a painter survives. Poulet was in England by 1492, when he became librarian to Henry VII (1457–1509), a post he held until at least 1506. As such, he was the first appointed keeper of the Royal Library, which George II presented to the nation in 1757.[35]

A colophon and a record of payment from the king document Poulet's work as a scribe. At the royal residence at Sheen (later renamed Richmond) Poulet signed and dated a copy of the *Imaginacion de la vraie noblesse* (cat. no. 121) in 1496, which the Master of the Prayer Books of around 1500 illuminated for the king. A musical compilation that in part extols the union of York and Lancaster has been attributed to Poulet (London, British Library, Royal Ms. 11 E xi). In 1503 he wrote two rolls associated with the king's almshouses at Westminster, for which he received twenty-six shillings and eight pence, and another roll probably associated with the marriage of Margaret to James IV of Scotland (British Library, Lansdowne Roll 4). Between 1496 and 1502 he also received payment for books, bindings, and clasps.[36]

Among Poulet's personal correspondents was Jean de Blicque de Houpplines, French secretary at Calais.[37] In June 1506 Poulet was paid for having gone to Calais on the "Kinges busyness."[38] In 1506 Henry VIII replaced Poulet as librarian with Giles Duwes; Maurits Smeyers suggested that Poulet might have returned to Lille at that time.[39]

NICOLAS SPIERINC (act. ca. 1453–1499)

Originating in Zwijndrecht, near Rotterdam, Nicolas Spierinc became a favorite scribe of the Burgundian court.[40] The first mention of him is in the Ghent archives of 1453 and concerns rent on his house there.[41] He enrolled in the school of medicine at the university at Leuven on January 31, 1455, where in an unusual gesture, the school register identifies him as a "scriptor."[42] Spierinc was coordinating various aspects of book production by 1469 while working for Charles the Bold. Ducal accounts of January 1469 record payment to him as *escripvain* for having transcribed a prayer book (cat. no. 16), and again in August for having copied, illuminated, and bound eight books of ordinances, of which only the *Ordonnances du premier écuyer d'écuyerie* survives (Vienna, Österreichische Nationalbibliothek, Ms. Ser. N. 2616). During the 1450s and through the 1470s, Spierinc purchased and sold a variety of properties in Ghent, where he and Barbe Colfs (d. 1479/80) raised their children.[43] Although Spierinc's name appears regularly in the Ghent archives until June 1499, none of his identified work postdates the early 1480s.

Spierinc's distinctive calligraphic style of graceful cadelles arching into the borders of text pages is readily recognizable. The bold strokes and delicate arabesques resist the confines of the text block and form elaborate interlace patterns, which at times he shaded with gold and pale color. They sprout acanthus leaves, support drolleries, and charge the blank parchment with energetic bursts of pattern. Close examination reveals that he added the exuberant cadelles to the restrained strokes of the *bastarda* script, which he or others had already written. His finest *bastarda* exhibits a lightness, refinement, and level of invention that are rarely seen.

Spierinc's hand appears in books illuminated by the most noted illuminators of the day, especially Van Lathem and the Vienna Master of Mary of Burgundy. The three of them created the Prayer Book of Charles the Bold (cat. no. 16). Spierinc also collaborated with the two illuminators and Simon Marmion on the Trivulzio Hours (cat. no. 17) and the Hours of Mary of Burgundy (cat. no. 19). With the Vienna Master of Mary of Burgundy, Spierinc also produced the Hours of Engelbert of Nassau (cat. no. 18). He likely copied the Voustre Demeure Hours (cat. no. 20), illustrated by the Vienna Master of Mary of Burgundy and/or his followers, and also Van Lathem, Simon Marmion, and the Master of the Dresden Prayer Book. He may also have transcribed parts of a book of hours in Madrid (Madrid, Biblioteca Nacional, Ms. Vit. 24–10) and sections of the Sachsenheim Hours illuminated by Van Lathem (Stuttgart, Württembergische Landesbibliothek, Ms. brev. 162). Antoine de Schryver has argued that Spierinc was also an illuminator, specifically that he was the Master of Mary of Burgundy, but this identification has not gained acceptance.[44]

Notes

1. Only the ending of the Christian name is abbreviated. The signature is reproduced in Pächt and Thoss 1990, 2: fig. 200.
2. Pächt 1948: 66.
3. Lieftinck 1969: 153.
4. On Aubert's family, see Cockshaw 1968.
5. Known from archival evidence. For a transcription, see Straub 1995: 311.
6. Straub 1995: 311.
7. Straub 1995: 134, 312.
8. A possibility suggested by Scot McKendrick.
9. See Straub 1995 for lists sorted by type of inscription and by patron. Kren has added to this a further attribution (see cat. no. 50).
10. Paviot 1999: 16.

11. Straub 1995: 324.
12. For the guild's records, see Weale 1872–73a: 329, and Weale 1864–65a: 310.
13. *Author ac scriptor hui[us] operis presentis nomen est ei antonius van damme moran in trahes brugis an[n]o 1531*, fols. 128v–129.
14. Formerly Amsterdam, Bibliotheca Philosophica Hermetica; König 1991: 530–45, no. 34, and Sotheby's, London, July 6, 2000, lot 57.
15. *Aste librito iscribio autonyo van damme el qual viue en la calle delos sombrereros de tras el monesterio delos augustines a brujas 1545* (König 1991: 545).
16. For transcriptions of the accounts, see Steppe 1969: 501.
17. See Cambridge 1993: no. 29.
18. Brussels 1959: 178.
19. De Schryver 1969b: 438–39, 455. De Schryver identified Oxford, Bodleian Library, Ms. Hatton 13 as the manuscript. As Scot McKendrick has kindly pointed out, however, the script does not match that in other manuscripts by Du Quesne.
20. Pächt and Alexander 1966–73, 1: 25, no. 331.
21. Bossuat 1943: 268.
22. Suggested by Scot McKendrick.
23. Pinchart 1865: 476, 478, 485; Durrieu 1910a: 58–59.
24. Richmond 1979: 64, no. 131.
25. See Scot McKendrick, "Reviving the Past: Illustrated Manuscripts of Secular Vernacular Texts, 1467–1500" (this volume), n. 77.
26. For a list, see Trapp 1975: 80–96, which supplements Pächt 1944b: 137, n. 6.
27. Trapp 1991: 86; and Reeve 1983: 12–20.
28. Trapp, in Beitenholz and Deutscher 1985–87, 2: 421; Brown (A.) 1984: 352–56.
29. Trapp (1981–82: 30) lists the manuscripts.
30. Trapp, in Beitenholz and Deutscher 1985–87, 2: 421.
31. Trapp, in Beitenholz and Deutscher 1985–87, 2: 420.
32. Weale 1872–73a: 297.
33. Smeyers 1998: 467; Backhouse 1999: 272.
34. See Catherine Reynolds, "Illuminators and the Painters' Guilds" (this volume).
35. George II presented the Royal Library to the British Museum in 1757. Much of the groundwork on Poulet was laid by Janet Backhouse. See Backhouse 1987 and 1999.
36. For the records of payment and the Lansdowne roll, see Backhouse 1987: 32, n. 38, and 33, nn. 40–41. Campbell and Foister (1986: 722, n. 44) list payments by Henry VII to Poulet.
37. For their correspondence, see British Library, Add. Ms. 46455, fol. 115v, and British Library, Add. Ms. 46456, fols. 126, 127.
38. Poulet was paid forty shillings to go to Calais (Campbell and Foister 1986: 722, n. 44).
39. Smeyers 1998: 468.
40. Since Spierinc was a common name in the Netherlands, care must be taken not to make assumptions about the scribe's possible relatives or to confuse him with a Dutch illuminator of the same name. See de Schryver 1969b: 434–47; Byvanck and Hoogewerff 1925: xxiii, 63–65, nos. 151–56.
41. De Schryver, commentary for a facsimile of the Prayer Book of Charles the Bold (cat. no. 16), typescript.
42. Smeyers (1998: 280) suggested that Spierinc entered the school expressly to advance his career as *libraire*.
43. De Schryver, commentary (see note 41). Three of their five children were minors when the mother died. One son evidently became a physician and another a printer and binder. See de Schryver 1969a: 47.
44. De Schryver 1969a: 90–102.

BIBLIOGRAPHIES TO THE CATALOGUE ENTRIES

PART 1

CAT. NO. 1. Marrow 2002: 67–76

CAT. NO. 2. Schilling 1961: 211–36; Kraus 1962: 54–65, no. 25; Winkler 1964: 281; Marrow 1966: 67–68; Cologne 1968: no. D65; Delaissé 1968: 76–77; de Schryver 1969b: 444 n. 46; Gorissen 1973: 49, 51, 112, 148, 149, 154, 172, 173, 180, 181, 182, 183, 192, 211, 217, 397, 411, 452, 464, 629, 665, 1051–59, 1121; Kraus 1974: no. 36; Delaissé, Marrow, and De Wit 1977: 508; Harthan 1977: 37–38; Kraus 1978b: no. 61; Panhans-Bühler 1978: 19–20; Euw and Plotzek 1979–85, 2: 115–41, 148, 158; Karlowskiej-Kamzowej 1981: 77; Plotzek 1982: 35–36, fig. 2; Belting and Eichberger 1983: 95–96; Lemaire 1983: 9, 12–15; Pächt, Jenni, and Thoss 1983, 1: 54, 91, 103; Labuda 1984: 33–34 n. 16; Cardon, Lievens, and Smeyers 1985: 162; Liebaers et al. 1985: 162–63; Verdier 1985: 206; Los Angeles 1986: 78; Van Miegroet 1986: 38, fig. 44; Baltimore 1988: 150–56; Smeyers 1988: 70–71, 76, fig. 21; Upton 1990: 47, 49; Pickwoad 1991: 55–80; Smeyers and Cardon 1991: 91, 101, 103; Vermeersch 1992: 81; Châtelet 1993: 80–84; ; De Hamel 1994: 206, 208, 209; Faßbender 1994: no. 121, fig. 52; New York 1994a: 178–79, fig. 171; Steinmetz 1995: 209; Van Buren, Marrow, and Pettenati 1996: 298, 308 n. 6, 332, 335, 341 n. 79, 343, 346–48, 350, 351 n. 6, 352 nn. 26–27, 353 n. 42; Bousmanne 1997: 43, 62, 63, 72, 75, 96, 111, 198, 271–72, 377; Brinkmann 1997: 238 n. 15; Randall 1997: 174, 202, 208, 239, 249, 250, 260, 261, 351; König 1998b: 364–65; Smeyers 1998: 262; Allmand 1999: 270; Gesché and Scolas 1999: 67; Clark 2000: 112, 141; Leuven 2002: 299, no. 78

CAT. NO. 3. Waagen 1847: 177; Waagen 1862: 110–11; Pinchart 1865: 474–510; Dehaisnes 1882: 37; Reusens 1899: pl. 49; Schestag 1899: 207; Reinach 1903: 267; Doutrepont 1909: 414–18; Van den Gheyn (J.) 1909: 90–91; Lyna 1918: 184–85; Durrieu 1921a: 51–52; Post 1923: 171–74; Winkler 1925: 24, 41, 44, 69, 71, 164; Lyna 1933: 89; Gaspar and Lyna 1944: 10ff.; Panofsky 1953, 1: 268, 282 n. 3, 292–94, 462, 466, 475, 477; Delaissé 1955a: 21–55; Delaissé 1958: no. 27; Brussels 1959: 52–53, no. 42; Châtelet 1966: 11; Brussels 1967a: 125, no. 188; Friedländer 1967–76, 2: 25; Bruyn 1968: 92–96; Delaissé 1968: 64; Masai and Wittek 1968–82, 3: 108, no. A207; D'Ancona and Aeschlimann 1969: 225–26, no. 115; Brussels 1970: 26–27, nos. 17–19; Davies (M.) 1972: 208; Van Buren 1972: 249–68; de Schryver 1974: 46; Brussels 1977a: no. 5; Gilissen 1977: 455–62; Brussels 1979b: no. 36; Cockshaw 1979b; Euw and Plotzek 1979–85, 3: 252, 254; De Winter 1982: 139–40; Rouzet 1982; Brussels 1984: no. 71a; Gaspar and Lyna 1984–89, 3: 9–15; Cockshaw 1985: 27–31; Binding 1987: 123–27; Dogaer 1987a: 85; Kudorfer 1988: 121; Sint-Truiden 1988: no. 44; Brussels 1989b: 127–33, no. 48; Châtelet 1989: 18; Camille 1990: 112; Pächt, Jenni, and Thoss 1983: 53ff., 73ff.; Thomas (M.)

MASTER OF JAMES IV
OF SCOTLAND
Saint John the Baptist
(detail, ill. 125)

and Zink 1990: 217; Van den Bergen-Pantens 1990: 93; Alexander 1992: 165; Paris 1993: 87; Zimmermann and De Rentiis 1994: 226 n. 24, 273; Van Buren, Marrow, and Pettenati 1996: 321 n. 27, 342; New York 1998: 22; Smeyers 1998: 288, 290, 291, 301 no. 2, 352; De Vos 1999: 249–51; Kemperdick 1999: 58–59; Van den Bergen-Pantens 2000

CAT. NO. 4. Friedländer 1916: 21, 174; Folie 1963: 206; Friedländer 1967–76, 1: 84; Gellman 1970: 484–85; Upton 1972: 139–40, 142–43, 152, 154, 179, 180 n. 20, 368–72, no. 21, fig. 21; Richter 1974: 380–82; Schabacker 1974: 17, 42–43, 46, 73, 80–81, 129–30, no. 2, fig 2; Panhans-Bühler 1978: 11–16, fig. 1; Ringbom 1984: 148; Upton 1990: 1 n. 4, 56 n. 1, 57–59, 64–65, 70, fig. 58; Hand 1992: 7, 10, 16, 17 nn. 1–2, fig. 1; New York 1994a: 32, 34, 53, 71, 80 no. 4, 86–91, 105, 115, 178–79, pl. 87, figs. 19, 105, 106; New York 1998: 96–97, no. 3

CAT. NO. 5. London 1957: no. 22; Rowlands 1962: 419–23; Friedländer 1967–76, 1: 107; Hamburg 1969: 66, no. 24; Gellman 1970: 204, 428–30; Sterling 1971: 21, 24; Upton 1972: 109, 282–85; Richter 1974: 357–60; Schabacker 1974: 105–6; Panhans-Bühler 1978: 36–53; Ringbom 1984: 52; Upton 1990: 44–47, 55–57; Hand 1992: 7, 9–10; New York 1994a: 112–16, no. 9

CAT. NO. 6. Brussels 1969: 106, no. 84; Brussels 1970: nos. 44, 45, 47, 48; Büttner 1972: 99; Van Buren 1975: 300–302, n. 64; Panhans-Bühler 1978: 18–35; Bruges 1981: 273–74, no. 116; Pächt, Jenni, and Thoss 1983: 103; Van Buren 1983: 64; Sinclair 1987: nos. 1001, 1804; Pächt and Thoss 1990: 80; Brussels 1991: 124, no. 27; New York 1994a: 176–80, no. 21; Van Buren 1999: 17 n. 32; Leuven 2002: 315, no. 86

CAT. NO. 7. Hédouin 1847: 273; Friedländer 1923a: 167–70; Hulin de Loo 1942: 11–19; Davies (M.) 1968: 85–87; Davies (M.) 1970: 18–26; Hoffman 1978: 634–49; Grosshans 1991: 63–98; Ainsworth 1992: 244–45; Grosshans 1992: 233–42; Paris 1993: 80; Campbell 1998: 301–9

CAT. NO. 8. Agnew 1971: no. 24; Agnew 1979: 16–19, no. 13; Toronto 1980: 2–3; Sterling 1981b: 3–18; Ainsworth 1992: 248–49; Châtelet 1996: 152, 163 n. 18; DOA 1996, 20: 451; Nash 1999: 12, 231, 232

CAT. NO. 9. Backhouse 1993a: 18–22; Kren 1996: 193–220; The Hague 2002: 170, 212

CAT. NO. 10. *The Holy Virgins Entering Paradise:* De Ricci 1935–40, 2: 176; Hoffman 1958: 177; Cincinnati 1959: no. 340; New York 1968b: no. 10; Lawrence 1969: no. 24, pl. 58; Clark 1992: 207 n. 21; Hindman 1992: 223–32; Paris 1993: 80; Paris 1994: 2; Kren 1996: 219–20 n. 24; Hindman et al. 1997: 60–72, no. 8; Gil 1998a: 44, 47 n. 15; New York 1998: 25, 110; Van der Velden 2000: 52. *Scenes from the Life of Saint Denis:* Hindman 1992: 223–32; Paris 1994: 2; Hindman et al. 1997: 63–72; Van der Velden 2000: 52

CAT. NO. 11. Friedländer 1923a: 167–70; Michel 1927: 142, 145; Lehman 1928: no. 91; Sterling 1941: 48, no. 124, 125; Ring 1949b: 221; Hoffman 1958: 10–11, 37, 125, 178; New York 1959a: 27; Lehman 1964: 18; Hoffman 1969:

244; Szabo 1975: 84; Baetjer 1977: 341–42, 344; Baetjer 1980: 115; Sterling 1981b: 12 n. 28; Ainsworth 1992: 246–48; Baetjer 1995: 254; Châtelet 1996: 154, 164–65; New York 1998: 109–11; Sterling and Ainsworth 1998: 2–6, no. 1

CAT. NO. 12. Reinach 1919: 240; De Ricci 1935–40, 1: 102–3; Hoffman 1969: 245; Hoffman 1973: 274, 275; Thorpe 1976; Hindman 1977: 203 n. 45, 204; Malibu 1983a: 31, 32; Dutschke et al. 1989: 523–26; Ainsworth 1992: 244; Brinkmann 1992c: 119 n. 111, 120 n. 113, 125; Clark 1992: 196, 201–2, 204, 206 n. 3, 207 n. 19, 208 nn. 35, 40–41; de Schryver 1992: 173–74; Hindman 1992: 228; Kren 1992a: 24; Legaré 1992: 214; Paris 1993: 89 under no. 41; Kren 1996: 211–16; Nash 1999: 231, 242, 248–49 n. 104

CAT. NO. 13. Doutrepont 1909: 235 n. 2, 493; Cambridge, Mass., 1955: no. 89; Brussels 1959: no. 191; Faye and Bond 1962: 273; Baltimore 1965: no. 35; Gilissen 1969: 161; Hoffman 1969: 245; Unterkircher and de Schryver 1969: 152; Hoffman 1973: 273, 275; Hindman 1977: 191–93, 204; Kraus 1978b: 198, no. 79; Hellinga 1981: 21 n. 14; Dogaer 1987a: 143; Kren and Wieck 1990: 33; Barstow 1992: 258; Blockmans 1992: 40, 42, 44; Clark 1992: 201, 204; Cockshaw 1992: 58–60, 62 n. 25; de Schryver 1992: 177; Eichberger 1992: 129; Kren 1992a: 18–19, 23–24; Lewis (S.) 1992: 77, 86; Morgan 1992: 65, 67; Smith (J.) 1992: 51; Wieck 1992: 119, 126; Paris 1993: 89; Paris 1994: 6; Schmitt 1994: fig. 9; Brinkmann 1997: 163; Schmitt 1998: fig. 5; Charron and Gil 1999: 95, 100; Paviot 1999: 14, 16 n. 68

CAT. NO. 14. Doutrepont 1909: 235, 493; Cambridge, Mass., 1955: no. 88; Brussels 1959: 153; Baltrušaitis 1960: 362 n. 29; Jackson 1960: 151–64; Faye and Bond 1962: 273; Baltimore 1965: 53; McGrath 1968: 46; Cuttler 1969b: 318–19; Hoffman 1969: 245; Hoffman 1973: 273, 275; Hindman 1977: 193, 204; Kraus 1978b: 198, no. 79; Hellinga 1981: 21 n. 14; Palmer 1982: 17 n. 26; Kren and Wieck 1990; Legaré 1991: 80–81; Barstow 1992: 258; Blockmans 1992: 40, 42, 51; Clark 1992: 201, 204; Cockshaw 1992: 58–60, 62 n. 25; de Schryver 1992: 174–76; Dinzelbacher 1992: 111, 115–16; Eichberger 1992: 129–34, 137–38; Hindman 1992: 227–29; Kren 1992a: 13–14, 16–18, 20, 23–24; Kren 1992b: 141–42, 147–51; Legaré 1992: 212; Lewis (S.) 1992: 77, 84, 86; Lowry 1992: 103; Morgan 1992: 65, 67; Wieck 1992: 119–26; Baschet 1993: 429 n. 78; Paris 1993: 89; Paris 1994: 6; Utrecht 1994: 67; Wieck 1994: 134 n. 2; Zürich 1994: 339, no. 130, and passim; Smeyers 1995: 240–50; Brinkmann 1997: 163, 222; Hindman et al. 1997: 67; Los Angeles 1997: 84–85; Charron and Gil 1999: 95, 100; Lisbon 2000: 428–29, no. 119

CAT. NO. 15. Durrieu 1903a: 64; Beissel (S.) 1904: 53–56; De Mély 1913: 305–6; Winkler 1915: 295; Winkler 1925: 71; Kraus 1957: no. 46; Kraus 1978b: 170, no. 65; Euw and Plotzek 1979–85, 2: 142–59; Török 1985: 20, fig. 17; Verdier 1985: 206; Büttner 1987: 316 n. 7, 326; Cologne 1987: 182; Dogaer 1987a: 103, fig. 57; Baltimore 1988: 150–52; Cambridge 1993: 130; De Hamel 1994: 170, 184; Paris 1995: 28–29, fig. 12; Steinmetz 1995: 247, 273–74 nn. 570–81; Van Buren,

Marrow, and Pettenati 1996: 155, 160 n. 29, 347, 352
n. 29, 544, 549 n. 29; Bousmanne 1997: 39, 43, 79, 82,
98, 100–101, 106, 109–10, 112, 115, 117, 121, 147, 149, 165,
176, 180, 183, 187, 192, 219, 272–74, 377; Brussels 1997:
6, 8, 37, 59, 64; Randall 1997: 202, 247, 248, 249, 259,
264, 269, 274, 281, 288, 310, 311, 324, 347, 415; Stroo
et al. 1999: 229, 233 n. 50, fig. 124

PART 2

Cat. no. 16. Durrieu 1910a: 70–71; Durrieu 1910b:
68–69; Winkler 1915: 302, 304; Durrieu 1916: 100–101,
107 n. 1, 112–18, 120 n. 1, 121–30; Smital 1924: 10, 30;
Winkler 1925: 90, 196; Pächt 1948: 55 n. 26; de
Schryver 1957: 338–42; Brussels 1959: no. 242;
Deuchler 1963: 235; Boon 1964: 249–50, no.4; de
Schryver 1969a: 26–27; de Schryver 1969b: 444 n. 44,
453, 454; Duverger 1969: 99; Lieftinck 1969: 27, 29–30,
33–35, 41, figs. 54, 55; Unterkircher and de Schryver
1969: 26–27, 44–46, 49, 52, 53, 79, 87–88, 136, 160;
Dumon 1973: 4; de Schryver 1974: 73–74; Ghent 1975,
2: 369, 377; Van Buren 1975: 294, 297, 300 n. 62;
Thomas (M.) 1976: 88–90; Brussels 1977a: 12–13;
London 1980: fig. 6; Thoss 1982: 20, 115, figs. 10, 83;
Dogaer 1987: 133, 137; Kren and Wieck 1990: 14, fig. 8;
Pächt and Thoss 1990: 38, 80, 83, 84; Brinkmann and
König 1991: 91, 93, 314, 316; Kren 1992a: 55 n. 6, 179
n. 15; Inglis 1995: 11; Van Buren 1996a: 92 n. 75; Wolf
(E.) 1996: 15–16, 20, 100, 101, 103, 134, 230, 280–81, 294,
299, 306; Bousmanne 1997: 139; Brinkmann 1997, 1:
110 n. 46, 238 n. 16; Los Angeles 1997: 91, 92–93;
Randall 1997: 352; Campbell 1998: 298; Bruyère 1999:
843–45; Van der Velden 2000: 124, 127, 129, 130, 146,
147; Bousmanne and Voelkle 2001: 73

Cat. no. 17. Porro 1884: 331–32, no. 472; Durrieu 1916:
106–7

Cat. no. 18. Waagen 1854–57, 3: 82–84; Oxford
1895–1953, 4: 559–60, nos. 21793–94; Durrieu 1921a:
66, pl. 85; Winkler 1925: 104, 113, 190; Antwerp 1930;
Hulin de Loo 1939b: 162–63, 174–75; Winkler 1942:
265–66, figs. 8, 9, 11; Pächt 1944a: 299–300, pls. 3d,
4e; Pächt 1948: 20–21, 28, 30–34, 37, 38b, 41b, 43, 48,
no. 14, pls. A–D, pl. 16; Lyna 1949: 151–55; London
1953–54: nos. 596, 597; Brussels 1959: 190–91, nos. 267,
268; Wescher 1959: 126–35; Lieftinck 1964: 257–94,
figs. 4, 15; Ringbom 1965: 204; Pächt and Alexander
1966–73, 1: 27, no. 361, pl. 29, figs. 61a–b; Lieftinck
1969, 1: 39–76; Alexander 1970: passim; Backhouse
1973b: 684–85; Van Buren 1975: 286–92, 297, 302;
Malibu 1983b: 3, 49, 56, 63 n. 2, 120; Markl 1983: 189;
Oxford 1984: 159–63, no. 230; Testa 1986: 157; Dogaer
1987a: 17, 137, 145, 149; Pächt and Thoss 1990: 38, 84;
Brinkmann and König 1991: 12, 91, 93, 103, 104, 105,
106, 145, 151, 204, 234, 314, 316, 326, 328, 329, 368, 374;
Kaufmann (T.) and Kaufmann (V.) 1991: 49, 54;
Inglis 1995: 11; König 1995: 42 n. 3, 61 n. 27, 120–22,
pls. 29–33, 36, 37, 138–43 n. 41, 153–54 nn. 89–93;
Brinkmann 1997: 26, 186 n. 143, 187 n. 149, 238 n. 16;
Berlin 1998: 31, 77, 120–22, 138, 139–41, 153–54;
Brinkmann 1998: 31, 77, 138, 139–41, 153–54; Smeyers
1998: 393, 397, 416 n. 75, 444, 483 n. 56; Daems 1999: 8

Cat. no. 19. Gottlieb (Th.) 1900: 27; Thieme-Becker
1907–50, 22: 418–19; Lindner 1912: 230; Winkler 1915:
279–306; Durrieu 1916: 91–97, 107; Durrieu 1921a: 58;
Winkler 1925: 103–13, 203f.; Hulin de Loo 1939b: 178;
Winkler 1942: 265; Pächt 1944a: 295, n. 8, 296, n. 15;
Wescher 1946: 191ff; Gaspar 1947: 113–24; Pächt 1948:
64ff., no. 7, pls. 10–13, 19, 40b, c, 45; Lyna 1949: 151–55;
Ring 1949a: 86–87; Colding 1951: 171f.; Vienna 1952:
no. 206; de Schryver 1957: 338–42; Anzelewsky 1959:

114–25; Brussels 1959: 184; Vienna 1959: 36; Bergström
1960: 335–43; Brussels 1962: no. 1; Boon 1964: 241–54;
Brayer 1964: 39, no. 5; Lieftinck 1964b: 254–92; de
Schryver 1969b: 435, 444; Duverger 1969: 97–104;
Lieftinck 1969: 24–36; Unterkircher and de Schryver
1969; Alexander 1970; Büttner 1972: 92–126; Dogaer
1972: 97–104; Hoffman 1973: 284f.; Unterkircher 1974;
Biermann 1975: 15–311; Ghent 1975, 2: 326–29; Van
Buren 1975: 286, 288, 293–302; Farquhar 1976: 26;
Pächt 1976: 28–32; Harthan 1977: 110–13; Büttner
1978: 290–303; Bruges 1981: 245; De Winter 1981:
342–427, fig. 10; Jenni and Thoss 1982: 25–29;
Bonsanti 1983: 22, fig. 17a; Büttner 1983: 72; Malibu
1983a: 5, 7–8, 63, 64; Markl 1983: 17, 18, 28, 112, 201;
Pächt, Jenni, and Thöss 1983: 103; Hansen 1984: 233f.;
Testa 1984: 189–236; Büttner 1987: 317, 325, 334, 340;
Dogaer 1987a: 133–36; Vienna 1987b: 52–56;
Brinkmann 1987–88: 142; Pächt and Thoss 1990:
69–85; Thoss 1991; Brinkmann 1992a: 191 n. 6; de
Schryver 1992: 171–73, 177; Kren 1992a: 25 n. 33, Lewis
(S.) 1992: 80; Smith (J.) 1992: 54; Van Elslande 1992:
127–69; Spreitzer 1994; Inglis 1995; Smeyers and Van
der Stock 1996: 21–22; Smeyers 1999: 395, fig. 52;
Vöhringer 2002: 63

Cat. no. 20. *Voustre Demeure Hours*: Durrieu 1893: 34;
Paz Y Meliá 1901: passim; Van den Gheyn (J.) 1906:
305; Winkler 1913a: 274; Winkler 1914: 238; Winkler
1925: 183; Domínguez Bordona 1933: no. 983; Hulin de
Loo 1939b: 177; Winkler 1942: figs. 15, 16; Pächt 1944a:
300; Pächt 1948: 38–40, 67–68, no. 15; Brussels 1964:
no. 113; Janini and Serrano 1969: no. 221; Lieftinck
1969: 77–108; Ghent 1975: 377–78; no. 615; Malibu
1983a: 27, 29, 31, 36, 38 n. 17; Berlin 1987: 113; Dogaer
1987a: 17, 131, 137, 145, 149; Brinkmann 1988: 94; Kren
and Rathofer 1988: 37, 38, 40, 229, 232, 355, 356, 358;
Brinkmann and König 1991: 149, 372; Brinkmann
1992a: 186–90; Brinkmann 1992c: 106 n. 102, 133
n. 124; Clark 1992: 206 nn. 1, 3, 5, 207 n. 18; de
Schryver 1992: 173; Paris 1993: 300; Brinkmann 1997:
13–14, 183–98, 279, 306, 344, 370; Smeyers 1998: 341,
352 n. 101, 395, 397, 416 n. 77. *Album of Miniatures from
the Voustre Demeure Hours*: Winkler 1913c: 268ff.;
Winkler 1925: 103, 159, 189; Wescher 1936: 167ff.;
Hulin de Loo 1939b: 158ff.; Winkler 1943: 55–64, figs.
17, 18; Pächt 1948: 68, no. 16; Brussels 1951: no. 112;
Boese 1966: 209; Hoffman 1969: 245; Lieftinck 1969:
77–108; Van Buren 1975: 290–92, 297; Berlin 1987:
113–14; Pächt and Thoss 1990: 89, 96–97; Ainsworth
1992: 244; Brinkmann 1992a; 186–90; Brinkmann
1992c: 133 n. 124, 142; Clark 1992: 206 nn. 1, 3, 5, 207
n. 18; de Schryver 1992: 173; Brinkmann 1997: 13–14,
183–96. *The Pietà*: Winkler 1923: 255; Antwerp 1930:
no. 14; Ford and Vickers 1939: 12 n. 30; Hulin de Loo
1939b: 177; Worcester 1939: 24, no. 17; Philadelphia
1941: 31, no. 343; Philadelphia 1953: no. 343, pl. 96;
Cleveland 1967: 306, no. VII 7; Hoffman 1969: 274;
Unterkircher and de Schryver 1969: 155, n. 272;
Sweeny 1972: 52–53, no. 343; Hoffman 1973: 245 n. 8;
Malibu 1983a: 39 n. 27; Ringbom 1984: 136, 139;
Brinkmann 1992a: 187 n. 26, 193; Clark 1992: 207 n. 18,
208 n. 40; Legaré 1992: 214–15; Brinkmann 1997; 188
nn. 154, 155, 390–91, no. 31b; Sterling and Ainsworth
1998: 4 n. 9

Cat. no. 21. Hind and Popham 1915–32, 5: 65–66;
Popham 1928: 134; Pächt 1948: 70, no. 25; Lieftinck
1969: 91–92; Mazal and Thoss 1993: 39; DOA 1996,
20: 727; Buck 2001: 160–61

Cat. no. 22. James 1913: 244–45, no. 215; Pächt 1948: 64,
no. 6; London 1953–54: 159, no. 594; Amsterdam 1959:

no. 198; Lieftinck 1964b: 286; Lieftinck 1969: 1–7, 191;
Roosen-Runge and Roosen-Runge 1981: 65; Malibu
1983a: 20 n. 3; Hughes (M.) 1984a: 58–59; Testa 1986;
Dogaer 1987a: 30; Thoss 1987: 57; Pächt and Thoss
1990: 89; Barstow 1992: 261, no. 20; Blockmans 1992:
41; Kren 1992a: 14; Morgan 1992: 65; Smith (J.) 1992:
58; Cambridge 1993: 150–51; Brinkmann 1997: 189
n. 163; Brown (M.) 1998: 288; Smeyers 1998: 386, 387,
416, no. 61

Cat. no. 23. Winkler 1942: 268; Pächt 1948: 51; Ring
1949a: 87; Brussels 1959: 189, no. 265; Deuchler 1963:
fig. 373; Ghent 1975, 2: 374–75, no. 610; Van Buren
1975: 290, n. 30; Hughes (M.) 1984a: 72–73, no. 23;
Dhanens 1987: 116; Dogaer 1987a; Trio 1990: 125–32;
Blockmans 1992: 38–39; Brinkmann 1992c: 20 n. 3;
Smeyers 1998: 385, 387

Cat. no. 24. Lieftinck 1964a: no. 37a; Lieftinck 1964b:
cols. 255–92; Lieftinck 1969: xiii–xiv, 13–23; Brussels
1975: no. 45; Malibu 1983a: 17, 18, 20; Dogaer 1987a:
149; Brinkmann 1997: 123 n. 84, 343 n.2; Brinkmann
1998: 132–33, n. 28

Cat. no. 25. London 1862: 584, no. 6834; Paris 1907, 1:
58, pl. 73; Winkler 1925: 196; Pächt 1948: 68, no. 17;
Lieftinck 1969: xv, 109–25; Van Buren 1975: 307; Pächt
1976; De Winter 1981: 353, 424, n. 20; Malibu 1983a:
18, 21, 23, 27, 29 n. 8, 30 n. 22; Testa 1986: 128, 130,
134, 169; Dogaer 1987a: 149; Tudor-Craig 1987: 356ff.
Brinkmann 1988; Pächt and Thoss 1990: 89, 96, 97;
Brinkmann and König 1991: 12, 135, 136, 149, 151, 152,
218, 219, 229, 234, 358, 359, 372, 374, 375; Brinkmann
1992c: 133, n. 124; Kren 1992a: 18; Brinkmann 1997: 124
n. 93; Brinkmann 1998: 119, 125; Smeyers 1998: 468

Cat. no. 26. Popham 1928: 134; Pächt 1948: no. 26;
Lieftinck 1969: 136

Cat. no. 27. Waagen 1854–57, 3: 113; London 1911:
no. 232; James 1931: 73; New York 1934: 49; De Ricci
1935–40, 2: 1457–58; Pächt 1944a: 295; Pächt 1948:
62–63; D'Ancona and Aeschlimann 1949: 26; Lyna
1949: 151 n. 1; Ring 1949a: 87; Brussels 1959: 156,
no. 199; Poesch 1964: 84; Gilissen 1969: 160; Ghent
1975, 2: 370–71, no. 606; Van Buren 1975: 289 n. 21;
Haussherr 1977: 233; Voelkle 1980: 2; Hughes (M.)
1984a: 56; Emmerson and Lewis 1985: 396, no. 89;
Dogaer 1987a: 149; New York 1988b: nos. 799–803;
Schuppisser 1991: 187; Barstow 1992: 257 no. 19, 261;
Blockmans 1992: 40; Cockshaw 1992: 60; Kren 1992a:
17, 19; Lewis (S.) 1992; Morgan 1992: 65–67, 70, 73
n. 41; Wieck 1992: 125; Lemaire 1994: 54; Straub 1995:
122, no. 2.2.4.12; Randall 1997: 369; Smeyers 1998: 12,
387–88; Charron and Gil 1999: 95, 100

Cat. no. 28. Waagen 1847: 177–78; Waagen 1862;
Doutrepont 1909: 235–36, n. 1; Durrieu 1927: 64;
Gaspar and Lyna 1944: 10; Delaissé 1955: 21–55;
Brussels 1959: 155, no. 196; Delaissé 1955: pl 45;
Brussels 1967b: 25, 30, no. 6; Davies (M.) 1972: 208,
pl. 74; Gorissen 1973: 411; Dogaer 1975: 102–3; Ghent
1975: no. 604; Van Buren 1975: 289, n. 21; Brussels
1977: 97, no. 17; Malibu 1983a: 27, 28, 29; Hughes (M.)
1984a: 68; Gaspar and Lyna 1984–89, 3: 1: 290–94; 2:
440–41; 3: no. 290; Brussels 1986: 44–45, no. 22;
Smeyers 1998: 376, 377, 416 n. 48; Barstow 1992: 261,
no. 21; Blockmans 1992: 36, 40, 45 n. 46; Cockshaw
1992: 58–61, 62 n. 11; Lewis (S.) 1992: 77, 84, 86, 87
n. 6, 87 n. 9, 88 n. 32, 88 n. 43; Morgan 1992: 63,
67–70; Smith (J.) 1992: 51–52, 54, 55 n. 6; Laurent
1993; Debae 1995: 272–74, no. 155; Steinmetz 1995:
232–33; Kren 1996: 206–8; Lemaire 1996: 77–78;
Randall 1997: no. 276; Sutton and Visser-Fuchs 1997b:

36–39; Smeyers 1998: 376–77, 416 n. 47; Bousmanne and Van Hoorebeeck 2000: 119–22

CAT. NO. 29. Pinchart 1865: 503; Winkler 1925: 117, 163; Pächt 1948: 47 n. 3; Brussels 1951: no. 106; Brussels 1959: 155–56, no. 197; Gilissen 1969: 160; Lieftinck 1969; Dogaer 1975: 109; Ghent 1975: 329–31, no. 605; Van Buren 1975: 289, n. 21; Brussels 1977a: 99–100, no. 20; Euw and Plotzek 1979–85, 3: 248–49; Hughes (M.) 1984a: 53–78; Hughes (M.) 1984b: 3–17; Dogaer 1987a: 149; Sinclair 1988: nos. 5822, 5898; Gaspar and Lyna 1984–89, 3: 168, no. 288; Barstow 1992: 261–62, no. 22; Blockmans 1992: 40, 42; Cockshaw 1992: 58, 60; Lewis (S.) 1992: 78, 87 n. 6; Morgan 1992: 65, 66–68, 70; Laurent 1993, 1, part 2: 367, nos. 85–87; Debae 1995: 164, no. 152; Straub 1995: 105–7; Châtelet 1996: 151–55; Kren 1996: 193–220; Vanwijnsberghe 1996: 169–79; Sutton and Visser-Fuchs 1997b: 36–39; Smeyers 1998: 376–77, 416 n. 48; Charron and Gil 1999:100; Queruel 1999: 100; Bousmanne and Van Hoorebeeck 2000: 90–93

CAT. NO. 30. Friedländer 1935: 99–104; Wescher 1946: 199; Panofsky 1953: 334 n. 3, 500; Wescher 1959: 128; Winkler 1964: 165–66, 171–75, fig. 127, 267; Friedländer 1967–76, 4: 85; Seilern 1969: 39–42, no. 314, pls. 26, 27; Seilern 1971: 66, no. 314; Byam Shaw 1976: 320; Braham 1981: 118–19, no. 167, fig. 167, pl. 20; London 1981: 65, no. 197; Reynolds (C.) 1981: 563; Campbell 1985: 49–50; Farr 1987: 122; Sander 1989: 49 n. 2; London 1991b: 82–83, 181, no. 37; Dhanens 1998: 105, 106–7 n. 66; Martens (D.) 2002: 116–18, fig. 8

CAT. NO. 31. Destrée 1914: 118–20; London 1935; Schöne 1938: 18, no. 120; Van Puyvelde 1948: pl. 70; London 1949; Panofsky 1953: 337, 501; Van Puyvelde 1953: 225; Winkler 1964: 212–15; Friedländer 1967–76, 4: 33, 70–71, no. 16; Wilton 1968: 55–56, no. 149; Ringbom 1984: 96, 98–100, 102; Sander 1992: 225; Dhanens 1998: 161–62

CAT. NO. 32. *Emerson-White Hours*: Quaritch 1887: 3458–60, no. 35696; Quaritch 1892: 14, pls. 208–12; London 1912b: 17; Antwerp 1930, 1: 16–17, no. 33; 2: 47, pl. 65, fig. 91; De Ricci 1935–40, 1: 1056, no. 3; 2: 1205, 2306–7, no. 6; Hulin de Loo 1939b: 167, 179, 180; Pächt 1948: 71–72, no. 204; Baltimore 1949: 74–75, no. 204; Panofsky 1953: 410 n. 12; Wescher 1959: 128–30; Faye and Bond 1962: 278; Cambridge, Mass., 1964–66: 3–4; Cambridge, Mass., 1967: pl. opp. 187; Hoffman 1969: 245; Lieftinck 1969: 9, 56, 88, 170; Hoffman 1973: 273; Ghent 1975: 385; Van Buren 1975: 306–7; Hindman 1977: 189–91, 187 n. 8, 204; De Winter 1981: 424 n. 16, 425 n. 30; Cambridge, Mass., 1983: 50–51, 134, no. 24; Malibu 1983a: 31, 33–34, 37–39, 39 n. 30, 47 n. 11; Dogaer 1987a: 131, 141, 149; Brinkmann 1992a: 189, 193 n. 39; Brinkmann 1992c: 106–10; Clark 1992: 206 n. 3, 207 n. 18; Brinkmann 1997: 196–201, 233, 370; Ainsworth 1998: 220. *The Annunciation to the Shepherds*: Brinkmann 1997: 197, fig. 192; Los Angeles 1997: 100, 101, no. 42; Alexander 1988: 123–24. *The Mass of Saint Gregory*: Lieftinck 1969: 37–38; Leuven 1975: 114–16, fig. 37; Gaspar and Lyna 1984–89, 3: 442; Brussels 1986: 38–39, no. 19; Dogaer 1987a: 145–49; Brinkmann 1997: 197–98; Leuven 1998: 502–3, no. 196; Smeyers 1998: 148 no. 79, 172; Weniger 2001: 144–46

CAT. NO. 33. Huth, Ellis, and Hazlitt 1880, 2: 723–24; Weale 1894: 162, 165–66; Thieme-Becker 1907–50, 26: 123; Kenyon 1912: 16–19, no. 13; London 1912a: 38, no. 9; Millar 1914–20: 96–97, 103, 105, 106, 107; London 1923: 37–38, no. 8; Winkler 1925: 40, 170; Winkler

1943: 60; Ring 1949b: no. 174; Turner 1967: 50–51, no. 68; de Schryver 1969a: 152 n. 263; Hoffman 1969: 245, 268–70; Hoffman 1973: 273, 274; Hindman 1977: 188–90, 204; Sterling 1981b: 10–11, 13–14, 17; Büttner 1983: 77 n. 40, 97, 108, 217; Malibu 1983a: 31–39, no. 4; Ringbom 1984: 196–98, 200, 202; Backhouse 1985: 28; Dogaer 1987a: 131, 141, 166; Kren and Rathofer 1988: 26, 238, 364, 365; Brinkmann and König 1991: 87, 311; Ainsworth 1992: 250, 255 n. 14 n. 15; Brinkmann 1992a: 188–90; Brinkmann 1992c: 140–42; Clark 1992: 199–201, 205, 206 n. 1, 206 n. 3, 207 n. 18, 208 n. 14; Hindman 1992: 228, 232 n. 27; Legaré 1992: 214–15, 218; Saint Petersburg 1996: 18, 22; Backhouse 1997a: 203; Brinkmann 1997: 17 n. 48, 172–83, 192, 198, 201–2, 223, 230, 232, 370, 388; Ainsworth 1998: 217, 220; Weniger 2001: 143–47; Paris 2002: 149, no. 48

CAT. NO. 34. Brinkmann 1997: 311, fig. 81

CAT. NO. 35. Popham 1928: 143; Bock and Rosenberg 1930: 4; Pächt 1948: 71, no. 29; Brinkmann and König 1991: 108, 331 n. 43; Berlin 1998: 120 fig. 27, 128; Buck 2001: 159–63, no. I 21

CAT. NO. 36. Cibulka and Matějček 1924–25: 31–37, 40; Pächt 1948: 65, no. 9; Dokoupil 1959: no. 3, 11; Dogaer 1987a: 131, 149; Brinkmann 1997: 392, no. 35, pls. 22–24, figs. 107–11; Brinkmann 1998: 132–33, n. 28

CAT. NO. 37. Hoffman 1969: 245; Hoffman 1973: 273; Van Buren 1975: 307; Pächt 1976: 30 fig. 3; Brinkmann 1992c, 133–35, fig. 41; Clark 1992: 197 n. 10, 199 n. 19, 207; Brinkmann 1997: 314 n. 109; Berlin 1998: 129, n. 25, fig. 42; Brinkmann 1998: 129

CAT. NO. 38. Seidlitz 1885: 98f., no. 121; Dodgson 1910–11: 4–7; Schenk zu Schweinsberg 1922: 18; Winkler 1925: 104, 113, 158; Durrieu 1927: 41, 85f.; Popham 1928: 139; Wescher 1931: 172–74; Hulin de Loo 1939b: 162, 176; Winkler 1942: 266, 270; Pächt 1944a: 295–300; Wescher 1946: 192; Pächt 1948: 24, 66, no. 11; Lyna 1949: 154; Brussels 1951: no. 111; Wescher 1959: 132–35; Lieftinck 1964b: 268; Boese 1966: 158, no. 315; Lieftinck 1969: 126–47; Alexander 1970: 22; Backhouse 1973b: 684; Berlin 1975: 227–28, no. 154; Biermann 1975: 21, 37; Schaefer 1975: 405, 413; Schenk zu Schweinsberg 1975: 151–57; Van Buren 1975: 288–90, 294, 307, no. 6; De Winter 1981: 353; Cambridge, Mass., 1983: 50; Malibu 1983b: 17; Testa 1986: 123, 125, 135, 146, 151, 154, 176; Bartz and König 1987: 515; Dogaer 1987a: 145, 149; Thoss 1987: 121, 130; Brinkmann and König 1991: 130, 141, 151, 353, 363, 364, 374; Brinkmann 1992c: 133, n. 124; Inglis 1995: 20; Brinkmann 1997: 16 n. 40, 187 n. 149, 217, 229, 280 n. 21, 313–314; Berlin 1998

CAT. NO. 39. Lieftinck 1969, 1: xiii–xiv, xxviii, 14, 20–23; 2: figs. 45, 46; Dogaer 1972: 98; Hilger 1973: 40 n. 46; Van Buren 1975: 307; Malibu 1983a: 17–20 no. 2; Dogaer 1987a: 149; Brinkmann 1997: 343 n. 2

CAT. NO. 40. Waagen 1854–57, 3: 85–86; Oxford 1895–1953, 4: 606; Winkler 1925: 190; Hulin de Loo 1939b: 174; Pächt 1944a: 296–97; Pächt 1948: 65, no. 8; Lyna 1951–55; London 1953–54: no. 595; Brussels 1959: 191, no. 270; Lieftinck 1964b: 257–94; Pächt and Alexander 1966–73, 1: 27, no. 360; Lieftinck 1969: 157–64, figs. 271–83; Alexander 1970: 21; Ghent 1975, 2: 378–79, no. 616; Van Buren 1975: 307, no. 19; Oxford 1980, 4: 560–61, no. 21797; Oxford 1984: 49, no. 78; Testa 1986: 125; Dogaer 1987a: 131, 149; Brinkmann 1988: 95; Brinkmann 1992a: 189–90 n. 45; Clark 1992: 208 n. 41; Brinkmann 1997: 15 n. 32, 180 n. 114, 181 n. 121; Berlin 1998: 119, fig. 25

CAT. NO. 41. Warner (G.) 1920, 1: 236–40, no. 104; Winkler 1925: 113, 169; London 1953–54: no. 598; Alexander 1970: 47–48; Backhouse 1973b: 684; London 1973: no. 1; Van Buren 1975: 306–7; Pächt 1976; Scott (K.) 1976: 52–53, n. 194: 85; Kipling 1977: 34 n. 9; Backhouse 1979, pl. 60; Trenkler 1979: 81–82, 84; De Winter 1981: 347, 362–63, 369, 374, 397, 406, 408, 424 n. 20, 425 n. 26; Limentani Virdis 1981: 91; Alexander 1983: 161; Hidalgo Ogáyar 1983: 129, 131; Malibu 1983a: 21–30, no. 3; Turner 1983; Camille 1984: 508–14; Backhouse 1985: 39, 58; Dogaer 1987a: 149; Toronto 1987: 189; Tudor-Craig 1987; Barker 1988: 242, 244; Brinkmann 1988; Kren and Rathofer 1988: 5; Alexander 1989: 312–14; Meale 1989: 226 n. 33, 34; Steenbock 1990: 135–36, 141; Brinkmann and König 1991: 12, 134, 151, 234, 357, 374; Clark 1992: 199, 203; Kren 1992a: 18; Backhouse 1996; Saint Petersburg 1996: 41, 43, 147; Backhouse 1997a: 197; Brinkmann 1997: 86 n. 60, 124, 154 n. 24, 306, 311, 344 n. 4; Leuven 1998: 527; Smeyers 1998: 425, 468, 469; Visser-Fuchs 1998: 284

CAT. NO. 42. Winkler 1925: 113, 208; Vienna 1936: no. 40; Hulin de Loo 1939b: 162, 173; Pächt 1948: 66, no. 12; Lyna 1949; Vienna 1952: no. 209; Aurenhammer 1959: 56; Brussels 1959: no. 266; Brussels 1962: no. 5; Sulzberger 1962a: 46, n. 5; Mazal and Unterkircher 1963: 285; Köster 1965: 493; Dhanens 1969: 361–79; Lieftinck 1969: 152–56; Hilger 1973: 54: Van Buren 1975: 307, no. 2; De Winter 1981: 423–24, n. 16; Malibu 1983a: 23; Markl 1983: 178; Dogaer 1987a: 149; Thoss 1987: no. 19; Pächt and Thoss 1990: 98–101; Van Buren 1993: 1189; DOA 1996, 20: 727; Smeyers 1998: 397–98; Legaré 2001: 33–87

CAT. NO. 43. Waagen 1854–57, 3: 82; Meyer 1897: 305, n. 3; Oxford 1895–1953, 4: 606; Pächt 1944a: 295; Pächt 1948: 21–22, 47 n. 3, 63, no. 3; Chesney 1951: 11–39; London 1953–54: no. 592; Brussels 1959: 153–54, no. 192; Lieftinck 1964b: 257–94; Pächt and Alexander 1966–73, 1: 26, no. 352; Brussels 1967b: 32, no. 9; Lieftinck 1969: ix, 154; Alexander 1970: 21; Pollard 1970: 205–6; Ghent 1975: 369, no. 603; Van Buren 1975: 289 n. 21; Foot 1980: 198–99; Oxford 1980, 4: 606–7, no. 21940; Malibu 1983a: 29; Oxford 1984: 163; Dogaer 1987a: 149; Barstow 1992: 258, 260, no. 8; Blockmans 1992: 40; Cockshaw 1992: 58–60, n. 21; Kren 1992a: 16; Lewis (S.) 1992: 86 n. 3, 87 n. 6; Lowry 1992: 103, 107–8 n. 21; Morgan 1992: 63, 67–69; Smith (J.) 1992: 51; Smeyers 1998: 375 n. 42, 384–85, n. 60; Bousmanne and Van Hoorebeeck 2000: 92, 102

CAT. NO. 44. Backhouse 2002: 71–90

CAT. NO. 45. Kren and Wieck 1990: 33; Paris 1990: 227; Clark 1992: 207 n. 18; Eichberger 1992: 138 n. 2

CAT. NO. 46. Hulin de Loo 1902: no. 101; Friedländer 1903: 79; Weale 1903b: 329; Paris 1904: no. 120; Mather 1915: 267; Friedländer 1923a: 169–70; Michel 1927: 143; Foncke 1938: 185; Worcester 1939: no. 18; Philadelphia 1941: 31, no. 1329; Rosen 1941: 462–63, 466; Ring 1949b: no. 181; Godenne and Maes 1951; Philadelphia 1953: 98, no. 1329; Eisler 1961: no. 65; Sweeny 1972: 53; Ringbom 1984: 48 n. 45; Ainsworth 1992: 249–51; Philadelphia 1994: 71; Châtelet 1996: 166–67; New York 1998: 110; Sterling and Ainsworth 1998: 6

CAT. NO. 47. Thieme-Becker 1907–50, 24: 122–23; Friedländer 1923a: 167–70; Winkler 1923: 247–68; Popham 1926: 21–22; London 1927: 181, no. 503; Reinach 1931: 341–52; London 1932: 322–23, no. 637; Winkler 1934: 65–72; Mongan 1942: 115–20; New

York 1959a: 26–27; New York 1998: 110, 207, 208, no. 9; Sterling and Ainsworth 1998: 4, fig. 1.2, n. 8

Cat. no. 48. Guerlin 1894: 35–41; Brinkmann 1997: 264–74, 362, 370, 395, no. 50

Cat. no. 49. De Ricci 1935–40: 1660, no. 37; Los Angeles 1987: 172–74; Brinkmann 1991: 123; Van der Horst and Klamt 1991: 123; Legaré 1996: 220, 222; Brinkmann 1997: 288–90, 297, 304; Legaré 1998: 60–62

Cat. no. 50. Cologne 1960: 77, no. 13, figs. 94, 95; Cologne 1973: 83; Euw and Plotzek 1979–85, 3: 82–88; DOA 1996, 17: 455; Zimmermann 1998: 180–92, pl. 107a

Cat. no. 51. Pächt 1948: 13; Panofsky 1953, 1: 463 n. 4; London 1954: no. 2; Armstrong 1970: 41; Dogaer 1975: 110; London 1976: no. 9; Hellinga 1981: 21 n. 13, 24 n. 16; Büttner 1983: 11, 120, 216–17; Hughes (M.) 1984a: 62, 64 no. 13; Barstow 1992: 258 no. 2; Cockshaw 1992: 58, 60; Eichberger 1992: 129; Kren 1992a: 16; Lewis (S.) 1992: 86, 86 n. 3, 88 n. 41; Morgan 1992: 69–70; Backhouse 1994: 50 n. 12; New York 1994a: 174–75; Backhouse 1997a: 192; Smeyers 1998: 376; Smith (J.) 1998: 40, 50

Cat. no. 52. James 1895: no. 20; London 1953–54: 158, no. 590; Hoffman 1958: 66, 91, n. 12; Cambridge 1966: 46–47, 110, pl. 30; Cambridge 1976: no. 4; Wormald and Giles 1982: 211–15; Pächt and Thoss 1990, 2: 33; Brinkmann 1992a: 192 n. 17; Eichberger 1992: 134; Cambridge 1993: 76–77, no. 21; Brinkmann 1997: 22, 164–67, 272–74, 399, figs. 46, 76; de Schryver 1999: 67 n. 99

Cat. no. 53. London 1862: 583, no. 6833; Spitzer 1890–92, 5: 140, no. 25; London 1908: 114, no. 235; Winkler 1925: 180; Amsterdam 1959: no. 265; Hoffman 1969: 245 n. 8; Hoffman 1973: 273; Harthan 1977: 146–49; Hindman 1977: 192–93, 200–201, 204; Harthan 1983: 34, 37; Malibu 1983a: 31; Dogaer 1987a: 103, 131, 141; Brinkmann 1991: 119–22; Brinkmann 1992a: 184–86, 190; Brinkmann 1992c: 125–30, 133, n. 123; Clark 1992: 196–98 n. 8, 200 n. 19, 202, 203, 206, n. 8, 207; de Schryver 1992: 175; Eichberger 1992: 134; Hindman 1992: 227–29; Kren 1992a: 19; Palmer 1992: 161; Zürich 1994: 338–39, no. 130; Inglis 1995: 11; Bousmanne 1997: 17, n. 48, 59, 159–72, 239, 271–73, 359, 362; Smeyers 1998: 341, 352 n. 100; Nash 1999: 232

PART 3

Cat. no. 54. Rive 1782: no. 14; Pinchart 1860–61: 24–29; Pinchart 1865: 473–510; Doutrepont 1909: 179; Durrieu 1910a: 61; Van den Gheyn (J.) 1910: 14; Durrieu 1921a: 22, 48–49, pls. 25, 26; Winkler 1925: 75, 193; Bossuat 1946: 205 no. 8, 214 n. 6; Dijon 1950: no. 12; Brussels 1951: no. 96; Ross (D.) 1963: 70, no. 21; Lucas 1970: 238; Brussels 1977a: 8 n. 18, 60; de Schryver 1979b: 469, 472–73; Bruges 1981: 246; Prevenier and Blockmans 1986: 313, fig. 279; Dogaer 1987a: 108, 112; McKendrick 1988: 182, 187; Smith (J.) 1992: 52, fig. 20; Lemaire 1993: 247, n. 19; McKendrick 1996a: 18–20, 24, 27 n. 1, fig. 3; McKendrick 1996b: 133 n. 15, 136 n. 19, 141 n. 34; Smeyers 1998: 326, 357, 360–61, fig. 10; Wilson 1998: 29; Blondeau 2001: 731–52

Cat. no. 55. Pinchart 1865: 505–10; Doutrepont 1909: 32–35; Van den Gheyn (J.) 1910: passim; Durrieu 1921a: 21, 48; Winkler 1925: 75, 162; Brussels 1959: nos. 144–47; Brussels 1967a: no. 161; Masai and Wittek 1968–82, 4: 20–21, no. 411; Brussels 1977a: 82–83, no. 6; Kraus 1978, no. 71; Euw and Plotzek 1979–85, 3:

251–55; Pächt, Jenni, and Thoss 1983: 89; Gaspar and Lyna 1984–89, 3: 82–90, 425–27; Dogaer 1987a: 16, 108, 112; Kren and Wieck 1990: 10, fig. 5; Nuremberg 1993: 136, no. 102; Straub 1995: 17–26, 51–59, 192–242; Los Angeles 1997: 94, 95; Smeyers 1998: 309, 356–58

Cat. no. 56. Dehaisnes 1881: 234; Martin 1885–99, 5: 58; Doutrepont 1909: 314–18; Martin 1917: 155–72; Durrieu 1921a: 49–50, pls. xxviii, xxix; Winkler 1923: 394–95; Winkler 1925: 69, 194, pl. 34; Durrieu 1927: 26–27, 60–61; Lyna 1928: 182, 184; Martin and Lauer 1929: 51, pl. 67; Brussels 1951: no. 82; Brussels 1959: 149, no. 187; Samaran and Marichal 1959: 181; Van Leeuwen 1975: iv–v, 1–54; Brussels 1977a: 13; Paris 1980: 64, no. 112; Conell 1984; Dogaer 1987a: 85–86, figs. 44, 45; Randall 1992: 247, 249, 250; DOA 1996, vol. 20: 389; Smeyers 1998: 364, fig. 15; Leuven 2002: 312–13, no. 85; Paris 2002: 202–3, no. 90; Schandel 2002

Cat. no. 57. Toustain 1881: 1–26; Toustain 1881–82: 186–91; Thompson 1912: 41–44; Thompson 1916: 31–34, pls. 63–72; Brussels 1959: 143; Cockshaw 1979a: 120; Pächt, Jenni, and Thoss 1983: 52, 73–74, figs. 39, 80; DOA 1996, 17: 454–55; Backhouse 1997b: 9, pl. 3; Labory 1997–99, 28: 196–98

Cat. no. 58. Dibdin 1817, 1: cciii–cciv; Lacaita 1879, 4: 322; London 1908: no. 160, pl. 111; Doutrepont 1909: 43–49; Durrieu 1910a: 69–71; Lindner 1912: 53–54; Winkler 1915: 302–3; Winkler 1925: 90, 169; Smital 1930b: 46; Ham 1932: 66–77; Woledge 1954: no. 68; Brussels 1959: no. 160; Manchester 1976: 30, no. 51, pl. 12; Richmond 1979: no. 130; Dogaer 1987a: 136; Bruges 1992: 164–69 no. 4, pls. on 114, 118, 120, 165, 166, 168, 170, 197; Straub 1995: 113–16, 247, 251–67; Wolf (E.) 1996: 154–55, 252–55, no. 4; Smeyers 1998: 405–6, fig. 69

Cat. no. 59. Van Praet 1831: 175–76, no. 41; Paris 1836–48, 2: 336–40; Lindner 1912: 46–49, figs. 13–15; Winkler 1915: 301; Durrieu 1921a: 27, 55, pl. 46; Winkler 1925: 90, 192; Smital 1930b: 46; Brussels 1951: no. 83; Brussels 1959: no. 158, pls. 6, 51; de Schryver 1969b: 450 n. 64; Pinkernell 1971: 22–24; Pinkernell 1973: 295–301; Van Buren 1975: 300 n. 59; Van Buren 1979: 368–69, 371, figs. 18–21; Dogaer 1987a: 136; McKendrick 1988: 28, 43; Bruges 1992: 115–16 (figs.), 122, 125–26, 137–38, 199 no. 86, 200; Paris 1992: no. 49; Nieuwstraten 1994: 134–47; Lemaire 1996: 207; Wolf (E.) 1996: 182–91, 271–72; Smeyers 1998: 405, 416, n. 96

Cat. no. 60. Van Praet 1831: 136–37, no. 31; Paris 1836–48, 4: 344–47; Lindner 1912: 51–52, fig. 17; Winkler 1915: 301, fig. 17; Winkler 1925: 90, 192; Smital 1930b: 46; Brussels 1959: no. 159, pl. 50; de Schryver 1969a: 136–39, pl. 17; de Schryver 1969b: 449; Lieberman 1970: 471–72; Van Buren 1975: 299–300, fig. 13; Bruges 1981: no. 107, pl. 20; Monfrin 1982: 91; Dogaer 1987a: 136; McKendrick 1988: 182, 186; Pächt and Thoss 1990: 38, 83; Smeyers 1998: 405, fig. 68

Cat. no. 61. Van Praet 1831: 139–40, no. 33; Lucas 1970: 246; Bruges 1992: 198 no. 27, 200

Cat. no. 62. Van Praet 1829: 25; Van Praet 1831: 107–8, no. 8; Smital 1930a: 226–28, fig. 239; Smital 1930b: 47; Cockshaw and Vanden Bosch 1963: 22–35; Brussels 1973: 218–19; Bruges 1992: 121, 134, 142–43, 180–81 (figs.), 182–84 no. 13, 199 no. 105, 200; McKendrick 1996a: 44–46, fig. 13; Smeyers 1998: 411–13, fig. 83

Cat. no. 63. Kraus 1961: no. 21; Winkler 1961a; Ross (D.) 1963: 70, no. 14; Euw and Plotzek 1979–85, 4: 240–55;

Cologne 1987: 199; Dogaer 1987a: 113; Hoppe 1987; McKendrick 1988: 222; Kren and Wieck 1990: 14, fig. 7; Bruges 1992: 185; Kren 1992b: 155 n. 32; Vermeersch 1992: 220; Martens, in New York 1994a: 8; fig. 7; McKendrick 1996a; McKendrick 1996b: 131; Los Angeles 1997: 96, 97; Smeyers 1998: 357

Cat. no. 64. Dorez 1903: 159–60; Warner (G.) 1903: pl. 52; London 1912a: 27, no. 74; Winkler 1915: 302, no. 1; Durrieu 1921a: 25, 53, pl. 39; London 1923: 28, no. 77; London 1923–65, 4: 15, pl. 41; Winkler 1925: 90, 137, 178; Durrieu 1927: 66, 99; Hulin de Loo 1939b: 161; Pächt 1948: 50–51 n. 13; London 1953–54: no. 577; de Schryver 1969b: 440 n. 32; Vaughan 1973: 205 n. 1; London 1976: no. 8; Van Ettro 1976: col. 369, pl. 3; Brussels 1977a: 11; de Schryver 1979a: 142–43; Watson 1979: no. 374, pl. 774; Malibu 1983a: no. 1; Dogaer 1987a: 16, 121, 124; Brinkmann 1992a: 192 n. 17; Cambridge 1993: 76; Backhouse 1997a: 192, pl. 171; Brinkmann 1997: 134, 192 n. 17, 399; Smeyers 1998: 372, 373, fig. 26; de Schryver 1999: 59–62, figs. 14, 15

Cat. no. 65. New York 1934: no. 107; Brussels 1959: 112, no. 119; Preston and Tottle 1971: 115; Bornstein 1975: 66–71; New York 1975: 108, no. 114; Holbrook 1978: 819–26; Euw and Plotzek 1979–85, 4: 255; New York 1980: no. 4; Lawrence 1983: 150–52, no. 28; Calkins 1984: 143, 149; New York 1985: 20–21; Calkins 1986: 157–73; Dogaer 1987a: 113; New York 1988b: no. 876; Monks 1990: 56 n. 34; Brinkmann 1992a: 192 n. 17

Cat. no. 66. Omont 1891: 5, no. 2; Warner (G.) and Gilson 1921, 2: 262; Lucas 1970: 247; Schullian 1981: 708; Backhouse 1987: 40; Sutton and Visser-Fuchs 1995: 81, 84, 96 n. 138; Carley 2000: 6 H.1.2

Cat. no. 67. Brussels 1973: 189 n. 13; Brussels 1979a: 336; Pächt, Jenni, and Thoss 1983: 34, figs. 30–33; Lenger 1985: 100; Brinkmann 1997: 93, 101; Gil 1997: 20, 22, 25, 30 nn. 2, 3, 31 n. 3, figs. 4, 19, 20; Clark 2000: 47–51, 82–83, 87, 97–101, 129–30, 136, 172–75, 237–39, figs. 24, 219–26

Cat. no. 68. Shaw and Madden 1833: pl. 26; Humphreys 1844–49: 14; Coulton 1930: passim; Wright and Wright 1966: 354, 359, 363; Geneva 1976: 121; New York 1982: 65; Randall 1992: 137; Le Guay 1998: 31–34, 173, 180–82

Cat. no. 69. De Kèralio 1798–99; Van Praet 1831: 170–71, no. 57; Durrieu 1921a: 28, 56–57, pl. 50; Rosanbo 1929: 5–16; Smital 1930a: 227–28, fig. 240; Smital 1930b: 47, 65, 71; London 1953–54: no. 588; Zsuppan 1970: 23–24, 37; Bruges 1981: no. 110, pls. 24–26; Jung 1982: 238; Dogaer 1987a: 124, 136; Bruges 1992: 147, 199 no. 109, 200; Bruinsma 1992: 161–62; Chavannes-Mazel 1992: 144–47; Cambridge 1993: 154; Smeyers 1998: 412

Cat. no. 70. Cambridge 1856–67, 4: 473–74; London 1953–54: no. 587; Zsuppan 1970: 23, 37; Cambridge 1976: no. 2; Bruges 1981: 254; Jung 1982: 238; Lemaire 1983: 12–15; Dogaer 1987a: 124; Bruinsma 1992: passim, pl. 8; Chavannes-Mazel 1992: passim, pl. 5; Cambridge 1993: 154–55, no. 51; Smeyers 1998: 413, fig. 85

Cat. no. 71. Van Praet 1831: 235–39, no. 93; Durrieu 1921a: 28, 56, pl. 49; Winkler 1925: 75, 98, 192; Martin 1928: 72–73, 112, pls. 77, 78; Smital 1930a: 227–28, pl. 14a–d; Smital 1930b: 47, 65, 69–71, 98–99, figs. 16–19; Brussels 1951: nos. 99, 100; Brussels 1959: nos. 164, 165, pl. 52; Bruges 1981: no. 109, pls. 22, 23, 87; Dogaer 1987a: 124, 136; Brinkmann 1987–88: 127; Bruges 1992: 121, 129, 134, 135 (fig.), 139 (fig.), 140, 144, 146–47, 199 no. 120, 200; Brinkmann 1997: 75–79, 291–92, 296; Le Guay 1998: 30–31, 189–90; Smeyers 1998: 410–11; de Schryver 1999: 54, fig. 10

CAT. NO. 72. Lehrs 1902: 124–41; Leipzig and Stuttgart 1925: no. 4432; Rossiter 1951; Anzelewsky 1959: 114–23; London 1963: 132; Pellechet and Polain 1970: 2482; Brussels 1973: no. 102; Goff 1973: B-711; Kraus 1978a: 309–12; Paris 1981: B 509; Arnim 1984: 193–97, no. 63; Nuremberg 1987: no. 11; Hellinga 1991: 52–54; Cambridge 1993: no. 56; Brinkmann 1997: 113–21, pls. 94–100; New York 1999b: 42–43, no. 15

CAT. NO. 73. Montreal 1960: no. 167; Huyghebaert 1969: 237–38, 242; Dogaer 1987a: 131; Los Angeles 1992: 150; Brinkmann 1997: 106; Los Angeles 1997: 98, 99

CAT. NO. 74. Bradley 1887–89, 1: 227–28; Omont 1891: 9, no. 72; Warner (G.) and Gilson 1921, 2: 213; Bossuat 1943: 257; Keach 1969: passim; Lucas 1970: 234; Cahn and Marrow 1978: 256; Pächt 1978: 14, 16 n. 43; Watson 1979: no. 900, pl. 771; Shailor 1984: 317; Backhouse 1987: 26, 40, pl. 9; McKendrick 1988: 256–57; McKendrick 1996b: 141 n. 37; Sutton and Visser-Fuchs 1999: 295 n. 65; Carley 2000: 19 H.1.66

CAT. NO. 75. Shaw and Madden 1833: no. 27, fig. 2; Humphreys 1844–49: 14, 42; Waagen 1854–57, 1: 130; Omont 1891: 5, no. 12; Warner (G.) and Gilson 1921, 2: 176; Schofield 1923, 2: 453; Kekewich 1971: 484–85; London 1973: no. 99, pls. 18, 19; London 1976: 24–25, no. 6; Pächt 1978: 14, fig. 21; Bruges 1981: 220; Turner 1983: 99; Backhouse 1987: 24, 40, pl. 1; Dogaer 1987a: 105; McKendrick 1992: 159 n. 89; Sutton and Visser-Fuchs 1995: 85; Mahony 1996: 104–7, fig. 3; Payne and Jefferson 1996: 194, pl. 1; Backhouse 1997a: 196, pl. 173; Sutton and Visser-Fuchs 1999: 257–99, figs. 1, 2, 7–9, 16, 17; Carley 2000: 8 H.1.12

CAT. NO. 76. Shaw and Madden 1833: no. 27, fig. 1; Shaw 1843, 2: pl. 53; Humphreys 1844–49: 14; London 1912a: 27, no. 75; Durrieu 1921a: 29, pl. 58; London 1923–65, 3: 28, no. 78; Winkler 1925: 137, 180; Dogaer 1963: 5; Innsbruck 1969: no. 46; Wright 1972: 238, 359; London 1976: no. 7; Brussels 1977a: 61; Dogaer 1981: 105; Payne 1996: 45–46, figs. 1, 2; Backhouse 1997a: 200, pl. 178

CAT. NO. 77. Humphreys 1844–49: 14; Ross (D.) 1963: 21; Ross (D.) 1969: 177–86, passim; Pächt 1978: 3, 5, 8–9, 14–15, figs. 4, 20, pl. 1; Malibu 1983a: 6, fig. 2; Backhouse 1987: 40; Dogaer 1987a: 51, 55; Tite 1994: 13; Brown (M.) 1998: 284–85, fig. 166; Carley 2000: 10 H.1.23

CAT. NO. 78. Shaw and Madden 1833: no. 28, fig. 1; Omont 1891: 7, no. 33; London 1912a: 33, no. 116; Durrieu 1921a: 30–31, 61, pl. 66; Warner (G.) and Gilson 1921, 2: 141, pl. 87; Schofield 1923, 2: 454; Winkler 1925: 137, 179; Saxl and Meier 1953: 199–200, pl. 9, fig. 25; London 1953–54: no. 586; Kekewich 1971: 484; Mombello 1967: 186–87; Bozzolo 1973: 23, 136–37; London 1975: no. 34; Pächt 1978: 14; Backhouse 1979: 70, pl. 61; Backhouse 1987: 24, 27, 39; Dogaer 1987a: 125, pl. 73; Reynolds (C.) 1988: 153–59; McKendrick 1992: 159 n. 89; McKendrick 1994: 162–63, 165; Sutton and Visser-Fuchs 1995: 85; Sutton and Visser-Fuchs 1999: 275, fig. 13; Carley 2000: 12 H.1.33

CAT. NO. 79. Kraus 1974: no. 40; Kraus 1978b: no. 81; Euw and Plotzek 1979–85, 3: 257–66; Kren and Wieck 1990: 13, fig. 6; McKendrick 1994: 161 n. 67; Sutton and Visser-Fuchs 1995: 82, 96 n. 139; Rottier 1996: 89, 104; Brinkmann 1997: 295; Los Angeles 1997:

102, 103; Le Guay 1998: 39, 185; Sutton and Visser-Fuchs 1999: 278–79, 281 (fig. 18), 295 n. 65; Carley 2000: 13 H.1.37; Backhouse 2001: 156 n. 27

CAT. NO. 80. Shaw and Madden 1833: no. 27; Omont 1891: 6, no. 28; Herbert 1911: 314; London 1912a: 33, no. 112; Warner (G.) and Gilson 1921, 2: 315; Schofield 1923, 2: 453; Winkler 1925: 117, 137, 179; Smital 1930b: 53; London 1953–54: no. 585; Lucas 1970: 247; Kekewich 1971: 484; Watson 1979: no. 907, pl. 816; Schullian 1981: 709; Backhouse 1987: 39; Dogaer 1987a: 125, pl. 74; McKendrick 1988: 241, 255; McKendrick 1990: 110; McKendrick 1992: 159 n. 89; McKendrick 1994: 159, 161–63; Sutton and Visser-Fuchs 1995: 81, 84, 96 n. 138; Backhouse 1997a: 199–200, pl. 177; Brinkmann 1997: 155 n. 60; Sutton and Visser-Fuchs 1999: 284; Carley 2000: 11 H.1.28

CAT. NO. 81. Waagen 1854–57, 4: 126–27; Herbert 1911: 314; Millar 1914–20: 89–94; Parshall 1969: 335; Kekewich 1971: 482–83; Kipling 1977: 31; Bruges 1981: 220, 229; Deutsch 1986: 16 n. 49, 17 n. 57, 155 nn. 18, 19, 164–66, 169, 171, 173, 174 n. 14, 176, 188; Backhouse 1987: 24; Brinkmann 1987–88: 126 n. 22; McKendrick 1990: 124–25, 127; Bruges 1992: 110, 155, 186–89, no. 15; McKendrick 1992: 153–54; McKendrick 1994: 162, 164; Sutton and Visser-Fuchs 1995: 84; Vale 1995: 121; Brinkmann 1997: 295, 399; Smeyers 1998: 467; Carley 2000: 7 H.1.5; Backhouse 2001: 152

CAT. NO. 82. Shaw 1843, 2: pl. 55; Humphreys 1844–49: 14; Berger 1884: 162–63, 177, 179, 203, 296, 386, 389–90; Bradley 1887–89, 3: 151; Omont 1891: 6, no. 31; Warner (G.) and Gilson 1921, 2: 170–71, pl. 93a, b; Schofield 1923, 2: 453; Kekewich 1971: 483; Watson 1979: no. 896, pl. 742; Deutsch 1986: 136 n. 4, 137 n. 10, 144 n. 14, 155 n. 18; Backhouse 1987: 26, 28, 29; Brinkmann 1987–88: 126 n. 22; McKendrick 1992: 154, 159 n. 100; McKendrick 1994: 162, 164, 165; Sutton and Visser-Fuchs 1995: 85; Brinkmann 1997: 295, 399; Carley 2000: 11 H.1.31; Komada 2000, 1: chap. 4, sec. 4; 3: no. 38; Nackers 2002

CAT. NO. 83. Omont 1891: 7, nos. 47, 48; Winkler 1915: 336; Warner (G.) and Gilson 1921, 2: 313–14, pl. 106; Schofield 1923, 2: 453; Winkler 1925: 137, 179; Kekewich 1971: 483; Watson 1979: no. 906, pl. 815; Muñoz Delgado 1985: 328; Backhouse 1987: 26, 28, 39; Dogaer 1987a: 117; Thoss 1987: 94; Brinkmann 1987–88: 126 n. 22; McKendrick 1992: 154, 159 n. 100; McKendrick 1994: 162, 164, 165; Sutton and Visser-Fuchs 1995: 85; Smeyers and Van der Stock 1996: 141; Brinkmann 1997: 145, 295, 397, 399; Carley 2000: 15 H.1.45–46; Komada 2000, 1: chap. 4, sec. 4; 3: no. 38; Nackers 2002

CAT. NO. 84. Millar 1925: 15–19; James 1930–32: 15–18; Loomis and Loomis 1938: 128; London 1953–54: no. 583; Parshall 1969: 335, pl. 113b; Matheson 1979: 255; Meale 1989: 206, 216, 226–27 n. 38; Sutton and Visser-Fuchs 1995: 97 n. 146; Brinkmann 1997: 397; Matheson 1998: 298–99; Pickering and O'Mara 1999: 1

CAT. NO. 85. Kervyn de Lettenhove 1879, 1: v; Durrieu 1891; Dorez 1908: 89, pls. 54, 55; Winkler 1925: 113; Pächt 1944a: 295; Pächt 1948: 63–64, pls. 6–9; London 1953–54: 159, no. 593; Brussels 1959: 155, no. 195, pl. 60; Lieftinck 1969, 1: viii–ix; Alexander 1970: 21; Hassall 1970: 13–15, pls. 25–30; Van Buren 1975: 289 n. 25; Malibu 1983a: 22–23; Hughes (M.) 1984a: 73–74; Dogaer 1987a: 149; Thoss 1987: 60; Pächt and Thoss 1990, 2: 101; Barstow 1992: 257, 260, no. 11; Blockmans 1992: 41; Cockshaw 1992: 58, 60; Derolez 1992: 102 n. 7; Cambridge 1993: 148–49, no. 48;

Straub 1995: 117; Smeyers 1998: 388–89; Charron and Gil 1999: 95, 100

CAT. NO. 86. Durrieu 1892: 129; Leidinger 1920: 21, 32; Winkler 1925: 186; Olschki 1932: 14; Pächt 1948: 66–67, no. 13; Lieftinck 1969: x, xxv; Cologne 1970: 75, 86, no. 131; Dogaer 1972: 98 n. 3; Biermann 1975: 22; De Winter 1981: 380–81, 423–24 n. 16; Wolf (H.) 1981: 18; Kleve 1984: 241, 373 no. D42, 379–81 no. D55; Dogaer 1987a: 149; Franke 1997b: ill. 45; Randall 1997: 433; Smeyers 1998: 450

CAT. NO. 87. Warner (G.) and Gilson 1921, 2: 175; Winkler 1925: 117, 179; Smital 1930b: 53; Folda 1973: 94, no. 37; Backhouse 1987: 24–25, 39, pl. 2; Dogaer 1987a: 158; Sutton and Visser-Fuchs 1995: 85; Backhouse 1997a: 203 pl. 180; Carley 2000: 14 H.1.42

PART 4

CAT. NO. 88. Stevenson 1872: 335; Pächt 1944a: 295ff., pl. 4c; London 1953–54: no. 599; Manchester 1960: no. 36; Ker 1969–92, 4: 447–49, no. 60; Austin 1971: no. 12; Van Buren 1975: 307 no 20; Manchester 1976: no. 53; Pächt 1976: 31, fig. 7; De Winter 1981: 355 n. 20; 374 n. 37; fig. 53, cover pl.; Dogaer 1987a: 149; Brinkmann 1988: 94; Alexander 1989: 309–17, figs. 1, 2, 4, 6, 9, 11, 12, 14, 16; Pächt and Thoss 1990: 97; Trapp 1991: 113; Brinkmann 1997: 124 n. 93; Berlin 1998: 119, 125

CAT. NO. 89. Young and Aitken 1908: 23–25; London 1953–54: no. 602; Brussels 1963: 22, no. 37; Dublin 1964: 18, no. 51; Thompson and Campbell 1974: 16; De Winter 1981: 424 n. 20; Toronto 1987: 188–89, no. 125; Brinkmann 1997: 143 n. 50, 279

CAT. NO. 90. Coggiola 1908: 474; Riehl 1909; Clemen 1923, 1: 274; Winkler 1925: 187, 189; Leidinger 1936; Köster 1965: 469–71; Munich 1970a: 111 no. 57; Munich 1970b: 42 no. 57; Biermann 1975: passim; Kupfer-Tarasulo 1979a: 285–86; De Winter 1981: 355 n. 20, 373–77, fig. 51, 60; Wolf (H.) 1981: 49; Malibu 1983a: 39 n. 22, 47 n. 11, 56, fig. 6d; Munich 1983b: 156–57, no. 63; Hansen 1984: 212–14; Köster 1984: 535; Ringbom 1984: 174 n. 13; 197, 200, 202–4, 208 n. 60; Büttner 1985: 214, 233, pl. 216; Dogaer 1987a: 143, 160, 166; Kren and Rathofer 1988: 231; Pächt and Thoss 1990, 1: 97; Steenbock 1990: 135, 141 no. 5; Brinkmann 1991: 218; Brinkmann and König 1991: 137, 138, 147, 220, 360, 361, 370, 428; Kaufmann (T.) and Kaufmann 1991: 50, 53; Brinkmann 1992c: 114, n. 104; Clark 1992: 206 n. 1, 207 n. 21; Paris 1993: 384; Brinkmann 1997: 206–7, 306 n. 77, 314 n. 110

CAT. NO. 91. Coggiola 1908: 1, 74, 142, 161 n. 1, 185–86; London 1908: 81, no. 164, pl. 112; Michel 1924: 202; Winkler 1925: 190; Antwerp 1930: 19, 48, no. 38, fig. 94; Santos 1930: 18, 25, 30; Gaspar 1932: 56–77, 60–62, 64–66, 68, 70, 72–73, 76–77; New York 1934: 61–62, no. 131, pl. 88; De Ricci 1935–40, 2: 87; Wescher 1946: 194, 199–200; Baltimore 1949: 76; Lisbon 1958: 21, no. 28; Santos 1959: 36; Detroit 1960: 399, no. 212; Aguiar 1962: 134–37; Winkler 1962: 9; New York 1964: 36, no. 43, pl. 15; Winkler 1964: 175; Köster 1965: 467–68; Møller-Martindale 1966: 312, 355; Ricker and Saywell 1968: fol. 6, 258; Salmi and Mellini 1972: figs. 27, 28; Hurt 1973: 45 n. 9; Köster 1973: 116, no. B7, fig. 4; Biermann 1975: 25; Deswarte 1977: 207–8; Euw and Plotzek 1979–85: 253, 270–73, 275, 279–80, 282, 284, 306; New York 1980: 3–4; De Winter 1981: 346, figs. 7, 124; Bowles 1983: 132, pl. 100; Markl 1983: 9, 12, 13, 25–28, 30, 71, 112, 155, 172, 194, fig. 5; Köster 1984: 535, n. 16; Moxey 1986: 27–28, fig. 12; Testa 1986: 128, 130,

134, 169; Dogaer 1987a: 164, 166, 177; New York 1988b: nos. 1051, 1052, 1053, 1054, 1055, 1056; Buijsen 1989: 210, no. 3, fig. 2; Testa 1991: 109; Fitzgerald 1992: 53; Hindman 1992: 224, 231–32 nn. 12–13; Mazal and Thoss 1993: 207 n. 5, fig. 10; Paviot 1995; Brinkmann 1997: 133 n. 11; Hindman et al. 1997: 64; Calkins 1998: 59, 65, 66; Driver 1997: 85, 87, fig. 44; Lisbon 1998: 14, 20, 82; Smeyers 1998: 479, 483 n. 157, ill. 93; Willemsen 1998: 82, 109, 215, 216, 231, 232, 240; Boston 2000: 86; Goehring 2000: 167, 170 n. 49, 183 n. 34, figs. 163, 210; Lisbon 2000: 288–89, no. 70

CAT. NO. 92. Michel 1924: 193–204; De Figueiredo 1931: 16, 17, 63; Gaspar 1932; Beck 1933: 266–79; Winkler 1943: 60 n. 5; Winkler 1957: 285, 289; Wescher 1959: 133; Salmi and Mellini 1972: 32; Biermann 1975: 25; De Coo 1978: 168–74; Winkler 1978: 157–58; De Coo 1979: 49–51, 215–27; Euw and Plotzek 1979–85: 274–75; De Winter 1981: 358, 397, 415; Hindman 1981: 456; Markl 1983: 12, 13, 16, 24, 26, 27, 28, 51, 54, 55–59, 69, 83, 95, 96, 97, 109, 111, 112, 149, 159, 160, 178, 184, 189, 194–95, 199, 200, 201, 202, 203; Hansen 1984: 193–94; Dogaer 1987a: 164, 172; Brinkmann 1988: 93–94; Kren and Rathofer 1988: 41, 232, 359; Brinkmann and König 1991: 12, 134, 143, 234, 357, 366; Brinkmann 1992a: 193 n. 37; New York 1995: 56–59, 66–67, nos. 7–9, 13, 14; Brinkmann 1997: 175–76, 320; Dekeyzer and De Laet 1997; Nieuwdorp and Dekeyzer 1997; Smeyers 1997b: 188–89; Ainsworth 1998: 44; Willemsen 1998: 215, 231, 232, 237–40; Daems 1999: 62–65, 83–86, 89–92, 94, 103–4, 110–11, 114, 148, 157, 161, 167; Dekeyzer et al. 1999: 303–16; Vandenabeele et al. 1999: 169–72; Goehring 2000: 166–70; 186, 188, 214–15; Vandenabeele 2000: 147–57; Dekeyzer 2002; Vandenabeele and Moens 2002; Vöhringer 2002: 52, 53, 58, n. 45, 64, 66, 72; Watteeuw 2002

CAT. NO. 93. Winkler 1925: 189; Courcelle-Ladmirant 1939; Rome 1953: 455–56; Naples 1967: 15–17; Benevento 1968: 43, pls. 24–28; Hoffman 1969: 245 n. 8; Hoffman 1973: 273 n. 50; Guerrieri 1974: 33, 98; De Winter 1981: passim; Fossier 1982: 88; Malibu 1983a: 10, 31–32, 36–37, 48 n. 16, 85 n. 4; Ringbom 1984: 51, 96 n. 92, 196–201, 206, 208–9; Testa 1986: 137, 174; Brinkmann 1988: 95; Brinkmann and König 1991: 12, 137, 138, 221, 234, 360, 361, 362; Ainsworth 1992: 250–52; Clark 1992: 200–201, 204–5, 206 n. 3; De Maio 1992; Hindman 1992: 223–25, 228; Kren 1992a: 20, 24; Legaré 1992: 214–22; Paris 1993: 384; Boni 1994: 223–68; Rome 1994: 52–53; Naples 1995: 31, no. 41; Boni and Garofalo 1997: 99–128; Brinkmann 1997: 149, 187, 201–11, 305, 344; Milan 1999: 131–32

CAT. NO. 94. De Ricci 1935–40, 1: 800, no. 277; Randall 1997: 381–87, no. 275; Smeyers 1998: 338–45; Legaré 1999a: 450, 454, no. 9; Leuven 2002: 319, no. 88

CAT. NO. 95. Brussels 1962: no. 48, pl. 12; Brussels 1971: 28ff.; Thoss 1987: no. 62, pl. 5; Pächt and Thoss 1990: 101–3, pls. 201–4; De Hamel 1994: 228, 231, pl. 208; Brinkmann 1997: 398; Smeyers 1998: 444

CAT. NO. 96. Paris Vita Christi: Rive 1782: no. 17; Van Praet 1831: 120; Saint Remy 1944: 54, 67, 68, pl. 7; Lemaire 1993: 243, 246, 247; Smeyers 1998: 450 fig. 51, 452. Morgan Vita Christi: Van Praet 1831: 120; Pierpont Morgan Library 1960: 12–15; Parshall 1969: 336; Pierpont Morgan Library 1969: 7, pl. 13; New York 1974: no. 46; New York 1980: no. 23; Dogaer 1987a: 117; New York 1988b: nos. 872, 873; Lemaire 1993: 243, 246, 247; Brinkmann 1997: 397; Smeyers 1998: 450, 452, 483, n. 80

CAT. NO. 97. Martin 1885–99, 5: 152–54; Martin and Lauer 1929: 5, pl. 76; Samaran and Marichal 1959: 189; Lieberman 1970: 367–74, 475; Bruges 1981: 237; Pächt and Thoss 1990: 103; Bousmanne 1997: 40–41; Brinkmann 1997: 374; Charron and Gil 1999: 92–93

CAT. NO. 98. Hart Collection 1964: no. 16; Ker 1969–92, 2: 93–94; Manchester 1976: 30–31, no. 54, pl. 13; Blackburn 1985: pl. 7; Brinkmann 1997: 294, 297, 397

CAT. NO. 99. Escorial Hours: Antolín 1910–23, 4: 276, 603; Hulin de Loo 1931: 42; Toledo 1992: 469; Brinkmann 1997: 143–48; Hindman et al. 1997: 90. Salvator Mundi: Dobschütz 1899: 197–262, 306–9; Hulin de Loo 1931: 42; De Ricci 1935–40, 2: 1716; Schöne 1937: 170–74; Van de Walle de Ghelcke 1952: 402–6; Réau 1955–59, 2, part 2: 17–19; Schiller 1971–72, 2: 78–79; Scillia 1975: 165–73, 282, 286–87; Thoss 1986: 131–45; Dogaer 1987a: 166; Thoss 1987: 117–18, no. 77; Van Miegroet 1989: 77–79, 326–27, no. 84; Hand 1992: 10, no. 11; Hindman et al. 1997: 84–92, no. 11; New York 1998: 286–87, no. 74

CAT. NO. 100. Dibdin 1817, 1: clxiii–clxviii; Waagen 1854–57, 1: 131; London 1873–83, 2: 174, 175; Warner (G.) 1903: pl. 53; Coggiola 1908: 149; London 1910: 15–16; Herbert 1911: 318–19; Winkler 1913a: 276–77; Destrée 1914: 145–46; Winkler 1914: 232–38, 243; Durrieu 1921a: 35, 65; Lázaro 1922: 138–39; London 1923–65, 3: pls. 45, 46; Winkler 1925: 95, 98, 176–77; Lázaro 1928; Winkler 1943: 59–61, 63; Wescher 1946: 198; London 1953–54: no. 606; Lieftinck 1957: 12–13; Winkler 1964: 189; Turner 1967: 49–50, no. 65; Backhouse 1968: 86–87; Delaissé 1968: 73; Biermann 1968–69: 63 n. 77; Lieftinck 1969: 160; Friedländer 1967–76, 6, part 2: 91–92, 103, no. 181; Munby 1972: 10, 75–76; Scillia 1975: 182–84, 190–94, 212–13, 282, 288–89; McKinnon 1976; De Winter 1981: 344–47, 422 n. 4; Limentani Virdis 1981: 90, 91; Cleveland 1982: 153; Malibu 1983a: 40–48, no. 5; McKinnon 1984; Brussels 1985: 74, 79, no. 53; Hughes (A.) 1985: 13; Liebaers et al. 1985: 170, 172; Muñoz Delgado 1985: 149; Washington 1986b: 134; Dogaer 1987a: 131, 149, 166; Kren and Rathofer 1988: 38, 230, 257; Van Miegroet 1989: 80–84, 327–28, 330–31, no. 85; De Kesel 1992: 193; Hindman 1992: 224–25; Lewis (S.) 1992: 87 n. 17; Backhouse 1993b; Cambridge 1993: 136, 156; Paris 1993: 299; De Hamel 1994: 215; Saint Petersburg 1996: 37, 39; Backhouse 1997a: 217; Brinkmann 1997: 13, 113, 131–43, 239 n. 18, 242, 264, 298–99, 307, 314, 315 n. 113, 317, 345, 357, 370–71, 387–88; Ainsworth 1998: 107, 109; Calkins 1998: 54, 56, 57–58; Dhanens 1998: 214–15; New York 1998: 277, 282; Smeyers 1998: 477, 478; Daems 1999: 69; London 1999: 94–95, no. 23

CAT. NO. 101. Friedländer 1967–76, 4, part 2: 102, no. 168; Mundy 1980: 34, 52, n. 56; Silver 1984: 99; Van Miegroet 1989: 125, 130, 282–83, no. 11; Ainsworth 1998: 272–76; New York 1998: 289–90; Valencia 1999: 32, 173

CAT. NO. 102. Bermejo Martínez 1975: 259–61; Ainsworth 1998: 274–75; Valencia 1999: 32, no. 2

CAT. NO. 103. De Ricci 1935–40: 95; Dutschke et al. 1989: 437–40

CAT. NO. 104. Gottlieb (Th.) 1900: 136; Wormald 1951: 118–19; Vienna 1959: 49, no. 156; Brussels 1962: 12, no. 17; Innsbruck 1969: 103, no. 391; Van Buren 1975: 307, 308, n. 13; Schramm, Fillitz, and Mütherich 1978: 89f., no. 132; Winkler 1978: 127, 207, pl. 73; Unterkircher 1983: 15; Dogaer 1987a: 166; Thoss 1987: 106, no. 68;

Van Miegroet 1989: 85, 328–29; Innsbruck 1992: 147–48, 282–84, no. 100; Smeyers and Van der Stock 1996: 30–31; Hindman et al. 1997: 83; Smeyers 1998: 434, 436, 437

CAT. NO. 105. Weale 1883: 35; Coggiola 1908: 201; Lázaro 1922: 138–39; Michel 1924: 202; Lázaro 1928: 7, no. 3; Cleveland 1963: 269–71; Wixom 1964: 60–63; Biermann 1975: 22, 24–25, 50, 64, 83; Scillia 1975: 228–32; De Winter 1981; Cambridge, Mass., 1983: 56; Lawrence 1983: 143–45; Malibu 1983a: 9, 40, 56 n. 22; Markl 1983: 16–18, 69, 71, 76, 93, 126, 131–32, 145, 172, 184, 189; Testa 1986: 58 n. 12, 115, 123, 137, 138, 142 n. 4, 151, 154, 155 n. 2, 160, 165, 176 n. 2; Dogaer 1987a: 129, 131, 159, 166; Brinkmann 1988: 93, 94, 95, 100; London 1989: 16, 17; Cleveland 1990: 6; Brinkmann and König 1991: 117, 118, 119, 138, 139, 141, 146, 340, 341, 361, 364, 369; Scillia 1991: 1–7; Backhouse 1993b: 17, 21, 50; Testa 1994: 419; Evans and Brinkmann 1995: 123, 428–29, 575; Brinkmann 1997: 15 n. 32, 133 n. 8, 148 n. 69, 186 n. 143, 210; Krieger 2000: 215–33

CAT. NO. 106. Bruges 1949: 30, no. 48; Lugt 1968: 20, no. 57; Van Miegroet 1989: 322–23, no. 75c; Ainsworth 1998: 13–14, 16, 21, 36, 319

CAT. NO. 107. Locker-Lampson 1886: 221; New York 1934: 63, no. 133; De Ricci 1935–40, 2: 1480, no. 659; New York 1939: 14, no. 48; Detroit 1960: 399, no. 212; Winkler 1962; Dogaer 1969: 340; Tokyo and Kyoto 1976: no. 21; De Winter 1981: 363, 405, fig. 135; Malibu 1983a: 46–47; Oklahoma City 1985: 287–88, no. 109; Dogaer 1987a: 177; Van Miegroet 1989: 83, 328, no. 86, pl. 78; Brinkmann 1997: 143, 398; Hindman et al. 1997: 95; Ainsworth 1998: 13, 20–21, 23; New York 1998: 277–78; Krieger 2000: 215, 231

CAT. NO. 108. Manchester, Rylands ms. 39: James 1921, 1: 97–102, no. 39, 2: pls. 90–100; Wolf (H.) 1985: 32, pls. 35–37; Manchester 1993: 7. Morgan 1046: De Ricci 1935–40, 2: 1841, no. 9; Ryskamp 1984: 30

CAT. NO. 109. Herbert 1911: 320–21; London 1912a: 35, no. 4; Winkler 1913a: 275–76; Winkler 1913b: 52; Millar 1914–20: 96–101; Winkler 1915: 284 n. 2; Durrieu 1921a: 36, 71; London 1923: 35, no. 4; London 1923–65, 2: pl. 36; Winkler 1925: 127, 178, 197; Hulin de Loo 1939a: 16, 17; Winkler 1943: 60, 61; Pächt 1948: 59 n. 39; Colding 1953: 65; Lieftinck 1957: 16; Winkler 1962: 11; Turner 1967: 50; Ringbom 1969: 164–65; Biermann 1975: 25; Trenkler 1979: 79–80; Euw and Plotzek 1979–85, 2: 275, 279, 282–84; De Winter 1981: 417; Murdoch et al. 1981: 4; Malibu 1983a: 63–68, no. 8; Markl 1983: 170; Backhouse 1985: 18–20; Dogaer 1987a: 164, 166, 177; Toronto 1987: 189; Brinkmann 1988: 94; Büttner 1993–94: 118; De Kesel 1992: 192; De Hamel 1994: 170, 195–96; Saint Petersburg 1996: 32; Backhouse 1997a: 219; Brinkmann 1997: 187 n. 149, 326; Calkins 1998: 49, 54, 63, 66, n. 2; Smeyers 1998: 421, 441; London 1999: 97, no. 25

CAT. NO. 110. Durrieu 1921a: 70; Durrieu 1921b: 206–12; Winkler 1925: 119–20, 127–29, 205; Hulin de Loo 1939b: 171, 174; Winkler 1943: 56, 58–59, 63; Wescher 1946: 198; Macfarlane 1960: 3–20; Brussels 1962: no. 65; Winkler 1964: 75; Unterkircher 1967: 244–47; Ringbom 1969: 166–67; Thompson and Campbell 1974: 15; De Winter 1981: 407, 423 n. 10, 424 n. 21; Malibu 1983a: 68 n. 2; Markl 1983: 18, 28, 143, 145; Ringbom 1984: 21–22; Testa 1986: 58 n. 12, 61, 111, 130 n. 3, 138, 153, 155–56; Dogaer 1987a: 166; Thoss 1987: 113–14, no. 74; Unterkircher 1987: 9–78; Brinkmann 1988: 95; Kren and Rathofer 1988: 232; Mazal and Thoss 1993: 49, 69 n. 13, 70 n. 14, 217, 237 n. 13, 238

n. 14; De Hamel 1994: 170, 195; Testa 1994: 419; Brinkmann 1997: 26; Dhanens 1998: 314–15; Smeyers 1998: 466; Willemsen 1998: 268; Vöhringer 2002: 70

CAT. NO. 111. Durrieu 1921b: 203; Winkler 1943: 61, figs. 10ff.; Salmon 1971: 181f., nos. 566ff.; Gorissen 1973: 105; Vatican City 1979: 34f., no. 67ff., pl. 12; Euw and Plotzek 1979–85, 2: 256ff.; Malibu 1983a: 63ff., 113ff.; Kleve 1984: 374f., 383f., Dogaer 1987a: 166; Brinkmann 1988: 93; Vatican City 1988: 36ff.; Cologne 1992: 286–309, nos. 61–63

CAT. NO. 112. Berlin 1931: no. 51; Düsseldorf 1967: 122–23, no. 472; Berlin 1975: no. 158; Berlin 1978: 42–43, no. 15; Malibu 1983a: 39 n. 30, 67; Berlin 1987: 114–15, no. 77; Cologne 1987: 225–26; Brinkmann 1987–88: 151; Brinkmann 1997: 143 n. 50, 279

CAT. NO. 113. *Berlin Leaves nos. 641, 667*: Kurth 1925: 40–41; Winkler 1925: 159; Wescher 1931: 181–84; Anzelewsky 1964: 43–59; Brinkmann 1987–88: 127, 151; Smeyers 1998: 430. *Morgan G46*: New York 1959b: 32, no. 49; New York 1968: 48, no. 68; New York 1980: no. 37; Brinkmann 1987–88: 151. *Marlay Cuttings*: London 1886: nos. 39–42; London 1908: nos. 201–3; Winkler 1925: 159, 181; Wormald and Giles 1982: 144–46; Brinkmann 1987–88: 151, 152, 158–59; Cambridge 1993: 86–87, no. 27

CAT. NO. 114. Waagen 1854–57, 1: 131–32; London 1862: 583; Herbert 1911: 319 n. 1; Durrieu 1921a: 41, 87; Durrieu 1921b: 202, 204; London 1923–65, 4: 17; Ferrandis 1943: 222–23; Winkler 1943: 59; Schwarz 1959: 94; Winkler 1964: 175; Köster 1965: 468–69, 478, 483–84, 492, 494, 503; Turner 1967: 48–49, no. 63; Backhouse 1968: 85–86; Munby 1972: 10; Pächt 1973: 88, 90 n. 9; Kren 1974: 10, 21–27; Cahn and Marrow 1978: 261; De Winter 1981: 346–47, 394; Pächt 1981: 23; Cambridge, Mass., 1983: 58; Malibu 1983a: 59–68, no. 7; Markl 1983: 18, 26; Marrow 1983a: 156–58, 161; Backhouse 1985: 5, 15; Brussels 1985: no. 59; Brinkmann 1987–88: 134, 138; Barker 1988: 132, 141; Calkins 1989: 11–12; Brinkmann and König 1991: 90, 313; Brinkmann 1992a: 193 n. 47; Brinkmann 1992b: 207; Brinkmann 1992c: 46, 49ff., 72–80, 102, 106, 139, 144, 172–76; De Kesel 1992: 201 n. 40; Backhouse 1993b: fig. 5; Nash 1995: 437; Saint Petersburg 1996: 31; Stroo and Syfer-d'Olne 1996: 170; Brinkmann 1997: 180, 322–23; Smeyers 1999: 435, 438

CAT. NO. 115. Previously unpublished

CAT. NO. 116. London 1862: 583, no. 6829

CAT. NO. 117. Herbert 1911: 319; London 1912a: 28, no. 78; Winkler 1913a: 276–77; Winkler 1914: 241; London 1923: 28, no. 81; London 1923–65, 1: pl. 37; Winkler 1925: 98, 176; Jenni and Thoss 1982: 118; Backhouse 1985: 31; Dogaer 1987a: 129, 131, 158; Brinkmann 1987–88: 138, 139; Kren 1992b: 145, 146; Backhouse 1993–94; Saint Petersburg 1996: 31; Brinkmann 1997: 13, 186 n. 143, 275–80, 289, 302, 313, 387; Smeyers 1998: 435, 438; Alexander 1999: 95–96, no. 24

CAT. NO. 118. Monasticon Belge 1890–1993, 2: 404; Dorez 1908: 77–83, pls. 50–52; Winkler 1925: 187; Saxl 1937–38: 61–62; London 1953–54: no. 610; Delaissé 1955b: 114–15; Huyghebaert 1969; Hassall 1970: 32–33 n. 5, pls. 158–60; Brussels 1973: 22; Bruges 1981: 183, 184, 185–86, 188–92 no. 87, 204; Malibu 1983a: 56, fig. 6e; Courcelle 1984, 2: 250–52, fig. 488; Dogaer 1987a: 113, 131, 159, 160; Kren and Rathofer 1988: 239; McKendrick 1988: 112; Brinkmann 1992a: 192 n. 17; De Kesel 1992: 189 n. 39; Geirnaert 1992: 174, 176–78; Cambridge 1993: no. 71; Saint Petersburg 1996: 44;

Brinkmann 1997: 15 n. 32, 167–68 fig. 49, 225 n. 333, 297; Smeyers 1998: 413, 456, 457 fig. 58, 459; Bruges 2002: 183; Vöhringer 2002: 75–77

CAT. NO. 119. Shaw and Madden 1833: no. 34; Waagen 1854–57, 1: 118–19; Omont 1891: 10, no. 84; Warner (G.) 1903: pl. 54; Herbert 1911: 317–18; Warner (G.) and Gilson 1921, 2: 203–4; London 1923–65, 4: pl. 46; London 1953–54: 453, no. 615; Genet 1977: 174–219; Kipling 1977: 42–43, 46, pls. 3, 4; London 1983: 34–35, no. 1; Malibu 1983a: 56, 58 n. 19, 168 n. 2; Strong 1983: 13–14, pl. 4; Backhouse 1987: 36–37, pls. 15–17, 19; Dogaer 1987a: 159, 160; Hobbs 1989: 49–62; Meale 1989: 205, 225 n. 29; De Kesel 1992: 186, 195, 199 n. 27; Backhouse 1993c: 8, 14 fig. 4; Brook 1993: 1–33; Backhouse 1994: 52; Backhouse 1995: 176, pl. 43; Sutton and Visser-Fuchs 1995: 97 n. 145; Smeyers and Van der Stock 1996: 41; Backhouse 1997a: 214–15, pl. 189; Backhouse 1997b: 11, pl. 6; Smeyers 1998: 467; Backhouse 2000: 157–63; Carley 2000: 21 H.1.77

CAT. NO. 120. Dibdin 1817, 1: cxxvii, cxxviii, ccx–ccxiv; Shaw 1843, 2: pls. 56, 57, 58; Humphreys 1844–49: 15; Waagen 1854–57, 1: 117–18; Ward and Herbert 1883–1910, 1: 892–94; Bourdillon 1906: 12; Langlois 1910: 144–45; Herbert 1911: 318; Kuhn 1913–14: 40, 65, pl. 14; Winkler 1915: 338–41, figs. 53, 54; Durrieu 1921a: 32, 62, pl. 72; London 1923–65, 3: 16, pl. xlvii; Winkler 1925: 128–29, pl. 77; Loomis and Loomis 1938: 129; Pächt 1948: 56, n. 27; Saxl and Meier 1953: 171–73; London 1953–54: no. 609; Knaus 1960: cols. 577–78; Tuve 1966: 257 n. 15, 324, figs. 94, 107; Wright and Wright 1966, 2: 403 n. 7; Fleming 1969: 28, 42, 71, 208; Alexander 1970; Hassall 1970: 33; Munby 1972: 142–43; Wright 1972: 145–46, 152, 238, 358–59, 444; Geneva 1976: 171; Scott (M.) 1980: 196, 197, figs. 135–37; Bruges 1981: 192; Madou 1981: 111; Malibu 1983a: 49–58, no. 6; The Hague 1984: 26; Liebaers et al. 1985: 172 (pl.), 173; Dogaer 1987a: 159, 160; De Kesel 1992: 186; Wieck 1992: 127 n. 22; Cambridge 1993: 207; Smeyers and Van der Stock 1996: 34, 35, fig. 36; Backhouse 1997a: 215, pl. 190; Korteweg 1998: 22, 47, cover pl., fig. 12; Smeyers 1998: 445 fig. 37, 447; Lisbon 2000: no. 68; Paris 2002: 100–101, no. 27

CAT. NO. 121. Shaw 1843, 2: pl. 65; Humphreys 1844–49: 14; Bradley 1887–89, 3: 92; Omont 1891: 10, no. 98; Warner (G.) 1903: text to pl. 54; Herbert 1911: 317; Warner (G.) and Gilson 1921, 2: 336; London 1954: no. 17; Kipling 1977: 37, 43, frontis., pl. 5; Backhouse 1979: 72–74, pl. 63; Watson 1979: no. 913, pl. 882; Murdoch et al. 1981: 26–29, pls. 40, 41; Malibu 1983a: 168 n.2; Strong 1983: 13–14, pl. 5; Backhouse 1987: 35–36, pl. 11; Meale 1989: 205; De Kesel 1992: 186; Backhouse 1993c: 7–8; Backhouse 1995: 176; Smeyers and Van der Stock 1996: 41; Smeyers 1998: 467–68, fig. 72; Backhouse 1999: 272, fig. 12.2; Backhouse 2000: 161; Carley 2000: 23 H.1.88

CAT. NO. 122. Delaissé, Marrow, and De Wit 1977: 348–73; Brussels 1996: 44, 46, 51 n. 10, 64

CAT. NO. 123. Rive 1782: nos. 19, 20; Woledge 1954: 129, no. 181; Aeschbach 1987: 24, 47, 87–89, 92; Legaré, Tesson, and Roy 1991: 84, 86, 87, 94, figs. 13–15; Legaré 1992: 212, 217, 219, no. 18, figs. 243, 246; Lemaire 1993: 243, 246; Jung 1996: 590; Legaré 1996: 207–8; Brinkmann 1997: 220–22; Smeyers 1998: 448–49 fig. 46, 452, 483 n. 73

PART 5

CAT. NO. 124. Neugass 1976: 2504; Kraus 1978a: 105f.; Kraus 1978b: no. 91; Euw and Plotzek 1979–85, 2:

256–85; De Winter 1981: 387, 417, 426 n. 44, fig. 145; Plotzek 1982: 35–36; Malibu 1983a: 8–9, 46, 48 n. 19, 63, 67, 68, 120; Büttner 1987: 320, 326 n. 20, 336, 339 n. 45, 341; Brinkmann 1987–88: 144–49; Kren and Rathofer 1988: 40, 51, 232, 242, 359, 369; Calkins 1989: 6, 7, 9, 12–14; Pächt and Thoss 1990: 82, 83, 89, 96; Brinkmann and König 1991: 139, 362; Van der Horst and Klamt 1991: 120–21, 152; Brinkmann 1992b: 204–5; Cologne 1992: 287; De Kesel 1992: 188; Cambridge 1993: 86; Erlande-Brandenburg 1993: 172; Backhouse 1993–94: 49 n. 16; Zürich 1994: 206; Steinmetz 1995: 230, 254–56; Rottier 1996: 6, 147, 170; Saint Petersburg 1996: 14–16, 19, 26–27, 32; Smeyers and Van der Stock 1996: 14; Brinkmann 1997: 186 n. 143, 246 n. 4, 304, 311, 325–29, 336, 360, 371; Hindman et al. 1997: 90; Los Angeles 1997: 117, 118–19; Ainsworth 1998: 39, 42, 235, 237; Calkins 1998: 49–51, 54, 61, 65; Castiñeiras 1998: 43 n. 5, 202; Jacobs 1998: 2, 7, 37, 46, 110–11, figs. 6, 59; Mellinkoff 1998: 47, fig. 14; Willemsen 1998: 78, 109, 215, 231–32, 240, 268, ill. 40; Daems 1999; Henisch 1999: 66, 88–90, 101, 128, 170, pls. 6–15, 7–6; Raguin and Zakin 2002: 97; Vöhringer 2002: 52, 64, 72; Wisse 2002: 1670–74

CAT. NO. 125. Priest 1940: 237–38; Tokyo 1972: no. 51; New York 1990: no. 78; Wisse 2002

CAT. NO. 126. Michiels 1845–49, 2: 371–75; Reichhard 1852; Harzen 1858; Zanotto 1862; Förster 1867: 25–53; Grimm 1875; Baes 1889; Chmelarz 1889; Durrieu 1891; Destrée 1892; Destrée 1894a; Destrée 1894b; Destrée 1900; Durrieu 1903a: 321–28; Ongania 1903; Vries and Mopurgo 1903–7; Vries 1904–10; Coggiola 1908; Fierens-Gevaert 1908; Mély 1909; Duclos 1910: 387; Durrieu 1910b; Winkler 1913a; Winkler 1915; Durrieu 1921a: 82–84; Durrieu 1921b: 203–6, 209; Winkler 1925: 200–202; Lyna 1933: 126–28; Duverger 1938; Hulin de Loo 1939a: 15; Winkler 1943: 56; Lanckoronska 1958; Charensol 1959; Denis, Knuttel, and Meischkel 1961; Diringer 1963; Lieftinck 1964b: 286; Winkler 1964: 198; Köster 1965: 473–74; Salmi and Mellini 1972; Biermann 1975: 15, 25, 27, 31, 38, 43, 44, 45, 46, 51, 57, 58, 63, 74, 87, 95, 103, 104, 108, 112, 115, 120, 122, 124, 126, 131–33, 135, 136, 138, 140, 144; Hurt 1975–76; Drigsdahl 1977: 38–41; Wolf (E.) 1982; Malibu 1983a: 6, 8, 27, 40, 48 n. 28, 61, 67, 80, 83, 85 n. 4, 120, 122 nn. 25, 33; Markl 1983: 18–19, 21, 26, 59, 69, 71, 80, 83, 92, 94, 96, 97, 98, 99, 103, 132, 145, 149, 160, 162, 165, 170, 172, 178, 189, 192, 194, 200, 201, 205; Testa 1986: 43, 114, 117–18, 126, 144, 162, 173; Dogaer 1987a: 17, 164, 166, 172, 177; Mariani Canova 1987; Thoss 1987: 103, 107, 121, 125, 128; Brinkmann 1987–88: 138; Brinkmann 1988: 93, 94, 95; Kren and Rathofer 1988: 22–24, 26, 39, 44, 45, 50–54, 56–61, 64–68, 70, 91, 99, 103, 115, 117, 215, 217, 218, 230, 235, 236, 240–45, 247–51, 253–58, 279, 286, 290, 301, 303, 341, 342, 343, 344, 357, 362, 363, 367, 368–72, 374–77, 378, 379, 381, 382, 384–86, 408, 416, 420, 431, 434; Brinkmann and König 1991: 12, 31, 52, 53, 57, 66, 129, 134, 234, 253, 275, 280, 289, 351, 352, 357; De Hamel 1994: 215, 218; Saint Petersburg 1996: 19, 20, 26, 39–41, 55, 114; Brinkmann 1997: 133 n. 12, 179 n. 109, 200, 201 n. 258, 299, 304, 328; Ainsworth 1998: 40, 42, 44, 143, 220; Calkins 1998: 50, 53, 54, 55, 60–61, 63; Smeyers 1998: 475, 476, 483 n. 148; Willemsen 1998: 112, 215, 240; As-Vijvers 1999: 251, n.16; Daems 1999: 62–65, 83–84, 89–92, 103–5, 125–27, 130–33, 141–43, 147–49, 157, 159, 161, 163, 167; Vöhringer 2002: 52, 60, 63, 64, 67, 72

CAT. NO. 127. Dibdin 1817, 1: 168–71; Waagen 1854–57, 2: 214–15; London 1908: no. 165, 82; Winkler 1925: 181; Köster 1965: 474–76; Deswarte 1977; Kaufmann (T.)

and Kaufmann 1991: 55, fig. 20; Lisbon 2000: 159, 160, 418, no. 113

CAT. NO. 128. London 1965: 7, no. 5; Manchester 1976: no. 31, 56

CAT. NO. 129. Warner (G.) 1894; Robinson 1895; Warner (G.) 1903, pl. 58; Herbert 1911: 298–300, 321–22, pl. 47; Durrieu 1921a: 36, 72; London 1923–65, 3: 13–14; Winkler 1925: 151, 177; Duverger 1930: 87–90; Hind 1938–48, 5: 73–81; Hulin de Loo 1939a: 16–19; Winkler 1943: 61–64; Colding 1953: 59; Wescher 1960: 80; Schoutteten 1967: 91–92; Sawicka 1973: 308; Euw and Plotzek 1979–85, 2: 268; Büttner 1983: 11, 136, 217; De la Mare 1983: 402; Malibu 1983a: 113–22, no. 15; Liebaers et al. 1985: 166, 172; Campbell and Foister 1986: 720; Evans 1986; Dogaer 1987a: 17, 161, 166; Brinkmann 1987–88: 146–47; Evans 1992; Evans and Brinkmann 1995; London 1996: 10; Saint Petersburg 1996: 26, 32; Backhouse 1997a: 231; Brinkmann 1997: 16 n. 36, 328 n. 53; Calkins 1998: 52, 56, 63; Smeyers 1998: 440–41

CAT. NO. 130. Shaw 1843, 2: pl. 62; Humphreys 1844–49: 14; Ward and Herbert 1883–1910, 1: 81–82, 90–91; Warner (G.) and Gilson 1921, 2: 308–10, pl. 105a–c; Saxl and Meier 1953: 215–16, figs. 36, 45, 46; London 1954: no. 28; Dickens 1955; Croft-Murray 1956: 123–24; Parkes 1969: 15; Lawton 1983: 55–69, pl. 4; Edwards and Pearsall 1989: 265, 266; Meale 1989: 215; Mooney 1989: 256, 263, 274–75; Scott (K.) 1996, 2: no. 102, 282–85, pls. 386–89; Backhouse 1997a: 229, pl. 207; Backhouse 1997b: 14–16, pls. 9, 10, 12

CAT. NO. 131. Brewer 1862–1932, 4, part 1: no. 2152; Auerbach 1954b: 39–46; London 1983: no. 2; Strong 1983: 30; Campbell and Foister 1986: 721; Backhouse 1989: 7, n. 29; Gunn and Lindley 1991: 40–41; Starkey 1991: V.37.1

CAT. NO. 132. Royal Commission 1883–1976, 13: 7; Trapp 1975: 89, no. 9; London 1977–78: no. 38; Murdoch et al. 1981: no. 10; Trapp 1981–82: 30, 33; Gibaud 1982: 26–27, 50–51, 54–55, 72–74; Strong 1983: 14–15 n. 6, fig. 6; Brown (A.) 1984: 360–61, 370–71, pl. 5; Beitenholz and Deutscher 1985–87: 420–21, fig. 8; Trapp 1991: 90–92, fig. 35

CAT. NO. 133. Colding 1953: 64; Auerbach 1961: 50–51, 287, no. 2; Murdoch et al. 1981: 32; Murrell 1983: 4–7; Strong 1983: 34, 189, no. 4; London 1991a: no. V.45, 91; Reynolds (G.) 1999: 45–48, no. 2

CAT. NO. 134. Strong 1983: 189–90; Cordellier 1995: n.p.; Paris 1997: 238, no. 194

CAT. NO. 135. Brewer 1862–1932, 4, part 1: no. 297; Foister 1983: 635; Bayne-Powell 1985: 130; Campbell and Foister 1986: 722, n. 41; Backhouse 1989: 11; Coombs 1998: 19, fig. 5; Reynolds (G.) 1999: 47

CAT. NO. 136. Winkler 1925: 175; Stockholm 1952: no. 161; Hammer-Tugendhat 1981: 16; Brinkmann 1992c: 36, 73, n. 70; Copenhagen 1999: 100–101; Daems 1999; As-Vijvers 2002

CAT. NO. 137. Waagen 1854–57, 3: 84–85; Oxford 1895–1953, 4: 525, no. 21686; Millar 1914–20, 4, part 2: 106, pl. 38; Durrieu 1921a: 70–71, pl. 98; Winkler 1925: 190; Taranco 1951: 124–25, pls. 38, 39; London 1953–54: no. 603; Macfarlane 1960: 16; Pächt and Alexander 1966–73, 1: 30 no. 396, pl. 31, figs. 396a–c; Malibu 1983a: 60, fig. 7b; Ringbom 1984: 172, fig. 141; Dogaer 1987a: 131; Brinkmann 1992c: 36–38, 77, 102; Brinkmann 1997: 15 n. 32, 179 n. 109, 323; As-Vijvers 2002

CAT. NO. 138. Millar 1914–20: 95–108; Borenius 1930: frontis.; Winkler 1943: 60; Köster 1959: 40–45; Köster 1965: 472–73; Lieftinck 1969, 1: 117; Harthan 1977: 150–53; De Winter 1981: 424 n. 21, 427 n. 63; Malibu 1983a: 39 n. 35; Dogaer 1987a: 166; Brinkmann 1992a: 194 n. 47; Brinkmann 1992c: 139–43; De Hamel 1994: 196, 198; Brinkmann 1997: 177–80, 251 n. 22; Randall 1997: 147; As-Vijvers 2002

CAT. NO. 139. Lieftinck 1957: 1–28; Winkler 1962: 22, n. 6; Biermann 1975: 28–29; Euw and Plotzek 1979–85, 2: 279; Marrow 1984: 559; Testa 1986: 42–43, 125; Dogaer 1987a: 177; London 1989: 17–18; Brinkmann and König 1991: 13, 30, 31, 235, 253; Testa 1994: 419, 422–24; Washington 2002: 37, no. 28

CAT. NO. 140. Quaritch 1905; Destrée and Bautier 1924; Wescher 1959: 126–35; Winkler 1962: 9, 13; New York 1964: 48–49, no. 64; Stewart 1966: 49; Gail 1968: 8; Ricker and Saywell 1968: 250, 252, 253, 254, 257, 266; Cuttler 1969a: 273; Hurt 1973: 45, n. 9; Bornstein 1975: 65, 72; New York 1975: 21; Warner (M.) 1976: 26, pl. 1; Degering and Steenbock 1977: figs. 4, 7; Delaissé, Marrow, and De Wit 1977: 593; Kupfer-Tarasulo 1979a: 275, 285 n. 41, 287 n. 48, 49, 288 n. 51, 289 n. 55; Kupfer-Tarasulo 1979b: 209, 211; Euw and Plotzek 1979–85, 2: 253, 274, 279, 298; New York 1980: no. 33; Voelkle and Passela 1980: 21–22; Strayer 1982, 1: 297; Wolf (E.) 1982: figs. 2, 3, 6, 7, 10, 11; Bowles 1983: 143; Büttner 1983: 113 n. 146; Cambridge, Mass., 1983: 80; Malibu 1983a: 79–81, 84, 85 n. 4; Markl 1983: 71, 88, 150, 152; Hansen 1984: 216–28; Marrow 1984: 455, 545–46, 549; Marrow 1986: 159–60; Testa 1986: 128, 154; Dogaer 1987a: 17, 177; Baltimore 1988: 51, 219–20, no. 106; Kren and Rathofer 1988: 205–7, 213–16, 221, 222, 232–33, 235–41, 243–44, 247, 249, 250–55; New York 1988b: nos. 1041, 1042, 1043, 1044; Alexander 1990: 450; Gross 1990: 169; Brinkmann 1991: 121; Brinkmann and König 1991: 32, 53, 115, 130, 140, 146, 208, 214, 254, 276, 338, 353, 363, 368; Leesti 1991: 116–17, 123; Mayberry 1991: 212–13; Fitzgerald 1992: 48a; Scailliérez 1992: 28; New York 1993: 109–10, no. 31; Testa 1994: 418, 424; DOA 1996, 3: 727; Brinkmann 1997: 40 n. 10, 336 n. 75; Driver 1997: 79–80, 86; Hindman et al. 1997: 117; Randall 1997: 518, 538; Wieck 1997: 32, no. 17; Kren 1998: 216, 223, 225; New York 1998: 392; Smeyers 1998: 479–80, 483 n. 159; Henisch 1999: 208–9; Testa 2000: n. 32; Wieck, Voelkle, and Hearne 2000: 12; Evanston 2001: 221; Vöhringer 2002: 53, 59, 64, 66, 67, 70, 72, 73, 75

CAT. NO. 141. Weale 1872–73b: 195–97; Warner (G.) 1903: pl. 55; London 1912a: 28, pl. opp. 28, no. 79; London 1923: 28–29, no. 82; London 1923–65, 1: pl. 39; Winkler 1925: 139, 140, 180, pl. 82; London 1929: no. 30, pl. 5; Colding 1953: 65; Lieftinck 1957: 24; McKinnon 1978: 40, 42, fig. 8b; Backhouse 1979: pl. 67; Marrow 1984: 542–43 n. 27; Testa 1986: 47, 51, 148; Dogaer 1987a, p. 177; Saint Petersburg 1996: 44, 45; Backhouse 1997a: no. 203; Smeyers 1998: 462, fig. 64, 463

CAT. NO. 142. Conway 1921: 286; Friedländer 1921: 191; Friedländer 1924–37, 4: 154, no. 212c; Wehle and Salinger 1947: 97–98; Bologna (F.) 1956: 29 n. 18; Marlier 1957: 109; Larsen 1960: 7; Eisler 1964: 100; Friedländer 1967–76, 6, part 2: 107, no. 212c; Mundy 1980: 33; Ainsworth 1998: 286–88; New York 1998: 312–13, no. 98; Ainsworth 2002: 1–25

CAT. NO. 143. Hatchard 1905; Steer 1961: 4; Testa 1994: 416–26; Bruges 1998: 103, no. 72

CAT. NO. 144. Cambridge 1966: 46–47, no. 110; Kupfer-Tarasulo 1979b; Wormald and Giles 1982: 186–87; Marrow 1984: 541; Testa 1986: 50 n. 28, 173 n. 4; Dogaer 1987a: 177; London 1989: 17; König 1991: 542; Cambridge 1993: pp. 90–91, no. 29; Testa 1994: 418

CAT. NO. 145. Göpfert 1827–34: no. 2936; Ellis and Weale 1883: 15; Kaemmerer and Ströhl 1903: 20, no. 24; Durrieu 1910b: 168; Winkler 1925: 121, 140, 209; Winkler 1961b: 70–78; Van Puyvelde 1963: 386; Adolph 1964: 251; Steinmann 1964: 139–77; Winkler 1964: 22, 43; Winkler 1966: 385–414: 7–82; Schmitz-Cliever and Grimme 1967: 229–31; Grimme and Ludwig 1968: 54, no. 96, pls. 15, 16; Biermann 1968–69: 49, 65; Biermann 1975: 18, 48–106; Mainz 1975: no. 39; Brussels 1977c: 163–64, no. 349; Delaissé, Marrow, and De Wit 1977: 593; Marrow 1977: 174 nn. 57, 58, 175 n. 63; Kraus 1978b: no. 97; Kupfer-Tarasulo 1979a: 274–75, 285 n. 41, 286–88 nn. 49, 52, 289 n. 55, 291 n. 29, 292 n. 61, 293–95; Kupfer-Tarasulo 1979b: 209–10 n. 4, 211, 214, 217, 219; Marrow 1979: 37–38, nos. 161, 167; Nordenfalk 1979: no. 26; Peters 1979: 362–67, 381, nos. 16, 17; Euw and Plotzek 1979–85, 2: 286–313; Mainz 1980; Malibu 1983: 9; Périer-D'Ieteren 1984: 128; Verdier 1985: 207; Testa 1986: 46–47, n. 13, 51, 130, 142, 154, 162; Büttner 1987: 332, n. 37; Brinkmann 1988: 93, 95; Kren and Rathofer 1988: 217–18, n. 13; Müller Hofstede 1988: 17; Calkins 1989: 13; Mainz 1990: 189; Brinkmann and König 1991: 13, 24, 25, 31, 120, 122, 126, 129, 131, 132, 133, 136, 137, 140, 141, 142, 155, 212, 222, 223, 235, 246, 253, 343, 344, 345, 349, 352, 354, 355, 360, 363, 364, 365, 377, 378; Testa 1991: 89–115, esp. 97 n. 23, 105–6 n. 41, 110 n. 56, fig. 13; Van der Horst and Klamt 1991: 120, n. 22; Alexander 1992: 34; New York 1992: 100; Scailliérez 1992: 25; Testa 1992b: 59 n. 31, 60, 61 n. 33; Büttner 1993: 31, 44–49, 55; Backhouse 1993–94, 1: 49 n. 16; Steinmetz 1995: 206; Rottier 1996: 111; Saint Petersburg 1996: 47; Brinkmann 1997: 16 n. 36, 361 n. 54; Hindman et al. 1997: 99, 108; Los Angeles 1997: 120, 121; Ainsworth 1998: 39, 42, 235, 237; Kren 1998: 225; Lisbon 2000: 65, 67, no. 8; Testa 2000: 108–11, n. 7, n. 21

CAT. NO. 146. Destrée 1898: 80–85; Kaemmerer and Ströhl 1903: 20; Destrée 1923: 19–23; Winkler 1925: 139–40, 184; De Ricci 1935–40, 1: 809, no. 324; 2: 2291; Worcester 1939: no. 50; Baltimore 1949: no. 212; Wescher 1959: 133; Winkler 1962: 12; Reynaud 1967: 346, 349; Biermann 1975: 31, 103–4, 268, nn. 135–38; Marrow, 1975: 177, 264, n. 40; Washington 1975: 190, no. 49; Rose 1976: 135, n. 12; Kupfer-Tarasulo 1979a: 274–98; Kupfer-Tarasulo 1979b: 209–26; Marrow 1979: n. 316, 106 n. 448; Euw and Plotzek 1979–85, 2: 282, 284, 298, 300, 302, 306, 311; Büttner 1983: 119, n. 165; Malibu 1983a: 9, n. 29, 10; Marrow 1983b, 101, n. 19; Marrow 1984: 539, n. 13; Ringbom 1984: 205–9; Liebaers et al. 1985: 169; Testa 1986: 42, n. 1, 56, 69, n. 3, 118, 142; Dogaer 1987a: 171, 172, 177; Kren and Rathofer 1988: 9, 25, 26, 203, 218, 209, 329, 344, 345, fig. 13; Baltimore 1989: 14; London 1989: 17; Steenbock 1990: 142, n. 14; Brinkmann and König 1991: 12, 28, 110, 115, 120, 234, 250, 333, 338, 342–43; Leesti 1991: 125, n. 26; Testa 1991: 111, n. 3; Cambridge 1993: 86; Saint Petersburg 1996: 28; Randall 1997: 539–48; Bruges 1998: 161, 164–65; Smeyers 1998: 430, 432, 483 n. 21; Testa 2000: n. 27, n. 43

CAT. NO. 147. Góis 1566, 2: 59; Shaw 1843: pls. 79, 80, 81; Figanière 1853: 268–76; Waagen 1854–57, 1: 133–35; Kaemmerer and Ströhl 1903; Weale 1903a; Thieme-Becker 1907–50, 1: 596; Durrieu 1910b: 166–67; Durrieu 1921a: 37, 69; Destrée 1923: 23–28; Winkler

1925: 139–40, 176; Durrieu 1927: 43, 90; Santos 1930: 23, 25–26, 30, 32; Santos 1939: 11–14; Wescher 1946: 209; Colding 1953: 26, 56; London 1953–54: no. 626; London 1955–56: no. 567; Lisbon 1958: no. 19; Aguiar 1959: 119–20, 127, 129, 142, 144; Santos 1959; Aguiar 1962; Smith (R.) 1968: 200; Innsbruck 1969: no. 16; Santos 1970, 3: 312–20; Segurado 1970: 12, 54, 142, 175–77, 228, 454, 460, 503–5, 512; Baumgarten 1972; Baumgarten 1975; Biermann 1975: 40, 42, 269–70; Segurado 1975: 157; Kupfer-Tarasulo 1979a: 274–75 n. 5, 298 n. 73; Malibu 1983a: 69–78, no. 9; Markl 1983: 9, 20, 25, 30, 33–40, 103–4, 127, 149, 151, 155; Albuquerque and Abreu e Lima 1984; Marrow 1984: 558; Ringbom 1984: 75; Liebaers et al. 1985: 168, 172; Testa 1986: 47–48; Kren and Rathofer 1988: 27, 31, 219, 223, 345, 350; Brinkmann and König 1991: 18, 25, 26, 187, 240, 247, 248; Washington 1991: 146–47, no. 27; Saint Petersburg 1996: 39; Lisbon 2000: 340–41, no. 92

CAT. NO. 148. Weale 1895: 70; Destrée 1923: 45–47; Baltimore 1949: 79; Stewart 1966: 49; Dogaer 1969: 340; Euw and Plotzek 1979–85, 2: 293; New York 1980: no. 35; Marrow 1984: 559; Testa 1986: 48, 128; Dogaer 1987a: 177; Kren and Rathofer 1988: 57, 247, 346, fig. 16; Brinkmann and König 1991: 32, 254; König 1991: no. 34; Scailliérez 1992: 28; Testa 1994: 419, 424; DOA 1996, 3: 727; Driver 1997: 86, 92 n. 25; Hindman et al. 1997: 98 n. 1, 119 n. 26; Randall 1997: 259, 499, 529; Wieck 1997: 116, no. 91

CAT. NO. 149. Bruges 1908: 54; Friedländer 1924–37: 160, no. 55; Benesch 1929: 209; March 1949: 219–21; Staring 1952: 144–49; Bruyn 1961: 124; Osten 1961: 469; Herzog 1969: 355–57, no. 78; Steppe 1969: 485–506; Berlin 1996: 90, 556; Toledo 2001: nos. 184, 185; Mensger 2002: 198

CAT. NO. 150. Destrée 1896; London 1911; Ghent 1913: 211, no. 1422; Durrieu 1921a: 68; Durrieu 1921b: 203, 206; Destrée 1923; Winkler 1925: 139, 140, 167; Gaspar 1943; Brussels 1958a: 80–82, no. 47; Delaissé 1958: no. 50; Hurt 1973: 43–46; Meiss 1974: 323; Biermann 1975: passim; Brussels 1977b: 87, no. 80; Delaissé, Marrow, and De Wit 1977: 592–93; Thomas (H.) 1978: 12; Malibu 1983a: 79, 80, 85, n. 4; Markl 1983: 16, 70, 82, 83, 87, 88, 94, 96, 99, 149–50, 159, 168, 172; Brussels 1984: no. 30a; Marrow 1984: 537–59; Gaspar and Lyna 1984–89, 3: 76–82; Büttner 1985: 197–233; Testa 1986: 49–50, 142; Dogaer 1987a: 17, 171, 177; Dogaer 1987b: 173; Kren and Rathofer 1988: 247; Brussels 1989b: 52–53, no. 44; Brinkmann and König 1991: 12, 17, 32, 67, 140, 234, 239, 254, 255, 290, 363; Kren 1998: 224, n. 48; Smeyers 1998: 430; Testa 2000: 109, 112, 114–18, 120, nn. 14, 15, 30; Vöhringer 2002: 50, 56, 61, 63, 72, 75

CAT. NO. 151. Winkler 1925: 140; De Ricci 1935–40, 1: 100; Biermann 1975: 266 n. 943; Marrow 1984: 540; Testa 1986: 48; Dutschke et al. 1989: 497–501

CAT. NO. 152. London 1994: 69, 70

CAT. NO. 153. Weyer 1852: no. 45; Sauzay 1861: no. 1064; Parthey 1863–64, 1: 367, no. 345; Wescher 1946: 208; Colding 1953: 62, 179 n. 40, fig. 102; Vey 1966: no. 39; Biermann 1975: 31, 36; Roberts 1979: 67, no. 56; Scailliérez 1992: 26 and passim, n. 28; Hindman et al. 1997: 116–17, 119 n. 22; Bruges 1998: 104–5, no. 74

CAT. NO. 154. *Munich, Bayerische Staatsbibliothek, Clm. 23683*: Riehl 1909: 438; Leidinger 1912a; Leidinger 1912b: 37; Winkler 1925: 187; Gaspar 1932: 56; Munich 1959: 11; Wescher 1959: 130; Munich 1970a: 45–46; Munich 1970b: 42, no. 58; Biermann 1975: 38 and

passim; Euw and Plotzek 1979–85: 302, 310; Malibu 1983a: 79, 81, 85; Munich 1983b: 160, no. 65; Hansen 1984: 17–28; Hansen 1985: 24–29; Kren and Rathofer 1988; Brinkmann and König 1991: 12, 32, 33, 47, 48, 56, 66, 191, 234, 255, 270, 279, 289; Kren 1998: 209, 210, 212, 213, 216, 218; Willemsen 1998: 111, 215; Testa 2000: 110; Vöhringer 2002: 54, 60, 63, 67, 68, 70, 71, 73, 74. *Monserrat, Abbey, Ms. 53*: Albareda 1917: 71–76, no. 53; Mundó 1959: 221–23; Olivar 1969: 31–34; Kren 1998: 209–16, 219–20, 223–25, 226–28. *Los Angeles, JPGM, Ms. 3*: Drawing 1985: 43; Los Angeles, 1985: p. 201; De Hamel 1986: 195; Kren 1998: 209, 214, 227; Daems 1999: 10

CAT. NO. 155. London 1884–94, 2: pls. 135, 136; London 1910: 16, no. 49; Herbert 1911: 322, 323; London 1911; Durrieu 1921a: 37, 68–69; Durrieu 1921b: 206; London 1923–65, 3: 15; Winkler 1925: 139, 140, 177; Winkler 1962: 13; Hindman 1981: 456–57; Malibu 1983a: 79, 85 nn. 4, 10; Dogaer 1987a: 17, 171, 177; Kren and Rathofer 1988: 268, n. 21; Brinkmann and König 1991: 33, 47, 66, 67, 100, 140, 194, 255, 270, 289, 290, 323, 363; Saint Petersburg 1996: 15; Backhouse 1997a: 231; Smeyers 1998: 420; Willemsen 1998: 67, 76, 79, 81, 110, 128, 215, 217, 218, 231–33; Vöhringer 2002: 60, 61

CAT. NO. 156. Kugler 1854: 18–19; Kaemmerer and Ströhl 1903: 1, 24, n. 1; Thieme-Becker 1907–50, 24: 86; London 1927: 239; Dublin 1955: no. 28; Bieler 1961; Princeton 1967, no. 34; Testa 1984: 189–236; Testa 1986: 29; Dogaer 1987a: 177; Kren and Rathofer 1988: 30, 31, 223, 349, 350; Brinkmann and König 1991: 12, 32, 113, 130, 134, 135, 234, 255, 336, 352, 357, 358; Testa 1991: 103–4; Brinkmann 1992c: 79, n. 75; Ainsworth 1998: 44, 235, 237; Berlin 1998: 70 n. 37; Daems 1999: 11; Testa 2000: 108, n. 7

CAT. NO. 157. Artemis 1990: no. 3

CAT. NO. 158. Previously unpublished

Cat. no. 159. London 1862: 584–85, no. 6836a, b; London 1908: no. 231; London 1910: 16; Herbert 1911: 323; Delisle 1913: 26; Destrée 1923: 40–41; London 1923: 30–31; London 1923–65, 3, pl. 50; Winkler 1925: 140, 177; Gaspar 1932: 56; Gaspar 1943: 5, 15; Winkler 1962: 13; Backhouse 1968: 85–86; Munby 1972: 10; Biermann 1975: 42; Malibu 1983a: 79–85, no. 10; Markl 1983: 88; Dogaer 1987a: 177; Kren and Rathofer 1988: 29, 30, 43, 65–68, 71, 72, 74, 75, 85; 221, 222, 235, 255, 256, 257, 259, 260, 263, 273; 347, 348, 362, 382, 383, 384, 385, 388, 390, 391, 401; see also: 13, 38, 39, 206, 332; Brinkmann and König 1991: 30, 252; Paris 1993: 320; De Hamel 1994: 195; Hindman et al. 1997: 117; Kren 1998: 216; Testa 2000: 120; Vöhringer 2002: 60

CAT. NO. 160. Los Angeles 1997: 122; Vöhringer 2002: 56 n. 41, 73–74

CAT. NO. 161. Weale 1905–6: 355–57; London 1908: 118, no. 241; Durrieu 1921a: 67; Destrée 1923: 52–56; Winkler 1925: 1978: 180; Wescher 1946: 208; D'Ancona and Aeschlimann 1949: pl. 12; Colding 1953: 62–63, 179, n. 43; Euw and Plotzek 1979–85, 2: 293; Murdock et al. 1981, pl. 99; Malibu 1983a: 30, no. vi; Malibu 1983a: 85, n. 14, under no. 10; Marrow 1984: 553, 558; Brinkmann and König 1991: 26, 27, 28, 248, 249, 250; Hindman et al. 1997: 98, 113–15, 117; Coombs 1998: 24; Smeyers 1998: 501, 504, no. 20

CAT. NO. 162. London 1912a: 36, no. 6; London 1923: 36, no. 6; Winkler 1925: 120, 178; Colding 1953: 25, 64, 65; Murdoch et al. 1981: 3–4, 30; London 1983: 35, no. 3; Backhouse 1985: 49, 51; Backhouse 1997a: 220; Brinkmann 1997: 378; Coombs 1998: 16

CAT. NO. 163. Los Angeles 1989: 123, no. 30; Parker 1999: 159; Köhler 2000: 9–10; Toledo 2001: 388

CAT. NO. 164. Brussels 1866–, 14: 631; Friedländer 1967–76, 13: 21, pl. 25; Franz 1969: 94; Liebaers et al. 1985: 269–70; Grosshans 1996: 248, no. 735; New York 1998: 266

CAT. NO. 165. Van Mander 1604: 234; Hofmann 1872: 67, no. 271; Friedländer 1921a: 100; Michel 1931: 64–65, no. 30; Tolnay 1935, 1: 41, 91; Auner 1956: 96–97; Grossmann 1966: 204; Arpino 1967: 111, no. 77; Friedländer 1967–76, 14: 29, 46, pl. 53; Bott 1968: 38, no. 11; Stechow 1968: 144, 155; Marijnissen and Seidel 1971: 51, 314–27, no. 43; Alpers 1972–73, 168 n. 18; Gibson 1977: 190–91 fig. 144, 193–94; Brumble 1979: 125, 127, 130, 134–36; Genaille 1980: 143–52; Liebenwein 1985: 126–29; Kren and Rathofer 1988: 68, 256, 257, 385; Gibson 1989: 67, 75; Hagen and Hagen 1990: 112–16, 119; Gibson 1991: 45–46, 52 n. 160; Delevoy 1994: 106; Wied 1994: 34, 35, 163, no. 51; Francastel 1995: 125, 144, 174, 181; 184–85, 187, 196, 197, 212; Tokyo 1995: 64, 241, no. B1; DOA 1996, 4: 905; Meadow 1997: 183; Simonson 1998: 71–92; New York 2001: 8–10, 75, 83 n. 38; Meadow 2002: 102, 122

CAT. NO. 166. De Ricci 1935–40, 2: 1459; New York 1964: 49, no. 65; Liechtenstein 1976: 66–68; Voelkle and Passela 1980: 27; Testa 1984: no. 231 n. 78; Dogaer 1987a: 167–70; Vienna 1987b: 134; Irblich 1988: 23; New York 1988b: nos. 1033, 1034; London 1991: 150; Fitzgerald 1992: 30a

CAT. NO. 167. London 1881: 53, no. 82; Falke 1912: no. 1, pl. 1; The Hague 1923: 5; Antwerp 1930: 22, 48–49, no. 47; New York 1934: 69, no. 145; De Ricci 1935–40, 2: 1483; Voelkle and Passela 1980; 41; Büttner 1983: 202; New York 1988b: nos. 1048, 1049; Fitzgerald 1992: 30a; Wieck 1997: 18, 108

CAT. NO. 168. Previously unpublished.

CAT. NO. 169. *Epistle-Lectionary*: Dibdin 1817, 1: clxxxiii; Waagen 1854–57, 3: 49; London 1908: 86; London 1953–54: no. 623; Auerbach 1954a: 52; Paget 1959: 400–401, figs. 43, 45; Trapp 1975: 92, no. 15; London 1977–78: no. 43 pl.; Murdoch et al. 1981: 30; Trapp 1981–82: 28–33, app. fig. 9; Hardie 1982: 80–85; Strong 1983: 30, fig. 13; Brown (A.) 1984: 354–55; Alexander and Temple 1985: no. 827, fig. 827a, b; Pächt 1985: 83, no. 827, pl. 57, figs. 827a, b; Trapp, in Bietenholz and Deutscher 1985–87, 2: 421, fig. 11; Dogaer 1987a: 166; Gunn and Lindley 1991: 41, figs. 10, 11; Starkey 1991: 84; Trapp 1991: 92, 96; Smeyers 1998: 468; Carley 2000: 267. *Gospel-Lectionary*: Dibdin 1817, 1: clxxxiii; London 1908: no. 173; London 1953–54: no. 624; Auerbach 1954a: 52; Auerbach 1954b: 45; Paget 1959: 400; Trapp 1975: 91, no. 14; Murdoch et al. 1981: 30; Trapp 1981–82: 28–33, app. fig. 8; Hardie 1982: 80–85; Strong 1983: 30; Brown (A.) 1984: 354–55; Hardie 1984; Alexander and Temple 1985: no. 828, fig. 828a, b; Trapp in Bietenholz and Deutscher 1985–87, 2: 421, fig. 10; Dogaer 1987a: 166; Gunn and Lindley 1991: 41; Trapp 1991: 92, 96; Smeyers 1998: 468, 483 n. 125; Carley 2000: 267

CAT. NO. 170. Beissel (S.) 1904: 50; Winkler 1925: 140, 151, 168; Lemaire 1984: 105; Dogaer 1987a: 170; Saint Petersburg 1996: 44

CAT. NO. 171. Bock and Rosenberg 1930: 47; Held 1933: 277–79; Bevers 1998: 46–48; Koch 1998: 15–18; Muller 1998: 29

CAT. NO. 172. Bock and Rosenberg 1930: 38; Held 1933: 279; Bevers 1998: 46; Koch 1998: 18

REFERENCES

ADOLPH 1964: R. Adolph. "Bericht zur Ausstellung im Suermondt-Museum, Aachen: Bibliophile Kostbarkeiten aus Privatbesitz, Aachen 1963." *Aachener Kunstblätter 29* (1964): 251–52.

AESCHBACH 1987: Marc Aeschbach, ed. *Raoul Lefèvre: Le Recueil des histoires de Troyes*. New York, 1987.

AGNEW 1971: Thos. Agnew & Sons Ltd. *Old Masters: Recent Acquisitions, 2nd November–10th December, 1971*. London, 1971.

AGNEW 1979: Thos. Agnew & Sons Ltd. *Old Master Paintings: Recent Acquisitions, June 7–July 27 1979*. London, 1979.

AGUIAR 1959: António de Aguiar. "Acerca de António de Holanda, um dos autores da Genealogia de D. Manuel Pereira, 3º Conde da Feira." *Arquivo do Distrito de Aveiro 25* (1959): 117–45.

AGUIAR 1962: António de Aguiar. *A Genealogia iluminada do Infante Dom Fernando por António de Holanda e Simão Bening*. Lisbon, 1962.

AINSWORTH 1992: Maryan W. Ainsworth. "New Observations on the Working Technique in Simon Marmion's Panel Paintings." In *Margaret of York, Simon Marmion and The Visions of Tondal*, edited by T. Kren: 243–56. Malibu, 1992.

AINSWORTH 1997: Maryan W. Ainsworth. "Old Assumptions Reconsidered through Revised Methodologies." In *Le Dessin sous-jacent dans la peinture: Colloque XI, 1995*, edited by R. Van Schoute and H. Verougstraete: 103–8. Louvain-la-Neuve, 1997.

AINSWORTH 1998: Maryan W. Ainsworth. *Gerard David: Purity of Vision in an Age of Transition*. New York, 1998.

AINSWORTH 2002: Maryan W. Ainsworth. "Was Simon Bening a Panel Painter?" In *"Als Ich Can": Liber Amicorum in Memory of Professor Dr. Maurits Smeyers*: 1–25. Leuven, 2002.

AINSWORTH 2003: Maryan W. Ainsworth. "'Diverse Patterns Pertaining to the Crafts of the Painters or Iluminators . . .': Gerard David and the Bening Workshop." *Master Drawings 41* (March 2003). Forthcoming.

ALBAREDA 1917: P. A. M. Albareda. "Les Manuscrits de la Bibliotheca de Montserrat." *Analecta Montserratensia 1*, no. 53 (1917): 71–77.

ALBUQUERQUE 1990: Martim de Albuquerque. *A Torre do Tombo e os seus tesouros*. Lisbon, 1990.

ALBUQUERQUE AND ABREU E LIMA 1984: Martim de Albuquerque and João Paulo de Abreu e Lima. *António de Holanda e Simão Bening: A Genealogia do Infante Dom Fernando de Portugal. Fac-símile do MS. da British Library, Add. 12531*. Porto and Lisbon, 1984.

ALEXANDER 1970: J. J. G. Alexander. *The Master of Mary of Burgundy: A Book of Hours for Engelbert of Nassau. The Bodleian Library, Oxford*. Oxford, 1970.

ALEXANDER 1983: J. J. G. Alexander. "Painting and Manuscript Illumination for Royal Patrons in the Later Middle Ages." In *English Court Culture in the Later Middle Ages*, edited by V. J. Scattergood and J. W. Sherborne: 141–62. London, 1983.

ALEXANDER 1988: J. J. G. Alexander. "Constraints on Pictorial Invention in Renaissance Illumination: The Role of Copying North and South of the Alps in the Fifteenth and Sixteenth Centuries." *Miniatura 1* (1988): 123–35.

ALEXANDER 1989: J. J. G. Alexander. "Katherine Bray's Flemish Book of Hours." *The Ricardian 8*, no. 107 (1989): 308–17.

ALEXANDER 1990: J. J. G. Alexander. "Labeur and Paresse: Ideological Representations of Medieval Peasant Labor." *Art Bulletin 72* (1990): 436–52.

ALEXANDER 1992: J. J. G. Alexander. *Medieval Illuminators and Their Methods of Work*. New Haven and London, 1992.

ALEXANDER 1999: J. J. G. Alexander. "Foreign Illuminators and Illuminated Manuscripts." In *The Cambridge History of the Book in Britain. Vol. III: 1400–1557*, edited by Lotte Hellinga and J. B. Trapp: 47–64. Cambridge, 1999.

ALEXANDER AND TEMPLE 1985: J. J. G. Alexander and Elżbieta Temple. *Illuminated Manuscripts in Oxford College Libraries, The University Archives and the Taylor Institution*. Oxford, 1985.

ALLMAND 1999: Christopher Allmand. "War and the Non-Combatant in the Middle Ages." In *Medieval Warfare: A History*, edited by Maurice Keen: 253–72. Oxford, 1999.

ALPERS 1972–73: Svetlana Alpers. "Bruegel's Festive Peasants." *Simiolus 6* (1972–73): 163–76.

AMSTERDAM 1959: *La Miniature flamande à l'époque bourguignonne*. Exh. cat. Rijksmuseum, Amsterdam, 1959.

AMSTERDAM 1982: *A Flowery Past: A Survey of Dutch and Flemish Flower Painting from 1600 until the Present*. Exh. cat. by Sam Segal. Amsterdam, Gallery P. de Boer, 1982.

AMSTERDAM 1984: *Willem van Oranje: Om vrijheid van geweten*. Exh. cat. Rijksmuseum, Amsterdam, 1984.

AMSTERDAM 1994: *The Art of Devotion in the Late Middle Ages in Europe, 1300–1500*. Exh. cat. by Henk van Os et al. Amsterdam, Rijksmuseum; Princeton, 1994.

ANTOLÍN 1910–23: Guillermo Antolín. *Catálogo de los códices latinos de la Real Biblioteca del Escorial*. 5 vols. Madrid, 1910–23.

ANTWERP 1930: *Trésor de l'art flamand du Moyen Âge au XVIIIème siècle: Mémorial de l'exposition d'art flamand ancien à Anvers 1930 par un groupe de spécialistes*. Exh. cat. preface by Paul Lambotte. 2 vols. Brussels and Paris, 1932.

ANZELEWSKY 1959: Fedja Anzelewsky. "Die drei Boccaccio-Stiche von 1476 und ihre Meister." In *Festschrift Friedrich Winkler*, edited by Hans Möhle et al.: 114–25. Berlin, 1959.

ANZELEWSKY 1964: Fedja Anzelewsky. "Der Meister der Lübecker Bibel von 1494." *Zeitschrift für Kunstgeschichte 27* (1964): 43–59.

ANZELEWSKY 1998: Fedja Anzelewsky. "Maria von Burgund, Maximilian und das Stundenbuch im Berliner Kupferstichkabinett." In *Das Berliner Stundenbuch der Maria von Burgund und Kaiser Maximilians: Handschrift 78 B 12 im Kupferstichkabinett der Staatlichen Museen zu Berlin Preussischer Kulturbesitz*. Exh. cat. by Eberhard König, with Fedja Anzelewsky, Bodo Brinkmann and Frauke Steenbock: 11–28. Berlin, Kupferstichkabinett der Staatlichen Museen zu Berlin, Preussischer Kulturbesitz, 1998.

APPUHN AND HEUSINGER 1965: H. Appuhn and C. von Heusinger. "Der Fund kleiner Andachtsbilder des 13. bis 17. Jahrhunderts in Kloster Wienhausen." *Niederdeutsche Beiträge zur Kunstgeschichte 4* (1965): 157–238.

ARMSTRONG 1979: C. J. Armstrong. "L'Échange culturel entre les cours d'Angleterre et de Bourgogne à l'époque de Charles le Téméraire." In *Cinq-centième Anniversaire de la bataille de Nancy, 1477: Actes du colloque organisé par l'Institut de Recherche régionale en Sciences sociales, humaines et économiques de l'Université de Nancy II* (Nancy, 22–24 septembre 1977): 35–49. Nancy, 1979.

ARNIM 1984: Manfred von Arnim. *Katalog der Bibliothek Otto Schäfer, Schweinfurt*. Stuttgart, 1984.

ARNOULD 1988: Alain Arnould. "The Iconographical Sources of a Composite Manuscript from the Library of Raphael de Mercatellis." *Journal of the Warburg and Courtauld Institutes 51* (1988): 197–209.

ARNOULD 1998: Alain Arnould, O.P. *De la production de miniatures de Cornelia van Wulfschkercke au couvent des Carmélites de Sion à Bruges*. Elementa historiae Ordinis Praedicatorum, 5. Brussels, 1998.

ARNOULD 2002: Alain Arnould. "Boethius op de Drempel van een nieuw Tijperk van Handschrift naar Druk en van Druk naar Handschrift: De Productie van Boethius' *De consolatione philosophie* als Voorbeeld van de Overgang van Geschreven naar gedrukte Boek in het laat 15de-eeuws Vlaanderen." In *"Als Ich Can": Liber Amicorum in Memory of Professor Maurits Smeyers*. Leuven, 2002.

ARPINO 1967: Giovanni Arpino. *L'opera completa di Bruegel*. Milan, 1967.

ARRAS 2000: *Fragments d'une splendeur: Arras à la fin du Moyen Âge*. Exh. cat. edited by Annick Notter. Arras, Musée des Beaux-Arts, 2000.

ARTEMIS 1990: Artemis Fine Art Limited. *Master Prints and Drawings: 15th to 20th Centuries*. London, 1990.

ASAERT 1972: G. Asaert. "Documenten voor de geschiedenis van de beeldhouwkunst te Antwerpen in de XVe eeuw." *Jaarboek van het Koninklijk Museum voor Schone Kunsten Antwerpen*, 1972: 43–86.

ASAERT 1985: G. Asaert. *Documenten voor de gecshiedenis van de Antwerpse scheepvaart voornamelijk de Engelandvaart (1404–1485)*. Brussels, 1985.

AS-VIJVERS 1999: Anne Margreet W. As-Vijvers. "Marginal Decoration in Ghent-Bruges Manuscripts." In *Sources for the History of Medieval Books and Libraries*, edited by Rita Schlusemann, Jos M. M. Hermans, and Margriet Hoogvliet: 245–56. Groningen, 1999.

AS-VIJVERS 2002: Anne Margreet W. As-Vijvers. "Randversiering in Gents-Brugse Manuscripten: De Meester van de Davidscènes en andere Verluchters als Specialisten in Margedecoratie." Doctoral thesis, Universiteit van Amsterdam, 2002.

AUERBACH 1954a: Erna Auerbach. "Notes on Flemish Miniaturists in England." *Burlington Magazine 96* (1954): 51–53.

AUERBACH 1954b: Erna Auerbach. *Tudor Artists*. London, 1954.

AUERBACH 1957: Erna Auerbach. "Some Tudor Portraits at the Royal Academy." *Burlington Magazine* 99 (1957): 9–13.

AUERBACH 1961: Erna Auerbach. *Nicholas Hilliard*. London, 1961.

AUNER 1956: Michael Auner. "Pieter Bruegel: Umrisse eines Lebensbildes." *Jahrbuch der Kunsthistorischen Sammlungen in Wien* 52 (1956): 51–122.

AURENHAMMER 1959: H. Aurenhammer. *Lexikon der christlichen Ikonographie: Band I. Alpha und Omega – Christus und die vierundzwanzig Ältesten*. Vienna, 1959.

AUSTIN 1971: *Gothic and Renaissance Illuminated Manuscripts from Texas Collections*. Exh. cat. Austin, University of Texas, 1971.

AVRIL 1969: François Avril. "Trois Manuscrits napolitains des collections de Charles V et de Jean de Berry." *Bibliothèque de l'École des Chartes* 127 (1969): 291–328.

AVRIL 1989: F. Avril. *Heures à l'usage de Rome*. Tours, Bibliothèque municipale, ms. 218. [Tours, 1989.]

AVRIL 1993: François Avril. Review of Thomas Kren, *Margaret of York, Simon Marmion and The Visions of Tondal* (1992). *Bulletin du bibliophile* 1 (1993): 172–75.

AXTERS 1966: S. Axters. "De zalige Heinrich Seuse in nederlandse Handschriften." In *Heinrich Seuse. Studien zum 600. Todestag, 1366–1966*, edited by E. Filthaut: 343–96. Cologne, 1966.

BACKHOUSE 1968: Janet Backhouse. "A Victorian Connoisseur and His Manuscripts." *British Museum Quarterly* 32 (1968): 76–92.

BACKHOUSE 1973a: Janet Backhouse. "Bourdichon's 'Hours of Henry VII.'" *British Museum Quarterly* 37 (1973): 95–101.

BACKHOUSE 1973b: Janet Backhouse. Review of J. J. G. Alexander *The Master of Mary of Burgundy* (1970). *Burlington Magazine* 115 (1973): 684–85.

BACKHOUSE 1979: Janet Backhouse. *The Illuminated Manuscript*. London, 1979.

BACKHOUSE 1985: Janet Backhouse. *Books of Hours*. London, 1985.

BACKHOUSE 1987: Janet Backhouse. "Founders of the Royal Library: Edward IV and Henry VII as Collectors of Illuminated Manuscripts." In *England in the Fifteenth Century: Proceedings of the 1986 Harlaxton Symposium*, edited by Daniel Williams: 23–41. Woodbridge, 1987.

BACKHOUSE 1989: Janet Backhouse. "Illuminated Manuscripts and the Early Development of the Portrait Miniature." In *Early Tudor England: Proceedings of the 1987 Harlaxton Symposium*, edited by D. Williams: 1–18. London, 1989.

BACKHOUSE 1993a: Janet Backhouse. "Early Renaissance Miniatures: Illuminations from the Collection of Miss Violetta Harris." *National Art Collections Fund Review Year Ended 31 December 1992*, 1993: 18–22.

BACKHOUSE 1993b: Janet Backhouse. *The Isabella Breviary*. London, 1993.

BACKHOUSE 1993c: Janet Backhouse. "A Salute to the Tudor Rose." In *Miscellanea Martin Wittek: Album de codicologie et de paléographie offert à Martin Wittek*, edited by Anny Raman and Eugène Manning: 1–14. Paris, 1993.

BACKHOUSE 1993–94: Janet Backhouse. "The So-Called Hours of Philip the Fair. An Introductory Note on British Library Additional MS 17280." *Wiener Jahrbuch für Kunstgeschichte* 46–47, pt. 1 (1993–94): 45–54.

BACKHOUSE 1994: Janet Backhouse. "Sir John Donne's Flemish Manuscripts." In *Medieval Codicology, Iconography, Literature, and Translation: Studies for Keith Val Sinclair*, edited by Peter Rolfe Monks and D. D. R. Owen: 48–57. Leiden, 1994.

BACKHOUSE 1995: Janet Backhouse. "Illuminated Manuscripts Associated with Henry VII and Members of His Immediate Family." In *The Reign of Henry VII: Proceedings of the 1993 Harlaxton Symposium*, edited by Benjamin Thompson: 175–87. Stamford, 1995.

BACKHOUSE 1996: Janet Backhouse. *The Hastings Hours*. London, 1996.

BACKHOUSE 1997a: Janet Backhouse. *The Illuminated Page. Ten Centuries of Manuscript Painting in the British Library*. London, 1997.

BACKHOUSE 1997b: Janet Backhouse. *Pictures from the Past: Using and Abusing Medieval Manuscript Imagery*. Medieval Research Centre: Texts and Studies 1. Leicester, 1997.

BACKHOUSE 1999: Janet Backhouse. "The Royal Library from Edward IV to Henry VII." In *The Cambridge History of the Book in Britain*, edited by Lotte Hellinga and J. B. Trapp, vol. 3: 267–73. Cambridge, 1999.

BACKHOUSE 2000: Janet Backhouse. "Charles of Orleans Illuminated." In *Charles d'Orléans in England (1415–1440)*, edited by Mary-Jo Arn: 157–63. Woodbridge, 2000.

BACKHOUSE 2001: Janet Backhouse. "Memorials and Manuscripts of a Yorkist Elite." In *St. George's Chapel, Windsor, in the Late Middle Ages*, edited by C. Richmond and E. Scarff: 151–60. Historical Monographs Relating to St George's Chapel, Windsor Castle, 17. Windsor, 2001.

BACKHOUSE 2002: Janet Backhouse. "The Hours of Charlotte de Bourbon at Alnwick Castle." In *"Als Ich Can": Liber Amicorum in Memory of Professor Maurits Smeyers*: 71–90. Leuven, 2002.

BAES 1889: Edgar Baes. "Notes sur le Bréviaire Grimani et les manuscrits à miniatures du commencement du XVIe siècle." *Bulletin des Commissions royales d'Art et d'Archéologie de la Belgique* 28 (1889): 135–80.

BAETJER 1977: Katharine Baetjer. "Pleasures and Problems of Early French Painting." *Apollo* 106 (1977): 340–49.

BAETJER 1980: Katharine Baetjer. *European Paintings in The Metropolitan Museum of Art by Artists Born in or before 1865: A Summary Catalogue*. 3 vols. New York, 1980.

BAETJER 1995: Katharine Baetjer. *European Paintings in The Metropolitan Museum of Art by Artists Born before 1865: A Summary Catalogue*. New York, 1995.

BAIER 1977: Walter Baier. *Untersuchungen zu den Passionsbetrachtungen in der Vita Christi des Ludolf von Sachsen: Ein quellenkritischer Beitrag zu Leben und Werk Ludolfs und zur Geschichte der Passionstheologie*. 2 vols. Analecta Cartusiana, 44. Salzburg, 1977.

BALTIMORE 1949: *Illuminated Books of the Middle Ages and Renaissance: An Exhibition Held at the Baltimore Museum of Art*. Exh. cat. by Dorothy E. Miner. Baltimore, Baltimore Museum of Art, 1949.

BALTIMORE 1965: *Two Thousand Years of Calligraphy*. Exh. cat. by Dorothy Miner, Victor I. Carlson, and P. W. Filby. Baltimore, Baltimore Museum of Art, 1965.

BALTIMORE 1988: *Time Sanctified: The Book of Hours in Medieval Art and Life*. Exh. cat. edited by Roger S. Wieck. Baltimore, Walters Art Gallery, 1988.

BALTIMORE 1989: Walters Art Gallery. *Bulletin of the Walters Art Gallery*, 1989.

BALTRUŠAITIS 1960: Jurgis Baltrušaitis. *Réveils et prodiges: Le Gothique fantastique*. Paris, 1960.

BARKER 1988: Nicolas Barker, et al. *Treasures of the British Library*. London, 1988.

BARROIS 1830: J. Barrois. *Bibliothèque prototypographique; ou, Librairies des fils du roi Jean, Charles V, Jean de Berri, Philippe de Bourgogne, et les siens*. Paris, 1830.

BARSTOW 1992: Kurtis A. Barstow. "Appendix: The Library of Margaret of York and Some Related Books." In *Margaret of York, Simon Marmion and The Visions of Tondal*, edited by T. Kren: 257–63. Malibu, 1992.

BARTELINK 1994: G. J. M. Bartelink, ed. *Athanase d'Alexandrie: Vie d'Antoine*. Sources chrétiennes, 400. Paris, 1994.

BARTSCH 1978–: Adam Ritter von Bartsch. *The Illustrated Bartsch*. 175 vols. planned. Edited by Walter L. Strauss. New York, 1978–.

BARTZ AND KÖNIG 1987: Gabriele Bartz and Eberhard König. "Die Illustration des Totenoffiziums in Stundenbüchern." In *Im Angesicht des Todes. Ein interdisziplinäres Kompendium*, edited by Von Hansjakob Becker: 487–528. 2 vols. Pietas Liturgica, vols. 3–4. Saint Ottilien, 1987.

BASCHET 1993: Jérôme Baschet. *Les Justices de l'au-delà*. Paris, 1993.

BASEL 1966: Öffentliche Kunstsammlung Basel. *Katalog*. Vol. 1, Die Kunst bis 1800. Basel, 1966.

BAUMGARTEN 1972: Sandor Baumgarten. "Saint Étienne et sa 'descendance' vus par Simon Bening." *Acta Historiae Artium* 18 (1972): 137–41.

BAUMGARTEN 1975: Sandor Baumgarten. "Présence de la Hongrie." *Acta Historiae Artium* 21 (1975): 83–85.

BAYNE-POWELL 1985: Robert Bayne-Powell. *Catalogue of Portrait Miniatures in the Fitzwilliam Museum, Cambridge*. Cambridge, 1985.

BAYOT 1907: A. Bayot. "Observations sur les manuscrits de l'Histoire de la Toison d'or de Guillaume Fillastre." *Revue des bibliothèques et archives de Belgique* 5 (1907): 425–38.

BEAUMONT 1971: Maria Alice Beaumont. "Livro de Horas de D. Manuel." *Observador* 16 (June 4, 1971): 61.

BEAUMONT 1972: Maria Alice Beaumont. "Livro de Horas." *Observador* 64 (May 5, 1972): 61.

BECK 1933: E. Beck. "The Mayer van den Bergh Breviary." *Burlington Magazine* (1933): 266–79.

BEISSEL (E.) 1905: E. Beissel. "Exposition de l'histoire de l'art à Düsseldorf, 1904." *Les Arts anciens de Flandre* 1 (1905): 49–51.

BEISSEL (S.) 1904: S. Beissel. "Exposition de l'histoire de l'art à Düsseldorf 1904. II. Les Manuscrits flamands." *Les Arts anciens de Flandre* 1 (1904): 49–56.

BELL 1988: S. G. Bell. "Medieval Women Book Owners: Arbiters of Lay Piety and Ambassadors of Culture." Reprinted in *Women and Power in the Middle Ages*, edited by M. Erler and M. Kowaleski: 149–87. Athens, Ga., 1988.

BELTING AND EICHBERGER 1983: H. Belting and D. Eichberger. *Jan van Eyck als Erzähler*. Worms, 1983.

BENESCH 1929: Otto Benesch. "Jan Vermeyen als Bildnismaler." *Münchner Jahrbuch der bildenden Kunst*, n.s., 6 (1929): 204–15.

BENEVENTO 1968: Mario Rotili. *Miniatura francese a Napoli*. Benevento, Museo del Sannio, 1968.

BERGER 1884: Samuel Berger. *La Bible française au Moyen Âge: Étude sur les plus anciennes versions de la Bible écrites en prose de langue d'oïl*. Paris, 1884.

BERGSTRÖM 1960: Ingvar Bergström. "On Religious Symbolism in European Portraiture of the XVth and XVIth Centuries." In *Umanesimo et esoterismo*: 335–43. Padua, 1960.

BERGSTRÖM 1985: Ingvar Bergström. "On Georg Hoefnagel's Manner of Working with Notes on the Influence of the Archetypa Series of 1592." In *Netherlandish Mannerism: Papers Given at a Symposium in Nationalmuseum, Stockholm, September 21–22, 1984*, edited by Görel Cavalli–Björkman: 177–87. Nationalmusei Skriftserie, n.s., 4. Stockholm, 1985.

BERLIN 1931: *Schöne Handschriften aus dem Besitz der Preussischen Staatsbibliothek*. Exh. cat. by Albert Boeckler and Hans Wegener. Berlin, Preussische Staatsbibliothek, 1931.

BERLIN 1975: *Zimelien: Abendländische Handschriften des Mittelalters aus den Sammlungen der Stiftung Preussischer Kulturbesitz*. Exh. cat. by T. Brandis et al. Berlin, Staatliche Museen, 1975.

BERLIN 1978: *Kostbare Handschriften und Drucke: Ausstellung zur Eröffnung des Neubaus in Berlin*. Exh. cat. edited by T. Brandis. Wiesbaden, Staatsbibliothek Preussischer Kulturbesitz, 1978.

BERLIN 1986: Stiftung Preussischer Kulturbesitz. *Preussischer Kulturbesitz: 25 Jahre in Berlin: Sammeln—Forschen—Bilden. Aus der Arbeit der Stiftung Preussischer Kulturbesitz, 1961–1986*. Berlin, 1986.

BERLIN 1987: *Das christliche Gebetbuch im Mittelalter: Andachts– und Stundenbücher in Handschrift und Frühdruck*. Exh. cat. by Gerard Achten, with the assistance of Eva Bliembach. Austellungskataloge, Staatsbibliothek Preussischer Kulturbesitz, 13. Berlin, Staatsbibliothek, 1987.

BERLIN 1996: *Gemäldegalerie Berlin: Gesamtverzeichnis*. Berlin, Staatliche Museen zu Berlin, Preussischer Kulturbesitz, 1996.

BERLIN 1998: *Das Berliner Stundenbuch der Maria von Burgund und Kaiser Maximilians: Handschrift 78 B 12 im Kupferstichkabinett der Staatlichen Museen zu Berlin Preussischer Kulturbesitz*. Commentary by Eberhard König, with Fedja Anzelewsky, Bodo Brinkmann and Frauke Steenbock. Berlin, Kupferstichkabinett der Staatlichen Museen zu Berlin, Preussischer Kulturbesitz, 1998.

BERMEJO 1962: Elisa Bermejo Martínez. *Juan de Flandes*. Madrid, 1962.

BERMEJO MARTÍNEZ 1972: Elisa Bermejo Martínez. *Colecciones del Patrimonio Nacional. Pintura X. Primitivos flamencos*. 1972.

BERMEJO MARTÍNEZ 1975: Elisa Bermejo Martínez. "Gérard David y Ambrosius Benson, autores de dos pinturas inéditas de la 'Virgen con el Niño.'" *Archivo español de arte* 48, no. 190–91 (April–September 1975): 259–63.

BERN 1969: *Die Burgunderbeute und Werke burgundischer Hofkunst*. Exh. cat. Bern, Bernisches Historisches Museum, 1969.

BEVERS 1998: Holm Bevers. "The Antwerp Sketchbook of the Bles Workshop in the Berlin Kupferstichkabinett." In *Herri met de Bles: Studies and Explorations of the World Landscape Tradition*, edited by Norman Muller, Betsy Rosasco, and James Marrow: 39–50. Princeton, 1998.

BIBLIOTHECA SANCTORUM 1961–70: *Bibliotheca Sanctorum*. 12 vols. Rome, 1961–70.

BIELER 1961: L. Bieler. "The Chester Beatty Library Catalogue of Western Manuscripts." Typescript. Dublin, 1961.

BIERMANN 1968–69: Alfons W. Biermann. "Das verschollene Stundenbuch Kardinal Albrechts von Brandenburg (1514–1545)." *Mainzer Zeitschrift* 63–64 (1968–69): 47–66.

BIERMANN 1975: Alfons W. Biermann. "Die Miniaturenhandschriften des Kardinals Albrecht von Brandenburg (1514–1545)." *Aachener Kunstblätter* 46 (1975): 15–311.

BIETENHOLZ AND DEUTSCHER 1985–87: Peter Bietenholz and Thomas Deutscher, eds. *Contemporaries of Erasmus: A Biographical Register of the Renaissance and Reformation*. 3 vols. Toronto, 1985–87.

BILLINGE 1998: R. Billinge. "Links with Schongauer in Three Early Netherlandish Paintings in the National Gallery." *Leiden Kunsthistorisch Jaarboek* 11 (1998): 81–90.

BINDING 1987: Günther Binding, ed. *Der mittelalterliche Baubetrieb Westeuropas: Katalog der zeitgenössischen Darstellungen*. Cologne, 1987.

BLACKBURN 1985: *The Hart Collection: Coins, Manuscripts, Printed Books*. Blackburn, Blackburn Museum and Art Gallery, 1985.

BLAIR 1959: C. Blair. "New Light on Four Almain Armours: 2." *The Connoisseur* 144 (December 1959): 240–44.

BLOCKMANS 1992: Wim Blockmans. "The Devotion of a Lonely Duchess." In *Margaret of York, Simon Marmion and The Visions of Tondal*, edited by T. Kren: 29–46. Malibu, 1992.

BLOCKMANS 1998: W. Blockmans. "Manuscript Acquisition by the Burgundian Court and the Market for Books in the Fifteenth-Century Netherlands." In *Art Markets in Europe, 1400–1800*, edited by M. North and D. Ormrod: 7–18. Aldershot, 1998.

BLOCKMANS AND PREVENIER 1999: Wim Blockmans and Walter Prevenier. *The Promised Lands: The Low Countries Under Burgundian Rule, 1369–1530*. Translated by Elizabeth Fackelman; translated, revised, and edited by Edward Peters. Philadelphia, 1999.

BLONDEAU 2001: Chrystèle Blondeau. "Les Intentions d'une oeuvre (Faits et gestes d'Alexandre le Grand de Vasque de Lucène) et sa réception par Charles le Téméraire." *Revue du Nord* 83, no. 342 (2001): 731–52.

BOCK AND ROSENBERG 1930: Elfried Bock and Jakob Rosenberg. *Die niederländischen Meister: Staatliche Museen zu Berlin*. 2 vols. Die Zeichnungen alter Meister im Kupferstichkabinett. Berlin, 1930.

BODENSTEDT 1944: Sister Mary Immaculate Bodenstedt. *The Vita Christi of Ludolphus the Carthusian*. Washington, D.C., 1944.

BOESE 1966: H. Boese. *Die lateinischen Handschriften der Sammlung Hamilton zu Berlin*. Wiesbaden, 1966.

BOGDANOW 1964: Fanni Bogdanow. "The Fragments of *Guiron le Courtois* Preserved in Ms. Douce 383, Oxford." *Medium Aevum* 33 (1964): 89–101.

BOLOGNA (F.) 1956: Ferdinando Bologna. "Nuove attribuzioni a Jan Provost." *Musées royaux des Beaux-Arts de Belgique, Bulletin* 5 (1956): 13–31.

BOLOGNA (G.) 1973: Giulia Bologna. *Miniature lombarde della Biblioteca Trivulziana*. Milan, 1973.

BONI 1994: Vincenzo Boni. "Note e suggestioni della Biblioteca nazionale 'Vittorio Emanuele III.'" *Euresis* 10 (1994): 223–68.

BONI AND GAROFALO 1997: Vincenzo Boni and Anna Maria Garofalo. "La Sezione Manoscritti e Rari." In *La Biblioteca nazionale di Napoli: Memoria e orizzonti virtuali*: 99–128. Quaderni della Biblioteca nazionale di Napoli, ser. 9, no. 1. Naples, 1997.

BONSANTI 1983: G. Bonsanti. "Maria di Borgogna in un ritratto di Michael Pacher." *Paragone* 1 (1983): 13–39.

BOON 1946: K. G. Boon. *Gerard David*. Amsterdam, n.d. [1946].

BOON 1958: K. G. Boon. "Was Colard Mansion de Illustrator van 'Le Livre de la Ruyne des Nobles Hommes et Femmes'?" In *Amor Librorum. Bibliographic and Other Essays: A Tribute to Abraham Horodisch on His Sixtieth Birthday*: 85–88. Zürich and Amsterdam, 1958.

BOON 1964: Karel G. Boon. "Nieuwe Gegevens over de Meester van Katharina van Kleef en zijn Atelier." *Bulletin van de Koninklijke Nederlandsche Oudheidkundige Bond*, ser. 6, 17 (1964): cols. 241–54.

BOON 1978: K. G. Boon. *Netherlandish Drawings of the Fifteenth and Sixteenth Centuries*. 2 vols. Translated by Margot Muntz. Catalogus van de Nederlandse tekeningen in het Rijksmuseum te Amsterdam, 2. The Hague, 1978.

BORENIUS 1930: Tancred Borenius. *Mediaeval Pilgrims' Badges*. London, 1930.

BORNSTEIN 1975: Diane Bornstein. *Mirrors of Courtesy*. Hamden, Conn., 1975.

BOSSUAT 1943: Robert Bossuat. "Traductions françaises des *Commentaires* de César à la fin du XVe siècle." *Bibliothèque d'Humanisme et Renaissance: Documents et travaux* 3 (1943): 253–411.

BOSSUAT 1946: Robert Bossuat. "Vasque de Lucène, traducteur de Quinte-Curce (1468)." *Bibliothèque d'Humanisme et Renaissance: Documents et travaux* 8 (1946): 197–245.

BOSTON 1995: *Memory and the Middle Ages*. Exh. cat., edited by Nancy Netzer and Virginia Reinburg. Boston, Boston College Museum of Art, 1995.

BOSTON 2000: *The Art of the Book from the Early Middle Ages to the Renaissance: A Journey through a Thousand Years*. Exh. cat. Boston, Boston College, John J. Burns Library, 2000.

BOTT 1968: Gerhard Bott. *Die Gemäldegalerie des Hessischen Landesmuseums in Darmstadt*. Hannau, 1968.

BOUDET 1997: J.-P. Boudet. "Le Bel Automne de la culture médiévale (XIVe–XVe siècle)." In *Histoire culturelle de la France*, edited by J.-P. Rioux and J.-F. Sirinelli, vol. 1, *Le Moyen Âge*: 225–358. Paris, 1997.

BOURDILLON 1906: Francis William Bourdillon. *The Early Editions of the Roman de la Rose*. London, 1906.

BOUSMANNE 1997: Bernard Bousmanne. "*Item a Guillaume Wyelant aussi enlumineur*": Willem Vrelant, un aspect de l'enluminure dans les Pays-Bas méridionaux, sous le mécénat des ducs de Bourgogne Philippe le Bon et Charles le Téméraire. Brussels, 1997.

BOUSMANNE AND VAN HOOREBEECK 2000: Bernard Bousmanne and Céline van Hoorebeeck, eds. *La Librairie des ducs de Bourgogne: Manuscrits conservés à la Bibliothèque royale de Belgique*. Vol. 1. Turnhout, 2000.

BOUSMANNE AND VOELKLE 2001: Bernard Bousmanne and William Voelkle. *The Black Hours: MS M.493, The Pierpont Morgan Library, New York*. Lucerne, 2001.

BOWLES 1954: E. A. Bowles. "Haut and Bas: The Grouping of Musical Instruments in the Middle Ages." *Musica Disciplina, A Journal of the History of Music*, edited by A. Carapetyan, 8 (1954): 115–40.

BOWLES 1983: Edmund A. Bowles. *La Pratique musicale au Moyen Âge: Musical Performance in the Late Middle Ages*. Paris, 1983.

BOZZOLO 1973: C. Bozzolo. *Manuscrits des traductions françaises d'oeuvres de Boccace, XVe siècle*. Medioevo e Umanesimo 15. Padua, 1973.

BOZZOLO 1977: C. Bozzolo. "L'Humaniste Gontier Col et Boccace." In *Boccaccio in Europe: Proceedings of the Boccaccio Conference, Louvain, December 1975*, edited by Gilbert Tournoy: 15–22. Leuven, 1977.

BRADLEY 1887–89: John W. Bradley. *A Dictionary of Miniaturists, Illuminators, Calligraphers and Copyists from the Establishment of Christianity to the 18th Century*. 3 vols. London, 1887–89.

BRAHAM 1981AMI: Helen Braham. *The Princes Gate Collection: Courtauld Institute Galleries.* London, 1981.

BRAUN 1924: Joseph Braun. *Der christliche Altar in seiner geschichtlichen Entwicklung.* 2 vols. Munich, 1924.

BRAYER 1964: E. Brayer. "Livres d'heures contenant des textes en français." *Bulletin d'information de l'Institut de Recherche et d'Histoire des Textes* (Paris) 12 (1964): 39, no. 5.

BREJON DE LAVERGNÉE 1979: Arnauld Brejon de Lavergnée. *Catalogue sommaire illustré des peintures du Musée du Louvre I: Écoles flamande et hollandaise.* Paris, 1979.

BRESLAUER 1965: Martin Breslauer (Firm), London. *A 15th Century Manuscript of Valerius Maximus in French, Illuminated by the Bedford Master and an Outstanding Burgundian Painter-Illuminator.* The Hague.

BREWER 1862–1932: J. S. Brewer, ed. *Letters and Papers, Foreign and Domestic, of the Reign of Henry VIII.* 22 vols. in 35. London, 1862–1932.

BRINKMANN 1987–88: Bodo Brinkmann. "Neues vom Meister der Lübecker Bibel." *Jahrbuch der Berliner Museen* 29–30 (1987–88): 123–61.

BRINKMANN 1988: Bodo Brinkmann. "The Hastings Hours and the Master of 1499." *British Library Journal* 14 (1988): 90–106.

BRINKMANN 1991: Bodo Brinkmann. "Über den Meister des Dresdener Gebetbuchs und seine Beziehung zu Utrecht." In *Masters and Miniatures: Proceedings of the Congress on Medieval Manuscript Illumination in the Northern Netherlands* (Utrecht, 10–13 December 1989). Doornspijk, 1991.

BRINKMANN 1992a: Bodo Brinkmann. "The Contribution of Simon Marmion to Books of Hours from Ghent and Bruges." In *Margaret of York, Simon Marmion, and The Visions of Tondal*, edited by T. Kren: 181–94. Malibu, 1992.

BRINKMANN 1992b: Bodo Brinkmann. "Fitzwilliam 1058–1975 and the 'Capriccio' in Flemish Book Illustration." In *Fifteenth-Century Flemish Manuscripts in Cambridge Collections; Transactions of the Cambridge Bibliographical Society* 10, pt. 2 (1992): 203–14.

BRINKMANN 1992c: Bodo Brinkmann. *Offizium der Madonna: Der Codex Vat. lat. 10293 und verwandte kleine Stundenbücher mit Architekturbordüren.* Codices e Vaticanis selecti 72. Stuttgart and Zürich, 1992.

BRINKMANN 1997: Bodo Brinkmann. *Die flämische Buchmalerei am Ende des Burgunderreichs: Der Meister des Dresdener Gebetbuchs und die Miniaturisten seiner Zeit.* 2 vols. Turnhout, 1997.

BRINKMANN 1998: Bodo Brinkmann. "Der Maler und sein Kreis." In *Das Berliner Stundenbuch der Maria von Burgund und Kaiser Maximilians: Handschrift 78 B 12 im Kupferstichkabinett der Staatlichen Museen zu Berlin Preussischer Kulturbesitz*: 111–54. Exh. cat. by Eberhard König, with Fedja Anzelewsky, Bodo Brinkmann and Frauke Steenbock. Berlin, Kupferstichkabinett der Staatlichen Museen zu Berlin, Preussischer Kulturbesitz, 1998.

BRINKMANN AND KÖNIG 1991: Bodo Brinkmann and Eberhard König. *Simon Bening: Das Blumen-Stundenbuch Simon Bening: Le Livre d'heures aux fleurs, Clm 23637 Bayerische Staatsbibliothek München.* Lucerne, 1991.

BROOK 1993: Leslie Brook. *Two Late Medieval Love Treatises: Heloise's 'Art d'Amour' and a Collection of 'Demandes d'Amour.'* Oxford, 1993.

BROWN (A.) 1984: A. J. Brown. "The Date of Erasmus' Latin Translation of the New Testament." *Transactions of the Cambridge Bibliographical Society* 8 (1984): 351–80.

BROWN (D.) 1978: David A. Brown. "The London *Madonna of the Rocks* in the Light of Two Milanese Adaptations." In *Collaboration in Italian Renaissance Art*, edited by Wendy Steadman Sheard and John T. Paoletti: 167–77. New Haven, 1978.

BROWN (M.) 1990: Michelle P. Brown. *A Guide to Western Historical Scripts from Antiquity to 1600.* London, 1990.

BROWN (M.) 1998: Michelle P. Brown. "Sir Robert Cotton, Collector and Connoisseur?" In *Illuminating the Book: Makers and Interpreters: Essays in Honour of Janet Backhouse*, edited by Michelle P. Brown and Scot McKendrick: 281–98. London, 1998.

BRUGES 1908: *Les Chefs-d'oeuvre de l'art ancien à l'exposition de la Toison d'or à Bruges en 1907.* Exh. cat. edited by J. Van Der Gheyn. Bruges, 1908.

BRUGES 1927: *Tentoonstelling van miniaturen en boekbanden.* Exh. cat. Bruges, 1927.

BRUGES 1949: *Gerard David.* Exh. cat. with an introduction by M. J. Friedländer. Bruges, Musée Communal de Bruges; Brussels, 1949.

BRUGES 1962: *La Toison d'or: Cinq siècles d'art et d'histoire.* Bruges, Musée Communal des Beaux-Arts, 1962.

BRUGES 1965: *Jan Gossaert genaamd Mabuse.* Exh. cat. by H. Pauwels, H. R. Hoetink, S. Herzog. Bruges, Groeningemuseum, 1965.

BRUGES 1981: *Vlaamse Kunst op Perkament: Handschriften en miniaturen te Brugge van de 12de tot de 16de eeuw.* Exh. cat. Bruges, Gruuthusemuseum, 1981.

BRUGES 1985: *Juan de Flandes.* Exh. cat. by Ignace Vandevivere. Bruges, Memlingmuseum, Sint-Janshospitaal, 1985.

BRUGES 1992: *Lodewijk van Gruuthuse: Mecenas en europees Diplomaat, ca. 1427–1492.* Exh. cat. edited by Maximiliaan P. J. Martens. Bruges, Gruuthusemuseum, 1992.

BRUGES 1994: *Hans Memling.* Exh. cat. by Dirk de Vos et al. 2 vols. Bruges, Groeningemuseum, 1994.

BRUGES 1998: *Bruges et la Renaissance, de Memling à Pourbus.* Exh. cat. edited by Maximiliaan P. J. Martens. 2 vols. Bruges, Memlingmuseum, Sint-Janshospitaal, 1998.

BRUGES 2002: Laurent Busine and Ludo Vandamme et al. *Le Vaste Monde à livres ouverts: Manuscrits médiévaux en dialogue avec l'art contemporain.* Exh. cat. Bruges, Grand Séminaire, 2002.

BRUINSMA 1992: E. Bruinsma. "The *lettre bourguignonne* in Cambridge University Library Nn.3.2 and Other Flemish Manuscripts: A Method of Identification." *Transactions of the Cambridge Bibliographical Society* 10 (1992): 156–64.

BRUMBLE 1979: H. David Brumble. "Peter Bruegel the Elder: The Allegory of Landscape." *Art Quarterly* 2, no. 2 (spring 1979): 125–39.

BRUSSELS 1866–: Académie royale des Sciences, des Lettres et des Beaux-Arts de Belgique. *Biographie nationale.* Brussels, 1866–.

BRUSSELS 1931: *Exposition de reliures, II: Du XVIIe siècle à la fin du XIXe.* Exh. cat. Brussels, Bibliothéque royale de Belgique, 1931.

BRUSSELS 1951: *Le Siècle de Bourgogne.* Exh. cat. Brussels, Palais des Beaux-Arts, 1951.

BRUSSELS 1958: *Les Richesses de la bibliophilie belge.* Exh. cat. Brussels, Bibliothèque royale de Belgique, 1958.

BRUSSELS 1958a: *Trésors de la Bibliothèque royale.* Exh. cat. Brussels, Bibliothèque royale de Belgique, 1958.

BRUSSELS 1959: *La Miniature flamande: Le Mécénat de Philippe le Bon.* Exh. cat. by L. M. J. Delaissé. Brussels, Palais des Beaux-Arts, 1959.

BRUSSELS 1962: *Manuscrits et livres imprimés concernant l'histoire des Pays-Bas, 1475–1600.* Exh. cat. by Franz Unterkircher. Brussels, Bibliothèque royale Albert Ier, 1962.

BRUSSELS 1963: *Trésors des bibliothèques d'Écosse.* Exh. cat. Brussels, Bibliothèque royale Albert Ier, 1963.

BRUSSELS 1964: *Miniatures espagnoles et flamandes dans les collections d'Espagne.* Exh. cat. Brussels, Bibliothèque royale Albert Ier, 1964.

BRUSSELS 1967a: *La Librairie de Philippe le Bon: Exposition organisée à l'occasion du 500e anniversaire de la mort du duc.* Exh. cat. edited by G. Dogaer and M. Debae. Brussels, Bibliothèque royale Albert Ier, 1967.

BRUSSELS 1967b: *Marguerite d'York et son temps.* Exh. cat. Brussels, La Banque de Bruxelles, 1967.

BRUSSELS 1969: *Quinze Années d'acquisitions de la pose de la première pierre à l'inauguration officielle de la bibliothèque.* Exh. cat. Brussels, Bibliothèque royale Albert Ier, 1969.

BRUSSELS 1970: Bibliothèque royale Albert Ier. *La Librairie de Bourgogne et quelques acquisitions récentes de la Bibliothèque royale Albert Ier: Cinquante Miniatures.* Brussels, 1970.

BRUSSELS 1971: *Thomas a Kempis et la dévotion moderne.* Exh. cat. Brussels, Bibliothèque Royale Albert Ier, 1971.

BRUSSELS 1973: *Le Cinquième Centenaire de l'imprimerie dans les anciens Pays-Bas.* Exh. cat. Brussels, Bibliothèque royale Albert Ier, 1973.

BRUSSELS 1974: *Dit is West-Vlaanderen: Tentoonstelling Passage 44.* Exh. cat. Brussels, 1974.

BRUSSELS 1975: *Vijf jaar aanwinsten, 1969–1973.* Exh. cat. Brussels, Koninklijke Bibliotheek Albert Ier, 1975.

BRUSSELS 1977a: *Charles le Téméraire.* Exh. cat. edited by P. Cockshaw et al. Brussels, Bibliothèque royale Albert Ier, 1977.

BRUSSELS 1977b: *Le Livre illustré en Occident, du haut Moyen Âge à nos jours.* Exh. cat. Brussels, Bibliothèque royale Albert Ier, 1977.

BRUSSELS 1977c: *Albert Dürer aux Pays Bas: Son voyage (1520–1521), son influence.* Exh. cat. Brussels, Palais des Beaux-Arts, 1977.

BRUSSELS 1979a: *Cinq Années d'acquisitions, 1974–1978.* Exh. cat. Brussels, Bibliothèque royale Albert Ier, 1979.

BRUSSELS 1979b: *Rogier van der Weyden/Rogier de la Pasture: Peintre officiel de la ville de Bruxelles, portraitiste de la cour de Bourgogne.* Exh. cat. Brussels, Musée Communale, 1979.

BRUSSELS 1984: *Manuscrits et imprimés anciens en facsimilé de 1600 à 1984.* Catalogue by Claudine Lemaire and Elly Cockx-Indestege. Brussels, Bibliothèque royale Albert Ier, 1984.

BRUSSELS 1985: *Les Rois bibliophiles.* Exh. cat. edited by Amalia Sarriá. Brussels, Bibliothèque royale Albert Ier, 1985.

BRUSSELS 1986: *Miniaturen in Grisaille.* Exh. cat. by Pierre Cockshaw. Brussels, Bibliothèque royale Albert Ier, 1986.

BRUSSELS 1987a: *La Librairie de Marguerite d'Autriche.* Exh. cat. by Marguerite Debae. Brussels, Bibliothèque royale Albert Ier, 1987.

BRUSSELS 1987b: *Trésors de la Toison d'or.* Exh. cat. Brussels, Palais des Beaux-Arts, 1987.

BRUSSELS 1989a: *Cent cinquantième anniversaire de l'ouverture au public 21 mai 1839.* Exh. cat. edited Anny Raman and Pierre Cockshaw. Brussels, Bibliothèque royale Albert Ier, 1989.

BRUSSELS 1989b: *Manuscrits à peintures, 1460–1486*. Exh. cat. by Christiane Pantens. Brussels, Bibliothèque royale Albert Ier, 1989.

BRUSSELS 1991: *Isabelle de Portugal: Duchesse de Bourgogne, 1397–1471*. Exh. cat. edited by C. Lemaire and M. Henry. Brussels, Bibliothèque royale Albert Ier, 1991.

BRUSSELS 1992: Bibliothèque royale Albert Ier. "Acquisitions." *Bulletin d'information* 36, no. 1–2 (1992): 4–6.

BRUSSELS 1996: *L'Ordre de la toison d'or de Philippe le Bon à Philippe le Beau (1430–1505): Idéal ou reflet d'une société?* Exh. cat. edited by P. Cockshaw and C. van den Bergen-Pantens. Brussels, Bibliothèque royale Albert Ier, 1996.

BRUSSELS 1997: *Guillaume Wielant ou Willem Vrelant: Miniaturiste à la cour de Bourgogne au XVe siècle.* Exh. cat. edited by Bernard Bousmanne. Brussels, Bibliothèque royale de Belgique, 1997.

BRUYÈRE 1999: Paul Bruyère. "La Plus Ancienne Représentation connue de l'ex-voto offert par Charles le Hardi à la cathédrale de Liège (Circa 1584)." *Bulletin de la Société Royale, le Vieux–Liège* (13, no. 20), no. 284 (January–March 1999): 833–56.

BRUYN 1961: J. Bruyn. "Een drieluik van Aertgen van Leyden." *Koninklijk Museum voor Schone Kunsten, Jaarboek*, 1961: 113–29.

BRUYN 1968: J. Bruyn. "Een portret van Enguerrand de Monstrelet door Rogier van der Weyden." In *Miscellanea Jozef Duverger*, vol. 1: 92–101. Ghent, 1968.

BUCHANAN 1990: Iain Buchanan. "The Collection of Niclaes Jongelick: II, The 'Months' by Pieter Bruegel the Elder. *Burlington Magazine* 132 (1990): 541–50.

BUCHTHAL 1971: Hugo Buchthal. *Historia Troiana: Studies in the History of Mediaeval Secular Illustration.* Studies of the Warburg Institute, 32. London and Leiden, 1971.

BUCK 1995: Stephanie Buck. "Petrus Christus's Berlin Wings and the Metropolitan Museum's Eyckian Diptych." In *Petrus Christus in Renaissance Bruges: An Interdisciplinary Approach*, edited by Maryan W. Ainsworth: 65–83. New York, 1995.

BUCK 2001: Stephanie Buck. *Die niederländischen Zeichnungen des 15. Jahrhunderts im Berliner Kupferstichkabinett: Kritischer Katalog.* Turnhout, 2001.

BUCK 2003: Stephanie Buck. "The Impact of Hugo van der Goes as a Draftsman." *Master Drawings* 41, no. 3 (2003). Forthcoming.

BUETTNER 2001: B. Buettner. "Women and the Circulation of Books." *Journal of the Early Book Society* 4 (2001): 9–31.

BUIJNSTER-SMETS 1995: Leontine Buijnsters-Smets. *Jan Massys: Een Antwerps schilder uit de zestiende eeuw.* Zwolle, 1995.

BUIJSEN 1989: Edwin Buijsen. Review of R. L. Falkenburg, *Joachim Patinir: Landscape as an Image of the Pilgrimage of Life*. *Simiolus* 19 (1989): 209–15.

BURGIO 1998: Eugenio Burgio. "David Aubert e *La Vengeance de la mort Nostre Seigneur*. Contributo alla storia della tradizione." *Studi testuali* 5 (1998): 57–115.

BÜTTNER 1972: F. O. Büttner. "Mens divina liber grandis est. Zu einigen Darstellungen des Lesens in spätmittelalterlichen Handschriften." *Philobiblon* 16 (1972): 92–126.

BÜTTNER 1978: F. O. Büttner. "Zur französischen Buchmalerei um 1500. Bemerkungen anlässlich zweier Publikationen." *Scriptorium* 32 (1978): 290–303.

BÜTTNER 1979: F. O. Büttner. "*Ad Te, Domine, levavi animam meam.* Bildnisse in der Wortillustration zu Psalm 24:1." In *Miscellanea Codicologica F. Masai dicata MCMLXXIX*, edited by Pierre Cockshaw, Monique-Cécile Garand, and Pierre Jodogne, vol. 2: 331–43. Ghent, 1979.

BÜTTNER 1983: F. O. Büttner. *Imitatio Pietatis. Motive der christlichen Ikonographie als Modelle zur Verähnlichung.* Berlin, 1983.

BÜTTNER 1985: F. O. Büttner. "Ikonographisches Eigengut der Rondzier in spätmittelalterlichen Handschriften: Inhalte und Programme." *Scriptorium* 39 (1985): 197–233.

BÜTTNER 1987: F. O. Büttner. "Komposite Programme der Stundenbuchikonographie in den südlichen Niederlanden bis gegen 1480." In *Opstellen voor Dr. Jan Deschamps ter gelegenheid van zijn zeventigste verjaardag*, edited by Elly Cockx-Indestege and Frans Hendrickx, vol. 1: 311–41. Miscellanea Neerlandica, no. 1. Leuven, 1987.

BÜTTNER 1993: F. O. Büttner. "Andachtsbuch und Andachtsbild: Flämische Beispiele einer nichtnarrativen Ikonographie in Psalter, Stundenbuch und Gebetbuch." In *Miscellanea Martin Wittek: Album de codicologie et de paléographie offert à Martin Wittek*, edited by Anny Raman and Eugène Manning: 27–64. Leuven, 1993.

BÜTTNER 1993–94: F. O. Büttner. "Das Christusbild auf Niedrigster Stilhöhe. Aussichtigkeit und Körpersichtigkeit in Narrativen Passionsdarstellungen der Jahrzehnte um 1300." *Wiener Jahrbuch für Kunstgeschichte* 46–47 (1993–94): 99–130, 397–400.

BUZZATI AND CINOTTI 1966: Dino Buzzati and Mia Cinotti. *L'opera completa di Bosch.* Milan, 1966.

BYAM SHAW 1976: James Byam Shaw. *Drawings by Old Masters at Christ Church, Oxford.* Oxford, 1976.

BYVANCK 1924: A. W. Byvanck. *Les Principaux Manuscrits à peintures de la Bibliothèque royale des Pays-Bas et du Musée Meermanno-Westreenianum à La Haye.* Paris, 1924.

BYVANCK AND HOOGEWERFF 1925: A. W. Byvanck and G. J. Hoogewerff. *La Miniature hollandaise dans les manuscrits des 14e, 15e, et 16e siècle.* The Hague, 1925.

CAHN AND MARROW 1978: Walter Cahn and James Marrow. "Medieval and Renaissance Manuscripts at Yale: A Selection." *Yale University Library Gazette* 52 (1978): 173–283.

CALKINS 1984: Robert G. Calkins. *Programs of Medieval Illumination.* The Franklin D. Murphy Lectures, 5. Lawrence, Kans., 1984.

CALKINS 1986: Robert G. Calkins. "Piero de' Crescenzi and the Medieval Garden." In *Medieval Gardens*, edited by Elisabeth B. MacDougall: 157–73. Dumbarton Oaks Colloquium on the History of Landscape Architecture, 9. Washington, D.C., 1986.

CALKINS 1989: Robert G. Calkins. "Sacred Image and Illusion in Late Flemish Manuscripts." *Essays in Medieval Studies: Proceedings of the Illinois Medieval Association* 6 (1989): 1–29.

CALKINS 1998: Robert G. Calkins. "Gerard Horenbout and His Associates: Illuminating Activities in Ghent, 1480–1521." In *In Detail: New Studies of Northern Renaissance Art in Honor of Walter S. Gibson*, edited by Laurinda S. Dixon: 49–67. [Turnhout], 1998.

CAMBRIDGE 1856–67: University Library. *A Catalogue of the Manuscripts Preserved in the Library of the University of Cambridge.* 6 vols. Cambridge, 1856–67.

CAMBRIDGE 1966: *Illuminated Manuscripts in the Fitzwilliam Museum: An Exhibition to Commemorate the 150th Anniversary of the Death of the Founder Richard, 7th Viscount Fitzwilliam of Merrion.* Exh. cat. edited by F. Wormald and P. Giles. Cambridge, Fitzwilliam Museum, 1966.

CAMBRIDGE 1976: *William Caxton: An Exhibition to Commemorate the Quincentenary of the Introduction of Printing into England.* Exh. cat. edited by Brian Jenkins. Cambridge, University Library, 1976.

CAMBRIDGE 1993: *Splendours of Flanders: Late Medieval Art in Cambridge Collections.* Exh. cat. edited by Alain Arnould and Jean Michel Massing. Cambridge, Fitzwilliam Museum, 1993.

CAMBRIDGE, MASS., 1955: *Illuminated and Calligraphic Manuscripts.* Exh. cat. Cambridge, Mass., Fogg Art Museum and Houghton Library, Harvard University, 1955.

CAMBRIDGE, MASS., 1964–66: *The Houghton Library Reports XXIV and XXV Accessions for the Years 1964–1966.* Cambridge, Mass., Harvard College Library, 1967.

CAMBRIDGE, MASS., 1967: *The Houghton Library 1942–1967. A Selection of Books and Manuscripts in Harvard Collections.* Cambridge, Mass., Harvard College Library, 1967.

CAMBRIDGE, MASS., 1983: *Late Medieval and Renaissance Illuminated Manuscripts, 1350–1525, in the Houghton Library.* Exh. cat. by Roger S. Wieck. Cambridge, Mass., Houghton Library, Harvard University, 1983.

CAMBRIDGE, MASS., 1996: *Harvard's Art Museums: 100 Years of Collecting.* Exh. cat. by James Cuno et al. Cambridge, Mass., Harvard University, 1996.

CAMILLE 1984: Michael Camille. "The Hastings Hours: A 15th-Century Flemish Book of Hours Made for William, Lord Hastings, Now in the British Library, London" [book review]. *Art History* 7 (December 1984): 508–14.

CAMILLE 1990: Michael Camille. *The Gothic Idol: Ideology and Image-Making in Medieval Art.* Cambridge, 1990.

CAMPBELL 1976: Lorne Campbell. "The Art Market in the Southern Netherlands in the Fifteenth Century." *Burlington Magazine* 118 (1976): 188–98.

CAMPBELL 1979: Lorne Campbell. *Van der Weyden.* London, 1979.

CAMPBELL 1981a: Lorne Campbell. "Early Netherlandish Painters and Their Workshops." In *Le Dessin sous-jacent dans la peinture: Colloque III, 1979, le problème Maître de Flémalle-van der Weyden*, edited by D. Hollanders-Favart and R. van Schoute: 43–61. Louvain-la-Neuve, 1981.

CAMPBELL 1981b: Lorne Campbell. "Notes on Netherlandish Pictures in the Veneto in the Fifteenth and Sixteenth Centuries." *Burlington Magazine* 123 (1981): 467–73.

CAMPBELL 1985: Lorne Campbell. *The Early Flemish Pictures in the Collection of Her Majesty the Queen.* Cambridge, 1985.

CAMPBELL 1990. Lorne Campbell. *Renaissance Portraits.* New Haven, 1990.

CAMPBELL 1998: Lorne Campbell. *The Fifteenth Century Netherlandish Schools.* National Gallery Catalogues. London, 1998.

CAMPBELL AND FOISTER 1986: Lorne Campbell and Susan Foister. "Gerard, Lucas and Susanna Horenbout." *Burlington Magazine* 128 (1986): 719–27.

CARDON 1991: Bert Cardon. "Rogier van der Weyden and the Master of Amiens 200: Concerning the Relationships between Panel Painting and Book Illumination." In *Le Dessin sous-jacent dans la peinture: Colloque VIII, 8–10 septembre 1989: Dessin sous-jacent et copies*, edited by H. Verougstraete-Marcq and R. van Schoute: 43–55. Louvain-la-Neuve, 1991.

CARDON 1993: Bert Cardon. "Nouvelles Données concernant les relations artistiques entre le Maître d'Amiens 200 et Rogier van der Weyden." In *Le*

Dessin sous-jacent dans la peinture: Colloque IX, 12–14 septembre 1991: Dessin sous-jacent et pratiques d'atelier, edited by H. Verougstraete-Marcq and R. van Schoute: 51–57. Louvain-la-Neuve, 1993.

CARDON, LIEVENS, AND SMEYERS 1985: Bert Cardon, Robrecht Lievens, and Maurits Smeyers. *Typologische Taferelen uit het Leven van Jezus: A Manuscript from the Gold Scrolls Group (Bruges, ca. 1440) in the Pierpont Morgan Library, New York, Ms. Morgan 649*. Leuven, 1985.

CARLEY 2000: James P. Carley. *The Libraries of King Henry VIII*. Corpus of British Medieval Library Catalogues, 7. London, 2000.

CARTON 1847: C. Carton. "Colard Mansion et les imprimeurs brugeois du XVe siècle." *Annales de la Société d'émulation pour l'Étude de l'Histoire et des Antiquités de la Flandre*, ser. 2, 5 (1847): 370–71.

CARTON 1966: C. Carton. "Un Tableau et son donateur: Guillaume de Montbléru, premier escuyer d'escuyrie du comte de Charolais." *Annales de Bourgogne* 38 (1966): 172–87.

CASCIARO 1994: R. Casciaro. "Note su Antonio da Monza miniatore." *Prospettiva* 75–76 (1994): 109–23.

CASIER AND BERGMANS 1921: Joseph Casier and Paul Bergmans. *L'Art ancien dans les Flandres (Région de l'Escaut: Mémorial de l'exposition rétrospective organisée à Gand en 1913*. Brussels and Paris, 1921.

CASTIÑEIRAS 1998: Manuel Antonio Castiñeiras. *Introducción al método iconográfico*. Barcelona, 1998.

CAZELLES 1984: Raymond Cazelles. *The Très Riches Heures of Jean, Duke of Berry: Commentary to the Facsimile Edition of Manuscript 65 from the Collection of the Musée Condé, Chantilly*. Translated by T. Faunce. Lucerne, 1984.

CEPEDA 1994: Isabel Vilares Cepeda. *Inventário dos códices iluminados até 1500*. vol. 1. *Distrito de Lisboa*. Lisbon, 1994.

CHAMPION 1910: Pierre Champion. "Un 'Liber amicorum' du XVe siècle: Notice d'un manuscrit d'Alain Chartier ayant appartenu a Marie de Clèves, femme de Charles d'Orléans (Bibl. Nat., ms. français, 20026)." *Revue des bibliothèques* 20 (1910): 320–36.

CHAMPION 1911: Pierre Champion. *Vie de Charles d'Orléans (1394–1465)*. Paris, 1911.

CHANCEL 1987: Béatrice de Chancel. "Les Manuscrits de la *Bouquechardière* de Jean de Courcy." *Revue d'histoire des textes* 17 (1987): 219–90.

CHARENSOL 1959: Georges Charensol. "La Miniature flamande." *La Revue des deux mondes*, n.s., 20, no. 5 (1959): 718–23.

CHARRON 2000: Pascale Charron. "Les Peintres, peintres verriers et enlumineurs lillois au début du XVIe siècle d'après les statuts inédits de leur corporation." *Revue du Nord* 82 (2000): 723–38.

CHARRON AND GIL 1999: Pascale Charron and Marc Gil. "Les Enlumineurs des manuscrits de David Aubert." In *Les Manuscrits de David Aubert*, edited by Danielle Quéruel: 81–100. Cultures et civilisations médiévales 18. Paris, 1999.

CHÂTELET 1966: Albert Châtelet. "Roger van der Weyden et Jean van Eyck." *Jaarboek Koninklijk Museum voor Schone Kunsten Antwerpen*, 1966: 7–38.

CHÂTELET 1967: Albert Châtelet. *Heures de Turin. Quarante-cinq feuillets à peintures provenant des Très belles heures de Jean de France, duc de Berry*. Turin, 1967.

CHÂTELET 1989: Albert Châtelet. "Roger van der Weyden et le lobby polinois." *Revue de l'art* 84 (1989): 9–21.

CHÂTELET 1993: Albert Châtelet. *Jean van Eyck Enlumineur: Les Heures de Turin et de Milan-Turin*. Strasbourg, 1993.

CHÂTELET 1996: Albert Châtelet. "Simon Marmion, I. La Vie." In *Valenciennes aux XIVe et XVe siècles: Art et histoire*, edited by Ludovic Nys and d'Alain Salamagne: 151–67. Valenciennes, 1996.

CHÂTELET 1999: Albert Châtelet. "Jean de Pestien au service de Philippe le Bon et de son prisonnier le Roi René." *Artibus et historiae* 40 (1999): 77–87.

CHAVANNES-MAZEL 1988: Claudine A. Chavannes-Mazel. "The *Miroir Historial* of Jean le Bon: The Leiden Manuscript and Its Related Copies." Doctoral thesis, Rijksuniversiteit te Leiden, 1988.

CHAVANNES-MAZEL 1992: Claudine A. Chavannes-Mazel. "The Twelve Ladies of Rhetoric in Cambridge [CUL MS Nn.3.2]." In *Fifteenth-Century Flemish Manuscripts in Cambridge Collections: Transactions of the Cambridge Bibliographical Society* 10, pt. 2 (1992): 139–55.

CHESNEY 1951: Kathleen Chesney. "Notes on Some Treatises of Devotion Intended for Margaret of York (Ms. Douce 365)." *Medium Aevum* 20 (1951): 11–39.

CHMELARZ 1889: Eduard Chmelarz. "Ein Verwandter des Breviarium Grimani in der K. K. Hofbibliothek." *Jahrbuch des Kunsthistorischen Sammlungen des Allerhöchsten Kaiserhauses* 9 (1889): 429–45.

CIBULKA AND MATĚJČEK 1924–25: J. Cibulka and A. Matějček. "Francouzké a flámské iluminované v knihovne premonstrátske kanonie v Nové Říše." *Památky archeologické* 34 (1924–25): 22–40.

CINCINNATI 1959: *The Lehman Collection, New York*. Exh. cat. Cincinnati Art Museum, 1959.

CLARK 1992: Gregory T. Clark. "The Chronology of the Louthe Master and His Identification with Simon Marmion." In *Margaret of York, Simon Marmion and The Visions of Tondal*, edited by T. Kren: 195–208. Malibu, 1992.

CLARK 1997: Gregory T. Clark. *The Hours of Isabel la Católica, the Facsimile Edition: Commentary*. Madrid, 1997.

CLARK 2000: Gregory T. Clark. *Made in Flanders: The Master of the Ghent Privileges and Manuscript Painting in the Southern Netherlands in the Time of Philip the Good*. Turnhout, 2000.

CLEMEN 1923: Paul Clemen, ed. *Belgische Kunstdenkmäler*. 2 vols. Munich, 1923.

CLEVELAND 1963: "Year in Review for 1963." *Bulletin of The Cleveland Museum of Art* 50 (1963): 269–71.

CLEVELAND 1967: *Treasures from Medieval France*. Exh. cat. compiled by William D. Wixom. Cleveland Museum of Art, 1967.

CLEVELAND 1982: Cleveland Museum of Art. *Catalogue of Paintings. III: European Paintings of the 16th, 17th, and 18th Centuries*. Cleveland, 1982.

CLEVELAND 1990: Cleveland Museum of Art. *Handlist of Illuminated Manuscripts and Miniatures*. Cleveland, 1990.

COCKSHAW 1968: Pierre Cockshaw. "La Famille du copiste David Aubert." *Scriptorium* 22 (1968): 279–87.

COCKSHAW 1977: Pierre Cockshaw. "Les Manuscrits de Charles de Bourgogne et de ses proches." In *Charles le Téméraire: Exposition organisée à l'occasion du cinquième centenaire de sa mort*: 3–19. Exh. cat. Brussels, 1977.

COCKSHAW 1979a: Pierre Cockshaw. "La Miniature à Bruxelles sous le règne de Philippe le Bon." In *Rogier van der Weyden / Rogier de la Pasture, peintre officiel de la ville de Bruxelles, portraitiste de la cour de Bourgogne*: 116–25. Exh. cat. Brussels, Musée Communale, 1979.

COCKSHAW 1979b: Pierre Cockshaw. *Les Miniatures des Chroniques de Hainaut (15ème siècle)*. Mons, 1979.

COCKSHAW 1984: Pierre Cockshaw. "De la réalisation d'un livre à sa destruction: L'Exemplaire de l'histoire de la Toison d'Or de Charles le Téméraire." In *Liber amicorum Herman Liebaers*: 201–12. Brussels, 1984.

COCKSHAW 1985: Pierre Cockshaw. "Observations à propos du premier volume des *Chroniques de Hainaut*." In *Calames et Cahiers: Mélanges de codicologie et de paléographie offerts à Léon Gilissen*: 27–31. Brussels, 1985.

COCKSHAW 1992: Pierre Cockshaw. "Some Remarks on the Character and Content of the Library of Margaret of York." In *Margaret of York, Simon Marmion and The Visions of Tondal*, edited by T. Kren: 57–62. Malibu, 1992.

COCKSHAW 2000: Pierre Cockshaw. "Jean Wauquelin – documents d'archives." In *Les Chroniques de Hainaut; ou, Les Ambitions d'un prince bourguignon*, edited by Christiane Van den Bergen-Pantens: 45–46. Turnhout, 2000.

COCKSHAW AND VANDEN BOSCH 1963: Pierre Cockshaw and W. Vanden Bosch. "Acquisitions." *Bulletin Koninklijke Bibliotheek van België* 7, no. 3 (March 5, 1963): 22–35.

COGGIOLA 1908: Giulio Coggiola. *Il Breviario Grimani della Biblioteca Marciana di Venezia: Ricerche storiche e artistiche*. Leiden, 1908.

COLDING 1951: Torben Holck Colding. "Über die Beziehungen zwischen der Buchmalerei und der Kabinettminiatur." *Nordisk Tidskrift för Bok- och Biblioteksväsen* 38 (1951): 169–80.

COLDING 1953: Torben Holck Colding. *Aspects of Miniature Painting: Its Origins and Development*. Copenhagen, 1953.

COLEMAN 1996: J. Coleman. *Public Reading and the Reading Public in Late Medieval England and France*. New York, 1996.

COLOGNE 1960: *Grosse Kunst des Mittelalters aus Privatbesitz*. Exh. cat. edited by H. Schnitzler. Cologne, Schnütgen-Museum, 1960.

COLOGNE 1968: *Weltkunst aus Privatbesitz*. Exh. cat. edited by H. May. Cologne, Kunsthalle, 1968.

COLOGNE 1970: *Herbst des Mittelalters. Spätgotik in Köln und am Niederrhein*. Exh. cat. edited by G. von der Osten. Cologne, Kunsthalle, 1970.

COLOGNE 1973: *Rhein und Maas: Kunst und Kultur, 800–1400*. 2 vols. Exh. cat. Cologne, Schnütgen-Museum, 1973.

COLOGNE 1987: *Andachtsbücher des Mittelalters aus Privatsbesitz*. Exh. cat. by Joachim Plotzek. Cologne, Schnütgen Museum, 1987.

COLOGNE 1992: *Biblioteca Apostolica Vaticana: Liturgie und Andacht im Mittelalter*. Exh. cat. edited by J. M. Plotzek and U. Surmann. Cologne, Erzbischöfliches Diözesanmuseum, 1992.

COLOGNE 2002: *Ars vivendi, Ars moriendi: Die Handschriftensammlung Renate König*. Exh. cat. Cologne, Erzbischöfliches Diözesanmuseum, 2002.

CONELL 1984: J. Conell. "*L'Instruction d'un jeune prince*: A Critical Edition and Analysis." Ph.D. diss., Catholic University of America, Washington, D.C., 1984.

CONTAMINE 1997: P. Contamine. *La Noblesse au royaume de France de Philippe le Bel à Louis XII: Essai de synthèse*. Paris, 1997.

CONWAY 1916: William M. Conway. "Gerard David's Descent from the Cross." *Burlington Magazine* 29 (1916): 309–10.

CONWAY 1921: William Martin Conway. *The Van Eycks and Their Followers*. London, 1921.

COOLS 2001: Hans Cools. "Les Frères Henri, Jean, Antoine et Corneille de Glymes-Berghen: Les Quatre Fils Aymon des Pays-Bas bourguignons." In *Le Héros bourguignon: Histoire et épopée*, edited by Jean-Marie Cauchies et al. *Publication du centre européen d'études bourguignonnes (XIVe–XVIe s.)* 41 (2001): 123–33.

COOMBS 1998: Katherine Coombs. *The Portrait Miniature in England*. London, 1998.

COPENHAGEN 1999: *Living Words and Luminous Pictures: Medieval Book Culture in Denmark*. Exh. cat. edited by Erik Petersen. Copenhagen, Kongelige Bibliotek, 1999.

CORDELLIER 1995: Dominique Cordellier. "Portrait d'Henry VIII, Lucas Horenbaut (or Hornebolt)." *Bulletin de la Société des Amis du Louvre*, March 1995.

CORNELIS 1987: E. Cornelis. "De kunstenaar in het laatmiddeleeuwse Gent I, Organisatie en kunstproduktie van de Sint-Lucasgilde in de15de eeuw." *Handelingen der Maatschappij voor Geschiedenis en Oudheidkunde te Gent*, n.s., 41 (1987): 97–128.

CORNELIS 1988: E. Cornelis. "De kunstenaar in het laatmiddeleeuwse II. De sociaal-economische positie van de meesters van de Sint-Lucasgilde in de 15de eeuw." *Handelingen der Maatschappij voor Geschiedenis en Oudheidkunde te Gent*, n.s., 42 (1988): 95–138.

COULTON 1930: G. G. Coulton. *The Chronicler of European Chivalry*. London, 1930.

COURCELLE 1984: Pierre Courcelle. *Lecteurs païens et lecteurs chrétiens de l'Enéide: Les Manuscrits illustrés de l'Enéide du Xe au XVe siècle*. 2 vols. Vol. 2 by P. Courcelle and J. Courcelle. Paris, 1984.

COURCELLE-LADMIRANT 1939: Jeanne Courcelle-Ladmirant. "Le Bréviaire flamand dit 'La Flora' de la Bibliothèque nationale de Naples." *Bulletin de l'Institut historique belge de Rome* 20 (1939): 223–33.

CROFT-MURRAY 1956: E. Croft-Murray. "Lambert Barnard: An English Early Renaissance Painter." *Archaeological Journal* 113 (1956): 108–25.

CUNDALL 1916: H. M. Cundall. "The Buccleuch Miniatures." *The Connoisseur* 46 (September 1916): 37–40.

CUTTLER 1969a: Charles Cuttler. "Bosch and the Narrenschiff. A Problem in Relationships." *Art Bulletin* 51 (1969): 257–66.

CUTTLER 1969b: Charles Cuttler. "Two Aspects of Bosch's Hell Imagery." *Miscellanea F. Lyna; Scriptorium* 23 (1969): 313–19.

CUVELIER 1900: Joseph Cuvelier. "Inventaire analytique des archives de la chapelle du St-Sang à Bruges précédé d'une notice historique sur la chapelle." *Annales de la Société d'Émulation pour l'Étude de l'Histoire et des Antiquités de la Flandre* (Bruges) 50 (1900): 1–152.

D'ANCONA AND AESCHLIMANN 1949: Paolo D'Ancona and E. Aeschlimann. *Dictionnaire des miniaturistes du Moyen Âge et de la Renaissance*. 2nd ed. Milan, 1949.

D'ANCONA AND AESCHLIMANN 1969: Paolo D'Ancona and E. Aeschlimann. *The Art of Illumination*. London, 1969.

DAEMS 1999: Cindy Daems. "Het Spinola-getijdenboek (Los Angeles, J. Paul Getty Museum, Ms. Ludwig IX 18) Een Gents-Brugs handschrift van omstreeks 1510–1520." Doctoral thesis, Katholieke Universiteit Leuven, 1999.

DAVIES (H.) 1910: Hugh W. Davies. *Catalogue of a Collection of Early French Books in the Library of C. Fairfax Murray*. 2 vols. London, 1910.

DAVIES (M.) 1968: Martin Davies. *National Gallery Catalogues: Early Netherlandish School*. 3rd ed. London, 1968.

DAVIES (M.) 1970: Martin Davies. *Les Primitifs flamands, I: Corpus de la peinture des anciens Pays-Bas Méridionaux au XVe siècle*, 11. The National Gallery, London. Brussels, 1970.

DAVIES (M.) 1972: Martin Davies. *Rogier van der Weyden: An Essay, with a Critical Catalogue of Paintings Assigned to Him and to Robert Campin*. London, 1972.

DE BAETS 1958: J. De Baets. "Het drieluik 'De Kruisdood' in de Sint-Baafskatedraal te Gent." *Schets* 10, no. 4 (1958): 101–6.

DE BOISLISLE 1880: A. de Boislisle. "Inventaire des bijoux vêtements, manuscrits et objets précieux appartenant à la comtesse de Monpensier." *Annuaire-Bulletin de la Société de l'Histoire de France*, 1880: 269–309.

DE BUSSCHER 1859a: E. de Busscher. "Peinture murale à l'huile du XVe siècle à Gand.—Indices primordiaux de l'emploi de la couleur à l'huile, au XIVe siècle, à Gand. —Recherches sur les anciens peintres gantois." *Messager des sciences historiques*, 1859: 105–271.

DE BUSSCHER 1859b: Edmond de Busscher. *Recherches sur les peintres gantois des XIVe et XVe siècles*. Ghent, 1859.

DE BUSSCHER 1866: Edmond de Busscher. *Recherches sur les peintres et sculpteurs à Gand aux XVIe, XVIIe et XVIIIe siècles*. Ghent, 1866.

DE COO 1978: Jozef de Coo. "Breviarum genaamd Mayer van den Bergh." In *Museum Mayer van den Bergh Catalogus I: Schilderijen, verluchte handschriften, tekeningen*: 168–74. 3rd ed. Antwerp, 1978.

DE COO 1979: Jozef de Coo. *Fritz Mayer van den Bergh: The Collector, the Collection*. Schoten, 1979.

DE FIGUEIREDO 1931: José de Figueiredo. *L'Art portugais de l'époque des grandes découvertes jusqu'au XX siècle*. Paris, Exposition Coloniale Internationale, 1931.

DE HAMEL 1986: Christopher De Hamel. *A History of Illuminated Manuscripts*. Oxford, 1986.

DE HAMEL 1994: Christopher De Hamel. *A History of Illuminated Manuscripts*. 2nd ed. Revised, enlarged, and with new illustrations. London, 1994.

DE JONG ET AL. 1997: Jan de Jong, Mark Meadow, Herman Roodenburg, and Frits Scholten. *Pieter Bruegel. Nederlands Kunsthistorisch Jaarboek* 47 (1996). Zwolle, 1997.

DE KÈRALIO 1798–99: Louis Félix de Kèralio. "Notice d'un manuscrit de la Bibliothèque nationale, cote no. 7392. . . ." *Notices et extraits des manuscrits de la Bibliothèque nationale et autres bibliothèques* 5 (1798–99): 167–77.

DE KESEL 1992: Lieve De Kesel. "Cambridge University Library Ms. Add. 4100: A Book of Hours Illuminated by the Master of the Prayer Books of circa 1500." In *Fifteenth-Century Flemish Manuscripts in Cambridge Collections; Transactions of the Cambridge Bibliographical Society* 10, part 2 (1992): 182–202.

DE LA MARE 1983: Albinia C. De la Mare. "Script and Manuscripts in Milan under the Sforzas." In *Milano nell'età di Ludovico il Moro: Atti del Convegno internazionale 28 febbraio–4 marzo 1983*, vol. 2: 397–408. Milan, 1983.

DE MAIO 1992: Romeo de Maio. *Il Codice Flora: Una pinacoteca miniata nella Biblioteca nazionale di Napoli*. Naples, 1992.

De MÉLY 1909: Fernand De Mély. "Le Bréviaire Grimani et les inscriptions de ses miniatures." *Revue de l'art ancien et moderne* 25 (1909): 81–92, 225–36.

DE MÉLY 1913: Fernand De Mély. *Les Primitifs et leurs signatures*. Paris, 1913.

DE RAADT 1895: J.-Th. De Raadt. "Communications" (Gérard Horebout est-il le principal collaborateur du Bréviaire Grimani?: Paroles prononcées après une conférence de M. Joseph Destrée). *Annales de la Société d'Archéologie de Bruxelles* 9 (1895): 149–60.

DE RAM 1861: Pierre François Xavier de Ram. *Joannis Molani in Academia lovaniensi s. theologiae doctoris et professoris Historiae Lovaniensium libri XIV*. 2 vols. Brussels, 1861.

DE RICCI 1935–40: Seymour De Ricci, with the assistance of W. J. Wilson. *Census of Medieval and Renaissance Manuscripts in the United States and Canada*. 3 vols. New York, 1935–40. Reprint, New York, 1961.

DE SCHREVEL 1902: A. de Schrevel. "Statuts de la gilde des libraires, imprimeurs, maîtres et maîtresses d'école à Bruges, 19 janvier 1612." *Annales de la Société d'Émulation de Bruges* 52 (1902): 35–302.

DE SCHRYVER 1957: Antoine de Schryver. "Lieven van Lathem, een onbekende grootmeester van de Vlaamse miniatuurschilderkunst." In *Handelingen van het XXIIe Vlaams Filologencongres*: 338–42. Ghent, 1957.

DE SCHRYVER 1969a: Antoine de Schryver. "Étude de l'enluminure." In *Gebetbuch Karls des Kühnen vel potius, Stundenbuch der Maria von Burgund: Codex Vindobonensis 1857 der Österreichischen Nationalbibliothek*: 21–173. 2 vols. Codices selecti phototypice impressi, 14. Graz, 1969.

DE SCHRYVER 1969b: Antoine de Schryver. "Nicolas Spierinc, calligraphe et enlumineur des ordonnances des États de l'Hôtel de Charles le Téméraire." *Miscellanea F. Lyna; Scriptorium* 23 (1969): 434–58.

DE SCHRYVER 1974: Antoine de Schryver. "Pour une meilleure orientation des recherches à propos du Maître de Girart de Roussillon." In *Rogier van der Weyden en zijn tijd: Internationaal Colloquium, 11–12 Juni, 1964*: 43–82. Brussels, 1974.

DE SCHRYVER 1979a: Antoine de Schryver. "L'oeuvre authentique de Philippe de Mazerolles, enlumineur de Charles le Téméraire." In *Cinq-centième Anniversaire de la bataille de Nancy, 1477: Actes du colloque organisé par l'Institut de Recherche régionale en Sciences sociales, humaines et économiques de l'Université de Nancy II (Nancy, 22–24 septembre 1977)*: 135–44. Nancy, 1979.

DE SCHRYVER 1979b: Antoine de Schryver. "Prix de l'enluminure et codicologie: Le Point comme unité de calcul de l'enlumineur dans «Le Songe du viel pellerin» et «Les Faictz et gestes d'Alexandre». (Paris B.N., Fr. 9200–9201 et Fr. 22547)." In *Miscellanea Codicologica F. Masai dicata MCMLXXIX*, edited by Pierre Cockshaw, Monique-Cécile Garand, and Pierre Jodogne, vol. 2: 469–79. Ghent, 1979.

DE SCHRYVER 1992: Antoine de Schryver. "The Louthe Master and the Marmion Case." In *Margaret of York, Simon Marmion and The Visions of Tondal*, edited by T. Kren: 171–80. Malibu, 1992.

DE SCHRYVER 1999: Antoine de Schryver. "Philippe de Mazerolles: Le Livre d'heures noir et les manuscrits d'Ordonnances militaires de Charles le Téméraire." *Revue de l'art* 126 (1999): 50–67.

DE SCHRYVER 2000: Antoine de Schryver. "Jacques de Brégilles, responsable de la librairie des ducs de Bourgogne sous Charles le Téméraire." In *Les Chroniques de Hainaut; ou, Les Ambitions d'un prince bourguignon*, edited by Christiane van den Bergen-Pantens: 83–89. Turnhout, 2000.

DE SCHRYVER, DYKMANS, AND RUYSSCHAERT 1989: Antoine de Schryver, Marc Dykmans, and José

Ruysschaert. *Le Pontifical de Ferry de Clugny, cardinal et évêque de Tournai.* Vatican City, 1989.

DE SCHRYVER AND MARIJNISSEN 1961: Antoine de Schryver and Roger Marijnissen. "Materiële Geschiedenis." *Bulletin van het Koninklijk Instituut voor het Kunstpatrimonium* 4 (1961): 11–23.

DE SMEDT (C.) ET AL. 1883: Charles de Smedt et al., eds. "Appendix ad catalogum cod[icum] hagiog[raphicorum] civit[atis] Namurcensis." *Analecta bollandiana* 2 (1883): 130–60, 279–354.

DE SMEDT (R.) 2000: R. de Smedt. *Les Chevaliers de l'Ordre de la Toison d'or au XVe siècle. Notices bio-bibliographiques.* 2nd ed. Frankfurt am Main, 2000.

DE SMET 1845: J.-J. De Smet. "Note sur une petite chronique manuscrit de l'abbaye de St-Adrien, à Grammont." *Bulletin de l'Académie Royale des Sciences et Belles-Lettres de Bruxelles* 12 (1845): 154–60.

DE VAIVRE 1999: B. de Vaivre. "Les Armoires et devises des Rolin." In *La Splendeur des Rolin: Un Mécénat privé à la cour de Bourgogne,* edited by Brigitte Maurice-Chabard: 37–65. Paris, 1999.

DE VOS 1994: Dirk de Vos. *Hans Memling: The Complete Works.* Ghent, 1994.

DE VOS 1999: Dirk de Vos. *Rogier van der Weyden: The Complete Works.* New York, 1999.

DE WINTER 1981: Patrick M. de Winter. "A Book of Hours of Queen Isabel la Católica." *Bulletin of the Cleveland Museum of Art* 67 (1981): 342–427.

DE WINTER 1982: Patrick de Winter. "The Illustrations of the 'Chroniques de Hainaut' in the 15th Century." *Scriptorium* 36 (1982): 139–40.

DE WINTER 1985: Patrick de Winter. *La Bibliothèque de Philippe le Hardi, duc de Bourgogne (1364–1404): Étude sur les manuscrits à peintures d'une collection princière à l'époque du "style gothique international."* Paris, 1985.

DEBAE 1995: Marguerite Debae. *La Bibliothèque de Marguerite d'Autriche. Essai de Reconstitution d'après l'Inventaire de 1523–1524.* Leuven, 1995.

DEBES 1988: Dietmar Debes, ed. *Zimelien. Bücherschätze der Universitätsbibliothek Leipzig.* Leipzig, 1988.

DEGERING AND STEENBOCK 1977: Hermann Degering and Frauke Steenbock, eds. *Albrecht Glockendon, Kalendar von 1526: Ms. germ. oct. 9 der Staatsbibliothek Preussischer Kulturbesitz Berlin.* 2 vols. Stuttgart, 1977.

DEHAISNES 1881: C. Dehaisnes, ed. *Inventaire sommaire des archives départementales antérieures à 1790, Nord: Archives civiles, série B, Chambre des Comptes de Lille.* Vol. 4. Lille, 1881.

DEHAISNES 1882: C. Dehaisnes. "Documents inédits concernant Jean Le Tavernier et Louis Liédet, miniaturistes des ducs de Bourgogne." *Bulletin des Commissions royales d'Art et d'Archéologie* 21 (1882): 20–39.

DEHAISNES 1886: C. Dehaisnes. *Histoire de l'art dans La Flandre, l'Artois, et le Hainaut avant le XVe siècle.* Lille, 1886.

DEHAISNES 1892: C. Dehaisnes. *Recherches sur le retable de Saint-Bertin et sur Simon Marmion.* Lille and Valenciennes, 1892.

DEKEYZER 2002: Brigitte Dekeyzer. "A Distant Echo of the Breviarum Grimani: On Two Separate Illuminations from the Kasteel van Gaasbeek (Lennik, Belgium)." In *"Als Ich Can": Liber Amicorum in Memory of Professor Dr. Maurits Smeyers*: 445–73. Leuven, 2002.

DEKEYZER ET AL. 1999: Brigitte Dekeyzer, Peter Vandenabeele, Luc Moens, and Bert Cardon. "The Mayer van den Bergh Breviary (Ghent-Bruges, Early 16th Century): Hands and Pigments." In *La Peinture dans les Pays-Bas au 16e siècle: Pratiques d'atelier, infrarouges et autres méthodes d'investigation,* edited by

Hélène Verougstraete and Roger Van Schoute: 303–16. Leuven, 1999.

DEKEYZER AND DE LAET 1997: Brigitte Dekeyzer and Peter De Laet. *Breviarium Mayer van den Bergh.* Antwerp, 1997. CD-Rom.

DELAISSÉ 1953: L. M. J. Delaissé. Review of K. Chesney, "Notes on Some Treatises of Devotion Intended for Margaret of York." *Scriptorium* 7 (1953): 174.

DELAISSÉ 1955a: L. M. J. Delaissé. "Les 'Chroniques de Hainaut' et l'atelier de Jean Wauquelin à Mons, dans l'histoire de la miniature flamande." *Miscellanea Erwin Panofsky; Musées royaux des Beaux-Arts, Bulletin,* no. 1–3 (1955): 21–55.

DELAISSÉ 1955b: L. M. J. Delaissé. "L'Exposition 'Flemish Art' à Londres." *Scriptorium* 9 (1955): 112–15.

DELAISSÉ 1956: L. M. J. Delaissé. *Le Manuscrit autographe de Thomas à Kempis et "L'Imitation de Jésus-Christ": Examen archéologique et édition diplomatique du Bruxellensis 5855–61.* 2 vols. Paris and Brussels, 1956.

DELAISSÉ 1958: L. M. J. Delaissé. *Miniatures médiévales de la Librairie de Bourgogne au Cabinet des manuscrits de la Bibliothèque royale de Belgique.* Commentary by L. M. J. Delaissé, forewords by H. Liebaers and F. Masai. Geneva, 1958.

DELAISSÉ 1968: L. M. J. Delaissé. *A Century of Dutch Manuscript Illumination.* Berkeley and Los Angeles, 1968.

DELAISSÉ 1972: L. M. J. Delaissé. "The Miniatures Added in the Low Countries to the Turin-Milan Hours and Their Political Significance." In *Kunsthistorische Forschungen: Otto Pächt seinem 70. Geburtstag*: 135–49. Salzburg, 1972.

DELAISSÉ, LIEBAERS, AND MASAI 1965: L. M. J. Delaissé, H. Liebaers, and F. Masai. *Medieval Miniatures from the Department of Manuscripts (Formerly the "Library of Burgundy") The Royal Library of Belgium.* New York, 1965.

DELAISSÉ, MARROW AND DE WIT 1977: L. M. J. Delaissé, James Marrow, and John de Wit. *Illuminated Manuscripts: The James A. de Rothschild Collection at Waddesdon Manor.* Fribourg, 1977.

DELEVOY 1994: Robert L. Delevoy. *Bruegel.* Geneva, 1994.

DELISLE 1868–81: Léopold Delisle. *Le Cabinet des manuscrits de la Bibliothèque impériale/nationale.* 3 vols. plus atlas. Histoire générale de Paris. Paris, 1868–81.

DELUMEAU AND LIGHTBOWN 1996: Jean Delumeau and Ronald Lightbown. *Histoire artistique de l'Europe: La Renaissance.* Edited by George Duby, Michel Laclotte, and Philippe Sénéchal. Paris, 1996.

DENIS 1793–1802: M. Denis. *Codices manuscripti theologici Bibliothecae Palatinae Vindobonensis latini aliarumque occidentis linguarum.* 2 vols. Vienna, 1793–1802.

DENIS, KNUTTEL, AND MEISCHKEL 1961: Valentine Denis, Gerard Knuttel and Rudolf Meischkel. "Flemish and Dutch Art." *Encyclopaedia of World Art,* vol. 5: cols. 402–49. London, 1961.

DENUCÉ 1927: J. Denucé. *Museaum Plantin-Moretus: Catalogue des manuscrits.* Antwerp, 1927.

DENUCÉ 1928: J. Denucé. "Frans Horenbout. Geograaf en Ingenieur van Koning Filips II." *Antwerpsche Achievenbild,* ser. 2, 3 (1928): 261–67.

DEROLEZ 1979: A. Derolez. *The Library of Raphael de Marcatellis, Abbot of Saint Bavon's, Ghent, 1437–1508.* Ghent, 1979.

DEROLEZ 1992: Albert Derolez. "A Renaissance Manuscript in the Hands of Margaret of York." In *Margaret of York, Simon Marmion and The Visions of Tondal,* edited by T. Kren: 99–102. Malibu, 1992.

DEROLEZ 2001: A. Derolez, ed. *Corpus Catalogorum Belgii: The Medieval Booklists of the Southern Low Countries.* Vol. 4, *Provinces of Brabant and Hainaut.* 2nd ed. Brussels, 2001.

DERVAL 1935: Jean de Derval. "Un Bibliophile Breton du XVe siècle." In *Les Trésors des bibliothèques de France,* 5: 157–62. Paris, 1935.

DESBARREAUX-BERNARD AND BAUDOUIN 1872: Desbarreaux-Bernard and A. Baudouin. "Inventaire des livres et du mobilier de Bernard de Béarn, bâtard de Commenge (1497)." *Mémoires de l'Académie des Sciences, Inscriptions et Belles-lettres de Toulouse,* ser. 7, 4 (1872): 82–131.

DESOBRY 1970: Jean Desobry. "L'Histoire des Croisades de Guillaume de Tyr et ses continuateurs. Ms. 483 de la Bibliothèque municipale d'Amiens (entre 1450 et 1473)." *Bulletin trimestriel de la Société des antiquaires de Picardie,* 1970: 220–35.

DESTRÉE 1891: Joseph Destrée. "Recherches sur les enlumineurs flamands." *Bulletin des Commissions royales d'Art et d'Archéologie* 30 (1891): 263–98.

DESTRÉE 1892: Joseph Destrée. "Recherches sur les enlumineurs flamands." *Bulletin des Commissions royales d'Art et d'Archéologie* 31 (1892): 185–231.

DESTRÉE 1894a: Joseph Destrée. "Les Miniatures du Grimani et leur attribution aux Horenbout." *Annales de la Societé d'Archéologie de Bruxelles* 8 (1894): 492–515.

DESTRÉE 1894b: Joseph Destrée. "Recherches sur les miniaturistes du Bréviaire Grimani." *Revue de l'art chrétien* 37, 1 (1894): 1–17.

DESTRÉE 1895: Joseph Destrée. *Les Heures de Notre Dame dites de Hennessy.* Brussels, 1895.

DESTRÉE 1898: Joseph Destrée. "Recherches sur les enlumineurs flamands." *Bulletin des Commissions royales d'Art et d'Archéologie* 37 (1898): 80–137.

DESTRÉE 1900: Joseph Destrée. "Grimani." *Revue de l'art chrétien* 43, no. 1 (1900): 5–8.

DESTRÉE 1914: Joseph Destrée. *Hugo van der Goes.* Brussels and Paris, 1914.

DESTRÉE 1923: Joseph Destrée. *Les Heures de Notre-Dame dites de Hennessy.* Brussels, 1923.

DESTRÉE AND BAUTIER 1924: Joseph Destrée and Pierre Bautier. *Les Heures dites Da Costa, manuscrit de l'école Ganto-Brugeoise premier tiers du XVIe siècle.* Brussels, 1924.

DESWARTE 1977: Sylvie Deswarte. *Les Enluminures de la "Leitura Nova," 1504–1552: Étude sur la culture artistique au Portugal au temps de l'humanisme.* Cultura medieval e moderna 8. Paris, 1977.

DETROIT 1960: *Flanders in the Fifteenth Century: Art and Civilization.* Exh. cat. Detroit Institute of Fine Arts, 1960.

DEUCHLER 1963: F. Deuchler. *Die Burgunderbeute: Inventar der Beutestücke aus den Schlachten von Grandson, Murten und Nancy, 1476/1477.* Bern, 1963.

DEUTSCH 1986: Guy N. Deutsch. *Iconographie de l'illustration de Flavius Josèphe au temps de Jean Fouquet.* Arbeiten zur Literatur und Geschichte des hellenistischen Judentums, 12. Leiden, 1986.

DEVILLERS 1880: L. Devillers. "Le Passé artistique de la ville de Mons." *Annales du Cercle archéologique de Mons* 16 (1880): 289–522.

DHANENS 1969: Elisabeth Dhanens. "Le Scriptorium des hiéronymites à Gand." *Miscellanea F. Lyna; Scriptorium* 23 (1969): 361–79.

DHANENS 1980: Elisabeth Dhanens. *Hubert and Jan van Eyck.* New York, 1980.

DHANENS 1987: Elisabeth Dhanens. "Een 'Maagschap van de H. Anna' in het derde kwart van de 15de eeuw." *Academiae Analecta: Mededelingen van de*

Koninklijke Academie voor Wetenschappen, Letteren en Schone Kunsten van België. Klasse der Schone Kunsten 48 (1987): 113–21.

DHANENS 1998: Elisabeth Dhanens. Hugo van der Goes. Antwerp, 1998.

DHANENS AND DIJKSTRA 1999: Elisabeth Dhanens and Jeltje Dijkstra. Rogier de le Pasture van der Weyden: Introduction à l'oeuvre, relecture des sources. Tournai, 1999.

DI STEFANO 1963: G. Di Stefano. "Tradizione esegetica e traduzioni di Valerio Massimo nel primo umanesimo francese." Studi francesi 21 (1963): 403–6.

DI STEFANO 1965: G. Di Stefano. "Ricerche su Nicolas de Gonesse, traduttore di Valerio Massimo." Studi francesi 26 (1965): 210–13.

DIBDIN 1817: T. F. Dibdin. The Bibliographical Decameron, or Ten Days Pleasant Discourse upon Illuminated Manuscripts and Subjects Connected with Early Engraving, Typography and Bibliography. 3 vols. London, 1817.

DICKENS 1955: A. G. Dickens. "The Tudor-Percy Emblem in Royal 18 D ii." Archaeological Journal 112 (1955): 95–99.

DICKINSON 1861–83: F. H. Dickinson, ed. Missale ad usum insignis et praeclarae ecclesiae Sarum. Burntisland. Scotland, 1861–83.

DIERICX 1814–15: C.-L. Diericx. Mémoires sur la ville de Gand. 2 vols. Ghent, 1814–15.

DIJON 1950: Manuscrits des ducs de Bourgogne de la Bibliothèque nationale. Dijon, Musée de Dijon, 1950.

DINZELBACHER 1992: Peter Dinzelbacher. "The Latin Visio Tnugdali and Its French Translations." In Margaret of York, Simon Marmion and The Visions of Tondal, edited by T. Kren: 111–17. Malibu, 1992.

DIRINGER 1963: David Diringer. "La miniatura fiamminga del XV e XVI secolo; il Breviario Grimani." In "Miniatura: Il Rinascimento," in Enciclopedia universale dell'arte, vol. 9: esp. cols. 390–91. Venice and Rome, 1963.

DOA 1996: The Dictionary of Art. Edited by Jane Turner. 34 vols. London and New York, 1996.

DOBSCHÜTZ 1899: Ernst von Dobschütz. Christusbilder: Untersuchungen zur christlichen Legende. Leipzig, 1899.

DODGSON 1910–11: Campbell Dodgson. "Drei Studien II: Eine Darstellung des Jagdunfalls der Maria von Burgund." Jahrbuch der Kunsthistorischen Sammlungen des Allerhöchsten Kaiserhauses 29 (1910–11): 4–7.

DOGAER 1963: Georges Dogaer. "Des anciens livres des statuts manuscrits de l'ordre de la Toison d'or." Publications du Centre européen d'études burgondomédianes 5 (1963): 65–70.

DOGAER 1969: Georges Dogaer. "La Travée brugeoise dans quelques manuscrits de l'école Ganto-Brugeoise." Miscellanea F. Lyna; Scriptorium 23 (1969): 338–41.

DOGAER 1971: Georges Dogaer. "Miniatures flamandes ajouté à une «Légende dorée» enluminée en France." Revue des archéologues et historiens d'art de Louvain 4 (1971) 155–63.

DOGAER 1972: Georges Dogaer. "Miniature flamande vers 1475–1485. À propos de trois ouvrages récents." Scriptorium 26 (1972): 97–104.

DOGAER 1975: Georges Dogaer. "Margareta van York, bibliofiele." Handelingen van de Koninklijke Kring voor Oudheidkunde, Letteren en Kunst van Mechelen 79 (1975): 99–111.

DOGAER 1977: Georges Dogaer. "Einfluss der Randverzierung der sog. Gent-Brügger Schule auf die deutsche Buchmalerei um 1500." In Bibliothek-Buch-Geschichte: Kurt Köster zum 65. Geburtstag, edited by Gunther Pflug et al.: 211–17. Frankfurt am Main, 1977.

DOGAER 1979: Georges Dogaer. "L'"École Ganto-Brugeoise,' une fausse appellation." Miscellanea codicologica F. Masai dicata. In MCMLXXIX, edited by Pierre Cockshaw, Monique-Cécile Garand, and Pierre Jodogne, vol 2: 511–18. Ghent, 1979.

DOGAER 1981: Georges Dogaer. "Enkele Dateringsproblemen van Handschriften uit de zgn. Gents-Brugse School." In Archivum artis Lovaniense: Bijdragen tot de Geschiedenis van de Kunst der Nederlanden opgedragen aan Prof. Em. Dr. J. K. Steppe, edited by M. Smeyers: 99–109. Leuven, 1981.

DOGAER 1987a: Georges Dogaer. Flemish Miniature Painting in the 15th and 16th Centuries. Amsterdam, 1987.

DOGAER 1987b: Georges Dogaer. Review of "Ouvrages publiés par la Section l'Oeuvre nationale pour la reproduction de manuscrits à miniatures de Belgique," by Eugène Rouir (Le Livre et l'estampe 31 [1985]: 43–45). Scriptorium 41 (1987): 173–74, no. 739.

DOKOUPIL 1959: Vladislav Dokoupil. Catalogus codicum manu scriptorum in Bibliotheca Universitatis Brunensis asservatorum 3. Prague, 1959.

DOMÍNGUEZ BORDONA 1933: J. Domínguez Bordona. Manuscritos con pinturas. 2 vols. Madrid, 1933.

DOMÍNGUEZ RODRÍGUEZ 1973: Ana Domínguez Rodríguez. "Iconografía de los Signos dell Zodíaco en seis Libros de Horas de la Biblioteca Nacional." Homenaje a Gómez Moreno, II; Revista de la Universidad Complutense 22, no. 85 (1973): 27–80.

DOMÍNGUEZ RODRÍGUEZ 1976: Ana Domínguez Rodríguez. "El paisaje en un Libro de Horas del siglo." Bellas Artes 53 (1976): 11–15.

DOMÍNGUEZ RODRÍGUEZ 1979: Ana Domínguez Rodríguez. Libros de horas del siglo XV en la Biblioteca Nacional. Publicaciones de la Fundación Universitaria Española, Bellas Artes 3. Madrid, 1979.

DOMÍNGUEZ RODRÍGUEZ AND DOCAMPO CAPILLA 1995: Ana Domínguez Rodríguez and F. Javier Docampo Capilla. Diminuto Devocionario del Museo Arqueológico Nacional: Estudio del Códice y sus miniaturas. [Madrid], 1995.

DOREZ 1903: Léon Dorez. "Les Manuscrits à peintures du Musée Britannique," review of Illuminated Manuscripts in the British Museum Series I–IV, by George Frederic Warner. Revue de bibliothèques 13 (1903): 159–60.

DOREZ 1908: Léon Dorez. Les Manuscrits à peintures de la bibliothèque de Lord Leicester à Holkham Hall, Norfolk: Choix de miniatures et de reliures. Paris, 1908.

DÖRNHÖFFER 1907: Friedrich Dörnhöffer. Hortulus animae: Cod. bibl. pal. vindob. 2706: The Garden of the Soul. Facsimile ed. 3 vols. Utrecht, 1907.

DOUTREPONT 1906: G. Doutrepont. Inventaire de la "librairie" de Philippe le Bon (1420). Brussels, 1906.

DOUTREPONT 1909: Georges Doutrepont. La Littérature française à la cour des ducs de Bourgogne: Philippe le Hardi, Jean sans Peur, Philippe le Bon, Charles le Téméraire. Paris, 1909. Reprint, Geneva, 1970.

DRAWING 1985: "Museum Acquisitions." Drawing 8, no. 2 (July–August 1985): 43.

DRIGSDAHL 1977: Erik Drigsdahl. "Flamske illuminerede handskrifter." In Humaniora, 1974–76: 38–41. Copenhagen, 1977.

DRIVER 1997: Martha W. Driver. "Mirrors of a Collective Past: Reconsidering Images of Medieval Women." In Women and the Book: Assessing the Visual Evidence, edited by Lesley Smith and Jane H. M. Taylor: 75–93. London, 1997.

DUBLIN 1955: A Loan Collection of Western Illuminated Manuscripts from the Library of Sir Chester Beatty Exhibited in the Library of Trinity College, Dublin. Exh. cat. edited by R. Dougan. Dublin, 1955.

DUBLIN 1964: Treasures from Scottish Libraries. Exh. cat. Dublin, Trinity College Library, 1964.

DUCLOS 1910: Adolphe Julien Duclos. Bruges: Histoire et souvenirs. Bruges, 1910.

DUMON 1973: Pierre Dumon. L'Alphabet gothique dit de Marie de Bourgogne: Reproduction du Codex Bruxellensis II 845. Brussels, 1973.

DUMOULIN AND PYCKE 1993: Chanoine Jean Dumoulin and Jacques Pycke. "Comptes de la paroisse Sainte-Marguerite de Tournai au quinzième siècle: Documents inédits relatifs à Roger de la Pasture, Robert Campin et d'autres artisans tournaisiens." In Les Grands Siècles de Tournai (12e–15e siècles): 279–320. Tournai and Louvain-la-Neuve, 1993.

DUNBAR 1974–80: Burton L. Dunbar. "The Landscape Paintings of Cornelis Massys." Musées royaux des Beaux-Arts de Belgique, Bulletin 23–29, nos. 1–3 (1974–80): 97–122.

DUNBAR 1979: Burton Dunbar. "A 'View of Brussels' by Cornelis Massys." Master Drawings 17 (1979): 392–401.

DUPEUX 1991: Cécile Dupeux. "La Lactation de Saint Bernard de Clairvaux: Genèse et évolution d'une image." In L'Image et la production du sacré: Actes du colloque de Strasbourg, 20–21 janvier 1988, edited by Françoise Dunand, Jean-Michel Spieser, and Jean Wirth: 165–93. Paris, 1991.

DURRIEU 1891: Paul Durrieu. "Alexandre Bening et les peintres du Bréviaire Grimani." Gazette des Beaux-Arts, ser. 3, 33, 5 (1891): 353–67; 6 (1891): 55–69.

DURRIEU 1892: Paul Durrieu. "Notes sur quelques manuscrits français ou d'origine française conservés dans les bibliothèques d'Allemagne." Bibliothèque de l'École des Chartes 53 (1892): 115–43.

DURRIEU 1893: Paul Durrieu. "Manuscrits d'Espagne remarquables principalement par leurs peintures et par la beauté de leur exécution, d'après des notes prises à Madrid, à l'Exposition Historique pour le quatrième centenaire de Colomb, et complétés à la Biblioteca Nacional et à la Bibliothèque de l'Escurial." Bibliothèque de l'École des Chartes 54 (1893): 251–326.

DURRIEU 1902: Paul Durrieu, ed. Heures de Turin. Quarante-cinq feuillets à peintures provenant des Très belles heures de Jean de France, duc de Berry. Paris, 1902.

DURRIEU 1903a: Paul Durrieu. "L'Histoire du bon Roi Alexandre. Manuscrit à miniatures de la Collection Dutuit." Revue de l'art ancien et moderne 13 (1903): 49–64, 103–14.

DURRIEU 1903b: Paul Durrieu. "Les Très Riches Heures du duc de Berry conservées à Chantilly, au Musée Condé, et le Bréviaire Grimani." Bibliothèque de l'École des Chartes 64, no. 3–4 (1903): 321–28.

DURRIEU 1910a: Paul Durrieu. "Découverte de deux importants manuscrits de la 'librairie' des Ducs de Bourgogne." Bibliothèque de l'École des Chartes 71 (1910): 58–71.

DURRIEU 1910b: Paul Durrieu. "L'enlumineur flamand Simon Bening." Académie des inscriptions et belles-lettres, Comptes rendus des séances de l'année 1910: 162–69. Reprinted as L'Enlumineur flamand Simon Bening, Paris, 1910.

DURRIEU 1910c: Paul Durrieu. "Les 'Préfigures' de la passion dans l'ornementation d'un manuscrit du XVe siècle." Revue de l'art chrétien 60 (1910): 67–69.

DURRIEU 1916: Paul Durrieu. "Livre de prières peint pour Charles le Téméraire par son enlumineur en titre Philippe de Mazerolles (Le maître de 'La Conquête de la Toison d'Or')." *Monuments et mémoires de la Fondation Eugène Piot* 22, no. 1 (1916): 71–130.

DURRIEU 1921a: Paul Durrieu. *La Miniature flamande au temps de la cour de Bourgogne (1415–1530)*. Paris and Brussels, 1921.

DURRIEU 1921b: Paul Durrieu. "Les 'Heures' de Jacques IV roi d'Écosse." *Gazette des Beaux–Arts*, ser. 5, 3 (1921): 197–212.

DURRIEU 1927: Paul Durrieu. *La Miniature flamande au temps de la cour Bourgogne, 1415–1530*. 2nd ed. Paris and Brussels, 1927.

DÜSSELDORF 1904: *Kunsthistorische Ausstellung Düsseldorf, 1904: Katalog*. Exh. cat. Düsseldorf, 1904.

DÜSSELDORF 1967: *Preussischer Kulturbesitz*. Exh. cat. by V. Elbern. Düsseldorf, Städtische Kunsthalle, 1967.

DUTSCHKE ET AL. 1989: C. W. Dutschke et al. *Guide to Medieval and Renaissance Manuscripts in the Huntington Library*. 2 vols. San Marino, 1989.

DUVERGER 1930: J. Duverger. "Gerard Horenbault 1465?–1540: Hofschilder van Margareta van Oostenrijk." *Maandblad voor Oude en Jonge Kunst*, no. 4 (April 1930): 81–90.

DUVERGER 1938: J. Duverger. "Nieuwe gegevens betreffende het Breviarium Grimani." *Jaarboek der Koninklijke Musea voor Schoone Kunsten van België* 1 (1938): 19–30.

DUVERGER 1969: J. Duverger. "Hofschilder Lieven Van Lathem (ca. 1430–1493)." *Jaarboek van het Koninklijk Museum voor Schone Kunsten, Antwerpen*, 1969: 97–104.

EBERLEIN 1983: J. K. Eberlein. "The Curtain in Raphael's Sistine *Madonna*." *Art Bulletin* 65 (1983): 61–66.

EDINBURGH 1963: *Treasures of Belgian Libraries*. Exh. cat. Edinburgh, National Library of Scotland, 1963.

EDINBURGH 1968: *British Portrait Miniatures*. Exh. cat. Edinburgh, The Arts Council Gallery, 1968.

EDMOND 1983: Mary Edmond. *Hilliard and Oliver: The Lives and Works of Two Great Miniaturists*. London, 1983.

EDWARDS AND PEARSALL: A. S. G. Edwards and D. Pearsall. "The Manuscripts of the Major English Poetic Texts." In *Book Production and Publishing in Britain, 1375–1475*, edited by J. Griffiths and D. Pearsall: 257–78. Cambridge, 1989.

EECKHOUT 1959: Paul Eeckhout. "'De Predella' belangrijke aanwinst van het Museum voor Schone Kunsten." *Stad Gent* 26 (1959): 203–5.

EECKHOUT 1962: Paul Eeckhout. "Lieven van Pottelsberghe." *Oost-Vlaanderen*, no. 4 (1962): 93, 104.

EICHBERGER 1992: Dagmar Eichberger. "Image Follows Text? *The Visions of Tondal* and Its Relationship to Depictions of Hell and Purgatory in Fifteenth-Century Illuminated Manuscripts." In *Margaret of York, Simon Marmion, and The Visions of Tondal*, edited by T. Kren: 129–40. Malibu, 1992.

EICHBERGER 1998: Dagmar Eichberger. "Devotional Objects in Book Format: Diptychs in the Collection of Margaret of Austria and Her Family." In *The Art of the Book: Its Place in Medieval Worship*, edited by Margaret M. Manion and Bernard J. Muir: 291–323. Exeter, 1998.

EICHBERGER 2002: Dagmar Eichberger. *Leben mit Kunst, Wirken durch Kunst: Sammelwesen und Hofkunst unter Margarete von Österreich, Regentin der Niederlande*. Turnhout, 2002.

EISLER 1961: Colin Tobias Eisler. *New England Museums. Les primitifs flamands, I: Corpus de la peinture des anciens Pays-Bas méridionaux au quinzième siècle, 4*. Brussels, 1961.

EISLER 1964: Colin Eisler. Review of *Les Primitifs flamands au Musée Metropolitan de New York* by Erik Larsen. *Art Bulletin* 46 (1964): 99–106.

EISLER 1969: Colin Eisler. "The Golden Christ of Cortona and the Man of Sorrows in Italy." *Art Bulletin* 51 (1969): 107–18, 233–47.

ELLIS AND WEALE 1883: F. S. Ellis and W. H. James Weale. *The Hours of Albert of Brandenburg. . . . With a Notice of the Miniature Painters and Illuminators of Bruges, 1457–1523*. London, 1883.

EMMERSON AND LEWIS 1985: Richard Kenneth Emmerson and Suzanne Lewis. "Census and Bibliography of Medieval Manuscripts Containing Apocalypse Illustrations, ca. 800–1500. II." *Traditio* 41 (1985): 367–409.

LES ENLUMINURES 1997: Les Enluminures (Firm), Paris. *Catalogue 6: Heures me fault de Nostre Dame: A Book of Hours, Too, Must Be Mine*. Paris, 1997.

ERLANDE-BRANDENBURG 1993: Alain Erlande-Brandenburg. *Quand les cathédrales étaient peintes*. Paris, 1993.

ESCH 1995: A. Esch. "Roman Customs Registers 1470–80: Items of Interest to Historians of Art and Material Culture." *Journal of the Warburg and Courtauld Institutes* 58 (1995): 72–87.

ESCH AND ESCH 1978: A. Esch and D. Esch. "Die Grabplatte Martins V. und andere Importstücke in den römischen Zollregistern der Frührenaissance." *Römisches Jahrbuch für Kunstgeschichte* 17 (1978): 211–17.

EUW AND PLOTZEK 1979–85: Anton von Euw and Joachim M. Plotzek. *Die Handschriften der Sammlung Ludwig*. 4 vols. Cologne, 1979–85.

EVANS 1986: Mark L. Evans. "A Newly Discovered Leaf of 'The Sforza Hours.'" *British Library Journal* 12 (1986): 21–27.

EVANS 1991: Mark. L. Evans. "Die Miniaturen des Münchener Medici-Gebetbuchs CLM 23639 und verwandte Handschriften." In *Das Gebetbuch Lorenzos de' Medici 1485 : Handschrift Clm 23639 der Bayerischen Staatsbibliothek, München*: 169–275. Frankfurt am Main, 1991.

EVANS 1992: Mark Evans. *The Sforza Hours*. London, 1992.

EVANS AND BRINKMANN 1995: Mark L. Evans and Bodo Brinkmann, with a contribution by Hubert Herkommer. *The Sforza Hours, Add. MS. 34294 of the British Library, London*. Lucerne, 1995.

EVANSTON 2001: *Manuscript Illumination in the Modern Age: Recovery and Reconstruction*. Catalogue edited by Sandra Hindman and Nina Rowe. Evanston, Ill., 2001.

EVEN 1866–69: E. van Even. "Monographie de l'ancienne école de peinture de Louvain." *Messager des sciences historiques* 1866–69.

FAIETTI AND NESSELRATH 1995: M. Faietti and A. Nesselrath. "'Bizar più che reverso di medaglia': Un Codex avec grotesques, monstres et ornéments du jeune Amico Aspertini." *Revue de l'art* 107 (1995): 44–88.

FALKE 1912: Otto von Falke. *Die Kunstsammlung Eugen Gutmann*. Berlin, 1912.

FALKENBURG 1994: Reindert Falkenburg. *The Fruit of Devotion: Mysticism and the Imagery of Love in Flemish Paintings of the Virgin and Child, 1450-1550*. Oculi, vol. 5. Amsterdam and Philadelphia, 1994.

FARQUHAR 1976: James Douglas Farquhar. *Creation and Imitation: The Work of a Fifteenth-Century Manuscript Illuminator*. Fort Lauderdale, Fla., 1976.

FARQUHAR 1980: James Douglas Farquhar. "Identity in an Anonymous Age: Bruges Manuscript Illuminators and Their Signs." *Viator* 11 (1980): 371–83.

FARR 1987: Dennis Farr, ed. *100 Masterpieces: Bernardo Daddi to Ben Nicholson: European Paintings and Drawings from the 14th to 20th Century*. London, Courtauld Institute Galleries, 1987.

FAßBENDER 1994: Birgit Faßbender. *Gotische Tanzdarstellungen*. Europäische Hochschulschriften, ser. 28, vol. 192. Frankfurt am Main, 1994.

FAVRESSE 1946: F. Favresse. "Les premiers statuts connus des métiers bruxellois du duc et de la ville." *Bulletin de la Commission royale d'histoire* 3 (1946): 76–79.

FAYE AND BOND 1962: C. U. Faye and W. H. Bond. *Supplement to the Census of Medieval and Renaissance Manuscripts in the United States and Canada*. New York, 1962.

FERRANDIS 1943: José Ferrandis. *Datos documentales inéditos para la historia del arte español, III: Inventarios reales (Juan II a Juana la Loca)*. Madrid, 1943.

FEYS AND DE SCHREVEL 1896: Feys and De Schrevel. "Fondation de Guillaume de Montbléru en la chapelle de S. Luc et S. Eloi dite chapelle des peintres à Bruges." *Annales de la Société d'Émulation de Bruges pour l'étude de l'histoire et des antiquités de la Flandre*, ser. 5, 9, no. 46 (1896): 117–41.

FIERENS-GEVAERT 1908: Hippolyte Fierens-Gevaert. "La Flandre à Venise: Le Bréviaire Grimani à la Bibliothèque de S. Marc: Le Génie de nos miniaturistes, Les propriétaires successifs du manuscrit, Les enlumineurs du Bréviaire, Le libre échange artistique de le Flandre et de l'Italie. . . ." *Journal de Bruxelles*, November 9, 1908: 1–2, cols. 1–6 and 1–4.

FIFIELD 1972: M. Fifield. "The French Manuscripts of *La Forteresse de la Foy*." *Manuscripta* 16 (1972): 98–111.

FIGANIÈRE 1853: Frederico Francisco de la Figanière. *Catalogo dos manuscriptos portuguezes existentes no Museu britannico*. Lisbon, 1853.

FILEDT KOK 1996: Jan Piet Filedt Kok. "Over de Calvarieberg: Albrecht Dürer in Leiden, omstreeks 1520." *Bulletin van het Rijksmuseum* 44, no. 4 (1996): 335–59.

FINOT 1895: J. Finot, ed. *Inventaire sommaire des archives départementales antérieures à 1790, Nord: Archives civiles, série B, Chambre des Comptes de Lille*. Vol. 8. Lille, 1895.

FINSTEN 1981: J. Finsten. *Isaac Oliver, Art at the Courts of Elizabeth I and James I*. 2 vols. New York, 1981.

FITZGERALD 1992: Wilma Fitzgerald. *Ocelli Nominum: Names and Shelf Marks of Famous/Familiar Manuscripts*. Subsidia Mediaevalia 19. Toronto, 1992.

FLEMING 1969: John Vincent Fleming. *The Roman de la Rose: A Study in Allegory and Iconography*. Princeton, 1969.

FLETCHER 1981: John Fletcher. "A Portrait of William Carey and Lord Hunsdon's Long Gallery." *Burlington Magazine* 123 (1981): 304.

FLORENCE 1980: *L'Époque de Lucas de Leyde et Pierre Bruegel*. Exh. cat. Florence, Istituto Universitario Olandese di Storia dell'Arte, 1980.

FOISTER 1983: Susan Foister. Review of exhibition catalogue, *Artists of the Tudor Court: The Portrait Miniature Rediscovered*. *Burlington Magazine* 125 (1983): 635–36.

FOLDA 1973: J. Folda. "Manuscripts of the History of Outremer by William of Tyre: A Handlist." *Scriptorium* 27 (1973): 90–95.

FOLIE 1963: Jacqueline Folie. "Les Oeuvres authentifiées des primitifs flamands." *Institut royal du Patrimoine Artistique, Bulletin* 6 (1963): 183–256.

FOLSOM 1990: Rose Folsom. *The Calligraphers' Dictionary*. London, 1990.

FONCKE 1938: Elza Foncke. "Aantekeningen betreffende Hieronymus van Busleyden." *Gentsche Bijdragen tot de Kunstgeschiedenis* 5 (1938): 179–220.

FOOT 1980: Miriam M. Foot. "Monasteries and Dragons. A Selection of Dutch and Flemish Bindings of the Late Fifteenth and Early Sixteenth Centuries in the British Library, Cambridge University Library and the Bodleian Library, Oxford." In *Hellinga Festschrift. Forty-three Studies in Bibliography Presented to Prof. Dr. Wytze Hellinga on the Occasion of His Retirement from the Chair of Neophilology in the University of Amsterdam at the End of the Year 1978*: 193–204. Amsterdam, 1980.

FÖRSTER 1867: Ernst Förster, ed. "Der Codex Grimani in der St. Marcus-Bibliothek zu Venedig." In *Denkmale deutscher Baukunst, Bildnerei und Malerei von Einführung des Christenthums bis auf die neueste Zeit*, vol. 11. Leipzig, 1867.

FOSKETT 1972: Daphne Foskett. *A Dictionary of British Miniature Painters*. London, 1972.

FOSKETT 1984: Daphne Foskett. Review *The English Renaissance Miniature*. *Royal Society of Arts Journal* 132 (April 1984): 343–44.

FOSSIER 1982: François Fossier. *Le Palais Farnèse*. Vol. 3, part 2, *La Bibliothèque Farnèse: Étude des manuscrits latins et en langue vernaculaire*. Rome, 1982.

FOUREZ 1948: L. Fourez. "Jean Carondelet et Tournai." *Tournai, Reconstruction et Avenir* 31–32 (1948): 13–14.

FOX 1973: J. Fox. *Charles d'Orléans: Choix de Poésies*. Exeter, 1973.

FRANCASTEL 1995: Pierre Francastel. *Bruegel*. Paris, 1995.

FRANKE 1997a: B. Franke. "Ritter und Heroen der burgundischen Antike." *Städel Jahrbuch*, n.s., 16 (1997): 113–46.

FRANKE 1997b: B. Franke, ed. *Die Kunst der Burgundischen Niederlande*. Berlin, 1997.

FRANZ 1969: Heinrich Gerard Franz. *Niederländische Landschaftsmalerei im Zeitalter des Manierismus*. Graz, 1969.

FRIEDLÄNDER 1903: Max J. Friedländer. "Die Brügger Leihausstellung von 1902." *Repertorium für Kunstwissenschaft* 26 (1903): 66–91, 147–75.

FRIEDLÄNDER 1916: Max J. Friedländer. *Von Eyck bis Bruegel: Studien zur Geschichte der niederländischen Malerei*. Berlin, 1916.

FRIEDLÄNDER 1923a: Max J. Friedländer. "Einige Tafelbilder Simon Marmions." *Jahrbuch für Kunstwissenschaft* 1 (1923): 167–70.

FRIEDLÄNDER 1923b: Max J. Friedländer. *Die Lübecker Bibel*. Munich, 1923.

FRIEDLÄNDER 1924–37: Max J. Friedländer. *Die altniederländische Malerei*. 14 vols. Berlin and Leiden, 1924–37.

FRIEDLÄNDER 1935: Max J. Friedländer. "Eine Zeichnung von Hugo Van Der Goes." *Pantheon* 35, no. 3 (1935): 99–104.

FRIEDLÄNDER 1967: Max J. Friedländer. "Ein vlämischer Portraitmaler in England." *Gentsche Bijdragen tot de Kunstgeschiedenis* 4 (1937): 5–18.

FRIEDLÄNDER 1967–76: Max J. Friedländer. *Early Netherlandish Painting*. Trans. H. Norden. Comments and notes by N. Veronée-Verhaegen. 14 vols. New York, 1967–76.

FRIMMEL 1888: Theodor Frimmel. *Der Anonimo Morelliano (Marcanton Michiel's Notizia d'opere del disegno)*. Quellenschriften für Kunstgeschichte und Kunsttechnik des Mittelalters und der Neuzeit. Vienna, 1888.

GACHARD 1845: L. P. Gachard. *Notice des Archives de M. le duc de Caraman, précédée de recherches historiques sur les princes de Chimay et les comtes de Beaumont*. Brussels, 1845.

GAIER 1962: Claude Gaier. "À propos d'armes et d'armures de transition (1495–1500): Le Témoignage pictural du 'Siège de Jérusalem' du Musée de Gand." *Armi antichi: Bollettino dell'Accademia di S. Marciano, Torino* 1 (1962): 93–109.

GAIL 1968: Marzieh Gail. *Life in the Renaissance*. New York, 1968.

GALLET-GUERNE 1974: D. Gallet-Guerne. *Vasque de Lucène et la "Cyropédie" à la cour de Bourgogne (1470)*. Geneva, 1974.

GASPAR 1932: Camille Gaspar. *Le Bréviaire du Musée Mayer van den Bergh à Anvers: Étude du texte et des miniatures*. 2 vols. Brussels, 1932.

GASPAR 1943: Camille Gaspar. *Le Calendrier des Heures de Hennessy*. 2 vols. Brussels, 1943.

GASPAR 1947: Camille Gaspar. "Le Livre d'Heures de Charles le Téméraire." *Carnets du Séminaire des Arts: Les Arts plastiques* (Brussels) 1 (1947): 113–24.

GASPAR AND LYNA 1944: Camille Gaspar and Frédéric Lyna. *Philippe le Bon et ses beaux livres*. Brussels, 1944.

GASPAR AND LYNA 1984–89: Camille Gaspar and Frédéric Lyna. *Les principaux manuscrits à peinture de la Bibliothèque royale de Belgique*. 3 vols.: vol. 1 (2 parts, by Gaspar and Lyna), reprint of 1937 ed., Brussels, 1984; vol. 2 (by Gaspar and Lyna), reprint of 1945 ed., Brussels, 1987; vol. 3 (2 parts, by Lyna, posthumously edited by Christine van den Bergen-Pantens), Brussels, 1989.

GEIRNAERT 1992: Noel Geirnaert. "Classical Texts in Bruges around 1473: Cooperation of Italian Scribes, Bruges Parchment–Rulers, Illuminators and Book-Binders for Johannes Crabbe." In *Fifteenth-Century Flemish Manuscripts in Cambridge Collections: Transactions of the Cambridge Bibliographical Society* 10, no. 2 (1992): 173–81.

GEITH 1996: Karl-Ernst Geith. "Un Texte méconnu, un texte reconnu: La Traduction française de la *Vita Jesu Christi* de Michael de Massa." In *Le Moyen Âge dans la modernité: Mélanges offerts à Roger Dragonetti*, edited by Jean R. Scheidegger with Sabine Girardet and Eric Hicks: 237–49. Nouvelle Bibliothèque du Moyen Âge, 39. Paris, 1996.

GELLMAN 1970: L. B. Gellman. "Petrus Christus." Ph.D. diss., Johns Hopkins University, Baltimore, 1970.

GENAILLE 1980: Robert Genaille. "La Pie sur le gibet." In *Relations artistiques entre les Pays-Bas et l'Italie à la Renaissance: Études dédiées à Suzanne Sulzberger*: 143–52. Études d'histoire de l'art, 4. Brussels, 1980.

GENAILLE 1988: Robert Genaille. "Le Paysage dans la peinture des anciens Pays-Bas au temps de Bruegel." *Jaarboek van het Koninklijk Museum voor Schone Kunsten Antwerpen*, 1988: 137–87.

GÉNARD 1875: P. Génard. "Inventaire des manuscrits de Philippe de Hornes (1488)." *Le Bibliophile belge* 9 (1875): 21–30.

GENET 1977: J.-P. Genet, ed. *Four English Political Tracts of the Later Middle Ages*. Camden Society, ser. 4, 18. London, 1977.

GENEVA 1976: *L'Enluminure de Charlemagne à François Ier*. Exh. cat. by Bernard Gagnebin et al. Geneva, Musée Rath, 1976.

GERLACH 1969: Pater Gerlach. "De Nassauers van Breda en Jeroen Bosch's 'De Tuin der Lusten.'" *Brabantia* 18 (1969): 155–60.

GERLACH 1971: Pater Gerlach. "Hendrik III van Nassau, heer van Breda, veldheer, diplomaat en mecenas." *Brabantia* 20 (1971): 45–94.

GESCHÉ AND SCOLAS 1999: Adolphe Gesché and Paul Scolas, eds. *Dieu à l'épreuve de notre cri*. Paris, 1999.

GHENT 1913: *L'Art ancien dans les Flandres (Région de l'Escaut)*. Exh. cat. Ghent, 1913.

GHENT 1957: *Justus van Gent, Berruguete en het Hof van Urbino*. Exh. cat. Ghent, Museum voor Schone Kunsten, 1957.

GHENT 1975: *Gent, duizend jaar kunst en cultuur*. Exh. cat. compiled by Antoine de Schryver et al. 3 vols. Ghent, Museum voor Schone Kunsten, 1975.

GIBAUD 1982: Henri Gibaud, *Un Inédit d'Érasme: La Première Version du Nouveau Testament copiée par Pierre Meghen, 1506–1509: Contribution à l'établissement d'une édition critique du Novum Testamentum*. Angers, 1982.

GIBSON 1969: Walter S. Gibson. "The Paintings of Cornelis Engebrechtsz." Ph.D. diss., Harvard University, Cambridge, Mass., 1969.

GIBSON 1973: Walter S. Gibson. *Hieronymus Bosch*. London, 1973.

GIBSON 1977: Walter S. Gibson. *Bruegel*. London, 1977.

GIBSON 1989: Walter S. Gibson. *"Mirror of the Earth" The World Landscape in Sixteenth-Century Flemish Painting*. Princeton, 1989.

GIBSON 1991: Walter S. Gibson. "Bruegel and the Peasants: A Problem of Interpretation." In *Pieter Bruegel the Elder: Two Studies*: 11–52. The Franklin D. Murphy Lectures 11. Lawrence, Kans., 1991.

GIL 1997: Marc Gil. "Du manuscrit enluminé: Le Maître de la *Vita Christi* de Cambrai, successeur du Maître des Privilèges de Gand." *Bulletin du bibliophile*, 1997: 7–32.

GIL 1998a: Marc Gil. "Un Livre d'heures inédit de l'atelier de Simon Marmion à Valenciennes." *Revue de l'art* 121 (1998): 43–48.

GIL 1998b: Marc Gil. "Le Mécénat littéraire de Jean de Créquy, conseiller et chambellan de Philippe le Bon: Exemple singulier de création et de diffusion d'oeuvres nouvelles à la cour de Bourgogne." *Eulalie* 1 (1998): 69–93.

GIL 1999: Marc Gil. "Du Maître du Mansel au Maître de Rambures: Le Milieu des peintres et des enlumineurs de Picardie, ca. 1440–1480." 4 vols. Doctoral thesis, Université de la Sorbonne-Paris, Paris IV, 1999.

GILISSEN 1969: L. Gilissen. "Un Élément codicologique trop peu exploité: La Réglure." *Miscellanea F. Lyna; Scriptorium* 23 (1969): 150–62.

GILISSEN 1977: Léon Gilissen. "La Miniature en terre wallonne au temps des ducs de Bourgogne." *La Wallonie: Le Pays et les hommes* 1 (1977): 455–62.

GILLIODTS-VAN SEVEREN 1897: L. Gilliodts-van Severen. *L'Oeuvre de Jean Brito, prototypographie brugeois. . . .* Annales de la Société d'Émulation de Bruges, 47. Bruges, 1897.

GILLIODTS-VAN SEVEREN 1899: L. Gilliodts-van Severen. *Inventaire diplomatique des archives de l'ancienne École Bogaerde à Bruges*. 2 vols. Bruges, 1899.

GILLIODTS-VAN SEVEREN 1905: L. Gilliodts-van Severen. *Cartulaire de l'ancienne Estaple de Bruges*. Bruges, 1905.

GODENNE AND MAES 1951: W. Godenne and L. T. Maes. *Iconographie des Membres du Grand Conseil de Malines*. Brussels, [1951].

GOEHRING 2000: Margaret L. Goehring. "Landscape in Franco-Flemish Manuscript Illumination of the Late Fifteenth- and Early Sixteenth-Centuries." Ph.D. diss., Case Western Reserve University, Cleveland, 2000.

GOETHALS 1849: Félix-Victor Goethals. *Dictionnaire généalogique et héraldique des familles nobles du royaume de Belgique*. Brussels, 1849.

GOFF 1973: Frederick R. Goff, ed. *Incunabula in American Libraries*. Millwood, N.Y., 1973.

GÓIS 1566: Damião de Góis. *Crónica do Felicissimo Rei D. Manuel*. 4 vols. Lisbon, 1566. Reprint. Coimbra, 1955.

GOLDSCHMIDT 1901: Adolph Goldschmidt. "Rode und Notke, zwei Lübecker Maler des 15. Jahrhunderts." *Zeitschrift für bildende Kunst*, n.s., 12 (1901): 31–39, 55–60.

GOOVAERTS 1896: A. Goovaerts. "Les Ordonnances données en 1480, à Tournai, aux métiers des peintres et des verriers." *Compte rendu des séances de la Commission royale d'histoire*, ser. 5, 4 (1995): 97–182.

GÖPFERT 1827–34: Georg Andreas Göpfert. *Handschriftlicher Katalog der Schönborn'schen Schlossbibliothek, zusammengestellt vom Schlossgeistlichen*. 1827–34.

GORISSEN 1973: Friedrich Gorissen. *Das Stundenbuch der Katharina von Kleve: Analyse und Kommentar*. Berlin, 1973.

GOTTLIEB (C.) 1971: C. Gottlieb. "The Living Host." *Konsthistorisk tidskrift* 40 (May 1971): 30-46.

GOTTLIEB (TH.) 1900: Th. Gottlieb. *Büchersammlung Kaiser Maximilians I.* (Die Ambraser Handschriften): Beitrag zur Geschichte der Wiener Hofbibliothek 1. Leipzig, 1900.

GRANGE 1897: A. de La Grange. *Choix des testaments tournaisiens antérieurs au XVIe siècle*. Tournai, 1897.

GRANGE AND CLOQUET 1887–88: A. de La Grange and L. Cloquet. *Études sur l'art à Tournai et sur les anciens artistes de cette ville*. 2 vols. Mémoires de la Société historique et littéraire de Tournai, 20–21. Tournai, 1887–88.

GREENSLADE 1963: S. L. Greenslade, ed. *The West from the Reformation to the Present Day*. Cambridge History of the Bible 3. Cambridge, 1963.

GRIMM 1875: Herman Grimm. "Zur Entstehung des Breviarium Grimani." *Jahrbuch der Königlich preuszischen Kunstsammlungen, Berlin* 1 (1875): 242–44.

GRIMME AND LUDWIG 1968: Ernst Günther Grimme and Peter Ludwig, eds. "Grosse Kunst aus Tausend Jahren: Kirchenschätze aus dem Bistum Aachen." *Aachener Kunstblätter* 36 (1968): 1–335.

GROHN 1971: Hans Werner Grohn. *L'opera pittorica completa di Holbein il Giovane*. Introduction by Roberto Salvini. Milan, 1971.

GROSS 1990: Angelika Gross. *"La Folie": Wahnsinn und Narrheit im spätmittelalterlichen Text und Bild*. Heidelberg, 1990.

GROSSHANS 1991: Rainald Grosshans. "Simon Marmion, das Retabel von Saint-Bertin zu Saint Omer: Zur Rekonstruktion und Entstehungsgeschichte des Altares." *Jahrbuch der Berliner Museen* 33 (1991): 63–98.

GROSSHANS 1992: Rainald Grosshans. "Simon Marmion and the Saint Bertin Altarpiece: Notes on the Genesis of the Painting." In *Margaret of York, Simon Marmion and The Visions of Tondal*, edited by T. Kren: 233–42. Malibu, 1992.

GROSSHANS 1996: Rainald Grosshans, ed. *Gemäldegalerie Berlin: Gesamtverzeichnis*. Berlin: Staatliche Museen zu Berlin, Preussischer Kulturbesitz, 1996.

GROSSMANN 1966: F. Grossmann. *Bruegel: The Paintings*. 2nd ed. London, 1966.

GROTE 1973: Andreas Grote, ed. *Brevarium Grimani. Faksimileausgabe der Miniaturen und Kommentar*. Berlin, 1973.

GRUBER 1993: Alain Gruber, ed. *L'Art décoratif en Europe*. vol. 1: *Renaissance et Maniérisme*. Paris, 1993.

GUÉNÉE 1980: B. Guénée. *Histoire et culture historique dans l'Occident médiéval*. Paris, 1980.

GUERLIN 1894: Robert Guerlin. "Notes sur un livre d'heures du XVIe siècle, dit 'Manuscrit des Carpentin.'" *Le Manuscrit: Revue spéciale de documents-manuscrits* 1 (1894): 35–41.

GUERRIERI 1974: Guerriera Guerrieri. *La Biblioteca nazionale «Vittorio Emanuele III» di Napoli*. Milan and Naples, 1974.

GUICCIARDINI 1567: Lodovico Guicciardini. *Descrittione di . . . tutti I Paesi Bassi. . . .* Antwerp, 1567.

GUICCIARDINI 1588: Lodovico Guicciardini. *Descrittione di . . . tutti i Paesi Bassi. . . .* 2nd ed. Antwerp, 1588.

GUNN AND LINDLEY 1991: S. J. Gunn and P. G. Lindley, eds. *Cardinal Wolsey: Church, State and Art*. Cambridge, 1991.

GÜNTHER 1995: Jörn Günther. *Mittelalterliche Handschriften und Miniaturen*. Hamburg, 1995.

GUSMÃO [1954]: Adriano de Gusmão. "Século XVI Iluminura Manuelina." In João Barreira, *Arte Portuguesa: Pintura*, vol. 2: 195–221. Lisbon, [1954?].

GWYN 1990: P. Gwyn. *The King's Cardinal. The Rise and Fall of Thomas Wolsey*. London, 1990.

HAGEN AND HAGEN 1990: Rose-Marie Hagen and Rainer Hagen. "In friedlicher Landschaft das Gerät des ärgsten Todes." *Art: Das Kunstmagazin*, no. 10 (October 1990): 112–16, 119.

THE HAGUE 1980: *Schatten van de Koninklijke Bibliotheek*. Exh. cat. The Hague, Het Rijksmuseum Meermanno-Westreenianum / Museum van het Boek, 1980.

THE HAGUE 1984: *Boeken van en rond Willem van Oranje*. Exh. cat. The Hague, Koninklijke Bibliotheek, 1984.

THE HAGUE 2002: *Praal, ernst, en emotie: De wereld van het Franse middeleeuwse handschrift*. Exh. cat. by Anne S. Korteweg et al. The Hague, Museum Meermanno-Westreenianum, 2002. Eng. ed.: *Splendour, Gravity, and Emotion: French Medieval Manuscripts in Dutch Collections*. The Hague, 2002.

HAM 1932: Edward Billings Ham. "Le Manuscrit de Gillion de Trazegnies à Chatsworth." *Romania* 58 (1932): 66–77.

HAMBURG 1969: *Meister Francke und die Kunst um 1400*. Exh. cat. edited by Thomas Puttfarken with Heilwig von Bruchhausen. Hamburg, Kunsthalle, 1969.

HAMBURG 1997: Jeffrey Hamburger. *Nuns as Artists: The Visual Culture of a Medieval Convent*. Berkeley, 1997.

HAMMER-TUGENDHAT 1981: Daniela Hammer-Tugendhat. *Hieronymus Bosch: Eine historische Interpretation seiner Gestaltungsprinzipien*. Munich, 1981.

HAND 1992: John Oliver Hand. "*Salve sancta facies*: Some Thoughts on the Iconography of the *Head of Christ* by Petrus Christus." *Metropolitan Museum Journal* 27 (1992): 7–18.

HANSEN 1984: Wilhelm Hansen. *Kalenderminiaturen der Stundenbücher: Mittelalterliches Leben im Jahreslauf*. Munich, 1984.

HANSEN 1985: Wilhelm Hansen. "Zu den Stundenbüchern des Simon Bening aus Brügge." *Die Kunst* 97 (January 1985): 24–29.

HARBISON 1985: Craig Harbison. "Visions and Meditations in Early Flemish Painting." *Simiolus* 15, no. 2 (1985): 87–117.

HARBISON 1995: Craig Harbison. "Fact, Symbol, Ideal: Roles for Realism in Early Netherlandish Painting." In *Petrus Christus in Renaissance Bruges, An Interdisciplinary Approach*, edited by Maryan W. Ainsworth: 21-34. New York, 1995.

HARDIE 1982: S. M. Hardie. "Cardinal Wolsey's Patronage of the Arts." Master's thesis, University of Bristol, 1982.

HARPER 1991: John Harper. *The Forms and Orders of Western Liturgy From the Tenth to the Eighteenth Century: A Historical Introduction and Guide for Students and Musicians*. Oxford, 1991.

HARSGOR 1972: Mikhaël Harsgor. "Recherches sur le personnel du conseil du roi sous Charles VIII et Louis XII." Doctoral thesis, Université de Sorbonne-Paris, Paris IV, 1972.

HART COLLECTION 1964: *Illustrated Manuscripts and Early Printed Books from the Hart Collection*. Blackburn, 1964.

HARTHAN 1977: John Harthan. *Books of Hours and Their Owners*. London, 1977.

HARTHAN 1983: John Harthan. *An Introduction to Illuminated Manuscripts*. London, 1983.

HARZEN 1858: E. Harzen. "Gerhard Horebout von Gent, Illuminist des Breviars Grimani in der St. Markus-Bibliothek in Venedig." *Archiv für die zeichnenden Künste* 4 (1858): 3–20.

HASENOHR 1989: Geneviève Hasenohr. "L'Essor des bibliothèques privées aux XIVe et XVe siècles." In *Histoire des bibliothèques françaises, I: Les Bibliothèques médiévales du VIe siècle à 1530*, edited by A. Vernet: 215–63. Paris, 1989.

HASENOHR 1990: Geneviève Hasenohr. "Vers une nouvelle esthétique." In *Mise en page et mise en texte du livre manuscrit*, edited by H. J. Martin and J. Vézin: 349–52. Paris, 1990.

HASENOHR AND ZINK 1992: Geneviève Hasenohr and Michel Zink, eds. *Dictionnaire des lettres françaises. Le Moyen Âge*. Paris, 1992.

HASSALL 1970: W. O. Hassall, ed. *The Holkham Library: Illuminations*. Oxford, 1970.

HATCHARD 1905: *Catalogue of the Library of Arundel Castle*. London, 1905.

HAUSSHERR 1977: Reiner Haussherr. "Eine verspätete Apocalypsen-Handschrift und ihre Vorlage." In *Studies in Late Medieval and Renaissance Painting in Honor of Millard Meiss*, edited by Irving Lavin and John Plummer, vol. 1: 219–40. New York, 1977.

HÉDOUIN 1847: Pierre Hédouin. "Memling: Étude sur la vie et les ouvrages de ce peintre, suivie du catalogue de ses tableaux." *Annales archéologiques* 6 (1847): 256–78.

HEIDEN 1998: Rüdiger an der Heiden. *Die Alte Pinakothek: Sammlungsgeschichte, Bau und Bilder*. Munich, 1998.

HEITMANN 1981 K. Heitmann. "Die Antike-Rezeption am burgundischen Hof: Olivier de la Marche und der Heroenkult Karl des Kühnen." In *Die Rezeption der Antike*, edited by A. Buck: 97–118. Hamburg, 1981.

HELD 1933: Julius Held. "Notizen zu einem niederländischen Skizzenbuch in Berlin." *Oud Holland* (1933): 273–88.

HELLINGA 1981: Lotte Hellinga. "Caxton and the Bibliophiles." In *Eleventh International Congress of Bibliophiles, Brussels: Communications*, edited by P. Culot and E. Rouir: 11–38. Brussels, 1981.

HELLINGA 1991: Lotte Hellinga. "Illustration of Fifteenth-Century Books: A Bird's-Eye View of Changes and Techniques." *Bulletin du bibliophile*, no. 1 (1991): 42–61.

HÉNAULT 1907: Maurice Hénault. "Les Marmion (Jehan, Simon, Mille et Colinet): Peintres amiénois du XVe siècle." *Revue archéologique*, ser. 4, 9 (1907): 119–40, 282–304, 410–24; 10 (1907): 108–24.

HENDRIX 1988: Lee Hendrix. "An Introduction to Hoefnagel and Bocskay's *Model Book of Calligraphy* in the J. Paul Getty Museum." In *Prag um 1600: Beiträge zur Kunst und Kultur am Hofe Rudolfs II*: 110–17. Freren, 1988.

HENISCH 1999: Bridget Ann Henisch. *The Medieval Calendar Year*. University Park, Pa., 1999.

HERBERT 1911: J. A. Herbert. *Illuminated Manuscripts*. Bath, 1911.

HÉRON DE VILLEFOSSE 1959: René Héron de Villefosse. "En marge d'un rare livre d'heures." *Connaissance des arts* 87 (May 1959): 56–59.

HERZOG 1969: Sadja Herzog. "Jan Gossart Called Mabuse (ca. 1478–1532): A Study of His Chronology with a Catalogue of His Works." Ph.D. diss., Bryn Mawr College, 1969.

HIDALGO OGÁYAR 1983: Juana Hidalgo Ogáyar. "Libro de horas de William Hastings." *Goya* 177 (1983): 127–31.

HILGER 1973: Wolfgang Hilger. *Das ältere Gebetbuch Maximilians I: Kommentar zur Faksimile-Ausgabe*. Codices selecti 39. Graz, 1973.

HIND 1938–48: Arthur M. Hind. *Early Italian Engraving*. 7 vols. London, 1938–48.

HIND AND POPHAM 1915–32: Arthur M. Hind and A. E. Popham, eds. *Catalogue of Drawings by Dutch and Flemish Artists Preserved in the Department of Prints and Drawings in the British Museum*. 5 vols. London, 1915–32.

HINDMAN 1977: Sandra Hindman. "The Case of Simon Marmion: Attributions and Documents." *Zeitschrift für Kunstgeschichte* 40 (1977): 185–204.

HINDMAN 1981: Sandra Hindman. "Pieter Bruegel's *Children's Games*: Folly and Chance." *Art Bulletin* 63 (1981): 447–75.

HINDMAN 1992: Sandra Hindman. "Two Leaves from an Unknown Breviary: The Case for Simon Marmion." In *Margaret of York, Simon Marmion and The Visions of Tondal*, edited by T. Kren: 223–32. Malibu, 1992.

HINDMAN ET AL. 1997: Sandra Hindman et al. *The Robert Lehman Collection, IV: Illuminations*. New York, 1997.

HINDMAN AND SPIEGEL 1981: Sandra Hindman and Gabrielle M. Spiegel. "The Fleur-de-Lis Frontispieces to Guillaume de Nangis's Chronique Abrégée: Political Iconography in Late Fifteenth-Century France." *Viator* 12 (1982): 381–407.

HIRSCH 1967: Elisabeth Feist Hirsch. *Damião de Gois: The Life and Thought of a Portuguese Humanist, 1502–1574*. The Hague, 1967.

HOBBS 1989: T. Hobbs. "Prosimetrum in *Le Livre dit Grace Entière sur le fait du gouvernement d'un Prince*, the Governance of a Prince Treatise in British Library MS Royal 16 F ii." In *Littera et Sensus: Essays on Form and Meaning in Medieval French Literature Presented to John Fox*: 49–62. Exeter, 1989.

HOFFMAN 1958: Edith Hoffman. "Simon Marmion." Ph.D. diss., Courtauld Institute, London, 1958.

HOFFMAN 1969: Edith Hoffman. "Simon Marmion Re-considered." *Miscellanea F. Lyna*; *Scriptorium* 23 (1969): 243–71.

HOFFMAN 1973: Edith Warren Hoffman. "Simon Marmion or 'The Master of the Altarpiece of Saint-Bertin': A Problem in Attribution." *Scriptorium* 27 (1973): 263–90.

HOFFMAN 1978: Edith Warren Hoffman. "A Reconstruction and Reinterpretation of Guillaume Fillastre's Altarpiece of St.-Bertin." *Art Bulletin* 60 (1978) 634–49.

HOFMANN 1872: Rudolf Hofmann. *Die Gemälde-Sammlung des Grossherzoglichen Museums zu Darmstadt*. Darmstadt, 1872.

HOLANDA 1930: Francesco de Holanda. *Da pintura antigua, tratado de Francisco de Hollanda . . . commentada par Joaquim de Vasconcellos*. 2nd ed. Porto, [1930].

HOLBROOK 1978: S. E. Holbrook. "Clock Dials on a Fifteenth-Century Country Estate, and Other Burgundian Clocks." *Antiquarian Horology* 10, no. 7 (summer 1978): 819–26.

HONIG 1998: Elizabeth Alice Honig. *Painting and the Market in Early Modern Antwerp*. New York, 1998.

HOOGEWERFF 1936–47: G. J. Hoogewerff. *De Noordnederlandsche schilderkunst*. 5 vols. The Hague, 1936–47.

HOPPE 1987: Jody L. Hoppe. "*Les Fais d'Alexandre le Grant*: A Fifteenth Century Manuscript at the J. Paul Getty Museum." Master's thesis, University of California, Santa Barbara, 1987.

HOUDOY 1880: J. Houdoy. *Histoire artistique de la Cathédrale de Cambrai*. Paris, 1880.

HOWARD 1964: James W. Howard, Jr. "The Architectural Elements of the Malvagna Triptych by Jan Gossaert Called Mabuse." Ph.D. diss., New York University, 1964.

HUGHES (A.) 1985: A. Hughes. "Forty-seven Medieval Office Manuscripts in the British Museum. A Provisional Inventory of Antiphonals and Breviaries." Typescript, 1985.

HUGHES (M.) 1984a: Muriel J. Hughes. "The Library of Margaret of York, Duchess of Burgundy." *The Private Library*, ser. 3, 7 (1984): 53–78.

HUGHES (M.) 1984b: Muriel J. Hughes. "Margaret of York, Duchess of Burgundy: Diplomat, Patroness, Bibliophile, and Benefactress." *The Private Library*, ser. 3, 7 (1984): 3–17.

HULIN DE LOO 1902: Georges Hulin de Loo. *De l'identité de certains maîtres anonymes*. Extrait du Catalogue critique de l'Exposition de Bruges 1902. Bruges, 1902.

HULIN DE LOO 1911: Georges Hulin de Loo. *Heures de Milan: Troisième partie des Très-Belles Heures de Notre-Dame enluminées par les peintres de Jean de France, duc de Berry, et par ceux du duc Guillaume de Bavière, comte du Hainaut et de Hollande*. Brussels and Paris, 1911.

HULIN DE LOO 1925: Georges Hulin de Loo. "Quelques notes de voyage." *Académie royale de Belgique, Bulletins de la Classe des Beaux-Arts* 7 (1925): 100–106.

HULIN DE LOO 1931: Georges Hulin de Loo. "Quelques oeuvres d'art inédites rencontrées en Espagne." *Académie royale de Belgique, Bulletins de la Classe des Beaux-Arts* 13 (1931): 39–43.

HULIN DE LOO 1939a: Georges Hulin de Loo. "Comment j'ai retrouvé Horenbaut." *Annuaire des Musées royaux des Beaux-Arts de Belgique* 2 (1939): 3–21.

HULIN DE LOO 1939b: Georges Hulin de Loo. "La Vignette chez les enlumineurs gantois entre 1470 et 1500." *Académie royale de Belgique, Bulletins de la Classe Des Beaux–Arts* 21 (1939): 158–80.

HULIN DE LOO 1942: Georges Hulin de Loo. "Tableaux perdus de Simon Marmion." In *Aan Max J. Friedländer*: 11–19. The Hague, 1942.

HUMPHREYS 1844–49: H. N. Humphreys. *The Illuminated Books of the Middle Ages*. London, 1844–49.

HURT 1973: Jethro M. Hurt. "The Early Ownership of the Hennessy Hours." *Scriptorium* 27 (1973): 43–46.

HURT 1975–76: Jethro Hurt. "The Grimani Breviary, Reproduced from the Illuminated Manuscript Belonging to the Biblioteca Marciana, Venice" (book review). *Art Journal* 35 (winter 1975–76): 182–86.

HUTH, ELLIS, AND HAZLITT 1880: Henry Huth, Frederick Startridge Ellis, and William Carew Hazlitt. *The Huth Library: A Catalogue of the Printed Books, Manuscripts, Autograph Letters, and Engravings Collected by Henry Huth*. 5 vols. London, 1880.

HUYBENS 1975: G. Huybens. "Het muziekleven ten tijde van Dirk Bouts, Richard de Bellengues (1380[?]–1471), kannunik-musicus." *Arca Lovaniensis: Jaerboek vrienden Stedelijk Museum Leuven* 4 (1975): 312–33.

HUYGHEBAERT 1969: Nicolas Huyghebaert. "Trois Manuscrits de Jean Crabbe, abbé des Dunes." *Miscellanea F. Lyna*; *Scriptorium* 23 (1969): 232–42.

INGLIS 1995: Eric Inglis. *The Hours of Mary of Burgundy: Codex Vindobonensis 1857, Vienna Österreichische Nationalbibliothek*. London, 1995.

INNSBRUCK 1969: *Ausstellung Maximilian I., Innsbruck. (Zum 450. Todesjahr): Katalog*. Exh. cat. Innsbruck, Zeughaus, 1969.

INNSBRUCK 1992: *Hispania-Austria*. Exh. cat. Innsbruck, Schloss Ambras, 1992.

ISHIKAWA 1989: Chiyo Ishikawa. "The *Retablo de la Reina Católica* by Juan de Flandes and Michel Sittow." Ph.D. diss., Bryn Mawr College, 1989.

IRBLICH 1988: Eva Irblich. "Herrschaftsauffassung und persönliche Andacht Kaiser Friedrichs III., Maximilians I, und Karls V. im Spiegel ihrer Gebetbücher." *Codices Manuscripti* 14 (1988): 11–45.

JACKSON 1960: William A. Jackson. "Contemporary Collectors XXIV: Philip Hover." *The Book Collector* 9, no. 2 (1960): 151–64.

JACOBS 1998: Lynn F. Jacobs. *Early Netherlandish Carved Altarpieces, 1380–1550: Medieval Tastes and Mass Marketing*. Cambridge, 1998.

JAMES 1895: Montague Rhodes James. *A Descriptive Catalogue of the Manuscripts in the Fitzwilliam Museum*. Cambridge, 1895.

JAMES 1913: Montague Rhodes James. *A Descriptive Catalogue of the Manuscripts in the Library of St. John's College, Cambridge*. Cambridge, 1913.

JAMES 1921: Montague Rhodes James. *A Descriptive Catalogue of the Latin Manuscripts in the John Rylands Library at Manchester*. 2 vols. Manchester, 1921.

JAMES 1931: Montague Rhodes James. *The Apocalypse in Art*. London, 1931.

JAMES 1930–32: Montague Rhodes James. *A Descriptive Catalogue of the Manuscripts in the Library of Lambeth Palace*. Parts 1–5 in 2 vols. Cambridge, 1930–32.

JANINI AND SERRANO 1969: José Janini and José Serrano. *Manuscritos litúrgicos de la Biblioteca Nacional*. Madrid, 1969.

JENNI AND THOSS 1982: Ulrike Jenni and Dagmar Thoss. *Das Schwarze Gebetbuch (Gebetbuch des Galeazzo Maria Sforza) Codex 1856 der Österreichischen Nationalbibliothek in Wien*. Frankfurt am Main, 1982.

JONES 2000: Sue Jones. "The Use of Patterns by Jan van Eyck's Assistants and Followers." In *Investigating Jan van Eyck*, edited by S. Foister, S. Jones, and D. Coels: 197–208. Turnhout, 2000.

JUNG 1982: M. R. Jung. "Les 'Douze Dames de rhétorique.'" In *Du mot au texte: Actes du IIIème Colloque International sur le Moyen français, Düsseldorf, 17–19 septembre 1980*, edited by P. Wunderli: 229–40. Tübingen, 1982.

JUNG 1996: Marc-René Jung. *La Légende de Troie en France au moyen âge: Analyse des versions françaises et bibliographie raisonnée des manuscrits*. Basel; Tübingen: Francke, 1996.

JUNG 1997: M.-R. Jung. "*Ovide Metamorphose* en prose (Bruges, vers 1475)." In "*À l'heure encore de mon escrire": Aspects de la littérature de Bourgogne sous Philippe le Bon et Charles le Téméraire*, edited by C. Thiry: 99–115. Paris, 1997.

JUSTI 1887: C. Justi. "Juan de Flandes, ein niederländerischer Hofmaler Isabella der Katholischen." *Jahrbuch der Königlich preuszischen Kunstsammlungen* 8 (1887): 157–69.

KAEMMERER AND STRÖHL 1903: Ludwig Kaemmerer and Hugo Gerard Ströhl. *Ahnenreihen aus dem Stammbaum des portugiesischen Königshauses: Miniaturenfolge in der Bibliothek des British Museum zu London*. 2 vols. Stuttgart, 1903.

KARLOWSKIEJ-KAMZOWEJ 1981: Alicji Karlowskiej-Kamzowej, ed. *Les Relations artistiques entre la Pologne, la France, la Flandre et la Basse Rhénanie du XI-IIe au XVe siècle*. Uniwersytet im. Adama Mickiewicza w Poznaniu, Seńia Historia Sztuki, 13. Poznan, 1981.

KAUFMANN (T.) 1988: Thomas DaCosta Kaufmann. *The School of Prague: Painting at the Court of Rudolf II*. Chicago, 1988.

KAUFMANN (T.) AND KAUFMANN 1991: Thomas DaCosta Kaufmann and Virginia Roehrig Kaufmann. "The Sanctification of Nature: Observations on the Origins of Trompe l'oeil in Netherlandish Book Painting of the Fifteenth and Sixteenth Centuries." *The J. Paul Getty Museum Journal* 19 (1991): 43–64.

KAUFMANN (V.) 1992: Virginia Roehrig Kaufmann. "The Theme of Pilgrimage in the Miniatures of the *Hours of Engelbert of Nassau*." *Poznańskie Towarzystwo Przyjaciól Nauk*, no. 110 (1992): 33–42.

KAVALER 1999: Ethan M. Kavaler. *Pieter Bruegel: Parables of Order and Enterprise*. Cambridge, 1999.

KEACH 1969: G. Keach. "Two Flemish Manuscripts of Caesar's Commentaries." Master's thesis, Yale University, 1969.

KEKEWICH 1971: Margaret Kekewich. "Edward IV, William Claxton and Literary Patronage in Yorkist England." *Modern Language Review* 66, no. 3 (July 1971): 481–87.

KEMP-WELCH 1979: Alice Kemp-Welch. *Of Six Mediaeval Women, to Which Is Added a Note on Mediaeval Gardens*. Williamstown, Mass., 1979.

KEMPERDICK 1999: Stephan Kemperdick. *Rogier van der Weyden 1399/1400–1464*. Cologne, 1999.

KEMPERDICK 2000: Stephan Kemperdick. *Rogier Van der Weyden: 1399/1400–1464*. Cologne, 2000.

KENNEDY 1917: H. A. Kennedy. *Early English Portrait Miniatures in the Collection of the Duke of Buccleuch*. Edited by Charles Holme. London: The Studio, 1917.

KENYON 1912: Frederic George Kenyon. *Catalogue of The Fifty Manuscripts and Printed Books Bequeathed to the British Museum by Alfred H. Huth*. London, 1912.

KER 1969–92: N. R. Ker. *Medieval Manuscripts in British Libraries*. 4 vols. Vol. 4 by N. R. Ker and A. J. Piper. Oxford, 1969–92.

KERVYN DE LETTENHOVE 1879: Joseph M. B. C. Kervyn de Lettenhove. *Istore et croniques de Flandres, d'après les textes de divers manuscrits*. 2 vols. Brussels, 1879.

KESSLER 1977: Herbert L. Kessler. "The Chantilly *Miroir de l'humaine salvation* and Its Models." In *Studies in Late Medieval and Renaissance Painting in Honor of Millard Meiss*: 274–82. New York, 1977.

KIPLING 1977: Gordon Kipling. *The Triumph of Honour: Burgundian Origins of the Elizabethan Renaissance*. Leiden, 1977.

KIPLING 1981: Gordon Kipling. "Henry VII and the Origins of Tudor Patronage." In *Patronage in the Renaissance*, edited by Guy Fitch Lytle and Stephen Orgel: 117–64. Princeton, 1981.

KITZINGER 1975: Ernst Kitzinger. "The Role of Miniature Painting in Mural Decoration." In *The Place of Book Illumination in Byzantine Art*: 99–142. Princeton, 1975.

KLEVE 1984: *Land im Mittelpunkt der Mächte: Die Herzogtümer Jülich, Kleve, Berg*. Exhibition catalogue. Kleve, Städtisches Museum Haus Koekkoek, 1984.

KNAUS 1960: Hermann Knaus. "Handschriften der Grafen von Nassau-Breda." *Archiv für Geschichte des Buchwesens* 3 (1960): 567–80.

KOCH 1998: Robert Koch. "A Rediscovered Painting: *The Road to Calvary* by Herri met de Bles." In *Herri met de Bles: Studies and Explorations of the World Landscape Tradition*, edited by Norman Muller, Betsy Rosasco, and James Marrow: 9–21. Princeton, 1998.

KÖHLER 2000: Alfred Köhler. "Persönlichkeit und Herrschaft." In *Kaiser Karl V. (1500–1558): Macht und Ohnmacht Europas: 7–25*. Exh. cat. Vienna, Kunsthistorisches Museum, 2000.

KOMADA 2000: A. Komada. "Les Illustrations de la *Bible historiale*: Les Manuscrits réalisés dans le Nord." Doctoral thesis, Université de Sorbonne-Paris, Paris IV, 2000.

KOMADA 2002: A. Komada. "Particularités des manuscrits de la 'Bible Historiale' enluminés dans le Nord: Le Cas de la 'Bible' de Philippe de Croÿ, comte de Chimay." In *Richesses médiévales du Nord et du Hainaut*, edited by J.-C. Herbin: 185–98. Valenciennes, 2002.

KÖNIG 1982: Eberhard König. *Französische Buchmalerei um 1450*. Berlin, 1982.

KÖNIG 1991: Eberhard König. *Das goldene Zeitalter der burgundischen Buchmalerei, 1430–1560*. Leuchtendes Mittelalter 3. Antiquariat Heribert Tenschert, Katalog 27. Rotthalmünster, 1991.

KÖNIG 1998a: Eberhard König. "Text und Bild im Berliner Stundenbuch." In *Das Berliner Stundenbuch der Maria von Burgund und Kaiser Maximilians: Handschrift 78 B 12 im Kupferstichkabinett der Staatlichen Museen zu Berlin Preussischer Kulturbesitz: 39–110*. Exh. cat. by Eberhard König, with Fedja Anzelewsky, Bodo Brinkmann and Frauke Steenbock. Berlin, Kupferstichkabinett der Staatlichen Museen zu Berlin, Preussischer Kulturbesitz, 1998.

KÖNIG 1998b: Eberhard König. *Dreiunddreissig mittelalterliche Handschriften aus Byzanz, Italien, Frankreich, Deutschland, Flandern und den Niederlanden vom 11. bis zum frühen 16. Jahrhundert*. Leuchtendes Mittelalter, neue folge 2. Rotthalmünster, 1998.

KORTEWEG 1984: Anne S. Korteweg. "De bibliotheek van Willem van Oranje: De Handschriften." In *Boeken van en rond Willem van Oranje*. Exh. cat. The Hague, Koninklijke Bibliotheek, 1984.

KORTEWEG 1998: Anne S. Korteweg. *Boeken van Oranje-Nassau*. The Hague, Museum van het Boek, 1998.

KÖSTER 1959: Kurt Köster. "Wallfahrtsmedaillen und Pilgerandenken vom Heiligen Rock zu Trier." *Trierisches Jahrbuch*, 1959: 36–56.

KÖSTER 1965: Kurt Köster. "Religiöse Medaillen und Wallfahrts-Devotionalien in der Flämischen Buchmalerei des 15. und frühen 16. Jahrhunderts." In *Buch und Welt: Festschrift für Gustav Hofmann zum 65. Geburtstag dargebracht*: 459–504. Wiesbaden, 1965.

KÖSTER 1973: Kurt Köster. "Pilgerzeichen und Wallfahrtsplaketten von St. Adrian in Geraardsbergen: Zu einer Darstellung auf einer flämischen Altartafel des 15. Jahrhunderts im Historischen Museum zu Frankfurt am Main." *Städel–Jahrbuch*, n.s., 4 (1973): 103–20.

KÖSTER 1979: Kurt Köster. "Kollektionen metallener Wallfahrts-Devotionalien und kleiner Andachtsbilder, eingenäht in spätmittelälterliche Gebetbuch-Handschriften." In *Das Buch und sein Haus: Gerhard Liebers gewidmet zur Vollendung des 65. Lebensjahres*, edited by R. Fuhlrott and Bertram Haller, vol. 1: 77–130. Wiesbaden, 1979.

KÖSTER 1984: Kurt Köster. "Gemalte Kollektionen von Pilgerzeichen und religiösen Medaillen in flämischen Gebet- und Stundenbüchern des 15. und frühen 16. Jahrhunderts. Neue Funde in Handschriften der Gent–Brügger Schule." In *Liber Amicorum Herman Liebaers*): 485–535. Brussels, 1984.

KOTKOVÁ 1997: Olga Kotková. "The Prague Ecce Homo: An Early Work By Juan de Flandes?" In *Le Dessin sous-jacent et la technologie dans la peinture*, edited by Roger Van Schoute and Hélène Verougstraete: 185–92. Louvain-la-Neuve, 1997.

KRAUS 1956: H. P. Kraus. *Remarkable Manuscripts, Books, and Maps from the IXth to the XVIIIth Century*. Catalogue 80. New York, 1956.

KRAUS 1957: H. P. Kraus. *Distinguished Books and Manuscripts*. Catalogue 85. New York, 1957.

KRAUS 1961: H. P. Kraus. *Catalogue 95*. Vaduz, 1961.

Kraus 1962: H. P. Kraus. *Thirty-five Manuscripts*. Catalogue 100. New York, 1962.

KRAUS 1974: H. P. Kraus. *Monumenta codicum manu scriptorum*. Exh. cat. New York, 1974.

KRAUS 1978a: H. P. Kraus. *A Rare Book Saga*. New York, 1978.

KRAUS 1978b: H. P. Kraus. *In Retrospect: A Catalogue of 100 Outstanding Manuscripts Sold in the Last Four Decades*. New York, 1978.

KREN 1974: Thomas Kren. "A Book of Hours in the Beinecke Library (Ms. 287) and an Atelier from the Ghent–Bruges School." Master's thesis, Yale University, 1974.

KREN 1992a: Thomas Kren. "Introduction." In *Margaret of York, Simon Marmion and The Visions of Tondal*, edited by T. Kren: 13–27. Malibu, 1992.

KREN 1992b: Thomas Kren. "Some Illuminated Manuscripts of The Vision of Lazarus from the Time of Margaret of York." In *Margaret of York, Simon Marmion and The Visions of Tondal*, edited by T. Kren: 141–56. Malibu, 1992.

KREN 1996: Thomas Kren. "Some Newly Discovered Miniatures by Simon Marmion and His Workshop." *British Library Journal* 22, no. 2 (1996): 193–220.

KREN 1998: Thomas Kren. "Landscape as Leitmotif: A Reintegrated Book of Hours Illuminated by Simon Bening." In *Illuminating the Book: Makers and Interpreters*, edited by Michelle P. Brown and Scot McKendrick: 209–32. London, 1998.

KREN 1999: Thomas Kren. Review of *The Robert Lehman Collection, IV: Illuminations*, by Sandra Hindman et al. *Burlington Magazine* 141 (April 1999): 232–33.

KREN 2002: Thomas Kren. "Seven Illuminated Books of Hours Written by the Parisian Scribe Jean Dubreuil, c. 1475–1485." In *Reading Texts and Images: Essays on Medieval and Renaissance Art and Patronage in Honour of Margaret M. Manion*, edited by Bernard J. Muir: 157–200. Exeter, 2002.

KREN AND RATHOFER 1988: Thomas Kren and Johannes Rathofer. *Simon Bening. Flämischer Kalendar / Flemish Calendar: Clm. 23638 Bayerische Staatsbibliothek, München.* 2 vols. Lucerne, 1988.

KREN AND WIECK 1990: Thomas Kren and Roger S. Wieck. *The Visions of Tondal from the Library of Margaret of York.* Malibu, 1990.

KRIEGER 2000: Michaela Krieger. "Gerard David als Illuminator." *Festschrift für Konrad Oberhuber*: 215–33. Milan, 2000.

KRISTELLER 1905: Paul Kristeller. *Kupferstich und Holzschnitt in vier Jahrhunderten.* Berlin, 1905.

KUDORFER 1988: Dieter Kudorfer. Review of "Woodcut Presentation Scenes in Books Printed by Caxton, de Worde, Pynson," by Julie A. Smith (*Gutenberg-Jahrbuch*, 61 [1986]: 322–43). *Scriptorium* 42 (1988): 121, no. 474.

KUGLER 1854: Franz Kugler. Review of *Ueber das mit 33 Miniaturen gezierte Brevier Philipps II. Von Spanien. Im Besitze Ihrer Durchlaucht der Fürstin zu Putbus,* by F. von Schönholz. *Kunstblätter* 24 (1840). Reprinted in *Kleine Schriften und Studien zur Kunstgeschichte,* vol. 2: 18–19. Stuttgart, 1854.

KUHN 1913–14: Alfred Kuhn. "Die illustration des Rosenromans." *Jahrbuch der Kunsthistorischen Sammlungen des Allerhöchsten Kaiserhauses* 31 (1913–14): 1–66.

KUPFER-TARASULO 1979a: M. Kupfer-Tarasulo. "Innovation and Copy in the Stein Quadriptych of Simon Bening." *Zeitschrift für Kunstgeschichte* 42 (1979): 274–98.

KUPFER-TARASULO 1979b: M. Kupfer-Tarasulo. "A Rosary Psalter Illuminated by Simon Bening." *Quaerendo* 9 (1979): 209–26.

KURATH ET AL. 1952: *Middle English Dictionary.* Edited by H. Kurath et al. Ann Arbor and London, 1952–.

KURTH 1925: Willy Kurth. "Darstellungen aus dem Leben der Maria von einem niederrheinischen Meister um 1525." *Monatshefte für Bücherfreunde und Graphiksammler* 1 (1925): 40–41.

LABARTE 1879: J. Labarte. *Inventaire du mobilier de Charles V, roi de France.* Paris, 1879.

LABORDE (A. DE) 1934: A. de Laborde. "Les Principaux manuscrits à peintures du Musée des Princes Czartoryski à Cracovie." *Bulletin de la Société Française de reproductions de manuscrits à peintures* 18 (1934): 5–164.

LABORDE (A. DE) 1936–38. A. de Laborde. *Les Principaux Manuscrits à peintures conservés dans l'ancienne Bibliothèque impériale publique de Saint-Pétersbourg.* 2 vols. Paris, Société de Reproductions de Manuscrits à Peintures, 1936–38.

LABORDE (L. DE) 1849–52: L. de Laborde. *Les Ducs de Bourgogne: Études sur les lettres, les arts et l'industrie pendant le XVe siècle. . . . Seconde partie. Preuves.* 3 vols. Paris, 1849–52.

LABORY 1997–99: G. Labory. "Les Manuscrits de la Grande Chronique de Normandie du XIVe et du XVe siècle." *Revue d'histoire des textes* 27 (1997): 191–222; 28 (1998): 183–233; 29 (1999): 245–94.

LABUDA 1981: Adam S. Labuda. "La Prédelle de Philippe Bischof de l'église Notre Dame à Gdansk—Problèms de l'iconographie de la mort au bas moyen-âge." In *Les Relations artistiques entre la Pologne, la France, la Flandre et la Basse Rhenanie du XIIIe au XV siècle*: 67–79. Poznań, 1981.

LABUDA 1984: Adam S. Labuda. *Wroclawski oltarz sw. Barbary i jego twórcy: Studium o malarstwie Slaskim polowy XV wieku.* Poznań, 1984.

LACAITA 1879: J. P. Lacaita. *Catalogue of the Library at Chatsworth.* 4 vols. London, 1879.

LAFITTE 1997: M.-P. Lafitte. "Les Manuscrits de Louis de Bruges, chevalier de la Toison d'Or." In *Le Banquet du Faisan, 1454: L'Occident face au défi de l'Empire Ottoman,* edited by M.-T. Caron and D. Clauzel: 243–55. Arras, 1997.

LAING 1878. David Laing. *Facsimiles of Designs from Engraved Copperplates Illustrating 'Le Livre de la ruyne des nobles hommes et femmes,' par Jehan Bocace de Certald, Imprimé à Bruges par Colard Mansion, anno M.CCCC.LXXVI.* Edinburgh, 1878.

LANCKORONSKA 1958: Maria Lanckoronska. *Die christlich-humanistische Symbolsprache und deren Bedeutung in zwei Gebetbüchern des frühen 16. Jahrhunderts: Gebetbuch Kaiser Maximilians und Breviarium Grimani.* Studien zur deutschen Kunstgeschichte, 319. Baden-Baden, 1958.

LANDAU AND PARSHALL 1994: David Landau and Peter Parshall. *The Renaissance Print, 1470–1550.* New Haven, 1994.

LANE 1984: Barbara Lane. *The Altar and the Altarpiece: Sacramental Themes in Early Netherlandish Painting.* New York, 1984.

LANGLOIS 1910: Ernest Langlois. *Les Manuscrits du Roman de la Rose: Description et classement.* Travaux et mémoires de l'Université de Lille, n.s. 1, Droits, lettres 7. Paris and Lille, 1910.

LARSEN 1960: Erik Larsen. *Les primitifs flamands au Musée Metropolitian de New York.* Utrecht, 1960.

LAURENT 1993: René Laurent. *Les Sceaux des princes territoriaux belges du Xe siècle à 1482.* 2 parts in 3 vols. Brussels, 1993.

LAWRENCE 1969: *The Waning Middle Ages: An Exhibition of French and Netherlandish Art from 1350 to 1500, Commemorating the Fiftieth Anniversary of the Publication of The Waning of the Middle Ages.* Exh. cat. by J. L. Schrader. Lawrence, Kans., Spencer Museum of Art, University of Kansas, 1969.

LAWRENCE 1983: *Gardens of the Middle Ages.* Exh. cat. edited by Marilyn Stokstad and Jerry Stannard. Lawrence, Kansas, Spencer Museum of Art, University of Kansas, 1983.

LAWTON 1983: Lesley Lawton. "The Illustration of Late Medieval Secular Texts, with Special Reference to Lydgate's 'Troy Book.'" In *Manuscripts and Readers in Fifteenth-Century England: The Literary Implications of Manuscript Study,* edited by Derek Pearsall: 41–69. Cambridge, 1983.

LÁZARO 1922: José Lázaro. "Le Manuscrit du British Museum intitulé Isabella Book ou Bréviaire d'Isabelle la Catholique." In *Congrès d'histoire de l'art, Paris, 26 septembre–5 octobre 1921: Compte-rendu analytique*: 138–39. Paris, 1922.

LÁZARO 1928: José Lázaro. *Un supuesto breviario de Isabel la Católica.* Communicación al Congreso de Historia del Arte, celebrado en París en 1921, sobre el Manuscrito adicional núm. 18.851 del British Museum, llamado "Isabella Book" o Breviario de Isabel la Católica. Madrid, 1928.

LE GUAY 1998: Laetitia Le Guay. *Les Princes de Bourgogne lecteurs de Froissart: Les Rapports entre le texte et l'image dans les manuscrits enluminés du livre IV des Chroniques.* Turnhout, 1998.

LECOY DE LA MARCHE 1873: A. Lecoy de La Marche. *Extraits des comptes et mémoriaux du roi René pour servir à l'histoire des arts au XVe siècle.* Paris, 1873.

LEESTI 1991: Elizabeth Leesti. "A Depiction of Saint Sebald of Nuremberg by Simon Bening." *Oud Holland* 105, no. 2 (1991): 116–26.

LEGARÉ 1990: A.-M. Legaré. "Allégorie et arts de mémoire: Un Manuscrit enluminé de la librairie de Marguerite d'Autriche." *Bulletin du bibliophile,* n.s. (1990): 314–44.

LEGARÉ 1991: Anne-Marie Legaré. *Le Livre des Échecs amoureux.* Paris, 1991.

LEGARÉ 1992: Anne-Marie Legaré. "The Master of Antoine Rolin: A Hainaut Illuminator Working in the Orbit of Simon Marmion." In *Margaret of York, Simon Marmion and The Visions of Tondal,* edited by Thomas Kren: 209–22. Malibu, 1992.

LEGARÉ 1996: Anne-Marie Legaré. "L'Héritage de Simon Marmion en Hainaut (1490–1520)." In *Valenciennes aux XIVe et XVe siècles: Art et histoire,* edited by Ludovic Nys and Alain Salamagne: 201–24. Valenciennes, 1996.

LEGARÉ 1998: Anne-Marie Legaré. "Livres d'heures, livres de femmes: quelques exemples en Hainaut" In *Eulalie: Mediathèques, librairies et lecteurs en Nord-Pas-de-Calais* 1 (1998): 53–68.

LEGARÉ 1999: Anne-Marie Legaré. "Loyset Liédet: Un Nouveau Manuscrit enluminé." *Revue de l'art* 126 (1999): 36–49.

LEGARÉ 1999a: Anne-Marie Legaré. "La Pentecôte sous un porche . . . : Architecture et enluminure dans les provinces du Nord." In *Pierre, lumière, couleur: Études d'histoire de l'art du Moyen Âge en l'honneur d'Anne Prache,* edited by Fabienne Joubert and Dany Sandron: 441–55. Paris, 1999.

LEGARÉ 2001: Anne-Marie Legaré. "Charlotte de Savoie's Library and Illuminators." *Women and Book Culture in Late Medieval and Early Modern France,* edited by Martha W. Driver and Cynthia Brown; *Journal of the Early Book Society* 4 (2001): 33–87.

LEGARÉ 2002: Anne-Marie Legaré. "Le Rapports du Maître d'Antoine Rolin avec l'imprimé. L'exemple du *Pèlerinage de vie humaine* en prose (Genève, Bibliothèque publique et universitaire, Ms. Fr. 182)." In *Richesses médiévales du Nord et du Hainaut,* edited by J.-C. Herbin: 65–124. Valenciennes, 2002.

LEGARÉ, TESSON, AND ROY 1991: Anne-Marie Legaré, Françoise Guichard Tesson, and Bruno Roy. *Le livre des Échecs amoureux.* Paris, 1991.

LEGNER 1973: A. Legner. "Zur Präsenz der grossen Reliquienschreine in der Ausstellung Rhein und Maas." In *Rhein und Maas: Kunst und Kultur, 800–1200,* vol. 2: 65–94. Cologne, 1973.

LEHMAN 1928: Robert Lehman. *The Philip Lehman Collection, New York: Paintings.* Paris, 1928.

LEHMAN 1964: Robert Lehman. *The Lehman Collection at 7 West 54th Street.* New York, n.d. [1964].

LEHRS 1902: Max Lehrs. "Der Meister der Boccaccio-Bilder." *Jahrbuch der Königlich preuszischen Kunstsammlungen* 23 (1902): 124–41.

LEIDINGER 1912a: Georg Leidinger. *Miniaturen aus Handschriften der Königlichen Hof- und Staatsbibliothek München.* Vol. 2, *Flämischer Kalender (Cod. lat. 23638).* Munich, 1912.

LEIDINGER 1912b: Georg Leidinger. *Verzeichnis der wichtigsten Miniaturen-Handschriften der Klg. Hof- und Staatsbibliothekin in München.* Munich, 1912.

LEIDINGER 1920: Georg Leidinger. *Meisterwerke der Buchmalerei aus Handschriften der Bayerischen Staatsbibliothek München.* Munich, 1920.

LEIDINGER 1936: Georg Leidinger. *Flämischer Kalender des XVI. Jahrhunderts gemalt vom Meister des «Hortulus animae».* Munich, 1936.

LEIPZIG AND STUTTGART 1925: *Gesamtkatalog der Wiegendrucke.* 7 vols. Leipzig and Stuttgart, 1925.

LELOUX 1977: H. Leloux. "Noordoostnederlands in Keulen." *Driemaandelijkse Bladen* 29 (1977): 11–31.

LEMAIRE 1983: Claudine Lemaire. "Quatre fermoirs de reliure armoriés d'origine laïque provenant des

Pays-Bas méridionaux datant du XVe siècle." *Le Livre et l'estampe* 29 no. 113–14 (1983): 7–16.

LEMAIRE 1984: Claudine Lemaire. "La Bibliothèque des ducs d'Arenberg, une première approche." In *Liber Amicorum Herman Liebaers*: 81–106. Brussels, 1984.

LEMAIRE 1993: Claudine Lemaire. "Les manuscrits de Jean II, Comte d'Oettingen ou la fin d'une légende." In *Miscellanea Martin Wittek: Album de codicologie et de paléographie offert à Martin Wittek*, edited by Anny Raman and Eugène Manning: 243–51. Leuven and Paris, 1993.

LEMAIRE 1994: Claudine Lemaire. "Remarques relatives aux inventaires de la librairie de Bourgogne réalisés en 1467–69, 1477, 1485, 1487 et aux manuscrits des duchesses." *Scriptorium* 48 (1994): 294–98.

LEMAIRE 1996: Claudine Lemaire. "La Bibliothèque de Louis de Gruuthuse." In *L'Ordre de la Toison d'or de Philippe le Bon à Philippe le Beau (1430–1505): Idéal ou reflet d'une société?*: 206–8. Exh. cat. Brussels, Bibliothèque royale de Belgique, 1996.

LENGER 1985: Marie-Thérèse Lenger. "Contribution de la codicologie à l'étude des incunables." In *Calames et Cahiers: Mélanges de codicologie et de paléographie offerts à Léon Gilissen*: 99–106. Brussels, 1985.

LEPROUX 1998: Guy-Michel Leproux. "Un Peintre anversois à Paris sous le règne de François Ier: Noël Bellemare." *Cahiers de la Rotonde* 20 (1998): 125–54.

LEPROUX 2001: Guy-Michel Leproux. *La Peinture à Paris sous le règne de François Ier*. Paris, 2001.

LEROQUAIS 1927: Victor Leroquais. *Les Livres d'heures manuscrits de la Bibliothèque nationale*. 2 vols. Paris, 1927.

LEROQUAIS 1934: Victor Leroquais. *Les Bréviaires manuscrits de bibliothèques publiques de France*. 5 vols. Paris.

LEUVEN 1975: *Dirk Bouts en zijn tijd*. Exh. cat. Leuven, Sint-Pieterskerk, 1975.

LEUVEN 1990: *Bernardus en de Cisterciënzerfamilie in België, 1090–1990*. Exh. cat. edited by M. Sabbe, M. Lamberigts, and F. Gistelinck. Leuven, Bibliotheek van de Faculteit der Godgeleerdheid, 1990.

LEUVEN 1993: *Vlaamse miniaturen voor Van Eyck (ca. 1380–ca. 1420): Catalogus*. Exh. cat. edited by Maurits Smeyers. Leuven, 1993.

LEUVEN 1998: *Dirk Bouts (ca. 1410–1475), een Vlaams primitief te Leuven*. Exh. cat. edited by Maurits Smeyers. Leuven, Sint-Pieterskerk en Predikherenkerk te Leuven, 1998.

LEUVEN 1999: *The Treasury of Petrus Alamire: Music and Art in Flemish Court Manuscripts, 1500–1535*. Exh. cat. Leuven, Sint-Pieterskerk en Predikherenkerk te Leuven, 1999.

LEUVEN 2002: *Medieval Mastery. Book Illumination from Charlemagne to Charles the Bold: 800–1475*. Exh. cat. Leuven, Stedelijk Museum Vander Kelen-Mertens, 2002.

LEWIS (F.) 1992: Flora Lewis. "Rewarding Devotion: Indulgences and the Promotion of Images." In *The Church and the Arts: Papers Read at the 1990 Summer Meeting and the 1991 Winter Meeting of the Ecclesiastical History Society*, edited by Diana Wood: 179–94. Oxford, 1992.

LEWIS (S.) 1992: Suzanne Lewis. "The *Apocalypse* of Margaret of York." In *Margaret of York, Simon Marmion, and The Visions of Tondal*, edited by T. Kren: 77–88. Malibu, 1992.

LIEBAERS ET AL. 1985: Herman Liebaers, Valentin Vermeersch, Leon Voet, et al. *Flemish Art from the Beginning till Now*. Antwerp, 1985.

LIEBENWEIN 1985: Renate Liebenwein. "Pieter Bruegel d. Ä.: Die Elster auf dem Galgen." In *Entdeckungen in hessischen Museen: Vom "Paradiesgärtlein" zum "Westhafen,"* edited by Hansgeorg Dickmann and Kurt Zimmermann: 126–29. Frankfurt am Main, 1985.

LIEBERMAN 1970: Max Lieberman. "Autour de l'iconographie Gersonienne: Les Miniatures et les manuscrits qui les contiennent." *Romania* 91 (1970): 341–77, 467–90.

LIECHTENSTEIN 1976: Prinz Heinrich Karl von Liechtenstein. *Das Gebetbuch Karls V: Kommentarband*. Graz, 1976.

LIEFTINCK 1957: Gerard Isaac Lieftinck. "Kunstwerk of juweel? Het gebedenboek van de heer C. H. Beels te Hilversum." *Nederlands Kunsthistorisch Jaarboek* 8 (1957): 1–28.

LIEFTINCK 1964a: Gerard Isaac Lieftinck. *Manuscrits datés conservés dans les Pays-Bas: Catalogue paléographique des manuscrits en écriture latine portant des indications de date*. 2 vols. Amsterdam, 1964.

LIEFTINCK 1964b: Gerard Isaac Lieftinck. "De Meester van Maria van Bourgondië en Rooclooster bij Brussel." *Bulletin en nieuws-bulletin, Koninklijke Nederlandse Oudheidkundige Bond* 17 (1964): cols. 254–96.

LIEFTINCK 1969: Gerard Isaac Lieftinck. *Boekverluchters uit de omgeving van Maria van Bourgondië c. 1475–c. 1485*. 2 vols. Verhandelingen van de Koninklijke Vlaamse Academie Voor Wetenschappen, Letteren en Schone Kunsten van België. Klasse der Letteren 31, no. 66. Brussels, 1969.

LIMENTANI VIRDIS 1981: Caterina Limentani Virdis. *Codici miniati fiamminghi e olandesi nelle Biblioteche dell'Italia nord-orientale*. Vicenza, 1981.

LINDNER 1912: Arthur Lindner. *Der Breslauer Froissart: Festschrift des Vereins für Geschichte der bildenden Künste zu Breslau, zum fünfzigjährigen Jubiläum verfasst im Auftrage des Vereins*. Berlin, 1912.

LISBON 1882: *Catalogo illustrado da Exposição retrospectiva de arte ornamental portugueza e hespanhola celebrada em Lisboa em 1882*. Lisbon, 1882.

LISBON 1895: *Catalogo da Sala de Sua Magestade El-Rei: Exposição de arte sacra ornamental promovida pela Commissão do centenario de Santo Antonio em Lisboa no anno de 1895*. Exh. cat. by Ramalho Ortigão. Lisbon, 1895.

LISBON 1958: *A Rainha D. Leonor*. Exh. cat. Lisbon, Mosteiro da Madre de Deus, 1958.

LISBON 1983: *Os Descobrimentos portugueses e a Europa do renascimento: XVII Exposição Europeia de arte, ciência e cultura*. Exh. cat. Lisbon, Museu Nacional de Arte Antiga, 1983.

LISBON 1990: *A Iluminura em Portugal: Catálogo da exposição inaugural do Arquivo Nacional da Torre do Tombo*. With essays by F. M. Esteves Pereira and Francisco de Macedo, notes and preface by Martim de Albuquerque. Exh. cat. Lisbon, Arquivo Nacional da Torre do Tombo, 1990.

LISBON 1992: *No Tempo das Feitorias: A arte portuguesa na Época dos Descobrimentos*. 2 vols. Exh. cat. Lisbon, Museu Nacional de Arte Antiga, 1992.

LISBON 1998: Ivo Carneiro de Sousa. *V Centenário das Misericordias portuguesas, 1498–1998*. Lisbon, 1998.

LISBON 2000: *The Image of Time: European Manuscript Books*. Exh. cat. Lisbon, Calouste Gulbenkian Museum, 2000.

LOCKER-LAMPSON 1886: Frederick Locker-Lampson. *The Rowfant Library: A Catalogue of the Printed Books, Manuscripts, Autograph Letters, Drawings and Pictures Collected by Frederick Locker-Lampson*, 1886.

LONDON 1862: *Special Exhibition of Works of Art of the Mediaeval, Renaissance, and More Recent Periods, on Loan at the South Kensington Museum, June 1862*. Exh. cat. edited by J. C. Robinson. London, South Kensington Museum, 1862.

LONDON 1865: *Catalogue of the Special Exhibition of Portrait Miniatures on Loan at the South Kensington Museum, June 1865*. Exh. cat. London, South Kensington Museum, 1865.

LONDON 1873–83: Palaeographical Society. *Facsimiles of Manuscripts and Inscriptions*. 1st series. Edited by E. A. Bond and E. M. Thompson. 3 vols. London, 1873–83.

LONDON 1881: *Catalogue of the Special Loan Exhibition of Spanish and Portuguese Ornamental Art*. Exh. cat. edited by J. C. Robinson. London, South Kensington Museum, 1881.

LONDON 1884–94: *Facsimiles of Manuscripts and Inscriptions*. 2nd series. Edited by Edward Augustus Bond, Edward Maunde Thompson, and George Frederic Warner. 2 vols. London, Palaeographical Society, 1884–94.

LONDON 1886: *Catalogue of a Series of Illuminations from Mss. Principally of the Italian and French Schools*. London, Burlington Fine Arts Club, 1886.

LONDON 1908: *Exhibition of Illuminated Manuscripts*. Exh. cat. Burlington Fine Arts Club, London, 1908.

LONDON 1909: *Exhibition Illustrative of Early English Portraiture*. Exh. cat. by Lionel Cust, Charles Francis Bell, and Max Rosenheim. London, Burlington Fine Arts Club, 1909.

LONDON 1910: *British Museum: Reproductions from Illuminated Manuscripts*. 3rd series, 2nd ed. London, 1910.

LONDON 1911: British Museum. *Miniatures and Borders from a Flemish Horae, British Museum Add. MS. 24098, Early Sixteenth Century: Reproduced in Honour of Sir George Warner*. Oxford, 1911.

LONDON 1912a: British Museum. *Guide to the Exhibited Manuscripts. Part III: Illuminated Manuscripts and Bindings of Manuscripts Exhibited in the Grenville Library*. London, 1912.

LONDON 1912b: British Museum. *Catalogue of the Fifty Manuscripts & Printed Books Bequeathed to the British Museum by Alfred H. Huth*. London, 1912.

LONDON 1916–17: *Ninety-Six Miniatures from the Collection Lent by the Duke of Buccleuch, 1916-1917*. Exh. cat. London, Victoria and Albert Museum, 1916–17.

LONDON 1923: Victoria and Albert Museum. *Catalogue of Miniatures, Leaves and Cuttings from Illuminated Manuscripts*. London, 1923.

LONDON 1923–65: British Museum. *Reproductions from Illuminated Manuscripts. Series I–V*. 5 vols. London, 1923–65.

LONDON 1927: *Catalogue of the Loan Exhibition of Flemish and Belgian Art: A Memorial Volume*. Exh. cat. edited by Sir Martin Conway. London, Burlington House, 1927.

LONDON 1929: *A Guide to the Exhibition of Some Part of the Egerton Collection of Manuscripts in the British Museum 1929*. Compiled by Julius P. Gilson. London, 1929.

LONDON 1932: Royal Academy of Arts. *Exhibition of French Art, 1200–1900*. Exh. cat. edited by W. G. Constable. London, Burlington House, 1932.

LONDON 1935: *Exhibition of Masterpieces through Four Centuries (1400–1800)*. Exh. cat. London, M. Knoedler & Co., 1935.

LONDON 1949: *Masterpieces of Dutch and Flemish Painting*. Exh. cat. by R. Warner. London, Eugene Slatter Gallery, 1949.

LONDON 1953–54: *Flemish Art 1300–1700*. Exh. cat. London, Royal Academy of Arts, 1953–54.

LONDON 1954: "Anglo-Flemish Art under the Tudors." Typescript. Exh. cat. London, British Museum, 1954.

LONDON 1955–56: *Portuguese Art, 800–1800*. Exh. cat. London, Royal Academy of Arts, 1955–56.

LONDON 1956–57: *British Portraits*. Exh. cat. London, Royal Academy of Arts, winter 1956–57.

LONDON 1957: *Loan Exhibition of Pictures from the City Art Gallery, Birmingham*. Exh. cat. London, Thos. Agnew & Sons Ltd., 1957.

LONDON 1959a: *Treasures of Cambridge*. Exh. cat. London, Goldsmith's Hall, 1959.

LONDON 1959b: Review of *Treasures of Cambridge*. Exhibition at Goldsmith's Hall. *The Connoisseur* (American ed.) 143 (April 1959): 102–5.

LONDON 1963: *Catalogue of Books Printed in the XVth Century Now in the British Museum*. Corrected reprint. 12 vols. London: British Museum, 1963.

LONDON 1965: *Treasures from Private Libraries in England*. Exh. cat. London, National Book League, 1965.

LONDON 1967: *Illuminated Manuscripts Exhibited in the Grenville Library*. London, The British Museum, 1967.

LONDON 1973: *Richard III*. Exh. cat. compiled by Pamela Tudor-Craig. London, National Portrait Gallery, 1973.

LONDON 1975: *Giovanni Boccaccio*. Exh. cat. London, British Library, 1975.

LONDON 1976: *William Caxton: An Exhibition to Commemorate the Quincentenary of the Introduction of Printing into England*. Exh. cat. London, British Library, 1976.

LONDON 1977–78: *"The King's Good Servant": Sir Thomas More 1477/8–1535*. Exh. cat. London, National Portrait Gallery, 1977–78.

LONDON 1978–79: *Holbein and the Court of Henry VIII*. Exh. cat. London, The Queen's Gallery, Buckingham Palace, 1978–79.

LONDON 1980: *The Gold Reliquary of Charles the Bold*. Exh. cat. compiled by M. Campbell. London, Victoria and Albert Museum, 1980.

LONDON 1981: *Drawing: Technique and Purpose*. Exh. cat. by S. Lambert. London, Victoria and Albert Museum, 1981.

LONDON 1983: *Artists of the Tudor Court: The Portrait Miniature Rediscovered, 1520–1620*. Exh. cat. compiled by R. Strong, with contributions by V. J. Murrell. London, Victoria and Albert Museum, 1983.

LONDON 1989: Sandra Hindman. *Four Miniatures by Simon Bening*. Exh. cat. London, Hazlitt, Gooden & Fox, 1989.

LONDON 1991a: *Henry VIII: A European Court in England*. Exh. cat. edited by David Starkey. London, 1991.

LONDON 1991b: *Master Drawings from the Courtauld Collection*. Exh. cat. edited by William Bradford & Helen Braham. London, Courtauld Institute Galleries, 1991.

LONDON 1994: *Kingston Lacy, Dorset*. London, 1994.

LONDON 1995: *German Renaissance Prints, 1490–1550*. Exh. cat. by G. Bartrum. London, British Museum, 1995.

LONDON 1996: *Old Master Drawings from the Malcolm Collection*. Exh. cat. by Martin Royalton-Kisch, Hugo Chapman, and Stephen Coppel. London, British Museum, 1996.

LONDON 1998: British Library. *Catalogue of Additions to the Manuscripts, New Series, 1966–1970*. 2 vols. London, 1998.

LONDON 1999: *The Apocalypse and the Shape of Things to Come*. Exh. cat. edited by Frances Carey. London, British Museum, 1999.

LOOMIS AND LOOMIS 1938: Roger Sherman Loomis and Laura Hibbard Loomis. *Arthurian Legends in Medieval Art*. New York, 1938.

LOS ANGELES 1985: J. Paul Getty Museum. "Acquisitions 1984: Manuscripts." *The J. Paul Getty Museum Journal* 13 (1985): 199–204.

LOS ANGELES 1986: J. Paul Getty Museum. *The J. Paul Getty Museum: Handbook of the Collections*. Malibu, 1986.

LOS ANGELES 1987: J. Paul Getty Museum. "Acquisitions 1986: Manuscripts." *The J. Paul Getty Museum Journal* 15 (1987): 172–74.

LOS ANGELES 1989: J. Paul Getty Museum. "Acquisitions 1988." *The J. Paul Getty Museum Journal* 17 (1989): 123.

LOS ANGELES 1992: J. Paul Getty Museum. "Acquisitions 1991: Manuscripts." *The J. Paul Getty Museum Journal* 20 (1992): 148–50.

LOS ANGELES 1997: J. Paul Getty Museum. *Masterpieces of the J. Paul Getty Museum: Illuminated Manuscripts*. Los Angeles, 1997.

LOUF 1992: André Louf. "Un Triptyque de Simon Bening, commandité par Pierre van Onderberghen, abbé des Dunes (1515–1519)." *Cîteaux* 43 (1992): 221–37.

LOWRY 1992: Martin Lowry. "Sister or Country Cousin? The Huntington Recuyell and the Getty Tondal." *Margaret of York, Simon Marmion and The Visions of Tondal*, edited by T. Kren: 103–10. Malibu, 1992.

LUCAS 1970: Robert H. Lucas. "Medieval French Translations of the Latin Classics to 1500." *Speculum* 45 (1970): 225–53.

LUGT 1968: F. Lugt. *Inventaire général des dessins des écoles du nord: Maîtres des anciens Pays-Bas nés avant 1550*. Paris, 1968.

LYNA 1928: Frederik Lyna. "Onbekende Miniaturen van den Girary meester (Jehan Dreux) (Brussel, k Hss. 10976 en 9017)." *Het Boek* 17 (1928): 179–91.

LYNA 1933: Frédéric Lyna. *De Vlaamsche miniatuur van 1200 tot 1530*. Brussels, 1933.

LYNA 1949: Frédéric Lyna. "Un Livre sur le maître de Marie de Bourgogne." *Scriptorium* 3 (1949): 151–55.

MACFARLANE 1960: Leslie Macfarlane. "The Book of Hours of James IV and Margaret Tudor." *The Innes Review* 11 (1960): 3–21.

MACHARIS 1965: M. Macharis. "Geeraard Horenbout, zijn wapen en waagschap." *Ons Heem* 19 (1965) 219–23.

MACINGHI NEGLI STROZZI 1877: Alessandra Macinghi negli Strozzi. *Lettere di una gentildonna fiorentina del secolo XV ai figliuoli esuli*, edited by C. Guasti. Florence, 1877.

MACLAREN AND BRAHAM 1970: Neil MacLaren. *The Spanish School*. 2nd ed., revised by Allan Braham. London, 1970.

MADOU 1981: Mireille Madou. "Die Leidse 'Kroniek van Enguerrand de Monstrelet' Bijdrage in het onderzoek naar een exacte datering van de codex." In *Archivum Artis Lovaniense: Bijdragen tot de geschiedenis van de kunst der Nederlanden opgedragen aan Prof. Em. J. K. Steppe*, edited by Maurits Smeyers: 111–22. Leuven, 1981.

MADRID 1993: *Santiago, Camino de Europa: Culto y cultura en la peregrinación a Compostela*. Exh. cat. compiled by Serafín Moralejo and Fernando López Alsina. Madrid, Fundación Caja; Santiago de Compostela, Monasterio de San Martín Pinario, 1993.

MAHONY 1996: Dhira B. Mahony. "Courtly Presentation and Authorial Self-Fashioning: Frontispiece Miniatures in Late Medieval French and English Manuscripts." *Mediaevalia* 21 (1996): 104–7.

MAINZ 1975: *1000 Jahre Mainzer Dom (975–1975): Werden und Wandel*. Exh. cat. by Wilhelm Jung. Mainz, Bischöfliches Dom- und Diozesanmuseums, 1975.

MAINZ 1980: *Das Gebetbuch des Kardinals Albrecht von Brandenburg*. Exh. cat. compiled by J. M. Plotzek. Mainz, Mittelrheinisches Landesmuseum, 1980.

MAINZ 1990: *Albrecht von Brandenburg: Kurfürst, Erkanzler, Kardinal, 1490–1545*. Exh. cat. compiled by H. Reber, et al. Mainz, Landesmuseum, 1990.

MALIBU 1983a: *Renaissance Painting in Manuscripts: Treasures from the British Library*. Exh. cat. edited by Thomas Kren. Malibu, J. Paul Getty Museum, 1983.

MALIBU 1983b: *Master Drawings from the Woodner Collection*. Exh. cat. by George R. Goldner. Malibu, J. Paul Getty Museum, 1983.

MALIBU 1991: *A Thousand Years of the Bible: An Exhibition of Manuscripts from The J. Paul Getty Museum, Malibu, and Printed Books from The Department of Special Collections, University Research Library, UCLA*. Exh. cat. Malibu, J. Paul Getty Museum, 1991.

MANCHESTER 1960: *Works of Art from Private Collections in Lancashire, Cheshire, Cumberland, Westmorland, Parts of Shropshire, Staffordshire and Derbyshire, North Wales and Anglesey*. Exh. cat. Manchester, City Art Gallery, 1960.

MANCHESTER 1976: *Medieval and Early Renaissance Treasures in the North West*. Exh. cat. ed. J. Alexander and P. Crossley. Manchester, Whitworth Art Gallery, 1976.

MANCHESTER 1993: *Through Painted Windows: Visions of Medieval Life in Books of Hours*. Exhibition guide by Sarah Lawrance. Manchester, John Rylands University Library, 1993.

MANN 1998: N. Mann. "Petrarch and Portraits." In *The Image of the Individual: Portraits in the Renaissance*, edited by N. Mann and L. Syson: 15–20. London, 1998.

MARCH 1949: José March. "Juanín Gossart. Nota sobre el retrato de Don Juan de Zúñiga y Avellaneda." *Boletín de la Sociedad Española de Excursions* 53 (1949): 219–21.

MARIANI CANOVA 1969: Giordana Mariani Canova. *La miniatura veneta del Rinasciment, 1450–1500*. Venice, 1969.

MARIANI CANOVA 1987: Giordana Mariani Canova. "Fiori fiamminghi a Venezia: Benedetto Bordon e il Breviario Grimani." *Per ricordo di Sonia Tiso: Scritti di storia dell'arte fiamminghi e olandese*: 5–12. Ferrara, 1987.

MARIJNISSEN AND SEIDEL 1971: Roger-H. Marijnissen and Max Seidel. *Bruegel*. Brussels, 1971.

MARKL 1983: Dagoberto Markl. *Livro de horas de D. Manuel*. Lisbon, 1983.

MARLIER 1957: Georges Marlier. *Ambrosius Benson et la peinture à Bruges au temps des Charles-Quint*. Damme, 1957.

MARLIER 1966: Georges Marlier. *La Renaissance flamande: Pierre Coeck d'Alost*. Brussels, 1966.

MARROW 1966: James Marrow. "Pictorial Reversals in the Turin-Milan Hours." *Scriptorium* 20 (1966): 67–69.

MARROW 1973: James Marrow. "Dutch Illumination and the Devotio Moderna." *Medium Aevum* 42, no. 3 (1973): 251–58.

MARROW 1975: James Marrow. "From Sacred Metaphor to descriptive Narrative: Transformations of Passion iconography in the Late Middle Ages." Ph.D. diss., Columbia University, New York 1975.

MARROW 1977: James Marrow. "Circumdederunt me canes multi: Christ's Tormentors in Northern European Art of the Late Middle Ages and Early Renaissance." *Art Bulletin* 59 (1977): 167–81.

MARROW 1979: James Marrow. *Passion Iconography in Northern European Art of the Late Middle Ages and Early Renaissance.* Kortrijk, 1979.

MARROW 1983a: James Marrow. "'In desen speigell': A New Form of *Memento mori* in Fifteenth-Century Netherlandish Art." In *Essays in Northern European Art Presented to Egbert Haverkamp–Begemann*: 154–63. Doornspijk, 1983.

MARROW 1983b: James Marrow. "Nikolaus Glockendon and Simon Bening: German Copies of the Evangelist Portraits in Bening's Stockholm Book of Hours." *Nationalmuseum Bulletin* 7, no. 2 (1983): 93–101.

MARROW 1984: James Marrow. "Simon Bening in 1521: A Group of Dated Miniatures." In *Liber Amicorum Herman Liebaers*: 537–59. Brussels, 1984.

MARROW 1986: James Marrow. "Symbol and Meaning in Northern European Art of the Late Middle Ages and the Early Renaissance." *Simiolus* 16 (1986): 159–60.

MARROW 1991: James B. Marrow. "Dutch Manuscript Painting in Context: Encounters with the Art of France, the Southern Netherlands and Germany." In *Masters and Miniatures: Proceedings of the Congress on Medieval Manuscript Illumination in the Northern Netherlands*, edited by Koert van der Horst and Johann-Christian Klamt: 53–88. Doornspijk, 1991.

MARROW 1994: James Marrow, with a contribution by François Avril. *The Hours of Simon de Varie.* Malibu and The Hague, 1994.

MARROW 2002: James Marrow. "Une Page inconnue des Heures de Turin." *Revue de l'art* 135 (2002): 67–76.

MARTENS (D.) 2002: Didier Martens. "Transmission et métamorphose d'un modèle: La Descendance au XVIème siècle de la 'Virgo inter virgenes' attribuée à Hugo van der Goes." In *Annales de la Société Royale d'Archéologie de Bruxelles* 65 (2002): 105–88.

MARTENS (M.) 1992: Maximiliaan P. J. Martens. "Artistic Patronage in Bruges Institutions, ca. 1440–1482." Ph.D. diss., University of California, Santa Barbara, 1992.

MARTENS (M.) 1999: Maximiliaan P. J. Martens. "The Position of the Artist in the Fifteenth Century: Salaries and Social Mobility." In *Showing Status: Representation of Social Positions in the Late Middle Ages*, edited by W. Blockmans and A. Janse: 387–414. Turnhout, 1999.

MARTENS (M.) 2000: Maximiliaan P. J. Martens. "De Portretten van Lieven van Pottelsberghe en Livina van Steelant." In *200 Jaar Verzamelen: Collectieboek Museum voor Schone Kunsten Gent*: 52–56. Ghent, 2000.

MARTIN 1885–99: H. Martin. *Catalogue des manuscrits de la Bibliothèque de l'Arsenal.* Vol. 5. Paris, 1889. Reprint, Paris, 1979.

MARTIN 1917: Henry Martin. "Jean Hennecart: peintre de Charles le Téméraire." *Gazette des Beaux-Arts* 59 (1917): 155–72.

MARTIN 1928: Henry Martin. *Les Joyaux de l'enluminure à la Bibliothèque Nationale.* Paris / Brussels, 1928.

MARTIN AND LAUER 1929: H. Martin and P. Lauer. *Les principaux manuscrits à peintures de la Bibliothèque de l'Arsenal à Paris.* Paris, 1929.

MARTINDALE 1966: Andrew Martindale. "The Rise of the Artist: The Changing Status of the Craftsman." In *The Flowering of the Middle Ages*: 281–314. London, 1966.

MARTINDALE 1988: A. Martindale. *Simone Martini.* Oxford, 1988.

MASAI AND WITTEK 1968–82: F. Masai and M. Wittek. *Manuscrits datés conservés en Belgique.* 4 vols. Brussels, 1968–82.

MATHER 1915: Frank Jewett Mather, Jr. "Three Early Flemish Tomb Pictures." *Art in America* 3 (1915): 261–72.

MATHESON 1979: Lister M. Matheson. "The Middle English Prose *Brut*: A Location List of the Manuscripts and Early Printed Editions." *Analytical and Enumerative Bibliography* 3/4 (1979): 254–66.

MATHESON 1998: Lister M. Matheson. *The Prose Brut: The Development of a Middle English Chronicle.* Medieval and Renaissance Texts and Studies, 180. Tempe (Arizona), 1998.

MATHIEU 1953: C. Mathieu. "Le Métier des peintres à Bruxelles aux XIVème et XVème siècles." In *Bruxelles au XVème siècle*: 221–35. Brussels, 1953.

MAURICE-CHABARD 1999: Brigitte Maurice-Chabard, ed. *La Splendeur des Rolin: Un Mécénat privé à la cour de Bourgogne.* Picard, 1999.

MAYBERRY 1991: Nancy Mayberry. "The Controversy over the Immaculate Conception in Medieval and Renaissance Art, Literature, and Society." *Journal of Medieval and Renaissance Studies* 21 (fall 1991): 207–24.

MAZAL AND THOSS 1991: O. Mazal and D. Thoss. *Das buchaltärchen / Livre-autel Herzog Philipps des Guten von Burgund, Codex 1800 der Österreichiscen Nationalbibliothek in Wien.* Lucerne, 1991.

MAZAL AND THOSS 1993: Otto von Mazal and Dagmar Thoss. *Das Croy-Gebetbuch: Codex 1858 der Österreichischen Nationalbibliothek in Wien.* Lucern, 1993.

MAZAL AND UNTERKIRCHER 1963: Otto Mazal and Franz Unterkircher. *Katalog der abendländischen Handschriften der Österreichischen Nationalbibliothek. "Series Nova."* 5 vols. Vienna, 1963.

MCGRATH 1968: Robert L. McGrath. "Satan and Bosch: *The Visio Tundali* and the Monastic Vices." *Gazette des Beaux-Arts* 71 (1968): 45–50.

MCKENDRICK 1988: Scot McKendrick. "Classical Mythology and Ancient History of Works of Art at the Courts of France, Burgundy, and England, 1364–1500." The Courtauld Institute, London, 1988.

MCKENDRICK 1990: Scot McKendrick. "*La Grande Histoire Cesar* and the Manuscripts of Edward IV." *English Manuscript Studies, 1100–1700* 2 (1990): 109–38.

MCKENDRICK 1991: Scot McKendrick. "The *Great History of Troy*: A Reassessment of the Development of a Secular Theme in Late Medieval Art." *Journal of the Warburg and Courtauld Institutes* 54 (1991): 43–82.

MCKENDRICK 1992: Scot McKendrick. "Lodewijk van Gruuthuse en de Librije van Edward IV." In *Lodewijk van Gruuthuse, Mecenas en Europees Diplomaat ca. 1427–1492*, edited by Maximiliaan P. J. Martens: 153–59. Bruges, 1992.

MCKENDRICK 1994: Scot McKendrick. "The *Romuléon* and the Manuscripts of Edward IV." In *England in the Fifteenth Century: Proceedings of the 1992 Harlaxton Symposium*, edited by Nicholas Rogers: 149–69. Stamford, 1994.

MCKENDRICK 1996a: Scot McKendrick. *The History of Alexander the Great: Illuminated Manuscript of Vasco da Lucena's French Translation of the Ancient Text by Quintus Curtius Rufus.* Los Angeles, 1996.

MCKENDRICK 1996b: Scot McKendrick. "Illustrated Manuscripts of Vasco da Lucena's Translation of Curtius's Historiae Alexandri Magni: Nature Corrupted by Fortune?" In *Medieval Manuscripts of the Latin Classics: Production and Use. Proceedings of

the Seminar in the History of the Book to 1500, Leiden, 1993*: 131–49. Los Altos Hills, Ca., 1996.

MCKENDRICK 2003: Scot McKendrick. *Flemish Illuminated Manuscripts, 1400–1550.* London, 2003.

MCKINNON 1976: James W. McKinnon. "Canticum Novum in 'The Isabella Book.'" *Medievalia* 2 (1976): 207–22.

MCKINNON 1978: James W. McKinnon. "Representations of the Mass in Medieval and Renaissance Art." *Journal of the American Musicological Society* 31 (1978): 21–52.

MCKINNON 1984: James W. McKinnon. "The Fifteen Temple Steps and the Gradual Psalms." *Imago musicae* 1 (1984): 29–49.

MEADOW 1997: Mark A. Meadow. "Bruegel's 'Procession to Calvary,' Aemulatio and the Space of Vernacular Style." In *Pieter Bruegel*, edited by Jan de Jong et al.: 181–205. *Nederlands Kunsthistorisch Jaarboek* 47 (1996). Zwolle, 1997.

MEADOW 2002: Mark A. Meadow. *Pieter Bruegel the Elder's "Netherlandish Proverbs" and the Practice of Rhetoric.* Zwolle, 2002.

MEALE 1989: Carol Meale. "Patrons, Buyers and Owners: Book Production and Social Status." In *Book Production and Publishing in Britain, 1375–1475*, edited by Jeremy Griffiths and Derek Pearsall: 201–38. Cambridge, 1989.

MEISS 1968: Millard Meiss. *French Painting in the Time of Jean de Berry. The Boucicaut Master.* London, 1968.

MEISS 1974: Millard Meiss. *French Painting in the Time of Jean de Berry: the Limbourgs and Their Contemporaries.* 2 vols. New York, 1974.

MELLEN 1971: P. Mellen. *Jean Clouet.* London, 1971.

MELLINKOFF 1998: Ruth Mellinkoff. "Sarah and Hagar: Laughter and Tears." In *Illuminating the Book: Makers and Interpreters*, edited by Michelle P. Brown and Scot McKendrick: 35–51. London, 1998.

MENÉNDEZ PIDAL DE NAVASCUÉS 1996: F. Menéndez Pidal de Navascués. *El libro de la cofradía de Santiago: Caballería medieval burgalesa.* [Cádiz].

MENSGER 2002: Missing text to be inserted here.

MERKL 1999: Ulrich Merkl. *Buchmalerei in Bayern in der ersten Hälfte des 16. Jahrhunderts: Spätblüte und Endzeit einer Gattung.* Regensburg, 1999.

MESSAGER DES SCIENCES HISTORIQUES 1833: "Diptique peint par Gerard Horenbout." *Messager des sciences historiques; ou, Archives des arts et de la bibliographie de Belgique,* 1833: 12–16.

MESTAYER 1991: M. Mestayer. "La Bibliothèque de Charles II, comte de Lalaing, en 1541." In *Les Sources littéraires et leurs publics dans l'espace bourguignon (XIVe–XVIe s.)*: 199–216. Publication du Centre européen d'Études bourguignonnes, 31. Neuchâtel, 1991.

MEYER 1885: Paul Meyer. "Les Premières Compilations françaises d'histoire ancienne. I. Les Faits des Romains; II. Histoire ancienne jusqu'à César." *Romania* 14 (1885): 1–81.

MEYER 1897: Paul Meyer. "Recherches sur l'épopée française." *Bibliothèque de l'école des chartes*, ser. 6, 3 (1897): 29–63, 304–42.

MICHEL 1924: Édouard Michel. "Le Bréviaire de la Collection Mayer van den Bergh à Anvers." *Gazette des Beaux-Arts* 66 (April 1924): 193–204.

MICHEL 1927: Édouard Michel. "À propos de Simon Marmion." *Gazette des Beaux-Arts*, ser. 5, 16 (1927): 141–54.

MICHEL 1931: Édouard Michel. *Bruegel.* Paris, 1931.

MICHEL (H.) 1925: Henri Michel. *L'Imprimeur Colard Mansion et le Boccace de la Bibliothèque d'Amiens.* Paris, 1925.

MICHIELS 1845–49: Alfred Michiels. *Histoire de la peinture flamande et hollandaise*. Vols. 1–4. Brussels, 1845–49.

MIÉLOT 1881: Jean Miélot. *Vie de Ste. Catharine d'Alexandrie*. Edited by Marius Sepet. Paris, 1881.

MILAN 1999: *I Santi Patroni: Modelli di santita, culti e patronati in Occidente*. Exh. cat. by Leonardi Claudio and Antonella Degl'Innocenti. Milan, Biblioteca nazionale centrale Vittorio Emanuele III di Napoli, 1999.

MILLAR 1914–20: Eric George Millar. "Les Manuscrits à peintures des bibliothèques de Londres." *Bulletin de la Société française de Reproductions de Manuscrits à peintures* 4 (1914–20): 89–108.

MILLAR 1925: Eric George Millar. "Les Principaux Manuscrits à peintures du Lambeth Palace à Londres." *Bulletin de la Société française de Réproductions de Manuscrits à peintures* 9 (1925): 5–81.

MODENA 1987: *Biblioteca Estensa Modena*. Florence, 1987.

MODENA 1997: *Gebet und betrachtungen des Lebens des mitlers Gottes und des menschen unsers Herrens Jesu Christi von Anfang seiner heyligen menschwerdung von alle seinem Leyden bis in das Endt seines aller bittersten sterbens an dem holtz des heiligen Creutzes menschlichs gemuet bewegend und reytzend zu Andacht*. Modena, 1997.

MOMBELLO 1971: G. Mombello. "I manoscritti delle opere di Dante, Petrarca, e Boccaccio nelle principali libréria francesi del secolo XV." In *Il Boccaccio nella cultura francese*. Edited by C. Pellegrini: 81–209. Florence, 1971.

MONASTICON BELGE 1890–1993: *Monasticon Belge*. Edited by Ursmer Berlière and Centre national de Recherches d'Histoire réligieuse. 8 vols. Bruges and Liège, 1890–1993.

MONFRIN 1967: J. Monfrin. "Le Goût des lettres antiques à la cour de Bourgogne au XVe siècle." *Bulletin de la Société nationale des Antiquaires de France*, 1967: 285–89.

MONFRIN 1972: J. Monfrin. "La Connaissance de l'antiquité et le problème de l'humanisme en langue vulgaire dans la France du XVe siècle." In *The Late Middle Ages and the Dawn of Humanism outside Italy*, edited by G. Verbeke and J. Ijsewijn: 131–70. Leuven, 1972.

MONFRIN 1982: J. Monfrin. "La Place du *Secret des Secrets* dans la littérature française médiévale." In *Pseudo-Aristotle, The Secret of Secrets: Sources and Influences*, edited by W. F. Ryan and Charles B. Schmitt: 73–113. Warburg Institute Surveys, 9. London, 1982.

MONGAN 1942: Agnes Mongan. "A *Pietà* by Simon Marmion." *Bulletin of the Fogg Museum of Art* 6, no. 6 (1942): 115–20.

MONKS 1990: Peter Rolfe Monks. The *Brussels Horloge de Sapience: Iconography and Text of Brussels, Bibliothèque Royale, MS. IV 111*. Leiden, 1990.

MONKS 1994: Peter Rolf Monks. "Some Doubtful Attributions to the Master of Jean Rolin II." In *Medieval Codicology, Iconography, Literature, and Translation: Studies for Keith Val Sinclair*, edited by Peter Rolfe Monks and D. D. R. Owen: 143–50. Leiden, 1994.

MONTREAL 1960: Museum of Fine Arts. *Canada Collects: European Paintings, 1860–1960*. Montreal, 1960.

MOONEY 1989: L. R. Mooney. "Lydgate's 'Kings of England' and Another Verse Chronicle of the Kings." *Viator* 20 (1989): 255–75.

MORELLO AND MADDALO 1995: Giovanni Morello and Silvia Maddalo. *Liturgia in Figura. Codici liturgici rinascimentali della Biblioteca Apostolica Vaticana*. Rome, Biblioteca Apostolica Vaticana, Salone Sistino, 1995.

MORGAN 1992: Nigel Morgan. "Texts of Devotion and Religious Instruction Associated with Margaret of York." In *Margaret of York, Simon Marmion, and The Visions of Tondal*, edited by T. Kren: 63–76. Malibu, 1992.

MOSCOW 1990: *Dekorativno-prikladnoe iskusstvo ot pozdnei antichnosti do pozdnei gotiki iz: sobranii Muzeia Metropoliten, N'iu-Iork, i Khudozhestvennogo instituta, Chikago: Kratkii katalog vystavki*. Exh. cat. by E. R. Kan'kovskaia. Moscow, 1990.

MOXEY 1986: Keith P. F. Moxey. "A New Look at Netherlandish Landscape and Still-Life Painting." *Arts in Virginia* 26, no. 2 (1986): 27–28.

MULLER 1998: Norman Muller. "Technical Analysis of the Princeton *Road to Calvary*." In *Herri met de Bles: Studies and Explorations of the World Landscape Tradition*, edited by Norman Muller, Betsy Rosasco, and James Marrow: 23–37. Princeton, 1998.

MÜLLER HOFSTEDE 1988: Justus Müller Hofstede. "Artificial Light in Honthorst and Terbrugghen: Form and Iconography." In *Hendrick ter Brugghen und die Nachfolger Caravaggios in Holland*, edited by Rüdiger Klessman: 13–43. Braunschweig, 1988.

MUNBY 1972: A. N. L. Munby. *Connoisseurs and Medieval Miniatures, 1750–1850*. Oxford, 1972.

MUNDÓ 1959: Anscari M. Mundó, Dom. "Les Collections de manuscrits en Catalogne, et celle de Montserrat en particulier." *Archives, Bibliothèques et musées de Belgique* 30 (1959): 221–23.

MUNDY 1980: E. James Mundy. "Gerard David Studies." Ph.D. diss., Princeton University, 1980.

MUNICH 1959: *Buchkunst und Bibliophile in Spätgotik und Renaissance*. Munich, Bayerische Staatsbibliothek, 1959.

MUNICH 1970a: *Cimelia Monacensia: Wertvolle Handschriften und frühe Drucke der Bayerischen Staatsbibliothek, München*. Wiesbaden, Bayerische Staatsbibliothek, 1970.

MUNICH 1970b: *Treasures of the Bavarian State Library: An Exhibition of Manuscripts, Incunabula and Block-Books*. Exh. cat. by Fridolin Dressler; translated by Malcolm Turner. Munich, Bayerische Staatsbibliothek, 1970.

MUNICH 1983a: *Alte Pinakothek München: Erläuterungen zu den ausgestellten Gemälden*. Munich, Bayerische Staatsgemäldesammlungen, 1983.

MUNICH 1983b: *Thesaurus librorum: 425 Jahre Bayerische Staatsbibliothek*. Exh. cat., Munich, Bayerische Staatsbibliothek, 1983.

MUÑOZ DELGADO 1985: Concepción Muñoz Delgado. "Un manuscrito inédito de la Real Biblioteca de el Escorial." *Archivo español de arte* 58 (April–June 1985): 144–56.

MURDOCH ET AL. 1981: John Murdoch, V. J. Murrell, P. J. Noon, and R. Strong. *The English Miniature*. London, 1981.

MURRELL 1983: Jim Murrell. *The Way Howe to Lymne: Tudor Miniatures Observed*. London, 1983.

MUSÉE DU LOUVRE 1988: "Les Récentes Acquisitions de musées nationaux." *La Revue du Louvre* 2 (1988): 155.

MUSÉE DU LOUVRE 1991: *Nouvelles Acquisitions du département des peintures, 1987–90*. Paris, 1991.

MUYLLE 1981: J. Muylle. "Pieter Bruegel en Abraham Ortelius. Bijdrage tot de literaire receptie van Pieter Bruegels werk." In *Archivum Artis Lovaniense: Bijdragen tot de geschiedenis van de kunst der Nederlanden, opgedragen aan Prof. Em. Dr. J. K. Steppe*: 319–37. Leuven, 1981.

NACKERS 2002: S. Nackers. "The 'Eloquence' of Grisaille in the *Bible historiale* of Edward IV (Mss. Royal 15 D I, 18 D IX and 18 D X)." M.A. thesis, Courtauld Institute of Art, London, 2002.

NAPLES 1967: *Arte francese a Napoli*. Naples, 1967.

NAPLES 1995: *Al campo d'oro con gli azzurra gigli: Libri di casa Farnese*. Exh. cat. Naples, Biblioteca nazionale, 1995.

NASH 1995: Susie Nash. "A Fifteenth-Century French Manuscript and an Unknown Painting by Robert Campin." *Burlington Magazine* 137 (1995): 428–37.

NASH 1999: Susie Nash. *Between France and Flanders: Manuscript Illumination in Amiens*. London, 1999.

NEUGASS 1976: F. Neugass. "Neu entdecktes Stundenbuch in Amerika." *Weltkunst* 46 (December 15, 1976): 2504.

NEW YORK 1934: *Exhibition of Illuminated Manuscripts Held at the New York Public Library, November 1933–April 1934*. Exh. cat. by Belle Da Costa Greene and Meta P. Harssen. New York, New York Public Library, 1934.

NEW YORK 1939: *Illustrated Catalogue of an Exhibition Held on the Occasion of the New York's World's Fair*. Exh. cat. New York, Pierpont Morgan Library, 1939.

NEW YORK 1959a: Columbia University. *Great Master Drawings of Seven Centuries*. Exh. cat. New York, M. Knoedler and Company, 1959.

NEW YORK 1959b: *Manuscripts from the William S. Glazier Collection*. Compiled by John Plummer. New York, Pierpont Morgan Library, 1959.

NEW YORK 1964: *Liturgical Manuscripts for the Mass and Divine Office*. Exh. cat. by John Plummer. New York, Pierpont Morgan Library, 1964.

NEW YORK 1968a: *The Glazier Collection of Illuminated Manuscripts*. Compiled by John Plummer. New York, Pierpont Morgan Library, 1968.

NEW YORK 1968b: *Medieval Art from Private Collections. A Special Exhibition at the Cloisters*. Exh. cat. by Carmen Gómez-Moreno. New York, The Cloisters, Metropolitan Museum of Art, 1968.

NEW YORK 1974: *Mediaeval and Renaissance Manuscripts: Major Acquisitions of the Pierpont Morgan Library, 1924–1974*. New York, Pierpont Morgan Library, 1974.

NEW YORK 1975: *The Secular Spirit: Life and Art and the End of the Middle Ages*. Exh. cat. with foreword by Thomas Hoving and introduction by Timothy B. Husband and Jane Hayward. New York, The Cloisters, Metropolitan Museum of Art, 1975.

NEW YORK 1980: *Flowers in Books and Drawings, ca. 940–1840*. Exh. cat. New York, Pierpont Morgan Library, 1980.

NEW YORK 1982: *The Last Flowering: French Painting in Manuscripts, 1420–1530, from American Collections*. Compiled by John Plummer and Gregory Clark. New York, 1982.

NEW YORK 1985: *Wine: Celebration and Ceremony*. Exh. cat. compiled by Hugh Johnson, Dora Jane Janson, and David Revere McFadden. New York, Cooper-Hewitt Museum, 1985.

NEW YORK 1988a: *Painting in Renaissance Siena, 1420–1500*. Exh. cat. New York, Metropolitan Museum of Art, 1988.

NEW YORK 1988b: Research Center for Musical Iconography. *Inventory of Musical Iconography 3: The Pierpont Morgan Library, New York, Medieval and Renaissance Manuscripts*. Compiled by T. Ford and A. Green. New York, 1988.

NEW YORK 1992: *The Bernard H. Breslauer Collection of Manuscript Illuminations*. Edited by W. Voelkle and R. Wieck. Exh. cat. New York, Pierpont Morgan Library, 1992.

NEW YORK 1993: *In August Company: The Collections of the Pierpont Morgan Library.* New York, 1993.

NEW YORK 1993–95: *Facsimile in Early Netherlandish Painting: Dieric Bouts's Virgin and Child.* Exh. cat. by Mary W. Ainsworth. New York, Metropolitan Museum of Art, 1993.

NEW YORK 1994a: *Petrus Christus: Renaissance Master of Bruges.* Exh. cat. by Maryan W. Ainsworth, with contributions by Maximiliaan P. J. Martens. New York, The Metropolitan Museum of Art, 1994.

NEW YORK 1994b: *The Painted Page: Italian Renaissance Book Illumination, 1450–1550.* Exh. cat. edited by Jonathan J. G. Alexander. London, Royal Academy of Arts, 1994.

NEW YORK 1995: *The Luminous Image: Painted Glass Roundels in the Lowlands, 1480–1560.* Exh. cat. by Timothy B. Husband. New York, Metropolitan Museum of Art, 1995.

NEW YORK 1998: *From Van Eyck to Bruegel: Early Netherlandish Painting in the Metropolitan Museum of Art.* Exh. cat. edited by Maryan Ainsworth and Keith Christiansen. New York, Metropolitan Museum of Art, 1998.

NEW YORK 1999a: *Mirror of the Medieval World.* Exh. cat. edited by W. Wixom. New York, Metropolitan Museum of Art, 1999.

NEW YORK 1999b: *The Wormsley Library: A Personal Selection by Sir Paul Getty, K. B. E.* Exh. cat. Edited by H. George Fletcher. New York, Pierpont Morgan Library, 1999.

NEW YORK 2001: *Pieter Bruegel the Elder: Drawings and Prints.* Exh. cat. edited by Nadine M. Orenstein. New York, Metropolitan Museum of Art, 2001.

NEW YORK 2002: *Tapestry in the Renaissance: Art and Magnificence.* Exh. cat. by Thomas Campbell. New York, Metropolitan Museum of Art, 2002.

NEWMAN 1991: J. Newman. "Cardinal Wolsey's Collegiate Foundations." In *Cardinal Wolsey: Church, State, and Art*, edited by S. J. Gunn and P. G. Lindley: 103–15. Cambridge, 1991.

NIEUWDORP AND DEKEYZER 1997: Hans Nieuwdorp and Brigitte Dekeyzer. *Breviarium Mayer Van den Bergh: Alle miniaturen.* Ghent, 1997.

NIEUWSTRATEN 1994: Rineke Nieuwstraten. "Vervaardigers en bezitters van Raoul Lefèvre's *Histoire de Jason*: Kanalen voor de verbreiding van een idee." *Millennium: Tijdschrift voor middeleeuwse studies 8* (1994): 134–47.

NORDENFALK 1979: Carl Nordenfalk. *Bokmålningar från medeltid och renässans i Nationalmusei samlingar: en konstbok från Nationalmuseum.* Stockholm, 1979.

NUREMBERG 1987: *Fünf Jahrhunderte Buchillustration: Meisterwerke der Buchgraphik aus der Bibliothek Otto Schäfer.* Exh. cat. compiled by Eduard Isphording, Manfred von Arnim, and Ursula Timann. Nuremberg, Germanisches Nationalmuseum, 1987.

NUREMBERG 1993: *Ludwigslust: Die Sammlung Irene und Peter Ludwig.* Exh. cat. compiled by M. Eissenhauer. Nuremberg, Germanisches Nationalmuseum, 1993.

NYS 1991: L. Nys. "Un Petit Triptyque sculpté de prestation de serment tournaisien du début du XVe siècle conservé au Musée des Arts Décoratifs de Paris." *Revue des archéologues et historiens d'art de Louvain* 24 (1991): 47–56.

NYS AND SALAMAGNE 1996: Ludovic Nys and d'Alain Salamagne, eds. *Valenciennes aux XIVe et XVe siècles: Art et histoire.* Valenciennes, 1996.

OBREEN 1903: H. G. A. Obreen. *Geschiedenis van het geslacht van Wassenaer.* Leiden, 1903.

OETTINGER 1938: K. Oettinger. "Das Rätsel der Kunst des Hugo van der Goes." *Jahrbuch der Kunsthistorischen Sammlungen in Wien* 12 (1938): 43–76.

OKLAHOMA CITY 1985: *Songs of Glory: Medieval Art from 900–1500.* Exh. cat. by David Mickenberg. Oklahoma City, Oklahoma Museum of Art, 1985.

OKUBO 1995: Masami Okubo. "Les Traditions apocryphes dans la littérature mariale du Moyen Âge: Étude et édition de textes français des XIIIe–XVe siècles." Doctorale thesis, Université de Sorbonne-Paris, Paris IV, 1995.

OLIVAR 1969: Alexandre Olivar. *Els manuscrits litúrgics de la Biblioteca de Montserrat.* Scripta et Documenta, 18. Barcelona, 1969.

OLSCHKI 1932: Leonardo Olschki. *Manuscrits français à peintures des bibliothèques d'Allemagne.* Geneva, 1932.

OMONT 1891: H. Omont. In "Les Manuscrits français des rois d'Angleterre au château de Richmond." *Études romanes dédiées à Gaston Paris*: 1–13, Paris, 1891. Reprint, Geneva, 1976.

ONGANIA 1903: Ferdinand Ongania, ed. *Le Bréviaire Grimani à la Bibliothèque Marciana de Venise.* Venice, 1903.

ONGHENA 1968: M. J. Onghena. "Enkele gegevens en Opmerkingen betreffende twee zestiende eeuwse Handschriften van het gulden Vlies." In *Miscellanea Jozef Duverger; Bijdragen tot de Kunstgeschiedenis der Nederlanden*, vol. 1: 187–215. Ghent, 1968.

ORTH 1996: Myra D. Orth. "What Goes Around: Borders and Frames in French Manuscripts." *Journal of the Walters Art Gallery* 54 (1996): 189–201, 277–78.

ORTH 1997: Myra D. Orth. "Deux Enluminures françaises de la Renaissance au Musée des Beaux-Arts de Lyon." *Bulletin des musées et monuments lyonnais* 3 (1997): 20–33.

OSTEN 1961: Gert Von der Osten. "Studien zu Jan Gossaert." In *Essays in Honor of Erwin Panofsky*, edited by Millard Meiss: 454–475. New York, 1961.

OTTOSEN 1993: Knud Ottosen. *The Responsories and Versicles of the Latin Office of the Dead.* Aarhus, 1993.

OXFORD 1895–1953: Bodleian Library. *A Summary Catalogue of Western Manuscripts in the Bodleian Library at Oxford.* 7 vols. Oxford, 1895–1953. Reprint, Munich, 1980.

OXFORD 1980: Bodleian Library. *A Summary Catalogue of Western Manuscripts in the Bodleian Library at Oxford.* 7 vols. Munich, 1980.

OXFORD 1984: *The Douce Legacy: An Exhibition to Commemorate the 150th Anniversary of the Bequest of Francis Douce (1757–1834).* Exh. cat. Oxford, Bodleian Library, 1984.

PÄCHT 1944a: Otto Pächt. "The Master of Mary of Burgundy." *Burlington Magazine* 85 (1944): 295–300.

PÄCHT 1944b: Otto Pächt. "Holbein and Kratzer as Collaborators." *Burlington Magazine* 85 (1944): 134–39.

PÄCHT 1948: Otto Pächt. *The Master of Mary of Burgundy.* London, 1948.

PÄCHT 1973: Otto Pächt. "René d'Anjou—Studien I." *Jahrbuch der Kunsthistorischen Sammlungen in Wien* 69 (1973): 85–126.

PÄCHT 1976: Otto Pächt. "Die niederländischen Stundenbücher des Lord Hastings." In *Essays Presented to G. I. Lieftinck*, vol. 4, *Miniatures, Scripts, Collections*: 28–32. Litterae textuales. Amsterdam, 1976.

PÄCHT 1978: Otto Pächt. "La Terre de Flandres." *Pantheon* 36 (1978): 3–16.

PÄCHT 1979: Otto Pächt. "'Simon Mormion myt der handt.'" *Revue de l'art* 46 (1979): 7–15.

PÄCHT 1981: Otto Pächt. "Dévotion du roi René pour sainte Marie-Madeleine et le sanctuaire de Saint-Maximin." *Chronique Méridionale: Arts du Moyen Âge et de la Renaissance*, 1981: 15–28.

PÄCHT 1986: Otto Pächt. *Book Illumination in the Middle Ages: An Introduction.* London, 1986.

PÄCHT AND ALEXANDER 1966–73: Otto Pächt and J. J. G. Alexander. *Illuminated Manuscripts in the Bodleian Library, Oxford.* 3 vols. Oxford, 1966–73.

PÄCHT, JENNI, AND THOSS 1983: Otto Pächt, Ulrike Jenni, and Dagmar Thoss. *Flämische Schule I.* 2 vols. Veröffentlichungen der Kommission für Schrift- und Buchwesen des Mittelalters, ser. 1, Die illuminierten Handschriften und Inkunabeln der Österreichischen Nationalbibliothek, 6. Vienna, 1983.

PÄCHT AND THOSS 1990: Otto Pächt and Dagmar Thoss. *Flämische Schule II.* 2 vols. Veröffentlichungen der Kommission für Schrift- und Buchwesen des Mittelalters, ser. 1, Die illuminierten Handschriften und Inkunabeln der Österreichischen Nationalbibliothek, vol. 7. Vienna, 1990.

PAGET 1959: H. Paget. "Gerard and Lucas Horenbolt in England." *Burlington Magazine* 101 (1959): 396–402.

PALMER 1982: Nigel F. Palmer. "*Visio Tnugdali*": The German and Dutch Translations and Their Circulation in the Later Middle Ages. Munich and Zürich, 1982.

PALMER 1992: Nigel F. Palmer. "Illustrated Printed Editions of *The Visions of Tondal* from the Late Fifteenth and Early Sixteenth Centuries." In *Margaret of York, Simon Marmion, and The Visions of Tondal*, edited by T. Kren: 157–70. Malibu, 1992.

PANHANS-BÜHLER 1978: U. Panhans-Bühler. *Eklektizismus und Originalität im Werk des Petrus Christus.* Wiener Kunstgeschichtliche Forschungen, 5. Vienna, 1978.

PANOFSKY 1953: E. Panofsky. *Early Netherlandish Painting: Its Origins and Character.* 2 vols. Cambridge, Mass., 1953.

PARAVICINI 1975: W. Paravicini. *Guy de Brimeu: Der burgundische Staat und seine adlige Führungsschicht unter Karl dem Kühnen.* Bonn, 1975.

PARAVICINI 1978: W. Paravicini. "Soziale Schichtung und soziale Mobilität am Hof der Herzöge von Burgund." *Francia* 5 (1977): 127–82.

PARAVICINI AND PARAVICINI 2000: A. Paravicini and W. Paravicini. "L'Arsenal intellectuel d'un homme de pouvoir: Les Livres de Guillaume Hugonet, chancelier de Bourgogne." In *Penser le pouvoir au Moyen Âge (VIIIe–XVe siècle): Études d'histoire et de littérature offertes à Françoise Autrand*, edited by D. Boutet and J. Verger: 261–325. Paris, 2000.

PARAVICINI BAGLIANI 1990: Agostino Paravicini Bagliani. *Les Manuscrits enluminés des comtes et ducs de Savoie: Études publieées.* Turin, 1990.

PARIS 1836–48: Paulin Paris. *Les Manuscrits françois de la bibliothèque du roi. . . .* 7 vols. Paris, 1838–48.

PARIS 1868: Bibliothèque nationale. *Catalogue des manuscrits français.* vol. 1. Paris, 1868.

PARIS 1904: *Les Primitifs français.* Exh. cat. by Henri Bouchot et al. 3 vols. Paris, Musée du Louvre, 1904.

PARIS 1907: *Catalogue of the Rodolphe Kann Collection: Objets d'art.* 2 vols. Paris, 1907.

PARIS 1955: *Manuscrits à peintures du XIIIe au XVIe siècle.* Paris, Bibliothèque nationale de France, 1955.

PARIS 1962: *Catalogue général des manuscrits des bibliothèques publiques de France.* Vol. 3. Paris, 1962.

PARIS 1968: *Manuscrits à peintures XIIe, XIVe, XVe, XVIe siècles.* Exh. cat. Paris, Palais Galliera, 1968.

PARIS 1975: *Boccace en France: De l'humanisme à l'érotisme.* Exh. cat. by Florence Callu and François Avril. Paris, Bibliothèque nationale de France, 1975.

PARIS 1980: *Trésors de la Bibliothèque de L'Arsenal.* Exh. cat. Paris, Bibliothèque nationale de France, 1980.

PARIS 1981: *Catalogue des incunables de la Bibliothèque nationale de France.* Paris: Bibliothèque nationale de France, 1981.

PARIS 1990: *St. Bernard et le monde cistercien.* Exh. cat. compiled by L. Pressouyre and T. N. Kinder. Paris, 1990.

PARIS 1992: *Des livres et des rois. La Bibliothèque royale de Blois.* Exh. cat. edited by Ursula Baurmeister and Marie-Pierre Laffitte. Paris, Bibliothèque nationale de France, 1992.

PARIS 1993: *Les Manuscrits à peintures en France, 1440–1520.* Exh. cat. by François Avril and Nicole Reynaud. Paris, Bibliothèque nationale de France, 1993.

PARIS 1994: *The Renaissance in France: Drawings from the École des Beaux-Arts, Paris.* Exh. cat. by E. Brugerolles and D. Guillet. Paris, École nationale supérieure, 1994. Eng. ed.: Cambridge, Mass., 1995.

PARIS 1995: *Hans Memling au Louvre.* Exh. cat. by P. Lorentz and T. Borchert. Paris, Musée du Louvre, 1995.

PARIS 1997: *Des mécènes par milliers: Un Siècle de dons par les Amis du Louvre.* Exh. cat. Paris, Musée du Louvre, 1997.

PARIS 1998: *L'Art au temps des rois maudits, Philippe le Bel et ses fils.* Paris, Galeries nationales du Grand Palais, 1998.

PARIS 2002: *Sur la terre comme au ciel: Jardins d'Occident à la fin du Moyen Âge.* Exh. cat. edited by Élisabeth Antoine. Paris, Musée national du Moyen Âge, 2002.

PARKER 1999: Geoffrey Parker. "The Political World of Charles V." In *Charles V, 1500–1558, and His Time,* edited by Hugo Soly: 113–225. Antwerp, 1999.

PARKES 1969: M. B. Parkes. *English Cursive Book Hands, 1250–1500.* Oxford, 1969.

PARMENTIER 1937: R. A. Parmentier. "Bescheiden omtrent Brugsche schilders van de 16e eeuw. I. Ambrosius Benson." *Annales de la Société d'Émulation pour l'étude de l'histoire et des antiquités de la Flandre* 80 (1937): 92–94.

PARMENTIER 1942: R. A. Parmentier. "Bronnen voor de geschiedenis van het Brugsche schildersmilieu in de XVIe eeuw. Gerard David." *Revue belge d'archéologie et d'histoire de l'art* 12 (1942): 5–19.

PARSHALL 1969: Peter W. Parshall. "A Dutch Manuscript of ca. 1480 from an Atelier in Bruges." *Miscellanea F. Lyna; Scriptorium* 23 (1969): 333–37.

PARTHEY 1863–64: Gustav Parthey. *Deutscher Bildersaal: Verzeichniss der in Deutschland vorhandenen Oelbilder verstorbener Maler aller Schulen.* 2 vols. Berlin, 1863–64.

PASSAVANT 1860–64: J. D. Passavant. *Le Peintre-graveur.* 6 vols. in 3. Leipzig, 1860–64.

PASTOREAU 1989: "Présences héraldiques dans le livre médiéval." In *Les Bibliothèques médiévales du VIe siècle à 1530,* edited by André Vernet: 215–63. Histoire des bibliothèques françaises, 1. Paris, 1989.

PAVIOT 1995: Jacques Paviot. *Portugal et Bourgogne au XVe siècle, 1384–1482.* Lisbon, 1995.

PAVIOT 1999: Jacques Paviot. "David Aubert et la cour de Bourgogne." In *Les Manuscrits de David Aubert,* edited by Danielle Quéruel: 9–18. Cultures et Civilisations Médiévales, 18. Paris, 1999.

PAYNE 1996: Ann Payne. "Statutes and Armorial of the Order of the Golden Fleece, British Library, Harley Ms 6199." In *L'Ordre de la Toison d'or, de Philippe le Bon à Philippe le Beau (1430–1505): Idéal ou reflet d'une société?,* edited by Christiane van den Bergen-Pantens: 45–46. Brussels, 1996.

PAYNE AND JEFFERSON 1996: Ann Payne and Lisa Jefferson. "Edward IV: The Garter and the Golden Fleece." In *L'Ordre de la Toison d'or, de Philippe le Bon à Philippe le Beau (1430–1505): Idéal ou reflet d'une société?,* edited by Christiane van den Bergen-Pantens: 194–97. Brussels, 1996.

PAZ Y MÉLIA 1901: A. Paz y Mélia. "Codices más notables de la Biblioteca Nacional." *Revista de archivos, bibliotecas y museos* 5 (1901): 289–94.

PELLECHET AND POLAIN 1970: Marie Pellechet and Louis Polain. *Catalogue général des incunables des bibliothèques publiques de France.* Reprint. 26 vols. Nendeln, 1970.

PERDRIZET 1907: P. Perdrizet. "Jean Miélot, l'un des traducteurs de Philippe le Bon." *Revue d'histoire littéraire de la France* 14 (1907): 472–82.

PEREIRA 1984: Fernando António Baptista Pereira. *Livro de Horas dito de D. Fernando.* Lisbon, 1984.

PÉRIER-D'IETEREN 1984: C. Périer-D'Ieteren. *Les Volets peints des retables bruxellois conservés en Suède et le rayonnement de Colyn de Coter.* Stockholm: Kungliga Vitterhets Historie och Antikvitets Akademien, 1984.

PERROT AND LASTEYRIE 1904: Georges Perrot and Robert de Lasteyrie. "Un Manuscrit de la Bibliothèque de Philippe le Bon." In *Fondation Eugène Piot: Monuments et mémoires publiés par l'Académie des inscriptions et belles-lettres:* 7–90. Paris, 1904.

PETERS 1979: J. S. Peters. "Early Drawings of Augustin Hirschvogel." *Master Drawings* 17 (1979): 362–81.

PETRUCCI 1977: A. Petrucci. "La concezione cristiana del libro fra VI e VII secolo." In *Libri e lettori nel Medioevo: Guida storica e critica,* edited by G. Cavallo: 5–26. Bari, 1977.

PHILADELPHIA 1941: The Johnson Collection. *Catalogue of Paintings.* Philadelphia, 1941.

PHILADELPHIA 1953: The Johnson Collection. *Two Hundred and Eighty-Eight Reproductions: Italian, Dutch, Flemish, German, Spanish, French, English and 19th Century Paintings.* Philadelphia, 1953.

PHILADELPHIA 1994: Philadelphia Museum of Art. *Paintings from Europe and the Americas in the Philadelphia Museum of Art: A Concise Catalogue.* Edited by Curtis R. Scott, Owen Hess Dugan, and John Paschetto. Philadelphia, 1994.

PICKERING AND O'MARA 1999: O. S. Pickering and V. M. O'Mara. *The Index of Middle English Prose, Handlist XIII: Manuscripts in Lambeth Palace Library, Including Those Formerly in Sion College Library.* Cambridge, 1999.

PICKWOAD 1991: N. Pickwoad. "Italian and French Sixteenth-Century Bookbinding." *Gazette of the Grolier Club,* n.s., 43 (1991): 55–80.

PIERPONT MORGAN LIBRARY 1960. *Tenth Report to the Fellows of the Pierpont Morgan Library.* Compiled by Frederick B. Adams Jr. New York, 1960.

PIERPONT MORGAN LIBRARY 1969. *The Pierpont Morgan Library: A Review of Acquisitions, 1949–1968.* New York, 1969.

PINCHART 1860–81: Alexandre Pinchart. *Archives des Arts, Sciences, et Lettres. Documents inédits.* 3 vols. Ghent, 1860–81.

PINCHART 1865: Alexandre Pinchart. "Miniaturistes, enlumineurs et calligraphes employés par Philippe le Bon et Charles le Téméraire et leurs oeuvres." *Bulletin des Commissions royales d'Art et d'Archéologie* 4 (1865): 473–510. Also published as a monograph with the same title, Brussels, 1865.

PINKERNELL 1971: Raoul Lefèvre. *L'Histoire de Jason.* Edited by G. Pinkernell. Frankfurt am Main, 1971.

PINKERNELL 1973: Gert Pinkernell. "Die Handschrift B. N., Ms Fr. 331 von Raoul Lefèvres 'Histoire de Jason' und das Wirken des Miniaturisten Lievin van Lathem in Brügge." *Scriptorium* 27 (1973): 295–301.

PŁONKA-BAŁUS 2001: Katarzyna Płonka-Bałus. "Tak Zwany Modlitewnik Króla Władysława IV Wazy: Metamorfoza tredniowiecznych Godzinek 2945 Z Biblioteki Czartoryskich." In *Ars graeca—Ars latina: Studia dedykowane Profesor Annie Różyckiej Bryzek:* 351–64. Kraków, 2001.

PŁONKA-BAŁUS 2002a: Katarzyna Płonka-Bałus. "Pomiędzy Koncepcją artysty a Funkcjądziela sztulki: Miniatura ze Scenami męki Pańskiej w Rękopisie *Vita Christi* w Bibliotece Czartoryskich." In *Magistro et amico amici discipuli: Lechowi Kalinowskiemu w osiemdziesięciolecie urodzin:* 505–19. Kraków, 2002.

PŁONKA-BAŁUS 2002b: Katarzyna Płonka-Bałus. "*Vita Christi, La Vengeance de la mort Jhesu Christ Nostre Seigneur:* Remarks on the Decoration of a 15th-Century Flemish Manuscript in Czartoryski Library." In *"Als Ich Can": Liber Amicorum in Memory of Professor Maurits Smeyers.* Leuven, 2002.

PLOTZEK 1982: Joachim Plotzek. "Die Stundenbücher der Sammlung Ludwig." *Museen der Stadt Köln Bulletin* 3 (1982): 25, 35–36.

PLUMMER 1964: John Plummer. *Liturgical Manuscripts for the Mass and the Divine Office.* New York, 1964.

POESCH 1964: Jessie Poesch. "Sources for Two Dürer Enigmas: The Four Naked Women or The Choice of Paris." *Art Bulletin* 46 (1964): 78–86.

POLLARD 1970: Graham Pollard. "The Names of Some English Fifteenth-Century Binders." *The Library* 25 (1970): 193–218.

POPHAM 1926: A. E. Popham. "Simon Marmion (after)." *Old Master Drawings: A Quarterly Magazine for Students and Collectors* 1, no. 2 (1926): 21–22.

POPHAM 1928: A. E. Popham. "Drawings by a Flemish Miniaturist. *Art in America* 16 (1928): 134–43.

POPLIMONT 1863: Charles Poplimont. *La Belgique héraldique: Recueil historique, chronologique, généalogique et biographique complet de toutes les maisons nobles, reconnues de la Belgique.* Brussels, 1863.

PORRO 1884: Giulio Porro. *Catalogo dei codici manoscritti della Trivulziana.* Biblioteca storica italiana, 2. Turin, 1884.

POST 1923: Paul Post. "Die Darbringungsminiatur der Hennegauchronik in der Bibliothek zu Brüssel." *Jahrbuch für Kunstwissenschaft,* 1923: 171–74.

PRESTON AND TOTTLE [1971]: Ralph C. Preston, John Tottle, et al. "The Growth of European Culture." In *Culture Regions in the Eastern Hemisphere:* 114–51. Heath Social Studies Series. Lexington, Mass., [1971].

PREVENIER AND BLOCKMANS 1983: Walter Prevenier and Wim Blockmans. *De Bourgondische Nederlanden.* Antwerp, 1983.

PREVENIER AND BLOCKMANS 1986: Walter Prevenier and Wim Blockmans. *The Burgundian Netherlands.* English ed. Cambridge, 1986. First published Antwerp, 1983.

PRIEST 1940: Alan Priest. "Loans from the Collection of George D. Pratt." *Bulletin of the Metropolitan Museum of Art* 35 (December 1940): 237–40.

PRINCETON 1967: *Selected Manuscripts from the Chester Beatty Library.* Exh. cat. Princeton, University Library, 1967.

PROCTER AND WORDSWORTH 1879: Francis Procter and Christopher Wordsworth. *Breviarium ad usum insignis ecclesiae Sarum. Fasciculus II.* Cambridge, 1879.

PROST 1902–13: B. Prost. *Inventaires mobiliers et extraits des comptes des ducs de Bourgogne de la maison de Valois*. 2 vols. Paris, 1902–13.

QUARITCH 1887: Bernard Quaritch. *A General Catalogue of Books Offered to the Public at the Affixed Prices*. Vol. 6. London, 1887.

QUARITCH 1891: Bernard Quaritch. *Facsimiles of Choice Examples Selected from Illuminated Manuscripts, Unpublished Drawings and Illustrated Books of Early Date*. Part 5. London, 1891.

QUARITCH 1892: Bernard Quaritch. *Facsimiles of Illustrations in Biblical and Liturgical Manuscripts Executed in Various Countries during the XI–XVI Centuries now in the Possession of Bernard Quaritch. Facsimiles of Choice Examples Selected from Illuminated Manuscripts, Unpublished Drawings and Illustrated Books of Early Date*. Part 6–10. London, 1887–92.

QUARITCH 1905: Bernard Quaritch. *Description of a Very Beautiful Book of Hours Illuminated Probably by Hans Memling and Gérard David*. London, 1905.

QUÉRUEL 1999: Danielle Quéruel, ed. *Les Manuscrits de David Aubert*. Cultures et civilisations médiévales, 18. Paris, 1999.

RAGUIN AND ZAKIN 2002: Virginia Chieffo Raguin and Helen Jackson Zakin, with contributions from Elizabeth Carson Pastan. *Stained Glass before 1700 in the Collections of the Midwest States*. Vol. 1. Corpus Vitrearum, part 7. London and Turnhout, 2002.

RAGUSA AND GREEN 1961: Isa Ragusa and Rosalie B. Green, trans. and ed. *Meditations on the Life of Christ: An Illustrated Manuscript of the Fourteenth Century by Saint Bonaventure*. Princeton, 1961.

RANDALL 1992: Lilian M. C. Randall. *Medieval and Renaissance Manuscripts in the Walters Art Gallery*. Vol. 2, *France, 1420–1540*. 2 vols. Baltimore and London, 1992.

RANDALL 1997: Lilian M. C. Randall. *Medieval and Renaissance Manuscripts in the Walters Art Gallery*. Vol. 3, *Belgium, 1250–1530*. 2 vols. Baltimore, 1997.

RÉAU 1955–59: Louis Réau. *Iconographie de l'art chétien*. 3 vols. in 6 parts. Paris, 1955–59.

REEVE 1983: M. D. Reeve. "Manuscripts Copied from Books." In *Manuscripts in the Fifty Years after the Invention of Printing: Some Papers Read at a Colloquium at the Warburg Institute on 12–13 March 1982*, edited by J. B. Trapp: 12–20. London.

REICHHARD 1852: Gottfried Reichhard. "Das schönste Brevier und dessen treuer Hüther." *Oesterreichischer Volksfreund* (Vienna), no. 40 (April 17, 1852): 383–85.

REINACH 1903: S. Reinach. "Un Manuscrit de Philippe le Bon à la bibliothèque de Saint-Pétersbourg." *Gazette des Beaux-Arts*, ser. 3, 29 (April 1903): 265–78; 30 (July 1903): 53–63; (November 1903): 371–80.

REINACH 1919: S. Reinach. "Une Miniature de Simon Marmion." *Revue archéologique*, ser. 5, 10 (1919): 240.

REINACH 1931: S. Reinach. "Les Portes du Trésor de St. Bertin." *Gazette des Beaux-Arts* 6 (1931): 341–52.

REUSENS 1899: Edmond Henri Reusens. *Éléments de paléographie*. Leuven, 1899.

REYNAUD 1967: Nicole Reynaud. "Le Couronnement de la Vierge de Michel Sittow." *La Revue du Louvre et des musées de France* 17, no. 1 (1967): 345–52.

REYNAUD 1977: Nicole Reynaud. "Georges Trubert, enlumineur du roi René et de René II de Lorraine." *Revue de l'art* 35 (1977): 52.

REYNOLDS (C.) 1981: Catherine Reynolds. "Courtauld Institute Galleries: Early Netherlandish Works in the Princes Gate Collection." *Burlington Magazine* 123 (1981): 562–64.

REYNOLDS (C.) 1988: Catherine Reynolds. "Illustrated Boccaccio Manuscripts in the British Library (London)." *Studi sul Boccaccio* 17 (1988): 113–81.

REYNOLDS (C.) 2000a: C. Reynolds. "The Function and Display of Netherlandish Cloth Paintings." In *The Fabric of Images: European Cloth Paintings on Textile Supports in the Fourteenth and Fifteenth Centuries*, edited by C. Villers: 89–98. London, 2000.

REYNOLDS (C.) 2000b: C. Reynolds. "The King of Painters." In *Investigating Jan van Eyck*, edited by S. Foister, S. Jones, and D. Coels: 1–16. Turnhout, 2000.

REYNOLDS (G.) 1983: G. Reynolds. "The English Miniature of the Renaissance: A 'Rediscovery' Examined." *Apollo* 68 (October 1983): 308.

REYNOLDS (G.) 1988: G. Reynolds. *English Portrait Miniatures*. Cambridge, 1988.

REYNOLDS (G.) 1998: G. Reynolds. *British Portrait Miniatures: Fitzwilliam Museum Handbooks*. Cambridge, 1998.

REYNOLDS (G.) 1999: G. Reynolds. *The Sixteenth and Seventeenth-Century Miniatures in the Collection of Her Majesty the Queen*. London, 1999.

RÉZEAU 1986: Pierre Rézeau. *Répertoire d'incipit des prières françaises à la fin du Moyen Âge: Addenda et corrigenda aux répertoires de Sonet et Sinclair, Nouveaux incipit*. Publications romanes et françaises, 174. Paris, 1986.

RICHMOND 1979: *Treasures from Chatsworth: The Devonshire Inheritance*. Exh. cat. edited by Sir A. Blunt. Organized and circulated by the International Exhibitions Foundation. Richmond, Virginia Museum of Fine Arts, 1979.

RICHTER 1974: Bernhard Richter. "Untersuchungen zum Werk des Petrus Christus." Doctoral thesis, Universität Heidelberg, 1974.

RICKER AND SAYWELL 1968: John C. Ricker and John T. Saywell. *The Emergence of Europe. The Story of Western Man*. Toronto, 1968.

RIEHL 1909: Berthold Riehl. "Studien über Miniaturen niederländischer Gebetbücher des 15. und 16. Jahrhunderts im Bayerischen National-Museum und in der Hof- und Staatsbibliothek [sic] zu München." *Abhandlungen der Historischen Klasse der Königlich Bayerischen Akademie der Wissenschaften* (Munich) 24 (1909): 435–60.

RIETSTAP 1972: J. B. Rietstap. *Armorial général*. 2 vols. Reprint, Baltimore, 1972. First published Gouda, 1884–87.

RING 1949a: Grete Ring. "Review of Otto Pächt, *Master Mary of Burgundy* (1948)." *Burlington Magazine* 91 (1949): 86–87.

RING 1949b: Grete Ring. *A Century of French Painting, 1400–1500*. London, 1949. Reprint, New York, 1979.

RING 1979: Grete Ring. *A Century of French Paintings*. New York, 1979.

RINGBOM 1962: Sixten Ringbom. "Maria in Sole and the Virgin of the Rosary." *Journal of the Warburg and Courtauld Institutes* 25 (1962): 326–30.

RINGBOM 1966: Sixten Ringbom. "Nuptial Symbolism in Some Fifteenth-Century Reflections of Roman Sepulchral Portraiture." *Temenos* 2 (1966): 72–97.

RINGBOM 1969: Sixten Ringbom. "Devotional Images and Imaginative Devotions: Notes on the Place of Art in Late Medieval Private Piety." *Gazette des Beaux-Arts* 73 (March 1969): 159–70.

RINGBOM 1984: Sixten Ringbom. *Icon to Narrative: The Rise of the Dramatic Close-up in Fifteenth-Century Devotional Painting*. Davaco, 1984.

RIVE 1782: Abbé J. J. Rive. "Essai sur l'art de vérifier l'âge des miniatures peintes dans des manuscrits depuis le XIVe jusqu'au XVIIe siècle inclusive...." [Paris, 1782].

ROBERTET 1970: Jean Robertet. *Oeuvres*. Edited by C. Margaret Zsuppán. Textes littéraires français, 159. Geneva, 1970.

ROBERTS 1979: Jane Roberts. *Holbein*. London, 1979.

ROBERTS-JONES AND ROBERTS-JONES 1997: Philippe Roberts-Jones and Françoise Roberts-Jones. *Pierre Bruegel l'ancien*. Paris, 1997.

ROBINSON 1895: J. C. Robinson. "The Sforza Book of Hours." *Bibliographica* 1 (1895): 428–36.

ROEDER 1955: Helen Roeder. *Saints and Their Attributes; with a Guide to Localities and Patronage*. London, [1955].

ROMBOUTS AND VAN LERIUS 1864–76: P. Rombouts and T. van Lerius. *De Liggeren en andere historische archieven der Antwerpsche Sint Lucasgilde / Les Liggeren et autres archives historiques de la Gilde Anversoise de Saint Luc*. 2 vols. Antwerp and The Hague, 1864–76.

ROME 1953: *Mostra storica nazionale della miniatura*. Rome, 1953.

ROME 1994: *Pregare nel segreto: Libri d'ore e testi di spiritualità nella tradizione cristiana*. Exh. cat. by Guglielmo Cavallo, Barbara Tellini Santoni and Alberto Manodori. Rome, Biblioteca Vallicelliana, 1994.

ROOSEN-RUNGE AND ROOSEN-RUNGE 1981: M. Roosen-Runge and H. Roosen-Runge. *Das spätgotische Musterbuch des Stephan Schriber in der Bayerischen Staatsbibliothek München*. Wiesbaden, 1981.

ROQUES 1938: M. Roques. "Le Livre de Melibée et Prudence par Renaut de Louhans." *Histoire littéraire de la France* 37 (1938): 493–503.

ROSANBO 1929: Cte de Rosanbo. "Notice sur les Douze Dames de Rhétorique (Manuscrit 1174 de la Bibliothèque Nationale de Paris)." In *Bulletin de la Société française de Reproduction des Manuscrits à peintures*, 1929: 5–16.

ROSE 1976: P. Rose. "The Iconography of the Raising of the Cross." *Tribute to Wolfgang Stechow*, edited by W. L. Strauss; *Print Review* 5 (spring 1976): 131–41.

ROSEN 1941: David Rosen. "Preservation versus Restoration." *Magazine for Art* 34, no. 9 (1941): 1–15.

ROSENTHAL 1982: J. T. Rosenthal. "Aristocratic Cultural Patronage and Book Bequests, 1350–1500." *Bulletin of the John Rylands University Library of Manchester* 64 (1982): 522–48.

ROSS (C.) 1974: Charles Ross. *Edward IV*. London, 1974.

ROSS (D.) 1963: D. J. A. Ross. *Alexander Historiatus: A Guide to Medieval Illustrated Alexander Literature*. London, 1963.

ROSS (D.) 1969: D. J. A. Ross. "Some Geographical and Topographical Miniatures in a Fragmentary *Trésor des Histoires*." *Scriptorium* 23 (1969): 177–86.

ROSSI AND CASCIARO 1990: M. Rossi and R. Casciaro. "Miniature rinascimentali inedite alla Biblioteca Braidense." *Rinascimento in miniatura dedicato a Stella Matalon; Quaderni di Brera* 6 (1990): 13–39.

ROSSITER 1951: Henry P. Rossiter. "Colard Mansion's Boccaccio of 1476." In *Beiträge für Georg Swarzenski*: 103–10. Berlin, 1951.

ROTHE 1966: Edith Rothe. *Buchmalerei aus zwölf Jahrhunderten*. Berlin, 1966.

ROTTIER 1996: Honoré Rottier. *Rondreis door middeleeuws Vlaanderen*. Leuven, 1996.

ROUSE AND ROUSE 2000: R. H. Rouse and M. A. Rouse. *Manuscripts and Their Makers. Commercial Book Producers in Medieval Paris, 1200–1500*. 2 vols. London, 2000.

ROUZET 1982: Anne Rouzet. *Les Chroniques de Hainaut de Jacques de Guise*. Liège, 1982.

ROWLANDS 1962: J. Rowlands. "A Man of Sorrows by Petrus Christus." *Burlington Magazine* 104 (1962): 419–23.

ROYAL COMMISSION 1883–1976: Historical Manuscripts Commission. *Calendar of the Manuscripts of the Most Hon. The Marquess of Salisbury, K.G., etc., Preserved at Hatfield House, Hertfordshire*. 24 vols. London, 1883–1976.

RYSKAMP 1984: Charles Ryskamp, ed. *Twentieth Report to the Fellows of The Pierpont Morgan Library, 1981–1983*. New York, Pierpont Morgan Library, 1984.

RYSKAMP 1989: Charles Ryskamp, ed. *Twentieth Report to the Fellows of The Pierpont Morgan Library, 1984–1986*. New York, Pierpont Morgan Library, 1989.

SAINT PETERSBURG 1996: *Flemish Illuminated Manuscripts, 1475–1550*. Exh. cat. edited by M. Smeyers and Jan Van der Stock. Saint Petersburg, State Hermitage Museum, 1996.

SAINT REMY 1944: See Surirey de Saint Remy 1944.

SALAMANCA 1988: *Las edades del hombre: El arte en la iglesia de Castilla y Leon*. Exh. cat. Salamanca, 1988.

SALMI AND MELLINI 1972: Mario Salmi and Gian Lorenzo Mellini. *The Grimani Breviary Reproduced from the Illuminated Manuscript Belonging to the Biblioteca Marciana, Venice*. London, 1972.

SALMON 1971: P. Salmon. *Les Manuscrits liturgiques de la Bibliothèque Vaticane IV*. Studi e testi, 267. Vatican City, 1971.

SAMARAN AND MARICHAL 1959: Ch. Samaran and R. Marichal. *Catalogue des manuscrits en écriture latine portant des indications de date, de lieu ou de copiste*. Musée Condé et Bibliothèque parisiennes. Paris, 1959.

SANDER 1989: Jochen Sander. "The Meeting of Jacob and Rachel: Hugo Van Der Goes' Drawing at Christ Church, Oxford." *Master Drawings* 27 (1989): 39–52.

SANDER 1992: Jochen Sander. *Hugo van der Goes: Stilentwickung und Chronologie (Berlin Schriften zur Kunst)*. Mainz, 1992.

SANDER 1997: Jochen Sander. "Ein unbekanntes Werk Gerard Davids: Die Beweinung Christi in Halbfigur." *Staedel-Jahrbuch*, n.s., 16 (1997): 159–70.

SANDERUS 1641–44: Antoine Sanderus. *Flandria illustrata; sive, Descriptio comitatus istius per totum terraru orbem celeberrimi*. 2 vols. Coloniae Agrippinae [Cologne], 1641–44.

SANDERUS 1725: Antonius Sanderus. *Flandria illustrata; sive, Descriptio comitatus istius per totum terrarum orbem celeberrimi*. 2 vols. New ed. Brussels and The Hague, 1725.

SANTOS 1930: Reynaldo dos Santos. "Les Principaux Manuscrits à peintures conservés en Portugal." *Bulletin de la Société française de Reproductions de Manuscrits à peintures* 14 (1930): 5–32.

SANTOS 1932: Reynald dos Santos. *Les Principaux Manuscrits à peintures conservés en Portugal*. Paris, 1932.

SANTOS 1939: Reynaldo dos Santos. *A Tomada de Lisboa nas illuminuras Manuelinas*. Lisbon, 1939. 2nd ed., 1970.

SANTOS 1950: Reynaldo dos Santos. "Un Exemplaire de Vasari annoté par Francisco de Olanda." In *Studi Vasariani, atti del Convegno internazionale per il IV. Centenario della prima edizione delle "Vite" del Vasari*. Firenze, Palazzo Strozzi (1950): 91–92.

SANTOS 1959: Reynaldo dos Santos. "O livro de Horas da Rainha D. Leonor de António de Hollanda." *Bellas Artes*, ser. 2, 13–14 (1959): 36.

SANTOS 1970: Reynaldo dos Santos. *Oito séculos de arte portuguesa; história e espirito*. 3 vols. Lisbon, 1970.

SAUZAY 1861: A. Sauzay. *Catalogue du Musée Sauvageot*. Paris: Musée du Louvre, 1861.

SAWICKA 1973: S. Sawicka. "À propos du catalogue de manuscrits enluminés de la Bibliotheque Bodléienne." *Scriptorium* 27 (1973): 306–8.

SAXL 1937–38: Fritz Saxl. "A Marsilio Ficino Manuscript written in Bruges, c. 1475, and the Alum Monopoly of the Popes." *Journal of the Warburg Institute* 1 (1937–38): 61–62.

SAXL AND MEIER 1953: Fritz Saxl and H. Meier. *Verzeichnis astrologischer und mythologischer illustrierter Handschriften des lateinischen Mittelalters, 3: Handschriften in englischen Bibliotheken*. 2 vols. London, 1953.

SCAILLIÉREZ 1992: Cécile Scailliérez. "Entre enluminure et peinture: À propos d'un paysage avec *St. Jerome Penitent* de l'école Ganto-Brugeoise récemment acquis par le Louvre." *La Revue du Louvre et des Musées de France* 42, no. 2 (June 1992): 16–31.

SCHABACKER 1974: Peter H. Schabacker. *Petrus Christus*. Utrecht, 1974.

SCHAEFER 1975: Claude Schaefer. "Un Livre d'heures Ganto-Brugeois, Ms. 16 de la Bibliotheca Nacional à Lisbonne." *Arquivos do Centro Cultural Português* 9 (1975): 399–414.

SCHANDEL 2002: Pascal Schandel. "Jean Hennecart, premier peintre du jardin du Coudenberg (XVe siècle)." *Revue de l'art* 135, no. 2 (2002).

SCHATBORN 1970: P. Schatborn. "39 Grisailles in the Book of Hours of Philip the Good in The Hague: An Attribution to the 'Gebetbuchmeister um 1500.'" *Oud Holland* 85 (1970): 45–48.

SCHELLER 1983: R. A. Scheller. "Ensigns of Authority: French Royal Symbolism in the Age of Louis XII." *Simiolus* 13 (1983): 75–141.

SCHENK ZU SCHWEINSBERG 1922: Eberhard Schenk zu Schweinsberg. *Die Illustrationen der Chronik von Flandern—Handschrift Nr. 437—der Stadtbibliothek zu Brügge und ihr Verhältnis zu Hans Memling*. Studien zur deutschen Kunstgeschichte, 224. Strasbourg, 1922.

SCHENK ZU SCHWEINSBERG 1975: Eberhard Schenk zu Schweinsberg. "Das Gebetbuch für Graf Engelbert II. von Nassau und sein Meister." *Nassauische Annalen* 86 (1975): 139–75.

SCHESTAG 1899: A. Schestag. "Die Chronik von Jerusalem." *Jahrbuch der Kunsthistorischen Sammlungen des allerhöchsten Kaiserhauses* 20 (1899): 195–216.

SCHILLER 1971–72: Gertrud Schiller. *Iconography of Christian Art*. 2nd ed. 2 vols. Translated by Janet Seligman. New York, 1971–72.

SCHILLING 1961: R. Schilling. "Das Llangattock-Stundenbuch; Sein Verhältnis zu van Eyck und dem Vollender des Turin-Mailänder Stundenbuches." *Wallraf-Richartz-Jahrbuch* 23 (1961): 211–36.

SCHMITT 1994: J.-C. Schmitt. *Les Revenants: Les Vivants et les morts dans la société médiévale*. [Paris], 1994.

SCHMITT 1998: J.-C. Schmitt. *Strigoii: Viii si mortii în societatea medievală*. Bucharest, 1998.

SCHMITZ-CLIEVER AND GRIMME 1967: E. Schmitz-Cliever and E. G. Grimme. "Repertorium medicohistoricum Aquense: Ein Beitrag zur medizinhistorischen Topographie." *Aachener Kunstblätter* 34 (1967): 194–251.

SCHÖNE 1937: Wolfgang Schöne. "Über einige altiederländische Bilder vor allem in Spanien." *Jahrbuch der Preuszischen Kunstsammlungen* 58 (1937): 153–81.

SCHÖNE 1938: Wolfgang Schöne. *Die grossen Meister der Niederländischen Malerei des 15. Jahrhunderts. Hubert van Eyck bis Quentin Massys*. Leipzig, 1938.

SCHOUTEET 1963: A. Schouteet. "Inventaris van het archief van het voormalige gild van de Librariërs en van de vereniging van schoolmeesters te Brugge." *Handelingen van het Genootschap voor Gechiedenis "Société d'Émulation"* 100 (1963): 228–69.

SCHOUTEET 1989: A. Schouteet. *De Vlaamse Primitieven te Brugge: Bronnen voor de schilderkunst te Brugge tot de dood van Gerard David*. Fontes Historiae Artis Neerlandicae 2. Brussels, 1989.

SCHOUTTETEN 1967: M. J. Schoutteten. "L'Iconographie de Marguerite d'Autriche." *Publications du Centre des européen d'études burgundomédianes* 9 (1967): 91–92.

SCHRAMM, FILLITZ, AND MÜTHERICH 1978: P. E. Schramm, H. Fillitz, F. Mütherich. *Denkmale der deutschen Könige und Kaiser, II: Ein Beitrag zur Herrschergeschichte von Rudolf I. bis Maximilian I.* Veröffentlichungen des Zentralinstituts für Kunstgeschichte in München, 7. Munich, 1978.

SCHULLIAN 1981: D. M. Schullian. "A Revised List of Manuscripts of Valerius Maximus." *Miscellanea Augusto Campana*, edited by R. Avesani, vol. 2; *Medioevo e Umanesimo* 45 (1981): 695–728.

SCHUPPISSER 1991: Fritz Oskar Schuppisser. Review of the J. Paul Getty Museum Symposium on Simon Marmion. *Kunstchronik* 44, no. 1 (1991): 185–91.

SCHWARZ 1959: Heinrich Schwarz. "The Mirror of the Artist and the Mirror of the Devout." *Studies in the History of Art Dedicated to William E. Suida*. London, 1959.

SCILLIA 1975: Diane Graybowski Scillia. "Gerard David and Manuscript Illumination in the Low Countries, 1480–1509." Ph.D. diss., Case Western Reserve University, Cleveland, 1975.

SCILLIA 1991: Diane Scillia. "Gerard David and Manuscript Illumination Reconsidered: The Cleveland Saint Elizabeth of Hungary (CMA 63.256,fol. 197v)." Paper presented at the International Congress on Medieval Studies, Western Michigan University, Kalamazoo, Michigan, May 9–12, 1991.

SCOFIELD 1923: Cora L. Scofield. *The Life and Reign of Edward the Fourth, King of England and of France and Lord of Ireland*. 2 vols. London, 1923. Reprint, New York, 1967.

SCOTT (K.) 1976: Kathleen L. Scott. *The Caxton Master and His Patrons*. Cambridge Bibliographical Society, Monograph, no. 8. Cambridge, 1976.

SCOTT (K.) 1996: Kathleen Scott. *Later Gothic Manuscripts, 1390–1490*. 2 vols. A Survey of Manuscripts Illuminated in the British Isles, 6. London, 1996.

SCOTT (M.) 1980: Margaret Scott. *The History of Dress Series: Late Gothic Europe, 1400–1500*. London, 1980.

SEGURADO 1970: Jorge Segurado. *Francisco d'Ollanda*. Lisbon, 1970.

SEGURADO 1975: Jorge Segurado. "Damião de Goes." *Belas artes* 28–29 (1975): 133–84.

SEIDLITZ 1885: W. V. Seidlitz. "Die illustrierten Handschriften der Hamilton-Sammlung zu Berlin. Livers d'Heures." *Repertorium für Kunstwissenschaft* 8 (1885): 94–110.

SEILERN 1955: Antoine Seilern. *Flemish Paintings and Drawings at 56 Princes Gate*. London, 1955.

SEILERN 1969: Antoine Seilern. *Flemish Paintings and Drawings at 56 Princes Gate London SW7: Addenda*. London, 1969.

SEILERN 1971: Antoine Seilern. *Corrigenda and Addenda to the Catalogues of Paintings and Drawings at 56 Princes Gate London SW7*. London, 1971.

SEUSE 1907: Heinrich Seuse. "Deutsche Schriften." In *Würtembergische Kommission für Landesgeschichte*, edited by K. Bihlmeyer: 7–195. Stuttgart, 1907.

SHAILOR 1984: Barbara A. Shailor. *Catalogue of Medieval and Renaissance Manuscripts in the Beinecke Rare Book and Manuscripts Library, Yale University*. vol. 1. Binghamton, N.Y., 1984.

SHAW 1843: Henry Shaw. *Dresses and Decorations of the Middle Ages*. 2 vols. London, 1843.

SHAW AND MADDEN 1833: Henry Shaw and Sir Frederic Madden. *Illuminated Ornaments Selected from Manuscripts and Early Printed Books from the Sixth to the Seventeenth Centuries*. London, 1833.

SILVER 1982: Larry Silver. "Early Northern European Paintings." *Saint Louis Art Museum Bulletin* 16, no. 3 (1982): 2–47.

SILVER 1984: Larry Silver. *The Paintings of Quinten Massys with Catalogue Raisonné*. Montclair, N.J., 1984.

SIMONSON 1998: Anne Simonson. "Pieter Bruegel's *Magpie on the Gallows*." *Konsthistorisk tidskrift* 67, no. 2 (1998): 71–92.

SINCLAIR 1987: K. V. Sinclair. *Prières en ancien français: Additions et corrections aux articles 1–2374 du Répertoire de Sonet: Supplément*. Townsville, 1987.

SINCLAIR 1988: K. V. Sinclair. *French Devotional Texts of the Middle Ages: A Bibliographical Manuscript Guide. Second Supplement*. New York and London, 1988.

SINT-TRUIDEN 1988: *Brustem 1467. Un Combat médiéval à l'aube des temps modernes*. Sint-Truiden, 1988.

SMEYERS 1988: MAURITS SMEYERS. "A Mid-Fifteenth Century Book of Hours from Bruges in the Walters Art Gallery (Ms. 721) and Its Relation to the Turin-Milan Hours." *Journal of the Walters Art Gallery* 46 (1988): 55–76.

SMEYERS 1994: Maurits Smeyers. "Het Marianum of Onze-Lieve-Vrouw-in-de-zon. Getuige van een lat-middeleeuwse devotie." *Nederlands kunsthistorisch jaarboek* (1994): 271–99.

SMEYERS 1995: Maurits Smeyers. "Flemish Miniatures for England." In *The Low Countries: Arts and Society in Flanders and the Netherlands, a Yearbook, 1995–96*. Bruges, 1995.

SMEYERS 1997a: Maurits Smeyers. "The Restoration of the Brevarium Mayer van den Bergh: A Multidisciplinary Project in Progress." In *Le Dessin sous—jacent et la technologie dans la peinture*: 38–41. Louvain-la-Neuve, Université Catholique de Louvain, Institut supérieur d'Archéologie et d'Histoire de l'Art, 1997.

SMEYERS 1997b: Maurits Smeyers. "Iluminuras flamengas executadas para Portugal (1440–1530)." *Revista de ciências históricas, Universidade Portucalense* 12 (1997): 169–200.

SMEYERS 1997c: M. Smeyers. "Analecta Memlingiana: From Hemling to Memling—From Panoramic View to Compartimented Representation." In *Memling Studies: Proceedings of the International Colloquium (Bruges, 10–12 November 1994)*: 186–94. Leuven, 1997.

SMEYERS 1998: Maurits Smeyers. *L'Art de la miniature flamande du VIIIe au XVIe siècle*. Tournai, 1998.

SMEYERS 1999: Maurits Smeyers. *Flemish Miniatures from the 8th to the mid-16th century: The Medieval World on Parchment*. Leuven, 1999.

SMEYERS ET AL. 1993: Maurits Smeyers et al. *Naer natueren Ghelike: Vlaamse miniaturen voor Van Eyck (ca. 1350–ca. 1420)*. Leuven, 1993.

SMEYERS AND CARDON 1984: Maurits Smeyers and Bert Cardon. "Vier eeuwen Vlaamse Miniatuurkunst in Handschriften uit het Grootseminarie te Brugge." In *De Duinenabdij en het Grootseminarie te Brugge*, edited by Adelbert Denaux and Eric van den Berghe. Weesp, 1984.

SMEYERS AND CARDON 1990: M. Smeyers and B. Cardon. "Merktekens in de Brugse miniatuurkunst." In *Merken Opmerken, Merk- en meestertekens op kunstwerken in de Zuidelijke Nederlanden en het Prinsbisdom Luik, Typologie en Methode*, edited by C. Van Vlierden and M. Smeyers. Leuven, 1990.

SMEYERS AND CARDON 1991: Maurits Smeyers and Bert Cardon. "Utrecht and Bruges—South and North 'Boundless' Relations in the 15th Century." In *Masters and Miniatures: Proceedings of the Congress on Medieval Manuscript Illumination in the Northern Netherlands (Utrecht, 10–13 December 1989)*, edited by Koert Van der Horst and Johann-Christian Klamt: 89–104. Ghent, 1991.

SMEYERS AND VAN DER STOCK 1996: Maurits Smeyers and Jan Van der Stock. *Flemish Illuminated Manuscripts, 1475–1550*. Ghent, 1996.

SMITAL 1924: O. Smital. *Die Chronik des Kreuzfahrerkönigreiches Jerusalem ("Les Croniques de Jherusalem abregies"): Facsimile der burgundisch-flämischen Miniaturhandschrift der wiener Nationalbibliothek Nr. 2533*. Munich, 1924.

SMITAL 1930a: O. Smital. "Der Meister des Louis de Bruges, Ein brügger Buchmaler aus den Siebzigerjahren des XV. Jahrhunderts." *Jahrbuch der kunsthistorischen Sammlungen in Wien*, n.s., 4 (1930): 223–30.

SMITAL 1930b: Ottokar Smital. *Das schwarze Gebetbuch des Herzogs Galeazzo Maria Sforza*. Vienna, 1930.

SMITH (J.) 1992: Jeffrey Chipps Smith. "Margaret of York and the Burgundian Portrait Tradition." In *Margaret of York, Simon Marmion and The Visions of Tondal*, edited by T. Kren: 47–56. Malibu, 1992.

SMITH (J.) 1998: Jeffrey Chipps Smith. "The Practical Logistics of Art: Thoughts on the Commissioning, Displaying, and Storing of Art at the Burgundian Court." In *New Studies in Northern Renaissance Art in Honor of Walter S. Gibson)*: 27–48. Turnhout, 1998.

SMITH (R.) 1968: Robert C. Smith. *The Art of Portugal, 1500–1800*. New York, 1968.

SNYDER 1960: J. E. Snyder. "The Early Haarlem School of Painting, I–II." *Art Bulletin* 42 (1960): 39–55, 113–32.

SOLTÉSZ 1985: Elizabeth Soltész. *Flemish Calendar. Introductory Essay to the Facsimile Edition of Cod. Lat. 389 of the National Széchényi Library, Budapest*. Budapest, 1985.

SOMMÉ 1998: M. Sommé. *Isabelle de Portugal, duchesse de Bourgogne: Une Femme au pouvoir au XVe siècle*. Villeneuve d'Ascq, 1998.

SONET 1956: Jean Sonet. *Répertoire d'incipit de prières en ancien français*. Société de Publications romanes et françaises, 54. Geneva, 1956.

SOUSA 1967: José de Campos e Sousa. *Livros de horas. Iluminuras*. São Paulo, 1967.

SPAMER 1930: A. Spamer. *Das kleine Andachtsbild vom XIV. zum XX. Jahrhundert*. Munich, 1930.

SPITZER 1890–92: Frédéric Spitzer. *La Collection Spitzer: Antiquité, Moyen-Âge, Renaissance*. 6 vols. Mâcon, 1890–92.

SPREITZER 1994: Jennifer Spreitzer. "Framing Mary of Burgundy." *Chicago Art Journal* 4, no. 1 (1994): 2–13.

STARING 1952: A. Staring. "Vraagstukken der Oranje-Iconographie, II: Rondom twee portretten door Jan Gossaert van Mabuse." *Oud Holland* 67 (1952): 144–56.

STARKEY 1991: David Starkey, ed. *Henry VIII: A European Court in England*. London, 1991.

STECHER 1882–91: Auguste J. Stecher. *Oeuvres de Jean Lemaire de Belges*. 4 vols. Leuven.

STECHOW 1966: Wolfgang Stechow. *Northern Renaissance Art, 1400–1600: Sources and Documents*. Sources and Documents in the History of Art. Englewood Cliffs, N.J., 1966.

STEENBOCK 1990: Frauke Steenbock. "LARGESSE—Münzen, Blüten, und Mannaregen: Eine Motivstudie." In *Festschrift für Peter Bloch*, edited by Hartmut Krohm and Christian Theuerkauff: 135–42. Mainz, 1990.

STEER 1961: F. Steer. *Bibliotheca norfolciana: A Catalog of Selected Manuscripts and Printed Books in the Library of His Grace, the Duke of Norfolk*. London, 1961.

STEINMANN 1964: U. Steinmann. "Das Andachts-Gebetbuch vom Leiden Christi des Kardinals Albrecht von Brandenburg." *Aachener Kunstblätter* 29 (1964): 139–77.

STEINMETZ 1995: A. S. Steinmetz. *Das Altarretabel in der altniederländischen Malerei*. Weimar, 1995.

STEPPE 1961: J. K. Steppe. "Vlaamse Kunstwerken in het Bezit van Doña Juana Enrìquez, Echtgenote van Jan II van Aragon en Moeder van Ferdinand de Katholieke." In *Scrinium Lovaniense: Mélanges historiques Étienne van Cauwenbergh; Université de Louvain Receuil de travaux d'histoire et de philologie*, ser. 4, 24 (1961): 301–30.

STEPPE 1969: J. K. Steppe. "Mencía de Mendoza et Jean-Louis Vives." In *Scrinium Erasmianum*, vol. 2: 451–506. Leiden, 1969.

STEPPE 1974: J. Steppe. "Onbekend werk van Schilders uit de Tweede Helft van de 15e Eeuw in de Voormalige Abdijkerk van Sint-Bertinus te Saint-Omar." In *XLIII Congres Sint-Niklaas-Waas 1974, Annalen*: 308–20.

STERLING 1941: Charles Sterling. *La Peinture française: Les Peintres du Moyen Âge*. Paris, 1941.

STERLING 1968: Charles Sterling. "Jean Hey, le Maître de Moulins." *Revue de l'art* 1–2 (1968): 27–33.

STERLING 1971: Charles Sterling. "Observations on Petrus Christus." *Art Bulletin* 53 (1971): 1–26.

STERLING 1981a: Charles Sterling. "La Peinture sur panneau picarde et son rayonnement dans le nord de la France au XVe siècle." *Bulletin de la Société de l'Histoire de l'Art français* (Paris), 1981: 7–49.

STERLING 1981b: Charles Sterling. "Un Nouveau Tableau de Simon Marmion." *Revue d'art canadienne/Canadian Art Review* 8 (1981): 3–18.

STERLING AND AINSWORTH 1998: Charles Sterling and Maryan W. Ainsworth. "France, Fifteenth and Sixteenth Centuries." In *The Robert Lehman Collection, II: Fifteenth- to Eighteenth-Century European Paintings: France, Central Europe, The Netherlands, Spain, and Great Britain*: 1–28. New York, 1998.

STEVENSON 1872: J. Stevenson. "Second Notice of the Manuscripts at Stonyhurst College." *Historical Manuscripts Commission*, 3rd report (1872): 334–41.

STEWART 1966: Stanley Stewart. *The Enclosed Garden*. Milwaukee, 1966.

STOCKHOLM 1952: *Gyllene Böcker*. Catalogue by Kåre Olsen and Carl Nordenfalk. Stockholm, National Museum, 1952.

STRAUB 1995: Richard E. F. Straub. *David Aubert, escripvain et clerc*. Études de langue et littérature françaises, 96. Amsterdam, 1995.

STRAUB 1998: Richard E. F. Straub. *La Tradition manuscrite de la Vie de Jésus-Christ en sept parties*. Inedita & Rara 15. Montreal, 1998.

STRAYER 1982: Joseph R. Strayer, ed. *Dictionary of the Middle Ages*. 13 vols. New York, 1982.

STRING 1996a: Tatiana Christine String. "Henry VIII and the Art of Royal Supremacy." Ph.D. diss., University of Texas at Austin, 1996.

STRING 1996b: Tatiana Christine String. "Henry VIII's Illuminated 'Great Bible.'" *Journal of the Warburg and Courtauld Institutes* 59 (1996): 315–24.

STROHM 1985: R. Strohm. *Music in Late Medieval Bruges*. Oxford, 1985.

STRONG 1969: Roy Strong. *Tudor and Jacobean Portraits in the National Portrait Gallery*. 2 vols. London, 1969.

STRONG 1983: Roy Strong. *The English Renaissance Miniature*. London, 1983.

STROO 1994: C. Stroo. "Bourgondische presentatietaferelen: Boeken en politiek ten tijde van Filips de Goede en Karel de Stoute." In *Boeken in de late Middeleeuwen: Verslag van de Groningse Codicologendagen 1992*, edited by J. M. M. Hermans and K. van der Hoek: 285–98. Groningen, 1994.

STROO ET AL. 1999: Cyriel Stroo et al. *The Flemish Primitives: Catalogue of Early Netherlandish Painting in the Royal Museums of Fine Arts of Belgium*. Vol. 2, *The Dirk Bouts, Petrus Christus, Hans Memling, and Hugo van der Goes Groups*. Brussels, 1999.

STROO ET AL. 2001: Cyriel Stroo et al. *The Flemish Primitives: Catalogue of Early Netherlandish Painting in the Royal Museums of Fine Arts of Belgium*. Vol. 3, *Hieronymous Bosch, Albrecht Bouts, Gerard David, Colijn de Coter, Goossen van der Weyden*. Turnhout, 2001.

STROO AND SYFER-D'OLNE 1996: Cyriel Stroo and Pascale Syfer-d'Olne. *The Flemish Primitives: Catalogue of Early Netherlandish Painting in the Royal Museums of Fine Arts of Belgium*. Vol. 1, *The Master of Flémalle and Rogier van der Weyden Groups*. Brussels, 1996.

SULZBERGER 1959: S. Sulzberger. "Gérard de Saint Jean et l'art de la miniature." *Oud Holland* 74 (1959): 167–69.

SULZBERGER 1962a: S. Sulzberger. "Jérôme Bosch et les maîtres de l'enluminure." *Scriptorium* 16 (1962): 46–49.

SULZBERGER 1962b: S. Sulzberger. "Notes sur la grisaille." *Gazette des Beaux-Arts*, ser. 6, 59 (February 1962): 119–20.

SURIREY DE SAINT REMY 1944: Henry de Surirey de Saint Remy. *Jean II de Bourbon, duc de Bourbonnais et d'Auvergne, 1426–1488*. Nouvelle collection d'études médiévales. Paris, 1944.

SUTTON AND VISSER-FUCHS 1995: Anne F. Sutton and Livia Visser-Fuchs. "Choosing a Book in Late Fifteenth-Century England and Burgundy." In *England and the Low Countries in the Late Middle Ages*, edited by Caroline Barron and Nigel Saul: 61–98. Stroud, 1995.

SUTTON AND VISSER-FUCHS 1997a: Anne F. Sutton and Livia Visser-Fuchs. "The Cult of Angels in Late Fifteenth-Century England: An Hours of the Guardian Angel Presented to Queen Elizabeth Woodville." In *Women and the Book: Assessing the Visual Evidence*, edited by Lesley Smith and Jane H. M. Taylor: 230–36. London, 1997.

SUTTON AND VISSER-FUCHS 1997b: Anne F. Sutton and Livia Visser-Fuchs. *Richard III's Books: Ideals and Reality in the Life and Library of a Medieval Prince*. Phoenix Mill, Stroud, Gloucestershire, 1997.

SUTTON AND VISSER-FUCHS 1999: Anne F. Sutton and Livia Visser-Fuchs. "Richard III and the Knave of Cards: An Illuminator's Model in Manuscript and Print, 1440s to 1990s." *Antiquaries Journal* 79 (1999): 257–99.

SWEENY 1972: Barbara Sweeny. *John G. Johnson Collection: Catalogue of Flemish and Dutch Paintings*. Philadelphia, 1972.

SZABO 1975: George Szabo. *The Robert Lehman Collection: A Guide*. New York, 1975.

SZÁNTÓ 1963: Tibor Szántó. "Ein grosser Schreibkünstler des XVI. Jahrhunderts." *Gutenberg-Jahrbuch*, 1963: 38ff.

TARANCO 1951: F. M. Garin Ortiz de Taranco. *Un libro de horas del Conde-Duque de Olivares*. Valencia, 1951.

TCHERNOVA 1960: G. A. Tchernova. *Miniatury Bolchikh Francuskikh Khronik*. Moscow, 1960.

TESTA 1984: Judith Anne Testa. "The Beatty Rosarium Reconstructed: A Manuscript with Excised Miniatures by Simon Bening." *Oud Holland* 98 (1984): 189–236.

TESTA 1986: Judith Anne Testa. *The Beatty Rosarium: A Manuscript with Paintings by Simon Bening*. Studies and Facsimiles of Netherlandish Illuminated Manuscripts, 1. Dornspijk, 1986.

TESTA 1991: Judith Anne Testa. "Fragments of a Spanish Prayerbook with Miniatures by Simon Bening." *Oud Holland* 105 (1991): 89–115.

TESTA 1992a: Judith Anne Testa. "Addendum: Fragments of a Spanish Prayerbook with Miniatures by Simon Bening." *Oud Holland* 106 (1992): 30.

TESTA 1992b: Judith Anne Testa. *The Stockholm-Kassel Book of Hours: A Reintegrated Manuscript from the Shop of Simon Bening*. Acta Bibliothecae Regiae Stockholmiensis, 53. Stockholm, 1992.

TESTA 1994: Judith Anne Testa. "An Unpublished Manuscript by Simon Bening." *Burlington Magazine* 136 (1994): 416–26.

TESTA 2000: Judith Anne Testa. "Simon Bening and the Italian High Renaissance: Some Unexplored Sources." *Oud Holland* 114 (2000): 107–24.

THIEME-BECKER 1907–50: Ulrich Thieme and Felix Becker, eds. *Allgemeines Lexikon der bildenden Künstler von der Antike bis zur Gegenwart*. 37 vols. Leipzig, 1907–50.

THIERRY 1835: A. Thierry. *Recueil des monuments inédits de l'histoire du tiers état, 1er série, Région du Nord*. 2 Paris, 1835.

THIERRY 1856–70: A. Thierry. *Recueil des manuscrits inédits de l'histoire du tiers état*. 4 vols. Paris, 1856–70.

THOMAS (H.) 1978: Hans Michael Thomas. Review of Biermann 1975. *Scriptorium* 32 (1978): 12, no. 60.

THOMAS (M.) 1976: M. Thomas. "Le Livre de prières de Philippe le Bon: Premier Bilan d'une découverte." *Les Dossiers de l'archéologie* 16 (May–June 1976): 84–95.

THOMAS (M.) AND ZINK 1990: Marcel Thomas and Michel Zink. *Girart de Roussillon, ou, L'Épopée de Bourgogne: Le Manuscrit de Vienne, Cod. 2549*. Paris, 1990.

THOMPSON (C.) AND CAMPBELL 1974: C. Thompson and L. Campbell. *Hugo van der Goes and the Trinity Panels in Edinburgh*. Edinburgh, 1974.

THOMPSON (H.) 1912: Henry Yates Thompson. *A Descriptive Catalogue of Fourteen Illuminated Manuscripts nos. XCV to CVIII*. Cambridge, 1912.

THOMPSON (H.) 1916: Henry Yates Thompson. *Illustrations from One Hundred Manuscripts in the Library of Henry Yates Thompson*. Vol. 6. London, 1916.

THORPE 1976: James Thorpe. *Book of Hours: Illuminations by Simon Marmion*. San Marino, 1976.

THOSS 1987: Dagmar Thoss. "Die Bebilderten Handschriften der Bibliothek des Prinzen Eugen von Savoyen." In *Bibliotheca Eugeniana: Die Sammlungen des Prinzen Eugen von Savoyen*. Exh. cat. Vienna, Österreichische Nationalbibliothek and Graphische Sammlung Albertina, 1987.

THOSS 1991: Dagmar Thoss. "Der Meister des Schwarzen Gebetbuchs—ein holländischer Buchmaler?" In *Masters and Miniatures: Proceedings of the Congress on Medieval Manuscript Illumination in the Northern Netherlands (Utrecht, 10–13 December 1989)*, edited by K. van der Horst and J.-C. Klamt: 149–60. Doornspijk, 1991.

THRUPP 1989: S. L. Thrupp. *The Merchant Class of Medieval London, 1300–1500*. Reprint of 1948 ed. Ann Arbor, 1989.

THURLEY 1993: S. Thurley. *The Royal Palaces of Tudor England: Architecture and Court Life, 1460–1547*. New Haven and London, 1993.

TITE 1994: Colin G.C. Tite. *The Manuscript Library of Sir Robert Cotton*. The Panizzi Lectures 1993. London, 1994.

TOKYO 1972: *Treasured Masterpieces of the Metropolitan Museum of Art*. Exh. cat. Tokyo, National Museum of Western Art, 1972.

TOKYO 1995: *The World of Bruegel: The Coppée Collection and Eleven International Museums*. Exh. cat. by Holm Bevers et al. Tokyo, Tobu Museum of Art, 1995.

TOKYO AND KYOTO 1976: *Masterpieces of World Art from American Museums: From Egyptian to Contemporary Art*. Tokyo, National Museum of Western Art, and Kyoto, National Museum, 1976.

TOLEDO 1992: *Reyes y mecenas: Los reyes católicos, Maximiliano I y los inicios de la casa de Austria en España*. Toledo, 1992.

TOLEDO 2000: *Carolus*. Exh. cat. Toledo, Museo de Santa Cruz, 2000.

TOLNAY 1934: Charles de Tolnay. Studien zu den Gemälden Pieter Bruegels der Ältere." *Jahrbuch der Kunsthistorischen Sammlungen in Wien* 8 (1934): 105–35.

TOLNAY 1935: Charles de Tolnay. *Pierre Bruegel l'Ancien*. 2 vols. Brussels, 1935.

TOLNAY 1965: Charles de Tolnay. "Newly Discovered Miniatures by Pieter Bruegel the Elder." *Burlington Magazine* 107 (1965): 110–14.

TOLNAY 1980: Charles de Tolnay. "Further Miniatures by Pieter Bruegel the Elder." *Burlington Magazine* 122 (1980): 616–23.

TÖRÖK 1985: Gyöngyi Török. "Beiträge zur Verbreitung einer niederländischen Dreifaltigkeitsdarstellung im 15. Jahrhundert: Eine Elfenbeintafel aus dem Besitze Philipps des Guten von Burgund." *Jahrbuch der Kunsthistorischen Sammlungen in Wien* 81 (1985): 7–31.

TORONTO 1980: Art Gallery of Ontario. *Annual Report 1979/1980*. Toronto, 1980.

TORONTO 1987: *The Glory of the Page: Medieval and Renaissance Illuminated Manuscripts from Glasgow University Library*. Exh. cat. by Nigel Thorp. Toronto, Art Gallery of Ontario, 1987.

TOUSTAIN 1881: Le comte de Toustain. *Chroniques de Normandie: Un Folio de 257 feuillets avec miniatures et lettres ornées*. Bayeux, 1881.

TOUSTAIN 1881–82: Le comte de Toustain. "Un Manuscrit des Chroniques de Normandie." *Bulletin de la Société des antiquaires de Normandie* 11 (1881–82): 186–91.

TRAPP 1975: J. B. Trapp. "Notes on Manuscripts Written by Peter Meghen." *Book Collector* 24 (1975): 80–96.

TRAPP 1980: J. B. Trapp. "Tommaso Moro e l'Utopia." *Academia Nazionale dei Linci*. Rome, 1980.

TRAPP 1981–82: J. B. Trapp. "Peter Meghen, 1466/7–1540, Scribe and Courier," and appendix: "Notes on Manuscripts Written by Meghen." *Erasmus in English* 11 (1981–82): 28–35.

TRAPP 1983: J. B. Trapp. "Pieter Meghen, Yet Again." In *Manuscripts in the Fifty Years after the Invention of Printing*, edited by J. B. Trapp: 23–28. London, 1983.

TRAPP 1991: J. B. Trapp. *Erasmus, Colet, and More: The Early Tudor Humanists and Their Books*. Panizzi Lectures 1990. London, 1991.

TRENKLER 1973: Ernst Trenkler. *Geschichte der Öster-reichischen Nationalbibliothek.* Vol. 2, *Die National-bibliothek (1923–1967).* Vienna, 1973.

TRENKLER 1979: Ernst Trenkler. *Rothschild-Gebetbuch: Codex Vindobonensis seria nova 2844 des Öster-reichischen Nationalbibliothek.* Codices selecti, 67. Graz, 1979.

TRIO 1990: P. Trio. *De Gentse broederschappen (1182–1580): Ontstaan, naamgeving, materiële uitrusting, structuur, opheffing, en bronnen.* Ghent, 1990.

TRIO 1995: P. Trio. "L'Enlumineur à Bruges, Gand et Ypres (1300–1435). Son Milieu socio-économique et corporatif." In *Flanders in a European Perspective: Manuscript Illumination c. 1400 in Flanders and Abroad,* edited by M. Smeyers and B. Cardon: 721–29. Leuven, 1995.

TUDOR-CRAIG 1987: P. Tudor-Craig. "The Hours of Edward V and William Lord Hastings: British Library Manuscript Additional 54782." In *England in the Fifteenth Century: Proceedings of the 1986 Harlaxton Symposium,* edited by D. Williams: 351–69. Wood-bridge, Suffolk, 1987.

TURIN 1997: *Jan van Eyck (1390 c.–1441): Opere a confronto.* Exh. cat. Turin, Galleria Sabauda, 1997.

TURIN 1999: *Boccaccio visualizzato.* Edited by V. Branca. 3 vols. Turin, 1999.

TURNER 1967: Derek H. Turner. *Illuminated Manuscripts Exhibited in the Grenville Library.* London, 1967.

TURNER 1983: Derek H. Turner. *The Hastings Hours: A Fifteenth-Century Book of Hours Made for William, Lord Hastings, Now in the British Library, London.* London, 1983.

TUVE 1966: Rosemund Tuve. *Allegorical Imagery: Some Mediaeval Books and Their Posterity.* Princeton, 1966.

UNTERKIRCHER 1963: Franz Unterkircher. "Ambraser Handschriften. Ein Tausch zwischen dem Kunsthis-torischen Museum und der Nationalbibliothek im Jahre 1936." *Jahrbuch der Kunsthistorischen Sammlungen im Wien* 59 (1963): 225–64.

UNTERKIRCHER 1967: Franz Unterkircher. *Abendländische Buchmalerei. Miniaturen aus Handschriften der Öster-reichischen Nationalbibliothek.* Graz, Vienna, and Cologne, 1967.

UNTERKIRCHER 1974: Franz Unterkircher. *Bürgundisches Brevier: Die schönsten Miniaturen aus dem Stundenbuch der Maria von Burgund, Codex Vindobonensis 1857.* Graz, 1974.

UNTERKIRCHER 1983: Franz Unterkircher. *Maximilian I: Ein kaiserlicher Auftraggeber illustrierter Handschriften.* Hamburg, 1983.

UNTERKIRCHER 1987: Franz Unterkircher. *Das Gebetbuch Jakobs IV von Schottland und seiner Gemahlin Margaret Tudor: Vollständige Faksimile-Ausgabe im Original-format des Codex 1897 des Österreichischen National-bibliothek Wien.* Codices selecti 85. Graz, 1987.

UNTERKIRCHER AND DE SCHRYVER 1969: Franz Unter-kircher and Antoine de Schryver. *Gebetbuch Karls des Kühnen vel potius, Stundenbuch der Maria von Burgund: Codex Vindobonensis 1857 der Österreichischen National-bibliothek.* 2 vols. Graz, 1969.

UPTON 1972: Joel Upton. "Petrus Christus." Ph.D. diss., Bryn Mawr College, 1972.

UPTON 1990: Joel M. Upton. *Petrus Christus: His Place in Fifteenth-Century Flemish Painting.* University Park, Pa., and London, 1990.

UTRECHT 1989: *The Golden Age of Dutch Manuscript Paint-ing.* Introduction by James H. Marrow. Exh. cat. by Henri Defoer, Anne Korteweg and Wilhelmina Wüstefeld. Utrecht, Rijksmuseum het Catharijne-convent, 1989.

UTRECHT 1994: *Duivels en demonen: De duivel in de Nederlandse beeldcultuur.* Exh. cat. by Petra van Boheemen and Paul Dirkse. Utrecht, Rijksmuseum het Catharijneconvent, 1994.

VALE 1981: Malcolm Vale. *War and Chivalry: War and Aristocratic Culture in England, France and Burgundy at the End of the Middle Ages.* Athens, Ga., 1981.

VALE 1995: Malcolm Vale. "An Anglo-Burgundian Nobleman and Art Patron: Louis de Bruges, Lord of La Gruthuyse and Earl of Winchester." In *England and the Low Countries in the Late Middle Ages,* edited by Caroline Barron and Nigel Saul: 115–31. Stroud, 1995.

VALENCIA 1999: *Pintura europea en colecciones valencianas.* Exh. cat. by Fernando B. Doménech et al. Valencia, Museo de Bellas Artes, 1999.

VALENCIA 1999a: Instituto de Valencia de Don Juan. *Status du Thoison.* Insigne Orden del Toison de Oro Valencia, 1999.

VALLESE 1983: Gloria Vallese. "Il tema della follia nell'arte di Bosch: Iconografia e stile." *Paragone* 34, no. 405 (November 1983): 3–49.

VAN ARENBERGH 1880–83: E. van Arenbergh. "Denis Harduyn, Hardwyn or Harduinus (Dionysius)." In *Biographie nationale* 8: cols. 714–17. Brussels, 1880–83.

VAN ASPEREN DE BOER ET AL. 1997: J. R. J. van Asperen de Boer et al., eds. *Jan van Eyck: Two Paintings of "Saint Francis Receiving the Stigmata."* Philadelphia, 1997.

VAN BASTELAER AND HULIN DE LOO 1907: René van Bastelaer and Georges Hulin de Loo. *Peter Bruegel l'Ancien, son oeuvre et son temps: Étude historique, suivie des catalogues raisonnés de son oeuvre dessiné et gravé.* 5 parts. Brussels, 1907.

VAN BUREN 1972: Anne Hagopian Van Buren. "New Evidence for Jan Wauquelin's Activity in the Chroniques de Hainaut and for the Date of the Miniatures." *Scriptorium* 26 (1972): 249–68.

VAN BUREN 1975: Anne Hagopian van Buren. "The Master of Mary of Burgundy and His Colleagues: The State of Research and Questions of Method." *Zeitschrift für Kunstgeschichte* 38 (1975): 286–309.

VAN BUREN 1979: Anne Hagopian van Buren. "The Model Roll of the Golden Fleece." *Art Bulletin* 61 (1979): 359–76.

VAN BUREN 1983: Anne Hagopian van Buren. "Jean Wauquelin de Mons et la production du livre aux Pay-Bas." *Publication du Centre Européen d'Études burgondo-médianes* 23 (1983): 53–66.

VAN BUREN 1984: Anne Hagopian van Buren. "London, British Library, Renaissance Painting in Manu-scripts." *Burlington Magazine* 126 (1984): 652–53, 661.

VAN BUREN 1993: Anne Hagopian van Buren. Review of Pächt and Thoss, *Die Illuminierten Handschriften und Inkunabeln der Österreichischen Nationalbibliothek: Flämische Schule II. Speculum* 68 (October 1993): 1187–90.

VAN BUREN 1996a: Anne Hagopian van Buren. "Images monumentales de la Toison d'or: Aux murs du château de Hesdin et en tapisserie." In *L'Ordre de la Toison d'or, de Philippe le Bon à Philippe le Beau (1430–1505): Idéal ou reflet d'une société?,* edited by Christiane van den Bergen-Pantens: 226–33. Brussels, 1996.

VAN BUREN 1996b: Anne Hagopian van Buren. "Philip the Good's Manuscripts as Documents of His Rela-tions with the Empire." In *Pays bourguignons et terres d'Empire (XVe–XVIe s.): Rapports politiques et institu-tionnels; Publication du Centre europé d'Études bour-guignonnes (XIVe–XVIe s.),* no. 36 (1996): 49–69.

VAN BUREN 1999: Anne Hagopian van Buren, "Willem Vrelant: Questions and Issues." *Revue belge d'archéol-ogie et d'histoire de l'art* 58 (1999): 3–30.

VAN BUREN 2002: Anne Hagopian van Buren. "Dreux Jehan and the *Grandes Heures* of Philip the Bold." In "Als Ich Can:" *Liber Amicorum in Memory of Professor Dr. Maurits Smeyers:* 1377–1414. Leuven, 2002.

VAN BUREN, MARROW, AND PETTENATI 1996: Anne H. van Buren, James H. Marrow, and Silvana Pettenati. *Heures de Turin-Milan, Inv. No. 47, Museo Civico d'Arte Antica, Torino: Kommentar, Commentary, Commentaire.* Lucerne, 1996.

VAN DE CASTEELE 1866: D. van de Casteele. "Docu-ments divers de la Société S. Luc à Bruges Keuren." *Annales de la Société d'Émulation pour l'Étude de l'Histoire et des Antiquités de la Flandre,* ser. 3, 1 (1866): 5–54.

VAN DE WALLE DE GHELCKE 1952: Thierry van de Walle de Ghelcke. "Y a-t-il un Gérard David miniaturist?" In *Studies over de kerkelijke en kunstgeschiedenis van West–Vlaanderen:* 399–422. Bruges, 1952.

VAN DEN BERGEN-PANTENS 1990: Christiane van den Bergen-Pantens. Review of *Das Epos des burgunder-reiches Girart de Roussillon,* by Dagmar Thoss. *Scripto-rium* 44 (1990): 93, no. 312.

VAN DEN BERGEN-PANTENS 1993: Christiane van den Bergen-Pantens. "Héraldique et bibliophilie; Le Cas d'Antoine, grand bâtard de Bourgogne (1421–1504)." In *Miscellanea Martin Wittek; Album de codicologie et de paléographie offert à Martin Wittek,* edited by A. Raman and E. Manning: 323–53. Leuven, 1993.

VAN DEN BERGEN-PANTENS 2000: Christiane van den Bergen-Pantens, ed. *Les Chroniques de Hainaut; ou, Les Ambitions d'un prince bourguignon.* Turnhout, 2000.

VAN DEN BERGEN-PANTENS 2001: Christiane van den Bergen-Pantens. "Étude et datation du 'Triptyque de Saint Hippolyte' (Cathédrale Saint-Sauveur à Bruges)." In *Bouts Studies,* edited by Bert Cardon et al. Leuven, 2001.

VAN DEN GHEYN (G.) 1889: G. van den Gheyn. *Les Cavaux polychromés en Flandre.* Ghent, 1889.

VAN DEN GHEYN (J.) 1906: J. van den Gheyn. "Notes sur quelques manuscrits à miniatures de l'école flamande conservés dans les bibliothèques d'Espagne." *Annales de l'Académie d'Archéologie de Belgique* 58 (1906): 305–30.

VAN DEN GHEYN (J.) 1909: J. van den Gheyn. "Note sur quelques scribes et enlumineurs de la Cour de Bour-gogne et d'après le compte de Gautier Poulain." *Bulletin de l'Académie de Belgique* (1909): 90–91.

VAN DEN GHEYN (J.) 1910: J. van den Gheyn. *Histoire de Charles Martel: Reproduction des 102 miniatures de Loyset Liédet (1470).* Brussels, 1910.

VAN DEN HAUTE 1913: C. van den Haute. *La Corporation des peintres de Bruges.* Bruges, 1913.

VAN DER HAEGHEN 1914: V. van der Haeghen. "Notes sur l'atelier de Gérard Horenbault ver la fin du XVe siècle." *Bulletijn der Maatschappij van Geschied-en Oudheidkunde te Gent* 22 (1914): 26–36.

VAN DER HOEK 1989: Klaas van der Hoek. "De Noord-hollandse verluchter Spierinck Haarlem en/of Bever-wijk, circa 1485–1519." *Middeleeuwse hand-schriftenkunde in de Nederlanden 1988; Verslag van de Groningse Codicologendagen, 28–29 april 1988,* edited by Jos. M. M. Hermans: 163–82. The Hague, 1989.

VAN DER HORST 1989: Koert van der Horst. *Illuminated and Decorated Medieval Manuscripts in the University Library, Utrecht: An Illustrated Catalogue.* The Hague, 1989.

VAN DER HORST AND KLAMT 1991: Koert van der Horst and Johann-Christian Klamt, eds. *Masters and Miniatures: Proceedings of the Congress on Medieval Manuscript Illumination in the Northern Netherlands (Utrecht, 10–13 December 1989)*. Ghent, 1991.

VAN DER STOCK 1983: Jan van der Stock. "Cornelis Matsys fecit (1510/11–1556): Leven en werk met speciale aandacht voor zijn grafisch oeuvre." Doctoral thesis, Katholieke Universiteit, Leuven, 1983.

VAN DER STOCK 1984: Jan van der Stock. "Enkele nieuwe gegevens over Cornelis Matsys (1510/11–april 1556/januari 1557)." *Jaarboek van het Koninklijk Museum voor Schone Kunsten Antwerpen* (1984): 103–21.

VAN DER STOCK 1985: Jan van der Stock. *Cornelis Matsys (1510/11–1556/57): Grafisch werk*. Exh. cat. Brussels, Bibliothèque royale Albert Ier, 1985.

VAN DER STRAELEN 1855: J. van der Straelen. *Jaarboek der vermaerde en kunstryke Gilde van Sint Lucas binnen de stad Antwerpen*. Antwerp, 1855.

VAN DER VELDEN 1995: Hugo van der Velden. "Cambyses Reconsidered: Gerard David's 'Exemplum Iustitiae' for Bruges Town Hall." *Simiolus* 23, no. 1 (1995): 40–60.

VAN DER VELDEN 2000: Hugo van der Velden. *The Donor's Image: Gerard Loyet and the Votive Portraits of Charles the Bold*. Turnhout, 2000.

VAN ELSLANDE 1992: R. van Elslande. "Lieven van Lathem, een onbekende belangrijke kunstenaar uit de 15de eeuw." In *Scheldeveld. Jaarboek*, 1992: 127–69.

VAN ETTRO 1976: F. J. van Ettro. "De oudste afbeelding van het wapen van Zeeland." *De Nederlandsche Leeuw* 93, nos. 10–12 (1976): 367–72.

VAN LEEUWEN 1975: C. G. van Leuwen. *Denkbeelden van een vliesridder: De Instruction d'un jeune Prince van Guillebert van Lannoy*. Amsterdam, 1975.

VAN MANDER 1604: Carel van Mander. *Het Schilder-Boeck*. . . . Haarlem, 1604. Reprint, Utrecht, 1969.

VAN MIEGROET 1986: Hans J. van Miegroet. *De invloed van de roege Nederlandse schilderkunst in de eerste helft van de 15de eeuw op Konrad Witz*. Verhandelingen van de Koninkligke Academie voor Wetenschappen, Letteren en Schone Kunsten van België, Klasse der Schone Kunsten 48, no. 42. Brussels, 1986.

VAN MIEGROET 1989: Hans J. Van Miegroet. *Gerard David*. Antwerp, 1989.

VAN PRAET 1829: J. B. B. van Praet. *Notice sur Colard Mansion*. Paris, 1829.

VAN PRAET 1831: J. B. B. van Praet. *Recherches sur Louis de Bruges, seigneur de la Gruthuyse, suivies de la notice des manuscrits qui lui ont appartenu, et dont la plus grande partie se conserve à la Bibliothèque de Roi*. Paris, 1831.

VAN PUYVELDE 1948: Leo van Puyvelde. *The Flemish Primitives*. Brussels, 1948.

VAN PUYVELDE 1953: Leo van Puyvelde. *La Peinture flamande au siècle des Van Eyck*. Paris, 1953.

VAN PUYVELDE 1963: Leo van Puyvelde. *Die Welt von Bosch und Bruegel*. Munich, 1963.

VAN UYTVEN 1992: R. van Uytven. "Splendour or Wealth: Art and Economy in the Burgundian Netherlands." *Transactions of the Cambridge Bibliographical Society* 10 (1992): 101–24.

VANDENABEELE 2000: Peter Vandenabeele. "Optimalisatie van Micro-Raman Spectroscopie en Totalereflectie X-Stralen Flourescentie vor de Analyse ven Kunstvoorwerpen." Doctoral thesis, Universiteit Gent, 2000.

VANDENABEELE AND MOENS 2002: Peter Vandenabeele and Luc Moens. "Spectroscopic Pigment Investigation of the Mayer van den Bergh Breviary." In

"Als Ich Can": Liber Amicorum in Memory of Professor Maurits Smeyers: 1443–55. Leuven, 2002.

VANDENABEELE ET AL. 1999: Peter Vandenabeele, Bernhard Wehling, Luc Moens, Brigitte Dekeyzer, Bert Cardon, Alex von Bohlen, and Reinhold Klockenkämper. "Pigment Investigation of a Late-Medieval Manuscript with Total Reflection X-ray Fluorescence and Micro-Raman Spectroscopy." *Analyst* 124 (1999): 169–72.

VANDERJAGT 1995. Arie Johan Vanderjagt. "Classical Learning and the Building of Power at the Fifteenth-Century Burgundian Court." In *Centres of Learning: Learning and Location in Pre-Modern Europe and the Near East*, edited by J. W. Drijvers and A. A. MacDonald: 267–77. Leiden, 1995.

VANWIJNSBERGHE 1995: Dominique Vanwijnsberghe. "Mise au point concernant l'enluminure tournaisienne au XVe siècle." *Mémoires de la Société d'Histoire et d'Archéologie de Tournai* 8 (1995): 33–60.

VANWIJNSBERGHE 1996: Dominique Vanwijnsberghe. "Simon Marmion, III: L'Oeuvre enluminé." In *Valenciennes aux XIVe et XVe siècles: Art et histoire*, edited by Ludovic Nys and d'Alain Salamagne: 169–79. Valenciennes, 1996.

VANWIJNSBERGHE 2001: Dominique Vanwijnsberghe. "De fin or et d'azur": Les Commanditaires de livres et le métier de l'enluminure à Tournai à la fin du Moyen Âge (XIVe–XVe siècles). Leuven, 2001.

VANWIJNSBERGHE 2002: Dominique Vanwijnsberghe. "At the Court as in the City: The Miniature in the Burgundian Netherlands in the Fifteenth Century." In *Medieval Mastery: Book Illumination from Charlemagne to Charles the Bold, 800–1475*: 263–71. Exh. cat. Leuven, Stedelijk Museum Vander Kelen-Mertens, 2002.

VASARI 1550: Giorgio Vasari. *Le vite de piu eccellenti architetti, pittori, et scultori italiani*. . . . Florence, 1550.

VASARI 1927: Giorgio Vasari. *The Lives of the Painters, Sculptors, and Architects*. 4 vols. Everyman's Library. London, 1927.

VATICAN CITY 1996: *Vedere i classici: L'illustrazione libraria dei testi antichi dall'età romana al tardo medioevo*. Exh. cat. edited by Marco Buonocore. Vatican City, Biblioteca Apostolica Vaticana, 1996.

VATICAN CITY 1979: *Libri manoscritti e stampati del Belgio nella Biblioteca Vaticana, secoli IX–XVII*. Exh. cat. Vatican City, Biblioteca Apostolica Vaticana, 1979.

VATICAN CITY 1988: *Die schönsten Stundenbücher aus der Biblioteca Apostolica Vaticana*. Exh. cat. by Giovanni Morello. Vatican City, Biblioteca Apostolica Vaticana, 1988.

VAUGHAN 1973: Richard Vaughan. *Charles the Bold: The Last Valois Duke of Burgundy*. London, 1973.

VERDIER 1985: P. Verdier. Review of *Die Handschriften der Sammlung Ludwig*. *Speculum* 60 (1985): 203–7.

VERGNE 1995: Frédéric Vergne. *A Princely Library: The Manuscript Collection of the Duke d'Aumale, Chateau de Chantilly*. Translated by Nina McPherson. Paris, 1995.

VERHAEGEN 1961: Nicole Verhaegen. "Het Calvarie-Drieluik Toegeschreven aan Justus van Gent den de Bijhorende Predella." *Bulletin van het Koninklijk Instituut voor het Kunstpatrimonium* 4 (1961): 6–10.

VERMEERSCH 1976: V. Vermeersch. *Grafmonumenten te Brugge voor 1578*. 3 vols. Bruges, 1976.

VERMEERSCH 1992: V. Vermeersch, ed. *Bruges and Europe*. Antwerp, 1992.

VEROUGSTRAETE, DE SCHRYVER, AND MARIJNISSEN 1995: Hélène Verougstraete, Antoine de Schryver and Roger H. Marijnissen. "Peintures sur papier et

parchemin marouflés aux XVe et XVIe siècles: L'Exemple d'une *Vierge et Enfant* de la suite de Gérard David." In *Le Dessin sous-jacent dans la peinture: Colloque X, 1993*, edited by H. Verougstraete and R. van Schoute: 96–105. Louvain-la-Neuve, 1995.

VEY 1966: Horst Vey. "Johann Peter Weyer: Seine Gemäldesammlung und Seine Kunstliebe." *Wallraf-Richartz-Jahrbuch* 28 (1966): 159–254.

VIENNA 1936: *Nationalbibliothek in Wien: Katalog der Ausstellung von Neuerwerbungen aus den Jahren 1930–1935*. Vienna, Nationalbibliothek, 1936.

VIENNA 1948: *25 Jahre Neuerwerbungen der Österreichischen Nationalbibliothek 1923–1948: Katalog der Ausstellung aus Anlass des 25 jährigen Dienstjubiläums des Generaldirektors Univ.–Prof. Dr. Joseph Bick*. Exh. cat. Vienna, Österreichische Nationalbibliothek, 1948.

VIENNA 1952: *Abendländische Buchmalerei*. Exh. cat. Vienna, Österreichische Nationalbibliothek, 1952.

VIENNA 1959: *Maximilian I (1459–1519)*. Exh. cat. Vienna, Österreichische Nationalbibliothek, 1959.

VIENNA 1967: *Schätze und Kostbarkeiten: Ausstellung der wertvollsten Erwerbungen (Handschriften, Inkunabeln, Autographen, Papyri, Bücher, Musicalia, Theatralia, Kartenwerke, Globen, Graphiken, Lichtbilder u.a.m.) und Bildschau der Leistungen der Österreichischen Nationalbibliothek in der zweiten Republik, 1947–1967*. Exh. cat. Vienna, Österreichische Nationalbibliothek, 1967.

VIENNA 1987a: *Bibliotheca Eugeniana: Die Sammlungen des Prinzen Eugen von Savoyen*. Exh. cat. Vienna, Österreichische Nationalbibliothek and Graphische Sammlung Albertina, 1987.

VIENNA 1987b: *Flämische Buchmalerei Handschriftenschätze aus dem Burgunderreich*. Exh. cat. by Dagmar Thoss. Vienna, Österreichische Nationalbibliothek, 1987.

VIENNA 1988: *Prag um 1600: Kunst und Kultur am Hofe Kaiser Rudolfs II.* 2 vols. Vienna, Kunsthistorisches Museum, 1988.

VIGNAU-SCHUURMAN 1969: Theodora Wilberg Vignau-Schuurman. *Die emblematischen Elemente im Werke Joris Hoefnagels*. Leiden, 1969.

VISSER-FUCHS 1998: Livia Visser-Fuchs. "Edward IV's Only Romance? Cambridge, Corpus Christi College MS 91, L'Histoire des Seigneurs de Gavre." *The Ricardian* 11 (1998): 278–87.

VOELKLE AND PASSELA 1980: William M. Voelkle and Charles V. Passela. *The Pierpont Morgan Library Masterpieces of Medieval Painting: The Art of Illumination*. Chicago, 1980.

VOGELAAR 1987: Christiaan Vogelaar. *Netherlandish Fifteenth and Sixteenth Century Paintings in The National Gallery of Ireland: A Complete Catalogue*. Dublin, 1987.

VÖHRINGER 2002: Christian Vöhringer. *Pieter Bruegels d. Ä. Landschaft mit pflügendem Bauern und Ikarussturz: Mythenkritik und Kalendermotivik im 16. Jahrhundert*. Munich, 2002.

VORONOVA 1980: Tamara Voronova. *Les Grandes Chroniques de France: Enluminures du XVe siècle*. Leningrad, 1980.

VORONOVA AND STERLIGOV 1996: Tamara Voronova and Andrei Sterligov. *Western European Illuminated Manuscripts of the 8th to the 16th Centuries*. Saint Petersburg, 1996.

VRIES 1904–10: Scato de Vries, ed. *Bréviaire Grimani de la Bibliothèque de S. Marco à Venise: Reproduction photographique complète*. 12 vols. Leiden, 1904–10.

VRIES AND MOPURGO 1903–7: Scato de Vries and S. Mopurgo, eds. *Das Breviarium Grimani*. Leiden and Leipzig, 1903–7.

WAAGEN 1847: Gustav Friedrich Waagen. "Nachträge zur Kenntnis der altniederländischen Malerschulen des 15. und 16. Jahrhunderts." *Kunstblatt*, 1847: 177–78.

WAAGEN 1854–57: Gustav Friedrich Waagen. *Treasures of Art in Great Britain*. 4 vols. London, 1854–57.

WAAGEN 1862: Gustav Friedrich Waagen. *Handbuch der deutschen und niederländischen Malerschulen*. 2 vols. Stuttgart, 1862.

WALLERT 1991: A. Wallert. "Instructions for Manuscript Illumination in a 15th Century Netherlandish Technical Treatise." In *Masters and Miniatures*, edited by K. van der Horst and J. C. Klamt: 447–56. Studies and Facsimiles of Netherlandish Illuminated Manuscripts, 3. Doornspijk, 1991.

WALZ 1994: D. Walz. *Das Falkenbuch Friedrichs II*. Graz, 1994.

WARD AND HERBERT 1883–1910: H. L. D. Ward and J. A. Herbert. *Catalogue of Romances in the Department of Manuscripts in the British Museum*. 3 vols. London, 1883–1910.

WARNER (G.) 1894: George Frederic Warner. *Miniatures and Borders from the Book of Hours of Bona Sforza, Duchess of Milan, in the British Museum*. London, 1894.

WARNER (G.) 1903: George Frederic Warner. *Illuminated Manuscripts in the British Museum: Miniatures, Borders and Initials*. Series I–IV. London, 1903.

WARNER (G.) 1910: George Frederic Warner. *Reproductions from Illuminated Manuscripts*. Series I–III. 2nd ed. 3 vols. London, 1910.

WARNER (G.) 1920: George Frederic Warner. *Descriptive Catalogue of Illuminated Manuscripts in the Library of C. W. Dyson Perrins*. 2 vols. Oxford, 1920.

WARNER (G.) AND GILSON 1921: George F. Warner and Julius P. Gilson. *Catalogue of Western Manuscripts in the Old Royal and King's Collections. British Museum*. 4 vols. London, 1921. Reprints, 1971; Munich, 1997.

WARNER (M.) 1976: Marina Warner. *Alone of All Her Sex: The Myth and Cult of the Virgin Mary*. New York, 1976.

WARSAW 1960: *Malarstwo Niderlandzkie w zbiorach Polskich, 1450–1550*. Exh. cat. by Jan Bialostocki. Warsaw, Muzeum Narodowe w Warszawie, 1960.

WASHINGTON 1975: *Medieval and Renaissance Miniatures from the National Gallery of Art*. Exh. cat. compiled by Carra Ferguson, David S. Stevens Schaff, Gary Vikan, under the direction of Carl Nordenfalk; edited by Gary Vikan. Washington, D.C., National Gallery of Art, 1975.

WASHINGTON 1986a: *The Age of Bruegel: Netherlandish Drawings in the Sixteenth Century*. Exh. cat. by John Hand et al. Washington, D.C., National Gallery of Art, 1986.

WASHINGTON 1986b: *Early Netherlandish Painting*. Exh. cat. by John Oliver Hand and Martha Wolff. Washington, D.C., National Gallery of Art, 1986.

WASHINGTON 1991: *Circa 1492: Art in the Age of Exploration*. Exh. cat. edited by J. A. Levenson. Washington, D.C., National Gallery of Art, 1991.

WASHINGTON 1995: *The Touch of the Artist: Master Drawings from the Woodner Collections*. Exh. cat. edited by Margaret Morgan Grasselli. Washington, D.C., National Gallery of Art, 1995.

WASHINGTON 2002: *Deceptions and Illusions: Five Centuries of Trompe l'Oeil Painting*. Exh. cat. Washington, D.C., National Gallery of Art, 2002.

WATSON 1979: Andrew G. Watson. *Catalogue of Dated and Datable Manuscripts c. 700–1600 in the Department of Manuscripts, the British Library*. 2 vols. London, 1979.

WATTEEUW 2002: Lieve Watteeuw. "In de ban van de band: Het Breviarium Mayer van den Bergh gebonden en gerestaureerd, een historische benadering." In *"Als Ich Can": Liber Amicorum in Memory of Professor Maurits Smeyers*: 1605–27. Leuven, 2002.

WAUTERS 1878: Alphonse Wauters. *Les Tapisseries bruxellois*. Brussels, 1878. Reprint, 1973.

WAUTERS 1890–91: Alphonse Wauters. "Lieven van Lathem." In *Biographie nationale publiée par l'Académie royale des Sciences, des Lettres, et des Beaux-Arts de Belgique*, vol. 11: cols. 421–23. Brussels, 1890–91.

WEALE 1863–65: W. H. J. Weale. "Inventaire des chartes et documents appartenant aux archives de la Corporation de Saint Luc et Saint Éloi à Bruges." *Le Beffroi* 1–2 (1863–65).

WEALE 1864–65a: W. H. James Weale. "Les enlumineurs de Bruges." *Le Beffroi* 2 (1864–65): 298–319.

WEALE 1864–65b: W. H. J. Weale. "Gerard David." *Le Beffroi* 2 (1864–65): 268–97.

WEALE 1866–70: W. H. J. Weale. "Le Couvent des Soeurs de Notre-Dame, dit de Sion, à Bruges." *Le Beffroi* 3 (1866–70): 46–53, 76–93, 213–30, 301–28.

WEALE 1872–73a: W. H. James Weale. "Documents inédits sur les enlumineurs de Bruges." *Le Beffroi* 4 (1872–73): 111–19, 238–337.

WEALE 1872–73b: W. H. James Weale. "Manuscrit enluminé de l'abbaye de Messines, c.1530." *Le Beffroi* 4 (1872–73): 195–97.

WEALE 1883: W. H. James Weale. *The Hours of Albert of Brandenburg*. London, 1883.

WEALE 1894: W. H. James Weale. *Bookbindings and Rubbings of Bindings in the National Art Library South Kensington*. 2 vols. London, 1894.

WEALE 1895: W. H. James Weale. *Gerard David, Painter and Illuminator*. London, 1895.

WEALE 1903a: W. H. James Weale. Review of *Ahnenreihen aus dem Stammbaum des portugiesischen Königshauses: Miniaturenfolge in der Bibliothek des British Museum*, by Ludwig Kaemmerer and H. G. Ströhl. *Burlington Magazine* 3 (1903): 321–24.

WEALE 1903b: "The Early Painters of the Netherlands as Illustrated by the Bruges Exhibition of 1902." *Burlington Magazine* 1 (1903): 326–33.

WEALE 1905–6: W. H. James Weale. "Simon Binnink, Miniaturist." *Burlington Magazine* 8 (1905–6) 355–57.

WEALE 1911: W. H. James Weale. "Peintres brugeoises, les Claeissins, 1500–1656." *Annales de la Société d'Émulation de Bruges* 61 (1911): 26–76.

WEHLE AND SALINGER 1947: Harry B. Wehle and Margaretta Salinger. *A Catalogue of Early Flemish, Dutch, and German Paintings*. New York, 1947.

WEISZ 1913: E. Weisz. *Jan Gossart gen. Mabuse: Sein Leben und seine Werke*. Parchim, 1913.

WEITZMANN 1975: Kurt Weitzmann. "The Study of Byzantine Book Illumination, Past, Present, and Future." In *The Place of Book Illumination in Byzantine Art*: 1–60. Princeton, 1975.

WENIGER 2001: Matthias Weniger. "Provost als Buchmaler – Versuch einer Nachlese." In *Aus Albrecht Dürers Welt*, edited by Bodo Brinkmann, Hartmut Krohm, and Michael Roth: 143–51. Turnhout, 2001.

WESCHER 1931: Paul Wescher. *Beschreibendes Verzeichnis der Miniaturen — Handschriften und Einzelblätter — des Kupferstichkabinetts der Staatlichen Museen Berlin*. Leipzig, 1931.

WESCHER 1936: Paul Wescher. *Miniaturen des Kupferstichkabinetts der Staatlichen Museen Berlin*. Leipzig, 1936.

WESCHER 1946: Paul Wescher. "Sanders and Simon Bening and Gerard Horenbout." *Art Quarterly* 9 (1946): 191–209.

WESCHER 1959: Paul Wescher. "Beiträge zu Sanders und Simon Bening und Gerard Horenbout." In *Festschrift Friedrich Winkler*: 126–35. Berlin, 1959.

WESCHER 1960: Paul Wescher. "Francesco Binasco, Miniaturmaler der Sforza." *Jahrbuch der Berliner Museen*, n.s., 2 (1960): 75–91.

WEYER 1852: Johann Peter Weyer. *Beschreibung des Inhaltes der Sammlung von Gemälden älterer Meister des Herrn Johann Peter Weyer in Coeln*. Cologne, 1852.

WIECK 1981: Roger Wieck. "The Rosenwald Scribe Miniature and Its Sister Miniatures." *Oud Holland* 95 (1981): 151–61.

WIECK 1992: Roger S. Wieck. "Margaret of York's Visions of Tondal: Relationship of the Miniatures to a Text Transformed by Translator and Illuminator." In *Margaret of York, Simon Marmion and The Visions of Tondal*, edited by T. Kren: 119–28. Malibu, 1992.

WIECK 1994: Roger S. Wieck. "Inventive Efficiency from the Master of the Ghent Privileges; or, A Little Bit of Hell Goes a Long Way." In *Medieval Codicology, Iconography, Literature, and Translation: Studies for Keith Val Sinclair*, edited by Peter Rolfe Monks and D. D. R. Owen: 134–42. Leiden, 1994.

WIECK 1996: Roger S. Wieck. "Folia fugitiva: The Pursuit of the Illuminated Manuscript Leaf." *Journal of the Walters Art Gallery* 54 (1996): 233–54.

WIECK 1997: Roger S. Wieck. *Painted Prayers: The Book of Hours in Medieval and Renaissance Art*. New York, 1997.

WIECK 1999: Roger S. Wieck. "The Death Desired: Books of Hours and the Medieval Funeral." In *Death and Dying in the Middle Ages*, edited by Edelgard E. DuBruck and Barbara I. Gusick: 431–76. Studies in the Humanities: Literature, Politics, Society, vol. 45. New York, 1999.

WIECK, VOELKLE, AND HEARNE 2000: Roger S. Wieck, William M. Voelkle, and K. Michelle Hearne. *The Hours of Henry VIII: A Renaissance Masterpiece by Jean Poyet*. New York, 2000.

WIED 1994: Alexander Wied. *Bruegel*. Milan, 1994.

WIESELGREN 1925: O. Wieselgren. "Skoklosterhandskriften av Vasco de Lucenas Curtius-Parafras." *Nordisk tidskft för bok- och biblioteksväsen* 12 (1925).

WIJSMAN 2002: H. Wijsman. "William Lord Hastings: Les Faits de Jacques de Lalaing et le 'Maître aux inscriptions blanches.' À propos du manuscrit français 16830 de la Bibliothèque nationale de France." In *"Als Ich Can": Liber Amicorum in Memory of Professor Dr. Maurits Smeyers*: 1641–64. Leuven, 2002.

WILLARD 1996: C. C. Willard. "Patrons at the Burgundian Court: Jean V de Créquy and His Wife, Louise de la Tour." In *The Search for a Patron in the Middle Ages and the Renaissance*, edited by D. G. Wilkins and R. L. Wilkins: 55–62. Lewiston, 1996.

WILLEMSEN 1998: Annemarieke Willemsen. *Kinderdelijt: Middeleeuws speelgoed in de Nederlanden*. [Nijmegen], 1998.

WILLIAMS 1987: Daniel Williams, ed. *England in the Fifteenth Century: Proceedings of the 1986 Harlaxton Symposium*. Woodbridge, Suffolk, 1987.

WILSON 1998: Jean C. Wilson. *Painting in Bruges at the Close of the Middle Ages*. Studies in Society and Visual Culture. University Park, Pa., 1998.

WILTON 1968: Sidney, 16th Earl of Pembroke. *A Catalogue of the Paintings and Drawings in the Collection at Wilton House, Salisbury, Wiltshire*. London and New York, 1968.

WINKLER 1913a: Friedrich Winkler. "Gerard David und die Brügger Miniaturmalerei seiner Zeit." *Monatshefte für Kunstwissenschaft* 6 (1913): 271–80.

WINKLER 1913b: Friedrich Winkler. "Miniaturen der Clara de Keysere?" *Mitteilungen der Gesellschaft für vervielfältigende Kunst: Beilage der graphischen Künste* 3 (1913): 49–53.

WINKLER 1913c: Friedrich Winkler. "Simon Marmion als Miniaturmaler." *Jahrbuch der Königlich preussischen Kunstsammlungen* 34 (1913): 251–80.

WINKLER 1914: Friedrich Winkler. "Der Brügger Meister des Dresdener Gebetbuches und seine Werke." *Jahrbuch der Königlich preussischen Kunstsammlungen* 35 (1914): 225–44.

WINKLER 1915: Friedrich Winkler. "Studien zur Geschichte der niederländischen Miniaturmalerei des XV. und XVI. Jahrhunderts." *Jahrbuch der Kunsthistorischen Sammlungen des allerhöchsten Kaiserhauses* 32, no. 3 (1915): 279–342.

WINKLER 1921: Friedrich Winkler. *Der Leipziger Valerius Maximus: Mit einer Einleitung über die Anfänge des Sittenbildes in den Niederlanden.* Leipzig, 1921.

WINKLER 1921a: Friedrich Winkler. "Die Anfänge Jan Gossarts." *Jahrbuch der Königlich preussischen Kunstsammlung* 42 (1921): 5–19.

WINKLER 1923: Friedrich Winkler. "Die nordfranzösische Malerei im 15. Jahrhundert und ihr Verhältnis zur altniederländischen Malerei." In *Belgische Kunstdenkmäler*, edited by Paul Clemen, vol. 1: 247–68. Munich, 1923.

WINKLER 1925: Friedrich Winkler. *Die flämische Buchmalerei des XV. und XVI. Jahrhunderts: Künstler und Werke von den Brüdern van Eyck bis zu Simon Bening.* Leipzig, 1925.

WINKLER 1934: Friedrich Winkler. "Simon Marmion." *Pantheon* 13 (1934): 65–72.

WINKLER 1942: Friedrich Winkler. "Neuentdeckte Altniederländer I: Sanders Bening." *Pantheon* 30 (1942): 261–71.

WINKLER 1943: Friedrich Winkler. "Neuentdeckte Altniederländer, II: Gerard Horenbaut." *Pantheon* 31 (1943): 55–64.

WINKLER 1957: Friedrich Winkler. "Buchmalereien von Jan Provost." In *Miscellanea Prof. Dr. D[omien] Roggen.* Antwerp, 1957.

WINKLER 1961a: Friedrich Winkler. "Quintus Curtius Rufus, Les fais d'Alexandre." Typescript, 1961.

WINKLER 1961b: Friedrich Winkler. "Simon Benings Gebetbuch des Kardinals Albrecht von Brandenburg." *Pantheon*, ser. 2, 19 (1961): 70–78.

WINKLER 1962: Friedrich Winkler. *Das Gebetbuch des Kardinals Albrecht von Brandenburg aus der Sammlung Ludwig: Aachen.* Aachen, 1962.

WINKLER 1964: Friedrich Winkler. *Das Werk des Hugo van der Goes.* Berlin, 1964.

WINKLER 1966: Friedrich Winkler. "Das Gebetbuch des Kardinals Albrecht von Brandenburg." In *Mainz und der Mittelrhein in der europäischen Kunstgeschichte: Studien für Wolfgang Fritz Volbach zu seinem 70. Geburtstag*: 385–414. Forschungen zur Kunstgeschichte und christlichen Archäologie 6. Mainz, 1966.

WINKLER 1978: Friedrich Winkler. *Die flämische Buchmalerei des XV. und XVI. Jahrhunderts: Künstler und Werke von den Brüdern van Eyck bis zu Simon Bening.* Reprint, with addenda by G. Dogaer. Amsterdam, 1978. First published Leipzig, 1925.

WISSE 2002: Jacob Wisse. "Question of Style: Two Illuminations by Gerard Horenbout in the the Metropolitan Museum of Art." In *"Als Ich Can": Liber Amicorum in Memory of Professor Maurits Smeyers*: 1665–85. Leuven, 2002.

WIXOM 1964: William D. Wixom. "Hours of Ferdinand V and Isabella of Spain." *Bulletin of The Cleveland Museum of Art* 51 (1964): 60–63.

WOERMANN 1896: Karl Woermann. *Katalog der Königlichen Gemäldegalerie zu Dresden.* Dresden, 1896.

WOLEDGE 1954: B. Woledge. *Bibliographie des romans et nouvelles en prose française antérieures à 1500.* Geneva, 1954.

WOLF (E.) 1996: Eva Wolf. *Das Bild in der spätmittelalterlichen Buchmalerei: Das Sachsenheim-Gebetbuch im Werk Lievin van Lathems.* Hildesheim, 1996.

WOLF (H.) 1978: Horst Wolf. *Niederländisch-flämische Buchmalerei des Spätmittelalters.* Berlin, 1978.

WOLF (H.) 1981: Horst Wolf. *Gent-Brügger Buchmalerei des Spätmitte-lalters.* Berlin, 1981.

WOLF (H.) 1982: Horst Wolf. *Die Meister des Breviarium Grimani.* Berlin, 1982.

WOLF (H.) 1985: Horst Wolf. *Kostbarkeiten flämischer Buchmalerei.* Berlin, 1985.

WOLFF 1998: Martha Wolff. "The Southern Netherlands, Fifteenth and Sixteenth Centuries." In *The Robert Lehman Collection, II: Fifteenth- to Eighteenth-Century European Paintings: France, Central Europe, The Netherlands, Spain, and Great Britain*, edited by Egbert Haverkamp-Begemann: 61–124. New York, 1998.

WOLFS 1966: S. Wolfs. "Zum Thema: Seuse und die Niederländen." In *Heinrich Seuse. Studien zum 600.Todestag, 1366–1966*, edited by E. Filthaut: 397–408. Cologne, 1966.

WOOD AND FYFE 1955: Casey A. Wood and F. Marjorie Fyfe, trans. and eds. *The Art of Falconry, Being the De arte venandi cum avibus of Frederick II Hohenstaufen.* Boston, 1955.

WORCESTER 1939: *The Worcester-Philadelphia Exhibition of Flemish Painting.* Exh. cat. Worcester, Worcester Art Museum, 1939.

WORMALD 1951: F. Wormald. "An Italian Poet at the Court of Henry VII." *Journal of Warburg and Courtauld Institutes* 14 (1951): 118–19.

WORMALD AND GILES 1982: F. Wormald and P. M. Giles. *A Descriptive Catalogue of the Additional Manuscripts in the Fitzwilliam Museum Acquired between 1895–1979 (Excluding the McClean Collection).* Cambridge, 1982.

WRIGHT 1972: Cyril Ernest Wright. *Fontes Harleiani: A Study of the Sources of the Harleian Collection of Manuscripts Preserved in the Department of Manuscripts in the British Museum.* London, 1972.

WRIGHT AND WRIGHT 1966: Cyril Ernest Wright and Ruth C. Wright, eds. *The Diary of Humfrey Wanley.* 2 vols. London, 1966.

WYSS 1955–56: R. L. Wyss. "Die Caesarteppiche und ihr ikonographisches Verhältnis zur Illustration der 'Faits des Romans' im 14. und 15. Jahrhundert." *Jahrbuch des Bernischen historischen Museums in Bern* 35–36 (1955–56): 103–232.

YARZA LUACES 1993: Joaquín Yarza Luaces. *Los reyes católicos: Paisaje artístico de una monarquía.* Madrid, 1993.

YOUNG AND AITKEN 1908: J. Young and P. Henderson Aitken. *A Catalogue of the Manuscripts in the Library of the Hunterian Museum in the University of Glasgow.* Glasgow, 1908.

ZANOTTO 1862: Francesco Zanotto. "Dissertazione intorno al Breviario Manoscritto posseduto dal cardinale Domenico Grimani da lui legato alla Repubblica di Venezia, ora custodito nella Biblioteca Marciana." Preface to Antonio Perini and Francesco Zanotto, *Fac-Simile delle miniature contenute nel Breviario Grimani, conservato nella Biblioteca di S. Marco*: iii–xlvi. Venice, 1862.

ZIMMERMANN AND DE RENTIIS 1994: Margarete Zimmermann and Dianna de Rentiis. *The City of Scholars: New Approaches to Christine de Pizan.* Berlin, 1994.

ZIMMERMANN 1998: W. Haio Zimmermann. *Pfosten, Ständer und Schwelle und der Übergang vom Pfosten-zum Ständerbau—eine Studie zu Innovation und Baharrung im Hausbau: zu Konstruktion und haltbarkeit prähistorischer bis neuzeitlicher Holzbauten von den Nord- und Ostseeländern bis zu den Alpen.* Oldenburg, 1998.

ZSUPPÁN 1970: C. Margaret Zsuppán, ed. *Jean Robertet: Oeuvres.* Textes littéraires français, no. 159. Geneva, 1970.

ZÜRICH 1994: *Himmel, Hölle, Fegefeuer: Das Jenseits im Mittelalter.* Exh. cat. compiled by Peter Jezler. Zürich, Schweizerische Landesmuseum, 1994.

ZWOLLO 1965: Annie Zwollo. "De landschapstekeningen van Cornelis Massys." *Nederlands kunsthistorisch jaarboek.* 16 (1965): 43–65.

INDEX OF NAMES

Note: Page numbers in italics refer to illustrations.

INDEX OF WORKS OF ART

ILLUSTRATION CREDITS

Alnwick Castle: ills. 44a–c, 168. Collection of the Duke
of Northumberland.
Antwerp, Koninklijk Museum voor Schone Kunsten:
fig. 7, © KIK/IRPA, Brussels.
Antwerp, Museum Mayer van den Bergh: fig. 10, ills.
92a–i. / ills. 92f–i. Photos: copyright IRPA-KIK,
Brussels.
Arundel Castle: ill. 143. Reproduced by kind permission
of His Grace the Duke of Norfolk.
Baltimore, The Walters Art Museum: fig. 26, ills. 94, 146.
Basel, Kunstmuseum: ill. 101. Öffentliche
Kunstsammlung Basel, Kunstmuseum; Bequest of
Max Geldner, Basel. Photo: Martin Bühler.
Berlin, Staatliche Museen zu Berlin, Preussischer
Kulturbesitz, Gemäldegalerie: figs. 42, 45, 58; ills.
149a–b, 164. Photos: Jörg P. Anders, Berlin.
Berlin, Staatliche Museen zu Berlin, Preussischer
Kulturbesitz, Kupferstichkabinett: figs. 55, 74; ills. 20a,
20c, 35, 38a–e, 113a, 113d, 171, 172. Photos: Jörg P.
Anders, Berlin.
Berlin, Staatsbibliothek zu Berlin, Preussischer
Kulturbesitz, Handschriftenabteilung: figs. 34, 37;
ill. 112.
Besançon, Bibliothèque municipale: fig. 33.
Birmingham Museums and Art Gallery: ill. 5. Presented
by the Trustees of the Feeney Charitable Trust to
Birmingham Museums and Art Gallery, 1935.
Blackburn, Blackburn Museum and Art Gallery:
ills. 98a–b.
Brussels, Bibliothèque royale de Belgique: figs. 18, 36d;
ills. 3, 6, 24, 28a–b, 29, 32c, 150a–h.
Brussels, Musée royaux des Beaux-Arts de Belgique: figs.
4, 6.
Bucks, Wormsley Library, Sir Paul Getty, K. B. E.: ills.
72a–b. Photos: British Library.
Cambridge, The Fitzwilliam Museum: ills. 52, 113c,
144a–b. By kind permission of the Syndics of the
Fitzwilliam Museum, Cambridge.
Cambridge, St John's College: ills. 22a–b. By permission
of the Master and Fellows of St John's College,
Cambridge.
Cambridge, University Library: ill. 70. By permission of
the Syndics of Cambridge University Library.
Cambridge, Mass., Fogg Art Museum, Harvard
University: ill. 47. Courtesy of the Fogg Art Museum,
Harvard University Art Museums, Francis H. Burr
Memorial Fund, Alpheus Hyatt Fund and William M.
Prichard Fund. Photo: Katya Kallsen,
© President and Fellows of Harvard College.
Cambridge, Mass., Houghton Library, Harvard
University: ills. 32a–b, 32e–f.
Chatsworth, Duke of Devonshire and the Chatsworth
Settlement Trustees: fig. 51; ills. 58a–b, 128.
Devonshire Collection, Chatsworth. Reproduced by
permission of the Duke of Devonshire and the
Chatsworth Settlement Trustees.
Cleveland, Cleveland Museum of Art: fig. 20; ills. 105a–b.
Leonard C. Hanna, Jr. Fund.
Copenhagen, Det Kongelige Bibliotek: ills. 136a–b.
Darmstadt, Hessisches Landesmuseum: ill. 165.
Dublin, Chester Beatty Library: ills. 156a–c.
El Escorial, Spain, Monasterio de San Lorenzo: figs. 15,
29; ill. 99a. © Patrimonio Nacional.
Frankfurt, Städelsches Kunstinstitut: fig. 11.
Ghent, Museum voor Schone Kunsten: figs. 14, 70.
Ghent, Saint Bavo Cathedral: fig. 48. Photo: © Paul M.
R. Maeyaert.

Glasgow University Library: ill. 89.
The Hague, Koninklijke Bibliotheek: fig. 49; ills. 17a–c.
Hamburg, Kunsthalle, Kupferstichkabinett: fig. 69.
Photo: Elke Walford.
Hatfield House, Marquess of Salisbury: ill. 132.
Holkham Hall, Earl of Leicester and Trustees of the
Holkham Estate: ill. 85. By kind permission of the Earl
of Leicester and Trustees of the Holkham Estate. /
ills. 118a–b. Collection of the Earl of Leicester,
Holkham Hall, Norfolk/Bridgeman Art Library.
Houston, Museum of Fine Arts: fig. 9. The Edith A. and
Percy S. Straus Collection.
Kew, Public Record Office: ill. 131.
Lancashire, Stonyhurst College: ill. 88.
Leipzig, Universitätsbibliothek: fig. 32.
Leuven, Collegiate Church of Saint Peter: fig. 60.
Copyright Scala/Art Resource, New York; St. Peter,
Leuven, Belgium.
Lisbon, Fundação Calouste Gulbenkian, Museu Calouste
Gulbenkian: ill. 127.
London, The British Library: figs. 25, 36a–b, 38, 52, 59;
ills. 9a–c, 33a–b, 39, 41a–b, 51, 57, 64, 66, 68, 74, 75a–b,
76a–b, 77, 78, 80, 82, 83a–c, 87, 100a–b, 109a–b,
114a–b, 117a–b, 119a–b, 120, 121a–b, 129a–f, 130a–b,
141, 147a–d, 155, 159a–c, 162a–b.
London, The British Museum: ill. 21.
London, The Courtauld Institute Gallery: ill. 30. Princes
Gate Collection 314.
London, Lambeth Palace Library: ill. 84.
London, The National Gallery: figs. 5, 27; ills. 7a–b.
London, Sir John Soane's Museum: ills. 81, 138. By
courtesy of the Trustees of Sir John Soane's Museum.
London, Victoria and Albert Museum: ills. 53a–b, 135,
158, 159d, 161.
Los Angeles, J. Paul Getty Museum: figs. 28, 46; ills. 1, 2a,
2b, 13, 14a–d, 15, 16a–d, 32d, 45, 49a–b, 50, 55a–c,
63a–b, 73, 79a–b, 124a–b, 145a–b, 154c, 160, 163.
Madrid, Biblioteca de la Fundación Lázaro Galdiano: ills.
25a–c.
Madrid, Biblioteca Nacional: figs. 30, 50, 64; ills. 20b, 20e.
Madrid, Museo del Prado: fig. 19.
Manchester, The John Rylands University Library of
Manchester: ills. 67, 108a. Reproduced by courtesy of
the Director and Librarian, The John Rylands
University Library.
Montserrat, Biblioteca de l'Abadia de Montserrat
(Montserrat Abbey): ill. 154b.
Munich, Bayerische Staatsbibliothek: ills. 86, 90a–c, 154a,
154d.
Munich, Bayerische Staatsgemäldesammlungen, Alte
Pinakothek: fig. 67.
Naples, Biblioteca Nazionale "Vittorio Emanuele III":
ills. 93a–b. By permission of the Ministero per i Beni e
le Attività Culturali–Italy.
New York, The Aurora Trust: fig. 12.
New York, The Metropolitan Museum of Art: figs. 62,
63. M. W. Ainsworth and A. Gilchrest, The
Metropolitan Museum of Art. / fig. 72. The Jules
Bache Collection, 1949. / ill. 4. Bequest of Lillian S.
Timken, 1959. Photo: © 1993 The Metropolitan
Museum of Art. / ill. 10b. The Robert Lehman
Collection, 1975. / ills. 11a–b. The Robert Lehman
Collection, 1975. Photos: © 1982 The Metropolitan
Museum of Art. / ill. 99b. The Robert Lehman
Collection, 1975. Photo: © 1986 The Metropolitan
Museum of Art. / ills. 125a–b. Bequest of George D.
Pratt, 1935. Photos: © 1994 The Metropolitan Museum

of Art. / ill. 142. The Friedsam Collection, Bequest of
Michael Friedsam, 1931. Photo: © 1998 The
Metropolitan Museum of Art.
New York, The Pierpont Morgan Library: ills. 107, 113b,
148b, 166b; ills. 27, 65, 91a–c, 96a, 108b, 140b, 148a,
167b. Photos: Joseph Zehavi. / ills. 140a, 167a. Photos:
David A. Loggie. / ill. 166a. Photo: Schecter Lee.
Nová Říše, Czech Republic, The Premonstratensian
Abbey of Nová Říše: ills. 36a–b
Oxford, Bodleian Library: figs. 36c, 56; ills. 18a–c, 40a–b,
43a–b, 137a–b. Bodleian Library, University of Oxford.
Oxford, Christ Church: ills. 169a, 169c. The Governing
Body of Christ Church, Oxford.
Oxford, Magdalen College: ill. 169b. The President and
Fellows of Magdalen College, Oxford.
Paris, Bibliothèque de l'Arsenal: figs. 23, 35; ills. 56a–b,
97. Photos: BnF. Arsenal.
Paris, Bibliothèque nationale de France: figs. 3, 54; ills.
54a–b, 59, 60, 61, 62, 69, 71a–b, 96b, 123.
Paris, École nationale supérieure des Beaux-Arts: ill. 26.
Paris, Musée du Louvre: fig. 22; ills. 106, 134, 154. Photos:
Réunion des Musées Nationaux / Art Resource, New
York. / fig. 24. Photo: Scala / Art Resource, New York.
Philadelphia, The Philadelphia Museum of Art: fig. 13.
The John G. Johnson Collection. Photo: Lynn
Rosenthal, 1997. / ills. 20d, 46. The John G. Johnson
Collection.
Private Collections: ills. 10a, 157. / ill. 34. Photo: Jochen
Beyer, Village Neuf, France. / ills. 48a–b. Courtesy of
Sam Fogg, Ltd. / ill. 139. Photo: © Board of Trustees,
National Gallery of Art, Washington, D.C. / ills.
170a–b. Courtesy of Dr. Jörn Günther, Antiquariat,
Hamburg.
Ramsen, Switzerland, Heribert Tenschert: ills. 115a–b.
Rouen, Musée des Beaux-Arts: fig. 68.
Rome, Santa Croce di Gerusalemme: fig. 43
Salisbury, Wilton House: ill. 31. By kind permission of
the Earl of Pembroke and the Trustees of Wilton
House Trust, Wilton House, Salisbury, United
Kingdom.
San Marino, The Huntington Library: fig. 47; ills. 12a–c,
103, 151.
Toledo, The Toledo Museum of Art: fig. 21. Gift of
Edward Drummond Libbey.
Toronto, Art Gallery of Ontario: ill. 8
Turin, Biblioteca Nazionale: fig. 40.
Turin, Museo Civico: fig. 39.
Valencia, Serra de Alzaga Collection: ill. 102.
Vatican City, Biblioteca Apostolica Vaticana: ills. 111a–d.
Venice, Biblioteca Nazionale Marciana: figs. 31, 71; ills.
126a–b.
Vienna, Kunsthistorisches Museum: fig. 16.
Vienna, Österreichische Nationalbibliothek: figs. 8, 17,
61, 65, 73; ills. 19a–b, 42, 95, 104, 110a–b.
Waddesdon Manor: ill. 122. Waddesdon, The Rothschild
Collection (The National Trust). Photo: Mike Fear.
Ware, St Edmund's College: ills. 116a–b. Photos:
davemorgan.
Washington, D.C., National Gallery of Art: fig. 41.
Andrew W. Mellon Collection. Photo: © Board of
Trustees, National Gallery of Art, Washington.
Wimborn, Kingston Lacy (The National Trust): ill. 152.
National Trust Photographic Library/Derrick E.
Witty.
Windsor Castle, Her Majesty Queen Elizabeth II, The
Royal Library: ills. 23, 133. The Royal Collection
© 2002, Her Majesty Queen Elizabeth II.

ABOUT THE AUTHORS

Maryan W. Ainsworth is curator of early Netherlandish, French, and German paintings at The Metropolitan Museum of Art and adjunct professor at Barnard College and Columbia University. She specializes in the integration of technical examination of paintings with art-historical research. Among her many publications is *Gerard David: Purity of Vision in an Age of Transition*.

Mari-Tere Alvarez is senior project coordinator at the J. Paul Getty Museum and recently received her Ph.D. in art history from the University of Southern California with a dissertation entitled "The Art Market in Renaissance Spain: From Flanders to Castile." She has published on polychrome sculpture and is currently working on the Renaissance collection and patronage of Mencía de Mendoza.

Brigitte Dekeyzer is a member of the Study Centre of Flemish Miniaturists (Belgium, K. U. Leuven). She has published on Ghent-Bruges manuscript illumination, especially on the Mayer van den Bergh Breviary (Antwerp, Museum Mayer van den Bergh, Inv. Nr. 946), the central topic of her Ph.D thesis.

Richard Gay, assistant curator in the Department of Manuscripts at the J. Paul Getty Museum, specializes in French manuscript illumination. He has organized diverse exhibitions on medieval illumination at the Getty Museum, and has taught at Cornell University.

Thomas Kren is curator of manuscripts at the J. Paul Getty Museum and adjunct professor of art history at the University of Southern California. His publications on Flemish and French manuscript illumination include *Simon Bening's Flemish Calendar*; *Margaret of York, Simon Marmion, and the Visions of Tondal*; and *Renaissance Painting in Manuscripts: Treasures from the British Library*.

Scot McKendrick is curator of manuscripts at the British Library and a Fellow of the Courtauld Institute of Art. He has lectured and published extensively on late-medieval illuminated manuscripts and art and is the author of *The History of Alexander the Great*.

Elizabeth Morrison is assistant curator in the Department of Manuscripts at the J. Paul Getty Museum. She is a specialist in French Gothic and Flemish Renaissance manuscript illumination and has curated various exhibitions at the Getty Museum.

Catherine Reynolds, formerly a lecturer in art history at the Universities of Reading and London, is currently a consultant on manuscripts for Christie's, London. Her publications include contributions to *Boccaccio Visualizzato* and to volumes on Robert Campin, Jan van Eyck, and Hans Memling.